Handbook of Prevention and Treatment with Children and Adolescents

Handbook of Prevention and Treatment with Children and Adolescents

Intervention in the Real World Context

Edited by

Robert T. Ammerman, Ph.D.
Michel Hersen, Ph.D.

JOHN WILEY & SONS, INC.

New York • Chichester • Weinheim • Brisbane • Singapore • Toronto

Library of Congress Cataloging-in-Publication Data:

Handbook of prevention and treatment with children and adolescents :
    intervention in the real world context / edited by Robert T.
    Ammerman, Michel Hersen.
        p.   cm.
    Includes bibliographical references and index.
    ISBN 0-471-12163-0 (cloth : alk. paper)
    1. Socially handicapped children—Mental health services.
    2. Socially handicapped teenagers—Mental health services. 3. Child
    psychopathology—Prevention.   4. Adolescent psychopathology—
    Prevention. 5. Child psychotherapy. 6. Adolescent psychotherapy.
    I. Ammerman, Robert T. II. Hersen, Michel.
    RJ499.H3326   1997
    618.92′89—dc21   96-51877

To Blanca Uribe and Richard Wilson—RTA

To Vicki, Nathaniel, and Jonathan—MH

Contributors

Robert T. Ammerman, Ph.D.
Associate Professor of Psychiatry
MCP◆Hahnemann School of Medicine
Allegheny University of the Health Sciences
Pittsburgh, Pennsylvania

Arthur D. Anastopoulos, Ph.D.
Associate Professor
Department of Psychology
University of North Carolina at Greensboro
Greensboro, North Carolina

J. Xavier Apodaca
SDSU/UCSD Joint Doctoral Program in
   Clinical Psychology
Department of Psychology
San Diego State University
San Diego, California

Michael W. Arthur, Ph.D.
Project Director, Six State Risk Assessment
   Project and National Center for the
   Advancement of Prevention Projects
Social Development Research Group
School of Social Work
University of Washington
Seattle, Washington

Frank Barry, M.S.
Senior Extension Associate
Family Life Development Center
College of Human Ecology
Cornell University
Ithaca, New York

Gerald S. Berenson, M.D.
Professor of Medicine
School of Public Health and Tropical
   Medicine
Tulane University Medical Center
New Orleans, Louisiana

G. Anne Bogat, Ph.D.
Professor of Psychology
Michigan State University
East Lansing, Michigan

Robert H. Bradley, Ph.D.
Professor
Center for Research on Teaching and
   Learning
University of Arkansas at Little Rock
Little Rock, Arkansas

Deborah Brown, M.A.
Department of Psychology
University of Missouri-Columbia
Columbia, Missouri

Richard F. Catalano, Ph.D.
Associate Professor of Sociology and
   Associate Director
Social Development Research Group
School of Social Work
University of Washington
Seattle, Washington

Kristin Cole, M.S.
Associate Research Scholar
Columbia University School of Social Work
New York, New York

Christian M. Connell
Department of Psychology
University of South Carolina
Columbia, South Carolina

Mark R. Dadds, Ph.D.
Director of Clinical Training & Deputy Dean
  (Research)
School of Applied Psychology
Griffith University
Nathan, Queensland, Australia

Michael D. DeBellis, M.D.
Assistant Professor of Psychiatry
University of Pittsburgh Medical Center
Director, Developmental Traumatology
  Laboratory
Western Psychiatric Institute and Clinic
Pittsburgh, Pennsylvania

Rhonda D'Imperio, Ph.D.
Assistant Professor of Psychiatry
Louisiana State University Medical Center
New Orleans, Louisiana

Eric F. Dubow, Ph.D.
Professor of Psychology
Bowling Green State University
Department of Psychology
Bowling Green, Ohio

Carl J. Dunst, Ph.D.
Research Scientist
Orelena Hawks Puckett Institute
Asheville, North Carolina

John P. Elder, Ph.D.
Professor and Chair, Division of Health
  Promotion
Graduate School of Public Health
San Diego State University
San Diego, California

James Garbarino, Ph.D.
Professor of Human Development and Family
  Studies
Director of Family Life Development Center
College of Human Ecology
Cornell University
Ithaca, New York

Alan M. Gross, Ph.D.
Professor of Psychology
University of Mississippi
University, Mississippi

Louis P. Hagopian, Ph.D.
Assistant Professor, Department of
  Psychiatry and Behavioral Sciences
The Johns Hopkins University School of
  Medicine
Department of Behavioral Psychology
Kennedy Krieger Institute
Baltimore, Maryland

J. David Hawkins, Ph.D.
Professor and Director
Social Development Research Group
School of Social Work
University of Washington
Seattle, Washington

Robert L. Hendren, D.O.
Professor of Psychiatry
Director, Child and Adolescent Psychiatry
University of Medicine and Dentistry New
  Jersey
Robert Wood Johnson Medical School
Piscataway, New Jersey

Michel Hersen, Ph.D.
Professor and Dean
School of Professional Psychology
Pacific University
Forest Grove, Oregon

Ruth C. Jampol, Ph.D.
Clinical Director, Crestwood Program
Woods Resources, Incorporated
Langhorne, Pennsylvania

Leonard A. Jason, Ph.D.
Professor of Psychology
DePaul University
Chicago, Illinois

Carolyn C. Johnson, Ph.D.
Research Associate Professor
School of Public Health and Tropical
  Medicine
Tulane University Medical Center
New Orleans, Louisiana

Richard Kosterman, Ph.D.
Research Consultant
Social Development Research Group
School of Social Work
University of Washington
Seattle, Washington

Carol Larroque, M.D.
Assistant Professor of Psychiatry
Director of Pediatric Consultation Liaison
University of New Mexico School of
  Medicine
Albuquerque, New Mexico

Eugene Maguin, Ph.D.
Program Manager
Research Institute on Addictions
Buffalo, New York

J. Scott Mizes, Ph.D.
Department of Psychology
Philadelphia College of Osteopathic
  Medicine
Philadelphia, Pennsylvania

Donna Moreau, M.D.
Associate Clinical Professor of Child
  Psychiatry
New York State Psychiatric Institute
Columbia University College of Physicians
  and Surgeons
New York, New York

Laura Mufson, Ph.D.
Assistant Professor of Clinical Psychology
Division of Clinical and Genetic
  Epidemiology
Department of Psychiatry
New York State Psychiatric Institute
College of Physicians & Surgeons of
  Columbia University
New York, New York

Theresa A. Nicklas, Dr.P.H., L.D.N.
Research Associate Professor
School of Public Health and Tropical
  Medicine
Tulane University Medical Center
New Orleans, Louisiana

Thomas H. Ollendick, Ph.D.
Professor of Psychology
Virginia Polytechnic Institute and State
  University
Blacksburg, Virginia

Tonya Mizell Palermo, M.A.
Department of Psychology
Case Western Reserve University
Cleveland, Ohio

Deborah Parra-Medina, MPH
SDSU/UCSD Joint Doctoral Program in
  Public Health
Graduate School of Public Health
San Diego State University
San Diego, California

Lizette Peterson, Ph.D.
Professor of Psychology
University of Missouri-Columbia
Columbia, Missouri

Ronald J. Prinz, Ph.D.
Carolina Distinguished Professor
Department of Psychology
University of South Carolina
Columbia, South Carolina

Carolyn E. Roecker, Ph.D.
Assistant Professor of Psychology
University of Dayton
Dayton, Ohio

Steven P. Schinke, Ph.D.
Professor of Social Work
Columbia University School of Social Work
New York, New York

Scott Spreat, Ed.D.
Clinical Director, Woodland Center
Woods Services, Incorporated
Langhorne, Pennsylvania

Carol M. Trivette, Ph.D.
Research Scientist
Orelena Hawks Puckett Institute
Morganton, North Carolina

G. Stennis Watson, M.A.
Department of Psychology
The University of Mississippi
University, Mississippi

Larry S. Webber, Ph.D.
Professor and Department Chair,
    Biostatistics and Epidemiology
School of Public Health and Tropical
    Medicine
Tulane University Medical Center
New Orleans, Louisiana

Joseph Westermeyer, M.D., Ph.D.
Professor of Psychiatry
University of Minnesota
Chief of Psychiatry Service
Minneapolis Veterans Administration
    Medical Center
Minneapolis, Minnesota

Leanne Whiteside-Mansell, Ed.D.
Adjunct Assistant Professor
Center for Research on Teaching and
    Learning
University of Arkansas at Little Rock
Little Rock, Arkansas

Sandy K. Wurtele, Ph.D.
Associate Professor of Psychology
University of Colorado
Colorado Springs, Colorado

Preface

In the past decade, numerous sociodemographic forces have converged to undermine children's development and psychosocial adjustment: poverty, child maltreatment and other forms of family violence, dissolution of traditional family structures, crime and violence in the community, and substance abuse, to name a few. In isolation, each of these problem areas adversely affects social, emotional, and behavioral functioning in children. In aggregation, however, potential outcomes for children and families can be devastating. It is against this background that clinicians strive to prevent and treat psychopathology and behavioral disorders in children and adolescents. Yet, the negative social influences on children and their families are often out of the direct control of clinicians, and the quantity of time spent in actual treatment pales in comparison with that spent in settings which promoted psychosocial dysfunction in the first place. Because this disparity subverts the effectiveness of interventions, clinical programs must be designed and carried out that take into account those factors in the child's social ecology interfering with optimal outcomes.

The overarching purpose of this book, evident in the subtitle, is to address the problems encountered when intervening with children, adolescents, and their families who face poverty, violence, substance abuse, and other social ills. We contend that the success of prevention and treatment programs depends on understanding and appreciating those social forces that can profoundly impact children's development and adjustment. The 23 chapters in this book are divided into five parts. Following an introductory chapter by the editors (Part One), the importance of poverty and community influences is covered in General Issues (Part Two). Part Three contains chapters describing levels of intervention (Intervention Formats and Settings): individual and group, restrictive settings, and school and community. Part Four is entitled Preventive Interventions, and describes prevention approaches for early intervention, smoking, substance use and abuse, conduct disorders and antisocial behavior, mental health, health promotion, unintentional injury and child abuse and neglect, sexual abuse, and AIDS and sexually transmitted diseases. Finally, Part Five (Treatment Interventions) addresses treatment of child and adolescent disorders. Topics covered include depressive disorders, anxiety disorders, posttraumatic stress disorder, mental retardation and developmental disabilities, conduct disorder, attention-deficit/hyperactivity disorder, eating disorders, and substance abuse disorders.

Authors have emphasized state-of-the-art clinical practice that has been empirically evaluated. Moreover, the authors of Chapters 7–23 followed a predetermined format that includes the following headings: Description of the Problem (or Disorder), Scope of the Problem (or Epidemiology), Causes and Consequences, Impediments to Intervention in the Real World Context, Prevention (or Treatment), subheadings of Assessment Strategies and Prevention (or Treatment) Approaches, and Summary. Each chapter considers the challenges faced by both clinicians and researchers in working with children and adolescents living under adverse social circumstances.

We acknowledge the assistance and support provided to us by numerous individuals in bringing this book to fruition. We are especially grateful to the contributors for sharing their expertise and insights. We also thank our editor at John Wiley & Sons, Jo Ann Miller, for her encouragement and patience throughout the publication process. Cindy DeLuca and Burt Bolton provided invaluable clerical support, and we were also assisted by Beth Boerger, Nancy Baldwin, Christine C. Apple, Christopher M. Brooks, and Stacey L. Sanders. Finally, we thank our families (especially our children!) for their inspiration in and support of our efforts.

ROBERT T. AMMERMAN
MICHEL HERSEN

Pittsburgh, Pennsylvania
Forest Grove, Oregon

Contents

PART ONE

Introduction

CHAPTER 1

Prevention and Treatment with Children and Adolescents in the Real World Context

ROBERT T. AMMERMAN and MICHEL HERSEN

In the past decade, considerable attention has been focused on the efficacy and effectiveness of psychological and psychiatric interventions for children and adolescents. The scientific literature on this issue has blossomed and we are now in a unique position to address the utility of treatments and programs that have been developed for this population. Indeed, several meta-analyses specifically tackle the question of treatment and outcome in childhood disorders. For example, Casey and Berman (1985) examined 75 studies (published between 1952 and 1983) of psychotherapy outcome in children and adolescents aged 3 to 15 years. Specific goals of the meta-analysis were to determine: (a) whether some forms of psychotherapy were superior to others; (b) whether the efficacy of psychotherapy varied as a function of outcome measures used; and (c) what child characteristics mediate outcome. Studies reviewed had an average $N = 42$ at posttreatment, looked at children who were primarily male (60%) and had a mean age of 8.9 years, and included treatments that were carried out for an average of 9.5 weeks (range = 1–37 weeks). Behavior therapy was the most common form of treatment represented (56%); 21% of studies examined cognitive-behavior therapy. Client-centered therapy was evaluated in 28% of studies, and dynamic therapy was represented in 9%.

Results indicated an overall effect size of 0.71: Children receiving psychotherapy had an outcome more than two-thirds of a standard deviation better than controls. This finding is consistent with meta-analyses of adult psychotherapy (e.g., Shapiro & Shapiro, 1982). Behavioral interventions were more effective than their nonbehavioral counterparts, with effect sizes of 0.91 and 0.40, respectively. No differences were found between play versus nonplay therapies, individual versus group approaches, parent-involved versus child-only interventions, or as a function of age. Treatment effectiveness was greater in children displaying impulsivity, phobia, and somatic problems (these were also most likely to be targeted in those studies evaluating behavior therapy). Problems of social adjustment were less responsive to treatment.

Shapiro and Shapiro (1982) argued that the relative superiority of behavior therapy was tempered by the fact that behavioral and nonbehavioral treatment outcome studies tended to target different problems. Moreover, they contended that assessment measures used in behavioral studies were often directly linked to treatment targets, as opposed to more global indices of functioning utilized in nonbehavioral studies. When these therapy-specific measures (which the authors believed led to an artificially inflated effect size for behavior therapy) were excluded from the analysis, behavior therapy was no longer superior to nonbehavioral interventions.

In a second meta-analysis, Weisz, Weiss, Alicke, and Klotz (1987) examined 105 outcome studies (see Weiss & Weisz, 1990) of behavioral and nonbehavioral interventions with children and adolescents aged 4 to 18 years. Studies were selected only if they contrasted a treatment condition with a nontreatment or minimally treated (i.e., attention) control group. As in Casey and Berman (1985), the authors sought to identify overall treatment effectiveness as well as correlates of positive treatment outcome. However, Weisz et al. cogently argued that the direct link between assessment approaches to treatment targets in most behavioral evaluations is not necessarily a confound in determining effect size of behavior therapy versus nonbehavioral interventions. For example, in the case of phobia, the most clinically meaningful indication of fear and its reduction is degree of approach to the feared stimulus (typically used to assess behavioral interventions for phobia). In this case, global measures of child adjustment are tangentially, not primarily, relevant. In their meta-analysis, Weisz and associates distinguished between outcome "measures similar to the training procedures [that] are appropriate and necessary for a fair test of treatment success" (1987, p. 546) and those assessments intricately linked to treatment that were deemed "unnecessary."

Findings revealed a mean effect size of 0.79 for treatment versus control comparisons. Once again, behavior therapy was found to be more effective than nonbehavioral interventions (0.88 versus 0.44). This superiority remained when "appropriate and necessary" assessments were retained (0.93 versus 0.45), but it disappeared when *all* therapy-like measures were eliminated. Overall effect size did not significantly change as a function of problem type (i.e., overcontrolled versus undercontrolled behavioral disorders). Children (ages 4 to 12) were more likely to improve when contrasted with adolescents (ages 13 to 18). Also, investigations using nonclinical samples obtained equivalent findings to those recruiting subjects from clinics. Finally, treatment gains were likely to be maintained at 6-month follow-up.

A third meta-analysis (Durlak, Fuhram, & Lampman, 1991), albeit more circumscribed in scope, examined the effectiveness of and mediating factors in cognitive-behavior therapy for children. Specifically, 64 studies published between 1970 and 1987 were selected for analysis. Criteria for inclusion consisted of the use of a control group, treatment of behaviorally disordered children, and implementation of cognitive-behavioral treatment *without* concurrent family therapy or other form of treatment. Results indicated that treatment effectiveness was mediated by age and, presumably, level of cognitive development. The effect size was greater for children aged 11 to 13 years (0.92) relative to children aged 5 to 10 years (0.57 and 0.55). The authors concluded that cognitive-behavior therapy is more effective for children in the formal operations stage of cognitive development than for children in the preoperational and concrete operations stages. Other factors (e.g., type of problem, methodological features) did not emerge as significant influences on effect size.

The preceding meta-analyses yield several important conclusions. First, psychotherapy is an effective intervention for a variety of social, emotional, and behavioral problems in children and adolescents with psychiatric disorders. Moreover, treatment effects are durable at short-term follow-up. Second, behavior therapy in particular is an especially effective intervention. And third, effect sizes are similar in meta-analyses of both the child and adult treatment literatures.

It is a common complaint among clinicians, however, that the "experimental" research literature has limited generalizability to actual clinic cases because of features inherent to laboratory studies that purportedly limit external validity. This sentiment is widely held among clinicians (e.g., Raw, 1993), and indeed, the limited research of outcome in "natural" clinic settings (without the methodological control of laboratory studies) has yielded less positive results in contrast to that of more empirically rigorous evaluations (Weisz & Weiss, 1989). Weisz et al. explored 10 hypotheses as to why there are such disparities between laboratory and clinic findings. Meta-analysis revealed that research treatment differed from clinic treatment in that clinic samples were more pathologically disturbed, research settings had superior resources, and behavior therapy (which was more likely to be part of research studies but is less likely to employed by the clinical community as a whole) is more effective than nonbehavioral treatments. The analysis did not support other hypotheses (e.g., superior methodologies in recent research, research clinicians are superior to community clinicians, research therapists are more carefully trained, research psychotherapy is more circumscribed in terms of clinical presentations, and research therapy is more highly structured).

The majority of interventions, particularly those designed to treat existing psychopathology, intervene at the level of the individual child or adolescent and/or the child's family. Yet, as reflected in the widely accepted ecological model and its derivatives (Belsky, 1993; Werkele & Wolfe, 1993), the child is influenced by forces at multiple levels, including the community and the broader society and culture. These influences, which include poverty, violence, inadequate education, and other factors, conspire to undermine the child's development and psychosocial adjustment. Furthermore, they offer considerable challenges to clinicians who must contend with forces mitigating the impact of treatment, and which are often out of their direct control. Treatment that is carried out in the community, therefore, is intervention in the "real world," where children reside in settings that are potentially deleterious to their long-term adaptation, health, and well-being. The less than optimal outcomes found in community treatment studies must be understood within the context of these powerful factors that threaten the child's and the family's overall psychosocial functioning.

The following sections briefly describe four areas (poverty, family and community violence, substance abuse, and access to health and special services) that have risen to the fore as particularly important threats to child development and adjustment. Although not inclusive, these areas must be addressed by clinicians and researchers alike in designing and evaluating interventions because they can be expected to moderate the impact and long-term effectiveness of treatment and prevention programs.

POVERTY

In 1993, the Bureau of the Census (1994) reported that 15,727,000 children in the United States (23% of this population) lived in poverty. This is the highest proportion of children living in poverty in 20 years, and represents a steady increase from the 14% identified in 1969 (poverty was defined as a family income below $11,890 for a family of three). Poverty eludes a simple definition, and it is likely that the preceding criterion results in an underestimation of the number of children who suffer economic hardship and deprivation. Poverty brings with it a host of health risks, including mal-nutrition, exposure to environmental toxins, vulnerability to asthma, and increased ac-cidental injuries. Additional risks to psychosocial development include depression, loneliness, and other internalizing and externalizing disorders (McLoyd, 1990).

The mechanisms by which poverty affects psychosocial development in children and adolescents are complex and multidetermined. Biological impacts of poverty inter-fere with optimal growth and development. Low birth weight, malnutrition, and con-stant hunger compromise a host of physiological systems which, in turn, adversely impact psychological development. The stressors associated with economic hardship, particularly if they are chronic and long-standing, tax family emotional and psycho-logical resources and have a debilitating effect on the child. Many children who are poor live in crowded, crime-ridden neighborhoods that provide pressures to conform to antisocial influences (e.g., gang membership). The clustering of risk factors in con-junction with poverty exacerbates and contributes to the potential negative conse-quences of severe economic hardship.

FAMILY AND COMMUNITY VIOLENCE

Few topics in childhood have received as much attention in the past decade as abuse and neglect. The reasons for this are clear. In a recent summary of statistics on child maltreatment, Curtis, Boyd, Liepold, and Petit (1995) noted the following yearly phys-ical consequences of child abuse and neglect: 2,000 fatalities, 18,000 serious disabili-ties, and 141,700 serious injuries. In 1993, there were almost 2 million reports of maltreatment, involving approximately 3 million children. In 1984, 28 of every 1,000 children were involved in maltreatment reports, but this number increased to 43 per thousand children in 1993. According to the National Committee to Prevent Child Abuse (1995), there was a 4.5% rise in reported maltreatment from 1993 to 1994, and a 63% increase in total reports from 1985 to 1994. Of reports in 1993 (U.S. Depart-ment of Health and Human Services, 1995), 7% of maltreated were under the age of one year, 33% were between 1 and 5 years, 39% were between 6 and 12 years, and 21% were 13 years and older. In 80% of cases, parents were the perpetrators. Forty-five percent of cases involved neglect, 22% physical abuse, 13% sexual abuse, 13% other, 5% emotional neglect, and 2% medical neglect. Although not all reported cases of mal-treatment are substantiated, many cases of abuse and neglect are thought to go unde-tected, particularly those in which there are few overt signs of mistreatment (i.e., physical injury).

These statistics document the pervasiveness of maltreatment in children and ado-lescents. The potential short- and long-term consequences of maltreatment are equally troubling. They include disruptions in social and emotional development, and increased risk for aggression, anxiety and mood disorders, substance abuse, educa-tional underachievement, and maltreating one's own children in adulthood (see Briere, Berliner, Bulkley, Jenny, & Reid, 1996). In addition, maltreated children often reside in homes in which other forms of family violence occur. As many as 10 million children are witnesses to acts of violence between parents or their partners (Straus, 1991). Evidence has accrued suggesting that witnessing violence between adults in the family can have the same damaging effects to children's psychosocial development as being directly victimized (Wolfe, Zak, Wilson, & Jaffe, 1986). Taken together, family violence has become pandemic, and it is essential that assessment and intervention strategies take these issues into account.

Community violence, too, affects children's social and emotional functioning. Safety is a critical ingredient to optimal development, and a constant threat to life and well-being (which characterizes many inner-city and impoverished neighborhoods in the United States) undermines family functioning and child adjustment. Community violence aggregates with other sociodemographic risks, including poverty, crowding, hunger, exposure to environmental toxins, inadequate economic opportunities, and family violence, to name a few. Each of these factors, in isolation and in combination, has potentially deleterious consequences for children and their families. Once again, interventions are doomed to failure if they do not reflect an appreciation and understanding of the negative forces that impact children and adolescents living in these settings.

SUBSTANCE ABUSE

Substance abuse has also emerged as a major societal problem. Parental substance abuse has been cited as the primary contributor to child neglect (Dore, Doris, & Wright, 1995), and an important etiologic feature of other forms of maltreatment toward children. Moreover, parents involved with both substance abuse *and* child maltreatment are more likely to have their children removed from the home and placed in temporary adoption services, and are thought to be less responsive to remedial treatments designed to enhance parenting skills (Murphy et al., 1991). The offspring of parental substance abusers (fathers in particular) are more likely to have substance abuse problems themselves (see Hawkins, Catalano, & Miller, 1992).

Alcohol and drug use among American adolescents is so widespread that it has come to be viewed as almost normative. In a survey of high school seniors, Johnston, O'Malley, and Bachman (1995) found that 80% had used alcohol at some point in their lives, while 63% had been drunk as a result of excessive use. Lewinsohn, Hops, Roberts, Seely, and Andrews (1993) reported that 10.8% of 9th to 12th graders had a lifetime occurrence of a substance dependence or abuse disorder. Evidence shows that early onset of substance use is associated with substance abuse later in development, and that alcohol and drug problems in youth are likely to extend into adulthood. The etiology of adolescent substance abuse is complicated, and involves genetic, biophysiological, behavioral, family, and social ecological influences (Tarter & Vanyukov, 1994). Risk pathways to drug and alcohol abuse and dependence involve both the additive and interactive effects of these multiple systems.

The potential negative consequences of substance abuse and dependence are numerous. They include, but are not limited to, health problems, poor academic achievement, delinquency, increased risk for unwanted pregnancies and sexually transmitted diseases, and suicide and affective disorders (see Wagner & Kassel, 1995). As with poverty and violence, important etiologic influences are difficult to access and control by clinicians. In early to middle adolescence, the peer group becomes especially influential, and the presence of other risk factors (parental substance abuse, family dysfunction) sets the stage for the adolescent's vulnerability to that influence. Despite the acknowledged importance of peers in the emergence of substance abuse (Oetting & Beauvais, 1987), the majority of treatment programs for adolescent substance abusers do not actively involve the peer group in which substance abuse was originally promoted and encouraged. Although there are practical, logistical, and ethical barriers to routinely including peers in treatment, individual and family interventions are subverted because treated adolescents return to environments that are likely to elicit relapses and a return to previous patterns of abuse.

HEALTH AND SPECIAL SERVICES

As mentioned in the discussion of poverty, a significant proportion of children are at great risk for acute and chronic health problems. A survey by Wenger, Kaye, and La-Plante (1996) found that 6.1% (about 4 million) of children in the United States had some type of chronic illness or disability, although other estimates are as high as 10% to 15% (Newacheck & McManus, 1988). These children require continuous and long-term health care, but they may also require additional educational, psychological, and social supports. From the perspective of health care, considerable concern has been expressed about current health care reforms (which control access to services) and their impact on children with chronic medical needs (Newacheck & McManus, 1988; Perrin et al., 1994). Perrin et al. note, "The child who is assisted by technology may need a complex array of specialty and primary care physicians, specialized home nursing, social and mental health services, and respiratory therapy, among many others" (p. 504). They go on to call for an integration of services for children with special needs, particularly in today's climate of cost control and restricted access to specialized services.

The special needs of children and adolescents with disabilities and chronic illnesses have important implications for mental health clinicians. In designing interventions (either remedial or preventive), they must keep in mind the unique limitations associated with a given condition. Children with learning disabilities, especially nonverbal learning disability (Rourke, 1995), are at considerable risk for psychosocial maladaptation, and are unlikely to benefit from traditional interventions without substantial modification to materials and presentation formats. Furthermore, clinicians must work with a variety of systems involved in the child's life, including physicians, physical and occupational therapists, and educators to bring about meaningful and durable gains in functioning.

SUMMARY

Intervention in the real world context necessitates an understanding of and appreciation for the many forces and systems that impact the development and adaptation of children and adolescents. These influences are typically not the targets of intervention—individual and family-based treatments predominate in mental health. Yet, factors such as poverty and family violence undermine clinicians' best efforts limiting the effectiveness of interventions and may, in fact, partially account for the decreased success of treatments in "natural" (as opposed to laboratory) clinical settings (Weisz & Weiss, 1989). Efforts by mental health professionals to intervene at the community level (particularly to prevent the development of mental health problems) are essential to overcoming the impact of adverse social forces (see Mrazek & Haggerty, 1994). At the same time, however, individual and family treatment remains an important form of intervention, made more efficacious by taking into account the social ecology in which the child develops and lives.

REFERENCES

Belsky, J. (1993). Etiology of child maltreatment: A developmental-ecological analysis. *Psychological Bulletin, 114*, 413–434.

Briere, J., Berliner, L., Bulkley, J. A., Jenny, C., & Reid, T. (Eds.). (1996). *The APSAC handbook on child maltreatment*. Thousand Oaks, CA: Sage.

Casey, R. J., & Berman, J. S. (1985). The outcome of psychotherapy with children. *Psychological Bulletin, 98*, 388–400.

Curtis, P. A., Boyd, J. D., Liepold, M., & Petit, M. (1995). *Child abuse and neglect: A look at the states*. Washington, DC: Child Welfare League of America.

Dore, M. M., Doris, J. M., & Wright, P. (1985). Identifying substance abuse in maltreating families: A child welfare challenge. *Child Abuse & Neglect, 19*, 531–543.

Durlak, J. A., Fuhrman, P., & Lampman, C. (1991). Effectiveness of cognitive-behavior therapy for maladapting children: A meta-analysis. *Psychological Bulletin, 110*, 204–214.

Hawkins, J. D., Catalano, R. F., & Miller, J. Y. (1992). Risks and protection factors for alcohol and other drug problems in adolescence and early adulthood: Implications for substance abuse prevention. *Psychological Bulletin, 112*, 64–105.

Johnston, L. D., O'Malley, P. M., & Bachman, J. G. (1995, December 11). *Drug use rises again in 1995 among American teens* [News release]. Ann Arbor: University of Michigan News and Information Services.

Lewisohn, P. M., Hops, H., Roberts, R. E., Seely, J. R., & Andrews, J. A. (1993). Adolescent psychopathology: 1. Prevalence and incidence of depression and other *DSM-III-R* disorders in high school students. *Journal of Abnormal Psychology, 102*, 133–144.

McLoyd, V. C. (1990). The impact of economic hardship on Black families and children: Psychological distress, parenting, and socioemotional development. *Child Development, 61*, 311–346.

Mrazek, P. J., & Haggerty, R. J. (Eds.). (1994). *Reducing risks for mental disorders: Frontiers for preventive intervention research*. Washington, DC: National Academy Press.

Murphy, J. M., Jellinik, M. S., Quinn, D., Smith, G., Poitrast, F. G., & Goshkorn, M. (1991). Substance abuse and serious child mistreatment: Prevalence, risk, and outcome in a court sample. *Child Abuse & Neglect, 15*, 197–211.

National Committee to Prevent Child Abuse. (1995). *NCPCA's annual fifty state survey*. Chicago: Author.

Newacheck, P. W., & McManus, M. A. (1988). Financing health care for disabled children. *Pediatrics, 81*, 385–394.

Oetting, E. R., & Beauvais, F. (1987). Peer cluster therapy, socialization characteristics and adolescent drug use: A path analysis. *Journal of Counseling Psychology, 34*, 205–213.

Perrin, J., Kahn, R. S., Bloom, S. R., Davidson, S., Guyer, B., Hollinshead, W., Richmond, J. B., Walker, D. K., & Wise, P. H. (1994). Health care reform and the special needs of children [commentary]. *Pediatrics, 90*, 504–508.

Raw, S. D. (1993, March). Does psychotherapy research teach us anything about psychotherapy? *Behavior Therapist, 16*, 75–76.

Rourke, B. P. (Ed.). (1995). *Syndrome on nonverbal learning disabilities: Neurodevelopmental manifestations*. New York: Guilford Press.

Shapiro, D. A., & Shapiro, D. (1982). Meta-analysis of comparative therapy outcome studies: A replication and refinement. *Psychological Bulletin, 92,* 581–604.

Straus, M. A. (1991, September). *Children as witnesses to marital violence: A risk factor for lifelong problems among nationally representative sample of American men and women.* Paper presented at the Ross Roundtable on Children and Violence, Washington, DC.

Tarter, R. A., & Vanyukov, M. (1994). Alcoholism: A developmental disorder. *Journal of Consulting and Clinical Psychology, 62,* 1096–1107.

U.S. Bureau of the Census. (1994). *Income, poverty, and health insurance: 1993 supplemental tables.* Washington, DC: U.S. Department of Commerce.

U.S. Department of Health and Human Services, National Center on Child Abuse and Neglect. (1995). *Child maltreatment 1993: Reports from the states to the national center of child abuse and neglect.* Washington, DC: Government Printing Office.

Wagner, E. F., & Kassel, J. D. (1995). Substance use and abuse. In R. T. Ammerman & M. Hersen (Eds.), *Handbook of child behavior therapy* (pp. 367–388). New York: Wiley.

Weiss, B., & Weisz, J. R. (1990). The impact of methodological factors on child psychotherapy outcome research: A meta-analysis for researchers. *Journal of Abnormal Child Psychology, 18,* 639–670.

Weisz, J. R., Donenberg, G. R., Han, S. S., & Weiss, B. (1995). Bridging the gap between laboratory and clinic in child and adolescent psychotherapy. *Journal of Consulting Clinical Psychology, 63,* 688–701.

Weisz, J. R., & Weiss, B. (1989). Assessing the effects of clinic-based psychotherapy with children and adolescents. *Journal of Consulting and Clinical Psychology, 57,* 741–746.

Weisz, J. R., Weiss, B., Alicke, M. D., & Klotz, M. L. (1987). Effectiveness of psychotherapy with children and adolescents: A meta-analysis for clinicians. *Journal of Consulting Clinical Psychology, 55,* 542–549.

Wekerle, C., & Wolfe, D. A. (1993). Prevention of child physical abuse and neglect: Promising new directions. *Clinical Psychology Review, 13,* 501–540.

Wenger, B. L., Kaye, H. S., & LaPlante, M. P. (1996). Disabilities among children. *Disability Statistics Abstract,* No. 15. Washington, DC: National Institute on Disability and Rehabilitation Research.

Wolfe, D. A., Zak, L., Wilson, S., & Jaffe, P. (1986). Child witnesses to violence between parents: Critical issues in behavioral and social adjustment. *Journal of Abnormal Child Psychology, 14,* 95–104.

PART TWO

General Issues

CHAPTER 2

Children in Poverty

ROBERT H. BRADLEY and LEANNE WHITESIDE-MANSELL

When people encounter reports indicating that 22% of American children live in poverty, the first reaction is likely to be disbelief. How is it possible that so many poor children live in a country that, with a median family income of almost $40,000 per year, is one of the most affluent in the world? In 1992, six million children (26%) under the age of 6 officially lived in poverty. Such statistics are especially dismaying because the effects of living in poverty are severe and families move out of poverty only with great difficulty. The costs of poverty to the child, to the family, and to society at large are immense. The "safety net," which is supposed to protect children from the ravages of poverty, is stretched thin against such numbers, with each poverty program reaching only a fraction of those in poverty, and then—as a rule—for only a short time.

As alarming as the facts about poverty are for children in the United States, circumstances facing children in Third World countries are even more alarming. It is now estimated that over 1,000,000,000 children under the age of 15 live in poverty. Many of these children lack such basic necessities as adequate nutrition and clean water. They are often racked by disease, and about one-third will not survive until their fifth birthday (Lewis, 1992).

The purpose of this chapter is to examine what poverty means in the lives of children. Because poverty has been defined variously for research and policy analysis, and has been used interchangeably with employment status, socioeconomic status, and a number of other concepts indicative of economic well-being, it is first necessary to define poverty in a way that delineates its role in the lives of children. The process of defining poverty will lead directly to the ecological and psychological factors related to poverty, followed by a discussion of the impact of economic hardship and the mechanisms through which its negative impacts are achieved. The chapter closes with sections that briefly look at resilience and at interventions that may be efficacious in reducing both poverty and its consequences.

DEFINING POVERTY

It would be easier to understand economic hardship if there were a single clear definition for poverty. Knowing the various ways in which poverty is defined is important because each definition carries with it a different set of processes through which poverty may potentially affect the lives of children, a different set of outcomes for children living in poverty, and a different set of potential solutions to the hardships imposed by poverty. That said, two aspects of poverty seem to have remained consistent with historic understandings. At extreme levels, poverty is still a survival issue, and limitations in economic resources lead to hardships in the lives of the poor. Being poor means being at risk.

Poverty is most often defined with reference to standards established by the U.S. Bureau of the Census. These standards reflect only pretax cash income for the family, with poverty thresholds based on number of family members living in the household. These thresholds are adjusted annually in accordance with the Consumer Price Index. The standards reflect a definition of poverty the Social Security Administration developed in 1964 using an analysis of the cost of a nutritionally adequate food plan for a family of four done by the U.S. Department of Agriculture. It was determined that the poverty threshold should be established at three times the amount of the minimal cost of obtaining a nutritionally adequate family food plan, since families, on average, spent about one-third of their budget on food in the 1950s.

Although this definition of poverty is commonly employed in research and public policy analysis, it has numerous limitations. It no longer reflects the original conception of poverty as having too little income to meet a family's minimal daily living requirements because it has not been adjusted for the change in the proportion of total income families now spend on food. Families now spend only about one-sixth of their income on food rather than the one-third estimated in 1964 by the Department of Agriculture (Constance & Michael, 1995).

The census definition has other limitations as well. For example, no adjustments are made for actual differences in the cost of living from one locale to another. There are substantial differences in the costs of such basic items as food, housing, and transportation across geographic regions in the United States. Relatedly, circumstances of rural and urban life tend to be dramatically different, in terms of both costs for housing and basic commodities and resources available to assist with family life (alternative means of obtaining food, transportation costs, access to a network of kin, access to health care and social services, etc.). Neither are census-based poverty guidelines adjusted for noncash income such as food stamps or Medicaid, for family debt, for other family resources, or for any other contextual or personal circumstances related to a family's economic conditions. The current poverty thresholds do not take into account that at the lower end of the income scale, basic costs (e.g., for food, housing, and child care) consume a greater proportion of family income than is the case for middle-income families (Wilson, 1991). Finally, the pretax-based definition ignores the rising tax burden shared by lower income families.

Thresholds based on the census guidelines are often not good proxies for the actual level of material hardship reported by families (Huston, McLoyd, & Coll, 1994; Mayer & Jencks, 1989). This fact has long been recognized by the U.S. Department of Health and Human Services in setting poverty guidelines to be used to determine eligibility for various assistance programs. For example, eligibility for free lunch at school is often established at 185% of the poverty threshold because it is well known that many families with incomes above the poverty threshold still have times during the month when they have insufficient money to purchase enough food. According to Huston et al. (1994), poverty ". . . is a conglomerate of conditions and events that amount to a pervasive rather than a bounded stressor. Poor children and families are often exposed to poor health conditions, inadequate housing and homelessness, environmental toxins, and violent or unsupportive neighborhoods . . . poverty is not a unitary variable or distinct event" (p. 277). Many children whose family income to family size would not place them below the census thresholds for poverty still face the conglomerate of unfavorable circumstances related to insufficient income (e.g., living in a high-crime neighborhood, inadequate access to health care and social services, living with a single parent, frequent moves of residence, racism).

Most centrally, census definitions tend to underestimate the number of persons actually experiencing economic hardship. Using a newly proposed index of poverty that adjusts for many of the limitations of the census definition, the Panel on Poverty and Family Assistance (Constance & Michael, 1995) identified an additional 10 million people whose incomes are too low to take care of basic daily requirements. This proposed measure is a hybrid of the traditional *absolute* census definition and what is called a *relative* definition of poverty. A relative poverty threshold can be determined by an examination of income for a population. For example, a relative threshold might be set as one-third of the median income for a specific year. A definition based on cash income alone may lead one to think that by simply raising family income above some absolute poverty level, the difficulties associated with poverty will be resolved and the consequences of poverty ameliorated. The evidence suggests otherwise: There is no simple relationship between family income and children's development, except perhaps at the most extreme levels. The confluence of circumstances that pervade the lives of children in extreme poverty also tend to invade the lives of children whose families have incomes above the poverty threshold but below the median income for families in the United States. This evidence suggests that a relative definition of poverty may be more useful in identifying children at risk. Poverty is a continuum, with families whose incomes are up to 50% of the median income in the United States still subject to much of the hardship experienced by families whose incomes fall below the official absolute poverty threshold (Bane & Ellwood, 1989; Hernandez, 1993).

In effect, part of what economic hardship brings to a family is a feeling of being at risk and of being deprived. Obtaining enough income to reach the poverty threshold, by itself, may do little to relieve that sense of risk or the negative consequences such a feeling brings. Having enough income to reach the census-based poverty threshold does not even mean a family has enough money to meet such basic requirements as adequate health care, adequate transportation, adequate housing, or adequate education. It is an arbitrary standard that may not accurately convey a family's economic conditions; nor does it allow for an appreciation of a family's economic circumstances across time (i.e., the accumulating impact of persistent poverty).

A relative definition of poverty respects that individual reactions to one's level of income reflect the total context in which one lives. Being poor when all around you are poor and when living in a culture where material goods are given only moderate value means one thing. Being poor when many around you are not poor and when material possessions are highly valued means quite another. *The relation between economic hardship and psychological distress is contingent on the context in which economic hardship occurs.*

Even a family whose income allows it to meet basic survival needs may feel poor because the members see themselves as deprived, as unable to acquire what is accepted in society as basic needs. According to Galbraith (1958), individuals in such families may come to see themselves as degraded and as lacking worth. Correspondingly, they may come to view their communities as unresponsive, as places full of risks. In effect, members of families with incomes significantly below what is average for the society at large frequently experience psychological hardship that is a direct outgrowth of their inability to acquire resources they view as basic to life in their society.

Such negative attitudes associated with one's economic status become quite prevalent in a society with a highly monetarized economy, a highly materialistic set of values, and a disdain for certain subgroups within the society. The phenomenology of family economic life is only partly connected to the meeting of basic survival needs. It relates to the value one associates with certain goods and services. In a highly monetarized economy, a low-paying job may be seen as an affront to one's dignity, a service such as child care (because it commands little if any pay) to be of little worth. In the United States, fewer and fewer families are able to attain the lifestyle that has become the cultural standard, reinforced nightly via mass media: owning a home, taking vacations, sending one's children to college, and the like. As a consequence, more and more people feel poor, feel at risk, feel deprived with all the attendant negative consequences. Garbarino (1992) argues, "Any realistic conception of poverty must deal with the fact that human beings tend to evaluate their surroundings in relativistic terms" (p. 229). In effect, people judge their own circumstances in comparison to the circumstances of others and with reference to standards or ideals present in the culture. A definition of poverty tied strictly to cash income is not realistic because the feeling of hardship that accompanies low income is not limited to concerns about physical survival but includes concerns about worth, hope, efficacy, and a host of other factors tied to long-term well-being. These concerns, with their attendant negative consequences, impact not only the individuals experiencing them but reverberate to the community and to the broader society as well (e.g., criminality, attitudes toward employment where low wages are paid, attitudes about marriage and child rearing). The discrepancy between the cultural standard and what seems attainable is likely to be even greater for minorities and members of other out-groups in society (Hernandez, 1993; Spencer, 1993).

Another reason not to tie notions of poverty too closely to the census definition is that many of those just above the poverty threshold are subject to loss or diminishment of employment. Many of the families with economic stresses are employed but in marginal, low-paying jobs. These families are at constant risk of unemployment and are often unable to pay for child care (Phillips, 1995). They have limited access to health care and transportation (Harvey, 1991). These families are not in a position to make sound long-term decisions or to take advantage of the short-term opportunities. For example, they do not have the option to stock up on goods on sale because they do not have adequate cash reserves to afford such a purchase. In effect, families living in poverty are doubly disadvantaged. They do not have sufficient resources to meet life's needs, and because they lack some resources, poor families are unable to make best use of the resources they have. The stress of constant uncertainty and lack of control is psychologically debilitating. Men, especially, have much of their own sense of worth tied to employment that is sufficient to provide for the family (Garbarino, 1992).

A flexible definition of poverty tied to the notion of economic hardship and reflective of the broader family context is likely to be more useful in understanding the psychological processes that produce negative impacts in the lives of poor children, and in constructing effective interventions. It is also important to develop definitions that coincide with the particular purposes of scientific inquiry or policy.

The census definition is often used as a base to compute other indices of economic hardship. For example, eligibility for public programs is based on a multiple of the base threshold (e.g., 185% of the census poverty threshold). For research and data analysis purposes, a continuous ratio measure is favored. The "income-to-needs ratio" is calculated by dividing family income by its appropriate poverty threshold. An income-to-needs ratio of 1.0 indicates that a family is exactly at the poverty threshold. A ratio less than 1.0 indicates that a family is below the threshold; a ratio greater than 1.0 that a family is above poverty.

Socioeconomic Status and the Underclass

Understanding poverty and how it affects children's lives has been complicated because such poverty has been used interchangeably with other economic notions, most notably socioeconomic status (SES) and employment (or occupational) status. This practice contributes to confusion regarding the effects of low income per se.

In child development research, it has been more common to use some index of socioeconomic status than to use family income. Part of the reason is that it is often easier to obtain information about such factors as parental education, parental occupation, and area of residence than precise figures on household income. Researchers also posit that SES indices capture more of the contextual influences on children's health and development than income alone. Families with near equal incomes, but different levels of parental education, tend to provide different patterns of caregiving and different living environments for their children. The literature on the relationship between poverty and development has been somewhat difficult to interpret not only because SES measures have often been used as proxies for poverty but because different SES measures have been used in different studies. There is considerable debate on which index provides the most accurate appraisal of family living conditions (see Entwisle & Astone, 1994; Hauser, 1994, for a discussion of some of the issues). These arguments underscore two facts: (a) There is a complex relationship between proxies used to estimate family resources and child development; and (b) different means of estimating those resources may lead to different findings and recommendations about solutions. When investigating the impact of family poverty on children, the distinction between SES and poverty may be very important. The co-occurrence of an undereducated mother or a father employed in an occupation of low status adds to, but does not replace, the impact of lack of adequate economic resources.

Poverty has also been used interchangeably with the notion of an underclass (Bane & Ellwood, 1989). This notion, however, connotes the kinds of conditions prevalent in urban ghettos, and particularly conditions prevalent in families who have been impoverished for more than a single generation. Most poor families do not live in ghettos and most poverty is not persistent. In addition, most individuals who live in persistent poverty are not the stereotypes portrayed in the media (e.g., criminals, drug abusers, the mentally ill). They are much more likely to be elderly, disabled, or simply reside in a rural area (Corcoran, Duncan, Gurin, & Gurin, 1985). Attributing problems of the underclass to all children who live in poverty fails to disentangle issues of persistence and the concentration of poverty in one's area of residence from low income per se.

Duration of Poverty

The seriousness of the physical and psychological hardships plaguing low-income families depends on how long poverty lasts. The constant drain on a family in persistent poverty causes a depletion in economic, psychological, and physical resources. There are no financial savings to draw on that to provide a psychological buffer against the threat of additional loss of income. Constant stress and anxiety weaken the individual's ability to cope. The network of social support becomes exhausted from the continuous demands for help. The chronic stress and coping necessary to deal with ongoing problems associated with the lack of financial resources carry over into the interactions among family members. The capacity of poor parents to be supportive, sensitive, and involved with their children is diminished (McAdoo, 1988). At the other extreme are families that experience periodic short-term financial shortfalls. These families may not actually fall below the poverty threshold when income over the entire year is taken into account, even though there may be significant need during that part of the year when income is reduced. Many low-income families live in constant fear of losing their jobs; thus, they suffer from the stress associated with knowing there is no income to buffer them from the imminent fall into poverty.

Families that live in persistent poverty are demographically distinct from families that live in more transitory poverty (McLoyd, 1990; U.S. Bureau of the Census, 1992). African-American children are more likely to experience persistent poverty (McLoyd, 1990) and to reside in economically depressed neighborhoods. More African-American families also live near the borderline of poverty than do European American families. So, circumstances that result in income loss more frequently cause African-American families to fall below the poverty line. This includes medical expenses because many families just above the cut-point for poverty lack money to purchase health insurance and do not have access to adequate medical care (Bradley & Kelleher, 1992).

Not only are the outcomes for the children living in persistent poverty expected to differ from those of children in more transitory poverty, but the processes are also thought to differ. The hardships associated with transitory poverty include gaps in eligibility due to fluctuations in income. For example, 42.9% of families below the poverty threshold at least 2 months during 1990–1991 received public assistance at least once during that time compared with 78.9% of families in poverty every month of the 2 years. Families in persistent poverty have a constricted range of options available to them. They are trapped in neighborhoods that are unsafe for their children. These families experience more conflict and suffer psychological distress associated with long-term stress.

Identifying children in persistent poverty is complicated because family composition often changes, and the number of persons residing in the household at any given time point determines whether a child is designated as living in poverty. What constitutes persistent also depends on the way persistence is operationalized. The most frequently used definition of persistent poverty gives substantial weight to the instability of the family's income. Persistent poverty, by this "instability" definition, only requires that a family's annual income be below the poverty cutoff *most* of the time (e.g., at least 4 of 6 years). By this definition, families that move in and out of poverty are considered to be living in persistent poverty if they are below the designated level for enough years, even though the family's income during the other years may be substantially above the poverty threshold. Such circumstances are not rare when family members are employed in "boom and bust" occupations, and occupations characterized by cyclical trends. By contrast, persistence is sometimes equated with duration of poverty. Such a definition requires that a family's annual income fall below some poverty cutoff for some substantial number of *consecutive* years (or consecutive months). The problem with both definitions is that they are dependent on minor fluctuations in income, particularly around the poverty threshold. A family may not be regarded as being in persistent poverty if it has $1,000 in extra income one year or if a family member moves out of the household for a year.

An index of persistent poverty that is less sensitive to a poverty line cut and to the fluctuations in income is based on the income-to-needs ratio (Duncan & Rodgers, 1991). A ratio is formed as the family's aggregate income over some specified period of years divided by the family's aggregate poverty threshold for the same years. The result is a continuous measure, similar to the annual ratio, with 1.0 reflecting the poverty line. Such a measure is likely to be a more reliable indicator of the general level of economic hardship faced by a family over that period.

Summary

The most useful method of identifying families in poverty depends on the researcher's purpose. For example, to evaluate lack of material resources on development of children, the best measure of poverty may be a conservative absolute threshold, below which it would be impossible to purchase the necessary shelter, food, and clothing. However, to evaluate the impact of economic hardship and its associated psychological, social, and physical deprivation, a more sensitive measure of poverty is probably better. The Panel on Poverty and Family Assistance (Constance & Michael, 1995) proposed a revision of the official U.S. census definition to include not only food but clothing and shelter as essential family needs. The measure reflects differences in family types and geographic regions. The measure would also be revised yearly to adjust for changes in spending patterns of the population. The proposed measure has been criticized by Cogan (1995) because it fundamentally changes the official measure of poverty from an *absolute* standard to a *relative* standard. When the current census definition was compared with the proposed index, different families were identified as living in poverty. In one comparison, 4.2 million people were no longer classified as being in poverty, whereas 13.3 million others were moved into poverty. The greatest effect was to reduce the number of families receiving welfare from poverty status and to increase the number of working families designated as living in poverty.

Although this new approach to measuring poverty appears to more accurately identify families experiencing true economic hardship, it is complicated and time consuming to collect the data necessary to evaluate the needs of individual families. In addition, because the proposed measure includes as income assistance from government programs, the needs standards for these programs would require some adjustment to utilize this new measure. For this reason, it may not be the best method for determining program eligibility.

Researchers and policy makers have not reached consensus on the best method to measure long-term poverty. Be that as it may, there is considerable agreement that low income places children at risk. Further research needs to be carried out to determine how best to measure persistent poverty.

The Effects of Poverty on Health and Development

From before they are born, the children of poverty are at higher risk for a host of developmental problems. They are far more likely to be born prematurely and of low birth weight due to inadequate prenatal care and characteristics of the mother's lifestyle. They are also likely to be exposed to toxic substances in utero that can damage their rapidly growing nervous systems with lifelong consequences. Many poor children begin life biologically insulted (e.g., interuterine growth retardation, fetal alcohol syndrome, AIDS) and vulnerable. Relatedly, they have higher rates of childhood morbidity and mortality, including from continued exposure to parental smoking (Klerman, 1991) and environmental teratogens such as lead (Tesman & Hills, 1994). Throughout childhood, poor children are also more likely to confront other risks, such as maltreatment and crime (Zuravin, 1989).

Poverty exposes children to an array of potentially harmful substances, experiences, and conditions (National Research Council, 1993). This includes direct exposure to violence in the family (Garbarino, 1992; Gelles, 1992). Moreover, stresses and injuries produced by those circumstances leave children more vulnerable to subsequent exposures than is the case for children living in affluent circumstances (Parker, Greer, & Zuckerman, 1988). In a study of poor children who were also born low birthweight, the children were assessed at age 3 years in four domains of function: intellectual, behavioral, growth, and health (Bradley et al., 1994a). In each domain, cut-points were established and used to identify children as exhibiting a developmental problem. Of the 223 children born low birthweight and who lived in chronic poverty, only 26 escaped having a developmental problem in at least one of the four domains. Children of poverty are often born at multiple risk, and they continue to be exposed to conditions that pose additional risks so long as they remain in poverty.

There is substantial evidence that poor children more often manifest symptoms of psychiatric disturbance and maladaptive social functioning (Baldwin, Baldwin, & Cole, 1990; Bolger, Patterson, Thompson, & Kupersmidt, 1995; McLeod & Shanahan, 1993; Moore, Morrison, Zaslow, & Glei, 1994; Patterson, DeBaryshe, & Ramsey, 1989; Sameroff, Seifer, Zax, & Barocas, 1987; Takeuchi, Williams, & Adair, 1991). Economic hardship contributes to a wide variety of social and emotional problems, from internalizing problems such as depression to externalizing problems such as delinquent behavior and teenage pregnancy (Patterson et al., 1989; Sum & Fogg, 1991). However, strength of the relationship between economic hardship and mental disorders varies as a function of type of disorder. The relationship is strongest and most consistent with schizophrenia and personality disorders, reasonably consistent with mild depression, and inconsistent with neuroses and affective disorders (Ortega & Corzine, 1990). In a study of 1,733 four- to eight-year-old children drawn from the National Longitudinal Study of Youth, McLeod and Shanahan (1993) found that living in poverty was associated with both internalizing and externalizing symptoms. Takeuchik et al., (1991) observed that depressive symptoms, impulsive behavior, and antisocial behavior were more common in 7- to 11-year-old children from the National Survey of Children if those children spent some time living in poverty over the 5 years covered by the Survey. Lempers, Clark-Lempers, and Simons (1989) also found that in families where parents described themselves as suffering economic hardship adolescents exhibited more depression and loneliness. They also exhibited more drug use and delinquent behavior. Not surprisingly, the poor have a lower level of psychological well-being than more affluent individuals (Dohrenwend & Dohrenwend, 1974).

Poor children suffer disproportionately from nearly all diseases and have higher rates of injury and mortality than more affluent children (Durkin, Davidson, Kuhn, O'Connor, & Barlow, 1994; Haan, Kaplan, & Syme, 1989; Hughes & Simpson, 1995;

Klerman, 1991; Rosenbaum, 1992; Syme & Berkmann, 1976). For example, poor children are twice as likely to receive accidental injuries and 4.5 times as likely to be the victim of an intentional assault (Durkin et al., 1994; U.S. Department of Health & Human Services, 1991). Compared with children who are not poor, frequency of asthma and bacterial meningitis are twice as high, rheumatic fever more than twice as high, and lead poisoning three times as high (Wilson, 1993).

Perhaps of greater importance, poor children's health problems are often more severe. Preterm and low birth weight poor children are far more likely to suffer health and developmental consequences than their more affluent counterparts (Parker et al., 1988). Children from low-income families are two to three times as likely to suffer complications from appendicitis and bacterial meningitis. They are also twice as likely to have impaired vision and iron deficiency anemia (Starfield, 1989, 1992; Wilson, 1993). Poor children are more likely to die from injuries, infections, and other problems at every age than children who are not poor; and the average length of stay for poor children in acute care hospitals (as a measure of severity of illness) is longer than the average stay of nonpoor children (Bradley & Kelleher, 1992). House fires, motor vehicle injuries, and homicides are all higher for children living in poverty (Santer & Stocking, 1991; Wise & Meyers, 1988).

In the National Health and Nutrition Examination Surveys (NHANES), poor children were found to be shorter, lighter, and had smaller skinfold thickness; factors presumably related to less nutritious diets (Kotch & Shackelford, 1989). Information from the NHANES I and NHANES II studies indicated that poor children have greater rates of impaired hemoglobin and hematocrit levels. In a review of nutrition in low-income children, Kotch and Shackleford (1989) concluded that poor children consume less calories than more affluent children and poor children more often suffer from nutritional deficiencies. Cross-sectional studies have shown that impoverished children are more likely than affluent children to suffer from health problems such as prematurity, intrauterine growth retardation, poor vision, anemia, lead poisoning, and injuries that affect their physical functioning (Starfield, 1982). They are also more likely to experience morbidities that affect their mental health and social functioning (Danziger & Stern, 1990). Economic factors are so strongly implicated in the health status of children and adolescents that Birt Harvey (1991), in his presidential address to the American Academy of Pediatrics said, "Child health is a socioeconomic problem with health consequences."

For over 50 years, findings on the relationship between income and academic competence has accumulated. Relatedly, a large literature has accumulated on the relationship between poverty and intelligence. By the early 1960s, sufficient data had accumulated on this relationship for Head Start to become a centerpiece of federal legislation aimed at countering the negative effects of poverty on children's school achievement. In the intervening years, data have continued to mount linking poverty with lower levels of school achievement and intelligence test scores (Alexander & Entwisle, 1988; Bloom, 1964; Escalona, 1982; Pianta, Egeland, & Sroufe, 1990; Walberg & Marjoribanks, 1976). In an analysis of data from the Infant Health and Development study, Duncan, Brooks-Gunn, and Klebanov (1994) found that family income-to-needs ratio was strongly related to 5-year IQ. In their study, persistent poverty was twice as important as transient poverty in predicting IQ. Hess, Holloway, Price, and Dickson (1982) found that family occupational status was associated with letter recognition and vocabulary for preschool-age children. Kennedy, Van de Riet, and White (1963) reported results from a stratified random sample of 1,800 first-through sixth-grade black children selected to represent the black population of south-eastern United States. The mean IQ of the highest SES group was 25 points higher than the mean IQ of the lowest SES group.

There is substantial evidence that poverty is associated with less optimal outcomes in every area of functioning. Many of the studies reviewed focus on only a single outcome. Or, when multiple outcomes are at issue, data are only examined at the group level, with no attention to whether individual children experience multiple bad outcomes in conjunction with living in poverty. This is true even though it is well known that certain types of undesirable outcomes (teenage pregnancy, criminality, school failure) often occur in concert with other types of undesirable outcomes. In an analysis of data from the Infant Health and Development study, 40% of children born prematurely who lived in chronic poverty showed deficiencies in at least two areas of functioning (Bradley et al., 1994a).

Poverty and Development—A Complex Relationship

Most studies on the effects of poverty leave undeterminable the precise relationship between economic hardship and development (Phillips & Bridgman, 1995). Most studies only measure income at one point in time. Thus, estimates of the relationship leave unclear whether the influence of poverty is contemporaneous, cumulative, lagged, or some combination. Moreover, when a one-time measure of poverty is used, the relationship between economic hardship and poor development is often underestimated because "there is substantial movement across the poverty line from year to year" (Duncan & Rodgers, 1991, p. 538). Miller and Korenman (1994) found that prevalence of stunting (low height-for-age) and wasting (low weight-for-height) were higher for children living in persistent poverty. Differentials in nutritional status between poor and nonpoor children were larger for long-term poverty than for current-year poverty.

Duncan, Brooks-Gunn, and Klebanov (1994) examined the timing and duration of poverty for children from the Infant Health and Development Program. They had measures of family income when children were 12, 24, 36, and 48 months of age. They determined that both persistent and transitory poverty were useful in predicting IQ and behavior problems but that persistence was the more powerful predictor. The timing of poverty during this early period of life did not matter. Using data from the National Longitudinal Study of Youth, McLeod and Shanahan (1993) found that persistent poverty predicted internalizing symptoms of 4- to 8-year-old children; but current poverty status predicted externalizing symptoms. Using a slightly older group of children from the Charlotte Longitudinal Study (7 to 14 years), Bolger et al. (1995) found that children who experienced persistent economic hardship were more likely to have difficulties in peer relations, show conduct problems at school, and report low self-esteem than children who did not experience economic hardship. Children whose families experienced intermittent hardship fell in between. Results on the impact of persistent versus current poverty on maladaptive behavior are mixed, but the problem of explicating the relationship may well hinge on how persistent poverty is operationalized (Takeuchi et al., 1991).

The effects of poverty are best understood if one considers both family level poverty and neighborhood level poverty (Durkin et al., 1994; Mayer & Jencks, 1989). Although poor families are far more likely than affluent families to live in impoverished surroundings, the relative impact of family poverty on children's development is a function of the degree of saturation of poor people in the neighborhood. Brooks-Gunn, Duncan, Klebanov, and Sealand (1993) found that the effects of neighborhood income on childhood IQ were significant beyond what was contributed by family poverty. Relatedly, Zuravin (1989) shows evidence that the likelihood of maltreatment is greater in poor families living in poor neighborhoods compared with poor families living in more affluent neighborhoods. Overall, deteriorating neighborhoods, with a high concentration of poverty, welfare dependency, and crime create a "context for disengagement and violence" (Gelles, 1992; Goldstein, 1990).

The effects of poverty on well-being also do not seem constant across geographic settings. In a comparison of urban and rural poverty, Amato and Zuo (1992) found that rural poor had significantly lower levels of perceived health than did urban poor. The relationship was even more complex when differences in gender, race, and family status were considered. Poor African-Americans from rural areas reported higher levels of happiness, whereas poor whites in urban areas reported higher levels of happiness. African-American males were more likely to be depressed in urban than rural areas, whereas other males were more likely to be depressed in rural than urban areas. Single men without children in rural areas showed high levels of depression, whereas married women without children in urban areas showed low levels of depression.

In their review of studies linking socioeconomic status and mental disorders, Ortega and Corzine (1990) identify a number of other factors that complicate researchers' understanding of the relationship between poverty and development. For example, the two leading theories about the relationship between SES and mental disorders (i.e., social causation, and social selection/drift) imply opposite causation. The social causation explanation holds that mental disorder results from poverty and its cofactors; whereas the social selection explanation holds that those with mental disorder gradually drift into lower SES strata. Data taken from the Panel Study of Income Dynamics indicates that the low motivation to achieve and limited view of personal efficacy that frequently characterize poor adults are not so much the cause of poverty as the result of economic hardship (Corcoran et al., 1985). Lempers et al. (1989) examined the effects of a downturn in the agricultural economy on farm families in the Midwest. They found that economic hardship was associated with reduced parental nurturance and increased use of negative parental discipline. Adolescents in these families showed increased depression, loneliness, and juvenile delinquency. This study was particularly interesting in that the economic downturn often affected many families in the same community; thus, the associations may partially represent an *aggregation effect* (i.e., the impact may have been greater than would have occurred had only a single farm family in the community been hit by economic hardship). Research on more serious mental disorders provides some support for both the social causation and the social selection hypotheses—somewhat more for the drift hypothesis (Ortega & Corzine, 1990). Just as importantly, however, there is evidence that the poor are more likely to be defined as mentally ill even when they manifest the same level of symptomatology as do more affluent individuals; and they are perceived as exhibiting a greater level of impairment. De facto, there is bias in both labeling and treatment of persons from the lower social classes.

Modeling the Effects of Poverty

The impact of poverty (i.e., lack of access to money, material goods, and services that money can buy) on children's health and development is difficult to gauge because poverty so frequently co-occurs with other conditions (e.g., single parenthood, minority status, residence in a poor, crime-ridden neighborhood, exposure to teratogens) associated with poor developmental outcomes. These co-occurring conditions tend to have their own negative effect on development; and they operate with poverty to further limit normal development. A good example is lead exposure. Lead exposure is more common in poor children; and several studies have shown that blood lead level has a particularly negative impact on cognitive and motor abilities in low-income children (Harvey, Hamlin, Kumar, & Delves, 1984; Tesman & Hills, 1994; Winneke & Kramer, 1984). A disproportionate number of poor children are also born to unmarried teenage mothers (Klerman, 1991). Research on children born to such mothers shows that the children perform less well on cognitive and social-emotional measures than their peers (Furstenberg, Brooks-Gunn, & Morgan, 1987). Poor adolescent mothers are also more likely to live in deteriorating, crime-ridden neighborhoods, which contributes to low-quality parenting and developmental problems (Luster, Perlstadt, McKinney, & Sims, 1995). Research on delinquency and criminal behavior points to the problem of having only a single parent (Steinberg, 1987). Cochran, Larner, Riley, Gunnarsson, and Henderson (1990) also found that poor families have smaller social networks, less organizational involvement, and less frequent contact with family and friends. Mother's lack of social support was associated with teacher ratings of externalizing behavior for children in primary grades (Dodge, Pettit, & Bates, 1994). Perhaps most importantly, family income plays a major role in determining where children live and the institutions they have access to; and these conditions exert a powerful influence on both child and family (National Research Council, 1993).

The impact of these other factors (collectively referred to as poverty cofactors) is difficult to disentangle from poverty because they are naturally confounded. As the following examples show, sometimes poverty contributes to the likelihood that one of its co-factors will happen; sometimes co-factors will increase the likelihood of living in poverty:

- Being of minority status has historically meant having less access to educational and employment opportunities; the result is increased likelihood of low income.
- Chronic poverty decreases the likelihood of getting married and staying married, and single parents have more difficulty obtaining sufficient economic resources and using them efficiently.
- The stresses of economic hardship often lead to depression, with chronic depression decreasing the likelihood of stable employment and exploitation of available resources.

Poverty cofactors often exacerbate the risks imposed by economic hardship. In some instances (e.g., low education, parental mental illness), they may also account for the inability of adult family members to earn sufficient income to avoid poverty. They often make it more difficult to escape from poverty.

The relationship between poverty, its cofactors, and children's development is often quite complex, and is variable across individuals. For a particular outcome, the driving force may be poverty, may be a specific poverty cofactor, may be a combination, or may be a third variable that influences all three (e.g., family conflict). A good example is early motherhood. Conditions associated with poverty in childhood and adolescence, such as devastated, crime-ridden neighborhoods, inadequate health care and education, school and legal problems, and growing up in a female-headed household, contribute to the likelihood of early motherhood (Chase-Lansdale, 1993). Young mothers are less likely to get married or have stable employment, and they are more likely to experience acrimonious relationships with family members and spouses. There is evidence that adolescent mothers are more restrictive with their children, manifest fewer positive interactions, provide less stimulation and nurturance, and are more inclined to maltreat them. Adolescent mothers also model harsh behavior and limited problem-solving skills (Bolton & Belsky, 1986; Cichetti & Carlson, 1989; Grynch & Fincham, 1990; Luster & Middelstadt, 1993; Simmons, Lorenz, Conger, & Wu, 1992). These parental behaviors, in turn, lead to fear, distress, poor health, and psychological maladjustment on the part of the children (Emery, 1982; Gottman & Katz, 1989). The impact of such mediating factors was observed on psychomotor functioning in 2- to 5-year-old children from Uruguay (Bernardi et al., 1992).

Across the life span, the importance of particular poverty cofactors can change (Moen, Elder, & Luscher, 1995). A good example is the likely impact of deteriorated neighborhoods on children's attitudes and behavior. For preschoolers, such neighborhoods may mean a lack of organized, stimulating resources and recreational opportunities; for adolescents, such neighborhoods may mean frequent contacts with socially maladjusted peers. Wilson (1995) argues, "In neighborhoods with a paucity of regularly employed families, the chances of children interacting on a sustained basis with people who are employed or with families that have a steady breadwinner are slim. The net effect is that the youths are more likey to see joblessness as normative and perceive a weak relationship between schooling and postschool employment" (p. 538).

As a rule, research designs and analytic strategies used in poverty research do not adequately capture the complexity of the relationships between poverty, poverty cofactors, and children's development (e.g., cross-sectional data analyzed using simple linear models). What seems clear is that the larger number of such cofactors (i.e., risks) present, the worse the likely outcome for the child (Sameroff, Seifer, Baldwin, & Baldwin, 1993). Sameroff and his colleagues found, "It was the number of risk factors not the kind of risk factor that was the determining influence" (p. 81). Interpreting the research is made more difficult because of the imprecise use of technical terms such as "interact with," "mediate," and "moderator." The verb *interact* is used to denote both simple summative relationships involving poverty and its cofactors and true statistical interactions between poverty and its cofactors, even though only the latter use is appropriate. If being poor and being of minority status each contributes independently to nonoptimal development (a summative relationship), that is one thing. If being poor is a whole lot more devastating if you are of minority status than of majority status (an interactive relationship), that is quite another.

Baron and Kenny (1986) offer a particularly useful discussion of the distinction between mediators and moderators and of the analytic procedures required to verify moderating and mediating processes. Specifically, a variable (Variable b) can be said to moderate the effects of poverty on development (i.e., act as a moderator variable), if the effects of poverty (Variable a) on the target outcome (Variable c) is different at different levels of the moderator. To declare that Variable b acts as a moderator variable for Variable a with respect to Variable c requires a statistical interaction between Variable a and Variable b with respect to Variable c. A mediator variable (Variable y) is one that is influenced by poverty (Variable x) and that in turn influences the target outcome variable (Variable z). Establishing that Variable y mediates the relationship between Variable x and Variable z is somewhat complicated. It is necessary to show that relationships exist between Variable x and Variable y, Variable y and Variable z, and Variable x and Variable z. It is then necessary to show that part of the relationship between Variable x and Variable z is directed through Variable y. Baron and Kenny (1986) describe the basic statistical procedures needed to verify mediation. For more complicated mediational processes, structural equation modeling can be useful.

The impact of poverty is not constant; it is moderated by other factors affecting family life. For example, the negative consequences of poverty on adaptive social behavior may be moderated by access to a strong social support network, a cohesive two-parent unit, residence in a stable neighborhood where most other families are not poor, and the like. The research on divorce suggests that, for girls, being raised by a step-father increases the likelihood of antisocial behavior (Kulka & Weingartner, 1979). Another example is that the link between poverty and abusive violence depends on the ages of the child, and caregiver, and whether there are one or two adult parents (Gelles, 1992). These other conditions help to determine the effects of poverty.

To understand the link between poverty and poor development, it is important to consider three other issues. First, it is important to distinguish between environmental risk factors and environmental risk mechanisms. As Rutter, Champion, Quinton, Maugan, and Pickles (1995) argue, "The origins of a risk factor and the mode of operation of the risk mechanism have no necessary connection with one another" (p. 64). Second, not everyone who is poor is exposed to the same number of risk factors. The recent work in behavioral genetics suggests that genes may play a role in determining the environments that people experience (Plomin, 1994). Third, many of the analyses aimed at clarifying the relationship between poverty, its cofactors, and development do not examine the relationships using statistical models consistent with a view of human beings as dynamic, integrated organisms. For the most part, researchers have used some type of linear regression procedure that dissects the variance in a dependent (developmental) variable into components that are attributable to some set of behavioral, biological, and environmental variables whose contributions to the prediction of the developmental outcome are treated statistically as independent of other variables in the model—ignoring the role of moderation and mediation. Magnusson (1995) argues that such linear, summative analyses betray a misconception about the process of development. He states "that the total process cannot be understood by studying one aspect (variable) after the other in isolation from the other, simultaneously operating elements" (p. 26).

The most accepted perspective on development views the process as dynamic and systemic. All the mental, behavioral, biological, and environmental factors operating to influence development, do so through a process of reciprocal interactions. They do not operate as independent "causes." Thus, they may not be fully and accurately modeled using linear statistical procedures such as regression analysis where the effect of poverty is examined while controlling for other variables in the model. A good example of linear models that produce misleading results can be found in the work of Durkin and her colleagues (1994). They found that a low-income neighborhood was a slightly more important risk factor for unintentional injuries than assault injuries using linear regression analysis. When they used rate ratio estimation, however, they found that a low-income neighborhood was a far more significant factor in assault injuries than unintentional injuries, perhaps due to a threshold effect. Somewhat more holistic treatments of the data, such as structural equation modeling and partial-least squares, may more accurately capture the relationships of poverty variables and outcomes.

Methods that look at natural co-occurences of variables within individuals such as cluster analysis and log-linear analysis may help identify the way that poverty, poverty cofactors, and other personal and contextual factors operate in combination to influence development. For example, findings from a cluster analysis of young parents identified five types of parenting patterns (Whiteside-Mansell, Pope, & Bradley, 1996). The strongest discriminator among the five patterns was maternal intelligence. Poverty status did not appear the same for all groups either. One group of mothers showed an improvement in parenting from the time their children were infants to the time these children were toddlers, even though more of the mothers were living in poverty during the toddler period than during the infancy period. These young mothers differed from other mothers living in poverty in that they also moved into independent living arrangements by the time their children were toddlers, thereby actually increasing their likelihood of living in poverty.

Mediating Processes

Poverty and its cofactors degrade development through a variety of intervening mechanisms. For example, poor families are more often headed by a single adult caregiver, have adult members who are mentally ill or who have less education, have access to smaller network of social support, and are of minority status (Baldwin & Cain, 1981; Belle, 1990; Duncan & Rodgers, 1987). These cofactors, taken as a whole, mean that poor families often have less personal (psychological) resources to handle the needs of children, have less access to external material and emotional resources to assist with daily living and the stresses imposed by poverty, and may be subject to victimization by the larger society. These mediating conditions are the proximal "causes" of poor health and development. One good example is the process of mediation linking poverty and malaptive behavior for children of adolescent mothers described earlier (Chase-Lansdale, 1993). Neglect, understimulation, and harsh treatment by adolescent mothers, together with intraparental conflict and poor use of community resources, lead to poor health and maladjustment on the part of the children.

Families living in poverty experience more threatening and uncontrollable life events. Poor women, for example, are disproportionately exposed to crime and violence, incarceration of husbands, illness and death of children, and inadequate housing (Belle, 1990). Such chronic strains lead to stress and frustration (Kessler, 1979). Poverty and conflict over economic resources are associated with marital dissolution. In general, adults living in poverty experience increased stress attempting to deal with external demands as well as crises within their own family (spousal abuse, children who are noncompliant or present problems). Economic hardship not only co-occurs with exposure to such negative events but decreases the likelihood that families can move away from areas where such conditions, (e.g., crime and violence) are prevalent. Persistent poverty also tends to divorce families from support networks. When poverty persists, families are likely to gradually deplete the limited resources they can get from networks. They do this at the same time that their needs for the resources from social networks increase.

Stress is frequently cited as a mediator between economic hardship and poor health and development. Families living in poverty are more often exposed to stressful life events and the chronic strains associated with economic hardship (e.g., frustrated aspirations, family conflicts arising from inadequate resources, and job dissatisfaction). These experiences tend to lower self-esteem and diminish one's sense of control over daily life (Amato & Zuo, 1992; Pearlin, Menaghan, Lieberman, & Mullan, 1981). The stress associated with poverty frequently leads to depression (Belle, 1990). Economic hardship may also limit a parent's ability to engage in health-promoting activities (National Center for Children in Poverty, 1990). Lempers et al. (1989) found that economic hardship had both direct and indirect effect on adolescent distress. Poverty was associated with less nurturance on the part of parents and inconsistent, rejection-oriented discipline. For both boys and girls, these parental behaviors were associated with greater depression and loneliness; inconsistent discipline was also implicated in drug use. One of the more interesting findings of this study is that poverty had both a direct effect on adjustment and an indirect effect, through parenting, on child adjustment reactions

Ross and Huber (1985) have shown that the link between stress and depression is mediated by gender-based role obligations in the family (Belle, 1990). For men, it is the inability to provide for the financial needs of the family. Wolf (1987) observed that for low-income mothers negative role identifications, such as "bad mother," "bad provider," or "poor spouse" precipitated depression. For both men and women, the stress associated with chronic poverty results in a higher rate of divorce (Cherlin, 1979). The stress from economic hardship reduces parents' ability to draw effectively on their support networks (social or institutional) and makes it more difficult for them to extricate themselves from bad relationships. This, in turn, reduces the likelihood of effective parenting (McLoyd, 1990).

Although actual stress seems to be a likely mediator of the link between poverty and poor development, what is not yet clear is how much the exposure to stressful circumstances, per se, contributes to maladaptive functioning (the *stress exposure hypothesis*) (Ortega & Corzine, 1990). Ability to cope with stress and to deal with it resourcefully may well mediate the relationship and account for more of the variance in maladaptive outcomes than exposure itself (the *coping hypothesis*). A sense of fatalism and perceived inability to control life's circumstances engenders more passive coping strategies in the poor, including taking less advantage of available community resources (health, social service, education). Stress related to economic hardship also leads to conflicts between parents. Young children observing parental discord often retreat into isolation. Adolescents may seek the company of peers, too often delinquent peers, the result being behavioral problems and even illegal activities (Takeuchi et al., 1991). These actions (or lack of them) may be the more direct influences on poor adaptive functioning.

Parenting is one of the most consistently cited mediating processes. There are SES-associated differences in parental expectations for children; middle-class parents tend to have higher expectations for children's mastery of developmental tasks and school-related skills (Hoff-Ginsberg & Tardif, 1995). There also are SES-related differences in what parents tend to value as goals for their children, with lower SES families valuing conformity more and higher SES families valuing self-direction more (Kohn, 1969). These differences in ideas and values result in different styles of parenting. Higher SES parents tend to be more egalitarian and accepting, lower SES parents more authoritarian and punitive (Gecas, 1979; Hoffman, 1963). Moore and her colleagues (1994) found that children who never experienced poverty were 5.3 times more likely to live in homes characterized by warmth and stimulation. In their review of research on socioeconomic status and parenting, Hoff-Ginsberg and Tardif (1995) drew three conclusions regarding parenting behavior:

> Finding 1: In interacting with their young children, lower SES mothers are more controlling, restrictive, and disapproving than higher SES mothers. . . . Finding 2: There are more SES-associated differences on language measures of (mother-child) interaction than on nonverbal measures. . . . Finding 3: The nature of the SES-associated language differences is that higher SES mothers talk more, provide more object labels, sustain conversational topics longer, respond more contingently to their children's speech, and elicit more talk from their children than lower SES mothers. (pp. 175–177)

Research shows that such differences are associated with both cognitive and social development, including coping skills (Bradley & Caldwell, 1995). There are also SES-differences in how parents structure and monitor children's experiences. Bronfenbrenner and Crouter (1983) concluded that mothers can "encourage and shape the child's psychological growth by structuring the settings the child experiences so as to evoke certain kinds of activities and discourage others" (p. 379). The value of parents in structuring their children's learning experiences is becoming well documented (Feuerstein & Feuerstein, 1991). So is the value of monitoring, in that research shows monitoring to be related to injury prevention (Peterson, Ewigman, & Kivlahan, 1993), antisocial behavior (Brown, Mounts, Lamborn, & Steinberg, 1993; Patterson et al., 1989), and school achievement (Dornbusch, Ritter, Leiderman, Roberts, & Fraleigh, 1987).

Poverty is connected to a web of interrelated conditions and processes that negatively affect well-being. Research indicates that economic hardship leads to poor developmental outcomes in four basic ways: (a) less access to material resources and social services; (b) increased likelihood of encountering other adverse conditions; (c) depletion of psychological resources; and (d) dissolution of connections with other supportive agents (internal and external). There remains a need for substantially more research on alternative explanations for the link between economic hardship and poor development. Research to date provides only modest support for the stress exposure hypothesis, somewhat more for the coping hypothesis. However, in the case of mental disorders, the *biological vulnerability hypothesis* may even prove more satisfactory (Laucht, Esser, & Schmidt, 1993; Ortega & Corzine, 1990). Biological vulnerabilty may contribute strongly to other developmental problems as well (e.g., growth retardation) (Kelleher et al., 1993).

Delineating the role of poverty and its cofactors becomes important because each cofactor may be presumed to operate in a different way to affect health and development. Each is connected with a specific set of more proximal processes (i.e., actions and conditions) that determine what a child directly experiences and how a child interprets those experiences. Some cofactors (e.g., inadequate social support) also determine what adult family members experience, and, in turn, how they behave toward their children, toward each other, and toward other persons and institutions (Pascoe, Loda, Jeffries, & Earp, 1981). Duncan, Brooks-Gunn, and Klebanov (1994) found that both being in poverty and having a female head of household contributed to the likelihood of behavior problems in 5-year-olds. In the same group of 5-year-olds, having a female head of household did not contribute to the prediction of IQ, whereas poverty status did. Brooks-Gunn et al. (1993), in an analysis of the PSID data, found family income effects on out-of-wedlock births and dropping out of high school for 20-year-olds, even after controlling for maternal education, female head of household, and minority status. For out-of-wedlock births, mother's education and minority status also contributed. For dropping out of high school, mother's education and female head of household also contributed. The precise set of intervening mechanisms is not clear from any of these studies, but the results suggest a variety of different more proximal influences on development.

Social support can moderate the effects of poverty on children's development (Zuravin, 1989). For purposes of illustrating how the negative consequences of economic hardship may be mediated, consider how poverty may operate with this moderator, this cofactor, in the process (e.g., what Baron & Kenny, 1986, refer to as mediated moderation). Many poor families have inadequate connections to formal (organizations, institutions) and informal (kin, friends, neighbors) social networks that provide material resources (e.g., child care, nutritional supplements, special opportunities for children), emotional supports (encouragement, comforting, friendship), and informational supports (knowledge of child-rearing techniques, knowledge of community services). Such supports can be valuable in meeting basic needs (e.g., child care during times when a single parent is working the late shift in a minimum wage job or transportation to the clinic for a sick child) and in dealing with stress. Single parents and homeless families are especially vulnerable to social isolation (Parker et al., 1988). Furthermore, poor adults find their relationships less helpful in coping with the stresses of everyday life. In fact, poor adults are at higher risk of family dissolution and express greater dissatisfaction with family life (Conger et al., 1990).

By contrast, children from families that find themselves temporarily in poverty but who retain good connections to support networks tend to show few negative effects of economic hardship (Furstenberg et al., 1987). Access to social support enables parents to continue providing appropriate kinds of stimulation and nurturance for children (Pascoe et al., 1981). According to theories about stress, coping, and adaptation (Lazarus, 1993), coping with stress is easier with adequate support from others. Children living with families well connected to social support networks also are more likely to have access to good adult role models and opportunities that benefit them developmentally (Parker et al., 1988). Social support (networks) are important because they help buffer families against the ravages of poverty. They also enable adults to maximally utilize their own resources. In effect, social support not only moderates the effects of poverty but also sets in motion a number of processes that mediate the link between poverty and outcome. For example, it helps alleviate distress, which in turn enables mothers to be responsive and stimulating caretakers.

Models of Mediating Processes

The literature dealing with poverty offers a variety of proposed mechanisms linking economic conditions, economic hardship, and children's development. Most of these hypothesized mechanisms have not been adequately explored; they have verisimilitude, not established credibility. In effect, the literature mostly provides bits and pieces of the larger person-process-context-time tableaux. Bronfenbrenner (1995) eloquently argues for a more complete accounting and analysis of this total set of factors across time. The last subsection of this section on poverty and development includes information on several relatively elaborate models linking economic hardship to children's health and development. These models come closer to representing a complete ecological/developmental framework as described by Bronfenbrenner and his colleagues.

McLoyd (1990) presented a model linking economic hardship to poor adjustment and achievement in African-American children. The model identifies a set of mediational processes through which the link is established (see Figure 2.1). Economic hardship produces distress in adults that in turn may lead to conflicts between family members and non-optimal parenting strategies (e.g., the overuse of negative control strategies and failure to adequately monitor children's behavior). These processes result in low self-esteem and poor adaptive functioning among black youth. McLoyd has argued that a distressed parent may also react by becoming too restrictive, which leads to rebelliousness on the part of children and bonding with peers rather than parents. By contrast, social support and control help to moderate effects of distress on family relations and parenting, the result being a less negative cascade of behavior. Luster, Reischl, Gassaway, and Gomaa (1995) tested McLoyd's model in a sample of low-income African-American children. Parents who experienced difficult life circumstances reported more psychological distress. Psychological distress, in turn, had a negative impact on parenting which was related to children's PPVT-R scores and teacher perceptions of social skills. McLoyd, Jayaratne, Ceballo, and Borquez (1994) also tested this model using 241 single African-American mothers and their seventh- and eighth-grade children. They found that economic stressors affected adolescent

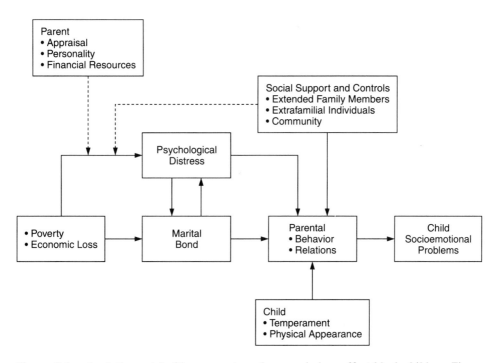

Figure 2.1. Analytic model of how poverty and economic loss affect black children. Figure appeared in V. C. McLoyd, (1990). The impact of economic hardship on black families and children: Psychological distress, parenting, and socioemotional development. *Child Development, 61,* 311–346.

socioemotional functioning indirectly through their impact on mothers' psychological functioning and, in turn, through parenting behavior and mother-child relations. In a more culturally diverse sample, Conger and his colleagues (1992) tested a model showing that economic loss led to parental rejection and harsh discipline. These, in turn, affected adjustment of boys during early adolescence.

Elder, Caspi, and Van Nguyen (1985) observed that income loss increases irritability and moodiness of fathers and that these changes led to more punitive, arbitrary, and rejecting parental behavior. The result was more temper tantrums and difficult behavior for the children. McLeod and Shanahan (1993) used structural equation techniques to test a model that included both current and persistent poverty, family stress, parental emotional responsiveness, the number of times the child was spanked, and children's internalizing and externalizing symptoms. Results showed that currently poor mothers more frequently spanked their children and were less emotionally responsive to them. These negative parenting behaviors were implicated in children's maladaptive symptoms. Bolger and colleagues (1995) also used structural equation models to determine the extent to which maternal involvement mediated the link between economic hardship and children's adjustment. They found that maternal involvement mediated 34% of the variance for externalizing behavior problems, 31% of the variance for self-esteem, and 14% of the variance for popularity. Studies by Elder and his colleagues (1985) indicated that one way that poverty influences maladjustment is by decreasing respect and dependence on parents while increasing dependence on peers. For older children, especially girls, it appears to lower feelings of self-adequacy and goal aspirations.

The general model linking economic hardship to parental distress, inadequate parenting, and child maladaptive functioning has substantial theoretical and empirical support. This model may well be supplemented by notions on stress, such as those offered by Garbarino (1977): It may not be the experience of low income per se but the perceived unmanageability of stress related to it that triggers negative parenting behavior. Furthermore, the experience of stress may increase the likelihood of a dysfunctional lifestyle (e.g., drug use) on the part of the parent. Paltiel (1988) concluded that low-income mothers were more likely to cope by engaging in risky health behaviors to provide comfort or relief from stressful lives.

Klerman (1991) proposed a model whereby the link between poverty and poor health is mediated through seven classes of variables (see Figure 2.2):

1. Inability to purchase goods and services essential for health.
2. Time constraints.
3. Stress and depression.
4. Inability to secure appropriate personal health services.
5. Inappropriate health service packages.
6. Unhealthy lifestyles and limited practice with health-promoting activities.
7. Limited motivation (see Figure 2.2).

Williams (1990) presents a similar model in which poverty is conceptualized as being mediated through four types of psychosocial factors and the quality of medical care available. Those psychosocial factors include: (a) health practices, such as smoking, alcohol consumption, and nutrition; (b) social ties; (c) perceptions of control; and

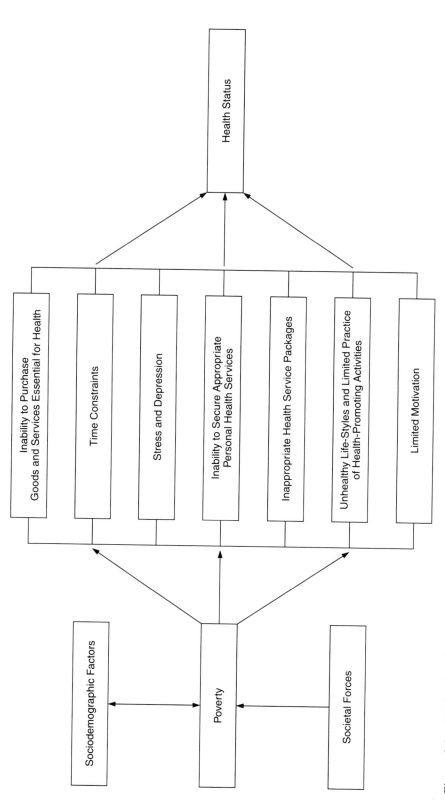

Figure 2.2. Mechanisms by which poverty affects health. Figure appeared in L. V. Klerman (1991). *Alive and well?* New York: Columbia University, National Center for Children in Poverty.

(d) stress. Both of these models also include demographic and biomedical factors as part of the array of influences on both economic status and developmental outcome.

By contrast, Mortorell (1980) constructed a model that places more emphasis on biological/nutritional factors and mechanisms. Poverty is seen as contributing directly to inadequate dietary intake as well as indirectly to inadequate dietary intake because of infection. Inadequate dietary intake results in deterioration of nutritional status caused by defective nutrient absorption, defective nutrient utilization, and poor defenses against infection. Poor nutrional status, in turn, contributes to an array of morbidities and mortality (see Figure 2.3).

Each model was constructed based on a review of medical literature, with some aspects having only limited current empirical support. There has been nothing approaching a full test of any of these models. There is reasonably good evidence, however, that children's health is related to their access to quality health care, and that such access ameliorates the effects of biological and social risks connected to economic hardship (Wise & Meyers, 1988). There are also good data showing lower health care utilization by members of impoverished families, both adults and children. Poor children are less

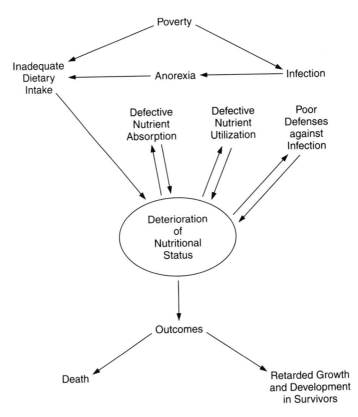

Figure 2.3. Biological mechanisms through which poverty affects nutritional status. Figure appeared in R. Martorell (1980). Interrelationships between diet, infectious disease, and nutritional status. In H. S. Greene & F. E. Johnston (Eds.), *Social and biological predictors of nutritional status. Physical growth and neurological development* (pp. 188–213). New York: Academic Press.

likely to have a regular source of care, less likely to receive preventive health services, and use fewer acute care services relative to their needs for medical care. Many poor families lack money to purchase needed health care services. But lack of money is not all that stands in the way of a low-income family's utilization of health services. The generally inadequate educational backgrounds of many poor adults (and the greater prevalence of ethnic minorities and recent immigrants among the poor) may make them less likely to seek help for symptoms of illness because of beliefs about the causes and cures for symptoms that do not square with modern medical practice. In effect, there may be both a lack of money to purchase service and a lack of fit between the care that is available and the care that is wanted (Bradley & Kelleher, 1992).

With increasing concerns about teenage pregnancy and gangs, several theories have been proposed to account for how heavily impoverished neighborhoods may increase the likelihood of poor developmental outcomes, particularly among adolescents (National Research Council, 1993). The general ecological hypothesis is that the larger the number of stresses and the fewer the number of supports in a neighborhood, the greater the distress among those living in the neighborhood. The greater the level of stress, the greater the likelihood of negative behavior and failure. According to Zuvarin (1989), "High risk neighborhoods are characterized by demographic, social, and physical characteristics that negatively impact on family and individual stress levels by decreasing the availability as well as the adequacy of support systems" (p. 102).

Wilson (1991) argues that neigborhoods with high rates of joblessness and single-parent families tend to produce a feeling of "social isolation" for adults caring for children. Over time, this results in socialization practices and family lifestyles that are not conducive to adaptive functioning (e.g., future orientation, active problem solving, household organization, warm and stimulating parenting, a focus on schooling and skill development, adequate monitoring). It also results in a loss of self- and group identification that sustains customary behavior and prevents deviant behavior (Harrell & Peterson, 1992). Klebanov, Brooks-Gunn, and Duncan (1994) conducted a limited test of this theory using data from the Infant Health and Development Program (1990). They tested a model in which both neighborhood resources and family resources and characteristics (various poverty co-factors) were conceptualized as influencing maternal characteristics (depression, social support, active coping) which, in turn, affect maternal behaviors directed toward the child. The results provided partial support for this model.

Young and Gately (1988) found that the rates of maltreatment by females was lower when substantial numbers of women with access to material resources were available for support. Overall, there is evidence that cohesion within the community affects how much children are likely to participate in neighborhood activities and utilize community resources. Participation, in turn, was positively related to happiness, social skills, and school adjustment (Homel, Burns, & Goodnow, 1987). Garbarino and Kostelny (1993) also demonstrated a relationship between social cohesion and abuse rates.

Although available evidence is consistent with ecological models proposed by Wilson, Garbarino, and others, it is important to remember the admonition offered by Bronfenbrenner, Moen, and Garbarino: "The task of demonstrating true ecological or community effect is no simple matter" (1984, p. 285). Several potentially confounding factors make interpretations about neighborhood effects difficult. Most notably, any differences observed in the incidence of negative behaviors or outcome may be due to the characteristics of those people who selected themselves to live there (a *selection effect*). Also, major social stressors may have a direct effect on a large proportion of neighborhood residents (an *aggregation effect*).

Jencks and Mayer (1990) identify four different kinds of theories relating neighborhood poverty to maladaptive social behavior:

1. Contagion theories—the idea that peers influence the spread of problem behaviors.
2. Collective socialization theories—the idea that role models and monitoring are critical to healthy and adaptive functioning.
3. Competition theories—the concept that people compete for scarce resources.
4. Relative deprivation theories—the belief that individuals evaluate their standing relative to the standing of their neighbors.

Brooks-Gunn and colleagues (1993) operationalized these notions in simple models linking neighborhood resources to child and adolescent outcomes via a variety of mediators, such as economic resources, parental characteristics, parenting behaviors, school environments, peer groups, and economic opportunities. They examined aspects of these theories with both very young children and adolescents. Affluent neighbors had a positive effect on IQ, teenage births, and school leaving. This suggests the influence of adult role models and monitoring as mediating variables. Evidence in favor of the contagion effect occurred only for adolescents. For example, Zuvarin (1989) discusses how particular feedback and sanctions present in low-income communities contribute to higher rates of maltreatment. Although these hypothesized mediational processes are consistent with research findings, it remains methodologically difficult to establish causal relationships between complex social settings and individual behavioral outcomes since results are often consistent with more than one explanation (National Research Council, 1993).

Shumow (1995) more fully delineates how neighborhoods, as physical contexts, affect developmental processes and psychological adjustment. She reviewed research showing that children engage in particular types of activities as a function of housing in a neighborhood. Low-income children living in high-rise urban dwellings spent more time "hanging out," whereas children in affluent suburban neighborhoods engaged in social pretend play and games more often. Entwisle, Alexander, and Olson (1994) found evidence that mathematics reasoning skills of school-age boys were related to the neighborhood in which the boys lived. They speculated that this difference may derive from differential opportunities to participate in complex rule-based games with peers. There are numerous variations on a basic hypothesis that physical aspects of the residential area determine the activities children engage in and that the type of activity, in turn, affects development of competence and psychological adjustment. Although these hypotheses are plausible, little direct evidence exists for most of them. A companion set of hypotheses relates to how the physical quality of neighborhoods affects parent-child relationships. Both the physical quality of housing and adult perceptions of the neighborhood characteristics (e.g., traffic, noise, esthetics, level of crime) seem related to parental depression and anger, each of which affects parental behavior. The extent of a child's home range (and the variety within it) affect how much children can explore their environments, with consequences for the acquisition of competence. Parental decisions as to how far children are allowed to travel from home without supervision depends on the parent's appraisal of potential harm present in the neighborhood (Jacobs & Bennett, 1993).

Hess and his colleagues (1982) have proposed models linking socioeconomic status to achievement. They argue that factors, such as a press for achievement, the family verbal environment, and values about schooling mediate the relationship. More concretely, they discuss how reading to the child, providing verbal stimulation and eliciting verbal responses, exposure to a variety of activities, direct teaching, provision of reading, writing, and other learning materials, and regulation in the use of television function are mechanisms by which more affluent, better educated parents enhance the achievement of their children. These researchers did not test their full model but found evidence linking most of the mediators to reading achievement. Others have presented and tested similar models of intellectual and academic achievement. Bradley, Caldwell, Rock, Casey, and Nelson (1987) found that the relationship between SES and 18-month Bayley MDI scores was mediated through the variety of stimulation offered the child and the degree to which the child's home environment was organized. The quality of the home learning environment appeared to function as a mediator for child IQ during early childhood (Bradley & Caldwell, 1980). Walberg and Marjoribanks (1976) report on a study of schoolchildren in the primary grades in which they found that most of the relationship between SES, family size, and achievement test scores was mediated through the home environment.

Morrison and Eccles (1995) took a somewhat different approach to exploring the relationship between economic hardship and children's achievement. They tested a model based more on the work of McLoyd (1990) and the work of Conger and his colleagues (1992). They looked at mediators, such as perceived neighborhood problems, parental depression, family cohesion, parental involvement, proactive prevention, parent-child conflict, and proactive encouragement. Results indicated that parental depression mediates the relation between parental income and parent-child conflict. However, neither family cohesion, parental depression, nor perceived neighborhood problems mediated the relationship with more direct parent actions such as parental involvement, proactive prevention, and proactive encouragement. Finally, direct parenting behaviors mediated the relationship between family income and adolescent GPA. Brody and his colleagues (1994) did not examine neighborhood effects, but they found that the relationship between a family's financial resources was mediated through parental depression and parental optimism. These parental psychological factors affected the quality of marital interactions, conflict between caregivers, and the amount of support received from cocaregivers. In turn, these behaviors influenced the youth's self-regulatory behavior, which contributed to not only school performance but to psychological problems as well.

Moving toward a Bioecological Analysis of Poverty

The history of research on poverty and its effects has moved from looking at simple associations between family income and various aspects of health and development to reasonably elaborate models designed to include moderator variables and mechanisms (mediators) of specific outcomes. Although this is movement in the right direction, most conceptions of poverty effects and most designs for examining those effects have not yet reached the level of analysis recommended by Bronfenbrenner (1995) and his colleagues. They offer a new paradigm, the bioecological paradigm, which integrates information from multiple levels of ecological systems through time (what is referred to as a process-person-context-time model). Belsky (1995) nicely summarizes what this model means and what it offers by way of clarifying how environments operate through development. The bioecological paradigm encourages "investigators to do more than investigate the mechanisms of mediation or moderator effects . . . [to look at the] interaction of moderators and mediators" (p. 550). In effect, future analyses should examine what Baron and Kenny (1986) have described as moderated mediation and mediated moderation. What are the potential advantages of research designs that include process, person, context, and time? Consider the probable pathways linking poverty to conduct disorders or school failure. It is likely that the pathway linking neighborhood factors, family structure and adult relationship factors, peer relationship factors, and parent-child relationship factors will be different for girls and boys and different for middle childhood and adolescence.

RESILIENCE

Although economic hardship works through several mechanisms to impede development and impair health, not all poor children succumb. Some remain resilient. The research of Sameroff, Seifer, Baldwin, and Baldwin (1993) makes clear that as risk factors pile up the probability of a positive outcome diminishes. Nonetheless, sufficient protective factors operate in the lives of some children so that they are able to resist the effects of economic hardship (Garmezy, 1993; Luthar & Zigler, 1991; Masten, Best, & Garmezy, 1990; Pellegrini, 1990; Rutter, 1987; Wang, Haertal, & Walberg, 1995; Zimmerman, & Arunkumar, 1994).

Egeland, Carlson, and Sroufe (1993) define resilience as the capacity for successful adaptation, positive functioning, and competence despite high-risk status. Resiliency means that a child can face stress or adversity without being debilitated (Zimmerman & Arunkumar, 1994). Resiliency does not mean the absence of risk; rather, it involves fending off the maladaptive response to risk. To understand how children from low-income homes avoid the negative consequences of poverty, Garmezy (1993) argues, "It is necessary to search for the presence of 'protective' factors that presumably compensate for those 'risk' elements that inhere in the lives and in the environments of many underprivileged children" (p. 129). Protective factors are those attributes of individuals or features of the environment that reduce exposure to adversity or minimize the effects of exposure (Wang et al., 1995).

Garmezy (1993) recognizes three broad categories of variables that can operate as protective factors: (a) personality/dispositional features, such as self-esteem, self-efficacy, optimism, internal locus of control, moderate to high activity level, even temperament, reflectiveness, cognitive competence, humor, active coping strategies, communicative skills, predictable behavior, mild to moderate emotional reactions, positive responsiveness to others, and the ability to choose and identify with resilient models; (b) family characteristics such as cohesion, shared values, warmth, patience, absence of conflict, stability, consistent rules and regulations, orderliness, high expectations, and presence of a supportive adult; and (c) availability of external support systems that encourage and reinforce a child's coping efforts (see also Hauser & Bowlds, 1990; Luthar & Zigler, 1991; Rutter, 1985; Werner, 1989). In her synthesis of research, Benard (1991) concluded that resilient children have strong interpersonal skills, respond well to others, engage in a high level of activity, set goals, maintain healthy expectations, and have a clear sense of purpose about their capacity to control their own destiny.

Research on resiliency is quite limited, and much of it has not focused on identifying the mechanisms that protect children from economic hardship nor on the developmental processes that activate such mechanisms (Garmezy, 1993). Werner's (1989) longitudinal study of children from Kuaii is an exception. So, too, is an analysis of data from the National Education Longitudinal Study conducted by Peng, Lee, Wang, and Walberg (1992). These researchers found that low SES students from urban communities whose combined scores in math and reading were in the top quartile had higher self-concepts and aspirations, a greater sense of internal control, interacted more with their parents, and were encouraged to do their best. A study of 243 premature, low birthweight children living in chronic poverty was designed to determine whether protective factors in the home environment of the child at 1 year of age and at 3 years of age increased probability of resiliency. Resiliency was operationalized as being in good to excellent health, being within the normal range for growth, not being below clinically designated cutoffs for maladaptive behavior on the Child Behavior Checklist, and having an IQ of 85 or greater. Six home environment factors were considered potentially protective: (a) low household density; (b) availability of a safe play area; (c) parental acceptance/lack of punitiveness; (d) availability of learning materials; (e) parental responsivity; and (f) variety of experiences. Among the children aged 1 year with three or more protective factors present in the home, 15% were classified as resilient. By contrast, only 2% of children with two or fewer protective factors were classified as resilient. Similarly, 20% of children aged 3 years with three or more protective factors present in the home were classified as resilient, whereas only 6% of children with two or fewer protective factors were resilient (Bradley, Whiteside, Mundfrom, Casey, Kelleher, & Pope, 1994a).

Although Chess's (1989) work was not directed to poor children, her identification of "adaptive distancing" as a means whereby children protect themselves from disordered families seems pertinent. In effect, children from high-risk families are sometimes able to be successful by distancing themselves from their immediate families, setting goals, then enlisting the support of peers and adults outside the family. Family involvement in schools and community institutions also seems to afford children protection from economic hardship, as does the availability of role models within the community (Wang, Haertal, & Walberg, 1995; Wilson, 1987). Strong schools with positive climates and other community facilities also seem protective (Garmezy, 1993; Rutter, 1987).

Although research and theory related to resiliency offers promise to those interested in designing useful preventive and interventive strategies for poor children, the field is still in a nascent stage with limited numbers of replicated findings about protective mechanisms. Several conclusions can be drawn from this research. First, resiliency, or the capacity to fend off the potential harm from risk, is relative, not absolute. Resilient does not mean perfectly adapted, just good enough to continue reasonably normal functioning. Second, to say a child is resilient does not mean that the child is invulnerable to all forms of risk. A child can be resilient to one risk condition, but susceptible to another. Third, resiliency does not mean that a child does not experience distress, only that the stress does not debilitate the child to the point of being unable to move on with life's tasks. Fourth, resiliency is not fixed. A child can be resilient for awhile but later succumb to the forces of adversity.

According to Garmezy, Masten, and Tellegran (1984), three basic models have been proposed to describe resilient reactions to risk: *compensatory, challenge,* and *protective.*

A compensatory factor is a variable that neutralizes exposure to risk. It has a direct and independent effect on the outcome variable of interest. Both risk and compensatory factors contribute to outcome, but their contributions are independent. There is evidence, for example, that responsive, stimulating caregiving compensates for some of the stresses created by economic hardship (Bradley et al., 1994b). In the challenge model, a stressor (or risk factor), if experienced in small amounts, may actually serve to steel a child against the negative consequences of larger exposures. This is precisely what happens with immunizations (i.e., small exposures enhance adaptation). The key is that a child must first successfully cope with the stress produced by limited exposure to the risk factor. A protective factor interacts with a risk factor in reducing the probability of harm. It works by moderating the effect of exposure. A protective factor may have a direct effect on outcome, but its effect is stronger in the presence of the stressor. Social support appears to moderate the effects of economic adversity; responsive caregivers appear to moderate the effect of a chaotic, conflictual family environment; good role models appear to moderate the effects of an impoverished, crime-ridden neighborhood. Understanding how these models operate with respect to different developmental processes should help in the design of potentially useful prevention and intervention strategies.

Thus far, support for applying these three resiliency models to particular outcomes is quite limited, and it will not be easy to achieve. As Zimmerman and Arunkumar (1994) argue, "Any particular study may fail to capture the resiliency process at the point in a child's or youth's development when it is most crucial; alternatively, a resiliency process may operate differently at different phases of development" (p. 10). Relatedly, it is difficult to specify for most outcomes which protective factors go with which risk factors. Most bad outcomes are not yoked to a single risk mechanism, and many risk factors do not occur in isolation.

Particularly important to the development of effective preventive and interventive efforts is the identification not just of protective factors but protective mechanisms (i.e., the processes through which protection against risk is actually afforded). Rutter (1987) discusses four basic types of processes that appear to protect children against adversity:

1. Reduction of risk impact—alteration of the risk and alteration of exposure to the risk.
2. Reduction of negative chain reactions.
3. Establishment and maintenance of self-esteem and self-efficacy.
4. Opening up of opportunities.

Governmental efforts to thwart the downward spiral connected with economic hardship have focused on the fourth process, but research on effectiveness of particular strategies based on any of the four processes is quite limited.

PROGRAMS TO ASSIST CHILDREN AND FAMILIES

It was with considerable optimism that President Johnson launched the "War on Poverty" in 1964 with the signing of the Equal Opportunity Act. Researchers and planners believed that increased educational and self-help opportunities offered by programs such as Head Start would substantially reduce the number of persons victimized by poverty. Although the percentage of persons living in poverty declined during the 1970s, the patchwork capacity of programs designed by the Office of Economic Opportunity to substantively change the lives of poor families came under increasing fire. Early evidence of the effectiveness of these programs was not encouraging (Zigler & Styfco, 1994). Indeed, centerpiece programs, such as Aid to Families with Dependent Children, began to be viewed as destructive rather than helpful. Many of the programs fell by the wayside, whereas others struggled with reduced or stagnant funding.

As the number of people, especially children, living in poverty began increasing again in the 1980s, there was renewed alarm and renewed calls for governmental and community action to deal with the ravages of economic hardship (Gomby, Larner, Stevenson, Lewit, & Behrman, 1995; Harvey, 1991; Klerman, 1991; National Research Council, 1993; Phillips & Bridgman, 1995; Smith, Blank, & Collins, 1992). Many of the ideas espoused were built on resiliency research (Zimmerman & Arunhumar, 1994) and an emergent science of prevention (Coie et al., 1993). They were also seasoned by reduced expectations (Zigler & Styfco, 1994) and recognition that funding from the government would be limited (Corbett, 1993). The purpose of this section is to highlight issues, ideas, and recommendations for programs designed to increase well-being and self-sufficiency of children facing economic hardship made by various researchers and study groups.

Many of the newer approaches for dealing with poverty derive from an understanding that "poverty is not a unitary variable or a distinct event" (Huston et al., 1994, p. 277). The meaning (and, therefore, effects) of low income and its related cofactors emerges from their ecological context (McLoyd et al., 1994). Moreover, the current pattern of governmental support programs may mean that economic hardship weighs as heavily on some of the working poor and near-poor as it does on those officially below the poverty line. For example, those with incomes just above the poverty line may have less access to high-quality child care than those with incomes below the poverty line, due to the child-care subsidies provided for some low-income mothers who are receiving education or job training (Phillips, 1995). As a result, the working poor and near-poor may be dependent on a patchwork of inexpensive and inconsistent child-care options, including care by relatives and neighbors who, themselves, may be experiencing economic hardship. Similarly, working poor may fail to receive adequate preventive health care or treatment for illnesses (Klerman, 1991).

Although many of the programs designed to address effects of poverty have been criticized for their failings, some programs have changed in response to those criticisms and to newer findings about how economic hardship operates to damage children. A good example is Head Start and Chapter 1 programs in public schools. These programs have evolved in terms of the ages of children they target, the goals they seek to achieve, program models and options used, and their emphasis on working with parents (Chimerine, Panton, & Russo, 1993; Zigler & Styfco, 1994). There is general agreement that if large-scale efforts, such as Head Start and Chapter 1, are to be effective, programs must include a broad array of services and there must be assurances of quality. Furthermore, since it is believed that the negative consequences of poverty are multiple and cumulative, there is reason to believe that preschool efforts like Head Start should be integrated more tightly with school-age efforts like Chapter 1, as is envisioned in the Head Start Transition Project (Kennedy, 1993).

There has been continued widespread interest in determining the effectiveness of programs designed for poor children. Head Start, the touchstone program, has been the most extensively evaluated social program in U.S. history. The results are mixed. In one of the better controlled studies, Lee, Brooks-Gunn, and Schnur (1988) found that Head Start children showed significantly larger gains on the Preschool Inventory and Motor Inhibition tests than comparison children who had other preschool experiences and children who had no preschool experience, after adjusting for initial group differences. The Head Start advantage was most notable in African-American children. Zigler and Styfco (1994) recently concluded that, although most Head Start evaluations have been plagued by technical difficulties, overall evidence suggests that Head Start "enhances school readiness and may have enduring effects on aspects of social competence" (p. 128). On the other hand, there is no compelling evidence that Head Start by itself can inoculate children against the long-term ravages of economic hardship. Like other large-scale governmental programs, there is wide variation in the quality of local programs. There has been a concerted effort to improve these local programs and to strengthen the family component based on evidence that below a certain threshold of quality Head Start has no positive impact on children. Recent funding of the Early Head Start initiative and the Head Start Transition Project is in keeping with research suggesting that the onset and duration of prevention efforts may be important for long-term effectiveness.

Historically, there have been two basic models of early childhood programs: *child-focused* and *family-focused*. There is evidence that high-quality child-care programs can result in IQ gains of about 8 points (on average) immediately after completion of the program (Barnett, 1995). The impact on social competence is less compelling. There is some evidence that such children may become more independent and socially confident and that they may have fewer out-of-wedlock births and be less reliant on social services (Boocock, 1995; Schweinhart, Barnes, & Weikart, 1993). Early childhood programs such as Head Start also may have a positive impact on health in that they require immunizations, they link children with health services, and they provide vision, hearing, and developmental screening.

Family-focused intervention programs have varied substantially in terms of intensity, type, and scope of services provided. Those whose focus has been almost exclusively on support services and parent education have shown limited effectiveness in improving children's cognitive or social competence. There is evidence, however, that programs designed to enhance parenting skills may reduce incidence of abuse and injuries (Olds & Kitzman, 1993). These programs have also been effective in modifying parenting behavior (Gomby et al., 1995). Linking parent support to job training and developmental child care seems to be key to obtaining robust, long-lasting effects. Ramey and Ramey (1990) argue strongly that long-lasting effects on academic achievement and social competence require early and intensive direct work with children living in conditions of economic hardship. Yoshikawa's (1995) review of 40 early childhood programs seems to buttress their argument. The four family-focused programs showing the greatest impact on children's functioning (High/Scope Perry Preschool Project, Syracuse University Family Development Research Program, Houston Parent Child Center, Yale Child Welfare Project) included high-quality center-based educational experiences for children beginning in infancy. Not only did these programs produce positive gains in intelligence, language, and parenting, but these changes preceded later impacts on delinquency and antisocial behavior.

A good example of how early childhood programs with a family focus may work to attain their effects can be seen from the evaluations of the Infant Health and Development Program (1990). IHDP was a multisite clinical trial involving 985 premature, low birthweight children. Families were enrolled in the study at the time of the target child's birth, with children randomly assigned to treatment and control groups. All participating received regular pediatric care and all families received referrals for needed social services. In addition, the treatment group received weekly home visits that included family support and parent education until the child was 12 months old. When children reached 12 months of age, they were enrolled in a high-quality child-care center where they received enriched educational child care 5 days a week until they were 3 years old. The families in the treatment group continued to receive biweekly home visits through age 3. Research on the program showed that treatment children performed better than control children on intelligence tests at ages 3 and 5. They also did better in adaptive behavior and on health measures at age 3 but not age 5 (Brooks-Gunn et al., 1994; Infant Health & Development Program, 1990). Research also showed that parents of children aged 3 years performed better on the HOME Inventory (Bradley, Whiteside, Mundfrom, Casey, Caldwell, & Barrett, 1994). Although a disproportionate number of the IHDP children were poor, not all children were in this category. Bradley, Whiteside, Mundfrom, Casey, Kelleher, and Pope (1994a) identified 223 IDHP children who lived in poverty from birth to age 3. Of those children, only 26 showed no signs of developmental problems: meaning they had IQ scores > 85, scores on the Child Behavior Checklist above the cutoff indicative of clinical problems, health rated as good to excellent, and growth within the normal range. To be considered resilient, a child had to be functioning well in all four areas. The children were then divided into four groups according to their intervention status (treatment vs. control) and the quality of their home environments (protective vs. nonprotective). Figure 2.4 shows the percentage of resilient children in each of the four groups. Only 6% of control children living in nonprotective environments were identified as resilient. This compares with 45% of children who had both the IHDP treatment and a protective home environment.

Evidence from research on early childhood programs indicates that the effectiveness of such programs is dependent on the quality and intensity of services provided. It is also related to the level of participation in the program (Ramey et al., 1992). Although evaluations of early intervention programs have moved away from near-exclusive reliance on IQ scores, school achievement, and parenting behavior as the indicators of program effectiveness, it is becoming evident that the impact of programs is generally restricted to the targets of the service. Center-based education programs mostly improve children's skills and behavior, but have little impact on the lives of parents. Conversely, family support programs tend to improve parenting and maternal life course, but the impact on child competence is limited (Yoshikawa, 1995). By not having an integrated package of services to promote the competence, self-sufficiency, and well-being of both parent and child, child-focused programs and family support programs tend to have a limited impact on the total family system that may not be sustained due to the continuing constraints and stresses imposed by economic hardship. For this reason, recent efforts to achieve broad-based and sustained effects that have focused on both parent and child are now referred to as *two-generation programs.* Two-generation programs differ from most programs previously labeled *child-focused* or *family-focused,* in that substantial programming efforts to develop self-sufficiency are directed at the parent and at the child.

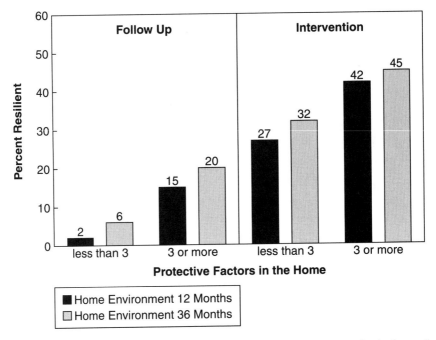

Figure 2.4.   Percent of resilient children by number of protective factors in the home for intervention and follow-up groups. Figure appeared in R. H. Bradley, L. Whiteside, D. J. Mundfrom, P. H. Casey, K. J. Kelleher, & S. K. Pope (1994). Contribution of early intervention and early caregiving experiences to resilience in low-birthweight, premature children living in poverty. *Journal of Clinical Child Psychology, 23,* 425–434.

Two-generation programs offer three key services: (a) early childhood education; (b) parenting education; and (c) adult education/job training. Very often two-generation programs also employ case managers to assist families with obtaining other services. Relatively few of these programs have been implemented because of the expense, and there have only been a few large-scale evaluations. St. Pierre, Layzer, and Barnes (1995) reviewed the limited literature available on two-generation programs and selected six exemplary programs for analysis: the Avance program in San Antonio, Texas, the Child Family Resource Program, the Comprehensive Child Development Program, Even Start, Head Start Family Service Centers, and New Chance. The last four of these programs have been operating less than seven years, so there is no long-term follow-up of participants. Two-generation programs vary considerably in the age of children who are targeted, the duration and intensity of services offered, and the particular ways that services are delivered. Some provide relatively low intensity educational services to children in the home, while others provide extensive services in child-care centers. Most provide parenting education and parent support. Again, however, programs vary considerably in terms of the amount and type of adult education and job training provided. In effect, there is not always that much difference between some programs previously labeled family-focused and some of the programs now referred to as two-generation. Overall, the two-generation programs seem to have a small, temporary effect on children's development and a short-term effect on parenting. As a general rule, the intensity of educational services provided to children was weak and the parenting education component was likewise somewhat weak (St. Pierre et al., 1995). Thus, it is not surprising that the average impact on both parent and child is marginal.

In effect, while current two-generation programs offer an extensive array of services targeted at a number of different outcomes (i.e., they are high in extensity), they are not always high in intensity and quality, two program attributes consistently associated with positive program impact. A major difficulty facing policy makers is the cost of providing such high-quality two-generation programs for children in poverty. Best estimates place such costs at $10,000 or more per child per year. The case for making such investments in poor people is a difficult one to win in the current political climate, despite the argument that $10,000 invested now will reduce the potential expenditures on special education, health services, incarceration, and the like, by a much greater amount. Partly in reaction to the current political climate, with its emphasis on moving poor parents from welfare to work (in effect, reducing the government's obligation for continued assistance), Smith et al. (1992) recommend that vehicles such as the JOBS program be expanded to offer a package of services for both parent and child. Their argument rests on two assumptions: First, the JOBS program already provides funding for an array of services, including education and job-readiness training, child care, transitional Medicaid, and case management to link to other support services; and second, the availability of these other support services seems to enhance the effectiveness of parent education and job training programs (Johnson, Walker, & Rodriguez, 1991). Smith and her colleagues (1992) also provide guidelines for how the JOBS program might be linked to other existing programs and services and case studies of eight JOBS programs where efforts to address the broader array of child and family needs are ongoing. As yet, there are few evaluations of these efforts because JOBS has been in operation for only a few years.

One of the governmental programs that Smith and her colleagues (1992) recommend linking to JOBS is the WIC program. WIC provides a monthly package of nutritious programs to meet part of the dietary needs of infants, children, and pregnant and postpartum women. The food packages are rich in nutrients frequently absent in the diets of poor people (e.g., iron, calcium, protein, vitamin A, vitamin B). Evaluations of this nutrient supplementation program have been plagued by methodological difficulties, with evidence suggesting limited success. There are indications of improved iron status (Kotch & Shackelford, 1989), but thus far there is not much evidence that participation in WIC can ameliorate the cognitive deficits sometimes associated with growth retardation (Pollitt, 1994). Reviews of research on nutrition supplementation programs carried out mostly in low-income countries suggest that early supplementary feeding may enhance motor and cognitive functioning during the first 2 years of life (Pollitt, 1994; Simeon & Grantham-McGregor, 1990). There was even some evidence that early nutritional supplements, especially if accompanied by early stimulation, improved achievement during the early school grades (Simeon & Grantham-McGregor, 1990).

Interventions designed to promote competence and well-being of young children and to strengthen their families have not, as a rule, targeted some of the key elements necessary to reduce the negative impact of economic hardship on adolescents (most notably neighborhood conditions and peer groups). Because adolescents who engage in one problem behavior frequently engage in multiple such behaviors, comprehensive services provided in a single location would appear most effective. The National Research Council (1993) recommended that four program strategies should be used with high-risk adolescents:

1. Sustained adult support, nurturance, and guidance.
2. Opportunities to be involved in the community through structured community learning and service experiences.
3. Opportunities to engage in structured experiences, including cooperative activities with peers aimed at learning how to cope productively with the stress and pressures of high-risk settings.
4. Demonstrations of respect and trust from adults.

Evaluation data attesting to the effectiveness of these program components, much less the entire package of services, are scarce. Mentoring programs, for example, have been used to help prevent teen pregnancy and delinquency, but little is known about the long-term value of such programs. There is somewhat more evidence showing that trained, professional case managers who work with teenage mothers can help reduce the incidence of repeat pregnancy (Brindis, Barth, & Loomis, 1987). Likewise, case workers who spend extensive time with delinquents appear to reduce recidivism (Davidson & Redner, 1988). The Teen Outreach program combines volunteer community service with after-school counseling. A 3-year evaluation indicated that participants in the program had fewer pregnancies and were less likely to drop out of school. The greatest impact was on those at highest risk and was related to the level of participation in the program (Philliber, Allen, Hoggson, & McNeil, 1988).

SUMMARY

Information about how poverty affects the lives of children has burgeoned during the past three decades. To some degree, it has become more integrated (the linkage is now stronger from child development literature to job training literature to criminal justice literature to school literature to family systems literature to mental health literature, etc.). The research on economic hardship has become more theory driven and is beginning to take advantage of large extant databases and more elaborate statistical modeling. Quantitative and qualitative approaches to data gathering and analysis are being usefully blended. Research has shifted from basically describing the factors associated with poverty to determining how and under what conditions economic hardship exerts its influence on human behavior, human development, and human institutions. In effect, it has moved in the direction of Bronfenbrenner's (1995) bioecological model. Mapping this terrain has a long way to go. Theories aimed at explaining how poverty impacts children's health and development have not yet demonstrated their adequacy. Most have not been fully tested; and critical tests between competing theories have not been made. To date, models based on theory have accounted for only a fraction of the variance in outcome measures.

There have been a few recent efforts to develop the kind of comprehensive database needed to understand the link between poverty, its cofactors, and children's behavior. A good example is the Project on Human Development in Chicago (Earls & Reiss, 1994). This elaborate project, funded by the National Institute of Justice and the MacArthur Foundation, is aimed at providing information that will be useful in the design of effective interventions.

Although efforts to prevent the negative consequences of poverty have a long history, prevention science is a newly emerging discipline. Coie and his colleagues (1993) offer some key principles for the new area of inquiry as well as some directions for the kinds of research needed to advance knowledge for devising successful prevention programs. This includes an admonition to collect the kinds of data needed to test competing developmental models and to track the process of impact through the mediating variables presumed to link poverty with specific bad outcomes. Until results from studies following these principles accumulate along with results from more basic science into the processes linking poverty and development, it will be difficult to fashion efficient, effective programs. Even so, current information would seem to recommend that programs should attempt to both reduce the risks associated with poverty and promote resilience. This knowledge has led many policy institutes and governmental bodies to recommend coordination of available services for such families—the increased emphasis on case management is a direct outgrowth of these new policies and prescriptions. Service coordination is de rigueur, part of the newly entrenched vocabulary of agency bureaucrats. There is, however, limited evidence that coordinated, brokered approaches to services are actually effective for multirisk families (Bradley & Kelleher, 1992). For multiproblem families—characterized by poverty, stress, disorganization, family members with limited personal capabilities, and poor social support—service coordination may not go deep enough in dealing with fundamental needs and problems. Such families need carefully interwoven services that guarantee an integrity of effect on the entire child/family system; there must be, in effect, a kind of "one stop shopping" approach to assistance. Multirisk families tend to have difficulty making and maintaining connections with the service system or moving from place to place to obtain needed services. They are not managers and they do not form networks. They are likely to connect only to a single service or to a single service provider. Multiproblem families facing economic hardship probably achieve most gains from a tightly meshed approach, something akin to what is envisioned for two-generation programs but even beyond current practice in some of those programs. Figure 2.5 displays the kinds of approaches that may be successful for families at different levels of risk.

Efforts to overcome the problems of economic hardship will probably benefit by also taking a developmental perspective. Many negative behaviors associated with poverty do not typically emerge until later in childhood (e.g., school dropout, substance abuse, serious psychopathology, teenage pregnancy, criminal acts). Nonetheless, many of these problems have developmental precursors that can be targeted earlier in the life span. As with risk factors, the same developmental precursors (e.g., inattentiveness, early acting out, difficulties in peer relationships) may be connected to several negative outcomes. Targeting these precursors may be more efficient than targeting an array of difficulties later in development. It is also true that different issues become more salient at different developmental points. Programs to promote certain components of resilience or to forestall certain developmental problems need to be carefully linked to those periods of particular salience—sometimes occurring before, sometimes occurring during that critical time. Although research is not strongly compelling about potential advantages of early intervention, there is enough information from intervention research, developmental theory, and risk research to suggest that an extensive array of services directed to child and family early in the child's life may be more cost-effective than providing similar services later in the life span (Klerman,

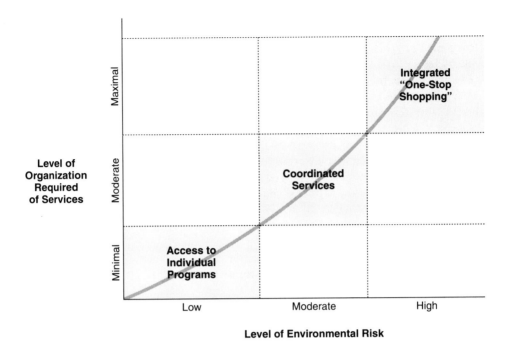

Figure 2.5. Levels of service delivery needed for different levels of environmental risk.

1991). As the child ages, services could be more targeted depending on family circumstances, the child's developmental needs, and the emergence of particular problems. At different points in childhood, service options could take advantage of appropriate resources (e.g., peer counseling, adult mentors, specific community facilities, and programs). It may also be beneficial (and reasonably inexpensive) to provide what are called *universal interventions* to groups of children who can be conveniently targeted because they are naturally concentrated and available (e.g., at school). Universal interventions are provided to all persons in a given context, although some may not be at risk, with the idea that it is not always easy to determine who may actually be at risk, it is cheaper to provide services in such contexts, and the intervention can focus not only on changing behavior in individuals (e.g., child, parent) but also on changing the context in which the child functions. One such effort is a school-based program being conducted by the Oregon Social Learning Center. In this program, parent training is being combined with student conflict resolution (Reid & Patterson, 1991). The school-wide option under Chapter 1 is a broad-based effort to provide universal interventions to school-age children. There are few data available on such universal interventions and how they may work in places with high concentrations of at-risk children.

REFERENCES

Alexander, K. L., & Entwisle, D. R. (1988). Achievement in the first 2 years of school: Patterns and progress. *Monographs of the Society for Research in Child Development, 53,* (2, Serial No. 218).

Amato, P. R., & Zuo, J. (1992). Rural poverty, urban poverty, and psychological well-being. *Sociological Quarterly, 33,* 229–240.

Baldwin, A. L., Baldwin, C., & Cole, R. E. (1990). Stress-resistant families and stress-resistant children. In J. Folf, A. S. Masten, D. Cicchetti, K. H. Nuechterlein, & S. Weintraub (Eds.), *Risk and protective factors in development of psychopathology* (pp. 257–280). Cambridge, England: Cambridge University Press.

Baldwin, W., & Cain, V. S. (1981). The children of teenage parents. In F. Furstenberg, R. Lincoln, & J. Menken (Eds.), *Teenage sexuality, pregnancy, and childbearing* (pp. 265–279). Philadelphia: University of Pennsylvania Press.

Bane, M. J., & Elwood, D. T. (1989). One fifth of the nation's children: Why are they poor? *Science, 245,* 1047–1052.

Barnett, W. S. (1995). Long-term effects of early childhood programs on cognitive and school outcomes. *The Future of Children, 5*(3), 25–50.

Baron, R., & Kenny, D. (1986). The moderator-mediator variable distinction in social psychological research. *Journal of Personality and Social Psychology, 11,* 1173–1182.

Belle, D. (1990). Poverty and women's mental health. *American Psychologist, 45,* 385–389.

Belsky, J. (1995). Expanding the ecology of human development: An evolutionary perspective. In P. Moen, G. Elder, & K. Luscher (Eds.), *Examining lives in context* (pp. 545–562). Washington, DC: American Psychological Association.

Benard, B. (1991). *Fostering resiliency in kids: Protective factors in the family, school and community.* Portland, OR: Northwest Regional Educational Laboratory.

Bernardi, R., Schwartzman, L., Canetti, A., Cerutti, A., Trenchi, N., & Rosenberg, S. (1992). Adolescent maternity: A risk factor in poverty situations? *Infant Mental Health Journal, 13,* 211–218.

Bloom, B. (1964). *Stability and change in human characteristics.* New York: Wiley.

Bolger, K. E., Patterson, C. J., Thompson, W. W., & Kupersmidt, J. B. (1995). Psychosocial adjustment among children experiencing persistent and intermittent family economic hardship. *Child Development, 66,* 1107–1129.

Bolton, F. G., & Belsky, J. (1986). The adolescent father and child maltreatment. In A. Elster & M. Lamb (Eds.), *Adolescent fatherhood* (pp. 123–140). Hillsdale, NJ: Erlbaum.

Boocock, S. J. (1995). Early childhood programs in other countries. *The Future of Children, 5*(3), 94–114.

Bradley, R. H., & Caldwell, B. M. (1980). The relation of the home environment, cognitive competence, and IQ among males and females. *Child Development, 51,* 1140–1148.

Bradley, R. H., & Caldwell, B. M. (1995). Caregiving and the regulation of child growth and development: Describing proximal aspects of caregiving systems. *Developmental Review, 15,* 38–85.

Bradley, R. H., Caldwell, B. M., Rock, S. L., Casey, P. H., & Nelson, J. (1987). The early development of low-birthweight infants: Relationship to health, family status, family context, family processes, and parenting. *International Journal of Behavioral Development, 10,* 301–318.

Bradley, R. H., & Kelleher, K. J. (1992, March). *Childhood morbidity and mortality: The growing impact of social factors.* Paper presented at the conference Social Science and Health Policy: Building Bridges Between Research and Action, Washington, DC.

Bradley, R. H., Whiteside, L., Mundfrom, D. J., Casey, P. H., Caldwell, B. M., & Barrett, K. (1994). The impact of the Infant Health and Development Program on the home environments of low-birth-weight, premature infants. *Journal of Educational Psychology, 86,* 531–541.

Bradley, R. H., Whiteside, L., Mundfrom, D. J., Casey, P. H., Kelleher, K. J., & Pope, S. K. (1994a). The contribution of early intervention and early caregiving experiences to resilience in low birthweight, premature children. *Journal of Clinical Child Psychology, 23,* 425–434.

Bradley, R. H., Whiteside, L., Mundfrom, D. J., Casey, P. H., Kelleher, K. J., & Pope, S. K. (1994b). Early indications of resilience and their relation to experiences in the home environments of low birthweight, premature children living in poverty. *Child Development, 65,* 346–360.

Brindis, C., Barth, R., & Loomis, A. (1987, March). Continuous counseling: Case management with teenage parents. *Social Casework: The Journal of Contemporary Social Work,* 164–172.

Brody, G. H., Stoneman, Z., Flor, D., McCrary, C., Hastings, L., & Conyers, O. (1994). Financial resources, parent psychological functioning, parent co-caregiving, and early adolescent competence in rural two-parent African-American families. *Child Development, 65,* 590–605.

Bronfenbrenner, U. (1995). Developmental ecology through space and time: A future perspective. In P. Moen, G. H. Elder, & K. Luscher (Eds.), *Examining lives in context* (pp. 619–648). Washington, DC: American Psychological Association.

Bronfenbrenner, U., & Crouter, A. (1983). The evolution of environmental models in developmental research. In W. Kessen (Ed.), *Handbook of child psychology* (4th ed.) (Vol. 1, pp. 357–414). New York: Wiley.

Bronfenbrenner, U., Moen, P., & Garbarino, J. (1984). Child, family, and community. In R. Parke (Ed.), *Review of child development research* (pp. 283–328). Chicago: University of Chicago Press.

Brooks-Gunn, J., Duncan, G., Klebanov, P., & Sealand, N. (1993). Do neighborhoods influence child and adolescent development? *American Journal of Sociology, 99,* 353–395.

Brooks-Gunn, J., McCarton, C. M., Casey, P. H., McCormick, M. C., Bauer, C. R., Bernbaum, J. C., Tyson, J., Swanson, M., Bennett, F. C., Scott, D. T., Tonasicia, J., & Meinert, C. L. (1994). Early intervention in low-birth-weight, premature infants. *Journal of the American Medical Association, 272,* 1257–1262.

Brown, R. B., Mounts, N., Lamborn, S. D., & Steinberg, L. (1993). Parenting practices and peer group affiliation. *Child Development, 64,* 467–482.

Chase-Lansdale, P. L. (1993). The impact of poverty on family processes. *Child, Youth, and Family Services Quarterly, 16,* 5–8.

Cherlin, A. (1979). Work life and marital dissolution. In G. Levinger & O. Moles (Eds.), *Divorce and separation: Context, causes and consequences* (pp. 151–166). New York: Basic Books.

Chess, S. (1989). Defying the voice of doom. In T. Dugan & R. Coles (Eds.), *The child in our times* (pp. 176–199). New York: Brunner/Mazel.

Chimerine, C. B., Panton, K. L., & Russo, A. W. (1993). *The other 91 percent: Strategies to improve the quality of out-of-school experiences of Chapter 1 students.* Washington, DC: U.S. Department of Education.

Cicchetti, D., & Carlson, V. (Eds.). (1989). *Research on the consequences of child maltreatment.* New York: Cambridge University Press.

Cochran, M., Larner, M., Riley, D., Gunnarsson, L., & Henderson, C. (1990). *Extending families. The social networks of parents and their children.* Cambridge, England: Cambridge University Press.

Cogan, J. F. (1995). Dissent. In C. F. Citro & R. T. Michael (Eds.), *Measuring poverty: A new approach* (pp. 385–390). Washington, DC: National Academy Press.

Coie, J. D., Watt, N. F., West, S. G., Hawkins, J. D., Asarnow, J. R., Markman, H. J., Ramey, S. L., Shure, M. B., & Long, B. (1993). The science of prevention: A conceptual framework and some directions for a national research program. *American Psychologist, 48,* 1013–1022.

Conger, R., Conger, K., Elder, G., Lorenz, F., Simons, R., & Whitbeck, L. (1992). A family process model of economic hardship and adjustment in early adolescent boys. *Child Development, 63,* 526–541.

Conger, R., Elder, G., Lorenz, F., Conger, K., Simons, R., Whitbeck, L., Huck, S., & Melby, J. (1990). Linking economic hardship to marital quality and instability. *Journal of Marriage and the Family, 52,* 642–656.

Constance, F. C., & Michael, R. T. (Eds.). (1995). *Measuring poverty: A new approach.* Washington, DC: National Academy Press.

Corbett, T. J. (1993). The Child Support Assurance System: New concept of old problems. *The Quarterly, 16,* 12–13.

Corcoran, M., Duncan, G., Gurin, G., & Gurin, P. (1985). Myth and reality: The causes and persistence of poverty. *Journal of Policy Analysis and Management, 4,* 516–536.

Danziger, S., & Stern, J. (1990). Economic factors. In *Innocenti occasional papers—No. 10: Special subseries—Child poverty in industrialized countries: The causes and consequences of child poverty in the United States.* Florence, Italy: UNICEF.

Davidson, W., & Redner, R. (1988). The prevention of juvenile delinquency: Diversion from the juvenile justice system. In R. Price, E. Cowen, R. Lorion, & J. Ramos-McKay (Eds.), *Fourteen ounces of prevention.* Washington, DC: American Psychological Association.

Dodge, K. A., Pettit, G. S., & Bates, J. E. (1994). Socialization mediators of the relation between socioeconomic status and child conduct problems. *Child Development, 65,* 649–665.

Dohrenwend, B. P., & Dohrenwend, B. (1974). Social and cultural influences on psychopathology. *Annual Review of Psychology, 25,* 417–452.

Dornbusch, S. M., Ritter, P. L., Leiderman, P. H., Roberts, D. F., & Fraleigh, M. J. (1987). The relation of parenting style to adolescent school performance. *Child Development, 58,* 1244–1257.

Duncan, G., Brooks-Gunn, J., & Klebanov, P. (1994). Economic deprivation and early-childhood development. *Child Development, 65,* 296–318.

Duncan, G., & Rodgers, W. (1987). Single parent families: Are their economic problems transitory or persistent? *Family Planning Perspectives, 19,* 171–178.

Duncan, G., & Rodgers, W. (1991). Has children's poverty become more persistent? *American Sociological Review, 56,* 538–550.

Durkin, M. S., Davidson, L. L., Kuhn, L., O'Connor, P., & Barlow, B. (1994). Low-income neighborhoods and the risk of severe pediatric injury: A small area analysis in Northern Manhattan. *American Journal of Public Health, 84,* 587–592.

Earls, F. J., & Reiss, A. J. (1994). *Breaking the cycle: Predicting and preventing crime.* Washington, DC: U.S. Department of Justice.

Egeland, B., Carlson, E., & Sroufe, L. A. (1993). Resilience as process. *Development and Psychopathology, 5,* 517–528.

Elder, G., Caspi, A., & Van Nguyen, T. (1985). Resourceful and vulnerable children: Family influences in hard times. In R. Silbereisen & H. Eyferth (Eds.), *Development as action in context* (pp. 167–186). Berlin: Springer-Verlag.

Emery, R. E. (1982). Interparental conflict and the children of discord and divorce. *Psychological Bulletin, 92,* 310–330.

Entwisle, D. R., Alexander, K., & Olson, L. (1994). The gender gap in math: Possible origin in neighborhood effects. *American Sociological Review, 59,* 822–838.

Entwisle, D. R., & Astone, N. M. (1994). Some practical guidelines for measuring youth's race/ethnicity and socioeconomic status. *Child Development, 65,* 1521–1540.

Escalona, S. (1982). Babies at double hazard: Early development of infants at biologic and social risk. *Pediatrics, 70,* 670–675.

Feuerstein, R., & Feuerstein, S. (1991). Mediated learning experience: A theoretical review. In R. Feuerstein, P. S. Klein, & A. Tannenbaum (Eds.), *Mediated learning experience* (pp. 3–52). London: Freund.

Furstenberg, F. F., Brooks-Gunn, J., & Morgan, S. P. (1987). *Adolescent mothers in later life.* Cambridge, England: Cambridge University Press.

Galbraith, J. K. (1958). *The affluent society.* Boston: Houghton Mifflin.

Garbarino, J. (1977). The human ecology of child maltreatment: A conceptual model for research. *Journal of Marriage and the Family, 39,* 721–735.

Garbarino, J. (1992). The meaning of poverty in the world of children. *American Behavioral Scientist, 35,* 220–237.

Garbarino, J., & Kostelny, K. (1993). Neighborhood and community influences. In T. Luster & L. Okagaki (Eds.), *Parenting: An ecological perspective* (pp. 203–226). Hillsdale, NJ: Erlbaum.

Garmezy, N. (1993). Children in poverty: Resilience despite risk. *Psychiatry, 56,* 127–136.

Garmezy, N., Masten, A. S., & Tellegen, A. (1984). The study of stress and competence in children: A building block for developmental psychopathology. *Child Development, 55,* 97–111.

Gecas, V. (1979). The influence of social class on socialization. In W. R. Burr, R. Hill, F. I. Nye, & I. L. Reiss (Eds.), *Contemporary theories about the family* (pp. 365–404). New York: Free Press.

Gelles, R. J. (1992). Poverty and violence toward children. *American Behavioral Scientist, 35,* 258–274.

Goldstein, S. J. (1990). Urban poverty and unavailable family members. *Journal of Strategic and Systemic Therapies, 9,* 35–48.

Gomby, D. S., Larner, M. B., Stevenson, C. S., Lewit, E. M., & Behrman, R. E. (1995). Long-term outcomes of early childhood programs: Analysis and recommendations. *The Future of Children, 5*(3), 6–24.

Gottman, J. M., & Katz, L. F. (1989). Effects of marital discord on young children's peer interactions and health. *Developmental Psychology, 25,* 373–381.

Grynch, J. H., & Fincham, F. D. (1990). Marital conflict and children's adjustment: A cognitive-contextual framework. *Psychological Bulletin, 108,* 267–290.

Haan, M. N., Kaplan, G. A., & Syme, S. L. (1989). Socioeconomic status and health: Old observations and new thoughts. In J. P. Bunker, D. S. Gomby, & B. H. Kehrer (Eds.), *Pathways to health: The role of social factors* (pp. 76–133). Palo Alto, CA: Henry J. Kaiser Foundation.

Harrell, A. V., & Peterson, G. E. (Eds.). (1992). *Drugs, crime, and social isolation: Barriers to urban opportunities.* Washington, DC: Urban Institute Press.

Harvey, B. (1991). We need a national child health policy. *Pediatrics, 87,* 1–6.

Harvey, P. G., Hamlin, M. W., Kumar, R., & Delves, H. T. (1984). Blood lead, behavior, and intelligence test performance in preschool children. *Science of the Total Environment, 40,* 45–60.

Hauser, R. M. (1994). Measuring socioeconomic status in studies of child development. *Child Development, 65,* 1541–1545.

Hauser, S. T., & Bowlds, M. K. (1990). Stress, coping, and adaptation. In S. S. Feldman & G. S. Elliott (Eds.), *At the threshold: The developing adolescent* (pp. 388–413). Cambridge, MA: Harvard University Press.

Hernandez, D. J. (1993). Childhood poverty: Trends, causes, and policies. *The Child, Youth, and Family Services Quarterly, 16*(1), 3–4.

Hess, R. D., Holloway, S., Price, G., & Dickson, W. P. (1982). Family environments and the acquisition of reading skills. In L. M. Loosa & I. E. Sigel (Eds.), *Families as learning environments of children* (pp. 87–113). New York: Plenum Press.

Hoff-Ginsberg, E. E., & Tardif, T. (1995). Socioeconomic status and parenting. In M. Bornstein (Ed.), *Handbook of parenting* (Vol. 2, pp. 161–188). Mahweh, NJ: Erlbaum.

Hoffman, M. L. (1963). Personality, family structure, and social class as antecedents of parental power assertion. *Child Development, 34,* 869–884.

Homel, R., Burns, A., & Goodnow, J. (1987). Parental social networks and child development. *Journal of Social and Personal Relationships, 4,* 159–177.

Hughes, D., & Simpson, L. (1995). The role of social change in preventing low birth weight. *The Future of Children, 5,* 87–102.

Huston, A. C., McLoyd, V. C., & Coll, C. G. (1994). Children and poverty: Issues in contemporary research. *Child Development, 65,* 275–282.

Infant Health and Development Program. (1990). Enhancing the outcomes of low-birth-weight, premature infants. *Journal of the American Medical Association, 263,* 3035–3070.

Jacobs, J., & Bennett, M. (1993). Decision making in one-parent and two-parent families: Influence and information selection. *Journal of Early Adolescence, 13,* 245–266.

Jencks, C., & Mayer, S. (1990). The social consequences of growing up in a poor neighborhood. In L. Lynn & M. McGeary (Eds.), *Inner city poverty in the United States.* Washington, DC: National Academy Press.

Johnson, D. L., Walker, T. B., & Rodriguez, G. (1991, April). *Enhancing the vocational prospects of low-income Hispanic mothers: Results of a family support program.* Paper presented at the biennial meeting of the Society for Research in Child Development, Seattle, WA.

Kelleher, K. J., Casey, P. H., Bradley, R. H., Pope, S. K., Whiteside, L., Barrett, K. W., Swanson, M. E., & Kirby, R. S. (1993). Risk factors and outcomes for failure to thrive in low-birth-weight, preterm infants. *Pediatrics, 91,* 181–201.

Kennedy, E. M. (1993). The Head Start Transition Project: Head Start goes to elementary school. In E. Zigler & S. J. Styfco (Eds.), *Head Start and beyond: A national plan for extended childhood intervention* (pp. 97–109). New Haven, CT: Yale University Press.

Kennedy, W., Van de Riet, V., & White, J. A. (1963). A normative sample of intelligence and achievement of Negro elementary school children in southeastern United States. *Monographs of the Society for Research in Child Development, 28* (Whole No. 6).

Kessler, R. C. (1979). Stress, social status, and psychological distress. *Journal of Health and Social Behavior, 20,* 259–272.

Klebanov, P. K., Brooks-Gunn, J., & Duncan, G. J. (1994). Does neighborhood and family poverty affect mothers' parenting, mental health, and social support? *Journal of Marriage and the Family, 56,* 441–455.

Klerman, L. V. (1991). *Alive and well?* New York: Columbia University, National Center for Children in Poverty.

Kohn, M. (1969). *Class and conformity: A study in values.* Homewood, IL: Dorsey Press.

Kotch, J., & Shackelford, J. (1989). *The nutritional status of low-income preschool children in the United States: A review of the literature.* (ERIC Document Reproduction Service No. ED 308 965 PS 018 152.)

Kulka, R. A., & Weingartner, H. (1979). The long-term effects of parental divorce in childhood on adult adjustments. *Journal of Social Issues, 35,* 50–78.

Laucht, M., Esser, G., & Schmidt, M. H. (1993). Adverse temperamental characteristics and early behavior problems in 3-month-old infants born with different psychosocial and biological risks. *Acta Paedopsychiatrica, 56,* 19–24.

Lazarus, R. S. (1993). From psychological stress to emotions: A history of changing outlooks. *Annual Review of Psychology, 44,* 1–21.

Lee, V. E., Brooks-Gunn, J., & Schnur, E. (1988). Does Head Start work? A 1-year follow-up comparison of disadvantaged children attending Head Start, no preschool, and other preschool programs. *Developmental Psychology, 24,* 210–222.

Lempers, J. D., Clark-Lempers, D., & Simons, R. L. (1989). Economic hardship, parenting, and distress in adolescence. *Child Development, 60,* 25–39.

Lewis, S. (1992). Food security, environment, poverty and the world's children. *Journal of Nutrition Education 24,* 38–58.

Luster, T., & Middelstadt, M. (1993). Adolescent mothers. In T. Luster & L. Okagaki (Eds.), *Parenting: An ecological perspective* (pp. 69–99). Hillsdale, NJ: Erlbaum.

Luster, T., Perlstadt, H., McKinney, M., & Sims, K. (1995, March). *Factors related to the quality of the home environment adolescent mothers provide for their infants.* Paper presented at the biennial meeting of the Society for Research in Child Development, Indianapolis, IN.

Luster, T., Reischl, T., Gassaway, J., & Gomaa, H. (1995, March). *Factors related to early school success among African-American children from low income families.* Paper presented at the biennial meeting of the Society for Research in Child Development, Indianapolis, IN.

Luthar, S. S., & Zigler, E. (1991). Vulnerability and competence: A review of research on resilience in childhood. *American Journal of Orthopsychiatry, 61,* 6–22.

Magnusson, D. (1995). Individual development: A holistic, integrated model. In P. Moen, G. Elder, & K. Luscher (Eds.), *Examining lives in context* (pp. 19–60). Washington, DC: American Psychological Association.

Masten, A. S., Best, K. M., & Garmezy, N. (1990). Resilience and development: Contributions from the study of children who overcome adversity. *Development and Psychopathology, 2,* 425–444.

Mayer, S. E., & Jencks, C. (1989). Growing up in poor neighborhoods: How much does it matter? *Science, 243,* 1441–1445.

McAdoo, H. P. (1988). *Black families* (2nd ed.). Newbury Park, CA: Sage.

McLeod, J. D., & Shanahan, M. J. (1993). Poverty, parenting, and children's mental health. *American Sociological Review, 58,* 351–366.

McLoyd, V. C. (1990). The impact of economic hardship on black families and children: Psychological distress, parenting, and socioemotional development. *Child Development, 61,* 311–346.

McLoyd, V. C., Jayaratne, T. E., Ceballo, R., & Borquez, J. (1994). Unemployment and work interruption among African American single mothers: Effects on parenting and adolescent socioemotional functioning. *Child Development, 65,* 562–589.

Miller, J. E., & Korenman, S. (1994). Poverty and children's nutritional status in the United States. *American Journal of Epidemiology, 140,* 233–242.

Moen, P., Elder, G. H., & Luscher, K. (Eds.). (1995). *Examining lives in context.* Washington, DC: American Psychological Association.

Moore, K. A., Morrison, D. R., Zaslow, M., & Glei, D. A. (1994, December). *Ebbing and flowing, learning and growing: Family economic resources and children's development.* Paper presented at research briefing of the Board on Children and Families, Child Trends, Inc., Washington, DC.

Morrison, L. A., & Eccles, J. (1995, March). *Poverty, parenting, and adolescents' achievement.* Paper presented at the biennial meeting of the Society for Research in Child Development, Indianapolis, IN.

Mortorell, R. (1980). Interrelationships between diet, infectious disease, and nutritional status. In H. S. Greene & F. E. Johnston (Eds.), *Social and biological predictors of nutritional status, physical growth and neurological development.* New York: Academic Press.

National Center for Children in Poverty. (1990). *Five million children: A statistical profile of our poorest young citizens.* New York: Columbia University School of Public Health.

National Research Council. (1993). *Losing generations.* Washington, DC: National Academy Press.

Olds, D. L., & Kitzman, H. (1993). Review of research on home visiting for pregnant women and parents of young children. *The Future of Children, 3*(3), 53–92.

Ortega, S. T., & Corzine, J. (1990). Socioeconomic status and mental disorders. *Research in Community Mental Health, 6,* 149–182.

Paltiel, F. L. (1988). Is being poor a mental health hazard? *Women's Health, 12,* 189–211.

Parker, S., Greer, S., & Zuckerman, B. (1988). Double jeopardy: The impact of poverty on early child development. *Pediatric Clinics of North America, 35,* 1127–1241.

Pascoe, J., Loda, F., Jeffries, V., & Earp, J. (1981). The association between mothers' social support and the provision of stimulation to their children. *Developmental and Behavioral Pediatrics, 2,* 15–19.

Patterson, G., DeBaryshe, B., & Ramsey, E. (1989). A developmental perspective on antisocial behavior. *American Psychologist, 44,* 329–335.

Pearlin, L. I., Menaghan, E. G., Lieberman, M. A., & Mullan, J. T. (1981). The stress process. *Journal of Health and Social Behavior, 22,* 337–356.

Pellegrini, D. S. (1990). Psychosocial risk and protective factors in childhood. *Developmental and Behavioral Pediatrics, 11,* 210–219.

Peng, S. S., Lee, R. M., Wang, M. C., & Walberg, H. J. (1992). Demographic disparities of inner-city eighth graders. *Urban Education, 26,* 441–459.

Peterson, L., Ewigman, B., & Kivlahan, C. (1993). Judgments regarding appropriate child supervision to prevent injury. *Child Development, 64,* 934–950.

Philliber, S., Allen, J., Hoggson, N., & McNeil, W. (1988). *Teen Outreach: A three-year evaluation of a program to prevent teen pregnancy and school dropout.* Washington, DC: Junior Leagues of America.

Phillips, D. (1995). *Child care for low income families.* Washington, DC: National Academy Press.

Phillips, D., & Bridgman, A. (Eds.). (1995). *New findings on children, families, and economic self-sufficiency.* Washington, DC: National Academy Press.

Pianta, R. C., Egeland, B., & Sroufe, L. A. (1990). Maternal stress and children's development: Prediction of school outcomes and identification of protective factors. In J. Rolf, A. Masten, D. Cicchetti, K. Nuechterlein, & S. Weintraub (Eds.), *Risk and protective factors in the development of psychopathology* (pp. 215–235). New York: Cambridge University Press.

Plomin, R. (1994). *Genetics and experience.* Newbury Park, CA: Sage.

Pollitt, E. (1994). Poverty and child development: Relevance of research in developing countries to the United States. *Child Development, 65,* 283–295.

Ramey, C. T., Bryant, D. M., Wasik, B. H., Sparling, J. J., Fendt, K. H., & LaVange, L. M. (1992). Infant Health and Development Program for low birth weight, premature infants: Program elements, family participation, and child intelligence. *Pediatrics, 3,* 454–465.

Ramey, C. T., & Ramey, S. L. (1990). Intensive educational intervention for children of poverty. *Intelligence, 14*, 1–9.

Reid, J. B., & Patterson, G. R. (1991). Early prevention and intervention with conduct problems: A social interactional model for the integration of research and practice. In G. Stoner, M. R. Shinn, & H. M. Walker (Eds.), *Interventions for achievement and behavior problems.* Silver Springs, MD: National Association of School Psychologists Publishers.

Rosenbaum, S. (1992). Child health and poor children. *American Behavioral Scientist, 35*, 275–289.

Ross, C. E., & Huber, J. (1985). Hardship and depression. *Journal of Health and Social Behavior, 26*, 312–327.

Rutter, M. (1985). Resilience in the face of adversity: Protective factors and resistance to psychiatric disorder. *British Journal of Psychiatry, 147*, 598–611.

Rutter, M. (1987). Psychosocial resilience and protective mechanisms. *American Journal of Orthopsychiatry, 57*, 316–331.

Rutter, M., Champion, L., Quinton, D., Maugan, B., & Pickles, A. (1995). Understanding individual differences in environmental-risk exposure. In P. Moen, G. Elder, & K. Luscher (Eds.), *Examining lives in context* (pp. 61–93). Washington, DC: American Psychological Association.

St. Pierre, R. G., Layzer, J. I., & Barnes, H. V. (1995). Two-generation programs: Design, cost, and sort-term effectiveness. *The Future of Children, 5*(3), 76–93.

Sameroff, A. J., Seifer, R., Baldwin, A., & Baldwin, C. (1993). Stability of intelligence from preschool to adolescence: The influence of social and family risk factors. *Child Development, 64*, 80–97.

Sameroff, A. J., Seifer, R., Zax, M., & Barocas, R. (1987). Early indicators of developmental risk: The Rochester longitudinal study. *Schizophrenia Bulletin, 13*, 383–394.

Santer, L., & Stocking, C. B. (1991). Safety practices and living conditions for low-income urban families. *Pediatrics, 88*, 1112–1118.

Schweinhart, L. J., Barnes, H. V., & Weikart, D. P. (1993). Significant benefits: The High/Scope Perry Preschool study through age 27. *Monograph of the High/Scope Educational Research Foundation,* No. 10. Ypsilanti, MI: High/Scope Press.

Shumow, L. B. (1995). *Neighborhoods as contexts for child development.* Unpublished manuscript.

Simeon, D. T., & Grantham-McGregor, S. M. (1990). Nutritional deficiencies and children's behaviour and mental development. *Nutrition Research Reviews, 3*, 1–24.

Simmons, R. L., Lorenz, F. O., Conger, R. D., & Wu, C.-I. (1992). Support from spouses as a mediator of the disruptive influence of economic strain on parenting. *Child Development, 63*, 1282–1301.

Smith, S., Blank, S., & Collins, R. (1992). *Pathways to self-sufficiency for two generations: Designing welfare-to-work programs that benefit children and strengthen families.* New York: Foundation for Child Development.

Spencer, M. B. (1993). Personality and social adjustment of children in poverty, or character development in a combative context. *The Child, Youth, and Family Services Quarterly, 16*(1), 8–9.

Starfield, B. (1982). Family income, ill health and medical care of U.S. children. *Journal of Public Health Policy, 3*, 244–259.

Starfield, B. (1989). Child health care and social factors: Poverty, class, race. *Bulletin of the New York Academy of Medicine, 65*, 299–306.

Starfield, B. (1992). Effects of poverty on health status. *Bulletin of the New York Academy of Medicine, 68,* 17–24.

Steinberg, L. (1987). Single parent, stepparents, and the susceptibility of adolescents to anti-social peer pressure. *Child Development, 58,* 269–275.

Sum, A. M., & Fogg, N. (1991). The adolescent poor and the transition to early adulthood. In P. Edelman & J. Ladner (Eds.), *Adolescence and poverty: Challenge of the 1990s* (pp. 37–110). Washington, DC: University Press of America.

Syme, L. S., & Berkmann, L. F. (1976). Social class, susceptibility, and sickness. *American Journal of Epidemiology, 104,* 1–8.

Takeuchi, D. T., Williams, D. R., & Adair, R. K. (1991). Economic stress in the family and children's emotional and behavioral problems. *Journal of Marriage and the Family, 53,* 1031–1041.

Tesman, J. R., & Hills, A. (1994). Developmental effects of lead exposure in children. *Social Policy Report, Society for Research in Child Development, 8*(3), 1–16.

U.S. Bureau of the Census. (1992). *Poverty in the United States, 1992.* Current population reports, series P-60, No. 185. Washington, DC: U.S. Government Printing Office.

U.S. Department of Health and Human Services. (1991). *Health status of minorities and low-income groups* (3rd ed.). Washington, DC: U.S. Government Printing Office.

Walberg, H. J., & Marjoribanks, K. (1976). Family environment and cognitive development: Twelve analytic models. *Review of Educational Research, 46,* 527–551.

Wang, M. C., Haertal, G. D., & Walberg, H. J. (1995, April). *Educational resilience: An emergent construct.* Paper presented at the annual meeting of the American Educational Research Association, San Francisco, CA.

Werner, E. E. (1989). High-risk children in young adulthood: A longitudinal study from birth to 32 years. *American Journal of Orthopsychiatry, 59,* 72–81.

Whiteside-Mansell, L., Pope, S., & Bradley, R. H. (1996). Patterns of parenting behavior in young mothers. *Family Relations, 45,* 273–281.

Williams, D. R. (1990). Socioeconomic differentials in health: A review and redirection. *Social Psychology Quarterly, 53,* 81–99.

Wilson, A. L. (1993). Poverty and children's health. *The Child, Youth, and Family Services Quarterly, 16,* 14–16.

Wilson, W. J. (1987). *The truly disadvantaged.* Chicago, IL: University of Chicago Press.

Wilson, W. J. (1991). Studying inner-city social dislocation: The challenge of public agenda research. *American Sociological Review, 56,* 1–14.

Wilson, W. J. (1995). Jobless ghettos and the social outcome of youngsters. In P. Moen, G. Elder, & K. Luscher (Eds.), *Examining lives in context* (pp. 527–544). Washington, DC: American Psychological Association.

Winneke, G., & Kramer, U. (1984). Neuropsychological effects of lead in children: Interactions with social background variables. *Neuropsychobiology, 11,* 195–202.

Wise, P. H., & Meyers, A. (1988). Poverty and child health. *Pediatric Clinics of North America, 35,* 1169–1187.

Wolf, B. (1987). *Low-income mothers at risk: The psychological effects of poverty-related stress.* Unpublished doctoral dissertation, Harvard Graduate School of Education, Cambridge, MA.

Yoshikawa, H. (1995). Long-term effects of early childhood programs on social outcomes and delinquency. *The Future of Children, 5*(3), 51–75.

Young, G., & Gately, T. (1988). Neighborhood impoverishment and child maltreatment. *Journal of Family Issues, 9,* 240–254.

Zigler, E., & Styfco, S. J. (1994). Head Start: Criticisms in a constructive context. *American Psychologist, 49,* 127–132.

Zimmerman, M. A., & Arunkumar, R. (1994). Resiliency research: Implications for schools and policy. *Social Policy Report, 8*(4).

Zuravin, S. J. (1989). The ecology of child abuse and neglect: Review of the literature and presentation of data. *Violence & Victims, 4,* 101–120.

CHAPTER 3

Children and the Community

FRANK BARRY and JAMES GARBARINO

Since Rachel Carson published her book *Silent Spring* in 1962, our society has become very aware of the importance of environmental factors in ensuring survival of various species of wildlife. As a result, we have legislated procedures to determine which species of wildlife are endangered and to protect their habitats from alteration (Bean, Fitzgerald, & O'Connell, 1991). We have come to realize that the danger to the survival of wildlife from habitat destruction is at least as great as the threat to individuals from poachers, predators, disease, and shortages of food.

Impressed by this realization, the U.S. Advisory Board on Child Abuse and Neglect[1] wrote in 1993:

> The Children who live in dangerous neighborhoods are surely no less important to the survival of our civilization than the snail darter fish or spotted owl. The Board believes that it is now time to ensure at least minimally suitable environments for our families and children. Neighborhoods in which children are at high risk should receive special attention, just as the discovery of a high level of pollution brings special attention to a body of water. (p. 18)

While geometric rates of population growth suggest that the human race is hardly in danger of extinction, its ability to maintain and carry on the civilization to which we have become accustomed is on far shakier ground.[2] High juvenile crime rates and child abuse reporting rates, children who do not do well in school, premature family formation, and other negative social indicators suggest a serious threat to the ability of future generations to maintain and improve the various institutions they will inherit (Garbarino, 1995; National Commission on Children, 1991; Whittaker, 1975).

From an environmental perspective, human communities of one sort or another have traditionally formed the habitat in which individuals of our species have grown and developed, just as the forest serves as the habitat for spotted owls, and wetlands serve as the habitat for a large variety of birds, fish, and mammals. In fact, biologists even use the same term—*community*—to describe a geographically discrete "system of organisms living together and linked together by their effects on one another and their responses to the environment they share" (Whittaker, 1975, p. 2).

---

[1] Author Frank Barry served on the U.S. Advisory Board on Child Abuse and Neglect from 1989 to 1993.

[2] After taking approximately 2,000 years to double before the time of Christ, the world human population has doubled since 1950—in less than 50 years.

As important as individualism is for the human species, particularly in this country, communities nevertheless provide the setting and context within which individuals perform their roles and functions. For human beings, communities have particular relevance for children and adolescents because these settings provide the place and the context for children to develop as they begin to form their identity and create a place and role for themselves beyond their family. As a result, community characteristics are as critical to a child's successful development as the nature of the forest cover is for the successful mating and survival of spotted owls in the Pacific Northwest.

But unlike wildlife, human beings have the unique ability to shape their own habitat and environment. If children are at risk from poor environments, adult humans have the power to alter the latter because in most cases they are responsible for creating it.

All of this raises difficult questions for clinicians accustomed to providing individual counseling and therapy. How do the environmental characteristics of the community actually affect children? How does one recognize environmentally caused effects as opposed to individual characteristics? Does it make sense to focus on individual treatment and counseling when people are clearly being damaged on a large scale by their surroundings? What can clinicians and other human service providers do to strengthen and restore a community's vitality? How should a clinician counsel a child in a dysfunctional community where "normal" behavior required for survival may be viewed as patently antisocial by the larger society? How should a clinician work with a child in a setting where the level of violence is beyond anything the clinician has experienced? This chapter and those that follow will address some of these questions.

CHANGES IN THE COMMUNITY

The environmental movement to protect wildlife arose from major changes that threatened the existence of various species of wildlife. Some of these changes, such as widespread use of DDT and other pesticides, represented changes in technology. Other changes included widespread destruction of wildlife habitats by developers, loggers, and other economic interests. Today, changes in the human community are seriously affecting our own species, and their effects are seen most readily by those who work with children and youth.

In much of the United States, and in other industrialized countries, the function of "the neighborhood" has diminished over the past 25 to 50 years (Wellman, 1979). The telephone, the automobile, television, and now the computer have enabled people to develop relationships, networks, and economic transactions that go far beyond the geographic area in which they live. At the same time, changes in employment patterns have radically altered patterns of interaction. Many women who in earlier times would have chatted with neighbors over the back fence today spend most of their waking time working outside the home, and have much less opportunity for neighborly interaction. As a result, the idea of a strong geographic neighborhood often seems nostalgic, even obsolete (Barry, 1994).

These changes have led to the emergence of individualized nongeographic networks to perform functions once fulfilled by formal and informal networks and institutions in sharply defined geographic areas. At the same time, traditionally defined communities are less able to provide nurturance, challenging roles, and social controls for children and youth.

These developments make it necessary to consider "communities without propinquity," that is, communities not limited by their geographic boundaries (Wellman, 1979). Sociologist Lloyd Street asserts simply that many professional people (including those in positions to make policy regarding the allocation of public and private resources) no longer really need a geographic neighborhood in the traditional sense (Powers, 1995). Support networks are formed at work or through various associations with people who live in entirely different communities—or with family members and associates who live hundreds of miles away. Because of the demands of their lifestyle, such people may know their geographic neighbors barely, if at all. For them it is important that the neighborhood not impede their lifestyle, but they do not depend on it for support in the way people depended on community institutions 50 to 100 years ago.

Such relative independence makes it easy for middle-class professionals and policy makers to underestimate the importance of neighborhood factors for others. It is easy to forget that a geographic neighborhood can still be very important for those who cannot so easily escape or transcend its boundaries, and it may be more important than we realize even for those who can. People still likely to be affected by factors within the neighborhood include not only the poor, but also children who are left alone after school while both their parents are working elsewhere. Mary Larner (1990) points out, "The neighborhood is especially important to young children during the elementary school years, when they begin to establish independent relationships in the several block area that lies within walking or bicycle distance" (p. 215). Its influence is also especially strong for people without cars, jobs, telephones, computers or extended personal networks. And Cochran and colleagues found that single-parent support networks were more dependent on neighbors than the networks of two-parent families (Cochran, Larner, Riley, Gunnarson, & Henderson, 1990).

Since people likely to be dependent on the neighborhood make up a significant proportion of the recipients of today's human services delivery system, healthy neighborhoods should be a matter of concern to human service professionals. Decisions made affecting the quality of neighborhood directly affect the environment "for developing human beings" (Cochran et al., 1990, p. 177).

FORCES THAT WEAKEN COMMUNITIES

The loss of industry in urban areas in the United States, particularly in cities, has dealt a devastating blow to inner-city neighborhoods. Disappearance of the jobs once held by male wage earners has been a major factor in the deterioration of both family and community life. At the same time, removal of many discriminatory housing barriers has allowed well-educated middle- and upper-income minority families to leave inner-city neighborhoods where they once served as role models, providing stability and leadership. This has resulted in virtual isolation of young inner-city blacks, particularly males, from successful role models and even information about jobs (Wilson, 1987). Construction of interstate highways around cities has accelerated suburbanization trends by making long distance commuting easier (Garbarino, 1982).

The closing of factories in small towns and cities across the country has deprived many rural families of adequate income, which has weakened rural communities as well (Fitchen, 1991). In rural areas and in some urban ones, the vitality of neighborhoods has been weakened by the loss of physical supports for a social infrastructure.

The school consolidation movement of the 1940s and 1950s deprived many small villages of a major social institution. The more recent closings of churches, neighborhood stores, factories, and post offices have had similar effects. "There is no longer a community here at all, just people" (Fitchen, 1981, p. 46; also Annie E. Casey Foundation, 1994).

Besides these losses, the past 30 years or so have witnessed the creation of a new rural phenomenon: the trailer park. Trailer parks often bring a relatively large number of low-income families into close propinquity, yet fail to provide any physical setting that would allow development of social infrastructures. As a result, there are often few if any social organizations within trailer parks that bring people together for a common purpose. The combined loss of social institutions and creation of new "communities" without them has seriously weakened the viability of neighborhoods in many rural areas (Fitchen, 1981). Such deterioration is not unlike what has occurred in many urban areas that have fallen on hard times.

And in neighborhoods of all economic levels in rural, urban, and suburban areas, the large-scale entry of women into the workforce has left many homes without adult supervision during the day. As a result, there is no longer a large pool of adults to look after the children of the community when they come home from school.

Results of these and other changes have not been evenly distributed. Both wealth and poverty have become more concentrated in recent decades, as poverty has become more frequent in both inner cities and some rural towns and villages (Fitchen, 1991; Wilson, 1987). For example, in Cleveland, the likelihood of poor families living in neighborhoods that were predominantly poor increased from 23% in 1960 to 60% in 1990 (Coulton & Tandy, 1992). In 1994, Kids Count determined that nearly 4 million children (6.2% of all U.S. children) lived in "Severely Distressed" neighborhoods, which existed in all but one state. These are neighborhoods where rates of poverty, female-headed families, high school dropouts, unemployment, and reliance on welfare are more than one standard deviation above the national mean in at least four of these five categories (Annie E. Casey Foundation, 1994, p. 9). Conversely, wealth has become more concentrated among a shrinking proportion of the population. In the 1980s, while income for the 40% of U.S. families at the bottom of the income scale actually declined in real terms, income for the top 20% rose by 29% and for the top 1% by 74% (U.S. Advisory Board, 1993, p. 7).

RESULTS

Along with major changes in communities, sweeping changes have occurred in many families and children. Since 1980, the number of reported cases of child abuse and neglect in the United States has almost tripled, going from 1.1 million to nearly 3 million in 1992 (U.S. Advisory Board on Child Abuse and Neglect, 1993, p. 8). In addition, the teen unmarried birth rate jumped by 62% from 1980 to 1992 (Children's Defense Fund, 1995, p. 102), while the percentage of children in single-parent families grew by 11% in just 6 years, from 1985 to 1991 (Annie E. Casey Foundation, 1994). The suicide rate among adolescents roughly tripled between the 1960s and 1980s (National Commission on Children, 1991, p. 35). Each of these changes reflects increasing difficulty for children and youth in meeting developmental needs. It would appear that a growing number of families are somehow not adequately performing their main task—raising their children.

In its 1993 report, the U.S. Advisory Board on Child Abuse and Neglect discussed the futility of attempting to "patch up" dysfunctional families using traditional mental health and social work models that are individually oriented and remedial in nature. These conceptual models assume that the problem lies within the individual and generally results from the individual's inability to adjust to society (Levine & Levine, 1992). Such models may work relatively successfully in traditional well-functioning communities. But they seem incapable of responding to the sheer magnitude of child maltreatment cases and other social problems besetting our society today, particularly in distressed neighborhoods that themselves have become dysfunctional. As the U.S. Advisory Board stated: "in these communities, CPS agencies have become overwhelmed by families with serious problems; too many children need help and there are not enough resources to provide it" (U.S. Advisory Board, 1990, p. 45).

Are these problems the result of disintegration of community—or are they responsible for disintegration of community? Or do both of these trends result from something else, such as a weakening of the family, or the economy? These questions are difficult to answer and perhaps they miss the point altogether. The fundamental issue is that these negative trends reinforce each other. Weak families weaken communities, and weak communities weaken families still further. Weak families and weak communities discourage economic activity, and reduced economic opportunity undermines families and communities even more (Halpern, 1995). Once this pernicious cycle begins, its initial cause becomes less important than finding ways to stop and reverse it. Changing whatever started it in the first place may not be enough to solve it now because so many new problems will have developed in the interim.

How Community Affects Children

Identifying which factor started the process of decline—important as that may be—is less critical than understanding how the sum total of all the various interactions affect children. For example, Rosenbaum and colleagues (1993) studied a sample of children whose families were given Section 8 housing certificates which allowed them to move out of Chicago public housing projects into private housing both elsewhere in the inner city and in the suburbs. They found that youth whose families were relocated to suburbs were more than twice as likely as youth who were relocated elsewhere in the inner-city to attend college (54% vs. 21%), and 75% vs. 41% found employment. The two groups were considered comparable because their destination was determined by the availability of housing, not by the families' choice. Consequently this result suggests that a functional community exerts a powerful social support effect on important life course events such as attending college and finding employment, even among some children who seemed destined to become dysfunctional adults while they lived in the projects.

Garbarino and Crouter (1978) developed a multiple regression scale for predicting child abuse reporting rates according to socioeconomic characteristics of the community. They and others used this method in Chicago, Omaha, and Spokane to examine the relationship between community characteristics and actual and predicted child abuse and neglect reporting rates. (Deccio, Horner, & Wilson, 1994; Garbarino & Kostelny, 1992; Garbarino & Sherman, 1980). In each case, investigators determined that communities with higher than predicted reporting rates had more community problems than neighborhoods with similar predicted levels but lower actual reporting rates. Community problems included higher unemployment levels, high mobility of residence, lack of telephones, (all indicators of poor social integration), as well as poor leadership by elected officials. Community institutions were weaker and residents had less hope. The general malaise even affected people in human services who were there to help. In short, community problems affected children both directly through the treatment they received from their parents and indirectly through the characteristics of the community (Garbarino & Kostelny, 1992).

William Julius Wilson (1987) conducted a thorough study of very disadvantaged neighborhoods in Chicago and concluded that the loss of manufacturing jobs from Chicago's inner-city neighborhoods had profound and negative effects on families, communities, and children. Wilson blamed the losses in jobs for a drastic increase in single-parent families, as men no longer had meaningful economic roles when welfare payments became the major source of income. Many men who are unable to find a job do not want to take on the responsibility of a family, and many of the women who bear their children do not want to link up permanently with men who offer poor long-term prospects. However, while these bleak realities tend to discourage formation of two-parent families, they have not stopped childbearing activity, and many one-parent families are the result (National Commission on Children, 1991).

In New York City's South Bronx, Roderick Wallace found that a large increase in homelessness, homicide, substance addiction, cirrhosis, suicide, AIDS, and low birth-weight babies resulted from closure of a number of fire stations. This action allowed more fires to burn out of control, which resulted in more damage and ultimately led to abandoned buildings and empty shells. These attracted criminal elements and also led to overcrowding elsewhere, which resulted in more fires. Many residents left, weakening informal and formal community and family networks. The strain of having to double up with other families for long periods severely taxed and sometimes ended supportive relationships. People who stayed as well as those who left lost many of their attachments, and this was reflected in various types of social pathology. In this instance, a clear, identifiable destructive change in the community produced extraordinarily negative results for children and families (Wallace, 1989, 1990; Wallace & Wallace, 1990).

While much of the relevant research documents trends in urban settings, Janet Fitchen (1981) traced similar patterns in depressed rural neighborhoods. She blames neighborhoods that have lost their economic and social institutions for the failure of many children to break the mold of families profoundly shaped by economic and social failure. Poor school performance and low self-esteem and behavior problems can all result when there are few positive role models accessible to children, just as deficits in this area have a pernicious effect in low-income urban neighborhoods.

Suburban communities have issues of their own. Although poverty is less likely to be a factor, many parents lack time for sufficient involvement with their children, and there may be few if any other adults available to fill this need.

BASIC NEEDS PROVIDED BY THE ENVIRONMENT

In spite of our increasingly individualistic lifestyle in the United States, human families and their children still depend on their community for many functions. Some are so basic they are often taken for granted, at least in healthy communities, but they do not always exist in dysfunctional communities. Here are the basic community assets which we believe are necessary for most children to be able to grow up satisfactorily.

Safety

Safety is fundamental. In neighborhoods without it, people live in isolation, afraid of their neighbors, afraid sometimes even to go outside (Cochran et al., 1990; National Commission on Children, 1991). Children fall behind in social development because they have limited opportunities to play with other children. And when a state of constant paranoia is required simply for survival, children do not have much emotional energy left for learning the fundamental social and cognitive skills they will need as adults (Garbarino, 1994).

Safety is a community problem. It is not something one family can handle in isolation. It has at least three parts—the formal infrastructure, usually represented most prominently by law enforcement, but also including the physical features of the community; informal mechanisms of social control, consisting of the things people in the community do individually and collectively to maintain order; and finally exterior influences, including economic forces and legislative changes as well as outside agents such as drug dealers who may enter the community from somewhere else.

Police in many cities are finding that neighborhood policing brings them into closer contact with neighborhood residents, and this can build positive attitudes among both police and residents. Better management of police resources and close attention to crime hot spots can have a major impact. Murders fell by 50% between 1992 and 1996 in New York and Houston and by 62% in Boston. Improved performance by police, with more emphasis on community problem solving and attention to seemingly minor "gateway" or quality of life crimes, have been given much of the credit for deterring much more serious crimes in these cities (Butterfield, 1997).

Design of streets and buildings can affect safety as well. Oscar Newman found that closing off streets to through traffic reduced crime in New York, but that locating housing projects at some distance from the street increased it. Designing buildings with private or semipublic areas tended to encourage residents to become protective of their space and of children playing in it. Designing visibility into buildings and surrounding areas was important as well (Newman, 1972).

Neighborhood residents can affect safety by keeping watch on areas surrounding their home, by intervening when children get into fights, and by questioning strangers who enter private or semiprivate space (Newman, 1972). Finally, community safety depends in part on what the community is willing to tolerate. Community norms and parental expectations are important. Much depends on the "degree of social cohesion on behalf of prosocial goals among residents" (Garbarino, 1982). Children interviewed in a school in Binghamton, New York, noted that when nothing of serious negative consequence happens to students and youths who cause repeated and serious disorders, other students tend to follow their example (Wahl, 1995).

Access to Economic Opportunity

Although safety may be the most immediate concern, economic opportunity provides the foundation for meeting most family needs. The ability of families to raise their children successfully depends on their ability to earn an adequate income (Zigler & Stevenson, 1993). As indicated earlier, lack of economic opportunity is associated with increasing proportions of single-parent families and increasing proportions of single teen mothers (Wilson, 1987). Much if not most neighborhood and rural community deterioration can probably be traced to economic losses—the closing of a local plant, mine, or other industry; long-term market changes for agricultural commodities or other locally produced goods; or technological changes that reduce local economic opportunities. Not all neighborhoods and communities need to have a major employer; some are bedroom communities by design, others by necessity. But if employment is not available in the community itself, then residents need access to jobs or economic activity nearby. If the economic opportunities are adequate and available to all, most of the other needs listed here can be fairly easily met.

Adequate and Affordable Housing

Families need adequate housing at prices they can afford. When it is not available, families tend to move frequently, either because they are unable to afford the rent, or because they hope to find a better place. Frequent moves can be hard on children, particularly when they involve transferring between schools. One study estimates that each time a family moves, a child's chance of completing high school diminishes by 2% (Edelman, 1994). Communities that make it easy for people to buy homes are likely to have greater residential stability than those with high levels of rental housing, especially if rents are high and quality is poor. In neighborhoods where people move frequently, it is hard to get to know one's neighbors and there is less emotional investment, or feeling of responsibility than in more stable neighborhoods. Those who have recently arrived are unlikely to be able to exert much control or influence, as they often still feel like strangers themselves. Even those who have lived for some time in the same house are likely to feel a lack of control and influence when their neighbors move frequently (Larner, 1990). In such a "stranger" environment, disorder can thrive.

Access to Health Care

Lack of health care can have tragic long-term effects. Simple ear infections in toddlers can lead to loss of hearing if not treated, and this can result in children being mistreated by parents, teachers, and other children who are unaware of their hearing problem. This can lead to school failure, social isolation, and behavior problems, with predictable consequences later on. Perhaps even more tragic are the unnecessary premature births that occur because of inadequate or nonexistent prenatal care. Such births can bring long-term problems for the child and high medical costs for society (Schorr, 1988).

A Warm, Loving Family Environment

Children of all ages, and adults too, need a warm loving family environment. Bronfenbrenner has described eloquently a child's need for a totally devoted, caring adult (Bronfenbrenner, 1988). For children to develop their potential, someone needs to love them, respond to their needs, and stimulate their development. Children learn trust when their own needs are met; children who do not learn to trust find it very difficult to establish successful relationships as they grow older (Erikson, 1963; National Commission on Children, 1991). There is considerable research indicating that children's chances for successful development are significantly greater when two parents are in the home compared with one. Lack of the birth father in the home appears to be related to discipline problems in school, juvenile delinquency, and crime (Horn, 1995; National Commission on Children, 1991). Although the need for a strong family environment is normally met by family rather than community, families need at least minimal levels of the kinds of support outlined here to provide their children with adequate attention.

NEEDS AT DIFFERENT AGES

In addition to the preceding general needs, children and families have special needs at different stages. These are described in the following subsections.

Infants and Toddlers—Support for Parents and Good Child Care

Infants are totally dependent on their parents, so a good family environment is critical. Their later development will depend in many ways on the skill and effectiveness of the parents during the first few months. Bonding normally occurs during the first few months after birth, and the quality of the bond will profoundly affect what happens later (Cole & Cole, 1993; National Commission on Children, 1991).

Home visiting programs have become an important tool for helping at-risk families through this critical period, especially with their firstborn child. In its second annual report, in 1991, the U.S. Advisory Board on Child Abuse and Neglect stated, "While not a panacea, the Board believes that no other single intervention has the promise that home visitation has" (p. 145). Many communities are implementing Healthy Families home visiting programs which begin work with at-risk parents at the birth of their first child. This is the time when they are most likely to be receptive to outside help, and involvement begins before negative child-rearing patterns become established (U.S. Advisory Board on Child Abuse and Neglect, 1993).

Since mothers today so often work outside the home, good child care is a critical need during their parents' working hours. If young children are to develop their potential, this must be interactive care with plenty of activity supervised by adults—not custodial care in which the main communication comes from a television set. Often care is provided by family day-care mothers, among whom the quality of child care may vary considerably (National Commission on Children, 1991; Cole & Cole, 1993). Some communities have day care councils and other organizations that make special efforts to support day-care mothers in providing quality care. Some employers now provide day care on or near their premises. This can dramatically reduce absenteeism and improve employee performance as well as simplifying life for parents. All of these things are examples of community support for families and children.

School-Age Children—Effective Schools Integrated into the Community

Since children spend so much of their time in school, the quality of their school experience is critical to their development. And since schools are usually created by the communities they serve, a school represents in many ways a collective statement by each community about its children.[3] Although there are obviously other influences as well, schools represent what the community has decided its children should have: They are a minienvironment or habitat for children, created by the larger community of adults to prepare those who will eventually replace them.

In kindergarten and the early grades, the teacher plays an extremely important role in determining how children feel about themselves. Teachers influence children's school performance in part by communicating their expectations in both nonverbal and verbal ways (Zigler & Stevenson, 1993). As the child grows older, the influence of the school continues: peer groups are likely to be established through relationships formed in school or at least with acquaintances made in school. And teachers, coaches, and other adults perform important roles as role models, mentors, and advisors (National Commission on Children, 1991; Zigler & Stevenson, 1993).

Schools can provide superior education through quality teaching, good interaction with the children, encouragement, and high expectations. But, there is growing evidence that very large schools may make both education and social development difficult, especially for at-risk children (Garbarino, 1982, 1995).

Beyond all this, the school can also play a major role in the community. In fact, it is unlikely that any other community institution will so profoundly influence as many families as the school their children attend—(even to the point of determining what time family members get up in the morning). Typically, the school is the one institution that nearly all families in a neighborhood experience in common. When schools operate in a closed fashion, the common experience is limited to sending one's child off in the morning and periodically receiving report cards. But schools that operate in a more open fashion have the potential to become the "Center of the Community," at least as far as families with children are concerned.

In discussing child development, Bronfenbrenner (1979) talks of the importance of links between the major arenas in the child's life. Children are likely to do best when there are strong links rather than barriers between home and school—the two primary components of the day-to-day world that most school-age children experience. And research bears this out; children do perform better when their parents become involved with the school (Zigler & Stevenson, 1993). James Comer's work in turning around unsuccessful schools in New Haven, Connecticut, and Prince Georges County, Maryland, dramatically emphasizes the importance of parent and teacher involvement (Comer, 1980; Schorr, 1988).

Many schools sponsor activities—from basketball games to class events and trips, that involve parents, volunteers, and local businesses. Beyond this, some schools invite parents and other community members in to tell stories to children, and some provide homework assignments that require children to interact with community members. Some schools are involved with internships and apprenticeships with local employers, and some host after-school programs and health clinics. Many require their students to perform community services as part of their curricula. Some even employ outreach workers to work with and involve parents (Garbarino, 1982; National Commission on Children, 1991; Ray, 1994; Schorr, 1988).

---

[3] "Community" is used here in a broad sense, since many urban and some rural neighborhoods in large school districts have little influence over the nature and quality of their schools.

Most communities have some form of day care for infants and preschoolers, but many schoolchildren, even when fairly young, are left to their own devices after school until their parents return from work. Leaving children unsupervised and alone for long periods has resulted in fearfulness in some children, and some researchers have found higher incidences of adolescent pregnancy, delinquency, and substance abuse as well (Zigler & Stevenson, 1993). Providing constructive activities for children after school is a challenge in most communities because it is very difficult for most parents to address this on an individual basis, especially when they are working most of the day. In some communities, activities are organized at community or youth centers; in others the school facilities are used for other activities after classes— even though school personnel may not be involved (National Commission for Children, 1991).

Adolescents—Constructive Opportunities for Youth

During adolescence, youth are developing their own goals and identity and reaching beyond their immediate families to establish themselves in the broader community. The supports and opportunities they find there play an important role in the success of their transition from school to work and from childhood to adulthood. To accomplish this transition successfully, they need positive role models—adults and other youth who can interact with them and influence them positively. In particular, boys need male role models—especially if they have grown up in a single-mother household. Adolescents need a place outside their home where they personally can belong, such as a sports team, a part-time job, or a group of friends (National Commission on Children, 1991). Providing a positive place where they matter—where their presence makes a difference—will help each youth make the transition between two types of social control: that provided by their childhood family and that which comes through holding a job and starting a new family of their own. The period of transition between these two webs of involvement and accountability is perhaps the time of greatest risk for antisocial behavior (Tonry, Ohlin, & Farrington, 1991).

Sports, art, and theater activities, other recreational organizations, apprenticeships, part-time jobs, and community volunteering opportunities are all constructive responses to this need. Adolescents need to become involved in constructive ways with adults outside their family, as well as with other youths their own age. If the community does not provide constructive opportunities for youth to socialize and develop, youth may create their own opportunities, which will not necessarily be constructive. The proliferation of gangs illustrates what can happen in the absence of positive opportunities. Halpern (1995) comments that "perhaps for the first time in the history of any community, adults have abdicated community leadership to youth" (p. 81). Since teenagers are responsible for a high proportion of the crime and disorder in any community, providing positive opportunities for them is a critical need, to say the least.

During the 1960s, youth became a "social barometer," as their behavior often turned out to be the "earliest visible expression of frustration in the inner city" (Halpern, 1995, p. 86). Problems exhibited by children and youth can provide early warnings of a community environment in distress, just as canaries were used by miners to warn of poisonous gases that would threaten their own existence.

Parents—Networks of Support

Parents are responsible for raising their children and creating a healthy home environment in which they will grow, but to do this successfully they must meet needs of their own. Beyond the basics—a safe neighborhood environment, opportunity to earn an adequate income, and adequate housing and health care, they also need to be able to develop their own support networks. These typically include relatives, friends, and neighbors, who help them by providing information, resources (exchanging child care or transportation), and emotional support. Parents also need to belong to something. If they do not work outside the home, the support network becomes even more important, as its absence will lead to isolation. Finally, parents need child-rearing information. Whereas many will get this naturally from family and friends, some—often from deprived backgrounds themselves—will need special outside information and help to provide adequate child care (Cochran et al., 1990).

In healthy communities, most families develop these supports naturally through religious organizations, social and recreational groups, colleagues at work, neighbors, and other friends. Public education by organizations such as Cooperative Extension can help provide child-rearing information. In some communities, family resource centers offer educational and social activities for parents. Some communities have developed hotlines for parents to call with questions on child-rearing issues.

Successful child development also requires access to services by all groups. A community in which some key services are denied to families that need it because they are of a different culture, or because doctors will not treat children on Medicaid, sacrifices development of the children affected. And participation by residents in the organizational life of the community is important. Halpern (1995) found that participation in community planning, improvement, and implementation activities brought positive results for those involved.

Historical Perspective

Clinicians have been working to heal physical, spiritual, mental, and emotional problems of individuals for thousands of years—possibly for as long as human beings have been able to communicate. Practitioners have carried different titles through the ages, and various bodies of knowledge in both scientific and spiritual realms—(medicine, psychology, religion)—have developed over the centuries.

But we have far less tradition and history with respect to healing sick communities. The first identifiable efforts to strengthen neighborhoods in this country are usually considered to have been the settlement houses that started in New York and Chicago in the late 1880s—barely over a century ago. At that time, major changes were taking place in many American cities as hundreds and thousands of immigrants came from parts of Europe, including some southern and eastern European countries that had not previously contributed to mass immigration in the United States (Halpern, 1995; Levine & Levine, 1970).

Inadequate life experience and unemployment were not major problems for most of them, as it took considerable energy and resourcefulness to find their way to this country at that time. Many had been skilled craftsmen in their own communities. By today's standards, jobs were plentiful, albeit at very low pay. But these immigrants overwhelmed neighborhood institutions and facilities, and they brought different customs and outlooks. And despite hard work, they often were unable to earn enough to live comfortably or even adequately (Halpern, 1995).

The settlement houses that sprang up on both sides of the Atlantic did much to strengthen neighborhoods. They formed clubs and brought people together for cultural, educational, social, and recreational purposes including young people who had previously caused trouble on the streets. They provided opportunities for people to build their own networks of friends and supports. While they responded to individual needs and emergencies, they also did neighborhood research, collecting data on community problems, and then advocated, educated, and organized. They focused on housing, garbage collection, lighting, education, sanitation, and other community issues. Many school programs taken for granted today—kindergarten, school lunches, evening classes, school nurses and visiting teachers (who later became school social workers), college extension classes, and classes for the physically and mentally disabled—were developed by settlement houses. Later these were adopted by the schools, often as a result of strenuous advocacy (Brieland, 1990; Levine & Levine, 1992).

Stanton Coit, who started the first settlement house in the United States, developed a plan for a "neighborhood guild" in 1891. Coit was concerned by the tendency to form single-purpose organizations that "did not encourage people to know one another in more than a single dimension" (Levine & Levine, 1992, p. 61). His neighborhood guild would pull people of all classes together to focus on all issues affecting their neighborhood. Even then, Coit saw the futility of organizing an agency to help people individually. "If we consider the vast amount of personal attention and time needed to understand and deal effectively with the case of any one man or family that has fallen into vice, crime, or pauperism, we shall see the impossibility of coping with even these evils alone, unless the helpers be both many and constantly at hand" (Coit, 1891, p. 27, quoted in Levine & Levine, 1992, p. 61). Coit saw the neighborhood guilds as a way to strengthen the neighborhood's ability to help its residents.

However World War I overwhelmed efforts to strengthen the community and divided the movement because some of its leaders, including Jane Addams, who founded Hull House in Chicago, devoted their attention to peace and antiwar movements. This made them controversial, even earning some the label "subversive." Money became hard to raise. According to the Levines, "The conservative atmosphere that would not support criticism of the United States during the war years persisted and intensified in the immediate postwar period. Efforts to change social conditions were therefore no longer acceptable" (Levine & Levine, 1992, p. 75).

In the decade that followed, the "Settlements—the former 'spearheads of reform'—became social work agencies in the narrower, contemporary sense" (Levine & Levine, 1992, p. 75). Community improvement efforts took a back seat to a much more individualistic approach fueled by the growing popularity of psychoanalysis developed by Sigmund Freud (Halpern, 1995). This approach appealed to people in upper economic brackets, which offered a new source of income for psychiatrists and counselors. And, "The availability of psychoanalytic theory to the social work profession . . . accelerated the ongoing shift in social workers' attention from community to individual maladjustment" (Halpern, 1995, p. 159). Social workers gradually accepted the idea that if a person was not functioning effectively, it was his or her own fault—not the result of a community or societal problem (Levine & Levine, 1992).

At the same time, the seeds of our modern categorical human services system were being planted, as social service workers, mental health clinicians, and educators focused on making their work more professional. Individual case investigations and records became the primary tool of professional social workers, replacing the neighborhood work and clubs of earlier years. Even the settlement houses established different departments and specialties to deal with different problems (Halpern, 1995). Competition and differences sprang up between the various helping professions, and the doctrine of confidentiality began to impede joint efforts. Sarason described a new phenomenon that he called "professional preciousness," the idea that only certain professionals were fit to work with people with mental problems (Levine & Levine, 1970, p. 5).

The Depression that followed the prosperity of the 1920s led to the Social Security Act and the beginnings of our present welfare system. Much of the federal focus was to implement laws on a national level to establish income streams for people who had little opportunity to work to escape poverty, especially widowed mothers and their children. The resulting programs effectively involved the government in human services at the local level to an unprecedented degree, eventually replacing many private charity agencies (Levine & Levine, 1992).

In the 1940s, World War II took precedence over social programs and temporarily created major new employment opportunities. Industrial jobs in northern and midwestern cities attracted hundreds of thousands of low-income people—both black and white—from the South in search of better opportunity. Mechanization of agriculture, discrimination, poverty, and in some cases violence, kept the migration going long after the jobs in the North began to dry up in the 1950s and 1960s. As jobs became scarce, they went to European Americans rather than African-Americans creating the basis for community problems evident today. Many social agencies in these communities adapted poorly to the change in neighborhood composition. Some reduced their services or closed completely, while others followed their former clients to the suburbs (Halpern, 1995; Levine & Levine, 1992).

In the 1950s, as in the 1920s, a prosperity ethic prevailed, and most energy went into helping individuals adjust to a negative environment rather than attempting to change it (Halpern, 1995; Levine & Levine, 1992). At the same time however, the foundation was being laid for the next major effort to strengthen communities, which occurred in the 1960s. In South Chicago, in 1939, Saul Alinsky had started an indigenous neighborhood organization to advocate the interests of the community and its residents (Halpern, 1995). Later several colleges and universities initiated community development programs to assist communities in strengthening their own institutions, both in this country and in developing countries elsewhere in the world.

In 1961, the Ford Foundation funded Community Progress Inc. to improve conditions in New Haven, Connecticut, through its Gray Areas program, and the following year New York's Henry Street Settlement House initiated Mobilization for Youth. Both involved comprehensive neighborhood efforts to improve education and conditions for youth, and both were intended to change the practices of existing agencies, which were viewed as part of the problem. Both involved neighborhood residents, although initially not in decision-making roles. And both became models for a renewed interest in neighborhood development by the federal government (Halpern, 1995).

These innovations culminated in the Kennedy-Johnson "War on Poverty" in the 1960s, which resulted from strong convictions—based in part on the civil rights movement—that poverty resulted from community conditions that needed to be changed. In passing the Economic Opportunities Act of 1964, the federal government went so far as to create a new local institution, the *community action agency,* which deliberately by-passed state and local governments to bring about changes on the local level. This was considered necessary, as local governments, human service agencies, and schools were seen as perpetuators of the community problems rather than part of the solution (Halpern, 1995).

But this effort resulted in a militancy and clash of values that generated political opposition, and ultimately community action agencies lost much of their freedom as change agents, as well as their funding and political support. Although most of these agencies continue to perform useful functions today, they have been stripped of many of their initial programs and most no longer see their main mission as reforming other institutions in their local communities.

The reformist agenda of the 1960s, fueled by the civil rights and antiwar move-ments, receded during the 1980s, as emphasis shifted back to individual problems. As concern grew about the federal deficit, federal willingness to undertake bold new ini-tiatives diminished, particularly in the area of improving neighborhoods.

Levine and Levine (1992) have described our pendulumlike approach to human problems in the United States as a contest between two diametrically opposed views of human motivation. On the one hand is the view that "people are basically 'good' but have been exposed to poor conditions and therefore have not reached their full poten-tial" (p. 8). The solution is to improve their situation by improving community condi-tions and services provided by community institutions. The countervailing view holds that "people are in difficulty not because of the situation but because of personal weaknesses and failings. . . . What must be changed is not the circumstance but the per-son" (p. 8).

According to the Levines, the predominant view during each period depends on the political and economic outlook at that time. During conservative eras, the second, in-dividualistic view has tended to prevail. Such periods have often been characterized by relative prosperity and dominance by conservative interests, with little desire to enter-tain notions of problems in society. The result, for mental health and human service workers, has been a focus on helping clients to adjust. The opposite view has gained support when economic conditions were not perceived positively and when there was a recognized need for reform. This emerged as conditions deteriorated in urban neigh-borhoods in connection with massive migrations in the late 19th century. It arose again after massive migration and loss of economic activity in the cities converged with the civil rights movement of the 1960s to both raise expectations of African-Americans and educate others about the consequences of racial discrimination (Halpern, 1995; Levine & Levine, 1992).

Whichever point of view predominated during any given period, there were never-theless voices advocating the opposite approach, and in every instance the seeds for the eventual resurgence of the latter were sown as the first view gained strength (Levine & Levine, 1992). During the conservative 1980s, William Lofquist (1983), who has done extensive consulting on youth issues, wrote a practice manual which incorporates both views, but strongly advocates more emphasis on changing community conditions that lead youth to develop problems.

Lofquist advocates a balance between preventive and remedial treatment efforts ad-dressing both community and individual issues. To help with conceptual understand-ing, he developed a matrix for classifying efforts according to whether they are preventive or remedial, and oriented toward the individual or community. He believes that efforts of each type are necessary, but that most communities overemphasize remedial efforts to undo problems exhibited by individuals after the fact. He notes that such remediation requires specialized skills, such as counseling, group work, and crisis intervention; whereas prevention requires broader skills, such as community assessment, community education, and planning. Prevention, he says, essentially means changing community conditions that breed individual problems. Such conditions could include lack of work opportunity, lack of opportunity for meaningful interaction with adults, lack of structured activity after school, lack of effective communication between youth and school officials, and lack of clear communication and training within the school (Lofquist, 1983).

Even so, changing community conditions is not necessarily easy. Lofquist notes that as long as the individual client can be blamed for his or her problem or condition, the onus for change lies entirely with him or her. But when the focus turns to community conditions, the onus for change spreads throughout the community. Instead of the client bearing the entire responsibility for change, some of this responsibility may even find its way to the human service professionals! The frequent instinctive negative reaction to change on the part of many professionals may provide insight into why clients do not always welcome suggestions for change either (Lofquist, 1983).

Robert Halpern (1995) carries this view a step farther, noting that most efforts to change distressed inner-city communities have focused on mobilizing those who live there, rather than addressing deeper societal causes of community decline. People who live in very distressed communities typically have a dearth of the skills and experience needed to bring about the changes required to make a difference, and their day-to-day struggle to survive often consumes what energy they have (Halpern, 1995).

Economic factors have led to the deterioration of most inner city neighborhoods, Halpern says, and these factors are beyond the ability of people living in poor neighborhoods to control. Therefore, he says, it is unfair to lay the entire onus for change at the community level. He believes that this responsibility must be borne at higher levels. Some of the forces affecting inner-city minority neighborhoods since World War II include not only loss of the manufacturing base, but deliberate destruction and/or isolation of low income neighborhoods by highway construction and "urban renewal." Deteriorated schools, public housing, and other services as a result of budget cutbacks, redlining by banks, and direct political decisions to weaken support for minority communities were also important factors (Halpern, 1995; Wallace, 1990).

Although Halpern and Wilson have limited their analyses to urban settings, Janet Fitchen (1981, 1991) reached similar conclusions with respect to rural areas. In short, it is naive to expect a deprived community to be able to undo all the damage done by forces that are well beyond its control. This does not mean that efforts should not be made to strengthen communities locally, or that local people should not be mobilized in connection with such efforts. Halpern credits community strengthening efforts with modest success. The difficulty, he believes, is a matter of scale. The Community Development Corporations, one of the most successful mechanisms developed during the 1960s, have at most been able to create only a few dozen jobs when thousands were needed (Halpern, 1995). To really solve the problem, it is necessary to go beyond victimized communities to get at far deeper societal causes and influences.

Halpern (1995) believes that larger society must stop excluding inner-city African-Americans from access to career opportunities that other Americans take for granted. Wilson (1987) advocates a national policy of full employment as the only way to reach the people in these neighborhoods. Fitchen (1991) notes that government policies drawn up on the basis of metropolitan needs often negatively affect rural communities. Many rural communities have also been particularly impacted by international market forces, which have led to mergers and buyouts, loss of local control, and ultimately the loss of many local manufacturing plants altogether.

Halpern, Wilson, and Fitchen identify the deeper causes as society myths, prejudices, and values. Myths include the conventional wisdom that anyone can "make it" in our society if he or she tries hard enough. Fitchen's books (1981, 1991) contain ample documentation that most of the rural poor work very hard, sometimes at two and three jobs—but still remain poor. Halpern (1995) and Wilson (1987) describe the futility of looking for work in inner cities with unemployment rates at 50% for young men.

Prejudices include our attitudes toward the poor, whether black or white. Fitchen (1981), and Halpern (1995), describing white and black rural and inner city poor, respectively, come to similar conclusions: The cards are stacked against them; they must play a game which it is almost impossible for them to win, yet they are blamed for their failures.

Values chiefly concern our high regard for individualism and capitalism. According to Halpern, those who benefit from these values have shown themselves unwilling to see their negative implications for those who do not benefit. The growth of large corporations has meant that decisions vital to the economic survival of communities are now made in offices hundreds or even thousands of miles away. Halpern describes manufacturing as having become "rootless" (1995, p. 144). The effects on families and children of business decisions to close a plant rank far lower than bottom line corporate financial considerations, even though profits may often be very short term.

Transportation policy provides a similar example. *USA Today* recently published a front-page article describing a long-term trend of reducing air service to small and mid-sized cities in the United States (Jones & Overberg, 1995). This reduction posed a clear threat to the ability of these cities to attract and maintain industry. The airlines have taken the action not because they were necessarily losing money, but because they could make more money using their planes on routes between major cities. As a result of airline deregulation, they are under no obligation to consider the environmental impact of their actions on the communities affected. Some cities have retained service by paying for it directly—presumably using funds that might otherwise go to schools, recreation, hospitals, or other community needs.

This might not be so harmful if there were more effective public mechanisms to ameliorate the effects of corporate decisions on the communities. Ironically, one of Richard Nixon's contributions in this regard was the Revenue Sharing Program, under which the federal government made payments to local governments, which they could use as they wished with few restrictions. This provided a way of at least returning tax revenues from some of the earnings of corporations to communities that may have been negatively affected by their decisions. But even that small concession has largely fallen victim to more recent federal budget cutting. Efforts of the federal and state governments to push responsibility for taxation and meeting social needs down to local governments simply increases the inequity between localities with a strong property tax base and those without it. Those with the weakest tax base are often those with the highest level of need, and from a child's perspective, such policies in effect increase the penalty for getting born in the wrong locale.

In the end, society cannot ignore the consequences of undermining environments for children any more than it can countenance destruction of rain forests in South America, or pollution of rivers and lakes. Continuing to carry out policies that deprive children of a suitable environment will have a devastating and very visible effect where it hurts most—in the nation's pocket book. As this is being written, much attention is being given by the media to the ability of the Social Security and pension plans to support citizens when they retire. The ratio of children to older people is changing dramatically. In 1940, there were only 11 people over 65 for every 100 people of working age (between 19 and 64). In 1990 there were 20; by 2020, there are expected to be 27; by 2040, 37 (U.S. Bureau of the Census, 1993). For those who are now working to be economically secure in retirement, it is essential that every child today become a successful, productive adult. But this will not happen if a large proportion of them end up in prisons, drug treatment centers, or on welfare.

To solve the problem of poverty-ridden neighborhoods, America needs to develop a more humane and equitable paradigm for the distribution of wealth. There has to be a reasonable balance to the overarching goal of allowing a business to make money or a unit of government to save money. Success at becoming more "efficient" has gone so far that Americans must face up to the real possibility that there may simply no longer be enough jobs for everyone; technological advances now allow the production of everything people want or need without everyone having to work. If this is so, how should the jobs be divided up? Should those who work the longest hours work less? Or should those who make the most scale back? Or should everyone retire earlier? Or should society continue to have what Halpern calls an "economically superfluous" class (Halpern, 1995, p. 224)?

In the end, Americans must come to terms with policies that deprive minorities in inner cities (and some rural whites) of society's benefits. Although the visible trappings of discrimination—the segregated buses and restaurants of the 1940s and 1950s—are gone—de facto economic segregation and discrimination remain very real, particularly in inner-city neighborhoods walled off from job opportunities in the suburbs (Halpern, 1995; Wilson, 1987). This must end. In the long run, it is questionable whether civilization will be able to survive under such shortsighted values and assumptions.

HISTORICAL EFFORTS TO STRENGTHEN INNER CITY COMMUNITIES

Halpern (1995) chronicles the efforts to rebuild inner cities in a manner similar to that of the Levines, and his work touches on many of the same themes. According to Halpern, designs to strengthen the inner city have become progressively more sophisticated, although they have never quite measured up to the level of need. While the early settlement houses did the right things for the period, Halpern notes that the inner city of the 1880s was not nearly as devastated as it is today. Lack of stability, social control, and community institutions were problems, but the basic need for jobs was being met, even though wages were less than adequate. Today that can no longer be said.

The phenomenon of long-term joblessness had become apparent by the 1960s and the title of the War on Poverty's flagship program—Office of Economic Opportunity—suggests a recognition of that. The community action agencies established to implement this act at the local level focused on helping disenfranchised people into the economy as well as on involving local residents in decision making and advocacy.

While their militancy generated a negative reaction instead of sympathy in some quarters, Halpern (1995), believes the CAAs did achieve a modest level of success in helping individuals into economically successful positions in society. Its requirement for "maximum feasible participation" of those to be served gave people experience in decision making and planning. Their biggest success probably lay in generating some successful long-lasting programs—particularly Head Start.

But neither Community Action Agencies of the War on Poverty nor other programs of the 1960s received sufficient funding to really do the job, as they were essentially overwhelmed by the country's war in Vietnam (Halpern, 1995).

Another relatively successful model did emerge from the 1960s—the Community Development Corporation—a locally controlled effort to strengthen the financial health of the community. Frequently, these projects arose from community organizations and many began with housing, spreading later to other areas, including day care, medical care, supermarkets, other retail outlets, light manufacturing, and other needs. Halpern (1995) credits these also with modest success in improving the community environment. As indicated earlier, they have lacked sufficient resources to compensate for disinvestment by both private and public sources, but by being locally controlled and investing their earnings in the community, they have served as an important symbol of hope and success. Perhaps most significant in the long run, they constitute business enterprises motivated by something other than the quest to maximize profits. As a result, they may be able to provide leadership in any effort to develop a new paradigm.

The newest effort described by Halpern (1995) is also the most sophisticated. It is an attempt to pull together public, private, and indigenous resources to develop a long-term comprehensive strategic plan to improve some of the most needy inner-city neighborhoods. These have resulted in major collaborative efforts to bring about action that has involved public, private and voluntary sectors and the community itself. An example is the Atlanta Project, started in 1991 by former President Jimmy Carter, who became alarmed that there are really two Atlantas—"one rich and successful, the other impoverished and desperate" (Hochman, 1992, p. 1; see also, The America Project, 1995).

The Atlanta Project has raised $10 million entirely from private sources for an effort to revitalize 20 distressed neighborhoods. Each neighborhood has been adopted by a major business or corporation located in Atlanta, and a local project coordinator and assistant who reside in the community have been employed in each. Each neighborhood has set goals, and each corporation is providing assistance, including loaned staff, to develop methods to achieve the goals. Many goals involve children and youth. The Atlanta Project effort is large in scale, comprehensive in nature, and it has begun on many fronts at once, in recognition of the seriousness and complexity of the problems it confronts. It relies on many volunteers and collaboration from existing agencies. It has so far carried out a massive immunization program, formed two youth organizations, created an $11 million loan fund for small businesses, established two literacy and reading centers, and placed over 100 volunteers in schools. While it involves top-level community and corporate leaders in policy making, it has undertaken extensive efforts to involve local people in priority setting and planning for their neighborhoods (The Atlanta Project, 1995; Hochman, 1992). It has in a sense attempted to function both from the top down and the bottom up.

A number of other cities, including Baltimore, Boston, Minneapolis, and New York, have developed somewhat similar efforts. The comprehensive multisector approach exposes high-level corporate executives directly to the realities faced by those who for one reason or another are not enjoying the benefits of our economic system—putting them face to face with the "other America." By creating an awareness that was lacking before, this may in the long run help to lay the foundation for a new paradigm. Questions to be answered include discovering whether a complex approach will work for the multiple problems that now exist, or whether such an approach will sink from its own complexity. And again, as always, will there be sufficient funds to make a difference? Halpern (1995) poses other provocative questions, including how one measures success: Is it best to benefit many people a little bit, or far fewer people a lot? How does one decide? Is it possible to revive the inner city economically? If not, what can be substituted? Retailing? Cultural institutions and identity? Recreation?

The jury is not yet in on this approach, since in most places it has been in operation for only a short time.

THE HUMAN SERVICE WORKER AND THE COMMUNITY

What are the roles of the clinician and the human services agency with respect to the community? This depends a good deal on the community one serves. Although this chapter has focused on very distressed communities, these are in fact a small minority of communities in this country. Most readers will probably be serving families and children in communities with far more resources and connections than some of those referred to here. Some may be working in communities with few if any perceived problems. At worst, many readers may be functioning in communities with deteriorating indicators (rates of crime, teen pregnancy, substance abuse, etc.).

As with individuals, it is much easier to prevent a community from declining than to try to provide remedial services after it has become severely distressed. In the early stages of deterioration, people with positive abilities and connections will still be on hand, and many will feel a dedication to the community and a desire to do something to preserve what they feel is valuable. Also, the community may still be able to attract outsiders in a position to help (bankers, investors, potential employers, or homeowners). It is much easier to reverse the process of decline early on than it will be later on if nothing is done. When a community has become truly devastated—when it has lost its ability to exert social control—its pathology affects human service workers as well as residents, and they also can become caught up in fear for their own safety and in reacting to seemingly unending crises.

Human service workers can undertake the following steps to strengthen their own communities. (Some will need to be adapted according to conditions in the community.)

1. *Look for evidence of environmental effects on children and youth you serve.* If many of your clients exhibit negative behaviors, substance abuse, or other similar problems, look for the elements they share in common. Think about environmental solutions. Find out how the problems started; think about community characteristics that could have prevented it. It is common to blame the family for the problems of children, but in many instances the families are also affected by negative community conditions. Or the problems may result from the interaction between weak families and serious community problems.

2. *Identify community issues and solutions from the perspective of those who live in the community.* Although you may feel you have good insights into causes and even

solutions, history can provide many examples of educated people who tried unsuccessfully to impose well-intended solutions on community people—sometimes as a result of failing to recognize unintended consequences. It is always important to "start where the people are." You can get a sense of "where people are" by talking to people individually, or in discussion or focus groups.

A simple question such as the following can help: "What would have to happen in this community for it to become an easier community to raise children in?" or ". . . an easier place to grow up in?" Note that the wording does not stigmatize either people or the community; it simply encourages people to focus on what would make their most important task easier. It also focuses on solutions.

3. *Incorporate community intervention into your approach.* Ascertain what you can do to intervene at a community level. This might involve getting funding to address the problem (if you are an administrator), moving away from an individual focus toward build groups and networks (if you are a frontline worker), or pulling together people who share concerns about the problem (if you are a community activist).

Sometimes it can be extremely helpful just to bring people in a community together to talk about what they see happening and what they wish to do about it. Until this happens, people tend to make important decisions on an individual basis, often to the detriment of the community. Coming together can allow people in a community to develop shared goals and make collective decisions that build commitment to improving their community. Coming together is the first step toward community empowerment.

In down-to-earth terms, intervention at the community level involves strengthening the ability of the whole community to raise its children effectively. It means reinventing ways to allow and encourage people in the community to take responsibility for things that were once done there (e.g., taking care of children; organizing and leading activities for youth; helping with education; mentoring; providing information and support to parents; exerting social controls on parents, children and youth). This can be done by encouraging or training individuals, getting existing groups or organizations to take on new community tasks, or organizing completely new community efforts.

4. *Encourage your clients to give something back.* Giving to someone else can be a big boost to one's self-respect, and it can also strengthen one's own community. This is particularly true for youth. Young people should be encouraged and organized to do positive things for their community. This can include anything from fixing up a vacant lot to visiting shut-in senior citizens or acting as big brother or sister to younger children, or, helping them with their homework. Whenever someone—a youth or adult—begins to volunteer for the first time in a way that helps to improve the community environment for children, this literally increases the capacity of the community to raise its children.

Where possible, challenge individuals to work positively to change negative community conditions. Don't just teach them to cope with a bad situation.

5. *Build linkages outside the community.* Because the community must depend on outside forces and resources, helping people in it to develop connections outside can effectively increase community capacity. If you are working in a community with serious problems, it is important to establish links with people outside the community who have resources the community needs. When members of a community are completely isolated from others, even well-intentioned outsiders can make wrong decisions simply from lack of information. And it is equally important to help people inside the community to develop connections that help them understand the "real world" outside.

6. *Think big but start small.* Unless you are very well connected (e.g., a former president, the mayor, the CEO of a corporation, or the head of a major organization), your initial efforts will probably start on a relatively small scale. Regardless of size in the beginning, however, it is important to achieve some success early so people do not lose interest and hope. But even if one starts small, it is important to think on a comprehensive scale. What are the various problems, what are the causes, and what would it take to address each of them? Do you know anyone who could help provide what is needed? How can you involve the people who have the resources and power to help, wherever they may be?

7. *Look for strengths and potential, not just problems.* Even the most distressed community will have strengths, and even people who appear to be without resources can surprise you with what they are able and willing to give. The process of improving a distressed community will be much slower and more difficult than for a more functional one, but the qualities needed for effective intervention are similar to those needed to work successfully with individuals—look for strengths, in both people and in institutions. When you find them, nurture them and build on them. McKnight & Kretzmann (1990) have developed a useful guide for mapping community assets.

8. *Remember that symbols are important.* You may not be able to organize an effort that will solve the major or underlying causes of a community's deterioration. But if you can start even a small effort that motivates people to do something positive about perceived community needs, and if people begin to see results, these efforts may do more than you realize. In bleak situations, symbols that allow people to hope are vitally important. Your efforts and those of others who become involved will inspire other individuals in ways you cannot initially imagine. They may, for example, influence a person's decision on whether to stay or leave the neighborhood, or inspire someone to make a positive personal choice or take a positive action (Ray, 1994; Slinski, 1990).

9. *Link up with others.* While no one person or agency is likely to be able to solve all of the problems, an effective collaboration between public and private efforts can have a significant impact. True collaboration takes a lot of time and work, but the payoff can be substantial. It is typical in such efforts, for agencies to go to great length to protect their current functions and their turf. But true effectiveness may result from their coming together to identify needs not being addressed and new creative ways to address them, which go beyond traditional conceptions of turf and function.

10. *Advocate at state and national levels.* Given the interconnectedness of forces that affect communities, do not limit your efforts to the community itself. Work on the big picture as well. Your efforts may be as simple as informing your Congressman or state legislator of needs and conditions in the community you are concerned with, or you may speak at conferences or write Op. Ed. pieces for newspapers. You might even take an active role in state or national organizations, depending on your connections and your level of functioning. Better yet, you may be able to help people you are working with in the community to do the same.

Program Reviews

Following are reviews of several human service programs that have played significant roles in strengthening the community.

- *Family Resource Centers* now being developed and promoted by the Family Resource Coalition in Chicago, might be described as today's version of the pioneer settlement houses of a century ago. While automobiles and mass transit lines may have reduced the need for staff and volunteers to actually live on the site today, the Resource Centers have many similar goals and sponsor many activities similar to those of the settlement houses. The principal goal is to strengthen the ability of families to raise and nurture their children successfully. However like the settlement houses, they do this by scheduling educational and social activities, activities to support parents, and activities to help parents network. They also advocate for better conditions and services for their community. A major principle of Family Resource Centers is to make their activities available to whoever needs them without the stringent eligibility standards that lead to "deficit based" screening and selection in many publicly operated services. Family Resource Centers build on the strengths of the individuals who participate in their programs viewing their customers as resources as well as participants (Family Resource Coalition, 1994).

- The *Master Teacher* program, developed by Cooperative Extension agent Margaret Slinsky, in Springfield, Massachusetts, identifies and recruits natural leaders in low-income urban neighborhoods and their rural counterparts. Participants take part in a series of informational and discussion sessions related to problems and needs they encounter among those they interact with. The purpose is to both provide information and to build a network of natural leaders. According to its founder, the process injects hope, encouragement, and empowerment into neighborhoods where they are in short supply. Results are very individualized, different for each community and individual. They have included a neglectful mother who decided to free herself of drugs, dispute resolution training that later averted a playground fight, a suicide averted, removal of drug dealers from a housing project, development of a youth leadership and a school dropout prevention program, and election of a neighborhood resident to the city council. The end result appears to be a higher degree of empowerment for the people in participating neighborhoods (Slinski, 1990).

- *The Neighborhood Parenting Support Project* was developed in 1988 in two neighborhoods in Winnipeg that had three to four times the city average of child maltreatment cases. The premise of the program was that strengthening social support for parenting at the neighborhood level would reduce the risk for child maltreatment.

    After identifying and mapping neighborhood and parent social networks, project staff initiated a social network intervention which consisted of "consulting, connecting, convening, constructing, and coaching." Through a neighborhood parenting support worker, parents were helped to change their personal social networks—reinforcing positive connections and weakening destructive connections. For example, to help parents reduce high family stress, the parent would be helped to weaken the stressful ties with family members and to reinforce ties with neighbors who might be less critical of the parent and better able to provide child care support in emergencies or emotional support in a crisis.

    The neighborhood parenting support worker provided social support in problem identification and solving, networking skills, parenting skills, support and help-seeking skills, communication skills, and support-giving skills. The support worker joined with and supported neighborhood central figures, natural helpers, and network "connectors" in developing a referral network and neighborhood parenting support network structures. She "connected" with people in settings frequented by parents and children, such as family centers, day care centers, and playgrounds, as well as coffee shops, laundromats, and churches (Garbarino, 1994).

- *The Community Lifelines Project,* operated by Cornell University's Family Life Development Center in Chemung County, New York, undertook to strengthen neighborhoods and community by working through local schools. This was accomplished by employing parents from the target neighborhood to work part time as paraprofessionals to strengthen parent involvement with the school, with each other and with their children.

  The paraprofessionals, known as Parent Partners, began simply by introducing themselves to parents waiting outside the school to pick up their children, inviting them in for coffee, listening to their concerns and interests, and developing activities in response. Activities have been educational (e.g., parenting classes), recreational (e.g., health fairs, family dances), and child oriented (e.g., an alternative playground and more family-friendly procedures for orientation and report card conferences).

  A program evaluation (Ray, 1994) determined that a large number of parents had become active volunteers in school, including many who had never done so previously; that many had gone back to get their General Equivalency Diploma (GED); that many had expanded their support system by making new friends; and that the behavior and academic performance of many of their children had improved. Having parents coming into the elementary school seemed to do much for both their children's self-image and the child-parent relationship. As a result of all this, at least a few parents who had to move out of their apartments for various reasons told the parent partners that they would not relocate outside the school neighborhood because the activities with the school had become too important to give up. In neighborhoods with high rates of mobility, this was a strong indication that these parents at least had begun to feel rooted in their neighborhood in a way that was previously lacking.

  In a rural community on the edge of the county, outreach workers have organized volunteer activities through the school, including a volunteer-run after-school program for children and several support groups for parents. All grew out of needs expressed by parents.

- Boston's *Violence Prevention Project* (Prothrow-Stith, 1991) is a community-based primary prevention program that seeks to change individual behavior and community attitudes about violence through outreach and education. The effort is designed to reduce the incidence of violent behavior and associated social and medical hazards for adolescents. The project is presently concentrating its efforts in Boston's two poorest neighborhoods.

  A supportive network of secondary therapeutic services and a hospital-based secondary prevention service project, directed toward patients with intentional injuries, supplement the primary prevention activities to provide a comprehensive program. A violence prevention curriculum used in high schools is at the core of the intervention. The project is geared to individual behavior modification using descriptive information on the risks of violence and homicide. It also provides alternative conflict resolution techniques and implements a nonviolent classroom ethos.

In addition, the school curriculum is also presented in less traditional educational settings (e.g., alternative schools, recreational programs, public housing developments, Sunday schools, boys and girls clubs, YMCAs, and neighborhood health centers) in the community. Clergy and police have also been recruited to spread violence prevention education through their contact with adolescents, their families, and other significant adults in the community. By using many and varied community settings to communicate the messages of violence prevention, the community becomes "saturated."

Because some youth need more than primary prevention efforts and the medical setting is often the only place that troubled youth go for help, the project has begun working with adolescents admitted to the Boston City Hospital with intentional injuries. Because adolescents do not return for follow-up services and are difficult to contact, a new strategy has been developed that uses pediatric nurses trained to work with seriously injured adolescents, their friends, and family during hospitalization and afterward. Support groups are also conducted for young people and their parents.

Limitations of this project centered around the notion among the general public that violence is inevitable and not preventable. To counteract this attitude, it was necessary to educate everyone in the community, not just the targeted adolescents. Media-based efforts and peer education strategies were essential in this process (Garbarino, 1994).

Evaluation of some of the more generic preventive approaches has been challenging because it can be difficult to quantify results. The Community Lifelines and Master Teacher program found many different individualized results that reflected the condition of each person who participated. Some people were encouraged to further their education, others developed more friends, while still others became active volunteers—and some did several of these things. Such an approach cannot be evaluated solely by counting the number of people who received a particular benefit; it must be evaluated in terms of its effect in helping to make the community an easier place for its families to raise their children and to carry out their other primary tasks in life. Empowering new people as volunteer helpers and providing opportunities, training, and support for them, as many of the preceding programs have done, appear quite literally to strengthen the community's capacity to raise its children. However, evaluators are only beginning to develop the tools and techniques to measure this kind of accomplishment.

Finally, strategic planning is being applied more and more frequently in community situations. The Heartland Center for Leadership Development in Lincoln, Neb., has produced a manual on developing the "Entrepreneurial Community" (Luther & Wall, 1989). William Lofquist of Development Publications, in Tucson, Ariz., distributes a manual called *Discovering the Meaning of Prevention* (Lofquist, 1983), which describes an approach to identifying and addressing conditions that prevent youth from reaching their potential. *The Search Conference,* (Emery & Purser, 1966) describes a weekend retreat methodology that effectively empowers community participants to develop a bottom up strategic plan in one weekend.

SUMMARY

Children are vitally affected by the quality of their community environment. It constitutes their introduction to the world beyond their family. And it constitutes the setting in which the family will provide for them. We have a responsibility for the characteristics of that environment, because unlike other animal species, humans create their own community environment.

However, although inner cities and some depressed rural environments are profoundly detrimental to children, it has not been easy to rectify some of the problems they present. At varying times during the past century, well-intentioned efforts have focused on involving the people living in such communities. However, the causes of community decline typically go beyond the community, and it is unrealistic to expect those who often have the fewest resources to do the most to change things that are beyond their control. Most community-based efforts over the years have only achieved modest success. (Halpern, 1995). However new comprehensive approaches in several communities that are heavily involving corporate leadership may achieve more.

Human services providers can help by "thinking environmentally"—by becoming aware of the link between individual problems and community conditions—and then by working through whatever means they have at their disposal to change those conditions. It can be very helpful to bring community residents together for this purpose. And although residents cannot be expected to solve the entire problem, it is important and empowering for them to be involved in efforts to improve their community.

While some efforts, such as those in Atlanta, began on a large scale, many others of necessity start small. However, it is important to plan on a large scale and expand as the opportunity arises. In the end, one of the biggest casualties of some communities has been hope. Restoring hope can be difficult, but it is not impossible. Sometimes small, symbolic acts that affect only a few individuals can have as much impact as much larger efforts that are impressive but seem farther removed.

What is critical is to involve as many people as possible thinking and acting in ways that will strengthen the ability of their community to raise its children.

REFERENCES

The America Project. (1995). *Because there is hope: Gearing up to renew urban America: A Report of the America Project.* Atlanta: Carter Collaboration Center.

Annie E. Casey Foundation. (1994). *Kids count data book.* Greenwich, CT: Author.

The Atlanta Project. (1995). *The Atlanta Project, 1991–1994: Program status summary.* Atlanta: Author.

Barry, F. D. (1994). *A neighborhood-based approach: What is it?* In G. B. Melton & F. D. Barry (Eds.), *Protecting children from abuse and neglect: Foundations for a new national strategy* (pp. 14–39). New York: Guilford Press.

Bean, M. J., Fitzgerald, S. G., & O'Connell, M. A. (1991). *Reconciling conflicts under the endangered species act: The habitat conservation planning experience.* Washington, DC: World Wildlife Fund.

Brieland, D. (1990). The Hull-House tradition and the contemporary social worker: Was Jane Addams really a social worker? *Social Work, 35,* 134–138.

Bronfenbrenner, U. (1979). *The ecology of human development: Experiments by nature and design.* Cambridge, MA: Harvard University Press.

Bronfenbrenner, U. (1988). Strengthening family systems. In M. Frank & E. F. Zigler (Eds.), *The parental leave crisis: Toward a national policy* (pp. 143–159). New Haven, CT: Yale University Press.

Butterfield, F. (1997, January 19). Crimefighting's about face. *New York Times,* D1, D6.

Carson, R. (1962). *Silent spring.* Boston: Houghton Mifflin.

Children's Defense Fund. (1995). *The state of America's children yearbook.* Washington, DC: Children's Defense Fund.

Cochran, M., Larner, M., Riley, D., Gunnarson, L., & Henderson, C. (1990). *Extending families: The social networks of parents and their children.* New York: Cambridge University Press.

Coit, S. (1891). *Neighborhood guilds: An instrument of social reform.* London: Swan Sonenschein.

Cole, M., & Cole, S. (1993). *The development of children* (2nd ed.). New York: Scientific American Books.

Comer, J. (1980). *School power: Implications of an intervention project.* New York: Free Press.

Coulton, C., & Tandy, S. (1992). Geographic concentration of poverty and risk to children in urban neighborhoods. *American Behavioral Scientist, 35,* 238–257.

Deccio, G., Horner, W., & Wilson, D. (1994). High-risk neighborhoods and high-risk families: Replication research related to the human ecology of child maltreatment. *Journal of Social Service Research, 18*(3/4), 123–137.

Edelman, M. W. (1994). *Wasting America's future.* Boston: Beacon Press.

Emery, M., & Purser, R. (1966). *The search conference: A powerful method for planning organizational change and community action.* San Francisco: Jossey-Bass.

Erikson, E. (1963). *Childhood and society* (2nd ed.). New York: Norton.

Family Resource Coalition. (1994). *Best Practices Project: Addendum to the progress report.* Chicago: Author.

Fitchen, J. (1981). *Poverty in rural America: A case study.* Boulder, CO: Westview Press.

Fitchen, J. (1991). *Endangered spaces, enduring places: Change, identity and survival in rural America.* Boulder, CO: Westview Press.

Garbarino, J. (1982). *Children and families in the social environment.* New York: Aldine de Gruyter.

Garbarino, J. (1994). Neighborhood-based programs. In F. Barry & G. Melton (Eds.), *Protecting children from abuse and neglect* (pp. 304–352). New York: Guilford Press.

Garbarino, J. (1995). *Raising children in a socially toxic environment.* San Francisco: Jossey-Bass.

Garbarino, J., & Crouter, A. (1978). Defining the community context of parent-child relations. *Child Development, 49,* 604–616.

Garbarino, J., & Kostelny, K. (1992). Child maltreatment as a community probelm. *Child Abuse and Neglect, 16,* 455–464.

Garbarino, J., & Sherman, D. (1980). High-risk neighborhoods and high-risk families: The human ecology of child maltreatment. *Child Development, 51,* 188–198.

Halpern, R. (1995). *Rebuilding the inner city: A history of neighborhood initiatives to address poverty in the United States.* New York: Columbia University Press.

Hochman, S. H. (1992). The Atlanta Project. In *Buying America back: Economic choices for the 1990's.* Tulsa, OK: Council Oak Books.

Horn, W. (1995). *Fatherhood facts.* Lancaster, PA: National Fatherhood Initiative.

Jones, D., & Overberg, P. (1995, August 11–13). Airline service bailout grounds mid-sized cities. *USA Today,* 1A–2A.

Larner, M. (1990). Local residential mobility and its effects on social networks. In M. Cochran, L. Gunnarson, C. Henderson, M. Larner, & D. Riley (Eds.), *Extending families: The social networks of parents and their children* (pp. 205–229). New York: Cambridge University Press.

Levine, M. L., & Levine, A. (1970). *A social history of helping services: Clinic, court, school and community.* New York: Appleton-Century-Crofts.

Levine, M. L., & Levine, A. (1992). *Helping children: A social history.* New York: Oxford University Press.

Lofquist, W. (1983). *Discovering the meaning of prevention: A practical approach to positive change.* Tucson, AZ: AYD.

Luther, V., & Wall, M. (1989). *The entrepreneurial community—A strategic approach to community survival.* Lincoln, NE: Heartland Center for Leadership Development.

McKnight, J., & Kretzmann, J. (1990). *Mapping community capacity.* Evanston, IL: Northwestern University, Center for Urban Affairs and Policy Research.

National Commission on Children. (1991). *Beyond rhetoric: A new agenda for children and families.* Washington, DC: Author.

Newman, O. (1972). *Defensible space: Crime prevention through urban design.* New York: Macmillan.

Powers, M. (1995). The hidden strengths of communities. *Human Ecology Forum, 23*(3), 13–16.

Prothrow-Stith, D. (1991). *Deadly consequences.* New York: HarperCollins.

Ray, M. (1994). *Community Lifelines Program evaluation report.* Ithaca, NY: Cornell University, Family Life Development Center.

Rosenbaum, J., Fishman, N., Brett, A., & Meaden, P. (1993). Can the Kerner commission's housing strategy improve employment, education, and social integration for low income blacks? *North Carolina Law Review, 71,* 1519–1556.

Schorr, L. B. (1988). *Within our reach: Breaking the cycle of disadvantage.* New York: Doubleday.

Slinski, M. D. (1990). *Building communities of support for families in poverty: Master teacher in Family Life Program.* Amherst, MA: University of Massachusetts, Cooperative Extension.

Tonry, M., Ohlin, L. E., & Farrington, D. P. (1991). *Human development and criminal behavior: New ways of advancing knowledge.* New York: Springer-Verlag.

U.S. Advisory Board on Child Abuse and Neglect. (1990). *Child abuse and neglect: Critical first steps in response to a national emergency.* Washington, DC: U.S. Department of Health and Human Services, Administration for Children and Families.

U.S. Advisory Board on Child Abuse and Neglect. (1991). *Creating caring communities: Blueprint for an effective federal policy on child abuse and neglect.* Washington, DC: U.S. Department of Health and Human Services, Administration for Children and Families.

U.S. Advisory Board on Child Abuse and Neglect. (1993). *Neighbors helping neighbors: A new national strategy for the protection of children.* Washington, DC: U.S. Department of Health and Human Services, Administration for Children and Families.

U.S. Bureau of the Census. (1993). *Current population reports: Population estimates and projections.* (Series P-25, Nos. 311, July 2, 1965; 519, April 1974; 917, July 1982; and 1095, February 1993). Washington, DC: U.S. Government Printing Office.

Wahl, B. (1995, June 22). [Verbal report on student survey from Broome County Probation Department] Presented at the meeting of Partnership for Peace, Binghamton, NY.

Wallace, R. (1989). Homelessness, contagious destruction of housing, and municipal service cuts in New York City: Demographics of a housing deficit. *Environment and Planning, 21,* 1585–1603.

Wallace, R. (1990). Urban desertification, public health and public order: 'Planned shrinkage,' violent death, substance abuse and AIDs in the Bronx. *Social Science Medicine, 31,* 801–813.

Wallace, R., & Wallace, D. (1990). *The burning begins again: Preliminary analysis of recent New York City fire statistics* (Social report). New York: New York City Council.

Wellman, B. (1979). The community question: The intimate networks of East Yonkers. *American Jounal of Sociology, 84,* 1201–1231.

Whittaker, R. H. (1975). *Communities and ecosystems.* Washington, DC: Macmillan.

Wilson, W. J. (1987). *The truly disadvantaged: The inner city, the underclass and public policy.* Chicago: University of Chicago Press.

Zigler, E., & Stevenson, M. F. (1993). *Children in a changing world: Developmental and social issues.* Pacific Grove, CA: Brooks/Cole.

PART THREE

Intervention Formats and Settings

CHAPTER 4

Individual and Group Interventions

CAROL LARROQUE and ROBERT L. HENDREN

Perhaps more than in any other profession, those who choose to work in the field of mental health do so because of their desire to help other human beings. Drawn by a strong desire to alleviate emotional pain in children and adolescents, professionals in this field find intervention to be paramount. Mental health professionals have as their armamentarium interventions with individuals, interventions with groups, and a combination of individual and group treatment.

The ability to diagnose mental illness and to understand what is necessary for the well-being of youngsters is greater than ever before. Treatment choices become increasingly more sophisticated and better understood. Yet, we live at a time when stressors in society are severe, and many children and adolescents grow up in an environment that places them at high risk for emotional problems. Nearly one in five youngsters will experience an emotional or behavioral disorder at some time during their youth, regardless of their socioeconomic background or the location of their home (National Advisory Mental Health Council, 1990).

Ironically, despite both substantial knowledge of mental illness and a grave need for treatment, resources for intervention are becoming increasingly scarce. As we approach the 21st century, it becomes increasingly obvious that child and adolescent mental health professionals need to provide psychological intervention to children and their families in a creative, multifaceted, integrated, and cost-effective manner. Intervention spans a continuum from prevention, to treatment of disorders, to rehabilitation, lending itself to the creative endeavors of the leaders in this field.

GROUP VERSUS INDIVIDUAL INTERVENTION

Certain principles must be considered in deciding to make an individual or group intervention. Individual interventions involve the therapist working directly with one client or patient. The choice of individual interventions are many and varied and the emotional health of the individual can range from minimal problems to severe mental illness. Group interventions run a spectrum from providing educational information and support to a large, healthy population (primary prevention), to providing specific therapy to a small select group of people with similar diagnoses or experiences (e.g., group therapy for incest survivors).

If group psychotherapy is to be employed as the form of group intervention, members of the group usually are carefully selected. The process of selection, however, often occurs through "deselection"; that is, group therapists exclude certain patients from consideration and include all others. With adults seeking group psychotherapy, the primary exclusion criteria are group deviancy and pervasive life crisis (Yalom, 1985). An individual who is deviant in a group is one who cannot participate in the group task of examining one's self and one's relationship with others. Individuals in acute crisis are excluded if they can be more efficiently treated by another therapy format. If conflicts are too extreme, the patient likely will choose to leave or be extruded from the group. Yalom (1985) believes that there is no exclusion marker for adult patients and that the vast majority can be treated in group therapy.

While Yalom's principles of group therapy can be adapted for youngsters, other factors also must be considered: (a) the goals of the intervention, (b) severity or type of problem or illness, (c) age of the youngster, and (d) available resources.

Goals of Intervention

When the goals of the intervention are to assist an emotionally healthy subgroup of the population in coping with a life circumstance problem, a group approach to intervention can be very useful.

Vignette 1

The counselor at a suburban middle school was aware that 40% of the student population was from homes in which the parents were separated or divorced. Many students referred to her were having some difficulty coping with the lifestyle required of them. To address the problem, the counselor established a group for children of separated or divorced parents. Meetings took place after school on the school campus, and several students became active leaders helping other children with similar problems. For example, when Jacob, a 12-year-old honor student, found it difficult to concentrate and saw his grades drop during his parents' divorce settlement, he began attending the group. He felt less isolated and blamed himself less for his family's problems. In time, he was able to adjust to his difficult and painful family situation and again began to find interest in his academic work and extracurricular activities.

Severity of Illness

Group interventions are generally targeted toward a group of individuals who are relatively healthy (although often at risk for emotional problems), or a group of individuals who are diagnosed with an emotional or behavioral disorder but who are stable and not severely impaired at the time of intervention. Patients who are psychotic, suicidal, severely depressed, or otherwise unstable should be carefully evaluated and treated with a specific individualized treatment plan geared toward promoting stabilization and recovery as safely and as quickly as possible. At times, individuals who are still in the recovery phase of severe, acute psychiatric illness participate in group therapy while in the protected and carefully monitored environment of a psychiatric hospital's inpatient unit. Not only are acutely or severely psychiatrically ill patients likely to interfere with the process of the group and the progress of the other members, but they can also become dangerously destabilized. Therefore, it is important that a qualified professional participate in the screening of potential participants in a group intervention and be actively involved in the group itself.

Vignette 2

Joseph, aged 17, was hospitalized for the second time with the diagnosis of schizoaffective disorder. While initially acutely psychotic with bizarre delusions of the FBI spying on him and planning to kill him, he stabilized with medication and the safe and structured environment of the hospital. He began attending group therapy sessions with the other patients as he planned for discharge. Two days prior to discharge, his biological father, who had been aloof and unpredictable in the past, abruptly told Joseph that he could not take him to his home and that Joseph would have to return to his anxious, intrusive, and poverty-stricken mother. The next morning, Joseph was confronted by two group members about his inappropriate relationship with his mother. Later that day, Joseph's condition deteriorated. He attempted to barricade himself in his room as he felt the FBI was closing in on him. In a state of delusion, he perceived others on the unit as "demons" who were planning to attack him because of his worthlessness. In a state of despair, he planned a suicide attempt. Close surveillance by the hospital staff who were aware of the patient's acute stressors—including confrontation during group therapy—protected the patient from self-harm. He was treated individually by his psychiatrist who offered security, support, and appropriate medication. The patient gradually recovered and was discharged 3 weeks later.

Because it is difficult to determine which youngsters may become destablized by a group intervention, members of a potential group must be screened carefully before admission. When an intervention is planned for a group of youngsters who are felt to be healthy, such as in a school setting where the intervention is part of an educational program, it is best for the instructor to consult a mental health professional in planning the program. Only a professional who is well trained in understanding all the ramifications of emotional disorders can foresee the potential problems that can arise from such intervention. The mental health professional can help select the material to be presented as well as offer advice for the best manner of presentation. Without these consultations and precautions, well-meaning interventions can become disruptive and even dangerous. They can precipitate a decompensation in seemingly healthy individuals and even cause youngsters to feel suicidal.

Vignette 3

Mary K. is a 15-year-old high school student who, 3 months prior, was assaulted and sexually molested while on vacation in a neighboring city. Her family discreetly took her to see a rape crisis counselor at a private hospital. Mary attended two sessions but did not feel a need to continue further even though her counselor recommended additional treatment. Unknowingly, Mary's health teacher, in an effort to prevent sexual abuse in teenagers, presented a program to her class that included a brief but detailed movie telling the story of a youngster who was sexually assaulted. Although circumstances in the movie were different from her own, Mary became very anxious during the class. Afterward, she experienced flashbacks and recurrent thoughts of her own assault. She was unable to sleep, became afraid to go out of her house, and felt as though she was about to "fall apart." With the assistance of her parents, she returned to see her counselor. After several daily meetings, she was able to return to school.

In Mary's case, the group intervention offered was not planned out carefully. The abrupt presentation of explicit and detailed material provoked and triggered symptoms of posttraumatic stress disorder. Without a previous knowledge of the dynamics of posttraumatic stress disorder, the instructor did not realize the impact of her intervention on this seemingly healthy young student. For Mary to function effectively again, her destablized condition required an intense individual intervention. Very often, individuals who have been sexually abused or traumatized in other ways require significant individual treatment before being able to join group treatment for the same disorder.

Age

Groups can be very successful interventions when used with youngsters who are in their preteen or adolescent years. During this period of development, youngsters are engaged in the process of separating from their parents and families and discovering their own identity. Peers provide a powerfully important influence.

Vignette 4

Georgette is a 17-year-old high school dropout who was admitted to an inpatient psychiatric unit following a suicide attempt with an overdose of Tylenol. Georgette, who expressed anger and distrust toward all adults, would not permit herself to engage with her doctor or therapist. She rejected every effort offered to her. It was not until after several group meetings with the other adolescents on the unit that she was able to be open to suggestions and accept observations about her own self-destructive and self-defeating behavior.

Availability of Resources

The availability of resources has a profound influence on an intervention. Providers need to consider indirect costs (i.e., office space, electrical bills, custodial services, insurance) as well as the financial and time constraints of professionals. Often creativity and the combination of services are necessary to provide needed intervention.

Vignette 5

At the University of New Mexico Woman's Health Center, a special Obstetrical Clinic was designed to address the needs of pregnant teens. The team of professionals (nurse-midwives, ob-gyn resident, social worker, nurse specialist, nutritionist, and child psychiatrist) quickly recognized that many pregnant adolescents are trying to cope with multiple psychological and social issues besides their premature parenthood. Adolescent girls who become pregnant and give birth are reported to frequently experience problems at home as well as substance abuse and psychopathology, in addition to increased socioeconomic deprivation (Trad, 1995). Taking into account available resources, several specific interventions were implemented by the clinic team. A brief screening questionnaire completed by each patient is reviewed by the social worker and diagnostic interviews are arranged with the social worker or child psychiatrist based on information in the questionnaire or by referral from other members of the team who are concerned about a patient's psychological status. High-risk or emotionally ill teens are referred for individualized assessment and treatment through this process.

In addition, each week a "Pizza Group" is conducted by the child psychiatrist. The group is open to any patient who wishes to attend as well as a partner, friend, or family member (usually the patient's mother or sister). The group provides the opportunity for the teens to discuss their concerns and fantasies about their pregnancy and delivery, to provide support to each other and to ask questions of the child psychiatrist. In a comfortable, fun setting with pizza and juice, the teens psychologically prepare for their delivery and for their new role as parents.

In addition to providing education and support, the one-hour group provides a mechanism by which high-risk teens can be monitored for symptoms of depression, abuse, and severe social problems. Problems such as homelessness, lack of food, and severe family stresses are mentioned in the group. Adolescents who demonstrate a need for additional help are directed to the appropriate team member to assist them or make referrals for needed resources.

The professionals on the multidisciplinary team treating these pregnant youngsters meet weekly for an hour to discuss any patients about whom they have concerns. The young women thus receive holistic, coordinated health care and appropriate mental health intervention from professionals, who need to offer only a few hours of service per week.

With a combination of both group and individual intervention and the use of a medical clinic and a multidisciplinary team, comprehensive medical and mental health services are provided to a high-risk group of teens.

PREVENTION AS AN INTERVENTION

The prevention of emotional disorders is particularly pertinent for young people. Preventive interventions at an early age offer a special opportunity to change the course of an individual's life. These preventive interventions are categorized as primary, secondary, and tertiary. Primary prevention is aimed at an entire population or at high-risk groups with the intent of strengthening an individual's ability to cope with specific types of stress, to reduce the stress itself, or to prevent the transmission of a disorder. The goal of secondary prevention is to identify a disorder early and to treat it promptly with the hope of decreasing the prevalence of a disorder. Finally, tertiary intervention attempts to reduce the prevalence of residual defects or disabilities due to an illness or disorder (Grant, 1991).

Preventive intervention targets a group or groups of youngsters rather than individuals. Group/environment-centered interventions aim to alter the "living and learning climate" in a particular setting. The intervention attempts to change the identified system. Illustrative is promoting the use of condoms among sexually active youth to prevent the spread of sexually transmitted diseases. Individual/child-centered interventions, on the other hand, focus on high-risk groups with individual approaches. The intervention attempts to change the risk factors impinging on the individual's attempts to cope successfully. Supportive therapy for a child whose parents are in the process of a divorce is an example of this type of intervention.

The participation of mental health professionals in the prevention of mental disorders in children is not a new concept. Anna Freud (1974) wrote of developmental lines and pointed out that child analysts need to be experts in the normal development of children as preparation for providing consultation to patients and other professionals in their interactions with healthy young children. The concept of primary prevention was also the guiding light of the Child Guidance Clinics developed earlier in this century. Gerald Caplan (1961; Simmons, 1987) and later Irving Berlin (1979; Simmons, 1987) encouraged the consultant-consulter model for preventive psychiatry. By providing psychiatric or psychological consultation to other health care providers or other professionals in the community, mental health professionals can touch the lives of many more youngsters than they would by individual therapy.

The use of primary prevention as an intervention may be more relevant than ever before. Rapid change in cultural values and family stability present a significant challenge to parents and professionals who work closely with children and youth. Although we now inhabit a world of sophisticated global communication, exciting electronic machinery, and computerized technology, emotional stability and opportunities for warm interpersonal relationships seem compromised more than ever. It is in this climate of exciting scientific discovery and weakened, interpersonal relationships that children and adolescents must accomplish the crucial task of human emotional and social development. Many families are challenged even further. They can no longer rely on the support of extended families, church, or community, which have become weakened in recent generations.

TREATMENT AS INTERVENTION

Another way of conceptualizing intervention is based on the medical model, which targets individuals rather than groups. In this model, an individual is considered to suffer from symptoms or to deviate from normality. A diagnosis of a particular disease or disorder leads to the prescription of individualized treatment. This model is utilized by most psychiatrists and mental health professionals today. It is also the model most likely to get reimbursed by insurance companies and other third-party payers. An individual is often already significantly impaired at the time of treatment. Frequent modes of treatment consist of medications, individual psychotherapy, group therapy, and family therapy. Variations and combinations of treatment are often useful. Inpatient hospitalization, partial hospitalization, and intensive day treatment programs are utilized for the most severe cases.

This model has several limitations. A significant number of youngsters with emotional disorders never get referred and remain untreated. Others, by the time they receive treatment, are extremely impaired due to environmental as well as biological factors. Hopes for recovery are modest. Although effectiveness is improving, treatments are far from curative. Preventive interventions are desirable in addition to direct treatment intervention.

DEVELOPMENTAL APPROACH TO INTERVENTION

Infancy

The arrival of a new infant into the home can be an opportune time to apply measures of primary prevention. During this period of transition, family members often are open to information that will assist them in caring for their new child. It also is a time when parents are more likely to accept and appreciate support from others.

Misunderstanding an infant's developmental needs and capacities can lead to unhealthy patterns of interaction that might be prevented or corrected with education and support. For decades, pediatricians have taken advantage of the first year of an infant's life to teach parents what to expect in normal development. They have called such interventions "anticipatory guidance." For better understanding of interactional patterns during infancy, intervention should involve the primary caregivers and the baby together.

Winnecott (1964) once remarked that "there is no such thing as a baby," dramatically highlighting the infant's dependency on adults for survival. While infants are indeed dependent on caregivers, they are not purely passive and "moldable" creatures, but play an important role in interactional patterns.

Sameroff and Emde (1989) reviewed past models of development and developed their "transactional" model. Past models have stressed that the child's development is determined biologically and realized through maturation. Other models have stressed the impact of the environment on the child's development (i.e., changes in the environment cause changes in the child).

A more valuable model is the transactional model. In this model, the child develops through a continuous dynamic interaction between the child and the experience provided by his or her family or social context. The child's effect on the environment is emphasized as well as the environment's effect on the child. For example, the child reacts to a stimulus in the environment; in return, the environment (caregiver) responds to the specific reaction of the infant; this causes, in turn, a possibly new reaction from the child, and so forth. In such a way, both constitutional factors and changes in the environment affect the infant's development (Sameroff & Emde, 1989).

The transactional model points out that caregivers and their infants each have special characteristics of relating that they bring into their relationships and these characteristics alter the interaction in a dynamically reciprocal manner. Such a formulation provides opportunities for intervention in the environment, with caregivers, and with the infant.

Vignette 6

Jacob is a 4-month-old infant who enjoys being held and appears to need a great deal of physical stimulation and interpersonal interaction. He becomes upset and will cry when left alone in his crib or playpen and seems to need less sleep than the average baby. When he is carried about, spoken or sung to, or taken on trips in his carriage, he is pleasant and enjoyable. Jacob's mother, on the other hand, is a quiet person who enjoys sedentary activities such as reading, sewing, and watching television. She needs periods of time in which she can be alone in a subdued environment. Jacob's demands on her feel extreme; and she wishes he would not seek attention so often. Over the past month, Jacob's need to be picked up and held has increased. Such demands on her have felt intrusive and overwhelming. In response to her baby's request for physical contact, she has become less available and has withdrawn from him. Experiencing the withdrawal and lack of availability of his mother, Jacob has responded by increased fussiness and irritability to the point that he appears to be whining "all the time" and never playing by himself. Jacob's mother now interprets his irritability as anger and rejection causing her to feel angry with him even during those moments of close contact such as feeding. Interactions between Jacob and his mother have become less and less pleasurable and have begun to seriously interfere with their relationship.

It was important to provide an intervention that would interrupt the vicious cycle of their unpleasant interaction. The intervention conceptualized the transactional experience of mother and baby. The therapist helped Jacob's mother see the infant's irritability and demands not as anger and rejection but rather as a desire to be with the person he knows to be the most important in his life. For Jacob, being held by his mother is a pleasure he wishes to experience more often. When Jacob's mother accepted this reinterpretation of Jacob's actions, she found holding him to be more pleasurable. She relaxed and enjoyed his company more often when she held "the baby who adored her." Being held and responded to more often helped Jacob feel more secure and loved, making it easier for him to spend brief periods quietly contented. The change in interactions between Jacob and his mother paved the way for a healthy relationship in the future.

For many parents, a primary prevention approach to intervention can ensure a smooth interaction with mutually gratifying reciprocity between caregivers and child. Taking a group approach and targeting new parents with education in the form of books, magazines, and newsletters, community lectures or talks by mental health professionals, and guidance from pediatricians and nursery school teachers can provide valuable primary intervention. Even TV shows with audience participation can be an exciting educational intervention for eager new parents. Neighborhood get-togethers with mothers and their new infants, as well as toddler and preschool play groups, can provide a wonderful source of information and support for young families.

It is, however, increasingly difficult for young families to take advantage of such primary prevention opportunities. In many families, both parents are working and their infant spends most of the day in a child-care center (frequently miles away from the parent's place of employment). This situation is made more difficult because many mobile, young families live a distance from relatives and do not have access to members of the extended family nor to the advice and support of the older generation. Mental health professionals, therefore, must not only provide education and guidance to young families, they must find creative ways to relay this information through nursery school parent meetings, weekend activities, or even TV shows.

"Family centered" places of employment are desperately needed in our society today. This includes places that facilitate "family leave," flexibility of work schedule, and on-site day care. In many European countries, nurseries and day-care centers are provided for the children of employees on work premises. Parents, especially mothers, can maintain contact and even nurse their very young children in the course of a workday. Such centers are few in the United States. Therefore, even parents who themselves received good parenting, are emotionally healthy, and understand the needs of young children, become very challenged as parents in today's world. A group intervention provided by mental health workers could be the education of the general public, especially parents, about the importance of flexibility in the work lives of parents as well as the importance of quality day care near the parent's place of work. Consultation to existing day-care programs can be another group intervention to impact the psychological development and care of the young child.

There are infants and parents who experience more serious emotional or behavioral difficulties and, therefore, require more intense intervention. This intervention may take the form of group therapy in which infants or toddlers and their parents attend therapeutic nursery programs two or more times a week. During the program, parents and child have the opportunity to interact while participating in developmentally relevant age-specific, growth-enhancing activities for the youngster. Parents are guided in these interactions and supported in a positive way while learning helpful techniques in relating to their child. Time may be set aside for parents to meet alone with a therapist for a process-oriented group intervention. Finally, an individual therapist may work alone on the special needs and interactions of the child and his or her parents.

Most of our current diagnostic mental health manuals primarily describe conditions as they are experienced by adults. However, to address the needs of the infant and young child, the Zero to Three/National Center for Clinical Infant Programs (1995) recently recognized the need for a systematic, developmentally based approach to the classification of mental health and developmental difficulties in the first four years of life. This organization developed a Diagnostic Classification of Mental Health and Developmental Disorders of Infancy and Early Childhood (Grant, 1991). This classification takes into account the infant's biological proclivities: his or her ability to self-regulate, to process information, to communicate, and to interact with others, particularly caregivers. The system of classification can help guide individual interventions focusing on the child's ability to interact and communicate feelings. These interventions may be taught by the therapist to the parents, who may be the ones to implement them.

Even with our improved ability to identify emotional and behavioral problems affecting infants, and with professionals better trained to address those problems, there still remains those multiproblem, chaotic families who do not access available resources. These families, along with a thoughtful and effective model of intervention of support and outreach, are aptly and beautifully described in Selma Fraighberg's classic article "Ghosts in the Nursery" (Fraighberg, Adelson, & Shapiro, 1975). Fraighberg points out that "babies can't wait" for their parents to receive long-term psychotherapy to correct destructive or ineffective interactional patterns. Fraighberg, therefore, presents her model of "kitchen psychotherapy": A trained therapist goes to the home of the infant at risk and warmly supports the parent while modeling appropriate care and interaction with the child. Most importantly, the therapist progressively helps the parent (usually the mother) link the relationship with her baby to her own past experiences, and allows the mother to affectively share past traumas, hurts, and disappointments. In this manner, the therapist drives away the "old ghosts" of the past and releases the mother to love and nurture her own baby.

For intervention during infancy, services must include education, day care, therapeutic nurseries, and individualized therapy through home visits to meet the wide range of parents, infants, and interactive patterns. While such individualized interventions can be costly in terms of therapists' time and emotional energy, it provides an opportunity to reach and provide intervention to those who would otherwise not receive it. For many families, it is through the development of trust that mental health professionals can provide guidance and support. This progressive intervention carries the potential of significantly changing the course of a child's life.

School-Age Child

Until recently, the school-age child was considered by adults and even mental heath professionals to be "innocent" and free from the psychological and social concerns experienced by adults. Freud, in developing his theories of psychosexual development, thought little occurred during this particular stage and referred to it as "latency." He did not elaborate about the conflicts or complexities that face children during the elementary school years. Writers, poets, and artists for the most part perpetuate the myth of a carefree childhood.

Children were considered to be psychologically and cognitively lacking in the maturity necessary to experience mental illnesses such as major depression. Thoughtful research has demonstrated, however, that the school-age years can indeed be a time of significant turmoil with the presence of psychological problems and psychiatric illness. In fact, many disorders are identified for the first time during the early school-age years such as attention-deficit hyperactivity disorder, learning disabilities, behavioral problems, and the depression of low self-esteem. One reason for the identification of problems at this age is the presentation to a youngster—perhaps for the first time—of age-specific tasks in a classroom setting. But another reason is that the youngster can now be observed in contrast to same-age peers by a professional who is outside the family setting. The child then can be observed in an objective fashion by teachers who are experienced in the usual behaviors of children of specific age groups.

Schools are in an ideal position to provide preventive intervention to our youngsters and schools have an unprecedented opportunity to improve the lives of young people (Hendren, Birrell, & Orley, 1994). Schools are currently the best place to develop a comprehensive mental health program because:

- Almost all children attend school sometime during their lives.
- Schools are often the strongest social and educational institution available for intervention.
- Young people's ability and motivation to stay in school, to learn, and to utilize what they learn is affected by their mental well-being.
- Schools can act as a safety net, protecting children from hazards that affect their learning, development, and psychosocial well-being.
- In addition to the family, schools are crucial in building or undermining self-esteem and a sense of competence.
- School mental health programs are effective in improving learning, mental well-being, and in treating mental disorders.
- When teachers are actively involved in metal health programs, the interventions can reach generations of children.
- Teachers have often received some training in developmental principles, making them potentially well-qualified to identify and remedy mental health difficulties in school-age children.

School-based mental health interventions may be group/environment-centered or individual/child-centered and one may lead to the other. Group approaches aim to improve the educational climate and to provide opportunities for children to connect with a healthy school program where they will find healthy role models. This positive mental health atmosphere includes the structure of the school day, the structuring of playground activities, the physical structure of the school, and the classroom decoration. Group-centered approaches also strive to enhance the ability of administrators, teachers, and support staff to deal with the specific areas of emotional or behavioral disturbance they encounter, and, when necessary, to understand how to make use of other agencies serving children.

Individual-centered activities include mental health consultations and specific problem-focused interventions as well as more general classroom programs to improve coping skills, social support, and self-esteem. With mental health interventions, the mental health professional usually provides a consultation for a particular child and family having difficulty. The result of the consultation may involve recommendations to the parents, the teacher, and in some cases, referral for treatment outside the classroom.

School-age youngsters often adapt easily to individual therapy. While some may be articulate and ready to discuss problems most prefer to use less direct means of communication. Play therapy using puppets or art, drawing and painting, or the use of games can all be successful media through which the children communicate their concerns and conflicts.

Vignette 7

Raymond, at age 7, had difficulty adjusting to his new foster home. He isolated himself in his room, argued with the other children in the home and would not comply with family rules. Neglected by his depressed and substance abusing biological mother, Raymond had learned to retreat from social interaction. He was described by his school teacher as being timid, withdrawn and fearful of new situations. The new foster home was bustling with noise and activity. Two very active, younger children vied for attention. His foster mother, a vivacious, competent woman, was experienced by Raymond as being overly intrusive.

Raymond's behavior and poor academic performance led his teacher to contact his foster mother and arrange a school based psychological assessment of him. The school psychologist subsequently provided weekly psychotherapy to Raymond, assisting him in his adjustment to his new home and school. In addition, the psychologist collaborated with Raymond's teacher in suggesting techniques to help him function in his classroom. Once a month Raymond's foster mother had a session with the school psychologist during which she learned strategies for interacting with Raymond. She was taught "floor time" as a method of giving Raymond undivided attention while learning about him as an individual. She could thus interact in a sensitive and less threatening manner.

With such interventions, Raymond gradually became more confident and socially adept. He demonstrated a marked improvement academically, flourished in peer relationships and began to interact in a more involved, affectionate manner in his home.

At this age, children are still very dependent on their parents for material and emotional support as well as for their identity in the larger world. Therefore, family therapy or regular meetings with the child's parents or guardian are crucial.

Greenspan (Greenspan & Salmon, 1993) believes that even during the grade school years "floor time" is essential. This is a special period of at least 30 minutes per day specifically set apart for a parent and child to interact and connect with each other through unstructured talk or play in which the parent follows the child's lead. The key concepts of floor time are that the child determines the direction of the play or conversation and the adult is fully and actively involved with the child. Shared but passive activities such as watching a TV show or reading a book together do not count. Floor time can function as a wonderful primary prevention intervention by enhancing communication between parent and child. It can also serve as a treatment intervention with the parent being the prime facilitator for the expression of important ideas and feelings. When used as a treatment modality, the parent-child floor time is guided by a mental health professional.

As the child matures, peer relationships become more important, making group therapy a relevant mode of intervention during the last years of elementary school and throughout middle school. Between 11 and 14 years of age, most youngsters begin to think about their individual identity. They are uncertain who they are now and who they will be in the future. However, as they begin to separate and attempt to become more independent of their parents, these youngsters are certain of one thing—they are *not* their parents. Their individuation process often leads them to be critical of even the most elemental aspects of their parents' behavior; they may criticize a parent's attire, walk, speech, or mannerisms. The young adolescent may feel embarrassed by a parent's company during social events. The awareness that he or she is still deeply dependent on a parent, can bring on strong feelings of frustration and anger to an adolescent. To survive this transition to independence, the adolescent seeks support from peers. Identifying with each other, young adolescents frequently dress and talk alike and enjoy the same music and activities. In light of the dynamics of early adolescence, group therapy with peers can be a very effective form of treatment. Also, such dynamics can explain some of the difficulties that might arise if a child in therapy identifies the therapist too closely with his or her parents or feels parents and therapist are collaborating and not understanding the youngster as an individual. The middle or junior high school years may be a time when group therapy is relevant and effective but work with families and individuals remains vitally important.

Adolescence

There is an old saying that points out, "It takes a village to raise a child." As children develop the physical and psychological skills necessary for explaining and negotiating the world, they require the opportunity and place to try out these abilities. An adolescent requires a relatively protected environment to try out new skills, take risks, and discover his or her individual identity. While parents and family remain important, the task of the adolescent is to separate adequately from them to ensure individuality. Peers and "soul-buddies" become agents of support, confidantes, and companions in risk taking.

Living in a village, young men or women could try out their independence and take risks outside the immediate family yet be protected by the shared traditional values of the community and the guidance of neighbors, friends, and extended family members. Special traditions would offer challenges and not only validate, but herald, their adulthood. In the United States today, "village" life is hard to come by. Communities are weakened more than ever before, and nuclear families are often isolated, perhaps not understanding or even knowing the values of those who live next door.

Primary prevention, group interventions offer adolescents the opportunity to spend their free time in a constructive manner. Mental health professionals can provide intervention by encouraging and organizing community youth programs and serving as consultants to such programs creating a village, or protected place, for adolescents to experiment and discover where their talents lie while learning about responsibility and interpersonal relationships. Such opportunities can exist in the context of sports programs, drama, journalism, and community service programs. As discussed earlier, schools are an ideal place for mental health intervention. However such "villages" must also exist in communities outside the school setting to reach the ever growing number of teenagers leaving school prematurely. Although not a traditional role for mental health professionals, they must encourage active community recruitment of adolescents into creative programs that will foster continued development. Those who care about youngsters, their mental health, their futures, and even their survival must support and implement strong community programs that offer teenagers opportunities to develop their talents and be identified as valued adults. Without sports, jobs, educational programs, and other such activities, young men and women cannot develop self-esteem and are left with a terrible void that they attempt to fill by drug abuse, gang activity, vandalism, and premature pregnancy.

Several urban mental health centers are already providing timely interventions by holding groups for adolescents who are gang members and have suffered emotionally prior to joining the gang, as well as from gang activity. These youngsters are supported and taught skills to allow them to develop a healthy cultural identity that may include gang membership without violence or delinquent behavior. They are also given opportunities to participate in constructive activities.

Besides the difficulties that arise for teenagers due to environmental and societal factors, significant mental disorders that are more biologically rooted, such as depression, bipolar disorders, and schizophrenia frequently manifest for the first time during adolescence. Adolescence is also a time when many youngsters experiment with alcohol or drugs and may become addicted or abusive of substances. Individual treatment is required in the initial evaluation of such adolescents, but due to the importance of peers during this developmental stage, group therapy is often a valuable treatment component.

Vignette 8

Carlos had been an excellent student in elementary school but during his middle school years, his home life became more and more dysfunctional with an increasing use of alcohol and drugs by the adults in his family. He spent more time on the streets, felt despairing of his situation and his future, and by his sophomore year in high school, he attended few classes. He felt hopeless, found no real pleasure in life, and, as a member of a local gang, frequently engaged in dangerous activities. As Carlos began to experience more severe symptoms of depression, he used more alcohol and drugs in an effort to cope with his feelings. It was only after Carlos got into trouble with the law that his psychiatric problems were recognized. The consulting child psychiatrist at the detention center diagnosed Carlos's severe depression as well as his substance abuse disorder. He was hospitalized on an adolescent unit where his psychiatric disorders were treated with a combination of therapy, the milieu, and medication. Upon discharge, a treatment plan for Carlos included a substance abuse treatment program for teenagers with group, individual, and family therapy as well as psychiatric monitoring and treatment of his depression with antidepressant medication.

SUMMARY

There are multiple approaches to providing psychological intervention to children and adolescents. A spectrum that includes prevention, treatment of disorders, and rehabilitation can be offered as individual interventions, as group interventions, or in combination. In choosing a particular intervention, the mental health professional must consider the goals of intervention, severity and type of problem or illness, age, and available resources. In general, individual interventions are necessary for youngsters who are acutely and significantly impaired. For infants and preschoolers, one must work not only with the child but also with the primary caregivers. School-age children do well with interventions that occur in the school setting. That age group also responds well to individual and family therapy. As adolescence approaches, the value of group therapy becomes more evident.

Contemporary society, with a weakening of institutions and extended families, demands that mental health professionals take an active role in providing opportunities for young people to explore their talents and establish their identity in sports programs, drama, the arts, mechanics, and other creative modalities.

With limited resources and a diversity of social and emotional problems in today's society, the mental health professional is indeed challenged. However, creative ideas and innovative approaches are more welcome than ever before; and, as always, the personal rewards of providing a service to young people remain deeply gratifying.

REFERENCES

American Psychiatric Association. (1994). *Diagnostic and statistical manual of mental disorders* (4th ed.). Washington, DC: Author.

Bemporad, J. R. (Ed.). (1980). *Child development in normality and psychopathology.* New York: Brunner/Mazel.

Berlin, I. N. (1979). Mental health consultation to child-serving agencies as therapeutic intervention. In J. D. Noshpitz (Ed.), *Basic handbook of child psychiatry* (pp. 353–364). New York: Basic Books.

Brazelton, T. B., & Cramer, B. G. (1990). *The earliest relationship.* New York: Addison-Wesley.

Caplan, G. (1961). Concluding discussion. In G. Caplan (Ed.), *Prevention of mental disorders in children* (pp. 398–416). New York: Basic Books.

Cohen, J. J., & Fish, M. C. (1993). *Handbook of school-based interventions.* San Francisco: Jossey-Bass.

Fraighberg, S., Adelson, E., & Shapiro, V. (1975). Ghosts in the nursery. *Journal of the American Academy of Child Psychiatry, 14,* 387–421.

Freud, A. (1974). The concept of developmental lines. In S. Harrison & J. McDermott (Eds.), *Childhood psychopathology* (pp. 133–156). New York: International Universities Press.

Grant, N. I. (1991). Primary prevention. In M. Lewis (Ed.), *Child and adolescent psychiatry* (pp. 918–929). Baltimore: Williams & Wilkins.

Greenspan, S. I., & Salmon, J. (1993). *Playground politics.* New York: Addison-Wesley.

Hendren, R., Birrell, W., & Orley, J. (1994). *Mental health programmes in schools.* Geneva, Switzerland: World Health Organization, Division of Mental Health.

Kaminer, Y. (Ed). (1994). *Adolescent substance abuse.* New York: Plenum Medical.

National Advisory Mental Health Council. (1990). *National plan for research on child and adolescent mental disorders.* Rockville, MD: U.S. Department of Health and Human Services, Public Health Service.

Sameroff, A. J., & Emde, R. N. (Eds.). (1989). *Relationship disturbances in early childhood.* New York: Basic Books.

Simmons, J. E. (1987). Consultations. In *Evaluation of children* (pp. 219–235). Philadelphia: Lea & Febiger.

Trad, P. V. (1995). Mental health of adolescent mothers. *Journal of the American Academy of Child and Adolescent Psychiatry, 34,* 130–142.

Tyson, P., & Tyson, R. L. (1990). *Psychoanalytic theories of development.* New Haven, CT: Yale University Press.

Wiener, J. M. (Ed). (1991). *Textbook of child and adolescent psychiatry.* Washington, DC: American Psychiatric Press.

Winnicott, D. W. (1964). *The child, the family, and the outside world.* Ontario, Canada: Penguin Books.

Yalom, I. (1985). *The theory and practice of group psychotherapy.* New York: Basic Books.

Zeanah, C. H., Jr. (1993). *Handbook of infant mental health.* New York: Guilford Press.

Zero to Three/National Center for Clinical Infant Programs. (1995). *Diagnostic classification: 0–3; Diagnostic classification and developmental disorders of infancy and early childhood.* Arlington, VA: Author.

CHAPTER 5

Residential Services for Children and Adolescents

SCOTT SPREAT and RUTH C. JAMPOL

Many children are unable to live with their natural families. In some cases, the family is unable to provide the structure and nurturance that is needed to raise the child, despite efforts by the social service system to support the family. The absence of structure and nurturance, often combined with medical and physical challenges to the child, may result in behavior problems for some children that preclude successful integration into community and family life. Isett, Roszkowski, and Spreat (1980) defined behaviors such as aggression and property destruction as barrier behaviors, because they effectively bar the child from meaningful prosocial integration. Children with such behavioral barriers are often placed outside the family for treatment that will, ostensibly, minimize the barriers to integration. *Residential treatment centers* are one option for such service.

Residential treatment center is a broad term that includes a wide range of potential services. The federal government (Redick, Witkin, Atay, & Manderscheid, 1994) defines a residential treatment center for emotionally disturbed children as an organization, not licensed as a psychiatric hospital, whose primary purpose is the provision of individually planned programs of mental health services for persons in residential care. The definition further notes that the children must be under 18 years of age and that the primary reason for placement for over half the children must be some form of mental illness, but not mental retardation, substance abuse, or alcoholism. A more inclusive definition would delete the exclusion for mental retardation and broaden the mental illness requirement to include behavior disorders of various types.

The preceding definition, with this modification, places residential treatment centers on a continuum of care between community-based services provided in a biological family, a foster family, or a group home, and long-term hospitalization. This broader definition of residential treatment centers will be used in the present chapter, which will consider residential services offered to children with emotional disorders and/or mental retardation. Clinical and administrative trends will also be examined.

Who Lives in Residential Treatment Centers?

Residential treatment centers serving children and adolescents with mental retardation and/or emotional disorders have been affected by trends to treat and educate children in the least restrictive setting possible. As a result, residential placement for children with mental retardation has become less popular. Paradoxically, however, residential treatment of emotionally disturbed children is being used more frequently.

The number of children with mental retardation who are being served in residential settings has declined dramatically over the past 20 years. Amado, Lakin, and Menke (1990) report that the residential population of children with mental retardation was 90,942 in 1977. This figure decreased to 60,391 in 1982, and 45,747 in 1988. They also noted that the average age at which a person first enters residential care has increased substantially over this time, and theorized that the Education of All Handicapped Children Act (PL 94-142) and programs to assist families in raising children in their home have contributed substantially to this change in population. The number of children who receive special education has increased every year since 1976 (Amado et al., 1990). The dramatic increase in school- and community-supplied services implies that those individuals who do enter the residential system will generally have greater behavioral and/or medical complexities than in the past.

Data on emotionally disturbed children placed in residential treatment centers are confusing and misleading, due to changes over time in how residential treatment centers are classified (Wells, 1991a, 1991b) and a lack of clarity about whether data refer to all children in out-of-home placements, children in nonfamily homes (group homes, residential treatment centers, and hospitals), or children in residential treatment centers as defined by this chapter. When children are counted by the system originating placement, as is often done, the numbers can be greatly inflated because children are often known to several systems simultaneously (Yelton, 1993). Nonetheless, studies have consistently found large increases in the number of children served in residential treatment centers over the past 20 years, and there is some consensus that the number of children in these placements has approximately doubled (Manderscheid & Sonnenshein, 1994; Tuma, 1989; Yelton, 1993). The U.S. Department of Health and Human Services reports that 27,785 individuals were living in residential treatment centers for emotionally disturbed children in 1990, representing slightly more than double the numbers of 1969 (Manderscheid & Sonnenshein, 1994).

These figures are particularly striking given the concurrent development, during the same period, of numerous resources that allow seriously emotionally disturbed children to remain in their home communities, including wraparound services and family preservation programs. At the same time, however, the use of state and county hospitals has dramatically declined (Manderscheid & Sonnenshein, 1994; Tuma, 1989). Apparently, the movement of some children from residential treatment centers into their home communities has been more than compensated for by the shifting of other children from long-term hospitalizations to residential treatment.

As a result of these trends, children with mental retardation and/or emotional disorders who are placed in residential treatment settings will tend to have a multiplicity of behavior problems and will exhibit significant barriers (e.g., aggression, property destruction, self-injurious behaviors) to placement in less restrictive settings. This chapter will include a critical review of broad clinical and administrative trends affecting the treatment of these challenging populations.

TRENDS AFFECTING RESIDENTIAL TREATMENT CENTERS FOR CHILDREN WITH MENTAL RETARDATION

Three major themes affect the delivery of residential services to children who have mental retardation. The practice of behavior therapy is evolving into a broader and more complex art; regulations, particularly those addressing the practice of behavior therapy, are becoming more limiting; and the role of medications continues to be scrutinized. Each of these three trends will be examined.

The Evolution of Behavior Therapy

The practice of behavior therapy has undergone significant changes over the past 15 years. In particular, there is greater emphasis on assessing the function of behavior and a recognition that the process of behavior change involves more than "catching them when they are bad." Several trends will be discussed.

Functionally Derived Treatment

In the 1970s, there was consensus that behavior modification programs could be implemented with little regard to the factors responsible for the initial development or subsequent maintenance of target behaviors (Griffith & Spreat, 1989; Iwata, Vollmer, Zarcone, & Rodgers, 1993). With powerful enough reinforcers and/or punishers, behaviors were changed without attention to their functional properties. Tremendous successes were evident in the treatment of individuals living in impoverished environments, and as Griffith and Spreat (1989) suggested, perhaps behavior modifiers were shaped away from their scientific heritage of the analysis of behavior by these successes. It was evident in the 1960s and early 1970s that while Skinner's (1953) cautions about antecedent and consequential events were being taught in graduate school, they were not widely applied in a systematic manner in real world clinical settings. Attention was largely directed toward consequence-based programming.

Despite the successes, not all procedures worked all the time for all the people being treated. Even punishment procedures were not always successful (Donnellan & LaVigna, 1990). This situation led some behavior analysts to return to the underpinnings of the profession—the analysis of behavior and the contingencies that maintain it. Iwata, Dorsey, Slifer, and Richman (1982) reminded clinicians that an analysis of the contingencies maintaining a behavior is an essential component of an efficient and humane treatment process. Other clinicians followed the lead of Iwata et al. (1982), and by the mid-1980s, the assessment of functional properties of target behaviors was considered the standard of the field (Axelrod, Spreat, Berry, & Moyer, 1993).

The renewed attention to functional properties of behavior resulted in a shift in the treatment focus away from the topography of target behaviors. Clinicians no longer were treating aggression, but rather escape-motivated aggression or attention-motivated aggression. A number of clinical benefits resulted from this shift in focus, including the ready identification of a likely reinforcer, identification of the contingency that will be the basis of treatment, identification of irrelevant approaches, and selection of interventions that are efficient for changing specific behaviors.

Iwata (1994) identified four basic functional classes of behavior:

1. *Attention Seeking* Behavior that is socially mediated and maintained by positive reinforcement.
2. *Escape* Behavior that is socially mediated and maintained by negative reinforcement.
3. *Stimulation* Behavior that is automatically (or perhaps internally) mediated and maintained by positive reinforcement.
4. *Terminating Aversives* Behavior that is automatically mediated and maintained by negative reinforcement.

Other models have also been developed to describe common functional properties of behavior. Most notable, Carr and Durand (1985) have proposed that many behaviors serve a communicative function. Others (cf. Aide to Functional Analysis, Willis & LaVigna, 1987) identify an emotional expression function to behavior, although this might be considered a communication function as well.

Having identified the functional properties of a target behavior, the clinician then helps the client develop alternative behaviors that will serve the function equally well. By understanding the variables that maintain target behaviors, the clinician can suggest treatment strategies that have some rational and systematic relationship with these variables (Repp, Felce, & Barton, 1988). Carr, Robinson, and Palumbo (1990) refer to this process as the development of functionally equivalent responses.

The use of functionally derived treatments requires the clinician to distinguish between the asocial target behavior and the usually reasonable needs that the behavior serves. For example, most individuals seek a certain level of social attention from others and have learned socially appropriate ways to obtain that attention. Problems arise when individuals have not learned socially acceptable ways of getting desired levels of attention. Thus, the goal of treatment is to teach better and more efficient alternatives, not simply to decrease asocial ways of meeting needs.

Functionally equivalent behaviors are those behaviors that enable the individual to achieve the same outcome as socially inappropriate behaviors. When these functionally equivalent responses are more efficient at producing reinforcement than the asocial behaviors, the functionally equivalent behavior will replace the less efficient asocial behavior (Billingsley & Neel, 1985; Horner & Billingsley, 1988). Some individuals have even suggested that the goal of treatment is solely to develop alternative responses (Carr et al., 1990). The actual reduction of target behaviors is considered a side effect, albeit a very important one, of treatment. In this sense, functionally derived treatments can be viewed as part of a package to enhance an individual's life, not merely a means of changing a behavior. One should note, however, that Response Contingent Electric Shock also can be considered part of a package to enhance an individual's life.

Examples of functionally derived treatments are appearing with greater frequency in the professional literature. Favell, McGimsey, and Schell (1982) successfully treated self-injury that appeared to be maintained by self-stimulation by providing individuals with alternate, more benign forms of self-stimulation. In a similar manner, Sigafoos and Kerr (1994) provided alternative leisure activities as a program to reduce a variety of challenging behaviors that tended to occur in the absence of engaging activities.

Escape-motivated behavior has been treated by reducing the aversiveness of the situation from which the subject seeks to escape (Carr, Newsom, & Binkoff, 1976). Similarly, Weeks and Gaylord-Ross (1981) reduced the complexity (and apparently the aversiveness) of tasks by substituting easier tasks for more difficult ones. Of course, it may be necessary to reintroduce the more aversive forms of the stimulus in a manner similar to desensitization. Luiselli, Mederios, and Cameron (1993) reported a differential reinforcement-based program to increase the time between toileting requests that were believed to function as escape behaviors.

A variant of the functionally derived treatment approach assumes that many behavior problems are attempts to communicate specific or general wants and needs (Carr & Durand, 1985; Donnellan, Mirenda, Mesaros, & Fassbender, 1984). Behavior problems are considered nonverbal communication classes (mands); thus the student who throws a task on the floor may be communicating, "I don't want to do this task." Treatment is then focused on teaching the child to communicate his or her wishes in more socially acceptable ways. A considerable body of literature supports the use of augmentative communication strategies to reduce socially and intrapersonally unacceptable behaviors.

Carr and Durand (1985) demonstrated that preemptive verbal strategies can be effective in reducing target behaviors. Children whose target behaviors were thought to be maintained by attention were taught more acceptable ways to solicit adult attention, and the rates of target behaviors decreased immediately. Similarly, Durand and Carr (1987) found that high task difficulty and low levels of adult attention were associated with increased rates of target behaviors. By teaching their subjects alternative ways to solicit help and/or attention, they reduced rates of target behaviors. Day, Rea, Schussler, Larsen, and Johnson (1988) obtained similar reductions in self-injurious behaviors (SIB) by teaching two developmentally disabled children to make requests as an alternative to SIB. Such programs will be successful only if the communication strategy is addressed by the adults and the function of the misbehavior is to obtain attention.

Teaching functionally equivalent behaviors (whether communicative or other) is not the only option for hypothesis-driven treatment. Iwata (1994) delineated a number of functionally derived treatments that are not specifically designed to teach functionally equivalent responses. For example, Iwata has recommended noncontingent reinforcement, extinction, time-out, and differential reinforcement as appropriate approaches with which to address attention-maintained behaviors. Similarly, escape-motivated behaviors might be addressed by noncontingent removal of the aversive event, demand desensitization, blocking the escape (extinction), or compliance training. Thus, functionally derived treatments do not necessarily involve the teaching of functionally equivalent behaviors. At this point, the relative efficacy of the various approaches remains an empirical question, and selection among alternatives might best follow the guidelines suggested by Axelrod et al. (1993).

Functional analysis does not always yield one specific function (Sturmey, 1994), and the identification of a specific function of a target behavior does not necessarily guarantee successful treatment (Scotti, Schulman, & Hojnacki, 1994). Axelrod (1987) provides a thorough discussion of the limitations to functional analysis.

Broader Focus of Treatment

The focus of many behaviorally oriented clinicians is shifting from isolated demonstrations of the ability to control and change behavior to more holistic demonstrations of improved life quality. Montrose Wolf (1978) was perhaps most responsible for encouraging behavior analysts to more broadly construe the concept of social importance. Building on Wolf's (1978) concerns about the social validity of our clinical actions, Horner, Sprague, and Flannery (1993) were led to postulate the "so what" question. "So what" if Gracie's head banging has decreased as a result of behavioral programming, if she still lives in a barren, understimulating environment and if she still leads an empty, segregated life? While this example is perhaps a bit extreme, the challenge to behavior analysts is to show that they can produce changes that affect the overall lifestyle of the individual (Sprague & Horner, 1991). Thus the social validation of our clinical work comes not merely from decreasing behavior, but from improving life quality. These approaches are not necessarily mutually exclusive, nor do all accept responsibility for improving their clients' lives by any means other than changing specific target behaviors.

The adoption of a broader approach to applied behavior analysis is an evolutionary process. Horner et al. (1993) note that there is still need for accurate measurement of target behaviors and scientifically valid demonstration of control. They simply urge that these scientific values be broadened to consider indices of life quality in addition to the reduction of behavior. While the reduction of traditional target behaviors remains important, the strategies of applied behavior analysis can also be used to address broader concerns of life quality, and this newer application may also result in behavior change.

Cameron and Kimball (1995) suggest that stimulus control methods that emphasize personal choice-making, communication competencies, and strategies that prevent the occurrence of target behaviors are viable treatment options. They note that options focusing on issues other than consequences have several advantages. They capitalize on existing behavior-environment relations so that new behaviors do not have to be taught. Stokes and Baer (1977) point out that establishing behavior change through methods of stimulus control enhances maintenance and generalizability, a significant benefit.

McFalls (1995) suggests that lack of choice is a frequent cause for socially unacceptable behaviors, and that programming should address ways to incorporate greater levels of choice into an individual's life. McFalls suggests that rather than reinforcing an individual for adapting to an environment perceived as unpleasant, we should help create an environment that is more acceptable to that individual. For example, if an individual hates his or her roommate, the appropriate response may simply be to enable one of the individuals to move, rather than attempting to program either one into a friendship.

Behavioral supports can be incorporated into programming in a number of ways, and perhaps the term itself is not precisely descriptive. In one of the earlier works in this area, Horner (1980) examined the effects of environmental enrichment on "adaptive" and "maladaptive" behavior of persons with profound mental retardation who lived in an institution. He found a higher incidence of adaptive object-directed behaviors and a lower incidence of "maladaptive" behaviors under environmentally rich conditions. Similarly, Sigafoos and Kerr (1994) reported that by providing individuals with opportunities to participate in leisure activities, they were able to increase adaptive behavior and decrease problem behaviors. Iwata and others have been conducting research on noncontingent reinforcement, which is essentially a form of environmental enrichment. Although one might expect the development of superstitious behaviors, this strategy often seems to be successful in reducing inappropriate behavior (Hagopian, Fisher, &

Legacy, 1994; Luiselli, 1994; Vollmer, Marcus, Bethany, & Ringdahl, 1995). It would be interesting to monitor the development of any superstitious behaviors to determine whether they became behavioral alternatives to target behaviors.

Staff in residential programs are essentially behavioral supports for the individuals who live there. A considerable body of literature suggests that staff behavior can directly affect consumer behavior. Wehby, Symons, and Shores (1995) observed that low rates of positive social interactions characterized classrooms in which students engaged in aggressive behavior. Hastings and Remington (1994) reported that empirical evidence exists that staff spend little time interacting with consumers, that they respond intermittently to challenging behaviors, and that these responses often inadvertently reinforce the challenging behaviors. A variety of behavior programs for staff have been demonstrated to change both staff and (indirectly) consumer behavior (cf. Hollander, Plutchik, & Horner, 1973; Montegar, Reid, Madsen, & Ewell, 1977; Spreat et al., 1985).

One type of staff behavior receiving considerable attention relates to making requests of consumers. At the simplest level (and probably the one we should try first), Tustin (1995) reported that by simply giving advance notice of transitions, he was able to reduce stereotypy in a man with autism. It is hardly surprising that how one requests a person to do a specific task affects that person's willingness to perform that task. Mace and colleagues have conducted a line of research on consumer compliance to requests, and they have found that higher probability requests (i.e., requests with which the consumer is likely to comply) can be used to prepare the consumer for lower probability requests, and that this process can increase cooperation with difficult or unpleasant requests (Mace et al., 1988).

Focus on Proactive Treatment Strategies

Cameron and Kimball (1995) offer an interesting challenge to behavior analysts. While noting that the manipulation of consequent events is generally positive in nature, they suggest that clinicians limit the diversity and richness of treatment options by focusing solely on consequences to target behaviors.

There is broad recognition that deficits in social skills are often associated with asocial behavior. Matson and Frame (1986) noted that deficits in social skills, while not pathological in themselves, were often correlated with pathologies such as depression, anxiety, and schizophrenia. By providing individuals with additional training in deficit areas, we may be helping to prepare them for future interactions with environmental stimuli that once elicited asocial behavior. When confronted with a stimulus that formerly elicited a socially inappropriate response, the individual may be able to make an alternative response subsequent to training.

Matson and Adkins (1980) used audiotapes to help teach appropriate forms of social interaction to two individuals with mental retardation. This training in social skills resulted in decreases in inappropriate social interactions. Similarly, Matson and Stephens (1978) reduced the explosive behavior of chronic psychiatric patients through social skill training. Kelly, Wildman, Urey, and Thurman (1979) taught students to ask questions and give positive feedback. The development of these skills was associated with gains in appropriate behavior. Bay-Hinitz, Peterson, and Quilitch (1994) demonstrated that cooperative games were more likely to be followed by increased cooperation and decreased aggression than were competitive games. Foxx, McMorrow, and Schloss (1983) adapted a game-playing approach to social skill development. Game players move around a game board by answering questions with socially appropriate responses. The authors report that individuals increased their social skills over a range of situations; however, generalization of these skills should probably not be assumed. Muscott and Gifford (1994) suggest that the virtual reality interface with computers could serve as a mechanism for enhanced training in social skill development.

A considerable amount of research has addressed instructional sequencing. Gunter, Shores, Jack, Denny, and DePaepe (1994) decreased disruptive behavior by employing an instructional sequence that provided the consumer with all information necessary to complete a task prior to being asked to complete that task. Kennedy, Itkonen, and Lindquist (1995) employed social comments interspersed with requests for compliance, and found that compliance was increased.

Movement from Free Operant

The types of behaviors that place individuals in residential treatment centers are not generally high in terms of absolute frequency. While 30 aggressive behaviors per month certainly make someone a poor neighbor, they cannot be considered frequent. Programs that rely on punishing misbehavior are doomed to, if not failure, at least limited success because they simply do not permit a sufficient number of stimulus-response connections. The movement from reactive programs to proactive programming has been a hallmark of the late 1980s and early 1990s.

In most cases, proactive programming has been largely oriented toward the development of functionally equivalent behaviors or enhanced communicative responses, but many clinicians consider punishment to be a valid tool for the treatment of behaviors (Axelrod & Apsche, 1983; Griffith & Spreat, 1989). Van Houten and Rohlider (1988) developed an interesting technique called "Recreating the Scene" which permits greater opportunity to build stimulus-response connections. In essence, this method permits the use of punishment procedures in an analogue situation. The client is prompted to perform the target behavior repeated times, and the consequence of that behavior is applied each time. This approach provides massed practice in learning consequences. The approach has been extended to the treatment of pica by Spreat, Axelrod, and Thompson (1995) by pairing it with the concept of the "baited" environment (Rojahn, McGonigle, Curcio, & Dixon, 1987).

The (Over) Regulation of Behavior Therapy

The practice of behavior therapy with children who have mental retardation and who live in residential settings has become a highly regulated clinical art. Spreat and Lipinski (1986) reviewed the mental retardation behavior modification policies of 38 states, and noted that while the regulatory procedures were varied, the elements of peer review, human rights review, and consent were typically present. In contrast, minimal attention was directed to the training of the staff who either develop or implement the program.

Griffith and Spreat (1989) suggested that the regulation of behavioral psychology was a direct outgrowth of earlier abuses of persons under the misnomer of behavior modification. Wexler (1975) provided a number of examples of such abusive practices, where procedures were used to punish people rather than to change behavior. Griffith and Spreat (1989) suggested that the use of the term "behavior modification" to describe these practices was inaccurate, and slandered a clinical art, rather than focusing on the behavior of individual therapists who designed such programs.

There have been several attempts to prevent the misuse of behavior modification techniques (cf. *Lake v. Cameron,* 1966; *Wyatt v. Stickney,* 1972). In these efforts, the courts established a variety of due process mechanisms to protect individuals from indiscriminate treatment. Consent and peer review were key components of these safeguards.

Acting to avoid further court involvement in the practice of behavioral psychology, individuals and organizations within the field lobbied successfully for a form of self-regulation that would offer effective protection for individuals (see Friedman, 1975; Martin, 1975; Risley & Sheldon-Wildgen, 1980; Sheldon-Widgen & Risley, 1982; Wexler, 1975). Although there was considerable opposition to the imposition of behavioral guidelines and regulations (cf. Goldiamond, 1976; Stolz, 1977), some common procedures, such as those noted above by Spreat and Lipinski (1986), have emerged over time.

Regulatory procedures for behavioral psychology appear unique compared with those of other professions. Behavioral psychology is regulated by the proposed treatment act, rather than by the qualification of the person developing the treatment strategy. Thus, while a dentist must have appropriate licensing and training before instituting possibly painful therapeutic acts, each specific act does not require peer review or human rights review. In contrast, no particular qualifications are needed to develop a behavior modification program involving the use of overcorrection, but the plan must be approved by several committees which also may have little or no expertise in clinical treatment (Spreat & Lanzi, 1989). With respect to behavioral psychology, the system regulates the art, rather than the artist. In Pennsylvania, an individual without even a bachelor's degree can develop an overcorrection program for a person with mental retardation, and if appropriate approvals are obtained, the program can be implemented. The licensing standard for the actual practice of psychology in Pennsylvania is a doctorate; this standard is obviously not applied to the treatment of persons with mental retardation who live in residential settings. Griffith and Spreat (1989) referred to this discrepancy as a subtle form of handicappism.

In addition to the possibility of handicappism, the regulation of the art, rather than the artist, appears to be in direct conflict with *Youngberg versus Romeo* (1982), which established the standard of professional judgment for clinical treatment of persons with mental retardation. According to this ruling, decisions made by professionals, within the scope of their credentialed and licensed experience, is presumptively valid. This standard offers a compelling argument for broader latitude in the selection and development of treatment approaches.

With such increased latitude would come obvious responsibilities. Only professionals are entitled to make professional judgments. Behavior modification procedures fall within the province of psychology or psychiatry, two fields in which the professional standard is a doctorate and a professional license. Only individuals with these credentials should be entitled to make professional judgments about the use of behavior modification procedures.

One might argue that psychology has allowed the deprofessionalization of its field. By encouraging the use of paraprofessionals (cf. Bijou & Ruiz, 1981), the practice of behavior modification has become the province of no one. There is no way to ensure that the person developing a restrictive behavior modification program for a client has any particular expertise in the area. Although the use of nonprofessional behavior therapists may be fiscally rewarding at a superficial level, the practice of pooling the knowledge of individuals who would be unable to exercise professional judgments with the general public provides little real protection of the client. The additional cost of credentialed professionals might be offset by the savings in time by significantly reducing peer review and human rights review components, as suggested by Spreat and Lanzi (1989).

Regulation has gone wrong with respect to behavioral psychology. While peer review and human rights review certainly have some limited role (Spreat & Lanzi, 1989), professional judgment must not be overridden by regulation. To meet the standard of professional judgment, we must ensure that appropriately credentialed professionals are making those judgments. With such recognition of professionalization must come a more autonomous form of practice. If regulations were to pay more attention to the qualifications of the artists, perhaps there would be less need to regulate the art itself.

Continuing Scrutiny of the Use of Psychoactive Medications

Continuing skepticism about the role of medications in mental retardation programs has resulted in increased insistence that these programs justify and empirically support their use of psychotropic medications. Such skepticism is probably warranted, as the use of psychotropic medications with persons who have mental retardation appears often to be guided by extrapolation from studies using intellectually average individuals with different treatment needs. It appears further justified by the existence of programs, such as Au Clair in Delaware, that treat individuals with serious behavioral disorders without use of psychoactive medications.

Medication reduction trials are a consistent theme in various regulations under which mental retardation programs operate (cf. Federal Regulations for Intermediate Care Facilities for the Mentally Retarded). Amado et al. (1990) note that the Intermediate Care Facilities for the Mentally Retarded (ICF/MR) regulations require that individuals who receive psychotropic medication must undergo frequent medication reduction trials, unless justified by a physician. The spirit of this regulation is laudable; persons should not continue to receive medication without evidence of benefit. On the other hand, it can be argued that these regulations minimize the chronicity of emotional disturbance. Behar (personal communication, 1994) notes that no one suggests giving a diabetic a medication holiday from insulin. The success of such medication reduction trials is questionable. Spreat, Serafin, Behar, and Leiman (1993) studied mandated medication reduction trials in an ICF/MR and found that the net amount of medication dispensed following such trials was essentially unchanged. Some clients received less medication following reduction trials, while others actually received more. On the other hand, May, London, Zimmerman, Thompson, and Mento (1994) reported that they were able to completely eliminate the use of Thioridazine in 22 persons with profound mental retardation who lived in a state developmental center. In support of this finding, the Au Clair program in Delaware serves extremely behaviorally disordered individuals without use of psychotropic medication (Shine, personal communication, 1991).

There is considerable disagreement within the field of psychiatry regarding the use of medications with persons with mental retardation. Some (Bishop, 1992) suggest that better diagnostic workups are essential to the prescriptive use of psychotropic medication. Through careful diagnosis, the psychiatrist may be better able to identify the medication most likely to help an individual. Other psychiatrists (Behar, 1993) express reservations about the reliability and validity of the diagnostic process when applied to persons with mental retardation. Their approach is more empirical, selecting medications relative to broad diagnostic needs and related safety factors and evaluating them on objective data.

More significant than the argument over approach may be the basic question of efficacy. Aman and Singh (1985) concluded that after 35 years of drug research, little is really known about efficacy. In their summary article, they noted that antipsychotics do seem to suppress stereotypy and in turn permit increases in adaptive behavior. The effects of antipsychotics on aggression, property destruction, and hyperactivity are still subject to debate, although it is evident that some individuals respond favorably. Spreat and Behar (1993) reported similar findings with respect to lithium. While certain individuals responded favorably to lithium, it was not possible to demonstrate efficacy in a group study.

Distinguishing responders from nonresponders appears to be the most difficult aspect of using psychotropic medications with persons with mental retardation. Some of the problem may be that psychopharmacology for persons with mental retardation is often directed toward the suppression of specific symptoms, rather than toward matching pharmacological agents to well-defined syndromes as in other aspects of psychiatry.

TRENDS AFFECTING RESIDENTIAL TREATMENT CENTERS FOR CHILDREN WITH EMOTIONAL DISTURBANCES

Trends in the use of residential treatment centers for emotionally disturbed children have been greatly affected by shifts in national policy, as well as by outcome studies conducted by the treatment centers themselves. Each of these areas will be briefly reviewed. Then three topics related to current practice in the residential treatment of emotionally disturbed children will be examined: who are currently served by these programs and who should be served; appropriate goals for residential treatment; and involvement of families in the treatment process.

Policy Trends Affecting Residential Treatment

Residential treatment centers for severely emotionally disturbed children operate at the intersection of the child welfare system and the child and adolescent mental health system. Residential treatment centers function within a continuum of mental health services as a restrictive service modality for youngsters whose symptoms cannot be managed or treated effectively within a community setting. However, a large proportion of children and adolescents in residential treatment centers are referred not through the community mental health system but through the child welfare system, in its attempts to meet the needs of abused and neglected children. A recent survey by the National Mental Health Association found that 47.6% of children in out-of-state mental health placements were placed by the child welfare system, compared with 7.2% by a mental health agency. The remainder were placed by educational (21.6%) or juvenile justice (17.6%) agencies (Yelton, 1993). Current trends in residential treatment of emotionally disturbed children and adolescents therefore can only be understood in the context of how recent changes in both the child welfare system and the child and adolescent mental health system have affected the residential treatment center's mission and population.

In the 1960s and 1970s, growing awareness of child abuse as a significant problem, accompanied by the passage of child abuse reporting laws, resulted in a huge increase in the numbers of children placed in foster care by the child welfare system (Yelton, 1993). Many of these children were found to "drift" within the child welfare system, without progressing toward either reunification with their biological families or adoption. Concern over how this rootlessness was affecting children led to the concept of "permanency planning." As defined by Maluccio and Fein (1983, p. 195), permanency planning refers to "the process of taking prompt, decisive action to maintain children in their own homes or place them permanently with other families." The ideological underpinnings of the permanency planning movement include core beliefs in the value of having children in a family setting, the primacy of the parent-child attachment, and the significance of the biological family in human connectedness (Maluccio & Fein, 1983). Permanency planning became a legal obligation of child welfare agencies with the passage of the federal Adoption Assistance and Child Welfare Act of 1980 (PL96-272), which required child welfare agencies to provide preventive services for children at risk for placement, reunification services as soon as possible when such a plan is feasible, and termination of parental rights when children cannot be returned home (Allen, Golubock, & Olson, 1987).

The child and adolescent mental health system has been undergoing a parallel transformation in recent years. Critics have long noted the lack of coordination among agencies that serve children with mental health needs (the child welfare, mental health, education, and juvenile justice systems). This failing has contributed to serious deficiencies in the delivery of mental health services to children. Between 15% and 19% of the nation's 63 million children have been estimated to need mental health treatment, and 70% to 80% of these children may not be getting appropriate care (Tuma, 1989). This problem is hardly new; statistics describing the need for improved delivery of children's mental health services have not changed significantly since the early 1900s (Tuma, 1989). This lack of appropriate services has been particularly acute for children and adolescents with severe emotional disturbances (Knitzer, 1982). In 1984, the federal CASSP (Child and Adolescent Service System Program) initiative was established to assist state mental health agencies in coordinating care for seriously emotionally disturbed children and adolescents. By 1993, all 50 states had developed CASSP projects (Yelton, 1993). The philosophical underpinnings of the CASSP initiative, articulated by Stroul and Friedman (1986), include beliefs that treatment should, ideally, take place in the context of one's family and community, and that families should be directly involved in planning and decision making for their children.

These parallel trends in child welfare and child and adolescent mental health have converged to underscore several principles that are reshaping residential treatment of emotionally disturbed children in the 1990s. First and foremost is the belief that the least restrictive, most community-based setting is always the preferred treatment setting for emotionally disturbed children and adolescents. Ideally, this setting should be the biological family, but if this is not possible then a substitute family or familylike setting within the community is preferable to residential treatment. Second, if residential treatment is absolutely necessary, it should be brief, with the goal of returning the child to the family, or at least to a community setting, as quickly as possible. Third, families should be involved in all aspects of residential treatment, from the admission decision to setting the goals for discharge.

For many practitioners of residential treatment, these principles have profoundly challenged their work. Residential treatment centers have traditionally provided long-term, rather than brief, treatment. Removing the child from the family for treatment has presented both practical and philosophical roadblocks to family involvement in residential treatment centers. The mandate for least restrictive settings has created a perception among many mental health professionals and child advocates that residential treatment is a poor substitute for community-based care and should be avoided at all costs. Advocates for residential treatment as a viable treatment option have felt compelled to justify the value of residential treatment centers in the continuum of child and adolescent mental health services (Whittaker, 1978) or search for the "phoenix" amid the "ashes" of residential treatment (Fein, 1986).

Compounding the threats to residential treatment from the ideological shifts within the child welfare and mental health systems are the increasingly difficult tasks being required of residential treatment centers. Young, Dore, and Pappenfort (1988) conducted two national surveys of residential treatment centers in 1966 and 1981, and concluded that over the 15-year period, facilities shifted to caring for more seriously disturbed youngsters in much shorter periods of time. There continues to be a broad consensus among researchers and practitioners that the children with mental health problems entering residential treatment in recent years have become increasingly disturbed and come from families that are more disorganized and fragmented than in the past (Balcerzak, 1991; Bernstein, 1987; Carlo 1985; Grellong, 1987; Small, Kennedy, & Bender, 1991). Not infrequently, families of children in residential treatment are virtually nonexistent (Balcerzak, 1991; Bernstein, 1987). As Small et al. (1991) commented: "The challenge to current practice in residential treatment is not that some of our clients act out so severely, but that these days almost all of them do" (p. 329). These changes may, in part, reflect worsening social conditions among families living in poverty, but are certainly also related to the movement to serve children in the least restrictive setting: Youngsters who were previously hospitalized for long periods in state and county institutions are now being served in residential treatment centers whereas those who were previously admitted to residential treatment centers are more likely to receive intensive services within their families and communities. At the same time that residential treatment centers are adjusting to the needs of this more difficult, aggressive, and disturbed population, they are also being asked to provide services in briefer time frames and with more involvement by increasingly fragmented families.

Trends within Residential Treatment Centers

In addition to the pressures created by shifting ideologies outside the residential treatment center, dissatisfaction with residential treatment as an effective setting for the treatment of emotionally disturbed children and adolescents has also sprung from developments within the institutions themselves. The history of residential treatment centers has been amply documented elsewhere (see Whittaker & Maluccio, 1989; Wilson & Lyman, 1983) and will not be repeated here. In brief, from the late 1940s until the early 1970s, innovative models of residential treatment were developed, resulting in vibrant programs whose concepts and techniques enriched and helped shape the field of children's mental health. Pioneers like Bruno Bettelheim (Bettelheim &

Sylvester, 1948), Fritz Redl (Redl & Wineman, 1957), and Albert Trieschman (Trieschman, Whittaker, & Brendtro, 1969) developed and refined the concept of the therapeutic milieu, thereby providing a theoretical rationale for the value of residential treatment as a uniquely effective modality. Nicholas Hobbs's (1966) psychoeducational model of residential treatment introduced an ecological framework for child treatment well before this approach became a mainstay of the children's mental health field. Other innovative approaches included the development of residential treatment programs based wholly on the principles of behavior analysis (Phillips, Phillips, Wolf, & Fixsen, 1973) and the Positive Peer Culture Model (Vorrath & Brendtro, 1974), which mobilized the power of the peer group to create positive change within an adolescent residential setting.

Despite the apparent successes of these programs during the time children attended them, outcome research has generally failed to establish that meaningful gains are necessarily maintained after discharge. Two landmark studies of children's postdischarge functioning at two well-established residential treatment centers found little relationship between children's adjustment during residential placement and their functioning after discharge (Allerhand, Weber, & Haug, 1966; Taylor & Alpert, 1973). Instead, these studies found that factors such as the child's active participation in the community during residential treatment, parents' participation in their child's residential treatment, and the degree of stability and perceived support in the child's postdischarge environment were associated with positive outcomes. Twenty years later, these sobering assessments of the long-term effectiveness of residential treatment still stand: continued research has confirmed that severity of the presenting problem, specific treatment modality employed, and status at discharge are, at best, weakly associated with functioning after discharge, while the supportiveness of the postdischarge environment and the involvement of the family in residential treatment are more strongly associated with long-term positive adjustment (Curry, 1991; Whittaker & Pfeiffer, 1994).

In light of these findings, it has been difficult to generate continued excitement about clinical innovations within residential treatment centers. Instead of focusing on treatment modalities, researchers and theorists have shifted their attention to the role of residential treatment within a continuum of mental health services for children. More energy is expended on justifying the entry into this setting (e.g., for whom is residential treatment necessary and/or effective?) and exit back into the community (e.g., how can residential treatment centers improve linkage with aftercare services?) than on improving service delivery in the centers. Though necessary and important, these lines of inquiry have done little to enrich the clinical interventions of residential treatment programs. In response to the ideological shifts, the failure to demonstrate long-term gains through residential treatment, and the high cost of residential treatment compared with efforts at family preservation, public funding to pilot-test new residential programs has been withdrawn, leading to further deterioration of these programs (Whittaker & Pfeiffer, 1994).

Three core issues currently face residential treatment providers. First, if less restrictive is better, under what circumstances should residential treatment be the treatment setting of choice—whom should residential treatment centers be serving? Second, what are the appropriate goals for residential treatment that are both achievable and consistent with CASSP principles and permanency planning, and in what time frames should these goals be achieved? In other words, what should residential treatment centers be trying to accomplish? Third, how can a treatment setting that takes over physical and psychological responsibility for a family's "problem child," often creating a large geographic separation between child and family, productively involve families in treatment? The first two issues involve attempts to redefine the contemporary mission of residential treatment centers and their position in the continuum of mental health services for children and adolescents; they do not directly address clinical practice within the treatment programs themselves. The third issue—involving families in residential treatment—represents the only major new clinical innovation in residential treatment of emotionally disturbed children over the past 15 years. Each of these three issues will be discussed in turn.

Whom Do Residential Treatment Centers Serve and Whom Should They Serve?

From studies and clinical descriptions of children referred for residential treatment, some broad, general characteristics of this population can be delineated. In a study of youths referred for residential treatment at one private, nonprofit mental health agency over a 12-month period, Wells and Whittington (1993) found that, compared with the general population, these youths were more impoverished, suffered more family breakdown, came from families that were less cohesive and adaptable than nonclinical families, and had experienced more stress. The youths' problems were characterized as diverse, severe, and diffuse, began at an early age, and included significant deficits in social competencies. The youths were found to have used extensive services throughout their lives and to have been "in crisis" during the year preceding referral to residential treatment. Based on these data, Wells and Whittington concluded that short-term treatments were unlikely to succeed with at least some of this population, and that, for some, even long-term programs could prove unsuccessful. Small et al. (1991) found that 60% of preadolescent boys admitted to one residential treatment center between 1985 and 1991 had histories of abuse, and that a sharp increase in the number of boys with reported histories of sexual abuse had occurred. Cates (1991a) described a high frequency of disrupted relationships between child and caretaker in children referred for residential treatment and stated that family dysfunction has repeatedly been found to be a primary factor leading to placement in residential treatment. Cates argued that the history of family disruptions may render these children unable to adapt to a familial system such as a foster home. Several studies have documented a higher level of physical aggression in children referred for residential treatment, compared with those referred to less restrictive treatment settings (Gabel, Finn, & Ahmed, 1988; Gabel & Shindledecker, 1992; Zimet, Farley, & Zimet, 1994). Others have noted a high degree of complicating factors in children referred for residential treatment, including the frequent presence of specific learning disabilities or intellectual limitations (Grellong, 1987) and increasing numbers of youths who are dually diagnosed with substance abuse and psychiatric disorders (Ponce & Jo, 1990).

Studies conducted in individual agencies, however, may mask differences across agencies. Workers in the field have long been aware that such factors as bed availability, funding, caseworker and agency bias, referral source, and the availability of less restrictive options strongly influence the decision to refer for residential treatment (Gabel, Stadler, & Bjoin, 1995; Guterman & Blythe, 1986; Maluccio & Marlow, 1972; Whittaker & Maluccio, 1989). In a recent comparison of boys referred for either residential placement or a less restrictive day hospital setting, Gabel et al. (1995) found that neither degree of psychopathology nor level of family dysfunction predicted what type of placement recommendation was made. Instead, the setting in which the boys were currently enrolled (day treatment versus residential) was the strongest predictor of future recommendations. The authors speculate that factors such as the availability of alternative levels of care and the referral sources (school district versus social service agency) may be influencing professionals' decisions more than the child's or family's level of functioning.

In practice, two conflicting phenomena seem to be occurring simultaneously. Many children are being referred for residential treatment only after less restrictive alternatives have been extensively tried. These children have usually been removed from their families by child welfare agencies due to serious abuse or neglect, and have been moved unsuccessfully from foster home to foster home, being repeatedly ejected because of their disruptive behavior in much the same way Fritz Redl bemoaned 30 years ago (Redl, 1966). As Martin, Pozdnjakoff, and Wilding (1976) prophesied 20 years ago, when these children finally enter residential treatment centers, they are even more difficult to treat because of the effects of multiple community failures. As a result, residential treatment centers have increasingly become the repositories for, in Yelton's (1993) words, "the children who no one wants" (p. 184).

On the other hand, a number of children continue to enter residential treatment when other less restrictive alternatives, had they been available, might have been successful. In the authors' experience, this is often the case with referrals from school districts, where interventions prior to referral for residential treatment only targeted the child in the school environment. Many times, family therapy—let alone more intensive interventions aimed at family preservation—may never have been tried. (Likewise, child welfare agencies may not have accessed appropriate less restrictive educational interventions prior to referral for residential treatment.) Intensive family services aimed at maintaining the child in the home are simply unavailable to professionals in the schools as a less restrictive treatment option. Despite the federal CASSP initiative of 1984, the lack of coordinated treatment and planning among agencies who serve seriously emotionally disturbed children remains a major stumbling block to the appropriate use of residential treatment.

Neither the overuse of community interventions when failure is inevitable nor the underuse of community resources that might successfully prevent out-of-home placement represents a satisfactory approach to residential placement. A more rational approach would require referring agencies, governmental policy makers, and residential treatment centers to put aside ideological generalizations (e.g., that seriously emotionally disturbed children should be rescued from "bad" parents and communities, or that a family environment is always healthier for a child than a more impersonal, institutional environment) and look carefully at what actually works for whom. As Whittaker (1978) has argued for years, children's mental health services require a total continuum of care, and both smaller, community-based services and larger, more secure settings need to be a part of it.

Efforts at utilizing residential treatment appropriately as part of a continuum of care are hampered not only by lack of coordination among agencies and by practical problems such as funding and bed availability, but by a lack of knowledge about what works for whom. Asking whether residential treatment is effective is analogous to asking whether psychotherapy works; the question is so broad that it is meaningless.

Studies instead need to determine what programs and treatment settings are effective for which youngsters. Currently, no information is available on this issue (Cates, 1991b; Wells, 1991b). Guterman and Blythe (1986) identify several unique strengths of residential treatment centers, including attenuated emotional relationships with a variety of adults, ability to handle more aggressive behavior, greater structure, and extensive peer exposure. It is relatively straightforward to determine when a child requires the structure and behavioral containment of a residential treatment center, and when placement decisions are made rationally, they are usually based on these considerations. Rarely is attention paid to whether a child is likely to benefit from extensive peer interactions or, instead, may be harmed by constant exposure to other seriously emotionally disturbed children.

The potential harm or benefit from attenuated emotional relationships with caregivers may be the most important consideration in determining whether residential treatment is appropriate, but it is also generally overlooked. Given the disrupted family histories of most children referred for residential treatment, there is likely to be great variability in their capacity for attachment. Those who retain this capacity will probably adjust best to a nurturing family environment and may be harmed by institutional care. Those who are impaired in this capacity are likely to find the expectations and emotional burdens of a family environment to be overwhelming and frustrating, and may actually thrive in an institutional setting. In addition, the concept of loyalty to one's family of origin, familiar to family therapists (Boszormenyi-Nagy & Krasner, 1986; Boszormenyi-Nagy & Spark, 1973), could help professionals understand and predict the optimal residential setting for a particular child. A child who feels intensely loyal to his or her parents is likely to sabotage attempts of others to provide structure, nurturance, and discipline. In the child's mind, the substitute caregiver's success would mean the natural parent was bad, incompetent, or irresponsible. While child-care workers in residential treatment centers have all felt the effects of these kinds of expressions of family loyalty, the disruptive impact will be more severe when a single caregiver substitutes for the natural parent. Thus, children with intense feelings of loyalty to their natural parents are likely to adjust better to the multiple caregivers in a residential treatment center than to a single caregiver in a foster home.

Too often, the child's developmental needs are also overlooked in placement decisions. Older children and adolescents may adjust poorly to new family environments not only because of their own family histories, but because of their normal developmental needs to question authority, affiliate with peers, and establish separate identities. If these tasks can sometimes overwhelm families that have been intact since the child's birth, they would certainly be likely to interfere with the establishment of new family bonds. Research is needed to determine how developmental issues may affect the likelihood of success in foster homes versus residential treatment centers for children of varying ages.

Residential treatment centers also need to develop specialized treatment programs for specific populations. Most residential treatment centers are differentiated from one another only by the level of care they provide: community-based, unlocked but intensively staffed and/or geographically isolated, and locked. Usually, the child's level of aggression, potential for self-harm, and potential for elopement will determine the type of program to which he or she is referred, without regard to the underlying clinical issues. It is possible that the development of specialized programs for specific populations such as sexual abuse victims, dually diagnosed substance abusers with psychiatric problems, and more vulnerable youngsters with impaired reality testing would lead to better treatment outcomes after discharge.

The Goals of Residential Treatment

In light of the failure of many children to maintain gains made in residential treatment after discharge, and the lack of correlation between progress within residential treatment and postdischarge status, a shift has occurred in the way proponents of residential treatment view this modality. While the therapeutic milieu remains a cornerstone of residential treatment (Wilson & Lyman, 1983), the conceptual emphasis has shifted to an ecologically based model of treatment (Guterman & Blythe, 1986; Whittaker, 1978; Whittaker & Maluccio, 1989). An ecological perspective considers not only the child within the treatment setting, but also "the complex interplay of many different elements both within and outside of the formal service context" (Whittaker & Maluccio, 1989, p. 96).

From an ecological perspective, the purpose of residential treatment is not to rescue children from their environment, but to link children with the appropriate services and systems within their home communities (Guterman & Blythe, 1986). Residential treatment centers are thus no longer expected to replace families and communities, but to be a part of those communities (Yelton, 1993). In fact, the entire residential treatment process can be conceived as a family support system rather than an intervention targeting the child (Whittaker, 1978). The goals of treatment then shift from remediation of psychiatric disorders to improving social supports through environmental helping (e.g., material aid, behavioral assistance, and guidance) and improving personal competencies through teaching life skills (e.g., social skills, conflict resolution skills, and skills for mastering the physical environment) (Whittaker, Schinke, & Gilchrist, 1986).

Implicit in the ecological model is the questioning of the notion of "cure." The expectation that children will be relieved of psychiatric symptoms and function well after discharge, regardless of the postdischarge environment, is replaced by an attempt to build up both the child's skills and the environment's resources so there will be a better fit between the child's needs and the environment's responsive capacity. Sound discharge planning may even supersede the achievement of treatment goals as an indicator that residential treatment should be terminated. Residential treatment and community-based support systems form a partnership in working to support the child. For severely impaired children who are currently being treated in residential treatment centers, such an alliance is certainly more likely to allow successful reintegration into the community than psychoanalytically based notions of working through symptoms to achieve a cure.

If the residential treatment center is reconceptualized as a temporary support available to a child and family, and not a place where a child goes to be cured, then multiple admissions to these programs would not necessarily indicate failure of either the residential treatment program or the aftercare plan. In the same way that a person suffering from a chronic medical illness such as severe diabetes might require periodic hospitalizations for stabilization, a seriously emotionally disturbed child might require periodic returns to a residential treatment center at times of increased stress. Treatment goals would need to be rewritten to place less emphasis on the child maintaining full behavioral control and more emphasis on developing necessary community supports. This approach would not only allow for more of a partnership between the residential treatment center and the community, but would also be likely to reduce the need for more costly hospitalizations.

Involving Families in Residential Treatment

The ecological model of residential treatment has brought about a major change in clinical practice within residential treatment centers. In the past 15 to 20 years, theoretical and practical approaches to residential treatment have dramatically shifted their emphasis away from perfecting the therapeutic milieu and toward developing models for inclusion of families in the treatment process.

For those clinicians familiar with the wealth of theoretical and practical knowledge generated in the family therapy field, it has been clear that inclusion of families in residential treatment entails much more than initiating family therapy, developing parent support groups, and planning "Family Days" at the residential treatment center. Many family members of children in residential treatment have long histories of feeling powerless, which can seriously impair their ability to provide appropriate structure and discipline for their children. Watching one's child progress in residential treatment can increase the parent's sense of failure (Finkelstein, 1974). In reaction to these increased feelings of powerlessness and failure, families may appear—from the staff's perspective—to be "sabotaging" the child's treatment, thereby increasing tension between families and residential staff.

Although family therapy sessions can be useful, they may not help and may even make matters worse if staff continue to make all the treatment decisions for the child. For families to feel empowered, they must be fully involved in the child's treatment (Martone, Kemp, & Pearson, 1989); they must function as "full partners" in the assessment, treatment planning, and discharge planning for their child (Krona, 1980). To fully involve parents without making them feel blamed or incompetent requires a paradigm shift on the part of the residential staff. The principles and techniques of strategic/systemic family therapy have provided a useful framework for making this shift (Brown, 1991; Kagan, 1983; Matthews & Roberts, 1988). To be successful, this paradigm shift must transcend the boundaries of family therapy sessions and be incorporated into the entire child-care practice, for example by calling on parents to design and enforce consequences when their children misbehave (Durrant, 1993; Greene & Holden, 1990). Parents can thus begin to see themselves as part of the solution, instead of part of the problem, and feel empowered to take control of the family. At the same time, they can learn useful parenting skills that will be necessary for postdischarge success.

Although the principles of strategic/systemic therapy have provided a useful model for the engagement of families in residential treatment, a number of impediments can interfere with successful implementation. Many practitioners emphasize the importance of involving the family in the intake process (Durrant, 1993; Greene & Holden, 1990; Kagan, 1983; Krona, 1980; Menses & Durrant, 1990). Family involvement at intake helps to set the expectation that residential treatment will be family-centered and can relay a message of empowerment to counteract the sense of failure and self-blame that often accompanies placement. Family involvement at intake also provides an opportunity to reframe the meaning of the placement in terms that are conducive to positive change (Durrant, 1993; Menses & Durrant, 1990). In reality, however, residential treatment is often one more step in a whole series of placements; the family may not have been responsible for the child in years, making it difficult for the residential treatment center to engage the parents as full partners in treatment. In some cases, the family may not be in agreement with the need for residential treatment. It then becomes obvious (although this is also true but unrecognized in many other cases) that the treatment contract is actually between the residential treatment center and the referring agency, and not between the treatment program and the family. In some cases, the family may not even be present at intake, vividly demonstrating how little power the parents now have over their child's life.

The ongoing involvement of the referring agency, so necessary for facilitating responsive aftercare, may also impede productive family involvement in residential treatment. In many cases, the referring agency has removed the child from the family due to abuse or neglect. Thus the very presence of the agency worker can exacerbate feelings of failure and self-blame. Often, the worker's style and belief system compound the problem: After all, the worker's role involves rescuing "innocent" children from "bad" or "incompetent" parents. Residential treatment staff must seek a delicate balance between maintaining a positive professional relationship with the referring agency and forging an empowering alliance with the family. This difficult balancing act is made even harder when families view the residential treatment staff as a part of the system that removed their child from their care and continues to give them messages that they are incompetent parents.

Along with the general sense of incompetence and powerlessness engendered when a child is removed from the home and cared for by others, parents may also develop the belief—almost always unspoken—that caring for their child is optional. If the child left the home years before he or she came to the residential treatment center, it can be difficult to help parents see their child-care responsibilities as mandatory. The process of reintegrating the child back into the family can be derailed if parents have come to see work responsibilities, responsibility to other family members, the child's disruptive behavior, or the child's stated wish to return to surrogate caregivers as reasons to avoid family visitation or discharge. The messages of responsibility and empowerment relayed by the residential treatment staff may have little impact when the larger community systems communicate to the family that others can and should be raising their child.

In addition, there is a strong possibility, especially when working with inner-city African-American families, that family members who do become involved in the treatment process may not be the ones who have the power to make changes. Many African-American families within inner-city communities include complex systems of both blood and nonblood relatives (e.g., neighbors, church members, clergy, friends); immediate family members who are traditionally engaged in treatment may not be the ones who hold the power to make treatment successful (Boyd-Franklin, 1989). Extended family systems may play significant roles for members of other ethnic minority groups as well. Although this issue affects family therapy with ethnic minority groups in all treatment settings, the problems can be magnified in residential treatment because of the geographic distance from the extended family system.

The process of involving families in residential treatment can be impeded by the practical obstacles resulting from the location of many residential treatment centers at a distance from the families they serve. For children who have been involved in dangerous peer-related activities such as gangs and drug-dealing, and for those at high risk of running away and placing themselves in danger, a geographic separation from the home community may be necessary to keep them safe and allow them to be engaged in the treatment process. However, it also presents a major obstacle to engaging families in the treatment process on a regular basis, particularly for families with few financial resources, little access to transportation, or burdensome work or child-care responsibilities. Innovative responses to these logistical problems include conducting family therapy sessions by telephone (Springer, 1991) and housing families in apartments at the residential treatment center to allow fuller participation in treatment (Falk, 1990). Such approaches, while useful, only partially compensate for the family's active, hands-on involvement on a regular basis.

Finally, residential treatment centers that commit to fuller family involvement in the treatment process must be prepared to accept and respond to the regression that often occurs when children spend time with family members with whom they do not live (Finkelstein, 1974). In the past, residential treatment centers have tended to interpret this regression as proof of the noxious influence of families and often have responded by further limiting the child's access to the family. Such responses are likely only to exacerbate the regression following the more infrequent family contacts. Although certain parents (e.g., chronic substance abusers and the seriously mentally ill) may indeed be so unreliable or damaging in their interactions with their children that their contact must be carefully monitored, in most instances the child's behavioral regression will be eased through more, rather than less, contact with family members. Even when parents are severely impaired, children may benefit from regular, carefully supervised contact (e.g., conference telephone calls with the child's therapist present, as well as supervised visits) followed by "debriefing" sessions to help the child reality-test and cope with emotional reactions. These controlled contacts can allow the child to gradually resolve family issues and can help curb the child's tendency to idealize the parent and project blame onto the residential staff. Residential staff need to be helped to see that limiting family involvement may result in short-term improvement in the child's behavior, but in the long run may have serious negative consequences.

SUMMARY

Residential treatment centers serving children and adolescents with emotional disturbances and/or mental retardation have been affected by recent trends to provide services in the least restrictive settings and by the increasing availability of educational and family supports in the community. These treatment programs now serve children and adolescents with more complex and challenging behavior problems including severe aggression, property destruction, and self-injurious behaviors. While the population in residential treatment centers serving children with mental retardation has declined, the population in treatment programs serving emotionally disturbed children has increased, due to the greatly reduced use of state and county facilities for long-term hospitalization.

In residential treatment programs for children with mental retardation, behavior therapy is becoming a more complex art. Attention to the functions of behavior, the client's overall quality of life, and proactive amelioration of skills deficits are augmenting traditional behavioral interventions aimed at reducing target behaviors. In many cases, these broader approaches are also successfully reducing target behaviors.

However, the practice of behavior therapy in residential treatment centers is hampered by burdensome regulations that do not adequately protect clients, since neither those who develop behavior modification programs nor those who approve them are necessarily qualified by training and licensure to make professional judgments. Use of psychoactive medications in treating people with mental retardation in residential treatment centers remains a controversial issue. Empirical evidence has not clearly demonstrated efficacy of these medications in group studies. While some psychiatrists believe efficacy can be improved through better diagnostic workups, others question the reliability and validity of the diagnostic process when applied to persons with mental retardation and propose a more empirical approach to prescribing psychoactive medications.

Residential treatment programs for emotionally disturbed children and adolescents have been greatly affected by converging ideological shifts within the child welfare and mental health systems, resulting in increased emphasis on community-based services and family preservation. Within the treatment centers, the consistent finding that postdischarge outcome is less related to progress in residential treatment than to family involvement in treatment and the availability of community supports after discharge has shifted the focus of residential providers. Much energy is now focused on determining who is appropriate to treat in a residential setting. Treatment goals are being reconceptualized to become more achievable and consistent with successful community reintegration. Methods of involving families productively in residential treatment represent the only major clinical innovation in residential treatment of emotionally disturbed children in recent years. The principles of strategic/systemic therapy provide a useful framework for engaging and empowering families, but numerous practical impediments may interfere with successful implementation of a family-centered residential treatment program.

REFERENCES

Allen, M., Golubock, C., & Olson, L. (1987). A guide to the Adoption and Child Welfare Act of 1980. In D. Ratterman, G. D. Dodson, & M. Hardin (Eds.), *Reasonable efforts to prevent foster placement* (pp. 576–610). Washington, DC: American Bar Association National Legal Resource Center for Child Advocacy and Protection.

Allerhand, M. E., Weber, R. E., & Haug, M. (1966). *Adaptation and adaptability: The Bellefaire follow-up study.* New York: Child Welfare League of America.

Amado, A., Lakin, C., & Menke, J. (1990). *1990 chart book on services for people with developmental disabilities.* Minneapolis: University of Minnesota, Center for Residential and Community Service.

Aman, M., & Singh, N. (1985). Pharmacological intervention. In J. Matson & J. Mulick (Eds.), *Handbook on mental retardation* (2nd ed., pp. 347–372). New York: Pergamon Press.

Axelrod, S. (1987). Functional and structural analyses of behavior: Approaches leading to reduced use of punishment procedures? *Research in Developmental Disabilities, 8,* 165–178.

Axelrod, S., & Apsche, J. (1983). *The effects of punishment on human behavior.* New York: Academic Press.

Axelrod, S., Spreat, S., Berry, B., & Moyer, L. (1993). A decision-making model for selecting the optimal treatment procedure. In R.Van Houten & S. Axelrod (Eds.), *Behavior analysis and treatment* (pp. 183–202). New York: Plenum Press.

Balcerzak, E. A. (1991). Toward the year 2000: Strategies for the field of residential group care. *Residential Treatment for Children and Youth, 8,* 57–70.

Bay-Hinitz, A., Peterson, R., & Quilitch, H. (1994). Cooperative games: A way to modify aggressive and cooperative behaviors in young children. *Journal of Applied Behavior Analysis, 27,* 435–446.

Behar, D. (1993). *Mental retardation and psychiatric illness.* Presentation at Carrier foundation COMED/Colloqium series. Belle Mead, NJ: Carrier Foundation.

Belcher, T. (1994). Behavioral change with environmental change. *Psychological Reports, 74,* 362.

Bernstein, J. (1987). Residential treatment and aftercare: Protecting our investment. *Residential Treatment for Children and Youth, 4,* 45–58.

Bettelheim, B., & Sylvester, E. (1948). A therapeutic milieu. *American Journal of Orthopsychiatry, 18,* 191–206.

Bijou, S., & Ruiz, R. (1981). *Behavior modification: Contributions to education* (pp. 239–240). Hillsdale, NJ: Erlbaum.

Billingsley, F., & Neel, R. (1985). Competing behaviors and their effects of skill generalization and maintenance. *Analysis and Intervention in Developmental Disabilities, 5,* 357–372.

Bishop, A. (1992). Empirical approach to psychopharmacology for institutionalized individuals with severe or profound mental retardation. *Mental Retardation, 30*(5), 283–288.

Boszormenyi-Nagy, I., & Krasner, B. R. (1986). *Between give and take: A clinical guide to contextual therapy.* New York: Brunner/Mazel.

Boszormenyi-Nagy, I., & Spark, I. M. (1973). *Invisible loyalties.* New York: Harper & Row.

Boyd-Franklin, N. (1989). *Black families in therapy: A multisystems approach.* New York: Guilford Press.

Brown, J. E. (1991). Family involvement in the residential treatment of children: A systemic perspective. *Australian and New Zealand Journal of Family Therapy, 12,* 17–22.

Cameron, M., & Kimball, J. (1995). Beyond consequences. *Mental Retardation, 33,* 268–270.

Carlo, P. (1985). The children's residential treatment center as a living laboratory for family members: A review of the literature and its implications for practice. *Child Care Quarterly, 14,* 156–170.

Carr, E. (1988). Functional equivalence as a means of response generalization. In R. Horner, G. Dunlap, & R. Koegel (Eds.), *Generalization and maintenance: Life style changes in applied settings* (pp. 221–241). Baltimore: Brookes.

Carr, E., & Durand, V. (1985). Reducing behavior problems through functional communication training. *Journal of Applied Behavior Analysis, 19,* 111–126.

Carr, E., Newsom, C., & Binkoff, J. (1976). Stimulus control of self-destructive behavior in a psychotic child. *Journal of Abnormal Child Psychology, 4,* 139–153.

Carr, E., Robinson, S., & Palumbo, L. (1990). The wrong issue: Aversive versus nonaversive treatment. The right issue: Functional treatment versus nonfunctional treatment. In A. Repp & N. Singh (Eds.), *Perspectives on the use of nonaversive and aversive interventions for persons with developmental disabilities* (pp. 361–379). Sycamore, IL: Sycamore.

Cates, J. A. (1991a). Residential treatment in the 1980s—Part 1: Characteristics of children served. *Residential Treatment for Children and Youth, 9,* 75–84.

Cates, J. A. (1991b). Residential treatment in the 1980s—Part 2: Characteristics of treatment centers. *Residential Treatment for Children and Youth, 9,* 75–84.

Curry, J. F. (1991). Outcome research on residential treatment: Implications and suggested directions. *American Journal of Orthopsychiatry, 61,* 348–357.

Day, R., Rea, J., Schussler, N., Larsen, S., & Johnson, W. (1988). A functionally based approach to the treatment of self-injurious behavior. *Behavior Modification, 12,* 565–589.

Donnellan, A., & LaVigna, G. (1990). Myths about punishment. In A. Repp & N. Singh (Eds.), *Perspectives on the use of nonaversive and aversive interventions for persons with developmental disabilities* (pp. 33–57). Sycamore, IL: Sycamore.

Donnellan, A., Mirenda, P., Mesaros, R., & Fassbender, L. (1984). Analyzing the communicative functions of aberrant behavior. *Journal of Association for Persons with Severe Handicaps, 3,* 201–212.

Durand, V., & Carr, E. (1987). Social influences on "self-stimulatory" behavior: Analysis and treatment application. *Journal of Applied Behavior Analysis, 20,* 119–132.

Durrant, M. (1993). *Residential treatment: A cooperative competency-based approach to therapy and program design.* New York: Norton.

Falk, R. (1990). Family reunification in a residential facility. *Residential Treatment for Children and Youth, 7,* 39–49.

Favell, J., McGimsey, J., & Schell, R. (1982). Treatment of self-injury by providing alternate sensory activities. *Analysis and Intervention in Developmental Disabilities, 2,* 83–104.

Fein, E. (1986). If there are ashes, there may be a phoenix. *Residential Treatment for Children and Youth, 4,* 31–43.

Finkelstein, N. E. (1974). Family participation in residential treatment. *Child Welfare, 53,* 570–575.

Foxx, R., McMorrow, M., & Schloss, C. (1983). Stacking the deck: Teaching social skills to retarded adults with a modified table game. *Journal of Applied Behavior Analysis, 16,* 157–170.

Friedman, P. (1975). Legal regulation of applied behavior analysis in mental institutions and prisons. *Arizona Law Review, 17,* 39–104.

Gabel, S., Finn, M., & Ahmed, A. (1988). Day treatment outcome with severely disturbed children. *Journal of the American Academy of Child and Adolescent Psychiatry, 176,* 323–331.

Gabel, S., & Shindledecker, R. (1992). Adolescent psychiatric inpatients: Characteristics, outcome, and comparison between discharged patients from specialized and nonspecialized adolescent units. *Journal of Youth and Adolescence, 21,* 1–17.

Gabel, S., Stadler, J., & Bjorn, J. (1995). Behavioral and family characteristics of boys in day hospital and residential settings: Is there a relationship to placement recommendations? *Continuum, 2,* 57–69.

Goldiamond, I. (1976). Singling out self-administered behavior therapies for professional review. *American Psychologist, 31,* 142–147.

Greene, J. R., & Holden, M. M. (1990). A strategic-systemic family therapy model: Rethinking residential treatment. *Residential Treatment for Children and Youth, 7,* 51–55.

Grellong, B. A. (1987). Residential care in context: Evaluation of a treatment process in response to social change. *Residential Treatment for Children and Youth, 4,* 59–70.

Griffith, R., & Spreat, S. (1989). Aversive behavior modification procedures and the use of professional judgement. *The Behavior Therapist, 12,* 143–146.

Gunter, P., Shores, R., Jack, S., Denny, R., & DePaepe, P. (1994). A case study of the effects of altering instructional interactions on the disruptive behavior of a child identified with severe behavior disorders. *Education and Treatment of Children, 17,* 435–444.

Guterman, N. B., & Blythe, B. J. (1986). Toward ecologically based intervention in residential treatment for children. *Social Service Review, 60,* 633–643.

Hagopian, L., Fisher, W., & Legacy, S. (1994). Schedule effects of noncontingent reinforcement on attention maintained destructive behavior. *Journal of Applied Behavior Analysis, 27,* 317–325.

Hastings, R., & Remington, B. (1994). Staff behaviour and its implications for people with learning disabilities. *British Journal of Clinical Psychology, 33,* 423–438.

Health Care Financing Administration. (1988). *Interpretive guidelines for intermediate care facilities for the mentally retarded or persons with related conditions (ICFs/MR).* Washington, DC: Author.

Hobbs, N. (1966). Helping disturbed children: Psychological and ecological strategies. *American Psychologist, 21,* 1105–1115.

Hollander, M., Plutchik, R., & Horner, V. (1973). Interaction of patient and attendant reinforcement programs: The "piggyback" effect. *Journal of Consulting and Clinical Psychology, 41,* 43–47.

Horner, R. (1980). The effects of an enrichment program on the behavior of institutionalized profoundly retarded children. *Journal of Applied Behavior Analysis, 13,* 473–491.

Horner, R., & Billingsley, F. (1988). The effect of competing behavior on the generalization and maintenance of adaptive behavior in applied settings. In R. Horner, R. Koegel, & G. Dunlap (Eds.), *Generalization and maintenance: Life style changes in applied settings* (pp. 197–220). Baltimore: Brookes.

Horner, R., Sprague, J., & Flannery, K. (1993). Building functional curricula for students with severe intellectual disabilities and severe problem behaviors. In R. Van Houten & S. Axelrod (Eds.), *Behavior analysis and treatment* (pp. 47–71). New York: Plenum Press.

Isett, R., Roszkowski, M., & Spreat, S. (1980). Where shall they live? A criterion-referenced approach to service planning. *Training Quarterly, 1*(2), 35–48.

Iwata, B. (1994). *Self-injury and related behavior disorders* [Workshop presentation] Philadelphia, PA: Behavior Intervention Specialists.

Iwata, B., Dorsey, M., Slifer, K., & Richman, P. (1982). Toward a functional analysis of self-injury. *Analysis and Intervention in Developmental Disabilities, 2,* 3–10.

Iwata, B., Vollmer, T., Zarcone, J., & Rodgers, T. (1993). Treatment classification and selection based on behavioral function. In R. Van Houten & S. Axelrod (Eds.), *Behavior analysis and treatment* (pp. 101–126). New York: Plenum Press.

Kagan, R. M. (1983). Engaging family competence to prevent repetitive and lengthy institutionalization of acting-out youth. *Residential Group Care and Treatment, 1,* 55–70.

Kelly, J., Wildman, B., Urey, J., & Thurman, C. (1979). Group skills to increase the conversational repertoire of retarded adolescents. *Child Behavior Therapy, 1,* 323–326.

Kennedy, C., Itkonen, T., & Lindquist, K. (1995). Comparing interspersed request and social comments as antecedents for increasing student compliance. *Journal of Applied Behavior Analysis, 28,* 97–98.

Knitzer, J. (1982). *Unclaimed children.* Washington, DC: Children's Defense Fund.

Krona, D. A. (1980). Parents as treatment partners in residential care. *Child Welfare, 59,* 91–96.

Lake v. Cameron, 364 F.2d 657 (DC Cir. 1966).

Luiselli, J. (1994). Effects of noncontingent sensory reinforcement on stereotypic behaviors in a child with posttraumatic neurological impairment. *Journal of Behavior Therapy and Experimental Psychiatry, 25,* 325–330.

Luiselli, J., Mederios, J., & Cameron, M. (1993). Behavioral treatment of high-rate toileting requests. *Habilitative Mental Healthcare Newsletter, 12,* 10–11.

Mace, F., Hock, M., Lalli, J., West, B., Belfiore, P., Pinter, E., & Brown, D. (1988). Behavioral momentum in the treatment of noncompliance. *Journal of Applied Behavior Analysis, 21,* 123–141.

Maluccio, A. N., & Fein, E. (1983). Permanency planning: A redefinition. *Child Welfare, 62,* 195–201.

Maluccio, A. N., & Marlow, W. D. (1972). Residential treatment of emotionally disturbed children: A review of the literature. *Social Service Review, 46,* 230–251.

Manderscheid, R., & Sonnenshein, M. (1994). *Mental health, United States, 1994.* Rockville, MD: U.S. Department of Health and Human Services.

Martin, L. H., Pozdnjakoff, I., & Wilding, J. (1976). The uses of residential care. *Child Welfare, 55,* 269–278.

Martin, R. (1975). *Legal challenges to behavior modification.* Champaign, IL: Research Press.

Martone, W. P., Kemp, G. F., & Pearson, S. J. (1989). The continuum of parental involvement in residential treatment: Engagement-participation-empowerment-discharge. *Residential Treatment for Children and Youth, 6,* 11–37.

Matson, J., & Adkins, J. (1980, October). A self-instructional social skills training program for mentally retarded persons. *Mental Retardation, 18*(5), 245–248.

Matson, J., & Frame, C. (1986). *Psychopathology among mentally retarded children and adolescents.* Beverly Hills, CA: Sage.

Matson, J., & Stephens, R. (1978). Increasing appropriate behavior of explosive chronic psychiatric patients with a social skills training package. *Behavior Modification, 2,* 242–245.

Matthews, W. J., & Roberts, J. (1988). The entrance of systems family therapy into a residential treatment center. *Children and Youth Services, 11,* 77–91.

May, P., London, E., Zimmerman, T., Thompson, R., & Mento, T. (1994). *Determination of indications for the use of neuroleptic medication in patients with profound mental retardation.* Unpublished manuscript.

McFalls, J. (1995). Beyond treatment acceptability: A comment. *Mental Retardation, 33,* 57–58.

Menses, G., & Durrant, M. (1990). Contextual residential care: Applying the principles of cybernetic therapy to the residential treatment of irresponsible adolescents and their families. *Residential Treatment of Children and Youth, 7*(3), 11–32.

Montegar, C., Reid, D., Madsen, C., & Ewell, M. (1977). Increasing institutional staff to resident interactions through in-service training and supervisor approval. *Behavior Therapy, 8,* 533–540.

Muscott, H., & Gifford, T. (1994). Virtual reality and social skills training for students with behavioral disorders: Applications, challenges, and promising practices. *Education and Treatment of Children, 17,* 417–434.

Phillips, E. L., Phillips, E. A., Wolf, M. M., & Fixsen, D. L. (1973). Achievement place: Development of the elected manager system. *Journal of Applied Behavior Analysis, 6,* 541–561.

Ponce, D. E., & Jo, H. S. (1990). Substance abuse and psychiatric disorders: The dilemma of increasing incidence of dual diagnosis in residential treatment centers. *Residential Treatment for Children and Youth, 8,* 5–15.

Redick, R., Witkin, M., Atay, J., & Manderscheid, R. (1994). *The evolution and expansion of mental health care in the United States between 1990 and 1995.* Washington, DC: U.S. Department of Health and Human Services/Public Health Service/Substance Abuse and Mental Health Services Administration.

Redl, F. (1966). *When we deal with children: Selected writings.* New York: Free Press.

Redl, F., & Wineman, D. (1957). *The aggressive child.* New York: Free Press.

Repp, A., Felce, D., & Barton, L. (1988). Basing the treatment of stereotypic and self-injurious behaviors on hypothesis of their causes. *Journal of Applied Behavior Analysis, 21,* 281–289.

Risley, T., & Sheldon-Wildgen, J. (1980). Suggested procedures for human rights committees of potentially controversial treatment programs. *The Behavior Therapist, 3,* 9–10.

Rojahn, J., McGonigle, J., Curcio, C., & Dixon, M. (1987). Suppression of pica by water mist and aromatic ammonia: A comparative analysis. *Behavior Modification, 11,* 65–74.

Scotti, J., Schulman, D., & Hohnacki, R. (1994). Functional analysis and unsuccessful treatment of Tourette's syndrome in a man with profound mental retardation. *Behavior Therapy, 25,* 721–738.

Sheldon-Wildgen, J., & Risley, T. (1982). Balancing clients' rights: The establishment of human rights and peer review committees. In A. Bellack, M. Hersen, & A. Kazdin (Eds.), *International handbook of behavior modification.* New York: Plenum Press.

Sigafoos, J., & Kerr, M. (1994). Provision of leisure activities for the reduction of challenging behavior. *Behavioral Interventions, 9,* 43–53.

Skinner, B. (1953). *Science and human behavior.* New York: Macmillan.

Small, R., Kennedy, K., & Bender, B. (1991). Critical issues for practice in residential treatment: The view from within. *American Journal of Orthopsychiatry, 61,* 327–338.

Sprague, J., & Horner, R. (1991). Determining the acceptability of behavior support plans. In M. Wang, H. Wahlberg, & M. Reynolds (Eds.), *Handbook of special education* (pp. 125–142). London: Pergamon Press.

Spreat, S., Axelrod, S., & Thompson, R. (1995, May). *Treatment of pica by recreating the scene.* Presentation at a meeting of the Delaware Valley Association of Behavior Analysts, Philadelphia, PA.

Spreat, S., & Behar, D. (1993). Final grant report (NIMH) (Contract No.MH-43851). Washington, DC: U.S. Government Printing Office.

Spreat, S., & Lanzi, F. (1989). Role of human rights committees in the review of restrictive/aversive behavior modification procedures: A national survey. *Mental Retardation, 27,* 375–382.

Spreat, S., & Lipinski, D. (1986). A survey of state policies regarding the use of restrictive/aversive behavior modification procedures. *Behavioral Residential Treatment, 1,* 137–152.

Spreat, S., Piper, T., Deaton, S., Savoy-Paff, D., Brantner, J., Lipinski, D., Dorsey, M., & Baker-Potts, J. (1985, September). The impact of supervisory feedback on staff and client behavior. *Education and Training of the Mentally Retarded, 20*(3), 196–203.

Spreat, S., Serafin, C., Behar, D., & Leiman, S. (1993). Tranquilizer reduction trails in a residential program for persons with mental retardation. *Hospital and Community Psychiatry, 44,* 1100–1102.

Springer, A. K. (1991). Telephone family therapy: An untapped resource. *Family Therapy, 18,* 123–128.

Stokes, T., & Baer, D. (1977). An implicit technology of generalization. *Journal of Applied Behavior Analysis, 10,* 349–367.

Stolz, S. (1977). Why no guidelines for behavior modification. *Journal of Applied Behavior Analysis, 10,* 541–547.

Stroul, B. A., & Friedman, R. M. (1986). *A system of care for severely emotionally disturbed children and youth.* Washington, DC: National Institute of Mental Health, Child and Adolescent Service System Program.

Sturmey, P. (1994). Assessing the functions of self-injurious behavior: A case of assessment failure. *Journal of Behavior Therapy and Experimental Psychiatry, 4,* 331–336.

Taylor, D. A., & Alpert, S. W. (1973). *Continuity and support following residential treatment.* New York: Child Welfare League of America.

Trieschman, A. E., Whittaker, J. K., & Brendtro, L. K. (1969). *The other 23 hours: Child-care work with emotionally disturbed children in a therapeutic milieu.* Chicago: Aldine de Gruyter.

Tuma, J. M. (1989). Mental health services for children: The state of the art. *American Psychologist, 44,* 188–199.

Tustin, R. (1995). The effects of advance notice on activity transitions on stereotypic behavior. *Journal of Applied Behavior Analysis, 28,* 91–92.

Van Houten, R., & Rohlider, A. (1988). Recreating the scene: An effective way to provide delayed punishment for inappropriate motor behavior. *Journal of Applied Behavior Analysis, 21,* 187–192.

Vollmer, T., Marcus, B., & LeBlanc, L. (1994). Treatment of self injury and hand mouthing following inconclusive functional analysis. *Journal of Applied Behavior Analysis, 27,* 331–344.

Vorrath, H. V., & Brendtro, L. K. (1974). *Positive peer culture.* New York: Aldine de Gruyter.

Weeks, E., & Gaylord-Ross, R. (1981). Task difficulty and aberrant behavior in severely handicapped students. *Journal of Applied Behavior Analysis, 14,* 327–338.

Wehby, J., Symons, F., & Shores, R. (1995). A descriptive analysis of aggressive behavior in classrooms for children with emotional and behavioral disorders. *Behavioral Disorders, 20,* 87–105.

Wells, K. (1991a). Long-term residential treatment for children: Introduction. *American Journal of Orthopsychiatry, 61,* 324–326.

Wells, K. (1991b). Placement of emotionally disturbed children in residential treatment: A review of placement criteria. *American Journal of Orthopsychiatry, 61,* 339–347.

Wells, K., & Whittington, D. (1993). Characteristics of youths referred to residential treatment: Implications for program design. *Children and Youth Services Review, 15,* 195–217.

Wexler, D. (1975). Reflections on the legal regulation of behavior modification in institutional settings. *Arizona Law Review, 17,* 132–143.

Whittaker, J. K. (1978). The changing character of residential child care: An ecological perspective. *Social Service Review, 52,* 21–36.

Whittaker, J. K., & Maluccio, A. N. (1989). Changing paradigms in residential services for disturbed/disturbing children: Retrospect and prospect. In R. P. Hawkins & J. Breiling (Eds.), *Therapeutic foster care: Critical issues* (pp. 81–102). Washington, DC: Child Welfare League of America.

Whittaker, J. K., & Pfeiffer, S. I. (1994). Research priorities for residential group child care. *Child Welfare, 73,* 583–601.

Whittaker, J. K., Schinke, S. P., & Gilchrist, L. D. (1986). The ecological paradigm in child, youth, and family services: Implications for policy and practice. *Social Service Review, 60,* 483–503.

Willis, T., & LaVigna, G. (1987). *Aide to functional analysis.* Los Angeles: Institute for Applied Behavior Analysis.

Wilson, D. R., & Lyman, R. D. (1983). Residential treatment of emotionally disturbed children. In C. E. Walker & M. C. Roberts (Eds.), *Handbook of clinical child psychology* (pp. 1069–1088). New York: Wiley.

Wolf, M. (1978). Social validity: The case for subjective measurement, or how applied behavior analysis is finding its heart. *Journal of Applied Behavior Analysis, 11,* 203–214.

Wyatt v. Stickney, 344 F. Supp. 373, 344 F. Supp., 387 (M.D. Alabama 1972).

Yelton, S. (1993). Children in residential treatment—Policies for the '90s. *Children and Youth Services Review, 15,* 173–193.

Young, T. M., Dore, M. M., & Pappenfort, D. M. (1988). Residential group care for children considered emotionally disturbed, 1966–1981. *Social Service Review, 62,* 158–170.

Youngberg v. Romeo, 102 S. Ct. (1982).

Zimet, S. G., Farley, G. K., & Zimet, G. D. (1994). Home behaviors of children in three treatment settings: An outpatient clinic, a day hospital, and an inpatient hospital. *Journal of the American Academy of Child and Adolescent Psychiatry, 33,* 56–59.

CHAPTER 6

Interventions in the School and Community

G. ANNE BOGAT and LEONARD A. JASON

Children and adolescents in the latter part of the 20th century face serious problems. Twenty percent of American children drop out prior to graduating from high school (Parker & Asher, 1987), and some inner-city schools have dropout rates of more than 50%. Levine and Perkins (1987) note that problems of education and delinquency are inextricably linked—surveys estimate "that perhaps 30% of all juvenile delinquents are learning disabled" (p. 16). Approximately 21% of all persons arrested and charged with a crime are under the age of 18 (U.S. Department of Census, 1981, as cited by Levine & Perkins, 1987).

The home life of a significant number of children and adolescents is also stressful and problematic. More than a million children each year live in families where the parents will divorce (Levine & Perkins, 1987); nearly that many are born to single, unmarried women in the same time period (Whitehead, 1993). Research indicates that divorce has negative effects on children, resulting in heightened levels of psychological and physiological distress (e.g., Garfinkel & McLanahan, 1986; Wallerstein & Blakeslee, 1989), in part because they live in single-parent families where the economic situation runs "between precarious and desperate" (Whitehead, 1993) and, in part, because children do not adjust easily to major life changes. If the divorce involves a prolonged custody battle, children will suffer greater adjustment problems (Emery, 1982; Luepnitz, 1982).

Finally, increased sexual activity in the United States has resulted in high rates of adolescent pregnancy. Many pregnant adolescents choose to keep the child rather than undergo an abortion or give up the baby for adoption (Popovich, 1990; Resnick, Blum, Bose, Smith, & Toogood, 1990). Becoming a mother at an early age has negative consequences for the teen. Because an adolescent's schooling is either disrupted briefly (she stops attending school during the latter stages of the pregnancy and after the birth, but then returns) or permanently (many teens drop out of school altogether), studies show that parenting adolescents suffer long-term economic and vocational problems compared with their nonparenting cohorts (e.g., Moore & Waite, 1977).

Given such statistics, it is not difficult for professionals to find serious social problems that need solving and large numbers of community members who want to collaborate in such endeavors. Productive relationships between researchers and the community are surprisingly rare; the good intentions of both groups are often unrealized. This chapter describes how researchers and community members can best collaborate with one another. Although the chapter is generally written from the perspective of research, the problems we delineate, and their solutions, are equally relevant and applicable to persons called on to conduct program evaluations of their interventions.

The chapter is divided into two main sections. The first describes how one initiates a good working collaboration; that is, what model should be used for the collaboration and what broad stages will occur once the collaboration is established. The second section focuses on how to develop the best possible evaluation to measure the impact of an intervention. Throughout both sections, we have provided examples of research collaborations in our own work to illustrate the typical problems and pitfalls, as well as successes, that the community intervener should expect.

COLLABORATIVE RESEARCH

Models of Collaboration

Conducting research in the community will necessarily involve collaboration with community residents and/or leaders. In treatment settings, where professionals more easily take an "expert stance," collaborations are less democratic. Prevention research and community research, which values the expertise of key community personnel, the importance of examining individual behavior in an ecological context, and the "principle of cultural pluralism," will be more genuinely collaborative (Kelly, 1988). Thus, models of collaboration range from those in which the recipients of programs and the ensuing evaluations are completely passive to those in which "the researcher seeks community assistance in setting the direction and focus of the research" (Hatch, Moss, Saran, Presley-Cantrell, & Mallory, 1993, p. 28).

More passive approaches to collaboration include those in which the researcher merely consults with persons who are "at the periphery of community cultural systems" (Hatch et al., 1993) or consults with community leaders and residents but fails to involve them in all stages of the research process. Wood and Gray (1991), writing from an organizational psychology perspective, argue that the more passive collaborations are not true collaborations. For these writers, "collaboration occurs when a group of autonomous stakeholders of a problem domain engage in an interactive process, using shared rules, norms, and structures, to act or decide on issues related to that domain" (p. 146). Problems are inherent in any approach to collaboration.

In research collaborations in which community stakeholders take a more passive approach, the problem(s) of focus, generated by the researcher, may not be the one(s) of most pressing importance to the community; outcome data may be used to promote an agenda that is not consonant with community values; and continuation of the project is unlikely because there are no formal or informal community organizations in place to continue the work (Hatch et al., 1993).

True collaborations between the researcher and the community are rare. They involve working together to set the research agenda: defining the problem of interest, designing the research methodology, discussing data analysis and data dissemination, and planning for the continuation of those interventions which prove useful and important. When such collaborations exist, they are, for several reasons, time-consuming.

First, community residents and researchers may hold different values about the community and its problems: "The community is most likely to be attracted to the potential of using research to solve immediate social problems, whereas the researcher and the funding agency seek information for scientific or policy purposes" (Hatch et al., 1993, p. 29). It is often difficult for researchers and community residents to find mutual arenas of interest in which to conduct their inquiry. Each stakeholder must secure some benefit from the collaboration, whether the initial interests are shared, differing, or opposing (Lax & Sebenius, 1986). However, successful collaborations develop "rules governing resource use" (Wood & Gray, 1991) wherein all parties generate a "shared understanding of the problem domain and their relationships to it. In so doing, participants create and agree on rules for managing their relationships and for seeking solutions to their collective problems" (p. 158).

Second, most researchers are trained in and rely on traditional, logical positivist scientific methodologies. Thus, they often have difficulty explaining to community groups the utility of experimental/control group designs, random assignment, blind interviewers, and standardized measures (to name only a few of the thorny issues). Community residents often feel that they are serving as guinea pigs for researchers. In part, this may be due to personal bad experiences with research or knowledge of prior misconduct. For example, The Tuskegee Study, conducted between 1932 and 1972, took blood samples from hundreds of African-American men suffering from syphilis. These men were informed that they were receiving treatment for "bad blood"; in fact, they were merely being observed by researchers to determine the long-term effects of their (treatable) disease (Thomas, 1991). The details of this study are well-known within the African-American community and the result has been widespread mistrust of the government and its health policies. For example, many African-Americans believe that HIV/AIDS is a disease spread by the government for the purpose of their genocide (Thomas, 1991). The first author, in conducting a longitudinal study with low-income pregnant adolescents, found that many African-American teens refused to use birth control, particularly Norplant, because they believed it could lead to permanent health problems, including sterility—a goal some believed was endorsed by the U.S. government.

Personal experiences with previous research collaborators may dramatically influence the current researcher's relationship to the setting. Reyes and Jason (1993) describe a consultation with a high school in which suspicion was paramount early in the relationship because a previous researcher had publicized negative information about the school.

Regardless of the community's prior experience or bias, most collaborative research involves the researcher providing the community with a minicourse in experimental design. This is only right. Because collaboration involves autonomous partners (according to Wood and Gray's, 1991, definition cited earlier), any compromise or loss of autonomy by one stakeholder should be done knowingly. As explained later in this chapter, no research design can answer every research question; thus, the choice of design (and the choice of instruments, etc.) will ultimately represent a compromise.

The explanations that occur in community/scientist or program evaluator research partnerships, however, are not solely one-way. Community residents may not have taken a research methods course, but they usually have a research agenda that may stipulate (sometimes by default) the methods of data collection and the use of the resultant program evaluation. For example, community residents often desire more qualitative measures of success, such as unstructured interviews with program recipients.

Although there are numerous pitfalls in a true, collaborative relationship, there are also mutual benefits. "Partners in a collaboration have the potential to understand the problem domain more fully and in a transformative way" (Wood & Gray, 1991, p. 159). In the process of educating each other, researchers and evaluators are faced with the dilemma of "to what extent the rigor of science must be protected" (Hatch et al., 1993, p. 30). But, as Hatch et al. (1993) note:

> By including the community as a coparticipant in the definition of the problem and in the formulation of hypotheses, the researcher can meet the real world, perhaps to the enrichment of science. Conversely, community members' own concerns can [often] best be served by logical hypotheses and "clean" methodology. (p. 30)

Stages in a Research Collaboration

In summarizing the consultation literature, Reyes and Jason (1993) note that five stages are common in any consultation: "(1) gaining entry into the system; (2) identifying goals; (3) defining goals; (4) planning and implementing the intervention; and (5) assessing the impact" (p. 306). In large part, because a collaborative research project involves some degree of consultation, these five stages are generally applicable to it as well.

Entry

Snowden, Munoz, and Kelly (1979) eloquently detail the manner in which a research collaboration is an "interpersonal process as a context for delivering psychological services" (p. 20). It cannot be emphasized enough that contact between the researcher or evaluator and those in the community must be face-to-face. Both stakeholders need to know whether the other is competent, trustworthy, and dependable. The process of entry is a feeling-out between the players, a courtship in which each decides whether or not to proceed with the relationship.

There seem to be several personal characteristics associated with researchers who engage in successful community interventions. Kelly, Munoz, and Snowden (1979) note that community researchers must be willing to make "a clear commitment of time and energy" (p. 349) to the process. They must also be flexible. Every stage in the process involves negotiation, to create a shared vision and understanding. It is not clear whether members of community groups must also possess these same personal characteristics, but one would assume that they would be valuable. In other words, both stakeholders must believe that "science and social action can blend in a manner that benefits both" (Kelly et al., 1979, p. 349).

The process of gaining entry and/or establishing a good working relationship can be accomplished in various ways. In his seminal treatise on consultation, Caplan (1970) emphasized the importance of identifying "key persons"; those who are integral to the network of relationships that one will need to negotiate. It can happen that the person most receptive to the research collaboration has no power to enact it.

For example, in school settings, interventions and evaluations often fail because a principal agrees to the project without soliciting the input of his or her teachers. Because teachers maintain high levels of control in their individual classrooms, their collaboration and cooperation is essential. The first author had obtained the support and cooperation of teachers, parents, and school board members at several preschools to evaluate a program to educate preschoolers about sexual abuse prevention. At one small preschool, the sole teacher left the program and was hurriedly replaced by a new teacher close to the start of the school year. In conversations with this new teacher, it became clear that she was not particularly comfortable with the idea of teaching the curriculum, and she did not seem to grasp the protocol of the evaluation procedures. But because she was concerned about asserting her opinions so soon after garnering the job, she was reluctant to back out of the project, even though the researcher gave her ample opportunity to do so. What happened on the first day of pretesting was typical of how the teacher served to undermine the intervention and evaluation. Arriving at the school on the day and at the appointed time the pretesting was to begin, the author saw, on the sidewalk, in the distance, the teacher taking all the students on a (spontaneous) field trip to the local ice cream shop.

Once key persons are identified, Kelly et al. (1979) suggest that early contacts should be "tentative" and "nonthreatening." They advocate approaching community members with an open agenda focused on the mutual benefits that might result from a collaboration. Some writers have emphasized the importance of respecting the expertise of organizational members and integrating their suggestions into the program and evaluation (e.g., Reyes & Jason, 1993; Shure, 1979). Holahan (1979) discussed being cognizant of the traditional hierarchies within the organization. Other researchers have negotiated the inclusion of services or programs peripheral to the evaluation into the contract for the research evaluation. In a large school transition/tutoring project implemented by the second author, schools assigned to the control condition were given information (e.g., psychological referral services) and supportive services as a means of compensating the school personnel for their activities in the evaluation (Jason et al., 1992).

Most of the problems and strengths of the future collaborative relationship are present from the beginning. In a recent program, developed and evaluated by the first author, several colleagues, and a school staff member, the administration's lack of commitment (and ultimate sabotage of the program) should have been obvious when school personnel failed to write their portions of the initial grant in a timely fashion and when, upon receiving the grant, they failed to expedite the hiring of a half-time staff person. On a positive note, the program and its evaluation persisted for several years despite these problems as a direct result of the excellence of the school staff person, who had a deep commitment to the program and its participants.

Identifying Goals

Shadish (1990) notes that there is an important trade-off between an intervention's importance and the possibility that it can be implemented:

> The more important the social problem, the more difficult it is to solve, because, by definition, important problems tend to involve more people, more money, and more vested interests. . . . the bigger the proposed intervention, the more likely it is to have big effects, but the less likely it is to be feasible [and] although interventions are more implementable if they are consistent with the beliefs and structures of the system that has to implement them, the more consistent an intervention is with the system, the less likely it is to be different enough to make a real difference. (p. 12)

In other words, if your goal is to create change in the short term, you have to think small; but thinking small works against thinking big and making a big difference (Shadish, 1990). Small goals are not always insignificant, however. Weick (1984) illustrated this by discussing some of the large-scale failures of the women's movement (e.g., failure to ratify the Equal Rights Amendment), and contrasting those with efforts aimed at achieving adoption of nonsexist language. This latter goal has met with widespread acceptance; it might be considered a "small win" that had large repercussions because it influenced the thinking (if not the actions) of large numbers of people.

Definition of Goals

Once the goals of the intervention and evaluation have been established, a working definition (or operational definition) of these goals is necessary. Boruch and Shadish (1983) summarized the types of questions posed by evaluation studies conducted in various fields. Outcome studies (whether the program worked or not) rarely accounted for more than one-fourth of all published research in a given field. Questions regarding consumer satisfaction, needs assessments, and cost of services studies predominated. Although questions regarding outcomes are the most difficult to measure, they have obvious importance.

Extraordinary amounts of time and energy are required to develop and evaluate most interventions. Persons involved in the research collaboration develop strong feelings about the program as a result of this investment. On the one hand, such attitudes may be necessary to mobilize sufficient energy for implementing the intervention and evaluation; on the other hand, such personal investments make it more likely that collaborators will maintain positive biases about the intervention, regardless of its objective effectiveness. Outcome studies, carefully planned to uncover both benefits and drawbacks (intended and unintended ones) to the intervention, can facilitate the objectivity of all participants. However, outcome research in and of itself cannot guarantee objectivity. Gensheimer, Mayer, Gottschalk, and Davidson (1986) found that the only factor that consistently explained whether or not juvenile diversion projects showed positive effects was whether the primary investigator was an author on the paper; if the primary investigator was an author, the intervention was more likely to show positive effects.

The definition of research goals is also affected by technical considerations and theoretical issues. These will be discussed in the second section of this chapter.

Planning and Implementing the Intervention

Interventions can be planned and implemented in two basic ways. First, some researchers or evaluators approach a setting, even their own, with a preexisting intervention.

> The danger of having such a plan is that of creating a false aura of wisdom and power, when many of the key factors are outside the realm of influence of the research. The benefits include the possibility of testing a specific program and thus being able to determine its effectiveness and being able to export it to other settings. (Kelly et al., 1979, p. 352)

Second, researchers and evaluators can develop an intervention, collaboratively, with setting personnel or community residents. That is, researchers or evaluators might approach the setting with some general ideas about the problem and ways of solving it, but the intervention is developed through lengthy conversations between all participants. The clear benefit of this approach is that if persons in a setting feel as if they own (or co-own) the intervention, they are more likely to continue it when the researcher or evaluator's involvement ends. Another benefit might be the development of a "truly innovative" intervention (Kelly et al., 1979). However, participants often have a vested interest in the way their organization functions, which might make it less likely that collaborators from the setting will help develop a true innovation. Some research with social program dissemination indicates that settings often adopt innovative programs and modify them in ways that conform to more traditional practices (e.g., Blakely, Mayer, & Davidson, 1986; Blakely et al., 1987). Familiarity with a setting often means that one is too conscious of (and thus inhibited by) the politics of that setting, the financial problems, and the various personalities of those who might oppose change.

Such problems in innovation are particularly true of preventive interventions. Most existing organizations are treatment focused; it is hard to ignore the press of existing problems to develop and implement prevention programs, particularly when resources are limited and choices must be made between the two approaches. For example, Bogat, Sullivan, and Grober (1993) describe child abuse prevention programs implemented in the State of Michigan that cost, on average, $597 per parent, per year. Compare this to the

> immediate per child costs [of abuse that] could include foster care ($450 per month), hospital costs (about $1,690 per hospital stay), and special education services ($655 per year) . . . Long term costs might include those related to court and detention, long-term foster care, and drug/alcohol rehabilitation programs . . . (Daro, 1988) (Bogat et al., 1993, p. 220)

Although clear benefits would result from preventing child abuse (financial benefits for the community and psychological benefits for the victims), relatively few preventive programs have been implemented.

Jason et al. (1995) document the minimal costs involved in implementing various smoking cessation programs and compare these to the staggering costs in health care expenditures and lost productivity that result from continued smoking. In the three worksites in which these authors implemented interventions, the cost of the different programs were approximately $4,700, $7,000, and $27,000; respectively. However, if those participants who were abstinent at the 12-month follow-up remained so for 20 years, the authors estimate the economic benefits of quitting to range from about $130,000 to $1.9 million, depending on the site.

When interventions are finally implemented, a new set of problems arise. Conducting good field research is a process of continual problem-solving and crisis management. For example, the authors of this chapter developed and evaluated a school transition program for elementary school transfer students (Bogat, Jones, & Jason, 1980). The program and its evaluation (including randomized treatment and control groups) were developed in collaboration with the school principal. We naively believed every possible problem and eventuality had been planned for; therefore, it was with stunned disbelief that we arrived at the school on the first day of the program to find that children in the experimental group had brought many of their friends, who were, unfortunately, in the control group. (Of course, we let all the children participate in the intervention, to do otherwise would have seemed mean-spirited.)

Jason et al.'s (1992) description of a tutoring project for transfer students underscores the importance of flexibility when implementing a school intervention. Elementary school calendars are busy and rarely consistent; special events are frequent, some are scheduled in advance and others are not. As the authors noted, "More than once, a tutor was left waiting for a child who was in an unannounced dress rehearsal for the school's Christmas pageant, or left with the single option of tutoring two children at the same time because of parties, holidays, or a shortened school day" (p. 132).

The intervention itself, which may have been agreed on by all parties, may be impossible to implement as conceived. Pilot work often can illuminate intervention difficulties. We discuss the importance of pilot work more thoroughly in the second section of this chapter.

Assessing the Impact

The final stage of consultation, and in this case a research collaboration, is assessing the impact of the intervention. It is somewhat misleading to think about assessment as the last stage in the process. Good assessment should inform the previous three stages; it is a process that begins early in the planning of the research collaboration.

As stated earlier, most evaluation questions tend to focus on issues of needs assessment, costs, and consumer satisfaction; the impact of an intervention is rarely assessed: "Questions about impact are less frequent, probably because public interest in them is low and costs of answering them are high" (Boruch & Shadish, 1983, p. 77). Elias (1991), in describing the implementation and evaluation of a school-based "social decision-making and problem-solving curriculum," noted that not only does each constituency that participates in the research team have a different perception of program success, but some constituencies are diverse, they are composed of (sub)constituencies, each of whose perceptions may vary as well. For example, within the school constituency, "Students make many of their evaluative judgments on the basis of less formal and less quantitative information, focusing on vivid, dramatic, clinical, and anecdotal examples of the program's functioning" (p. 399). This type of information as well as more pragmatic issues interests school officials. Other constituencies have other interests. As Elias (1991) noted, "External funding sources have required our evaluation process to include multiple indices of many constructs, . . . [and such requirements often increase] resentment among all school-based constituents" (p. 399).

This section has focused primarily on the human interactions inherent in establishing collaborative research relationships, whether those are instigated by researchers or evaluators. The next section is devoted to the technical complexities of conducting good evaluations—how best to assess the impact of an intervention.

ASSESSING THE IMPACT: ISSUES OF RESEARCH DESIGN IN COLLABORATIVE RELATIONSHIPS

There are many important considerations when assessing interventions including, what are the appropriate questions to ask and to evaluate; what research design is appropriate; and to what use will research results be put?

Decisions about all these questions are ultimately related to the research perspective one takes. Debates among community researchers have often centered on the value of a traditional, logical positivist approach versus other research strategies (e.g., an ecological perspective). A logical positivist approach rests on the foundation that knowledge results from the collection of empirical data using the scientific method; over time enough data accrues to reveal specific truths. Alternatively, an ecological approach suggests that knowledge is not gained in a linear fashion; the act of observation changes the phenomenon of interest and there are few generalizable "truths" about the social world (e.g., Kelly & Hess, 1987; Kingry-Westergaard & Kelly, 1990). A thorough discussion of these epistemological issues (and the relative values of each perspective) is beyond the scope of this chapter; however, we believe that the following sections represent important research considerations from any perspective.

Posing the Best Questions to Evaluate an Intervention

Levels of Research

Early in the planning stages of the evaluation, the research team must consider which entity they wish to effect. The targets for evaluation may be individuals, multiple individuals, groups or organizations, settings, mesosystems, and intersystems (Shinn, 1990). For example, in a school intervention, one might focus on particular students (individual-level), classrooms of students (multiple individuals-level), a school (groups or organizations-level), or classrooms of students and their interactions with teachers (settings-level).

Most often, psychologists pose questions that focus on the individual or groups of individuals, usually to the exclusion of more contextual variables. Sometimes it is easy to become overwhelmed with higher levels of analysis because they are more complex and operate as entities with distinct rules and regulations (Rousseau, 1985). There are also less articulated theories about these higher level systems to guide the development of relevant research questions (Shinn, 1990).

However, the level at which one pitches a research question has implications for understanding the phenomenon of interest. For example, current political discourse puts the blame for many of society's problems, particularly those involving youth, on a deterioration in family values. Parents of young offenders are often chastised for not being more integrally involved in the lives of their children. Such a "theory" might lead to the development of parenting programs for parents of at-risk youth (primary prevention) or those of youthful offenders (early, secondary prevention). However, when higher-order levels, beyond the individual, are examined, the problem (and hence its solution) becomes more complicated. Mason, Cauce, and Gonzales (1994) found that there were no substantive differences on typical measures of "good" parenting between parents whose children were engaging in delinquent behavior and those who were not. What seemed to matter most was the peer context of the adolescents: The parents of adolescents in neighborhoods with a "negative peer context" had no room for error in their parenting; small deviations in consistency or rule-setting, had negative effects on their children. For adolescents living in neighborhoods with more positive peer groups, parents had more latitude in their parenting behavior before it resulted in negative consequences for their children.

A number of researchers have offered suggestions for moving conceptualization beyond the individual. Seidman (1988, 1990) suggests the importance of focusing on social regularities—"a dynamic, temporal pattern of transactions . . . between at least two units or entities that constitute a social system or setting" (1990, p. 92). As an example, he notes that the ratio of teacher to student questions remains fairly constant throughout secondary school, even though, as students age, they are capable of more active participation and collaboration in the high school classroom. He suggests that many adolescents' disenfranchisement from academics may be a result of this particular teacher/student transaction (Seidman, 1990). Kelly's work on ecological models (discussed earlier) also emphasizes the importance of focusing on levels other than the individual, as does the work of Bronfenbrenner (e.g., 1979), Sarason (e.g., 1978, 1981, 1982), and Sameroff and Chandler (1975).

Finally, community psychologists have often promoted the importance of conducting cross-level research (e.g., Rousseau, 1985; Shinn, 1990). Conducting research evaluations that integrate a cross-level perspective also requires measurement instruments and statistical analyses that preserve the integrity and interaction of these levels. It is paradoxical that most attempts at cross-level research "measure extraindividual pheonomena by questioning individuals" (Shinn, 1990, p. 115). For example, evaluations of school interventions typically randomly assign classrooms to experimental or control groups, but analyze the data at the level of the individual (i.e., number of students), not the classroom.

Evaluations of community interventions rarely examine multiple levels of variables, the relative independence or nonindependence of each level of variable, and the influence that these different cross-level variables have on the measured outcome. A notable exception is a smoking cessation study conducted by Jason and his colleagues (1995).

Many statistical problems beyond the scope of this chapter are related to conducting cross-level research. The following sources provide more information: Bock, 1989; Bryk and Raudenbush, 1987; Burstein, 1980; Dansereau, Alutto, Markham, and Dumas, 1982; Dansereau, Alutto, and Yammarino, 1984; Dansereau and Markham, 1987; DeLeeuw and Kreft, 1986; Glick and Roberts, 1984; Goldstein, 1987; Hedeker, Gibbons, and Flay, 1994; Hedeker, McMahon, Jason, and Salina, 1994; Hopkins, 1982; Jason et al., 1995; Kenny, 1985; Kenny and LaVoie, 1985.

Theory

As stated earlier, most evaluation research circumvents the crucial question of whether the program worked (Boruch & Shadish, 1983). For those evaluators and researchers who decide to answer this important question, the assessment is often structured to provide a not particularly interesting answer. For example, many interventions are educational: A program is implemented to teach a group of individuals skills or knowledge about a particular topic (e.g., birth control), and the evaluation measures whether an increase in knowledge or skills occurs after participation. Obviously, it is important to know whether an intervention worked, but it is also important to understand why it either succeeded or failed. Theory is a useful tool for developing evaluations; it allows the researcher to answer "why" questions.

Lorion has long advocated the utility of a developmental perspective in the conduct of community research (Lorion, 1983, 1990; Lorion & Allen, 1989; Lorion, Price, & Eaton, 1988). He argues that social phenomena can be best studied by attending to how they change and develop over time. To some extent, the developmental perspective (see Sroufe & Rutter, 1984) encompasses many of the principles inherent in a cross-level approach to problem/program conceptualization and evaluation discussed above. Thus, it is important to consider implementing research that attends to levels as well as time. Within a developmental perspective, however, developmental psychology itself has substantive theories that might usefully aid researchers in understanding how participants experience interventions and the outcomes that result. [Other fields, such as organizational psychology, also have substantive theories that are useful for conceptualizing community interventions and evaluations (e.g., Bartunek, Foster-Fishman, & Keys, 1996; Foster-Fishman, & Keys, 1995).]

For example, much research has accumulated indicating that preschoolers do not learn as many concepts in sexual abuse education programs as do school-age children (e.g., Conte, Rosen, Saperstein, & Shermack, 1985; Wurtele & Miller-Perrin, 1992), and younger preschoolers learn less than older preschoolers (Borkin & Frank, 1986; Liang, Bogat, & McGrath, 1993). When program evaluations of sexual abuse education programs are not theoretically driven, there is no way of understanding this differential learning. Attention to basic developmental research could point to issues that should or should not be taught to preschoolers, show how best to teach each concept, and, finally, provide a framework to evaluate the manner in which children comprehend program concepts. McGrath and Bogat (1995) argue that to help children achieve competence on sexual abuse knowledge and skills, evaluators must become less concerned with what children learn and more concerned with what children think about what they learn (and what they do not learn). Research taking this approach has begun to fit a problem-solving model to children's mastery of sexual abuse education skills (Grober & Bogat, 1994) and to focus on preschoolers' differential understanding of adult authority in sexual abuse and benign situations (Bogat & McGrath, 1993).

Theory, then, can help formulate good research questions, but it is often applied in a post hoc fashion to explain research results. Care should be taken when doing so. For example, Berrick and Gilbert (1991) have been vocal critics of programs to educate preschoolers about sexual abuse. In their writing, they "apply, without caveat, selective findings from developmental research that examine benign, frequently occurring situations to sexual abuse education with preschoolers and conclude that programs can never be made age appropriate" (McGrath & Bogat, 1995, p. 172). Theory (in this case, developmental theory) cannot offer authoritative, post hoc explanations for research results that were not framed with those specific questions in mind.

Finally, theory may be of interest only to the researcher; practitioners and setting personnel may have a greater interest in pragmatic questions (Elias, 1991). The applied researcher should remember that theory and pragmatism need not be in conflict. Research evaluations can be designed to accomplish both aims, and will be more substantive as a result.

Research Design Issues

Shadish's (1990) admonition—"No perfect method exists for answering any given question" (p. 17)—should be taken to heart as the researcher or evaluator searches for the best methodology to answer research questions. The accuracy of the investigator's results will always be a trade-off between bandwidth and fidelity. "Bandwidth refers to the number of different kinds of questions that method answers, and fidelity refers to the accuracy of the answer provided" (Shadish, 1990, p. 17). The trade-off occurs because when one is improved, the other declines. What follows is a discussion of several important and recurrent issues that arise in school and community research.

True Experiments versus Alternative Approaches

The central hallmark of an experimental approach to evaluation involves randomly assigning entities (e.g., children, classrooms, or schools) to experimental or control groups. This is often a controversial procedure in community research. Galinsky,

Turnbull, Meglin, and Wilner (1993) speak for many practitioners when they write, "Designs that use a control group necessarily exclude some clients from the intervention and hence are problematic for practitioners who have service provision for their goal" (p. 443). Often, when persons in the community endorse a trial intervention they do so with great hope; they would not have agreed to the intervention unless they believed that positive outcomes were likely and would justify the inconvenience and hard work necessitated by a change in practice and protocol.

Scientists, on the other hand, are often well aware of highly touted interventions whose "miraculous" impact becomes less so when placed under the scrutiny of strict scientific methodology. For example, in the not-so-distant-past heart bypass surgery was considered a panacea, saving the lives of millions who would have died if treated with standard drug treatments. Funding agencies refused to grant monies to researchers wishing to conduct randomized trials with bypass procedures because they felt it would be unethical to deny persons a lifesaving procedure. When the randomized trials were conducted (through the Veterans Administration), it was found that only men with severe blood flow constriction into the heart benefited significantly from the surgical procedure. Men with less severe heart problems, who had the bypass operation, lived no longer than those men taking standard medications.

Randomized trials become more palatable to all collaborators when delayed-treatment control groups (rather than no-treatment control groups) are employed. The first author, in conducting interventions aimed at educating preschoolers about sexual abuse prevention (e.g., Liang et al., 1993), randomly assigned children within each classroom to experimental or delayed-treatment control groups. All children received the pretest, then the experimental group received the intervention, and finally, all children received the posttest. Upon completion of the posttest, the delayed-treatment control group received the program. Not only was this good experimental design, but using this approach resulted in several unanticipated benefits. For example, the curriculum was, of necessity, taught with smaller groups of children; many teachers felt that the extra time required to teach the program on two separate occasions was justified because the lessons were more effective with smaller groups.

Often, parents, teachers, and school officials are nervous about control groups, delayed treatment or not. Educating consumers about research and evaluation is the best policy. When implementing the sexual abuse education curriculum in various preschools, the first author found that the concept of control groups seemed to generate skepticism about the overall utility of the program ("If the program was good, you wouldn't need to evaluate it, would you?"). The evaluation team talked to parents about the importance of not deluding ourselves (parents, teachers, and evaluators) that simply because we were teaching children sexual abuse prevention skills, they were actually learning those skills. Also, we talked to parents about our own philosophy of field research: that participation in research is participation in a "favor bank." Current participants in the program were the beneficiaries of an improved curriculum that had resulted from information collected from children in previous years; the information obtained from this year's participants would benefit other children in the future.

Pilot Work

The importance of pilot work has been mentioned previously, but it cannot be emphasized enough the usefulness of pilot-testing the intervention as well as the evaluation prior to implementing a full-scale research program.

The first author and her colleagues spent four years implementing a mentoring project for low-income, pregnant teens. The first few months of the project served as a "practice" for the full-scale project. The project trained community women, who were themselves mothers, to serve as mentors for pregnant teens for a 9-month period, starting in the teen's last trimester and ending when the baby was 6 months old. Mentors were trained to provide social support to the teen and increase the teen's social network. The average age of the adolescents in this study was 15. Several problems emerged during the early pretesting, and three design issues were revised as a result of pilot work.

First, many of the teens were unreliable informants as to their due date, many gave birth to premature babies, and many stopped attending school in the last trimester due to medical complications. We wanted teens in the experimental group matched with mentors before the birth of the baby, as we believed that the birth could be an important bonding experience for the mentor and teen. But, in practice, we found that we were losing possible participants because they gave birth prior to the pretest interview and the subsequent random assignment, or they were not attending school and could not be located. To rectify these problems, we moved the pretest interview slightly earlier than we had originally planned. The two subsequent interviews (conducted one month and six months after the birth of the baby) were less problematic because the project staff had accurate information about the date of birth of each infant and could schedule interviews accordingly.

Second, the project coordinator (a person knowledgeable about research design) had agreed to assign teens randomly to the experimental or control groups after the initial phase of data collection. However, after completing a number of initial school intakes, and getting to know some of the teens quite well, the project coordinator began to have strong "gut" feelings about which teens could benefit most from a mentoring project. She knew that pure random assignment could mean that the teens she perceived to be "most deserving" of services would be assigned to the control group. In writing about social workers, Galinsky et al. (1993) noted that "when social work practitioners believe that a service is beneficial, they are likely to place service objectives above research objectives . . ." (p. 443). In this project, the program coordinator knew that her perceptions of which teens needed the program most might tempt her to compromise the research design and also might cause her to have negative feelings about the program. We solved this dilemma by assigning the randomization task to a research assistant who did not have responsibilities for any aspect of the intervention.

Third, researchers and practitioners alike have to be flexible with regard to the intervention as well as the research design. Again, pilot work enables changes to be made before all concerned become overly invested in a particular approach. In the mentoring study, our original plan was to conduct three, 3-hour training sessions for our mentors. Feedback from trainers and trainees following our piloting work resulted in reducing the number of sessions to two: Most of the essential information we hoped to convey to mentors could be covered in two sessions and mentors were anxious to be matched with their teens, rather than attend more training sessions.

It would be disingenuous to suggest that pilot work solves all or even most of the problems associated with a research project. In the mentoring project, every teen had a unique set of life circumstances that provided distinctive challenges for the mentor/mentee relationship. Whether the teen had a permanent domicile; whether her parents were supportive of the intervention or undermined it; whether her boyfriend was abusive, drug-dealing, or supportive; whether she was a good student or a borderline one—all these factors (and more) meant that the "basic mentoring intervention" was, ultimately, individually tailored for each pair. Mentors received weekly group supervision to keep their morale as high as possible, but mentor supervisors also participated in weekly meetings where strategizing and brainstorming took place in a supportive context. Bolstering the morale of our supervisors helped them to bolster the morale of our mentors (cf. Jason et al., 1992).

Finally, pilot work enabled our research group to develop a truly humane and realistic intervention. As we learned more about our population, we tweaked our intervention in ways that made it more valuable and more connected to the teens. We learned from our program coordinator that serving food to our mentors and teens at every meeting created a more positive environment for sharing and connection. We learned to create arenas for interaction between mentors and mentees that were not solely talking-based (our bias as middle-class psychologists); fun activities cemented many of the mentor/mentee relationships. Most importantly, we learned to keep our expectations for the project high, but accept the small gains that occurred for any individual teen.

Statistical Sensitivity

In an experimental or quasi-experimental design, issues related to statistical sensitivity are important. The ability to detect the significant results in an experiment is termed "statistical power." Boruch and Shadish (1983) detail two problems that can diminish statistical power in community interventions. First, "Programs are often not delivered as conceptualized or as advertised, . . . they are not "fixed" in the same sense that treatments are fixed in the physical sciences, and [thus] . . . their implementation is difficult to measure well" (p. 81). Good interventions are, in effect, tailor-made for every participant; however, the band in which such improvisation takes place needs to be defined. Specifying the minute variations within the intervention for every participant is probably unnecessary; however, collecting "dosage" information is relatively easy. Dosage (how much, for how long, and how intensely each participant received the intervention) can help specify the integrity of the intervention and determine issues related to cost/benefit ratios (how much treatment at what level of intensity is necessary to register an effect). Collecting dosage variables also attunes researcher and setting personnel to the process of the intervention and allows researchers to conduct time series analyses.

A second category of problems also can reduce statistical power in community research: The variables used to measure the outcomes are often "measured poorly or are irrelevant to the treatment . . . The reasons for this range from poor craftsmanship to wishful thinking about what the effects of intervention will be" (Boruch & Shadish, 1983, p. 81). One problem, recurrent in community research evaluations, is the confusion of manipulation checks with outcome measures. For example, a number of parenting programs bolster social support among high-risk parents to achieve positive physical and mental health outcomes for both mothers and children. To evaluate these interventions adequately, the researcher or evaluator must document that participants actually received increased support (a manipulation check); assessing the outcome of the intervention requires documenting change on one or more variables that measure physical and mental health (Bogat et al., 1993).

Assessing the manipulation and its impact on the outcome can lead to important information for developing cost-effective interventions. McMahon, Jason, and Hedeker

(1995) describe a social support smoking cessation intervention. The results showed that only one aspect of support was related to quitting (appraisal support), whereas others were not related (belonging, tangible, and self-esteem).

As Boruch and Shadish (1983) note: "The problem of maintaining power is exacerbated in community research because conventional approaches [to solving the problem], such as increasing sample size, are not always feasible" (p. 81). First, there may not be adequate resources to increase the number of persons participating in the intervention. Second, the intervention may be attempting to modify a very low base-rate behavior or event. Detecting changes in such events is difficult. Often, researchers attempt to compensate for the low base-rate problem by selecting only those persons who are at risk for a particular type of behavior (e.g., perpetrating child abuse). Caldwell, Bogat, and Davidson (1988) demonstrated that using screening instruments to select a population at risk to commit abuse actually led to relatively small increases in program efficiency. In this case, "sensitivity" is an instrument's capacity to identify abusive families, and "specificity" is its ability to identify nonabusive families. Suppose a researcher used a screening instrument to detect "risk to commit abuse" with a sensitivity of 85% and a specificity of 82.5% (the ratings of the best instruments currently available), and only delivered services to those persons identified as "at risk." Given the low base-rate of child abuse (about 1%), "over 95% of the families [identified] would be receiving services unnecessarily. If persons were not screened . . . 99% of the sample would receive services unnecessarily" (p. 618).

Qualitative Research

For various reasons, randomized trials are not always possible to execute, often because of logistical difficulties and high costs. Furthermore, control group designs rely on statistical techniques that compare mean scores of groups. Such designs are useful, but they may obscure real differences between different types of project participants. Of particular interest are those participants who do not benefit or may be harmed by an intervention. Other types of designs may be more practical as a first step, including the variants described by Campbell and Stanley (1963) and Cook and Campbell (1979). However, the search for alternatives has virtually ignored qualitative data techniques such as "experiential, phenomenological, clinical, case study, field work, participant observation, . . . [and] process evaluation" (Campbell, 1974, p. 1).

Qualitative approaches to research may, at times, be more valid than experimental, quantitative approaches. In writing about the experimental studies of mutual help groups, Tebes and Kramer (1991) noted:

> Random assignment, professional training of group leaders, the time-limited nature of the intervention, and extensive professional support and direction may make these [groups developed by researchers] unrepresentative of the essential characteristics of mutual support groups (Lieberman, 1986). In the case of quasi-experimental studies that have been conducted, their small number coupled with the failure to control for numerous threats to validity (e.g., participant selection factors, diffusion of treatments) have made it difficult to establish a cumulative scientific knowledge base. (p. 743)

As many writers have noted, the integration of qualitative and quantitative methods of research inquiry would be useful and complementary. The following sources can provide more information regarding qualitative approaches to research: Berg, 1989;

Bogdan and Bilken, 1992; Campbell, 1974; D'Aunno, Klein, and Susskind, 1985; Denzin and Lincoln, 1994; Maton, 1990; Patton, 1987, 1990; Tebes and Kramer, 1991.

Use of Research Results

Leviton and Hughes (1981) differentiate three types of use for the results of research and evaluation: instrumental, conceptual, and persuasive. Shadish (1990) explains each of these as follows:

> Instrumental use is the use of research results to dictate direct changes in programs; conceptual use aims to change the way that people think about problems and their solutions; and persuasive use tries to marshall convincing evidence to support a particular position. (p. 13)

The "use" agenda of the researcher and the community collaborators should be made clear in early conversations. How one plans on using the research results will affect the type of data collected, who participates in data collection, and the ultimate impact (narrow or broad) of the study (Shadish, 1990).

When the research project is completed, the researcher or evaluator and site personnel should meet to discuss the results and decide how the data will be used. One approach to communication may be modeled on the adversary hearing proposed by Levine (1974; Levine et al., 1978). This procedure is advocated as a way to integrate qualitative and quantitative research approaches. Research participants meet with researchers to hear the quantitative results of the evaluation. Participants then discuss whether their own experiences validate these findings. The approach can be highly structured, for example, resembling a "trial by jury" (Wolf, 1975, as cited in Tebes & Kramer, 1991), or, in the model advocated by Tebes and Kramer (1991), "an informal town meeting." Such an approach has utility for all collaborators:

> The adversary hearing pits two sorts of knowledge claims against one another: the professional knowledge of the researcher versus the experiential knowledge of the program participant. Experiential knowledge is pragmatic and concrete, and is derived from "lived experience"; whereas professional knowledge is university-based, analytical, and theory-driven (Borkman, 1990). (Tebes & Kramer, 1991, p. 750)

Once all collaborators agree about the validity of the study's results, then it is more likely that they will agree with how those results are implemented or disseminated.

SUMMARY

In this chapter we have described the types of collaborations that researchers, evaluators, and community members might effect and some of the practical considerations inherent in developing evaluations that truly assess the impact of an intervention. Although productive collaborations and valid and reliable evaluations are demanding, this should not discourage persons new to this endeavor. For all the difficulties inherent in field research, there are also tremendous satisfactions—the most rewarding, ultimately, is developing a program that has a positive effect on its participants.

Finally, the climate today in the United States is very favorable to evaluation. Most granting agencies (whether at the local, state, or federal level) require some type of evaluation to document the effectiveness of the proposed project. We hope that this chapter has inspired neophyte and experienced evaluators alike to consider conducting evaluations that reflect excellence, not merely ease.

REFERENCES

Bartunek, J. M., Foster-Fishman, P. G., & Keys, C. B. (1996). Using collaborative advocacy to foster intergroup cooperation. *Human Relations, 49*(6), 701–733.

Berg, B. L. (1989). *Qualitative research methods.* Boston: Allyn & Bacon.

Berrick, J. D., & Gilbert, N. (1991). *With the best of intentions: The child sexual abuse prevention movement.* New York: Guilford Press.

Blakely, C. H., Mayer, J. P., & Davidson, W. S., II. (1986). Social program innovation and dissemination: A study of organizational change processes. *Policy Studies Review, 6,* 273–286.

Blakely, C. H., Mayer, J. P., Gottschalk, R. G., Schmitt, N., Davidson, W. S., II, Roitman, D., & Emshoff, J. G. (1987). The fidelity-adaptation debate: Implications for the implementation of public sector social programs. *American Journal of Community Psychology, 15,* 253–268.

Bock, R. D. (1989). Measurement of human variation: A two-stage model. In R. D. Bock (Ed.), *Multilevel analysis of educational data* (pp. 319–342). New York: Academic Press.

Bogat, G. A., Jones, J. W., & Jason, L. A. (1980). School transitions: Preventive intervention following an elementary school closing. *Journal of Community Psychology, 8,* 343–352.

Bogat, G. A., & McGrath, M. P. (1993). Preschoolers' cognitions of authority, and its relationship to sexual abuse education. *Child Abuse & Neglect, 17,* 651–662.

Bogat, G. A., Sullivan, L., & Grober, J. (1993). Applications of social support to preventive interventions. In D. S. Glenwick & L. A. Jason (Eds.), *Promoting health and mental health in children, youth, and families* (pp. 205–232). New York: Springer.

Bogdan, R. C., & Bilken, S. K. (1992). *Qualitative research for education: An introduction to theory and methods.* Boston: Allyn & Bacon.

Borkin, J., & Frank, L. (1986). Sexual abuse prevention in preschoolers: A pilot program. *Child Welfare, 65,* 75–82.

Borkman, T. (1990). Experiential, professional, and lay frames of reference. In T. Powell (Ed.), *Working with self-help* (pp. 3–30). Silver Spring, MD: National Association of Social Workers.

Boruch, R. F., & Shadish, W. R. (1983). Design issues in community intervention research. In E. Seidman (Ed.), *Handbook of social intervention* (pp. 73–98). Beverly Hills, CA: Sage.

Bronfenbrenner, U. (1979). *The ecology of human development.* Cambridge, MA: Harvard University Press.

Bryk, A. S., & Raudenbush, S. W. (1987). Application of hierarchical linear models to assessing change. *Psychological Bulletin, 101,* 147–158.

Burstein, L. (1980). The analysis of multilevel data in educational research and evaluation. In D. Berliner (Ed.), *Review of research in education* (Vol. 8, pp. 158–233). Washington, DC: American Educational Research Association.

Caldwell, R. A., Bogat, G. A., & Davidson, W. S., II. (1988). The assessment of child abuse potential and the prevention of child abuse and neglect: A policy analysis. *American Journal of Community Psychology, 16,* 609–624.

Campbell, D. T. (1974, August). *Qualitative knowing in action research.* Paper presented at the meeting of the American Psychological Association, New Orleans.

Campbell, D. T., & Stanley, J. C. (1963). *Experimental and quasi-experimental designs for research.* Chicago: Rand McNally.

Caplan, G. (1970). *The theory and practice of mental health consultation.* New York: Basic Books.

Conte, J. R., Rosen, C., Saperstein, L., & Shermack, R. (1985). An evaluation of a program to prevent the sexual victimization of young children. *Child Abuse & Neglect, 9,* 319–328.

Cook, T. D., & Campbell, D. T. (1979). *Quasi-experimentation: Design and analysis issues for field settings.* Chicago: Rand McNally.

Dansereau, F., Jr., Alutto, J. A., Markham, S. E., & Dumas, M. (1982). Multiplexed supervision and leadership: An application of within and between analysis. In J. G. Hunt, U. Sekaran, & C. A. Schriesheim (Eds.), *Leadership: Beyond establishment views* (pp. 81–103). Carbondale: Southern Illinois University Press.

Dansereau, F., Jr., Alutto, J. A., & Yammarino, F. J. (1984). *Theory testing in organizational behavior: The variant approach.* Englewood Cliffs, NJ: Prentice-Hall.

Dansereau, F., Jr., & Markham, S. E. (1987). Levels of analysis in personnel and human resources management. *Personnel and Human Resources Management, 5,* 1–50.

Daro, D. (1988). *Confronting child abuse: Research for effective program design.* New York: Free Press.

D'Aunno, T., Klein, D. C., & Susskind, E. C. (1985). Seven approaches for the study of community phenomena. In E. C. Susskind & D. C. Klein (Eds.), *Community research: Methods, paradigms, and applications* (pp. 421–495). New York: Praeger.

DeLeeuw, J., & Kreft, I. (1986). Random coefficient models for multilevel analysis. *Journal of Educational Statistics, 11,* 57–85.

Denzin, N. K., & Lincoln, Y. S. (1994). *Handbook of qualitative research.* Thousand Oaks, CA: Sage.

Elias, M. (1991). An action research approach to evaluating the impact of a social decision-making and problem-solving curriculum for preventing behavior and academic dysfunction in children. *Evaluation and Program Planning, 14,* 397–401.

Emery, R. E. (1982). Interparental conflict and the children of discord and divorce. *Psychological Bulletin, 92,* 310–330.

Foster-Fishman, P. G., & Keys, C. B. (1995). The inserted pyramid: How a well-meaning employee empowerment initiative ran afoul of the culture of a public bureaucracy. In D. P. Moore (Ed.), *Academy of Management Best Paper Proceedings 1995* (pp. 364–368).

Galinsky, M. J., Turnbull, J. E., Meglin, D. E., & Wilner, M. E. (1993). Confronting the reality of collaborative practice research: Issues of practice, design, measurement, and team development. *Social Work, 38,* 440–449.

Garfinkel, I., & McLanahan, S. S. (1986). *Single mothers and their children: A new American dilemma.* Washington, DC: Urban Institute Press.

Gensheimer, L. K., Mayer, J. P., Gottschalk, R., & Davidson, W. S., II. (1986). Diverting youth from the juvenile justice system: A meta-analysis of intervention efficacy. In S. J. Apter & A. P. Goldstein (Eds.), *Youth violence: Programs & prospects* (pp. 39–57). New York: Pergamon Press.

Glick, W. H., & Roberts, K. H. (1984). Hypothesized interdependence, assumed independence. *Academy of Management Review, 13,* 133–147.

Goldstein, H. (1987). *Multilevel models in educational and social research.* New York: Oxford University Press.

Grober, J., & Bogat, G. A. (1994). Social problem solving in unsafe situations: Implications for sexual abuse education programs. *American Journal of Community Psychology, 22,* 399–414.

Hatch, J., Moss, N., Saran, A., Presley-Cantrell, L., & Mallory, C. (1993). Community research: Partnership in black communities. *American Journal of Preventive Medicine, 9,* 27–31.

Hedeker, D., Gibbons, R. D., & Flay, B. R. (1994). Random-effects regression models for clustered data: With an example from smoking prevention research. *Journal of Consulting and Clinical Psychology, 62,* 757–765.

Hedeker, D., McMahon, S. D., Jason, L. A., & Salina, D. (1994). Analysis of clustered data in community psychology: With an example from a worksite smoking cessation project. *American Journal of Community Psychology, 22,* 595–615.

Holahan, C. J. (1979). Redesigning physical environments to enhance social interactions. In R. F. Munoz, L. R. Snowden, & J. G. Kelly (Eds.), *Social and psychological research in community settings* (pp. 243–258). San Francisco: Jossey-Bass.

Hopkins, K. D. (1982). The unit of analysis: Group means versus individual observations. *American Educational Research Journal, 19,* 5–18.

Jason, L. A., McMahon, S. D., Salina, D., Hedeker, D., Stockton, M., Dunson, K., & Kimball, P. (1995). Assessing a smoking cessation intervention involving groups, incentives, and self-help manuals. *Behavior Therapy, 26,* 393–408.

Jason, L. A., Weine, A. M., Johnson, J. H., Warren-Sohlberg, L., Filippelli, L. A., Turner, E. Y., & Lardon, C. (1992). *Helping transfer students: Strategies for educational and social readjustment.* San Francisco: Jossey-Bass.

Kelly, J. G., with Dassoff, N., Levin, I., Schreckengost, J., Stelzner, S. P., & Altman, B. E. (1988). *A guide to prevention research in the community: First steps.* New York: Haworth Press.

Kelly, J. G., & Hess, R. E. (1987). *The ecology of prevention: Illustrating mental health consultation.* New York: Haworth Press.

Kelly, J. G., Munoz, R. F., & Snowden, L. R. (1979). Characteristics of community research projects and the implementation process. In R. F. Munoz, L. R. Snowden, & J. G. Kelly (Eds.), *Social and psychological research in community settings* (pp. 343–363). San Francisco: Jossey-Bass.

Kenny, D. A. (1985). The generalized group effect model. In J. R. Nesselroade & A. von Eye (Eds.), *Individual development and social change: Exploratory analysis* (pp. 343–357). Orlando, FL: Academic Press.

Kenny, D. A., & LaVoie, L. (1985). Separating individual and group effects. *Journal of Personality and Social Psychology, 48,* 339–348.

Kingry-Westergaard, C., & Kelly, J. G. (1990). A contextualist epistomology for ecological research. In P. Tolan, C. Keys, F. Chertok, & L. A. Jason (Eds.), *Researching community psychology: Issues of theory and methods* (pp. 23–31). Washington, DC: American Psychological Association.

Lax, D. A., & Sebenius, J. K. (1986). *The manager as negotiator.* New York: Free Press.

Levine, M. (1974). Scientific method and the adversary model: Some preliminary thoughts. *American Psychologist, 29,* 661–677.

Levine, M., Brown, E., Fitzgerald, C., Gopelrud, E., Gordon, M. E., Jayne-Lazarus, C., Rosenberg, N., & Slater, J. (1978). Adapting the jury trial for program evaluation. *Evaluation and Programming Planning, 1,* 177–186.

Levine, M., & Perkins, D. V. (1987). *Principles of community psychology: Perspectives and applications.* New York: Oxford University Press.

Leviton, L. C., & Hughes, E. F. X. (1981). Research on the utilization of evaluations: A review and synthesis. *Evaluation Review, 5,* 525–548.

Liang, B., Bogat, G. A., & McGrath, M. P. (1993). Differential learning of sexual abuse prevention concepts among preschoolers. *Child Abuse & Neglect, 17,* 641–650.

Lieberman, M. A. (1986). Self-help groups and psychiatry. *American Psychiatric Association Annual Review, 5,* 744–760.

Lorion, R. P. (1983). Evaluating preventive interventions: Guidelines for the serious change agent. In R. D. Felner, L. A. Jason, J. Moritsugu, & S. S. Farber (Eds.), *Preventive psychology: Theory, research and practice in community interventions* (pp. 251–268). New York: Pergamon Press.

Lorion, R. P. (1990). Developmental analyses of community phenomena. In P. Tolan, C. Keys, F. Chertok, & L. A. Jason (Eds.), *Researching community psychology: Issues of theory and methods.* (pp. 32–41). Washington, DC: American Psychological Association.

Lorion, R. P., & Allen, L. (1989). Preventive services in mental health. In D. Rochefort (Ed.), *Handbook on mental health policy in the United States* (pp. 403–434). Westport, CT: Greenwood Press.

Lorion, R. P., Price, R. H., & Eaton, W. W. (1988). The prevention of child and adolescent disorders: From theory to research. In D. Shaffer & I. Phillips (Eds.), *Project prevention* (pp. 55–96). Washington, DC: American Academy of Child and Adolescent Psychiatry.

Luepnitz, D. A. (1982). *Child custody: A study of families after divorce.* Lexington, MA: Lexington Books.

Mason, C. A., Cauce, A. M., & Gonzales, N. (1994, August). *One size fits all? Parental control with African-American youth.* Paper presented at the annual convention of the American Psychological Association, New York.

Maton, K. I. (1990). Toward the use of qualitative methodology in community psychology research. In P. Tolan, C. Keys, F. Chertok, & L. A. Jason (Eds.), *Researching community psychology: Issues of theory and methods* (pp. 153–156). Washington, DC: American Psychological Association.

McGrath, M. P., & Bogat, G. A. (1995). Motive, intention, and authority: Relating developmental research to sexual abuse education for preschoolers. *Journal of Applied Developmental Psychology, 16,* 171–191.

McMahon, S. D., Jason, L. A., & Hedeker, D. (1995). *Social support in a worksite smoking intervention: A test of theoretical models.* Unpublished manuscript.

Moore, K. A., & Waite, L. J. (1977). Early childbearing and educational attainment. *Family Planning Perspective, 9,* 220–225.

Parker, J. G., & Asher, S. R. (1987). Peer relations and later adjustment: Are low-accepted children at risk? *Psychological Bulletin, 102,* 357–389.

Patton, M. Q. (1987). *How to use qualitative methods in evaluation.* Beverly Hills, CA: Sage.

Patton, M. Q. (1990). *Qualitative evaluation and research methods* (2nd ed.). Newbury Park, CA: Sage.

Popovitch, S. N. (1990). *The relationship of family environment, mothers' influence, and pregnant adolescents' decisions to keep or release their babies for adoption.* Unpublished doctoral dissertation, Michigan State University, East Lansing.

Resnick, M. D., Blum, R. W., Bose, J., Smith, M., & Toogood, R. (1990). Characteristics of unmarried adolescent mothers: Determinants of child rearing versus adoption. *American Journal of Orthopsychiatry, 60,* 577–585.

Reyes, O., & Jason, L. A. (1993). Collaborating with the community. In J. E. Zins, T. R. Kratochwill, & S. N. Elliott (Eds.), *Handbook of consultation services for children: Applications in educational and clinical settings* (pp. 305–316). San Francisco: Jossey-Bass.

Rousseau, D. M. (1985). Issues of level in organizational research: Multi-level and cross-level perspectives. In L. L. Cummings & B. M. Staw (Eds.), *Research in organizational behavior* (Vol. 7, pp. 1–37). Greenwich, CT: JAI Press.

Sameroff, A. J., & Chandler, M. J. (1975). Reproductive risk and the continuum of caretaking causality. In F. D. Horowitz, M. Hetherington, S. Scarr-Salapatek, & G. Siegel (Eds.),

Review of child development research (Vol. 4, pp. 187–244). Chicago: University of Chicago Press.

Sarason, S. B. (1978). The nature of problem solving in social action. *American Psychologist, 33,* 370–380.

Sarason, S. B. (1981). *Psychology misdirected.* New York: Free Press.

Sarason, S. B. (1982). *The culture of the school and the problem of change.* Boston: Allyn & Bacon.

Seidman, E. (1988). Back to the future, community psychology: Unfolding a theory of social intervention. *American Journal of Community Psychology, 16,* 3–24.

Seidman, E. (1990). Pursuing the meaning and utility of social regularities for community psychology. In P. Tolan, C. Keys, F. Chertok, & L. A. Jason (Eds.), *Researching community psychology: Issues of theory and methods* (pp. 91–100). Washington, DC: American Psychological Association.

Shadish, W. (1990). Defining excellence criteria in community research. In P. Tolan, C. Keys, F. Chertok, & L. A. Jason (Eds.), *Researching community psychology: Issues of theory and methods* (pp. 9–22). Washington, DC: American Psychological Association.

Shinn, M. (1990). Mixing and matching: Levels of conceptualization, measurement, and statistical analysis in community research. In P. Tolan, C. Keys, F. Chertok, & L. A. Jason (Eds.), *Researching community psychology: Issues of theory and methods* (pp. 111–126). Washington, DC: American Psychological Association.

Shure, M. B. (1979). Training children to solve interpersonal problems: A preventive mental health program. In R. F. Munoz, L. R. Snowden, & J. G. Kelly (Eds.), *Social and psychological research in community settings* (pp. 30–58). San Francisco, CA: Jossey-Bass.

Snowden, L. R., Munoz, R. F., & Kelly, J. G. (1979). The process of implementing community-based research. In R. F. Munoz, L. R. Snowden, & J. G. Kelly (Eds.), *Social and psychological research in community settings* (pp. 14–29). San Francisco, CA: Jossey-Bass.

Sroufe, L. A., & Rutter, M. (1984). The domain of developmental psychopathology. *Child Development, 55,* 17–29.

Tebes, J. K., & Kramer, D. T. (1991). Quantitative and qualitative knowing in mutual support research: Some lessons from the recent history of scientific psychology. *American Journal of Community Psychology, 19,* 739–756.

Thomas, S. B. (1991). The Tuskegee Study, 1932–72: Implications for HIV education and AIDS risk education programs in the black community. *American Journal of Public Health, 81,* 1498–1505.

U.S. Department of the Census. (1981). *Statistical abstract of the United States, 1981* (102nd ed.). Washington, DC: U.S. Department of Commerce.

Wallerstein, J. S., & Blakeslee, S. (1989). *Second chances: Men, women, and children a decade after divorce.* New York: Ticknor & Fields.

Weick, K. E. (1984). Small wins: Redefining the scale of social problems. *American Psychologist, 39,* 40–49.

Whitehead, B. D. (1993). Dan Quayle was right. *Atlantic Monthly, 271,* 47–84.

Wolf, R. (1975). Trial by jury. *Phi Delta Kappa, 57,* 185–187.

Wood, D. J., & Gray, B. (1991). Toward a comprehensive theory of collaboration. *Journal of Applied Behavioral Science, 27,* 139–162.

Wurtele, S. K., & Miller-Perrin, C. L. (1992). *Preventing child sexual abuse: Sharing the responsibility.* Lincoln: University of Nebraska Press.

PART FOUR

Preventive Interventions

CHAPTER 7

Early Intervention with Young At-Risk Children and Their Families

CARL J. DUNST and CAROL M. TRIVETTE

Early intervention is a term now used broadly to refer to a wide range of experiences and supports provided to children, parents, and families during the pregnancy, infancy, and/or early childhood periods of development (Dunst, 1996). With few exceptions, these interventions are intended to compensate for or correct problems and conditions that place young children at risk for any number of poor outcomes. These problems or conditions include, but are not limited to, those that are environmental (e.g., poverty), biological (e.g., prematurity), genetic (e.g., chromosomal abnormalities), or any combination of these or other factors.

The conditions that place young children and their parents/families at risk for poor outcomes are now recognized as multiple and complex (Huston, 1995). More importantly, the ecology of these conditions has changed considerably since the early 1960s when the first wave of mission-oriented early intervention programs was implemented (see Condry, 1983; Dunst, 1996). Three recent reports (Children's Defense Fund, 1995; Farley, 1995a, 1995b; Marshall, 1991) illustrate dramatically that more and more of America's families have been placed at multiple risk for economic, societal, and political reasons (see especially Hanson & Carta, 1996). According to Halpern (1990, 1993), these risk factors can "take over" a child and family's life, undermine parents' ability to attend to their children's needs, and rob parents of the time and energy to perform effectively in their child-rearing roles. The most recent *Kids Count Data Book* (Annie E. Casey Foundation, 1994) contends that forces placing children at risk for poor outcomes have become so numerous and concentrated for so many families that the chances of children overcoming the odds have decreased considerably.

DESCRIPTION AND SCOPE OF THE PROBLEM

Despite calls for an expanded perspective of early childhood intervention (e.g., Dunst, 1985; Smith & Zaslow, 1995; Zigler & Berman, 1983), the largest majority of early intervention programs and practices both historically and contemporaneously can be characterized as having primarily *compensatory* underpinnings. Whether stated implicitly or

Appreciation is extended to Eileen Byrnes for typing the chapter, and both Eileen Byrnes and Carol Whitacre for compiling and verifying the references.

explicitly, early intervention directed at a child or his/her parents/family, or both, aims to impact in a positive direction the behavior(s) being influenced in a negative way by risk factors. Additionally, it is assumed that interventions will be potent enough to compensate for effects of the risk factors or correct problems resulting from risk factors. These kinds of interventions typically include early education and enrichment activities for young children or different kinds of parent training and support aimed at influencing child-rearing capabilities, or both. Herein lies the problem addressed in this chapter: If increasingly more prospective parents and young children and their families participating in early intervention programs are experiencing more numerous, more complex, more persistent, and increasingly intense risk factors, can early intervention as it has typically been designed and implemented (see Meisels & Shonkoff, 1990) produce effects that can meaningfully alter the course of child, parent, and family development? This problem was articulated by Halpern (1993) when he stated:

> We expect too much, or at least hope, that discrete interventions in one or a few domains of a child's or adult's life can somehow help that child or adult . . . escape his or her [at-risk] history or situation, beat the overwhelming odds of a marginal future, and set [the child and family] off on a different [life] path. (p. 162)

Cohort Differences and Effects

The scope of the problem is further understood by asking whether early intervention practices of the 1960s, 1970s, and 1980s—even successful ones—would be beneficial to children at risk for poor outcomes and their families now the targets of early intervention? The crux of the problem is that successive generations of early intervention program participants constitute different cohorts, with each cohort having different life circumstances and experiences influencing individual and family development.

A *cohort* is defined as those "people within a geographically or otherwise delineated population" (Glenn, 1977, p. 8) "born in a particular time and therefore exposed to a specific succession of social and historical changes [experiences, events, etc.] at certain ages" (Datan, 1975, p. 7). Evidence from life-span developmental psychology indicates that different birth cohorts have different life experiences, which can and often do have differential developmental consequences (Datan & Ginsberg, 1975; Datan, Greene, & Reese, 1986). Elder and Liker (1980), for example, found that for women who lived during the Great Depression, the influences of financial adversity continued to have lasting effects some 30 to 40 years later.

Potential influences of cohort differences on the effects of early intervention have generally been overlooked or ignored despite evidence indicating that the ecologies of successive generations of program participants have differed considerably (see Halpern, 1990, 1993, for an exception). Hernandez (1993), tracing changes in the structure, composition, and resources of American families during different decades over the past 200 years, concluded, "Revolutionary changes in the life course, the economy, and society have transformed childhood, and the resources available to children, during the past 150 years" (Hernandez, 1993, p. 417). Of particular relevance is that those conditions which place children at greatest risk for poor outcomes have actually become increasingly prevalent over the past 30 to 35 years, the period during which early intervention programs began and expanded. For example, whereas single-parent households increased at a rate of only 1% between 1940 and 1960, the rate increased by 9% between 1960 and 1990. One consequence of this change has been the increase in the percentage of children in single-parent households living in poverty (Bianchi, 1993, 1995). Even cursory inspection of available evidence (e.g., Annie E. Casey Foundation, 1994; Bianchi, 1993, 1995; Children's Defense Fund, 1995; Farley, 1995a, 1995b; Hernandez, 1993; Marshall, 1991) leads one to conclude the following: Different cohorts of children and families participating in early intervention programs since the early 1960s until the present have had different histories and life experiences, with the most recent cohorts of families constituting targets of early intervention experiencing more frequent, persistent, and intense risk conditions (see especially Garbarino, 1988).

AN ECOLOGICAL FRAMEWORK FOR UNDERSTANDING THE STRENGTHS AND LIMITATIONS OF EARLY INTERVENTION

Both the strengths and limitations of early intervention as a compensatory, problem-reduction or even a prevention enterprise are best understood within the context of an ecological perspective of behavior and development (Bronfenbrenner, 1979, 1992; Garbarino, 1992). According to Bronfenbrenner (1992), ecological theory is premised on the contention that "variations in developmental processes and outcomes are a *joint* function of the characteristics of the environment and a [developing] person" (p. 197). Such a perspective indicates that influences of any one particular environmental experience (e.g., early intervention) are best understood in relation to other environmental influences (e.g., poverty) and characteristics of the people experiencing these environmental influences.

For purposes of this chapter, an ecological perspective of environment views a child and family as embedded within any number of social systems and community settings or contexts, where both historical and contemporaneous experiences and events in these ecological niches (Bronfenbrenner, 1992) reverberate and either or both directly and indirectly influence child, parent, and family functioning (Cochran, 1990; Cochran & Brassard, 1979). Accordingly, early intervention programs may be thought of as one such ecological niche, and experiences emanating from this setting are one influence potentially affecting child behavior and development. Likewise, any number of other settings (day-care programs, community centers, neighborhoods, family resource programs, etc.) may be thought of as other sources of experiences that can as well potentially influence child, parent, and family functioning. Also, in this chapter, person characteristics are considered to be those intrapersonal and interpersonal factors that cause individuals to respond differentially to environmental influences and/or to alter the properties of environments in ways that increase or decrease the effects of participation in different ecological settings and niches (Bronfenbrenner, 1979, 1992).

Risk and Opportunity Factors

According to Garbarino and Abramowitz (1992), the kinds of settings that children and their families experience, whether directly or indirectly, either impede or enhance development. Those conditions that are development-impeding are described as *risk factors,* and those that are development-enhancing are described as *opportunity factors.*

Risk factors refer to conditions associated with increased likelihood of onset of any number of problems, greater severity of the problems, longer duration or more frequent episodes of dysfunction, or any number of other poor outcomes; whereas opportunity factors refer to any number of experiences and conditions that enhance, promote, or otherwise contribute to positive outcomes or optimal functioning.[1]

A simple but useful framework for showing the relationship between risk and opportunity factors and their consequences may be stated as follows:

$$B = f(R,O)$$

where B is behavior (development, competence, performance, etc.), R is risk factors, O is opportunity factors, and the relationship among the variables is stated: Behavior is related to either or both risk and opportunity factors, their combination, interaction, and so on. For example, whereas poverty, socially impoverished neighborhoods, and parent drug use constitute risk factors contributing to poor developmental prospects for young children (Hanson & Carta, 1996), early intervention—depending on how it is conceptualized and operationalized—constitutes an opportunity factor for positively influencing child, parent, and family functioning (Dunst, 1995c, 1996).

Person–Environment Relationships

Usefulness of the $B = f(R,O)$ paradigm for understanding early intervention as an ecological niche and source of opportunities is further understood by considering the relationship between risk and opportunity factors and the personal characteristics of parents and their children. According to Bronfenbrenner (1992), behavior and development are shaped by two sets of forces: (a) the environments experienced by a developing person (e.g., risk and opportunity factors); and (b) characteristics of the person experiencing environmental influences at any given point in time. By incorporating the latter, an expanded paradigm can be stated as:

$$B = f(R,O)(P)$$

when B, R, and O are as defined earlier, and P is person factors (characteristics), and the relationship among the variables is stated: Behavior is related to either or both risk and opportunity factors and person characteristics, their combination, interactions, and so on. Accordingly, the extent to which opportunity or risk factors have, respectively, "favorable or unfavorable [influences] on the development of individuals [depends on that person's] particular personal characteristics" (Bronfenbrenner, 1992, p. 194). Consequently, whether early intervention as an opportunity factor proves effective can be expected to differ according to any number of personal characteristics

---

[1] The term opportunity factor rather than the more widely used term protective factor (e.g., Pellegrini, 1990; Werner, 1990) is preferred for two reasons. First, in contrast to risk–protective factor frameworks that emphasize factors contributing to poor outcomes or protecting individuals from negative consequences associated with risk factors, the risk–opportunity factor frameworks emphasize positive outcomes associated with the presence of opportunity factors. Second, opportunity factors provide a wider lens for understanding the conditions associated with optimal developmental outcomes and for translating research into practice in a manner that promotes and enhances positive functioning, rather than just preventing poor outcomes.

of a child and/or his or her parents and family (Guralnick, 1997). Likewise, whether risk factors do or do not translate into poor outcomes depends on any number of person characteristics that make individuals vulnerable or resilient to adverse conditions (Rhodes & Brown, 1991).

CONSEQUENCES OF RISK AND OPPORTUNITY FACTORS

A large and corroborative body of evidence indicates that presence of *multiple risk factors* is related to increased probability of poor outcomes (see Greenbaum & Averbach, 1992), and that any combination of three or more risk factors places a child at substantial risk for a number of problem behaviors (e.g., Baracos, Seifer, & Sameroff, 1985; Dunst, 1995c; Dunst & Trivette, 1992, 1994; Sameroff, Seifer, Baracos, Zax, & Greenspan, 1987). An emerging literature indicates that presence of *multiple opportunity factors* is related to increased positive outcomes in both child and family functioning (Dunst & Trivette, 1992, 1994; Rhodes & Brown, 1991; Rolf, Masten, Cicchetti, Nuechterlein, & Weintraub, 1990; Werner & Smith, 1992).

In a now seminal paper by Sameroff and colleagues (1987), these investigators report findings from a study demonstrating cumulative negative effects of risk factors on child IQ at 4 years of age. Risk factors included maternal depression and anxiety, maternal locus of control (external), maternal education (<11 years), parenting style (nonresponsive), occupation of the head of the household (unskilled), negative life events, family size (three or more children), absence of a spouse or partner, and race. For each subject, a total risk score was computed by adding the risk factors present in the family and relating these to child IQ. The findings were both clear-cut and convincing. Whereas presence of one or two risk factors had no negative influences on child mental development status, presence of three or more risk factors has cumulative negative effects on child IQ. That is, the more risk factors that were present, proportionally the lower the children's IQs. Also, the combined influence of risk factors proved to be a more powerful predictor of child IQ than did the cumulative influence of any individual risk factors.

In a prospective, longitudinal study by Dunst and Trivette (1992, 1994), the investigators both replicated and extended the Sameroff et al. (1987) findings by examining influence of both risk and opportunity factors on child mental development at 12 and 18 months of age. The independent measures in this study were taken prenatally and at 1 and 6 months postpartum, and 12- and 18-month Bayley scale mental development indices (MDIs) were used as the dependent measure. Variables and criteria used to establish risk status were essentially the same as those used by Sameroff et al. (1987), whereas opportunity status was ascertained using maternal positive well-being and psychosocial health, maternal locus of control (internal), maternal education (>15 years), occupation of the head of household (professional), positive life events, presence of a spouse or partner, and parenting style (facilitative). Total risk and total opportunity factor scores were computed for each mother by summing number of times a family was assigned to a risk or opportunity group, respectively, based on the combination of measures of the same construct obtained on multiple occasions (see Dunst & Trivette, 1994). Results (see Figure 7.1) showed that both 12- and 18-month MDIs were negatively related to the number of risk factors, and were positively related to the number of opportunity factors. These findings both replicate results reported by

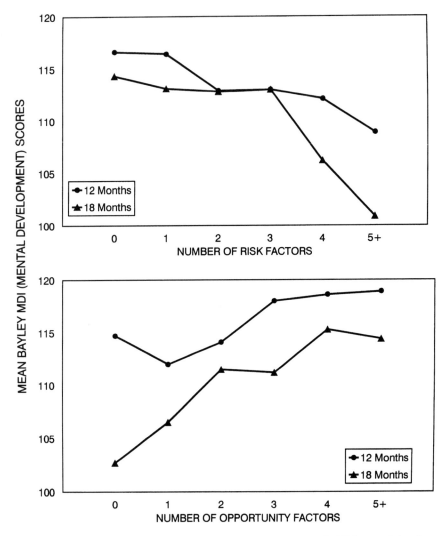

Figure 7.1. Relationship between risk and opportunity factors and child mental development.

Sameroff et al. (1987) and extend the findings by demonstrating the development-enhancing qualities of opportunity factors.

Results, although revealing, are partly confounded by the fact that some families were simultaneously characterized by the presence of both risk and opportunity factors. A composite score was therefore computed for each subject by subtracting cumulative risk scores from cumulative opportunity scores. For both the 12- and 18-month data, composite scores showed a linear relationship with child MDI. The more risk and fewer the opportunity factors, the more negative the impact, and the more opportunity and fewer the risk factors, the more positive the consequences. Where opportunity factors co-occurred with risk factors, negative effects of the risk factors were lessened and the positive influences of the opportunity factor heightened, with magnitude of the buffering or development-enhancing effects proportional to the ratio of risk-to-opportunity factors.

Research indicating that risk and opportunity factors have negative and positive influences, respectively, on behavior functioning is not limited to child mental development. There is a body of evidence demonstrating that accumulated risk has negative effects in other domains of child functioning, including emotional and behavioral problems, self-esteem, school achievement, and social competence (see especially Haggerty, Sherrod, Garmezy, & Rutter, 1994; Nelson, 1994; Rolf et al., 1990). Emerging evidence indicates that presence of multiple risk factors negatively affects parent and family functioning as well (e.g., Turner & Avison, 1985), and some data indicate that opportunity factors positively influence a number of aspects of parent and family functioning. For example, Dunst and Trivette (1992) found that multiple risk factors had negative effects on maternal psychological well-being and that accumulated opportunity factors had positive effects on well-being.

The finding that risk and opportunity factors are related in a manner consistent with the previously described ecological paradigm is also consistent with evidence indicating that despite apparent odds (risk factors), many children and their families succeed and do well even in the face of adversity (Rhodes & Brown, 1991). The research of Emmy Werner and her colleagues (Werner, Bierman, & French, 1971; Werner & Smith, 1977, 1982, 1992) is exemplary in this regard. In the now famous Kauai study of children and their families followed longitudinally from 1955 to the late 1980s, it was found that despite being "born and reared in chronic poverty, exposed to higher than average rates of prematurity and perinatal stress, and reared by mothers with little formal education" (Werner & Smith, 1992, p. 190), many children did exceedingly well and "escaped from childhood adversity" (Werner & Smith, 1992, p. 190). Careful examination of the factors associated with advantageous outcomes in the face of adversity found that both environment and person characteristics accounted for the positive benefits. Among the environmental factors were a personal social network of nurturing relatives and friends and a more extended, informal network consisting of neighborhood, community, and school members serving as sources of support, advice, and guidance to the developing child. Personal characteristics of the children who did well in spite of the odds included a behavioral style that "elicited positive responses from persons in their caregiving environments (such as an 'easy' infant temperament characterized by high activity, sociability, and freedom from distressing habits); [and] autonomy and social competence as a toddler" (Werner & Smith, 1992, p. 199). Still further, Werner and her colleagues found that for children experiencing positive outcomes, the links between the personal characteristics of the children and a supportive social environment were often reciprocal and transactional in nature and consequence. "Individuals [with engaging] dispositions led them to select or construct environments that, in turn, reinforced and sustained their active, outgoing dispositions and rewarded their competence" (Werner & Smith, 1992, p. 199).

Parenthetically, it is of interest and importance to point out that the conditions Werner and her colleagues found associated with positive outcomes are the very same ones that child development and family-oriented early intervention programs aim to create so as to positively influence child, parent, and family functioning. For example, promoting contingent caregiver social responsiveness to influence child competence is often a primary focus of child development-oriented early intervention programs. Likewise, provision and mobilization of social support so that parents have the time and energy, and knowledge and skills, to carry out parenting responsibilities are a major focus of family-support-oriented early intervention programs. The conditions that support parents' efforts to carry out child-rearing responsibilities as well as employ competency-enhancing international styles are, however, often difficult to mirror in many early intervention programs because of the presence of competing risk factors (e.g., Haskins, 1989; Kagan, 1991; U.S. General Accounting Office, 1995a). Programs which do successfully create conditions that mirror optimizing environments either explicitly or implicitly appreciate the interplay between risk and opportunity factors.

Some Sources of Risk and Opportunity in the Real World of Early Intervention

Although the terms risk and opportunity (as well as protective, potentiating, resilient, invulnerability, etc.) factors have been principally the nomenclature of researchers (see, e.g., Dunst, 1993), concepts embodied in these terms seem useful as unifying themes for understanding both the strengths and limitations of early intervention. This seems especially the case when one considers the "varieties" of early intervention being practiced in applied settings throughout the United States (Dunst, 1996) and other countries (see, e.g., Bambring, Beelman, & Rauh, 1996; Marfo, 1991). The value of these concepts is enhanced by considering that person and environment factors can operate independently and in combination as either risk or opportunity factors at different levels of ecological influence (Bronfenbrenner, 1979; Garbarino & Abramowitz, 1992). This section highlights some but certainly not all of the real world sources of risk and opportunity that children and families experience and practitioners and program builders face as they go about their business of "doing" early intervention. *Starting Points: Meeting the Needs of Our Youngest Children* (Carnegie Task Force on Meeting the Needs of Young Children, 1994) provides an extensive review and discussion of both the child/family and environmental factors that constitute sources of either risk or opportunity. We expand on these two categories by considering how early intervention programs and practices can function as sources of risk and opportunity as well.

Child and Family Factors

Early intervention as a development-influencing enterprise is explicitly premised on the belief that the benefits accruing from such practices are exceedingly better than if no intervention is provided at all. Early intervention is implicitly premised on the belief that most if not all children and families will benefit equally if "treatment dose" is constant across program participants. Evidence now indicates, however, that early intervention is differentially effective depending on any number of child and family (as well as other) factors (Guralnick, 1997; Marfo, 1991).

Knapp (1994), commenting on pregnancy-related biological factors as risk conditions (exposure to toxic agents, maternal use of drugs, vulnerable genetic background, etc.), noted that the earlier the onset and the longer the duration of the risk factors, the more likely embryonic, fetal, and child development are compromised. This would suggest that there are potentially some limitations of early intervention depending on the advent, severity, and complexity of risk conditions. The Infant Health and Development Program (1990), for example, produced evidence indicating that the effects of a standard set of interventions (home visits, child participation at a child development center, and parent group meetings) provided to low birth-weight premature infants and their mothers were more effective for infants weighing between 2001 and 2500 grams at birth compared with infants born weighing 2000 grams or less.

Similar findings were reported by Dunst (in press) for nine groups of biologically and/or environmentally at-risk children participating in an early intervention program. Children were assessed longitudinally using the Uzgiris and Hunt (1975) scales as outcome measures, and growth modeling (Willett, 1989) was employed for ascertaining the growth rates for individual children. Although all nine groups of children demonstrated developmental progress between birth and 48 months of age, change rates differed considerably as a function of source of risks (biologically at-risk children showed slower growth rates compared with those at risk for environmental reasons), with children having multiple biological risks and physical and sensory impairments showing the slowest rates of progress.

Although biological conditions function as risk factors negatively influencing child behavior and development, child intrapersonal and interpersonal characteristics have been found to influence the extent to which increased benefits accrue from early intervention. For example, Dunst and Lingerfelt (1985) found that effectiveness of an intervention designed to enhance the acquisition of infant response-contingent behavior was related to two dimensions of child temperament (rhythmicity and persistence). Infants who had more rhymatic behavioral styles and who demonstrated more persistence in interactions with their social and nonsocial environment showed the greatest amounts of infant operant learning. Huntington and Simeonsson's (1993) review of the temperament literature also found that different child behavioral styles functioned as either risk or opportunity factors mediating either nonadaptive or adaptive responses, respectively, to various kinds of environmental demands.

The preceding as well as other evidence (see especially Kopp, 1983, 1994) indicates that a number of child-related risk conditions can compromise child development, whereas certain child behavior characteristics can have competency-enhancing qualities. Evidence also indicates that personal characteristics of children's parents can function as opportunity or risk factors as well. In a study of children with either chromosomal abnormalities or physical impairments, who participated in an early intervention program, Dunst and Trivette (1994) found that mother's education was associated with child growth rates. In both samples, children of more educated mothers made the greatest progress while participating in an early intervention program. Dichtelmiller et al. (1992) reported much the same results in terms of parent knowledge of infant development. Both the mental and motor development of extremely low birth-weight infants was found to be related to mother's knowledge of infant development; the more knowledgeable the mothers, the more advanced the infant's development.

A finding that the effects of early intervention differ according to the personal characteristics of children's parents and families was also reported by Maisto and German (1981). These investigators found, after controlling for family socioeconomic status (SES) and mothers' education, that maternal external locus-of-control functioned as a risk factor and maternal internal locus-of-control functioned as an opportunity factor influencing child benefits associated with early intervention. Similarly, Dunst, Trivette, Hamby, and Pollock (1990) found that maternal positive well-being functioned as an opportunity factor and maternal negative well-being functioned as a risk factor. The same kind of relationship was found by Hannan and Luster (1991) between high and low family risk and the provision of, respectively, unsupportive or supportive home environments influencing child behavior and development.

Environmental Factors

Children and families participating in early intervention programs experience, in addition to the services provided by such programs, other life events and conditions that either compete with or complement early intervention. Environmental factors that compete with early intervention, thus functioning as risk factors, include family financial adversity, poor community economic conditions, family and community violence, parent drug use, neighborhood crime, and single parenting, to mention a few. These as well as other risk factors can compete with and interfere with early intervention in any number of ways. For example, a community characterized by high levels of violence and crime is often associated with higher rates of child maltreatment and parenting styles resistant to modification by early intervention. Likewise, high or concentrated levels of neighborhood crimes and violence are often cited by practitioners as factors lessening their desire to work with families living in these kinds of environments.

A concept useful for understanding whether and how environmental factors function as either sources of risk or opportunity is *environmental press:*

> Environmental press is the combined influence of forces working in a setting to shape the behavior and development of people in that setting. Environmental press arises from the circumstances confronting and surrounding an individual that creates psychosocial momentum and tends to guide that individual in a particular direction. (Garbarino & Abramowitz, 1992, p. 12)

The *combined influence* of risk factors has negative consequences on behavioral functioning, and the *combined influence* of opportunity factors has positive consequences on behavioral functioning. Additionally, it has been found that a preponderance of opportunity over risk factors has development-enhancing qualities. Consequently, it is not surprising that any number of environmental factors can and do impinge on children's and families' lives in ways that promote or impede participation in early intervention, their level and type of involvement, and responsiveness to different kinds of practices.

Recruiting families of children who are at risk for poor outcomes to participate in early childhood intervention programs must first occur if any benefits from intervention practices are to accrue. Practitioners, however, often state that children and families most in need of early intervention are generally the most difficult to reach. Recent evidence supports this claim. The results of a national study conducted by the U.S. General Accounting Office (1994) found that the combined influences of poverty (children living in a poor or near-poor family) and parent education (children whose most educated parent had less than a high school diploma) best predicted lack of participation in early childhood intervention programs. Thus, at least these two risk conditions combined to decrease parent enrollment of their children and families in early intervention.

A common complaint often voiced by early intervention practitioners is that it is difficult to engage "at-risk" parents and other caregiving family members in different kinds of interventions. Environmental press suggests that the at-risk conditions faced by these families divert attention away from child-rearing concerns, and rob parents of the time and energy to attend to their children as well as attend to recommendations or prescriptions made by early intervention professionals. For example, Powell (1993) noted that it is difficult for a mother or any other caregiver to give a child needed attention when the family is worried about how it will feed or shelter its members because of exceedingly limited financial or physical resources.

Dunst and his colleagues (Dunst, Leet, & Trivette, 1988; Dunst, Vance, & Cooper, 1986) used environmental press as a conceptual framework for testing the relationship between adequacy of families' resources in areas unrelated to child development and adherence to professionally prescribed regimens among parents of children with or at risk for disabilities and teenage mothers participating in several different early intervention programs. The participants completed both the Family Resource Scale (FRS; Dunst & Leet, 1987) and a measure of the extent to which parents had the time, physical and emotional energy, and a personal commitment and belief about the importance of child-level interventions prescribed or suggested by early intervention program staff. The FRS is a 30-item instrument measuring the availability of both physical and human resources (food, shelter, time, money, health care, etc.) in households with young children. In both studies, lack of adequate family resources was associated with energy-draining effects and the lack of perceived importance of child-level interventions. Moreover, the greater inadequacies in domains of family life unrelated to early intervention involving the child, the less likely parents indicated they found professional advice and recommendations about child development useful or helpful.

Based on both research and practice, there is now an increased appreciation for the match between parents' indicated need for resources and the effectiveness of intervention practices used to influence child, parent, and family functioning (Dunst, Trivette, & Deal, 1988, 1994). This was dramatically demonstrated by Affleck, Tennen, Rowe, Rosche, and Walker (1989) in a study of neonatal intensive care units (NICU) graduates and their mothers participating in a postdischarge home-based, early intervention program. The participants were 94 mothers randomly assigned to a control group or a group receiving support from professionally trained consultants who offered advice, assistance, and other kinds of support. The practitioners working with the experimental group were instructed to "deliver" early intervention in response to mother-requested support, and where mothers indicated no need for support, staff offered advice and assistance they, but not the mothers, deemed necessary for the benefit of either or both the mothers and children. Affleck and colleagues found that the effects of the interventions differed as a function of the conditions under which they were provided:

> Positive effects of the [intervention] program on mother's sense of competence, perceived control, and responsiveness were evident for mothers who [indicated] a need for support the most. But *at low levels of need for support, participation in the program had negative effects on these outcomes.* (Affleck et al., 1989, p. 488, emphasis added)

Thus, under one condition, early intervention functioned as an opportunity factor, and under another condition operated as a risk factor depending on whether the practices were family or professionally directed. Practically, the findings from the Affleck et al. study as well as other investigations (see Dunst, Trivette, & Jodry, 1997) indicate that intervention practices are most likely to function as an opportunity factor and have optimal positive effects under conditions where there is a match between such practices and a family's unique need for different kinds of support, resources, and services.

Recognition that accumulated risk operates in a negative way on child, parent, and family behavior forms the basis of many contemporary comprehensive early childhood intervention and two-generation programs (see, e.g., Halpern, 1990, 1993; St. Pierre, Layzer, & Barnes, 1995; Smith, 1995). These kinds of programs are premised on the assertion that intensive child development interventions coupled with interventions directed at the parents can more adequately compensate for influences of the risk conditions faced by program participants. Comprehensive intervention programs typically include some set of "core" child and family services delivered to all program participants, whereas two-generation intervention programs include "self-sufficiency services designed to improve the parent's education level, vocation skills, and employment status, and child development services that include preventive health care, parenting education, and high quality child care or early childhood education" (Smith & Zaslow, 1995, p. 1).

A recent analysis of the effectiveness of these programs by St. Pierre et al. (1995) indicated modest results at best. Examination of program characteristics and patterns of results obtained from these various initiatives from an environmental press perspective indicates that the failure to produce anything approaching robust findings can at least in part be accounted for by two sets of factors. The first factor is that what these (as well as other kinds of) early intervention programs offer and provide, in some cases, will match participant desires and needs, but in other cases will be inconsistent or incompatible with the forces influencing participant behavior; hence mixed results. The second factor has to do with the failure to recognize that it matters as much *how* interventions are done as *what* is done if early intervention is to have optimal positive benefits among the largest number of program participants. The latter has to do with the manner in which program factors can and do function as sources of either risk or opportunity.

Program Factors

Early intervention programs are generally thought of as *only* sources of opportunity. However, both quantitative and qualitative research indicates that depending on how early intervention is conceptualized and operationalized, and how staff practice their crafts, early intervention, like both child/family and environmental factors, can function as either sources of risk or opportunity (Dunst, Trivette, Gordon, & Starnes, 1993; Dunst, Trivette, & Hamby, 1996; Dunst, Trivette, & LaPointe, 1992; Dunst, Trivette, Starnes, Hamby, & Gordon, 1993; Trivette, Dunst, Boyd, & Hamby, 1996; Trivette, Dunst, & Hamby, 1996a, 1996b; Trivette, Dunst, Hamby, & LaPointe, 1996).

A review and synthesis of the human development intervention literature in general and the early intervention literature more specifically finds that program approaches and practitioner characteristics differ according to any number of paradigms and models (Dunst, 1995a, 1995b). Table 7.1, for example, shows five sets of contrasting models that are either explicitly or implicitly used to guide the conceptualization, development, and implementation of early intervention programs and practices. Each model provides a different lens for defining problems and strategies for solving them, or setting goals and developing plans for achieving stated intentions (see Dunst, 1995a, 1995b; Dunst, Trivette, & Thompson, 1990; and Trivette, Dunst, & Deal, 1997 for in-depth descriptions of the contrasting models). Collectively, sets of paradigms aligned at one end of the continuum or the other constitute the key characteristics of different "world views" of conceptually and procedurally distinct approaches to intervention (see Bond, 1982; Cowen, 1985, 1994; Dunst, Johanson, Trivette, & Hamby, 1991;

Table 7.1   Defining Features of Contrasting Approaches for Conceptualizing and Implementing Early Intervention

◄─────────────────── Contrasting Paradigms ───────────────────►

Promotion Models Focus on enhancement and optimization of competence and positive functioning	*Treatment Models* Focus on remediation of a disorder, problem, or disease, or its consequences
Empowerment Models Create opportunities for people to exercise existing capabilities as well as develop new competencies	*Expertise Models* Depend on professional expertise to solve problems for people
Strengths-Based Models Recognize the assets and talents of people, and help people use these competencies to strengthen functioning	*Deficit-Based Models* Focus on correcting peoples' weaknesses or problems
Resource-Based Models Define practices in terms of a broad range of community opportunities and experiences	*Service-Based Models* Define practices primarily in terms of professional services
Family-Centered Models View professionals as agents of families and responsive to family desires and concerns	*Professionally-Centered Models* View professionals as experts who determine the needs of people from their own as opposed to other people's perspectives

Dunst et al., 1992; Dunst et al., 1990; Hoke, 1968; Katz, 1984; Rappaport, 1981, 1987; Seeman, 1989; Trivette et al., 1997; Zautra & Sandler, 1983).

Evidence now indicates that early intervention programs can be characterized as falling along any number of continua depicted in Table 7.1 (Dunst et al., 1991; Dunst et al., 1996; Trivette et al., 1996); that practitioner attitudes, beliefs, and behavior vary depending on the paradigmatic bases of the programs in which they work (Dunst et al., 1996; Trivette et al., 1996, Trivette et al., 1996a); and that differences in both program models and practitioner helpgiving behaviors are associated with variations in numerous aspects of child and family functioning (Dunst, 1995b; Dunst et al., 1996, Trivette et al., 1996a, 1996b). Trivette et al. (1996a) for example, found that in programs adopting a family-centered philosophy, one was more likely to find practitioners employing empowering help-giving practices, and that parents who experienced these kinds of practices were more likely to indicate they had control over needed supports and resources from a target help-giver and his or her program. Similarly, Dunst et al. (1993) found that parents' descriptions of the benefits (or lack of) associated with intervention practices were reliably associated with *how* practitioners interacted with their families. Whereas positive outcomes were associated with practices that meaningfully involved parents in the help-giving/help-receiving relationship, negative outcomes were more likely to be found in situations in which practitioners were prescriptive and directive with families, and where there was a mismatch between what families desired and what practitioners offered.

Findings of this sort indicate that the manner in which programs are conceptualized and translated into practice matters in terms of whether certain kinds of benefits are realized. Although it is generally recognized that early intervention programs differ in any number of ways and that early intervention staff do not practice their crafts in an identical manner, it has not been the case that these differences are viewed as sources of either risk or opportunity. In both our research and experiences with literally hundreds of early intervention programs, we have encountered programs and practitioners who ought not to be in the business of working with young children and their families because what they do and how they do it is much more a source of risk than opportunity. Fortunately, most programs are primarily sources of opportunity and consequently produce many positive benefits.

CONCEPTUALIZING AND IMPLEMENTING EARLY INTERVENTION

Examination of both the early intervention efficacy literature and descriptions of early intervention programs and practices from a risk–opportunity perspective provides a unique vantage point for further understanding the strengths and limitations of different ways of conceptualizing and implementing early intervention. Based on what is known about the relationships between risk factors and negative outcomes and between opportunity factors and positive outcomes, and what is also known about sources of risks and opportunities (child/family, environment, program/practitioner), the professional can organize early intervention into one of three approaches or models. The first, the *compensatory model,* considers the manner in which early interventions directed at the child or family, or both, are expected to compensate for the influences of any number of extrafamily environmental risk factors. The second, the *eradication model,* directly considers the reduction or elimination of environmental risk factors as a primary focus of intervention practices. The third, the *ecological model,* considers both the reduction/elimination of environmental risk factors and the use of child/family focused interventions as conditions contributing to positive outcomes. Figure 7.2 shows each of these models in graphic form depicting early intervention as directed primarily toward child/family or risk factors, or both. Whether or not early intervention functions as an opportunity factor is assumed to vary depending on how such practices are conceptualized and operationalized.

Compensatory Model

Compensatory early intervention is premised on the assumption that interventions provided directly to children (or to children through their parents/caregivers) or directly to the parents, or both, can counter the negative effects of a high-risk ecology on the children's development. These kinds of interventions typically include efforts that provide children with experiences that focus specifically on influencing child behavior and development or the provision of any number of services or supports to the children and their families, or both. It is either implicitly or explicitly contended that such efforts can compensate for the adverse effects of environmental risk factors, and that the more that is done, the greater the compensatory value or influence. (The latter is typically described as program or service intensity.)

Many early intervention programs can be characterized as primarily compensatory in focus and orientation. They include a diverse array of both child-focused and family-focused early childhood intervention programs (see Dunst, 1996). These kinds of programs typically include a combination of either home- or center-based child

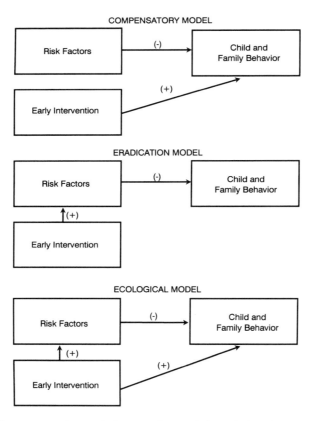

Figure 7.2.   Three contrasting early intervention models depicting the relationship between risk factors, intervention, and child and family outcomes.

development-oriented interventions and parenting and adult education of various kinds. They are increasingly, but not always, supplemented by child and family support services such as preventive health care, family planning, and social services. When the latter is the case, the programs are typically described as comprehensive early childhood intervention programs.

Developers of compensatory early intervention programs recognize that numerous environmental risk factors operate to impede child and family development, but only *indirectly* address the elimination or reduction of these risk factors. For example, Smith and Zaslow (1995) commented that two-generation early intervention programs "do not directly address neighborhood [environmental] risk factors, but have the potential to address them indirectly" (p. 19). If risk factors are addressed directly, they tend to be limited primarily to parent and family factors. Specifically, family poverty and parent education are often the major focus of compensatory early intervention, with the expectation that completing high school, job training, and the like will result in parent employment leading the family to a path out of poverty.

The strengths of compensatory early intervention programs and practices include that they have been widely tried and tested (Barnett, 1995; Yoshikawa, 1995), and we know a lot about the conditions that produce positive outcomes in both children and their parents or families (see, e.g., Gomby, Larner, Stevenson, Lewit, & Behrman,

1995; Ramey & Ramey, 1992). Limitations of these kinds of programs include that if a greater percentage of families now being targeted for early intervention experience more numerous and more intense risk factors at different levels of ecological influence, compensatory approaches seem unlikely to produce robust effects. At a minimum, researchers must be cautious in terms of the effects that would be expected as a result of these kinds of interventions.

Eradication Model

Eradication models place primary emphasis on the elimination or reduction of the environmental risk conditions associated with poor or detrimental outcomes. These kinds of approaches are premised on the assumption that the absence of environmental risks, or even the prevention of poor outcomes by removal of these risk factors, may be taken as evidence for the presence of positive functioning or the optimization of development (Dunst, Trivette, & Thompson, 1990). It is assumed that if environmental risk factors are absent or removed, child and family development as measured on any number of behavioral or developmental tasks will represent optimal performance.

Early intervention programs that are characterized as having an eradication orientation *directly* address the reduction and elimination of environmental risk factors by implementing strategies that improve housing conditions, create jobs, prevent crime, improve neighborhood safety and appearance, and the like. A recent U.S. General Accounting Office (1995b) report includes descriptions of eradication programs that have successfully altered the economic, physical, housing, and social fabric of communities in ways that have eliminated or significantly reduced a host of environmental risk factors (see also Ashley, 1991; Puls, 1991). Similarly, Kretzmann and McKnight (1993) describe an asset-based approach to eradicating risk conditions that emphasizes the capacity of communities to develop and mobilize resources leading to neighborhood regeneration.

Strengths of eradication models include that they directly attack the roots of the poverty, crime, violence, poor housing, and other environmental risk factors found in distressed neighborhoods and communities. They include such diverse activities as community and neighborhood watches, job placement and creation activities, economic development, purchasing and renovation of vacant homes, and financial assistance in the form of low interest loans to purchase homes or start businesses. The primary limitation of eradication models includes the implicit assumption that in the absence of environmental risks, parenting behavior will change in ways that provide children with experiences and opportunities optimizing developmental outcomes. Available evidence, however, indicates that parenting attitudes and behaviors are shaped and influenced by ecological influences in addition to those associated with neighborhood and community risk factors (Cochran, 1993; Garbarino & Kostelny, 1993). Consequently, directly reducing or eliminating environmental risks is a necessary but probably not sufficient condition for optimally influencing parent, child, and family development and functioning.

Ecological Model

Ecological models are premised on the assumption that behavior and development are multiply determined, and that multiple kinds of experiences and interventions must simultaneously be directed at reducing risk factors and creating opportunities that will optimally influence positive aspects of child and family functioning. These kinds of models have a three-pronged emphasis:

1. They directly address reduction or elimination of environmental risk conditions.
2. They use a wide range of child and family learning opportunities and experiences that positively influence parenting attitudes and behaviors and have child development enhancing qualities.
3. They explicitly employ program practices that are consistent with the premises, principles, and paradigms of community-based family support programs (Dunst, 1995a).

Elimination or reduction of environmental risk factors is typically accomplished using a variety of interventions, drawing from community development, economic development, sociology, epidemiology, and community psychology. Enhancement and promotion of child and family behavior and development is accomplished using different kinds of child-focused and family-focused interventions, drawing from human ecology, social support, child and family development, and related fields. The elimination and reduction of environmental risk factors and the use of child- and family-level interventions are accomplished using family-centered help-giving practices (Dunst & Trivette, 1996) that base intervention practices on the choices and priorities of families. Practitioners deliver interventions in an individualized, flexible, and responsive manner, display dignity and respect for families; and meaningfully involve families in ways that have empowering and family-strengthening influences.[2] The ecological model basically brings to bear the strengths of both compensatory and eradication approaches together with concern about *how* interventions are implemented as a way of producing positive outcomes in not only the child and family but the community as well.

Ecological approaches to early intervention, at least as defined from a risk–opportunity perspective, represent a "new breed" of programs and practices. The best examples of these kinds of early intervention are found in many of the community-based, family support programs and initiatives that have emerged during the past 10 to 15 years (see Weiss, 1995). At this point in their development and implementation, however, blending of key features of both compensatory and eradication approaches to early intervention is just beginning to occur. Nonetheless, many programs that are characterized by the elements of both approaches also include concern for program and practitioner factors. Bowen and Sellers (1994), as part of case studies of three programs serving families and children living in socially vulnerable communities, found that strengths of these programs included the broad-based approaches for reducing risks and creating opportunities, an emphasis on both family and community empowerment, and the use of program practices that emphasize participant involvement and responsibility

---

[2] This is not to say that developers and implementers of compensatory approaches or eradication approaches to early intervention are not concerned with how program practices and practitioner attitudes and behaviors influence program outcomes; however, they are rarely explicitly discussed as factors producing variation in child, parent, and family functioning.

for shaping program policy, deciding program foci, and determining solutions to problems and attainment of desired goals. *Starting Points* (Carnegie Task Force on Meeting the Needs of Young Children, 1994), an initiative of the Carnegie Corporation, represents a blueprint for how features of both compensatory and eradication approaches to early intervention can be combined with family support program practices resulting in a truly ecological approach to early intervention.

Among the strengths of the ecological approach are that it both makes intuitive sense and is highly consistent with research evidence about the multiple sources of risk and the need for operationalization of opportunity factors to both reduce/eliminate risk conditions and create opportunities that will optimally influence positive child and family outcomes. A limitation is that evidence demonstrating the effects and value-added benefits of this approach, in comparison to either compensatory or eradication models, is "not yet in." This limitation in part stems from the difficulty in evaluating these kinds of flexible, individualized programs and practices with traditional research methodologies (Powell, 1987). Nonetheless, the value of these kinds of early intervention programs and practices must be established if increased calls for adoption of ecological approaches are to be answered.

SUMMARY

The purpose of this chapter was to describe both the strengths and limitations of early intervention using a risk–opportunity framework (Garbarino & Abramowitz, 1992) for understanding how child/family, environmental, and program/practitioner factors function as either development-enhancing or development-impeding determinants of child, parent, and family functioning. Relevant research for both the intervention and nonintervention literatures was used to illustrate that the effects of risk and opportunity factors are often complex, cumulative, and interactive. The chapter took as a starting point that more and more families now being targeted for early intervention have experienced more frequent, persistent, and intense risk conditions, and that depending on how early intervention is conceptualized and implemented, the influences of certain kinds of contemporary interventions would be expected to be meager at best.

Both the risk–opportunity framework and the description of sources of both risks and opportunities were used for describing three approaches to early intervention. Each approach has both strengths and limitations, although the ecological model, at least as described in this chapter, would appear to hold the greatest promise for producing positive benefits among children and families at highest risk for poor outcomes. This seems to be the case not only because this approach attempts to both eliminate or reduce risk factors and create multiple child- and family-learning opportunities, but also explicitly considers how program practices and practitioner attitudes and behaviors function as opportunity factors having value-added benefits (Dunst & Trivette, 1996).

The approach described in this chapter for examining strengths and limitations of early intervention intentionally differed from the efforts of others who also have been concerned with the ecology of early intervention (e.g., Halpern, 1990; Powell, 1993; Zigler & Berman, 1983) and how different paradigms influence the methods and outcomes of interventions (Bond, 1982; Cowen, 1994; Kretzmann & McKnight, 1993; Rappaport, 1981; Seeman, 1989). The framework in this chapter provides a different lens for understanding the strengths and limitations of early intervention at a number of levels of analysis (theoretical, conceptual, procedural, operational). On the one hand, we believe that the risk–opportunity framework provides a unique vantage point for more fully understanding and appreciating the real world contexts of early intervention, and on the other hand, provides a new perspective for dialogue about how best to improve early intervention programs and practices so as to optimally benefit children, families, and communities.

REFERENCES

Affleck, G., Tennen, H., Rowe, J., Rosche, B., & Walker, L. (1989). Effects of formal support on mothers' adaptation to the hospital-to-home transition of high-risk infants: The benefits and costs of helping. *Child Development, 60,* 488–501.

Annie E. Casey Foundation. (1994). *Kids count data book: State profiles of child well-being.* Greenwich, CT: Author.

Ashley, D. (1991). *Constructing local solutions: Affordable housing.* Washington, DC: National Conference of State Legislators.

Bambring, M., Beelman, A., & Rauh, H. (Eds.). (1996). *Intervention in early childhood: Theory, evaluation, and practice.* New York: Aldine de Gruyter.

Baracos, R., Seifer, R., & Sameroff, A. (1985). Defining environmental risks: Multiple dimensions of psychological vulnerability. *American Journal of Community Psychology, 13,* 433–447.

Barnett, W. S. (1995). Long-term effects of early childhood programs on cognitive and school outcomes. *The Future of Children, 5*(3), 25–50.

Bianchi, S. (1993). Children of poverty: Why are they poor? In J. Chafel (Ed.), *Child poverty and public policy* (pp. 91–125). Washington, DC: Urban Institute Press.

Bianchi, S. (1995). The changing demographic and socioeconomic characteristics of single-parent families. *Marriage and Family Review, 20*(1/2), 71–97.

Bond, L. (1982). From prevention to promotion: Optimizing infant development. In L. Bond & J. Joffe (Eds.), *Facilitating infant and early childhood development* (pp. 5–39). Hanover, NH: University Press of New England.

Bowen, L., & Sellers, S. (1994). *Family support and socially vulnerable communities.* Chicago: Family Resources Coalition.

Bronfenbrenner, U. (1979). *The ecology of human development: Experiments by nature and design.* Cambridge, MA: Harvard University Press.

Bronfenbrenner, U. (1992). Ecological systems theory. In R. Vasta (Ed.), *Six theories of child development: Revised formulations and current issues* (pp. 187–249). London: Jessica Kingsley.

Carnegie Task Force on Meeting the Needs of Young Children. (1994). *Starting points: Meeting the needs of our youngest children.* New York: Carnegie Corporation.

Children's Defense Fund. (1995). *The state of America's children yearbook.* Washington, DC: Author.

Cochran, M. (1990). Personal networks in the ecology of human development. In M. Cochran, M. Larner, D. Riley, L. Gunnarson, & C. Henderson (Eds.), *Extending families: The social networks of parents and their children* (pp. 3–33). New York: Cambridge University Press.

Cochran, M. (1993). Parenting and personal social networks. In T. Luster & L. Okagaki (Eds.), *Parenting: An ecological perspective* (pp. 149–178). Hillsdale, NJ: Erlbaum.

Cochran, M., & Brassard, J. (1979). Child development and personal social networks. *Child Development, 50,* 601–616.

Condry, S. (1983). History and background of preschool intervention programs and the consortium for longitudinal studies. In The Consortium for Longitudinal Studies (Ed.), *As the twig is bent . . . Lasting effects of preschool programs* (pp. 1–31). Hillsdale, NJ: Erlbaum.

Cowen, E. L. (1985). Person-centered approaches to primary prevention in mental health: Situation-focused and competence-enhancement. *American Journal of Community Psychology, 13,* 31–48.

Cowen, E. L. (1994). The enhancement of psychological wellness: Challenges and opportunities. *American Journal of Community Psychology, 22,* 149–179.

Datan, N. (1975). Normative life crises: Academic perspectives. In N. Datan & L. H. Ginsberg (Eds.), *Life-span developmental psychology: Normative life crises* (pp. 3–16). New York: Academic Press.

Datan, N., & Ginsberg, L. H. (Eds.). (1975). *Life-span developmental psychology: Normative life crises.* New York: Academic Press.

Datan, N., Greene, A. L., & Reese, H. W. (Eds.). (1986). *Life-span developmental psychology: Intergenerational relations.* Hillsdale, NJ: Erlbaum.

Dichtelmiller, M., Meisels, S. J., Plunkett, J. W., Bozynski, M. E., Chaflin, C., & Mangelsdorf, S. C. (1992). The relationship of parental knowledge to the development of extremely low-birth-weight infants. *Journal of Early Intervention, 16*(3), 210–220.

Dunst, C. J. (1985). Rethinking early intervention. *Analysis and Intervention in Developmental Disabilities, 5,* 165–201.

Dunst, C. J. (1993). Implications of risk and opportunity factors for assessment and intervention practices. *Topics in Early Childhood Special Education, 13,* 143–153.

Dunst, C. J. (1995a). *Key characteristics and features of community-based family support programs.* Chicago: Family Resource Coalition.

Dunst, C. J. (1995b). Lenses through which we view our work (and our world). *Pennsylvania Early Intervention Newsletter, 6*(4), 1–5.

Dunst, C. J. (1995c, June). *Risks and opportunity factors influencing child and family behavior and development.* Presentation made at the Fourth National Early Intervention Conference, Coimbra, Portugal.

Dunst, C. J. (1996). Early intervention in the USA: Programs, models and practices. In M. Brambring, A. Beelmann, & H. Rauh (Eds.), *Intervention in early childhood: Theory, evaluation and practice* (pp. 11–52). New York: Aldine de Gruyter.

Dunst, C. J. (in press). Sensorimotor development and developmental disabilities. In B. Hodapp, E. Zigler, & J. Burack (Eds.), *Handbook of mental retardation and development.* New York: Cambridge University Press.

Dunst, C. J., Johanson, C., Trivette, C. M., & Hamby, D. (1991). Family-oriented early intervention policies or practices: Family-centered or not? *Exceptional Children, 58,* 115–126.

Dunst, C. J., & Leet, H. (1987). Measuring the adequacy of resources in households with young children. *Child: Care, Health and Development, 13,* 111–125.

Dunst, C. J., Leet, H., & Trivette, C. M. (1988). Family resources, personal well-being, and early intervention. *Journal of Special Education, 22,* 108–116.

Dunst, C. J., & Lingerfelt, B. (1985). Maternal ratings of temperament and operant learning in two- to three-month-old infants. *Child Development, 56,* 555–563.

Dunst, C. J., & Trivette, C. M. (1992, March). *Risk and opportunity factors influencing parent and child functioning.* Paper presented at the Ninth Annual Smoky Mountain Winter Institute, Asheville, NC.

Dunst, C. J., & Trivette, C. M. (1994). Methodological considerations and strategies for studying the long-term follow up of early intervention. In S. Friedman & H. C. Haywood (Ed.), *Developmental follow-up: Conceptus, domains and methods* (pp. 277–313). San Diego, CA: Academic Press.

Dunst, C. J., & Trivette, C. M. (1996). Empowerment, effective helpgiving practices, and family-centered care. *Pediatric Nursing, 22,* 334–337, 343.

Dunst, C. J., Trivette, C. M., & Deal, A. G. (1988). *Enabling and empowering families: Principles and guidelines for practice.* Cambridge, MA: Brookline Books.

Dunst, C. J., Trivette, C. M., & Deal, A. G. (Eds.). (1994). *Supporting and strengthening families: Vol. 1. Methods, strategies and practices.* Cambridge, MA: Brookline Books.

Dunst, C. J., Trivette, C. M., Gordon, N. J., & Starnes, A. L. (1993). Family-centered case management practices: Characteristics and consequences. In H. Singer & L. E. Powers (Eds.), *Families, disability, and empowerment: Active coping skills and strategies for family interventions* (pp. 88–118). Baltimore: Brookes.

Dunst, C. J., Trivette, C. M., & Hamby, D. (1996). Measuring the helpgiving practices of human services program practitioners. *Human Relations, 49,* 35–54.

Dunst, C. J., Trivette, C. M., Hamby, D., & Pollock, B. (1990). Family systems correlates of the behavior of young children with handicaps. *Journal of Early Intervention, 14,* 204–218.

Dunst, C. J., Trivette, C. M., & Jodry, W. (1997). Influences of social support on children with disabilities and their families. In M. Guralnick (Ed.), *The effectiveness of early intervention* (pp. 499–522). Baltimore: Brookes.

Dunst, C. J., Trivette, C. M., & LaPointe, N. (1992). Toward clarification of the meaning and key elements of empowerment. *Family Science Review, 5*(1/2), 111–130.

Dunst, C. J., Trivette, C. M., Starnes, A. L., Hamby, D. W., & Gordon, N. J. (1993). *Building and evaluating family support initiatives.* Baltimore: Brookes.

Dunst, C. J., Trivette, C. M., & Thompson, R. (1990). Supporting and strengthening family functioning: Toward a congruence between principles and practice. *Prevention in Human Services, 9*(1), 19–43.

Dunst, C. J., Vance, S. D., & Cooper, C. S. (1986). A social systems perspective of adolescent pregnancy: Determinants of parent and parent-child behavior. *Infant Mental Health Journal, 7,* 34–48.

Elder, G., & Liker, J. (1980). Hard times in women's lives: Historical influences across 40 years. *American Journal of Sociology, 88,* 241–269.

Farley, R. (Ed.). (1995a). *State of the union: America in the 1990s: Vol. 1. Economic trends.* New York: Sage.

Farley, R. (Ed.). (1995b). *State of the union: America in the 1990s: Vol. 2. Social trends.* New York: Sage.

Garbarino, J. (1988). *The future as if it really mattered.* Longmont, CO: Bookmasters Guild.

Garbarino, J. (1992). *Child and families in the social environment* (2nd ed.). New York: Aldine de Gruyter.

Garbarino, J., & Abramowitz, R. H. (1992). The ecology of human development. In J. Garbarino (Ed.), *Children and families in the social environment* (2nd ed., pp. 11–34). New York: Aldine de Gruyter.

Garbarino, J., & Kostelny, K. (1993). Neighborhood and community influences on parenting. In T. Luster & L. Okagaki (Eds.), *Parenting: An ecological perspective* (pp. 203–226). Hillsdale, NJ: Erlbaum.

Glenn, N. (1977). *Cohort analysis.* Newbury Park, CA: Sage.

Gomby, D., Larner, M., Stevenson, C., Lewit, E., & Behrman, R. (1995). Long-term outcomes of early childhood programs: Analysis and recommendations. *The Future of Children, 5*(3), 6–24.

Greenbaum, C., & Averbach, J. (Eds.). (1992). *Longitudinal studies of children at psychological risks: Cross-national perspectives.* Norwood, NJ: ABLEX.

Guralnick, M. (1997). *The effectiveness of early intervention.* Baltimore: Brookes.

Haggerty, R., Sherrod, L., Garmezy, N., & Rutter, M. (Eds.). (1994). *Stress, risks, and resilience in children and adolescents.* New York: Cambridge University Press.

Halpern, R. (1990). Poverty and early childhood parenting: Toward a framework for intervention. *American Journal of Orthopsychiatry, 60,* 6–18.

Halpern, R. (1993). The societal context of home visiting and related services for families in poverty. *The Future of Children, 3*(3), 158–171.

Hannon, K., & Luster, T. (1991). Influences of parent, child, and contextual factors on the quality of the home environment. *Infant Mental Health Journal, 12,* 17–27.

Hanson, M., & Carta, J. (1996). Addressing the challenges of families with multiple risks. *Exceptional Children, 62,* 201–212.

Haskins, R. (1989). Beyond metaphor: The efficacy of early childhood education. *American Psychologist, 44,* 274–282.

Hernandez, D. J. (1993). *America's children: Resources from family, government and the economy.* New York: Sage.

Hoke, B. (1968). Promotive medicine and the phenomenon of health. *Archives of Environmental Health, 16,* 269–278.

Huntington, G., & Simeonsson, R. (1993). Temperament and adaptation in infants and young children with disabilities. *Infant Mental Health Journal, 14,* 49–59.

Huston, A. C. (1995, August). *Children in poverty and public policy.* Paper presented at the 103rd annual meeting of Division 7 of the American Psychological Association, New York.

Infant Health and Development Program. (1990). Enhancing the outcomes of low-birth-weight, premature infants: A multisite, randomized trial. *Journal of the American Medical Association, 263*(22), 3035–3042.

Kagan, S. L. (1991). Excellence in early childhood education: Defining characteristics and next decade strategies. In S. L. Kagan (Ed.), *The care and education of America's young children* (pp. 237–258). Chicago: University of Chicago Press.

Katz, R. (1984). Empowerment and synergy: Expanding the community's healing process. In J. Rappaport, C. Swift, & R. Hess (Eds.), *Studies in empowerment: Steps toward understanding and action* (pp. 201–226). New York: Haworth Press.

Kopp, C. (1983). Risk factors in development. In P. Mussen (Ed.), *Handbook of child psychology: Vol. 2. Infancy and developmental psychobiology* (pp. 1081–1188). New York: Wiley.

Kopp, C. (1994). Trends and directions in studies of development risk. In C. Nelson (Ed.), *Threats to optimal development: Integrating biological, psychological, and social risk factors* (pp. 1–33). Hillsdale, NJ: Erlbaum.

Kretzmann, J., & McKnight, J. (1993). *Building community from the inside out.* Evanston, IL: Northwestern University, Center for Urban Affairs and Policy Research.

Maisto, A. A., & German, M. L. (1981). Maternal locus of control and developmental gain demonstrated by high-risk infants: A longitudinal analysis. *Journal of Psychology, 109,* 213–221.

Marfo, K. (Ed.). (1991) *Early intervention in transition.* New York: Praeger.

Marshall, R. (1991). *The state of families: 3. Losing direction. Families, human resource development, and economic performance.* Milwaukee, WI: Family Service America.

Martin, S. L., Ramey, C. T., & Ramey, S. (1990). The prevention of intellectual impairment in children of impoverished families: Findings of a randomized trial of educational day care. *American Journal of Public Health, 80*(7), 844–847.

Meisels, S. J., & Shonkoff, J. P. (Eds.). (1990). *Handbook of early childhood intervention.* New York: Cambridge University Press.

Nelson, C. (Ed.). (1994). *Threats to optimal development: Integrating biological, psychological, and social risk factors.* Hillsdale, NJ: Erlbaum.

Pellegrini, D. S. (1990). Psychosocial risk and protective factors in childhood. *Developmental and Behavioral Pediatrics, 11*(4), 201–209.

Powell, D. (1987). Methodological and conceptual issues in research. In S. L. Kagan, D. Powell, B. Weissbourd, & E. Zigler (Eds.), *America's family support programs* (pp. 311–328). New Haven, CT: Yale University Press.

Powell, D. (1993). Inside home visiting programs. *The Future of Children, 3*(3), 23–38.

Puls, B. (1991). *Building communities that work: Community economic development.* Washington, DC: National Conference of State Legislators.

Ramey, C. T., & Ramey, S. L. (1992). Early educational intervention with disadvantaged children—To what effect? *Applied and Preventative Psychology, 1,* 131–140.

Rappaport, J. (1981). In praise of paradox: A social policy of empowerment over prevention. *American Journal of Community Psychology, 9,* 1–25.

Rappaport, J. (1987). Terms of empowerment/exemplars of prevention: Toward a theory for community psychology. *American Journal of Community Psychology, 15*(2), 121–128.

Rhodes, W. A., & Brown, W. K. (Eds.). (1991). *Why some children succeed despite the odds.* New York: Praeger.

Rolf, J., Masten, A., Cicchetti, D., Nuechterlein, K., & Weintraub, S. (Eds.). (1990). *Risk and protective factors in the development of psychopathy.* New York: Cambridge University Press.

St. Pierre, R., Layzer, J., & Barnes, H. (1995). Two-generation programs: Design, cost, and shared-term effectiveness. *The Future of Children, 5*(3), 76-93.

Sameroff, A. J., Seifer, R., Baracos, R., Zax, M., & Greenspan, S. (1987). Intelligence quotient scores of 4-year-old children: Social-environment risk factors. *Pediatrics, 79*(3), 343–350.

Seeman, J. (1989). Toward a model of positive health. *American Psychologist, 44,* 1099–1109.

Smith, S. (Ed.). (1995). *Two-generation programs for families in poverty.* Norwood, NJ: ABLEX.

Smith, S., & Zaslow, M. (1995). Rationale and policy context for two-generation interventions. In S. Smith (Ed.), *Two-generation programs for families in poverty* (pp. 1–38). Norwood, NJ: ABLEX.

Trivette, C. M., Dunst, C. J., Boyd, K., & Hamby, D. (1996). Family-oriented program models, helpgiving practices, and parental control appraisals. *Exceptional Children, 62,* 197–199.

Trivette, C. M., Dunst, C. J., & Deal, A. G. (1997). Resource-based early intervention practices. In S. K. Thurman, J. R. Cornwell, & S. R. Gottwald (Eds.), *The contexts of early intervention: Systems and settings* (pp. 73–92). Baltimore: Brookes.

Trivette, C. M., Dunst, C. J., & Hamby, D. (1996a). Characteristics and consequences of helpgiving practices in contrasting human services programs. *American Journal of Community Psychology, 24,* 273–293.

Trivette, C. M., Dunst, C. J., & Hamby, D. (1996b). Factors associated with parental control appraisals in a family-centered early intervention program. *Journal of Early Intervention, 20,* 165–178.

Trivette, C. M., Dunst, C. J., Hamby, D. W., & LaPointe, N. (1996). Key elements of empowerment and their implications for early intervention. *Infant-Toddler Intervention: The Transdisciplinary Journal, 6,* 59–73.

Turner, R., & Avison, W. (1985). Assessing risk factors for parenting problems: The significance of social support. *Journal of Marriage and the Family, 47,* 881–891.

U.S. General Accounting Office. (1994). *Early childhood programs: Parent education and income best predict participation* (GAO/HEHS-95-47). Washington, DC: Author.

U.S. General Accounting Office. (1995a). *Early childhood centers: Services to prepare children for school often limited* (GAO/HEHS-95-21). Washington, DC: Author.

U.S. General Accounting Office. (1995b). *Community development: Comprehensive approaches address multiple needs but are challenging to implement* (GAO/RCED/HEHS-95-69). Washington, DC: Author.

Uzgiris, I. C., & Hunt, J. McV. (1975). *Assessment in infancy: Ordinal scales of psychological development.* Urbana: University of Illinois Press.

Weiss, H. (Ed.). (1995). *Raising our future: Families, schools, and communities joining together.* Cambridge, MA: Harvard Family Research Project.

Werner, E. (1990). Protective factors and individual resilience. In S. J. Meisels & J. P. Shonkoff (Eds.), *Handbook of early childhood intervention* (pp. 97–116). New York: Cambridge University Press.

Werner, E., Bierman, J., & French, F. (1971). *The children of Kauai.* Honolulu: University of Hawaii Press.

Werner, E., & Smith, R. (1977). *Kauai's children come of age.* Honolulu: University of Hawaii Press.

Werner, E., & Smith, R. (1982). *Vulnerable but invincible: A longitudinal study of resilient children and youth.* New York: McGraw-Hill.

Werner, E., & Smith, R. (1992). *Overcoming the odds: High-risk children from birth to adulthood.* Ithaca, NY: Cornell University Press.

Willett, J. B. (1989). Some results on reliability for the longitudinal measurement of change: Implications for the design of studies of individual growth. *Educational and Psychological Measurement, 49,* 587–602.

Yoshikawa, H. (1995). Long-term effects of early childhood programs on social outcomes and delinquency. *The Future of Children, 5*(3), 51–75.

Zautra, A., & Sandler, I. (1983). Life event needs assessments: Two models for measuring preventable mental health problems. In A. Zautra, K. Bachrach, & R. Hess (Eds.), *Strategies for needs assessment in prevention* (pp. 35–58). New York: Haworth Press.

Zigler, E., & Berman, W. (1983). Discerning the future of early childhood intervention. *American Psychologist, 38*(8), 894–906.

CHAPTER 8

Smoking

JOHN P. ELDER, DEBORAH PARRA-MEDINA, and J. XAVIER APODACA

DESCRIPTION OF THE PROBLEM

In 1987, 34% of people with less than a high school education and who were 20 years old or older smoked, as well as 36% of blue-collar workers, 42% of military personnel, 34% of African-Americans, 33% of Latinos, and 55% of Southeast Asian male immigrants.

The picture among adolescents is even less optimistic. Initiation of smoking climbs steadily between early junior high grades and the end of high school. Although the number of high school seniors who are regular smokers dropped from the mid-1970s to the early 1980s, it has since leveled off stubbornly at about 20% and has recently begun to climb again (Johnston, 1995). Experimentation with smoking occurs almost entirely during adolescence. The 1987 National Student Health Survey showed 51% of eighth graders and 63% of tenth graders to have smoked at least one cigarette in their lifetime.

For years preceding adolescence, children are barraged by a variety of media and adult role models indicating that smoking is associated with fun, glamour, adventure and even health. These images come from advertisements presented by cigarette companies featuring Joe Camel, film stars, and other media idols. In more subtle promotions, "good guys" in movies or videos are often seen with a cigarette or cigarette ads are displayed in the background of movies. Prosmoking influence comes even from parents or other adults who may not want their children to be smokers, a value belied by their own behavior.

Adolescence, however, represents the crucial developmental period for many and varied interpersonal skills that play a vital role in the acquisition of social, cultural, and economic reinforcement (Elder & Stern, 1986). Acceptance by one's peers tends to be a major reinforcer driving much of adolescents' behavior. It is during adolescence that the interpersonal temptation to take up the tobacco habit becomes strongest, as same-age or older peers and siblings increase the pressure on nonsmoking youth. Within a short time, adolescents can develop a physiological and psychological addiction to cigarettes and may be well on their way to becoming regular smokers. Ongoing peer reinforcement for cigarette smoking may no longer be necessary, as the negative reinforcement derived from smoking to counteract withdrawal symptoms may be sufficient to maintain the habit. From parents who leave cigarettes around the house, to unsupervised cigarette machines in public places, to the sales of single cigarettes by convenience stores and other retailers (most of whom do not check IDs), ready availability facilitates regular smoking (Erickson, Woodruff, Wildey, & Kenney, 1993). In short, it seems more remarkable that nearly 80% of high school seniors do *not* smoke rather than that 20% do.

Smoking represents a particular problem for youth of lower socioeconomic groups. In 1987, 40% of these youth (as measured by young adults who had a less than high school education) were regular cigarette smokers. The Surgeon General hopes that this percentage will be reduced to 27% by the year 2000 among low socioeconomic status youth. However, given the special advertising focus and apparent relatively more aggressive retailing that occurs in ethnic and blue-collar communities (Erickson et al., 1993), it seems questionable whether this ambitious goal can be reached.

Scope of Problem

Smoking is the most important behavioral risk factor associated with cardiovascular disease, many forms of cancer, bronchitis, and many other illnesses. In the United States alone, tobacco use is responsible for more than one out of every six deaths and is considered to be the most important single preventable cause of death and disease in our society (U.S. Department of Health & Humans Services [USDHHS], 1989).

Nearly one-third of all adults in the United States continue to smoke, even though total per capita cigarette consumption has declined dramatically over the past 25 years. Onset of this decline can be traced directly to the release of the Surgeon General's Report (U.S. Public Health Service [USPHS], 1964), which outlined the dangers of smoking uncovered by various chronic disease researchers in the United States, United Kingdom, and other Western countries over the prior 15 years (Doll & Hill, 1964; Doll & Peto, 1976). This decline, however, has been less pronounced among women than among men. Smoking remains relatively high among African-Americans and people of lower socioeconomic strata.

Causes and Consequences

Causes

Despite an apparent continued decline in adult smoking since 1965, adolescent smoking has remained virtually unchanged and now is going through an apparent increase (Eckhardt, Woodruff, & Elder, 1994; Klesges & Robinson, 1995). The critical question is, Why are 3,000 new adolescents experimenting with tobacco everyday (Centers for Disease Control [CDC], 1994a; Eckhardt et al., 1994).

Although many studies have been conducted to determine the cause of adolescent smoking onset, no single variable predominates. Many studies indicate peer pressure (Bettes, Dusenbury, Kerner, James-Ortiz, & Botvin, 1990; Newman, 1984), parental modeling and prompting (de Moor, Elder, Young, Wildey, & Moolgaard, 1989; de Moor et al., 1994; Klesges & Robinson, 1995; Moreno et al., 1994; Sallis et al., 1994), and perceived prevalence (Collins et al., 1987; Iannotti & Bush, 1992; Klesges & Robinson,

1995; Sussman et al., 1988) as powerful predictors of adolescent tobacco use. Significant predictors of adolescent smoking include variables such as media influence (CDC 1994c; Di Franza et al., 1991; Pierce et al., 1991); age (Eckhardt et al., 1994; Headen, Bauman, Deane, & Koch, 1991; McGee & Stanton, 1993); ethnicity and gender (Bettes et al., 1990; de Moor et al., 1994; Eckhardt et al., 1994; Sabogal, Otero-Sabogal, Perez-Stable, Marin, & Marin, 1989; Sussman, Dent, Flay, Hansen, & Johnson, 1987); acculturation (Sabogal et al., 1989); socioeconomic status (SES; Collins et al., 1987; Eckert, 1983; Elder, Amick, Sleet, & Senn, 1987; Headen et al., 1991); intent (Eckhardt et al., 1994); school performance and activities (Eckert, 1983; Karle et al., 1994; McGee & Stanton, 1993; Meyers & Brown, 1994); risk taking and rebelliousness (Klesges & Robinson, 1995), home use (Salomon, Stein, Eisenberg, & Klein, 1984); image (Bettes et al., 1990; Klesges & Robinson, 1995; Newman, 1984; Sussman, Dent, Burton, Stacy, & Flay, 1995); intrapersonal factors, such as low self-esteem and psychological distress (Bettes et al., 1990; CDC, 1994c; Klesges & Robinson, 1995); and use of other substances (Eckhardt et al., 1994; Meyers & Brown, 1994).

Theoretical Perspectives on Smoking Etiology

An examination of theoretical systems frequently invoked to explain smoking will assist in integrating these potential predictors. Those theories most frequently referred to in health, psychology, and public health promotion are the Health Belief model (HBM), social learning theory (SLT), theory of reasoned action (TRA), and applied behavior analysis (ABA).

Health Belief Model

The Health Belief model (HBM) holds that individuals take health action or fail to do so based on whether they (a) perceive themselves to either be susceptible or not susceptible to a particular health problem; (b) see the problem as serious; (c) perceive prevention or treatment as effective at little personal cost; and (d) receive a prompt or cue to take health action (Becker, 1979). When developed as a model for smoking, it suggests that aspects of smoking onset may be directly implicated by this model, not in its ability to predict onset but rather to indicate why onset may occur.

This model simplifies the cognitive processes that lead to a decision to first experiment with tobacco. Further, it complements the results of many studies that report knowledge of health consequences as a poor predictor and peer influence as a strong predictor of adolescent smoking.

Applied Behavior Analysis and Social Learning Theory

An applied behavior analytic or operant perspective considers smoking onset and maintenance in terms of the various contingencies influencing this initially social behavior. Children may seek the positive reinforcement that they assume will be forthcoming in the form of a more adult image, heightened heterosocial attractiveness, and even improved physical and intellectual abilities. In addition to these images projected in cigarette ads, the would-be smoker may be seeking positive reinforcement in the form of peer group acceptance, or conversely may be influenced by the negative reinforcement of avoiding rejection by peers who already smoke.

Additional operant explanations distinguish between performance and skill deficits. Performance deficits may result from a lack of reinforcement for nonsmoking (coupled with reinforcement for smoking), whereas skill deficits relate to insufficient interpersonal skills necessary to "say no" to tobacco. The latter perspective retains primacy in smoking prevention programs today, although it is more commonly associated with Bandura's social learning theory, which initially derived many of its principal tenets from operant psychology.

Social learning theory[1] (SLT) stresses the interrelationships between people, their behavior, and the environment through a process known as "reciprocal determinism." That is, although behavior is largely determined by the environment, an individual has the capacity to act in order to change his or her environment. Additionally, SLT purports that behavior is affected through the process of modeling. The social network with which one is in contact, either through preference or circumstance, manifests the behaviors most often observed and therefore most thoroughly learned (Bandura, 1977b).

The many studies that document the effect of parental smoking on adolescent experimentation with tobacco exemplify the concept of behavior initiation through modeling (de Moor et al., 1989; Evans et al., 1978; Moreno et al., 1994; Sallis et al., 1994). Evans, de Moor, and others have found evidence that effectively correlates smoking parents with a greater likelihood of smoking children compared with children in a non-smoking household.

Furthermore, SLT holds that performance of a behavior depends on a person's self-efficacy, the personal judgment of one's capabilities to organize and execute courses of action required to attain designated types of performances (Bandura, 1977b, 1995). Self-efficacy can both affect the decision to quit smoking as well as be the determinant of initial experimentation. In the latter case, adolescents with low self-esteem may have a greater need to be defined as "tough" or "cool" (Klesges & Robinson, 1995). If a child determines that tobacco use will result in such an image, his or her perceived self-efficacy will be directed to achieving the behavior. A more proximal example stems from the advent of peer pressure to smoke. Here, resistance self-efficacy to "just say no" is pitted against the strength of interpersonal relationships and the pressure to group compliance.

Theory of Reasoned Action

The theory of reasoned action (TRA) postulates that beliefs are at the basis of the attitudes that determine whether a behavior will occur. These attitudes can be affected by either "behavioral beliefs," "normative beliefs," or a combination of the two.

A behavioral belief is an assumption that performing a behavior that results in a positive outcome leads to a positive attitude toward that behavior. The beginning of adolescence is often accompanied by changes in peer relations, social activities, self-concepts, and experimentation. Additionally, the young adolescent experiences a perceived need for peer acceptance that may require compliance to group behavior standards including dares to perform maladaptive behaviors, such as smoking (Bettes et al., 1990). In turn, the adolescent is rewarded with social support, status, affection, and other reinforcers that indicate acceptance into the group. According to TRA, these anticipated positive outcomes to group compliance will motivate an adolescent to initiate smoking.

---

[1] Now reformulated as social cognitive theory, SLT historically (and to some extent currently) has exerted a far greater influence on the field of health promotion and particularly smoking prevention.

A normative belief refers to inferences individuals make about key individuals in their social network. A person who believes that individuals held in esteem think that he or she should perform the behavior, will be likely to do so (Ajzen & Fishbein, 1980). Stated another way, Sussman et al. (1995) describes normative influence as the perceived pressure placed on an individual by his or her peers to behave in a certain way (peer pressure).

An often cited variable associated with smoking onset is the inflated perception of tobacco use by one's peers (Bush & Iannotti, 1992; Collins et al., 1987; de Moor et al., 1989; Elder et al., 1987; Elder et al., 1989; Evans et al., 1978; Headen et al., 1991; Klesges & Robinson, 1995; Sussman et al., 1988). Collins et al. (1987) note that children of smokers had the highest levels of misperception of smoking prevalence among adolescent smokers, and Klesges and Robinson (1995) report that in high-risk adolescents, perceived smoking by teens was estimated to be twice as high as it actually was. Such misperception of tobacco use prevalence may lead adolescents to believe that smoking is an approved behavior and will result in positive peer reaction. The resulting behavior, according to TRA, is experimentation and continued and escalated tobacco use (Collins et al., 1987).

Media Influences

One of the main concerns of the public health community is that the themes and images used by the tobacco companies are attractive to and promote the use of tobacco by minors (Pierce et al., 1991). There is accumulating evidence that implicates the tobacco companies' concerted efforts to target adolescents with three promotional campaigns. One of the more blatantly controversial advertising campaigns is RJR Nabisco's introduction of "Joe Camel," the "smooth character" cartoon camel modeled after James Bond and Don Johnson of "Miami Vice." Di Franza et al. (1991) estimates an increase from $6 million per year prior to "Joe Camel" to $476 million per year in illegal sales to children.

In further support of Di Franza et al.'s (1991) findings, a study by Pierce et al. (1991) indicated that an inverse relationship existed between age and product recognition. Among subjects aged 12 through 65 years, the Camel advertising campaign was most recognized by those children aged 12 through 13 years (34.2%) and steadily declined to less than 10% in respondents 45 years and older. This inverse relationship was not demonstrated for all tobacco company advertising. Pierce and colleagues conclude that tobacco advertising, particularly of Camel cigarettes, effectively targets adolescents in the United States.

Since the 1971 ban on television and radio advertising of tobacco products, tobacco companies have become very clever in their promotional strategies.[2] This ultimately proved to be a major setback to tobacco control efforts. Targeting youth, they sponsor sports and entertainment events such as the "Camel Mud and Monster" series and rely on poster advertisements strategically placed near theaters, record stores, video arcades, and in malls where minors are apt to go and gather. Specialty items with a youth

---

[2] Throughout the latter half of the 1960s, the tobacco industry was reeling from aggressive anti-tobacco televised ads authored by health agencies who demanded at least some "equal time" to tell the public about the dangers of smoking. The TV-ban legislation, sponsored by tobacco state congressmen, allowed the industry to withdraw from television with the proviso that the antitobacco ads, be pulled as well. This ultimately proved a major setback to tobacco control efforts.

appeal are also used. These include baseball caps, posters, T-shirts, and candy cigarettes—all emblazoned with an appealing logo such as "Joe Camel." Magazine advertisements are also effective, utilizing images of young, healthy, independent, thrill-seeking men and women. This type of advertising reaches the adolescent who is in the process of developing a self-image (CDC, 1994c; Di Franza et al., 1991).

In all, the tobacco companies' efforts to hook children appear to have been very effective. However, the industry's efforts do not stop at just creating the habit, Di Franza et al. (1991) reported that, "the purpose of one tobacco industry study was to assess the feasibility of marketing low-tar brands to teens as an alternative to quitting." Furthermore, the study found that "the most commonly voiced reason for quitting among those who had done so . . . was sports." Sporting event sponsorships by the tobacco industry should be considered in relation to promoting continued tobacco use as well as initiation. Although it is unlikely that a direct link between smoking onset and media can be drawn, there seems to be little doubt that leaders in the industry believe they are capable of promoting smoking among youth.

Consequences

Adolescent Smoker

Reports indicate that nearly all onset of tobacco use occurs before high school graduation and can begin as early as seventh grade (CDC, 1994c; Elder & Stern, 1986; Klesges, & Robinson, 1995). In fact, about one-third of 14- to 18-year-olds use tobacco (CDC, 1994c). This period of development is associated with pronounced physiological, psychological, and sociological changes. This is a period when peer acceptance, compliance to group behavior standards, and experimentation with substances, including tobacco, occurs (Bettes et al., 1990).

Because the most severe health consequences of smoking are insidious, they do not manifest themselves until long after an individual is thoroughly behaviorally and physically addicted. Nevertheless, even in the early stages of the habit, detrimental health effects can occur. There can be a reduction in the rate of lung growth and function, increase in respiratory illnesses, and unfavorable effects on blood lipid levels (CDC, 1994a; Meyers & Brown, 1994). Compared with nonsmoking adolescents, smokers report that they are more likely to experience shortness of breath, coughing spells, phlegm production, and wheezing. Furthermore, researchers note an inverse relationship between frequency and duration of cigarette use and physical fitness (CDC, 1994c).

Additionally, the added burden of trying to quit stems from a positive association between frequency and intensity of tobacco use and symptoms of nicotine withdrawal in both younger and older smokers. Reported withdrawal symptoms include difficulty concentrating, irritability, hunger, restlessness, feeling sad, blue, or depressed, and craving cigarettes during previous quit attempts. Thus, even those adolescent smokers who intend to quit generally cannot (CDC, 1993).

Although severe, health-related consequences should not overshadow the social and psychological impact of adolescent smoking. Experimentation with tobacco is strongly associated with use of other substances (CDC, 1994c; Meyers & Brown, 1994). Tobacco is considered to be a "gateway drug" that leads to or precedes use of other substances (CDC, 1994c; Kaplan, Sallis, & Patterson, 1993). It has been established that smoking either precedes or is used concurrently with alcohol and marijuana and is a good predictor of future use of other illegal substances (Eckhardt et al., 1994). Thus, one of the consequences of tobacco use is introduction into a "drug culture": the first step to substance abuse may be the first cigarette smoked.

Poor school performance is also associated with adolescent smoking. It has been established that smokers generally are low achievers in academics and are nonparticipants in extracurricular activities, such as sports (Bush & Iannotti, 1992; Eckert, 1983; McGee & Stanton, 1993). Meyers and Brown (1994) also report a strong association between substance (including tobacco) abuse and low school attendance.

Additionally, there is a reported relationship between drug use and delinquency or unconventional behavior (Meyers & Brown, 1994). This unconventional behavior can include polydrug abuse, unsafe sex practices, and other negative health-related behaviors. Thus, the relationship between smoking, substance abuse, and delinquent behavior places the adolescent into a high-risk category for other health-related problems.

The Adult Smoker

Since 80% of adult smokers began smoking as adolescents, the most damaging consequence of tobacco experimentation lies in the future. Causes of death attributed to tobacco use include cancers of the lung, larynx, oral cavity, esophagus, urinary bladder, and pancreas. Twenty-one percent of all coronary heart disease deaths and 80% of all chronic pulmonary disease fatalities have been attributed to cigarette use (CDC, 1994e; Sussman et al., 1995). In a report by the Centers for Disease Control (1994e), 20% of all deaths in the United States were attributed to cigarette smoking. This proportion tallies to over 400,000 deaths annually with over five million years of potential life lost (YPLL; CDC, 1993; 1994e).

Additionally, women are at greater health risks due to smoking. Not only do they succumb to the same complications as men, but they are subject to a host of other problems as well. They are more likely to experience irregular menstrual periods and aggravated symptoms of menopause. They are at an increased risk for cervical cancer and osteoporosis. When using oral contraceptives, women who smoke increase their risk of heart attack tenfold and run a greater risk of strokes and blood clots in the lower extremities. Women who smoke during pregnancy increase their risk of having a miscarriage or delivering a low birth-weight infant (Minorities & Tobacco, 1994).

African-Americans also appear to suffer greater risk of smoking-related complications. Among ethnic groups, African-Americans have one of the highest mortality and morbidity rates related to cardiovascular disease and cancers caused by tobacco use (Klesges & Robinson, 1995). They are, in fact, 30% more likely to die from smoking-related diseases than the general population (Minorities & Tobacco, 1994).

Family, Friends, and Neighbors: The Passive Smokers

Environmental tobacco smoke (ETS), also known as *secondhand smoke* or passive smoke, comprises sidestream and exhaled smoke. ETS can also lead to serious health consequences. Secondhand smoke exposure has been linked to lung cancer in the general population. Three thousand lung cancer deaths of nonsmokers are attributed to ETS each year. Nonsmokers exposed to ETS in the workplace are 34% more likely to develop lung cancer. A nonsmoker living with a heavy smoker (more than 20 cigarettes a day) is 30% more likely to die of heart disease and twice as likely to die of lung cancer than a person who lives with a nonsmoker. Prolonged lifetime exposure may result in chronic obstructive pulmonary disease, such as emphysema. Women exposed to secondhand smoke are at a higher risk for developing breast cancer (Minorities & Tobacco, 1994).

Children exposed to ETS are at an increased risk for respiratory problems, such as bronchitis and pneumonia. Asthma, ear infections, coughing, wheezing, and phlegm are also more frequent in children whose parents smoke. ETS has also been linked to a greater increase in sudden infant death syndrome (SIDS). Likelihood of SIDS is three times greater for babies whose mothers smoked during pregnancy and twice as high for children whose mothers quit smoking during pregnancy but resumed smoking following birth (Minorities & Tobacco, 1994).

Another problem associated with passive exposure is the reaction experienced by 15% of those people with allergies. Symptoms include skin and/or mucous membrane sensitivity as well as asthma attacks. Furthermore, both bronchitis and pneumonia have been linked to passive smoke exposure (Sussman et al., 1995). ETS has recently been classified a Group A carcinogen by the Environmental Protection Agency. The Group A category includes such products as asbestos, benzene, and arsenic. These carcinogens have been shown to cause cancer in humans (Minorities & Tobacco, 1994; *Tobacco on Trial*, 1990).

Society Foots the Bill

Society as a whole feels the impact of tobacco users, whether it is in lost loved ones (400,000 premature lives lost every year as a result of tobacco use) or higher national health-care costs (reported at $50 billion). In relationship, this astronomical figure breaks down at $2.06 for each of the 24 billion packages of cigarettes sold with $.89 of that $2.06 being paid by the taxpayer (CDC, 1994b). Including costs due to lost productivity, total direct and indirect costs of tobacco use exceed $68 billion (CDC, 1994a).

IMPEDIMENTS TO INTERVENTION IN THE REAL WORLD CONTEXT

Schools have become the venue of choice for much of prevention work in tobacco use. There are probably two very different reasons for this emphasis. First, schools remain the best place to capture the majority of children and adolescents, given regular attendance and second, the general cooperation of school officials in combating health problems affords a positive environment for the health official. Unfortunately, schools are now becoming the focal point for all too much of community health behavior change efforts, including those emphasizing tobacco and drug use, violence, pregnancy, and other problems. At the same time, a growing number of Americans from conservative religious groups seem determined to limit strictly the breadth and depth of health promotion interventions in schools by getting elected to school boards and altering, reversing, or limiting health-related education carried out with children and adolescents.

Nevertheless, the struggle continues. Historically, more aggressive tobacco control measures, such as closing down retailers who sell cigarettes to minors without checking IDs and eliminating advertisement directed at youth (e.g., Joe Camel) have been seen as less politically feasible because the tobacco industry has extraordinary financial and political power. Therefore, arguably more effective interventions outside the schools were probably less palatable to health agencies and others responsible for tobacco control. But on August 10, 1995, President Clinton approved Food and Drug Administration (FDA) proposals that would: (a) prohibit the sale of cigarettes to minors; (b) severely limit advertising; (c) ban cigarette vending machines; (d) eliminate mail order sales and free sample promotions; and (e) require the tobacco industry to fund a $150 million per year antismoking education campaign. This action was immediately challenged in a lawsuit brought by the "Big 5" tobacco companies, and the issue currently is in the court's hands (Cimons, 1995).

At this time, a resurgence of political power among lawmakers friendly to the tobacco industry and gun lobby portend difficult times for researchers and program developers responsible for the major killers and cripplers of America's youth. The coming years promise decisive battles for school-based smoking prevention and community tobacco control.

PREVENTION

Assessment Strategies

Assessment of adolescent smoking not only emphasizes actual smoking behavior but also generally includes measures of influence variables relatively distal or proximal to onset of smoking. Some investigators also examine physical health outcomes secondary to tobacco use (see Figure 8.1).

Distal Influence Variables

Among typical measures of distal influence are physical-environmental, social-environmental, sociodemographic, and related variables. Physical-environmental variables include measures of opportunities to access tobacco, especially through stores that sell tobacco in the area near the school. Other variables in this category are the amount of media (e.g., billboards, free samples, newspaper ads), presentation of tobacco products in the communities, as well as other promotional influences.

Social-environmental measures primarily include a look at extracurricular activities that the school provides. Other extracurricular activities provided by the community (e.g., YMCA-YWCA; Boy Scouts/Girl Scouts) are included in this variable category. Sociodemographic and related variables will include measures of ethnicity, age, gender, family mean income, and parents' occupations (Arkin, Roemhild, Johnson, Luepker, & Murray, 1981; Best et al., 1984; Bonaguro, Pugh, & Bonaguro, 1986; Flay, 1985).

Proximal Influence Variables

Proximal influence variables include measures falling into the familial, peer, teacher, personal, and operant categories. These relatively salient influences include measures of parental modeling, sibling modeling, and parental attitudes toward tobacco use in the familial category. Peer variables include measures of the number of peers using tobacco (i.e., "peer modeling"), peer pressure or perceived "normative" pressure to engage in tobacco use behavior, and the normative beliefs of the subject with respect to

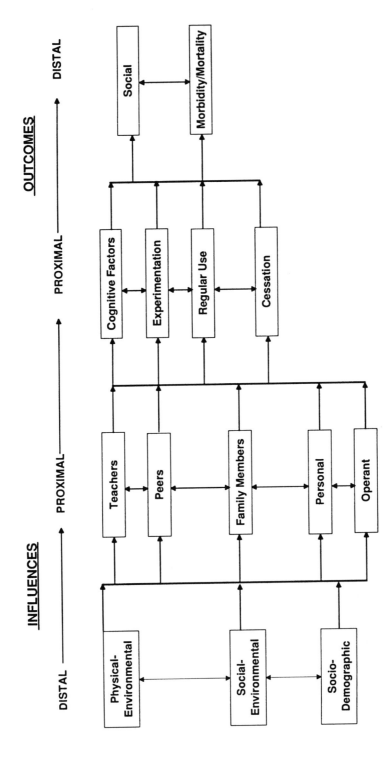

Figure 8.1. Assessment categories related to adolescent tobacco use and prevention.

the number of peers who use tobacco (Bonaguro et al., 1986; Friedman, Lichtenstein, & Biglan, 1985).

Finally, measures of actual and (student-) perceived teachers' tobacco use are often included in the assessment protocols. "Personal" variables include measures of adolescent behavior related to delinquency, aggressiveness, apathy, external locus of control, social competence (Botvin, G., Renick, & Baker, 1983; DuPont & Jason, 1984; McCaul & Glasgow, 1985; Schinke & Blythe, 1981; Schinke & Gilchrist, 1983), and stage of acquisition of tobacco use. The Stages of Change model looks at whether each student is a "precontemplator," "contemplator," "action-taker," or "maintainer" with respect to smokeless tobacco and cigarette use. Youth who have experimented with tobacco are asked at what age they did so (Stern, Prochaska, Velicer, & Elder, 1987).

Operant variables include consequences that may be material (Elder & Stern, 1986; Skinner, 1953; Sulzer-Azaroff & Mayer, 1977) or social (Bandura, 1977a; Bonaguro et al., 1986; Friedman et al., 1985; Perry & Jessor, 1985; Thoresen & Mahoney, 1974) and externally (Elder, Edelstein, & Narick, 1979; Patterson, 1971; Skinner, 1953; Sulzer-Azaroff & Mayer, 1977) or self-delivered (Bandura, 1977a, 1977b; Baranowski & Nader, 1985; Thoresen & Mahoney, 1974). These influences include a wide variety of potential "reinforcers" and "punishers," such as peer acceptance/rejection, physical gratification/revulsion, and keeping to or breaking a public commitment (Arkin et al., 1981; Carpenter, Lyons, & Miller, 1985; Elder & Stern, 1986; Flay, d'Avernas, Best, Kersell, & Ryan, 1983; Friedman et al., 1985; McCaul & Glasgow, 1985; O'Neill, Glasgow, & McCaul, 1983).

Proximal Outcome Measures (POVs)

Proximal outcome measures include both cognitive and behavioral categories. Cognitive change measures include the knowledge of various factors related to tobacco use (Botvin, A., & Eng, 1982; Botvin, A., Eng, & Williams, 1980; Botvin, G., Baker, Renick, Filazzola, & Botvin, 1984; Botvin, G. et al., 1983; Evans et al., 1981; Flay et al., 1983; McCaul & Glasgow, 1985; Perry & Jessor, 1985; Perry, Killen, Slinkard, & McAlister, 1980; Schinke & Blythe, 1981; Schinke & Gilchrist, 1983) as well as relevant attitudes (Ajzen & Fishbein, 1980; Botvin, G. et al., 1984; Henderson, 1979), beliefs (Ajzen & Fishbein, 1980; Henderson, 1979), values (Perry & Jessor, 1985), emotions (Perry & Jessor, 1985), and intentions (Ajzen & Fishbein, 1980; Evans et al., 1981; Henderson, 1979; McCaul & Glasgow, 1985; Schinke & Blythe, 1981; Schinke & Gilchrist, 1983) related to tobacco use.

The critical behavioral measure for this field is that of actual smoking and chewing tobacco and snuff use. Researchers look at a variety of behaviors (Arkin et al., 1981; Best et al., in press; Bonaguro et al., 1986; Flay, 1985; Friedman et al., 1985; Leventhal & Cleary, 1980), such as whether students initially experiment with tobacco, experiment with it on an irregular basis, regularly use tobacco, are attempting to quit, or have generalized their use to other forms of tobacco use (e.g., smokeless tobacco generalizing to cigarette use). Data on frequency, rate, duration, situational determinants, amounts, and type/brand of smokeless (as well as cigarette) tobacco use are also collected. Behavioral measures are often physiologically verified with saliva cotinine or other indices that may validate or enhance self-report through a "bogus pipeline" effect (Evans, Hansen, & Mittlemark, 1977). Murray, O'Connell, Schmid, and Perry (1987), however, have argued that such validation may be unnecessary given adequate assurances of confidentiality and anonymity.

PREVENTION APPROACHES

"Prevention" in the context of health promotion refers to any organized effort used to keep people from becoming dependent, regular tobacco users. Over the past two decades, the basic design and designated target groups of prevention efforts have changed, shifting from information-oriented prevention efforts to social skills based curricula. There has also been a developmental shift in the target groups from high school and college students to younger adolescents in junior high, middle, and elementary schools. Prevention efforts can include "educational" (emphasizing face-to-face behavior change efforts in classrooms or other group settings), media, and public policy/activism approaches. Educational approaches are the most rigorously evaluated and most commonly used prevention strategy.

Prevention programs can be placed in the context of stages of behavior change (Prochaska & Diclemente, 1983) in the acquisition of smoking (Elder & Stern, 1986; Flay et al., 1983). The stages generally can be broken down as follows:

1. Precontemplation (not even considering smoking),
2. Preparation and anticipation; contemplation (to smoke),
3. Initiation or experimentation (with smoking),
4. Action or transition (becoming a smoker), and
5. Regular smoking or maintenance (Elder & Stern, 1986; Flay et al., 1983).

Within the stages of change context, prevention involves disrupting the transition from one stage of acquisition to the next. Thus interventions attempt to deter onset of "regular smoking" by reducing the number of young adolescents who "initiate or experiment" with smoking (USDHHS, 1989). It has been shown that smoking is typically initiated or experimentation with tobacco begins in younger adolescents at about Grades 6 through 9 (Glynn, 1989). Although different influences are at play at these various ages, commonalties do exist; in particular, social influences and associated social skills that are responses to, or actually modifiers of these influences. Peers, siblings, parents, and media are sources of social influence that exert considerable pressure on adolescents to use tobacco. In many cases, young adolescents do not have the skills necessary to identify these influences and lack the knowledge and skills to resist these and other pressures to use tobacco (Flay, 1985).

Educational Approaches

Skills-based educational curricula are at the forefront of attention in tobacco control efforts (USDHHS, 1989), replacing previous traditional pedagogical approaches. These programs vary substantially in content, design, and delivery, as some emphasize social skills or resistance skills training, whereas others concentrate on clarifying misperceptions of the prevalence and consequences of tobacco use. There are, however, some common features to those programs that are effective (USDHHS, 1994). First, most assume that initiation of tobacco use results from peer pressure. Second, most prevention programs disseminate information on prevalence and short-term consequences of tobacco use. The goal of these programs is to teach adolescents the skills necessary to resist pressures to use tobacco while enhancing reinforcement for non-smoking and reducing reinforcement for smoking (Elder & Stern, 1986).

Many programs utilizing the social skills approach are hybrids of social inoculation theory (Evans, 1976; McGuire, 1964) and social learning theory (Bandura, 1977b). This theory asserts that the ability to resist smoking can be equated to the ability to resist disease. "Social inoculation" suggests that by giving individuals the tools (or "antibodies") necessary to resist social pressure (the "infection"), they will then be better able to resist pressures to use tobacco (the eventual "disease"). By inoculating adolescents against social pressures to use tobacco, development of smoking acquisition can be interrupted by preventing initiation and/or experimentation and subsequent regular use of tobacco.

School-based tobacco prevention programs in the United States have consistently had positive, although often modest, effects. Effects have been primarily in delaying initiation of regular tobacco use rather than preventing it (Biglan, Glasgos & Ary, 1987; Botvin, G., Batson & Witts-Vitale, 1989; Elder et al., 1993; Evans et al., 1978; Flay et al., 1985). The difference in prevalence between adolescents who receive the intervention program and those who do not ranges from 25% to 60% and persists from one to four years (USDHHS, 1994). Effects dissipate over time, however, particularly if intervention activities do not extend throughout the middle school, junior high, and high school years (Botvin, G. et al., 1992; Elder et al., 1993; Flay et al., 1989; Murray, Pirie, Luepker, & Pallonen, 1989; Pentz et al., 1989). This is particularly true for educational programs delivered through schools that include limited or no "boosters" (follow-up) or community or media activities, suggesting that additional efforts are needed for long-term success.

Another limitation is that social skills prevention programs have been tested almost exclusively on white, middle-class adolescents in classroom settings. Results from interventions not designed to be culturally specific indicate that broadly targeted interventions are not as effective in the ethnic minorities represented. Few psychosocial prevention curricula have been implemented or evaluated in high-risk or minority populations. Examples include Project S.H.O.U.T. (Student Helping Others Understand Tobacco) based in San Diego, California (Elder et al., 1993), and a study by Botvin conducted in New Jersey (Botvin, G. et al., 1992). Project S.H.O.U.T. works with an adolescent population that is 35% minority with a sister program in Tijuana, Mexico. The Botvin et al. (1989) program targeted urban Hispanic and black youth. These interventions used a multicultural approach. An important consideration in developing and implementing tobacco prevention programs is to show respect for cultural differences in our society and acknowledge that our communities are made up of individuals from varying ethnic, cultural, and linguistic backgrounds. To be effective, it is important for a health message to seem personally relevant to the individual receiving it. Cultural sensitivity in educational programs can be positive by including words, images, or situations that are common to the audience's daily life. Program implementers must avoid showing ignorance of or insensitivity toward the intended audience.

Effective Ingredients

Based on social skills curricula and the social inoculation approach, several sources have cited elements that are essential to the development of an effective tobacco use prevention program (Flay, 1985; Glynn, 1989; Guidelines, 1994; USDHHS, 1989).

First, prevention programs should, if at all possible, concentrate solely on tobacco use, prevention, and cessation, and be kept separate from other drug or general health issues. One concern is that tobacco control as one component of a multicomponent health education curriculum may be obscured by other health issues receiving more publicity. A few studies, however, suggest that tobacco use prevention can be effective when appropriately embedded within broader curricula for preventing drug and alcohol abuse (Hansen & Graham, 1991) or within curricula for general school health education (Walter & Wynder, 1989). An expert advisory panel convened by the National Cancer Institute concluded that school-based tobacco prevention conducted within a broad general health curricula appeared as effective as programs with an exclusive emphasis on tobacco, provided that the tobacco use component received at least five classroom sessions in each of two years between Grades 6 and 9 (Glynn, 1989). These more general health education curricula may be more attractive to schools that are already faced with many health education requirements (USDHHS, 1989).

The program should contain at least three different informational components. First, information on the immediate physiological effects of tobacco use such as bad breath, smelly clothes, and shortness of breath should be discussed. This type of information should clarify misperceptions as to the social consequences and significance of tobacco use. The goal is to make it "cool" not to smoke. Second, information on family, peer, and media influences on tobacco use and ways of recognizing them should also be provided. Once adolescents increase their awareness on this issue, they will be better able to resist these and other social influences. Third, learning of specific behavioral skills, such as refusal skills to resist offers to use tobacco, decision making, and problem-solving techniques should always be practiced using modeling and role playing.

The minimum length of the program should be one 5-session block delivered within the same year between the ages of 10 and 16 years. Ideally, intervention should begin prior to experimentation with tobacco and should continue through high school.

Finally, the target population should have the information, motivation, and skills necessary to act on this health issue. Peers, parents, teachers, and the community should be involved in prevention efforts to have an environment that is conducive to long-term change.

Media-Based Approach

Mass-media based messages and programs are included among the earliest smoking prevention efforts of federal agencies and voluntary health organizations. Much of this early programming was in response to the first Surgeon General's Report on Smoking and Health in 1964, the Fairness Doctrine Act (1967–1970), and the ban on broadcast advertising of cigarettes. For the purpose of this discussion, "mass media" is any form of communication that uses print, electronic, interpersonal, or display media. Messages range from antismoking exhortations delivered through the newspapers, television, and radio, to educational brochures and more comprehensive educational curricula that make use of media.

Early programs assumed that if health educators told people about the hazards of tobacco use, recognition of the negative consequences involved would scare them away from regular tobacco use. These health promotion campaigns were based roughly on the Health Belief model, which implies a knowledge-attitude-behavior paradigm or information deficit model. This explanatory model suggests that if people are given information about a behavior they will develop attitudes about the behavior, and those attitudes will lead to a change in their behavior.

Founded on social modeling and social support, it is postulated that behavior can be elicited through presentation of a role model who serves both as an example of, and a cue for, a desired behavior (Ramirez & McAlister, 1988). The mass media have tremendous capacity for modeling desired behaviors and can contribute to the redefining of social norms in support of prevention (e.g., making it "cool" not to smoke). Radio and television are the optimal channels, since electronic media reach the largest number of people in our society and are heavily used by all socioeconomic groups, all educational levels, and all racial/ethnic minorities (Bettinghaus, 1988). A mediating factor is that media be played at optimal viewing or listening times by target audience members.

In a 1986 review of media-based tobacco control efforts, Flay concluded that media programs alone are not effective. Instead, the most effective role of mass media in tobacco prevention is in the dissemination of other prevention resources of proven efficacy such as the social skills approaches (Flay, 1986). There have been several studies of mass-media based prevention programs (Bauman et al., 1988; Biglan et al., 1987; Flay, 1986; Ramirez & McAlister, 1988). These prevention approaches range from videotapes and paid spots, to messages delivered in different languages. These studies do not represent all that is known about general health promotion through mass media, but show how mass media can be helpful in tobacco use prevention and how to make use of communication and behavioral science theory in planning effective media materials (Bettinghaus, 1988).

Perhaps educational and media approaches to smoking prevention are guilty of a common fault: They place the onus of responsibility for resisting tobacco on the young nonsmoker. Social activism and policy enactment, in contrast, look first at what communities and the society as a whole should do to protect vulnerable youth.

Activism and Policy

Social activism can be viewed as one approach to organizing a community's tobacco control activities. Although there are several models of activism, the social action model implies grass roots participation by the entire community. The goal of social action is to make basic changes in community practices or norms (Rothman, 1979). Within the realm of social action, members of the community become activists and advocates who take direct action against a specific target—in this case, the marketing of tobacco.

Many communities are currently involved in activism projects aimed at changing community acceptance of tobacco use and tobacco promotion. This type of community-oriented activism can produce changes at both the individual and community level. Promoting behavior change on a community level can produce the type of environmental changes necessary to sustain a permanent reduction in tobacco use in a particular community. Although there have been few formal evaluations of social activism efforts, the few that have been evaluated have shown promising results.

Merchant education is a social action tool that has recently received national attention as an effective method for changing the practices of the retail industry. Merchant education has two purposes: first, to educate merchants regarding the laws restricting the sale of tobacco products to minors, and second, to reduce adolescent tobacco use by restricting access to tobacco. Merchants work with families and individuals in the community to counteract tobacco industry efforts to encourage adolescent tobacco use. In California, the Altman project in Santa Clara (Stop Teenage Addiction to Tobacco [STAT], 1992) and San Diego State University's Merchant Education program (Erickson et al., 1993), use adolescents who have the permission of both their parents and law enforcement officials to purchase tobacco at stores in an effort to identify stores not in compliance with the law. Stores that sell tobacco to these minors are then targeted for an educational and training effort directed at the store managers and clerks. In Santa Clara, stores selling tobacco to minors decreased by 34% following a community-wide merchant education effort (STAT, 1992). In San Diego, illegal sales to minors decreased almost 50% (Kaey, Woodruff, Wildey, & Kenney, 1993).

SUMMARY

From the early reports linking smoking and cancer over 40 years ago, to the release of the Surgeon General's report in 1964, to the increased popularity of the social inoculation model and school-based health promotion of the past two decades, efforts to keep teens from smoking have received increasing attention. In each successive iteration of prevention programs, the onus of resistance to the mounting pressures to smoke has been more squarely placed on the shoulders of 13-year-olds. The Health Belief model and theory of reasoned action deal extensively with how the individual *thinks* and how that impacts behavior, the implication being that altering perceptions of the social environment should constitute a major building block for a full repertoire of adaptive behaviors. Social learning theory, initially somewhat more environmentally focused, has been supplanted by the more intrapersonal social cognitive theory. At the cognitive extreme, the Stages of Change model essentially has virtually no reference to the environment, whereas applied behavior analysis, the most environmentally focused of relevant theories, still stresses *individual* behavior-consequence relationships.

Assessment of adolescent smoking emphasizes cognition in the context of one or more of the preceding theories, specific self-reported behaviors, and physiological validation of these reports. What the adolescent does, thinks, and secretes has been of paramount importance in virtually all research into the effectiveness of prevention efforts. Only recently has measurement expertise moved to the convenience store, vending machine, billboard, and other community locations and away from the individual.

In American culture, children learn much of their responsibilities and role behaviors in the schools. To these behaviors, health promoters and educators have added the importance of not smoking or using other drugs. Naturally, most smoking prevention programs have gravitated to the school as the ideal venue for accomplishing their mission. Yet school systems are being swamped with challenges from contentious school boards, voucher initiatives, and campus crime and are being held accountable for weak student performance on standardized tests. In the face of these issues, even if prevention programs were truly proven effective, administrators and teachers might question the priority of investing considerable time and resources in teaching students to avoid the use of a legal substance.

Although social activism and policy interventions hold the greatest promise for taking on the adolescent smoking problem, national efforts of this genre have only begun to take shape. Perhaps the best evidence how relatively more threatening vending machine and advertising control are to leaders in the tobacco industry is their willingness to support new standard school-based prevention efforts in tandem with an all-out attack against the more aggressive controls.

In the meantime, teen smoking rates continue to rise (Johnston, 1995).

REFERENCES

Ajzen, I., & Fishbein, M. (1980). *Understanding attitudes and predicting social behaviors.* Englewood Cliffs, NJ: Prentice-Hall.

Arkin, R. M., Roemhild, H. F., Johnson, C. A., Luepker, R. V., & Murray, D. M. (1981). The Minnesota smoking prevention program: A seventh grade health curriculum supplement. *Journal of School Health, 51*(9), 611–616.

Bandura, A. (1977a). Self-efficacy: Toward a unified theory of behavioral change. *Psychology Review, 84,* 191–215.

Bandura, A. (1977b). *Social learning theory.* Englewood Cliffs, NJ: Prentice-Hall.

Bandura, A. (1995). *Self-efficacy in changing societies.* Cambridge, England: Cambridge University Press.

Baranowski, T., & Nader, P. (1985). Family behavior. In D. C. Turk & R. D. Kerns (Eds.), *Health, illness, and families* (pp. 51–80). New York: Wiley.

Bauman, K. E., Brown, J. D., Bryan E. S., Fisher, L. A., Padgett, C. A., & Sweeney, J. M. (1988). Three mass media campaigns to prevent adolescent cigarette smoking. *Preventive Medicine, 17,* 510–533.

Becker, M. (1979). Psychosocial aspects of health-related behavior. In H. E. Freeman et al. (Ed.), *Handbook of medical sociology.* Englewood Cliffs, NJ: Prentice-Hall.

Best, J. A., Flay, B. R., Towson, S. M. J., Ryan, K. B., Perry, C. L., Brown, K. S., Kersell, M. W., & d'Avernas, J. R. (1984). Smoking prevention and the concept of risk. *Journal of Applied Social Psychology, 14*(3), 257–273.

Bettes, B. A., Dusenbury, L., Kerner, J., James-Ortiz, S., & Botvin, G. J. (1990). Ethnicity and psychosocial factors in alcohol and tobacco use in adolescence. *Child Development, 61,* 557–565.

Bettinghaus, E. P. (1988). Forum: A mass media campaign. *Preventive Medicine, 17,* 503–509.

Biglan, A., Glasgos, R., & Ary, D. (1987). How generalizable are the effects of smoking prevention programs? Refusal skills training and parent messages in a teacher administered program. *Journal of Behavioral Medicine, 10,* 613–628.

Bonaguro, J., Pugh, M., & Bonaguro, E. (1986). Multivariate analysis of smokeless tobacco use by adolescents in grades four through twelve. *Health Education, 17*(2), 4–7.

Botvin, A., & Eng, A. (1982). The efficacy of a multicomponent approach to the prevention of cigarette smoking. *Preventive Medicine, 11,* 199–211.

Botvin, A., Eng, A., & Williams, C. L. (1980). Preventing the onset of cigarette smoking through life-skills training. *Preventive Medicine, 9,* 135–143.

Botvin, G., Baker, E., Renick, N., Filazzola, A. D., & Botvin, E. M. (1984). A cognitive-behavioral approach to substance abuse prevention. *Addictive Behaviors, 9,* 137–148.

Botvin, G., Batson, H. W., & Witts-Vitale, S. (1989). A psychosocial approach to smoking prevention for urban black youth. *Public Health Reports, 104,* 573–582.

Botvin, G., Dusenbury, L., Baker, E., James-Ortiz, S., Botvin, E. M., & Kerner, J. (1992). Smoking prevention among urban minority youth: Assessing effects on outcome and mediating variables. *Health Psychology, 11*(5), 290–299.

Botvin, G., Renick, N. L., & Baker, E. (1983). The effects of scheduling format and booster sessions on a broad-spectrum psychosocial approach to smoking prevention. *Journal of Behavioral Medicine, 6,* 359–379.

Bush, P. J., & Iannotti, R. J. (1992). Elementary schoolchildren's use of alcohol, cigarettes, and marijuana and classmates attribution to socialization. *Drug and Alcohol Dependence, 30,* 275–287.

Carpenter, R., Lyons, C., & Miller, W. (1985). Peer-managed self-control program for prevention of alcohol abuse in American Indian high school students. *International Journal of Addictions, 20,* 299–310.

Centers for Disease Control, USDHHS, Public Health Service. (1993). Cigarette smoking-attributable mortality and years of potential life lost—United States, 1990. *Morbidity & Mortality Weekly Report, 42*(33), 645–649.

Centers for Disease Control, USDHHS, Public Health Service. (1994a, February). Guidelines for school health programs to prevent tobacco use and addiction. *Morbidity & Mortality Weekly Report, 43*(RR-2), 1–15.

Centers for Disease Control, USDHHS, Public Health Service. (1994b, July). Medical-care expenditures attributable to cigarette smoking—United States, 1993. *Morbidity & Mortality Weekly Report, 43*(26), 470–472.

Centers for Disease Control, USDHHS, Public Health Service. (1994c, March). Preventing tobacco use among young people. A report of the Surgeon General. *Morbidity & Mortality Weekly Report, 43*(RR-4), 1–10.

Centers for Disease Control, USDHHS, Public Health Service. (1994d, October). Reasons for tobacco use and symptoms of cigarette withdrawal among adolescent and young adult tobacco users—United States, 1993. *Morbidity & Mortality Weekly Report, 43*(41), 746–750.

Centers for Disease Control, USDHHS, Public Health Service. (1994e, June). Surveillance for smoking-attributable mortality and years of potential life lost, by state—United States, 1990. *Morbidity & Mortality Weekly Report, 44*(SS-1), 1–8.

Cimons, M. (1995, August 12). Legal battle looms over rules to curb teen smoking. *Los Angeles Times*, p. 24.

Collins, L. J., Sussman, S., Rauch, M. J., Dent, C. W., Johnson, C. J., Hansen, W. B., & Flay, B. R. (1987). Psychosocial predictors of young adolescent cigarette smoking: A sixteen-month, three-wave longitudinal study. *Journal of Applied Social Psychology, 17*(6), 554–573.

de Moor, C., Elder, J. P., Young, R. L., Wildey, M. B., & Molgaard, C. A. (1989). Generic tobacco use among four ethnic groups in a school age population. *Journal of Drug Education, 19*(3), 257–270.

de Moor, C., Johnston, D. A., Werden, D. L., Elder, J. P., Senn, K., & Whitehorse, L. (1994). Patterns and correlates of smoking and smokeless tobacco use among continuation high school students. *Addictive Behaviors, 19*(2), 175–184.

Di Franza, J. R., Richards, J. W., Jr., Paulman, P. M., Wolf-Gillespie, N., Fletcher, C., Jaffe, R. D., & Murray, D. (1991). RJR Nabisco's cartoon camel promotes Camel cigarettes to children. *Journal of the American Medical Association, 266*(22), 3149–3153.

Doll, R., & Hill, A. B. (1964). Mortality in relation to smoking: Ten years' observations of British doctors. *British Medical Journal, 1,* 1399–1410, 1460–1462.

Doll, R., & Peto, R. (1976). Mortality in relation to smoking: 20 years' observation on male British doctors. *British Medical Journal, 2,* 1525–1536.

DuPont, P., & Jason, L. (1984). Assertiveness training in a preventive drug education program. *Journal of Drug Education, 14,* 369–378.

Eckert, P. (1983). Beyond the statistics of adolescent smoking. *American Journal of Public Health, 13,* 446–461.

Eckhardt, L., Woodruff, S., & Elder, J. P. (1994). A longitudinal analysis of adolescent smoking and its correlates. *Journal of School Health, 64*(2), 67–72.

Elder, J. P., Amick, T., Sleet, D., & Senn, K. (1987). Potential consumer participation in a boycott of tobacco company-owned nontobacco products. *American Journal of Preventive Medicine, 3*(6), 323–326.

Elder, J. P., Atkins, C., de Moor, C., Edwards, C. C., Golbeck, A., Hovell, M. F., Nader, P. R., Sallis, J. F., Shulkin, J. J., Sleet, D. A., Wildey, M. B., Young, R. L., & Wendt, G. (1989). Prevention of tobacco use among adolescents in public schools in San Diego County, U.S.A. *Soz Praeventimed, 34,* 24–29.

Elder, J. P., Edelstein, B. A., & Narick, M. N. (1979). Adolescent psychiatric patients: Modifying aggressive behavior with social skills training. *Behavior Modification, 3*(2), 161–178.

Elder, J. P., & Stern, R. A. (1986). The ABCs of adolescent smoking prevention: An environment and skills model. *Health Education Quarterly, 13,* 181–191.

Elder, J. P., Wildey, M., de Moor, C., Sallis, J., Eckhardt, L., & Edwards, C. (1993). Long-term prevention of tobacco use among junior high school students through classroom telephone interventions. *American Journal of Public Health, 83*(9), 1239–1244.

Erickson, A. D., Woodruff, S. I., Wildey, M. B., & Kenney, E. (1993). A baseline assessment of cigarette sales to minors in San Diego, California. *Journal of Community Health, 18*(4), 213–224.

Evans, R. I. (1976). Smoking in children: Developing a social psychological strategy of deterrence. *Journal of Preventive Medicine, 5,* 122–127.

Evans, R. I., Hansen, W., & Mittlemark, M. (1977). Increasing the validity of self-reports of smoking behavior in children. *Journal of Applied Psychology, 62*(4), 521–523.

Evans, R. I., Rozelle, R. M., Maxwell, S. E., Raines, B. E., Dill, C. A., Guthrie, T. J., Henderson, A. H., & Hill, P. C. (1981). Social modeling films to deter smoking in adolescents: Results of a three-year field investigation. *Journal of Applied Psychology, 66*(4), 399–414.

Evans, R. I., Rozelle, R. M., Mittlemark, M. B., Hansen, W. B., Bane, A. L., & Havis, J. (1978). Deterring the onset of smoking in children: Knowledge of immediate physiological effects and coping with peer pressure, and parent modeling. *Journal of Applied Social Psychology, 8*(2), 126–135.

Flay, B. R. (1985). Psychosocial approaches to smoking prevention: A review of findings. *Health Psychology, 4,* 449–488.

Flay, B. R. (1986). Mass media linkages with school-based programs for drug abuse prevention. *Journal of School Health, 56,* 402–406.

Flay, B. R., d'Avernas, J. R., Best, J. A., Kersell, M. W., & Ryan, K. B. (1983). Cigarette smoking: Why young people do it and ways of preventing it. In P. J. McGrath & P. Firestone (Eds.), *Pediatric and adolescent behavioral medicine: Issues in treatment* (pp. 132–183). New York: Springer.

Flay, B. R., Koepke, D., Thomson, S. J., Santi, S., Best, J. A., & Brown, K. S. (1989). Six year follow-up of the first Waterloo school smoking prevention trial. *American Journal of Public Health, 79*(10), 1371–1376.

Flay, B. R., Ryan, K. B., Best, J. A., Brown, K. S., Kersell, M. W., d'Avernas, J. R., & Zanna, M. P. (1985). Are social psychological smoking prevention programs effective?: The Waterloo Study. *Journal of Behavioral Medicine, 8*(1), 37–59.

Friedman, L., Lichtenstein, E., & Biglan, A. (1985). Smoking onset among teens: An empirical analysis of situations. *Addictive Behaviors, 10,* 1–13.

Glynn, T. J. (1989). Essential elements of school-based smoking prevention programs. *Journal of School Health, 59,* 181–188.

Guidelines for school health programs to prevent tobacco use and addiction. (1994). *Journal of School Health, 64*(9), 353–360.

Hansen, W. B., & Graham, J. W. (1991). Preventing alcohol, marijuana, and cigarette use among adolescents: Peer pressure resistance training verses establishing conservative norms. *Preventive Medicine, 20,* 414–430.

Headen, S. W., Bauman, K. E., Deane, G. D., & Koch, G. G. (1991). Are the correlates of cigarette smoking initiation different for black and white adolescents? *American Journal of Public Health, 81*(7), 854–857.

Henderson, A. H. (1979). *Examination of a multivariate social-psychological model of adolescent smoking decisions and of the impact on antismoking messages.* Unpublished doctoral dissertation, University of Houston.

Iannotti, J. R., & Bush, P. J. (1992). Perceived versus actual use of alcohol, cigarettes, marijuana, and cocaine: Which has the most influence? *Journal of Youth and Adolescents, 21*(3), 375–389.

Johnston, L. (1995). *Monitoring the future survey.* Ann Arbor: University of Michigan.

Kaey, K. D., Woodruff, S. I., Wildey, M. B., & Kenney, E. M. (1993). Effect of a retailer intervention on cigarette sales to minors in San Diego County, California. *Tobacco Control, 2,* 145–151.

Kaplan, M. R., Sallis, J. F., Jr., & Patterson, T. L. (1993). *Health and human behavior.* New York: McGraw-Hill.

Karle, H., Shennasa, E., Edwards, C., Werden, D., Elder, J., & Whitehorse, L. (1994). Tobacco control for high-risk youth: Tracking and evaluation issues. *Family Community Health, 16*(4), 10–17.

Klesges, R. C., & Robinson, L. A. (1995). Predictors of smoking onset in adolescent African-American boys and girls. *Journal of Health Education, 26*(2), 85–91.

Leventhal, H., & Cleary, P. D. (1980). The smoking problem: A review of the research and theory in behavioral risk modification. *Psychological Bulletin, 88,* 370–405.

McCaul, K., & Glasgow, R. (1985). Preventing adolescent smoking: What have we learned about treatment construct validity? *Health Psychology, 4*(4), 361–388.

McGee, R., & Stanton, W. R. (1993). A longitudinal study of reasons for smoking in adolescence. *Addiction, 88,* 265–271.

McGuire, W. J. (1964). Inducing resistance to persuasion. *Advances in Experimental Social Psychology, 1,* 191–229.

Meyers, M. G., & Brown, S. A. (1994). Smoking and health in substance-abusing adolescents: A two-year follow-up. *Pediatrics, 93,* 561–566.

Minorities and tobacco. (1994, May). *American Association of World Health.*

Moreno, C., Laniado-Laborin, R., Sallis, J. F., Elder, J. P., de Moor, C., & Deosaransingh, K. (1994). Parental influences to smoke in Latino youth. *Preventive Medicine, 23,* 48–53.

Murray, D., O'Connell, C., Schmid, L., & Perry, C. (1987). The validity of smoking self-reports by adolescents: A reexamination of the bogus pipeline procedure. *Addictive Behaviors, 12,* 7–15.

Murray, D., Pirie, P., Luepker, R. V., & Pallonen, U. (1989). Five- and six-year follow-up results from four seventh grade smoking prevention strategies. *Journal of Behavioral Medicine, 12*(2), 207–218.

Newman, M. I. (1984). Capturing the energy of peer pressure: Insights from a longitudinal study of adolescent cigarette smoking. *Journal of School Health, 61,* 557–565.

O'Neill, H. K., Glasgow, R. E., & McCaul, K. D. (1983). Component analysis in smoking prevention research: Effects of social consequences information. *Addictive Behaviors, 8,* 419–423.

Patterson, G. (1971). *Families: Applications of social learning to family life.* Champaign, IL: Research Press.

Pentz, M., MacKinnon, D. P., Dwyer, J. H., Wang, E. Y. I., Hansen, W. B., & Flay, B. R. (1989). Longitudinal effects of the Midwestern prevention project on regular and experimental smoking in adolescents. *Preventive Medicine, 18*(2), 304–321.

Perry, C., & Jessor, R. (1985). The concept of health promotion and the prevention of adolescent drug use. *Health Education Quarterly,* 169–184.

Perry, C. L., Killen, J., Slinkard, L. A., & McAlister, A. L. (1980). Peer teaching and smoking prevention among junior high students. *Adolescence, 15,* 277–281.

Pierce, J. P., Gilpin, E., Burns, D. M., Whalen, E., Rosbrook, B., Shopland, D., & Johnson, M. (1991). Does tobacco advertising target young people to start smoking? *Journal of the American Medical Association, 226*(22), 3154, 3158.

Prochaska, J. O., & DiClemente, C. C. (1983). Stages and processes of self-change of smoking: Toward an integrative model of change. *Journal of Consulting and Clinical Psychology, 51,* 390–395.

Ramirez, A. G., & McAlister, A. L. (1988). Mass media campaign—A Su Salud. *Preventative Medicine, 17,* 608–621.

Rothman, J. (1979). Three models of community organization. In F. J. Cox et al. (Eds.), *Strategies of community organization* (3rd ed.). Itasca, IL: Peacock.

Sabogal, F., Otero-Sabogal, R., Perez-Stable, E. J., Marin, V. B., & Marin, G. (1989). Perceived self-efficacy to avoid smoking and addiction: Differences between Hispanics and non-Hispanic whites. *Hispanic Journal of Behavioral Sciences, 11*(22), 136–147.

Sallis, J. F., Deosaransingh, K., Woodruff, S. I., Vargas, R., Laniado-Laborin, R., Moreno, C., & Elder, J. P. (1994). Parental prompting of smoking among adolescents in Tijuana, Mexico. *International Journal of Behavioral Medicine, 1*(2), 122–136.

Salomon, G., Stein, Y., Eisenberg, S., & Klein, L. (1984). Adolescent smokers and nonsmokers: Profiles and their changing structures. *Preventive Medicine, 13,* 446–461.

Schinke, S. P., & Blythe, B. J. (1981). Cognitive-behavioral prevention of children's smoking. *Child Behavior Therapy, 3*(4), 25–42.

Schinke, S. P., & Gilchrist, L. D. (1983). Primary prevention of tobacco smoking. *Journal of School Health, 53,* 416–419.

Skinner, B. (1953). *Science and human behavior.* New York: Macmillan.

Stern, R., Prochaska, J., Velicer, W., & Elder, J. (1987). Stages of adolescent cigarette smoking acquisition: Measurement and sample profiles. *Addictive Behaviors, 12,* 319–329.

Stop teenage addiction to tobacco: Results of Teen Tobacco Purchase Survey. (1992). Unpublished data. San Jose, CA: Standford Center for Research in Disease Prevention.

Sulzer-Azaroff, B., & Mayer, E. (1977). *Applied behavior analysis procedures with children and youth.* New York: Holt, Rinehart and Winston.

Sussman, S., Dent, C. W., Burton, D., Stacy, A. W., & Flay, B. R. (1995). *Developing school-based tobacco use prevention and cessation programs.* Thousand Oaks, CA: Sage.

Sussman, S., Dent, C. W., Flay, B. R., Hansen, W. B., & Johnson, C. A. (1987). Psychosocial predictors of smoking onset by white, black, Hispanic, and Asian adolescents in Southern California. *Morbidity & Mortality Weekly Report, 36*(Suppl.), 11S–16S.

Sussman, S., Dent, C. W., Mestel-Rauch, J., Johnson, C. A., Hansen, W. B., & Flay, B. R. (1988). Adolescent nonsmokers, triers, and regular smokers' estimates of cigarette smoking prevalence: When do overestimations occur and by whom? *Journal of Applied Social Psychology, 18*(7), 537–551.

Thoresen, C., & Mahoney, M. (1974). *Behavioral self-control.* New York: Holt, Rinehart and Winston.

Tobacco on Trial. (1990, December). Boston: Tobacco Control Resource Center.

U.S. Department of Health and Human Services. (1989). *Reducing the health consequences of smoking: 25 years of progress. A report of the Surgeon General* (DHHS Publication No. CDC 89-8411). Washington, DC: Author.

U.S. Department of Health and Human Services. (1994). *Preventing tobacco use among young people: A report of the Surgeon General.* Washington, DC: Author.

U.S. Public Health Service. (1964). *The consequences of smoking. Report of the Advisory Committee to the Surgeon General of the Public Health Service* (PHS Publication No. 1103). Washington, DC: U.S. Department of Health Education and Welfare, Public Health Service, Centers for Disease Control.

Walter, H. J., & Wynder, E. L. (1989). The development, implementation, evaluation, and future directions of a chronic disease prevention program for children: The Know Your Body studies. *Preventive Medicine, 18,* 59–71.

CHAPTER 9

Substance Use and Abuse

J. DAVID HAWKINS, RICHARD KOSTERMAN, EUGENE MAGUIN,
RICHARD F. CATALANO, and MICHAEL W. ARTHUR

DESCRIPTION OF THE PROBLEM

The use, misuse, and abuse of psychoactive substances by children and adolescents poses important and difficult problems for our society. Among other problems, substance use increases risk for motor vehicle accidents (Perrine, Peck, & Fell, 1988), suicide (Berman & Schwartz, 1990), violence (Miczek et al., 1994), and pregnancy and high-risk sexual behavior (Leigh & Stall, 1993).

Since the late 1970s, important gains have been made in reducing the prevalence of use and misuse of substances among adolescents and adults. For example, from 1979 to 1993 the number of Americans using illicit drugs declined 50%, from 24.3 million to 11.7 million (Substance Abuse and Mental Health Services Administration, 1994). From 1984 to 1994, the proportion of alcohol-related traffic fatalities declined from 43% to 33% (National Highway Traffic Safety Administration, 1994). Yet, trends such as increases in the prevalence of alcohol, tobacco, and marijuana use among secondary school students in the United States since 1992 (Johnston, O'Malley, & Bachman, 1995), continuing increases in arrests for drug-related offenses, and continuing increases in drug treatment program admissions and emergency room visits for drug-related crises (Center for Substance Abuse Research, 1996) have revitalized national concern and the debate about how to combat substance abuse (Hawkins, Arthur, & Catalano, 1995).

This chapter focuses on prevention of substance misuse, abuse, and dependence disorders before they emerge. It does not discuss intervention or treatment of individuals diagnosed as having a substance abuse or dependence disorder or responses to alcohol misuse. The chapter summarizes recent trends in prevalence of substance use and abuse among children and adolescents. Next, approaches to the prevention of substance misuse, abuse, and disorders are surveyed. Using a risk and protective factor focused approach to substance abuse prevention, predictors of substance abuse identified in prospective longitudinal studies are examined as potential foci for preventive interventions. Prevention approaches that have shown efficacy in reducing risks and enhancing protective factors against substance abuse are reviewed. Finally, challenges and directions for implementing effective preventive interventions in real world settings are discussed.

Currently, in the United States over 80% of high school seniors have consumed alcohol (Johnston et al., 1995). In this respect, substance use is nearly universal in this society by late adolescence, well before it is legal. There are a number of psychoactive substances with potential for abuse with different pharmacological properties (Julien, 1981; Siegel, 1989). There is evidence that adolescents initiate use of these substances in a sequence typically beginning with alcohol or tobacco, and proceeding through a period of alcohol use before progressing to the use of marijuana. Marijuana use typically occurs before progressing to the use of other illegal drugs (Abbott et al., 1994; Kandel, Kessler, & Margulies, 1978). This sequence of drug use initiation reflects the normative perception of the social acceptability of these different substances rather than their specific pharmacological properties. In fact, as tobacco use has become less socially acceptable among American teens, it has dropped from the sequence of "gateway drugs" in some samples (Abbott et al., 1994). However, individuals who use cocaine, crack, opiates like heroin, or other illegal drugs usually began their drug experiences with alcohol, or in some cases, tobacco and alcohol. Use of alcohol in moderation by adults in this society is socially acceptable and legal. But an early initiation of the use of alcohol during childhood or adolescence increases risk for later problems related to substance use (Hawkins, Graham, Maguin, Abbott, & Catalano, in press).

When substance use becomes substance misuse, it is a problem of concern to health and mental health professionals. Substance misuse is such that it causes harm to self or others. Such harm may follow a single event of excessive use or result from prolonged use over a period of years. The misuse of substances has been associated with motor vehicle accidents (Perrine et al., 1988); with increased suicide risk (Berman & Schwartz, 1990; U.S. Department of Health and Human Services, 1992); with consensual sexual behavior resulting in unwanted or unplanned pregnancies or high risk of HIV infection (Chaiken & Chaiken, 1990; Leigh & Stall, 1993; Schroeder, 1993); and with increased involvement in interpersonal violence and crime (Campbell & Gibbs, 1986; Center for Substance Abuse Prevention, 1993; Fagan & Browne, 1994; Haberman & Baden, 1974; Ladecour & Temple, 1985; Miczek et al., 1994). Alcohol misuse is associated with child abuse, husband-to-wife marital violence, (including domestic homicide), and sexual assault (Campbell & Gibbs, 1986; Fagan & Browne, 1994; Haberman & Baden, 1974; Ladecour & Temple, 1985).

Continued use of substances during adolescence has been found to negatively affect educational performance and attainment. Newcomb, Maddahian, and Bentler (1986) found that use of cigarettes and hard drugs was associated with dropping out of high school, even after controlling for prior achievement, and that high scores on a composite measure of substance use predicted less college involvement after controlling for academic potential, conformity, and income.

Substance use has also been linked with increased job instability (Bachman, O'Malley, & Johnston, 1978; Kandel, Davies, Karus, & Yamaguchi, 1986; Kandel & Yamaguchi, 1987; Newcomb & Bentler, 1988), though effects on job performance may vary with specific substances involved and groups studied. White, Aidala, and Zablocki (1988) found that quantity-frequency, duration, and recency of marijuana use were not related to work, livelihood, or social functioning measures in a sample of well-educated, white, former residents of communes.

Although comorbidity of substance use and psychiatric disorders is often encountered clinically, the research evidence is mixed as to the role of substance use in this relationship. Newcomb and Bentler (1988) found that substance use had a direct effect on a psychoticism measure but not on measures of depression, suicidal ideation, and generalized emotional distress. Kandel et al. (1986) also found no relationship between substance use and depression. However, Johnson and Kaplan (1990) reported that longer periods of daily substance use were associated with increased anxiety and depression, especially for females in their panel.

When substance use becomes abuse or dependence, it is itself a diagnosable psychiatric disorder. Substance abuse is recurrent use of one or more substances resulting in a failure to fulfill major role obligations at work, school, or home; use in physically hazardous situations; use related to legal problems; or use causing or exacerbating persistent social or interpersonal problems. Substance dependence criteria include increased tolerance; withdrawal symptoms; quantity of use exceeding intentions; unsuccessful efforts to cut down use; excessive time spent obtaining, using, or recovering from the substance; interference with other important activities; and continued use despite knowledge of a problem related to the substance (*Diagnostic and Statistical Manual of Mental Disorders [DSM-IV]*, American Psychiatric Association, 1994, pp. 181–183).

It is important to note that the majority of alcohol-related problems in the United States involve individuals who are not dependent or addicted but who misuse alcohol by drinking to excess on some occasions (Institute of Medicine [IOM], 1990).

The ultimate goal of substance abuse prevention efforts is to reduce the prevalence of substance misuse, abuse, and dependence. Though the latter problems are typically manifested first in late adolescence and adulthood, substance use often begins in childhood or early adolescence, and misuse and abuse are observable in adolescent populations.

SCOPE OF THE PROBLEM

The best epidemiological data on prevalence of substance use and misuse among adolescents in the United States come from the Monitoring the Future Study (MTF) conducted by Drs. Lloyd Johnston, Patrick O'Malley, and Gerald Bachman (1995) at the University of Michigan. They have surveyed representative samples of high school seniors in the United States annually since 1975 with funding from the National Institute on Drug Abuse. Representative samples of 8th- and 10th-grade students attending public or private high schools in the continental United States excluding Alaska also have been surveyed annually since 1991 (Johnston et al., 1995). Table 9.1 shows the prevalence of use of illegal drugs in the lifetime, in the past year, and the past 30 days, excluding alcohol use, for 8th-, 10th-, and 12th-grade students in the United States in 1995. Separate estimates are provided for illegal drug use excluding marijuana and cocaine and for alcohol use and having been drunk.

In addition to current prevalence estimates, the MTF provides evidence of changes in substance use among successive cohorts of 12th-grade students. From 1975 to 1995, the lifetime prevalence of alcohol use has remained relatively constant among high school seniors. It increased slightly from 90.4% to 93.2% by 1980 and then decreased gradually to 87.0% in 1993. It appears to have remained relatively constant since that time, although a change in measurement to exclude those who have had only a few sips of alcohol puts the MTF lifetime prevalence among high school seniors in 1995 at 80.7%. Lifetime marijuana use prevalence rose from 47.3% in 1975 to a peak of 60.4% in 1979, fell uninterruptedly to 32.6% in 1992, and then rose continuously to 41.7% in 1995. The prevalence of lifetime cocaine use among high school seniors rose from

Table 9.1   Lifetime, 12-Month, and 30-Day Prevalence of Substance Use among U.S. Students in 1995

Drug Category	Grade		
	8	10	12
Lifetime Prevalence			
Any illicit drug, excluding . . .			
. . . alcohol	38.1%	45.9%	51.5%
. . . marijuana	19.9	34.1	41.7
. . . cocaine	4.2	5.0	6.0
Alcohol, any use	54.5	70.5	80.7
Alcohol, been drunk	25.3	46.9	63.2
12-Month Prevalence			
Any illicit drug, excluding . . .			
. . . alcohol	27.1	35.6	40.2
. . . marijuana	15.8	28.7	34.7
. . . cocaine	2.6	3.5	4.0
Alcohol, any use	45.3	63.5	73.7
Alcohol, been drunk	18.4	38.5	52.5
30-Day Prevalence			
Any illicit drug, excluding . . .			
. . . alcohol	16.1	21.6	24.8
. . . marijuana	9.1	17.2	21.2
. . . cocaine	1.2	1.7	1.8
Alcohol, any use	24.6	38.8	51.3
Alcohol, been drunk	8.3	20.8	33.2
Alcohol, 5+ drinks in past 2 weeks	14.5	24.0	29.8

Note. From Monitoring the Future. Johnston, O'Malley, & Bachman (1995).

9.0% in 1976 to a high of 17.3% in 1985, fell, uninterruptedly, to its 1994 value of 5.9% before increasing slightly to 6.0% in 1995.

Generally, the annual, past 30-day, and daily use prevalences of marijuana, cocaine, tobacco and alcohol show similar patterns—a prolonged uninterrupted decline in the late 1980s and early 1990s, followed by a recent rise in the prevalence of use. Figure 9.1 shows the changing prevalence of substance use in the past 30 days among high school seniors in the United States since 1975.

The Monitoring the Future survey data also reveal evidence of substance misuse among adolescents. Over 33% of 12th graders and over 20% of 10th graders report having been drunk in the past month.

Data on the prevalence of substance abuse and dependence among adolescents in the United States have only recently begun to be reported. Lewinsohn, Hops, Roberts, Seely, and Andrews (1993) reported prevalence of substance abuse or dependence for a sample 1,710 students in 9th to 12th grade attending schools in two urban metropolitan areas and three rural areas of Oregon. They found a lifetime prevalence of 8.3% for all substance use disorders at initial assessment and a lifetime prevalence of 10.8% at the 1-year follow-up. Lifetime prevalence of substance disorders was 4.6% for alcohol and 6.3% for all other drugs at initial assessment and 6.2% for alcohol and 8.2% for other drugs at follow-up.

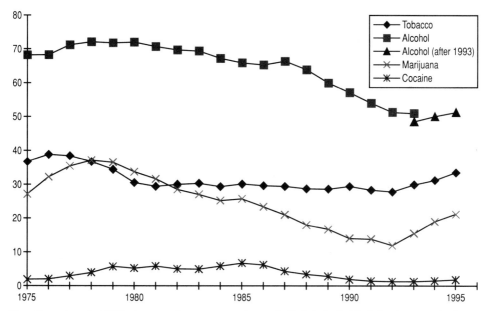

For all grades: In 1993, the question text was changed slightly in half of the forms to indicate that a "drink" meant "more than a few sips." The data in the upper line for alcohol came from forms using the original wording, while the data in the lower line came from forms using the revised wording. In 1993, each line of data was based on one of two forms for the 8th and 10th graders and on three of six forms for the 12th graders. N is one-half of N indicated for all groups. Data for 1994–1995 were based on all forms for all grades.

Figure 9.1. Trends in high school senior monthly use. *Sources:* Johnston, O'Malley, and Bachman (1991); Johnston, Bachman, and O'Malley (1993); and Johnston, O'Malley, and Bachman (1995).

The National Comorbidity Survey (Kessler et al., 1994), provided nationally representative data showing that lifetime prevalence of drug dependence excluding alcohol dependence among 15- to 24-year-olds was 9.1% for males and 5.5% for females. Prevalence of drug dependence in the past 12 months, excluding alcohol dependence, for the same age group was 4.5% for males and 2.1% for females. By early adulthood, substantial numbers of individuals in the United States have experienced drug abuse problems. Substantially larger proportions have misused substances. Interestingly, the probability of exhibiting abuse or dependence disorders for drugs other than alcohol 90% is higher than for alcohol (8.2% for other drugs vs. 6.2% for alcohol), even though the prevalence of alcohol use (80.7% lifetime prevalence in the MTF surveys) is much greater than is the prevalence of use of all other substances excluding alcohol (51.5% lifetime prevalence).

Consistent research evidence has emerged that an early age of initiation of substance use is an important predictor of later problems, such as abuse and dependence (Hawkins et al., 1995; Hawkins, Catalano, & Miller, 1992; Kandel, Simcha-Fagan, & Davies, 1986; Robins, 1992; Robins & Przybeck, 1985). Recent analyses have suggested that predictors of alcohol misuse operate indirectly, by affecting the age at which young people begin drinking alcohol. The same study found a strong direct effect of the age of alcohol initiation on alcohol misuse at age 18, with an earlier age of alcohol use initiation predicting greater alcohol misuse (Hawkins, Graham, et al., in press). These data suggest that delaying age of alcohol use initiation could prevent alcohol misuse by age 18. If efforts are to succeed in delaying initiation of alcohol and other drug use, it is important to know at what age that initiation begins.

The MTF study reports that, in 1995, 9.5% of 8th graders and 5.5% of 10th graders report having used alcohol by the 4th grade. Among 12th graders, in 1995, 9.8% reported that they first used alcohol by the 6th grade. About 2% of students first used marijuana by 6th grade in all three samples. Figure 9.2 shows the age of onset for tobacco, alcohol, and marijuana use reported by 12th-grade students in 1995.

APPROACHES TO SUBSTANCE ABUSE PREVENTION

There are numerous views of substance abuse with implications for how one might approach its prevention. Disease models, for example, conceptualize chemical dependency as a physiological illness with a genetic or heritable basis. These models have been the foundation of many substance abuse treatment efforts but have been used less frequently to guide prevention. Attempts to identify children of alcoholics and addicts in order to discourage or delay their initiation of any substance use are examples of preventive efforts guided by the disease model.

Harm reduction models, in contrast, seek to prevent specific harmful consequences of substance use, rather than substance use itself. Prevention efforts based on this model are likely to focus on preventing driving after drinking or other risky patterns of use, or on preventing violence associated with intoxication.

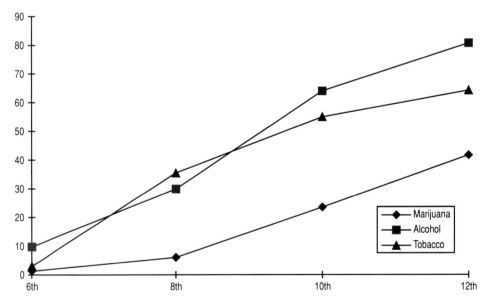

Figure 9.2. Incidence of use for marijuana, alcohol, and tobacco for 12th graders, 1995. *Source:* Johnston, O'Malley, and Bachman (1995).

Community systems models focus on the effects of laws, regulations, policies, and practices of systems in the community that affect availability of substances, community norms regarding substance use, and sanctions against undesired substance use. Preventive interventions grounded in these models include policy and legislative activities that encourage various systems to adopt and enforce laws, regulations, policies, and practices that seek to affect rates of consumption, misuse, and abuse.

The most comprehensive work in substance abuse prevention has been guided by a public health model of prevention that seeks to reduce risk factors for disease or disorder and promote processes that protect or buffer against risk (IOM, 1994). Prevention efforts guided by attention to risk and protective factors are derived from results of longitudinal studies that show relationships between characteristics of individuals, their environments, and their interactions with those environments, and the later development of substance abuse problems. Risk factors are characteristics of individuals and their environments that have been shown to predict a greater likelihood of future substance misuse, abuse, or dependence. Although the concept of protective factors is the subject of some controversy, there is evidence that the effects of exposure to risk can be mitigated by a variety of individual and environmental characteristics and by processes of interaction between individuals and their environments (Werner, 1989). Protective factors may directly decrease dysfunction; they may interact with a risk factor to moderate dysfunction; they may mediate the relationship through which a risk factor operates to cause dysfunction; or they may prevent the initial occurrence of a risk factor (Coie et al., 1993).

Longitudinal studies have identified risk factors for substance abuse within individuals, in the environments within which they develop, including families, schools, peer groups, and the broader community, and in the interactions of individuals and their environments (see Hawkins et al., 1995; Hawkins, Catalano, & Miller, 1992; Newcomb et al., 1986; Robins, 1992; Simcha-Fagan, Gersten, & Langer, 1986 for reviews). Knowledge about the causal status of many of these factors in the etiology of drug abuse is incomplete. The causal pathways linking risk factors to later drug use and abuse are not well understood, nor are the dynamic interactions among various risk and protective factors and behavior at different developmental stages (Clayton, 1993). Some risk factors may be markers along a pathway toward drug use, but not causal, in that their removal would not reduce drug use. Even if causal, some risk factors, like a family history of alcoholism, may be unchangeable though they still may be used for identifying subgroups at risk for preventive attention. Despite these limitations in understanding the causal pathways linking specific risk and protective factors to subsequent drug misuse, abuse, and dependence, the risk and protective factors derived from longitudinal research represent the most promising targets available for preventive intervention (Coie et al., 1993; IOM, 1994; Lorion & Ross, 1992). The risk and protective focused approach to prevention includes attention to factors of concern in both disease models and community systems models mentioned earlier.

RISK AND PROTECTIVE FACTORS FOR SUBSTANCE ABUSE

Individual Factors

Some children appear to be at greater risk for substance abuse by virtue of their family histories, prenatal and birth experiences, temperament, and early and persistent displays of problem behaviors. Perinatal complications (including preterm delivery, low birth weight, and anoxia) and brain damage (e.g., from infectious disease, traumatic head injury, or pre-postnatal exposure to toxins such as heavy metals, alcohol, tobacco, or cocaine) predispose children to later aggressive behavior and substance abuse (Brennan, Mednick, & Kandel, 1991; Michaud, Rivara, Jaffe, Fay, & Dailey, 1993).

A family history of alcoholism or other drug abuse is also a risk factor for alcoholism and substance abuse (Merikangas, Rounsaville, & Prusoff, 1992; Schukit, 1987; Tarter, 1988). Studies of twins and of adoptees have suggested that some individuals have a genetic predisposition to alcoholism (Blum et al., 1990; Cadoret, Cain, & Grove, 1980; Hrubec & Omenn, 1981; Kendler, 1992; Merikangas, 1990; Murray, Clifford, & Gurling, 1983; Pickens et al., 1991) and other drug abuse (Grove et al., 1990). However, these studies also indicate that most children of alcoholics do not themselves become alcoholics.

Some studies suggest that inherited biological traits and temperament link genetics and behavior (Blum et al., 1990; Schukit, 1987; Tarter, 1988). High behavior activity level (Tarter, Laird, Kabene, Bukstein, & Kaminer, 1990) and sensation seeking (Cloninger, Sigvardsson, & Bohman, 1988) have been identified as predictors of early drug initiation and abuse. Attention deficit/hyperactivity disorder in childhood has been found to predict substance abuse disorders in late adolescence, especially when combined with aggressive behaviors or conduct disorders (Gittelman, Mannuzza, & Bonagura, 1985).

A pattern of persistent conduct problems in multiple settings in childhood is an early behavioral predictor of risk for substance abuse. Aggressive behavior in boys at age 5 years has been found to predict frequent drug use in adolescence (Brook, Brook, Gordon, Whiteman, & Cohen, 1990; Kellam & Brown, 1982) and drug problems in adulthood (Lewis, Robins, & Rice, 1985).

Alienation from the dominant values of society (Jessor & Jessor, 1977; Penning & Barnes, 1982; Shedler & Block, 1990), low religiosity (Brunswick, Messeri, & Titus, 1992; Jessor, Donovan, & Windmer, 1980), and rebelliousness (Bachman, Johnston, & O'Malley, 1981; Block, Block, & Keyes, 1988; Kandel, 1982) also have been shown to predict greater drug use in adolescence. Attitudes favorable to drug use precede substance use initiation and predict use (e.g., Kandel et al., 1978; Krosnick & Judd, 1982).

As noted earlier, initiation of alcohol or other drug use at an early age has been found to strongly predict later alcohol misuse and drug abuse (Hawkins, Graham, et al., in press; Kandel, Single, & Kessler, 1976; Rachal et al., 1982; Robins & Pryzbeck, 1985). The younger the child is when alcohol or other drug use is first initiated, the greater the frequency of drug use (Fleming, Kellam, & Brown, 1982), the greater the probability of extensive and persistent involvement in the use of illicit drugs (Kandel, 1982), and the greater the risk of alcohol misuse (Hawkins, Graham, et al., in press) and drug abuse (Robins & Pryzbeck, 1985). Conversely, a later age of drug use onset has been shown to predict lower drug involvement and a greater probability of discontinuation of use (Kandel et al., 1976).

Family Factors

Beyond the genetic transmission of a propensity to alcoholism, family modeling of drug use behavior by parents and older siblings and permissive parental attitudes toward children's drug use predict greater risk of alcohol and other drug abuse (Barnes

& Welte, 1986; Brook, Gordon, Whiteman, & Cohen, 1986; Brook, Whiteman, Brook, & Gordon, 1988; Johnson, Shontz, & Locke, 1984). The more members of a household who use a drug, the greater is a child's risk of early initiation of use of that drug, and involving children in parental alcohol or drug-using behaviors (such as getting a beer for a parent) also increases risk for early initiation of drug use (Ahmed, Bush, Davidson, & Iannotti, 1984).

Risk for drug abuse is increased by family management practices characterized by permissive or unclear expectations for behavior, lax monitoring of children, and excessively severe and inconsistent punishment (Baumrind, 1983; Kandel & Andrews, 1987; Penning & Barnes, 1982). Both permissiveness and extremely authoritarian parenting practices predict later drug abuse in children (Baumrind, 1983; Shedler & Block, 1990).

The strength of family relationships—involvement and attachment between adult caretakers and children—also affects levels of risk and protection. Shedler and Block (1990) found that quality of mothers' interaction with their children at age 5 distinguished children who became frequent users of marijuana by age 18 from those who had only experimented with marijuana. Mothers of children who became frequent users were relatively cold, underresponsive, and underprotective with their children at age 5, giving them little encouragement but pressuring them to perform in tasks. Brook, Cohen, Whiteman, and Gordon (1992) found that low attachment to mother and paternal permissiveness predicted movement from low to moderate levels of alcohol and marijuana use.

Conversely, positive family relationships appear to discourage youths' initiation into drug use (Brook et al., 1986; Jessor & Jessor, 1977; Kim, 1979; Norem-Hebeisen, Johnson, Anderson, & Johnson, 1984; Selnow, 1987). Bonding to family may inhibit drug involvement during adolescence in a manner similar to the way in which family bonding inhibits delinquency (Hirschi, 1969). However, this is likely only when family members hold norms that are not permissive to alcohol and other drug use. Brook et al. (1990) reported observing a clear causal parental pathway to nondrug use among adolescents in their sample. Parental internalization of traditional values led to the development of strong parent-child attachment. Such mutual attachment led to the child's internalization of traditional norms and to prosocial behaviors, which in turn led the child to associate with non-drug-using peers, leading to abstinence from drug use during adolescence. It appears that parental norms and family bonding interact in influencing drug use or nonuse behaviors in adolescents. It is likely that family management practices and sibling norms and substance-related behaviors also interact in this process.

Peterson, Hawkins, Abbott, and Catalano (1994) found that parental norms against involving children in parental alcohol use (opening or pouring drinks for parents) and good family management practices mediated the effects of parental drinking on alcohol use of children at age 15. Good family management practices and refraining from involving children in adult alcohol use inhibited alcohol consumption among 15-year-olds, even when adults in the family drank alcohol.

High levels of family conflict also appear to contribute to risk for higher levels of substance use during adolescence (Simcha-Fagan et al., 1986). Rutter and Giller noted that parental conflict contributes to risk for antisocial behavior in children whether or not the parental dyad is intact. Needle, Su, and Doherty (1990) found that children who experienced divorce during their adolescence were more likely to use drugs than other adolescents (see also Penning & Barnes, 1982).

School Factors

Though the relationship between intelligence and drug abuse may be unclear, school experiences appear to contribute to drug nonuse, use, and misuse. Kandel and Davies (1992) reported that successful school performance is a protective factor mitigating against escalation to a pattern of regular marijuana use. Similarly, Hundleby and Mercer (1987) found that outstanding performance in school reduced likelihood of frequent drug use in adolescence. Conversely, poor school performance has been found to predict the early initiation of drug use (Bachman et al., 1991), levels of use of illegal drugs, and drug misuse (Holmberg, 1985).

Peer Factors

Peer use of substances has consistently been found to be among the stronger predictors of substance use among adolescents (Barnes & Welte, 1986; Brook et al., 1990; Brook et al., 1992; Elliott, Huizinga, & Ageton, 1985; Kandel, 1978, 1986; Kandel & Andrews, 1987). This relationship has been confirmed across racial groups (Byram & Fly, 1984; Dembo, Farrow, Schmeidler, & Burgos, 1979; Harford, 1985; Newcomb & Bentler, 1986).

Contextual Factors

Factors in the broader social environment also affect rates of drug abuse. Patterns of substance use in the neighborhood and community predict individual substance use behaviors (Robins, 1984). Similarly, availability and price of alcohol and other drugs affect rates of substance use, misuse, and abuse. (Gorsuch & Butler, 1976; Gottfredson, 1988; Maddahian, Newcomb, & Bentler, 1988). Gorsuch and Butler (1976) found that increased availability of alcohol was related to increased drinking prevalence, consumption, and the heavy use of alcohol. Availability and price are influenced by legal restriction or regulation on purchase, by excise taxes, and by market forces. Legal restriction significantly limits the prevalence of use of substances (Goldstein & Kalant, 1990). Changes in laws to be more restrictive on alcohol availability (raising the legal drinking age, raising excise taxes on alcohol, limiting alcohol outlets and liquor-by-the-drink sales) have been found to be followed by decreased alcohol consumption and auto fatalities (Cook & Tauchen, 1982; Holder & Blose, 1987; Saffer & Grossman, 1987).

Broad social norms regarding the acceptability and risk of use of alcohol or other drugs also appear to affect the prevalence of substance use and misuse (Flasher & Maisto, 1984; Robins, 1984; Vaillant, 1983; Watts & Rabow, 1983). Changes in social norms among students across the country regarding the social acceptability and risks associated with marijuana and cocaine use have been followed closely by changes in the prevalence of marijuana and cocaine use among high school seniors (Johnston, 1991).

There is conflicting evidence about the role of poverty as a risk factor for substance abuse. Robins and Ratliff (1979) found that extreme economic deprivation increased risk for alcohol and drug abuse in adulthood among antisocial children. Others, however (e.g., Bachman, Johnston, & O'Malley, 1981; Murray, Richards, Luepker, & Johnson,

1987), have found a positive correlation between parental education and occupational measures and alcohol and drug use among students.

Nevertheless, there is evidence that children who grow up in disorganized neighborhoods with high population density, high residential mobility, physical deterioration, and low levels of neighborhood cohesion or attachment to neighborhood face greater risk for a range of health and behavior problems, including drug trafficking and drug abuse (Fagan, 1988; Simcha-Fagan & Schwartz, 1986).

Protective Factors

Many adolescents avoid substance abuse and dependence despite exposure to multiple risk factors. Some investigators have identified factors and processes that protect against substance abuse. Individual characteristics including resilient temperament, positive social orientation, high intelligence, and skills have been identified (Radke-Yarrow & Sherman, 1990). Development of warmth, supportive relationships, and social bonding to adults during childhood is another important type of protection (Garmezy, 1985; Rutter, 1979; Werner & Smith, 1992). Bonding first develops in relationships with family members, but social bonds of commitment and attachment can develop in relationships with teachers, other relatives, and other adults in the community. Strong bonds to prosocial adults inhibit substance abuse. In addition, as noted earlier, if social groups such as peer groups, schools, and communities emphasize norms, beliefs, or behavioral standards that are in opposition to the use of substances by teenagers, these norms also serve a protective role in reducing the prevalence of drug use by adolescents (Hansen & Graham, 1991; Johnston, 1991).

Generalizations and Implications from Research on Risks and Protection

Research on risk and protective factors for substance abuse has shown that a number of factors in the individual and multiple social environments interact during development to affect an individual's degree of risk. The greater the number of risk factors to which an individual is exposed during development, the greater is that individual's risk for drug abuse (Bry, McKeon, & Pandina, 1982; Newcomb, Maddahian, Skager, & Bentler, 1987). Moreover, different risk factors appear to be particularly salient at different developmental stages (Bell, 1986; Flay, d'Avernas, Best, Kersell, & Ryan, 1983). Family and individual factors are the earliest consistent predictors of adolescent substance misuse and abuse (Baumrind, 1983; Kellam & Brown, 1982; Loeber & Stouthamer-Loeber, 1986; Yoshikawa, 1994), whereas school factors become significant predictors of later drug use during the mid- to late elementary years (Gottfredson, 1988). Peers who use substances increase in both prevalence and predictive power in adolescence.

In combination, this evidence suggests that effective prevention of substance abuse may require coordinated preventive actions that reduce risk factors and enhance protection in multiple domains across all phases of development among those at greatest risk by virtue of exposure to multiple risk factors. Preventive resources should be invested in populations of children exposed to multiple risk factors from early in life.

Interventions that reduce multiple risk factors while enhancing protective factors in family, school, peer, and community environments over the course of infant, child, and adolescent development hold great promise for preventing many adolescent health and behavior problems. Multifaceted interventions that support enduring community-level change to reduce risk and develop protective factors may be needed to achieve sustained reductions in substance abuse (Biglan, 1995; Flay et al., 1989; IOM, 1994). Ideally, the preventive interventions used in a specific community should be approaches shown in controlled studies to be efficacious for reducing targeted risks and enhancing known protective factors and processes. Further, in choosing interventions, it would be desirable to address the most prevalent or elevated risk factors in each community, with special attention to areas where multiple risk exposure is most prevalent.

Many of the risk factors reviewed here are common precursors of a number of health and behavior problems in adolescence including violent behavior, delinquency, teen pregnancy, and school dropout (Brewer, Hawkins, Catalano, & Neckerman, 1995; Developmental Research and Programs, 1994; Hawkins, Lishner, Jenson, & Catalano, 1987). Effective strategies for reducing these shared risk factors and enhancing protection against them should have beneficial effects on a number of health and behavior problems and lead, overall, to a more healthy population.

Theory

Because multiple risk and protective factors predict substance abuse, preventive interventions should be guided by theory that suggests the causal mechanisms linking risk and protective factors to future abuse (Hawkins, Catalano, Morrison, et al., 1992). Theory is critical for specifying how different risk and protective factors interrelate as well as how they are expressed developmentally, and in providing additional clues to the most promising points of intervention. Theory about the ways in which predictive factors fit into causal models of drug abuse can inform prevention design (Kazdin, 1990). Combined with a thorough assessment of needs and resources, theory can help indicate precisely which intervention components, as well as which comprehensive programs, are best suited to particular individuals, families, schools, or communities at specific developmental periods.

We have suggested that knowledge of empirically derived risk and protective factors for substance abuse, and a theoretical framework that organizes this knowledge into a causal model are necessary foundations for substance abuse prevention. Two additional bodies of information are needed to guide effective substance abuse prevention planning: knowledge of efficacious interventions for preventing substance abuse, and strategies for assessing existing levels of risk and protection to guide the selection and design of preventive interventions. Assessment issues will be considered next, followed by a discussion of the interventions for reducing risk and enhancing protection.

DIMENSIONS OF ASSESSMENT AND INTERVENTION

Preventive interventions must reach those exposed to multiple risk factors if they are to affect those at greatest risk of substance abuse. Interventions can be targeted to a greater or lesser degree. Thorough assessment strategies can help determine the optimal breadth of preventive interventions to be applied, given the population of concern and resources available. Adapting Gordon's (1983) classification system for prevention of disease, the Institute of Medicine's Committee on the Prevention of Mental

Disorders (1994) described three categories of preventive interventions. At the broadest level, *universal interventions* target the general public or entire population groups without distinguishing those exposed to high levels of risk from those who are not. Examples are media campaigns like "This is your brain on drugs," drug abuse prevention curricula in schools, and laws raising the legal drinking age to 21 years. These interventions may be most appropriate when the cost per individual is low, the intervention is widely acceptable to the population, and there is little risk of deleterious consequences from the intervention itself. *Selective interventions,* on the other hand, attempt to target those whose risk for developing substance use problems is significantly higher than average. Examples include home visitation by public health nurses to single, low-income, pregnant mothers to discourage substance use during pregnancy and promote good nutrition and healthy births, and early childhood training in emotional and behavioral self-regulation for children evidencing problems with impulse control. These types of interventions may be most appropriate when the cost per individual is low to moderate, and when the potential for negative effects is minimal. The most narrowly targeted prevention programs are *indicated interventions,* aimed at those having early detectable signs or symptoms foreshadowing substance abuse, or those with significant biological markers indicating predisposition for abuse or dependence. Interventions to encourage children and adolescents who have already initiated alcohol use to stop drinking are an example. Indicated interventions may be reasonable even if costs per individual are higher.

Epidemiological assessments of the prevalence of substance use, misuse, abuse, and dependence, and of the prevalence of risk and protective factors in populations or geographic areas are important for determining the most efficient combination of interventions at different levels, as well as the specific interventions to be applied.

Another important dimension in substance abuse prevention planning is the unit of assessment and intervention. Adolescent substance use prevention programs may be designed for entire communities, states, or even larger geographic areas. Assessment at this level is a relatively new development, often involving diverse data from public records (e.g., census data, health department, law enforcement, school district records) brought together and overlaid to provide a profile of levels and trends in risks and protection in the area of interest. At the other extreme, preventive interventions may be designed for specific individuals. Assessment strategies need to encompass this range, including epidemiologically based assessment tools for communities and larger areas, surveys of risks and protection in schools and other institutions, family-oriented assessment strategies, and tools for pediatricians, teachers, parents, and others to assess risk and protection levels in individual children and adolescents (e.g., Developmental Research and Programs, 1994; Hawkins & Fitzgibbon, 1993).

PREVENTION APPROACHES

Initiatives to reduce substance abuse are conventionally, if misleadingly, said to focus on drug supply and drug demand. The former consist mostly of foreign policy, domestic policy, and law enforcement activities. The latter typically encompass prevention and treatment interventions (Hawkins et al., 1995). In this chapter, we review preventive interventions with respect to their effects on risk and protective factors for substance abuse as well as for effects in preventing substance use, misuse, abuse, and dependence. This review provides selected examples of preventive interventions and their effects on risk and protective factors derived from adequately controlled studies. The purpose here is to illustrate the range of interventions that hold promise for preventing substance misuse and abuse (for more comprehensive reviews of substance abuse prevention, see Hawkins, Catalano, & Miller, 1992; Hawkins et al., 1995).

Reducing the Availability of Drugs through Laws, Law Enforcement, and Interdiction

Foreign policy and interdiction efforts that focus on stopping the flow of illegal drugs into the country seek to reduce the availability and increase the price of illegal drugs, particularly marijuana, heroin, and cocaine (Moore, 1990). Similarly, mandatory prison sentences for drug trafficking and for those found to be in possession of certain types and quantities of illegal substances, attempt, in part, to disrupt the sale of illegal drugs through existing distribution networks. These efforts have not been particularly effective in eliminating supplies or raising retail prices of illegal drugs, confirming that interdiction and law enforcement efforts cannot, in the face of strong demand, eliminate illegal drug supplies, or significantly raise the price of illegal drugs (Polich, Ellickson, Reuter, & Kahan, 1984).

What these efforts have accomplished is to convey a strong message about the unacceptability of illegal drug possession and behaviors such as drinking alcohol and driving. Well-publicized enforcement actions communicate social norms of disapproval against illegal drug possession or drinking and driving. Those with a stake in their roles in the school, workplace, or community may be deterred by such actions from illegal drug involvement or drinking and driving by perceptions that these behaviors could be risky. However, those with less commitment to roles in the larger society are less likely to be deterred by legal sanctions (Sherman, Smith, Schmidt, & Rogan, 1992). Enforcement efforts may deter some from using drugs, but they are most likely to deter those who are least likely to engage in drug abuse.

In contrast, regulatory efforts to limit availability of alcohol through changes in policies and laws governing taxes (Levy & Sheflin, 1985), liquor sales outlets (Wagenaar & Holder, 1991), and the legal drinking age (Saffer & Grossman, 1987), have been followed by reductions in rates of alcohol consumption, including rates of alcohol abuse as indicated by liver cirrhosis, and alcohol-related traffic accidents (Blose & Holder, 1987; Decker, Graitcer, & Schaffner, 1988; Krieg, 1982; O'Malley & Wagenaar, 1991). Thus, regulation of substances, like alcohol, that are distributed by legal channels through policies, laws, and enforcement approaches can affect levels of consumption, misuse, and abuse.

Preventive Interventions in Developmental Perspective

The principles of prevention in developmental perspective are to reduce risk factors, to enhance protective factors, to address these factors at appropriate developmental stages, to intervene early before the behavior stabilizes, and to address multiple risks with multiple strategies. The following interventions illustrate prevention approaches at different developmental stages that have been found to reduce risk factors and enhance protective factors for drug abuse in adequately controlled longitudinal studies.

Perinatal Interventions

A number of risk factors can be addressed prenatally. Prenatal drug exposure, premature birth and low birthweight, and poor early infant-caregiver relationships are each associated with behavior problems in childhood (Bates, Bayles, Bennet, Ridge, & Brown, 1991; Telzrow, 1990), which in turn may increase the likelihood of later substance abuse, given certain environmental conditions (McGee, Silva, & Williams, 1984; Sameroff & Chandler, 1975; Werner, 1987). Thus, interventions designed to promote healthy births and improve infant parenting can be viewed as promising approaches to prevention of alcohol and other drug abuse (Hawkins, Catalano, & Associates, 1992).

One such intervention, the Prenatal/Early Infancy Project, focused on low-income single pregnant women and consisted primarily of nurse home-visitation during pregnancy and the first two years of the infant's life, referral for services, early developmental screening of children, and transportation to well-child-care clinics. Compared with a control group that received all these services except nurse home-visitation, mothers who received home visitation were significantly more likely to improve their diets and stop smoking during pregnancy; teen mothers in the program were also 75% less likely to deliver prematurely and had 75% fewer verified reports of child abuse or neglect than control group mothers (Olds, Henderson, Chamberlin, & Tatelbaum, 1986; Olds, Henderson, Tatelbaum, & Chamberlin, 1988).

The Yale Child Welfare Project also focused on disadvantaged parents during pregnancy and early childhood. The intervention included home visits from social service professionals, pediatric care, day care, and developmental exams. A 10-year follow-up showed that mothers who had participated in the program had significantly higher levels of education, fewer children, greater likelihood of full-time employment, and had more contact with their children's teachers than a matched comparison group, and children in the program were rated less negatively by teachers in terms of their behavior, had fewer unexcused absences, received fewer referrals for school services (e.g., for emotional problems), and demonstrated significantly better overall adjustment to school (Seitz, Rosenbaum, & Apfel, 1985), suggesting that the intervention reduced risks and enhanced protection against future substance abuse.

Other studies of early family interventions have demonstrated similar results on functioning and cognitive and social development (Horacek, Ramey, Campbell, Hoffman, & Fletcher, 1987; Lally, Mangione, & Honig, 1988; Rauh, Achenbach, Nurcombe, Howell, & Teti, 1988). These results suggest that improving access to care and support services for pregnant and postpartum mothers can have enduring effects for early developmental risk reduction (IOM, 1994).

Preschool Interventions

Effective preschool interventions have targeted risk factors, such as poor family management practices, academic failure, and early problem behavior, as well as protective factors such as cognitive and social skills, and family bonding.

The Houston Parent-Child Development Center sought to address these factors among low-income Mexican-American families with children aged 1 to 2 years. The intervention involved home visits by trained female paraprofessionals from the barrios where the participants lived, providing information on how to promote healthy child development. The intervention also offered family workshops to encourage participation by fathers and siblings, English as a Second Language classes for mothers, and contact with community workers to provide additional social, health, and informational services. In addition, mothers and their children attended multiple sessions at the center where children were taught cognitive and social skills.

Follow-up assessments showed that, at 4 to 7 years of age, boys in the intervention group were rated as better behaved by their mothers than those in a control group, and at 7 to 10 years of age, teachers rated the intervention children as better behaved than controls (Johnson & Breckenridge, 1982). Children in the intervention condition were also one-fourth as likely as controls to be referred for special services, and more likely to score significantly higher on a basic skills test. These results suggest positive effects on conduct problems and achievement, which are predictors of later substance abuse. The intervention was successful at improving parent-child interactions and children's subsequent behavior and academic competence up to 8 years following intervention.

The Perry Preschool Project, serving low-income African-American families, included involvement of 3- to 4-year-old children in planned preschool activities, coupled with home visits by preschool teachers. Follow-ups revealed that children who had participated in the program were better behaved in school, and by age 19, were significantly less likely to have received poor grades, to have dropped out of school, to have been placed in special education, to report fighting, to have been on welfare, or to have been arrested, compared with a control group (Berrueta-Clement, Schweinhart, Barnett, Epstein, & Weikart, 1984; Schweinhart, 1987). While neither of these studies measured substance use outcomes directly, they demonstrate the effects of early childhood interventions on risk and protective factors predictive of substance abuse and on co-occurring problem behaviors including delinquency.

Interventions in the Elementary School Years

Social and academic competence become increasingly important as predictors of later health and behavior problems during the elementary grades. Persistent conduct problems, peer rejection, school failure and low commitment to school during this period are risk factors for later substance abuse (Hawkins, Catalano, & Miller, 1992). Preventive interventions during this period focus on enhancing parenting and family functioning, enhancing social and academic competence, and changing the school environment to be more supportive and inclusive of children who are having academic or social difficulties.

To address these risks, the Seattle Social Development Project trained elementary school teachers in techniques of classroom management and instruction designed to increase opportunities for student participation, to enhance skills for classroom involvement, and to increase rewards for positive involvement in the classroom. Parents were also offered programs that taught and encouraged use of proactive family management practices to reduce risks for substance abuse.

By 5th grade, intervention students reported more commitment and attachment (bonding) to school and higher levels of family communication, involvement, and bonding. They were also significantly less likely to have initiated alcohol use or delinquent behavior (Hawkins, Catalano, & Miller, 1992). By the end of Grade 6, boys in the intervention group from low-income families had significantly better academic achievement, better teacher-rated behavior, and lower rates of delinquency initiation than did control boys from low-income families, while girls in the intervention group from low-income families had lower rates of substance use initiation than did control girls from low-income families (O'Donnell, Hawkins, Catalano, Abbott, & Day, 1995).

The School Development Program, created by James Comer and his associates at the Yale Child Study Center (Comer, 1985, 1988) also targets risk factors in elementary schools and their environments. This program joins parents, teachers, school administrators, and mental health professionals into school teams for school management, mental health, and parent involvement. These teams meet regularly to review and improve the atmosphere of the school, to increase commitment of students and parents, and to strengthen the ties between the school and the community.

Quasi-experimental evaluations of the program in two inner-city schools serving low-income African-American children reported positive effects on student grades, achievement scores, and social competence scores, and decreased truancy and disciplinary problems (Cauce, Comer, & Schwartz, 1987; Comer, 1988).

Results of these two multicomponent interventions with schools and parents during the elementary grades suggest that addressing factors which emerge and stabilize as predictors of substance abuse during the elementary years holds promise for reducing later substance misuse and abuse. Preparing for the Drug Free Years (PDFY) is a universal (IOM, 1994) prevention program targeted at parents of preadolescents and adolescents. The curriculum was field-tested for two years in 10 diverse Seattle public schools. In addition, the curriculum has been tested as part of a regional broadcast media program, tested in different statewide implementations, tested within a health maintenance organization, and implemented in a project focusing on families of color. The goal of the PDFY curriculum is to empower parents of children aged 8 to 14 to reduce the risk that their children will develop problems with drugs and alcohol in adolescence. PDFY teaches parents how to reduce risk factors and enhance protective factors that are especially important during the late elementary and middle school years. PDFY consists of five 2-hour sessions. Sessions are typically conducted by two trained workshop leaders from the community.

Findings from large-scale nonexperimental pre-post designed studies (Hawkins, Catalano, & Kent, 1991; Heuser, 1990; Holcomb & Schulte, 1993) demonstrate that PDFY has been successful in targeting the intended audience and that parents find the program acceptable and of high value. In each case, high percentages of parents participated who had not attended parent workshops previously. In addition, these studies demonstrated that PDFY sessions improved parents' knowledge and changed important attitudes and behaviors relevant to later adolescent substance use. Further, the program was found to be acceptable to families of color in a study specifically designed to examine the acceptability of the program content to African-American, Hispanic, Samoan, and Native American communities. Finally, in experimental tests of the program using random assignment of families to PDFY or a control group, analysis of parent outcome measures indicated significant overall improvement on intervention-targeted parenting behaviors, general child management, and parent-child affective quality, for both mothers and fathers in the intervention group compared with the control group (Spoth & Redmond, 1995; Spoth, Redmond, Haggerty, & Ward, 1995). These significant differences favoring the PDFY intervention group were produced using observational and self-report measures of outcomes (Kosterman, Hawkins, Haggerty, Spoth, & Redmond, 1996; Kosterman, Hawkins, Spoth, Haggerty, & Zhu, in press). Finally, in another experimental study, intervention-targeted parenting behaviors showed significant improvement for both mothers and fathers, consistent with PDFY objectives (Spoth et al., 1995).

Interventions in the Middle and High School Years

The middle and high school years are characterized developmentally by the increased influence of peers (Tao Hunter & Youniss, 1982). Important risk factors that have been targeted by preventive interventions at this stage include social influences to use substances and attitudes favorable to substance use.

Interventions to change norms and to teach resistance strategies were implemented extensively in the 1980s. The Red Ribbon week of the National Federation of Parents for Drug Free Youth, the Reagan administration's "Just say NO!" campaign, and the National Media Partnership's "This is your brain on drugs" advertising campaign are examples of universal prevention strategies focused on changing norms for drug use. Though methodologically limited, one study indicates that such saturation advertising is associated with less favorable public attitudes toward marijuana and cocaine use (Black, 1989).

Well-controlled studies of efforts to change adolescent norms favorable to drug use and to teach skills to resist social influences to use drugs have been implemented in schools and communities. School curricula focusing on these goals typically teach children through instruction, modeling, and role play to identify and resist influences to use drugs and, in some cases, to prepare for associated stresses anticipated with such resistance (Botvin, 1986). Most of these curricula also seek to promote norms negative toward drug use (Hansen, Johnson, Flay, Graham, & Sobel, 1988; Perry, 1986). These normative change components typically include efforts to depict drug use as socially unacceptable, identify short-term negative consequences of drug use, provide evidence that drug use is not as widespread among peers as children may think, encourage children to make public commitments to remain drug free, and in some instances, use peer leaders to teach the curriculum (Botvin, 1986; Klepp, Halper, & Perry, 1986).

The Adolescent Alcohol Prevention Trial presented seventh graders with different combinations of information about drug use, training in skills to resist social influences to use drugs, and normative change components. Normative change appeared to be the strongest component of this intervention, resulting in significantly less onset and prevalence of heavy drinking, marijuana use, and cigarette smoking (Hansen & Graham, 1991). Other studies have also suggested that establishing clear social norms against substance use is an important component of prevention efforts at this developmental stage (e.g., Ellickson & Bell, 1990).

Social influence resistance training has been shown to be promising as part of broader instruction in social competence (Botvin, 1990). When adolescents are taught skills to resist social influences to use drugs along with an array of other social competencies, studies indicate that they are less likely to use alcohol or to engage in heavy drinking (Caplan et al., 1992); other promising effects on risk and protective factors for abuse have also been observed (Botvin, Baker, Dusenbury, Tortu, & Botvin, 1990; Botvin, Baker, Renick, Filazzola, & Botvin, 1984; Botvin & Eng, 1982). Botvin's long-term follow-up of his Life Skills training curriculum found a combination of social influence resistance and general life skills training in the 7th grade (with 8th and 9th grade boosters) resulted in up to 44% fewer drug users and 66% fewer polydrug users by 12th grade (Botvin, Baker, Dusenbury, Botvin, & Diaz, 1995). School curricula that promote norms antithetical to drug use and teach developmentally life skills and social influence resistance skills can reduce the incidence of substance use during adolescence.

Perhaps the most ambitious substance abuse preventive interventions that have been adequately evaluated have been efforts to address influence to use drugs and norms favorable to drug use in multiple social environments affecting adolescents. The Midwestern Prevention Project (Pentz et al., 1989) was a multilevel school and community intervention to prevent substance abuse using mass media programming, social influence resistance and normative change curricula in middle or junior high schools, parent education and organization, community organization, and health policy.

After the first year of mass media and school curriculum intervention, prevalence rates for monthly and weekly use of cigarettes, alcohol, and marijuana were significantly lower for students in schools exposed to both media programming and school curricula than for schools in a control condition that received the media intervention only. The net increase in drug use prevalence among intervention schools was half that of delayed intervention (control) schools (Pentz et al., 1989). In analyses examining eight schools randomly assigned to study condition 3 years following initiation of the interventions, significant differences between conditions were found for cigarette and marijuana use, but not alcohol use. The Midwestern Prevention Project was effective at preventing the onset of substance use among both high-risk and general population students (Johnson, Williams, Dei, & Sanabria, 1990).

Another series of studies of combined school and community interventions to prevent adolescent smoking and alcohol use has been conducted by Perry and her colleagues (Perry, Kelder, Murray, & Klepp, 1992; Perry et al., 1993). The Class of 1989 study was part of the Minnesota Heart Health Program (MHHP), a research and demonstration project to reduce cardiovascular disease in three communities from 1980 to 1993 (Perry et al., 1992). The Class of 1989 study was designed to evaluate the combined impact of a classroom-based social-influences smoking prevention curriculum delivered to the Class of 1989 during their 6th, 7th, and 8th grades, and the community-wide cardiovascular health promotion activities of the MHHP. Community-wide activities included seven strategies:

1. Cardiovascular risk factor screening for adults.
2. Grocery and restaurant point-of-purchase food labeling for health education.
3. Community mobilization for annual risk factor education campaigns.
4. Continuing education of health professionals to promote community awareness of cardiovascular disease risk factors and prevention.
5. Mass media education campaigns.
6. Adult education.
7. Youth education.

Using a quasi-experimental design, a single intervention community was matched with a reference community. The intervention community received both the school-based social influences curriculum and the community-wide intervention to improve diet, exercise, and reduced smoking patterns among the entire population, whereas the reference community received neither.

Analyses revealed significant differences in smoking prevalence between the intervention and comparison communities. When these students were seniors in high school, 14.6% of the cohort in the intervention community smoked, compared with 24.1% of the cohort in the reference community (Perry et al., 1992). The findings suggest that the combined school and community interventions can reduce smoking among middle and high school youths.

A second project, Project Northland, is using a similar combination of community-based and classroom interventions, along with a parent intervention component, to prevent alcohol use among adolescents in several small communities in northeastern Minnesota. This section of the state was targeted because alcohol-related problems were prevalent in the region (Perry et al., 1993). The project compares 20 school districts blocked by size and randomized to treatment and delayed-treatment control conditions (Perry et al., 1993; Perry, Williams, et al., in press).

After 3 years of intervention, students in the intervention school districts reported significantly lower scores on a Tendency to Use Alcohol scale, and significantly lower prevalence of monthly and weekly alcohol use (Perry, Williams, et al., in press). Significant differences in the hypothesized direction were also observed for survey scales measuring peer influences to use alcohol, perceived norms regarding teen alcohol use, parents communicating sanctions for their child's alcohol use, and reasons for teens not to use alcohol (Perry, Williams, et al., in press). These effects on alcohol-related attitudes and behaviors are noteworthy, given the wide prevalence of alcohol use among adolescents and the strong research design of the study.

Results reviewed in this chapter show the promise of substance abuse prevention. Several universal and selected interventions have been shown to be effective in reducing risks and enhancing protection against substance abuse across development from before birth through adolescence. Combinations of these interventions have shown the greatest effects in reducing substance use among adolescents.

It is likely that prevention strategies that link efficacious interventions to reduce risk and enhance protection in multiple domains across development hold the most promise for reducing cumulative risk for substance abuse. Such strategies require coordination of resources of many distinct health, education and service organizations. In addition, such prevention strategies should be tailored to the risk and protective profile of the populations or communities involved. To make such comprehensive strategies work and to ensure that they are institutionalized, community "ownership" of prevention initiatives is important.

IMPEDIMENTS TO INTERVENTION IN THE REAL WORLD CONTEXT

Until relatively recently, one of the major impediments to effective intervention was the absence of a framework for empirically based prevention. Preventive efforts often failed because they were based on naive, erroneous models of the problem of adolescent substance use that were inconsistent with the empirical evidence. This history gave rise to a perception that drug use prevention was not rigorous, but rather an amorphous aggregation of information and activities from "feel good" programs to "scared straight" tactics. As progress has been made in identifying risk and protective factors for substance use, misuse, and abuse in epidemiological and etiologic studies, a science of prevention has emerged (Coie et al., 1993; IOM, 1994). Preventive interventions at any level, from individual through community, can now be targeted at known predictors and inhibitors of substance use identified in empirical studies. Yet even with the emergence of an empirical framework for prevention, and despite the evidence of the efficacy of a range of interventions in reducing risks and enhancing protection, impediments still hinder widespread adoption and use of these advances.

The interventions reviewed here require the involvement of schools, communities, parents, legislative bodies, and law enforcement officials as agents of prevention. Attitudes of community residents and leaders regarding substance use and prevention affect a community's degree of readiness to put in place research-based prevention strategies. Moreover, to the extent that the goal is to involve multiple organizations, groups, and agencies in a community in a collaborative effort to address elevated risks and fill gaps in community protection, the ability of the community's various elements to work together also affects readiness for prevention.

Perceptions of Substance Use

Substance misuse, abuse, and dependence must be recognized as problems if preventive interventions are to be implemented and supported (e.g., Armenakis, Harris, & Mossholder, 1993; Haglund, Weisbrod, & Bracht, 1990; Prochaska, DiClemente, & Norcross, 1992; Rogers & Shoemaker, 1971). In a suburban community, residents may believe that drug use is an inner-city problem and not a relevant concern. Perhaps more commonly, adolescent substance use, particularly alcohol use, may be recognized, but accepted as a relatively normal, harmless part of growing up.

Peter Bell, former director of the Institute for Black Chemical Abuse, has suggested that families or communities confronted with multiple problems of poverty, violence, and transition, may not prioritize substance abuse as a problem in the face of other crises perceived to be more pressing. Bell has suggested that in some neighborhoods, the brutalizing everyday realities of crime, violence, and lack of opportunities increase acceptance and tolerance for emotional pain. Such tolerance of emotional pain may create a situation where substance use is normalized or at least tolerated (Developmental Research and Programs, 1994).

In some neighborhoods, the drug trade is a viable economic activity that brings in significant resources. As a result, the behavior of persons involved in this activity may be tolerated or accepted. Young people who become involved in the drug trade as lookouts or runners can provide income for themselves and their families. Drug use may follow. Bell has suggested that when families and communities perceive positive economic benefits from the drug trade they are unlikely to support prevention efforts, particularly when they see few economic alternatives (Developmental Research and Programs, 1994).

Bell has also argued that prevention efforts may be impeded by the perception that certain social or political forces encourage substance use among minority racial or cultural groups as a means of oppression or even genocide. Substance use prevention programs may be distrusted by those who hold such views.

Perceptions about substance abuse also can interfere with participation in substance abuse prevention programs. Some families, schools, or communities may fear that publicly acknowledging and becoming involved in efforts to prevent substance abuse will increase negative perceptions that they are "high risk" or "dysfunctional" social units.

Some groups have tried to avoid these problems by advertising preventive interventions such as parenting education programs using positive images of promoting development or health. Others have sought to ensure acceptance by first involving recognized community leaders as participants before seeking out families with multiple risks. Several other strategies for overcoming the impediments identified here have been suggested (see Developmental Research and Programs, 1991a, 1991b). Many communities make preventive interventions, such as school curricula or parenting programs, available universally to all students or parents. This avoids stigma associated with participation.

Perceptions of Prevention

Even if the misuse and abuse of substances by adolescents is viewed as a problem, if community members do not believe it can be prevented, it is difficult to generate enthusiasm for prevention activities. A sense of hopelessness and skepticism about the effectiveness of prevention itself can be an impediment to preventive intervention.

In families, schools, or communities that have failed to make improvements despite numerous attempts, a feeling of being overwhelmed by problems may emerge (Haglund et al., 1990). When people come to believe that change is impossible and their situation is hopeless, they are unlikely to invest in preventive actions that seek to improve things in the future. In communities where parents fear that their children may be shot before they reach adulthood, safety issues may be preeminent. In such situations, it is important to work on priority issues so that success is viewed as possible and a sense of efficacy develops. To become active in prevention, one must believe that one can play a significant role in what happens, and that one's efforts will produce positive results (e.g., Cottrell, 1976; Eng & Parker, 1990). Prevention is an investment in the future. Such an investment requires belief that the future is possible.

Similarly, if families, schools, and communities do not believe that it is possible to prevent substance abuse, they are unlikely to invest resources or effort in prevention activities. Individuals who believe that addiction is an unpreventable disease, for example, may resist involvement and refuse to support preventive efforts. In this regard, it is important to disseminate recent progress in prevention science. The potential agents of prevention must understand the evidence that risk for substance abuse is, to some degree, predictable; that risk and protective factors for substance abuse can be changed by preventive interventions; and that multicomponent intervention strategies targeting multiple risk and protective factors can be successfully implemented to prevent substance use and misuse among adolescents (Hawkins, Arthur, & Catalano, 1995; Hawkins, Arthur, & Olson, in press; Hawkins, Catalano, & Miller, 1992).

Ability to Work Together

Unlike treatment interventions, preventive interventions are not, of necessity, implemented in response to a crisis. Thus, they require proactive involvement of parents, teachers, neighborhood residents, health workers, law enforcement personnel and other community members over time. Research suggests that before people will be interested in organizing and working together on problems, they require a sense of psychological attachment to the community or group (e.g., Ahlbrandt & Cunningham, 1979; Chavis & Wandersman, 1990; McMillan & Chavis, 1986). Prevention efforts may be impeded when individuals perceive little similarity or interdependence with others in their family, school, or community. Active involvement in prevention requires a recognition that what happens to a group or community has a vital impact on one's life or cherished values. Thus, the creation of a sense of bonding to the family, school, neighborhood, or community may be an important part of launching a successful preventive initiative at a given level of intervention.

Equally important is a willingness to collaborate with diverse groups and individuals from a broad range of organizations and backgrounds toward the reduction of risk and enhancement of protection across development. Polarization and criticism inhibit the development of coordinated preventive strategies in which component elements work in a complementary fashion, or perhaps even synergistically, to prevent substance abuse.

Identification or creation of organizational structures to plan and guide prevention is important. Without an organizational structure, well-intentioned prevention programs may encounter a number of stumbling blocks (Andrews, 1990; Marrett, 1971; Schermerhorn, 1981; Zeira & Avedisian, 1989). As diverse individuals and organizations seek to work together to prevent substance abuse and related health and behavior problems, organizational structure can play a critical role in helping to clarify ambiguities, to establish a decision-making process, to manage conflicts so that open communication is not inhibited, to facilitate a clear and creative exchange of ideas, and to develop and achieve goals (e.g., Cottrell, 1976; Covin & Kilmann, 1990; Price & Lorion, 1989).

Finally, effective leadership is crucial for the success of prevention. A strong leader can help ignite a sense of attachment and commitment and facilitate the smooth operation of an organization. A recognized and widely respected individual with an appropriate leadership style can be an important asset in overcoming impediments and can work to enhance the immediacy, magnitude, and durability of intervention success (e.g., Fawcett, Paine, Francisco, & Vliet, 1993; Zeira & Avedisian, 1989).

SUMMARY

This chapter has reviewed the prevalence of substance use, misuse, abuse and dependence among adolescents. Over the past few years, use of substances, particularly marijuana, by adolescents has been increasing in prevalence, partially as a result of decreasing perceptions of social disapproval and risks associated with marijuana use (Johnston et al., 1995). The chapter also reviewed prevention approaches associated with disease models, harm reduction models, community systems models and risk and protective factor models of substance abuse. A risk and protective factor approach provides the framework for the remainder of the chapter. The chapter reviewed risk and protective factors in individuals, families, and school, peer, and community contexts. Next, illustrative preventive interventions shown to be efficacious in reducing risk and enhancing protection and preventing substance abuse were reviewed. These include policies and enforcement practices that regulate the legally available substance of alcohol; home visitation during pregnancy and the child's infancy to single low-income mothers; early childhood education programs that involve both parents and children; interventions that help teachers and parents during the elementary-grade years to be more effective in creating opportunities, skills, and reinforcement for positive social and academic development during childhood; school and community interventions that promote norms against substance use, misuse, and abuse, and skills to resist social influences to use drugs; and multicomponent interventions that seek to reduce risks simultaneously in multiple domains. Impediments to prevention have been identified, including perceptions that adolescent substance abuse is not a problem, perceptions that substance abuse cannot be prevented, and an inability of groups and individuals to work together. Suggestions for overcoming some of these impediments have been offered.

REFERENCES

Abbott, R. D., Hawkins, J. D., Catalano, R. F., Peterson, P. L., O'Donnell, J., Day, L. E., & Cheney, D. (1994). *Structure of problem behavior during transition from childhood to adolescence: A multigroup longitudinal analysis.* Manuscript submitted for publication.

Ahlbrandt, R., & Cunningham, J. (1979). *A new policy for neighborhood preservation.* New York: Praeger.

Ahmed, S. W., Bush, P. J., Davidson, F. R., & Iannotti, R. J. (1984, November). *Predicting children's use and intentions to use abusable substances.* Paper presented at the annual meeting of the American Public Health Association, Anaheim, CA.

American Psychiatric Association. (1980). *Diagnostic and statistical manual of mental disorders* (3rd ed.). Washington, DC: Author.

American Psychiatric Association. (1994). *Diagnostic and statistical manual of mental disorders* (4th ed.). Washington, DC: Author.

Andrews, A. (1990). Interdisciplinary and interorganizational collaboration. In A. Minahan (Ed.), *Encyclopedia of social work* (18th ed.). Silver Springs, MD: National Association of Social Workers.

Armenakis, A. A., Harris, S. G., & Mossholder, K. W. (1993). Creating readiness for organization change. *Human Relations, 46,* 681–703.

Bachman, J. G., Johnston, L. D., & O'Malley, P. M. (1981). *Monitoring the future: Questionnaire responses from the nation's high school seniors.* Ann Arbor, MI: Survey Research Center.

Bachman, J. G., Johnston, L. D., & O'Malley, P. M. (1991). How changes in drug use are linked to perceived risks and disapproval: Evidence from national studies that youth and young adults respond to information about the consequences of drug use. In L. Donohew, H. E. Sypher, & W. J. Bukoski (Eds.), *Persuasive communication and drug abuse prevention* (pp. 133–135). Hillsdale, NJ: Erlbaum.

Bachman, J. G., O'Malley, P. M., & Johnston, J. (1978). *Youth in transition: Vol. 6. Adolescence to adulthood—Change and stability in the lives of young men.* University of Michigan, Survey Research Center, Institute for Social Research, Ann Arbor, MI.

Barnes, G. M., & Welte, J. W. (1986). Patterns and predictors of alcohol use among 7–12th grade students in New York State. *Journal of Studies on Alcohol, 47,* 53–62.

Bates, J. E., Bayles, K., Bennet, D. S., Ridge, B., & Brown, M. M. (1991). Origins of externalizing behavior problems at eight years of age. In D. J. Pepler & K. H. Rubin (Eds.), *The development and treatment of childhood aggression* (pp. 93–120). Hillsdale, NJ: Erlbaum.

Baumrind, D. (1983, October). *Why adolescents take chances—And why they don't.* Invited address for the National Institute for Child Health and Human Development, Bethesda, MD.

Bell, R. Q. (1986). Age-specific manifestations in changing psychosocial risk. In D. C. Farran & J. D. McKinney (Eds.), *The concept of risk in intellectual and psychosocial development.* New York: Academic Press.

Berman, A. L., & Schwartz, R. H. (1990). Suicide attempts among adolescent drug users. *American Journal of Diseases of Children, 144*(3), 310–314.

Berrueta-Clement, J. R., Schweinhart, L. J., Barnett, W. S., Epstein, A. S., & Weikhart, D. P. (1984). *Changed lives: The effects of the Perry Preschool Program on youths through age 19.* Ypsilanti, MI: High/Scope Press.

Biglan, A. (1995). Translating what we know about the context of antisocial behavior into a lower prevalence of such behavior. *Journal of Applied Behavior Analysis, 28,* 479–492.

Black, G. S. (1989). *The attitudinal basis of drug use—1987 and changing attitudes toward drug use—1988: Reports from the Media Advertising Partnership for a Drug-Free America, Inc.* Rochester, NY: Gordon S. Black.

Block, J., Block, J. H., & Keyes, S. (1988). Longitudinally foretelling drug usage in adolescence: Early childhood personality and environmental precursors. *Child Development, 59,* 336–355.

Blose, J. O., & Holder, H. D. (1987). Liquour-by-the-drink and alcohol-related traffic crashes: A natural experiment using time-series analysis. *Journal of Studies on Alcohol, 48,* 52–60.

Blum, K., Noble, E. P., Sheridan, P. J., Montgomery, A., Ritchie, T., Jagadeeswonan, P., Nogami, H., Briggs, A. H., & Cohen, J. B. (1990). Allelic association of human dopamine D_2 receptor gene in alcoholism. *Journal of the American Medical Association, 263,* 2094–2095.

Botvin, G. J. (1986). Substance abuse prevention research: Recent developments and future directions. *Journal of School Health, 56,* 369–374.

Botvin, G. J. (1990). Substance abuse prevention: Theory, practice, and effectiveness. In M. Tonry & J. Q. Wilson (Eds.), *Crime and justice: A review of research: Vol. 13. Drugs and crime.* Chicago: University of Chicago Press.

Botvin, G. J., Baker, E., Dusenbury, L., Botvin, E. M., & Diaz, T. (1995). Long-term follow-up results of a randomized drug abuse prevention trial in a white middle-class population. *Journal of the American Medical Association, 273,* 1106–1112.

Botvin, G. J., Baker, E., Dusenbury, L., Tortu, S., & Botvin, E. M. (1990). Preventing adolescent drug abuse through a multimodal cognitive-behavioral approach: Results of a 3-year study. *Journal of Consulting and Clinical Psychology, 58,* 437–446.

Botvin, G. J., Baker, E., Renick, N. L., Filazzola, A. D., & Botvin, E. M. (1984). A cognitive-behavioral approach to substance abuse prevention. *Addictive Behaviors, 15,* 47–63.

Botvin, G. J., & Eng, A. (1982). The efficacy of a multicomponent approach to the prevention of cigarette smoking. *Preventive Medicine, 11,* 199–211.

Brennan, P., Mednick, S., & Kandel, E. (1991). Congenital determinants of violent and property offending. In D. Pepler & K. H. Rubins (Eds.), *The development and treatment of aggression* (pp. 81–92). Hillsdale, NJ: Cambridge University Press.

Brewer, D. D., Hawkins, J. D., Catalano, R. F., & Neckerman, H. J. (1995). Preventing serious, violent, and chronic juvenile offending: A review of selected strategies in childhood, adolescence, and the community. In J. C. Howell, B. Krisberg, J. D. Hawkins, & J. J. Wilson (Eds.), *A sourcebook: Serious, violent, and chronic juvenile offenders* (pp. 61–141). Thousand Oaks, CA: Sage.

Brook, J. S., Brook, D. W., Gordon, A. S., Whiteman, M., & Cohen, P. (1990). The psychosocial etiology of adolescent drug use: A family interactional approach. *Genetic, Social, and General Psychology Monographs, 116*(Whole No. 2).

Brook, J. S., Cohen, P., Whiteman, M., & Gordon, A. S. (1992). Psychosocial risk factors in the transition from moderate to heavy use or abuse of drugs. In M. Glantz & R. Pickens (Eds.), *Vulnerability to abuse* (pp. 359–388). Washington, DC: American Psychological Association.

Brook, J. S., Gordon, A. S., Whiteman, M., & Cohen, P. (1986). Some models and mechanisms for explaining the impact of maternal and adolescent characteristics on adolescent stage of drug use. *Developmental Psychology, 22,* 460–467.

Brook, J. S., Whiteman, M., Brook, D. W., & Gordon, A. S. (1988). *Sibling influence on adolescent drug abuse: Older brothers on younger brothers.* Unpublished manuscript.

Brunswick, A. F., Messeri, P. A., & Titus, S. P. (1992). Predictive factors in adult substance abuse: A prospective study of African American adolescents. In M. Glantz & R. Pickens (Eds.), *Vulnerability to abuse* (pp. 419–472). Washington, DC: American Psychological Association.

Bry, B. H., McKeon, P., & Pandina, R. J. (1982). Extent of drug use as a function of number of risk factors. *Journal of Abnormal Psychology, 91,* 273–279.

Byram, O. W., & Fly, J. W. (1984). Family structure, race, and adolescents' alcohol use: A research note. *American Journal of Drug and Alcohol Abuse, 10,* 467–478.

Cadoret, R. J., Cain, C. A., & Grove, W. M. (1980). Development of alcoholism in adoptees raised apart from alcoholic biologic relatives. *Archives of General Psychiatry, 37,* 561–563.

Campbell, A., & Gibbs, J. (Eds.). (1986). *Violent transactions.* New York: Blackwell.

Caplan, M., Weissberg, R. P., Grober, J. S., Sivo, P. J., Grady, K., & Jacoby, C. (1992). Social competence promotion with inner-city and suburban young adolescents: Effects on social adjustment and alcohol use. *Journal of Consulting and Clinical Psychology, 60,* 56–63.

Catalano, R. F., & Hawkins, J. D. (1996). The social development model: A theory of antisocial behavior. In J. D. Hawkins (Ed.), *Delinquency and crime: Current theories.* New York: Cambridge University Press.

Cauce, A. M., Comer, J. P., & Schwartz, D. (1987). Long-term effects of a systems-oriented school prevention program. *American Journal of Orthopsychiatry, 57,* 127–131.

Center for Substance Abuse Prevention (CSAP). (1993). *Signs of effectiveness in preventing alcohol and other drug problems.* Washington, DC: Author.

Center for Substance Abuse Prevention (CSAP). (1995). *Monitoring alcohol, tobacco, and other drug use in the community: Prototype and guide.* Washington, DC: Author.

Center for Substance Abuse Research (CESAR). (1996, July 1). National DAWN data show significant increases in drug-related emergency department episodes [Weekly FAX]. *CESAR FAX, 5,* 25. University of Maryland at College Park: Author.

Chaiken, J. M., & Chaiken, M. R. (1990). Drugs and predatory crime. In M. Tonry & J. Q. Wilson (Eds.), *Crime and justice: A review of research: Vol. 13. Drugs and crime* (pp. 203–239). Chicago: University of Chicago Press.

Chavis, D. M., & Wandersman, A. (1990). Sense of community in the urban environment: A catalyst for participation and community development. *American Journal of Community Psychology, 18,* 55–81.

Clayton, R. R. (1993). *Basic/etiology research: Drug use and its progression to drug abuse and drug dependence.* Unpublished manuscript, University of Kentucky, Center for Prevention Research.

Cloninger, C. R., Sigvardsson, S., & Bohman, M. (1988). Childhood personality predicts alcohol abuse in young adults. *Alcoholism: Clinical and Experimental Research, 12,* 494–505.

Coie, J. D., Watt, N. F., West, S. G., Hawkins, J. D., Asarnow, J. R., Markman, H. J., Ramey, S. L., Shure, M. B., & Long, B. (1993). The science of prevention: A conceptual framework and some directions for a national research program. *American Psychologist, 48,* 1013–1022.

Comer, J. P. (1985). The Yale-New Haven Primary Prevention Project: A follow-up study. *Journal of the American Academy of Child and Adolescent Psychiatry, 24,* 154–160.

Comer, J. P. (1988). Educating poor minority children. *Scientific American, 259,* 42–48.

Cook, P. J., & Tauchen, G. (1982). The effect of liquor taxes on heavy drinking. *Bell Journal of Economics, 13,* 379–390.

Cottrell, L. S., Jr. (1976). The competent community. In B. H. Kaplan, R. N. Wilson, & A. H. Leighton (Eds.), *Further explorations in social psychiatry* (pp. 195–211). New York: Basic Books.

Covin, T. J., & Kilmann, R. H. (1990). Implementation of large-scale planned change: Some areas of agreement and disagreement. *Psychological Reports, 66,* 1235–1241.

Decker, M. D., Graitcer, P. L., & Schaffner, W. (1988). Reduction in motor vehicle fatalities associated with an increase in the minimum drinking age. *Journal of the American Medical Association, 260,* 3604–3610.

Dembo, R., Farrow, D., Schmeidler, J., & Burgos, W. (1979). Testing a causal model of environmental influences on early drug involvement of inner-city junior high school youths. *American Journal of Drug and Alcohol Abuse, 6,* 313–336.

Developmental Research and Programs. (1991a). *Preparing for the drug free years planning guide.* Seattle, WA: Author.

Developmental Research and Programs. (1991b). *Guidelines for adapting preparing for the drug free years for diverse communities.* Seattle, WA: Author.

Developmental Research and Programs. (1994). *Communities that care: Community planning kit.* Seattle, WA: Author.

Ellickson, P. L., & Bell, R. M. (1990). Drug prevention in junior high: A multi-site longitudinal test. *Science, 247,* 1299–1305.

Elliott, D. S., Huizinga, D., & Ageton, S. S. (1985). *Explaining delinquency and drug use.* Beverly Hills, CA: Sage.

Eng, E., & Parker, E. (1990, October). *Community competence and health: Definitional, conceptual and measurement issues.* Paper presented at the annual meeting of the American Public Health Association, New York.

Fagan, J. (1988). *The social organization of drug use and drug dealing among urban gangs.* New York: John Jay College of Criminal Justice.

Fagan, J., & Browne, A. (1994). Violence between spouses and intimates: Physical aggression between women and men in intimate relationships. In A. J. Riess, Jr., & J. A. Roth (Eds.), *Understanding and preventing violence: Social influences* (Vol. 3, pp. 115–292). Washington, DC: National Academy Press.

Fawcett, S. B., Paine, A. L., Francisco, V. T., & Vliet, M. (1993). Promoting health through community development. In D. S. Glenwick & L. A. Jason (Eds.), *Promoting health and mental health in children, youth and families* (pp. 233–255). New York: Springer.

Flasher, L. V., & Maisto, S. A. (1984). A review of theory and research on drinking patterns among Jews. *The Journal of Nervous and Mental Disease, 172,* 596–603.

Flay, B. R., d'Avernas, J. R., Best, J. A., Kersell, M. W., & Ryan, K. B. (1983). Cigarette smoking: Why young people do it and ways of preventing it. In P. McGrath & P. Firestone (Eds.), *Pediatric and adolescent behavioral medicine* (pp. 132–183). New York: Springer-Verlag.

Flay, B. R., Koepke, D., Thomson, S. J., Santi, S., Best, J. A., & Brown, K. S. (1989). Six-year follow-up of the first Waterloo school smoking prevention trial. *American Journal of Public Health, 79,* 1371–1376.

Fleming, J. P., Kellam, S. G., & Brown, C. H. (1982). Early predictors of age of first use of alcohol, marijuana, and cigarettes. *Drug and Alcohol Dependence, 9,* 285–303.

Garmezy, N. (1985). Stress-resistant children: The search for protective factors. In J. E. Stevenson (Ed.), Recent research in developmental psychopathology. *Journal of Child Psychology and Psychiatry, 4* (Suppl.), 213–233.

Gittelman, R. S., Mannuzza, R. S., & Bonagura, N. (1985). Hyperactive boys almost grown up: 1. Psychiatric status. *Archives of General Psychiatry, 42,* 937–947.

Goldstein, A., & Kalant, H. (1990). Drug policy: Striking the right balance. *Science, 249,* 1513–1521.

Gordon, R. (1983). An operational classification of disease prevention. *Public Health Reports, 98,* 107–109.

Gorsuch, R. L., & Butler, M. C. (1976). Initial drug abuse: A review of predisposing social psychological factors. *Psychological Bulletin, 83,* 120–137.

Gottfredson, D. C. (1988). An evaluation of an organization-development approach to reducing school disorder. *Evaluation Review, 11,* 739–763.

Grove, W. M., Eckert, E. D., Heston, L., Bouchard, T. J., Segal, N., & Lykken, D. T. (1990). Heritability of substance abuse and antisocial behavior: A study of monozygotic twins reared apart. *Society of Biological Psychiatry, 27,* 1293–1304.

Haberman, H. E., & Baden, M. H. (1974). Alcoholism and violent death. *Quarterly Journal of Studies on Alcohol, 35,* 221–231.

Haglund, B., Weisbrod, R. R., & Bracht, N. (1990). Assessing the community: Its services, needs, leadership, and readiness. In N. Bracht (Ed.), *Health promotion at the community level* (pp. 91–108). Newbury Park, CA: Sage.

Hansen, W. B., & Graham, J. W. (1991). Preventing alcohol, marijuana, and cigarette use among adolescents: Peer pressure resistance training versus establishing conservative norms. *Preventive Medicine, 20,* 414–430.

Hansen, W. B., Johnson, C. A., Flay, B. R., Graham, J. W., & Sobel, J. (1988). Affective and social influences approaches to the prevention of multiple substance abuse among seventh-grade students: Results from Project SMART. *Preventive Medicine, 17,* 135–154.

Harford, T. C. (1985). Drinking patterns among black and nonblack adolescents: Results of a national survey. In R. Wright & T. D. Watts (Eds.), *Prevention of black alcoholism: Issues and strategies* (pp. 122–139). Springfield, IL: Thomas.

Hawkins, J. D., Arthur, M. W., & Catalano, R. F. (1995). Preventing substance abuse. In M. Tonry & D. Farrington (Eds.), *Crime and justice: A review of research: Vol. 19. Building a safer society: Strategic approaches to crime prevention* (pp. 343–427). Chicago: University of Chicago Press.

Hawkins, J. D., Arthur, M. W., & Olson, J. J. (in press). Community interventions to reduce risks and enhance protection against anti-social behavior. In D. S. Stoff, J. Brelining, & J. D. Masers (Eds.), *Handbook of antisocial behaviors.* New York: Wiley.

Hawkins, J. D., Catalano, R. F., & Associates. (1992). *Communities that care. Action for drug abuse prevention.* San Francisco: Jossey-Bass.

Hawkins, J. D., Catalano, R. F., & Kent, L. A. (1991). Combining broadcast media and parent education to prevent teenage drug abuse. In L. Donohew, H. E. Sypher, & W. J. Bukoski (Eds.), *Persuasive communication and drug abuse prevention* (pp. 283–294). Hillsdale, NJ: Erlbaum.

Hawkins, J. D., Catalano, R. F., & Miller, J. Y. (1992). Risk and protective factors for alcohol and other drug problems in adolescence and early adulthood: Implications for substance abuse prevention. *Psychological Bulletin, 112,* 64–105.

Hawkins, J. D., Catalano, R. F., Morrison, D. M., O'Donnell, J., Abbott, R. D., & Day, L. E. (1992). The Seattle Social Development Project: Effects of the first four years on protective factors and problem behaviors. In J. McCord & R. Tremblay (Eds.), *The prevention of anti-social behavior in children* (pp. 139–161). New York: Guilford Press.

Hawkins, J. D., & Fitzgibbon, J. J. (1993). Risk factors and risk behaviors in prevention of adolescent substance use. *Adolescent Medicine: State of the Art Reviews, 4,* 249–262.

Hawkins, J. D., Graham, J. W., Maguin, E., Abbott, R. D., & Catalano, R. F. (in press). Exploring the effects of age of alcohol use initiation and psychosocial risk factors on subsequent alcohol misuse. *Journal of Studies on Alcohol.*

Hawkins, J. D., Lishner, D. M., Jenson, J. M., & Catalano, R. F. (1987). Delinquents and drugs: What the evidence suggests about prevention and treatment programming. In B. S. Brown & A. R. Mills (Eds.), *Youth at high risk for substance abuse* (DHHS Publication No. ADM 87-1537, pp. 81–131). Washington, DC: U.S. Government Printing Office.

Heuser, J. P. (1990). *A preliminary evaluation of the short-term impact of the "Preparing for the Drug (Free) Years" community service program in Oregon.* Unpublished manuscript, Oregon Department of Justice, Crime Analysis Center, Salem, OR.

Hirschi, T. (1969). *Causes of delinquency.* Berkeley: University of California Press.

Holcomb, A. K., & Schulte, D. (1993). *Kansas family initiative evaluation 1992–1993.* Unpublished manuscript, DCCCA Center Evaluation Services, Lawrence, KS.

Holder, H. D., & Blose, J. O. (1987). Impact of changes in distilled spirits availability on apparent consumption: A time-series analysis of liquor-by-the-drink. *British Journal of Addiction, 82,* 623–631.

Holmberg, M. B. (1985). Longitudinal studies of drug abuse in a fifteen-year-old population: 1. Drug career. *Acta Psychiatrica Scandinavica, 71,* 67–79.

Horacek, H. J., Ramey, C. T., Campbell, F. A., Hoffman, K. P., & Fletcher, R. H. (1987). Predicting school failure and assessing early intervention with high-risk children. *Journal of the American Academy of Child and Adolescent Psychiatry, 26,* 758–763.

Hrubec, Z., & Omenn, G. S. (1981). Evidence of genetic predisposition to alcoholic cirrhosis and psychosis: Twin concordance for alcoholism and biological endpoints by zygosity among male veterans. *Alcoholism: Clinical and Experimental Research, 5,* 207–215.

Hundleby, J. D., & Mercer, G. W. (1987). Family and friends as social environments and their relationship to young adolescents' use of alcohol, tobacco, and marijuana. *Journal of Marriage and the Family, 49,* 151–164.

Institute of Medicine, Committee on Drug Use in the Workplace. (1990). *Under the influence: Drugs and the American work force.* Washington, DC: National Academy Press.

Institute of Medicine, Committee on Prevention of Mental Disorders. (1994). *Reducing risks for mental disorders: Frontiers for preventive intervention research.* Washington, DC: National Academy Press.

Jessor, R., Donovan, J. E., & Windmer, K. (1980). *Psychosocial factors in adolescent alcohol and drug use: The 1980 National Sample Study, and the 1974–1978 Panel Study.* Unpublished final report, University of Colorado, Institute of Behavioral Science, Boulder.

Jessor, R., & Jessor, S. L. (1977). *Problem behavior and psychosocial development: A longitudinal study of youth.* New York: Academic Press.

Johnson, B. D., Williams, T., Dei, K. A., & Sanabria, H. (1990). Drug abuse in the inner city: Impact on hard-drug users and the community. In M. Tonry & J. Q. Wilson (Eds.), *Crime and justice: A review of research: Vol. 13. Drugs and crime* (pp. 9–67). Chicago: University of Chicago Press.

Johnson, D. L., & Breckenridge, J. N. (1982). The Houston Parent-Child Development Center and the primary prevention of behavior problems in young children. *American Journal of Community Psychology, 10,* 305–316.

Johnson, G. M., Shontz, F. C., & Locke, T. P. (1984). Relationships between adolescent drug use and parental drug behaviors. *Adolescence, 19,* 295–299.

Johnson, R. J., & Kaplan, H. B. (1990). Stability of psychological symptoms: Drug use consequences and intervening processes. *Journal of Health and Social Behavior, 31,* 277–291.

Johnston, L. D. (1991). Toward a theory of drug epidemics. In L. Donohew, H. E. Sypher, & W. J. Bukoski (Eds.), *Persuasive communication and drug abuse prevention* (pp. 93–131). Hillsdale, NJ: Erlbaum.

Johnston, L. D., O'Malley, P. M., & Bachman, J. G. (1991). *Trends in drug use and associated factors among American high school students, college students, and young adults.* Rockville, MD: National Institute on Drug Abuse.

Johnston, L. D., O'Malley, P. M., & Bachman, J. G. (1993). *National survey results on drug abuse from the Monitoring the Future study 1975–1992: Vol. 1. Secondary school students.* Ann Arbor: University of Michigan, Institute for Social Research.

Johnston, L. D., O'Malley, P. M., & Bachman, J. G. (1995, December 11). *Drug use rises again in 1995 among American teens* [News Release]. University of Michigan News and Information Services, Ann Arbor.

Julien, R. M. (1981). *A primer of drug action.* San Francisco: Freeman.

Kandel, D. B. (1978). Covergences in prospective longitudinal surveys of drug use in normal populations. In D. B. Kandel (Ed.), *Longitudinal research on drug use: Empirical findings and methodological issues* (pp. 3–38). Washington, DC: Hemisphere.

Kandel, D. B. (1982). Epidemiological and psychosocial perspectives on adolescent drug use. *Journal of the American Academy of Clinical Psychiatry, 21,* 328–347.

Kandel, D. B. (1986). Processes of peer influence in adolescence. In R. Silberstein (Ed.), *Development as action in context: Problem behavior and normal youth development* (pp. 203–228). New York: Springer-Verlag.

Kandel, D. B., & Andrews, K. (1987). Processes of adolescent socialization by parents and peers. *International Journal of the Addictions, 22,* 319–342.

Kandel, D. B., & Davies, M. (1992). Progression to regular marijuana involvement: Phenomenology and risk factors for near-daily use. In M. Glantz & R. Pickens (Eds.), *Vulnerability to abuse* (pp. 211–253). Washington, DC: American Psychological Association.

Kandel, D. B., Davies, M., Karus, D., & Yamaguchi, K. (1986). The consequences in young adulthood of adolescent drug involvement. *Archives of General Psychiatry, 43,* 746–754.

Kandel, D. B., Kessler, R. C., & Margulies, R. Z. (1978). Antecedents of adolescent initiation into stages of drug use: A developmental analysis. *Journal of Youth and Adolescence, 7,* 13–40.

Kandel, D. B., Simcha-Fagan, O., & Davies, M. (1986). Risk factors for delinquency and illicit drug use from adolescence to young adulthood. *Journal of Drug Issues, 16,* 67–90.

Kandel, D. B., Single, E., & Kessler, R. (1976). The epidemiology of drug use among New York State high school students: Distribution, trends, and change in rates of use. *American Journal of Public Health, 66,* 43–53.

Kandel, D. B., & Yamaguchi, K. (1985). Developmental patterns of the use of legal, illegal, and medically prescribed psychotropic drugs from adolescence to young adulthood. In C. L. Jones & R. J. Battjes (Eds.), *Etiology of drug abuse: Implications for prevention* (NIDA Research Monograph No. 56). Washington, DC: U.S. Government Printing Office.

Kazdin, A. E. (1990, June). *Prevention of conduct disorder.* Paper presented to the National Conference on Prevention Research, National Institute of Mental Health, Bethesda, MA.

Kellam, S. G., & Brown, H. (1982). *Social adaptational and psychological antecedents of adolescent psychopathology ten years later.* Baltimore: Johns Hopkins University.

Kendler, K. F. (1992). A population-based twin study of alcoholism in women. *Journal of the American Medical Association, 268,* 1877–1882.

Kessler, R. C., McGonagle, K. A., Zhao, S., Nelson, C. B., Hughes, M., Eshleman, S., Wittehen, H. U., & Kendler, K. S. (1994). Lifetime and 12-month prevalence of *DSM-III-R* psychiatric disorders in the United States: Results from the National Comorbidity Study. *Archives of General Psychiatry, 51*, 8–19.

Kim, S. (1979). *An evaluation of ombudsman primary prevention program on student drug abuse*. Charlotte, NC: Charlotte Drug Education Center.

Klepp, K.-I., Halper, A., & Perry, C. L. (1986). The efficacy of peer leaders in drug abuse prevention. *Journal of School Health, 56*, 407–411.

Kosterman, R., Hawkins, J. D., Haggerty, K. P., Spoth, R., & Redmond, C. (1996). *Preparing for the Drug Free Years: Session-specific effects of a universal parent-training intervention with rural families*. Unpublished manuscript submitted for review. University of Washington, Social Development Research Group, Seattle, WA.

Kosterman, R., Hawkins, J. D., Spoth, R., Haggerty, K. P., & Zhu, K. (in press). Effects of a preventive parent-training intervention on observed family interactions: Proximal outcomes from preparing for the Drug Free Years. *Journal of Community Psychology*.

Krieg, T. L. (1982, December). Is raising the legal drinking age warranted? *The Police Chief,* 32–34.

Krosnick, J. A., & Judd, C. M. (1982). Transitions in social influence at adolescence: Who induces cigarette smoking? *Developmental Psychology, 18*, 359–368.

Ladecour, P., & Temple, M. (1985). Substance use among rapists. *Crime and Delinquency, 31,* 269–294.

Lally, J. R., Mangione, P. L., & Honig, A. S. (1988). The Syracuse University Family Development Research Program: Long-range impact on an early intervention with low-income children and their families. In D. R. Powell & I. Sigel (Eds.), *Advances in applied developmental psychology: Vol. 3. Parent education as early childhood intervention: Emerging directions in theory, research, and practice* (pp. 79–104). Norwood, NJ: ABLEX.

Leigh, B. C., & Stall, R. (1993). Substance use and risky sexual behavior for exposure to HIV: Issues in methodology, interpretation, and prevention. *American Psychologist, 48*(10), 1035–1045.

Levy, D., & Sheflin, N. (1985). The demand for alcoholic beverages: An aggregate time-series analysis. *Journal of Public Policy and Marketing, 4*, 47–54.

Lewinsohn, P. M., Hops, H., Roberts, R. E., Seely, J. R., & Andrews, J. A. (1993). Adolescent psychopathology: 1. Prevalence and incidence of depression and other *DSM-III-R* disorders in high school students. *Journal of Abnormal Psychology, 102*, 133–144.

Lewis, C. E., Robins, L. N., & Rice, J. (1985). Association of alcoholism with antisocial personality in urban men. *Journal of Nervous and Mental Disease, 173*, 166–174.

Loeber, R., & Stouthamer-Loeber, M. S. (1986). Family factors as correlates and predictors of juvenile conduct problems and delinquency. In M. Tonry & N. Morris (Eds.), *Crime and justice: An annual review of research* (Vol. 7, pp. 29–149). Chicago: University of Chicago Press.

Lorion, R. P., & Ross, J. G. (1992). Programs for change: A realistic look at the nation's potential for preventing substance involvement among high-risk youth [OSAP Special Issue]. *Journal of Community Psychology*, 3–9.

Maddahian, E., Newcomb, M. D., & Bentler, P. M. (1988). Risk factors for substance use: Ethnic differences among adolescents. *Journal of Substance Abuse, 1*, 11–23.

Marrett, C. (1971). On the specification of interorganizational dimensions. *Sociology and Social Research, 56*, 83–99.

McGee, R., Silva, P. A., & Williams, S. (1984). Perinatal, neurological, environmental and developmental characteristics of seven-year-old children with stable behavior problems. *Journal of Child Psychology and Psychiatry, 25*, 573–586.

McKnight, J. L., & Kretzman, J. (1990). *Mapping community capacity.* Chicago: Northwestern University, Center for Urban Affairs and Policy Research.

McMillan, D. W., & Chavis, D. M. (1986). Sense of community: A definition and theory. *Journal of Community Psychology, 14,* 6–23.

Merikangas, K. R. (1990). The genetic epidemiology of alcoholism. *Psychological Medicine, 20,* 11–22.

Merikangas, K. R., Rounsaville, B. J., & Prusoff, B. A. (1992). Familial factors in vulnerability to substance abuse. In M. Glantz & R. Pickens (Eds.), *Vulnerability to abuse* (pp. 75–97). Washington, DC: American Psychological Association.

Michaud, L. J., Rivara, F. P., Jaffe, K. M., Fay, G., & Dailey, J. L. (1993). Traumatic brain injury as a risk factor for behavioral disorders in children. *Archives of Physiological and Medical Rehabilitation, 74,* 368–375.

Miczek, K. A., DeBold, J. F., Haney, M., Tidey, J., Vivian, J., & Weerts, E. M. (1994). Alcohol, drugs of abuse, aggression, and violence. In A. J. Riess, Jr., & J. A. Roth (Eds.), *Understanding and preventing violence: Social influences* (Vol. 3, pp. 377–570). Washington, DC: National Academy Press.

Moore, M. H. (1990). Supply reduction and drug law enforcement. In M. Tonry & J. Q. Wilson (Eds.), *Crime and justice: A review of research: Vol. 13. Drugs and crime* (pp. 109–157). Chicago: University of Chicago Press.

Murray, D. M., Richards, R. V., Luepker, R. V., & Johnson, C. A. (1987). The prevention of cigarette smoking in children: Two- and three-year follow-up comparisons of four prevention strategies. *Journal of Behavioral Medicine, 10,* 595–611.

Murray, R. M., Clifford, C. A., & Gurling, H. M. D. (1983). Twin and adoption studies: How good is the evidence for a genetic role? *Recent Developments in Alcoholism, 1,* 25–48.

National Highway Traffic Safety Administration. (1994). *Traffic safety facts 1994: Alcohol, Table 2. 1984–1994.* Washington, DC: Author.

Needle, R. H., Su, S. S., & Doherty, W. J. (1990). Divorce, remarriage, and adolescent substance use: A prospective longitudinal study. *Journal of Marriage and the Family, 52,* 157–169.

Newcomb, M. D., & Bentler, P. M. (1986). Substance use and ethnicity: Differential impact of peer and adult models. *Journal of Psychology, 120,* 83–95.

Newcomb, M. D., & Bentler, P. M. (1988). *Consequences of adolescent drug use: Impact on the lives of young adults.* Newbury Park, CA: Sage.

Newcomb, M. D., Maddahian, E., & Bentler, P. M. (1986). Risk factors for drug use among adolescents: Concurrent and longitudinal analyses. *American Journal of Public Health, 76,* 525–530.

Newcomb, M. D., Maddahian, E., Skager, R., & Bentler, P. M. (1987). Substance abuse and psychosocial risk factors among teenagers: Associations with sex, age, ethnicity and type of school. *American Journal of Drug and Alcohol Abuse, 13,* 413–433.

Norem-Hebeisen, A., Johnson, D. W., Anderson, D., & Johnson, R. (1984). Predictors and concomitants of changes in drug use patterns among teenagers. *Journal of Social Psychology, 124,* 43–50.

O'Donnell, J., Hawkins, J. D., Catalano, R. C., Abbott, R. D., & Day, L. E. (1995). Preventing school failure, drug use, and delinquency among low-income children: Effects of a long-term prevention project in elementary schools. *American Journal of Orthopsychiatry, 65,* 87–100.

Olds, D. L., Henderson, C. R., Chamberlin, R., & Tatelbaum, R. (1986). Preventing child abuse and neglect: A randomized trial of nurse home visitation. *Pediatrics, 78,* 65–78.

Olds, D. L., Henderson, C. R., Tatelbaum, R., & Chamberlin, R. (1988). Improving the life-course development of socially disadvantaged mothers: A randomized trial of nurse home visitation. *American Journal of Public Health, 78,* 1436–1445.

O'Malley, P. M., & Wagenaar, A. C. (1991). Effects of minimum drinking age laws on alcohol use, related behaviors and traffic crash involvement among American youth: 1976–1987. *Journal of Studies on Alcohol, 52,* 478–491.

Penning, M., & Barnes, G. E. (1982). Adolescent marijuana use: A review. *International Journal of the Addictions, 17,* 749–791.

Pentz, M. A., Dwyer, J. H., MacKinnon, D. P., Flay, B. R., Hansen, W. B., Wang, E. Y. I., & Johnson, C. A. (1989). A multi-community trial for primary prevention of adolescent drug abuse: Effects on drug use prevalence. *Journal of the American Medical Association, 261,* 3259–3266.

Perrine, M. W., Peck, R. C., & Fell, J. C. (1988). Epidemiologic perspectives on drunk driving. In U.S. Department of Health and Human Services (Ed.), *Background papers of Surgeon General's workshop on drunk driving* (pp. 35–76). Washington, DC: U.S. Department of Health and Human Services.

Perry, C. L. (1986). Community-wide health promotion and drug abuse prevention. *Journal of School Health, 56,* 359–363.

Perry, C. L., Kelder, S. H., & Komro, K. (in press). *The social world of adolescents: Family, peers, schools, and culture.* Washington, DC: Carnegie Council on Adolescents, Carnegie Corporation.

Perry, C. L., Kelder, S. H., Murray, D. M., & Klepp, K.-I. (1992). Community-wide smoking prevention: Long-term outcomes of the Minnesota Heart Health Program and Class of 1989 study. *American Journal of Public Health, 82,* 1210–1216.

Perry, C. L., Williams, C. L., Forster, J. L., Wolfson, M., Wagenaar, A. C., Finnegan, J. R., McGovern, P. G., Veblen-Mortenson, S., Komro, K. A., & Anstine, P. S. (1993). Background, conceptualization and design of a community-wide research program on adolescent alcohol use: Project Northland. *Health Education Research, 8,* 125–136.

Perry, C. L., Williams, C. L., Veblen-Mortenson, S., Toomey, T. L., Komro, K. A., Anstine, P. S., McGovern, P. G., Finnegan, J. R., Forster, J. L., Wagenaar, A. C., & Wolfson, M. (in press). Outcomes of a community-wide alcohol use prevention program during early adolescence: Project Northland. *American Journal of Public Health.*

Peterson, P. L., Hawkins, J. D., Abbott, R. D., & Catalano, R. F. (1994). Disentangling the effects of parental drinking, family management, and parental alcohol norms on current drinking by Black and White adolescents. *Journal of Research on Adolescence, 4,* 203–227.

Pickens, R. W., Svikis, D. S., McGue, M., Lykken, D. T., Heston, L. L., & Clayton, P. J. (1991). Heterogeneity in the inheritance of alcoholism: A study of male and female twins. *Archives of General Psychiatry, 48,* 19–28.

Polich, J. M., Ellickson, P. L., Reuter, P., & Kahan, J. P. (1984). *Strategies for controlling adolescent drug use.* Santa Monica, CA: RAND Corp.

Price, R. H., & Lorion, R. P. (1989). Prevention programming as organizational reinvention: From research to implementation. In *Prevention of mental disorders.* Rockville, MD: National Clearinghouse for Alcohol and Drug Information.

Prochaska, J. O., DiClemente, C. C., & Norcross, J. C. (1992). In search of how people change: Applications to addictive behaviors. *American Psychologist, 47,* 1102–1114.

Rachal, J. V., Guess, L. L., Hubbard, R. L., Maisto, S. A., Cavanaugh, E. R., Waddell, R., & Benrud, C. H. (1982). Facts for planning: No. 4. Alcohol misuse by adolescents. *Alcohol Health and Research World,* 61–68.

Radke-Yarrow, M., & Sherman, T. (1990). Children born at medical risk: Factors affecting vulnerability and resilience. In J. Rolf, A. S. Masten, D. Cicchetti, K. H. Nuechterlein, & S. Weintraub (Eds.), *Risk and protective factors in the development of psychopathology.* Cambridge, England: Cambridge University Press.

Rauh, V. A., Achenbach, T. H., Nurcombe, B., Howell, C. T., & Teti, D. M. (1988). Minimizing adverse effects of low birth weight: Four-year results of an early intervention program. *Child Development, 59,* 544–553.

Robins, L. N. (1984). The natural history of adolescent drug use. *American Journal of Public Health, 74,* 656–657.

Robins, L. N. (1992). *Synthesis and analysis of longitudinal research on substance abuse.* Unpublished report for the Robert Wood Johnson Foundation.

Robins, L. N., & Przybeck, T. R. (1985). Age of onset of drug use as a factor in drug and other disorders. In C. L. Jones & R. J. Battjes (Eds.), *Etiology of drug abuse: Implications for prevention* (National Institute on Drug Abuse Research Monograph No. 56, DHHS Publication No. ADM 85-1335, pp. 178–192). Washington, DC: U.S. Government Printing Office.

Robins, L. N., & Ratcliff, K. S. (1979). Risk factors in the continuation of childhood antisocial behavior into adulthood. *International Journal of Mental Health, 7,* 76–116.

Rogers, E. M., & Shoemaker, F. F. (1971). *Communication of innovations: A cross-cultural approach* (2nd ed.). New York: Free Press.

Rutter, M. (1979). Protective factors in children's responses to stress and disadvantage. In M. W. Kent & J. E. Rolf (Eds.), *Primary prevention of psychopathology: Vol. 3. Social competence in children* (pp. 49–74). Hanover, NH: University Press of New England.

Saffer, H., & Grossman, M. (1987). Beer taxes, the legal drinking age, and youth motor vehicle fatalities. *Journal of Legal Studies, 16,* 351–374.

Sameroff, A. J., & Chandler, M. J. (1975). Reproductive risk and the continuum of caretaking casualty. In F. D. Horowitz, M. Hetherington, & S. Scarr-Salopatek (Eds.), *Review of child development research* (Vol. 4, pp. 187–244). Chicago: University of Chicago Press.

Schermerhorn, J. R. (1981). Open questions limiting the practice of interorganizational development. *Group and Organizational Studies, 6,* 83–95.

Schroeder, S. A. (1993). Substance abuse (President's message). In *Substance Abuse, the Robert Wood Johnson Foundation Annual Report 1992.*

Schukit, M. A. (1987). Biological vulnerability to alcoholism. *Journal of Consulting and Clinical Psychology, 55,* 301–309.

Schweinhart, L. J. (1987). Can preschool programs help prevent delinquency? In J. Q. Wilson & G. C. Loury (Eds.), *From children to citizens: Families, schools, and delinquency prevention.* New York: Springer-Verlag.

Seitz, V., Rosenbaum, L. K., & Apfel, N. H. (1985). Effects of family support intervention: A ten-year follow-up. *Child Development, 56,* 376–391.

Selnow, G. W. (1987). Parent-child relationships and single- and two-parent families: Implications for substance usage. *Journal of Drug Education, 17,* 315–326.

Shedler, J., & Block, J. (1990). Adolescent drug use and psychological health: A longitudinal inquiry. *American Psychologist, 45,* 612–630.

Sherman, L. W., Smith, D. A., Schmidt, J. D., & Rogan, D. A. (1992). Crime, punishment, and stake in conformity: Legal and informal control of domestic violence. *American Sociological Review, 52,* 680–690.

Siegel, R. K. (1989). *Intoxication.* New York: Dutton.

Simcha-Fagan, O., Gersten, J. C., & Langer, T. S. (1986). Early precursors and concurrent correlates of patterns of illicit drug use in adolescence. *Journal of Drug Issues, 16,* 7–28.

Simcha-Fagan, O., & Schwartz, J. E. (1986). Neighborhood and delinquency: An assessment of contextual effects. *Criminology, 24,* 667–704.

Spoth, R., & Redmond, C. (1995). Parent motivation to enroll in parenting skills programs: A model of family context and health belief predictors. *Journal of Family Psychology, 9*(3), 294–310.

Spoth, R., Redmond, C., Haggerty, K., & Ward, T. (1995, May). A controlled outcome study examining individual difference and attendance effects. *Journal of Marriage and the Family, 57,* 449–464.

Substance Abuse and Mental Health Services Administration (SAMHSA). (1994, Summer). Statistics paint the picture of mental health. *SAMHSA News, 2*(3), 3–5, 14.

Tao Hunter, F. T., & Youniss, J. (1982). Change in functions of three relations during adolescence. *Developmental Psychology, 18,* 806–811.

Tarter, R. (1988). Are there inherited behavioral traits which predispose to substance abuse? *Journal of Consulting and Clinical Psychology, 56,* 189–196.

Tarter, R., Laird, S., Kabene, M., Bukstein, O., & Kaminer, Y. (1990). Drug abuse severity in adolescents is associated with magnitude of deviation in temperament traits. *British Journal of Addiction, 85,* 1501–1504.

Telzrow, C. F. (1990). Impact of perinatal complications on education. In J. W. Gray & R. S. Dean (Eds.), *Neuropsychology of perinatal complications* (pp. 161–185). New York: Springer.

U.S. Department of Health and Human Services. (1992). *Position papers from the Third National Injury Control Conference: Setting the national agenda for injury control in the 1990's.* Washington, DC: Author.

Vaillant, G. (1983). *The natural history of alcoholism.* Cambridge, MA: Harvard University Press.

Wagenaar, A. C., & Holder, H. D. (1991). A change from public to private sale of wine: Results from natural experiments in Iowa and West Virginia. *Journal of Studies on Alcohol, 52,* 162–173.

Watts, R. K., & Rabow, J. (1983). Alcohol availability and alcohol-related problems in 213 Californian cities. *Alcoholism: Clinical and Experimental Research, 7,* 47–58.

Werner, E. E. (1987). Vulnerability and resiliency in children at risk for delinquency: A longitudinal study from birth to adulthood. In J. D. Burchard & S. N. Burchard (Eds.), *Primary prevention of psychopathology: Vol. 10. Prevention of delinquent behavior.* Newbury Park, CA: Sage.

Werner, E. E. (1989). High-risk children in young adulthood: A longitudinal study from birth to 32 years. *American Journal of Orthopsychiatry, 59,* 72–81.

Werner, E. E., & Smith, R. S. (1982). *Vulnerable but invincible: A longitudinal study of resilient children and youth.* New York: McGraw-Hill.

White, H. R., Aidala, A., & Zablocki, B. (1988). A longitudinal investigation of drug use and work patterns among middle-class, white adults. *Journal of Applied Behavioral Science, 24,* 455–469.

Yoshikawa, H. (1994). Prevention as cumulative protection: Effects of early family support and education on chronic delinquency and its risks. *Psychological Bulletin, 115,* 28–54.

Zeira, Y., & Avedisian, J. (1989). Organizational planned change: Assessing the chances for success. *Organizational Dynamics, 17,* 31–45.

CHAPTER 10

Conduct Disorders and Antisocial Behavior

RONALD J. PRINZ and CHRISTIAN M. CONNELL

Conduct disorder is a disruptive behavior disorder that occurs in late childhood and adolescence. According to the Diagnostic and Statistical Manual of Mental Disorders (*DSM-IV;* APA, 1994), the main features of conduct disorder are: (a) "a repetitive and persistent pattern of behavior in which the basic rights of others or major age-appropriate societal norms or rules are violated"; and (b) significant impairment of social and academic functioning. Behaviors that interfere with the rights of others or violate societal norms include a broad range of actions. For example, harm or threat of harm toward other people can include bullying, frequent physical fights, use of a weapon (e.g., knife, club, gun), physical cruelty, confrontational theft, or rape. Other manifestations of conduct disorder can include deliberate vandalism, theft and deceit, running away from home overnight (other than to avoid physical or sexual abuse at home), and chronic school truancy.

Unlike prior versions of the *DSM, DSM-IV* (APA, 1994) distinguishes between childhood-onset and adolescent-onset conduct disorder. Diagnosis of the childhood-onset version of conduct disorder requires that at least one of the criterion characteristics begins prior to age 10 years and usually means that the full set of diagnostic criteria are met prior to puberty. The early-onset distinction is based on empirical findings on developmental precursors and pathways of conduct disorder. Youth with the highest risk for serious delinquency and associated aggression or violence typically begin to display conduct problems in early childhood. This early-onset group evidences pronounced cross-situational behavior problems between ages 4 and 8 (Dumas, 1992; Loeber, 1988, 1990; Loeber & LeBlanc, 1990; Patterson, DeBaryshe, & Ramsey, 1989).

Estimates of the prevalence of conduct disorder vary somewhat as a function of strictness of diagnostic criteria as well as other factors such as setting (e.g., urban versus rural) and socioeconomic status. Kazdin (1995) notes that prevalence estimates for conduct disorder in youth aged 4 to 18 years vary from 2% to 6%.

CAUSES AND CONSEQUENCES

Our causal understanding of the ontogeny of conduct disorder is based on extensive research regarding significant risk factors and to a lesser extent on work related to protective factors that may mitigate risk. One particularly well-supported set of approaches to understanding the develpment of early-onset conduct disorder is found in the social-interactional perspective. This approach maintains that social-environmental variables interact with child characteristics (including biological features) to influence trajectories toward, or away from, antisocial outcomes. Many of the implicated risk factors for conduct disorder are in fact embedded in the social environment and unfold in a developmental progression.

Preschool Years

Parenting difficulties play a major role in the development of oppositional-aggressive behavior during the preschool years that increases risk for later conduct problems (Patterson, 1982; Patterson, Reid, & Dishion, 1992; Wahler & Dumas, 1987). Such parenting difficulties mainly include poor discipline (Farrington & West, 1981; McCord, 1988; Patterson et al., 1992), coercive family processes (Patterson, 1982), and insufficient positive teaching (Loeber & Stouthamer-Loeber, 1986; Wadsworth, 1980). These parenting difficulties may more adversely affect children with early temperament problems (Bates, Bayles, Bennett, Ridge, & Brown, 1991; Campbell, Breaux, Ewing, & Szumowski, 1986; Offord, Boyle, & Racine, 1991) in a transactional manner that escalates oppositional behavior with parents and siblings and aggravates attentional problems (Dumas, 1992; Loeber & Stouthamer-Loeber, 1986; Moffitt, 1990).

In addition to parenting difficulties, a second set of family risk factors may exert influence during the preschool years (and later as well). This second set pertains to sources of family adversity and includes parental social insularity and social disadvantage (Dumas, 1986a; Wahler & Dumas, 1987), parental alcohol and illicit drug abuse (West & Prinz, 1987), parental criminality and psychopathology (Offord, 1982; Robins, 1981), and marital discord (Offord & Boyle, 1986; Rutter & Giller, 1983). In terms of likely pathway, family adversity during the preschool years affects child behavior primarily because high stress disrupts parenting and heightens parenting difficulties that are already present (Capaldi & Patterson, 1991; Dumas, 1986b; Snyder, 1991; West & Prinz, 1987). Over time, transactions between child temperament and parenting difficulties, especially in the presence of family adversity, are likely to further undermine parenting and escalate child conduct problems, setting the stage for a difficult transition to first grade.

Early Elementary School

Conduct problems in first grade (often manifested as cross-situational aggression) place a child at increased risk for subsequent learning difficulties (Offord & Waters, 1983; Rutter & Giller, 1983) and future delinquency (Dumas, 1992; Loeber, 1988, 1990; Patterson et al., 1989). Children who enter first grade already exhibiting high rates of aggressive and oppositional behavior are at risk for classroom behavior problems such as ignoring teacher instructions, hitting classmates, disrupting class, and destroying property (Prinz, Connor, & Wilson, 1981). This type of classroom behavior brings about two new risk factors—negative classroom experiences and disturbed peer relations—adding to risk already generated by exposure to parenting difficulties. Children exhibiting disruptive and inattentive behaviors in class tend to develop learning difficulties related to reading and language-related skills (Moffitt, 1993a, 1993b), which further frustrates them, making classroom experiences more aversive. Furthermore, disruptive classroom behaviors tend to provoke aversive responses from teachers, resulting in negative feedback from teacher to parent that puts a strain on parent-school relations and further taxes parents who are struggling with other sources of family adversity on top of child management problems (Campbell, 1991; Patterson et al., 1992).

Disturbed peer relations also emerge as a risk factor in the early elementary school years. Children exhibiting aggressive and disruptive behavior in school often have underdeveloped social skills that lead to peer rejection and social isolation as early as second or third grade (Bierman, 1986; Cantrell & Prinz, 1985; Dodge, 1989; Parker & Asher, 1987).

Late Childhood and Early Adolescence

An escalating spiral of aggressive and aversive interactions with teachers, peers, and family members is accelerated by negative classroom experiences and peer rejection (Conduct Problems Prevention Research Group [CPPRG], 1992; Reid, 1993). If family-, peer-, and school-related risk factors predominate, this pattern continues through late childhood and into adolescence (Moffitt, 1993a). Around fourth or fifth grade, the impact of rejection by mainstream peers is magnified (Dishion, Patterson, Stoolmiller, & Skinner, 1991; Snyder, Dishion, & Patterson, 1986). In the family domain, insufficient parental monitoring and supervision (Patterson et al., 1992) along with marked family conflict (Dishion et al., 1991; Prinz, Foster, Kent, & O'Leary, 1979) make matters worse. In school, a history of learning difficulties, classroom misconduct, and rejection by teachers and classmates leads to poor "bonding" to the school context, which is a prelude for future school failure and dropout or expulsion (Hawkins & Lishner, 1987; Hawkins & Weis, 1985; Hirschi, 1969).

Although less well understood, protective factors increase the likelihood that some children desist from this negative spiral over time. Two such putative protective factors, family social support and positive school climate, may provide some offsetting effects to mitigate risk from the aforementioned factors. Even when parents are ineffective at discipline and other parenting skills, children may still derive a critical amount of social support from family relationships (Rutter, 1978; Zelkowitz, 1987). Growing evidence points to family support as a significant variable for positive adjustment in childhood and adolescence, and indirect evidence suggests that family support is a protective factor for conduct disorder and adolescent substance abuse (Cauce, Reid, Landesman, & Gonzales, 1990; Cohen & Wills, 1985; Rutter, 1979; Werner & Smith, 1982; Wills, Vaccaro, & McNamara, 1992).

Positive school climate may also be a mitigating influence. Some evidence has accrued suggesting that school climate impacts school-wide conduct problems, truancy, and school dropout, and is related to bonding with school (Hawkins & Lam, 1987; Reynolds, Jones, St. Leger, & Murgatroyd, 1980; Rutter & Giller, 1983).

IMPEDIMENTS TO INTERVENTION

Compared with outpatient treatment, preventive interventions with children at risk for conduct disorder are generally harder for several reasons. Generally, families seek outpatient treatment, whereas preventionists may approach families, raising the issues associated with engagement and recruitment. Prevention programs, particularly the ones developed very recently, are more likely to involve simultaneous multiple interventions that, by definition, involve greater implementation difficulties. Prevention programs are more likely to target whole systems, such as families, peer groups, classrooms, and entire schools. Finally, prevention outcomes are not as quickly detectable as treatment outcomes, and preventionists are forced to settle for evidence of risk reduction while awaiting long-term indications of impact.

PREVENTION

Prevention programs can be divided along a continuum based on the target population to be served by the program. Universal interventions are targeted at an entire population rather than a specific subgroup. Selected interventions, on the other hand, narrow this focus by targeting individuals based on identified risk factors related to the development of a given disorder. Finally, indicated interventions are targeted at individuals who already demonstrate detectable symptoms that foreshadow the development of a disorder.

Assessment Strategies

Screening plays a significant role primarily in selected and indicated but not universal preventive interventions. Prevention researchers choose among risk factors, select informants, and create specific procedures for screening.

Risk-Factor Selection

A first consideration for screening is to identify the marker variables or risk factors that will define the inclusion criteria (Lochman & CPPRG, 1995). The family, school, and peer risk factors discussed earlier are prime candidates for selection criteria. For early-onset conduct disorder, aggressive behavior is a commonly used criterion for indicated interventions, but poor school performance and peer rejection have also received consideration (Coie, Lochman, Terry, & Hyman, 1992; Kupersmidt & Coie, 1990). Vitaro, Tremblay, Gagnon, and Pelletier (1994) used hyperactivity and impulsivity as selection variables. For late-onset conduct disorder, viable selection criteria have been based on parent management style, school performance, and peer group behavior (Dishion et al., 1991; Loeber & Dishion, 1983).

Informant Selection

After one or more risk factors are chosen for screening criteria, there are choices of which types of informants to deploy. Possible informants include observers, parents, teachers, peers, and target children. Three considerations are whether an informant has access to the relevant information, avoidance of possible source bias, and the cost for screening. The latter consideration lessens the utility of direct observation for screening, although the methodological advantages of observation have been demonstrated (Charlebois, LeBlanc, Gagnon, & Larivee, 1994).

To address the informant issue, Loeber, Green, and Lahey (1990) surveyed clinicians and researchers as to the relative usefulness of teachers, mothers, and child self-report as informants on child problem behavior. Mothers and teachers were rated as more desirable informants than children on a number of externalizing behaviors including hyperactivity, oppositional behavior, and conduct problems, whereas children were seen as better informants for internalizing behaviors. Domain appears to be a major reason for choosing informants, as teachers were rated as more useful for screening school-based behaviors related to externalizing problems (e.g., hyperactivity), and mothers were rated as more useful in reporting home-based concerns (e.g., oppositional behavior). Results of a study comparing youth, parent, and teacher report of behavior in 177 adolescent males referred for disruptive behavior reinforce clinicians' and researchers' views of appropriate informants. Youth appear to be inappropriate informants for their own hyperactive and oppositional behaviors, while self-report of conduct problems appears to add to the assessment process (Loeber, Green, Lahey, & Stouthamer-Loeber, 1989).

Source bias or informant perception can also play a role in the utility of a particular behavioral report (Kazdin, 1988). Children tend to report fewer symptoms than parents or other informants, possibly because they perceive their behavior as less problematic than those who experience its effects. There is some discrepancy in the literature as to when children are most effective as self-reporters. Some researchers argue that younger children tend to agree more with other informants (Achenbach, McConaughy, & Howell, 1987), while others argue that older children are more effective at describing their behavior (Edelbrock, Costello, Dulcan, Kalas, & Conover, 1985). Kazdin (1988) noted that parental perceptions of child symptoms can also be influenced by parental psychopathology, marital discord, behavioral expectations, self-esteem, stressors, and external social support.

Because various informants contribute different information relevant to risk, multiple informants may lead to more effective screening. Verhulst, Koot, and Ende (1994) found that teacher report of child behavior was a stronger predictor of poor outcome than parent report, but that the combination of parent and teacher information increased predictive power significantly, particularly among females. Other studies have examined the predictive accuracy of behavioral measures (e.g., teacher ratings of aggressiveness and hyperactivity) with sociometric categorization (e.g., peer rejection). In a comparison of the two screening procedures, behavioral ratings appear to be stronger predictors of later problem behavior, both teacher-rated and self-report (Vitaro et al., 1994), although this finding contradicts findings by Parker and Asher (1987). Vitaro et al. (1994) suggested that for younger children behavioral ratings may be better predictors than peer rejection, which may not hold for older children. While teacher ratings may be more powerful predictors of conduct disorder than peer ratings, the combination may be event stronger. In a longitudinal sample of children starting at first grade, Tremblay, LeBlanc, and Schwartzman (1988) found that teacher and peer ratings (of aggression and sociability) equally predicted delinquency in boys, but the combination did not improve the prediction. For girls, however, the combination of teacher and peer ratings significantly increased predictive utility.

Screening Procedures

Deployment of multiple informants can be expensive, particularly when screening for low-base-rate behaviors in the general population. Multiple gating addresses this problem. Multiple gating typically involves a stepwise approach to assessment in which an inexpensive screening measure is applied to a general or specified population to determine first level of risk, followed by more expensive and extensive assessments (or "gates") to select for higher levels of risk. Proponents of multiple gating (Loeber, Dishion, & Patterson, 1984) suggest that this process maximizes accuracy by decreasing the number of false positives and negatives and minimizes cost. In a conduct-disorder prevention program, maximizing accuracy is an important goal in terms of minimizing the chance of iatrogenic effects for youth who do not need the intervention.

One common approach used teacher behavioral ratings as a first gate, followed by parent behavioral ratings as a second gate. Studies by Lochman et al. (1995) and August, Realmuto, Crosby, and MacDonald (1995) adopted this approach and also added a third gate related to parenting practices. Lochman et al. found that the second gate (parent ratings) significantly increased the predictive accuracy of the first gate (teacher ratings), while the third gate (parenting practices) provided little additional power. August et al. (1995) suggested that the three gates add predictive utility for specific child disorders and found that the first gate was predictive of later diagnoses of attention-deficit/hyperactivity disorder (ADHD) and oppositional defiant disorder (ODD). The second gate significantly improved the prediction of ADHD but added little to the prediction of ODD. Finally, the third gate, parent management style, contributed significantly to the prediction of ODD but not ADHD.

Others have examined whether adding more intensive screening mechanisms as additional gates improves high-risk selection. A study by Charlebois et al. (1994) utilized teacher ratings as a first gate followed by a second gate that incorporated direct observation in cross-setting behaviors to assess the severity and specificity of negative behaviors. Addition of severity and more precise labeling of negative behaviors, particularly task-inappropriate behavior, improved prediction of later delinquent behaviors.

Mediational screening is another assessment strategy that may improve selection accuracy and increase cost-effectiveness (Pillow, Sandler, Braver, Wolchik, & Gersten, 1991). Rather than a stepwise screening based on "marker" or risk variables, mediational screening involves selecting individuals who have been exposed to a given stressor and who show deficiencies in critical skills. Pillow et al. (1991) used this method to successfully screen children of divorced parents at risk for subsequent depression, but others have criticized this approach. Brown (1991) suggests that mediational screening, while effectively isolating some high-risk subgroups within a given population, may ignore other equally high-risk groups. Caldwell (1991) questions the actual cost-benefit of such a screening mechanism. In response, Sandler, Braver, Wolchik, Pillow, and Gersten (1991) suggest that mediational screening is best used for disorders with a low base rate in the population, for disorders requiring intense intervention to alter identified mediators, for programs with potential iatrogenic effects, and for disorders that can be screened with a high degree of sensitivity and specificity. These recommendations suggest that mediational screening may be an appropriate assessment strategy for prevention programs dealing with antisocial behavior in children.

Prevention Approaches

Prevention of conduct problems in children and adolescents includes a broad spectrum of programming based mainly on the extensive literature pertaining to risk and protective factors. Prevention programs in the research literature vary on two important dimensions. The first dimension concerns the type of conduct problem targeted in the intervention. Preventive programs may address the development of early-onset conduct problems or late-onset conduct problems. Some of the prevention work with adolescents focuses on the prevention of delinquency or recidivism in delinquents, whereas other work focuses on the prevention of conduct disorder.

A second important dimension concerns the levels of intervention. Programs may deal with individuals, families, classrooms, schools, or community systems in trying to prevent conduct disorder and delinquency. Additionally, recent programs have begun to emphasize cross-setting or multicomponent programming as a more extensive mode of intervention.

Early Intervention

Most research on the prevention of conduct disorder has targeted the early-onset population. Such preventive interventions encompass the broad range of focal points from individual and family, to community and multicomponent interventions. Individual-focused interventions target a variety of behaviors in at-risk children including peer relations (Lochman, Coie, Underwood, & Terry, 1993), problem-solving ability (Spivak & Shure, 1989), and early achievement (Schweinhart & Weikart, 1988).

Interventions that target peer relations derive from findings that aggressive and rejected children are at increased risk for developing long-term behavioral deficits (Parker & Asher, 1987). Promoting acquisition of appropriate social skills is intended to normalize peer relations and avert later consequences such as rejection and gravitation to deviant peers. Such programming has been successful at demonstrating significant impact on the level of aggressive behavior, particularly for children identified as aggressive and rejected by their peers (Lochman et al., 1993). Vitaro and Tremblay (1994) found that social-skill focused interventions were associated with subsequent changes in the best friends that the youth selected. In an alternative approach called peer coping-skills training, Prinz, Blechman, and Dumas (1994) tested an intervention involving cooperative learning activities in small groups composed of both high-risk and socially competent children. Prinz et al. (1994) reported that high-risk children showed significant reductions in aggression and increases in prosocial functioning, without the socially competent children showing any iatrogenic effects. The peer coping-skills approach was designed for inclusion in a multicomponent prevention program.

Closely linked to peer-related programs are those preventive strategies that focus on social or interpersonal-cognitive problem-solving ability development. In a meta-analysis of 49 studies (1981 to 1990) targeting social competence training (SCT), Beelman, Pfingsten, and Lösel (1994) found that social problem-solving was a particularly effective form of prevention of social problems, especially in at-risk children. Social problem-solving programs are based on the premise that aggressive children have cognitive-processing deficits that mediate aggressive behavior, supported by findings that aggressive children demonstrate distorted cognitive appraisals of social situations and utilize aggressive schemata for acting on these appraisals (Lochman & Curry, 1986).

Social problem-solving (SPS) programs have produced positive results. Lochman and Curry (1986) report significant reductions in parent ratings of aggression and on-task behavior in the classroom for children completing an 18-week intervention. Social relations interventions (SRI) that incorporate SPS and prosocial skills training are particularly effective in dealing with the most at-risk population for early-onset conduct disorder. Aggressive-rejected children are at greater risk for developing conduct disorder or delinquency than aggressive-only or rejected-only children (Coie et al., 1992). Following completion of a SRI program with African-American third graders, aggressive-rejected children had lower levels of aggression and rejection than aggressive-rejected controls as well as increased positive social acceptance, while rejected-only children did not differ following the program. Interestingly, children completing the intervention rated themselves as having lower self-worth than control students after completion of the program.

Teacher-led curricula based on SPS have also been shown to have lasting impacts on children's academic and behavioral problems (Elias, Gara, Schuyler, Branden-Muller, & Sayette, 1991). In a 5-year follow-up of a 2-year curriculum for children in late elementary school a number of interesting findings emerged. Children undergoing a general and intensive SPS program exceeded controls in academic ability with students in the intensive program doing significantly better in math and language arts and having fewer absences from school. Children in the SPS condition reported less alcohol and tobacco use, vandalism, and aggression against both parents and students. Finally, boys in the control group displayed significantly more unpopularity, self-destructiveness, depression, and delinquency.

Interpersonal cognitive problem-solving (ICPS) differs from SPS in that the theory behind the program suggests an emphasis on how children logically solve problems in social situations rather than on their cognitive appraisals of those situations. Results for ICPS are positive, but the program is not without its critics. Spivak and Shure (1989) summarize their findings over the past two decades as indicating significant improvements in positive behaviors, peer acceptance, and academic achievement, with decreases in negative behaviors such as aggression and impatience. Such findings have been shown to be stable at 1-year follow-up periods. Efforts to replicate ICPS findings have not found such positive results. When teacher-raters of behavior were kept blind to the intervention status of children, many of the effects reported by Spivak and Shure were not found including changes in behavioral adjustment, alternate solution generation, and the role of problem-solving skills in mediating behavioral outcomes (Rickel, Eshelman, & Loigman, 1983).

Poor early achievement has been linked to both depression and antisocial behavior in children (Kellam, Rebok, Ialongo, & Mayer, 1994; Kellam, Rebok, Mayer, Ialongo, & Kalodner, 1994). While promotion of early achievement in children has been added to several multicomponent programs that will be examined later in this chapter, one line of research has examined the impact of programming solely focused on that end in the reduction of antisocial behavior in later life. Follow-ups to the Perry Preschool program in Ypsilanti, Michigan suggested that early educational programming to increase achievement can have significant impact on the development of antisocial behavior in adolescence and adulthood (Schweinhart & Weikart, 1988; Weikart, 1989). Program children were more likely to have positive outcomes related to achievement, graduation rates, and post secondary enrollment at 20-year follow-up. In addition, children were less likely to engage in high-risk behaviors or delinquent acts. Children in the program had lower rates of arrest, less serious offenses among those who committed crimes, and lower rates of pregnancy among teens (Berrueta-Clement, Schweinhart, Barnett, & Weikart, 1987). The authors suggested that such long-term effects were the result of increased school readiness leading to positive reaction from teachers, greater school commitment, and higher achievement. Others have suggested that the home-visitation component of the program resulted in parents becoming better child socializers and providing more home-school linkages and a more supportive home environment (Seitz, 1990; Zigler, Taussig, & Black, 1992).

Parent and family-focused interventions have developed under the assumption that changes in parenting style or family functioning will lead to noticeable changes in child behavior. Parent education, or parent training, represents the primary focus of parent-driven programming. Parent training has long been used as a highly successful means of treating conduct disordered and highly aggressive children (Dumas, 1989). Research on the role parent training may play in primary and secondary prevention strategies has been growing. This increased emphasis is due, in part, to its cost-effectiveness and ease of administration, as well as its overall effectiveness as a possible intervention in the development of conduct disorder (Webster-Stratton, 1994; Wright, Stroud, & Keenan, 1993).

Parent-training programs typically train parents to use attention and reinforcement when children are behaving appropriately, and to use behavioral discipline strategies when children behave inappropriately (Sanders, 1995). Many studies have demonstrated the effectiveness of parent training both alone (Sheeber & Johnson, 1994; Webster-Stratton, 1985, 1994) as well as in conjunction with school-based programming (Hawkins, Von Cleve, & Catalano, 1991; O'Donnell, Hawkins, Catalano, Abbott, & Day, 1995). Behavioral improvement in children has been observed by teachers at 1-year follow-up for parent training programs (Strayhorn & Weidman, 1991).

There are, however, some challenges to using parent training as a preventive intervention with at-risk families. Webster-Stratton (1985) reports that nonresponders to treatment tend to come from low SES backgrounds and have a higher proportion of negative life-events following exposure to intervention. Dumas and Albin (1986) found that a number of adverse social and material conditions predicted treatment success in parent training workshops including maternal psychopathology, previous need of child services, absence of a father figure, source of referral, and maternal education.

An additional problem during parent training is sporadic attendance and dropout. Prinz and Miller (1994) reported a significant reduction in treatment dropout as a result of an enhanced family treatment component that focused on parental concerns not directly related to the parent-child intervention (e.g., job stress, health problems, family disputes, personal worries). Differential dropout effects for the enhanced versus traditional approach to parent training were particularly pronounced among families having multiple sources of distress.

While many programs focus on individual and family factors in the development of conduct disorder, a growing number of programs recognize the important role of the school and greater community in the development, and by implication prevention, of conduct disorder. School-based programming has been developed utilizing both curricular and environmental changes. One such program is the Good Behavior Game, a classroom-based behavior management program in which classrooms are divided into teams of students (Kellam, Rebok, Ialongo, & Mayer, 1994). Teams are rewarded following periods of positive behavior, the underlying goal being the fostering of self- and peer-based management of behavior through group reinforcement. Follow-up at six years suggests that the Good Behavior Game is effective at reducing aggression among males rated as showing above-average aggressiveness in the first grade. In other words, the program improved the aggressive level of more aggressive males.

The PATHS curriculum represents a curricular approach to teaching children how to appropriately recognize, express, and regulate their emotions that focuses on teaching children self-control and problem-solving (Greenberg, Kusche, Cook, & Quamma, 1995). This program has been used both in standard classrooms, as well as special education classrooms and appears to be effective at helping children manage emotional outbursts. This program may also be effective as a targeted intervention because children with high and moderate levels of behavioral problems appear to be more affected by the curriculum than children with low levels of behavioral problems as rated by teachers.

Olweus's work with bullies in Norwegian elementary schools is also relevant to the discussion of school-based prevention of conduct disorder. While conduct-disordered youth are not necessarily bullies, Olweus (1994) acknowledges the conceptual similarity between the two populations. The Bullying Program attempts to create a school environment that fosters warm, positive involvement from adults while establishing firm limits on unacceptable behavior. Violation of limits is met with nonphysical sanctions against the offender. This model is based, in part, on an authoritative view of adult-child interactions. Evaluations of the program suggest a marked decrease in levels of bullying at school with no observed displacement of bullying activities on the way to and from school. Olweus reports a general decline in other areas of antisocial behavior such as vandalism, fighting, stealing, truancy, and drunkenness. Students exposed to the program report more positive school climate and higher satisfaction with school life. Finally, Olweus reports that the Bullying Program reduced both the number of existing victimization problems in school as well as the number of new victims.

Community-based prevention programs, which have been included less often than school-based programs in prevention studies, are typically implemented through a neighborhood group or housing project. For example, the Modello/Homestead Gardens Program (described in Kelley, 1993) implemented several prevention activities in two low-income housing projects, including parenting classes, leadership training courses, teacher training, and individual or family counseling for residents. Reported evaluation following the second year of implementation pointed to decreases in truancy rates, school failure, discipline referrals, and teen-age pregnancy, and improvement in school achievement (see Kelley, 1993). In community-based programs that focus on nonschool skill development (e.g., recreational involvement; Jones & Offord, 1989), little spillover effects were observed on school performance or home behavior, although community measures of antisocial behavior (e.g., police and security records) did show some improvement.

A growing number of prevention research researchers are investigating multicomponent interventions. Such programs seek to combine a number of different prevention approaches and to address multiple systems affecting the child's development. Because there is little evidence of short-term single-level interventions producing positive outcomes with children at pronounced risk for early-onset conduct disorder, it is not surprising that the field has moved toward comprehensive multi-system interventions that extend into multiple years (Weissberg, Caplan, & Harwood, 1991).

One such effort is the Montreal Prevention Experiment (McCord, Tremblay, Vitaro, & Desmarais-Gervais, 1994; Vitaro & Tremblay, 1994). The Montreal project employed a parent-training program, based on procedures developed at the Oregon Social Learning Center, plus a school-based skills training program for identified children that lasted 2 years. Skill training focused on development of self-control as well as social skills. This bimodal approach, which simultaneously addressed parent and child skills, produced minimal initial effects but yielded better academic performance and less delinquent involvement at 3 to 5 year follow-up (McCord et al., 1994). According to Vitaro and Tremblay (1994), youth who had received the intervention were more likely to select best friends who were significantly less disruptive, and these authors have argued that the bimodal approach produces more durable effects than either a parent-focused or child-focused unimodal approach because behavior change in each context is reinforced by accompanying changes in the other context.

Like the Montreal project, the Seattle Social Development Project (SSDP) also combined interventions. SSDP wedded a focus on classroom-based social skills with parent training plus teacher training in classroom management and interactive instruction (O'Donnell et al., 1995). This intervention is based on Hirschi's (1969) social control theory and assumes that delinquent behavior is less likely to occur when high levels of conventional social bonding are present in the family and at school. Participation in the intervention program led to lower use of tobacco, alcohol, and marijuana by at-risk females, and higher academic achievement with lower initiation rates of delinquent acts, but not less drug use, by at-risk males (O'Donnell et al., 1995), while youth in the nonintervention condition escalated their aggressive behavior (Hawkins et al., 1991). Hawkins et al. (1991) and O'Donnell et al. (1995) reported that prevention effects were stronger for European American youth than for other ethnic groups in the sample.

The FAST Track Project (CPPRG, 1992) has taken the multicomponent approach even further by combining five intervention components (parent training, home visiting, social skills training, academic tutoring, and the PATHS curriculum) to promote family, child, and school competence. Preliminary results indicate that participation in the FAST Track program led to increased parent involvement, improved child social-cognitive problem-solving skills, and improved reading, and positive distal outcomes such as decreased problem behavior at school, fewer incidents of peer-initiated aggression, and improved sociometric peer ratings (McMahon & CPPRG, 1995). The investigators noted that their confidence in these preliminary findings was tempered by equivocal mediational results. Clear conclusions about this study must await the final results to be gleaned from combining three cohorts in four sites over multiple years of intervention (CPPRG, 1992).

Unlike the two previous multicomponent programs, the Positive Parenting Program (Triple P) reported by Sanders and Markie-Dadds (1995) is entirely parent and family focused but still takes a comprehensive multilevel approach. The Triple P consists of five levels of intervention and parents can penetrate the model based on their level of need: (1) low-cost self-help programs; (2) brief-support interventions; (3, 4) variations of parent-training programs; and (5) intensive behavioral family therapy addressing issues such as marital conflict, parental depression, and parenting stress. Families participating in the Triple P interventions reported lower levels of oppositional and aggressive child behavior, decreased parental negativity, and increased parental sense of competence (Sanders, 1995).

Later Intervention

Compared with efforts targeting early-onset conduct disorder, fewer programs have addressed the prevention of late-onset conduct disorder and related adolescent problems. This may be because late-onset conduct disorder tends to be more transitory or developmentally normative (e.g., via adolescent rebellion) or perhaps because the two versions of conduct disorder are harder to distinguish at the later stages.

Preventive programs for late-onset antisocial behavior often utilize the established family-based technologies associated with early-onset prevention programs. Parent-focused interventions emphasize parental monitoring, positive reinforcement, limit setting, and problem-solving. For example, the Adolescent Transistions Project (Dishion & Andrews, 1995) employed such a parent-focused intervention, along with a teen-focused intervention that was designed to promote self-regulation of prosocial and disruptive behaviors. When compared across four groups (parent group, teen group, parent and teen group, and no group), the parent group fared best at reducing parent-child conflict and subsequent behavior problems (i.e., externalizing behavior and tobacco use). In fact, involvement in the teen group actually appeared to have an negative impact on tobacco use, as usage increased over the 1-year follow-up period (Dishion & Andrews, 1995). Based on their experience, Dishion and Andrews (1995) cautioned against aggregating deviant youth in homogeneous groups. Consistent with this concern, Prinz et al. (1994), described earlier, formed heterogeneous peer intervention groups to circumvent this problem with the younger age group, but the heterogeneous approach is not yet widely used with adolescents.

Other efforts have focused exclusively on school-based interventions. For example, Weissberg and Caplan (1991, as cited in Weissberg, Caplan, & Harwood, 1991) reported that a school-based curriculum focusing on impulse control, stress management, problem-solving, and social skills training during middle school had significant results on early adolescent's behavior. Participants demonstrated improved problem-solving abilities, prosocial views on conflict resolution, improved teacher ratings on impulsivity and sociability, as well as decreased delinquent behavior. Students with 2 years of training demonstrated significant gains over those with 1 year or no training.

Another school-based approach, the Teen Outreach Program is an intervention designed to prevent a number of problematic adolescent behaviors including school failure, suspension, and teenage pregnancy (Allen, Kuperminc, Philliber, & Herre, 1994). This school-based program involves adolescents in community-based volunteer positions and links this extracurricular involvement with a classroom curriculum emphasizing group discussion. Findings suggest that the degree to which the program promotes student autonomy and relatedness or connection between students was predictive of lower levels of problem behavior. For middle school students, the quality of volunteer experience was also predictive of lower rates of problem behavior. Whereas few programs address the broad issues of primary prevention of late-onset conduct disorder, a number of programs deal with the prevention of juvenile delinquency, particularly the issue of recidivism among first-time offenders. Although such programs are technically outside the realm of the prevention of conduct disorder, they are included in this chapter because of their conceptual similarity to prevention programs for adolescents at risk for future antisocial behavior problems. Tolan and Guerra (1994) provide an excellent review of universal, selected, and indicated interventions designed to prevent delinquency. Generally speaking, universal interventions tend to overlap with those programs aimed at preventing the broad spectrum of antisocial behavior including conduct disorder and juvenile delinquency. Selected programs focus intervention efforts on those individuals who already demonstrate some tendency toward involvement in delinquent activities. Indicated programs cover the spectrum from individual to family-focused interventions and on to community-based programming.

Individual and family-based programs targeting selected populations frequently employ behavioral skills training and/or family-based therapeutic and skills-training approaches (Mulvey, Arthur, & Reppucci, 1993). Although several evaluations have been conducted on individually focused interventions, evidence from controlled research endeavors appears to be lacking (Tolan & Guerra, 1994). Family-based approaches, on the other hand, appear to have strong support, particularly when combining programs that address parenting style as well as family relations. Such programs frequently suffer from poor engagement. One program with demonstrated efficacy in dealing with the families of more serious delinquent offenders is multisystemic therapy (MST). Although this program has largely been applied to serious offenders, results suggest that this intensive therapeutic effect can lead to significant reductions in recidivism. Juveniles sent through MST programs demonstrate improved family functioning and fewer repeat offenses than youth treated with individual therapy or processed by the Department of Youth Services (Borduin, Mann, Cone, Henggeler, 1995; Henggeler, Melton, & Smith, 1992).

Other programs have taken a more community-based approach to dealing with the prevention of juvenile antisocial behavior. Davidson and Wolfred (1977) evaluated the short- and long-term outcomes of a community-based residential behavioral treatment program for predelinquents. Short-term outcomes suggested that such a program impacted behavior of youths in the residential setting. Classroom performance and behavior improved while youth participated in the program. Follow-up results suggest that gains were not maintained after completion of the residential program. Compared with matched controls, participants were more likely to have been institutionalized and less likely to have been placed back in their own homes. In addition, participants had increased contact with the juvenile justice system.

Because programs that separate individuals from their natural environments often have decreased efficacy, some programs have attempted instead to alter the way in which community-based institutions deal with delinquent children. Scholte (1992) trained Dutch detectives to assess for the presence of psychosocial risk factors during juvenile police contact. Children found to be at risk for psychosocial problems were referred to local mental health professionals who investigated the risk factors and sought to resolve problems on behalf of the youth. A quasi-experimental evaluation reveals that participants demonstrated improved family functioning, decreased school difficulties, and marked decreases in recidivism rates. Tolan, Perry, and Jones (1987) undertook a consultation program with a rural juvenile court to implement a psychoeducational program for first-time offenders. Prior to the consultation program, the working relationship between the court system and the local community mental health center was largely "unproductive" (p. 44). Consultation focused on roles of several community agencies in the development of a first-time offender program. Participants in the program had significantly lower rates of recidivism than nonparticipants. The authors suggested three possible reasons for the reduction in recidivism: (a) change in participants' views based on the educational focus of the program; (b) changes in the judicial process; and (c) changes in the agency workers' perceptions of juvenile delinquents.

Diversion programs represent another class of prevention programs for altering the way court and police systems deal with juvenile offenders. The Adolescent Diversion Project (ADP; Davidson & Redner, 1988) employs a two-pronged intervention action model consisting of behavioral contracting and child advocacy. Results from over 15 years of research suggest that when ADP is delivered by paraprofessionals outside the realm of the court system, it is an effective program in both suburban and urban settings. Diversion appears to work best when accompanied by the action model described earlier or when volunteers develop empathic interpersonal relationships with assigned youth. Diversion does not appear to be effective when delivered by professionals or within the confines of the court system (Davidson, Redner, Blakely, Mitchell, & Emshoff, 1987).

SUMMARY

Conduct disorder is a disruptive behavior disorder, occurring in late childhood and adolescence, marked by a pattern of violating societal norms and significant impairment of social and academic functioning. The *DSM-IV* (APA, 1994) distinguishes two types of conduct disorder based on the age of onset: childhood and adolescence. Extensive research focusing on risk and, to a lesser extent, protective factors suggests a number of causal pathways including early parenting difficulties, the development of oppositional-aggressive behaviors, academic difficulty, and peer relationship problems. Family support and positive school climate are possible mediating factors that minimize risk for conduct disorder.

Compared with outpatient treatment, preventive interventions with children at risk for conduct disorder are generally harder to implement because of engagement and recruitment issues, simultaneous multiple interventions, targeting of whole systems, and delayed impact.

Interventions within prevention programs fall into three general categories based on the target population: universal (the general population), selected (individuals with identified risk factors), and indicated (individuals already demonstrating symptoms suggesting the development of the disorder). Screening is particularly important for selected and indicated interventions, and involves selecting risk factors that will define inclusion, determining the types of informants to deploy, and selecting a screening procedure. Although multiple informants generally increase the predictive utility of the screening process, this approach can be cost-prohibitive. Multiple gating and mediational screening are two techniques that address the issue of selecting high-risk samples while remaining cost-effective.

Prevention programs differ on two important dimensions: the type of conduct disorder targeted and the levels of intervention being provided. Programs may deal with individuals, families, classrooms, schools, or community systems, as well as combinations of levels (an approach made popular by a number of multicomponent interventions).

Early-onset interventions targeting individual-level change including social-skills interventions or problem-solving ability have demonstrated efficacy at reducing behavioral problems in young children. School-based curricular programs or achievement-building interventions have also reduced subsequent delinquent behavior when used at an early age. Parent-based interventions (e.g., parent training) while effective, tend to work only for restricted ranges of parents (based on SES) and suffer from poor rates of attendance and high attrition. Community-based efforts at preventing delinquency have been less well documented, but represent a promising approach at intervention. Finally, several multicomponent preventive interventions are currently being studied; initial results are encouraging, but their long-term effectiveness remains to be seen.

Interventions during adolescence and for prevention of late-onset conduct disorder vary considerably in approach. Family approaches focus on enhancing parental monitoring, appropriate discipline, and positive communication. School-based interventions are more diverse and focus on social problem-solving, social and academic skills training, and strengthening of alternatives to antisocial behavior. Diversion programs tend to focus on alternative ways of reaching adolescents who have begun to get into trouble; these efforts may provide family support and education via para-professionals.

At this stage in the development of conduct disorder prevention, the field has produced several intervention formats and modest long-term results.

REFERENCES

Achenbach, T. M., McConaughy, S. H., & Howell, C. T. (1987). Child/adolescent behavioral and emotional problems: Implications of cross-informant correlations for situational specificity. *Psychological Bulletin, 101,* 213–232.

Allen, J. P., Kuperminc, G., Philliber, S., & Herre, K. (1994). Programmatic prevention of adolescent problem behaviors: The role of autonomy, relatedness, and volunteer service in the Teen Outreach Program. *American Journal of Community Psychology, 22,* 617–638.

American Psychiatric Association. (1994). *Diagnostic and statistical manual of mental disorders* (4th ed.). Washington, DC: Author.

August, G. J., Realmuto, G. M., Crosby, R. D., & MacDonald, A. W. (1995). Community-based multiple-gate screening of children at risk for conduct disorder. *Journal of Abnormal Child Psychology, 23,* 521–544.

Bates, J. E., Bayles, K., Bennett, D. S., Ridge, B., & Brown, M. M. (1991). Origins of externalizing behavior problems at eight years of age. In D. J. Pepler & K. H. Rubin (Eds.), *The development and treatment of childhood aggression* (pp. 93–119). Hillsdale, NJ: Erlbaum.

Beelman, A., Pfingsten, U., & Lösel, F. (1994). Effects of training social competence in children: A meta-analysis of recent evaluation studies. *Journal of Clinical Child Psychology, 23,* 260–271.

Berrueta-Clement, J. R., Schweinhart, L. J., Barnett, W. S., & Weikart, D. P. (1987). The effects of early educational intervention on crime and delinquency in adolescence and early adulthood. In J. D. Burchard & S. N. Burchard (Eds.), *Primary prevention of psychopathology: Vol. 10. Prevention of delinquent behavior* (pp. 220–240). Newbury Park, CA: Sage.

Bierman, K. (1986). The relationship of social aggression and peer rejection in middle childhood. In R. J. Prinz (Ed.), *Advances in behavioral assessment of children and families* (pp. 151–178). Greenwich, CT: JAI Press.

Boyle, M. H., & Offord, D. R. (1990). Primary prevention of conduct disorder: Issues and prospects. *Journal of the American Academy of Child and Adolescent Psychiatry, 29,* 227–233.

Brown, C. H. (1991). Comparison of mediational selected strategies and sequential designs for preventive trials: Comments on a proposal by Pillow et al. *American Journal of Community Psychology, 19,* 837–846.

Caldwell, R. A. (1991). Mediational screening: Is the benefit worth the cost? *American Journal of Community Psychology, 19,* 847–851.

Campbell, S. B. (1991). Longitudinal studies of active and aggressive preschoolers: Individual differences in early behavior and outcome. In D. Cicchetti & S. L. Toth (Eds.), *Rochester Symposium on Developmental Psychopathology: Vol. 2. Internalizing and externalizing expressions of dysfunction* (pp. 57–90). Hillsdale, NJ: Erlbaum.

Campbell, S. B., Breaux, A. M., Ewing, L. J., & Szumowski, E. K. (1986). Correlates and predictors of hyperactivity and aggression: A longitudinal study of parent-referred problem preschoolers. *Journal of Abnormal Child Psychology, 14,* 217–234.

Cantrell, V. L., & Prinz, R. J. (1985). Multiple perspectives of rejected, neglected, and accepted children: Relationship between sociometric status and behavioral characteristics. *Journal of Consulting and Clinical Psychology, 53,* 884–889.

Capaldi, D. M., & Patterson, G. R. (1991). Relation of parental transitions to boys' adjustment problems: Linear hypothesis, and mothers at risk for transitions and unskilled parenting. *Developmental Psychology, 27,* 489–504.

Cauce, A. M., Reid, M., Landesman, S., & Gonzales, N. (1990). Social support in young children: Measurement, structure, and behavioral impact. In B. R. Sarason, I. G. Sarason, & G. R. Pierce (Eds.), *Social support: An interactional view* (pp. 64–94). New York: Wiley.

Charlebois, P., LeBlanc, M., Gagnon, C., & Larivee, S. (1994). Methodological issues in multiple-gating screening procedures for antisocial behaviors in elementary students. *RASE: Remedial and Special Education, 15,* 44–54.

Cohen, S., & Wills, T. A. (1985). Stress, social support, and the buffering hypothesis. *Psychological Bulletin, 98,* 310–357.

Coie, J. D., Lochman, J. E., Terry, R., & Hyman, C. (1992). Predicting early adolescent disorder from childhood aggression and peer rejection. *Journal of Consulting and Clinical Psychology, 60,* 783–792.

Conduct Problems Prevention Research Group. (1992). A developmental and clinical model for the prevention of Conduct Disorder: The FAST Track Program. *Development and Psychopathology, 4,* 509–527.

Davidson, W. S., & Redner, R. (1988). The prevention of juvenile delinquency: Diversion from the juvenile justice system. In R. H. Price, E. L. Cowen, R. P. Lorion, & J. Ramos-McKay (Eds.), *Fourteen ounces of prevention: A casebook for practitioners* (pp. 123–137). Washington, DC: American Psychological Association.

Davidson, W. S., Redner, R., Blakely, C. H., Mitchell, C. M., & Emshoff, J. G. (1987). Diversion of juvenile offenders: An experimental comparison. *Journal of Consulting and Clinical Psychology, 55,* 68–75.

Davidson, W. S., & Wolfred, T. R. (1977). Evaluation of a community-based behavior modification program for prevention of delinquency: The failure of success. *Community Mental Health Journal, 13,* 296–306.

Dishion, T. J., & Andrews, D. W. (1995). Preventing escalation in problem behaviors with high-risk young adolescents: Immediate and 1-year outcomes. *Journal of Consulting and Clinical Psychology, 63,* 538–548.

Dishion, T. J., Patterson, G. R., Stoolmiller, M., & Skinner, M. L. (1991). Family, school, and behavioral antecedents to early adolescent involvement with antisocial peers. *Developmental Psychology, 27,* 172–180.

Dodge, K. A. (1989). Enhancing social relationships. In E. J. Mash & R. J. Barkley (Eds.), *Behavioral treatment of childhood disorders* (pp. 222–244). New York: Guilford Press.

Dumas, J. E. (1986a). Indirect influence of maternal social contacts on mother-child interactions: A setting-event analysis. *Journal of Abnormal Child Psychology, 14,* 205–216.

Dumas, J. E. (1986b). Parental perception and treatment outcome in families of aggressive children: A causal model. *Behavior Therapy, 17,* 420–432.

Dumas, J. E. (1989). Treating antisocial behavior in children: Child and family approaches. *Clinical Psychology Review, 9,* 197–222.

Dumas, J. E. (1992). Conduct Disorder. In S. M. Turner, K. S. Calhoun, & H. E. Adams (Eds.), *Handbook of clinical behavior therapy* (2nd ed., pp. 285–316). New York: Wiley.

Dumas, J. E., & Albin, J. B. (1986). Parent training outcome: Does active parental involvement matter? *Behavior Research and Therapy, 24,* 227–230.

Edelbrock, C. S., Costello, A. J., Dulcan, M. K., Kalas, D., & Conover, N. (1985). Age differences in the reliability of the psychiatric interview of the child. *Child Development, 56,* 265–275.

Elias, M. J., Gara, M. A., Schuyler, T. F., Branden-Muller, L. R., & Sayette, M. A. (1991). The promotion of social competence: Longitudinal study of a preventive school-based program. *American Journal of Orthopsychiatry, 61,* 409–417.

Farrington, D. P., & West, D. J. (1981). The Cambridge study in delinquent development (United Kingdom). In S. A. Mednick & A. E. Baert (Eds.), *Prospective longitudinal research: An empirical basis for the primary prevention of psychosocial disorders* (pp. 90–110). New York: Oxford University Press.

Gottfredson, D. C. (1986). Environmental and individual interventions to reduce the risk of delinquent behavior. *Criminology, 24,* 705–731.

Greca, A. M., & Silverman, W. K. (1993). Parent reports of child behavior problems: Bias in participation. *Journal of Abnormal Child Psychology, 21,* 89–101.

Greenberg, M. T., Kusche, C. A., Cook, E. T., & Quamma, J. P. (1995). Promoting emotional competence in school-aged children: The effects of the PATHS curriculum. *Development and Psychopathology, 7,* 117–136.

Hawkins, J. D., & Lam, T. (1987). Teacher practices, social development and delinquency. In J. D. Burchard & S. N. Burchard (Eds.), *Prevention of delinquent behavior* (pp. 241–274). Newbury Park, CA: Sage.

Hawkins, J. D., & Lishner, D. (1987). Etiology and prevention of antisocial behavior in children and adolescents. In D. H. Crowell, I. M. Evans, & C. R. O'Donnell (Eds.), *Childhood aggression and violence: Sources of influence, prevention, and control* (pp. 263–282). New York: Plenum Press.

Hawkins, J. D., Von Cleve, E., & Catalano, R. F. (1991). Reducing early childhood aggression: Results of a primary prevention program. *Journal of the American Academy of Child and Adolescent Psychiatry, 30,* 208–217.

Hawkins, J. D., & Weis, J. G. (1985). The social development model: An integrated approach to delinquency prevention. *Journal of Primary Prevention, 6,* 73–97.

Henggeler, S. W., Melton, G. B., & Smith, L. A. (1992). Family preservation using multisystemic therapy: An effective alternative to incarcerating serious juvenile offenders. *Journal of Consulting and Clinical Psychology, 60,* 953–961.

Hirschi, T. (1969). *Causes of delinquency.* Los Angeles: University of California Press.

Jones, M. B., & Offord, D. R. (1989). Reduction of antisocial behavior in poor children by non-school skill development. *Journal of Child Psychology and Psychiatry, 30,* 737–750.

Kazdin, A. E. (1988). *Child psychotherapy: Developing and identifying effective treatments.* Needham Heights, MA: Allyn & Bacon.

Kazdin, A. E. (1995). *Conduct disorders in childhood and adolescence* (2nd ed.). Thousand Oaks, CA: Sage.

Kellam, S. G., Rebok, G. W., Ialongo, N., & Mayer, L. S. (1994). The course and malleability of aggressive behavior from early first grade into middle school: Results of a developmental epidemiologically based preventive trial. *Journal of Child Psychology and Psychiatry, 35,* 259–281.

Kellam, S. G., Rebok, G. W., Mayer, L. S., Ialongo, N., & Kalodner, C. R. (1994). Depressive symptoms over first grade and their response to a developmental epidemiologically based preventive trial aimed at improving achievement. *Development and Psychopathology, 6,* 463–481.

Kelley, T. M. (1993). Neo-cognitive learning theory: Implications for prevention and early intervention strategies with at-risk youth. *Adolescence, 28,* 439–460.

Kupersmidt, J. B., & Coie, J. D. (1990). Preadolescent peer status, aggression, and school adjustment as predictors of externalizing problems in adolescence. *Child Development, 61,* 1350–1362.

Lochman, J. E., Coie, J. D., Underwood, M. K., & Terry, R. (1993). Effectiveness of a social relations intervention program for aggressive and nonaggressive, rejected children. *Journal of Consulting and Clinical Psychology, 61,* 1053–1058.

Lochman, J. E., & the Conduct Problems Prevention Research Group. (1995). Screening of child behavior problems for prevention programs at school entry. *Journal of Consulting and Clinical Psychology, 63,* 549–559.

Lochman, J. E., & Curry, J. F. (1986). Effects of social problem-solving training and self-instruction training with aggressive boys. *Journal of Clinical Child Psychology, 15,* 159–164.

Loeber, R. (1988). The natural history of juvenile conduct problems, delinquency, and associated substance use: Evidence for developmental progressions. In B. B. Lahey & A. E. Kazdin (Eds.), *Advances in clinical child psychology* (Vol. 11, pp. 73–124). New York: Plenum Press.

Loeber, R. (1990). Development and risk factors of juvenile antisocial behavior and delinquency. *Clinical Psychology Review, 10,* 1–42.

Loeber, R., & Dishion, T. J. (1983). Early predictors of male delinquency: A review. *Psychological Bulletin, 94,* 68–99.

Loeber, R., Dishion, T. J., & Patterson, G. R. (1984). Multiple gating: A multistage assessment procedure for identifying youths at risk for delinquency. *Journal of Research on Crime and Delinquency, 21,* 7–32.

Loeber, R., Green, S. M., & Lahey, B. B. (1990). Mental health professionals' perception of the utility of children, mothers, and teachers as informants on childhood psychopathology. *Journal of Clinical Child Psychology, 19,* 136–143.

Loeber, R., Green, S. M., Lahey, B. B., & Stouthamer-Loeber, M. (1989). Optimal informants on childhood disruptive behaviors. *Development and Psychopathology, 1,* 317–337.

Loeber, R., & LeBlanc, M. (1990). Toward a developmental criminology. In M. Tonry & N. Morris (Eds.), *Crime and justice* (Vol. 12, pp. 375–473). Chicago: University of Chicago Press.

Loeber, R., & Stouthamer-Loeber, M. (1986). Family factors as correlates and predictors of juvenile conduct problems and delinquency. In N. Morris & M. Tonry (Eds.), *Crime and justice: An annual review of research* (Vol. 7, pp. 29–149). Chicago: University of Chicago Press.

McCord, J. (1988). Parental behavior in the cycle of aggression. *Psychiatry, 51,* 14–23.

McCord, J., Tremblay, R. E., Vitaro, F., & Desmarais-Gervais, L. (1994). Boys' disruptive behavior, school adjustment, and delinquency: The Montreal prevention experiment. *International Journal of Behavioral Development, 17,* 739–752.

McMahon, R. J. (1994). Diagnosis, assessment, and treatment of externalizing problems in children: The role of longitudinal data. *Journal of Consulting and Clinical Psychology, 62,* 901–917.

McMahon, R. J., & the Conduct Problems Prevention Research Group. (1995). The prevention of Conduct Disorders in school-aged children: The FAST Track Project. In M. R. Sanders (Chair), *Prevention of conduct disorders: An international perspective.* Symposium conducted at the meeting of the World Congress of Behavioural & Cognitive Therapies, Coppenhagen, Denmark.

Moffitt, T. E. (1990). Juvenile delinquency and attention deficit disorder: Boys' developmental trajectories from age 3 to age 15. *Child Development, 61,* 893–910.

Moffitt, T. E. (1993a). Adolescence-limited and life-course-persistent antisocial behavior: A developmental taxonomy. *Psychological Review, 100,* 674–701.

Moffitt, T. E. (1993b). The neuropsychology of conduct disorder. *Development and Psychopathology, 5,* 135–151.

Mulvey, E. P., Arthur, M. W., & Reppucci, N. D. (1993). The prevention and treatment of juvenile delinquency: A review of the research. *Clinical Psychology Review, 13,* 133–167.

O'Donnell, J., Hawkins, J. D., Catalano, R. F., Abbott, R. D., & Day, L. E. (1995). Preventing school failure, drug use, and delinquency among low-income children: Long-term intervention in elementary schools. *American Journal of Orthopsychiatry, 65,* 87–100.

Offord, D. R. (1982). Family backgrounds of male and female delinquents. In J. Gunn & D. P. Farrington (Eds.), *Delinquency and the criminal justice system* (pp. 129–152). New York: Wiley.

Offord, D. R., & Boyle, M. H. (1986). Problems in setting up and executing large-scale psychiatric epidemiological studies. *Psychiatric Developments, 3,* 257–272.

Offord, D. R., Boyle, M. C., & Racine, Y. A. (1991). The epidemiology of antisocial behavior in childhood and adolescence. In D. J. Pepler & K. H. Rubin (Eds.), *The development and treatment of childhood aggression* (pp. 31–54). Hillsdale, NJ: Erlbaum.

Offord, D. R., & Waters, B. G. (1983). Socialization and its failure. In M. D. Levine, W. B. Carey, A. C. Crocker, & R. T. Gross (Eds.), *Developmental-behavioral pediatrics* (pp. 111–133). Philadelphia: Saunders.

Olweus, D. (1994). Annotation: Bullying at school: Basic facts and effects of a school-based intervention program. *Journal of Child Psychology and Psychiatry, 33,* 1171–1190.

Parker, J. G., & Asher, S. R. (1987). Peer relations and later personal adjustment: Are low-accepted children at risk? *Psychological Bulletin, 102,* 357–389.

Patterson, G. R. (1982). *Coercive family process.* Eugene, OR: Castalia.

Patterson, G. R., DeBaryshe, B. D., & Ramsey, E. (1989). A developmental perspective on antisocial behavior. *American Psychologist, 44,* 329–335.

Patterson, G. R., Reid, J. B., & Dishion, T. J. (1992). *A social interactional approach: 4. Antisocial boys.* Eugene, OR: Castalia Press.

Pillow, D. R., Sandler, I. N., Braver, S. L, Wolchick, S. A., & Gersten, J. C. (1991). Theory-based screening for prevention: Focusing on mediating processes in children of divorce. *American Journal of Community Psychology, 19,* 809–836.

Prinz, R. J., Blechman, E. A., & Dumas, J. E. (1994). An evaluation of peer coping-skills training for childhood aggression. *Journal of Clinical Child Psychology, 23,* 193–203.

Prinz, R. J., Connor, P. A., & Wilson C. C. (1981). Hyperactive and aggressive behaviors in childhood: Intertwined dimensions. *Journal of Abnormal Child Psychology, 9,* 191–202.

Prinz, R. J., Foster, S., Kent, R. N., & O'Leary, K. D. (1979). Multivariate assessment of conflict in distressed and nondistressed mother-adolescent dyads. *Journal of Applied Behavior Analysis, 12,* 116–125.

Prinz, R. J., & Miller, G. E. (1994). Family-based treatment for childhood antisocial behavior: Experimental influences of dropout and engagement. *Journal of Consulting and Clinical Psychology, 62,* 645–650.

Reid, J. B. (1993). Prevention of conduct disorder before and after school entry: Relating interventions to developmental findings. *Development and Psychopathology, 5,* 243–262.

Reynolds, D., Jones, D., St. Leger, S., & Murgatroyd, S. (1980). School factors and truancy. In L. Hersov & I. Berg (Eds.), *Out of school: Modern perspectives in truancy and school refusal* (pp. 85–110). Chichester, England: Wiley.

Rickel, A. U., Eshelman, A. K., & Loigman, G. A. (1983). Social problem-solving training: A follow-up study of cognitive and behavioral effects. *Journal of Abnormal Child Psychology, 11,* 15–28.

Robins, L. N. (1981). Epidemiological approaches to natural history research: Children's antisocial disorders. *Journal of the American Academy of Child Psychiatry, 20,* 566–580.

Rutter, M. (1978). Early sources of security and competence. In J. S. Bruner & A. Garton (Eds.), *Human growth and development* (pp. 33–61). Oxford, England: Clarendon.

Rutter, M. (1979). Protective factors in children's responses to stress and disadvantage. In M. W. Kent & J. E. Rolf (Eds.), *Primary prevention of psychopathology: Vol. 3. Social competence in children* (pp. 49–74). London: University Press of England.

Rutter, M., & Giller, H. (1983). *Juvenile delinquency: Trends and perspectives.* New York: Penguin.

Sanders, M. R. (Ed.). (1995). *Healthy families, healthy nation: Strategies for promoting family mental health in Australia.* Brisbane, QLD: Australian Academic Press.

Sanders, M. R., & Markie-Dadds, C. (1995). Triple P: A multilevel family intervention program for children with disruptive behavior disorders. In P. Cotton & H. Jackson (Eds.), *Early intervention and preventive mental health applications of clinical psychology* (pp. 43–69). Melbourne: Australian Psychology Society.

Sandler, I. N., Braver, S. L, Wolchik, S. A., Pillow, D. R., & Gersten, J. C. (1991). Small theory and the strategic choices of prevention research. *American Journal of Community Psychology, 19,* 873–880.

Scholte, E. M. (1992). Identification of children at risk at the police station and the prevention of delinquency. *Psychiatry Interpersonal & Biological Processes, 55,* 354–369.

Schweinhart, L. J., & Weikart, D. B. (1988). The High/Scope Perry Preschool program. In R. H. Price, E. L. Cowen, R. P. Lorion, & J. Ramos-McKay (Eds.), *Fourteen ounces of prevention: A casebook for practitioners* (pp. 53–65). Washington, DC: American Psychological Association.

Seitz, V. (1990). Intervention programs for impoverished children: A comparison of educational and family support models. *Annals of Child Development, 7,* 73–103.

Sheeber, L. B., & Johnson, J. H. (1994). Evaluation of a temperament-focused, parent-training program. *Journal of Clinical Child Psychology, 23,* 249–259.

Snyder, J. (1991). Discipline as a mediator of the impact of maternal stress and mood on child-conduct problems. *Development and Psychopathology, 3,* 263–276.

Snyder, J., Dishion, T. J., & Patterson, G. R. (1986). Determinants and consequences of associating with deviant peers. *Journal of Early Adolescence, 6,* 29–43.

Spivak, G., & Shure, M. B. (1989). Interpersonal cognitive problem solving (ICPS): A competence-building primary prevention program. *Prevention in Human Services, 6,* 151–178.

Strayhorn, J. M., & Weidman, C. S. (1991). Follow-up one year after parent-child interaction training: Effects of behavior of preschool children. *Journal of the American Academy of Child and Adolescent Psychiatry, 30,* 138–143.

Tolan, P. H., & Guerra, N. G. (1994). Prevention of delinquency: Current status and issues. *Applied and Preventive Psychology, 3,* 251–273.

Tolan, P. H., Perry, S., & Jones, T. (1987). Delinquency prevention: An example of consultation in rural community mental health. *Journal of Community Psychology, 15,* 43–50.

Tremblay, R. E., LeBlanc, M., & Schwartzman, A. E. (1988). The predictive power of first-grade peer and teacher ratings of behavior: Sex differences in antisocial behavior and personality at adolescence. *Journal of Abnormal Child Psychology, 16,* 571–583.

Verhulst, F. C., Koot, H. M., & Van der Ende, J. (1994). Differential predictive value of parents' and teachers' reports of children's problem behaviors: A longitudinal study. *Journal of Abnormal Child Psychology, 22,* 531–546.

Vitaro, F., & Tremblay, R. E. (1994). Impact of a prevention program on aggressive children's friendships and social adjustment. *Journal of Abnormal Child Psychology, 22,* 457–475.

Vitaro, F., Tremblay, R. E., Gagnon, C., & Pelletier, D. (1994). Predictive accuracy of behavioral and sociometric assessments of high-risk kindergarten children. *Journal of Clinical Child Psychology, 23,* 272–282.

Wadsworth, M. E. J. (1980). Early life events and later behavioral outcomes in a British longitudinal study. In S. B. Sells, K. Crandell, M. Roff, J. S. Strauss, & W. Pollin (Eds.), *Human functioning in longitudinal perspective* (pp. 168–180). Baltimore: Williams & Wilkins.

Wahler, R. G., & Dumas, J. E. (1987). Stimulus class determinants of mother-child coercive interchanges in multidistressed families: Assessment and intervention. In J. D. Burchard & S. N. Burchard (Eds.), *Prevention of delinquent behavior* (pp. 190–219). Beverly Hills, CA: Sage.

Webster-Stratton, C. (1985). Predictors of treatment outcome in parent training for conduct-disordered children. *Behavior Therapy, 16,* 223–243.

Webster-Stratton, C. (1994). Advancing videotape parent training: A comparison study. *Journal of Consulting and Clinical Psychology, 62,* 583–593.

Weikart, D. P. (1989). Early childhood education and primary prevention. *Prevention in Human Services, 6,* 285–306.

Weissberg, R. P., Caplan, M., & Harwood, R. L. (1991). Promoting competent young people in competence-enhancing environments: A systems-based perspective on primary prevention. *Journal of Consulting and Clinical Psychology, 59,* 830–841.

Werner, E. E., & Smith, R. S. (1982). *Vulnerable but invincible.* New York: McGraw-Hill.

West, M. O., & Prinz, R. J. (1987). Parental alcoholism & childhood psychopathology. *Psychological Bulletin, 102,* 204–218.

Wills, T. A., Vaccaro, D., & McNamara, G. (1992). The role of life events, family support, and competence in adolescent substance use: A test of vulnerability and protective factors. *American Journal of Community Psychology, 20,* 349–374.

Wright, L., Stroud, R., & Keenan, M. (1993). Indirect treatment of children via parent training: A burgeoning form of secondary prevention. *Applied and Preventive Psychology, 2,* 191–200.

Zelkowitz, P. (1987). Social support and aggressive behavior in young children. *Journal of Applied Family and Child Studies, 36,* 129–134.

Zigler, E., Taussig, C., & Black, K. (1992). Early childhood intervention: A promising preventative for juvenile delinquency. *American Psychologist, 47,* 997–1006.

CHAPTER 11

Mental Health

ERIC F. DUBOW, CAROLYN E. ROECKER, and RHONDA D'IMPERIO

DESCRIPTION OF PROBLEM

The National Advisory Mental Health Council (1990) has estimated that between 12% and 22% of America's youth under age 18 are in need of mental health services for behavioral and/or emotional disorders that have reached clinically significant levels. The Consortium on the School-Based Promotion of Social Competence (1994) cites several factors as accounting for this "unprecedented health crisis in our nation":

> Increased poverty rates among children; the breakdown of traditional neighborhoods and extended families; reduced amounts of meaningful and supportive personal contact between young people and positive adult role models; inadequate housing and unsafe neighborhood environments; changing demographics so that large numbers of young children are entering school in a state of economic and educational disadvantage; the proliferation of health-damaging media messages; and societal attitudes and behaviors that hurt ethnic minorities. (p. 270)

Many youth, however, are not vulnerable to the potentially negative effects of these experiences. Garmezy (1994) has noted, "History is dotted with images of survivorship despite the most horrendous events" (p. 12). This quote exemplifies the essence of the resilience literature—the identification of risk and protective processes (personal and environmental) across the developmental period. Findings in the resilience literature have led to the design and implementation of intervention programs to prevent maladjustment and promote competent mental health outcomes.

We set forth to accomplish several objectives in this chapter:

1. To define, clarify, and attempt to untangle the major concepts in the resilience literature.
2. To discuss the scope of mental health problems among children and adolescents.
3. To explore the empirical evidence on risk and protective mechanisms contributing to child and adolescent behavioral, emotional, and academic adjustment.
4. To provide illustrative interventions, based on the findings in the risk and resilience literature, designed to prevent maladjustment and promote competence in children and adolescents.

Definitions of Terms in the Resilience Literature

Resilience refers to "the process of, capacity for, or outcome of successful adaptation despite challenging or threatening circumstances" (Masten, Best, & Garmezy, 1990, p. 426). To study resilience, it is necessary to review how researchers have conceptualized and operationalized several relevant concepts (a) "challenging or threatening circumstances," or "risk factors"; (b) "outcome of successful adaptation," or "competence"; and (c) "protective factors," those personal and environmental characteristics that promote resilience.

Risk factors are statistical correlates of poor mental health outcomes (Masten et al., 1990). By definition, a risk factor must occur prior to later negative outcomes (Loeber, 1990). For example, epidemiological studies have indicated that between 10% and 15% of children with one schizophrenic parent will be diagnosed with schizophrenia at some point in their lives (Richters & Weintraub, 1990). Because risk for schizophrenia in the general population is only 1%, children with a schizophrenic parent are at higher risk for the disorder. Other risk factors for mental health problems include poverty, family instability, low birth weight, and exposure to specific and cumulative stressful life events such as parental separation or divorce, loss of a loved one, and moving to a new home or school (Masten et al., 1990).

Several issues need to be considered in determining risk status. First, when examining risk rates, it is easy to overlook that, for an individual, the chances of overcoming psychopathology are influenced by specific experiences in his or her life, not by the frequencies of the disorder in the population or subpopulation (Richters & Weintraub, 1990). Second, it is necessary to consider the context, or the person's life circumstances, in which the risk factor operates. For example, Rutter (1990) described the notion of "risk trajectory"; that is, certain turning points in life exist (e.g., parent moving out of the home) that, unless modified by a protective factor, may lead to negative outcomes. In addition, the presence of risk factors may increase the likelihood of exposure to multiple acute stressors (Rutter, 1979). Thus, it may be important to examine the effects of changes in risk factors over time, rather than view risk factors as static. Third, it is not so much the distal risk factor (e.g., parental separation/divorce) that directly influences mental health outcomes, but rather the proximal processes (e.g., ineffective parenting) involved in risk exposure.

Competence has been conceptualized in a number of ways (see Coatsworth & Sandler, 1992). One model of competence, reflected in the research design of Project Competence (Garmezy, Masten, & Tellegen, 1984) and the work of Kellam and associates at the Prevention Research Center at Johns Hopkins University (Kellam & Rebok, 1992), defines social competence (or social adaptation) in terms of observable behavioral criteria. Kellam and Rebok (1992) note that social adaptation is measured by "the social task demands and the adequacy of behavioral responses of the individual in particular social fields at particular stages of life" (p. 166). According to this model, social adaptation is operationalized as "social adaptational status," or the judgment of the adequacy of the individual's performance by "natural raters" in the environment (e.g., parents, teachers, peers, supervisors). The natural raters both define the tasks and rate the individual's success in accomplishing the tasks. In contrast, Kellam and Rebok (1992) define "psychological well-being" in terms of the individual's internal states (e.g., anxiety, depression, self-esteem, physiological status). Thus, ratings of behaviors by parents, peers, and teachers, as well as academic performance, reflect competence or social adaptational status, whereas self-ratings of mood states reflect psychological well-being. The social adaptational status model of competence is more restrictive than the "quadripartite model" developed by Felner, Lease, and Phillips (1992) who argue that socially competent behavior has four required conditions: (a) adequate cognitive processing and decision-making skills; (b) emotion-focused regulation and coping strategies; (c) necessary behavioral skills; and (d) motivational sets and expectancies that are consistent with desirable behaviors. The Felner et al. (1992) model includes both social adaptational status and psychological well-being, as well as other cognitive characteristics under the umbrella of social competence.

Because of the conceptual differences among competence models, it becomes difficult to operationalize resilience. For example, Luthar (1991), using the social adaptational status approach to competence, found that resilient adolescents (those experiencing a high degree of life stress, but who were rated as competent by teachers and peers) exhibited higher levels of anxiety and depression than competent adolescents who had experienced low levels of life stress, and similar levels of anxiety and depression compared with low-competence adolescents exposed to high levels of stress. The resilient adolescents may have had an internal rather than an external response to high levels of stress. Others similarly reported that there may be a cost to externally manifested competence (e.g., Farber & Egeland, 1987; Parker, Cowen, Work, & Wyman, 1990). Luthar, Doernberger, and Zigler (1993) have also found that adolescents may simultaneously be competent in some areas (e.g., academic) but not others (e.g., social relationships), and that their competence may not be stable over time.

Protective factors are personal (e.g., temperament, coping skills) or environmental resources (e.g., supportive relationships with others, youth organizations) that modify the experience of a risk situation to increase the likelihood of a positive outcome for children with high levels of the resource, compared with those who have low levels of the resource, despite the presence of the risk factor (Rutter, 1990). A protective factor operates *only* in the presence of the risk factor and involves a change from a risk to an adaptive trajectory. For example, a *protective* role for social problem-solving skills would be indicated if these skills are beneficial to children's adjustment at high levels of risk but are unrelated to children's adjustment at low levels of risk. Alternatively, Garmezy et al. (1984) illustrate that a personal or environmental resource might play a *compensatory* role. In this case, the resource operates independently of the risk factor; Higher levels of the resource relate to higher levels of competence, holding the risk level constant. Thus, if higher levels of social problem-solving skills relate to higher levels of adjustment for groups of children with either low or high stress levels, the resource plays a compensatory role.

Luthar (1993) stresses that both compensatory and protective effects of resources have implications for the development of intervention programs to promote competence. If a resource is found to be equally beneficial at both high and low levels of risk exposure (i.e., a compensatory effect), it is just as important to enhance this resource as it would be if the resource was found to be more beneficial at high than low levels of risk exposure (i.e., a protective role). Knowledge of the processes by which protective factors operate is also critical to the design of interventions. According to Rutter (1987), protective factors might (a) reduce the child's exposure to the risk condition (e.g., stricter parental supervision might reduce the child's exposure to deviant peers); (b) reduce the likelihood of negative chain reactions (e.g., a supportive extended family network might reduce the snowballing of negative events associated with parental separation/divorce); (c) promote self-esteem and self-efficacy (e.g., supportive staff members in youth organizations in disadvantaged neighborhoods might help the child with academic tasks that increase his or her perceived competence); and (d) open up opportunities (e.g., volunteer/vocational programs in inner-city schools might alter the potentially negative outcomes associated with growing up in poverty).

SCOPE OF PROBLEM

Prevalence of Mental Health Problems and Risk Factors

As noted earlier, the National Advisory Mental Health Council (1990) estimates that nearly one in five children is in need of mental health services. In terms of the prevalence of specific disorders, Merikangas and Angst's (1995) review of studies estimated that approximately 5% of community samples of adolescents met the diagnostic criteria for major depression in the past 6 months, and 34% had recently experienced clinically significant *symptoms* (although not the syndrome characterizing the disorder). In a Canadian community sample, Offord, Boyle, and Racine (1989) found that 7% of males and 3% of females 12 to 16 years of age met the diagnostic criteria for conduct disorder within the past 6 months; in addition, 14% of the males and 8% of the females admitted to having destroyed property (one symptom of conduct disorder). In terms of substance use, Botvin, Schinke, and Orlandi's (1995) review of survey studies showed that 77% of high school seniors had used alcohol in the past year and 27% had used one or more illegal drugs in the past year; among eighth graders, 26% had used alcohol, 4% had used marijuana, and 5% had used inhalants in the past month. Compas and Hammen (1994) noted the high rates of comorbidity (co-occurrence of two or more diagnoses) of mental disorders among adolescents. For example, in their review of studies, 17% to 79% of depressed adolescents met criteria for conduct disorder, and 23% to 25% of depressed adolescents met criteria for attention-deficit/hyperactivity disorder.

Estimates of child and adolescent mental health problems are much higher for children who are exposed to risk factors. Consequently, it is important to examine prevalence estimates of a variety of relatively common childhood risk conditions. For example, Mrazek and Haggerty (1994) estimate that 20% of the adult population in the United States suffer from an active mental disorder. Severe and/or chronic parental psychiatric illness is associated with significant impairment in children's mental health (e.g., Beardslee, Bemporad, Keller, & Klerman, 1984). Keller et al. (1986) found that 65% of the children they examined had at least one diagnosed disorder *after* a parent had experienced a depressive episode; 46% had two or more diagnoses. Although their parents were diagnosed with a depressive disorder, the children's diagnoses included major depression, oppositional syndrome, conduct disorder, dysthymia, overanxious disorder, alcohol abuse, and phobic disorder.

Other risk factors for poor mental health outcomes in children have also been identified. For example, in Keller et al.'s (1986) study, the only variable more strongly associated with negative outcomes than parental mental illness was low socioeconomic status. Over 14.3 million children in the United States are currently living in poverty (Strawn, 1992), and the number is increasing. It is projected that by the year 2000, one in three children will be living in poverty. Poverty is associated with a variety of poor outcomes including low academic performance and antisocial behavior (Dubow & Ippolito, 1994).

Studies have also shown that children who are exposed to *specific individual* stressors are at risk for adjustment problems. Guidubaldi, Cleminshaw, Perry, and McLoughlin (1983) noted that 40% to 50% of children born during the 1980s would spend some time in a single-parent family, mostly due to parental divorce. Another relatively frequent event during childhood is geographic mobility. Researchers report that 20% to 30% of children experience school transfers each year, perhaps as high as 50% in low-income areas (Cappas & Dubow, 1988; Felner, Primavera, & Cauce, 1981). A third stressor experienced by a significant number of children is the loss of a loved one (Berlinsky & Biller, 1982; Felner, Ginter, Boike, & Cowen, 1981). Approximately 6% of children under age 18 are likely to experience the death of a parent. Among other significant losses, Dubow (1989) found that over two years, 23% of a sample of fifth through seventh graders experienced the death of a grandparent. Coleman and Coleman (1984) noted that schools cannot avoid experiencing the death of a student; thus, many children experience the death of a peer. In general, these studies have found that exposure to each of these stressors is associated with a range of adjustment problems including teacher and peer ratings of behavior problems, academic difficulties, and emotional disturbance.

Major Issues in Examining "Scope of the Problem"

Coie et al. (1993) point out that there is a nonspecificity between risk factor and mental health outcome. That is, a given risk factor may lead to a range of mental health problems rather than a specific outcome, and any specific disorder may be associated with numerous risk factors. Thus, it is necessary to decide whether an intervention should be targeted at (a) a group of children exposed to a *specific* risk factor; (b) a group of children exposed to a *range of diverse risk factors* given that risk factors across domains (e.g., individual, family, peer group, community) appear to be interdependent; or (c) an *entire population* of children who have not yet even experienced a risk factor, based on data showing that at some time during childhood and adolescence, they are likely to experience at least one identified risk factor.

Intervention programs are often categorized into one of three types according to the population targeted: universal, selected, and indicated (Gordon, 1983). *Universal* programs target all individuals in a given population; participants are not selected on the basis of their behavior or adjustment. These interventions can be targeted at specific populations who are at risk, by virtue of having recently experienced a specific stressor or stressors (e.g., children whose parents have recently separated), in order to prevent potential adjustment problems. Alternatively, universal interventions might be targeted at an entire population without regard to their experience of risk conditions; the notion here is that enhancing basic coping or problem-solving skills will serve to promote competence and build a foundation of skills to help "inoculate" individuals when they face stressors in the future. *Selected* programs target individuals who are currently displaying mild signs of vulnerability to the stressor; these programs are designed to curtail *current* problem responses. Finally, *indicated* programs target individuals who have been identified as displaying clinically significant difficulties. The interventions to be described later focus on universal intervention programs aimed at *preventing* poor mental health outcomes by either targeting children exposed to risk conditions but who are as yet unaffected, or targeting all children in a given population to promote competence.

Another critical issue in determining the scope of the problem is that risk factors should be viewed as distal or proximal. Distal factors (e.g., living in a high crime area, parental divorce) do not *directly* influence the child (Baldwin, Baldwin, & Cole, 1990). Instead, the effects of these distal factors are *mediated through* proximal processes (e.g., ineffective parental monitoring, presence of substances or weapons in the home, exposure to deviant peers) that are perhaps more under the control of the child or his or her family. To the degree that the proximal risk processes are present, the child will experience negative mental health outcomes. Therefore, interventions need to target the proximal risk processes that influence outcomes (Pillow, Sandler, Braver, Wolchik, & Gersten, 1991).

CAUSES AND CONSEQUENCES: EFFECTS OF RISK AND PROTECTIVE FACTORS ON BEHAVIORAL, EMOTIONAL, AND ACADEMIC ADJUSTMENT

It is beyond the scope of this chapter to review the extensive literature on stressors and protective factors in child and adolescent adjustment, which is based on a multitude of studies of both high-risk youth and community samples. The reader is referred to several volumes reviewing this research (Anthony & Cohler, 1987; Garmezy & Rutter, 1983; Haggerty, Sherrod, Garmezy, & Rutter, 1994; Mrazek & Haggerty, 1994; Rolf, Masten, Cicchetti, Nuechterlein, & Weintraub, 1990), a journal relevant to this broad topic area (i.e., *Developmental Psychopathology*), and a sampling of empirical research (e.g., Cohen, Burt, & Bjork, 1987; Compas, Howell, Phares, Williams, & Giunta, 1989; DuBois, Felner, Brand, Adan, & Evans, 1992; Dubow & Luster, 1990; Dubow & Tisak, 1989; Dubow, Tisak, Causey, Hryshko, & Reid, 1991; Garmezy et al., 1984; Nettles & Pleck, 1994; Quinn, 1995; Rutter, 1979; Seifer & Sameroff, 1987; Sterling, Cowen, Weissberg, Lotyczewski, & Boike, 1985; Stouthamer-Loeber, Loeber, Farrington, Zhang, Van Kammen, & Maguin, 1993; Werner & Smith, 1992; Wertlieb, Weigel, & Feldstein, 1987). In this section, we summarize some of the major findings relevant to the effects of stressors and protective factors.

Effects of Stressors

Many of the studies cited in the previous paragraph examined the relation between cumulative stressors (i.e., the experience of a number of stressors during a specified period of time) and child or adolescent adjustment. Cumulative stressful life events scales include "major events" such as parental separation or divorce, birth of a sibling, family member leaving home, death or hospitalization of a family member, parent loses job, parent arrested, and/or "daily hassles" such as arguments with family member or receiving a poor grade (see DeLongis, Coyne, Dakof, Folkman, & Lazarus, 1982). Compas (1987) reviewed 32 studies of children and adolescents, noting that most of the studies were cross-sectional in nature (i.e., based on data collected at one point in time) and thus were unable to shed light on the potential *causal* role of stressors. Since Compas's review, however, a number of prospective studies, in which individuals are assessed at more than one time point, have provided evidence that experiencing an accumulation of stressful events at one point in time is associated with *increases over time* (usually between 6 months and 2 years, across studies) in adjustment problems (e.g., Compas et al., 1989; DuBois et al., 1992). There is also evidence that poor academic or behavioral adjustment may lead to increases over time in the experience of stressful events (e.g., DuBois et al., 1992; Dubow et al., 1991), suggesting that having symptoms of psychopathology may affect ways of interacting with the environment that lead to the occurrence of more stressful life events.

Stressors appear to have a multiplicative rather than an additive relationship to predicting mental health problems. For example, Rutter (1979) reported on the effects of stressors experienced by a sample of 10-year-old children on the Isle of Wight and inner-city London. There was no risk of mental disorder for children who were exposed to only one of the six potential risk factors (marital discord, low socioeconomic status, overcrowding in the family, paternal criminality, maternal psychiatric disorder, and admission into an out-of-home placement). For children who experienced two or three risk factors concurrently, however, the risk of disorder increased fourfold, and for children who experienced four or more stressors, the risk of disorder increased tenfold (see also Garmezy, 1981).

There is a consensus in the literature that researchers need to focus not on the effects of isolated life events or risk factors, but on an "aggregated accumulation" of events during a specified time period (Luthar, 1993; Rutter, 1994). For example, Sameroff and Seifer (1990) reported on the results of their Rochester Longitudinal Study, an investigation of the effects of parental mental illness in over 300 families on the cognitive and social development of children beginning at 4 months of age. The authors developed a multiple risk index composed of ten risk factors across the family and cultural domains (e.g., chronicity of mother's mental illness, maternal education and occupation, maternal beliefs about child rearing, minority status, family size). This index predicted child IQ at age 4 years better than any single risk factor. The authors found, "When groups were formed based on cluster analyses of families with the same degree of overall risk, there were no differences among these groups on the outcomes even though there were distinct patterns of risk factors present in the groups" (p. 62).

Effects of Protective Factors

Garmezy and Rutter (1983) identified a triad of protective factors that are hypothesized to operate in youth who exhibit competent outcomes despite exposure to significant risk conditions. Cowen and Work (1988) and Luther and Zigler (1991) summarized and provided examples of this triad: (a) dispositional/temperamental attributes of the child (e.g., autonomy, responsiveness, intellectual ability); (b) a warm and secure family relationship; and (c) availability of extrafamilial support (e.g., teachers, peers, youth leaders). Many of the studies cited in the introductory paragraph of this section have examined the protective functions of elements within this triad; only a few studies are reviewed in this section.

Werner and colleagues (Werner, 1993; Werner & Smith, 1982, 1992) conducted a 30-year longitudinal study of 698 infants born on the island of Kauai in 1955. This cohort was chosen because of the higher than average rates of poverty and associated chronic stressors in the community. One-third of the cohort was designated as high risk because they had experienced four or more of the following risk factors by age 2: born into poverty, experienced moderate to severe degrees of perinatal stress, or lived in a family troubled by discord, divorce, parental alcoholism, or mental illness. Two-thirds of these high-risk children were stress-affected; they developed serious learning or behavior problems by age 10 or had delinquency records, mental health problems, or pregnancies by age 18. However, one-third of the high-risk children were labeled as "resilient"; they succeeded in school, managed their home life and social life well, and their vocational and educational accomplishments at age 32 were at least equal to those of their low-risk peers in the cohort who had grown up under more affluent, secure, and stable conditions. Werner and Smith (1992) described the three clusters of protective factors that distinguished the resilient group from their stress-affected high-risk peers at age 18:

> (1) at least average intelligence, and dispositional attributes that elicited positive responses from family members and strangers, such as robustness, vigor, and an active, sociable temperament; (2) affectional ties with parent substitutes such as grandparents and older siblings, which encouraged trust, autonomy, and initiative; and (3) an external support system (in church, youth groups, or school) which rewarded competence and provided them with a sense of coherence. (p. 192)

(See Werner, 1993; and Werner & Smith, 1992, for a description of the outcomes in adulthood for the resilient group.)

Cowen and colleagues (Cowen, Wyman, Work, & Parker, 1990; Parker et al., 1990) designed the Rochester Child Resilience Project to identify protective factors distinguishing between stress-resilient and stress-affected children. The researchers generated a high-risk sample of fourth through sixth grade urban children by selecting from a larger population only those who had experienced four or more stressful life events. Teachers and parents rated children on global items reflecting social and academic achievement; these ratings were used to categorize the children as stress-resilient and stress-affected. In terms of data relevant to the first triad of protective factors (individual characteristics), compared with stress-affected children, stress-resilient children rated themselves higher on school adjustment, perceived competence, self-esteem, empathy, a sense of realistic control over events, and exhibited effective problem-solving skills and positive coping strategies; parents rated stress-resilient children as having easier temperaments. Relevant to the second triad (family support), compared with parents of stress-affected children, parents of stress-resilient children rated themselves as having higher levels of perceived efficacy, indicated that the fathers were more involved in child care, and perceived more positive parent-child relationships with age-appropriate and consistent discipline practices. Data relevant to the third triad of protective factors (community support) were not collected.

As noted earlier, researchers have recommended the need to focus on the effects of an "aggregated accumulation" of risk factors; the same must be said for protective factors. Dubow and Luster (1990) analyzed data from the National Longitudinal Survey of Youth, a probability sample of over 6,000 women interviewed each year beginning in 1979. The authors examined risk and protective factors in a subsample of 721 children (ages 8–15) born to teenage mothers. Children were determined to be at risk for a behavior or academic problem if they experienced at least one risk condition (e.g., poverty, overcrowding in the home, low maternal education, low maternal self-esteem) shown to predict poorer adjustment in that domain. The effects of four protective factors (i.e., moderate or better levels of emotional and cognitive stimulation provided in the home, child self-esteem and IQ) were also examined. Whereas nearly half of the at-risk children with zero protective factors exhibited significant adjustment problems, children with two or more protective factors were far less likely to experience significant adjustment problems.

Cowen (1980) describes two important "strands" in the field of prevention. The "generative strand" is the phase during which researchers develop a knowledge base of information regarding processes that might account for the development of psychopathology and the promotion of competencies. The "executive strand" is the phase during which this knowledge is applied to the design and implementation of intervention programs. Thus, the generative studies reviewed in this section provide the foundation on which researchers have built the prevention programs to be discussed later.

IMPEDIMENTS TO INTERVENTION IN THE REAL WORLD

A major issue in implementing interventions for children and adolescents is deciding how best to reach youth in order to promote competencies, especially youth who are at risk for the development of mental health problems. Two settings have frequently been targeted for outreach: community youth organizations and schools. Community youth organizations rank second only to public schools in the number of children involved each year (Quinn, 1995). Thus, interventions based in community youth organizations (e.g., Boys and Girls Clubs, YMCA/YWCA) appear to be an excellent way to reach a number of youth, and studies have found that children and adolescents who feel they are active participants in their community and perceive community members as supportive exhibit more positive adjustment (Prevention Connection, 1994). Children who are particularly at risk (e.g., living in low-income or high-crime neighborhoods) are least likely to become involved in these settings (Quinn, 1995). In addition, Quinn (1995) noted that between the ages of 12 and 13, participation in youth organizations begins to decline, so it is even more difficult to reach at-risk adolescents. Implementation and evaluation of community-based programs are also problematic. Although the quality of adult leadership for these programs is cited as critical to program outcomes, program leaders often have little formal training in working with children and adolescents (Quinn, 1995). Additionally, program evaluation in these settings is compromised because budget priorities favor service provision over evaluation.

The school environment appears to be the most logical point of intervention because it serves the greatest number of children and is associated with the conveyance of information, influence of behavioral and attitude norms, and development of future skills (Botvin et al., 1995). Students and the general public perceive schools as a natural setting for building competencies and preventing the development of unhealthy behaviors; thus, school-based interventions are often accepted by the community (Consortium on the School-Based Promotion of Social Competence, 1994). Schools are also conduits for reaching parents and connecting students and their families with needed services (e.g., medical and mental health services, academic tutoring), extracurricular clubs, and organizations in the larger community (Botvin et al., 1995). Schools receive the largest proportion of state, federal, and local funding for children, and in the face of ever-diminishing mental health appropriations, programs that can be incorporated into the school system are more likely to access these funds (Consortium on the School-Based Promotion of Social Competence, 1994).

There are problems, however, implementing intervention programs in the schools. First, it is difficult to reach the subset of children and adolescents who drop out of school or are chronically truant. These children are at higher risk than the general school population to develop mental health problems; indeed, the very nature of these behaviors suggests that these youth are already an *indicated* population in need of more intense intervention. Second, schools are not the only environment in which social learning occurs (Botvin et al., 1995). Baldwin et al. (1990) found that for children at high risk for adjustment problems, a match between parental values and those of the larger community was related to better outcome. This suggests that coordination between the various environments in which children develop is more likely to result in the prevention of mental health problems.

Other impediments to program implementation are characteristic of the interventions themselves (Mrazek & Haggerty, 1994). Often, interventions are piloted on small groups of students and implemented by psychologists or research personnel; careful evaluation of this process is ongoing to maintain fidelity. Although this makes for sound research, transfer of these programs into the larger school setting requires special attention. For example, a decision must be made regarding who should present the program to the children. Program components must be user-friendly and compatible with the time and personnel commitments of the school (Mrazek & Haggerty, 1994). In addition, teachers and administrators must be educated regarding the curricular information presented and any innovative activities (e.g., small group projects, role-plays); it is critical to enlist the support of faculty and staff to ensure a "team approach." Efforts should also be made to inform and gain support from parents and the larger community through public forums.

Once the program is in place, ongoing evaluation must occur to establish whether the program was implemented as planned and is showing effectiveness (Linney, 1989). An important part of the implementation is the fidelity of the instruction; the program must be monitored to determine whether the material is being covered as intended. Methods of monitoring include the instructor's self-report, video- or audiotaping of sessions, and random visits from a supervisor. Such an evaluation can be intimidating to teachers who are implementing the program. Larger systemic factors must also be evaluated. For example, if a program was developed for a small group format, is it being used that way, or is it being implemented through lecture format for a class of 35 students? One way to address these issues and alleviate evaluation concerns is to enlist the assistance of teachers and administrators in program development and evaluation (Linney, 1989).

It is also necessary to obtain measures of desired student outcomes targeted by the intervention. This type of evaluation is aimed at establishing the efficacy of the program and identifying portions in need of revision. Although schools may be very invested in programs, it is often difficult to allocate large portions of time for administering outcome measures. Archival data (e.g., grade-point average, referrals to the principal, suspensions) and unobtrusive measures (e.g., behavioral observations in the classroom, videotaping) may be less prohibitive in terms of time constraints. An added benefit of obtaining such measures is that by including these types of data along with student self-report measures, convergent evidence of desired outcomes may be obtained, enhancing the validity of the program (Linney, 1989).

PREVENTIVE INTERVENTIONS

This section provides a description of programs designed to *prevent* poor mental health outcomes in universal populations by either targeting children who have been exposed to risk conditions but who are as yet unaffected, or targeting all children in a given population to promote competence. This is not an exhaustive review of these intervention programs; rather, we have chosen several representative programs that target different age groups, different risk conditions, and different domains of protective resources (personal and environmental), and have published data regarding program effectiveness. The description of each program includes why the targeted youth are believed to be at risk, the researchers' bases for enhancing the specific protective resources, and a brief summary of program evaluation data.

Programs of each type that focus on enhancing personal resources are in part based on the literature regarding social problem-solving (SPS) skills and modeled after social skills training (SST) programs (e.g., Allen, Chinsky, Larcen, Lochman, & Selinger, 1976; Caplan et al., 1992; Elias & Weissberg, 1990; Spivack, Platt, & Shure, 1976; Weissberg et al., 1981). Research has shown that SPS skills (i.e., cognitive skills such as sensing emotions of others, problem identification, generation of alternative solutions to social problems, consideration of the consequences of those solutions, self-monitoring one's performance of the chosen solution) are related to behavioral and academic adjustment in children. School-based competence-building intervention programs based on the SST model typically range from 10 to 20 forty-minute to one-hour sessions implemented during one semester, or repeated with booster sessions during subsequent semesters to consolidate the acquisition of skills. The programs include role-plays, videotape and live modeling, and small group discussions. Children receiving SST programs have exhibited increases in social problem-solving skills, and in many cases, improvement in self-concept and behavioral adjustment (e.g., reduced teacher-rated problem behaviors, delinquent acts, and substance use).

Preventive Interventions Targeting Children Exposed to Risk

Children of Divorce Intervention Program (Pedro-Carroll, 1985)

Perhaps the specific stressor receiving the most attention as the focus of preventive interventions is parental divorce or separation (e.g., Alpert-Gillis, Pedro-Carroll, & Cowen, 1989; Stolberg & Garrison, 1985). Hetherington (1989) notes that while many of the family members from divorced homes recover within three years, some children continue to exhibit intense, long-term behavioral and emotional problems. Researchers have identified a number of protective resources among children from divorced families: problem-solving skills within the child; positive post-divorce relationships with both the custodial and noncustodial parent; encouragement by parents to discuss divorce-related feelings; and available adult and peer support for the child (e.g., Hetherington, 1989; Wallerstein & Kelly, 1980; Wolchik, Ruehlman, Braver, & Sandler, 1989).

Pedro-Carroll and colleagues (Alpert-Gillis et al., 1989; Pedro-Carroll, 1985; Pedro-Carroll & Cowen, 1985; Pedro-Carroll, Cowen, Hightower, & Guare, 1986) developed the Children of Divorce Intervention Program (CODIP), a 16-session school-based support-group program that has been implemented with children in Grades 2 through 6.

During the first few sessions, children share common divorce-related experiences to reduce their feelings of isolation and stigmatization, and to gain support from other children with similar experiences. Activities include: a "feelings grab bag," in which children role-play feelings written on papers they draw from the grab bag; viewing a filmstrip about parental divorce, discussing issues raised in the film, and sharing personal common experiences; and developing a newsletter "for other kids" to help them cope with their parents' divorce. Several sessions focus on the development of coping skills to help children gain a sense of control in their lives. Specifically, group leaders instruct the children in a 5-step social problem-solving sequence. Children practice these steps by applying them to self-generated problems, role-playing problem vignettes, and acting as a panel of "experts" on a staged TV program designed to help children from divorced families. Children are also taught to distinguish between solvable and unsolvable problems (i.e., problems they can and cannot control). Additional sessions focus on dealing with anger and split loyalties between parents and recognizing different forms of family constellation (via storybooks).

In one study, 52 second- and third-grade urban children received the intervention, and were compared, through a pre- and posttest design, with children of divorced families and children from intact families who did not receive the intervention. Intervention children improved more than the comparison groups on a measure of self-ratings of feelings about their families, parents, themselves, and their coping skills; teacher ratings of social competence; and parent ratings of the children's feelings and problem-solving skills (Alpert-Gillis et al., 1989). Similar positive evaluations of the CODIP program have been reported in samples of fourth- to sixth-grade suburban children (Pedro-Carroll & Cowen, 1985; Pedro-Carroll et al., 1986).

The School Transitional Environment Project (STEP; Felner & Adan, 1988)

One of the more common life transitions that children typically face is the normative transition from elementary to junior high school, or from junior high to high school. Although school transitions may provide opportunities for positive development, they are often associated with negative effects on students' grade-point averages, attendance, and self-esteem, and increase the likelihood of substance use and delinquency (e.g., Blythe, Simmons, & Bush, 1978; Blythe, Simmons, & Carlton-Ford, 1983; Felner, Farber, & Primavera, 1983; Felner, Ginter, & Primavera, 1982; Felner, Primavera, & Cauce, 1981). Felner and Adan (1988) noted that these effects may lead to longer-term consequences such as school dropout and serious mental disorders. Resources that help students negotiate school transitions include coping and problem-solving skills, teacher and peer support, and positive perceptions of the school environment (e.g., Causey & Dubow, 1993; Crockett, Petersen, Graber, Schulenberg, & Ebata, 1989; Elias, Gara, & Ubriaco, 1985). Features of the school setting affect students' perceptions of the school environment and the social support they receive in school. Felner and Adan (1988) noted that two important school setting variables are the complexity of the new school environment and the environment's ability to meet the students' needs. For example, students need to adapt to a larger, older, and new peer group, and teachers must get to know and support many new students.

One approach to helping students cope with school transitions is to enhance their social problem-solving skills (see Elias et al., 1986). A second approach is to change aspects of the environment that might compromise students' efforts to negotiate the transition. The STEP program is targeted at students transitioning into a larger school, often from multiple feeder schools. The program has two major components: reorganizing the school's social system; and restructuring the roles of key support sources (i.e., homeroom teachers and guidance counselors). The social system is reorganized as follows: STEP students share their major academic classes (e.g., English, math, science) and homeroom only with other STEP students, eliminating the shifting peer groups in each period of the school day; and STEP classrooms are located in the same part of the building so as to enhance informal interactions with familiar peers, reduce feelings of being overwhelmed by the size of the school, and lessen the level of interaction with older peers who younger students may find intimidating (this also serves to reduce potentially negative social pressures from older students). Restructuring the roles of key support sources is accomplished as follows: homeroom teachers are trained to take the role of guidance counselor to each STEP student by helping him or her choose classes and discuss other school-related or personal concerns; homeroom teachers follow up any student absence with a phone call to the parents; STEP teachers provide personal STEP program orientations for each STEP student and parent prior to the school year; STEP teachers meet weekly as a group to discuss their common students and plan any extra support a student may need; and school guidance counselors act as consultants to the teachers in terms of both implementing the program and providing additional and more intensive services to students who have such needs.

Felner et al. (1982) evaluated the STEP program in a sample of primarily lower socioeconomic status minority students who made the transition to a large urban high school. A control group who made the transition to the same school but were not part of the program also participated. Students in the control group exhibited decreases in grade-point averages and self-esteem, and increases in absenteeism; whereas STEP students' scores were stable across the academic year. In addition, compared with control group students, STEP students perceived teachers as more supportive and the school environment as more stable. Across the high school years, there was a 43% dropout rate for the comparison group compared with a 21% dropout rate for STEP students; additionally, STEP students maintained their advantage over time in terms of academic achievement and lower rates of absenteeism (Felner & Adan, 1988). Finally, Felner and Adan (1988) reported findings from replications of the STEP program in other schools, noting program effects in preventing emotional and behavioral difficulties (e.g., depression, substance use, delinquent behavior).

The Ypsilanti Perry Preschool Project (Weikart, Bond, & McNeil, 1978)

Many studies have documented the effects of poverty on children's academic and behavioral adjustment (e.g., Entwisle & Alexander, 1992; Garbarino, 1992; Garmezy, 1991; Ramey & Ramey, 1990; Rycraft, 1990). Dubow and Ippolito (1994) found that the number of years children spent in poverty between the toddler and preschool years predicted decreases in math and reading achievement, and increases in antisocial behavior over the subsequent elementary school years. Researchers have also found a link between school failure (success during school and amount of schooling) and delinquency, perhaps because school failure weakens attachment bonds to the school and strengthens bonds to delinquent peers (see Farnworth, 1982). Preschool programs have demonstrated long-term effects on enhancing school success in terms of reducing dropout rates and placement in special education classes, and increasing academic achievement and school motivation (The Consortium for Longitudinal Studies, 1983).

The Ypsilanti Perry Preschool Project (see Berrueta-Clement, Schweinhart, Barnett, & Weikart, 1987; Schweinhart & Weikart, 1983; Weikart et al., 1978) began in 1962 in an Ypsilanti, Michigan, neighborhood whose residents were low-income

African-American families; half were single-parent families, only half had an employed adult male living in the home, and half of the families were receiving government assistance. Between 1962 and 1965, 123 three- and four-year-olds were randomly assigned to either the preschool program or a control group that received no treatment. Children attended the preschool program for 2 years (the 4-year-olds in 1962 attended only 1 year) from October through May, 5 days a week, 2½ hours per day, and teachers conducted 90-minute home visits each week. Each class was taught by a team of teachers. The curriculum (Hohmann, Banet, & Weikart, 1979; Weikart, Rogers, Adcock, & McClelland, 1971) focused on general cognitive growth based on Piagetian theory. The classroom was arranged into a number of separate work areas (e.g., blocks, art, a kitchen, music, sand and water). The 2½-hour preschool day was structured as follows: planning time (20 minutes) during which the teachers help the children choose a work area and plan an activity; work time (40 minutes) during which children implement their plan in that area; group meeting (10 minutes) during which teachers help children evaluate their plans; cleanup (15 minutes); juice and group time (30 minutes) during which teachers and children review their efforts and teachers reinforce specific cognitive goals as will be described; activity time (20 minutes) during which an indoor or outdoor motor activity is performed to further reinforce cognitive goals; and circle time (15 minutes) for reviewing the day's work. The curriculum was based on the development of four cognitive goals: classification (e.g., investigating and describing attributes of objects); seriation (e.g., arranging objects in a series according to a property of the objects); spatial relations (e.g., fitting objects together and taking them apart); and temporal relations (e.g., experiencing and describing different rates of speed). The development of these goals formed the centerpiece of the chosen plans and activities. Through weekly home visits, the teacher, parent, and child worked together on activities designed to reinforce these goals given each child's developmental level.

Program children increased more in standardized IQ tests compared with control children by the end of the 2 years. By fourth grade, differences between the program and control groups on standardized IQ tests decreased, but program children outperformed controls on reading and math tests, and 17% of the program children had been retained in grade or required special education classes compared with 38% of the control children. By eighth grade, there were no group differences in IQ scores, but program children continued to obtain higher scores on achievement tests and placed a higher value on education than did control children; program parents were more satisfied with their children's school performance and had higher educational aspirations for them. Program students were more likely to graduate from high school, obtain further education, and be employed by age 19. Program children also reported lower levels of delinquent behavior by eighth grade, and by age 19, 51% of the control students were arrested at least once compared with 31% of the program students.

Preventive Interventions Targeting All Children in a Given Population

I CAN DO Program (Dubow, 1995)

Our research group has conducted studies with elementary school children, their parents, and teachers focusing on the relation between stressful life events and academic and behavioral adjustment, and the role of a variety of potential protective factors (e.g., Cappas, 1991; Causey & Dubow, 1992; Dubow & Luster, 1990; Dubow & Tisak,

1989; Dubow et al., 1991; Dubow & Ullman, 1989). For example, in a sample of 361 third through fifth graders, Dubow and Tisak (1989) found that exposure to higher levels of stressful life events in the past year predicted poorer teacher- and parent-rated academic and behavioral adjustment. In addition, high levels of social support (particularly family and peer support) and social problem-solving skills acted as protective factors. In a 2-year follow-up study of these children, Dubow et al. (1991) found that increases over time in social support and social problem-solving skills predicted improvement over time in behavioral and academic adjustment. These results provided the framework for developing a preventive intervention designed to enhance children's social support and social problem-solving skills.

The I CAN DO program (Dubow, 1995; Dubow, Schmidt, McBride, Edwards, & Merk, 1993) is a 13-session (45 minutes per session) curriculum developed for fourth graders to teach children general coping skills. Children learn to practice these skills in relation to five stressful events/experiences that occur to a significant number of children: parental separation or divorce; loss of a loved one; move to a new home or school; spending significant amounts of time in situations without adult supervision (self-care); and feeling "different" (ethnically, physically, etc.) The program is designed for a universal population to teach children coping strategies that they could use if they were exposed to each stressor, and how they might be helpful to peers experiencing the stressor. The first three sessions focus on explaining the concept of problem-solving and presenting the 6-step "I CAN DO" problem-solving sequence (the first letter of each step spells I CAN DO: *I*dentify the problem; *C*hoices to solve it; *A*ttention to all information; *N*arrow down the choices to one; *D*o what you decide; and *O*utcome); and presenting two viable coping skills for hard (uncontrollable) problems (learning strategies to make oneself feel better and seeking social support). These skills are instructed through activities such as a bingo game to review the skill concepts; worksheets to identify social support network members in the family, peer group, and community; and role-plays. The next 10 sessions are divided into five units (two sessions each) devoted to each stressor, and focus on applying the general coping skills to each stressor. For example, in the coping with loss unit, a video is shown in which a child in school copes with the loss of the school's crossing guard; children apply the I CAN DO steps in reviewing how the boy and his classmates coped with the loss. In the moving unit, children participate in a "pretend" move activity; they also role-play several scenarios about a child who is new to the school and how they might make the newcomer feel welcome. In the differences unit, children perform a simulated blindness task requiring them to develop an appreciation for the special efforts of individuals with disabilities. In the self-care unit, children are instructed on how to complete with their parents a "Parent-Child Agreement" outlining house rules, emergency rules, and rules for opening the door and answering the phone if they are ever at home alone even for a very short period. In the parental separation/divorce unit, an actor role-plays a child who presents to the class many problems she is facing as a result of her parents' divorce (e.g., extra responsibilities such as food-shopping, caring for younger siblings). The children in the classroom provide this actor with suggestions based on the general coping skills.

Dubow et al. (1993) implemented the program using a sample of 88 fourth graders. Two classrooms received the program in the fall semester (immediate intervention), and two received it in the spring semester (but served as the comparison group in the fall semester; delayed intervention). Researchers conducted pre-, post-, and 5-month follow-up testing. The immediate intervention group improved significantly more than the delayed intervention group in solving problem vignettes about each stressor and in their comfort with implementing coping strategies taught in the program. The immediate intervention group maintained their improvement at 5-month follow-up on these measures. The delayed intervention group also improved on these measures after having received the program. Process evaluation indicated that the program was implemented as described in the training manual, and that children held very positive opinions about the program and the usefulness of the information they had learned.

Life Skills Training (Botvin & Dusenbury, 1987)

Substance use by children and adolescents is widely recognized as a significant problem facing families, schools, and communities. Apart from being problematic in itself, substance use by youth is related to poorer academic performance and increased behavior problems (see Botvin et al., 1995). Drug and alcohol education is mandated by many states; however, information-based programs modeled on traditional classroom instruction have been found to be rather limited in their effectiveness (Botvin & Dusenbury, 1987). Substance use appears to be multiply determined; both interpersonal and intrapersonal factors affect an individual's choice to use tobacco, alcohol, and other substances. Such factors include modeling by high-status role models, the desire to "fit in" with peers, low self-confidence, and rebelliousness (Botvin & Dusenbury, 1987). Therefore, programs that provide information but do not address these other factors are less likely to effect significant change in youth substance use.

Life Skills Training (LST) is a program developed to help youth develop the skills for coping with the social influences to use substances. Although the program is tailored specifically to address substance use issues, personal and social skills building are also taught. The program consists of five major conceptual components, taught in 16 sessions. Didactics, small group discussions, demonstrations (e.g., physiological effects of smoking demonstrated using biofeedback; use of effective coping techniques), and cognitive-behavioral modification techniques (e.g., making appropriate self-statements; diaphragmatic breathing) are used to provide youth with the information in each component; participants also spend time practicing the new skills of each component. The first two components (cognitive skills and decision making) focus on factors related to youth substance use. Youth are instructed about the short- and long-term effects of substance use, current prevalence rates, norms, decreasing social acceptability, and tactics used by advertisers to sell these products (e.g., alcohol and tobacco). An "inoculation" model is used that initially exposes students to mildly persuasive advertising and arguments for the use of substances, and as they develop and practice resistance and refusal skills, the level of persuasion is intensified. LST also targets more general skills such as critical thinking and decision making. A third component focuses on techniques to reduce anxiety (e.g., relaxation, mental rehearsal, and deep breathing). The fourth component, social skills training, addresses communication skills (verbal and nonverbal). In addition to communication skills, miscommunication, and ways to avoid it, is highlighted. Common social situations are discussed, and students role-play various social interactions (e.g., initiating social contacts, basic conversation skills, and interactions with the opposite sex). Participants are also instructed in verbal and nonverbal assertiveness skills regarding requests and open expression of their feelings. In a fifth component, self-improvement, each student designs a self-improvement project to improve one specific skill or behavior.

This ongoing project provides students with the opportunity to incorporate the personal skills they are learning, and the group discussions allow others to provide feedback during the project.

Botvin and Dusenbury (1987) reviewed a series of studies examining the effectiveness of LST. The initial evaluation of the LST was conducted using 281 eighth-, ninth-, and tenth-grade students in New York City suburbs; the primary focus was tobacco use. The program was implemented over 3 months by outside health professionals. Comparison of pretest and posttest questionnaires indicated that the LST produced a 75% reduction in new cigarette smoking during the 3 months. A 3-month follow-up study found that the treatment group still had 67% fewer new smokers than the no-treatment group. The effectiveness of LST in the prevention of alcohol and marijuana use has also been examined. In a study involving 1,200 seventh-grade students from New York City suburbs, several variations in the administration of the program were examined: (a) teacher-led; (b) peer-led; (c) teacher-led plus booster sessions; and (d) peer-led plus booster sessions. Both teacher- and peer-led programs had a significant effect on tobacco and alcohol use. In addition, compared with students in the control condition, students in the peer-led programs reported a 71% reduction in total marijuana use and an 83% reduction in regular marijuana use.

Teen Outreach Program (Philliber & Allen, 1992)

A critical task in adolescent development is to establish personal autonomy in social interactions while maintaining a sense of relatedness with significant others (Allen, Hauser, Bell, & O'Connor, 1994). For those adolescents who fail to accomplish this task, numerous problem behaviors can occur (e.g., pregnancy, school failure, school dropout). These behaviors are costly not only to the youth involved but also to society, and school-based intervention programs have been implemented, with limited success, to prevent these problems. One reason for the equivocal success of many of these programs may be that, although they directly address problem behaviors that adolescents are experiencing, enhancement of the critical tasks specific to adolescent development may be overlooked. Allen, Kuperminc, Philliber, and Herre (1994) suggested that one way to enhance the effectiveness of these programs is to match the intervention to the critical tasks in adolescent development.

Teen Outreach is a school-based student volunteer program implemented in schools across both the United States and Canada. The goals are to prevent early pregnancy and promote academic advancement by enhancing the autonomy and social relatedness of middle school participants. This program is a collaborative effort of school personnel and a local fund, most often the local Junior League. The program consists of two major components: a curriculum for small group discussions led by a facilitator; and community volunteer service. Although the core components are consistent throughout participating sites, the actual implementation of the program varies widely. Some sites offer the program as part of the school curriculum, whereas others offer it as an extracurricular activity. Participants meet at least once per week throughout the school year in discussion groups that address topics such as communication skills, human development, parenting and family relationships, and sex education; group exercises, films, and presentations are also used. Although the style of instruction differs across groups, the focus of the groups is on developing a supportive environment in which students can share their thoughts and feelings. The types of volunteer work performed by students also vary, both within and across sites; some volunteer activities include working as aides in hospitals and nursing homes, peer tutoring, and participating in fundraisers.

Teen Outreach has documented a consistent record of effectiveness. Using data from the academic school years 1984 to 1989, Philliber and Allen (1992) showed that students participating in Teen Outreach programs exhibited consistently lower incidence rates of teen pregnancy, school suspension, school failure, and school dropout relative to nonparticipating students. Because participation in Teen Outreach is voluntary, students who join the program are somewhat self-selected. However, pre- and post-involvement behavior ratings show that the *change* in problem behaviors decreased more for those students involved in the Teen Outreach program (Allen, Philliber, & Hoggson, 1990). Allen, Kuperminc, et al. (1994) investigated the process behind the success of Teen Outreach by examining how participation in the program affects the development of autonomy and relatedness. They found that for middle school children, involvement in Teen Outreach enhanced both autonomy and relatedness to other students and adults. Additionally, those sites where the program produced greater development of autonomy and relatedness reported better outcomes with respect to problem behaviors.

Seattle Social Development Project (Hawkins et al., 1992)

Coie et al. (1993) emphasize the interdependence of risk and protective factors across many contexts (e.g., individual, family, school, peer). They also stress that intervention needs to occur before risk factors stabilize. Because early conduct problems, low academic achievement, low commitment to school, and high levels of family conflict precede the development of adolescent delinquency and substance use (Farrington & Hawkins, 1991), intervention programs must occur early and encompass environments central to the child's development.

The Seattle Social Development Project is a 4-year intervention targeted at reducing risk factors related to the development of delinquency and substance use. Children in the first through fourth grades were chosen to participate in the project. The intervention was designed to promote the development of bonds between the children/family and schools because these bonds should act as protective factors by enhancing children's adherence to the behavioral norms of home and school, thus reducing the likelihood of deviant behaviors. The program takes a multifaceted approach with components addressing the following contexts: school, home, and the individual child. The school component (Grades 1–4) consists of workshops in which teachers are taught to implement the following adaptations:

1. *Proactive Classroom Management.* Establishing classroom environments that are conducive to learning by creating consistent patterns of expectations, promoting appropriate behavior, minimizing interruption of learning, and encouraging and rewarding students for appropriate effort and behavior.
2. *Interactive Teaching.* Children's grades are based on mastery of material and exhibited improvement over past performance, until mastery is obtained.
3. *Cooperative Learning.* Groups of students of differing abilities and backgrounds work together as "learning partners" for the team's mastery of material.

The home component (Grades 1–3) consists of a two-part parent training program. The first part is designed to increase positive parental involvement with the child by instructing parents to (a) monitor children and identify desired and undesired behaviors; (b) teach expectations for appropriate behavior; and (c) consistently provide children with positive reinforcement for desired behavior and negative consequences for inappropriate behavior. The second part is designed to enhance positive communication between the parent and child, and the parent and school. Additionally, parents are taught to support their children's academic progress by developing a positive learning environment in the home and assisting with reading and math skills. The child component (formally implemented in Grade 1, applied through Grade 4) consists of social problem-solving training designed to teach alternative solutions to interpersonal problems, and skills in communication, decision making, negotiation, and conflict resolution.

To evaluate program effectiveness, information was obtained on 199 entering fifth graders who had participated in the project for all four prior academic years; information was also obtained for 809 fifth graders who had little or no involvement in the project. Group differences were found on both family and school measures. Specifically, children and their families who participated in the project reported greater proactive family management, greater family communication, and greater family involvement than did children and families in the control group. Although significant group differences in academic achievement were not found, children who had participated in the project had a more positive perception of school than did control students; they perceived school as more rewarding, and they reported being more attached and committed to the school. Although children in both groups reported minimal alcohol use or delinquency, those children participating in the project endorsed significantly fewer of either problem behavior.

SUMMARY AND DIRECTIONS FOR THE FUTURE

A significant number of children and adolescents develop serious mental health problems each year (e.g., conduct problems, mood disorders, substance use). The resilience literature has identified processes that place youth at risk, and perhaps more important, those personal and environmental resources that may protect youth from developing mental health problems. These findings have begun to be successfully applied to the design of intervention programs focusing on single and multiple risk factors targeting universal populations (to promote competence and prevent disorder) and selected and indicated populations (to prevent further development of symptomatology). The preventive interventions described in this chapter show much promise; however, they also raise a number of issues that investigators are now addressing in prevention research.

First, in light of the findings that mental health outcomes are multiply determined by risk factors spanning diverse contexts, researchers have voiced the need for the development of comprehensive frameworks that identify the range of distal influences and proximal mediators and specify their effects on outcome variables over time. For example, Guerra and colleagues (Eron, 1994; Guerra, Eron, Huesmann, Tolan, & Van Acker, 1997; Guerra, Huesmann, Tolan, Van Acker, & Eron, 1995) describe a cognitive-ecological theory of the development of aggression that takes into account both contextual factors such as poverty and recent stressful life events, and cognitive factors such as self-efficacy, normative beliefs about aggression, and expectancies for outcomes. They have applied this theory to understanding the development of aggression and violence among inner-city youth. They posit that the child reared in a chaotic, disadvantaged environment is more frequently exposed to aggression and is thus more likely to develop aggressive scripts for behavior. Furthermore, this child is more likely to rely on these well-learned scripts when feeling overwhelmed in order "to keep the information-processing load within his or her capabilities during this chaos" (Guerra et al., in press). In support of their model, Guerra et al. (1995) found that in a sample of nearly 2,000 children from low-income neighborhoods, the distal factor of low income had an indirect influence on children's aggression, mediated by the proximal effects of stressful life events and normative beliefs about aggression.

Second, researchers have suggested that preventive interventions should be conceptualized as multimodal and long term (The Consortium on the School-Based Promotion of Social Competence, 1994). Guerra et al. (in press; see also Eron, 1994) have recently launched a large-scale longitudinal intervention program to reduce the development of aggressive and antisocial behavior and to enhance social competence among children in urban schools. The program intervenes at three different contextual levels: the individual, the peer group, and the family. All children in the intervention receive a general classroom enhancement program during Grades 2, 3, 5, and 6, with booster sessions in Grade 8; this curriculum targets the cognitions central to the cognitive-ecological model. A subsample of these children who have been identified as high-risk (i.e., higher levels of teacher- and peer-rated aggression) also receive more intensive small group training with peers in Grades 2, 3, 5, and 6. In addition, a subsample of these high-risk children also receive a small-group family training intervention consisting of 22 sessions during the second-grade year. Initial results are promising, suggesting that the most intensive level of intervention (which intervenes at the individual, peer, and family contexts) is associated with the largest decreases in peer-nominated aggression. Another recently begun large-scale multimodal intervention, the FAST Track Program (Conduct Problems Prevention Research Group, 1992), was designed to prevent the further development of conduct disorder symptoms in a selected population. The program targets first graders through the middle school years, and intervenes across the following settings: home (parent training, home visiting/case management), peers (friendship groups), and school (academic tutoring, teacher-led social skills enhancement). Initial evaluations of FAST Track have indicated positive changes in parenting, parent involvement, and children's social skills, and these changes appear to mediate the more long-term predictors of adjustment—early aggressive behavior and interpersonal interactions (Dodge & Conduct Problems Prevention Research Group, 1993).

Third, researchers are continuing to make advances in methodological approaches to prevention research. For example, in terms of a general model for conducting prevention research, Kellam and colleagues at the Johns Hopkins Prevention Research Center (Dolan et al., 1993; Kellam & Rebok, 1992; Kellam, Rebok, Ialongo, & Mayer, 1994) offer a developmental-epidemiological perspective. This framework is based on tracking trajectories of specific behaviors among an epidemiologically defined sample (e.g., all first graders in an entire community) "to explain variation in developmental paths including antecedents, moderators, and outcomes" (Kellam & Rebok, 1992, p. 165). This group of researchers advocates using a "multistage sampling" procedure by which smaller representative subsamples are drawn from the universal population to participate in microanalytic prevention studies and interventions testing specific aspects of their framework. These researchers also note the importance of understanding developmental trajectories to determine the most appropriate point of intervention. For example, intervention to prevent aggression should begin by first grade if first grade aggression predicts adolescent delinquency (Kellam et al., 1994). In terms of identifying the sample for intervention, researchers have noted that the benefits of targeting universal, selected, or indicated populations are largely unknown (Tolan, Guerra, & Kendall, 1995). Pillow et al. (1991) have suggested screening subjects on the basis of mediating variables as a method for enhancing the ability to detect program effects (e.g., screening out potential subjects who already have a high level of the resource). In addition, screening reduces the sample size by identifying those most likely to benefit from the program, thereby improving the cost-effectiveness of the intervention. Thus, future prevention research will likely benefit from further methodological refinements.

Finally, there has recently been an increase in attention to the moderating role of ethnicity in the relations among risk processes, resource variables, and children's adjustment. For example, although Nettles and Pleck (1994) reported higher rates of school-related and legal problems for African-American compared to white youth, they also stressed that there is variability within each ethnic group, and research has often confounded race and socioeconomic status. Furthermore, Guerra et al. (1995), in a study of elementary school children, found that normative beliefs about aggression, socioeconomic status, and stressful life events played different roles in the development of aggression among African-American, white, and Hispanic children. This suggests that researchers need to develop preventive interventions that are sensitive to cultural differences.

Theoretical and methodological advances are now charting the development of large-scale preventive intervention programs that address risk and protective processes across multiple contexts. Such programs are necessary to test the degree to which theoretical models and intervention approaches are generalizable across diverse groups of youth. The results of these efforts will no doubt both refine theoretical models, and in turn, reshape intervention approaches to building children's competencies.

REFERENCES

Allen, G. J., Chinsky, J. M., Larcen, S. W., Lochman, J. E., & Selinger, H. V. (1976). *Community psychology and the schools: A behaviorally oriented multilevel preventive approach.* Hillsdale, NJ: Erlbaum.

Allen, J. P., Hauser, S. T., Bell, K. L., & O'Connor, T. G. (1994). Longitudinal assessment of autonomy and relatedness in adolescent-family interactions as predictors of adolescent ego development and self-esteem. *Child Development, 65,* 179–194.

Allen, J. P., Kuperminc, G., Philliber, S., & Herre, K. (1994). Programmatic prevention of adolescent problem behaviors: The role of autonomy, relatedness, and volunteer service in the Teen Outreach program. *American Journal of Community Psychology, 22,* 617–638.

Allen, J. P., Philliber, S., & Hoggson, N. (1990). School-based prevention of teen-age pregnancy and school dropout: Process evaluation of the National Replication of the Teen Outreach Program. *American Journal of Community Psychology, 18,* 505–524.

Alpert-Gillis, L. J., Pedro-Carroll, J. L., & Cowen, E. L. (1989). The children of divorce intervention program: Development, implementation, and evaluation of a program for young urban children. *Journal of Consulting and Clinical Psychology, 57,* 583–589.

Anthony, E. J., & Cohler, B. J. (Eds.). (1987). *The invulnerable child.* New York: Guilford Press.

Baldwin, A. L., Baldwin, C., & Cole, R. E. (1990). Stress-resistant families and stress-resistant children. In J. Rolf, A. S. Masten, D. Cicchetti, K. H. Nuechterlein, & S. Weintraub (Eds.), *Risk and protective factors in the development of psychopathology* (pp. 257–280). New York: Cambridge University Press.

Beardslee, W. R., Bemporad, J., Keller, M. B., & Klerman, G. L. (1984). Children of parents with a major affective disorder: A review. In S. Chess & A. Thomas (Eds.), *Annual progress in child psychiatry and child development* (pp. 390–404). New York: Brunner/Mazel.

Berlinsky, E., & Biller, H. (1982). *Parental death and psychological development.* Lexington, MA: Heath.

Berrueta-Clement, J. R., Schweinhart, L. J., Barnett, W. S., & Weikart, D. P. (1987). The effects of early educational intervention on crime and delinquency in adolescence and early adulthood. In J. D. Burchard & S. N. Burchard (Eds.), *Prevention of delinquent behavior* (pp. 220–240). London: Sage.

Blyth, D. A., Simmons, R. G., & Bush, D. (1978). The transition into early adolescence: A longitudinal comparison of youth in two educational contexts. *Sociology of Education, 51,* 149–162.

Blyth, D. A., Simmons, R. G., & Carlton-Ford, S. (1983). The adjustment of early adolescents to school transitions. *Journal of Early Adolescence, 3,* 105–120.

Botvin, G. J., & Dusenbury, L. (1987). Life skills training: A psychoeducational approach to substance-abuse prevention. In C. A. Maher & J. E. Zins (Eds.), *Psychoeducational interventions in the schools: Methods and procedures for enhancing student competence* (pp. 46–65). New York: Pergamon Press.

Botvin, G. J., Schinke, S., & Orlandi, M. A. (1995). School-based health promotion: Substance abuse and sexual behavior. *Applied and Preventive Psychology, 4,* 167–184.

Caplan, M., Weissberg, R. P., Grober, J. S., Sivo, P. J., Grady, K., & Jacoby, C. (1992). Social competence promotion with inner-city and suburban young adolescents: Effects on social adjustment and alcohol use. *Journal of Consulting and Clinical Psychology, 60,* 56–63.

Cappas, C. L. (1991). *Evaluation of a prevention program for children experiencing a geographic relocation.* Unpublished doctoral dissertation, Bowling Green State University, Bowling Green, OH.

Cappas, C. L., & Dubow, E. F. (1988, May). *Moving, stress, and social support in elementary school children: Relations to adjustment.* Paper presented at the meeting of the Midwestern Psychological Association, Chicago.

Causey, D. L., & Dubow, E. F. (1992). Development of a self-report coping measure for elementary school children. *Journal of Clinical Child Psychology, 21,* 47–59.

Causey, D. L., & Dubow, E. F. (1993). Negotiating the transition to junior high school: The contributions of coping strategies and perceptions of the school environment. *Prevention in Human Services, 10,* 59–81.

Coatsworth, J. D., & Sandler, I. (1992). Defining and measuring children's competence: Issues for community psychology. *Community Psychologist, 26,* 16–17.

Cohen, L. H., Burt, C. E., & Bjorck, J. P. (1987). Life stress and adjustment: Effects of life events experienced by young adolescents and their parents. *Developmental Psychology, 23,* 583–592.

Coie, J. D., Watt, N. F., West, S. G., Hawkins, J. D., Asarnow, J. R., Markman, H. J., Ramey, S. L., Shure, M. B., & Long, B. (1993). The science of prevention: A conceptual framework and some directions for a national research program. *American Psychologist, 48,* 1013–1022.

Coleman, F. W., & Coleman, W. S. (1984). Helping siblings and other peers cope with dying. In H. Wass & C. A. Corr (Eds.), *Childhood and death* (pp. 129–150). Washington, DC: Hemisphere.

Compas, B. E. (1987). Coping with stress during childhood and adolescence. *Psychological Bulletin, 101*, 393–403.

Compas, B. E., & Hammen, C. L. (1994). Child and adolescent depression: Covariation and comorbidity in development. In R. H. Haggerty, L. R. Sherrod, N. Garmezy, & M. Rutter (Eds.), *Stress, risk, and resilience in children and adolescents: Process, mechanisms, and interventions* (pp. 225–267). Cambridge, England: Cambridge University Press.

Compas, B. E., Howell, D. C., Phares, V., Williams, R. A., & Giunta, C. T. (1989). Risk factors for emotional/behavioral problems in young adolescents: A prospective analysis of adolescent and parental stress and symptoms. *Journal of Consulting and Clinical Psychology, 57*, 732–740.

Conduct Problems Prevention Research Group. (1992). A developmental and clinical model for the prevention of Conduct Disorder: The FAST Track program. *Development and Psychopathology, 4*, 509–527.

The Consortium for Longitudinal Studies. (1983). *As the twig is bent: Lasting effects of preschool programs.* Hillsdale, NJ: Erlbaum.

The Consortium on the School-Based Promotion of Social Competence. (1994). The school-based promotion of social competence: Theory, research, practice, and policy. In R. H. Haggerty, L. R. Sherrod, N. Garmezy, & M. Rutter (Eds.), *Stress, risk, and resilience in children and adolescents: Process, mechanisms, and interventions* (pp. 268–316). Cambridge, England: Cambridge University Press.

Cowen, E. L. (1980). The wooing of primary prevention. *American Journal of Community Psychology, 8*, 258–284.

Cowen, E. L., & Work, W. C. (1988). Resilient children, psychological wellness, and primary prevention. *American Journal of Community Psychology, 16*, 591–607.

Cowen, E. L., Wyman, P. A., Work, W., & Parker, G. M. (1990). The Rochester Child Resilience Study: Overview and summary of first year findings. *Development and Psychopathology, 2*, 193–212.

Crockett, L. J., Petersen, A. C., Graber, J. A., Schulenberg, J. E., & Ebata, A. (1989). School transitions and adjustment during early adolescence. *Journal of Early Adolescence, 9*, 181–210.

Delongis, A., Coyne, J. C., Dakof, G., Folkman, S., & Lazarus, R. S. (1982). Relationship of daily hassles, uplifts, and major life events to health status. *Journal of Health Psychology, 1*, 119–136.

Dodge, K. A., & the Conduct Problems Prevention Research Group. (1993, March). *Effects of intervention on children at high risk for conduct problems.* Paper presented at the biennial meeting of the Society for Research in Child Development, New Orleans, LA.

Dolan, L. J., Kellam, S. G., Brown, C. H., Werthamer-Larsson, L., Rebok, G. W., Mayer, L. S., Laudolff, J., Turkkan, J. S., Ford, C., & Wheeler, L. (1993). The short-term impact of two classroom-based preventive interventions on aggressive and shy behaviors and poor achievement. *Journal of Applied Developmental Psychology, 14*, 317–345.

DuBois, D. L., Felner, R. D., Brand, S., Adan, A. M., & Evans, E. G. (1992). A prospective study of life stress, social support, and adaptation in early adolescence. *Child Development, 63*, 542–557.

Dubow, E. F. (1989). [A two-year longitudinal study of stressful life events, resources, and adjustment]. Unpublished raw data.

Dubow, E. F. (1995). *I CAN DO problem-solving training manual.* Bowling Green, OH: Bowling Green State University.

Dubow, E. F., & Ippolito, M. F. (1994). Effects of poverty and quality of the home environment on changes in the academic and behavioral adjustment of elementary school-age children. *Journal of Clinical Child Psychology, 23*, 401–412.

Dubow, E. F., & Luster, T. (1990). Adjustment of children born to teenage mothers: The contribution of risk and protective factors. *Journal of Marriage and the Family, 52,* 393–404.

Dubow, E. F., Schmidt, D., McBride, J., Edwards, S., & Merk, F. L. (1993). Teaching children to cope with stressful experiences: Initial implementation and evaluation of a primary prevention program. *Journal of Clinical Child Psychology, 22,* 428–440.

Dubow, E. F., & Tisak, J. (1989). The relation between stressful life events and adjustment in elementary school children: The role of social support and social problem-solving skills. *Child Development, 60,* 1412–1423.

Dubow, E. F., Tisak, J., Causey, D., Hryshko, A., & Reid, G. (1991). A two-year longitudinal study of stressful life events, social support, and social problem-solving skills: Contributions to children's behavioral and academic adjustment. *Child Development, 62,* 583–599.

Dubow, E. F., & Ullman, D. G. (1989). Assessing social support in elementary school children: The survey of children's social support. *Journal of Clinical Child Psychology, 18,* 52–64

Elias, M. J., Gara, M., & Ubriaco, M. (1985). Sources of stress and support in children's transition to middle school: An empirical analysis. *Journal of Clinical Child Psychology, 14,* 112–118.

Elias, M. J., Gara, M., Ubriaco, M., Rothman, P. A., Clabby, J. F., & Schuyler, T. (1986). Impact of a preventive social problem-solving intervention on children's coping with middle-school stressors. *American Journal of Community Psychology, 14,* 259–276.

Elias, M. J., & Weissberg, R. P. (1990). School-based social competence promotion as a primary prevention strategy: A tale of two projects. In R. P. Lorion (Ed.), *Protecting the children: Strategies for optimizing emotional and behavioral development* (pp. 177–200). New York: Haworth Press.

Entwisle, D. R., & Alexander, K. L. (1992). Summer setback: Race, poverty, school composition, and mathematics achievement in the first two years of school. *American Psychological Review, 57,* 72–84.

Eron, L. D. (1994, August). *Aggression is a learned behavior and therefore can be unlearned.* Paper presented at the annual meeting of the American Psychological Association, Los Angeles, CA.

Farber, E. A., & Egeland, B. (1987). Invulnerability among abused and neglected children. In E. J. Anthony & B. J. Cohler (Eds.), *The invulnerable child* (pp. 253–288). New York: Guilford Press.

Farnworth, M. (1982). *Schooling and self-reported delinquency: A longitudinal study.* Ypsilanti, MI: High/Scope Educational Research Foundation.

Farrington, D. P., & Hawkins, J. D. (1991). Predicting participation, early onset, and later persistence in officially recorded offending. *Criminal Behaviour and Mental Health, 1,* 1–33.

Felner, R. D., & Adan, A. M. (1988). The school transitional environment project: An ecological intervention and evaluation. In R. H. Price, E. L. Cowen, R. P. Lorion, J. Ramos-McKay, & B. Hitchins (Eds.), *Fourteen ounces of prevention: A casebook of exemplary primary prevention programs* (pp. 111–122). Washington DC: American Psychological Association.

Felner, R. D., Farber, S. S., & Primavera, J. (1983). Transitions and stressful life events: A model for primary prevention. In R. D. Felner, L. A. Jason, J. N. Moritsugu, & S. S. Farber (Eds.), *Preventive psychology: Theory, research, and practice* (pp. 199–215). New York: Pergaman Press.

Felner, R. D., Ginter, M. A., Boike, M. F., & Cowen, E. L. (1981). Parental death or divorce and the school adjustment of young children. *American Journal of Community Psychology, 9,* 181–191.

Felner, R. D., Ginter, M. A., & Primavera, J. (1982). Primary prevention during school transitions: Social support and environmental structure. *American Journal of Community Psychology, 10,* 227–240.

Felner, R. D., Lease, A. M., & Phillips, R. S. (1992). Ecological perspectives on social competence: Quadripartite aspects for assessment and change. *Community Psychologist, 26,* 17–18.

Felner, R. D., Primavera, J., & Cauce, A. M. (1981). The impact of school transitions: A focus for preventive efforts. *American Journal of Community Psychology, 9,* 449–459.

Garbarino, J. (1992). The meaning of poverty in the world of children. *American Behavioral Scientist, 35,* 220–237.

Garmezy, N. (1981). Children under stress: Perspectives on antecedents and correlates of vulnerability and resistance to psychopathology. In A. I. Rabin, J. Aronoff, A. M. Barclay, & R. A. Zucker (Eds.), *Further explorations in personality* (pp. 196–269). New York: Wiley.

Garmezy, N. (1991). Resiliency and vulnerability to adverse developmental outcomes associated with poverty. *American Behavioral Scientist, 34,* 416–430.

Garmezy, N. (1994). Reflections and commentary on risk, resilience, and development. In R. H. Haggerty, L. R. Sherrod, N. Garmezy, & M. Rutter (Eds.), *Stress, risk, and resilience in children and adolescents: Process, mechanisms, and interventions* (pp. 1–18). Cambridge, England: Cambridge University Press.

Garmezy, N., Masten, A. S., & Tellegen, A. (1984). The study of stress and competence in children: A building block for developmental psychopathology. *Child Development, 55,* 97–111.

Garmezy, N., & Rutter, M. (Eds.). (1983). *Stress, coping, and development in children.* New York: McGraw-Hill.

Gordon, R. (1983). An operational definition of prevention. *Public Health Reports, 98,* 107–109.

Guerra, N. G., Eron, L. D., Huesmann, L. R., Tolan, P., & Van Acker, R. (1997). A cognitive/ecological approach to the prevention and mitigation of violence and aggression in inner-city youth. In D. P. Fry & K. Bjorkqvist (Eds.), *Cultural variation in conflict resolution: Alternatives to violence* (pp. 199–214). Mahwah, NJ: Erlbaum.

Guerra, N. G., Huesmann, L. R., Tolan, P. H., Van Acker, R., & Eron, L. D. (1995). Stressful events and individual beliefs as correlates of economic disadvantage and aggression among urban children. *Journal of Consulting Psychology, 63,* 518–528.

Guidubaldi, J., Cleminshaw, H. K., Perry, J. D., & McLoughlin, C. S. (1983). The impact of parental divorce on children: Report of the nationwide NASP study. *School Psychology Review, 12,* 300–323.

Haggerty, R. J., Sherrod, L. R., Garmezy, N., & Rutter, M. (Eds.). (1994). *Stress, risk, and resilience in children and adolescents: Processes, mechanisms, and interventions.* Cambridge, England: Cambridge University Press.

Hawkins, J. D., Catalano, R. F., Morrison, D. M., O'Donnell, J., Abbott, R. D., & Day, L. E. (1992). The Seattle social development project: Effects of the first four years on protective factors and problem behaviors. In J. McCord & R. E. Tremblay (Eds.), *Preventing antisocial behavior: Interventions from birth through adolescence* (pp. 139–161). New York: Guilford Press.

Hetherington, E. M. (1989). Coping with family transitions: Winners, losers, and survivors. *Child Development, 60,* 1–14.

Hohmann, M., Banet, B., & Weikart, D. P. (1979). *Young children in action: A manual for preschool educators.* Ypsilanti, MI: High/Scope Press.

Kellam, S. G., & Rebok, G. W. (1992). In J. McCord & R. E. Tremblay (Eds.), *Preventing antisocial behavior: Interventions from birth through adolescence* (pp. 162–195). New York: Guilford Press.

Kellam, S. G., Rebok, G. W., Ialongo, N., & Mayer, L. S. (1994). The course and malleability of aggressive behavior from early first grade into middle school: Results of a developmental epidemiologically based preventive trial. *Journal of Child Psychology and Psychiatry, 35,* 259–281.

Keller, M. B., Beardslee, W. R., Dorer, D. J., Lavori, P. W., Samuelson, H., & Klerman, G. L. (1986). Impact of severity and chronicity of parental affective illness on adaptive functioning and psychopathology in children. *Archives of General Psychiatry, 43,* 930–937.

Linney, J. A. (1989). Optimizing research strategies in the schools. In L. A. Bond & B. E. Compas (Eds.), *Primary prevention and promotion in the schools* (pp. 50–76). Newbury Park, CA: Sage.

Loeber, R. (1990). Development and risk factors of juvenile antisocial behavior and delinquency. *Clinical Psychology Review, 10,* 1–42.

Luthar, S. S. (1991). Vulnerability and resilience: A study of high-risk adolescents. *Child Development, 62,* 600–616.

Luthar, S. S. (1993). Annotation: Methodological and conceptual issues in research on childhood resilience. *Journal of Psychology and Psychiatry, 34,* 441–453.

Luthar, S. S., Doernberger, C. H., & Zigler, E. (1993). Resilience is not a unidimensional construct: Insights from a prospective study of inner-city adolescents. *Development and Psychopathology, 5,* 703–713.

Luthar, S. S., & Zigler, E. (1991). Vulnerability and competence: A review of research on resilience in childhood. *American Journal of Orthopsychiatry, 61,* 6–22.

Masten, A. S., Best, K. M., & Garmezy, N. (1990). Resilience and development: Contributions from the study of children who overcome adversity. *Development and Psychopathology, 2,* 425–444.

Merikangas, K. R., & Angst, J. (1995). The challenge of depressive disorders in adolescence. In M. Rutter (Ed.), *Psychosocial disturbances in young people: Challenges for prevention* (pp. 131–165). Cambridge, England: Cambridge University Press.

Mrazek, P. J., & Haggerty, R. J. (1994). *Reducing risks for mental disorders: Frontiers for preventive intervention research.* Washington, DC: Institute of Medicine, National Academy Press.

National Advisory Mental Health Council. (1990). *National plan for research on child and adolescent mental disorders.* Washington, DC: National Institute of Mental Health.

Nettles, S. M., & Pleck, J. H. (1994). Risk, resilience, and development: The multiple ecologies of black adolescents in the United States. In R. H. Haggerty, L. R. Sherrod, N. Garmezy, & M. Rutter (Eds.), *Stress, risk, and resilience in children and adolescents: Process, mechanisms, and interventions* (pp. 147–181). Cambridge, England: Cambridge University Press.

Offord, D. R., Boyle, M. H., & Racine, Y. (1989). Ontario Child Health Study: Correlates of disorder. *Journal of the American Academy of Child and Adolescent Psychiatry, 28,* 856–860.

Parker, G. R., Cowen, E. L., Work, W. C., & Wyman, P. A. (1990). Test correlates of stress resilience among urban school children. *Journal of Primary Prevention, 11,* 19–35.

Pedro-Carroll, J. L. (1985). *The children of divorce intervention program: Procedures manual.* Rochester, NY: University of Rochester, Center for Community Study.

Pedro-Carroll, J. L., & Cowen, E. L. (1985). The children of divorce intervention program: An investigation of the efficacy of a school-based prevention program. *Journal of Consulting and Clinical Psychology, 53,* 603–611.

Pedro-Carroll, J. L., Cowen, E. L., Hightower, A. D., & Guare, J. C. (1986). Preventive intervention with latency-aged children of divorce: A replication study. *American Journal of Community Psychology, 53,* 277–289.

Philliber, S., & Allen, J. P. (1992). Life options and community service: Teen Outreach Program. In B. C. Miller, J. J. Card., R. L. Paikoff, & J. L. Peterson (Eds.), *Preventing adolescent pregnancy: Model programs and evaluations* (pp. 139–155). Newbury Park, CA: Sage.

Pillow, D. P., Sandler, I. N., Braver, S. L., Wolchik, S. A., & Gersten, J. C. (1991). Theory-based screening for prevention: Focusing on mediating processes in children of divorce. *American Journal of Community Psychology, 19,* 809–836.

Prevention Connection. (1994). *Piecing together the future: Promoting resilience in children and adolescents: Strategies for the prevention of alcohol and tobacco use.* Bowling Green, OH: Bowling Green State University.

Quinn, J. (1995). Positive effects of participation in youth organizations. In M. Rutter (Ed.), *Psychosocial disturbances in young people: Challenges for prevention* (pp. 274–304). Cambridge, England: Cambridge University Press.

Ramey, C. T., & Ramey, S. L. (1990). Intensive educational intervention for children of poverty. *Intelligence, 14,* 1–9.

Richters, J., & Weintraub, S. (1990). Beyond diathesis: Toward an understanding of high-risk environments. In J. Rolf, A. S. Masten, D. Cicchetti, K. H. Nuechterlein, & S. Weintraub (Eds.), *Risk and protective factors in the development of psychopathology* (pp. 67–96). New York: Cambridge University Press.

Rolf, J., Masten, A. S., Cicchetti, D., Nuechterlein, K. H., & Weintraub, S. (Eds.). (1990). *Risk and protective factors in the development of psychopathology.* New York: Cambridge University Press.

Rutter, M. (1979). Protective factors in children's responses to stress and disadvantage. In M. W. Kent & J. E. Rolf (Eds.), *Social competence in children* (pp. 49–74). Hanover, NH: University Press of New England.

Rutter, M. (1987). Psychosocial resilience and protective mechanisms. *American Journal of Orthopsychiatry, 57,* 316–331.

Rutter, M. (1990). Psychosocial resilience and protective mechanisms. In J. Rolf, A. S. Masten, D. Cicchetti, K. H. Nuechterlein, & S. Weintraub (Eds.), *Risk and protective factors in the development of psychopathology* (pp. 181–214). New York: Cambridge University Press.

Rutter, M. (1994). Stress research: Accomplishments and tasks ahead. In R. H. Haggerty, L. R. Sherrod, N. Garmezy, & M. Rutter (Eds.), *Stress, risk, and resilience in children and adolescents: Process, mechanisms, and interventions* (pp. 354–385). Cambridge, England: Cambridge University Press.

Rycraft, J. R. (1990). Behind the walls of poverty: Economically disadvantaged gifted and talented children. *Early Childhood Development and Care, 63,* 139–147.

Sameroff, A. J., & Seifer, R. (1990). Early contributors to developmental risk. In J. Rolf, A. S. Masten, D. Cicchetti, K. H. Nuechterlein, & S. Weintraub (Eds.), *Risk and protective factors in the development of psychopathology* (pp. 52–66). New York: Cambridge University Press.

Schweinhart, L. J., & Weikart, D. (1983). The effects of the Perry Preschool Program on youths through age 15—A summary. In The Consortium for Longitudinal Studies (Ed.), *As the twig is bent: Lasting effects of preschool programs* (pp. 71–101). Hillsdale, NJ: Erlbaum.

Seifer, R., & Sameroff, A. J. (1987). Multiple determinants of risk and vulnerability. In E. J. Anthony & B. J. Cohler (Eds.), *The invulnerable child* (pp. 51–69). New York: Guilford Press.

Spivack, G., Platt, J. J., & Shure, M. B. (1976). *The problem-solving approach to adjustment.* San Francisco: Jossey-Bass.

Sterling, S., Cowen, E. L., Weissberg, R. P., Lotyczewski, B., & Boike, M. (1985). Recent stressful life events and young children's school adjustment. *American Journal of Community Psychology, 13,* 87–98.

Stolberg, A. L., & Garrison, K. M. (1985). Evaluating a primary prevention program for children of divorce. *American Journal of Community Psychology, 13,* 111–124.

Stouthamer-Loeber, M., Loeber, R., Farrington, D. P., Zhang, Q., Van Kammen, W., & Maguin, E. (1993). The double edge of protective and risk factors for delinquency: Interrelations and developmental patterns. *Development and Psychopathology, 5,* 683–701.

Strawn, J. (1992). The states and the poor: Child poverty rises as the safety net shrinks. *Social Policy Report: Society for Research in Child Development, 6,* 1–19.

Tolan, P. H., Guerra, N. G., & Kendall, P. C. (1995). A developmental-ecological perspective on antisocial behavior in children and adolescents: Toward a unified risk and intervention framework. *Journal of Consulting and Clinical Psychology, 63,* 579–584.

Wallerstein, J. S., & Kelly, J. B. (1980). *Surviving the breakup: How children and parents cope with divorce.* New York: Basic Books.

Weikart, D. P., Bond, J. T., & McNeil, J. T. (1978). The Ypsilanti Perry Preschool project: Preschool years and longitudinal results through fourth grade. *Monographs of the High/Scope Educational Research Foundation* (Whole No. 3).

Weikart, D. P., Rogers, L., Adcock, C., & McClelland, D. (1971). *The cognitively oriented curriculum: A framework for preschool teachers.* Urbana, IL: National Association for the Education of Young Children.

Weissberg, R. P., Gesten, E. L., Carnrike, C. L., Toro, P. A., Rapkin, B. D., Davidson, E., & Cowen, E. L. (1981). Social problem-solving skills training: A competence building intervention with second- to fourth-grade children. *American Journal of Community Psychology, 9,* 411–413.

Werner, E. E. (1993). Risk, resilience, and recovery: Perspectives from the Kauai longitudinal study. *Development and Psychopathology, 15,* 503–515.

Werner, E. E., & Smith, R. S. (1982). *Vulnerable but invincible: A longitudinal study of resilient children and youth.* New York: McGraw-Hill.

Werner, E. E., & Smith, R. S. (1992). *Overcoming the odds: High-risk children from birth to adulthood.* Ithaca, NY: Cornell University Press.

Wertlieb, D., Weigel, C., & Feldstein, M. (1987). Stress, social support, and behavior symptoms in middle childhood. *Journal of Clinical Child Psychology, 16,* 204–211.

Wolchik, S. A., Ruehlman, L. S., Braver, S. L., & Sandler, I. N. (1989). Social support of children of divorce: Direct and stress buffering effects. *American Journal of Community Psychology, 17,* 485–501.

CHAPTER 12

Health Promotion

CAROLYN C. JOHNSON, THERESA A. NICKLAS, LARRY S. WEBBER, and GERALD S. BERENSON

DESCRIPTION OF THE PROBLEM

Evan died in an automobile accident on a state highway in Washington Parish, Louisiana. It was discovered during autopsy that his aorta and coronary arteries contained fatty streaks and fibrous placques, evidence of coronary artery disease—but Evan was only 17 years old. Evan had been a participant in the Bogalusa Heart Study when he was 15 years old, and it was noted that he was a regular smoker.

Information began to accumulate more than 40 years ago that young American men evidenced silent stages of coronary heart disease. Autopsies of 300 U.S. soldiers in Korea and 105 soldiers in Vietnam showed advanced coronary atherosclerosis (Enos, Holmes, & Beyer, 1953; McNamara, Molot, Stremple, & Cutting, 1971). The mean age of the soldiers in the Korea and Vietnam studies was 22 years.

These observations were reinforced by findings from 1,292 autopsies of black and white males in the New Orleans Community Pathology Study (Strong et al., 1984). Indications were that by the third and fourth decade of life, atherosclerosis and significant coronary artery disease involved almost 90% of the population studied.

It is now recognized that precursors of adult cardiovascular diseases begin in childhood, and early onset of atherosclerotic lesions occurs even in infancy. Of particular interest, pathology studies of the cardiovascular system show atherosclerosis has a tremendous variability in the severity of disease among individuals. Understanding factors that contribute to this variability, and to the silent onset of coronary artery disease at an early age, should provide directions for further reduction of cardiovascular disease in our nation.

The evolution of the risk factor concept from the Framingham Study, along with other major epidemiological programs, has shown the importance of risk factor identification and subsequent morbidity from cardiovascular diseases (Lenfant, Stone, & Castelli, 1987). The resolution of serum lipids into different lipoprotein classes with varying atherogenic potential has provided further impetus to the clinical study of asymptomatic individuals at cardiovascular risk (Frerichs, Srinivasan, Webber, & Berenson, 1976; Srinivasan, Frerichs, Webber, & Berenson, 1976). Cardiovascular

287

epidemiological studies in communities like the Bogalusa Heart Study (Berenson et al., 1980) and the Muscatine Study (Lauer, Connor, Leaverton, Reiter, & Clark, 1975) have provided methods for cardiovascular profiling of risk factors in children and young adults, and have shown that deleterious lifestyles, such as tobacco use and sedentary behavior, are associated with increased risk. These observations provide a strong rationale to begin health promotion and intervention programs at an early age (Downey, Cresanta, & Berenson, 1989; Perry et al., 1990).

Overview of the Bogalusa Heart Study

The Bogalusa Heart Study is a long-term epidemiological investigation into the early natural history of cardiovascular disease in a biracial (white/black) community. It has been ongoing for more than 20 years, and involves the population of Ward 4, Washington Parish, Louisiana, in which Bogalusa is the major incorporated area. The population is 65% white and approximately equal in gender. Since 1973, the consenting population has been examined through seven cross-sectional surveys of school-age children and adolescents and five post-high school longitudinal surveys (Webber, Srinivasan, & Berenson, 1993). In the most recent post-high school survey (1995), the oldest cohort had reached age 36 years. To date, 15,000 children, adolescents, and young adults have been examined in the Bogalusa study.

The Bogalusa cardiovascular screening comprised measurements of serum total cholesterol, high-density lipoprotein cholesterol (HDL-C), low-density lipoprotein cholesterol (LDL-C), very low-density lipoprotein cholesterol (VLDL-C), triglycerides, systolic and diastolic blood pressure, anthropometric indices (e.g., height, weight, subscapular and triceps skinfolds), Tanner scale criteria for maturation, and insulin and glucose levels. Lifestyles measured include diet; Type A behavior pattern; and tobacco, alcohol, and oral contraceptive use. All measurements have been conducted by rigorously trained examiners according to standardized protocols. The study has been enriched over time with various substudies conducted with specific hypotheses in mind. Measurement procedures and quality controls have been described in detail elsewhere (Berenson, 1986; Berenson et al., 1980).

SCOPE OF THE PROBLEM

Autopsy Studies: Bogalusa Heart Study

Evidence is clear that atherosclerotic lesions begin in early life (Holman, McGill, Strong, & Geer, 1958). Commonly studied sites in autopsies are the aorta and coronary arteries. Fatty streaks have been seen at both sites for children as young as 3 years of age. By the second decade of life, elevated lesions have been found. By young adulthood, lesions had progressed to set the stage for overt clinical manifestations in the fifth and sixth decades of life.

Of particular importance were findings from the Bogalusa Heart Study that have been able to relate antemortem risk factor levels to the extent of vascular disease. Deaths of individuals between the ages of 3 and 31 years that occurred from 1978 to 1987 included 66 individuals who had risk factors previously measured in the Bogalusa Heart Study. Intimal surface involvement of the aorta with fatty streaks was greater in blacks than in whites, and coronary artery fatty streaks were more extensive in males than females (Berenson et al., 1992; Newman et al., 1986). Fibrous plaque lesions in the aorta were less extensive than in the coronary arteries (0%–12% vs. 0%–22%), and prevalence of these lesions was higher in males, particularly white males, than in females.

Fatty streaks in the aortas of white males were significantly and positively correlated with antemortem serum total cholesterol, LDL-C levels, and ponderal index (PI; kg/m^3), while fatty streaks in the coronary vessels were associated with serum triglycerides, VLDL-C, systolic and diastolic blood pressure, and PI (Figure 12.1). These associations were in the same direction for black males (Figure 12.2). Risk factor levels by tertiles of fatty streaks in the aorta or coronary vessels are shown in Table 12.1. LDL-C relates positively and significantly with lesions in both locations.

Heart disease, expressed by arterial lipid deposition, is associated with well-known risk factors, such as serum cholesterol, triglycerides, and blood pressure (Table 12.2). Research indicates, however, that at the earliest stages of intracellular lipid deposition, when more advanced collagen-capping increases the lesion, regression can take place.

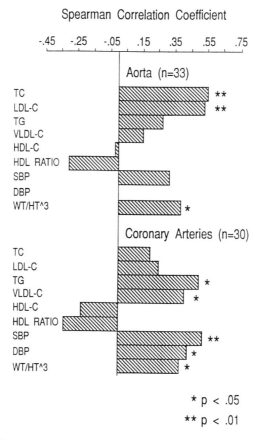

Figure 12.1.   Association between fatty streak involvement and risk factor levels in white males: The Bogalusa Heart Study.

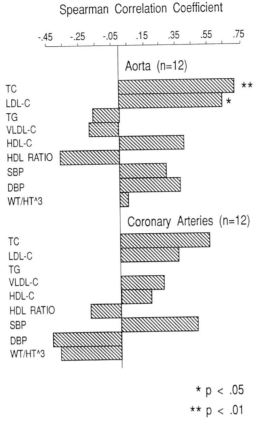

Figure 12.2. Association between fatty streak involvement and risk factor levels in black males: The Bogalusa Heart Study.

The assumption then is that control of risk factors in childhood might delay or attenuate the progression of atherosclerotic disease.

Physiological Risk Factors in Youth

The Bogalusa Heart Study has provided many interesting findings on distributions, levels, tracking, and determinants of obesity, blood pressure, serum lipids and lipoproteins, nutrition, and lifestyles of children, adolescents, and young adults.

Obesity

Interesting race and sex differences in obesity have been noted as children age. For example, white males exhibit a body mass index (BMI) 3–5 units greater than black males, but not until young adulthood. For females, however, blacks have higher BMI at all ages with the uppermost percentiles considerably greater by adolescence (Figure 12.3). Similar results were noted for subscapular skinfolds which also increase slowly with age. By young adulthood, white males have levels 4–8 mm greater than black males. The opposite is noted for females after adolescence, with blacks having levels

Table 12.1   Mean Age-Adjusted Risk Factor Levels by Tertiles of Fatty Streaks: The Bogalusa Heart Study

Risk Factor	Tertile of Lesions			p Value Significance
	Low	Middle	High	
Aorta ($n = 62$)				
Total cholesterol (mg/dl)	131	144	172	$p < 0.0001$
Triglycerides (mg/dl)	72	73	83	NS
Lipoprotein cholesterol (mg/dl)				
LDL	65	74	97	$p < 0.0001$
HDL	58	58	60	NS
VLDL	9	11	13	NS
HDL ratio	0.80	0.80	0.65	NS
Blood pressure (mm Hg)				
Systolic	103	107	107	NS
Diastolic	67	66	66	NS
Ponderal index (kg/m³)	11.8	12.2	13.0	NS
Coronary Artery ($n = 57$)				
Total cholesterol (mg/dl)	143	149	159	NS
Triglycerides (md/dl)	68	74	89	NS
Lipoprotein cholesterol (mg/dl)				
LDL	72	78	90	$p < 0.05$
HDL	61	61	55	NS
VLDL	9	9	14	$p < 0.05$
HDL ratio	0.82	0.81	0.61	NS
Blood pressure (mm Hg)				
Systolic	104	103	113	$p < 0.001$
Diastolic	66	66	69	NS
Ponderal index (kg/m³)	11.8	12.4	13.3	NS

HDL = high-density lipoprotein; LDL = low-density lipoprotein; NS = not significant; VLDL = very low density lipoprotein

Table 12.2   Risk Factors for Coronary Artery Disease

Age > 45 in a man

Age > 55 or menopause in a woman

Cigarette smoking

Diabetes mellitus

High-density-lipoprotein cholesterol level < 35 mg/dl

History of cerebrovascular or occlusive peripheral vascular disease

Hypertension

Low-density-lipoprotein cholesterol level 130 mg/dl or higher

Myocardial infarction or sudden death before age 55 in a parent or sibling

Obesity (30% or more overweight)

Total cholesterol level 200 mg/dl or higher

Note. Reprinted with permission, Berenson et al., *Patient Care* June 15, 1993, pp. 135–145.

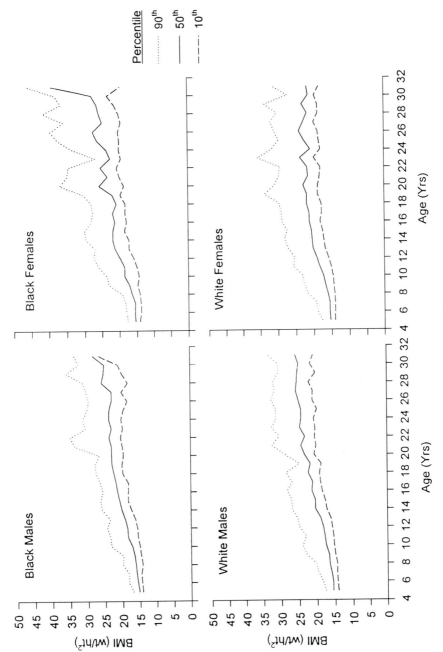

Figure 12.3. Percentile distributions for the BMI (weight/height²) for children and young adults.

up to 10 mm greater than whites. This reflects the early onset of obesity so prevalent in black female adults. Debate continues, however, whether obesity is a primary cardiovascular risk factor or whether it influences cardiovascular disease through its association with blood pressure and serum lipids and lipoproteins (Webber, Harsha, Nicklas, & Berenson, 1994).

Blood Pressure

Hypertension is the second most common cardiovascular disease in adults and its prevalence is highest in black populations. In children, a well-accepted absolute criterion for hypertension does not exist; therefore, blood pressure levels are scrutinized relative to peers. Children's blood pressure levels increase with chronological age from 5 to 18 years, at which time levels stabilize during young adulthood (Voors, Foster, Frerichs, Webber, & Berenson, 1976; Wattigney, Webber, Srinivasan, & Berenson, 1995). It is not until the fourth decade of life that blood pressure begins to rise again. Surprisingly, few racial differences in blood pressure levels between blacks and whites have been noted until late adolescence when levels at the upper percentiles were 2–4 mm Hg higher in blacks than whites. A difference in levels between boys and girls after age 12 years are noted, with boys' levels 4–6 mm Hg higher.

Blood pressure levels "track" from childhood to young adulthood (Bao, Threefoot, Srinivasan, & Berenson, 1995). About 50% of children with elevated systolic blood pressure (above the age-, race-, sex-specific 75th percentile) remained in this uppermost quartile over time. This finding, which has been supported by correlation and regression models as well as persistence in rankings over time, is about twice what would be expected by chance alone and was consistent for both black and white boys and girls. Another way to express this phenomenon is that, over a 12- to 15-year span, the best predictor of young adult blood pressure levels was childhood blood pressure levels. Interestingly, the next best predictor was change in BMI. Those children who gained more weight per height over time tended to have higher blood pressure levels as young adults. The Bogalusa Heart Study has documented evidence of hypertensive disease, cardiac enlargement, renal artery changes, and microalbuminuria in black males in childhood, and children persisting at the 90th percentile are apt to show these end organ changes (Jiang et al., 1994; Urbina & Berenson, 1994).

Serum Cholesterol

Serum lipid and lipoprotein levels have long been implicated as risk factors for cardiovascular disease. LDL-C shows a positive risk association with disease while HDL-C shows an inverse risk association. Autopsy evidence cited earlier indicates that these levels are related to lipid deposits in the aorta and coronary arteries.

Levels of serum total cholesterol rise rapidly after birth during the first two years of life, almost to those levels seen during young adulthood (Freedman, Srinivasan, Cresanta, Webber, & Berenson, 1987). During puberty, the opposite phenomenon occurs with a slight decline in serum total cholesterol, LDL-C, and HDL-C (Berenson, Srinivasan, Cresanta, Foster, & Webber, 1981). During later adolescence, LDL-C levels rise but HDL-C levels continue to decline, especially for white males, creating a rise in the LDL-C/HDL-C ratio (Figure 12.4). This has particular importance for white males because the greater the ratio of total cholesterol to HDL-C, the greater the risk for developing coronary artery disease. White children have higher levels of serum triglycerides and VLDL-C whereas black children have higher HDL-C, apolipoproteins B-1 and E, and lipoprotein(a) levels.

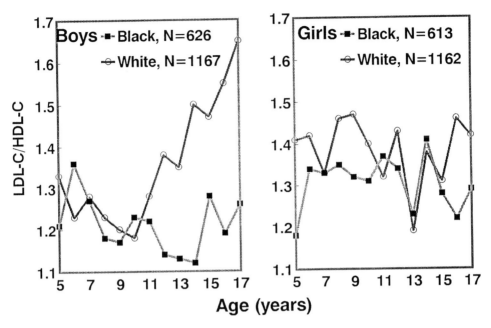

Figure 12.4.   Change of LDL-C/HDL-C in children with age: The Bogalusa Heart Study.

Tracking was very high for total cholesterol and LDL-C with up to 70% of those individuals in the uppermost quintile during childhood remaining there by young adulthood (Webber, Srinivasan, Wattigney, & Berenson, 1991). For all of the lipids and lipoproteins, as was observed for blood pressure, the best predictor of adult level was childhood level. Changes in BMI from childhood to adulthood were significant predictors of adult levels for serum total cholesterol, LDL-C, and VLDL-C, but were inversely associated with HDL-C.

Clustering of risk factors occurs during childhood and is similar to that observed for adults (Smoak et al., 1987; Webber, Voors, Srinivasan, Frerichs, & Berenson, 1979). A much greater than expected number of children have been observed with a clustering of obesity, high blood pressure, and serum cholesterol. This clustering was greater in white males than in white females and black children. Of importance, this clustering was associated with age, being greater for school-age children than preschool-age children. Evidence is clear that the race and sex differences noted in lipid and lipoprotein levels and the rather high tracking dictate the need for prevention models to start during youth. Further studies with apolipoproteins A and B show a stronger relationship than lipoproteins with parental heart disease and provide a surrogate measure of future heart disease (Srinivasan & Berenson, 1995).

Behavioral Risk Factors in Youth

Tobacco, Alcohol, and Oral Contraceptive Use

Information regarding the smoking behaviors of children and adolescents has been obtained in Bogalusa since 1973 by self-report questionnaire; however, plasma thiocyanate determination has been used as an objective validation of exposure to smoking (Dalferes, Webber, Radhakrishnamurthy, & Berenson, 1980).

Generally, it was found that white boys adopt cigarette smoking in the early teens, earlier than the other race/sex groups, while the percentage of white girls who smoked increased and surpassed the boys by the late teens. Black boys and girls, therefore, lagged behind white children in early smoking experience. Most of the children who experimented with smoking at a very early age (12–13 years) did not progress to regular smoking (Hunter, Webber, & Berenson, 1980).

Higher LDL-C and VLDL-C levels were observed for white boys and white and black girls who smoked, as well as for girls who used oral contraceptives. Even after adjusting cholesterol values for oral contraceptive use, smokers still had higher levels of VLDL-C and lower HDL-C (Webber et al., 1982; Webber, Hunter, Johnson, Srinivasan, & Berenson, 1991). Smokers' cholesterol and triglyceride levels were independent of age, sexual maturation, obesity, and alcohol consumption; however, it was not the initiate but the established smoker who was smoking three or more packs of cigarettes weekly who had higher mean lipid levels.

Social learning and diffusion theories were used to investigate the influences of tobacco use trial and subsequent adoption (Hunter, Baugh, Webber, Sklov, & Berenson, 1982). Parental approval and peer acceptance were major factors in both the trial and adoption of smoking. Interestingly, some racial effects also were observed. For example, white children were more inclined to smoke if their parents smoked and/or approved, while black children tried and adopted smoking if they had sibling and/or peer approval. In one cross-sectional survey, more than 60% of the children, 8 to 17 years old, said that they were given their first cigarette by someone else, and at least half of those who started smoking before age 12 said they smoked their first cigarette with a family member or an older friend. For those children who tried cigarettes by age 12, it appeared to take at least 2 years for regular maintenance of the habit (Baugh, Hunter, Webber, & Berenson, 1982).

Although the majority of children reported that their first cigarette was provided by someone else, a higher degree of adoption and maintenance was observed by those children who first purchased their own cigarettes (Croft, Hunter, Webber, Watson, & Berenson, 1985). Two other factors were associated with the transition from trial to maintenance: Adopters were more likely to have smokers as friends and family members, and were more likely to believe that smoking was pleasurable and not harmful.

Smoking attitudes and first use were examined more recently with third to sixth graders in 1993–1994, and essentially the results were consistent with those obtained more than 10 years earlier, that is, parental modeling, and sibling and/or peer influence dominated. One noticeable difference, however, was that more than 90% of these children were aware of the cancer and heart disease risk associated with smoking (Greenlund, Johnson, Webber, & Berenson, in press).

When a decline in cigarette smoking was observed nationally, a concurrent decline was noted in the Bogalusa population; however, Bogalusa was one of the first locations to note that this decline in cigarette smoking was accompanied by an increase in the use of smokeless tobacco by white boys (Hunter et al., 1986). Smoking was found to positively associate with alcohol use, and for white boys, this clustering was also associated with hostility (Johnson, Hunter, Amos, Elder, & Berenson, 1989).

Alcohol use data have been obtained from school-age children and adolescents in Bogalusa by a self-report instrument similar to the smoking questionnaire since 1981

(Johnson, Myers, Webber, Srinivasan, & Berenson, 1995). The highest percentage of regular drinkers (defined as an average of one drink a week) was among white males, and the lowest percentage was among black females. Although the legal purchasing age in Louisiana is 21 years, adolescents who drank reported drinking the equivalent of about a six-pack of beer once or twice a week (probably weekends). An average prevalence of 25% of school-age youth, aged 12 to 19, who reported regular alcohol consumption appeared to be lower in Bogalusa than that reported elsewhere, such as the Monitoring the Future Study (Johnston, O'Malley, & Bachman, 1993). Even so, one-fourth of the student population, Grades approximately 6 through 12, is a large proportion of children engaged in an activity that could lead to personal, social, economic, and health problems.

In 1993–1994, third to sixth graders were questioned regarding alcohol attitudes and first use. Children's attitudes were generally negative regarding drinking alcohol, and most of those who had experimented had family members who drank (Johnson, Greenlund, Webber, & Berenson, 1996).

Psychosocial Factors

Type A behavior, anger/hostility, learned helplessness, and other psychosocial factors have been investigated in Bogalusa relative to cardiovascular disease. The Hunter-Wolf Type A Behavior Scale was developed for children and adolescents, Grades 8 through 12 (Amos, Hunter, Zinkgraf, Miner, & Berenson, 1987; Hunter, Wolf, Sklov, Webber, Watson & Berenson, 1982; Wolf, Sklov, Wenzl, Hunter, & Berenson, 1982). Factors that contributed to the total Type A score were eagerness/energy, hostility, competitiveness, drive, and control. Generally, total Type A scores were found to increase with age, and were consistently higher for white males than the other race/sex groups. Consistent associations with cardiovascular risk factors in this age group, 8–17 years, have not been observed (Johnson, Hunter, & Berenson, 1989a).

Hostility, measured by the Hunter-Wolf Type A scale, was found to track at least as well as blood pressure, correlating over 3 years at .49 in the highest quintile of the population, and .40 for the lowest quintile (Johnson, Hunter, & Berenson, 1989b). This measure of hostility as a component of the Hunter-Wolf Type A questionnaire was found to decrease with age and was associated with smoking and drinking in white males in the 1981–1982 cross-sectional survey of school-age individuals. Anger was measured by the Jacobs Pediatric Anger Expression Scale in the 1981 and 1993 cross-sectional surveys. Once again, no relationships with risk factors could be found, except for an inverse association of denied or repressed anger and a positive association of overtly expressed anger with alcohol consumption for white females in 1981 (Johnson, Webber, Myers, & Berenson, 1994). Some interesting demographics, however, reflected that overt anger was higher in whites and repressed anger was higher in blacks.

Learned helplessness, a cognitive and behavioral response set to repeated failure, was studied in 1993 (Johnson et al., 1995). It was found that learned helplessness was significantly associated with all indices of obesity for white females and with waist/hip ratio for black females at the high school level.

Diet

Dietary data have been collected from six cohorts of 10-year-olds ($n = 1,439$) and two cohorts of 13-year-olds ($n = 360$) since 1973 (Nicklas, 1995; Nicklas, Farris, Srinivasan, Webber, & Berenson, 1989). Data also were collected on a cohort of infants from 6 months to 4 years of age and again at age 10, a cohort of teens biannually from 10 years to 17 years of age, and young adults, aged 19 to 28 years (Nicklas, Johnson, Myers, Webber, & Berenson, 1995).

Dietary Intakes of Children and Adolescents.   The percentage of energy from selected dietary components is presented in Table 12.3. Total energy intake exceeded the Recommended Dietary Allowances (Weidman, Kwiterovich, Jesse, & Nugent, 1983) at all ages. Child and adolescent diets had similar macronutrient composition: 13% protein, 38% fat, and 49% carbohydrate, including a large sucrose intake. The low polyunsaturated/saturated fat ratio (< 0.5) at all ages reflected a high saturated fat (14%–16%) and low polyunsaturated fat (5.7%) diet. Mean dietary cholesterol intake reached levels observed in adolescents by 2 years of age (i.e. 300 mg/day).

Concurrent with a rapid increase in energy intake was an increase in sodium intake. Sodium intakes ranged from 0.88 to 4.0 grams ($\bar{x} = 3.33$ gm). A fourfold increase in mean daily sodium intake from 6 months to 4 years, and a 3- to 4-gram sodium intake between ages 10 to 17 years were observed.

Secular Trends in Dietary Intakes of Children.   Energy, macronutrients, and cholesterol intakes for each of the six survey years of 10-year-olds are presented in Table 12.4. Total energy intakes remained virtually the same from 1973 to 1988, and no detectable racial differences were found. Gender differences, however, indicated that boys had consistently higher energy intakes than girls at both ages from 1973 to 1988. A significant negative trend was noted in 10-year-olds for energy intake per kg body weight from 1973 to 1988.

Percentage of energy from protein increased significantly over the 15 years for 10-year-old children. In contrast, the percentage of energy from fat decreased significantly, reflected in a decrease in percent energy from saturated fatty acids from 1973 to 1988.

Trends in macronutrient intakes of Bogalusa children from 1973 to 1988 are similar to trends noted in children's intakes reported from four national studies. A negative trend in percent energy from fat and saturated fat has persisted from 1987 to 1993; likewise, an increasing trend in percent energy from carbohydrate and protein has also continued.

Contribution of School Meals to Dietary Intakes of Children.   The nutrient contribution of school meals was assessed for a subsample of children who consumed school breakfast ($n = 200$) in 1984–1985 and 1987–1988, and school lunch ($n = 197$) in 1973 to 1988 (Table 12.5; Farris, Nicklas, Webber, & Berenson, 1992; Nicklas, 1995). For 10-year-old children, school breakfast contributed 26% of the daily energy intake and provided about one-fourth to one-third of the day's total protein, carbohydrate, cholesterol, and sodium. Breakfast provided 15% and 18% of the children's total sucrose and total fat intake, respectively, came from breakfast. Energy intake from the breakfast meal averaged 577 kcal, 16% of which came from protein, 23% from fat, and 61% from carbohydrate. In the breakfast meal, 5% to 8% of the calories came from sucrose and saturated fat, respectively, and breakfast accounted for an average sodium intake of 1.02 grams.

The school lunch contributed 25% of daily energy intake, and provided about one-third of the day's total protein, fat, cholesterol, saturated fat, and sodium. Twenty-one percent of the day's total carbohydrate and 16% of total sucrose came from school

Table 12.3 Dietary Composition of Diets of Children and Adolescents by Age

	Age (Yr)								
Dietary Component (% kcal)	5 (n = 125) (1973–74)	1 (n = 99) (1974–75)	2 (n = 135) (1975–76)	3 (n = 106) (1976–77)	4 (n = 219) (1977–78)	10 (n = 871) (1973–82)	13 (n = 148) (1976–77)	15 (n = 108) (1978–79)	17 (n = 159) (1980–81)
Energy (kcal)	949	1356	1922	2162	2258	2144	2361	2334	2438
Protein	13	14	13	12	13	13	13	14	14
Carbohydrate	55	49	48	51	49	49	47	50	46
Fats	35	39	41	38	39	39	41	38	40
Saturated Fat	16	17	16	14	14	15	15	13	14
Cholesterol (mg)	110	247	376	347	390	302	306	336	378
mg/1000 kcal	106	183	193	164	172	138	129	146	151

Note. Reprinted with permission, Nicklas, *American Journal of Medical Sciences*, 310 (Suppl. 1): S101–S108, 1995.

Table 12.4 Secular Trends in Macronutrient Intakes of Children in the Bogalusa Heart Study (1973–1988) Compared with National Studies (1987–1994)

| Nutrients (% kcal) | National Studies (1987–1994) | | | |
	USDA Nationwide Food Consumption Survey (NFCS 1987–88) (6–11 yrs) n = 10172	The Dietary Intervention in Children Study (DISC) - Baseline 1987–90 (8–11 yrs) n = 652	National Health and Nutrition Examination Survey (NHANES III) (1988–91) (6–11 yrs) n = 1745	The School Nutrition Dietary Assessment Study (SNDAS) 1993 (6–10 yrs) n = 1383
Protein	15	15	14	15
Carbohydrate	50	53	53	53
Total Fat	36	34	34	34
Saturated Fat	14	13	13	13
Polyunsaturated Fat	6	6	6	NR
Monounsaturated Fat	13	13	13	NR
Cholesterol (mg)	252	202	225	270

Significant linear trend (1973 to 1988):
[a] p < 0.0001
[b] p < 0.001
[c] p < 0.01
[d] p < 0.05
NR = Not reported

Note. Reprinted with permission, Nicklas, 1995.

299

Table 12.5   Contribution of School Meals to Dietary Intakes of
Participating Children

Nutrients (% kcal)	% Daily Total	The Bogalusa Heart Study (1987–1988) % Total Meal
School Breakfast		
Calories, kcal	26	577
Protein	30	16
Carbohydrate	30	61
Fat	18	23
Saturated Fat	18	8
Cholesterol, mg	25	61
Sodium, mg	27	1002
School Lunch		
Calories, kcal	25	567
Protein	31	18
Carbohydrate	21	44
Fat	31	40
Saturated Fat	26	17
Cholesterol, mg	34	82
Sodium, mg	31	1003

Note. Reprinted with permission, Nicklas, 1995.

20   Ammerman Page Corrections

lunch. Energy intake from the lunch meal averaged 567 kcal, representing 18% from protein, 40% from fat, and 44% from carbohydrate. In the school lunch, 6% to 17% of the calories came from sucrose and saturated fat, respectively.

Together, the school breakfast and lunch contributed approximately 50% of the student's total daily intake of energy, protein, cholesterol, carbohydrate, and sodium. While 40% of the day's total fat came from the school breakfast and lunch, about one-third of the day's total sucrose came from school meals.

Comparison with American Heart Association Dietary Recommendations. The percentage of children exceeding the dietary recommendations for total fat, saturated fatty acids, and dietary cholesterol is presented in Figure 12.5 (Nicklas, Webber, Srinivasan, & Berenson, 1993; USDHHS, 1980, 1988; Weidman, Kwiterovich, Jesse, & Nugent, 1983). An apparent decrease in the percentage of children exceeding the dietary recommendations for total fat and saturated fatty acid from 1973 to 1985 can be seen. In 1973–1974, 74% of 10-year-old children exceeded the dietary cholesterol recommendations of 100 mg/1000 kcal. This percentage decreased to 51% in 1984–1985. This decrease in dietary cholesterol intake largely reflects a decrease in the consumption of eggs from 1973 to 1985. Although the diets of children have changed favorably from 1973 to 1988, a large percentage of children still exceed the current dietary recommendations for total fat, saturated fat, and sodium.

Comparison with National Surveys.   Data show that the nutrient composition of Bogalusa children and adolescents' diets are similar to those reported in national surveys (Nicklas, 1995; Nicklas, Farris, et al., 1989). What might be different, however, is the type of foods consumed and their contribution to intakes of specific nutrients

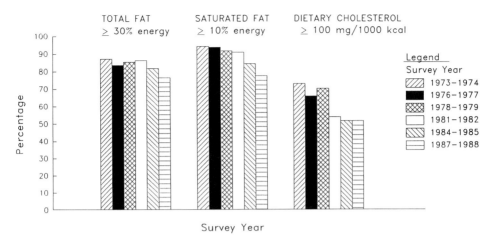

Figure 12.5.   The percent of 10-year-old children exceeding the AHA dietary recommendations.

because of regional variations. In Louisiana for example, red beans and rice with sausage is traditional Monday fare and fried seafood is commonly eaten on Friday.

Differences in food choices and nutrient intakes also reflect age and consumption patterns across the United States. For example, the percentage of saturated fat from milk decreases and percentage from meats increases as children get older; an overall decline in consumption of whole milk has been paralleled by an increase of 2% milk and skim milk; and decreased egg, red meat, and butter use has accompanied increased poultry, fish, and margarine use (Call & Sanchez, 1967; Nicklas, 1995; Park & Yetley, 1990).

Causes and Consequences

Adult Cardiovascular Disease

Cardiovascular diseases are the major causes of morbidity and mortality in the United States population. Although there has been a significant decline in coronary artery disease and hypertension, and reduced deaths from cardiovascular disease and stroke, adult heart diseases still account for almost half of the deaths in this country today (Jenkins, 1988).

Lifestyle Implications

Diet

Dietary intake is a major environmental determinant of cardiovascular risk (Kris-Etherton et al., 1988; Nicklas, 1995; Nicklas, Farris, et al., 1988; Weldman, Elveback, Nelson, Hodgson, & Ellefson, 1978). Information about its influence on cardiovascular disease early in life, however, is limited. Parallel variations across populations in the diets of adults and their cardiovascular risk are probably the strongest evidence showing the importance of diet. Intrapopulation studies, however, have not consistently shown such diet-risk relationships. Difficulty in documenting the types and amounts of foods in a complex food supply (Beaton et al., 1979; Farris & Nicklas, 1993; Jacobs, Anderson, & Blackburn, 1979; Liu, Stamler, Dyer, McKeever, & McKeever, 1978; Morgan et al., 1978; Thompson & Dennison, 1994), and limitations of nutrient databases (Hoover, 1983) are methodological constraints that often obscure associations of risk factors and diet.

Tobacco Use

Smoking kills close to half a million Americans each year and is considered to be the leading cause of premature morbidity and mortality in the United States (Schultz, 1991). Even though smoking among males dropped from 52% in 1965 to 38% in 1983, prevalence decreased only slightly among women, 34% to 30% (U.S. Public Health Service [USPHS], 1983). Smoking has been causally associated with lung, mouth, throat, bladder, and other cancers, cardiovascular disease, emphysema, chronic obstructive pulmonary disease, low birth weights, and other newborn abnormalities (USPHS, 1980, 1982, 1983). Of special concern, "One out of three adolescents is using tobacco by age 18 and adolescent users become adult users" (USPHS, 1994). Recent data show that earlier onset of smoking is associated with heavier smoking (Taioli & Wynder, 1991), and heavier smokers were least likely to quit (USPHS, 1989).

Alcohol Use

At least two-thirds of adult Americans drink alcohol, and about 18 million have problems due to alcohol use (National Institute on Alcohol Abuse and Alcoholism, 1987). Alcohol factors into approximately half of all homicides, suicides, and motor vehicle fatalities. It is also the leading preventable cause of birth defects, and contributes to liver disease mortality. Although the legal drinking age is 21 in most states, 90% of high school seniors report using alcohol at least once (Webber, Hunter, Johnson, Srinivasan, & Berenson, 1991).

Physical Activity

Low levels of physical activity are related to coronary heart disease, hypertension, noninsulin-dependent diabetes mellitus, osteoporosis, obesity, stroke, colon cancer, back injury, and mental health (Harris & Associates, 1989; Powell, Caspersen, & Koplan, 1989; Salonen, Puska, & Tuomilehto, 1982). Longer life, functional independence, and greater quality of life are expectations for the elderly who are physically active. It is estimated that only 22% of Americans engage in 30 minutes of light to moderate activity five or more times a week. Prevalence of sedentary behavior increases with advancing age, yet activity patterns are acquired in childhood, usually in response to parental attitudes and modeling (USPHS, 1990). Reports that the nation's children are getting fatter appear to be due to increased inactivity, since indications are that caloric consumption has remained stable (Shear et al., 1988). In the Bogalusa Heart Study evidence of increased body weight and fatness of children were documented over the past two decades. Although the average increase for schoolchildren was 1.5 kg, at the upper percentiles an increase of 4–6 kg was noted.

Anger/Hostility

For over one hundred years, anger/hostility has been viewed as a psychoemotional factor that may be related to cardiovascular disease (Osler, 1892; Suarez & Williams,

1992). Many epidemiological and clinical studies have found that anger/hostility are significant correlates of adult sympathetic nervous system arousal, elevated resting blood pressure and serum cholesterol, and coronary atherosclerosis (Barefoot, Dahlstrom, & Williams, 1983; Dembroski, MacDougall, Williams, Haney, & Blumenthal, 1985; Krantz & Manuck, 1984; MacDougall, Dembroski, Dimsdale, & Hackett, 1985; Manuck, Kaplan, & Matthews, 1986; Williams, 1992). It is believed that anger stylistics develop very early in life in response to modeling and vicarious and direct reinforcement (Ballard, Cummings, & Larkin, 1993).

Social Support

Social situations and interpersonal relationships play a large role in the etiology, maintenance, and cessation of smoking, alcohol consumption, cardiovascular function under stress, and impact of life changes, trauma, and stress (Kaplan, Sallis, & Patterson, 1993; Kaplan et al., 1988). Social support is difficult to define because of its dynamic nature, but might be viewed as the perceived or actual resources an individual has available at any point in time. On the other hand, poor social support precedes mortality, even when controlling for baseline health status (e.g., Berkman & Syme, 1979).

IMPEDIMENTS TO INTERVENTION IN THE REAL WORLD CONTEXT

Health Promotion in Schools

Advantages

It is consistently recognized that the school is an appropriate site for health education and promotion (Stone, 1990; Stone & Perry, 1990). Earlier efforts for health education began around 1975 to reduce smoking. These efforts have now evolved into more organized programs devoted to comprehensive health education (Hetzel & Berenson, 1987).

Greater than 90% of the nation's children and adolescents are in school. The schools are the primary educating facilities and are the major socializing environments in which children receive more than 15,000 hours of exposure during adolescence (Rutter, Maughan, Mortimore, & Ouston, 1979). Young people's experiences in school help to determine their vulnerability to adolescent health problems (Hawkins & Catalano, 1990).

School-based health promotion can be effected with well-trained educators within an existing and highly sanctioned group setting (Lytle et al., 1994). This results in cost-efficiency and normative support for behavioral change. The entire school infrastructure is amenable to integration of health promotion at all levels, including district and school administration, school faculty, food service, physical education, and access to parents. The school is, therefore, the ideal model for health behavior diffusion and adoption.

Today, the National School Lunch Program feeds more than 25 million children daily (Burghardt & Devaney, 1993). Approximately 99% of public schools, and 83% of all public and private schools combined participate in the program. On a typical school day, 66% of children 6 to 10 years of age participate. Recent studies reporting on the

National School Lunch Program impact on dietary intakes of children indicated that, for some 10-year-old children, approximately 50%–60% of the daily total energy intake comes from school meals (Devaney, Gordon, & Burghardt, 1995; Nicklas, 1995).

Barriers

The very aspects of the school setting that can make it desirable for health promotion can also present barriers to effective health promotion and especially health promotion research. To the researcher, the school presents a special set of challenges. School systems, already preexisting and depending on public funding, are typically highly structured with limited resources (Lytle et al., 1994). Teacher unions, staff availability, space restrictions, district-wide policies, state educational requirements, and either stable or erratic school scheduling can make incorporation of ongoing health promotion programs challenging and associated research taxing.

In some areas, teacher union contracts restrict teacher responsibilities and time, requiring careful negotiation for training for and incorporation of health promotion activities. Schools may not have funds for adequate physical education equipment, or space to ensure that physical education continues despite climactic conditions. District-wide policies regarding use of tobacco products, can hinder or help, and a health promotion activity that can be most useful is working with districts to strongly regulate tobacco-use policies. Often extracurricular activities, such as field trips, picture-taking, and fire drills, are required and will usually be scheduled during those times considered "expendable" (e.g., physical education or health classes). Exercise and physical education programs have declined in schools.

Probably the most difficult obstacle to overcome is the addition of health promotion curricula and activities into the classroom. State requirements regarding academic credits that must be delivered usually encompass most of the school day. Careful and sensitive planning and negotiation with teachers and administrators, however, can result in effective scheduling for health education. This has been accomplished in all three of the population-based programs described in this chapter: Health Ahead/Heart Smart, CATCH (Lytle et al., 1994), and Gimme 5.

Several factors affect program implementation and success of healthy modifications in school meals. Although a mandate from the U.S. Department of Agriculture (1994) states that school meals are to approach the dietary guidelines for Americans, several factors need to be considered for successful implementation to occur. Many food service staff have been preparing school meals the same way for 20 years and may be resistant to any change; therefore, changes need to be gradual and accompanied with adequate training, materials, and reinforcement. Many training programs are available that have been shown to be successful (Nicklas, O'Neil, Carroll, Shi, & Berenson, in press; Weldman, Elveback, Nelson, Hodgson, & Ellefson, 1978); yet, no mechanism exists to effectively disseminate those programs. One approach has been in the delivery of training programs to food service staff through a cooperative effort by the State Department of Education, university faculty, State Office of Public Health, and community organizations (Nicklas et al., 1995). In addition to training, staff need modified recipes and alternative preparation techniques, along with a wider selection of healthier vendor products and commodities, to support school meal changes. "Competitive foods" are no longer allowed for sale during school lunch period, and this positive change needs to be reinforced at the student and faculty levels.

Intervention with Families

Advantages

Development of healthy lifestyles in children requires family members' support and cooperation, and any school-based health education effort should involve the adults in the student's home. Children need to receive reinforcement through consistent rather than conflicting health messages from school and home. Health promotion interventions that change the health skills and habits of the household unit are more likely to promote long-lasting health behavior changes in the child (Johnson et al., 1994).

A body of research that identifies the development of behaviors within the home unit, such as smoking, eating, and sedentary or physically active lifestyles, offers a strong rationale for health promotion within families. Children's primary social learning environment, especially at very young ages, is the home (Baranowski & Nader, 1985). Even though it is difficult to determine genetic versus environmental contributions, cardiovascular risk factors, such as blood pressure and blood cholesterol levels, cluster within families (Bao, Srinivasan, Wattigney, & Berenson, 1995; Johnson et al., 1991; Nader et al., 1989; Sallis & Nader, 1988). Also, obese parents tend to have obese children, even when the children are adopted (Garn & Clark, 1976). Evidence exists that a child's attitude and behavior regarding physical activity are significantly correlated with those of his or her parents (Dowell, 1973; Griffiths & Payne, 1976; Perrier Corp., 1979; Waxman & Stunkard, 1980). A major factor related to adoption of tobacco use by very young children is smoking by household members (Greenlund, Johnson, Webber, & Berenson, 1995; Hunter, Webber, & Berenson, 1980; Hunter, Croft, Vizelberg, & Berenson, 1987).

Strong evidence exists for family influence on eating behaviors. Adults buy and prepare the food and determine how it is to be used. Correlations have been found between children's weight and parental food offers and encouragements to eat (Klesges et al., 1983). Even taste for salt seems to be a function of family food preference (Garn & Clark, 1976; Young, Leong, & Pennell, 1984). Recently, a strong association was found between parental and adolescent fat intake: The probability of having a low fat intake was five times higher if the mother had a low fat intake (Rossow & Rise, 1994). In addition, parental smoking and alcohol consumption appeared to have additive effects on the corresponding behaviors of their children. In the same study, it was found that the effect of parental health behaviors on that of their adolescent child does not seem to decrease with increasing age of the adolescent.

Parent interests, modeling and teaching, positive reinforcement for eating, and discipline through physical activity restriction have strong influences on children (Johnson et al., 1994). Not to be ignored, however, is the influence that children have on parents. For example, children have considerable leverage regarding food purchases and consumption (Ward & Wackman, 1972). It follows that the family unit is a viable target for cardiovascular intervention and is certainly an important target for health education/promotion efforts.

Barriers

How best to reach and involve families is not completely understood and barriers to family participation do exist. It is virtually impossible to expect entire families to attend risk-reducing behavioral training sessions at hospitals or clinics. Most health insurance programs do not pay for prevention efforts in this area. Funding for these programs would have to be shifted to the participants; therefore, cost, as well as difficult logistics, make these kinds of programs impractical. Workers in this field hope that insurance companies will begin to reimburse for prevention, business corporations will recognize the value of prevention as opposed to remediation for employees, and other funding sources will become available to make these kinds of prevention programs more accessible to families.

A more viable way to reach families for public health promotion, and even for more intense programs, is through the schools. The school is usually located within the family's neighborhood and becomes an access point of convenience and may attract families who would not be involved in the mainstream of clinical intervention. Achieving successful parent participation and involvement even at the school level has proved difficult. In the Health Ahead/Heart Smart Family Health Promotion, which will be described, a participation rate of 59% was considered exceptional. Research data have been obtained on difficulties in getting parents to attend school programs (Perry et al., 1988). For example, during development of the Minnesota school program, it was found that the most challenging and difficult aspect of the parent education program was parent involvement. Based on a needs survey, health promotion materials were developed for at-home use. In the CATCH program, the majority of the parent program involved materials developed for home use, such as home curricula, newsletters, and refrigerator tip sheets (Johnson et al., 1994). In-school activities that were successful at the third-grade level were less attended as the children progressed to higher grade levels.

An increasing number of programs aimed at reaching parents through churches are being developed (Lasater, Wells, Carleton, & Elder, 1986). These appear to be viable, but the target audience is narrow and a large number of churches would need to be recruited over long periods of time for any kind of a sustained effect. Experience has indicated that each church needs to be recruited on an individual basis.

Several observations can be made about the problem of parent participation. The modern trend for both parents to work, the increasing prevalence of single-parent families, and a shifting of responsibility for education, even in the area of physical and mental health, outside the home and into the schools, could account for a large proportion of the lack of parental involvement in children's health education.

PREVENTION

Medical advances have resulted in a rationale for the formation of education and community programs to promote health and prevent and reduce risk of chronic disease development (e.g., heart attack and stroke). Children and youth are natural targets for preventive efforts since the major risk factors for cardiovascular disease, hyperlipidemia, smoking, hypertension, and obesity along with sedentary behaviors, tend to begin early in life. Although most cardiovascular prevention trials have been conducted with adults (e.g., MRFIT), it would seem logical that prevention at early ages would have its greatest impact when behaviors are still being formed.

Compelling also are the numbers of children in the United States who are already affected by elevated risk factors. An estimated five million of our children have high blood pressure, more than 20 million are obese, five million are using tobacco, and about 20 million have elevated levels of serum total cholesterol (Calhoun & Oparil,

1995). Based on the serious implications of these statistics, it is imperative to begin prevention of heart disease, and indeed, of any chronic disease, early in life.

The most effective approach to prevention can be achieved through comprehensive health education and health promotion in schools. The most important information regarding behaviors and risk reduction of children and adolescents has been obtained through school health promotion programs, in which education and environmental changes have been demonstrated to be effective.

Assessment Strategies

Cardiovascular Screening

The current recommendations are to screen for cardiovascular risk only those children who have a positive family history (i.e., if young parents have a history of heart disease, then their children should be screened). Data from the Bogalusa Heart Study indicate that 50% of children judged at high risk based on parental history alone would not be screened. Parents of young children are generally too young for overt symptoms of heart disease. As would be expected, parental history increases as the schoolchildren age. Another obstacle is that single-parent families result in poor identification of fathers in some cases and fathers missing from the household in others.

A recommendation based on Bogalusa data would be to develop cardiovascular risk profiles on all children, generally at time of entry into elementary school. The high relationship of risk factors to underlying cardiovascular disease noted in autopsy studies emphasizes this need. Examination of children in pediatric and family practice settings should include observations for cardiovascular risk, family history, growth and development comparisons, obesity, blood pressure, selected lipids and lipoproteins, and behavioral factors (e.g., active or sedentary lifestyle, intention to use tobacco products, difficulties with anger and aggression, and low social support or social isolation).

Knowledge, Attitudes, and Behaviors

Knowledge. Four generations of health education research have indicated that knowledge is essential but not sufficient to bring about behavior change. It is a first step, however, in the health education/promotion process, and provides an opportunity to evaluate effectiveness of program components based on information-transfer, assess a baseline level at which children are beginning their health education, and determine the level of health information of a given population just through everyday exposure. When knowledge assessments are used to determine effectiveness of a program, questions should reflect the information provided in that program. For example, in Gimme 5, knowledge questions were focused on the attributes and consumption of fruit and vegetables and the advantages of five helpings a day. In the Heart Smart School and Family Health Promotion program, knowledge questions centered on risk factors and behaviors related to elevated risk, whereas in the Child and Adolescent Trial for Cardiovascular Health (CATCH) knowledge questions related to diet and physical activity.

Attitudes. The second generation of health education research included attitudes as well as knowledge. It was once believed that attitudes needed to be changed first in order for behaviors to change. We now have information indicating that attitude change can occur after behavior. Attitudes will usually be measured to understand those cognitive or psychosocial factors that could influence behavioral outcome. In any case, it is important to assess those factors that could mediate health behavior.

Factors that are important in health promotion and which might loosely be proscribed to the domain of attitudes are: health beliefs, self-efficacy, and perceptions of social support. For example, health beliefs that could be questioned are the importance of health, the relationship between lifestyles and cardiovascular risk, the relevance and usefulness of being more physically active, and the ability to manage stress. It is important to address beliefs that can help or hinder health promotion efforts.

Social support is difficult to define because the concept is so dynamic, but it can be viewed as access to social resources when needed (Cobb, 1976; Rimm & Masters, 1979). Social support through peer pressure, interpersonal relationships, family history, and social situations has been found to influence tobacco use/nonuse (Greenlund et al., 1995; Marlatt & Gordon, 1980; West, Graham, Swanson, & Wilkinson, 1977), dietary habits, and physical activity patterns. Perceived social support can help alleviate acute or chronic trauma and stress. Epidemiological studies of social support and mortality indicate that poor social support precede mortality even when controlling for baseline health status (e.g., Berkman & Syme, 1979). Friendly support during high-stress performance tasks has resulted in reduced heart rate during those tasks (Kamarck, Manuck, & Jennings, 1990). Social support has been most commonly measured with self-report questionnaires specific to behaviors that form the basis for change (e.g., increased physical activity). Interviews and observations, however, can add valuable verbal and nonverbal information to this assessment.

Self-efficacy (i.e., perceptions of personal capability to perform a specific behavior, or self-confidence) has been related to behavior change in many arenas. Just obtaining a response to one question, "How confident are you that you can . . . ?" has been found to correlate highly with the specific behavior questioned (Rimm & Masters, 1979).

Behaviors. The most familiar outcome behaviors of interest in health promotion are increased physical activity, nontobacco and alcohol use, and dietary habits. In CATCH, physical activity levels were measured with the Self-Administered Physical Activity Checklist (SAPAC), a self-report checklist for type, duration, and intensity of activity, including TV watching and video game playing (Sallis et al., 1995). Observations during physical education classes verified increased moderate to vigorous physical activity by students (McKenzie, Sallis, & Nader, 1991). Cardiovascular fitness was assessed by measuring distance covered in a nine-minute run/walk in CATCH and by measuring completion times for a one-mile run/walk in Health Ahead/Heart Smart (Arbeit et al., 1992; Turley et al., 1994). Strength and flexibility were also assessed in Health Ahead/Heart Smart with a series of maneuvers designed for that purpose (Serpas, Harsha, Virgilio, & Berenson, 1989).

In the Bogalusa Heart Study, Health Ahead/Heart Smart, and CATCH, smoking/nonsmoking was assessed with a self-report questionnaire that also requested information regarding kind of tobacco products used, and length and frequency of use. More objective assessments of smoking/nonsmoking are the plasma thiocyanate and saliva cotinine methods (Dalferes, Webber, Radhakrishnamurthy, & Berenson, 1980; Langone, Gjika, & Van Vunakis, 1973).

Diet. Most dietary assessments fall into two general groups. Those techniques that assess intake by recall, such as the 24-hour recall and food frequencies, are essentially retrospective; the subject has not been forewarned and has not modified behavior in anticipation. The second method involves ongoing record keeping. This method may elicit an increased awareness of eating behavior, such as time, place, and amount. Other techniques, such as diet histories, may be combinations of recall and record keeping.

Selection of a particular dietary assessment technique is governed by the purpose for which it will be used. Some methods are essentially for individual evaluations (e.g., the 7-day record and dietary history); others are designed for appraisal of groups (e.g., the 24-hour dietary recall). A major limitation of the 24-hour recall is the daily variability of foods consumed by a given person (Beaton et al., 1979; Jacobs, Anderson, & Blackburn, 1979; Liu, Stamler, Dyer, McKeever, & McKeever, 1978; Morgan et al., 1978). A single 24-hour period provides little information about an individual's usual dietary intake, but the accumulated data provide reasonably good estimates of the mean food intake of population groups.

In the Bogalusa Heart Study, the Child and Adolescent Trial for Cardiovascular Health, and Gimme 5, 24-hour dietary recalls were collected on a subsample of the population to assess dietary intakes of children, adolescents, and young adults. To obtain information on usual eating habits over a longer period of time, a food frequency questionnaire was used.

PREVENTION APPROACHES

Two strategies for the primary prevention of CHD in childhood are the population-based approach and the high-risk approach (Strong & Dennison, 1988). In the population strategy, the purpose is to displace the entire distribution of a variable in a more favorable direction (Kottke, Gatewood, Wu, & Park, 1988). Distribution displacement usually takes place slowly over time and could result from changes in dietary norms, through education, environmental modifications, or government and school policies. Screening for risk is selective in the population and is based on well-known criteria, such as a positive family history. On the other hand, the high-risk strategy involves screening the entire population to identify and select for intense prevention efforts those individuals who have elevated risk factors such as hyperlipidemia (Rose, 1981). Despite the controversy over who should be screened in the pediatric population (Buser, Riesen, & Mordasini, 1990; Chase, O'Quin, & O'Brien, 1974; Walter & Wynder, 1989), it is logical that both strategies are needed to prevent the development of a chronic illness as pervasive, persistent, and costly as cardiovascular disease.

Population-Based Strategies for Prevention through Health Promotion—Health Ahead/Heart Smart

The Health Ahead/Heart Smart elementary health promotion effort permeates all aspects of the school environment and encourages elementary schoolchildren beginning in kindergarten to adopt healthy lifestyles by promoting realistic judgments of personal ability and self-esteem. It was developed (1984–1987) with the following objectives:

• To increase knowledge in the areas of cardiovascular health, behaviors, and risk factors.

- To develop networks of peer support for cardiovascular healthy behaviors.
- To enable students to adopt eating behaviors that comply with USDA requirements for total fat (< 30% of total calories), saturated fat (< 10% of total calories), and sodium ($\approx$ 2 gr/24 hr).
- To develop knowledge, behavioral skills, and patterns of physical activity consistent with lifetime physical fitness.
- To empower students to resist peer pressure for nonhealthy behaviors (e.g., tobacco, alcohol or drug use).
- To enable students to manage stress utilizing coping skills, such as problem-solving, goals clarification, self-monitoring of behavior, and relaxation.

Heart Smart relies on theoretical constructs from research in adoption and diffusion of innovations, Precede Model for program development, and social cognitive theory for motivational concepts (Bandura, 1977; Green, Kreuter, Deeds, & Partridge, 1980).

The curricula, from kindergarten through Grade 6, has a scope and sequence that considers behavioral and cognitive development. The curricula cover the following major areas: (a) cardiovascular health, anatomy and physiology, infectious disease, and injury prevention; (b) nutrition and eating behavior; (c) physical activity and exercise behavior; and (d) behavioral and coping skills, including overcoming violent behavior. It was recommended that the Health Ahead/Heart Smart curricula, which consists of 15 to 35 hours per grade level, be taught by school faculty over the full school year as a part of general sciences and/or physical education.

Superkids-Superfit, the physical activity component, consists of a 12-lesson curriculum and aerobic activities integrated into physical education. The goal of Superkids-Superfit was to teach exercise as a lifestyle for fun and included many noncompetitive exercise protocols.

The goal of the school lunch program was to modify school meals for total fat, saturated fat, and sodium through menu planning, food purchasing, recipe modification, and food preparation and production techniques (Nicklas, Forcier, et al., 1989). The school cafeteria format was "Offer versus Serve" for experimental and intervention purposes in which students had a choice between regular school lunches and cardiovascular health menus.

Staff training and development were important for Heart Smart to be implemented effectively within the school system. Teachers, physical education specialists, and food service managers and technicians received specialized instruction, while resources were developed within the school for personnel to enhance their own health development (e.g., access to cardiovascular-healthy meals, aerobics classes after school, walking programs, and brief "stretch breaks" during class periods). Cardiovascular health screening was offered to students and teachers during the development and evaluation phases of the program. The schools are an ideal place for screening to occur, but because of the expense involved, most schools will not adopt this policy long-term. Even so, participants in screening showed greater improvement in health knowledge than nonparticipants (Arbeit et al., 1992). To round out Health Ahead/Heart Smart, a parent support program was informative in nature, mostly through newsletters, but it also included popular school health fairs. Parents also served on an Advisory Committee (the COR [heart] Committee) which included an administrator, teachers, and food service workers (Arbeit, Serpas, Johnson, Forcier, & Berenson, 1991).

As the first Center for National Research and Demonstration–Arteriosclerosis, funded by the National Heart, Lung and Blood Institute (NHLBI), of the National Institutes of Health, Heart Smart was designed to include four elementary schools in Jefferson Parish (County), Louisiana. Of the 870 eligible fourth and fifth graders, 530 (61%) received parental consent to participate. Data from Health Ahead/Heart Smart were certainly encouraging. School lunch choices were successfully altered, and children whose lunch choices were cardiovascular healthful evidenced the greatest cholesterol reduction. Improvements in run/walk performance were related in predicted directions to the overall cardiovascular risk profile; for example, increases in HDL-C were observed at intervention schools (Arbeit et al., 1992). These observations support the relationship between behavior change and physiological changes achieved through a total school health promotion.

The Health Ahead/Heart Smart program is continuing in New Orleans inner-city schools supported by the school district and provided by the Tulane Center for Cardiovascular Health as a public service. Training institutes directed to teachers, cafeteria managers, and school nurses are now being implemented to disseminate the program.

Child and Adolescent Trial for Cardiovascular Health (CATCH)

The Child and Adolescent Trial for Cardiovascular Health (CATCH) is an NHLBI-sponsored multisite (University of California at San Diego, University of Minnesota, University of Texas at Houston, and Tulane University School of Public Health and Tropical Medicine) longitudinal field trial for a multidisciplinary intervention for children in Grades 3, 4, and 5 (ages 8–11). The primary goal was to assess the effects of the intervention on changing the environment of schools (food services and physical education) and the lifestyles of children (eating and physical activity behaviors) to reduce subsequent cardiovascular disease risk.

The study involved 5,106 students initially in third grade (mean age 8.76 years at baseline) in 96 public schools. They represented 61.1% of the students enrolled in the third grade at those schools, and were those for whom blood analysis was completed for lipid assessment at baseline. At follow-up, 79% ($n = 4,019$) of these students also participated in blood assessment and formed the primary cohort for student-level study outcomes (Luepker et al., 1996). Subjects were 69% Anglo, 13% African-American, and 14% Latino.

Ninety-six elementary schools were randomized after baseline measurements to either an intervention group (56 schools; 14 per field center) or a control group (40 schools; 10 per field center). The intervention schools were further randomized such that half received a school-based program consisting of the school food service, physical education, and the CATCH curricula, and the other half received the same school-based program plus a home and family-based program. The control group received the usual health curricula, physical education, and food service programs.

The CATCH interventions involved all students in the third grade in the 1991–1992 school year in each of the 56 intervention schools and continued for three years as the children grew. The program included the following intervention components:

- *Food Service.* Eat Smart (Nicklas et al., 1994) was designed to provide children with tasty meals, lower in fat (to 30% of calories), saturated fat (10% of calories), and sodium (600–1,000 mg/serving), while maintaining recommended levels of essential nutrients in the school breakfast and lunch programs. Food service personnel attended a one-day training session at the beginning of each school year with monthly follow-up and group booster sessions each school year.

- *Physical Education.* CATCH PE (McKenzie et al, 1996) sought to increase the amount of moderate-to-vigorous physical activity (MVPA) to 40% of the class period at school and to encourage these activities outside school. CATCH PE included a curriculum, teacher training, and on-site follow-up. Physical education specialists and classroom teachers had one to one-and-a-half days of training each school year in the use of materials for CATCH PE.

- *Classroom.* The Adventures of Hearty Heart and Friends, the curriculum for third grade, focused on eating patterns and physical activity. It consisted of 15 classroom sessions of approximately 40 minutes each, taught over a five-week period. The Go for Health curricula were implemented in Grades 4 and 5 and consisted of two 30-minute lessons taught each week for 8 to 12 weeks. All curricula included skill-building activities on eating behaviors and physical activity patterns. Lessons included such topics as choosing healthful breakfast and lunch at school, preparing snacks, and increased MVPA at school and at home. F.A.C.T.S. for 5 (Facts about Chewing Tobacco and Snuff) was a four-lesson curriculum for fifth graders to assist in preventing the onset of tobacco use. The focus was on tearing down barriers to living in a smoke-free environment.

- *Family-Based Programs.* In those schools randomized to the family program for each grade level, five to seven activity packets were sent home at weekly intervals. Parents and children worked together on a variety of activities to improve eating and physical activity patterns (Johnson et al., 1994). Audiotapes of all the home curricula were available in both English and Spanish. During the third and fourth grades, students were invited with their parents and siblings to a school activity called Family Fun Night. This program consisted of aerobic dance performances by students, food booths emphasizing healthy snacks and recipes, tips regarding heart-health themes, and games and contests rewarding knowledge of heart health skills.

Measures and Results.   Program Implementation process measures were developed to monitor the degree of implementation of the interventions as well as potential confounding influences and policies within the schools (McGraw et al., 1994). These consisted of teacher interviews and classroom observations designed to measure the acceptability, compliance, and ease of use of the classroom-based lessons.

- *Outcome Measures at the School Level.* The Eat Smart Food Service Program was assessed by trained observers who collected recipes, menus, and vendor product information for five consecutive days from food service personnel (Ebzery et al., 1995). Student participation in school lunch programs did not change differently by intervention group, remaining between 71% and 78%. The percentage of calories from total fat in the meals was reduced from baseline significantly more in the intervention (−6.8%) than in the control schools (−2.7%; Luepker et al., 1995). Calories from saturated fat were also significantly reduced.

Involvement in CATCH PE was assessed by an instrument called the System for Observing Fitness Instruction Time (SOFIT; McKenzie, Sallis, & Nader, 1991). During each semester, every PE class was visited twice by trained observers who used SOFIT to observe the type and intensity of the children's activities and the behaviors of the physical education specialist or teacher. The measure provided a quantitation of lesson length and type of physical activity during classes. Although the length of PE class did not differ between control and intervention schools, intensity of physical activity increased significantly in intervention compared with control schools.

- *Outcome Measures at the Individual Level.* The Health Behavior Questionnaire (HBQ) was a 45-minute class-administered instrument to evaluate factors associated with diet, exercise, and smoking (Edmundson et al., 1996). Children in the intervention schools scored higher for dietary knowledge, intentions, and self-reported food choice. Perceived social support for healthful eating patterns also was significantly higher in the intervention groups.

  A food-record-assisted 24-hour dietary recall compared total daily food and nutrient intake in a sample of 30 students per school measured at both baseline (third grade) and follow-up (fifth grade) (Lytle et al., 1993). The increase in total daily kilocalorie intake was greater in the control schools. Fat intake was significantly lower in children in intervention schools (30.3% of calories) at follow-up compared with children in control schools (32.2% of calories) ($p < 0.01$). Concomitantly, there was a lower intake of saturated fatty acids (-1.1% of calories) in children in the intervention schools with little change for children in the control schools (-0.4%) ($p < 0.01$). Polyunsaturated and monounsaturated fat and cholesterol intake were also slightly lower in children in the intervention schools.

  The Self-Administered Physical Activity Checklist (SAPAC) was given in the fifth grade to assess type, duration, and intensity of selected leisure-time physical activities, television watching, and video games (Sallis et al., 1995). Vigorous physical activity where the student reported breathing hard was significantly higher in the intervention schools (Intervention = 58.5 min vs. Control = 46.5 min; $p < .003$).

- *Outcome Physiological Measures.* Nonfasting venipuncture samples were drawn for lipid determination at both baseline (third grade) and follow-up (fifth grade; Luepker et al., 1995; Webber et al., 1995). The students' total blood cholesterol showed a trend to decrease by 0.4 mg/dl (*SE* 1.0 mg/dl; $p = .68$) more in the intervention schools. Apo-B cholesterol also showed a trend to decrease to a greater extent, although not statistically significant, in the intervention group (-0.7 mg/dl; *SE* 0.8 mg/dl; $p = .40$).

Comments.   CATCH demonstrated that a school-based program involving school food service, physical education, classroom curricula, and the family can be successfully implemented in diverse populations in four areas of the country. The CATCH programs were delivered with a high degree of fidelity by teachers and staff after effective training programs. The school environment can be changed to allow children the practice of healthful behaviors without adding substantial cost and time to the busy school schedule. These changes, when continued for several years, have considerable potential for altering behaviors long-term and perhaps for producing cardiovascular health benefits.

Gimme 5: A Fresh Nutrition Concept for Students

Gimme 5 is an ongoing program designed to increase consumption of fruit and vegetables by high school students by using the 5-A-Day message propagated and funded by the National Cancer Institute (Havas et al., 1995; Havas et al., 1994). Twelve high schools (6 matched pairs) were selected to participate in the four-year nutrition intervention program. The cohort for this longitudinal study was defined as all 9th grade students enrolled in the 12 participating New Orleans archdiocesan high schools in 1993–1994 ($N = 2,339$) who responded to baseline questionnaires in spring 1993 (95% of enrollment; $N = 2,213$; 44% male, 77% white, 4% black, 7% Hispanic, 12% other including Asian and Indian). Questionnaires were designed to assess knowledge, frequency of fruit/vegetable consumption, awareness of the 5-A-Day Program, stages of behavior change, self-efficacy, self-perception, and social support.

Theoretical Framework.   Gimme 5 is designed to create an environment in which predisposing, enabling, and reinforcing factors, described in the PRECEDE Model of Health Education (Green et al., 1980), influence increased daily consumption of fruit/vegetables. Consistent with the PRECEDE model, the specific components of the program address the following steps to behavior change:

1. *Awareness Development.* Strategies for exposure and rationale for participation.
2. *Interest Stimulation.* Efforts to have the audience shift into an information-collecting mode.
3. *Skills Training.* Activities that provide practice of behaviors necessary for success.
4. *Reinforcement.* Provision for external and internal reward systems to increase the probability of behavior adoption.
5. *Application.* Problem-solving for in vivo application and mastery of relevant behaviors.
6. *Maintenance.* Self-management strategies and modeling opportunities for long-term continuance of behaviors.

Gimme 5 Intervention—Gimme 5 Workshops.   Five workshops are being implemented with the cohort from 1994 to 1997:

1. *Fresh Start.* An introduction to the benefits of eating fruits and vegetables.
2. *Body Works.* Eating healthy for appearance and athletic performance.
3. *Fresh Snax to the Max.* Snacking.
4. *Fast Food: Go for the Green.*
5. *Microwave Magic and Other Quick Fixes.*

These 55-minute interactive sessions were planned so that basic knowledge and skills build cumulatively. They are delivered by school staff trained by *Gimme* 5 personnel.

School Meal and Snack Modification.   The goal of Fresh Choices is to increase the availability, variety, and taste of fruits and vegetables meeting 5-A-Day standards and nutrient criteria in school meals, vending machines, and snack outlets. Included in this endeavor are monthly marketing activities to promote increased fruit and vegetable consumption.

Media and Marketing Campaign.   This campaign is the main thrust of the Gimme 5 program and will provide appealing pictures, messages, and activities relevant to teenage interests that will also increase awareness and reinforce concepts and positive attitudes toward fruit/vegetable consumption (Figure 12.6). Specific media materials and activities used in the monthly promotions are shown in Table 12.6.

Supplementary Subject Activities.   A booklet of approximately 85 activities in 10 academic subjects that highlight fruits and vegetables are planned to reinforce the program and complement the workshops. Faculty are asked to present at least one activity each semester in their subject matter area. All activities were designed to be consistent with high school textbook and academic requirements.

Parent Support Program.   Raisin' Teens includes materials such as refrigerator magnets, fruit and vegetable recipes, biannual newsletters, and other home activities to

Figure 12.6.   Gimme 5 marketing station for grapes.

Table 12.6   Gimme 5 Media/Marketing Components

Marketing Stations	Colorful 3-panel, 6-ft vertical stations displaying 5-A-Day messages, promotional materials, and other Gimme 5 events
Taste-Testings	Monthly giveaways of fruit/vegetables with recipes that meet 5-A-Day nutrient criteria
Point-of-Service Signs	Placards that advertise monthly taste-testings and fruit/vegetable cafeteria sales
Posters	Framed posters in high visibility school locations that depict teens in athletic and leisure activities with humorous prose
Table-Tents	Cafeteria table-tents featuring 5-A-Day messages and brain-teasers
Public Service Announcements	School-wide announcements regarding Gimme 5 events, contest deadlines, and winners
Power Lotto	Competitions by student clubs and sports teams for rewards of produce snacks for their club/team; demonstrations with recipes, nutrient information, and purchasing tips accompany snack delivery
Faculty Baskets	Fruit/vegetable baskets given to faculty each semester to encourage consumption
Faculty Tip Sheets	Nutritional information posted on faculty refrigerators encouraging support for students

stimulate parent support for student dietary improvement. Parent-Teacher Organization meetings are the site of taste-testings of Gimme 5 recipes, media displays, and literature distribution. Colorful commercial brochures featuring individual fruits and vegetables are mailed to parents each semester. The Gimme 5 Alive newsletter informs parents of Gimme 5 school and cafeteria activities and provides useful information concerning the at-home purchase and preparation of fruits and vegetables.

Baseline assessment indicated that only about one-third of the fruit/vegetable and Five-A-Day message knowledge questions were answered correctly, and correct responding was significantly higher for girls than boys (44% vs. 36%) and for whites compared with the other ethnic groups. Only 12% of students reported eating five or more daily servings of fruits and vegetables; the mean was 2.7 servings. The Five-A-Day program was unknown to 82% of students.

Assessing stages of behavior change indicated whether students were unaware of the necessity for change (precontemplation), were thinking about or preparing for dietary change (contemplation or preparation), and were making change (action or maintenance). More females than males were in preparation (61% vs. 38%), and more males than females were in precontemplation (44% vs. 24%). When questioned about self-efficacy, approximately 40% of students felt "very" or "extremely" confident that they could eat five daily servings of fruits/vegetables. Baseline social support was not associated with number of daily servings reported.

Impact measures determined that most of the cohort was aware of Gimme 5 media activities and were extremely impressed by the fruits/vegetable giveaways, cafeteria table-tents with puzzles, contests, posters, and marketing stations. Public address announcements received approval but were not quite as popular. Importantly, more than three-fourths of the students reported that the Five-A-Day message was personally relevant. It is obvious that the media activities were a useful strategy for reaching high school students, and will be continued. Baseline information, on the other hand, indicated a need for knowledge and intervention efforts in the area of fruit and vegetable consumption by high school students.

A High-Risk Strategy for Prevention through Health Promotion— The Health Ahead/Heart Smart Family Health Promotion Program

The Family Health Promotion program was implemented by a multidisciplinary team, including a physician, nurse specialist, physical educator, nutritionist, and behavioral scientist. The purpose of the initial program, funded by NHLBI, was a research and demonstration program in schools to evaluate the feasibility and effectiveness of a behavioral program with high-risk elementary schoolchildren and their families in a public school system (Johnson et al., 1991). Behaviors underlying physiological changes that could lead to cardiovascular pathology later in life had been identified in young children; therefore, the rationale of the program was that children and their families could be taught lifestyle modifications that could prevent disease development. Also, since cardiovascular risk factors cluster within families (Sallis & Nader, 1988), and since elementary schoolchildren would have less of a chance of maintaining improved lifestyle habits without parental support and involvement, the program included home adults as well. The program site was the child's school, a neighborhood location of each access and convenience.

The Family Health Promotion targeted eating, exercise, stress management, and smoking prevention in 12 weekly 90-minute group sessions and six concurrent individual family counseling sessions every other week (Table 12.7). Education, motivation, skills-building, and application through home practice were promoted through brief didactic presentations, group discussions and problem-solving, hands-on activities, and behavior modification strategies. Comprehensive screening took place before and after intervention, resulting in a 15-week program.

Cardiovascular Risk.   All third- and fourth-grade children of two elementary schools, whose parents provided written consent, were screened to identify those with elevated risk factors, namely, elevated levels of systolic and diastolic blood pressure, Rohrer Index (kg/m^3) (Keys, Fidanza, Karvonen, Kimura, & Taylor, 1972), total cholesterol, LDL-C, and low levels of HDL-C. Nineteen children (12 black, 7 white) and their parents ($n = 23$) agreed to participate. Parents were screened after recruitment, and were found to have multiple elevated cardiovascular risk factors as well (Johnson et al., 1987).

Even though changes in physiological risk factors would not be expected over a short time period, some impressive outcomes were noted (Table 12.8). Adults in the program significantly decreased systolic, diastolic, and mean arterial pressure, and triglyceride levels. Total serum cholesterol decreased by approximately 19 mg/dl, which was not statistically significant, but was impressive.

Desired trends were found for children in the program. A decrease in diastolic blood pressure of approximately 10 mm/Hg was not statistically significant, but was considered clinically significant. Children in the intervention gained no additional weight,

**Table 12.7   Heart Smart Family Health Promotion Program:
A Sample Intervention Program**

Week 1	Orientation to program Cardiovascular risk factors
Week 2	Cardiovascular screening*
Week 3	Family counseling* Cardiovascular screening feedback
Week 4	What is a heart-healthy eating pattern? Role of exercise in cardiovascular health
Week 5	Family counseling: Nutrition, exercise, smoking*
Week 6	Ordering healthy food when dining out
Week 7	Power-up with self-confidence
Week 8	Choosing healthy snacks
Week 9	Family counseling: Nutrition, exercise, smoking*
Week 10	Social support
Week 11	Reading labels at the grocery store Modifying recipes Behavioral shopping hints
Week 12	Family counseling: Nutrition, exercise, smoking* Heart-healthy group picnic
Week 13	Stress Management
Week 14	Maintenance planning Stimulus control
Week 15	Cardiovascular screening*

* Session with individual families rather than whole group.

Note. Reprinted with permission, Johnson et al., 1991.

**Table 12.8   Means and (Standard Deviations) for Selected Risk Factors Pre- and
Postintervention for Adults Participating in the Heart Smart Family Health Promotion**

Risk Factor	Assessment	n	mean ($\pm$ s.d.)	p
Ponderosity (kg/m^3)	Pre	14	18.1 (3.5)	NS
	Post	12	17.7 (4.0)	
Systolic BP (mm Hg)	Pre	14	123.5 (14.2)	< .02
	Post	12	109.8 (10.6)	
Diastolic BP (mm Hg)	Pre	14	91.3 (13.1)	< .02
	Post	12	75.8 (9.8)	
Mean Arterial Pressure (mm Hg)	Pre	14	102.0 (12.8)	< .02
	Post	12	87.2 (9.5)	
Total Cholesterol (mg/dl)	Pre	13	202.2 (35.8)	NS
	Post	11	183.6 (27.9)	
Triglycerides (mg/dl)	Pre	13	144.1 (73.4)	< .05
	Post	11	92.8 (41.0)	
Knowledge Score	Pre	8	15.1 (3.3)	< .008
	Post	8	17.9 (3.8)	

which was considered positive for those children who were recruited because of elevated Rohrer Index. The average weight of the parents did not change.

Nutrition. Six nutrition modules included topic areas such as planning a cardiovascular-healthy meal, snacking, dining out, food purchasing and preparation, and recipe modification (Nicklas, Arbeit, Johnson, Franklin, & Berenson, 1987; Nicklas, Arbeit, Johnson, Franklin, & Berenson, 1988; Nicklas, Johnson, Arbeit, Franklin, & Berenson, 1988). Learning activities and role-playing were reinforced with a variety of products (e.g., food samples, discount coupons, and recipe booklets). Evaluations included multiple 24-hour food records, questionnaires, and 24-hour urine samples to assess total fat, saturated fat, sugar, and sodium intake. Decreases in intake of each of these dietary components were observed in intervention families compared with control families. Urinary analyses reflected reduced sodium excretion for both adults and children. These decreases were not statistically significant, probably due to the small sample size.

Physical Activity. Taking advantage of group support and modeling, weekly meetings always included group physical activity and relaxation procedures prior to closure. During counseling, families were asked to design a program of physical activity that met or exceeded the American Heart Association recommendation to exercise at 60% to 75% of maximum heart rate for at least 15 minutes a minimum of three times a week (American Heart Association, 1978). Brisk walking and other aerobic exercises were encouraged for the entire family. Children's run times during a 1-mile run/walk improved by an average of 1.5 minutes ($p < 0.01$), reflecting enhanded cardiovascular fitness. Parents' physical activity was assessed by self-reported activities and activity levels. Adults who completed baseline and postintervention questionnaires reported substantial increases in leisure physical activity levels. The group average increase in activity was approximately 10 miles of jogging per person or its metabolic equivalent per week.

Behavioral Strategies. Behavioral strategies for change were based on social cognitive theory (Bandura, 1977) and behavioral learning theory (Skinner, 1953), and included social support, modeling, self-efficacy training, counseling, contracting, stimulus control and positive reinforcement (Mann, 1972; Rimm & Masters, 1979). A social support network for families was developed, and self-efficacy was enhanced by building skills and experiencing success one step at a time (shaping).

In a total of six family counseling sessions (three eating and three exercise), areas of improvement and obstacles to improvement were discussed. Contingency contracts (Figure 12.7) were voluntarily negotiated and rewards were offered for contract performance, such as theater tickets, YMCA passes, and sporting goods discounts (Johnson, Nicklas, Arbeit, Webber, & Berenson, 1992). In this program, contracts were negotiated between participants and staff, but it was explained that contracts could be made between children and parents, between participants and caregivers, and/or between adult family members.

Contracts targeted food preparations (e.g., salting habits) and consumption of foods high in fat, sugar, and sodium. Examples of common foods that were found to be a problem and contracted for change were regular soft drinks, bacon, deli meats, eggs, whole milk, cake, and cookies. Decreases in consumption of these foods paralleled increased consumption of foods and beverages contracted for substitution, such as diet

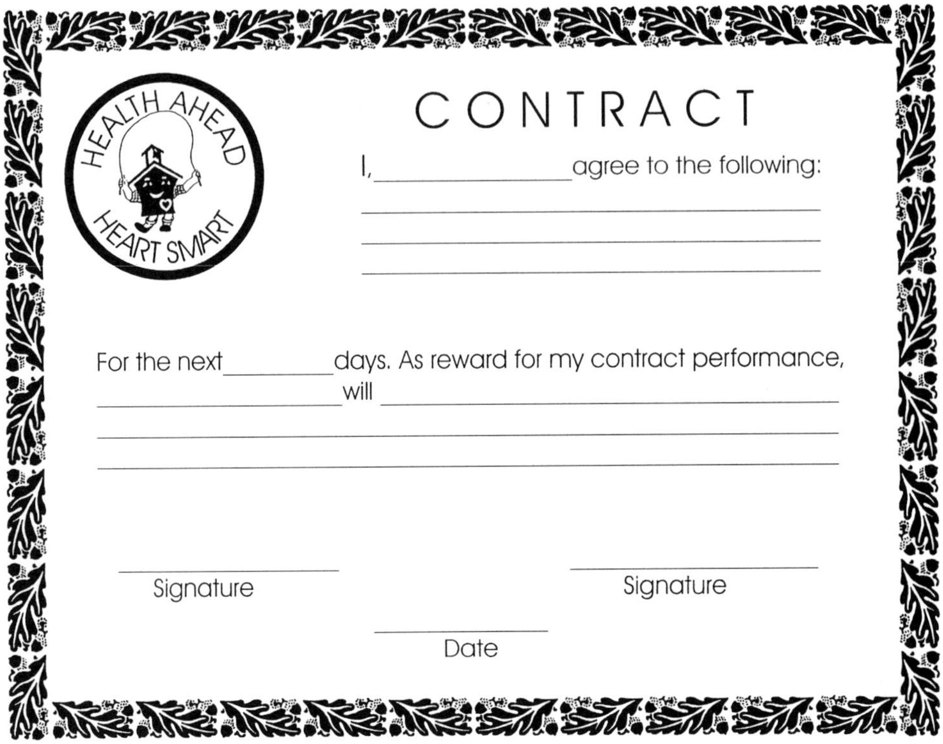

HEALTH AHEAD
HEART SMART

CONTRACT

I, ________________ agree to the following:

____

____

____

For the next ________ days. As reward for my contract performance,
________________ will ________________________________

____

____

________________ Signature

________________ Signature

________________ Date

Figure 12.7. Heart Smart Family Health Promotion Program: Sample contract.

soft drinks, fruit, turkey, or chicken. Families in the intervention indicated that food preferences also had changed considerably during the program.

Comments and Conclusions. The Heart Smart Family Health Promotion program was a high-risk strategy that demonstrated a school-based cardiovascular health model can be effective as a risk reduction program. The program drew on the strength of two societal systems—the family and the school—to promote healthy lifestyles among children who were at elevated disease risk. Program factors that could contribute to long-term change were:

- Addressing children in the early formative years before lifestyle habits are rigidly established.
- Including the entire family system, the strongest area of influence in a child's life.
- Teaching family members to use intrafamily social reinforcement.
- Encouraging a shift from extrinsic to intrinsic reinforcement.

It was concluded that counseling families in cardiovascular-healthy nutrition and to be more physically active is a viable way of reaching each individual in a family unit, especially if the formal contract is used. This program takes advantage of the principle that individuals are more likely to adopt healthier habits with family support when the necessary changes are expected from everyone, not just the family members with apparent risk or illness.

The Heart Smart Family Health Promotion at Ft. Polk, Louisiana

The high-risk approach to prevention is a versatile strategy because it can be modified to accommodate varied situations. The same principles in the high-risk program were applied to the worksite by engaging active military personnel and dependents at the U.S. Army base at Ft. Polk, Louisiana. Rather than select participants based on elevated cardiovascular risk factors, all families who were screened were invited to participate in the 10-week educational and skills-building program targeting eating, physical activity, smoking prevention, and personal management (Berenson et al., 1993; Johnson, Harsha, Powers, Webber, & Berenson, 1993; Nicklas, Webber, Kern, et al., 1993; Webber, Srinivasan, Harsha, Powers, & Berenson, 1993). Additional objectives of the program were formation of a social support network and development of a referral system for observed clinical problems, such as morbid obesity and excessive alcohol intake, to existing intervention programs on the base. An interesting outcome, noted by base medical personnel, was that the positive public relations generated by the program had considerable potential for enhanced use of military medical facilities and for reduced use of Champus payments for off-base medical services.

REFERENCES

American Heart Association. (1978). *Heart facts.* Dallas, TX: American Heart Association.

Amos, C. I., Hunter, S. M., Zinkgraf, S. A., Miner, M. H., & Berenson, G. S. (1987). Characteristics of a comprehensive Type A measurement for children in a biracial community: The Bogalusa Heart Study. *Journal of Behavioral Medicine, 10,* 425–439.

Arbeit, M. L., Johnson, C. C., Mott, D. S., Harsha, D. W., Nicklas, T. A., Webber, L. S., & Berenson, G. S. (1992). The Heart Smart cardiovascular school health program: Behavioral correlates of risk factor change. *Preventive Medicine, 21,* 18–32.

Arbeit, M. L., Serpas, D. C., Johnson, C. C., Forcier, J. E., & Berenson, G. S. (1991). The implementation of a cardiovascular school health promotion program: Utilization and impact of a school health advisory committee: The Heart Smart program. *Health Education Research, 6,* 423–430.

Ballard, M. E., Cummings, E. M., & Larkin, K. (1993). Emotional and cardiovascular responses to adults' angry behavior and to challenging tasks in children of hypertensive and normotensive parents. *Child Development, 64,* 500–515.

Bandura, A. (1977). *A social learning theory.* Englewood Cliffs, NJ: Prentice-Hall.

Bao, W., Srinivasan, S. R., Wattigney, W. A., & Berenson, G. S. (1995). The relation of parental cardiovascular disease to risk factors in children and young adults: The Bogalusa Heart Study. *Circulation, 91,* 365–371.

Bao, W., Threefoot, S., Srinivasan, S. R., & Berenson, G. S. (1995). Essential hypertension predicted by persistence of elevated blood pressure from childhood to adulthood: The Bogalusa Heart Study. *American Journal of Hypertension, 8,* 657–665.

Baranowski, T., & Nader, P. R. (1985). Family involvement in health-related behavior change programs. In D. Turk & R. Kerns (Eds.), *Health, illness and families: A lifespan perspective* (pp. 51–80). New York: Wiley.

Barefoot, J. C., Dahlstrom, W. C., & Williams, R. B. (1983). Hostility, CHD incidence, and total mortality: A 25-year follow-up study of 255 physicians. *Psychosomatic Medicine, 45,* 109–114.

Baugh, J. G., Hunter, S. M., Webber, L. S., & Berenson, G. S. (1982). Developmental trends of first cigarette smoking experience of children: The Bogalusa Heart Study. *American Journal of Public Health, 72,* 1161–1164.

Beaton, G. H., Milner, J., Corey, P., McGuire, V., Cousins, M., & Stewart, E. (1979). Sources of variance in 24-hour dietary recall data: Implications for nutrition study design and interpretation. *American Journal of Clinical Nutrition, 32,* 2546–2559.

Berenson, G. S. (Ed.). (1986). *Causation of cardiovascular risk factors in children: Perspectives on cardiovascular risk in early life.* New York: Raven Press.

Berenson, G. S., Harsha, D. W., Johnson, C. C., Nicklas, T. A. (1993, June 15). Teach families to be Heart Smart. *Patient Care, 135*–145.

Berenson, G. S., McMahan, C. A., Voors, A. W., Webber, L. S., Srinivasan, S. R., Frank, G. C., Foster, T. A., & Blonde, C. V. (1980). *Cardiovascular risk factors in children—The early natural history of atherosclerosis and essential hypertension.* New York: Oxford University Press.

Berenson, G. S., Schnakenberg, D., Harsha, D. W., Webber, L. S., Johnson, C. C., Nicklas, T. A., & Srinivasan, S. R. (1993). Fort Polk Heart Smart Program Part 1: Background design and significance. *Military Medicine, 158,* 304–308.

Berenson, G. S., Srinivasan, S. R., Cresanta, J. L., Foster, T. A., & Webber, L. S. (1981). Dynamic changes of serum lipoproteins in children during adolescence and sexual maturation. *American Journal of Epidemiology, 113,* 157–170.

Berenson, G. S., Wattigney, W. A., Tracy, R. E., Newman, W. P., III, Srinivasan, S. R., Webber, L. S., Dalferes, E. R., Jr., & Strong, J. B. (1992). Atherosclerosis of the aorta and coronary arteries and cardiovascular risk factors in person aged 6 to 30 years and studied at necropsy: The Bogalusa Heart Study. *American Journal of Cardiology, 70,* 851–858.

Berkman, L., & Syme, S. L. (1979). Social networks, host resistance, and mortality: A nine-year follow-up study of Alameda County residents. *American Journal of Epidemiology, 109,* 188–204.

Burghardt, J., & Devany, B. (1993). *The School Nutrition Dietary Assessment Study. Summary of findings.* Princeton, NJ: Mathematica Policy Research.

Buser, F., Riesen, W. F., & Mordasini, R. (1990). Lipid screening in paediatrics for early detection of cardiovascular risks. *Journal of Clinical Chemistry and Clinical Biochemistry, 28,* 107–111.

Calhoun, D. A., & Oparil, S. (1995). Racial differences in the pathogenesis of hypertension. *American Journal of the Medical Sciences, 310*(Suppl. 1), S86–S90.

Call, D. S., & Sanchez, A. M. (1967). Trends in fat disappearance in the United States, 1909–1965. *Journal of Nutrition, 93,* 1–28.

Chase, H. P., O'Quin, R. J., & O'Brien, D. (1974). Screening for hyperlipidaemia in childhood. *Journal of the American Medical Association, 230,* 1535.

Cobb, S. (1976). Social support as a moderator of life stress. *Psychosomatic Medicine, 38,* 300–313.

Croft, J. B., Hunter, S. M., Webber, L. S., Watson, R. B., & Berenson, G. S. (1985). Cigarette smoking behavioral distinctions between experimental nonadopters and adopters in children and adolescents—A consideration of transitional smoking experience: The Bogalusa Heart Study. *Preventive Medicine, 14,* 109–122.

Dalferes, E. R., Webber, L. S., Radhakrishnamurthy, B., & Berenson, G. S. (1980). Continuous-flow (AutoAnalyzer I) analysis for plasma thiocyanate as an index of tobacco smoking. *Clinical Chemistry, 26,* 493–495.

Dembroski, T. M., MacDougall, J. M., Williams, R. B., Haney, T., & Blumenthal, J. A. (1985). Components of Type A, hostility and anger-in: Relationship to angiographic findings. *Psychosomatic Medicine, 47,* 219–233.

Devaney, B. L., Gordon, A. R., & Burghardt, J. A. (1995). Dietary intakes of students. *American Journal of Clinical Nutrition, 26*(Suppl.), 205S–212S.

Dowell, L. J. (1973). A study of physical and psychological variables related to attitudes toward physical activity. *International Journal of Sports Psychology, 4,* 39.

Downey, A. M., Cresanta, J. L., & Berenson, G. S. (1989). Cardiovascular health promotion in children: "Heart Smart" and the changing role of physicians. *American Journal of Preventive Medicine, 5,* 279–295.

Ebzery, M. K., Montgomery, D. H., Evans, M. A., Hewes, L. V., Zive, M. M., Reed, D. B., Rice, R., Hann, B., & Dwyer, J. T. (1995). *School meal data collection and documentation methods in a multisite study.* Manuscript submitted for publication.

Edmundson, E., Parcel, G. S., Feldman, H. A., Elder, J., Perry, C. L., Johnson, C. C., Williston, B. J., Stone, E., Yang, M., & Lytle, L. (1996). The effects of child and adolescent trial for cardiovascular health upon psychosocial determinants of diet and physical activity behavior. *Preventive Medicine, 25,* 442–454.

Enos, W., Holmes, R., & Beyer, J. (1953). Coronary disease among United States soldiers killed in action in Korea. *Journal of the American Medical Association, 152,* 1090–1092.

Farris, R. P., & Nicklas, T. A. (1993). Characterizing children's eating behavior. In R. M. Suskind & L. L. Suskind (Eds.), *Textbook of pediatric nutrition* (2nd ed., pp. 505–516). New York: Raven Press.

Farris, R. P., Nicklas, T. A., Webber, L. S., & Berenson, G. S. (1992). Nutrient contribution of the school lunch program. Implications for Healthy People 2000. *Journal of School Health, 62,* 180–184.

Freedman, D. S., Srinivasan, S. R., Cresanta, J. L., Webber, L. S., & Berenson, G. S. (1987). Cardiovascular disease risk factors from birth to seven years of age: The Bogalusa Heart Study. 4. Serum lipids and lipoproteins. *Pediatrics Supplement, 80,* 789–796.

Frerichs, R. R., Srinivasan, S. R., Webber, L. S., & Berenson, G. S. (1976). Serum cholesterol and triglyceride levels in 3,446 children from a biracial community: The Bogalusa Heart Study. *Circulation, 54,* 302–308.

Garn, S. M., & Clark, D. C. (1976). Trends in fatness and the origins of obesity. *Pediatrics, 57,* 443–456.

Green, L. W., Kreuter, M. W., Deeds, S. G., & Partridge, K. L. (1980). *Health education planning: A diagnostic approach* (pp. 142–158). Palo Alto, CA: Mayfield.

Greenlund, K., Johnson, C. C., Webber, L. S., & Berenson, G. S. (in press). Smoking attitudes and initiation among third through sixth grade students: The Bogalusa Heart Study. *American Journal of Public Health.*

Griffiths, M., & Payne, P. R. (1976). Energy expenditure in small children of obese and nonobese parents. *Nature, 260,* 698.

Harris, L., & Associates, Inc. (1989). *The Prevention Index '89: Summary report.* Emmaus, PA: Rodale Press.

Havas, S., Heimendinger, J., Damron, D., Nicklas, T. A., Cowan, A., Beresford, S. A., Sorenson, G., Buller, D., Bishops, D., Baranowski, T. E., & Reynolds, K. (1995). Five-A-Day for better health—Nine community research projects to increase fruit and vegetable consumption. *Public Health Reports, 110,* 68–79.

Havas, S., Heimendinger, J., Reynolds, R., Baranowski, T., Nicklas, T. A., Bishop, D., Buller, D., Sorenson, G., Beresford, S. A. S., Cowan, A., & Damron, D. (1994). Five-A-Day for better health: A new research initiative. *Journal of the American Dietetic Association, 94,* 32–36.

Hawkins, J. D., & Catalano, R. F. (1990). Broadening the vision of education: Schools as health promoting environments. *Journal of School Health, 60,* 178–181.

Hetzel, B. S., & Berenson, G. S. (1987). *Cardiovascular risk factors in childhood: Epidemiology and prevention.* New York: Elsevier.

Holman, R. L., McGill, H. C., Strong, J. P., & Geer, J. C. (1958). The natural history of atherosclerosis: The early aortic lesions as seen in the middle of the 20th century. *American Journal of Pathology, 34,* 209–345.

Hoover, L. W. (1983). Computerized nutrient data bases: 1. Comparison of nutrient analysis systems. *Journal of the American Dietetic Association, 82,* 504–505.

Hunter, S. M., Baugh, J. G., Webber, L. S., Sklov, M. C., & Berenson, G. S. (1982). Social learning effects on trial and adoption of cigarette smoking in children: The Bogalusa Heart Study. *Preventive Medicine, 11,* 29–42.

Hunter, S. M., Croft, J. B., Burke, G. L., Parker, F. C., Webber, L. S., & Berenson, G. S. (1986). Longitudinal patterns of cigarette smoking and smokeless tobacco use in youth: The Bogalusa Heart Study. *American Journal of Public Health, 76,* 193–195.

Hunter, S. M., Croft, J. B., Vizelberg, I. A., & Berenson, G. S. (1987). Psychosocial influences on cigarette smoking among youth in a southern community: The Bogalusa Heart Study. *Morbidity & Mortality Weekly Report, 36*(Suppl), 17S–23S.

Hunter, S. M., Webber, L. S., & Berenson, G. S. (1980). Cigarette smoking and tobacco usage behavior in children and adolescents: The Bogalusa Heart Study. *Preventive Medicine, 9,* 701–712.

Hunter, S. M., Wolf, T. M., Sklov, M. C., Webber, L. S., Watson, R. M., & Berenson, G. S. (1982). Type A coronary-prone behavior pattern and cardiovascular risk factor variables in children and adolescents: The Bogalusa Heart Study. *Journal of Chronic Diseases, 35,* 613–621.

Jacobs, D. R., Jr., Anderson, J. T., & Blackburn, H. (1979). Diet and serum cholesterol. Do zero correlations negate the relationship? *American Journal of Epidemiology, 110,* 77–87.

Jenkins, C. D. (1988). Epidemiology of cardiovascular diseases. *Journal of Consulting and Clinical Psychology, 56,* 324–332.

Jiang, X., Srinivasan, S. R., Radhakrishnamurthy, B., Dalferes, E. R., Jr., Bao, W., & Berenson, G. S. (1994). Microalbuminuria in young adults related to blood pressure in a biracial (black-white) population: The Bogalusa Heart Study. *American Journal of Hypertension, 7,* 794–800.

Johnson, C. C., Greenlund, K., Webber, L. S., & Berenson, G. S. (1996). *What do young children think about drinking alcohol? A perspective from the Bogalusa Heart Study.* Manuscript submitted for publication.

Johnson, C. C., Harsha, D. W., Powers, C. R., Webber, L. S., & Berenson, G. S. (1993). Fort Polk Heart Smart Program Part 4: Lifestyles of military personnel and their families. *Military Medicine, 158,* 317–322.

Johnson, C. C., Hunter, S. M., Amos, C. I., Elder, S. T., & Berenson, G. S. (1989). Cigarette smoking, alcohol, and oral contraceptive use by Type A adolescents: The Bogalusa Heart Study. *Journal of Behavioral Medicine, 12,* 13–24.

Johnson, C. C., Hunter, S. M., & Berenson, G. S. (1989a, October). *Association of Type A behavior with cardiovascular risk factors: The Bogalusa Heart Study.* Paper presented at the 62nd Scientific Sessions of the American Heart Association, New Orleans, LA.

Johnson, C. C., Hunter, S. M., & Berenson, G. S. (1989b, October). *Tracking and age trends of global Type A and factor components: The Bogalusa Heart Study.* Paper presented at the 62nd Scientific Sessions of the American Heart Association, New Orleans, LA.

Johnson, C. C., Myers, L., Webber, L. S., Bonura, S. R., Hunter, S. M., & Berenson, G. S. (in press). A study of learned helplessness and cardiovascular health in children: The Bogalusa Heart Study. *American Journal of Health Behavior, Education & Promotion.*

Johnson, C. C., Myers, L., Webber, L. S., Srinivasan, S. R., & Berenson, G. S. (1995). Alcohol consumption among adolescents and young adults: The Bogalusa Heart Study, 1981 to 1991. *American Journal of Public Health, 85,* 979–982.

Johnson, C. C., Nicklas, T. A., Arbeit, M. L., Franklin, F. A., Cresanta, J. L., Harsha, D. W., & Berenson, G. S. (1987). Cardiovascular risk in parents of children with elevated blood pressure: "Heart Smart" Family Health Promotion. *Journal of Clinical Hypertension, 3,* 559–566.

Johnson, C. C., Nicklas, T. A., Arbeit, M. L., Harsha, D. W., Mott, D. S., Hunter, S. M., Wattigney, W., & Berenson, G. S. (1991). Cardiovascular intervention for high-risk families: The Heart Smart Program. *Southern Medical Journal, 84,* 1305–1312.

Johnson, C. C., Nicklas, T. A., Arbeit, M. A., Webber, L. S., & Berenson, G. S. (1992). Behavioral counseling and contracting as methods for promoting cardiovascular health in families. *Journal of the American Dietetic Association, 92,* 479–481.

Johnson, C. C., Osganian, S. K., Budman, S. B., Lytle, L. A., Barrera, E. P., Bonura, S. R., Wu, M. C., & Nader, P. R. (1994). CATCH: Family process evaluation in a multicenter trial. *Health Education Quarterly,* (Suppl. 2), S91–S106.

Johnson, C. C., Webber, L. S., Myers, L., & Berenson, G. S. (1994, April 13–16). *Demographic characteristics and cardiovascular risk of anger in children: The Bogalusa Heart Study.* Presented at the 15th anniversary meeting of the Society of Behavioral Medicine, Boston, MA.

Johnston, L. D., O'Malley, P. M., & Bachman, J. G. (1993). *National survey results on drug use from the Monitoring the Future Study, 1975–1992: Vol. 1. Secondary school students.* Washington, DC: U.S. Department of Health and Human Services, Public Health Service, National Institutes of Health.

Kamarck, T. W., Manuck, S. B., & Jennings, J. R. (1990). Social support reduces cardiovascular reactivity to psychological challenge: A laboratory model. *Psychosomatic Medicine, 52,* 42–58.

Kaplan, R. M., Sallis, J. F., Jr., & Patterson, T. L. (1993). *Health and human behavior* (pp. 132–155). New York: McGraw-Hill.

Kaplan, G. A., Salonen, J. T., Cohen, R. D., Brand, R. J., Syme, S. L., & Puska, P. (1988). Social connections and mortality from all causes and from cardiovascular disease: Prospective evidence from Eastern Finland. *American Journal of Epidemiology, 128,* 370–380.

Keys, A., Fidanza, F., Karvonen, M. J., Kimura, N., & Taylor, H. L. (1972). Indices of relative weight and obesity. *Journal of Chronic Disease, 25,* 329–343.

Klesges, R. C., Coates, T. J., Brown, G., Sturgeon-Tuillisch, J., Moldenhauer-Klesges, L. M., Holzer, B., Woolfrey, J., & Vollmer, J. (1983). Parental influences on children's eating behavior and relative weight. *Journal of Applied Behavioral Analysis, 16,* 371–378.

Kottke, T. E., Gatewood, L. C., Wu, S.-C., & Park, H.-A. (1988). Preventing heart disease: Is treating the high risk sufficient? *Journal of Clinical Epidemiology, 411,* 1083–1093.

Krantz, D. S., & Manuck, S. B. (1984). Acute psychophysiological reactivity and risk of cardiovascular disease: A review and methodologic critique. *Psychological Bulletin, 96,* 435–464.

Kris-Etherton, P. M., Krummel, D., Russell, M. E., Dreon, D., Mackey, S., Borchers, J., & Wood, P. D. (1988). The effect of diet on plasma lipids, lipoproteins, and coronary heart disease. National Cholesterol Education Program. *Journal of the American Dietetic Association, 88,* 1373–1400.

Langone, J. J., Gjika, H. B., & Van Vunakis, H. (1973). Nicotine and its metabolites. Radioimmunoassays for nicotine and cotinine. *Biochemistry, 112,* 5025.

Lasater, T. M., Wells, B. L., Carleton, R. A., & Elder, J. P. (1986). The role of churches in disease prevention research studies. *Public Health Reports, 101,* 125–131.

Lauer, R. M., Connor, W. E., Leaverton, P. E., Reiter, M. A., & Clarke, W. F. (1975). Coronary heart disease risk factors in school children—The Muscatine Study. *Journal of Pediatrics, 86,* 697.

Lenfant, C., Stone, E., & Castelli, W. (1987). Celebrating 40 years of the Framingham Heart Study. *Journal of School Health, 57,* 279–281.

Liu, K., Stamler, J., Dyer, A., McKeever, J., & McKeever, P. (1978). Statistical methods to assess and minimize the role of intraindividual variability in obscuring the relationship between dietary lipids and serum cholesterol. *Journal of Chronic Diseases, 31,* 399–418.

Luepker, R. V., Perry, C. L., McKinlay, S. M., Nader, P. R., Parcel, G. S., Stone, E. J., Webber, L. S., Elder, J. P., Feldman, H. A., Johnson, C. C., Kelder, S. H., & Wu, M. (1996). Outcomes of a field trial to improve children's dietary patterns and physical activity: The Child and Adolescent Trial for Cardiovascular Health (CATCH). *Journal of the American Medical Association, 275*(10), 768–776.

Lytle, L. A., Davidann, B. Z., Bachman, K., Edmundson, E. W., Johnson, C. C., Reeds, J. N., Wambsgans, K. C., & Budman, S. (1994). Challenges of conducting process evaluation in a multicenter trial. *Health Education Quarterly,* (Suppl. 2), S129–S142.

Lytle, L. A., Nichaman, M. Z., Obarzanek, E., Glovsky, E., Montgomery, D., Nicklas, T., Zive, M. E., & Feldman, H. (1993). Validation of 24-hour recalls assisted by food records in third-grade children. *Journal of the American Dietetic Association, 93,* 1431–1436.

MacDougall, J. M., Dembroski, T. M., Dimsdale, J. E., & Hackett, T. P. (1985). Components of Type A, hostility and anger-in: Further relationships to angiographic findings. *Health Psychology, 4,* 137–152.

Mann, R. A. (1972). The behavior-therapeutic use of contingency contracting to control an adult behavior problem: Weight control. *Journal of Applied Behavior Analysis, 5,* 99–109.

Manuck, S. B., Kaplan, J. R., & Matthews, K. A. (1986). Behavioral antecedents of coronary heart disease and atherosclerosis. *Arteriosclerosis, 6,* 2–14.

Marlatt, G. A., & Gordon, J. R. (1980). Determinants of relapse: Implications for the maintenance of behavior change. In P. O. Davidson & S. M. Davidson (Eds.), *Behavioral medicine: Changing health lifestyles* (pp. 410–452). New York: Brunner/Mazel.

McGraw, S. A., Stone, E. J., Osganian, S. K., Elder, J. P., Perry, C. L., Johnson, C. C., Parcel, G. S., Webber, L. S., & Luepker, R. V. (1994). Design of process evaluation within the Child and Adolescent Trial for Cardiovascular Health (CATCH). *Health Education Quarterly,* (Suppl. 2), S5–S26.

McKenzie, T. L., Nader, P. R., Strikmiller, P. K., Yang, M., Stone, E. J., Perry, C. L., Taylor, W. C., Epping, J. N., Feldman, H. A., Luepker, R. V., & Kelder, S. H. (1996). School physical education: Effect of the Child and Adolescent Trial for Cardiovascular Health. *Preventive Medicine, 25,* 423–431.

McKenzie, T. L., Sallis, J. F., & Nader, P. R. (1991). SOFIT: System for observing fitness instruction time. *Journal of Teaching in Physical Education, 11,* 195–205.

McNamara, J. J., Molot, M. A., Stremple, J. F., & Cutting, R. T. (1971). Coronary artery disease in combat casualties in Vietnam. *Journal of the American Medical Association, 216,* 1185–1187.

Montgomery, D. H., Zive, M. M., Raizman, D., Nicklas, T., Snyder, P., Evans, M., Baker, N., Hann, B., & Bachman, K. (1995). *Description and evaluation of a food service intervention: Eat Smart training.* Manuscript submitted for publication.

Morgan, R. W., Jain, M., Miller, A. B., Choi, N. W., Matthews, V., Munan, L., Burch, J. D., Feather, J., Howe, G. R., & Kelly, A. (1978). A comparison of dietary methods in epidemiologic studies. *American Journal of Epidemiology, 107,* 488–498.

Nader, P. R., Sallis, J. F., Patterson, T. L., Abramson, I. S., Rupp, J. W., Senn, K. L., Atkins, C. J., Roppe, B. E., Morris, J. A., Wallace, U. P., & Vega, W. A. (1989). A family approach to cardiovascular risk reduction: Results from the San Diego Family Health Project. *Health Education Quarterly, 16,* 229–244.

National Institute on Alcohol Abuse and Alcoholism. (1987). *Sixth special report to the U.S. Congress on alcohol and health.* Washington, DC: U.S. Department of Health and Human Services.

Newman, W. P., Freedman, D. S., Voors, A. W., Gard, P. D., Srinivasan, S. R., Cresanta, J. L., Williamson, G. S., Webber, L. S., & Berenson, G. S. (1986). Relation of serum lipoprotein levels and systolic blood pressure to early atherosclerosis: The Bogalusa Heart Study. *New England Journal of Medicine, 314,* 138–144.

Nicklas, T. A. (1995). Dietary studies of children and young adults (1973–1988): The Bogalusa Heart Study. *American Journal of Medical Sciences, 310*(Suppl. 1), S101–S108.

Nicklas, T. A. (1995). Dietary studies of children: The Bogalusa Heart Study Experience. *Journal of the American Dietetic Association, 95,* 1127–1133.

Nicklas, T. A., Arbeit, M. L., Johnson, C. C., Franklin, F. A., & Berenson, G. S. (1987). A family approach to cardiovascular risk reduction through diet (GEM No. 86). *Journal of Nutrition Education, 19,* 302A.

Nicklas, T. A., Arbeit, M. L., Johnson, C. C., Franklin, F. A., & Berenson, G. S. (1988). "Heart Smart" program: A family intervention program for eating behavior of children at high risk for cardiovascular disease. *Journal of Nutrition Education, 20,* 128–132.

Nicklas, T. A., Farris, R. P., Smoak, C. G., Frank, G. C., Srinivasan, S. R., Webber, L. S., & Berenson, G. S. (1988). Dietary factors relate to cardiovascular risk factors in early life: The Bogalusa Heart Study. *Arteriosclerosis, 8,* 193–199.

Nicklas, T. A., Farris, R. P., Srinivasan, S. R., Webber, L. S., & Berenson, G. S. (1989). Nutritional studies in children and implications for change: The Bogalusa Heart Study. *Journal of Advances in Medicine, 2,* 451–474.

Nicklas, T. A., Forcier, J. E., Farris, R. P., Hunter, S. M., Webber, L. S., & Berenson, G. S. (1989). Heart Smart School Lunch Program: A vehicle for cardiovascular health promotion. *Journal of Health Promotion, 4,* 91–100.

Nicklas, T. A., Johnson, C. C., Arbeit, M. L., Franklin, F. A., & Berenson, G. S. (1988). A dynamic family approach for the prevention of cardiovascular disease. *Journal of the American Dietetic Association, 88,* 1438–1440.

Nicklas, T. A., Johnson, C. C., Myers, L., Webber, L. S., & Berenson, G. S. (1995). Eating patterns, nutrient intakes and alcohol consumption patterns of young adults: The Bogalusa Heart Study. *Medicine, Exercise, Nutrition and Health, 4,* 316–324.

Nicklas, T. A., O'Neil, C., Carroll, A., Shi, R., & Berenson, G. S. (1996). Part 1. Training institute: An effective training program for implementing dietary guidelines in school meals. *School Food Service Research Review, 20*(1), 34–39.

Nicklas, T. A., Stone, E., Montgomery, D., Snyder, P., Zive, M., Ebzery, M. K., Clesi, A., Hann, B., & Dwyer, J. (1994). Meeting the dietary goals for school meals by the year 2000:

The CATCH Eat Smart School Nutrition Program. *Journal of Health Education, 25,* 299–307.

Nicklas, T. A., Webber, L. S., Kern, S. L., Powers, C. R., Harsha, D. W., & Berenson, G. S. (1993). Fort Polk Heart Smart Program Part 3: Assessment of dietary intake of military wives. *Military Medicine, 158,* 312–316.

Nicklas, T. A., Webber, L. S., Srinivasan, S. R., & Berenson, G. S. (1993). Secular trends in dietary intakes and cardiovascular risk factors of 10-year-old children, 1973–1988. *American Journal of Clinical Nutrition, 57,* 930–937.

Osler, W. (1892). *Lectures on angina pectoris and allied states.* New York: Appleton.

Park, Y. K., & Yetley, E. A. (1990). Trend changes in use and current intakes of tropical oils in the United States. *American Journal of Clinical Nutrition, 51,* 738–748.

Perrier Corp. (1979). *Fitness in America: The Perrier study.* Great Waters, NY: Author.

Perry, C. L., Luepker, R., Murray, D., Kurth, C., Mulis, R., Crockett, S., & Jacobs, D. (1988). Parent involvement with children's health promotion: The Minnesota Home Team. *American Journal of Public Health, 79,* 1156–1160.

Perry, C. L., Stone, E. J., Parcel, G. S., Ellison, R. C., Nader, P. R., Webber, L. S., & Luepker, R. V. (1990). School-based cardiovascular health promotion: The Child and Adolescent Trial for Cardiovascular Health (CATCH). *Journal of School Health, 60,* 406–413.

Powell, K. E., Caspersen, C. J., & Loplan, J. P. (1989). Physical activity and chronic disease. *American Journal of Clinical Nutrition, 49,* 999–1006.

Rimm, D. C., & Masters, J. C. (1979). *Behavior therapy: Techniques and empirical findings* (pp. 177–179). New York: Academic Press.

Rose, G. (1981). Strategy of prevention: Lessons from cardiovascular disease. *British Medical Journal, 282,* 1847–1851.

Rossow, I., & Rise, J. (1994). Concordance of parental and adolescent health behaviors. *Social Science Medicine, 38,* 1299–1305.

Rutter, M., Maughan, B., Mortimore, P., & Ouston, J. (1979). *Fifteen thousand hours: Secondary schools and their effects on children.* London: Open Books.

Sallis, J. F., Harsha, D., Strikmiller, P., Ehlinger, S., Williston, B. J., Davidann, B., Woods, S., Cribb, P., Osganian, V., & Stone, E. (1995). *Validation of interviewer- and self-administered physical activity checklists for fifth-grade students.* Manuscript submitted for publication.

Sallis, J. F., & Nader, P. R. (1988). Family determinants of health behaviors. In D. S. Gochman (Ed.), *Health behavior: Emerging Research Perspectives* (pp. 107–124). New York: Plenum Press.

Salonen, J. T., Puska, P., & Tuomilehto, J. (1982). Physical activity and risk of myocardial infarction, cerebral stroke and death: A longitudinal study in Eastern Finland. *American Journal of Epidemiology, 115,* 526–537.

Schultz, J. M. (1991). Smoking-attributable mortality and years of potential life lost: United States, 1988. *Morbidity and Mortality Weekly Report, 40,* 62–71.

Serpas, D. C., Harsha, D. W., Virgilio, S. J., & Berenson, G. S. (1989). *Heart Smart: Superkids-Superfit exercise curriculum for cardiovascular health* (2nd ed.). New Orleans: Louisiana State University Medical Center.

Shear, C. L., Freedman, D. S., Burke, G. L., Harsha, D. W., Webber, L. S., & Berenson, G. S. (1988). Secular trends of obesity in early life: The Bogalusa Heart Study. *American Journal of Public Health, 73,* 75–77.

Skinner, B. F. (1953). *Science and human behavior.* New York: Macmillan.

Smoak, C. G., Burke, G. C., Webber, L. S., Harsha, D. W., Srinivasan, S. R., & Berenson, G. S. (1987). Relation of obesity to clustering of cardiovascular disease risk factors in children and young adults: The Bogalusa Heart Study. *American Journal of Epidemiology, 125,* 364–372.

Srinivasan, S. R., & Berenson, G. S. (1995). Serum apolipoproteins A-1 and B as markers of coronary artery disease risk in early life: The Bogalusa Heart Study. *Clinical Chemistry, 4,* 159–164.

Srinivasan, S. R., Frerichs, R. R., Webber, L. S., & Berenson, G. S. (1976). Serum lipoprotein profile in children from a biracial community: The Bogalusa Heart Study. *Circulation, 54,* 309–318.

Stone, E. J. (1990). ACCESS: Keystones for school health promotion. *Journal of School Health, 60,* 298–300.

Stone, E. J., & Perry, C. L. (1990). United States: Perspectives in school health. *Journal of School Health, 60,* 363–369.

Strong, J. P., Oalmann, M. C., Newman, W. P., III, Tracy, R. E., Malcom, G. T., Johnson, W. D., McMahan, L. H., Rock, W. A., Jr., & Guzman, M. A. (1984). Coronary heart disease in young black and white males in New Orleans: Community Pathology Study. *American Heart Journal, 108,* 747–759.

Strong, W. B., & Dennison, B. A. (1988). Pediatric preventive cardiology: Atherosclerosis and coronary heart disease. *Pediatric Review, 9,* 303–314.

Suarez, E. C., & Williams, R. B., Jr. (1992). Interactive models of reactivity: The relationship between hostility and potentially pathogenic physiological responses to social stressors. In N. Schneiderman, P. McCabe, & A. Baum (Eds.), *Perspectives in behavioral medicine: Stress and disease processes* (pp. 179–195). Hillsdale, NJ: Erlbaum.

Taioli, E., & Wynder, E. L. (1991). Effect of the age at which smoking begins on frequency of smoking in adulthood [Letter]. *New England Journal of Medicine, 325,* 968–969.

Thompson, F. E., & Dennison, B. A. (1994). Dietary sources of fats and cholesterol in U.S. children aged 2 through 5 years. *American Journal of Public Health, 84,* 799–806.

Turley, K. R., Wilmore, J. H., Simons-Morton, B., Williston, J. M., Epping, J. R., & Dahlstrom, G. (1994). The reliability and validity of the 9-minute run in third-grade children. *Pediatric Exercise Science, 6,* 178–187.

U.S. Department of Agriculture. (1994). National school lunch program and school breakfast program: School meals initiative for healthy children. *Federal Register, 7,* CFR Parts 210, 220.

U.S. Department of Health and Human Services (USDHHS). (1980). *Promoting health/preventing disease objectives for the nation.* Washington, DC: U.S. Government Printing Office.

U.S. Department of Health and Human Services (USDHHS). (1988). *The Surgeon General's report on nutrition and health* (DHHS Publication No. 88-50210). Washington, DC: U.S. Government Printing Office.

U.S. Public Health Service. (1980). *The health consequences of smoking for women.* Washington, DC: U.S. Government Printing Office.

U.S. Public Health Service. (1982). *The health consequences of smoking: Cancer* (DHHS Publication No. 82-50179). Washington, DC: U.S. Government Printing Office.

U.S. Public Health Service. (1983). *The health consequences of smoking: Cardiovascular disease* (DHHS Publication No. 84-50204). Washington, DC: U.S. Government Printing Office.

U.S. Public Health Service. (1989). *Reducing the health consequences of smoking: 25 years of progress. A report of the Surgeon General* (DHHS Publication No. 89-8411). Washington, DC: U.S. Government Printing Office.

U.S. Public Health Service. (1990). *Healthy people 2000: National health promotion and disease prevention objectives.* Washington, DC: U.S. Government Printing Office.

U.S. Public Health Service. (1994). *Preventing tobacco use among young people: A report of the surgeon general* (Publication No. 017-001-00491-0). Washington, DC: U.S. Government Printing Office.

Urbina, E., & Berenson, G. S. (1994). Children, hypertension and hypertensive diseases. *Journal of Hypertension Control, 4,* 3–5.

Voors, A. W., Foster, T. A., Frerichs, P. R., Webber, L. S., & Berenson, G. S. (1976). Studies of blood pressure in children, ages 5–14 years, in a total biracial community: The Bogalusa Heart Study. *Circulation, 54,* 319–327.

Walter, H. J., & Wynder, E. L. (1989). The development, implementation, evaluation, and future directions of a chronic disease prevention program for children: The "Know Your Body" studies. *Preventive Medicine, 18,* 59–71.

Ward, S., & Wackman, D. (1972). Television advertising and intrafamily influences on children's purchase influence attempts and parental yielding. *Journal of Marketing Research, 9,* 316.

Wattigney, W. A., Webber, L. S., Srinivasan, S. R., & Berenson, G. S. (1995). The emergence of clinically abnormal levels of cardiovascular disease risk-factor variables in young adults: The Bogalusa Heart Study. *Preventive Medicine, 24,* 612–626.

Waxman, M., & Stunkard, A. J. (1980). Calorie intake and expenditure of obese boys. *Journal of Pediatrics, 96,* 187.

Webber, L. S., Harsha, D. W., Nicklas, T. A., & Berenson, G. S. (1994). Secular trends in obesity in childhood. In L. J. Filer, Jr., R. M. Lauer, & R. V. Luepker (Eds.), *Prevention of atherosclerosis and hypertension beginning in youth* (pp. 194–203). Philadelphia: Lea & Febiger.

Webber, L. S., Hunter, S. M., Baugh, J. G., Srinivasan, S. R., Sklov, M. C., & Berenson, G. S. (1982). The interaction of cigarette smoking, oral contraceptive use, and cardiovascular risk factor variables in children: The Bogalusa Heart Study. *American Journal of Public Health, 72,* 266–274.

Webber, L. S., Hunter, S. M., Johnson, C. C., Srinivasan, S. R., & Berenson, G. S. (1991). Smoking, alcohol, and oral contraceptives. Effects on lipids during adolescence and young adulthood: The Bogalusa Heart Study. Hyperlipidemia in childhood and the development of atherosclerosis. *Annals of the New York Academy of Sciences, 623,* 135–154.

Webber, L. S., Osganian, V., Luepker, R. V., Feldman, H. A., Stone, E. J., Elder, J. P., Perry, C. L., Nader, P. R., Parcel, G. S., Broyles, S. L., & McKinlay, S. M. (1995). Cardiovascular risk factors among third grade children in four regions of the United States. The CATCH Study. *American Journal of Epidemiology, 141,* 428–439.

Webber, L. S., Srinivasan, S. R., & Berenson, G. S. (1993). Epidemiology of early cardiovascular disease: Observations from the Bogalusa Heart Study. *American Journal of Human Biology, 5,* 433–450.

Webber, L. S., Srinivasan, S. R., Harsha, D. W., Powers, C. R., & Berenson, G. S. (1993). Fort Polk Heart Smart Program Part 2: Cardiovascular risk factor assessment. *Military Medicine, 158,* 308–311.

Webber, L. S., Srinivasan, S. R., Wattigney, W., & Berenson, G. S. (1991). Tracking of serum lipids and lipoproteins from childhood to adulthood: The Bogalusa Heart Study. *American Journal of Epidemiology, 133,* 884–899.

Webber, L. S., Voors, A. W., Srinivasan, S. R., Frerichs, R. R., & Berenson, G. S. (1979). Occurrence in children of multiple risk factors in coronary artery disease: The Bogalusa Heart Study. *Preventive Medicine, 8,* 407–418.

Weidman, W., Jr., Kwiterovich, P., Jesse, M. J., & Nugent, E. (1983). American Heart Association Committee Report—Diet in the healthy child. Task Force Committee of the Nutrition

Committee and the Cardiovascular Disease in the Young Council of the American Heart Association. *Circulation, 67,* 1411A–1414A.

Weldman, W. H., Elveback, L. R., Nelson, R. A., Hodgson, P. A., & Ellefson, R. D. (1978). Nutrient intake and serum cholesterol level in normal children 6 to 16 years of age. *Pediatrics, 61,* 354–359.

West, D. W., Graham, S., Swanson, M., & Wilkinson, G. (1977). Five-year follow-up of a smoking withdrawal clinic population. *American Journal of Public Health, 67,* 537–544.

Williams, D. R. (1992). Black-white differences in blood pressure: The role of social factors. *Ethnicity and Disease, 2,* 126–141.

Wolf, T. M., Sklov, M. C., Wenzl, P. A., Hunter, S. M., & Berenson, G. S. (1982). Validation of a measure of Type A behavior pattern in children: The Bogalusa Heart Study. *Child Development, 53,* 126–135.

Young, D. L., Leong, M., & Pennell, M. D. (1984). Relationship between sodium intake in infancy and at 4 years of age. *Nutrition Research, 4,* 553–560.

CHAPTER 13

Unintentional Injury and Child Abuse and Neglect

DEBORAH BROWN and LIZETTE PETERSON

Description of the Problem

Although it has been killing more than 142,000 Americans every year (National Committee for Injury Prevention and Control, 1989), there is a "neglected disease" (National Academy of Sciences, 1966) in this country that is only now beginning to receive critical attention. Facing its annual toll of $133 billion (National Committee for Injury Prevention and Control, 1989) to $158 billion (Rice & Mackenzie, 1989), national agencies such as the National Institute for Child Health and Human Development (NICHD), and the Centers for Disease Control (CDC) are calling for grant proposals to find ways of overcoming it. In fact, researchers from a variety of disciplines and a number of different countries convened in 1993 at the Second World Congress and in 1996 at the Third World Congress on Injury Control to discuss this looming health threat: unintentional injuries.

Unintentional injuries are responsible for the overwhelming majority of child fatalities (Baker, O'Neill, & Karpf, 1984; Dershewitz & Williamson, 1977). Although the mortality rate from AIDS continues to climb at an alarming rate (Bindels, Reijneueld, Mulder-Folkerts, Coutinho, & van den Hoek, 1994; Casabona, Blanch, Vall, & Salvador, 1993), unintentional injuries remain the leading cause of premature mortality in the United States (CDC, 1994a). Based on mortality data from 1980, a report from the *Journal of the American Medical Association* concluded, "For children aged 5 to 9 years [in 1985], the estimated risk of dying of injuries during the subsequent 15 years is 2.6 times the risk of dying of all other causes combined" (Budnick & Chaiken, 1985, p. 3351).

Unintentional injuries were previously termed "accidents," which erroneously suggested an etiology of chance or bad luck, and inherently precluded prevention efforts. One purpose of this chapter will be to review evidence that suggests other etiologies (e.g., characteristics of the caregiver, the child, and the environment) contribute to unintentional injuries, thereby marking potential points for intervention. This chapter will also review current prevention strategies, offer suggestions for future prevention strategies, and list important obstacles faced in implementing those strategies in the real world context.

SCOPE OF THE PROBLEM

One obstacle to establishing broad spectrum, effective preventive interventions should be presented at the outset; there has been a historic separation between the study of unintentional injuries and injuries due to child abuse and neglect, even though there are clear similarities between the etiologies and the consequences of these events, and it is often impossible to differentiate between the two types of injuries (Peterson & Brown, 1994). Like unintentional injuries, injuries due to child abuse and neglect in the United States extract a heavy price; almost $500 million has been spent annually on resulting medical and foster care for maltreated children (American Association for Protecting Children, 1985; Daro, 1988). Child abuse is also responsible for a significant percentage of American child fatalities; an unknown number of cases of fatal child abuse apparently go unreported (Ewigman, Kivlahan, & Land, 1993). Of the almost 3 million cases of maltreatment that are reported annually (National Committee to Prevent Child Abuse, 1994), 1,400 result in death (Daro & McCurdy, 1992). Like researchers who study unintentional injuries, researchers in the child abuse and neglect field have progressed from unidimensional models of parent pathology (Cohen, Raphling, & Green, 1966; Heins, 1969; Helfer, 1977) to multidimensional models that consider the entire context (e.g., Garbarino, 1977, 1981). This trend paralleled the progress of unintentional injury researchers from a focus on the injury (De Haven, 1942) to a focus that includes the person and his or her context (Scheidt, 1988).

Not only do child abuse and neglect and unintentional injury show notable similarities, but the two types of injury are sometimes indistinguishable. For example, the strange patterns of head injury described by physicians, such as John Caffey in 1946, were misdiagnosed as unintentional injuries until 1962, when the correct diagnosis of the *battered child syndrome* was introduced (Kempe et al., 1962). More recently, Ewigman et al. (1993) reported that as many as 32% of 384 child fatalities officially documented as unintentional injuries were due to maltreatment, and only 11% were clearly not due to abuse or neglect. Their findings underscore the large prevalence of cases in which an indisputable diagnosis is difficult, leading some authors to call for autopsies in these instances (Wilske & Eisenmenger, 1991).

The problem is compounded by the low utility of the term "neglect," when no guidelines for nonneglectful supervision have been established. Neglect is typically defined by a failure to provide supervision in accordance with community standards (Christoffel et al., 1992). However, research has shown that no such standards actually exist. For example, Peterson, Ewigman, and Kivlahan (1993) found an alarming range of opinions and a virtual absence of consensus across and within groups of mothers, physicians, and Division of Family Services (DFS) employees on what constituted the safe supervision of children from birth to the age 10 years. Not only are the criteria for physical neglect unclear, but physical neglect also remains undifferentiated from other types of neglect (e.g., physical neglect vs. emotional neglect; see Paget, Philip, & Abramczyk, 1993, for review). Both the lack of standard delineations among injuries due to neglect, abuse, or unintentional injury, and the inability of health professionals to make these delineations conclusively, argue for a common label. This argument is further strengthened by evidence presented later in this chapter, which will show the commonalities that exist when examining the etiologies of these different types of injury. Because of these blurred boundaries of definition and commonalities in etiology, this chapter will consider child injury as a whole when reviewing the literature, unifying the fields of child maltreatment and unintentional injury and presenting the consequent advantages.

CAUSES AND CONSEQUENCES

"Causes": Risk Factors Associated with Child Injury

Causal research with injury is logically implausible, because it would necessitate an experimental design that included highly undesirable conditions (e.g., injuring children). Previous research on injury prevention (e.g., Garbarino, 1977; Rappaport, 1977) has revealed that child injuries are significantly correlated with a number of risk factors. The current authors (Peterson & Brown, 1994) constructed a working model (see Figure 13.1) that organizes these risk factors into a 2 × 3 matrix. Although this working model incorporates empirical findings, its validity as a complete, independent paradigm has not yet been established.

First, risk factors were divided into "background contributors" and "immediate contributors." Background contributors are more chronic, global variables that characterize the context in which an injury is more likely to occur (e.g., where poverty and ongoing emotional disturbance of the caregiver are present). The immediate contributors are more acute, specific variables that characterize a rather brief period

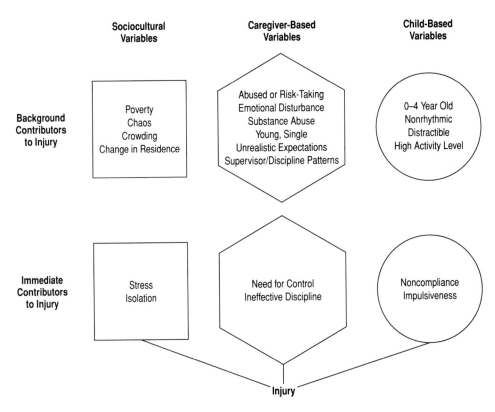

Figure 13.1.   Risk factors associated with child injury.

in which injury is more likely to occur (e.g., when the child behaves noncompliantly while the caregiver is experiencing an already high level of stress). In addition to this division between background and immediate contributors to injury, a second division separated sociocultural, caregiver-based, and child-based variables. Arguably, variables in the resulting cells of the 2 by 3 matrix could be placed in different cells (e.g., caregiver isolation may be a chronic rather than an acute stressor). Also, this matrix does not clarify interrelationships among variables (see McLoyd, 1990, for a model that focuses on interactions among etiological factors). However, this preliminary model offers both clinicians and researchers in the real world context a clear and empirically based conceptualization of the etiology of child injuries.

Sociocultural Variables

Poverty is the sociocultural variable that shows the strongest relationship with both unintentional injury (Gallagher, Finson, Guyer, & Goodenough, 1984) and injury resulting from maltreatment (Daro, 1988), with the most frequent injuries occurring in the most impoverished households. Westfelt (1982) reported that low income was a strong predictor of unintentional injury within a Swedish sample, and an American sample of children from low-income households had more than a 2.5 relative risk of suffering a fatal unintentional injury in comparison with middle-income children (Nersesian, Petit, Shaper, Lemieux, & Naor, 1985). Paralleling the findings from unintentional injury research, child maltreatment researchers reported that 65% to 81% of families accused of maltreatment earned less than $7,000 per year (American Humane Society, 1978; Pelton, 1977).

A second important sociocultural variable is chaos in the household, defined here as a loud, confusing, unpredictable family environment. A longitudinal twin study linked this type of chaos to unintentional injury (Matheny, 1987, 1993), and survey data from 2,083 people nationwide suggested a link between chaos and abuse (Straus, Gelles, & Steinmetz, 1980; Williams, 1978). Furthermore, a prospective study of 400 mothers showed that the women who were more likely to maltreat their children were those living in the most chaotic environments (Olds, Hendersen, Chamberlin, & Tatelbaum, 1986).

Crowding, both in the household and in the neighborhood or community, is a third sociocultural variable associated with injury. Consistent with an early review of the existing research (Parke & Collmer, 1975), Gray, Cutler, Dean, and Kempe (1977) reported that children born to women in crowded conditions had a greater risk of being hospitalized for maltreatment than children born to women with similar incomes but in less crowded environments. Also, more child injuries seem to be reported in areas documented by census data as crowded (Rivara & Barber, 1985).

Children who experience frequent changes in residence may be at greater risk for suffering unintentional injuries (Beautrais, Fergusson, & Shannon, 1982) or being maltreated (Altemeier, O'Connor, Vietze, Sandler, & Sherrod, 1984; Lauer, Ten Broeck, & Grossman, 1974). Like crowding and chaos, frequent changes in residence may be experienced more commonly by families living in poverty—adding to these children's already elevated risk of injury. Child injuries are not unique to lower-income families (Daro, 1988; Gallagher et al., 1984). However, poverty and the variables that often co-occur with it can create a riskier background context.

Against these background contributors, two immediate risk factors may occur at the sociocultural level: stress and isolation. Researchers have linked high levels of stress to unintentional injuries such as drownings (Pearn & Nixon, 1977), and fractures, burns, and injuries sustained in motor vehicle collisions (Beautrais et al., 1982). Other researchers have documented the link between stress and maltreatment (Daro, 1988; Green, Gaines, & Sangrund, 1974; Wolfe, 1988). Moreover, Garbarino (1977) pointed out that stress arising from a death or separation may be magnified by the resulting social isolation. Social isolation, in turn, may indirectly contribute to unintentional injuries (e.g., Pearn & Nixon, 1977), perhaps because less adult supervision is available, or perhaps because child maltreatment occurs (Giovannoni & Billingsley, 1970; Monaghan & Buckfield, 1981) occurring when there are fewer potential witnesses present. Isolation may also co-occur with caregiver problems such as emotional disturbance, substance abuse, or other variables associated with a maltreating caregiver (Garbarino, 1977), as reviewed in the next section.

Caregiver-Based Variables

Unintentional injury research has shown that the children of depressed caregivers may be as much as four times more likely to suffer unintentional injuries than children of nondepressed caregivers (Brown & Davidson, 1978), particularly in high-risk situations (Garbarino, Kostelny, & Dubros, 1991). Similarly, early research on the etiology of child abuse and neglect focused on the emotional disturbance of the caregiver (Cohen et al., 1966; Heins, 1969; Helfer, 1977). The risk of child injuries seems to be influenced not only by caregivers' current psychological health, but also by their histories. For example, caregivers' history has been linked with the unintentional injuries of their children; those who took greater risks as children seem to have children who experience more unintentional injuries (Rivara & Mueller, 1987). Also, research suggests that caregivers who were abused as children may be more likely to maltreat their own children (e.g., Kaufman & Zigler, 1987; Sroufe & Fleeson, 1986; Widom, 1989), although biological variables (DiLalla & Gottesman, 1991) and attachment style (Zeanah & Zeanah, 1989) have been proposed as mediators in this relationship.

Another caregiver-based variable related to child injury is substance abuse. Not only are substance-abusing caregivers more likely to unintentionally injure themselves (Wilson, Baker, Teret, Shock, & Garbarino, 1991), but also their children have a higher risk of being seriously injured than the children of caregivers who do not abuse alcohol or drugs (Bijur, Kurzon, Overpeck, & Scheidt, 1992; Westfelt, 1982). Furthermore, the National Clinical Evaluation Study (Berkeley Planning Associates, 1983) concluded that substance abuse is a key predictor of child abuse and neglect.

Demographically, caregivers' youth and status as single parents may be risk factors for child injury. Researchers have linked both caregivers' youth (Beautrais et al., 1982; McCormick, Shapiro, & Starfield, 1981) and single marital status (Rivara & Mueller, 1987) with unintentional injuries (e.g., pedestrian injuries, Rivara & Barber, 1985). In the same vein, child abuse and neglect seem to be associated with caregivers' youth (Lynch, 1975; Young, 1982) and single marital status (American Association for Protecting Children, 1986; Giovannoni & Billingsley, 1970).

Even older, married caregivers who are free of emotional disturbance, substance abuse, and a history of risk taking may have a child at higher risk of injury in a situation marked by immediate caregiver-based contributors, such as a temporarily high need for control or a disciplinary action that has not achieved quick satisfaction. A lack of critical parenting information, including realistic expectations and appropriate supervision and discipline strategies, has also been linked to both unintentional injury and injury due to abuse. Specifically, underestimating children's range of movement (Roberts & Wright, 1982) or overestimating children's ability to keep themselves safe (Peterson, 1989) may lead to inadequate supervision and the greater likelihood of injury (Wilson et al., 1991). On the other hand, parents who abuse their children frequently display both sporadically excessive supervision of their children's behavior (Herrenkohl, Herrenkohl, & Egolf, 1983; Monroe & Schellenbach, 1989) and harsh discipline when children fail to meet their unrealistic expectations (Azar & Rohrbeck, 1986), suggesting that a balance of parental expectation and intervention is optimal.

Child-Based Variables

Just as a caregiver's young age is a risk factor for child injury, children of younger ages (0–4) are more likely to die from unintentional injuries (Baker, O'Neill, & Karpf, 1984) or from maltreatment (American Association for Protecting Children, 1986) than older children. Infants are particularly vulnerable if they are nonrhythmic (i.e., if they show daily eating and sleeping cycles that are asynchronous with those of most caregivers). Children who show irregular sleeping and eating patterns are more likely than other family members to experience unintentional injuries (Matheny, 1987) or to be maltreated (Herrenkohl & Herrenkohl, 1979).

In addition to young age and irregular rhythms, children who have symptoms of attention-deficit/hyperactivity disorder (ADHD) and conduct disorder (see *DSM-IV*, American Psychiatric Association, 1994) are at special risk of injury. Distractibility has been linked with both unintentional injuries (Zuckerman & Duby, 1985) and child abuse and neglect (Egeland, Sroufe, & Erickson, 1983; Wolfe, 1988). Also, high activity levels seem to place children at greater risk of suffering unintentional injuries (Gayton, Bailey, Wagner, & Hardesty, 1986; Hartsough & Lambert, 1985) and child abuse and neglect (Daro, 1988). Similarly, conduct disorder symptoms, such as aggressive responding or rule breaking, seem to co-occur with unintentional injury (Bijur, Stewart-Brown, & Butler, 1986; see Taylor et al., 1986, for review) and abuse (Bousha & Twentyman, 1984; Lorber, Felton, & Reid, 1984; Reid, Taplin, & Loeber, 1981). When a child suddenly acts impulsively or argumentatively in a context of other risky sociocultural, caregiver-based, or child-based background variables, that child is at particularly high risk for injury.

Summary of Variables Related to Injury

On a sociocultural level, a risky background context for injury would be characterized by a low-income, chaotic household, where moves from one crowded area to another are common. If this household were at maximum risk of injury, at least two people would reside there. First, there would be a young, single caregiver with a history of risk taking or abuse. The caregiver would not have realistic expectations for children or appropriate supervision or disciplinary strategies, and he or she would be abusing alcohol or drugs in an effort to cope with feelings of depression or of being overwhelmed. Second, there would be a nonrhythmic, distractible toddler with a high energy level. Particularly at a time when there is tension in this high-risk household and other adults are absent, an acute situation would be characterized by the toddler's impulsive, noncompliant behavior despite the caregiver's attempts to supervise and discipline. If the caregiver surrenders control and becomes less vigilant of risks to the child, unintentional injury is more likely to occur. If the caregiver is feeling a high need for control, or does not manage his or her anger well, physical abuse is more likely to occur. Being able to identify high-risk chronic and acute situations in which children may be injured is critical for developing programs that prevent child injuries and their potentially fatal consequences.

Consequences of Child Injury

Researchers have documented significant short-term and long-term consequences of child maltreatment. Documented short-term consequences cover a wide range of children's functioning, including cognitive, social, emotional, behavioral, and physical problems. Many of these problems continue into adulthood, potentially contributing to other long-term problems such as substance abuse. Although the consequences of most unintentional injuries have not been researched as extensively or at as many levels of functioning as has child maltreatment, there is evidence linking unintentional head injury to cognitive problems and broader psychopathology as well. Furthermore, one of the most serious consequences of injury, traumatic brain injury, has been linked to psychosocial problems ranging from attention difficulties and impulsivity to peer problems and aggressiveness, outcomes similar to those seen in abused children. The reader must also realize that some of these factors may have existed premorbidly and may be the cause rather than the result of the trauma. Further, although a single event is usually identified as the source of traumatic brain injury, damage inflicted by parents may have existed, undiagnosed, as well. Finally, no differences were found between unintentionally injured children and maltreated children on any of the variables included in a rare study that compared the two (Friedman & Morse, 1974). Thus, there is some limited, preliminary evidence that unintentionally injured children may share maltreated children's vulnerability toward the problems discussed in the following subsections.

Cognitive Problems

Unintentional injuries that result in unconsciousness or posttraumatic amnesia are often followed by impaired intellectual performance (Klonoff, Crockett, & Clark, 1984). Similarly, maltreated children appear to score significantly lower on intelligence tests than do other children (see Ammerman, Cassisi, Hersen, & Van Hasselt, 1986, for review). This finding remained significant even in samples from which children with head injuries had been excluded (e.g., Appelbaum, 1980), helping to rule out traumatic brain injury per se as a cause (Brandwein, 1973). The corresponding academic performance of both children with traumatic brain injuries (Farmer & Peterson, 1995) and maltreated children (Hufton & Oates, 1977; Salzinger, Kaplan, Pelcovitz, Samit, & Krieger, 1984) appears to be compromised, as is their acquisition of verbal skills (see Jaffe et al., 1993, for review of unintentionally injured children, and Law & Conway, 1992, for review of maltreated children). Begali (1992) described a range of outcomes for children with traumatic brain injury, including employment difficulties as adults. Malinosky-Rummell and Hansen (1993) similarly reported that maltreated children also seem to be more likely to have vocational problems as adults, but they noted that little empirical data are available.

Social Problems

Unintentionally injured children who suffered brain trauma may have more difficulty maintaining peer relationships because these children often experience deficits in their ability to decode social cues, to maintain awareness of self and others, to avoid self-consciousness about obvious medical conditions, and to maintain a positive self-esteem (Ylvisaker, Urbanczyk, & Feeney, 1992). While noting the presence of numerous mediating variables and the need for further research, Conaway and Hansen (1989) similarly concluded their review of maltreated children's social behavior by stating, "The literature indicates that physically abused and neglected children are more likely than nonabused peers to have problems related to social behavior," (p. 650). For decades, maltreated children have been described as temperamental and needy (e.g., Gaensbauer & Sands, 1968; Johnson & Morse, 1968), with poor social skills and noted periods of withdrawal. In adulthood, a history of being maltreated may be significantly correlated with a negative attitude toward interpersonal interactions (see Malinosky-Rummell & Hansen, 1993).

Emotional Problems

Whether it is a direct outcome of the trauma or an emotional reaction to the social and cognitive challenges secondary to their condition, children who have sustained brain injury show a variety of emotional problems. Mood swings, depression, poor anger control, apathy, and low frustration tolerance are frequently reported in the literature (Fletcher & Levin, 1988; Mateer & Williams, 1991). It is noted, however, that premorbid levels of these characteristics are often unknown and may have contributed to the injuries in the first place. In childhood, maltreatment has also been associated with a host of emotional problems, ranging from low self-esteem and depression to uncontrolled temper tantrums (see Gelardo & Sanford, 1987). Studies of inpatient women, college women, and alcoholic men also indicate a relationship between childhood maltreatment and adult emotional problems such as those listed on the Symptom Checklist-90-Revised (see Malinosky-Rummell & Hansen, 1993). As with traumatic injury, however, a causal relationship between maltreatment and emotional difficulties cannot be assumed.

Behavioral Problems

The loss of certain "executive functions," which often occurs with frontal lobe brain injuries, can result in a host of behavioral problems, such as poor attention, impulsivity, and aggressiveness (Levin et al., 1994). Child maltreatment also may be correlated with aggressive behavior and juvenile delinquency, although the relationship seems to be influenced by variables such as socioeconomic status and the gender of the child (see Koski, 1988, for review). George and Main (1979) reported that abused children physically hurt other children twice as frequently as did their peers. Maltreated children appear to have less effective coping and self-soothing skills (Egeland, Sroufe, & Erickson, 1983; Gaensbauer & Sands, 1979). Adults who were abused as children also show maladaptive coping strategies (e.g., self-harm behaviors) more frequently than nonabused adults (see Malinosky-Rummell & Hansen, 1993). Also, maltreating behavior may be passed down to subsequent generations, such that abused children become abusive caregivers, as discussed later in this chapter.

Physical Problems

Ammerman et al. (1986) reviewed the rather shocking physical damage that can result from brain injuries sustained through child maltreatment. According to their review, the physical problems associated with abuse may include cerebral palsy (Diamond &

Jaudes, 1983), brain damage (Buchanan & Oliver, 1977), perceptual-motor deficits (Green, Voeller, Gaines, & Kubie, 1981), and restricted movement due to skeletal damage (Fontana, 1984). All of these outcomes are likely to be manifested by unintentionally injured children as well. Although some of these physical problems appear to be a precursor rather than a consequence of some injuries (Ammerman et al., 1986), caregivers should be fully aware of the potentially permanent damage that could result from a single serious injury. Brain damage may be the most frequently disabling or fatal outcome of injury, but burns or lacerations with subsequent scarring and injuries to bones, joints, and muscles which may limit motor abilities are also sources of potentially lifelong disability (Tarnowski, 1994). Indeed, many professionals may underestimate the damage that could result from some child injuries (Johnson, 1992).

Summary of Problems Related to Child Injury

This section has reviewed the potential consequences of child injury, which can have lasting effects through adulthood and even, in some cases, subsequent generations. Taken in conjunction with the information related to the millions of children who experience injuries annually, these problems highlight the need for appropriate interventions. However, as seen in the next section, many challenges need to be surmounted before effective intervention can take place.

IMPEDIMENTS TO INTERVENTION IN THE REAL WORLD CONTEXT

Schisms

As has been suggested thus far, one factor that has slowed progress in the area of treatment efforts has been the fractionation of research between the fields of unintentional injury and child abuse and neglect. In addition, both fields have been reluctant to move from a descriptive, epidemiological approach to a treatment orientation, and prevention has only recently benefited from a more person-focused, behavioral orientation.

Lack of Constituency

Both injury fields face the problem common to much of prevention: the absence of a clear constituency needed to lobby for change. Caregivers tend to worry about threats such as drugs and abduction rather than the much higher threat implied by the significantly greater base rate of injury (Eichelberger, Gotschall, Feely, Harstad, & Bowman, 1990). Few parents identify their children as a high-risk candidate for injury. The area of abuse and neglect is further hampered by the resistance to treatment that is frequently displayed by caregivers accused of maltreating their children. Indeed, individuals who are mandated to receive treatment seem to begin their participation with a strongly negative attitude and far less motivation to change than do parents prior to adjudication (Wolfe, 1988). In both types of injury, individuals who could benefit from treatment may avoid it because identifying the need for prevention requires an acknowledgment of both serious risk to one's child and one's own role in creating that risk. Lifting the stigma from those needing help with parenting and moving beyond the denial with which many parents approach injury risk are necessary for effective interventions.

Methodological Weaknesses

As was seen earlier, assessment devices in both areas tend to be inadequate. Interventions to avoid unintentional injury risk have typically been extremely molecular and specific, whereas interventions to prevent abuse and neglect have been generally molar and unfocused. Neither area seems to have identified the optimal point for intervention. In the past, both areas have adopted an "intervene and hope" philosophy rather than striving toward empirically validated solutions. "Quick fixes" (i.e., interventions that promised to do much but did little; Peterson & Roberts, 1992) have been prevalent in both areas.

Finally, identifying multiple points for intervention, ranging from populationwide applications to specific treatment of individuals in high-risk groups, will likely be necessary for effective prevention. Current programs tend to identify one focus or the other as desirable rather than unifying these approaches. Improved measurement tools, interventions with appropriate generality and specificity, and improved modes of implementation are all required to avoid past impediments.

Societal Ambivalence

There is a tension within the United States between personal freedoms and protection of children, which makes injury prevention in this country especially difficult. For example, the Consumer Product Safety Commission has shown great reluctance to ban dangerous toys and children's products, choosing instead to mandate warnings in small print (Berger, 1981). Striking children is maintained as a parental right in the United States, whereas it is illegal in some other industrialized countries. Further, the American culture tends to glamorize risk taking, which has been linked to unintentional injuries across generations.

Recently, however, there have been some changes in direction. Legislation requiring safety restraints and bicycle helmets has been passed, and the same automobile manufacturers are including safety features as part of their marketing strategies. Perhaps these changes signify a trend toward increased valuing of children, of safety, and of prevention and we optimistically look toward the future for further confirmation of this trend. In the meantime, we consider the tools and technologies that are available to identify effective avenues for prevention and to implement prevention programming.

PREVENTION

Assessment Strategies

To date, few assessment strategies have been designed that identify either children at high risk for injury or high-risk environmental contexts, in order to focus an intervention. There are a few notable exceptions in which environmental risks have been identified and effectively targeted. These exceptions include the installment of protective bars over windows in low-income housing to help prevent children's injuries from falling (Spiegel & Lindaman, 1977), and the manufacturing of refrigerator doors that may be opened from the inside, to help prevent asphyxiation deaths (Robertson, 1983). However, most assessment strategies in the injury research area have focused on post hoc assessment of the injury, either by identifying whether or not the injury was inflicted, or by trying to quantify the global etiology and severity of the injury. Neither of these approaches has provided reliable, valid, and sensitive assessment of injuries; indeed, both systems are currently undergoing rapid changes. Thus, each assessment area will receive only brief consideration here.

Differentiating Abuse from Other Forms of Injury

Since Kempe, Silverman, Steele, Droegemueller, and Silver's (1962) elucidation of the battered child syndrome, the medical literature has offered a number of physical demarcators that may be signs of physical abuse. For example, retinal hemorrhages (i.e., bleeding due to repeated bombardment of intracranial matter), in the absence of a history of severe trauma, is diagnostic of Shaken Impact syndrome (Bruce & Zimmerman, 1989). Similarly, Ammerman et al. (1986) suggested, "The classic signs of physical abuse are the unusual bone changes that infants exhibit under radiological examination" (p. 293). Unfortunately, physicians agree that many cases of physical abuse lack these classic signs (Fontana, Donovan, & Wong, 1963). Data from several recent studies (Bass, Kravath, & Glass, 1986; Downing, 1978; Ewigman et al., 1993; Jason, 1984) strongly suggest that the majority of child fatalities due to maltreatment are likely misdiagnosed as unintentional injury or illness (e.g., Sudden Infant Death syndrome). Consequently, cross-disciplinary child death review teams are being formed, which investigate the immediate caregiving antecedents to the fatality, and which may provide a better index of the extent to which child injury is related to human action or inaction.

Assessment of Etiology

One part of the International Classification of Diseases (ICD-9-CM, World Health Organization, 1989) is the E-codes, or codes for external causes of physical damage. The E-codes broadly categorize injuries due to Accident, Therapeutic Use, Suicide Attempt, Assault, or Undetermined cause. They were originally designed for documents, such as insurance claims and medical records, and they are often used when there has been an industrial or transportation-related injury. Although dated (e.g., offering highly detailed classification for the once-critical risk of railway injuries) and lacking precision in many critical areas, the E-codes are the only widely used mechanism for recording the source of an injury. In 1991, the National Committee of Vital and Health Statistics reported that the standardized use of E-codes could be beneficial to the study of injury. In 1993, the Second World Congress on Injury Control recommended that physicians should be required to use E-codes in hospital discharge data whenever the primary diagnosis is "injury." By April 1994, all American hospitals had included a place for E-codes on their billing forms, in conjunction with this national plan (CDC, 1992, 1994b). However, despite their widespread use and global orientation, E-codes are imprecise; they rely on outmoded terms such as "Accident" (implying an event that could not have been prevented), and they were created for coding purposes in official documents rather than for the identification of points of intervention.

Assessing Injury Severity

Most instruments used to measure injury severity have similarly emerged from the coding of medical chart data. The most commonly used index of severity is the Abbreviated Injury Scale (AIS; Petrucelli, 1981). The AIS rates the severity of medically attended injuries on a continuum from 0 to 6, with more severe injuries receiving higher numbers.

Of the other existing forms of the AIS (e.g., the Comprehensive Research Injury Scale, Committee on Medical Aspects of Automotive Safety, 1972; the Injury Severity Score, Baker, O'Neill, Hadden, & Long, 1974), all of them still offer only molar gradations of relatively serious injuries and require medical knowledge to complete.

Some investigators (e.g., Fisher, Well, Fulwider, & Edgerton, 1977) have created scales specific to injury type, such as burn severity. Other scales offer not only an index of immediate severity but also a prognosis. For example, Jaffe et al. (1993) reported that the severity and persistence of cognitive problems following head injury are related to scores on the Glasgow Coma Scale (Teasdale & Jennett, 1974), drawn from the hours and days following injury.

There have been a few attempts to measure the severity of child abuse injuries, but these attempts have tended to be imprecise and subjective. For example, Seaberg (1977) described a system by which coders were instructed to use equal units to measure gradations of severity, but they were given no specific criteria for how to differentiate among degrees of severity in order to assign the units. Similarly, many measures of minor injury have simply defined a minor injury as an injury that was not medically attended (Boyce, Sprunger, Sobolewski, & Schaefer, 1984). Allowing the mother or the child to determine what constitutes a minor injury is likely to result in wide discrepancies in data because of the large individual differences among children's responses to injury (e.g., some children cry at the slightest bump; other children pick themselves up and continue to play while bleeding) and differences in material judgments of what outcomes warrant the label of "injury."

The Minor Injury Severity Scale (Peterson, Saldana, & Heiblum, 1996) is a recently described tool that allows individuals with no previous medical experience to classify any injury resulting in lasting pain or a mark on the body. Injuries are scored on a continuum from 0 to 7, with a score of 7 indicating a fatality. This scale was designed to classify 22 types of minor injury, with enhanced sensitivity to more minor forms of injury (e.g., the severity required to change a low rating of 1 or 2 is far less than the severity required to change a 5 or 6, which indicates very serious injury). The Minor Injury Severity Scale can be used reliably and appears to be a valid strategy for quantifying minor injuries.

Assessing for Injury Process

It has been argued elsewhere (Peterson, Farmer, & Mori, 1987) that behavioral antecedents and consequences should be considered when investigating injuries to yield a more coherent picture of the process by which injuries occur. There have been several attempts to provide a methodology for such an assessment. For example, Christoffel et al. (1986) described an assessment system used to investigate pedestrian injuries. In this system, interviews with observers, parents, and the driver are supplemented by videotapes taken from the child's and the driver's perspective at the time of day when the injury occurred. Physical features such as traffic patterns and visibility are measured. Then, a multidisciplinary team of specialists (e.g., a psychologist, a social worker, a physician, and a traffic engineer) provides ratings of the Causal Sequence Reconstruction.

Our laboratory has described an alternative approach to the problem: Participant Event Monitoring (Peterson, Brown, Bartelstone, & Kern, 1996). In our study of Participant Event Monitoring, mothers and their children were trained to observe and record details of minor injury. Then, a highly trained interviewer gathered data from the mother or child, beginning with a request for an open-ended, stream-of-consciousness description of the event and ending with specific questions about the time of injury, including the child's activity and the mother's vigilance. Participant Event Monitoring appears to be a reliable and valid method of assessing minor injury events, and the interview process may have some applicability for investigating more major injuries.

The greatest utility of assessment strategies may be in the planning of prevention programs. Compared with post hoc measures that attempt to label either the intentionality or the severity of injuries, process levels of analysis may yield a richer understanding of how injuries occur and, therefore, how they could be prevented. As sweeping changes continue to be made in health professionals' approach to assessment, and improved methods of examining the human ecology of injuries are designed, it is likely that future prevention programs will improve accordingly. However, there are a number of impediments to these interventions.

Prevention Approaches

If an optimal prevention program were to be designed, based on the current authors' working model of the risk factors related to child injury, it would directly target the key variables at the sociocultural, caregiver, and child levels. To date, few such comprehensive and multidisciplinary programs have been empirically tested. Of the real world programs that have shown encouraging results in the prevention of unintentional injury or child maltreatment, most injury prevention interventions have targeted only one form of injury and most child abuse interventions have become corresponding and unfocused. Accordingly, the next section presents findings for unintentional injury prevention and prevention of abuse and neglect separately.

Current Unintentional Injury Prevention Programs

Because the field of unintentional injury was originally addressed by public health workers, many current prevention efforts are populationwide and focused on the environment. Examples of these and other types of programs will be reviewed, with information organized according to Peterson and Mori's (1985) Target by Method by Tactic matrix (see Table 13.1). As shown, the target may be the environment, the caregiver, or the child. The method is either legislative or educational, and the tactic describes the population in which injury is to be prevented: all children within a given area (populationwide prevention), children at specific points of development (milestone prevention), or children at elevated likelihood of injury (high-risk group prevention).

Targeting the Environment.   When the environment is the target of an unintentional injury prevention program, the method is usually legislative and the contingencies used to mandate change are typically strong. For example, the Poison Prevention Act (see Walton, 1982) required manufacturers to use child-resistant containers, thus significantly reducing the incidence of poisonings. Similarly, setting higher standards for the flammability of children's pajamas dramatically lowered the number of burns caused by sources other than house fires (Smith & Falk, 1987). Window guards significantly reduced fatalities due to children falling from buildings (Spiegel & Lindaman, 1977), and more restrictive safety standards for low-income housing have shown positive results as well (Gallagher, Hunter, & Guyer, 1985).

Table 13.1 Categorical Framework for Injury Prevention Interventions

	Method					
	Legislated/Mandated			Educational/Skill Building		
Target	Populationwide	Milestone	High Risk	Populationwide	Milestone	High Risk
Environment	Poison Prevention Packaging Act (Walton, 1982)	Safety requirements for crib manufacturers (Consumer Product Safety Commission, 1979)	Window barriers for low-income apartment dwellers (Spiegel & Lindaman, 1977)	Community bicycle paths (Organization for Economic Cooperation and Development, 1983)	Safe day care, safety inspection for day-care sites (Gallagher, Messenger, & Guyer, 1987)	Community efforts reduce child exposure to asbestos (Butler & Metrovich, 1987)
Parent	Bicycle helmet use laws (Rivara, 1985)	Safety seats for children who weigh less than 18 kg (40 lb) or who are less than 4 years old (Roberts & Turner, 1986)	In-home safety screen for neglectful families (Tertinger, Greene, & Lutzker, 1984)	Burn Prevention (Mackay & Rothman, 1982)	Physician anticipatory guidance regarding falls (Bass, Mehta, Ostrovsky, & Halperin, 1985)	Parent feedback (Gallagher, Hunter, & Guyer, 1985)
Child				Helmet use advertisements (Peterson & Roberts, 1992)	Street-crossing skills as children enter school (Yeaton & Bailey, 1978)	Latchkey home safety training (Peterson, 1984a, 1984b)

One noteworthy advantage of these interventions is that their success does not rely on the actions of either the caregiver or the child (Garbarino, 1988). Consequently, environmental interventions appear to be more effective than educational methods, although Garbarino (1988) noted the difficulty in demonstrating the effectiveness of many educational strategies (e.g., Project Burn Prevention; Mackay & Rothman, 1982). The key drawback to environmental interventions is the rather arduous process required to pass a public safety law mandating such change (Berger, 1981; Rivara, 1982), which ultimately addresses only one specific, accessible type of injury.

Targeting the Caregiver.   Laws that target the caregiver (e.g., mandated use of bicycle helmets; Rivara, 1985) are less effective than those which target the environment, for a number of reasons. First, the contingencies are often weak (e.g., many state safety restraint laws do not allow an officer to stop a car for a safety restraint violation, although a ticket can be given if the car is stopped for an unrelated reason). Second, the caregiver's compliance is required, and contacting individual caregivers is often difficult and costly. Finally, legislators are often reluctant to interfere with personal freedoms by mandating parental actions. Therefore, educational methods have been most often employed with caregivers, using populationwide, milestone, and high-risk group tactics. Populationwide educational messages with no contingencies have been communicated through the media, pamphlets, or town meetings, but they have not shown significant results in reducing child injuries (Colver, Hutchinson, & Judson, 1982; Mackay & Rothman, 1982; Pless, 1978). Although milestone educational interventions also have no contingencies, they generally have shown better results (e.g., teaching new parents about care safety; Roberts & Turner, 1986), suggesting that parents may have higher receptivity at certain milestones. Perhaps the most effective educational tactic targeted at the caregiver has been the high-risk group approach, where strong contingencies can be used. Teaching parenting skills to a group of high-risk caregivers has shown encouraging results, particularly when contingencies are strong because the caregiver is court mandated to participate (Tertinger, Greene, & Lutzker, 1984) or because the caregivers receive some type of compensation (Roberts & Turner, 1986).

Targeting the Child.   To date, there are no laws that assign children the responsibility for their own safety; focusing on children's role in keeping themselves safe may be viewed as only serving to "blame the victim" (Pless, Verreault, & Tenina, 1989, p. 998). Still, research has shown several one-on-one, educational programs with strong contingencies, which successfully build children's skills in avoiding kidnappings (Poche, Brouwer, & Swearingen, 1981), exiting buildings in the event of fire (Jones, Kazdin, & Haney, 1981), and practicing general safety at home (Peterson & Mori, 1985). Follow-up research on the effectiveness of these skills in future injury reduction remains necessary to determine the optimal method, tactic, and contingencies when targeting the child.

Summary.   Research has shown that prevention programs with the greatest potential to significantly reduce unintentional injuries include legislation targeting the environment, educational programs targeting high-risk groups of caregivers, and one-on-one educational programs targeting children, particularly when strong contingencies are present. The key weakness of these programs is that they are highly circumscribed, concentrating all efforts on one injury, one method, and one target. Conversely, the existing child maltreatment prevention programs have a global focus that might be more encompassing, but which might exclude equally important, discrete variables, as will be discussed.

Current Child Maltreatment Prevention Programs

With the exception of mandatory reporting legislation (American Association for Protecting Children, 1985) and a few authors' (e.g., Walker, Bonner, & Kaufman, 1988) innovative ideas for assisting children in avoiding abuse from caregivers, the vast majority of child maltreatment prevention programs target the caregiver. Populationwide tactics have been employed, such as the "It shouldn't hurt to be a child" campaign, national hotlines, and current billboards directing people to "Never hurt a child. Never, never, never." However, the primary tactic of most programs is provision of education, therapy, and support to high-risk groups.

Education.   Several researchers (e.g., Appelbaum, 1977; Azar & Twentyman, 1984; Lutzker & Rice, 1984) have documented the effectiveness of teaching healthy parenting skills to high-risk groups. For example, Wolfe, Kaufman, Aragona, and Sandler (1981) taught abusive parents stress reduction skills, anger management strategies, problem-solving techniques, and realistic developmental expectations for children. One-year follow-up data (Wolfe et al., 1982) suggested that these skills had been retained and the incidence of maltreatment had been reduced.

Therapy and Support.   Early psychiatric strategies focused on individual psychotherapy for high-risk groups (Helfer, 1975; Kempe & Helfer, 1972; Steele & Pollock, 1971), but outcome data did not show significant reductions in the incidence of maltreatment (Herrenkohl, Herrenkohl, Egolf, & Seech, 1979). Similarly, the sociological strategy of foster care placements showed some improvements in children's well-being (Kent, 1976) but only temporarily and at high cost to the nation (Daro, 1988). Consequently, programs such as the Intensive Crisis Counseling Program in Florida (Paschal & Schwann, 1986); Homebuilders in Washington (Kinney, Madsen, Fleming, & Haapala, 1977); Placement Prevention in Wisconsin (Landsman, 1985), and the Nebraska's Intensive Services Project (Leeds, 1984) developed a psychological case manager strategy. The strategy has a strong contingency because caregivers will lose their children to foster care homes if maltreatment occurs; such programs have shown encouraging results in reducing the need for out-of-home placement. However, Daro (1988) pointed out that a specific reduction in maltreatment incidence has not yet been demonstrated by these programs.

Interventions at the community level include group therapy (Bean, 1971), Parents Anonymous meetings (Blizinsky, 1982), lay therapy (Powell, 1986), and home visitor services. The significant impact of home visitors has been well documented (see Wekerle & Wolfe, 1993, for review), underscoring the importance of accessibility to professional help. However, programs that combine education with therapy and support are rare, and no programs currently incorporate interventions designed to address risk factors at the sociocultural and child levels.

Summary

The incidence, cost, and consequences of child injuries in the United States give testimony to the seriousness of this "neglected disease." Evidence suggests that an integrated approach to the problem, incorporating the work already done in both the child maltreatment field and the unintentional injury field, may be ideal. Having reviewed information from this unified perspective, it is recommended that efforts be directed toward five goals. First, future international research efforts must incorporate standardized definitions of injury that focus on process measures of etiology, rather than continuing to use subjective terms, such as "neglect," that foster attempts to blame someone. Second, relevant legislative and political changes will need to be made, despite obstacles such as a lack of constituency and an American culture that values individual freedom over safety considerations, accepts the striking of one's children, and glorifies risk taking. Third, based on results of research focused on etiological factors and informed by societal concerns, there needs to be expanded designing and implementation of populationwide universal prevention programs at the community, state, and national levels. Of primary importance would be the construction of environmental barriers to prevent injury where possible and educational programs that teach safety knowledge and caregiving skills. Fourth, for injuries that occur despite these primary prevention programs, the rapid improvements currently being made in approaches to assessment should be encouraged, completed, and then empirically examined to determine the degree to which they yield accurate identification of the etiology of injuries at the sociocultural, caregiver, and child levels. Finally, based on the results of these assessments, selected prevention programs need to be targeted at environmental contexts, groups of caregivers, or children identified as high-risk for child injury. The lessons learned in the past half-century from both the child maltreatment field and the unintentional injury field cannot effectively reduce child injury until they are united and applied at sociocultural, caregiver, and child levels within a real world context.

REFERENCES

Altemeier, W., O'Connor, S., Vietze, P., Sandler, H., & Sherrod, K. (1984). Prediction of child abuse: A prospective study of feasibility. *Child Abuse and Neglect, 8,* 393–400.

American Association for Protecting Children. (1985). *Highlights of official child neglect and abuse reporting, 1983.* Denver, CO: American Humane Society.

American Association for Protecting Children. (1986). *Highlights of official child neglect and abuse reporting.* Denver, CO: American Humane Society.

American Humane Society. (1978). *National analysis of official child neglect and abuse reporting.* Denver, CO: Author.

American Psychiatric Association. (1994). *Diagnostic and statistical manual of mental disorders* (4th ed.). Washington, DC: Author.

Ammerman, R. T., Cassisi, J. E., Hersen, M., & Van Hasselt, V. B. (1986). Consequences of physical abuse and neglect in children. *Clinical Psychology Review, 6,* 291–310.

Appelbaum, A. S. (1977). Developmental retardation in infants as a concomitant of physical child abuse. *Journal of Abnormal Child Psychology, 5,* 417–423.

Appelbaum, A. S. (1980). Developmental retardation in infants as concomitants of physical child abuse. In G. J. Williams & J. Money (Eds.), *Traumatic abuse and neglect of children at home* (pp. 304–310). Baltimore, MD: Johns Hopkins University Press.

Azar, S. T., & Rohrbeck, C. A. (1986). Child abuse and unrealistic expectations: Further validation of the parent opinion questionnaire. *Journal of Consulting and Clinical Psychology, 54,* 867–868.

Azar, S. T., & Twentyman, C. T. (1984, November). *An evaluation of the effectiveness of behaviorally versus insight-oriented group treatments with maltreating mothers.* Paper presented at the annual meeting of the Association for Advancement of Behavior Therapy, Philadelphia.

Baker, S. P., O'Neill, B., Hadden, W., Jr., & Long, W. B. (1974). The Injury Severity Score: A method for describing patients with multiple injuries and evaluating emergency care. *Journal of Trauma, 14,* 187–196.

Baker, S. P., O'Neill, B., & Karpf, R. S. (1984). *The injury fact book.* Lexington, MA: Lexington Books.

Bass, M., Kravath, R., & Glass, L. (1986). Death-scene investigations in sudden infant death. *New England Journal of Medicine, 315,* 100–128.

Bean, S. (1971). The parents' center project: A multi-service approach to the prevention of child abuse. *Child Welfare, 50,* 277–282.

Beautrais, A. L., Fergusson, D. M., & Shannon, D. T. (1981). Accidental poisoning in the first three years of life. *Australian Paediatric Journal, 17,* 104–109.

Beautrais, A. L., Fergusson, D. M., & Shannon, D. T. (1982). Childhood accidents in a New Zealand birth cohort. *Australian Paediatric Journal, 18,* 238–242.

Begali, V. (1992). *Head injury in children and adolescents: A resource and review for school and applied professionals* (2nd ed.). Brandon, VT: Clinical Psychology.

Berger, L. (1981). Childhood injuries: Recognition and prevention. *Current Problems in Pediatrics, 12,* 1–59.

Berkeley Planning Associates. (1983). *The exploration of client characteristics, services, and outcomes. Evaluation of the clinical demonstration projects on child abuse and neglect* (Contract No. 105–78-1108). Washington, DC: National Center on Child Abuse and Neglect.

Bijur, P. E., Kurzon, M., Overpeck, M. D., & Scheidt, P. C. (1992). Parental alcohol use, problem drinking, and children's injuries. *Journal of the American Medical Association, 267,* 3166–3171.

Bijur, P. E., Stewart-Brown, S., & Butler, N. (1986). Child behavior and accidental injury in 11,966 preschool children. *American Journal of Diseases of Children, 40,* 487–492.

Bindels, P. J., Reijneueld, S. A., Mulder-Folkerts, D. K., Coutinho, R. A., & van den Hoek, A. A. (1994). Impact of AIDS on premature mortality in Amsterdam. *AIDS, 8,* 233–237.

Blizinsky, M. (1982). Parents Anonymous and the private agency: Administrative cooperation. *Child Welfare, 61,* 305–311.

Bousha, D. M., & Twentyman, C. T. (1984). Mother-child interactional style in abuse, neglect, and control groups: Naturalistic observations in the home. *Journal of Abnormal Psychology, 93,* 106–114.

Boyce, W. T., Sprunzer, L. W., Sobolewski, S., & Schaefer, C. (1984). Epidemiology of injuries in a large, urban school district. *Pediatrics, 74,* 342–349.

Brandwein, H. (1973). The battered child: A definite and significant factor in mental retardation. *Mental Retardation, 11,* 50–51.

Brown, G. W., & Davidson, S. (1978). Social class, psychiatric disorder of mother, and accidents to children. *Lancet, 1,* 378.

Bruce, D. A., & Zimmerman, R. A. (1989). Shaken impact syndrome. *Pediatric Annals, 18,* 482–494.

Buchanan, A., & Oliver, J. E. (1977). Abuse and neglect as a cause of mental retardation: A study of 140 children admitted to subnormality hospitals in Wiltshire. *British Journal of Psychiatry, 131,* 458–467.

Budnick, L. D., & Chaiken, B. P. (1985). The probability of dying of injuries by the year 2000. *Journal of the American Medical Association, 254,* 3350–3352.

Caffey, J. (1946). Multiple fractures in the long bones of infants suffering from chronic subdural hematoma. *American Journal of Roentgenology, 56,* 163–173.

Casabona, B. J., Blanch, M. C., Vall, M. M., & Salvador, V. X. (1993). Premature mortality related to AIDS among men and women in Catalonia. *AIDS, 7,* 1099–1103.

Centers for Disease Control and Prevention. (1992). External cause-of-injury coding in hospital discharge data—United States, 1992. *Morbidity and Mortality Weekly Report, 41,* 249–251.

Centers for Disease Control and Prevention. (1993). Mortality patterns—United States, 1991. *Morbidity and Mortality Weekly Report, 42,* 891–900.

Centers for Disease Control and Prevention. (1994a, November). *Injury in the United States.* World Wide Web: URL http://www.cdc.gov/cgi-bin/includetext.p1?/General Information /injury/orginfo.txt.

Centers for Disease Control and Prevention. (1994b). Update: External cause-of-injury coding in hospital discharge data—United States, 1994. *Morbidity and Mortality Weekly Report, 43,* 465–468.

Christoffel, K. K., Scheidt, P. C., Agran, P. F., Kraus, J. F., McLoughlin, E., & Paulson, J. A. (1992). *Standard definitions for childhood injury research.* Washington, DC: U.S. Department of Health and Human Services.

Christoffel, K. K., Schofer, J. L., Lavigne, J. V., Jovanis, P. P., Brendt, B., & Tanz, R. (1986). Childhood pedestrian injury: A pilot study concerning etiology. *Accident Analysis and Prevention, 18,* 25–35.

Cohen, M., Raphling, D., & Green, P. (1966). Psychological aspects of the maltreatment syndrome of childhood. *Journal of Pediatrics, 69,* 279–284.

Colver, A. F., Hutchinson, P. J., & Judson, E. C. (1982). Promoting children's home safety. *British Medical Journal, 285,* 1177–1180.

Committee on Medical Aspects of Automotive Safety. (1972). Rating the severity of tissue damage: 2. The Comprehensive Scale. *Journal of the American Medical Association, 220,* 717–720.

Conaway, L. P., & Hansen, D. J. (1989). Social behavior of physically abused and neglected children: A critical review. *Clinical Psychology Review, 9,* 627–652.

Daro, D. (1988). *Confronting child abuse research for effective program design.* New York: Free Press.

Daro, D., & McCurdy, K. (1992). *Current trends in child abuse reporting and fatalities: The results of the 1990 annual fifty state survey.* Chicago: National Center on Child Abuse Prevention Research.

De Haven, H. (1942). Mechanical analysis of survival in falls from heights of fifty to one hundred and fifty feet. *War Medicine, 2,* 539–546.

Dershewitz, R. A., & Williamson, J. W. (1977). Prevention of childhood household injuries: A controlled clinical trial. *American Journal of Public Health, 67,* 1148–1153.

Diamond, L. J., & Jaudes, P. K. (1983). Child abuse in a cerebral-palsied population. *Developmental Medicine and Child Neurology, 25,* 169–174.

DiLalla, L. F., & Gottesman, I. I. (1991). Biological and genetic contributors to violence: Widom's untold tale. *Psychological Bulletin, 109,* 125–129.

Downing, D. (1978). A selective study of child mortality. *Child Abuse and Neglect, 2,* 101–108.

Egeland, B., Sroufe, A., & Erickson, M. (1983). The developmental consequence of different patterns of maltreatment. *Child Abuse and Neglect, 7,* 459–469.

Eichelberger, M. R., Gotschall, C. S., Feely, H. B., Harstad, P., & Bowman, L. M. (1990). Parental attitudes and knowledge of child safety: A national survey. *American Journal of Diseases of Children, 144,* 714–720.

Ewigman, B., Kivlahan, C., & Land, C. (1993). The Missouri Child Fatality Study: Under-reporting of maltreatment fatalities among children under five years of age, 1983–1986. *Pediatrics, 91*, 330–337.

Farmer, J. E., & Peterson, L. (1995). Pediatric traumatic brain injury: Promoting successful school reentry. *School Psychology Review, 24*, 228–241.

Fisher, J. C., Well, J. A., Fulwider, B. T., & Edgerton, M. T. (1977). Do we need a burn severity grading system? *Journal of Trauma, 11*, 252–255.

Fletcher, J. M., & Levin, H. S. (1988). Neurobehavioral effects of brain injury in children. In D. K. Routh (Ed.), *Handbook of pediatric psych. logy* (pp. 258–295). New York: Guilford Press.

Fontana, V. J. (1984). The maltreatment syndrome of children. *Pediatric Annals, 13*, 736–744.

Fontana, V. J., Donovan, D., & Wong, R. J. (1963). The "maltreatment syndrome" in children. *New England Journal of Medicine, 269*, 1389–1394.

Friedman, S. B., & Morse, C. W. (1974). Child abuse: A five-year follow-up of early case findings in the emergency department. *Pediatrics, 54*, 404–410.

Gaensbauer, T. J., & Sands, K. (1979). Distorted affective communication in abused/neglected infants and their potential impact on caretakers. *Journal of the American Academy of Child Psychiatry, 18*, 236–250.

Gallagher, S. S., Finson, K., Guyer, B., & Goodenough, S. S. (1984). The incidence of injuries among 87,000 Massachusetts children and adolescents. *American Journal of Public Health, 10*, 1340–1347.

Gallagher, S. S., Hunter, P., & Guyer, B. (1985). A home injury prevention program for children. *Pediatric Clinics of North America, 32*, 95–111.

Garbarino, J. (1977). The human ecology of child maltreatment: A conceptual model for research. *Journal of Marriage and the Family, 39*, 721–735.

Garbarino, J. (1981). An ecological approach to child maltreatment. In L. H. Pelton (Ed.), *The social context of child abuse and neglect* (pp. 228–267). New York: Human Sciences Press.

Garbarino, J. (1988). Preventing childhood injury: Developmental and mental health issues. *American Journal of Orthopsychiatry, 58*, 25–45.

Garbarino, J., Kostelny, K., & Dubrow, N. (1991). *No place to be a child: Growing up in a war zone.* Lexington, MA: Lexington Books.

Gayton, W. F., Bailey, C., Wagner, A., & Hardesty, V. A. (1986). Relationship between childhood hyperactivity and accident proneness. *Perceptual and Motor Skills, 63*(2, Pt 2), 801–802.

Gelardo, M. S., & Sanford, E. E. (1987). Child abuse and neglect: A review of the literature. *School Psychology Review, 16*, 137–155.

George, C., & Main, M. (1979). Social interactions of young abused children: Approach, avoidance, and aggression. *Child Development, 50*, 306–318.

Giovannoni, J. M., & Billingsley, A. (1970). Child neglect among the poor: A study of parental adequacy in families of three ethnic groups. *Child Welfare, 49*, 196–204.

Gray, J., Cutler, C., Dean, J., & Kempe, C. (1977). Prediction and prevention of child abuse and neglect. *Child Abuse and Neglect, 1*, 45–58.

Green, A. H., Gaines, R. W., & Sangrund, A. (1974). Child abuse: Pathological syndrome of family interaction. *American Journal of Psychiatry, 131*, 882–886.

Green, A. H., Voeller, K., Gaines, R., & Kubie, J. (1981). Neurological impairment in maltreated children. *Child Abuse and Neglect, 5*, 129–134.

Hartsough, C. S., & Lambert, N. M. (1985). Medical factors in hyperactive and normal children: Prenatal, developmental, and health history findings. *American Journal of Orthopsychiatry, 55*, 190–201.

Heins, M. (1969). Child abuse: Analysis of a current epidemic. *Michigan Medicine, 68,* 887–891.

Helfer, R. E. (1975). *The diagnostic process and treatment programs.* Washington, DC: U.S. Department of Health, Education, and Welfare.

Helfer, R. E. (1977). On the prevention of child abuse and neglect. *Child Abuse and Neglect, 1,* 502–504.

Herrenkohl, E. C., & Herrenkohl, R. C. (1979). A comparison of abused children and their nonabused siblings. *Journal of the American Academy of Child Psychology, 18,* 260–269.

Herrenkohl, R. C., Herrenkohl., E. C., & Egolf, B. P. (1983). Circumstances surrounding the occurrence of child maltreatment. *Journal of Consulting and Clinical Psychology, 51,* 242–431.

Herrenkohl, R. C., Herrenkohl., E. C., Egolf, B., & Seech, M. (1979). The repetition of child abuse: How frequently does it occur? *Child Abuse and Neglect, 3,* 67–72.

Hufton, I. W., & Oates, R. K. (1977). Non-organic failure to thrive: A long-term follow up. *Pediatrics, 59,* 73–77.

Jaffe, K. M., Fay, G. C., Polissar, N. L., Martin, K. M., Shurtleff, H., Rivara, J. B., & Winn, H. R. (1993). Severity of pediatric traumatic brain injury and neurobehavioral recovery at one year—A cohort study. *Archives of Physical Medicine and Rehabilitation, 74,* 587–595.

Jason, J. (1984). Centers for Disease Control and the epidemiology of violence. *Child Abuse and Neglect: The International Journal, 8,* 279–283.

Johnson, B., & Morse, H. A. (1968). Injured children and their parents. *Children, 15,* 147–152.

Johnson, D. A. (1992). Head injured children and education: A need for greater delineation and understanding. *British Journal of Educational Psychology, 62,* 404–409.

Jones, R. T., Kazdin, A. E., & Haney, J. I. (1981). Social validation and training of emergency fire safety skills for potential injury prevention and life saving. *Journal of Applied Behavior Analysis, 14,* 245–260.

Kaufman, J., & Zigler, E. F. (1987). Do abused children become abusive parents? *American Journal of Orthopsychiatry, 57,* 186–192.

Kempe, C., & Helfer, R. (1972). *Helping the battered child and his family.* Philadelphia: Lippincott.

Kempe, C., Silverman, F., Steele, B., Droegemueller, W., & Silver, H. (1962). The battered child syndrome. *Journal of the American Medical Association, 181,* 17–24.

Kent, J. (1976). A follow-up study of abused children. *Journal of Pediatric Psychology, 1,* 25–31.

Kinney, J., Madsen, B., Fleming, T., & Haapala, D. (1977). Homebuilders: Keeping families together. *Journal of Consulting and Clinical Psychology, 45,* 667–673.

Klonoff, H., Crockett, D. F., & Clark, C. (1984). Head trauma in children. In R. Tarter & G. Goldstein (Eds.), *Advances in clinical neuropsychology* (pp. 139–157). New York: Plenum Press.

Koski, P. R. (1988). Family violence and nonfamily deviance: Taking stock of the literature. *Marriage and Family Review, 12,* 23–46.

Landsman, M. (1985). *Evaluation of fourteen child placement prevention projects in Wisconsin.* Iowa City: University of Iowa, National Resource Center on Family-Based Services.

Lauer, B., Ten Broeck, E., & Grossman, M. (1974). Battered child syndrome: Review of 130 patients with controls. *Pediatrics, 54,* 67–70.

Law, J., & Conway, J. (1992). Effect of abuse and neglect on the development of children's speech and language. *Developmental Medicine and Child Neurology, 34,* 943–948.

Leeds, S. (1984). *Evaluation of Nebraska's Intensive Services Project.* Iowa City: University of Iowa, National Resource Center of Family-Based Services.

Levin, H. S., Mendelsohn, D., Lilly, M. A., Fletcher, J. M., Culhane, K. A., Chapman, S. B., Harward, H., Kusnerik, L., Bruce, K., & Eisenberg, H. M. (1994). Tower of London performance in relation to magnetic resonance imaging following closed head injury in children. *Neuropsychology, 8,* 171–179.

Loeber, R., Felton, D. K., & Reid, J. (1984). A social learning approach to the reduction of coercive processes in child abusive families: A molecular analysis. *Advances in Behavioral Research and Therapy, 6,* 29–45.

Lutzker, J. R., & Rice, J. M. (1984). A social learning approach to the reduction of coercive processes in child abusive families: A molecular analysis. *Advances in Behavioral Research and Therapy, 6,* 29–45.

Lynch, M. A. (1975). Ill-health and child abuse. *Lancet, 2,* 317–319.

Mackay, A. M., & Rothman, K. J. (1982). The incidence and severity of burn injuries following Project Burn Prevention. *American Journal of Public Health, 72,* 248–252.

Malinosky-Rummell, R., & Hansen, D. J. (1993). Long-term consequences of childhood physical abuse. *Psychological Bulletin, 114,* 68–79.

Mateer, C. A., & Williams, D. (1991). Effects of frontal lobe injury in childhood. *Developmental Neuropsychology, 7,* 359–376.

Matheny, A. P., Jr. (1987). Psychological characteristics of childhood accidents. *Journal of Social Issues, 4,* 45–60.

Matheny, A. P., Jr. (1993, May). *Gender differences for unintentional injuries of opposite-sex twins: Implications and injury control.* Paper presented at the Second World Conference on Injury Control, Atlanta, GA.

McCormick, M. C., Shapiro, S., & Starfield, B. H. (1981). Injury and its correlates among 1-year-old children. *American Journal of Diseases of Children, 135,*159–163.

McLoyd, V. C. (1990). The impact of economic hardship on Black families and children: Psychological distress, parenting, and socioemotional development. *Child Development, 61,* 311–346.

Monaghan, S. M., & Buckfield, P. M. (1981). Obstetrics and the family: Identification of mothers at risk for parenting failure and methods of support. *Child Abuse and Neglect, 5,* 27–32.

Monroe, L. D., & Schellenbach, C. J. (1989). Relationship of Child Abuse Potential Inventory scores to parental responses: A construct validity study. *Child and Family Behavior Therapy, 11,* 39–58.

National Academy of Sciences. (1966). *Accidental death and disability: The neglected disease of modern society.* Washington, DC: National Academy Press.

National Committee for Injury Prevention and Control. (1989). *Injury prevention: Meeting the challenge.* New York: Oxford University Press.

National Committee to Prevent Child Abuse. (1994). *A fact sheet on child abuse and neglect.* Chicago: Author.

Nersesian, W. S., Petit, M. R., Shaper, R., Lemieux, D., & Naor, E. (1985). Childhood death and poverty: A study of all childhood deaths in Maine, 1976 to 1980. *Pediatrics, 75,* 41–50.

Olds, D. L., Hendersen, C. R., Chamberlin, R., & Tatelbaum, R. (1986). Preventing child abuse and neglect: A randomized trial of nurse home visitation. *Pediatrics, 78,* 65–78.

Paget, K. D., Philip, J. D., & Abramczyk, L. W. (1993). Recent developments in child neglect. *Advances in Clinical Child Psychology, 15,* 121–174.

Parke, R., & Collmer, C. W. (1975). Child abuse: An interdisciplinary analysis. In E. M. Hetherington (Ed.), *Review of child development research* (pp. 509–590). Chicago: University of Chicago Press.

Paschal, J., & Schwann, L. (1986). Intensive crisis counseling in Florida. *Children Today, 15,* 12–16.

Pearn, J., & Nixon, J. (1977). Prevention of childhood drowning accidents. *Medical Journal of Australia, 1,* 616–618.

Pelton, L. (1977). *Child abuse and neglect and protective intervention in Mercer County, New Jersey: A parent interview and case record study.* Trenton, NJ: New Jersey Division of Youth and Family Services, Bureau of Research.

Peterson, L. (1989). Latchkey children's preparation for self-care: Overestimated, under-researched, and unsafe. *Journal of Clinical Child Psychology, 18,* 2–7.

Peterson, L., & Brown, D. (1994). Integrating child injury and abuse-neglect research: Common histories, etiologies, and solutions. *Psychological Bulletin, 116,* 293–315.

Peterson, L., Brown, D., Bartelstone, J., & Kern, T. (1996). Methodological consideration in participant event monitoring of low-baserate events in health psychology: Children's injuries as a model. *Health Psychology, 15,* 1–7.

Peterson, L., Ewigman, B., & Kivlahan, C. (1993). Judgments regarding appropriate child supervision to prevent injury: The role of environmental risk and child age. *Child Development, 64,* 934–950.

Peterson, L., Farmer, J., & Mori, L. (1987). Process analysis of injury situations: A complement to epidemiological methods. *Journal of Social Issues, 43,* 33–44.

Peterson, L., & Mori, L. (1985). Prevention of child injury: An overview of targets, methods, and tactics for psychologists. *Journal of Consulting and Clinical Psychology, 14,* 98–104.

Peterson, L., & Roberts, M. C. (1992). Complacency, misdirection, and effective prevention of children's injuries. *American Psychologist, 23,* 375–387.

Peterson, L., Saldana, L., & Heiblum, N. (1996). Quantifying tissue damage from childhood injury: The Minor Injury Severity Scale (MISS). *Journal of Pediatric Psychology, 21,* 251–267.

Petrucelli, E. (1981). *The Abbreviated Injury Sclae (AIS): Ten years of progress* (Technical Publication No. 810212). Warrendale, PA: Society of Automotive Engineers.

Pless, I. B. (1978). Accident prevention and health education: Back to the drawing board? *Pediatrics, 62,* 431–435.

Pless, I. B., Verreault, R., & Tenina, S. (1989). A case-control study of pedestrian and bicyclist injuries in childhood. *American Journal of Public Health, 79,* 995–998.

Poche, C., Brouwer, R., & Swearingen, M. (1981). Teaching self-protection to young children. *Journal of Applied Behavior Analysis, 14,* 169–176.

Powell, D. (1986, March). Parent education and support programs. *Young Children,* 47–53.

Rappaport, J. (1977). From Noah to Babel: Relationships between conceptions, values, analysis levels, and social intervention strategies. In I. Iscoe, B. L. Bloom, & C. D. Spielberger (Eds.), *Community psychology in transition* (pp. 175–184). New York: Hemisphere.

Reid, J. R., Taplin, P., & Loeber, R. (1981). A social interactional approach to the treatment of abusive families. In R. B. Stuart (Ed.), *Violent behavior: Social learning approaches to prediction, management, and treatment* (pp. 83–101). New York: Brunner/Mazel.

Rice, D. B., & Mackenzie, E. J. (1989). *Cost of injury in the United States: A report to Congress 1989.* San Francisco: University of California, Institute for Health and Aging.

Rivara, F. P. (1982). Epidemiology of childhood injuries: Review of current research and presentation of conceptual framework. *American Journal of Diseases of Children, 136,* 399–405.

Rivara, F. P. (1985). Traumatic deaths of children in the United States: Currently available prevention strategies. *Pediatrics, 75,* 456–462.

Rivara, F. P., & Barber, M. (1985). Sociodemographic determinants of childhood pedestrian injuries. *Pediatrics, 76,* 375–381.

Rivara, F. P., & Mueller, B. A. (1987). The epidemiology and causes of childhood injuries. *Journal of Diseases of Children, 136,* 502–506.

Roberts, M. C., & Turner, D. S. (1986). Rewarding parents for their children's use of safety seats. *Journal of Pediatric Psychology, 11,* 25–36.

Roberts, M. C., & Wright, L. (1982). Role of the pediatric psychologist as consultant to pediatricians. In J. Tuma (Ed.), *Handbook for the practice of pediatric psychology* (pp. 251–289). New York: Wiley-Interscience.

Robertson, L. S. (1983). *Injuries: Causes, control strategies, and public policy.* Lexington, MA: Lexington Books.

Salzinger, S., Kaplan, S., Pelcovitz, D., Samit, C., & Krieger, R. (1984). Parent and teacher assessment of children's behavior in child-maltreating families. *Journal of American Academy of Child Psychiatry, 23,* 458–464.

Scheidt, P. C. (1988). Behavioral research toward prevention of childhood injury. *American Journal of Diseases of Children, 142,* 612–617.

Seaberg, U. R. (1977). Predictors of injury severity in physical child abuse. *Journal of Social Service Research, 1,* 63–76.

Smith, G. S., & Falk, H. (1987). Unintentional injuries. In R. W. Ambler & N. B. Dold (Eds.), *Current pediatric therapy* (7th ed., pp. 102–104). Philadelphia, PA: Saunders.

Spiegel, C. N., & Lindaman, F. C. (1977). Children can't fly: A program to prevent childhood morbidity and mortality from window falls. *American Journal of Public Health, 67,* 1143–1147.

Sroufe, L. A., & Fleeson, J. (1986). Attachment and the construction of relationships. In W. W. Hartup & Z. Rubin (Eds.), *Relationships and development* (pp. 51–71). Hillsdale, NJ: Erlbaum.

Steele, B. F., & Pollock, C. B. (1971). A psychiatric study of parents who abuse infants and small children. In R. E. Helfer & C. H. Kempe (Eds.), *The battered child* (pp. 103–147). Chicago: University of Chicago Press.

Straus, M., Gelles, R., & Steinmetz, S. (1980). *Behind closed doors: Violence in the American family.* Garden City, NY: Anchor Press/Doubleday.

Tarnowski, K. J. (1994). *Behavioral aspects of pediatric burns.* New York: Plenum Press.

Taylor, E., Everitt, G., Thorley, R., Schachar, M., Rutter, M., & Wieselberg, M. (1986). Conduct disorder and hyperactivity: 2. *British Journal of Psychiatry, 149,* 768–777.

Teasdale, G., & Jennett, B. (1974). Assessment of coma and impaired consciousness. *Lancet, 2,* 81–84.

Tertinger, D. A., Greene, B. F., & Lutzker, J. R. (1984). Home safety: Development and validation of one component of an ecobehavioral treatment program for abused and neglected children. *Journal of Applied Behavior Analysis, 17,* 159–174.

Walker, C. E., Bonner, B., & Kaufman, K. (1988). *The physically and sexually abused child: Evaluation and treatment.* Elmsford, New York: Pergamon Press.

Walton, W. W. (1982). An evaluation of the Poison Prevention Packaging Act. *Pediatrics, 69,* 363–370.

Wekerle, C., & Wolfe, D. A. (1993). Prevention of child physical abuse and neglect: Promising new directions. *Clinical Psychology Review, 13,* 501–540.

Westfelt, J. A. (1982). Environmental factors in childhood accidents. *Acta Paediatrica Scandinavica, 291*(Suppl.), 1–75.

Widom, C. S. (1989). Does violence beget violence? A critical examination of the literature. *Psychological Bulletin, 106,* 3–28.

Williams, G. J. (1978). Child abuse. In P. R. Magrab (Ed.), *Psychological management of pediatric problems* (Vol. 1, pp. 253–291). Baltimore: University Park Press.

Wilske, J., & Eisenmenger, W. (1991). Unnatural causes of death in children. [English abstract]. *Offentliche Gesundheitswesen, 53,* 490–497.

Wilson, M., Baker, S., Teret, S., Shock, S., & Garbarino, J. (1991). *Saving children: A guide to injury prevention.* New York: Oxford University Press.

Wolfe, D. A. (1988). Child abuse and neglect. In E. J. Mash & L. G. Terdal (Eds.), *Behavioral assessment of childhood disorders* (2nd ed., pp. 627–669). New York: Guilford Press.

Wolfe, D. A., Kaufman, K., Aragona, J., & Sandler, J. (1981). *The child management program for abusive parents: Procedures for developing a child abuse intervention program.* Winter Park, FL: Anna.

Wolfe, D. A., St. Lawrence, J., Graves, K., Bethany, K., Bradlyn, D., & Kelly, J. (1982). Intensive behavioral parent training for a child abuse mother. *Behavior Therapy, 13,* 438–451.

World Health Organization. (1989, March). *The international classification of diseases, 9th revision: Clinical modification* (3rd ed., Vol. 2) (DHHS Publication NO. [PHS] 89–1260). Pittsburgh, PA: U.S. Department of Health and Human Services.

Ylvisaker, M., Urbanczyk, B., & Feeney, T. J. (1992). Social skills following traumatic brain injury. *Seminars in Speech and Language, 13,* 308–322.

Young, R. (1982). *Characteristics of families receiving services at Family and Children's Services of London/Middlesex: 1970–1980.* Unpublished manuscript.

Zeanah, C. H., & Zeanah, P. D. (1989). Intergenerational transmission of maltreatment: Insights from attachment theory and research. *Psychiatry, 52,* 177–196.

Zuckerman, B. S., & Duby, J. C. (1985). Developmental approach to injury prevention. *Pediatric Clinics of North America, 32,* 17–29.

CHAPTER 14

Sexual Abuse

SANDY K. WURTELE

DESCRIPTION OF THE PROBLEM

This chapter focuses on the serious and emotionally charged problem of child sexual abuse (CSA). Certainly, public and professional awareness of the CSA problem have increased in recent years. Many individuals, including several public figures, have disclosed their own childhood experiences of sexual abuse, and several institutions have come under fire for the sexual exploitation occurring within their walls. Public responses to these reports have ranged from outrage to disbelief. This chapter reviews what is known about the problem of CSA, starting out with definitional problems and information regarding the scope and consequences of CSA. Prevention programs for children are then described, as well as impediments to a broader prevention focus. Finally, the chapter will review how child-focused programs are assessed, and critically examine the evidence regarding their effectiveness.

Many aspects of the CSA problem make understanding, responding, and preventing it especially difficult. The first aspect is that the term *child sexual abuse* covers a wide range of behavior. According to state statutes, it can include penetration of the vagina, anus, or mouth, by any object; insertion of a finger in the vagina or anus; exposing one's sexual organs in an inappropriate way; vaginal or anal intercourse; touching or handling the genitals of another for the purpose of sexual arousal; intentionally masturbating in front of a child; oral-genital contact; promoting prostitution by minors; or forcing children to watch the sexual activities of others. A wide range of activities, varying in frequency, duration, and intensity, can meet the preceding definitions: a stranger exposing himself to a child; a single incident of inappropriate touching by a family friend; intercourse between a father and daughter occurring over several years.

Not only do the activities vary, but so do the perpetrators and victims. Unlike physical abuse, which is primarily perpetrated by parents or parental figures, children are sexually abused by strangers, babysitters, neighbors, family friends, parents, aunts/uncles, grandparents, cousins, siblings, teachers, clergy, daycare workers; the list goes on and on. There are, however, some common characteristics. Most studies indicate that among reported perpetrators, 90% or more are male, and approximately 75% of victims are abused by someone they know. Victims of CSA can include both girls and boys, of all ages. Although peak vulnerability for abuse of both boys and girls occurs between the ages of 7 and 13 (Finkelhor, 1994), there are disturbing data indicating that 25% to 35% of all sexually abused children are under the age of 7 (Cupoli & Sewell, 1988; Eckenrode, Munsch, Powers, & Doris, 1988).

The definition of CSA is also culture-specific. What is deemed acceptable sexual behavior varies by culture (see Korbin, 1990). In some societies, sexual contact between adults and children occurs during religious or ceremonial events. In other societies, sexualized behavior, such as fondling or kissing genitals, are normative child-rearing practices.

Definitions of CSA also vary by profession. Medical professionals tend to define CSA according to presence or absence of genital injuries or venereal disease. The legal perspective focuses on documentation and proof of existence of abusive acts by a perpetrator. Prohibited acts vary according to the activity, use of force or coercion, victim-perpetrator relationship, victim's age, and victim-perpetrator age discrepancy. Mental health professionals tend to endorse a broader definition of abuse and often consider a wider range of situations abusive (Atteberry-Bennett & Reppucci, 1986). Social service workers tend to define sexual abuse in terms of physical evidence or corroborating reports. For the purpose of this chapter, CSA is defined as sexual activities involving a child and an adult or significantly older child, where the activities are intended for the sexual stimulation of the perpetrator, and which constitute an abusive condition, such as when the child is coerced or tricked into the activity, or when there is a discrepancy in age between the participants, indicating a lack of consensuality.

SCOPE OF THE PROBLEM

Because sexual abuse is usually a secretive offense, there are no data telling us exactly how many cases occur each year. Instead, incidence data are based on cases that are disclosed to child protection or law enforcement agencies. Only a fraction of all cases makes it into these official databases. Two official sources for incidence data of CSA are the National Incidence Study (NIS), and surveys of state child protection agencies. The NIS was a federally funded study that counted official reports of abuse known to child protection agencies and unofficial reports of abuse known to professionals but not reported. Results showed that an estimated total of 133,619 children were reported as sexually abused in 1986, which represents an incidence rate of 2.11 per 1,000 children (Cappelleri, Eckenrode, & Powers, 1993). The National Committee to Prevent Child Abuse collects data from state child protection agency administrators. Data from their Fifty-State Survey of Child Abuse and Neglect (McCurdy & Daro, 1994) suggest that in 1993 approximately 150,000 children were sexually victimized, resulting in an incidence rate of 2.4 per 1,000 children. The National Center on Child Abuse and Neglect (U.S. Department of Health and Human Services, 1995) likewise reported that there were almost 140,000 victims of sexual abuse in 1993.

Deriving accurate incidence figures from the number of new cases reported is difficult because sexual abuse tends to be underreported. The discrepancy between reported cases and actual incidence was highlighted when the NIS revealed that less than half of the CSA cases identified by a sample of professionals across the country were formally reported (Sedlak, 1990). Victims, too, are unlikely to report. In Finkelhor's (1979) survey of college students, two-thirds of those who had been sexually abused as children did not tell anyone. Most professionals consider incidence figures to underestimate the scope of the problem, and a comparison of incidence figures with prevalence figures supports this proposition.

Prevalence studies determine the scope of the CSA problem by asking adults if they had experienced sexual abuse as children. Sexual abuse rates in retrospective studies range from 7% to 62% for females (with an average of 22% for contact abuse) and 3% to 16% for males (with an overall average of 7%) (Wurtele & Miller-Perrin, 1992). Such wide variations in reported prevalence reflect differences in the definitions of CSA used in various studies (e.g., whether abuse is limited to contact with the genitals), the ceiling age of abuse used (e.g., whether abuse occurred prior to age 16 or age 18), the types of samples used, and the methods for gathering data (e.g., via telephone, anonymously completed questionnaire). Even at the lower rates, these data imply that a significant number of women and men remember having been sexually victimized during the course of their development. Prevalence rates based on adult samples likely underestimate the actual extent of the problem, as there may be many more men and women who were victimized as children but do not remember their experiences. Indeed, Williams (1994) followed up 129 women who, as children, had been seen in an urban emergency room with a primary complaint of having been sexually abused. When these subjects were interviewed approximately 18 to 20 years later and asked whether they had ever been sexually abused as children, 38% did not recall having been sexually abused. These results suggest that retrospective studies may underestimate the extent of CSA.

Finkelhor (1994) has converted prevalence figures into annual rates, and asserted that if rates of sexual abuse among children today are comparable to what has been reported by adults, then approximately 500,000 new cases occur each year. Comparing this figure with the 140,000–150,000 incidence figures cited earlier suggests that less than one-third of all occurring cases are being identified and substantiated by child protection authorities. Much of the current interest in identifying and treating abuse victims, in addition to preventing CSA, can be attributed to this research, which confirms that sexual victimization during childhood is not a rare event.

CAUSES AND CONSEQUENCES

Causes

There is no simple answer to the question, "What causes child sexual abuse?" CSA is a complex phenomenon: Neither is there a single kind of act committed against children, nor is there a single cause that gives rise to the exploitation. Since no single risk factor has been identified that provides a necessary or sufficient cause of CSA, etiological models typically consider the individual, familial, and sociocultural risk factors that may contribute to this type of child maltreatment. Wurtele and Miller-Perrin (1992) compiled a list of risk factors thought to increase the likelihood of abuse occurring (see Table 14.1).

From this list it can be seen that there are factors in the potential offender that predispose some individuals toward using children sexually. Prominent in this list are a history of being abused, sexual attraction toward children, cognitions supporting sexual contact with children, and lack of empathic concern for children. Second, factors

Table 14.1 Possible Risk and Protective Factors Associated with Child Sexual Abuse

Components of CSA	Risk Factors	Protective Factors
Offender	Male Sexual attraction toward children Lack of empathic concern for children Cognitions or fantasies supporting sexual contact with children Poor impulse control Narcissistic identification with children Use of alcohol/drugs to lower inhibitions History of abuse or betrayal Feelings of inadequacy, loneliness, vulnerability, dependency Poor interpersonal (especially heterosocial) skills High stress (e.g., unemployment, financial problems) Need for power and control (possibly related to early life experience that resulted in feelings of helplessness)	If past history of abuse, has awareness of CSA History of a positive relationship with a good parental role model Good interpersonal skills Respect for children Empathy for, sensitivity to others Good decision-making skills High self-esteem Social support Good coping abilities
Child	Lack of knowledge of appropriate and inappropriate sexual behavior High need for attention or affection Overly trusting Low self-esteem, self-confidence Isolated Emotionally neglected Passive, unassertive Taught to be obedient Poor decision-making or problem-solving skills	Knowledgeable about appropriate and inappropriate sexual behavior Assertive High self-esteem, self-competence Have support persons Good problem-solving, decision-making skills
Child's Family	Emotional neglect of children Inappropriate expectations regarding child's responsibilities (e.g., role reversal) Inefficient or sporadic supervision Marital discord Family characterized by secretiveness, poor communication Over- or undersexualized home Lack of privacy; household crowding	Low stress Good social supports Economic security Supportive parents Age-appropriate sexual knowledge Efficient supervision Open climate; good communication patterns Child's sexual development promoted Child's self-esteem promoted

Table 14.1   *(Continued)*

Components of CSA	Risk Factors	Protective Factors
	Situations in which offenders have access to victims	Importance of personal safety stressed in home
	Power imbalance in marital dyad	Respect for each other's privacy by adults and children
	Self-protective behavior not modeled by parents	Affectionate parent-child relationship
	Inappropriately close or distant parent-child boundaries	Positive male/female relationships (mutual, symmetrical)
	Stressors in family (unemployment; poverty)	Effective problem-solving modeled by adults
	Socially or geographically isolated home	Positive sense of self modeled by adults
	Father substitute present	Appropriate boundaries between adults and children
	History of abuse in either parent	
	Exploitation of children to meet the needs of adults	
	Absence of natural parent	
Community/Society	View of children as possessions	Culture opposed to deriving sexual satisfaction from children
	Cultural acceptance for deriving sexual satisfaction from children	Quick prosecution and consistent punishment of offenders by legal system
	Easy access to victims	Cultural emphasis on equality between males and females
	Easy access to child pornography	Provision of sexuality education for children
	Portrayal of children as sexual beings in media and advertising	Community support for families
	Reluctance of legal system to prosecute	Children highly valued
	Sexually restrictive culture	Low tolerance for sexually coercive behaviors
	Lack of community support for families	Community awareness of the CSA problem and efforts devoted to its prevention
	Strong masculine sexualization (dominance, power in sexual relationships)	Research programs designed to further understanding of CSA and how to prevent it
	Patriarchal-authoritarian subcultures	
	Belief that children should always obey adults	
	Few opportunities for male/child nurturant interchanges that contain no sexual component	
	Lack of sexuality education in educational system	
	Devaluation of children	
	Community denial of the CSA problem	

Note. Reprinted from *Preventing Child Sexual Abuse: Sharing the Responsibility,* by Sandy K. Wurtele and Cindy L. Miller-Perrin, by permission of the University of Nebraska Press. Copyright 1992 by the University of Nebraska Press.

within a child make certain children more vulnerable than others. Notable here are lack of knowledge about inappropriate sexual behavior, low self-esteem, and high need for affection. Characteristics of the child's family may also contribute to the likelihood of abuse. Children who lack supervision, are emotionally estranged from their parents, or live in a home characterized by secretiveness, poor communication, or in one characterized as either over- or undersexualized, may be at higher risk. Finally, perpetrators' propensities to abuse may be enhanced by certain characteristics of the community or society in which they live. Societal risk factors include low value placed on children, absence of strong social norms prohibiting such kinds of sexual contact, low apprehension and conviction rates for molesters, or cultural supports for sexually coercive behavior.

Table 14.1 also contains possible protective, compensatory, or buffering factors. These factors may decrease the likelihood that a child would become a victim. Although no one factor predicts CSA, evidence exists to assume that the more risk factors involved across all systems, the higher the likelihood for abuse to occur. Conversely, the more protective factors involved across all systems, the lower the likelihood for abuse to occur. This multifactor conceptualization also suggests that reduction in the incidence of CSA will only be achieved by developing a comprehensive prevention approach, targeting the personal, familial, and environmental conditions that both increase and decrease the likelihood of abuse. Researchers hope to identify which risk and protective factors are correlated with abuse, so that more effective preventive approaches can be designed.

Consequences

Because both incidence and prevalence data suggest that many children experience sexual abuse, it is important to ask, "What are the effects of sexual abuse during childhood and does this childhood event have long-term consequences?" Research conducted over the past decade has shown that a wide range of psychological difficulties is more prevalent among those who have been sexually abused compared with those who have not. Given that this conclusion is based on studies utilizing a nomothetic approach (comparing groups of abused and nonabused children), the reader should avoid concluding that sexual victimization during childhood will have an inevitable, predictable, and negative impact on all victims. The reasons for this caution are that, first of all, a substantial minority of sexually abused children exhibit minimal or no sequelae: estimated proportions of victims found to be free of symptoms have ranged from 10% to 49% (Briere & Elliott, 1994; Kendall-Tackett, Williams, & Finkelhor, 1993). Second, it is impossible to predict precisely how a child will be impacted by the abuse experience. Actual impact may depend on abuse variables (who it was, what was done, for how long, whether force was employed), child characteristics (premorbid adjustment, age, gender, coping style), family functioning (family composition, parent-child relationship, reaction to disclosure), and community support (reactions to disclosure, availability of resources).

With these qualifiers in mind, the impact of sexual abuse on child victims across several developmental domains will be described (for reviews, see Beitchman, Zucker, Hood, daCosta, & Akman, 1991; Beitchman, Zucker, Hood, daCosta, Akman, & Cassavia, 1992; Briere & Elliott, 1994; Browne & Finkelhor, 1986; Kendall-Tackett et al., 1993; Miller-Perrin & Wurtele, 1990; Wolfe & Birt, 1995).

Emotional Development

Emotional distress is well documented in the research literature, and evidenced most commonly as depression, anxiety, and anger. Several studies have documented greater depressive symptomatology among child and adolescent victims, and depression also appears frequently in adults molested as children (Beitchman et al., 1992). Suicidal ideation or behavior also appear to be more common among victims of sexual abuse compared with nonabused controls. Given its threatening nature, it is no surprise that victims of CSA are also prone to chronic feelings of anxiety or fearfulness. Several studies have found a high percentage of CSA victims to have posttraumatic stress disorder (PTSD) symptomatology (e.g., reexperiencing the trauma; avoidance of trauma-related stimuli; hyperarousal). In Kendall-Tackett et al.'s (1993) review of the literature, 53% of sexually abused children exhibited PTSD symptomatology. Anxiety symptoms also appear among adult women molested as children (especially if they had been subjected to force during the abuse). Another common emotional sequel of CSA is anger. Briere and Elliott (1994) note that child victims often report chronic irritability, uncontrollable feelings of anger, and difficulties expressing anger appropriately. Anger can also be expressed in acting-out or behavioral problems (e.g., fighting, bullying), with abused children showing more difficulties in this area compared with nonabused children.

Sexual Development

Problems with sexuality have been found among sexually abused preschoolers, school-age children, adolescents, and adults molested as children. Oversexualized behavior (e.g., overt sexual acting out, compulsive masturbation, precocious sexual play or knowledge) consistently discriminates sexually abused children from other nonabused, clinic-referred children (Kendall-Tackett et al., 1993). Adolescents and adults molested as children are also prone to episodes of frequent, short-term sexual activity, often with a number of different partners (which puts them at risk for unintended pregnancies and contraction of sexually transmitted diseases). Other adult symptoms have included fear of or low interest in sex, having more sexual partners, and exhibiting compulsive sexual behavior.

Cognitive Development

Several studies have documented cognitive disturbances among child victims (e.g., poor concentration, inatttentiveness, dissociation) that can lead to behavioral and academic problems at school. School and learning problems are fairly prominent among school-age sexually abused children and adolescents. A recent study demonstrated that 31% of abused children, compared with 11% of controls, were one or more grades behind (Paradise, Rose, Sleeper, & Nathanson, 1994). Based on their review of the literature, Beitchman et al. (1991) found that between 32% and 85% of sexually abused school-age children exhibited behavioral and academic problems at school. Obviously, children who are in pain do not learn effectively and cannot develop to their full potential.

Physical Development

Physical sequelae of CSA can include genital injury, urinary tract infections, sexually transmitted diseases (including HIV), unintended pregnancies, and pain (headache, stomachache, pelvic pain, chronic pain). Researchers are also exploring the possible effects of CSA on hormonal, pubertal, and neuroendocrine changes. For example, Trickett, Putnam, and colleagues are finding that subgroups of sexually abused girls mature earlier, have different hormonal reactions, and possibly develop impaired immune functioning (DeAngelis, 1995).

Social Development

CSA is associated with both initial and long-term interpersonal difficulties (Briere & Elliott, 1994). Sexually abused children tend to be less socially competent, more aggressive, less trusting, and more socially withdrawn. As adults, survivors report more fears of men and women, more fear of intimacy, more difficulty trusting others, fewer friends, and more maladaptive interpersonal patterns.

IMPEDIMENTS TO INTERVENTION IN THE REAL WORLD CONTEXT

In response to the growing body of knowledge about the scope and consequences of CSA, many preventive programs have been developed and widely disseminated since the 1980s. Unlike efforts to prevent the physical abuse or neglect of children (which focus on modifying adult behavior), the focus of CSA prevention efforts has been primarily to alter the knowledge and skills of children, through group-based instruction on personal safety, usually conducted in educational settings. The primary focus of these programs is to strengthen a child's ability to recognize and resist assault (primary prevention), although they often have a secondary prevention focus as well (Miller-Perrin & Wurtele, 1988). The focus on secondary prevention of CSA is to encourage victims to disclose abuse and improve adults' responses to these disclosures so that children can receive early intervention and protection to reduce the negative consequences of sexual exploitation.

School-based personal safety programs have been adopted rapidly across the nation. In 1989, 36% of states mandated school-based CSA prevention (Kohl, 1993). National surveys of school administrators have found that 48% to 85% of school districts offer CSA prevention programs (Daro, 1994; Helge, 1992). Over 90% of teachers across the country viewed school-based CSA prevention programs as valuable and effective in one survey (Abrahams, Casey, & Daro, 1992), and in another, 96% of a national sample of elementary school principals rated the provision of CSA prevention education as average to above average in importance (Romano, Casey, & Daro, 1990). When asked as part of a national survey, parents of children in elementary school "strongly agreed" that CSA prevention should be part of all elementary school curricula (Conte & Fogarty, 1989). Our own local survey of parents of preschool children likewise found them to be supportive of including CSA prevention programs in preschools, with the majority (84%) indicating that they would be either somewhat or very likely to allow their children to participate in a CSA prevention program (Wurtele, Kvaternick, & Franklin, 1992). And children do participate in these programs. A telephone survey of 2,000 young people between the ages of 10 and 16 conducted in 1993 found that 67% of respondents reported having participated in a school-based victimization prevention program at some time in their educational careers (Finkelhor & Dziuba-Leatherman, 1995).

Child-centered CSA prevention programs have become the strategy of choice used by communities across the country to protect children from being sexually abused. This widespread adoption not withstanding, professionals who are considering offering these educational programs should be aware that there are still numerous challenges to choosing, implementing, evaluating, and maintaining a quality program for children.

In terms of choosing a program, the research cited is only now beginning to identify what the effective components of a CSA prevention program might be. A task force, sponsored by the American Professional Society on the Abuse of Children, is currently developing guidelines for program selection. In terms of implementing a program, several hurdles may exist, including resistance to the topic. Administrators, staff members, and/or parents may adhere to various myths (e.g., "We don't have a CSA problem here," "It's not the school's responsibility," or "My child is not at risk"), which will need to be debunked. Some school districts that anticipated resistance to CSA prevention programs involved the individuals early in program planning so that they would gain their support (see Helge, 1992). Training staff to teach these programs is imperative, so there must be agency support (e.g., providing release time for staff) for such training. Most typically, personnel in an organization are not trained in CSA identification and reporting techniques (e.g., Wurtele & Schmitt, 1992). Indeed, only three states require that teachers receive such training to be certified (Helge, 1992). Even if they are offered training, many have observed that school personnel are reluctant to report suspected cases, based on a fear of "causing trouble" (e.g., Hill & Jason, 1987). Even when they do report, oftentimes there is a lack of community and state agency support, which can be very frustrating for staff.

For prevention researchers who are attempting to evaluate these educational programs, several obstacles exist. First, there is a paucity of psychometrically sound, developmentally appropriate dependent measures. Researchers who intend to use behavioral measures face a host of ethical and logistical challenges, as will be described. Second, the setting may not support the requirements of an experimental design. For example, Ratto and Bogat (1990) describe how at one preschool where they were implementing a CSA education program, administrators requested that they provide the experimental condition to the control group. Furthermore, program evaluations are often considered a drain on resources that could be used for the programs themselves (Reppucci & Herman, 1991). And finally, to offer a school-based program on an ongoing basis requires administrative (including budgetary) support and commitment.

Paradoxically, a major impediment to the prevention of CSA may be the relatively exclusive focus on educating children. Providing a school-based program (which is most likely offered during one session of less than 2 hours duration; Helge, 1992; Kohl, 1993) is viewed as adequately equipping children to recognize and resist abuse. Such a "panacea" likely soothes parental anxieties. Yet this overly simplistic "solution" ignores that CSA is an extremely complex social problem. As noted earlier, prevention of CSA is best conceptualized as a process of altering risk and protective factors in the potential perpetrator, potential victim and his or her family, along with the environment in which they all exist.

So why do schools and the general public rely almost exclusively on this approach to preventing the sexual abuse of young children? First of all, because the primary function of school systems is to inform and educate, they have evolved as the obvious choice for educating children about sexual abuse. In addition to teachers' expertise as educators, their ongoing relationships with students and families enable them to play a key role in identifying and supporting abused children. School-based prevention programs also have appeal because of their ability to reach large numbers of children of every race, creed, ethnic, and socioeconomic group, in a relatively cost-efficient fashion. A universal primary prevention strategy likewise eliminates the stigma of identifying specific children or families as being at risk for sexual abuse, and thus avoids costly and intrusive interventions into family privacy (Daro, 1994). School-based personal safety programs also have appeal because they are "user friendly"; often canned packages requiring little input from the presenter. Use of scripted materials reduces the likelihood of inconsistent delivery of a program (a problem that has plagued some evaluations; e.g., Briggs, 1991; Conte, Rosen, Saperstein, & Shermack, 1985). By adhering to the script, teachers may also avoid the uncomfortable but important topic of sexuality.

Our society's reluctance to communicate openly and honestly about sexuality with children is another reason for the widespread acceptance of school-based CSA education programs. Most programs attempt to teach children about sexual abuse without discussing sexuality or even recognizing that children are sexual beings. Even though the implicit goal of these programs is to prevent *sexual* exploitation, the explicit goal is usually to teach personal safety, not sex education. This shift in emphasis is often done to reduce community opposition and avoid conflict with schools and parents. Thus, many CSA prevention programs avoid describing the sexual activities that are usually involved in this type of abuse, and few programs teach children anatomically correct terms for the genitals or provide them with instruction that promotes healthy sexuality. Making these programs void of information on sexuality has increased their acceptance and widespread adoption, but at what cost? Reppucci and Herman (1991) caution that "by avoiding sexuality, young children may get the message that sexuality is largely secretive and negative" (p. 146). The challenge for the next generation of CSA prevention programs is to incorporate this information into a broader context of normal sexuality and respect for self and others.

The strategy of targeting the general population of children also reflects the fact that we lack clear explanatory models for sexual abuse. While risk factors (both personal and environmental) have been identified for other types of child maltreatment, similar prediction models are not available for sexual abuse. Thus, instead of targeting potential victims or potential perpetrators, the majority of these programs view all children as potential victims and neglect to address those in the audience who are either offending or are in imminent danger of offending (Daro, 1994). There is one notable exception: The Committee for Children's *Second Step* curriculum teaches children skills to avoid becoming abusers and victimizers, by focusing on decreasing aggressive behavior and increasing empathy, problem-solving, social skills, and anger management.

To deal with the complexity of CSA, child-focused prevention programs should be only one of a range of prevention strategies. Programs must be expanded to include audiences other than potential victims. There are numerous ways to expand the efforts to prevent CSA and useful blueprints are available (e.g., Daro, 1994; Finkelhor, 1990; Tutty, 1991; Wurtele & Miller-Perrin, 1992). Several prevention strategies have been proposed (e.g., public awareness messages; treatment programs for male and female victims of CSA; comprehensive sexuality education for children and youth; training and education for professionals). One strategy frequently mentioned by prevention experts is to involve parents as "partners in prevention" (Wurtele & Miller-Perrin, 1992).

Parent-focused efforts have several potential advantages. For example, such efforts may indirectly affect the success of school-based prevention programs. The impact of prevention lessons taught at school depends on the support of parents at home, both to clarify concepts and to help children apply their new knowledge in daily life (Conte & Fogarty, 1989). Furthermore, if parents could be trained to be prevention educators, then children would receive repeated exposure to prevention information in the natural environment, thus providing a series of booster sessions to supplement other prevention efforts. Indeed, several studies have shown that parents (when adequately prepared) can be very effective instructors for their young children (Wurtele, 1993a, 1993b; Wurtele, Currier, Gillispie, & Franklin, 1991; Wurtele, Gillispie, Currier, & Franklin, 1992; Wurtele, Kast, & Melzer, 1992; Wurtele, Melzer, & Kast, 1992). Similarly, Finkelhor, Asdigian, and Dziuba-Leatherman (1995) found that children who had received victimization prevention instruction from their parents (in addition to information they received at school), had substantially more knowledge about CSA, made more use of self-protection strategies, were better able to thwart victimization attempts, and were more likely to disclose victimizations. As suggested by these results, discussing CSA with a parent might make it easier for a child to disclose to that parent if abuse has occurred, or occurs in the future. Finally, educated parents would be better able to identify child victims and respond appropriately to victim disclosures.

Despite the advantages of involving parents in prevention efforts, parent-centered efforts have been limited. Granted, most schools that offer prevention education to children also provide parents with the opportunity to preview curriculum materials and learn more about the CSA problem. Yet attendance at these parent informational meetings has been disappointingly low. For example, only one-third of the parents invited did so in Berrick (1988), and only one-fourth of parents attended a preview in Tutty (1993). Perhaps nonattendance is related to the topic; many parents have a difficult time talking to their children about sexual issues. Or they may think their children are not at risk for sexual victimization, perhaps (as one parent told me) because "they never interact with strangers" (indicating a lack of knowledge about CSA). Those parents who do attend informational meetings tend to be better informed and more likely to discuss this topic with their children anyway (e.g., Porch & Petretic-Jackson, 1986).

Nevertheless, researchers must focus on ways to encourage parents (especially fathers) to attend these orientation meetings. Focusing educational efforts on both mothers and fathers (or father substitutes) may also deter potential perpetrators. Perhaps parents would become more involved if creative prevention proponents employed numerous kinds of marketing techniques to reach parents (e.g., through schools, doctors, and counselors; see Elrod & Rubin, 1993), found more convenient meeting times and places for them (e.g., lunchtime meetings in the workplace, meetings at social or religious organizations), or used innovative instructional media to educate parents (e.g., television, videos, newspapers, or magazines). Although guidelines are available as to what should be included in the content of parent-centered materials (e.g., Wurtele & Miller-Perrin, 1992), further experimentation is needed to determine the most effective instructional technique to disseminate this information to parents. Examples of evaluations of parent education workshops are few in number (Berrick, 1988; McGee

& Painter, 1991; Porch & Petretic-Jackson, 1986). Another way to involve parents is by incorporating homework assignments that must be completed jointly by children and their parents. Although this tactic has worked in the health promotion area (e.g., Perry et al., 1988), few CSA prevention researchers have utilized parent-child workbooks, and when they are used, the problem of parental noncompliance has been noted (e.g., Ratto & Bogat, 1990). Thus, researchers have many impediments to overcome in their attempts to enlist parents as partners in prevention.

PREVENTION

Assessment Strategies

In the past decade, over 40 evaluations of child-focused CSA prevention programs have been published. Although this number is four times greater than the number of evaluations that were available for review almost 10 years ago (Wurtele, 1987), it is still far short of the number of programs being implemented across the country. Program development and dissemination are still far ahead of formal evaluations, although most schools report doing informal, in-house evaluations (Kohl, 1993). Several research designs and evaluation instruments have been employed to determine the effectiveness of these programs. In the following section, common measures used to assess program effectiveness will be reviewed.

Knowledge Acquisition

Most published evaluations employ some measure to assess the impact of school-based instruction on children's knowledge of CSA prevention concepts. The actual questions included in the measures depend on the content of the program, but children are usually asked what the names of body parts are, who strangers, perpetrators, and victims are, whether children should tell about inappropriate touching, what secrets should or should not be kept, whether children always have to obey grown ups, what is meant by sexual abuse, whether sexual abuse only happens to girls, and whether abuse is ever the child's fault.

Varied response formats have been utilized, including "yes/no/I don't know" (e.g., Saslawsky & Wurtele, 1986), true-false (e.g., Hazzard, Kleemeier, & Webb, 1990; Tutty, 1992), Likert-type scales (e.g., Kolko, Moser, Litz, & Hughes, 1987), multiple-choice (e.g., Conte et al., 1985), and open-ended questions (e.g., Harbeck, Peterson, & Starr, 1992). Although in the past, few studies included information on the psychometric properties of the scales, more recent research reports do. The 13-item Personal Safety Questionnaire (PSQ; Saslawsky & Wurtele, 1986) has adequate internal consistency (.78), but somewhat low test-retest reliability ($r = .64$). Tutty's (1992) 40-item Children's Knowledge of Abuse Questionnaire (CKAQ) evidences adequate test-retest reliability ($r = .76$) and correlates highly with the PSQ. The "What I Know about Touching" scale (Hazzard, Webb, Kleemeier, Angert, & Pohl, 1991) also has adequate internal consistency (.75) and test-retest reliability ($r = .77$).

Skill Gains

In addition to measuring knowledge gains, many researchers also assess children's gains in preventive skills. The major skill areas assessed have included children's ability to recognize unsafe situations, their self-report of their resistance skills in these unsafe situations (i.e., verbal and motoric responses), and their reporting skills.

The "What If" Situations Test (WIST) was developed to measure these preventive skills. The latest version of the WIST features six vignettes describing appropriate and inappropriate touch requests that are read to the child. One of the vignettes follows: What if you were playing at the park and a man you like said to you, "Hey [name of child], I'll go buy you an ice cream cone if you take off your pants and let me touch your private parts." A series of questions follows to determine children's abilities to recognize the appropriateness/inappropriateness of the request along with their abilities to utilize the primary prevention skills taught in personal safety programs (i.e., to verbally refuse, escape, report the incident, and make an informative disclosure). Test-retest reliability is high ($rs = .80$ to $.89$, depending on the skill), and these six skills have been shown to be conceptually and statistically distinct (Liang, Bogat, & McGrath, 1993). The advantage of an assessment of this kind is that the child is required to apply prevention knowledge to situations not presented in the educational program. In addition, by measuring several different preventive skills, the WIST allows researchers to determine whether certain skills are more easily learned than others.

Instead of orally presenting situations to child subjects, other researchers have successfully used videotapes of potential perpetrators making appropriate and inappropriate requests, and then asked the child subjects how they would or the person in the vignette should respond (e.g., Hazzard et al., 1990; Swan, Press, & Briggs, 1985). Encouragingly, few researchers today employ animal figures to measure children's protective responses, as was done early on (e.g., Gilbert, Berrick, Le Prohn, & Nyman, 1989).

The problems with self-report measures are well documented (Bellack & Hersen, 1988), and there is doubt whether children who report they would say "no," get away, and tell an adult about a sexually abusive situation would actually apply these skills if confronted with a potential perpetrator. Indeed, studies comparing what children say they will do and their actual behavior show poor verbal-nonverbal correspondence (e.g., Miltenberger, Thiesse-Duffy, Suda, Kozak, & Bruellman, 1990). Nevertheless, this method of program evaluation remains the most widely used because of the difficulties in employing behavioral measures (reviewed in following section).

Behavior Changes

Due to practical and ethical considerations, little research has studied whether children actually use the knowledge and skills in real-life abusive situations. Some studies have used confederates to simulate stranger abductions (e.g., Fryer, Kraizer, & Miyoshi, 1987a, 1987b; Miltenberger & Thiesse-Duffy, 1988; Poche, Yoder, & Miltenberger, 1988), but only a few have employed in vivo assessments to measure children's responses to a potential molester. For example, in Kraizer, Witte, and Fryer (1989), a confederate put his or her arm around the child and tried various techniques (flattery, bribery) to persuade the child to allow such touching. Scoring was based on the child's verbal response (e.g., saying "no") and body language (e.g., standing up, moving the confederate's hand). Harbeck et al. (1992) also used a behavioral measure in which a trained interviewer verbally described but did not physically act out the inappropriate touch. Children in this study had the opportunity to both verbally describe an action and also act out the response. Neither of these simulation techniques assessed whether children would reject sexual advances from familiar adults, who are the most common perpetrators.

Behavioral role plays are a rich source of data and have high external validity. But they are also time intensive and logistically difficult. In addition, these simulations are very difficult to construct without raising major human subject protection issues (see Conte, 1987). Ethical concerns about these strategies are whether such encounters would desensitize children to dangerous situations, along with the potential emotional upset these situations might cause. One also wonders whether consent rates would be affected by the inclusion of these tests, and if so, what this would do to the generalizability of findings.

Using an alternative strategy to measure impact on behavior, Finkelhor et al. (1995) conducted a national telephone survey inquiring about children's responses to actual or threatened sexual assaults. Children were asked: "Has there ever been a time when an older person tried to feel you, grab you or kiss you in a sexual way that made you feel afraid or bad?" (p. 144). Children who replied "yes" were then asked for more details about the assault and their reactions. Although this methodology still relies on self-report of victimization and self-protection strategies (no independent confirmation was obtained), and their findings apply only to older children (those aged 10 to 16), the researchers are to be commended for utilizing this innovative method of ascertaining whether children are applying what they are learning in the school-based prevention programs.

Disclosures

Very few researchers have reported on unsolicited disclosures, despite their importance as a secondary prevention outcome. This is perplexing, especially because this potential benefit seems easier to evaluate. Those who do report disclosures usually report only the actual number or percentage .and fail to provide additional information (e.g., type of abuse, past vs. ongoing, consequences of disclosure, disposition of case).

During their telephone interviews with young people who had participated in antivictimization programs, Finkelhor et al. (1995) asked the youth directly about their lifetime experience with a wide range of actual or attempted victimizations, including sexual victimizations. Such direct questioning of children's experiences is rare. Only one other study was found where children were asked directly about their own experiences with inappropriate touching (Kolko et al., 1987), although others have attempted to include these questions in their assessment battery but have met resistance from school district administrators (Theodore Henderson, personal communication, April 3, 1995). School administrators' concerns include the possible negative media attention if a "flood" of children disclose ongoing abuse, in addition to the impact such disclosures would have on school personnel and social service and law enforcement agencies.

Side Effects

Can children learn about sexual abuse and its prevention without becoming upset, frightened, or suspicious of nurturing touch? A few researchers have attempted to measure negative side effects, including elevated levels of fear and anxiety, acting out, negative sense of sexuality, and overgeneralization of concepts to benign touches.

To assess fear and anxiety, some researchers simply ask child subjects if the program made them feel worried or scared (e.g., Finkelhor & Dziuba-Leatherman, 1995;

Garbarino, 1987; Hazzard et al., 1990). Others have employed a standardized measure of anxiety (e.g., Hazzard et al., 1991). Still others have developed measures of anxiety specific to CSA prevention programs (e.g., Ratto & Bogat, 1990). For example, the Fear Assessment Thermometer Scale (FATS) assesses children's rated fears of various objects, people, and situations potentially affected by a personal safety program (Wurtele, Kast, Miller-Perrin, & Kondrick, 1989). Children rate their fear by moving a simulated column of mercury from 1 (not at all afraid) to 7 (very much afraid) on a cardboard representation of a thermometer. The instrument has an internal consistency of .74 and test-retest reliability of .69. It can be administered to both children and their parents (Wurtele & Miller-Perrin, 1987).

Children can also demonstrate upset by acting out. Some researchers simply ask parents if their children had shown any adverse reactions after participating in the programs (e.g., Nibert, Cooper, & Ford, 1989). Others ask parents to rate the frequency of certain behaviors thought to be indicative of emotional upset (e.g., Hazzard et al., 1991). It may also be useful to ask teachers to rate the same behaviors (e.g., Wurtele, 1990, 1993b; Wurtele, Gillispie, Currier, & Franklin, 1992; Wurtele, Kast, & Melzer, 1992; Wurtele et al., 1989).

Critics contend that CSA prevention programs might harm children's normal sexual development (e.g., Krivacska, 1990). Too few researchers have included measures of children's knowledge about and attitudes toward their own sexuality to be able to address this concern. Some preschoolers have been asked questions concerning body pride (e.g., "Do you like your private parts?"), knowledge of correct terminology for genitals, and whether the children believe that it is acceptable for them to touch their own genitals (Wurtele, 1993a, 1993b; Wurtele, Melzer, & Kast, 1992). The questions would be different for school-age children and adolescents, but the literature is void of examples.

Concern has also been expressed about another potential side effect: that program participants will overgeneralize the rules and concepts learned, and will become oversensitive to situations involving appropriate touch. The fear is that such overgeneralization could lead to false CSA allegations (Krivacska, 1989). To measure oversensitivity, Gilbert et al. (1989) asked program participants to place happy, sad, or confused faces on pictures of a bunny being bathed, tickled, told a secret, hit, and hugged. Information on the psychometric properties of this instrument was not provided, and the results are open to interpretation. Others have used touch discrimination measures to assess for oversensitivity involving appropriate touch. Examples of appropriate and inappropriate touching are presented, and children are asked to describe the touch as okay or not-okay. Some use videotaped vignettes to assess children's abilities to discriminate (e.g., Swan et al., 1985; Hazzard et al., 1990; Hazzard et al., 1991). More frequently, children listen to a description of a situation and are then asked to determine if the touch described was okay or not-okay (e.g., as measured by the WIST; see also Blumberg, Chadwick, Fogarty, Speth, & Chadwick, 1991).

The possibility of positive side effects has also been explored. For example, Binder and McNiel (1987) asked children if the program made them feel safer and better able to protect themselves. Others have inquired of children or parents (or both) if they discussed the contents of the program at home (Binder & McNiel, 1987; Hazzard et al., 1991; Kolko et al., 1987; Swan et al., 1985; Wurtele, 1990; Wurtele & Miller-Perrin, 1987; Wurtele et al., 1989).

Comment

Antivictimization prevention programs can be evaluated using proximal measures (i.e., immediately observable changes such as gains in knowledge or skills), and/or by measuring distal goals (i.e., long-term changes such as reduced incidence). An initial step is to evaluate proximal gains, and extant evaluations follow this strategy. Thus, assessment strategies have focused on determining whether children learn the information and skills conveyed in a personal safety program.

In my first review of CSA prevention programs (Wurtele, 1987), I noted several concerns about the dependent measures being employed. First, there were few measures in common across different studies. Today there is more consistency in the types of questions being asked of children. Second, information on psychometric properties of the tests was rarely provided. Recent reports are much more likely to include this information. Third, the problem of ceiling effects plagued some of the research (where many children are able to respond to simple pretest items). With some exceptions (e.g., Blumberg et al., 1991; Nibert, Cooper, Ford, Fitch, & Robinson, 1989), ceiling effects are not as much a problem in this decade's studies. Fourth, I noted the reluctance of researchers to measure behavioral changes resulting from program participation. Based on how few in vivo assessments are included in recent evaluations, this reluctance still apparently exists. Given the ethical problems associated with in vivo simulation techniques, I believe that they should be employed only when the benefit clearly outweighs the risks (e.g., to validate paper-pencil measures) and when proper ethical guidelines are followed (informed consent from parents and assent from children; debriefing of children after the procedure, etc.). Fifth, I encouraged researchers to use, as an additional dependent measure, reports of disclosure during or subsequent to a personal safety program. As noted earlier, still today few researchers provide this information. Researchers are urged to make this information available and to consider following the lead of some innovative researchers who have asked children directly about their victimization experiences. Finally, I urged prevention researchers to include measurements of negative side effects to better inform school administrators and parents about the potential adverse effects of these educational efforts. Encouragingly, several researchers have tested for negative effects, and have also provided us with valuable information about the positive side effects of these programs.

To close this section, here are two additional suggestions for prevention researchers. First, although average or composite scores may indicate the overall effect of a program, it would be helpful if researchers also reported item analyses. These would be useful in determining whether there are certain concepts or skills that children at certain ages or after participating in certain types of programs are not comprehending (see Liang et al., 1993; Tutty, 1992, for examples). Second, researchers are encouraged to use multiple sources (i.e., children, parents, teachers, child protective services/law enforcement) to fully determine the outcomes of these educational efforts.

Prevention Approaches

In this section, evidence as to the effectiveness of child-directed CSA prevention programs will be reviewed. Conclusions regarding effectiveness depend on the assessment strategy employed (knowledge vs. skill measures), characteristics of the target population (e.g., age, gender, SES), and type of program (e.g., active vs.

passive learning). Thus, the question of effectiveness will be answered from these different perspectives.

Knowledge Acquisition

Both school- and preschool-age children demonstrate enhanced knowledge about CSA prevention concepts following program participation. In their meta-analysis of CSA prevention evaluation studies, Berrick and Barth (1992) reported large effect sizes for both preschool-age children ($d = .86$) and elementary school-age children ($d = .98$). Furthermore, knowledge gains have been shown to be maintained for periods up to 3 months (Ratto & Bogat, 1990; Saslawsky & Wurtele, 1986; Wurtele, Saslawsky, Miller, Marrs, & Britcher, 1986), 5–6 months (Kolko et al., 1987; Kolko, Moser, & Hughes, 1989; Tutty, 1992; Wurtele, Kast, & Melzer, 1992), and 1 year (Briggs & Hawkins, 1994; Hazzard et al., 1991).

In the studies that compared responses of children from different age groups, older children knew more initially compared with younger children, and older children learned more of the concepts, even among school-age children (Binder & McNiel, 1987 [9–12 > 5–8 years]; Blumberg et al., 1991 [1–3 > K grades]; Borkin & Frank, 1986 [4, 5 > 3 years]; Conte et al., 1985 [6–10 > 4–5 years]; Harbeck et al., 1992 [11–16 > 4–7 years]; Hazzard et al., 1990 [4 > 3 grades]; Hazzard et al., 1991 [4 > 3 grades]; Nemerofsky, Carran, & Rosenberg, 1994 [4–6 > 3 years]; Saslawsky & Wurtele, 1986 [5, 6 > K,1 grades]; Tutty, 1992 [6 > 3 > 1 > K grades]; Wurtele, Currier, Gillispie, & Franklin, 1991 (4.5–5.5 > 3.5–4.5 years]; Wurtele et al., 1986 [5, 6 > K,1 grades]). The one exception was a study by Kraizer et al. (1989), which showed greater gains in knowledge among preschoolers and kindergartners compared with first, second, and third graders. With such consistent effects for age, it is imperative that programs and evaluation instruments be tailored to the developmental needs of the audience. Even if the same program is used for children aged 3 to 12, younger children will need supplementary materials and much more repetition (Tutty, 1992).

Critics of child-focused CSA prevention programs have asserted that preschoolers and kindergartners cannot learn CSA prevention concepts because of their limited cognitive abilities (Gilbert et al., 1989; Reppucci & Haugaard, 1989). Indeed, Krivacska (1990) claimed, "Below the age of 7, instruction in CSA concepts is contraindicated" (p. 67). Older studies did suggest that 3- to 5-year-old children achieved few, if any knowledge gains (e.g., Borkin & Frank, 1986; Christian, Dwyer, Schumm, & Coulson, 1988; Conte et al., 1985; Gilbert et al., 1989). However, more recent, methodologically rigorous studies amply demonstrate that they do indeed benefit from these programs in terms of knowledge acquisition (Harvey, Forehand, Brown, & Holmes, 1988; Nemerofsky et al., 1994; Peraino, 1990; Ratto & Bogat, 1990; Wurtele, 1990, 1993b; Wurtele et al., 1991; Wurtele, Gillispie, Currier, & Franklin, 1992; Wurtele, Kast, & Melzer, 1992; Wurtele et al., 1989; Wurtele, Marrs, & Miller-Perrin, 1987). Knowledge gains with young children are more likely to be achieved when programs teach concrete concepts, and include active learning (rehearsal, role play), repetition, multiple sessions, and teacher/parent education.

Along with age differences, gender differences have also been examined, with most studies finding no differences, especially with young children (Bogat & McGrath, 1993; Harvey et al., 1988; Kolko et al., 1989; Peraino, 1990; Saslawsky & Wurtele, 1986; Wolfe, MacPherson, Blount, & Wolfe, 1986; Wurtele, 1993b; Wurtele, Gillispie, Currier, & Franklin, 1992; Wurtele, Kast, & Melzer, 1992; Wurtele et al., 1989;

Wurtele et al., 1987; Wurtele et al., 1986). Three studies found school-age girls to be more knowledgeable than boys (Finkelhor et al., 1995; Hazzard et al., 1990; Sigurdson, Strang, & Doig, 1987).

The few studies examining the impact of socioeconomic status (SES) level on children's responses have produced conflicting results. Peraino (1990) reported a trend for lower-income preschoolers to learn more, whereas Briggs and Hawkins (1994) found that low-SES children knew less initially and gained less from the programs compared with middle-class children.

Skill Gains

The bulk of the research shows that preschool- and school-age children can learn certain preventive skills. Evidence for gains in the skills of recognizing, resisting, and reporting will be presented.

Recognize. The first major skill objective of a personal safety program is to help children recognize potentially abusive situations, so they will know when to apply their newly learned personal safety skills. Following program participation, children have improved in their ability to recognize inappropriate touches. This skill has been demonstrated with both school-age children (Blumberg et al., 1991; Hazzard et al., 1991; Swan et al., 1985) and 3- to 6-year-old children (Harvey et al., 1988; Peraino, 1990; Ratto & Bogat, 1990; Stilwell, Lutzker, & Greene, 1988; Wurtele, 1990, 1993b; Wurtele et al., 1991; Wurtele, Gillispie, Currier, & Franklin, 1992; Wurtele, Kast, & Melzer, 1992; Wurtele et al., 1989). With younger children, the ability to discriminate between appropriate and inappropriate touching of the genitals improves more when they are taught to use a concrete rule to protect their private parts as opposed to using feelings to guide their decision making (Blumberg et al., 1991; Wurtele et al., 1989).

Resist. The second skill objective of a personal safety program is to teach some form of self-protection, usually the verbal skill of refusing the sexual offer and the behavioral skill of escaping from the potential perpetrator. Based on findings obtained using written, verbal, or videotaped vignettes in which hypothetical abusive situations are described to the children and their responses to potential perpetrators are solicited, the data show that these programs can enhance children's resistance skills. After participating in a personal safety program, school-age children's scores on these measures (say "no," get away) improve significantly (Kolko et al., 1989; Saslawsky & Wurtele, 1986), as do scores for younger children (Harvey et al., 1988; Miltenberger & Thiesse-Duffy, 1988; Nemerofsky et al., 1994; Nibert et al., 1989; Ratto & Bogat, 1990; Stilwell et al., 1988; Wurtele, 1990, 1993b; Wurtele et al., 1991; Wurtele, Gillispie, Currier, & Franklin, 1992; Wurtele, Kast, & Melzer, 1992; Wurtele et al., 1989; Wurtele et al., 1987). As with knowledge gains, skill gains have been maintained at the follow-up conducted even a year after presentation of the programs (Hazzard et al., 1991). Preventive skill scores are higher when children participate in active-learning programs that provide multiple opportunities for children to practice the skills during the program (Blumberg et al., 1991; Wurtele et al., 1987).

There are some exceptions where children did not improve significantly either over time or in comparison with control children's scores (e.g., Borkin & Frank, 1986; Christian et al., 1988; Harbeck et al., 1992; Miltenberger et al., 1990), but this may be due to ceiling effects or to the instructional method (passive learning techniques; the

absence of examples of inappropriate touching in the educational program). Several researchers have noted that not all subjects evidence criterion performances (e.g., Fryer
et al., 1987a; Harbeck et al., 1992; Kraizer et al., 1989; Stilwell et al., 1988; Wurtele
et al., 1991), which highlights the need for more instruction.

Whether children can learn resistance skills has also been assessed by a few researchers through role plays. In general, children's performances during role plays
have been inconsistent and less effective (e.g., Harbeck et al., 1992; Stilwell et al.,
1988). In contrast, Kraizer et al. (1989) found strong effects on their skills measure for
younger children. The discrepancy most likely is due to the heavy emphasis on practicing these skills in the Kraizer et al. (1989) program as opposed to the passive instruction provided in the others. In the few studies that have compared what children say
they would do to what they actually do during role-play situations, their verbal responses are usually more effective than their behavioral responses (Harbeck et al.,
1992; Stilwell et al., 1988). These results suggest that children may be able to adequately verbalize prevention information and skills, but may have difficulty in actually
using the skills.

As noted, Finkelhor and his colleagues have addressed the question of skill utilization in real-life situations in their national survey of children aged 10 to 16 (Finkelhor
& Dziuba-Leatherman, 1995). Among their survey respondents, a surprisingly high
number (40%) of them reported specific instances where they used the information or
skills taught in the program to protect themselves. Victimized and threatened children
were more likely to use self-protection strategies if they had received comprehensive
prevention instruction, which included opportunities to practice the skills in class,
multiday presentations, and materials to take home to discuss with their parents. This
is the first study to suggest, "When children with prevention training do actually get
victimized or threatened after their program exposure, they can behave to some extent
in ways envisioned by prevention educators" (Finkelhor et al., 1995, p. 150).

Report. The third skill objective of most personal safety programs is to encourage children to report past or ongoing abuse. One method of assessing this skill is to
ask children if they would tell someone if they were involved in an abusive situation.
After participating in personal safety programs, children indicate a greater willingness to tell (Binder & McNiel, 1987; Kolko et al., 1987; Swan et al., 1985; Wolfe
et al., 1986; Wurtele, 1990, 1993b; Wurtele et al., 1991; Wurtele, Gillispie, Currier,
& Franklin, 1992). Not only are program participants more willing to tell, but they
also expand the type of resource person to whom they would report (Wurtele, 1993;
Wurtele, Kast, & Melzer, 1992). However, like others (Ratto & Bogat, 1990; Stilwell
et al., 1988), we consistently find that preschool children have difficulty accurately
describing the abusive situation to the resource person (Wurtele, 1990; Wurtele et al.,
1991).

As mentioned, very few researchers present information on unsolicited disclosures,
which is another way to determine if these programs are facilitating reporting. Published disclosure rates immediately following the program have varied from a low of
0% (Gilbert et al., 1989; Hill & Jason, 1987) to a high of 11% (Kolko et al., 1989). The
11% figure is impressive, given that sexually abused children rarely disclose purpose-
fully (Sorenson & Snow, 1991). Encouraging disclosure early in the abuse experience
is an important objective, as children are more seriously affected by long-lasting abuse
(e.g., Friedrich, Urquiza, & Beilke, 1986). Furthermore, telling or threatening to tell

has been suggested as an effective deterrent by both victims and offenders (Berliner & Conte, 1990; Budin & Johnson, 1989; Conte, Wolf, & Smith, 1989; Elliott, Browne, & Kilcoyne, 1995). Thus, emphasis in prevention programs on reporting is warranted, and it is incumbent on researchers to begin systematically documenting the frequency, type, and consequences of disclosures.

Side Effects

In this section, evidence for possible side effects of CSA prevention programs will be reviewed including whether these programs increase anxiety and acting out, affect sexual development, or result in suspiciousness of innocuous touching. In addition, the possibility of positive side effects will be explored. Other concerns about possible negative effects of these programs have been raised but have not been studied empirically; for example, what are the long-term effects on children's sexual attitudes/behaviors? What impact does prevention training have on family relationships? Do these programs affect adults' willingness to touch children?

Anxiety. When researchers have administered measures of anxiety to program participants (whether of general anxiety or anxiety specific to the program), none of them have found significant increases in anxiety (Hazzard et al., 1991; Ratto & Bogat, 1990; Wurtele et al., 1989; Wurtele & Miller-Perrin, 1987). When children have been asked directly if the program made them feel worried or scared, the percentages of children responding "yes" have ranged from 11.3% (Hazzard et al., 1990) to over half (Finkelhor & Dziuba-Leatherman, 1995; Garbarino, 1987). At face value, these latter statistics are alarming. The reader should note, however, that no pretests or control programs were used in these studies. Thus, we do not know what percentage of non-program children would report being afraid of being abused, but in today's violent world, chances are the percentages would be just as high, if not higher. Finkelhor and Dziuba-Leatherman (1995) also note that those children who reported increased levels of fear and anxiety also rated the programs most positively and were also the ones most likely to use the skills taught in the programs. They also suggest that these higher fear/anxiety ratings reflected that the children were taking the message of the training seriously. They conclude by urging professionals to "restrain from assuming that reports of increased fear and anxiety are a negative outcome of training programs" (p. 137).

Acting Out. When parents and teachers have been asked to report on adverse reactions seen among the children, few parents report observing problems (e.g., 3% in Finkelhor & Dziuba-Leatherman, 1995; 5% in Swan et al., 1985 and Hazzard et al., 1991; 7% in Nibert et al., 1989). Similarly, teachers and parents noticed few, if any, signs of increased emotional distress in several studies (Binder & McNiel, 1987; Wurtele, 1990, 1993b; Wurtele, Gillispie, Currier, & Franklin, 1992; Wurtele, Kast, & Melzer, 1992; Wurtele et al., 1989).

Negative Effects on Sexual Development. As noted previously, very few researchers have addressed the concern that these programs may be harming children's sexual development. Our research has addressed subsets of this question with one age group (3- to 5-year-old children). For example, in two studies (Wurtele, 1993a; Wurtele, Melzer, & Kast, 1992), we demonstrated that preschool children are largely unaware of the anatomically correct terminology for their genitals, but that they can learn the correct terms, especially when taught by their parents (vs. teachers; Wurtele, Melzer, & Kast, 1992). We also routinely ask children if they like their private parts (as a measure of body pride) and have found in four studies (Wurtele, 1993a, 1993b; Wurtele et al., 1991; Wurtele, Kast, & Melzer, 1992) that before the program, only about 70% of preschool children say "yes," whereas after the program, this figure increases significantly, to about 90%. When young children are asked during pretesting if it is acceptable for them to touch their own private parts, only 75% of children respond "yes," compared with an average of 90% after the program. Personal safety programs for young children can incorporate sexuality education by teaching young children: (a) correct terminology for their genitals; (b) that genital exploration is acceptable (in private); and (c) that their genitals are special and need to be protected. It is incumbent on researchers to expand the target population to determine how these programs affect older children and adolescents in terms of their sexual development.

Overgeneralization. An important question is whether these programs make children suspicious of innocuous touches. Information on children's abilities to recognize appropriate touches, both before and after a program, is necessary to address this concern. In two assessments of our personal safety program, we noted a tendency for young children to overgeneralize the rule to protect their private parts (Wurtele et al., 1989; Wurtele, Kast, & Melzer, 1992) and subsequently modified our program to include more opportunities to recognize the appropriateness of health professionals or parents touching the private parts for health or hygiene purposes. In our later studies, and in work by others where scores on appropriate-touch recognition have been reported, encouragingly, children's scores do not decrease significantly, and in some instances, these scores even increase significantly (Blumberg et al., 1991; Wurtele, 1993b). Thus, most children do not overgeneralize their recognition skills to hypothetical appropriate-touch requests, suggesting that program participants are not likely to misinterpret nurturing touches or make false accusations of CSA. This conclusion is bolstered by the fact that there have been no published accounts of false accusations following a personal safety program.

Positive Side Effects. Several researchers have found what might be considered positive side effects of program participation. For example, Binder and McNiel (1987) reported that 64% of the children in their study said that the program made them feel much safer (as did 71% of the children in Hazzard et al., 1990), and 72% felt better able to protect themselves. In Finkelhor and Dziuba-Leatherman (1995), 95% of youth who received a school-based victimization prevention program said they would recommend it to other children, and in general found the programs to be helpful and interesting (especially true of girls, younger children, African-American children, and low SES children). Children who reported being victimized or threatened and who had received comprehensive prevention programs perceived themselves as having been more effective in keeping themselves safe and minimizing their harm.

Several others have found that after participating in a program, children are more likely to discuss the contents of the program with their parents (Binder & McNiel, 1987; Finkelhor et al., 1995; Hazzard et al., 1991; Kolko et al., 1987; Wurtele, 1990; Wurtele et al., 1989; Wurtele & Miller-Perrin, 1987). Increasing parent-child communication about CSA not only reduces the secrecy surrounding this topic, but most likely increases the effectiveness of school-based personal safety instruction.

Comment

Using proximal measures, child-focused CSA prevention programs produce significant gains in knowledge and skills, among both school- and preschool-aged children. Older children obtain higher scores on the assessment instruments compared with younger children. These gains do not appear to vary depending on the gender of the child, but there may be differential effects according to parents' socioeconomic status. Gains are more notable when the programs are developmentally appropriate (e.g., avoid abstract, complex concepts with young children), occur on multiple occasions, offer periodic reviews, stimulate parent-child discussion about the topic, and give learners multiple opportunities to practice the skills being taught through role play and modeling. Encouragingly, these benefits are achieved with no or minimal short-term negative effects, and there is evidence of positive indirect effects (e.g., enhanced sexual development; increased parent-child discussion).

It is important to put these positive findings in perspective. First of all, as is true of any instructional endeavor, not all children score 100% on the instruments. There appear to be a small percentage of children who do not grasp prevention concepts and skills after training, and it becomes incumbent on researchers to offer additional/different instruction to these children (e.g., see Fryer et al., 1987a), and to identify needed modifications in the program. Furthermore, although increases in scores are statistically significant, in practical terms the gains are sometimes small, particularly on tests of preventive skills. As far as whether these programs produce changes in distal outcomes (i.e., delayed changes such as reduced incidence), the verdict is still out. There is preliminary evidence that children use the self-protection strategies taught in these programs when victimized or threatened (Finkelhor et al., 1995). Alternatively, there is at least one published account of 22 children (ages 6–10 years) who were abused by a school employee, despite having been exposed previously to a school-based CSA prevention program (Pelcovitz, Adler, Kaplan, Packman, & Krieger, 1992). Even though the program had serious limitations (it was a one-shot, brief filmed presentation), Pelcovitz et al. (1992) offer sound advice when they caution:

> We cannot assume that children are protected from possible victimization because we have presented them with some form of prevention programming. It is important that educators not be misled into believing that their responsibility to educate children regarding the prevention of sexual abuse is discharged through the presentation of a short film. (p. 891)

In attempting to answer the question, "Do these programs actually prevent sexual victimization?" researchers are faced with a measurement problem: How do we measure nonoccurrence? One way is to monitor incidence rates; if programs are effective, then incidence rates of CSA should decrease over time. To date, there is no evidence suggesting that these programs are helping to decrease the incidence of sexual abuse. Given the low base rate of sexual abuse, answering this important question would require following very large samples of trained and untrained children and documenting a lower incidence of abuse among the former. Although these are methodologically, pragmatically, and ethically difficult studies to conduct, demonstrating a reduction in the incidence of CSA represents the most demanding yet necessary challenge facing the prevention researcher.

In the interim, there is much work to be done to enhance existing programs, given the consistent finding that not all children benefit equally from the instruction. The charge for future researchers is to determine what kind of program works best with what type of children.

Summary

Child-focused personal safety programs play an important part in the effort to keep children safe from sexual victimization. Extant research demonstrates that children lack the knowledge and skills taught in these programs, that they are able to learn about sexual abuse concepts and prevention skills, and there is preliminary evidence that they are able to apply this information in real-life situations. Learning how to protect oneself is a valuable, lifelong lesson. At the same time, the responsibility for preventing CSA must be shared. The general public, professionals, and parents play important roles in this endeavor, but, these groups have not received the same attention as have children. It is time to extend preventive efforts and target others, particularly parents, to play a more active part in preventing CSA, so that children do not shoulder the full responsibility for prevention. This extension represents a logical and necessary next step toward the eradication of CSA.

References

Abrahams, N., Casey, K., & Daro, D. (1992). Teachers' knowledge, attitudes, and beliefs about child abuse and its prevention. *Child Abuse & Neglect, 16,* 229–238.

Atteberry-Bennett, J., & Reppucci, N. D. (1986, August). *What does child sexual abuse mean?* Paper presented at the annual convention of the American Psychological Association, Washington, DC.

Beitchman, J. H., Zucker, K. J., Hood, J. E., daCosta, G. A., & Akman, D. (1991). A review of the short-term effects of child sexual abuse. *Child Abuse & Neglect, 15,* 537–556.

Beitchman, J. H., Zucker, K. J., Hood, J. E., daCosta, G. A., Akman, D., & Cassavia, E. (1992). A review of the long-term effects of child sexual abuse. *Child Abuse & Neglect, 16,* 101–118.

Bellack, A. S., & Hersen, M. (1988). *Behavioral assessment: A practical handbook.* New York: Pergamon Press.

Berliner, L., & Conte, J. R. (1990). The process of victimization: The victims' perspective. *Child Abuse & Neglect, 14,* 29–40.

Berrick, J. D. (1988). Parental involvement in child abuse prevention training: What do they learn? *Child Abuse & Neglect, 12,* 543–553.

Berrick, J. D., & Barth, R. P. (1992). Child sexual abuse prevention: Research review and recommendations. *Social Work Research and Abstracts, 28,* 6–15.

Binder, R. L., & McNiel, D. E. (1987). Evaluation of a school-based sexual abuse prevention program: Cognitive and emotional effects. *Child Abuse & Neglect, 11,* 497–506.

Blumberg, E. J., Chadwick, M. W., Fogarty, L. A., Speth, T. W., & Chadwick, D. L. (1991). The touch discrimination component of sexual abuse prevention training: Unanticipated positive consequences. *Journal of Interpersonal Violence, 6,* 12–28.

Bogat, G. A., & McGrath, M. P. (1993). Preschoolers' cognitions of authority, and its relationship to sexual abuse education. *Child Abuse & Neglect, 17,* 651–662.

Borkin, J., & Frank, L. (1986). Sexual abuse prevention for preschoolers: A pilot program. *Child Welfare, 65,* 75–82.

Briere, J. N., & Elliott, D. M. (1994). Immediate and long-term impacts of child sexual abuse. *The Future of Children, 4,* 54–69.

Briggs, F. (1991). Child protection programs: Can they protect young children? *Early Child Development and Care, 67,* 61–72.

Briggs, F., & Hawkins, R. M. F. (1994). Follow-up data on the effectiveness of New Zealand's national school-based child protection program. *Child Abuse & Neglect, 18,* 635–643.

Browne, A., & Finkelhor, D. (1986). Impact of child sexual abuse: A review of the research. *Psychological Bulletin, 99,* 66–77.

Budin, L. E., & Johnson, C. F. (1989). Sex abuse prevention programs: Offenders' attitudes about their efficacy. *Child Abuse & Neglect, 13,* 77–87.

Cappelleri, J. C., Eckenrode, J., & Powers, J. L. (1993). The epidemiology of child abuse: Findings from the Second National Incidence and Prevalence Study of Child Abuse and Neglect. *American Journal of Public Health, 83,* 1622–1624.

Christian, R., Dwyer, S., Schumm, W. R., & Coulson, L. A. (1988). Prevention of sexual abuse for preschoolers: Evaluation of a pilot program. *Psychological Reports, 62,* 387–396.

Conte, J. R. (1987). Ethical issues in evaluation of prevention programs. *Child Abuse & Neglect, 11,* 171–172.

Conte, J. R., & Fogarty, L. A. (1989). *Attitudes on sexual abuse prevention programs: A national survey of parents.* (Available from J. R. Conte, School of Social Work, University of Washington, Mailstop 354900, 4101 15th Avenue N. E., Seattle, WA 98195-6299)

Conte, J. R., Rosen, C., Saperstein, L., & Shermack, R. (1985). An evaluation of a program to prevent the sexual victimization of young children. *Child Abuse & Neglect, 9,* 319–328.

Conte, J. R., Wolf, S., & Smith, T. (1989). What sexual offenders tell us about prevention strategies. *Child Abuse & Neglect, 13,* 293–301.

Cupoli, J. M., & Sewell, P. M. (1988). One thousand fifty-nine children with a chief complaint of sexual abuse. *Child Abuse & Neglect, 12,* 151–162.

Daro, D. (1994). Prevention of child sexual abuse. *The Future of Children, 4,* 198–223.

DeAngelis, T. (1995, April). New threat associated with child abuse. *The APA Monitor, 26,* 1, 38.

Eckenrode, J., Munsch, J., Powers, J., & Doris, J. (1988). The nature and substantiation of official sexual abuse reports. *Child Abuse & Neglect, 12,* 311–319.

Elliott, M., Browne, K., & Kilcoyne, J. (1995). Child sexual abuse prevention: What offenders tell us. *Child Abuse & Neglect, 19,* 579–594.

Elrod, J. M., & Rubin, R. H. (1993). Parental involvement in sexual abuse prevention education. *Child Abuse & Neglect, 17,* 527–538.

Finkelhor, D. (1979). *Sexually victimized children.* New York: Free Press.

Finkelhor, D. (1990). New ideas for child sexual abuse prevention. In R. K. Oates (Ed.), *Understanding and managing child sexual abuse* (pp. 385–396). Sydney, Australia: Harcourt Press.

Finkelhor, D. (1994). Current information on the scope and nature of child sexual abuse. *The Future of Children, 4,* 31–53.

Finkelhor, D., Asdigian, N., & Dziuba-Leatherman, J. (1995). The effectiveness of victimization prevention instruction: An evaluation of children's responses to actual threats and assaults. *Child Abuse & Neglect, 19,* 141–153.

Finkelhor, D., & Dziuba-Leatherman, J. (1995). Victimization prevention programs: A national survey of children's exposure and reactions. *Child Abuse & Neglect, 19,* 129–139.

Friedrich, W. N., Urquiza, A. J., & Beilke, R. L. (1986). Behavior problems in sexually abused young children. *Journal of Pediatric Psychology, 11*, 47–57.

Fryer, G. E., Kraizer, S. K., & Miyoshi, T. (1987a). Measuring actual reduction of risk to child abuse: A new approach. *Child Abuse & Neglect, 11*, 173–179.

Fryer, G. E., Kraizer, S. K., & Miyoshi, T. (1987b). Measuring children's retention of skills to resist stranger abduction: Use of the simulation technique. *Child Abuse & Neglect, 11*, 181–185.

Garbarino, J. (1987). Children's response to a sexual abuse prevention program: A study of the Spiderman comic. *Child Abuse & Neglect, 11*, 143–148.

Gilbert, N., Berrick, J. D., Le Prohn, N., & Nyman, N. (1989). *Protecting young children from sexual abuse: Does preschool training work?* Lexington, MA: Lexington Books.

Harbeck, C., Peterson, L., & Starr, L. (1992). Previously abused child victims' response to a sexual abuse prevention program: A matter of measures. *Behavior Therapy, 23*, 375–387.

Harvey, P., Forehand, R., Brown, C., & Holmes, T. (1988). The prevention of sexual abuse: Examination of the effectiveness of a program with kindergarten-age children. *Behavior Therapy, 19*, 429–435.

Hazzard, A., Kleemeier, C. P., & Webb, C. (1990). Teacher versus expert presentations of sexual abuse prevention programs. *Journal of Interpersonal Violence, 5*, 23–36.

Hazzard, A., Webb, C., Kleemeier, C., Angert, L., & Pohl, L. (1991). Child sexual abuse prevention: Evaluation and one-year follow-up. *Child Abuse & Neglect, 15*, 123–138.

Helge, D. (1992). *Child sexual abuse in America—A call for school and community action.* Bellingham, WA: National Rural Development Institute.

Hill, J. L., & Jason, L. A. (1987). An evaluation of a school-based child sexual abuse primary prevention program. *Psychotherapy Bulletin, 22*, 36–38.

Kendall-Tackett, K. A., Williams, L. M., & Finkelhor, D. (1993). Impact of sexual abuse on children: A review and synthesis of recent empirical studies. *Psychological Bulletin, 13*, 164–180.

Kohl, J. (1993). School-based child sexual abuse prevention programs. *Journal of Family Violence, 8*, 137–150.

Kolko, D. J., Moser, J. T., & Hughes, J. (1989). Classroom training in sexual victimization awareness and prevention skills: An extension of the Red Flag/Green Flag people program. *Journal of Family Violence, 4*, 25–45.

Kolko, D. J., Moser, J. T., Litz, J., & Hughes, J. (1987). Promoting awareness and prevention of child sexual vicitmization using the Red Flag/Green Flag program: An evaluation with follow-up. *Journal of Family Violence, 2*, 11–35.

Korbin, J. E. (1990). Child sexual abuse: A cross-cultural view. In R. K. Oates (Ed.), *Understanding and managing child sexual abuse* (pp. 42–58). Sydney, Australia: Harcourt Brace.

Kraizer, S., Witte, S. S., & Fryer, G. E., Jr. (1989). Child sexual abuse prevention programs: What makes them effective in protecting children? *Children Today, 18*, 23–27.

Krivacska, J. J. (1989). Child sexual abuse prevention programs and accusation of child sexual abuse: An analysis. *Issues in Child Abuse Accusations, 1*, 8–13.

Krivacska, J. J. (1990). *Designing child sexual abuse prevention programs: Current approaches and a proposal for the prevention, reduction, and identification of sexual misuse.* Springfield, IL: Thomas.

Liang, B., Bogart, G. A., & McGrath, M. P. (1993). Differential understanding of sexual abuse prevention concepts among preschoolers. *Child Abuse & Neglect, 17*, 641–650.

McCurdy, K., & Daro, D. (1994). *Current trends in child abuse reporting and fatalities: The results of the 1993 annual fifty state survey.* Chicago, IL: National Committee for the Prevention of Child Abuse.

McGee, R. A., & Painter, S. L. (1991). What if it happens in my family? Parental reactions to a hypothetical disclosure of sexual abuse. *Canadian Journal of Behavioural Science, 23,* 228–240.

Miller-Perrin, C. L., & Wurtele, S. K. (1988). The child sexual abuse prevention movement: A critical analysis of primary and secondary approaches. *Clinical Psychology Review, 8,* 313–329.

Miller-Perrin, C. L., & Wurtele, S. K. (1990). Reactions to childhood sexual abuse: Implications for Post-Traumatic Stress Disorder. In C. Meek (Ed.), *Post-Traumatic Stress Disorder: Assessment, differential diagnosis, forensic evaluation* (pp. 91–135). Sarasota, FL: Professional Resource Exchange.

Miltenberger, R. G., & Thiesse-Duffy, E. (1988). Evaluation of home-based programs for teaching personal safety skills to children. *Journal of Applied Behavior Analysis, 21,* 81–87.

Miltenberger, R. G., Thiesse-Duffy, E., Suda, K. T., Kozak, C., & Bruellman, J. (1990). Teaching prevention skills to children: The use of multiple measures to evaluate parent versus expert instruction. *Child and Family Behavior Therapy, 12,* 65–87.

Nemerofsky, A. G., Carran, D. T., & Rosenberg, L. A. (1994). Age variation in performance among preschool children in a sexual abuse prevention program. *Journal of Child Sexual Abuse, 31,* 85–102.

Nibert, D., Cooper, S., & Ford, J. (1989). Parents' observations of the effect of a sexual abuse prevention program on preschool children. *Child Welfare, 68,* 539–546.

Nibert, D., Cooper, S., Ford, J., Fitch, L. K., & Robinson, J. (1989). The ability of young children to learn abuse prevention. *Response, 12,* 14–20.

Paradise, J. E., Rose, L., Sleeper, L. A., & Nathanson, M. (1994). Behavior, family function, school performance, and predictors of persistent disturbance in sexually abused children. *Pediatrics, 93,* 452–459.

Pelcovitz, D., Adler, N. A., Kaplan, S., Packman, L., & Krieger, R. (1992). The failure of a school-based child sexual abuse prevention program. *Journal of the American Academy of Child and Adolescent Psychiatry, 31,* 887–892.

Peraino, J. M. (1990). Evaluation of a preschool antivictimization prevention program. *Journal of Interpersonal Violence, 5,* 520–528.

Perry, C. L., Luepker, R. V., Murray, D. M., Kurth, C., Mullis, R., Crockett, S., & Jacobs, D. R. (1988). Parent involvement with children's health promotion: The Minnesota Home Team. *American Journal of Public Health, 78,* 1156–1160.

Poche, C., Yoder, P., & Miltenberger, R. (1988). Teaching self-protection to children using television techniques. *Journal of Applied Behavior Analysis, 21,* 253–261.

Porch, T. L., & Petretic-Jackson, P. A. (1986, August). *Child sexual assault prevention: Evaluating parent education workshops.* Paper presented at the convention of the American Psychological Association, Washington, DC.

Ratto, R., & Bogat, G. A. (1990). An evaluation of a preschool curriculum to educate children in the prevention of sexual abuse. *Journal of Community Psychology, 18,* 289–297.

Reppucci, N. D., & Haugaard, J. J. (1989). Prevention of child sexual abuse: Myth or reality? *American Psychologist, 44,* 1266–1275.

Reppucci, N. D., & Herman, J. (1991). Sexuality education and child sexual abuse prevention programs in the schools. In G. Grant (Ed.), *Review of research in education* (Vol. 17, pp. 127–166). Washington, DC: American Educational Research Association.

Romano, N., Casey, K., & Daro, D. (1990). *Schools and child abuse: A national survey of principals' attitudes, beliefs, and practices.* Chicago: National Committee for the Prevention of Child Abuse.

Saslawsky, D. A., & Wurtele, S. K. (1986). Educating children about sexual abuse: Implications for pediatric intervention and possible prevention. *Journal of Pediatric Psychology, 11,* 235–245.

Sedlak, A. J. (1990). *Technical amendment to the study findings—National Incidence and Prevalence of Child Abuse and Neglect: 1988.* Rockville, MD: Westat.

Sigurdson, E., Strang, M., & Doig, T. (1987). What do children know about preventing sexual assault? How can their awareness be increased? *Canadian Journal of Psychiatry, 32,* 551–557.

Sorenson, T., & Snow, B. (1991). How children tell: The process of disclosure in child sexual abuse. *Child Welfare, 70,* 3–15.

Stilwell, S. L., Lutzker, J. R., & Greene, B. F. (1988). Evaluation of a sexual abuse prevention program for preschoolers. *Journal of Family Violence, 3,* 269–281.

Swan, H. L., Press, A. N., & Briggs, S. L. (1985). Child sexual abuse prevention: Does it work? *Child Welfare, 64,* 395–405.

Tutty, L. M. (1991). Child sexual abuse: A range of prevention options. In B. Thomlison & C. Bagley (Eds.), Child sexual abuse: Expanding the research base on program and treatment outcomes [Special issue]. *Journal of Child and Youth Care,* 23–41.

Tutty, L. M. (1992). The ability of elementary school children to learn child sexual abuse prevention concepts. *Child Abuse & Neglect, 16,* 369–384.

Tutty, L. M. (1993). Parents' perceptions of their child's knowledge of sexual abuse prevention concepts. *Journal of Child Sexual Abuse, 2,* 83–103.

U.S. Department of Health and Human Services, National Center on Child Abuse and Neglect. (1995). *Child maltreatment 1993: Reports from the states to the National Center on Child Abuse and Neglect.* Washington, DC: U.S. Government Printing Office.

Williams, L. M. (1994). Recall of childhood trauma: A prospective study of women's memories of child sexual abuse. *Journal of Consulting and Clinical Psychology, 62,* 1167–1176.

Wolfe, D. A., MacPherson, T., Blount, R., & Wolfe, V. V. (1986). Evaluation of a brief intervention for educating school children in awareness of physical and sexual abuse. *Child Abuse & Neglect, 10,* 85–92.

Wolfe, V. V., & Birt, J. (1995). The psychological sequelae of child sexual abuse. In T. H. Ollendick & R. J. Prinz (Eds.), *Advances in clinical child psychology* (Vol. 17, pp. 233–263). New York: Plenum Press.

Wurtele, S. K. (1987). School-based sexual abuse prevention programs: A review. *Child Abuse & Neglect, 11,* 483–495.

Wurtele, S. K. (1990). Teaching personal safety skills to four-year-old children: A behavioral approach. *Behavior Therapy, 21,* 25–32.

Wurtele, S. K. (1993a). Enhancing children's sexual development through child sexual abuse prevention programs. *Journal of Sex Education and Therapy, 19,* 37–46.

Wurtele, S. K. (1993b). The role of maintaining telephone contact with parents during the teaching of a personal safety program. *Journal of Child Sexual Abuse, 2,* 65–82.

Wurtele, S. K., Currier, L. L., Gillispie, E. I., & Franklin, C. F. (1991). The efficacy of a parent-implemented program for teaching preschoolers personal safety skills. *Behavior Therapy, 22,* 69–83.

Wurtele, S. K., Gillispie, E. I., Currier, L. L., & Franklin, C. F. (1992). A comparison of teachers vs. parents as instructors of a personal safety program for preschoolers. *Child Abuse & Neglect, 16,* 127–137.

Wurtele, S. K., Kast, L. C., & Melzer, A. M. (1992). Sexual abuse prevention education for young children: A comparison of teachers and parents as instructors. *Child Abuse & Neglect, 16,* 865–876.

Wurtele, S. K., Kast, L. C., Miller-Perrin, C. L., & Kondrick, P. A. (1989). A comparison of programs for teaching personal safety skills to preschoolers. *Journal of Consulting and Clinical Psychology, 57,* 505–511.

Wurtele, S. K., Kvaternick, M., & Franklin, C. F. (1992). Sexual abuse prevention for preschoolers: A survey of parents' behaviors, attitudes, and beliefs. *Journal of Child Sexual Abuse, 1,* 113–128.

Wurtele, S. K., Marrs, S. R., & Miller-Perrin, C. L. (1987). Practice makes perfect? The role of participant modeling in sexual abuse prevention programs. *Journal of Consulting and Clinical Psychology, 55,* 599–602.

Wurtele, S. K., Melzer, A. M., & Kast, L. C. (1992). Preschoolers' knowledge of and ability to learn genital terminology. *Journal of Sex Education and Therapy, 18,* 115–122.

Wurtele, S. K., & Miller-Perrin, C. L. (1987). An evaluation of side effects associated with participation in a child sexual abuse prevention program. *Journal of School Health, 57,* 228–231.

Wurtele, S. K., & Miller-Perrin, C. L. (1992). *Preventing child sexual abuse: Sharing the responsibility.* Lincoln: University of Nebraska Press.

Wurtele, S. K., Saslawsky, D. A., Miller, C. L., Marrs, S. R., & Britcher, J. C. (1986). Teaching personal safety skills for potential prevention of sexual abuse: A comparison of treatments. *Journal of Consulting and Clinical Psychology, 54,* 688–692.

Wurtele, S. K., & Schmitt, A. (1992). Child care workers' knowledge about reporting suspected child sexual abuse. *Child Abuse & Neglect, 16,* 385–390.

CHAPTER 15

AIDS and Sexually Transmitted Diseases

STEVEN P. SCHINKE and KRISTIN COLE

DESCRIPTION OF THE PROBLEM

Despite significant public health advances, AIDS and sexually transmitted diseases (STDs) continue to pose risks for millions of Americans. Consistently high prevalence rates are particularly disquieting because AIDS and STDs are almost completely preventable. Lingering technological and institutional impediments notwithstanding, many of the conditions necessary for widespread behavior modification have significantly improved. Recent developments in barrier and other forms of birth control, increased public awareness of the need for protected sex, and reduced obstacles to the distribution of information and devices for protecting oneself sexually have all contributed to positive behavior modification. In addition, American educational systems have begun to address sex education on a national level. Thus, the absence of concomitant sharp decreases in the rates of AIDS and STDs is counterintuitive, and worthy of closer analysis. This disparity between the ready access to the information about and tools for "safe" (protected) sex, on the one hand, and the high incidence rates of unsafe sexual contacts, on the other, is most striking among young Americans.

Female and male adolescents in this country experience the highest prevalence rates and the largest increases of AIDS and STDs relative to their numbers and proportional representation in the U.S. population. Adolescents are less informed about and frequently more susceptible to these health hazards. Young women and men are biologically capable of and inclined toward sexual activity but do not necessarily have the social or psychological skills to avoid its untoward consequences. Because of their youth, adolescents have more to lose by contracting an incurable disease. Based on their inordinate risk for HIV infection and other STDs and their potential for falling victim to extraordinary problems from early, unprotected sexual behavior, adolescents are the population focus of this chapter.

SCOPE OF THE PROBLEM

Of the 441,528 reported cases of AIDS in the United States as of December 1994, 1,965 were diagnosed among adolescents 13 to 19 years of age (Centers for Disease Control [CDC], 1994). This figure is even more alarming given the high rate of increase of adolescent AIDS. Whereas in 1981 only one case of adolescent AIDS was reported, this figure had ballooned to 417 cases reported in 1994 (CDC, 1994). Yet the typical 8-to-10-year incubation period between infection and overt symptomatology would indicate that relatively few HIV-infected youth will present with full-blown AIDS during adolescence. Indeed, although the prevalence of AIDS within this age group accounts for less than 1% of all AIDS cases, nearly 19% (or 81,646) of all AIDS cases have been diagnosed among adults in their 20s (CDC, 1994).

The delay in the disease's presentation, the absence of any population-wide HIV testing program, and the stigma still associated with HIV infection suggest that the actual rate of HIV infection among the adolescent population may be much higher than the records indicate. Rates of pregnancy and sexually transmitted diseases in the teenage population can be helpful in estimating truer rates of HIV infection among teenagers (DiClemente, 1989).

Because STD rates reflect high-risk sexual activity, high STD rates are generally believed to be indicative of similar levels of HIV infection (Stein, 1992). Higher rates of syphilis, gonorrhea, and pelvic inflammatory disease in the adolescent population place them at particular risk for HIV (Jemmett, Jemmett, Loretta, & Fong, 1992).

Nearly 3 million teenagers, or a quarter of the total yearly cases, contract an STD every year. Thus, one in eight 13- to 19-year-olds contracts an STD every year. That figure is double for 13- to 19-year-olds who have had intercourse (Alan Guttmacher Institute, 1993), and contraction rates for STD are on the rise among many adolescent populations (O'Reilly & Aral, 1985).

Teenage girls are at particular risk of contracting an STD. Adolescent girls have the highest rate of gonorrhea, cytomegalovirus, chlamydia, cervicitis, and pelvic inflammatory disease of any age group (Cates & Rauch, 1985; Mosher, 1985).

Minority communities, people of low socioeconomic status, and those living in urban areas are disproportionately affected by HIV and STDs (Holmes, Karon, & Kreiss, 1990). AIDS incidence rates are six times and three times higher, respectively, among African-American and Hispanics than among whites (CDC, 1994). Heterosexual HIV infection is also more prevalent among these urban groups than in any other group (Rolfs, Goldber, & Sharrar, 1990). The same population also reports the highest incidence of STDs, at rates between two and three times as high as the national average.

Epidemiological data puts African-American and Hispanic adolescents living in urban centers at highest risk for STDs and HIV infection (CDC, 1994). Rates of intravenous drug use, sexual intercourse, and sexually transmitted diseases are also higher for African-American and Hispanic adolescents than for majority culture adolescents (CDC, 1990, 1994).

CAUSES AND CONSEQUENCES

A major cause of soaring rates of HIV infection and other STDs is unprotected sexual intercourse. The percentage of American youth who have had intercourse by age 18 has risen progressively. In the past three decades, that percentage for young women more than doubled; for young men it rose by one-third (Alan Guttmacher Institute, 1993). Birth control among American youth, albeit improving, remains poor. Whereas about one-half of all sexually experienced young women aged 15 to 19 years report condom use at first intercourse, over one-third used nothing, and one in 10 relied on withdrawal (Forrest & Singh, 1990).

Although few adolescent AIDS cases are attributable to IV drug use (CDC, 1990), substance use of any kind places adolescents at risk for HIV infection by potentially impairing their reasoning and decision-making skills. Youths who use substances are less likely to practice safe sex. Unprotected sexual intercourse is reported by roughly half of all American teenagers by the age of 19 years (CDC, 1992). What is more, youths who use substances may be more inclined to have sex with multiple partners, thereby increasing their risk for contracting a sexually transmitted disease. Among sexually experienced people, adolescents have the highest rates of sexually transmitted diseases (Bell & Hein, 1984; Cates, 1990).

The tendency toward experimentation that occurs in adolescence also puts teenagers at increased risk for contracting an STD. Moreover, adolescents' limited ability to understand and anticipate the long-term consequences of such experimentation increases their risk for HIV infection and for contracting other STDs. Partly due to these characteristics, adolescent AIDS cases increased 77% between 1990 and 1992 (House Select Committee on Children, Youth & Families, 1992).

Impediments to Intervention in the Real World Context

The growing threat of AIDS to adolescents has particularly spurred the development and implementation of health behavior curricula. By 1990, 83% of students were receiving AIDS education—up from 52% in 1986 (Hingson & Strunin, 1992). The evaluation of health curricula has similarly become a national priority.

School-based health education programs have emphasized avoiding unprotected sex as their foremost goal. But success in this endeavor has been triply qualified: Programs have been blocked by local political initiatives; programs have done a better job of teaching facts than effecting behavior change; and programs have unevenly distributed information among the adolescent population.

The evaluation of school-based prevention efforts has yielded an enormous amount of data about the necessary components for encouraging safe, protected sex. These identified components include: (a) *knowledge* about disease transmission or conception, methods of prevention, and severity; (b) *perceived risk* in terms of increasing adolescents' understanding of their vulnerability to the condition; (c) *skills* pertaining to communication in high pressure situations that involve sex and drugs; (d) *perceived norms* of peers regarding high-risk behaviors; and (e) *substance abuse prevention* related to decreasing the use of alcohol and other drugs that may contribute to sexual risk taking and to IV drug use.

Early Educational Efforts

According to Kirby (1992), five major phases of modern sex education have occurred in the United States. The earliest sex education efforts emphasized the risks and consequences of pregnancy. These programs were built on the premise that if youth had the information to make an informed decision about pregnancy (or cancer or drug dependency), they would make it in favor of safe behavior. The next wave of instruction moved on to values clarifications, decision making, and communications skills, with the intention of helping students articulate their own priorities, comprehend the risks and advantages of a number of value-positions, and negotiate for their preferences by discussion.

While both of these approaches did increase students' knowledge about sexuality (Kirby, 1984) and STDs (Yarber, 1986), their effect on high-risk behavior was less successful (Whitley & Schofield, 1986). More recently, AIDS-prevention education has relied heavily on conceptual change theory through the Health Belief Model (if subjects are fully aware of the consequences of various possible actions, the subjects' choice will choose to be safe). These programs were widely implemented.

AIDS-prevention education has made considerable strides in disseminating important medical information. Using HIV knowledge as a rough indicator, a 1985 survey of adolescents living in a low AIDS-incidence area revealed very little knowledge about HIV (Price, Desmond, & Kukulka, 1985). Adolescents living in high-incidence urban areas were somewhat more informed. Yet in San Francisco, there was a high rate of awareness about sexual transmission of HIV, but not about the risks posed by intravenous drug use. Worse, only 60% of those surveyed understood that condom use could make sex safer (DiClemente, Zorn, & Temoshok, 1986).

Besides the problem of students who are uninformed, many students are seriously misinformed. One study (Strunin & Hingson, 1987) found that 60% of their respondents believed blood donation was a high-risk activity. More recent studies have indicated significant advances in young people's understanding about the virus, its related syndrome, and the basics of prevention (Anderson & Christenson, 1991; Brown, Fritz, & Barone, 1989; Dawson, Cynamon, & Fitti, 1987; Fisher & Moscovich 1991; Hingson, Strunin, Berlin, & Heeren, 1990; Malavaud, Dumay, & Malamaud, 1990; Roscoe & Kruger, 1990).

Despite the dissemination of vital health information to adolescent populations, several shortfalls remain. Health education initiatives are neither of long enough duration (the typical AIDS-education program in an American school lasts only 4 hours; Kirby, 1992) nor of effective enough content to reach even the most specific and captive audiences. One example of this was a university's intensive weeklong AIDS-awareness program that featured lectures, public discussions, free condoms, and heavy press coverage (Chervin & Martinez, 1987). Just a few weeks after the program, a survey found that more than a quarter of the students on the campus remained unable to define "safer sex." As Bandura (1992) points out, too often the language of these programs is so desexualized and euphemistic that few people can actually understand the messages with which they may be nonetheless quite consistently bombarded. Other studies have revealed that those students who did retain information from their health courses simultaneously retained a number of misconceptions about the subject matter, or continued to exhibit significant deficits in some key topics (Fisher & Fisher, 1991; Hingson et al., 1989; Miller & Downer, 1988).

The biggest shortfall of information-dissemination programs, however, may be that they have failed to reach those adolescents who have historically exhibited the highest rate of infection or pregnancy. Several studies (DiClemente, Lanier, Horan, & Lodico, 1991; Morris, Baker, Huscroft, Evans, & Zeljkovic, 1991; Nader, Wexler, Patterson, McKusick, & Coates, 1989) have shown that undereducation disproportionately affects delinquent adolescents—a population already prone to high-risk sexual and drug-related activity. Homeless and hard-core intravenous drug users (IVDUs) are also more frequently exposed to high-risk behavior than are most adolescents (Deisher, Robinson, & Boyer, 1982; Fullilove, Fullilove, Bowser, & Gross, 1990; Rahdert, 1988;

Rotheram-Borus, Koopman, & Erhardt, 1991; Stein, Jones, & Fisher, 1988; Stricof, Novick, Kennedy, & Weisfuse, 1988). Because members of both of these groups are more likely to switch schools or to drop out altogether, they are typically excluded from education efforts (Sondheimer, 1992), and few social programs exist for these populations.

Even when IVDUs can be reached by educational outreach, they are frequently blocked from receiving explicit and necessary information about how to clean needles. The political undesirability of addressing IV drug use in any way other than condemnation has seriously jeopardized prevention efforts with this population.

AIDS prevention campaigns have apparently also missed the majority of African-American and Hispanic adolescents. In contrast to the steady increase in the larger population's knowledge about HIV transmission and methods of prevention (Petosa & Wessinger, 1990), and despite the highest levels of perceived risk among these minority groups (DiClemente et al., 1988; Sonenstein, Pleck, & Ku, 1989), African-American and Hispanic adolescents consistently exhibit a knowledge level well below average (Bell, Feraios, & Bryan, 1990; DiClemente et al., 1988; DiClemente, Zorn, & Temoshok, 1987; Sonenstein, Pleck, & Ku, 1989). Their major areas of deficit include misconceptions regarding sexual transmission (failure to recognize that oral sex, vaginal sex, and asymptomatic partners may involve risk; DiClemente et al., 1988; Lesnick & Pace, 1990) and misconceptions regarding casual transmission (which can lead to prejudice and increased anxiety regarding perceived susceptibility (DiClemente et al., 1988)).

Compounding the problem of delivering effective school-based AIDS and STD prevention are the local political battles waged by school boards and community organizations who grapple with the fear that any discussion of adolescent sexual activity other than simple condemnation will serve merely to encourage it. Yet parents of schoolchildren express overwhelming support (94% in 1986) for HIV/AIDS education programs, with 80% in favor of safer sex instruction (Gallup, 1987). This pattern—in which unwarranted fear of opposition, rather than opposition itself, is the most important obstacle to the development and adoption of sex education programs—is a familiar one to health educators, and is consistent with the earlier findings of Scales and Kirby (1983).

Thus, the success of AIDS education programs is dependent not only on the quality, relevance, and accuracy of the information, but also on the mechanisms of social diffusion (Bandura, 1992). To date, the effectiveness of these programs has been heavily skewed in favor of mainstream school-attending white adolescents.

PREVENTION

Theories on the etiology of risk taking during adolescence have value for directing AIDS and STD prevention strategies. Rather than defining risk taking as pathological, early theorists viewed youthful deviance as the result of socially induced pressures and normal developmental needs to achieve socially desirable goals (Cloward & Ohlin, 1960). Later, theorists perceived risk taking among youth as the result of weak ties with conventional norms (Hirschi, 1969). Building on these tenets, theorists saw a pattern of risk taking that occurs when youths' conventional social bonds are neutralized through attenuating experiences (Elliot, Ageton, & Canter, 1979). To date, four major theories have guided interventions to reduce risk behaviors in the public health arena. These theories are social learning theory, conceptual change theory, problem behavior theory, and peer cluster theory.

Social learning theory specifically links individual behavior to the social environment. According to social learning theory, we learn how to behave by observing the actions of those around us, and modeling our own behavior after those we admire. As adolescents develop self-concepts and begin to mimic adult behavior, they are particularly keen observers of role models other than their parents, such as peers, older siblings, or high-profile media celebrities.

General susceptibility to social influences (Bandura, 1977) is related to low self-esteem, low self-satisfaction, low self-confidence, a greater need for social approval, a low sense of personal control, low assertiveness, and an impatience to assume adult roles or appear grown-up. Based on this theoretical formulation and existing empirical evidence, some researchers have hypothesized that resistance to social influences could be promoted by fostering the development of characteristics associated with low susceptibility to such influences. In particular, the inclusion of self-protective skills, problem-solving steps, interpersonal communication skills to enhance social proficiency and resiliency, and self-efficacy components in risk-reduction interventions for youth mirrors tenets of social cognitive theory. Not surprisingly, interventions grounded in social learning theory have rendered promising results in influencing youths' risk-reduction behavior (Bandura, 1990; Schinke, Moncher, & Holden, 1989; Schinke, Orlandi, Gordon, et al., 1990).

Conceptual change theory posits that youths' capacity for learning is not constrained by developmental stages (Piaget, 1954). Rather, according to conceptual change theory, cognitive development results from acquiring knowledge in particular content domains (Carey, 1985, 1990). Conceptual change theorists believe that learning occurs through cause-and-effect processes (Wellman & Gelman, 1992). For example, a youth may erroneously surmise that smokers become ill due to contagion. Traditional theory interprets such errors as the result of domain-general cognitive principles (Krister & Patterson, 1980; Kuhn, 1989). Conceptual change theorists, however, would suggest that the error stems from a lack of health knowledge. Conceptual change theory thus predicts that youths' misconceptions about health practices can be revised through accurate and germane learning about human functioning and health (Carey, 1985, 1990).

Problem behavior theory (Jessor & Jessor, 1977) begins by defining a "problem behavior" as one that is considered problematic within the context of a particular value system, and which typically elicits a social response designed to control it, whether informal (getting grounded), or formal and substantial (getting arrested). Many problem behaviors are age-graded; they are permissible for members of an older age group, but viewed as problems for younger individuals (e.g., smoking, sexual involvement). For these behaviors, age norms may serve as the defining characteristic.

Problem behavior theory recognizes the social function of problem behavior in the lives of many adolescents, and argues that an important reason adolescents engage in problem behaviors is that these behaviors help the adolescent achieve personal goals (i.e., acceptance from a particular peer group). Problem behaviors might also serve as a way of coping with failure (real or anticipated), boredom, social anxiety, unhappiness, rejection, social isolation, low self-esteem, or a lack of self-efficacy.

Peer cluster theory assumes that peer interactions largely determine risk-taking behavior (Oetting & Beauvais, 1986, 1987). Peer clusters include interactions among friends, dating dyads, and family constellations, as well as those within neighborhood settings, sports teams, and clubs. According to theorists, peer clusters and the norms they observe not only account for the presence and type of risk taking among adolescents, but may also help youths reduce pressures and influences toward deviance. The therapeutic use of peer clusters in an intervention context may enhance efforts to reduce adolescents' risk-associated lifestyle behaviors. By providing positive alternatives and by changing perceived social norms, therapeutic peer clusters can be a source of social development.

Peer cluster theory further emphasizes the role of anger as an important trait in predicting adolescent risk taking. Anger increases the chances of forming peer drug associations and probably increases chances of developing deviant norms (Oetting, in press). Peer cluster theory would indicate that preventive interventions should include the use of peer leaders to deliver information, components that address social norms, strategies to build and sustain positive peer clusters, and anger-management skills.

Assessment Strategies

Several categories of assessment methods can quantify risks for and evidence of AIDS and STDs among youth. Used appropriately, the following assessment methods will direct potentially effective programs.

Structured Clinical Interviews

Clinical interviews are helpful to isolate the individual and environmental context for HIV infection and other STDs. Because prevention services seek to help adolescents avoid HIV infection or other STDs entirely, assessment procedures in preparation for those services must search for prodromal conditions of the ultimate presenting problem. Effective structured clinical interviews will discover those conditions to direct subsequent prevention efforts. For the purposes of this chapter, a program seeking to prevent AIDS and other STDs will profit from interviews that compile not only information on high-risk sexual behavior among the target audience, but also that gather clinically relevant information on documented correlates of that behavior. Clinical interviews might thus ask youths and appropriate adult informants about IV drug and other substance use, prostitution, homosexuality, bisexuality, and other associated factors that prior research has shown helpful in predicting future risky sexual behaviors.

Clinical interviews to lay the foundation for AIDS and other STDs prevention programs should elicit empirically demonstrated correlates of these target problems and generate useful data for program design. Thus, in the earlier example of assessment procedures for an AIDS and STDs prevention program, structured clinical interviews should ask respondents about optimal conditions for delivering prevention services. Respondents might be asked about the timing, length, and situational context for prevention services. Should the prevention program be delivered in school or in after-school settings? Should the program engage both genders? How much time should be devoted to the program? Including these and similar questions in the structured clinical interview will increase the precision and responsiveness of the prevention effort.

Computerized Methods

Without offering significant advantages for the development of prevention programs, computerized assessment methods warrant inclusion in any comprehensive assessment system. Illustrative of the potential of these methods for prevention programs are findings from a study completed by Murray and Hannan (1990). Those investigators employed a computer-assisted telephone interviewing (CATI) system to follow youths involved in smoking prevention programs. Through the added precision and ease of use of the CATI system, Murray was able to track successfully several thousand youths for purposes of obtaining postintervention data on the efficacy of their prevention program. Absent the CATI systems, the investigators might not have gathered the rich follow-up data that allowed them to isolate the effects of their prevention program and suggest heuristic hypotheses to guide future research.

Self-Report Methods

Of all the extant assessment procedures, self-report methods remain the most heavily and frequently used. Self-report assessments continue to be popular for several reasons. Few other types of assessment methods offer the ease of administration, portability, low cost, and adaptability of self-report instruments. Self-report has the greatest diversity of existing psychometrically tested measures. Several thousand self-report instruments are accessible through the literature to reliably measure nearly any mental health, social, or behavioral topic imaginable. Consequently, the clinical and research literature contains myriad examples of self-reported indices as outcome variables for AIDS and STDs prevention programs.

Observational Methods

Assessment procedures that allow researchers to observe and collect data on behavioral interactions related to prevention outcomes offer distinct benefits. Among those benefits are the validity inherent in observing the behaviors targeted by the prevention program, the reduction in response bias as adolescents interact in naturalistic settings, and the ability to test interrater reliability within data collection teams. A researcher planning an HIV/STDs prevention program can gather through observational measures firsthand data on behaviors associated with increased protection, such as assertion skills or susceptibility to peer pressure. Her confidence in the veracity of the resulting data may be greater than her faith in parallel data gleaned from self-reported responses.

Observational data also lend themselves to archival retrieval and review through videotape recordings. Videotaped observational data have been employed to test the effectiveness of programs to prevent teenage pregnancy, child abuse, substance use, and other problems among adults and children (Schinke & Gordon, 1992; Schinke, Orlandi, Schilling, et al., 1990). Videotape recordings permit retrospective viewing and scoring in the laboratory setting. Data collected through videotape methods allow precise quantification of verbal and nonverbal parameters. And, relative to live behavioral observations, archival videotaped data are much easier to score for interrater reliability because they can be replayed again and again.

Physiological Measures

Representing a nascent type of assessment data, physiological measurements are most often adjuncts to self-report, observational, and other assessments. Typically, physiological assessment information is used as confirmatory evidence for the absence of a particular behavior or response targeted by a prevention program. For example, biochemical data collection is routinely part of evaluations to test the efficacy of interventions aimed at preventing tobacco, alcohol, or other drug use (Schinke, Orlandi, Schilling, et al., 1990). Past studies of these prevention programs have collected samples of expired alveolar air, blood, urine, saliva, or hair to determine whether clients were using the target substances.

Physiological measures are typically employed in prevention programs to enhance the veracity of self-reports. That enhancement occurs when clients believe biochemical samples can reveal true levels of physiological phenomena or functioning. For example, smoking prevention studies routinely inform youths that biochemical sampling will disclose whether they are using tobacco. Youths are then asked for biochemical samples and asked to self-report their smoking. Studies of such biochemical enhancement procedures for self-reported behavior confirm that the illusion of physiological verification increases the accuracy of youth reports (Patrick et al., 1994).

Prevention Approaches

Sex education interventions that deliver information regarding AIDS and STDs as part of a larger effort to change youths' attitudes and behavior have met with more success than information-only programs. Information alone cannot effect behavior change. Information must be tailored to the unique cultural, social, and psychological contexts within target populations. This conclusion is consistent with the results of similar efforts to curb behaviors associated with obesity, heart risk, and lung cancer (Bandura, 1992).

Several factors—knowledge, attitudes, beliefs, and practices—have been significantly associated with risk-reduction behavior. Some studies have found significant correlations between high levels of perceived risk and risk-reduction behavior (Goodman & Cohall, 1988; Hingson et al., 1990). Other more recent studies have not found perceived risk to be significantly associated with the reduction of AIDS risk behaviors when other socioenvironmental constructs (i.e., norms, self-efficacy) are controlled for (Brooks-Gunn & Furstenberg, 1990; Pendergrast, DuRant, & Gaillard, 1992; Walter et al., 1992; Weisman, Plichta, Nathanson, Ersminger, & Robinson, 1991). Consequently, perceived risk as a determinant for reducing AIDS risk behaviors is now being questioned in a fashion similar to knowledge. In short, perceived risk alone is not a sufficient motivator of the adoption and maintenance of reduced AIDS risk behaviors.

Social Skills and Communication

Recent studies have identified social skills efficacy, particularly communication with sexual partners, as a significant factor in sexual risk-reduction behavior among adolescents (Allen-Meares, 1984; DiClemente, 1991; Goodman & Cohall, 1989; Walter et al., 1992; Weisman et al., 1991). In a study of adolescent girls, a willingness to request condom use particularly predicted condom use consistency. High-school girls who were willing to request condom use during a sexual encounter were five times more likely than unwilling subjects to be consistent condom users.

Studies of effective contraceptors (Campbell & Barnland, 1977) have revealed several consistent personality traits. These traits include an ability to defy convention and disregard rules, which in turn suggests an ability to apply personal values to important situations. Effective contraceptors are also able to select contraceptives without regard to societal expectations. These adolescents also demonstrate self-efficacy, and do not experience individual setbacks as total failure. Self-efficacy has also been shown to predict safer sex practices in adolescents (Bandura, 1992).

In one illustrative social skills intervention, adolescents spent a day learning HIV/AIDS information, practicing interpersonal skills, and engaging in role plays. A control group received a similarly structured and equally informative intervention on career opportunities. At a 3-month follow-up measurement, adolescents who had received the AIDS intervention reported fewer occasions of coitus, fewer coital partners, greater use of condoms, and a lower incidence of heterosexual anal intercourse (Jemmett et al., 1992).

Drug Use

Studies have found that alcohol and marijuana use may reduce the likelihood that adolescents will use condoms (Fullilove et al., 1990; Hingson et al., 1990). Strong correlations were found between African-American youths who use crack and their rate of STDs (Fullilove et al., 1990). In the same study, stronger correlations between crack and STDs were found for those who combined crack use with sexual activity.

Peer Norms

Peer norms for condom use, contraception, and other risk-reduction behaviors have emerged as an important new arena in tracking and influencing risk behaviors (DiClemente, 1991; Lowe & Radius, 1987; Stanton, Black, Keane, & Feigelman, 1990; Walter et al., 1992). Younger adolescents may be particularly susceptible to peer pressure (Brooks-Gunn & Furstenberg, 1990). Youths' perceptions of peer norms are highly associated with both their age at first intercourse and their frequency of contraceptive use (Brooks-Gunn & Furstenberg, 1990). One study of incarcerated youth, for example, found them five times more likely to use condoms when they believed that activity to be supported among their peers (DiClemente, 1991).

Similarly, in a study of inner-city adolescents, perceived normative support increased by four times subjects' likelihood of condom use (DiClemente & Fisher, 1991). This and other data have convinced several researchers that effective interventions must include efforts to alter group norms (Miller, Turner, & Moses, 1990). Others additionally argue that prevention efforts would benefit from a community-based component (Coates & Greenblatt, 1989).

Both homosexual and heterosexual groups are sensitive to perceived social norms. Boyfriends particularly influence their girlfriends' contraceptive behavior. In one study, girls who perceived partner support were four times as likely to use contraception than those who did not (Weisman et al., 1991). Yet, both effective and ineffective contraceptors report that their birth control attitudes are influenced by peers. Effective contraceptors reported that their best female friends had the most influence on their birth control attitudes. Ineffective contraceptors cited boyfriends', parents', and self-influenced attitudes (Allen-Meares, 1984).

Parents also exert a significant social influence on their adolescent children. Predisposition to risky behaviors can be correlated to teens' experiences with parents during their adolescence (Abernathy, 1974). In addition, there is an association between daughters' responsible sexual behavior during adolescence and frequency of parental communication about sex (Fox & Inazu, 1980). Attitudinal and behavioral norms regarding reproductive behavior are transmitted through teens' interactions with parents (Sussman, 1974). Because the community and church can also play important roles in establishing social norms, some interventions have attempted to incorporate them. For one such program, the combination of parents, community, and the church was critical to its success. This program increased subjects' personally and socially responsible behavior and improved interpersonal and family communication skills (Alan Guttmacher Institute, 1994).

SUMMARY

Notwithstanding the relative lack of success of educational interventions to influence adolescent sexual risk-behavior thus far, there is significant reason for cheer. While sexual behavior is resistant to change, adolescents are a highly educable population. Adolescents are less set in their sexual habits than most adults. Further, intervention efforts targeted at such specific populations as drug users, adults in methadone maintenance, runaways, and gay youth have proven quite successful. And the nationwide increase in adolescent condom use in recent years suggests that better designed programs will yield even greater results.

Due to the range of psychosocial cofactors implicated in preventing risky sexual behaviors, and the frequently qualified successes of past efforts, developing effective content for sexual behavior interventions remains challenging. Yet health educators can profit from the close analyses of early intervention efforts.

The next generation of HIV and STD prevention curricula should continue to explain the major modes of disease transmission and conception. For this content to be effective, however, it must be joined with frank discussions of condom use (where to get them, how to use them), role-playing and imaging to encourage confidence and skill in safe sex negotiation, and reinforcement of the social normalcy and desirability of condom use. Intervention should be delivered through as many channels as possible (classroom, health program, counseling, peer leaders, community groups, and mass media) and, most importantly, with sensitivity to the distinct epistemological and cultural needs of the target population.

REFERENCES

Abernathy, V. (1974). Illegitimate conception among teenagers. *American Journal of Public Health, 64,* 622–665.

Alan Guttmacher Institute. (1993). *Facts in brief: Sexually transmitted diseases (STDs) in the United States.* New York: Author.

Alan Guttmacher Institute. (1994). *Sex and America's teenagers.* New York: Author.

Allen-Meares, P. (1984). Adolescent pregnancy and parenting: The forgotten adolescent father and his parents. *Journal of Social Work and Human Sexuality, 3,* 12–25.

Anderson, M. D., & Christenson, G. M. (1991). Ethnic breakdown of AIDS-related knowledge and attitudes from the National Adolescent Student Health Survey. *Journal of Health Education, 22,* 30–34.

Bandura, A. (1977). *Social learning theory.* Englewood Cliffs, NJ: Prentice-Hall.

Bandura, A. (1990). Perceived self-efficacy in the exercise of control over AIDS infection. *Evaluation and Program Planning, 13,* 9–17.

Bandura, A. (1992). A social cognitive approach to the exercise of control over AIDS infection. In R. DiClemente (Ed.), *Adolescents and AIDS: A generation in jeopardy* (pp. 89–116). Newbury Park, CA: Sage.

Bell, D., Feraios, A., & Bryan, T. (1990). Adolescent males' knowledge and attitudes about HIV in the context of their social world. *Journal of Applied Social Psychology, 20,* 424–448.

Bell, T., & Hein, K. (1984). The adolescent and sexually transmitted disease. In K. Holmes (Ed.), *Sexually transmitted diseases* (pp. 73–84). New York: McGraw-Hill.

Brooks-Gunn, J., & Furstenberg, F., Jr. (1990). Coming of age in the era of AIDS: Puberty, sexuality, and contraception. *Millbank Quarterly 1*(Suppl.1), 59–84.

Brown, L. K., Fritz, G. K., & Barone, V. J. (1989). The impact of HIV education on junior and senior high school students. *Journal of Adolescent Health Care, 10,* 386–392.

Campbell, B., & Barnland, D. (1977). Communication patterns and problems of pregnancy. *American Journal of Orthopsychiatry, 47,* 134–139.

Carey, S. (1985). Are children fundamentally different thinkers and learners from adults? In S. F. Chipman, J. W. Segal, & R. Glaser (Eds.), *Thinking and learning skills* (Vol. 2, pp. 485–575). Hillsdale, NJ: Erlbaum.

Carey, S. (1990). Cognitive development. In D. Osherson & E. Smith (Eds.), *Thinking: An invitation to cognitive science.* Boston: MIT Press.

Cates, W., Jr. (1990). The epidemiology and control of sexually transmitted diseases in adolescents. In M. Schydlower & M. Shafer (Eds.), *Adolescent medicine: State of the art reviews* (pp. 409–428). Philadelphia: Hanley & Belfus.

Cates, W., Jr., & Rauch, J. L. (1985). Adolescents and sexually transmitted diseases: An expanding problem. *Journal of Adolescent Health Care, 6,* 1–5.

Centers for Disease Control. (1990). HIV-related knowledge and behaviors among high school students: Selected U.S. sites in 1989. *Journal of the American Medical Association, 264,* 318–322.

Centers for Disease Control. (1992). Selected behaviors that increase risk for HIV infection among high school students—U.S., 1990. *Morbidity and Mortality Weekly Report, 41,* 231–240.

Centers for Disease Control. (1994). *HIV/AIDS surveillance report.* Atlanta, GA: Author.

Chervin, D. D., & Martinez, A. (1987, February 19). *Survey of the health of Stanford students.* Report to the Board of Trustees, Stanford University, Stanford, CA.

Cloward, R., & Ohlin, L. (1960). *Delinquency and opportunity.* New York: Free Press.

Coates, T. J., & Greenblatt, R. M. (1989). Behavioral change using community-level interventions. In K. Holmes (Ed.), *Sexually transmitted diseases* (pp. 1075–1080). New York: McGraw-Hill.

Dawson, D. A., Cynamon, M., & Fitti, J. E. (1987). AIDS knowledge and attitudes: Provisional data from the National Health Interview Survey. *Advance Data, 146,* 1–11.

Deisher, R. W., Robinson, G., & Boyer, D. (1982). The adolescent female and male prostitute. *Pediatric Annals, 11,* 812–825.

DiClemente, R. J. (1989). Prevention of human immunodeficiency virus infection among adolescents: The interplay of health education and public policy in the development of school-based AIDS education programs. *AIDS Education and Prevention, 1,* 70–78.

DiClemente, R. J. (1991). Predictors of HIV-preventive sexual behavior in a high-risk adolescent population: The influence of perceived peer norms and sexual communication on incarcerated adolescents' consistent use of condoms. *Society for Adolescent Medicine, 12,* 385–390.

DiClemente, R. J., Boyer, C. B., & Morales, E. (1988). Minorities and AIDS: Knowledge, attitudes and misconceptions among Black and Latino adolescents. *American Journal of Public Health, 1,* 55–57.

DiClemente, R. J., & Fisher, J. D. (1991). *Predictors of HIV-preventive sexual behavior among adolescents in an HIV epicenter: The influence of communication and perceived referent group norms on frequency of condom use.* Unpublished manuscript, University of California, San Francisco.

DiClemente, R. J., Lanier, M. M., Horan, P. F., & Lodico, M. (1991). Comparison of AIDS knowledge, attitudes, and behaviors among incarcerated adolescents and a public school sample in San Francisco. *American Journal of Public Health, 81,* 628–630.

DiClemente, R. J., Zorn, J., & Temoshok, L. (1986). A survey of knowledge, attitudes, and beliefs about AIDS in San Francisco. *American Journal of Public Health, 76,* 1443–1445.

DiClemente, R. J., Zorn, J., & Temoshok, L. (1987). The association of gender, ethnicity, and length of residence in the Bay area to adolescents' knowledge and attitudes about acquired immune deficiency syndrome. *Journal of Applied Social Psychology, 17,* 216–230.

Elliot, D., Ageton, S., & Canter, R. (1979). An integrated theoretical perspective on delinquent behavior. *Journal of Research in Crime and Delinquency, 16,* 3–27.

Fisher, J. D., & Fisher, W. A. (1991). *A general social psychological technology for changing HIV-risk behavior.* Unpublished manuscript.

Fisher, J. D., & Moscovich, S. J. (1991). Evolution of college students' HIV-related behavioral responses, attitudes, knowledge, and fear. *HIV Education and Prevention, 2,* 322–337.

Forrest, J. D., & Singh, S. (1990). The sexual and reproductive behavior of women, 1982–1988. *Family Planning and Perspectives, 22*(5), 206–214.

Fox, G. L., & Inazu, J. K. (1980). Patterns and outcomes of mother-daughter communication about sexuality. *Journal of Social Issues, 36,* 7–29.

Fullilove, R. E., Fullilove, M. T., Bowser, B. P., & Gross, S. A. (1990). Risk of sexually transmitted disease among Black adolescent crack users in Oakland and San Francisco, CA. *Journal of the American Medical Association, 263,* 851–855.

Gallup, A. (1987). *The 19th annual Gallup polls of the public's attitudes toward the public school.* Princeton, NJ: Author.

Goodman, E., & Cohall, A. T. (1989). Acquired immunodeficiency syndrome and adolescents: Knowledge, attitudes, beliefs, and behaviors in a New York City adolescent minority population. *Pediatrics, 84,* 36–42.

Hingson, R., & Strunin, L. (1992). Monitoring adolescents' response to the AIDS epidemic: Changes in knowledge, attitudes, beliefs, and behaviors. In R. DiClemente (Ed.), *Adolescents and AIDS: A generation in jeopardy* (pp. 17–33). Newbury Park, CA: Sage.

Hingson, R., Strunin, L., Berlin, B., & Heeren, T. (1990). Beliefs about AIDS, use of alcohol and drugs, and unprotected sex among Massachusetts adolescents. *American Journal of Public Health, 80,* 295–299.

Hingson, R., Strunin, L., Craven, D. E., Mofenson, L., Mangione, T., Berlin, B., Amaro, H., & Lamb, G. A. (1989). Survey of HIV knowledge and behavior changes among Massachusetts adults. *Preventive Medicine, 18,* 808–818.

Hirschi, T. (1969). *Causes of delinquency.* Berkeley: University of California Press.

Holmes, K. K., Karon, J. M., & Kreiss, J. (1990). The increasing frequency of heterosexuall acquired AIDS in the United States. *American Journal of Public Health, 80,* 858–862.

House Select Committee on Children, Youth & Families. (May, 1992). *A decade of denial: Teens and AIDS in America.* Washington, DC: Author.

Jemmett, J. B., III, Jemmett, S., Loretta, S., & Fong, G. T. (1992). Reduction in HIV-risk-associated sexual behaviors among Black male adolescents: Effects of an AIDS prevention intervention. *American Journal of Public Health, 82,* 372–377.

Jessor, R., & Jessor, S. L. (1977). *Problem behavior and psychosocial development: A longitudinal study of youth.* New York: Academic Press.

Kirby, D. (1984). *Sexuality education: An evaluation of programs and their effects.* Santa Cruz, CA: Network.

Kirby, D. (1992). School-based prevention programs: Design, evaluation, and effectiveness. In R. J. DiClemente (Ed.), *Adolescents and AIDS: A generation in jeopardy* (pp.159–180). Newbury Park, CA: Sage.

Krister, M. C., & Patterson, C. J. (1980). Children's conceptions of the causes of illness: Understanding of contagion and use of imminent justice. *Child Development, 51,* 839–849.

Kuhn, D. (1989). Children and adults as intuitive scientists. *Psychological Review, 96,* 674–689.

Lesnick, H., & Pace, B. (1990). Knowledge of AIDS risk factors in South Bronx Minority College students. *Journal of Acquired Immune Deficiency Syndromes, 3,* 173–176.

Lowe, C. S., & Radius, S. M. (1987). Young adults' contraceptive practices: An investigation of influences. *Adolescence, 22,* 291–304.

Malavaud, S., Dumay, F., & Malamaud, B. (1990). HIV infection: Assessment of sexual risk, knowledge, and attitudes towards prevention in 1,596 high school students in the Toulouse Education Authority Area. *American Journal of Health Promotion, 4,* 260–265.

Miller, H. G., Turner, C. F., & Moses, L. E. (Eds.). (1990). *HIV: The second decade.* Washington, DC: National Academy of Sciences.

Miller, L., & Downer, A. (1988). AIDS: What you and your friends need to know—A lesson plan for adolescents. *Journal of School Health, 58,* 137–141.

Morris, R., Baker, C., Huscroft, S., Evans, C. A., & Zeljkovic, S. (1991). Two-year variation in HIV-risk behaviors in detained minors. *VII International Conference on AIDS, 2,* 51. (Abstract No. W. D. 109)

Mosher, W. D. (1985). Reproductive impairments in the United States, 1965–1982. *Demography, 22,* 415–430.

Murray, D. M., & Hannan, P. J. (1990). Planning for the appropriate analysis in school-based drug-use prevention studies. *Journal of Consulting and Clinical Psychology, 58,* 458–468.

Nader, P. R., Wexler, D. B., Patterson, T. L., McKusick, L., & Coates, T. (1989). Comparison of beliefs about AIDS among urban, suburban, incarcerated, and gay adolescents. *Journal of Adolescent Health Care, 10,* 413–418.

Oetting, E. R. (in press). Drug abuse prevention with peer groups. In Z. Sloboda & W. J. Bukowski (Eds.), *Handbook for drug abuse prevention: Theory, science and practice.* New York: Plenum Press.

Oetting, E. R., & Beauvais, F. (1986). Peer cluster theory: Drugs and the adolescent. *Journal of Counseling Development, 65,* 17–22.

Oetting, E. R., & Beauvais, F. (1987). Peer cluster theory, socialization characteristics and adolescent drug use: A path analysis. *Journal of Counseling Psychology, 34,* 205–213.

O'Reilly, K., & Aral, S. (1985). Adolescents and sexual behavior: Trends and implications for STDs. *Journal of Adolescent Health Care, 6,* 262–270.

Patrick, D. L., Cheadle, A., Thompson, D. C., Diehr, P., Koepsell, T., & Kinne, S. (1994). The validity of self-reported smoking: A review and meta-analysis. *American Journal of Public Health, 84,* 1086–1093.

Pendergrast, R. A., DuRant, R. H., & Gaillard, G. L. (1992). Attitudinal and behavioral correlates of condom use in urban adolescent males. *Society for Adolescent Medicine, 13,* 133–139.

Petosa, R., & Wessinger, J. (1990). The HIV education needs of adolescents: A theory-based approach. *HIV Education and Prevention, 2,* 127–136.

Piaget, J. (1954). *The construction of reality in the child.* New York: Basic Books.

Price, J. H., Desmond, S., & Kukulka, G. (1985). High school students' perceptions and misperceptions of HIV. *Journal of School Health, 55,* 107–109.

Rahdert, E. R. (1988). Treatment services for adolescent drug abuse: Analysis of treatment research. In E. R. Rahdert & J. Grabowski (Eds.), *National Institute on Drug Abuse Monographs 77,* (pp. 1–3). Rockville, MD: National Institute on Drug Abuse.

Rolfs, R. T., Goldber, M., & Sharrar, R. G. (1990). Risk factors for syphilis: Cocaine use and prostitution. *American Journal of Public Health, 80,* 853–857.

Roscoe, B., & Kruger, T. L. (1990). HIV: Late adolescents' knowledge and its influence on sexual behavior. *Adolescence, 25,* 39–48.

Rotheram-Borus, M. J., Koopman, C., & Erhardt, A. A. (1991). Homeless youths and HIV infection. *American Psychologist, 46,* 1188–1197.

Scales, P., & Kirby, D. (1983). Important barriers to sex education: A survey of professionals. *Journal of Sex Research, 30,* 229–237.

Schinke, S. P., Botvin, G. J., Orlandi, M. A., Schilling, R. F., & Gordon, A. N. (1990). African-American and Hispanic-American adolescents, HIV infection, and preventive intervention. *AIDS Education and Prevention, 2,* 305–313.

Schinke, S. P., & Gordon, A. N. (1992). Innovative approaches to interpersonal skills training for minority adolescents. In R. DiClemente (Ed.), *Adolescents and AIDS* (pp. 181–193). Newbury Park, CA: Sage.

Schinke, S. P., Moncher, M. S., & Holden, G. W. (1989). Preventing HIV infection among Black and Hispanic adolescents. *Journal of Consulting and Clinical Psychology, 58,* 432–436.

Schinke, S. P., Orlandi, M. A., Gordon, A. N., Weston, R. E., Moncher, M. S., & Parms, C. A. (1990). AIDS prevention via computer-based intervention. *Computers in Human Service, 5,* 147–156.

Schinke, S. P., Orlandi, M. A., Schilling, R. F., Botvin, G. J., Gilchrist, L. D., & Landers, C. (1990). Tobacco use by American Indian and Alaska Native people: Risks, psychosocial factors, and preventive intervention. *Journal of Alcohol and Drug Education, 35,* 1–12.

Sondheimer, D. L. (1992). HIV infection and disease among homeless adolescents. In R. DiClemente (Ed.), *Adolescents and AIDS: A generation in jeopardy* (pp. 71–85). Newbury Park, CA: Sage.

Sonenstein, F., Pleck, J., & Ku, L. (1989). Sexual activity, condom use, and AIDS awareness among adolescent males. *Family Planning Perspectives, 21,* 152–158.

Stanton, B., Black, M., Keane, V., & Feigelman, S. (1990). HIV-risk behaviors in young people: Can we benefit from 30 years of social research? *HIV and Public Policy Journal, 5,* 17–23.

Stein, J. B., Jones, S. J., & Fisher, G. (1988). AIDS and IV drug use: Prevention strategies for youth. In M. Quackenbush, M. Nelson, & K. Clarck (Eds.), *The AIDS challenge* (pp. 273–295). Santa Cruz, CA: Network.

Stein, Z. A. (1992). The double bind in science policy and the protection of women from HIV infection. *American Journal of Public Health, 82,* 1471–1472.

Stricof, R. L., Novick, L. F., Kennedy, J. T., & Weisfuse, I. B. (1988, November). *HIV sero-prevalence of adolescents at Covenant House/under 21 in New York City.* Paper presented at the American Public Health Association Conference, Boston, MA.

Strunin, L., & Hingson, R. (1987). Acquired immunodeficiency syndrome and adolescents: Knowledge, beliefs, attitudes and behaviors. *Pediatrics, 79,* 825–832.

Sussman, M. (1974). The isolated nuclear family: Fact or fiction? In M. Sussman (Ed.), *Source book in marriage and the family* (pp. 25–30). Boston: Houghton Mifflin.

Walter, H. J., Vaughn, R. D., Gladis, M. M., Ragin, D. F., Kasen, S., & Cohall, A. T. (1992). Factors associated with AIDS-risk behaviors among high school students in an AIDS epicenter. *American Journal of Public Health, 82,* 528–532.

Weisman, C. S., Plichta, S., Nathanson, C. A., Ersminger, M., & Robinson, J. C. (1991). Consistency of condom use for disease prevention among adolescent users of oral contraceptives. *Family Planning Perspectives, 23,* 71–74.

Wellman, H. M., & Gelman, S. (1992). Cognitive development: Foundational theories of core domains. *Annual Review of Psychology, 43,* 337–375.

Whitley, B. E., Jr., & Schofield, J. W. (1986). Meta-analysis of research on adolescent contraceptive use. *Population and Environment, 8,* 173–203.

Yarber, W. (1986). *Pilot testing and evaluation of the CDC-sponsored STD curriculum.* Bloomington: Indiana University, Center for Health and Safety Studies.

PART FIVE

Treatment Interventions

CHAPTER 16

Depressive Disorders

LAURA MUFSON and DONNA MOREAU

DESCRIPTION OF THE DISORDERS

This chapter will provide an overview of depressive disorders seen in children and adolescents including the epidemiology, phenomenology, natural history, and associated impairments. The chapter will conclude with a discussion of impediments to intervention and assessment and treatment strategies commonly used for this disorder.

An important research and clinical task is to differentiate between normal adolescents and those with psychiatric disorders. Offer (1969) and Rutter, Graham, Chadwick, and Yule (1976) suggest that socially withdrawn adolescents with dramatic mood swings, cognitive distortions and increasing conflicts with parents and peers are not necessarily typical adolescents, but are more likely psychiatrically ill. While most adolescents pass through adolescence without prolonged periods of dysfunction, there is a group who find the age period difficult to traverse. For many such adolescents, this transition represents early manifestations of a psychiatric illness.

Due to the relatively late recognition of depression as a diagnostic entity in children, there is a paucity of information on children and adolescents when compared with information available on adult depression. Early studies of children and adolescents relied on reports from parents and teachers about the child. Introduction of systematic diagnostic assessment of children and adolescents in the mid-1970s increased the practice of obtaining information from the child as well as other informants. More recently, children and adolescents have been shown to be reliable informants about their mental states (Weissman, Wickmaratne, et al., 1987) and report more affective symptoms than their parents and teachers report about them (Angold, Weissman, John, & Merikangas, 1987).

The current *Diagnostic and Statistical Manual of Mental Disorders* (*DSM-IV;* American Psychiatric Association, 1994) has no separate diagnostic category for depression in children and adolescents; instead, the adult diagnostic criteria are minimally modified for application to the younger population. Specific modifications include substitution of irritability for depressed mood and minor changes in duration of symptoms for the diagnosis of dysthymic disorder from 2 years to 1 year.

Portions of this chapter were previously published in *Interpersonal Psychotherapy for Depressed Adolescents* by L. Mufson, D. Moreau, M. M. Weissman, and G. L. Klerman (1995), New York: Guilford Press.

Clinical Depression (Major Depressive Disorder)

Studies that have compared depressed adolescents with depressed adults conclude that, despite minor variations attributable to developmental stages, the symptom profile is the same (Carlson & Strober, 1979; Friedman, Hurt, Clarkin, Corn, & Aronoff, 1983; Inamdar, Siomopolous, Osborn, & Bianchi 1979). Both can have chronic or recurrent symptoms and/or episodes, significant psychosocial impairment, negative self-cognitions, problems with sleep and appetite, depressed mood, tearfulness, difficulty concentrating, and suicidal ideation (Kashani, Rosenberg, & Reigh, 1989; Ryan et al., 1987). They tend to differ, in that adolescents often do not report the pervasive anhedonia that is characteristic of adult depressives, and they appear to respond differently to tricyclic antidepressants (Carlson & Strober, 1979; Mitchell et al., 1988). Minor variations include adolescent reports of more hypersomnia, less terminal insomnia, and hyperphagia. They exhibit a more fluctuating course characterized by more interpersonal problems (Simeon, 1989); also, they make more suicide attempts than depressed adults.

The effects of developmental changes in cognition and emotional expression on presentation of depression over time have yet to be fully delineated. From childhood to adolescence, there appears to be a transition from predominantly vegetative symptoms to more inner psychological or cognitive ones. Adolescents (compared with children), begin to resemble adults in their depth of despair, sense of hopelessness, propensity for suicide, and accompanying anxiety and agitation (Bemporad & Lee, 1988). Ryan et al. (1987) conclude from their review of studies, that developmental changes across childhood and adolescence have only mild to moderate effects on the expression of a limited number of affective symptoms in children with major depression.

Studies using semistructured interviews and applying more rigorous diagnostic criteria to reported symptoms have yielded reduced but significant rates of depressive disorders in adolescents. There are six reported studies on prevalence rates of depressive disorders in adolescents, and four other studies on children and adolescents (Fleming & Offord, 1990). Prevalence rates for current major depression range from 0.4% to 5.7%, and 8.3% for lifetime rate of major depression (Fleming & Offord, 1990).

Dysthymic Disorder

Dysthymic disorder is distinguished from major depressive disorder (MDD) in that it requires a longer duration but milder constellation of depressive symptoms. Dysthymia has an earlier age of onset than MDD (Kovacs, Feinberg, Crouse-Novak, Paulauskas, & Finkelstein, 1984) and is frequently comorbid with major depression. Kovacs et al. followed children aged 8 to 13 years for approximately 5 years and found that 93% of the children diagnosed with dysthymia had other concurrently diagnosed conditions, the most common being MDD (57%) and anxiety (36%). For each year that the child has the disorder, the probability for remission decreased.

EPIDEMIOLOGY

Early epidemiological studies focused on depressive symptoms, while more recent studies have reported on depressive disorders. There is great variability in reports of prevalence rates of childhood depression due to variable diagnostic criteria, multiple populations (clinical versus community populations), different methods to obtain information (self-report questionnaires versus structured interviews), and varying informants (parents, teachers, and/or children). Thus, comparisons among studies is difficult. Depressive symptoms are common in prepubertal children, whereas depressive disorders are more commonly found in adolescents both in epidemiological samples and clinical populations (Angold, 1988a, 1988b; Fleming & Offord, 1990).

Depressive Mood/Symptoms

One of the earliest major studies of prevalence rates was Rutter's Isle of Wight study of children and the follow-up several years later of these same children. Rutter, Tizzard, Yule, Graham, and Whitmore (1976) found that among 2,303 children, aged 10 to 11 years, 13% expressed depressed mood and 9% were preoccupied with depressed topics at the initial interview. When reinterviewed at 14 to 15 years of age, 40% reported substantial feelings of misery and depression, 20% expressed feelings of self-depreciation and 7% to 8% expressed suicidal feelings (Rutter et al., 1976). Subsequent studies report prevalence rates, based on adolescent self-reports of depressive symptoms, of 8.6% to 55.6%.

The significance and prognosis of such high rates of depressive symptoms in multiple studies of adolescents are not clear. Some researchers suggest that adolescents report far more transitory symptoms of depression than adults. Schoenbach (1983) suggested that transitory symptoms may be part of normal development, while the more significant and persistent symptoms may be indicative of psychopathology.

Course of Adolescent Depression

Clinical experience suggests that the course of adolescent depression may differ from that of adult depression. Some adolescents tend to have more episodically intense periods of depression interspersed with periods of improved functioning (Angst, Merikangas, Scheidegger, & Wicki, 1990). The few follow-up studies that exist have indicated a generally poor prognosis, with a high risk for future episodes of affective illness and chronic psychosocial problems (Garber, Kriss, Koch, & Lindholm, 1988; Keller, Beardslee, Lavori, & Wunder, 1988; Macaulay et al., 1993). Kandel and Davies (1986) found, in their 9-year follow-up of a high school sample, that depressive symptoms in adolescence were the most significant predictive factor for depressive symptoms in adulthood.

Studies of recurrence rates of depression in adolescence include both community and clinic-referred samples. Lewinsohn, Clarke, Seely, and Rohde (1994) screened a large high school community sample of approximately 1,500 students for depression and identified 362 with a current or past episode of major depression. They found that 5% had relapsed in 6 months, 12% in 1 year, and 33% in 4 years. Factors associated with earlier recurrence included prior suicidal ideation and attempt, and later age at first onset of disorder.

Kovacs et al. (1984) have published the largest follow-up study on depressed children to date. They reported on 65 children, ages 8 to 13 years old, evaluated at intake and at 2-, 6-, and 12-month follow-ups. Semiannual interviews were conducted in later years. Two-thirds of subjects with major depression and dysthymic disorder had a subsequent episode by the end of 5 years. One year after onset of major depression, 41% still had not recovered, and 8% had not recovered at 2 years after onset. Kovacs et al. (1984) also found that, in children who did recover from their episode of major depression, 26% had a new episode within a year after their recovery, and 40% had a recurrence within 2 years after recovery from initial episode.

Keller et al. (1988) report results from a 2-year follow-up on 38 nonreferred adolescents who had been diagnosed with a current or past major depression. Median age of onset for depression in all 38 subjects was 14 years. The probability of persistent depression after 1 year was 21% and after 2 years was 10%. Keller et al. (1988) believe that these rates parallel the rates of chronicity and recovery that occur in adult depression. Harrington, Fudge, Rutter, Pickles, and Hill (1990) conducted a retrospective follow-up study on 52 subjects who had been seen in the hospital for depression 20 to 30 years previously. They found a strong continuity of depressive symptoms from adolescence to adulthood.

This body of research strongly suggests that children and adolescents with a major depression are at significant risk for future episodes of depression both in late adolescence and young adulthood. The studies conclude that chronic and significant psychosocial impairment and interpersonal difficulties are associated with adolescent depression, and these difficulties persist into adulthood.

CAUSES AND CONSEQUENCES

Risk factors associated with depression include age, gender, socioeconomic factors, birth cohort, family relationships, and family history.

Age

Prevalence rates of depressive symptoms and depressive disorders increase with age, marked by a sharp increase after puberty (Offord et al., 1987). Rates of depressive symptoms in children are approximately 9%, whereas by adolescence, such rates increase to 22% to 40%, depending on the study (Kaplan, Hong, & Weinhold, 1984; Offord et al., 1987; Rutter et al., 1976; Ryan, Puig-Antich, Cooper, et al., 1986). Prevalence rates of adolescent depression disorders range from 1.3% to 8% (Kashani et al., 1987; Rutter et al., 1976; Weissman, Gammon, et al., 1987).

Gender Differences

Increased rates of depression at puberty are accompanied by an acceleration in the rates in girls (Kashani et al., 1987; Rutter et al., 1976). Whereas prepubertally, rates in boys and girls are about equal, by adolescence, the sex ratio approaches 2:1 (Fleming, Offord, & Boyle, 1989; Kandel & Davies, 1982), which is the same as in adults.

Socioeconomic Factors

Low socioeconomic status has been associated with adult depressive symptoms (Cytryn, McKnew, Zahn-Waxler, & Gershon, 1986) and more recently, with depressive symptoms in children. Kaplan et al. (1984), in a study of high school students from diverse socioeconomic classes, found that lower SES adolescents had higher total Beck Depression Inventory Scores than those adolescents from higher SES. Similarly, Siegel and Griffin (1984) found that depressed adolescents tended to come from middle- or lower-class families, who also reported a higher incidence of divorce. Garrison, Schlucter, Schoenbach, and Kaplan (1989), reporting on a survey of 677 public school students, found that depressive symptoms were associated with minority race and lower socioeconomic status.

Family Relationships

Parental death and quality of family relationships have been associated with increased rates of depressive symptoms or major depression in adolescence. According to Wells, Deykin, and Klerman (1985), parental loss through death is a well-documented risk factor for depression in adolescence. Reinherz et al. (1989) conducted a 10-year longitudinal study of a lower-middle-class community and found that 21% of the 15-year-olds reported high levels of depressive symptoms on the Childrens Depression Inventory (CDI). Among the risk factors identified for these adolescents was the death of a parent, particularly for the girls. Although these and other studies have not demonstrated a robust link between early parental loss and later depression, this may be secondary to inadequate conceptualization of the association and resultant faulty methodology. Brown, Harris, and Bifulco (1986) have proffered an interactive model of depression related to early childhood loss that requires a current adverse event before there is "translation into an episode of depression."

In addition to early parental loss, the quality of family relationships in terms of warmth, cohesiveness, and punitiveness has been associated with childhood depression. Fendrich, Warner, and Weissman (1990), in a study of children at risk for psychiatric illness by virtue of major depression in the parents, found that those children reporting low family cohesion and affectionless control (punitive, nonsupportive control) had higher rates of major depression than those reporting more cohesive and warmer family relations. There is evidence that parents of depressed children are often angry, punitive, detached, and belittling (Kashani, Burbach, & Rosenberg, 1988), which may either increase the child's vulnerability to depression or exacerbate an existing episode.

Family History of Depression

There is increasingly strong evidence that major depression runs in families and that being the child of a depressed parent places one at increased risk for the development of major depression (Beardslee et al., 1983; Hammen, Burge, Burney, & Adrian, 1990; Weissman, Leckman, Merikangas, Gammon, & Prusoff, 1984; Weissman, Gammon, John, Merikangas, Warner, Prusoff, & Sckromskas, 1987). There is evidence that the earlier the age of onset of depression in the child or adolescent, the greater the familial loading in the relative (Weissman et al., 1987).

Weissman, Gammon, John, Merikangas, et al. (1987) found that children of depressed parents, compared with children of never mentally ill parents, are at threefold increased risk to develop school problems and suicidal behavior. Whether risk is due to a combination of genetic vulnerability, environmental stresses, and impaired parenting skills of depressed parents is unclear. These effects are most likely influenced by gender of the child and ill parent; age of child at time of parent's illness; nature of the relationship between child and depressed parent; course and recovery of parental illness; and psychiatric status of the other parent and other support figures (Beardslee et al., 1983; Downey & Coyne, 1990; Weissman et al., 1984; Weissman, Gammon, John, Merikangas, et al., 1987).

Comorbidity

Comorbidity is common in depressed children and adolescents. Disorders associated with major depression in adolescence include attention deficit disorder (Biederman et al., 1987), anxiety disorders (Alessi, Robbins, & Dilsaver, 1987; Bernstein & Garfinkel, 1986; Kovacs, Gatsonis, Paulauskas, & Richards, 1989), conduct disorders (Alessi & Robbins, 1984; Marriage, Fine, Moretti, & Haley, 1986), and eating disorders (Swift, Andrews, & Barklage, 1986). Ryan et al. (1987) found that mild conduct problems were present in 25% of adolescents but were disruptive in only 11% of the adolescents. Comorbidity with anxiety disorders and conduct disorder was found to be more frequent in children than adolescents with depression. Kovacs et al. (1989) found that depression comorbid with conduct disorder was associated with greater impairment in functioning. Researchers consistently find that among children and adolescents with a major affective disorder, about one-third also have a comorbid diagnosis of conduct disorder or a similar behavior problem (Carlson & Cantwell, 1980; Kashani et al., 1987; Kovacs et al., 1989; Puig-Antich, 1982).

Psychosocial Functioning

There is little question that major depression has an adverse effect on a child's academic performance, damages family and peer relationships, may increase alcohol and drug use, and may lead to suicide attempts. In a study of prepubertal depressives, Puig-Antich, Lukens, Davies, Goetz, Brennan-Quattrock, and Todak (1985a) found that mother-child relationships were markedly impaired in depressed children compared with children who had psychiatric and other medical disorders, and normal controls. The mother's pattern of low warmth, high irritability, and withdrawal were apparent not only in the parenting style but in the marital relationship as well. Depressed children were less able to make and maintain peer relationships. Age and sex of the children showed no association with psychosocial functioning. In another study of prepubertal children who had sustained recovery from their index episode, Puig-Antich et al. (1985) found that while school functioning had improved, they still suffered impairment in familial and peer relationships. Kandel and Davies (1986) found that adolescent dysphoric symptoms are associated with later difficulties in social functioning, such as increased school dropout, greater estrangement in personal relationships with parents and significant others, and more engagement in illegal activities. Garber et al. (1988) also found that depressed adolescents had significant adjustment difficulties in social activities, family relationships, and significant partner relationships. The aspects of psychosocial functioning that are most impaired during the depressive episode seem to either take longer to resolve or resolve only partially (Puig-Antich et al., 1985a).

IMPEDIMENTS TO INTERVENTION IN THE REAL WORLD CONTEXT

Although approximately 4% to 8% of adolescents are depressed, many go untreated (Keller, Lavori, Beardslee, Wunder & Ryan, 1991) or receive inadequate treatment (Whitaker, Johnson, Shaffer, et al., 1990). Epidemiological surveys suggest that less than 25% of adolescents who need mental health treatment receive it (Tuma, 1989). Studies indicate that contact with medical health professionals enhances one's chances of obtaining professional help for emotional problems (Saunders, Resnick, Hoberman, & Blum, 1994). However, research also suggests that adolescents are reluctant to discuss mental health problems with medical practitioners (Marks, Malizio, Hoch, Brody, & Fisher, 1983). There is a public health need to educate community and professionals about adolescent mental health disorders.

A literature search revealed no empirical data on barriers to treatment in adolescents. The following discussion of impediments is based on clinical experience working with inner-city adolescents of low SES in a large urban hospital. Some barriers may differ for other populations.

Parents

A significant barrier to treatment with children and adolescents can often be either the lack of parental involvement or parental refusal for treatment. Alternatively, some adolescents may not want their parents to know they are seeking services. Adolescents under the age of 18 are legal minors who need parental consent to receive certain services. Many hospitals and clinics will not see adolescents for treatment without parental consent. Causes of parental opposition to treatment include (a) disbelief that the adolescent has a problem he or she cannot solve him- or herself; (b) a mistrust for telling nonfamily members private details of family problems; (c) no access to resources due to financial constraints; (d) parent unable to miss work due to economic stresses; and (e) lack of knowledge that depression is a treatable disorder, not a stage of development.

To overcome parental resistance, it is crucial to make a strong alliance with family members to encourage treatment and to minimize the likelihood of its disruption. This involves individual sessions with parents to educate them about the therapeutic process and what the anticipated treatment will be with their child, to assess and address their concerns about the treatment, to gain perspective on their child's difficulties, and to educate them as to their own expected role in the treatment. Education about the process very often can alleviate a parent's anxiety about having offspring talk confidentially to a person outside the family.

Dysfunctional Families

Epidemiological studies demonstrate a high rate of psychiatric disorder, particularly depression, in the parents of children with depression diagnoses. Often the parents have comorbid alcohol or substance abuse disorder (Merikangas, Risch, & Weissman, 1994). Parents may refuse to participate in the child's treatment because they are too depressed and overwhelmed. There is a high incidence of disruptive communication patterns and poor relations among family members when one of them is depressed. The relationships have been characterized by the child's disengagement from the parents, social isolation, high levels of conflict, and lack of parental support and nurturance (Fendrich et al., 1991).

Having a psychiatrically ill parent can also affect an adolescent's sense of acceptability about seeking treatment. If the parent is not receiving treatment, the adolescent may feel unable to seek his or her own treatment. Adolescents in dysfunctional families have often taken on the parental role and act as caretaker to younger siblings. Such responsibility makes it difficult for the adolescent to attend regular therapy sessions and receive treatment. To overcome problems of dysfunctional families, the therapist should try to involve family members in the treatment services initially as much as possible and to refer them for their own treatment.

Poverty and Lack of Community Resources

Although some studies show that socioeconomic status is not necessarily an impediment to psychiatric intervention, poverty impacts on services provided in low SES communities and the means by which such services can be accessed. Recent health care reform has resulted in financial cuts to hospitals that have traditionally served the surrounding community and the newly created Medicaid HMOs, which are often located outside of the community. In addition, there are substantial numbers of people who are not eligible for Medicaid, but cannot afford to pay the standard fees of many hospitals and community mental health facilities. For those who cannot afford private treatment, being assigned to a lengthy wait list is a common procedure.

Budget cuts have also resulted in diminished resources, such as after-school programs and social service agencies. Enrichment programs that could prevent adolescents from engaging in risky activities are dwindling. Depressed mothers are finding it more difficult to receive home care so that older siblings are pressed into taking care of the home and the family. Sometimes, neither the depressed parent nor depressed adolescent is able to seek and obtain mental health services. The impact of current social policy on mental health services will have long-range effects for the individual, the family, and society.

Stigma

Despite educational efforts to decrease the stigma associated with psychiatric disorders, ignorance and denial persist. This results in delay in treatment or poor compliance with treatment recommendations. Implications are that educational and/or outreach programs are needed to facilitate adolescents' ability to seek and obtain services. A necessary solution is to educate the parents and families about the different treatment options available for depression.

Cultural Issues

Several problems have been identified in the delivery of mental health services to Hispanics and other ethnic minorities, including underutilization of traditional resources (Rodriguez, 1987) and premature dropout rates from psychotherapy (Sue, 1981). Rogler, Malgady, Constantino, and Blumenthal (1987) identified the following three approaches to provide culturally sensitive mental health services for Hispanics, but they would likely be of benefit to other ethnic minorities as well:

1. Increasing accessibility of treatments by recruiting bilingual and bicultural staff and developing networks in the minority community.
2. Selecting a treatment modality that is congruent with the population's perceived cultural values.
3. Introducing the patient's cultural values directly into the therapeutic modality and techniques to bridge cultural conflict.

When working with recent immigrants, it is important to be sensitive to issues of acculturation, differences between their customs and those of the host country, and differences in the roles of family members. The therapist must enhance the relevance of the therapy to the adolescents' cultural life, role in the family, and developmental stage. Such knowledge is crucial to avoid alienating these families, when working with them (Zayas & Bryant, 1984). The therapist's strategies will need to be congruent with the family's values, expectations, and natural coping style to gain acceptance with the participating family members. If it is not possible to match the family with a therapist of the same ethnicity, then it would still be important to have someone with whom the members could communicate in their own language. Above all, it is necessary to educate therapists about characteristics of other cultures who frequent the clinic so that they can increase their sensitivity to the values, morals, and customs intrinsic to the specific population. As Draguns (1981) suggests, it is helpful to use the patient as a source of information about his cultural experience rather than ignoring its influence on the treatment. The goal of culturally sensitive psychotherapy is to attenuate the cultural distance between patient and therapist, and thereby promote more effective therapeutic gains than would be achieved by standard treatments (Malgady, Rogler, & Costantino, 1990).

How to Work within the Real World Context of Service Delivery

The first and most important step a therapist can take when trying to ensure provision of services is to gain the support and/or cooperation of the significant family members or people in the child or adolescent's life. This can be done by meeting with the significant people, assessing their concerns, addressing them as best as possible, and then educating them about the treatment process. Where appropriate, referrals should be made for the parents' own treatment or for treatment of problematic siblings.

The second most important step therapists must take is to accept that they will need to be involved in more than just providing therapy once or twice a week. Instead, they must be involved as resource persons for the family's ills if they are to ensure compliance with treatment. To serve in this capacity, therapists must conduct a thorough assessment of environmental, cultural, and social aspects of the problem. Problems that need to be addressed include need for social service assistance, perhaps in the form of a home health attendant, need for housing, and need for safe organized after-school programs so that the adolescent can engage in peer relations and activities while in a safe environment. While much of the described activities sound like those of a case manager or social service person, it is rare to have clinic staff solely available to address those issues. Therefore, it is the therapist's job to place the adolescent's difficulties in the context of his or her family system, neighborhood system, and cultural system. By joining with the family in such a manner, the potential for change as a result of treatment should be significantly greater.

Practically speaking, prior to initiating the evaluation, the therapist should assess (a) the family's capacity to pay for the evaluation or treatment; and (b) any language barriers and how they can be addressed (i.e., through bilingual therapists or translators if necessary). If these issues cannot be addressed satisfactorily, the therapist must consider referring to another agency where there will be fewer obstacles to clear communication between patient and therapist. If the family will not give consent to treat the child or adolescent, the clinician must consult with risk management people in the agency and decide whether or not the situation necessitates accepting solely the adolescent's informed consent and whether or not to proceed with treatment. To ensure that one is providing the best treatment for the adolescent and his or her family, a thorough assessment of all comorbid disorders and possibility of abuse should be conducted so that the treatment is as informed as possible. Dealing with the environmental as well as the psychiatric difficulties of the adolescent will reduce the likelihood that the family will succumb to the many external influences working against receiving effective interventions.

TREATMENT

Assessment Strategies

The goal of a clinical diagnostic assessment is to confer the appropriate psychiatric disorder(s) to a given individual. The *DSM-III-R* and the more recently revised *DSM-IV,* a categorical diagnostic system, is the most commonly used in clinical practice and research. Assigning a *DSM-IV* diagnosis guides the clinician in educating the parents and adolescents about the natural history and course of a disorder and recommending clinically accepted treatment strategies.

Diagnostic procedures include clinical interviews as well as the use of structured and semistructured questionnaires and/or interviews with the adolescent and the parent(s). Information from ancillary sources, such as the school, pediatrician, and clergy can provide valuable supplemental information as well and can be obtained through direct interview or questionnaires. Psychological testing yields information on presence or absence of associated learning disabilities that may complicate a depressive episode. Medical tests will rule out the possibility of organic causes of depression, such as thyroid disease, neurological disease, diabetes, liver, or kidney disease.

Many assessment instruments are targeted for adolescents, parents, and teachers to assist the clinician in making an accurate diagnosis. To be useful, these instruments must have demonstrated reliability and validity in diagnosing depression. They range from structured and semistructured interviews to symptom scales and self-report inventories. Although most of these instruments were designed for research purposes (see Rutter, Tuma, & Lann, 1988, for full review), many have been incorporated into clinical assessment procedures. The latter will be briefly reviewed here.

The instruments provide the clinician with guidelines for a systematic review of symptoms for a given disorder. Such information is obtained from a variety of sources so that the quality and/or nature of the information can be compared and processed to make an accurate diagnosis. Changes in the adolescent's psychological status can also be monitored during the course of treatment. However, these are not a substitute for clinical acumen and are most effective when skillfully woven into the assessment and therapeutic relationship between the clinician and patient.

Sources of Information

To make a diagnosis and assess the psychosocial impairment associated with a disorder, the clinician must obtain information about the presence and severity of specific symptoms (Kazdin, French, Unis, & Esveldt-Dawson, 1983). The type of informant and the nature of information obtained must be taken into consideration during the assessment process. The therapist is interested in obtaining information about current and past depressive episodes, precipitants for the current episode, premorbid and current psychosocial functioning, and family history of psychiatric disorders.

Researchers have found that parents, teachers, and children report different types of symptoms or problems (Edelbrock, Costello, Dulcan, Conover, & Kalas, 1986; Kazdin, Esveldt-Dawson, Sherick, & Collbus, 1985). Discrepancies between parent and child reports are consistently found using a variety of diagnostic criteria and assessment instruments, including symptom scales and diagnostic interviews (Kashani, Orvaschel, Burke, & Reid, 1985; Lobovits, 1985; Moretti, Fine, Haley, & Marriage, 1985). Parents and children may employ different criteria of severity for determining when a behavior is worth mentioning, and as observers, they may be unable to perceive what is problematic for their child. In addition, they may have different areas of concern that are reflected in their responses (Kashani et al., 1985). Angold et al. (1987) found that parents are relatively unlikely to report symptoms which their children do not report, but children often report symptoms which their parents do not report. This is particularly true in the area of reports on suicidality, ideation or attempts (Velez & Cohen, 1988; Walker, Moreau, & Weissman, 1989).

Depressive symptoms can often be silent or misinterpreted. Some parents or teachers might consider the adolescent's silence and isolation as a "phase" or just a slight exacerbation of how the adolescent usually behaves. Social withdrawal may be so intense that the adolescent is basically ignored, particularly if there are other adolescents or events that immediately capture and demand the attention of adults. Irritability or anger may be the first symptom with which adolescents present, and they may be mislabeled as having a behavior problem.

Therefore, although it is important for the clinician to interview parents about their child, more accurate information about the child's internal state and altered mood is likely to be obtained directly from the adolescent. Angold et al. (1987) concludes that there appears to be a pattern of low sensitivity and high specificity for parental reports of children's depressive symptoms. For a full picture of the child's psychopathology, it appears prudent, however, to obtain information from as many sources as possible, including parents and teachers.

The clinician's ability to obtain and synthesize information is key to making an accurate assessment and diagnosis. The astute clinician will often reinterview someone with new information obtained from another informant. Discrepancies should be addressed directly with each informant in an attempt to clarify the point in question. The clinician needs to keep an open mind at all points of treatment to be able to integrate new information and reformulate diagnostic assessments accordingly.

Types of Interview

Types of interview used to make a diagnosis include the unstructured, semistructured, and structured. Unstructured interviews are conducted by skilled and experienced clinicians and do not follow specific patterns for questions or have delineated response options. Information gathered and the method for obtaining the information are a function of the clinician and his or her training.

Semistructured interviews are designed with specific questions to be asked by an interviewer who is presumed to be familiar with psychopathology and able to exercise clinical judgment in probing and making a diagnosis. Commonly used semistructured interviews are the Interview Schedule for Children (ISC; Kovacs, 1982), the Schedule for Affective Disorders and Schizophrenia, childhood version (Kiddie-SADS; Chambers et al., 1985) and the Child Assessment Schedule (CAS; Hodges, Kline, Stern, Cytryn, & McKnew, 1982). They all yield *DSM-III-R* diagnoses. The K-SADS has a present episode version and epidemiological lifetime version. The K-SADS and CAS have adequate reliability (see Compas, Ey, & Grant, 1993, for full review).

A structured interview can be administered by a trained lay interviewer. It uses questions that are to be read aloud exactly as written, has prescribed skip patterns, provides specific codes for recording responses, and thus diminishes the need for clinical judgment about problems (Edelbrock et al., 1986). Examples of structured interviews include the Diagnostic Interview Schedule for Children (DISC, version 2.3; Fisher, Wickes, Shaffer, Piacentini, & Lapkin, 1992) and the Diagnostic Interview for Children and Adolescents (DICA; Herjanic & Reich, 1982). Structured interviews permit diagnostic assessment according to systematic and specific criteria for psychiatric diagnosis and standardized methods for eliciting symptoms concerning a range of symptoms and behaviors (Gutterman, O'Brien, & Young, 1987). DISC diagnoses are generated by computer algorithms. For a complete review of interviews, see Rutter et al. (1988).

Structured interviews are commonly used in large epidemiological surveys, research protocols, and have a place in clinical practice as well. Semistructured interviews, commonly used in research, can aid in general clinical assessment. The format provides the clinician with a systematic guide for assessing all *DSM-III-R* or *DSM-IV* diagnoses ensuring a comprehensive assessment.

Self-Report Instruments

Self-report instruments are commonly used in clinical practice as well as for research purposes. The most commonly used self-report instruments to assess depression in children and adolescents include the Children's Depression Inventory (CDI), the Beck Depression Inventory (BDI), the Center for Epidemiological Studies Depression Scale (CES-D), the Reynolds Adolescent Depression Scale (RADS), and the Children's Depression Scale (CDS). These scales measure depressed mood and indicate core features of depressive disorders according to *DSM-III* criteria. Adequate internal consistency, reliability, test-retest reliability, and reliability over time have been established.

Clinician-Rated Instruments

Another type of measure that is used to assess adolescent depression is the clinician-rated instrument. The clinician rates the patient on a scale of items based on a clinical interview and observations of the patient. A frequently used clinician-rated symptom scale is the Hamilton Rating Scale for Depression. The scale is oriented toward the behavioral and somatic features of depression. It has been found to distinguish between three groups of subjects with a progressive increase in severity score of depressive symptomatology.

Treatment Approaches

Well-designed research protocols on the treatment of adolescent depression are sparse. Although numerous studies have demonstrated the efficacy of pharmacotherapy and short-term psychotherapies, alone and in combination, for acute and maintenance treatment of adults with major depression (see Weissman, Jarrett, & Rush, 1987, for review), results from comparable studies in depressed adolescents are disappointing. Pharmacological studies on the treatment of child and adolescent depression have attempted to replicate the adult treatment studies but failed to demonstrate efficacy. In addition, no published treatment study of any individual psychotherapy in the treatment of childhood or adolescent depression has employed minimum scientific standards (i.e., diagnostically homogeneous samples, specified treatment, random assignment to experimental and control groups). This section will review the peer-reviewed clinical trials as well as other treatments that are widely used clinically, but have not been tested empirically.

Pharmacotherapy

Numerous studies on the use of tricyclic antidepressants (TLAs) in children were published between the 1970s and 1980s (see Garfinkle, 1986, for a comprehensive review). All these studies were open clinical trials, and many studied children with disorders other than depression. The studies suggest the efficacy of imipramine for the treatment of depression in prepubertal children, but do not support its efficacy in adolescents (Ryan et al., 1986; Strober, Freeman, & Rigali, 1990). The studies, however, all have methodological problems, which leave open the question of whether or not antidepressants are efficacious for treatment of childhood depression. Most did not use specified diagnostic criteria or systematic assessment of diagnoses, used low doses of medication, or did not report on length of treatment. The overall positive response rate of 75% reported in these open clinical trials (Puig-Antich & Weston, 1983) was an impetus for further studies using more rigorous research design.

The recent controlled clinical trials of antidepressant medications in depressed adolescents, however, have not demonstrated efficacy. It is unclear whether this is due to methodological issues, such as small sample size, and diagnostic variability, or the biological uniqueness of adolescents (see Campbell & Spencer, 1988, for review). Medications used include the tricyclic antidepressants such as nortriptyline, imipramine, and desipramine, the serotenergic agent fluoxetine, and monoamine oxidase inhibitors. The study designs were open clinical trials, medication versus placebo, and double blind studies. The following studies reviewed used structured diagnostic interviews to yield *DSM-III* or *DSM-III-R* diagnoses. There are six published studies in children: two were placebo versus medication (Petti & Unis, 1981; Preskorn, Weller, Hughes, Weller, & Bolte, 1987), and four were double-blind (Geller, Cooper, Graham, Maistellar, & Bryant, 1990; Kashani, Hodges, & Shekim, 1980; Kashani, Whekim, & Reid, 1984; Puig-Antich et al., 1987). Seven studies on adolescents have been published: five were open clinical trials (Boulos, Kutcher, Gardner, & Young, 1992; Ryan, 1990; Ryan et al., 1986; Ryan, Puig-Antich, Rabinovich, Fried, et al., 1988; Strober et al., 1990) and three were double blind studies (Geller et al., 1990; Kramer & Feiguine, 1981; Simeon et al., 1990). In addition, there are two studies with adolescents that assessed lithium augmentation (Ryan, Meyer, Cahille, Mazzie, & Puig-Antich, 1988; Strober et al., 1990), and another open clinical trial using MAO inhibitors in nonresponders to tricyclic antidepressants (Ryan, Puig-Antich, Rabinovich, et al., 1988).

Kashani, Hodges, and Shekim (1980) and Petti and Unis (1981) reported on one child each, the former using amitriptyline in a double-blind placebo design and the latter using imipramine versus placebo. Kashani's subject became hypomanic, necessitating a dose reduction. Petti and Unis (1981) reported marked improvement with no reported side effects. Kashani et al. (1984) reported on nine prepubertal depressed children, who were randomly assigned to either amitriptyline or placebo after a 3- to 4-week baseline hospital evaluation for a 4-week trial and were then switched to the other. Depression scores decreased with both drug and placebo, but there was a greater nonsignificant decrease with the drug ($p = .09$). Puig-Antich et al. (1987) reported on 38 depressed prepubertal children who were given imipramine after a 2-week evaluation in a double-blind placebo control design. Placebo and drug response rate were similar (68% vs. 56%). However, in a complementary study in which 30 of the 38 subjects were tested for total serum drug level, combined levels of imipramine and desipramine predicted a positive response to the drug. Preskorn et al. (1987) reported that antidepressant medication was superior to placebo in children who did not suppress on the dexamethasone suppression test. Further study is needed to determine whether plasma levels or subtypes of depressive disorders predict a positive response to medication in depressed children. Geller et al. (1990) reported on 50 depressed children, who entered a 2-week single-blind placebo washout period followed by an 8-week random assignment, double-blind placebo controlled period. They found no significant differences in response between placebo or fixed level of nortriptyline.

Imipramine was given to 34 depressed adolescent inpatients in an open label trial (Ryan et al., 1986) at doses titrated to 5mg/kg/day as tolerated for 6 weeks. At the end of the trial, only 44% of the patients demonstrated diminution in depressive symptoms and most remained symptomatic. Plasma levels of drugs (combined imipramine and desipramine) did not correspond to improvement. Strober et al. (1990) described a similar study using imipramine at doses of 5 mg/kg/day for 6 weeks in 34 inpatient depressed adolescents with similar results. They reported that although serum levels did not correlate with improvement, all responders had levels greater than 180ng/ml. Ryan (1990) tried to distinguish placebo responders from medication responders in a study of 14 children and adolescents given nortriptyline ($n = 9$), imipramine ($n = 3$), or amitriptyline ($n = 2$). They used a technique proposed by Quitkin, Rabkin, Ross, and Stewart (cited in Ryan, 1990) in which it is hypothesized that responders have a pattern characterized by an initial lag in improvement followed by sustained improvement, and placebo responders demonstrate an immediate improvement followed by a variable course. They concluded that Quitkin's hypothesis (Ryan, 1990) was not supported in depressed adolescents. Boulos et al. (1992), in an open clinical trial, reported on the response of 15 depressed adolescents and young adults to fluoxetine in doses of 5 to 40 mgs a day for 6 to 7 weeks. The subjects had previously failed to respond to tricyclic antidepressant therapy. The authors concluded that fluoxetine in combination with psychosocial treatments may be an effective medication for those who have not responded to tricyclics.

Kramer and Feiguine (1981), Geller et al., (1990), and Simeon, Dinicola, Ferguson, and Copping (1990) reported on a total of 81 depressed adolescents treated with antidepressants in a double-blind design. Kramer and Feiguine (1981) gave amitriptyline or placebo to 20 depressed adolescent inpatients after a 2-day evaluation and reported that drug was no more effective than placebo after 6 weeks. Geller et al. (1990) randomly assigned 31 subjects to the nortriptyline or placebo 8-week trial after a 2-week single-blind placebo washout phase and reported that the study was terminated early because only one subject actively responded to drug. Twenty-one subjects improved during the placebo washout phase and were not assigned to the double-blind phase of the study. Simeon et al. (1990) assigned 40 subjects, 30 of whom completed the study, to a double-blind study of fluoxetine versus placebo. Although fluoxetine was more efficacious than placebo on all clinical measures except sleep, the differences were not statistically significant.

In an open clinical trial (determined by retrospective chart review), monoamine oxidase inhibitors (MAOI) either alone or in combination were used to treat 23 depressed adolescents who failed to respond to a 6-week course of TCAs (Ryan, Puig-Antich, Rabinovich, et al., 1988). Poor dietary compliance was a problem in the study, and the authors stated that risks of complications due to dietary indiscretion outweigh possible benefits of medication in impulsive unreliable adolescents or adolescents who use drugs or alcohol. Unstable families were also considered a contraindication to the use of MAOIs.

A total of 211 adolescents participated in these studies, 120 in open clinical trials and 91 in double blind design. The results thus far do not support efficacy of any of the standard antidepressant medications used for adult depression. Two additional studies reported on the efficacy of tricyclic antidepressants augmented with lithium for the treatment of depressed adolescents who failed to respond to TCA therapy alone. In an open treatment study of 14 depressed adolescents, 43% responded to the augmented treatment (Ryan, Meyer, et al., 1988). The adolescents had a trial of either amitriptyline, desipramine, or nortriptyline at adequate doses for a minimum of 6 weeks in most cases and exhibited only a partial response at best to the drug. There were no differences in baseline status or lithium level between responders and nonresponders. In the other study, only one adolescent showed improvement with the addition of lithium (Strober et al., 1990). Here again, further work is needed to determine whether lithium augmentation can play an effective role in the pharmacological treatment of adolescent depression.

The poor response of depressed children and adolescents to antidepressants in these studies poses significant research and clinical questions. If it is postulated that adolescent depression is the analog of adult depression, why do depressed adolescents fail to respond in these studies? Also, it is a well-held clinical belief that some depressed adolescents do respond to antidepressant medications; what are the characteristics that make them responsive? How can we predict which depressed adolescents will respond to medication? Several theories have been put forth to answer these questions (see Jensen, Ryan, & Prien, 1992, for a complete discussion). Three questions were posed at the 1990 NIMH workshop on medication studies to address the poor medication response of depressed children and adolescents (Jensen et al., 1992):

1. Can the design, methodology, or conduct of the studies explain the poor response?
2. Can the same diagnostic criteria used in adults be used in children?

3. Can quantitative and qualitative developmental differences in neurotransmitter and/or receptor systems between children and adults result in differential responses to medications?

Although the previously cited studies are far superior to the earlier studies in terms of design and methodology, inadequacies can be noted (see Jensen et al., 1992). Diagnostic measures are not necessarily reliable, and definitions of response are inconsistent or incomplete. Variables that could affect response are not controlled for consistently. In addition, samples suffer from small size and heterogeneity. Bipolar disorder, situational depression, psychosis, subtypes of depression, and comorbidity could account for the poor medication response in some adolescents (Jenson et al., 1992). Normal developmental processes and contextual factors may affect the onset, course, and treatment of adolescent depression (Strober, 1992). Conners (1992) outlines methodological suggestions for future studies to address these issues. In the meantime, it is standard clinical practice to treat depressed adolescents whose symptoms are persistent, impairing, and unremitting with the antidepressant medications demonstrated to be efficacious in adult depressives.

Psychosocial Treatments

In clinical practice, depressed adolescents frequently receive the psychotherapies that are efficacious in the treatment of adults (Hersen & Van Hasselt, 1987). Several thoughtful papers by leading clinicians have described their clinical experience and theoretical perspectives on psychotherapy for the depressed adolescent (Bemporad, 1988; Cytryn & McKnew, 1985; Kestenbaum & Kron, 1987; Liebowitz & Kernberg, 1988; Nissen 1986). In contrast to the small number of treatments that have been tested empirically in depressed adolescents, numerous ones are used clinically. These treatments include psychodynamic psychotherapy and psychoanalysis, cognitive-behavioral psychotherapy, behavior therapy, interpersonal psychotherapy, family therapy, and group therapy. The goal of all these treatments is to alleviate the psychological symptoms and improve functioning. Techniques consist of psychological interventions to alter the patient's behavior, thoughts, or attitudes that are felt to be contributing to the problems.

Although there are no published studies meeting all accepted scientific criteria for clinical trials, several studies have examined the efficacy of psychotherapy for the treatment of depression in adolescents: Reynolds and Coats (1986) cognitive-behavioral therapy; Robbins, Alessi, and Colfer (1989) and Mufson et al. (1994) interpersonal psychotherapy; Lewinsohn, Clarke, Hops, and Andrews (1990) Coping with Depression group psychotherapy. Clinical studies have demonstrated the feasibility of conducting controlled clinical trials with depressed adolescents and the possible efficacy of group psychotherapy based on trials in this population. As yet, however, there has not been one published controlled trial with random assignment, *DSM-III* or *DSM-IV* diagnoses, and individual psychotherapy for this population.

Cognitive Therapy

The defining characteristics of cognitive treatment are that it is directive, structured, and often time-limited, and emphasizes changing cognitions that are associated with behavioral events and problem-solving skills (Kovacs, 1979; Matson, 1989). There are various modifications of the general cognitive tenets developed by Aaron Beck.

Beck hypothesizes a three-part cognitive model of depression: negative view of self, the world, and the future (Beck, Rush, Shaw, & Emery, 1979). A person reacts to stress by activating this set of dysfunctional beliefs. Such negative cognitions are posited to be a result of faulty thought processes such as overgeneralization, personalization, absolute dichotomous thinking, and selective abstraction (Beck, 1967). Treatment focuses on correcting those misattributions and misperceptions through structured tasks in and out of sessions. Beck believes that the individual learns to master problems and situations by reevaluating and correcting his or her thinking (Beck et al., 1979).

The goals of cognitive therapy are (a) to obtain symptom relief, and (b) to uncover beliefs that lead to depression and subject them to reality testing (Emery, Bedrosian, & Garber, 1983). Techniques used to accomplish these goals include monitoring negative cognitions, helping the patient to make the connections between cognition, affect, and behavior, and learning to identify and alter dysfunctional beliefs (Beck et al., 1979). Emery et al. (1983), in their use of cognitive therapy with depressed children and adolescents, found it helpful to work with parents as well as adolescents to restructure parents' expectations for their children that result in decreased self-esteem. The goal of therapy is to decrease the reinforcement of the adolescent's dysfunctional cognitions.

Another model of cognitive therapy is based on Seligman's model of learned helplessness, which was derived from animal experimentation (Seligman & Maier, 1967). Seligman's model proposes that repeated experience with failure results in a sense of helplessness and hopelessness that the situation cannot change, which in turn results in depressive cognitions (Seligman & Maier, 1967). Treatment focuses on these feelings of helplessness and hopelessness by attempting to structure some success experiences to dissipate negative feelings and create a sense of hopefulness and mastery. Specific strategies include assistance in changing expectations for unpleasant events and relinquishing unattainable goals, acquisition of social or problem-solving skills, and changing attribution style (Petti, 1983).

Reynolds and Coats (1986) reported on a clinical trial comparing cognitive-behavioral therapy, relaxation training, and a wait-list control for the treatment of depressive symptoms in 30 adolescents. Treatment was conducted in 10 small group meetings of 50 minutes each over 5 weeks. Findings indicated superiority of the two active treatments in reduction of depressive symptoms when compared with wait-list control, with no differences between the two active treatments. This study, however, used depressive symptoms not diagnosis as the entrance criteria, so it obviously is not generalizable to treatment of adolescents with major depression disorder.

Behavioral Approaches

Although there are behavioral elements in cognitive therapy, another treatment modality more strictly focuses on the behavior of the individual as the root of the depression. One of the major behavioral models of depression is that of the loss of positive reinforcement. Lewinsohn, Weinstein, and Shaw (1969) found that depressed individuals appeared to lack access to sufficient schedules of positive reinforcement because of either the complete absence of reinforcement or the individual's inability to access them due to lack of appropriate skills. Low rate of positive reinforcement for one's behavior can lead to depression. In turn, depressive affect being displayed further decreases the individual's chances of receiving positive reinforcement for his or her behavior thereby exacerbating or increasing the depression. Lewinsohn's treatment for depression has focused on teaching adolescents skills necessary to obtain needed positive reinforcement to break the depressive feedback cycle.

A behavioral psychoeducational approach for coping with depression, with modifications for adolescents, has been developed by Clarke and Lewinsohn (1989). Lewinsohn et al. (1990) have conducted a clinical trial with 54 depressed adolescents comparing wait-list controls with two different presentations of the Coping with Depression Course for adolescents: group therapy with no treatment provided for their parents or group therapy with treatment provided for their parents. Patients in the two active treatments improved significantly more on the depressive measures than the wait-list group. There were no significant differences between the two active treatments. There was, however, a trend for greater improvement in the patients whose parents also participated in the treatment.

There has been an absence of formal use and/or testing in clinical trials of more strictly behavioral techniques with adolescents who have been diagnosed as depressed. The techniques have been used with depressive symptoms associated with other psychiatric disorders (Petti, 1983). Adolescents have been reported to respond to techniques focusing on self-control and social interactions (Petti, 1983). Some specific behavioral techniques that have been used in treatment of depressive symptoms and illustrated in case reports include modeling appropriate behavior, behavioral rehearsal, information giving, skills training, and homework regarding particular behaviors to be conducted outside the sessions (Petti, 1983).

Interpersonal Approach

Interpersonal psychotherapy is a time-limited brief psychotherapy based on the premise that depression occurs in the context of interpersonal relationships. Understanding the interpersonal context of depressive episodes can alleviate the depressive symptoms regardless of the etiology of the depressive episode. Emphasis is on issues in current rather than past relationships. The adult treatment manual (IPT) has been adapted for depressed adolescents (IPT-A; Mufson, Moreau, Weissman, & Klerman, 1993). The goals of IPT-A are to decrease the depressive symptomatology and improve social functioning by focusing on problems in the patient's interpersonal relationships. Five problem areas are identified as a possible focus: grief, interpersonal role disputes, role transitions, interpersonal deficits, and single-parent families. Techniques used include communication analysis, linkage of affect with events, expression of affect, and role playing. It is a 12-week treatment consisting of therapy sessions once a week.

Robbins and associates (1989), in a pilot treatment strategy for 38 adolescents hospitalized with major depression, conducted an open trial of psychotherapy that they described as similar to IPT. They noted that 47% of the patients responded with reduction of symptoms when treated with psychotherapy alone. The nonresponders were then treated with a combined tricyclic antidepressant and psychotherapy, and 92% responded. Interpreting results of this study is confounded because there appears to be a 50% placebo response rate in depressed adolescents regardless of type of treatment (i.e., medication or nonspecific psychotherapeutic intervention alone). Also, it is not possible to know whether responders in the second stage of the study improved because of medication, psychotherapy, or combined treatment.

Robbins et al. (1989) conducted this study without modifying the manual specifically for depressed adolescents; thus, procedures for the treatment are not defined.

Since this study was conducted, Mufson et al. (1993) have written a treatment manual of interpersonal psychotherapy for depressed adolescents (IPT-A), which is the basis of a completed open clinical trial of IPT-A and an ongoing randomized controlled clinical trial of IPT-A. Fourteen depressed adolescents were treated in an open clinical trial of IPT-A using the standardized treatment manual (Mufson et al., 1994). In general, results demonstrated feasibility and acceptability of the treatment and suggest a potential for efficacy (Mufson et al., 1994). A controlled clinical trial of IPT-A versus clinical management is underway to assess efficacy of the treatment. Further studies will need to address the issues of placebo response and differentiating positive responses among medication, IPT-A, and combined treatment.

Psychodynamic Psychotherapy

Psychodynamic psychotherapy is commonly used to treat depressed adolescents. The principles are derived from psychoanalytic theories. In the most simple terms, they are based on the premise that symptoms of distress are a result of unconscious conflicts. These symptoms can be addressed and decreased through such interventions as confrontation, clarification, and interpretation (Liebowitz & Kernberg, 1988). Within the psychodynamic psychotherapy framework, there are several types of psychodynamic psychotherapy: child psychoanalysis, expressive or exploratory child psychotherapy, supportive psychotherapy, and expressive supportive child psychotherapy. The specific applications and goals of each of these therapies are described in Liebowitz and Kernberg's (1988) excellent review of psychodynamic psychotherapies for children.

Psychodynamic theory understands depression as resulting from changes in the sense of self caused by a loss of relationships or achievements or constructs that were used to support a self-image or identity (Bemporad, 1988). The adolescent is particularly vulnerable to depression because the developmental task of adolescence is to change and solidify one's identity. Consequently, the adolescent may become vulnerable to losses that may occur in this process. Such vulnerabilities in character are believed to be a result of early childhood experiences that will not only shape adolescence but will affect adult personality and coping skills as well. Psychodynamic psychotherapists believe that psychological improvement will result from intrapsychic, characterological change.

The role of the therapist is to help the adolescent identify distortions about oneself and one's relationships, place them in the historical context of the relationship or situation, and help the adolescent have more realistic expectations and goals for relationships and self-concept. Symptom relief is achieved by bringing into conscious awareness unconscious conflicts and memories that the adolescent may have hidden from him- or herself. There is no manual standardizing the treatment, and therapists believe the treatment varies significantly with the specific patient-therapist alliance. To date, there have been no controlled clinical trials of psychodynamic psychotherapy with depressed adolescents.

Family Therapy

Family therapists conceptualize an individual's depression as occurring within the family system. The individual cannot be understood in isolation of some understanding of the larger social context or family system (Nichols, 1984). Disequilibrium among the family members, improper alliances, or communication difficulties can result in the creation of an identified patient who manifests the family's problems in his or her depression. Therefore, the therapist addresses the adolescent's depression by addressing the pathology in the family system. There is no one model of a dysfunctional family that has been linked to depression in children and adolescents. Specific issues typically addressed in family therapy that can be applied to depression as well as other psychiatric disorders include the concept of boundaries between family members, enmeshment of family members, and the importance of role relations in families. Family therapy is usually a brief action-oriented approach whose goal is to resolve the symptoms by changing the family members' behavior in the present (Nichols, 1984).

Within the family therapy modality, there are several different types of treatment, ranging from systems family therapy (Haley, 1976), structural family therapy (Minuchin, 1974) to contextual family therapy (Boszormenyi-Nagy & Krasner, 1986). These treatments differ in types of techniques and focus of treatment ranging from communication and interpersonal problem-solving skills (systems therapy), reframing interactions, altering boundaries and family hierarchy (structural therapy), to the use of paradoxical techniques such as prescribing the symptom that the therapist and patient are actually trying to eliminate. The guiding principle is that the most significant influence on an individual's behavior lies in the family relationships, the responses of the family system to the individual and vice versa. There have been several studies on the efficacy of family therapy for the treatment of family dysfunction and other disorders, but the studies have not been specifically for the treatment of adolescent depression.

Group Psychotherapy

One of the main goals of group therapy, for most any psychiatric problem, is to put the adolescent in contact with peers who have similar difficulties, who can provide support for each other, and who provide each other with opportunities to practice new skills for interpersonal relationships. The specific goals of group therapy can include: (a) enabling the individual to perceive similarity of one's needs with others; (b) generating alternative solutions to particular conflicts; (c) learning more effective social skills; and (d) increasing awareness of others' needs and feelings (Corey, 1981). Depressed adolescents have been treated in social skill training groups. In such a group, the focus of treatment is on identifying and practicing social skills that may alleviate conflict in relationships with family and friends. Within the group session, members will often role-play different communication skills, such as clarification of the problem, eliciting another person's point of view, and expression of their own feelings. Other groups may be less structured. Adolescents in these groups may use the sessions to discuss the problems they are having with family and friends, to learn whether or not their situation differs from that of many other adolescents, and together to generate solutions and gain confirmation of their feelings in the situation. Another significant aspect of these groups is that many of them are time-limited with set goals and programs to accomplish within that time.

SUMMARY

Depression is a serious psychiatric disorder for children and adolescents. Regrettably, Keller et al. (1991) found a significantly low rate of treatment in adolescents and children with major depression. Reasons for failure to adequately treat this population include lack of knowledge about the disorder and treatments and lack of availability of services. Recognition and treatment of depression is likely to increase if an effort is made to educate the community, and investigate and document efficacy of treatments for this population. Because exogenous factors are involved in adolescent depression, psychosocial treatments are likely to have their place as effective treatments either alone or in combination with pharmacological treatment. There is a clinical need for effective psychotherapeutic interventions with depressed adolescents and a scientific imperative to establish efficacy among the multitude of currently available therapies.

REFERENCES

Alessi, N., & Robbins, D. R. (1984). Symptoms and subtypes of depression among adolescents distinguished by the dexamethasone suppression test: A preliminary report. *Psychiatry Research, 11,* 177.

Alessi, N., Robbins, D. R., & Dilsaver, S. C. (1987). Panic and depressive disorders among psychiatrically hospitalized adolescents. *Psychiatry Research, 20,* 275–283.

American Psychiatric Association. (1987). *Diagnostic and statistical manual of mental disorders* (3rd ed., rev.). Washington, DC: Author.

American Psychiatric Association. (1994). *Diagnostic and statistical manual of mental disorders* (4th ed.). Washington, DC: Author.

Angold, A. (1988a). Childhood and adolescent depression: 1. Epidemiological and aetiological aspects. *British Journal of Psychiatry, 152,* 601–617.

Angold, A. (1988b). Childhood and adolescent depression: 2. Research in clinical populations. *British Journal of Psychiatry, 153,* 476–492.

Angold, A., Weissman, M. M., John, K., & Merikangas, K. R. (1987). Parent-child reports of depressive symptoms in children at low and high risk of depression. *Journal of Child Psychology and Psychiatry and Allied Disciplines, 28,* 901–915.

Angst, J., Merikangas, K., Scheidegger, P., & Wicki, W. (1990). Recurrent brief depression: A new subtype of affective disorder. *Journal of Affective Disorders, 19,* 87–98.

Beardslee, W., Bemporad, J., Keller, M. B., Klerman, G. L., Dorer, D. J., & Samuelson, H. (1983). Children of parents with Major Affective Disorder: A review. *American Journal of Psychiatry,140,* 825–832.

Beck, A. T. (1967). *Depression: Clinical, experimental and theoretical aspects.* New York: Harper & Row.

Beck, A. T., Rush, A. J., Shaw, B. F., & Emery, G. (1979). *Cognitive therapy of depression.* New York: Guilford Press.

Bemporad, J. (1988). Psychodynamic treatment of depressed adolescents. *Journal of Clinical Psychiatry, 49,*(9, suppl), 26–31.

Bemporad, J., & Lee, K. W. (1988). Affective disorders. In C. Kestenbaum & D. Williams (Eds.), *Handbook of clinical assessment of children and adolescents* (Vol. 2, pp. 626–650). New York: New York University Press.

Bernstein, G. A., & Garfinkel, B. D. (1986). School phobia: The overlap of affective and anxiety disorders. *Journal of the American Academy of Child and Adolescent Psychiatry, 25,* 235–241.

Biederman, J., Munir, K., Knee, D., Armentano, M., Autor, S., Waternaus, C., & Tsuang, M. (1987). High rate of Affective Disorder in probands with Attention Deficit Disorder and in their relatives: A controlled family study. *American Journal of Psychiatry, 144,* 330–333.

Boszormenyi-Nagy, I., & Krasner, B. R. (1986). *Between give and take: A clinical guide to contextual therapy.* New York: Brunner/Mazel.

Boulos, C., Kutcher, S., Gardner, D., & Young, E. (1992). An open naturalistic trial of fluoxetine in adolescents and young adults with treatment-resistant major depression. *Journal of Child and Adolescent Psychopharmacology, 2,* 103–111.

Brown, G. W., Harris, T. O., & Bifulco, A. (1986). Long-term effects of early loss of parent. In M. Rutter, C. E. Izard, & P. B. Read (Eds.), *Depression in young people: Developmental and clinical perspectives* (pp. 251–297). New York: Guilford Press.

Campbell, M., & Spencer, E. K. (1988). Psychopharmacology in child and adolescent psychiatry: A review of the past five years. *Journal of the American Academy of Child and Adolescent Psychiatry, 27,* 269–279.

Carlson, G., & Cantwell, D. (1980). Unmasking masked depression in children and adolescents. *American Journal of Psychiatry, 137,* 445–449.

Carlson, G., & Strober, M. (1979). Affective disorders in adolescence. *Psychiatric Clinics of North America, 2,* 511–526.

Chambers, W., Puig-Antich, J., Hirsh, M., Paez, P., Ambrosini, P., Tabrizi, M. A., & Davies, M. (1985). The assessment of affective disorders in children and adolescents by semistructured interview: Test-retest reliability of K-SADS-P. *Archives of General Psychiatry, 42,* 696–702.

Clarke, G., & Lewinsohn, P. M. (1989). The Coping with Depression course: A group psychoeducational intervention for unipolar depression. *Behavior Change, 6,* 554–569.

Compas, B., Ey, S., & Grant, K. (1993). Taxonomy, assessment, and diagnosis of depression during adolescence. *Psychological Bulletin, 114,* 323–344.

Conners, C. K. (1992). Methodology of antidepressant drug trials for treating depression in adolescents. *Journal of Child and Adolescent Psychopharmacology, 2,* 11–28.

Corey, G. (1981). *Theory and practice of group counseling* (2nd ed.). Monterey, CA: Brooks/Cole.

Cytryn, L., & McKnew, D. H. (1985). Treatment issues in childhood depression. *Psychiatric Annals, 15,* 401.

Cytryn, L., McKnew, D. H., Zahn-Waxler, C., & Gershon, E. S. (1986). Developmental issues in risk research: The offspring of affectively ill parents. In M. Rutter, C. E. Izard, & P. B. Read (Eds.), *Depression in young people: Developmental and clinical perspectives* (pp. 163–189). New York: Guilford Press.

Downey, G., & Coyne, J. (1990). Children of depressed parents: An integrated review. *Psychological Bulletin, 108,* 50–76.

Draguns, J. G. (1981). Counseling across cultures: Common themes and distinct approaches. In P. B. Pederson, J. G. Draguns, W. J., Conner, & J. E. Trimble (Eds.), *Counseling across cultures* (pp. 3–21). Hawaii: University of Hawaii.

Edelbrock, C., Costello, A. J., Dulcan, M. K., Conover, N. C., & Kalas, R. (1986). Parent-child agreement on child psychiatric symptoms assessed via structured interview. *Journal of Child Psychology, Psychiatry & Allied Disciplines, 27,* 181–190.

Emery, G., Bedrosian, R., & Garber, J. (1983). Cognitive therapy with depressed children and adolescents. In D. P. Cantwell & G. A. Carlson (Eds.), *Affective disorders in childhood and adolescence—An update* (pp. 445–471). New York: Spectrum.

Fendrich, M., Warner, V., & Weissman, M. M. (1990). Family risk factors, parental depression and psychopathology in offspring. *Developmental Psychology, 26,* 40–50.

Fisher, P., Wickes, J., Shaffer, D., Piacentini, J., & Lapkin, J. (1992). *National Institute of Mental Health Diagnostic Interview Schedule for Children (NIMH DISC, version 2.3): User's manual.* New York: New York State Psychiatric Institute, Division of Child and Adolescent Psychiatry.

Fleming, J. E., & Offord, S. R. (1990). Epidemiology of childhood depressive disorders: A critical review. *Journal of the American Academy of Child and Adolescent Psychiatry, 29,* 571–580.

Fleming, J. E., Offord, D. R., & Boyle, M. H. (1989). Prevalence of childhood and adolescent depression in the community: Ontario Child Health Study. *British Journal of Psychiatry, 155,* 647–654.

Friedman, R. C., Hurt, S. W., Clarkin, J. F., Corn, R., & Aronoff, M. S. (1983). Symptoms of depression among adolescents and young adults. *Journal of Affective Disorders, 5,* 37–43.

Garber, J., Kriss, M. R., Koch, M., & Lindholm, L. (1988). Recurrent depression in adolescents: A follow-up study. *Journal of the American Academy of Child and Adolescent Psychiatry, 27,* 49–54.

Garfinkle, B. D. (1986). Major affective disorders in children and adolescents. In G. Winokur & P. Clayton (Eds.), *The medical basis of psychiatry* (pp. 308–330). Philadelphia: Saunders.

Garrison, C. Z., Schlucter, M. D., Schoenbach, V. J., & Kaplan, B. K. (1989). Epidemiology of depressive symptoms in young adolescents. *Journal of the American Academy of Child and Adolescent Psychiatry, 28,* 343–351.

Geller, B., Cooper, T. B., Graham, D. L., Marsteller, F. A., & Bryant, D. M. (1990). Double-blind placebo-controlled study of nortriptyline in depressed adolescents using a "fixed plasma level" design. *Psychopharmacology Bulletin, 26,* 85–90.

Gutterman, E. M., O'Brien, J. D., & Young, J. G. (1987). Structured diagnostic interviews for children and adolescents: Current status and future directions. *Journal of the American Academy of Child and Adolescent Psychiatry, 26,* 621–630.

Haley, J. (1976). *Problem-solving therapy: New strategies for effective family therapy.* New York: Jossey-Bass.

Hammen, C., Burge, D., Burney, E., & Adrian, C. (1990). Longitudinal study of diagnoses in children of women with unipolar and bipolar affective disorder. *Archives of General Psychiatry, 47,* 1112–1117.

Harrington, R., Fudge, H., Rutter, M., Pickles, A., & Hill, J. (1990). Adult outcomes of childhood and adolescent depression. *Archives of General Psychiatry, 47,* 465–473.

Herjanic, B., & Reich, W. (1982). Development of a structured psychiatric interview for children: Agreement between child and parent on individual symptoms. *Journal of Abnormal Child Psychology, 10,* 307–324.

Hersen, M., & Van Hasselt, V. B. (1987). *Behavior therapy with children and adolescents: A clinical approach.* New York: Wiley.

Hodges, K., Kline, J., Stern, L., Cytryn, L., & McKnew, D. (1982). The development of a child assessment interview for research and clinical use. *Journal of Abnormal Child Psychology, 10,* 173–189.

Inamdar, S. C., Simopoulos, G., Osborn, M., & Bianchi, E. (1979). Phenomenology associated with depressed moods in adolescents. *American Journal of Psychiatry, 136,* 156–159.

Jensen, P., Ryan, N., & Prien, R. (1992). Psychopharmacology of child and adolescent major depression: Present status and future directions. *Journal of Child and Adolescent Psychopharmacology, 2,* 31–45.

Kandel, D. B., & Davies, M. (1982). Epidemiology of depressive mood in adolescents: An empirical study. *Archives of General Psychiatry, 39,* 1205–1212.

Kandel, D. B., & Davies, M. (1986). Adult sequelae of adolescent depressive symptoms. *Archives of General Psychiatry, 43,* 255–262.

Kaplan, S. L., Hong, G. K., & Weinhold, C. (1984). Epidemiology of depressive symptomatology. *Journal of the American Academy of Child and Adolescent Psychiatry, 23,* 91–98.

Kashani, J. H., Burbach, D. J., & Rosenberg, T. K. (1988). Perceptions of family conflict resolution and depressive symptomatology. *Journal of the American Academy of Child and Adolescent Psychiatry, 27,* 42–48.

Kashani, J. H., Carlson, G. A., Beck, N. C., Hoeper, E. W., Corcoran, C. M., McAllister, J. A., Fallahi, C., Rosenberg, T. K., & Reid, J. C. (1987). Depression, depressive symptoms, and depressed mood among a community sample of adolescents. *American Journal of Psychiatry, 144,* 931–941.

Kashani, J. H., Hodges, K. K., & Shekim, W. O. (1980). Hypomanic reaction to amitryptoline in a depressed child. *Psychosomatics, 21,* 867–872.

Kashani, J. H., Orvaschel, H., Burke, J. P., & Reid, J. C. (1985). Informant variance: The issue of parent-child disagreement. *Journal of the American Academy of Child and Adolescent Psychiatry, 24,* 437–441.

Kashani, J. H., Rosenberg, T. K., & Reigh, N. C. (1989). Developmental perspectives in child and adolescent depressive symptoms in a community sample. *American Journal of Psychiatry, 146,* 871–875.

Kashani, J. H., Shekim, W. O., & Reid, J. C. (1984). Amitriptyline in children with Major Depressive Disorder: A double-blind crossover pilot study. *Journal of the American Academy of Child and Adolescent Psychiatry, 23,* 348–351.

Kazdin, A. E., Esveldt-Dawson, K., Sherick, R. B., & Colbus, D. (1985). Assessment of overt behavior and childhood depression among psychiatrically disturbed children. *Journal of Consulting and Clinical Psychology, 53,* 201–210.

Kazdin, A. E., French, N. H., Unis, A. S., & Esveldt-Dawson, K. (1983). Assessment of childhood depression. *Journal of the American Academy of Child and Adolescent Psychiatry, 22,* 157–164.

Keller, M. B., Beardslee, W. R., Lavori, P. W., & Wunder, J. (1988). Course of major depression in nonreferred adolescents: A retrospective study. *Journal of Affective Disorders, 15,* 235–243.

Keller, M. B., Lavori, P. W., Beardslee, W. R., Wunder, J., & Ryan, N. (1991). Depression in children and adolescents: New data on "undertreatment" and a literature review on the efficacy of available treatments. *Journal of Affective Disorders, 21,* 156–171.

Kestenbaum, C. J., & Kron, L. (1987). Psychoanalytic intervention with children and adolescents with affective disorders: A combined treatment approach. *Journal of the American Academy of Psychoanalysis, 15,* 153–174.

Kovacs, M. (1979). The efficacy of cognitive and behavioral therapies for depression. *American Journal of Psychiatry, 137,* 1495–1501.

Kovacs, M. (1982). *The CDI.* Unpublished manuscript. University of Pittsburgh, Pittsburgh, PA.

Kovacs, M., Feinberg, T. L., Crouse-Novak, M. A., Paulauskas, S. L., & Finkelstein, R. (1984). Depressive disorders in childhood: 1. A longitudinal prospective study of characteristics and recovery. *Archives of General Psychiatry, 41,* 229–237.

Kovacs, M., Gatsonis, C., Paulauskas, S. L., & Richards, C. (1989). Depressive disorders in childhood: 4. A longitudinal study of comorbidity with and risk for anxiety disorders. *Archives of General Psychiatry, 46,* 776–782.

Kramer, A. D., & Feiguine, R. J. (1981). Clinical effects of amitryptiline in adolescent depression: A pilot study. *Journal of the American Academy of Child and Adolescent Psychiatry, 20,* 636–644.

Lewinsohn, P. M., Clarke, G. N., Hops, H., & Andrews, J. (1990). Cognitive-behavioral treatment for depressed adolescents. *Behavioral Therapy, 21,* 385–401.

Lewinsohn, P. M., Clarke, G. N., Seely, J. R., & Rohde, P. (1994). Major depression in community adolescents: Age at onset, episode duration, and time to recurrence. *Journal of the American Academy of Child and Adolescent Psychiatry, 33,* 809–818.

Lewinsohn, P. M., Weinstein, M., & Shaw, D. (1969). Depression: A clinical-research approach. In R. Rubin & C. Frank (Eds.), *Advances in behavior therapy* (pp. 231–240). New York: Academic Press.

Liebowitz, J. H., & Kernberg, P. F. (1988). Psychodynamic psychotherapies. In C. J. Kestenbaum & D. T. Williams (Eds.), *Handbook of clinical assessment of children and adolescents* (Vol. 2, p. 1045). New York: New York University Press.

Macaulay, E., Myersk, E., Mitchell, J., Calderone, R., Scholorek, K., & Treder, R. (1993). Depression in young people. *Journal of the American Academy of Child and Adolescent Psychiatry, 32,* 714–722.

Malgady, R. G., Rogler, L. H., & Constantino, G. (1990). Culturally sensitive psychotherapy for Puerto Rican children and adolescents: A program of treatment outcome research. *Journal of Consulting and Clinical Psychology, 58,* 704–712.

Marks, A. M., Malizio, J., Hoch, J., Brody, R., & Fisher, M. (1983). Assessment of health needs and willingness to utilize healthcare resources of adolescents in a suburban population. *Journal of Pediatrics, 102,* 456–460.

Marriage, K., Fine, S., Moretti, M., & Haley, B. (1986). Relationship between depression and Conduct Disorder in children and adolescents. *Journal of the American Academy of Child and Adolescent Psychiatry, 25,* 687–691.

Matson, J. L. (1989). *Treating depression in children and adolescents.* New York: Pergamon Press.

Merikangas, K. R., Risch, N. J., & Weissman, M. M. (1994). Comorbidity and co-transmission of alcoholism, anxiety, and depression. *Psychological Medicine, 24,* 69–80.

Minuchin, S. (1974). *Families and family therapy.* Cambridge, MA: Harvard University Press.

Mitchell. J., McCauley, E., Burke, P. M., & Moss, S. J. (1988). Phenomenology of depression in children and adolescents. *Journal of the American Academy of Child and Adolescent Psychiatry, 27,* 12–20.

Moretti, M., Fine S., Haley, B., & Marriage, K. (1985). Childhood and adolescent depression. *Journal of the American Academy of Child and Adolescent Psychiatry, 24,* 298–302.

Mufson, L., Moreau, D., Weissman, M. M., & Klerman, G. L. (1993). *Interpersonal psychotherapy for depressed adolescents.* New York: Guilford Press.

Mufson, L., Moreau, D., Weissman, M. M., Wickamaratne, P., Martin, J., & Samolov, A. (1994). The modification of interpersonal psychotherapy with depressed adolescents (IPT-A): Phase I and II studies. *Journal of the American Academy of Child and Adolescent Psychiatry, 33,* 695–705.

Nichols, M. (1984). *Family therapy: Concepts and methods.* New York: Gardner Press.

Nissen, G. (1986). Treatment for depression in children and adolescents. *Psychopathology, 19*(Suppl. 2), 152–161.

Offer, D. (1969). *The psychological world of the teenager: A study of normal adolescent boys. Adolescent turmoil* (pp. 174–193). New York: Basic Books.

Offord, D., Boyle, M. H., Szatmari, P., Rae-Grant, N., Links, P., Cadman, D. T., Byles, J. A., Crawford, J. W., Blum, H. M., Byrne, C., Thomas, H., & Woodward, C. A. (1987). Ontario Child Health Study: 2. Six-month prevalence of disorder and rates of service utilization. *Archives of General Psychiatry, 44,* 832–836.

Petti, T. A. (1983). Behavioral approaches in the treatment of depressed children. In D. P. Cantwell & G. A. Carlson (Eds.), *Affective disorders in childhood and adolescence—An update.* New York: Spectrum.

Petti, T. A., & Unis, A. (1981). Imipramine treatment of borderline children: Case reports with a controlled study. *American Journal of Psychiatry, 138,* 515–518.

Preskorn, S. H., Weller, E. B., Hughes, C. W., Weller, R. A., & Bolte, K. (1987). Depression in prepubertal children: Dexamethasone nonsuppression predicts differential response to imipramine versus placebo. *Psychopharmacology Bulletin, 23,* 128–133.

Puig-Antich, J. (1982). Major depression and Conduct Disorder in prepuberty. *Journal of the American Academy of Child and Adolescent Psychiatry, 21,* 118–128.

Puig-Antich, J., Lukens, E., Davies, M., Goetz, D., Brennan-Quattrock, J., & Todak, G. (1985a). Psychosocial functioning in prepubertal depressive disorders: 1. Interpersonal relationships during the depressive episode. *Archives of General Psychiatry, 42,* 500–507.

Puig-Antich, J., Lukens, E., Davies, M., Goetz, D., Brennan-Quattrock, J., & Todak, G. (1985b). Psychosocial functioning in prepubertal depressive disorders: 2. Interpersonal relationships after sustained recovery from affective episode. *Archives of General Psychiatry, 42,* 511–517.

Puig-Antich, J., Perel, M. P., Luputkin, W., Chambers, W. J., Tabrizi, M. A., King, J., Goez, R., Davies, M., & Stiller, R. L. (1987). Imipramine in prepubertal major depressive disorder in childhood. *Annual Review of Medicine, 34,* 231–245.

Puig-Antich, J., & Weston, B. (1983). The diagnosis and treatment of Major Depressive Disorder in childhood. *Annual Review of Medicine, 34,* 231–245.

Quitkin, F. M., Rabkin, J. G., Ross, D., & Stewart, J. W. (1984). Identification of true drug response to antidepressants: Use of pattern analysis. *Archives of General Psychiatry, 41,* 782–786.

Reinherz, H. Z., Stewart-Berghauer, G., Pakiz, B., Frost, A. K., Moeykens, B. A., & Holmes, W. M. (1989). The relationship of early risk and current mediators to depressive symptomatology in adolescents. *Journal of the American Academy of Child and Adolescent Psychiatry, 28,* 942–947.

Reynolds, W. M., & Coats, K. I. (1986). A comparison of cognitive-behavioral therapy and relaxation training for the treatment of depression in adolescents. *Journal of Consulting and Clinical Psychology, 44,* 653–660.

Robbins, D. R., Alessi, N. E., & Colfer, M. V. (1989). Treatment of adolescents with major depression: Implications of the DST and the melancholic clinical subtype. *Journal of Affective Disorders, 17,* 99–104.

Rodriguez, O. (1987). *Hispanics and human services: Help-seeking in the inner-city* (Monograph No. 14). New York: Fordham University, Hispanic Research Center.

Rogler, L., Malgady, R. G., Constantino, G., & Blumenthal, R. (1987). What do culturally sensitive mental health services mean? The case of Hispanics. *American Psychologist, 42,* 565–570.

Rutter M., Graham, P., Chadwick, F. D., & Yule, W. (1976). Adolescent turmoil: Fact or fiction. *Journal of Child Psychology & Psychiatry, 17,* 35–36.

Rutter, M., Tizzard, J., Yule, W., Graham, P., & Whitmore, K. (1976). Isle of Wight studies 1964–1974. *Psychological Medicine, 6,* 313–332.

Rutter, M., Tuma, A. H., & Lann, I. S. (Eds.). (1988). *Assessment and diagnosis in child psychopathology.* New York: Guilford Press.

Ryan, N. D. (1990). Pharmacotherapy of adolescent major depression: Beyond TCA's. *Psychopharmacology Bulletin, 26,* 75–79.

Ryan, N. D., Meyer, V., Cahille, S., Mazzie, D., & Puig-Antich, J. (1988). Lithium antidepressant augmentation in TCA refractory depression in adolescents. *Journal of the American Academy of Child and Adolescent Psychiatry, 27,* 371–376.

Ryan, N. D., Puig-Antich, J., Ambrosini, P., Rabinovich, H., Robinson, D., Nelson, B., Iyengar, S., & Twomey, J. (1987). The clinical picture of major depression in children and adolescents. *Archives of General Psychiatry, 44,* 854–861.

Ryan, N. D., Puig-Antich, J., Cooper, T., Rabinovich, H., Ambrosini, P., Davies, M., King, J., Torres, D., & Fried, J. (1986). Imipramine in adolescent major depression: Plasma level and clinical response. *Acta Psychiatrica Scandinavica, 73,* 275–288.

Ryan, N. D., Puig-Antich, J., Rabinovich, H., Fried, J., Ambrosini, P., Meyer, V., Torres, D., Dachille, S., & Mazzie, D. (1988). MAOIs in adolescent depression unresponsive to tricyclic antidepressants. *Journal of the American Academy of Child and Adolescent Psychiatry, 27,* 755–758.

Saunders, S. M., Resnick, M. D., Hoberman, H. M., & Blum, R. W. (1994). Formal help-seeking behavior of adolescents identifying themselves as having mental health problems. *Journal of the American Academy of Child and Adolescent Psychiatry, 33,* 718–728.

Schoenbach, V. J. (1983). Prevalence of self-reported depressive symptoms in young adolescents. *American Journal of Public Health, 73,* 1281–1287.

Seligman, M., & Maier, S. (1967). Failure to escape traumatic shock. *Journal of Experimental Psychology, 74,* 1–9.

Siegel, L., & Griffin, N. J. (1984). Correlates of depressive symptoms in adolescents. *Journal of Youth and Adolescence, 13,* 475–487.

Simeon, J. G. (1989). Depressive disorders in children and adolescents. *Journal of the University of Ottawa, 14,* 356–361.

Simeon, J. G., Dinicola, V. F., Ferguson, B. H., & Copping, W. (1990). Adolescent depression: A placebo-controlled fluoxetine study and follow-up. *Progress in Neuro-Psychopharmacology and Biological Psychiatry, 14,* 791–795.

Strober, M. (1992). The pharmacotherapy of depressive illness in adolescence: 3. Diagnostic and conceptual issues in studies of tricyclic antidepressants. *Journal of Child and Adolescent Psychopharmacology, 2,* 23–28.

Strober, M., Freeman, R., & Rigali, J. (1990). The pharmacotherapy of depressive illness in adolescence: 1. An open label trial of imipramine. *Psychopharmacology Bulletin, 26,* 80–84.

Sue, D. W. (1981). *Counseling the culturally different: Theory and practice.* New York: Wiley.

Swift, W. J., Andrews, D., & Barklage, N. E. (1986). The relationship between Addiction Disorder and Eating Disorder: A review of the literature. *American Journal of Psychiatry, 143,* 290–299.

Tuma, J. (1989). Mental health services for children: The state of the art. *American Psychologist, 44,* 188–189.

Velez, C., & Cohen, P. (1988). Suicidal behavior and ideation in a community sample of children: Maternal and youth reports. *Journal of the American Academy of Child and Adolescent Psychiatry, 27,* 349–356.

Walker, M., Moreau, D., & Weissman, M. M. (1989). Parents' awareness of children's suicide attempts. *American Journal of Psychiatry, 147,* 1363–1366.

Weissman, M. M., Gammon, D., John, K., Merikangas, K. R., Warner, V., Prusoff, B. A., & Sholomskas, D. (1987). Children of depressed parents: Increased psychopathology and early onset of major depression. *Archives of General Psychiatry, 44,* 847–853.

Weissman, M. M., Jarrett, R. B., & Rush, A. J. (1987). Psychotherapy and its relevance to the pharmacotherapy of major depression: A decade later (1976–1985). In H. Meltzer (Ed.), *Psychopharmacology: The third generation of progress.* New York: Raven Press.

430 Treatment Interventions

Weissman, M. M., Leckman, J. F., Merikangas, K. R., Gammon, D., & Prusoff, B. A. (1984). Depression and anxiety disorders in parents and children. *Archives of General Psychiatry, 41,* 845–851.

Weissman, M. M., Prusoff, B. A., Gammon, G. D., Merikangas, K. R., Leckman, J. F., & Kidd, K. K. (1984). Psychopathology in the children (ages 6–18) of depressed and normal parents. *Journal of the American Academy of Child and Adolescent Psychiatry, 23,* 78–84.

Weissman, M. M., Wickmaratne, P., Warner, V., John, K., Prusoff, B. A., Merikangas, K. R., & Gammon, G. D. (1987). Assessing psychiatric disorders in children: Discrepancies between mothers' and children's reports. *Archives of General Psychiatry, 44,* 747–753.

Wells, V. E., Deykin, E. Y., & Klerman, G. L. (1985). Risk factors for depression in adolescence. *Psychiatric Development, 3,* 83–108.

Whitaker, A., Johnson, J., Shaffer, D., Rapaport, J. L., Kalikow, K., Walsh, T. B., Davies, M., Braiman, S., & Dolinsky, A. (1990). Uncommon troubles in young people: Prevalence estimates of selected psychiatric disorders in a nonreferred adolescent population. *Archives of General Psychiatry, 47,* 487–496.

Zayas, L. H., & Bryant, C. (1984). Culturally sensitive treatment of adolescent Puerto Rican girls and their families. *Human Sciences Press, 1,* 235–253.

CHAPTER 17

Anxiety Disorders

LOUIS P. HAGOPIAN and THOMAS H. OLLENDICK

DESCRIPTION OF THE DISORDERS

In the most basic sense, anxiety can be described as a response to a stimulus perceived as threatening. The anxious response often occurs across modalities and may include behavioral avoidance, cognitions of impending harm and danger, increased physiological arousal, and feelings of dysphoria or terror. Such a response, when appropriate relative to the degree of danger, has obvious value in terms of maintaining safety and survival. An anxiety disorder is said to exist when the individual's functioning is impaired because the anxious response is extreme and out of proportion to the actual threat posed by the threatening stimulus. In the case of children, the developmental context is an additional factor that must be taken into consideration. That is, the anxiety must be of greater severity and duration than would be expected to occur in the course of normal development.

There is widespread agreement that transitory periods of fearfulness during childhood are a normal developmental phenomenon. Marks (1987a) described a developmental sequence of fearfulness that is relatively predictable and universal. Distress following sudden noises is common among infants. Fears and avoidance of novel stimuli, heights, separation from attachment figures, and of strangers emerge at around 6 months of age and usually diminish between the ages of 18 to 24 months. Fears of animals, imaginary creatures, and the dark are common during early childhood and usually decline prior to puberty. Fear of school is greatest when children enter school for the first time, and then later when starting junior or senior high school. During adolescence, fears related to social and interpersonal situations are predominant.

The most recent revision of the *Diagnostic and Statistical Manual of Mental Disorders* (*DSM-IV;* American Psychiatric Association, 1994) classifies anxiety disorders in children using essentially the same nosological framework as is used with adults (separation anxiety disorder is the only anxiety disorder that is exclusively diagnosed in childhood under the category, "disorders usually first diagnosed in infancy, childhood, or adolescence"). Overanxious disorder and avoidant disorder, which were included in this category in the *DSM-III-R* (American Psychiatric Association, 1987), have been eliminated as distinct diagnoses and subsumed in the *DSM-IV* under generalized anxiety disorder and social phobia, respectively. Although these revisions may represent progress toward an empirically based diagnostic system for anxiety-based disorders, the majority of concerns expressed about the validity and reliability of these specific disorders as defined in the *DSM-III-R* have not been addressed. The various anxiety disorders are defined essentially on the basis of the characteristics of the anxious response and/or the nature of the feared stimulus.

As noted earlier, distress and anxiety upon separation from a parent is a developmentally normal and transient phenomenon that is universally observed in infants between 6 and 18 months of age. Separation anxiety disorder, however, is characterized by persistent and extreme distress upon (or in anticipation of) separation, concerns about harm befalling a major attachment figure or oneself, reluctance to go to school (or elsewhere) to avoid separation, nightmares about separation, and physical complaints upon (or in anticipation of) separation (American Psychiatric Association, 1994).

Panic attacks are defined as sudden discrete periods of intense fear, characterized by symptoms such as palpitations and racing heart, sweating, trembling, shortness of breath, chest pain, nausea, dizziness, derealization and depersonalization, fear of losing control or going crazy, fear of dying, and paresthesias. Panic disorder with agoraphobia is characterized by recurrent panic attacks accompanied by persistent concern about additional attacks and anxiety and avoidance of situations from which escape may be difficult in the event of a panic attack. In panic disorder without agoraphobia, agoraphobic avoidance is absent. Agoraphobia without history of panic disorder is described as involving the presence of agoraphobic avoidance due to fear of experiencing paniclike symptoms, without a history of panic disorder (American Psychiatric Association, 1994). Although panic disorder is well established in adults, there are limited data (and considerable controversy) regarding the presence and nature of panic in children and adolescents (see Ollendick, Mattis, & King, 1994, for a review).

Persistent and excessive fear and avoidance of a specific object or situation (other than separation or embarrassment in social situations) is the essential feature of a phobia. Exposure to the feared object or situation typically provokes an immediate anxiety response that may lead to a panic attack (American Psychiatric Association, 1994). Another criterion for inclusion in this diagnostic category is an awareness by the individual that the response to the feared stimulus is excessive. As noted by Ollendick (1979) and reaffirmed by the *DSM-IV,* however, such an awareness may not be possible or at least not readily evident in younger children. Many young children believe quite strongly that their fear response is fully justified. As a result, the *DSM-IV* indicates that this criterion can be omitted for children.

Social phobia is characterized by excessive fear and avoidance of social situations or situations in which the individual may be scrutinized such that embarrassment may occur. As with specific phobia, exposure to the feared situation leads almost invariably to immediate anxiety, and possibly panic (American Psychiatric Association, 1994). In the *DSM-III-R,* children displaying these types of behaviors could be diagnosed with avoidant disorder of childhood or social phobia.

Obsessive-compulsive disorder involves the presence of obsessions and compulsions that are a source of distress and interfere with the child's functioning (American Psychiatric Association, 1994). Obsessions are defined as recurrent and intrusive thoughts or impulses (not simply excessive worries) that are a source of distress, which the child attempts to ignore or suppress with another thought or action. Compulsions are defined as repetitive behaviors or mental acts that the child feels compelled to perform, in response to an obsession, that relieve distress or prevent a dreaded event from occurring. Usually, compulsions are executed in a rigid, stereotypic fashion. Further, if the child's "ritual" or routine is interrupted, the child may escalate to the point of panic (Reed, Carter, & Miller, 1995).

Posttraumatic stress disorder in children has received considerable attention as a result of studies conducted on children who have survived accidents, natural disasters, and wars (Keppel-Benson & Ollendick, 1994). Other events can include physical or sexual abuse, invasive medical procedures, and the witnessing of domestic or community violence. In effect, any event that is outside the range of usual human experience that would be distressing to most individuals can lead to a traumatic response. The essential feature is that the traumatic event is reexperienced in ways such as (a) intrusive, distressing recollections of the event—including repetitive play; (b) distressing dreams (not necessarily of the event); (c) a sense of reliving the experience, often in the form of reenactment of the trauma; and (d) intense distress or physiological reactivity on exposure to internal or external cues associated with the event. There is also excessive avoidance of stimuli associated with the trauma, numbing of general responsiveness, and symptoms of increased arousal (American Psychiatric Association, 1994).

Generalized anxiety disorder is described as excessive and persistent anxiety and worry associated with difficulties such as restlessness, irritability, muscle tension, and sleep disturbance (American Psychiatric Association, 1994). The child's worries are about a variety of life events which are distressing to the extent that his or her functioning is impaired. In the *DSM-III-R,* this disorder was referred to as overanxious disorder of childhood.

Despite the recognized importance of developmental issues in the assessment and treatment of anxiety, few specific developmental considerations are made for the diagnosis of anxiety disorders in children in the *DSM-IV.* For panic disorder (with or without agoraphobia) and agoraphobia, there are no references to the diagnosis of these disorders in children. The number of associated symptoms required for the diagnosis of generalized anxiety disorder is decreased from three, to one of six for children. For specific phobia, social phobia, and obsessive-compulsive disorder, it is noted that the criterion specifying that the individual recognize his or her fear as excessive or unreasonable may be omitted for children. For specific phobia and social phobia, differences in children's expression of anxiety are noted (e.g., crying, tantrums, freezing, or clinging). For the diagnosis of social phobia in children, the child must have age-appropriate relationships with familiar people and the fear of social situations and unfamiliar people must occur with peers as well as adults.

The criteria for posttraumatic stress disorder specify the greatest number of developmental considerations to be made for the diagnosis of children. It is noted in the *DSM-IV* that the child's initial response to the trauma may be characterized by disorganization or agitation, in addition to an intense fearful reaction. Furthermore, the reexperiencing of the trauma may be expressed in children through repetitive play related to the trauma, frightening dreams (not necessarily of the traumatic event), and/or reenactment of the trauma.

EPIDEMIOLOGY

Before reviewing the epidemiology of anxiety disorders in children and adolescents, a number of methodological issues that have implications for interpretation of the available data should be noted. First, procedures and criteria for assessing symptoms and determining diagnoses tend to vary across studies making it difficult to make comparisons. Because of referral bias, prevalence estimates are typically higher among samples obtained from clinical populations than samples obtained from the general population or in community surveys. In addition, the age range of subjects in the sample is important to consider since the prevalence of certain anxiety disorders has been shown to differ between children and adolescents (Anderson, 1994; Bernstein & Borchardt, 1991).

Anxiety disorders are believed to be one of the most common types of psychiatric disorder experienced by children and adolescents (Anderson, 1994; Bernstein & Borchardt, 1991). Prevalence rates of clinically impairing anxiety disorders have ranged from 2.4% to 8.7% of children and adolescents in the general population. A significantly higher percentage of youngsters (6.8% to 17.3%) also meet diagnostic criteria for anxiety disorders without clinical impairment (Anderson, Williams, McGee, & Silva, 1987; Bird et al., 1988; Kashani & Orvaschel, 1988). Anxiety symptoms have been shown to be quite common in nondiagnosed children, occurring in as many as 20% of children sampled from the general population (Bell-Dolan, Last, & Strauss, 1990).

Rates of comorbidity between different anxiety disorders, and between anxiety and other psychiatric disorders are generally reported to be high. Comorbidity between anxiety disorders in general population samples have been reported to be as high as 39% among children and 14% among adolescents (Anderson, 1994). In a clinical sample, comorbidity among anxiety disorders ranged from 63% for panic disorder to 96% for overanxious disorder (Last, Perrin, Hersen, & Kazdin, 1992). Comorbidity between anxiety and depression has been found to be relatively high, with prevalence rates ranging from 17% to 69% of children in the general population (Anderson et al., 1987; Kashani & Orvaschel, 1988) and from 28% to 47% of children in clinical samples (Bernstein & Borchardt, 1991; Strauss, Lease, Last, & Francis, 1988). In a number of studies, the presence of an anxiety and depressive disorder has been shown to be associated with increased psychopathology and severity of both anxious and depressive symptoms (see Bernstein, 1991). Finally, high comorbidity between anxiety and other disorders, such as attention-deficit/hyperactivity disorder and conduct disorder, has been reported in a number of general population and clinical samples (see Anderson, 1994). In general, it has been shown that younger children with an anxiety disorder also show signs of attention-deficit/hyperactivity disorder, whereas older children and adolescents present with signs of major depression and conduct disturbances.

Although girls have been found to report more fears than boys in community samples (Ollendick, King, & Frary, 1989; Ollendick, Matson, & Helsel, 1985), few sex differences in the prevalence of anxiety disorders during childhood have been found in clinical samples (e.g., Last et al., 1992). During adolescence and early adulthood, sex differences in the prevalence of different types of anxiety disorders begin to emerge. Other than social phobia, which tends to be more common among boys, girls generally have higher rates of anxiety disorders during adolescence (see Anderson, 1994).

Separation anxiety disorder (SAD) is the most prevalent childhood anxiety disorder among young, prepubertal children, but is less common among adolescents. Overall prevalence rates of SAD in children and adolescents in the general population range from 2.0% to 5.4% (see Anderson, 1994). In a clinic-referred sample, Last and colleagues (Last, Francis, Hersen, Kazdin, & Strauss, 1987) found that children with SAD were mostly female, Caucasian, from lower socioeconomic families, and were brought in for treatment at a younger age in comparison with children with overanxious disorder. In another clinical sample, Francis, Last, and Strauss (1987) found no sex differences with respect to presentation of symptoms. However, younger children with SAD tended to report more symptoms, nightmares, and excessive distress on separation than did older children with SAD. Relative to children with school phobia, children with SAD had higher comorbidity with other disorders (92%), and were more likely to have mothers with psychiatric disorders suggesting more severe psychopathology among children with SAD (Last, Hersen, Kazdin, Francis, & Grubb, 1987).

Generalized anxiety disorder (GAD) in childhood (formerly overanxious disorder) is the most common anxiety disorder among older children and adolescents. Prevalence rates during childhood and adolescence have ranged from 2.6% to 5.9% (see Anderson, 1994). Relative to children with SAD, Last et al. (1992) found that children with overanxious disorder were brought in for treatment at a later age and tended to come from higher socioeconomic families. In another clinic sample, older children with overanxious disorder reported more symptoms and higher levels of depression than younger children (Strauss et al., 1988).

Probably one of the least prevalent anxiety disorders experienced by younger children is social phobia (formerly avoidant disorder). In a review of epidemiological studies using samples drawn from the general population, Anderson (1994) reported prevalence rates of approximately 1% for social phobia. In both general and clinical samples, social phobia in children is not usually found in isolation, but tends to co-occur with other anxiety disorders, usually GAD (Anderson et al., 1987; Francis, Last, & Strauss, 1992). Relative to children with specific phobia, children with social phobia were older, reported more phobias (particularly school phobia), had higher levels of loneliness and depression, and higher comorbidity for overanxious disorder (Strauss & Last, 1993).

The prevalence rates of specific phobias in children and adolescents in the general population have been reported to range from 2.4% to 3.6% (Anderson et al., 1987; McGee et al., 1990; Milne et al., 1995). In one study of adolescents (Milne et al., 1995), those with clinically significant phobias were more likely to be older, female, black, and have multiple phobias. Three-quarters of children diagnosed with specific phobia in a clinical sample were also diagnosed with another anxiety disorder, and about one-third were concurrently diagnosed with depression (Last et al., 1992).

Although there is limited epidemiological data, obsessive-compulsive disorder (OCD) appears to be one of the least prevalent anxiety disorders experienced by children, with only about 1% of adolescents sampled meeting diagnostic criteria (Flament et al., 1988). A number of studies have indicated that the onset of OCD is typically in early adolescence, with girls having a slightly later onset than boys (Hanna 1995; Last et al., 1992). Sex ratios have varied across studies, with some showing a higher prevalence among males and others showing an equal distribution across gender (see Hanna, 1995). Obsessions involving contamination and compulsions such as washing are most commonly reported across studies (see Bernstein & Borchardt, 1991). In a clinical sample, Hanna found that the majority of children and adolescents with OCD were Caucasian and from middle to upper-middle socioeconomic intact families, and had an age of onset ranging from 8 to 12 years. Lifetime comorbidity for other psychiatric disorders was 84%, and 26% had a lifetime tic disorder, supporting earlier studies suggesting a relationship between OCD and tics.

A number of general population studies have found that between 31% and 63% of children and adolescents report having experienced at least one panic attack (Macaulay & Kleinknecht, 1989; Warren & Zgourides, 1988). The prevalence rates of panic disorder using *DSM* criteria, however, are considerably lower with most estimates of children and adolescents in the general population being at approximately 1% (e.g., Whitaker et al., 1990). Rates of panic disorder have been reported to be much higher among clinical populations, with estimates ranging from 10% to 15% for children and adolescents. Both panic attacks and panic disorder are generally more common among females and adolescents than among males or younger children, respectively (see Ollendick et al., 1994).

The prevalence of posttraumatic stress disorder (PTSD) in children and adolescents in the general population is estimated to be approximately 1%; however, PTSD and posttraumatic symptoms have been reported to develop in as many as 37% of children and adolescents exposed to natural disasters (see Garrison et al., 1995). A number of studies have shown that the severity of posttraumatic symptoms are directly related to the level of exposure to the traumatic event, as well as the level of endangerment to one's life, the loss of loved ones, exposure to gruesome death, and the level of community devastation (Green & Lindy, 1994; Shaw et al., 1995). The range of posttraumatic symptoms following natural disaster varies widely and differs across race, gender, and age, with an increased risk for PTSD among African-Americans, females, and younger children (Shannon, Lonigan, Finch, & Taylor, 1994).

CAUSES AND CONSEQUENCES

There is a growing body of evidence suggesting that the development and maintenance of anxiety in children may occur as a function of a synergistic process involving familial, developmental, and environmental variables. Data supporting this position are derived from multiple sources including familial concordance studies, twin studies, longitudinal studies of anxiety and temperament, and behavioral studies. A number of familial concordance studies have demonstrated high concordance rates of anxiety disorders among first-degree relatives of anxiety-disordered patients (Crowe, Noyes, Pauls, & Slymen, 1983; Harris, Noyes, Crowe, & Chauldry, 1993). In addition, children of anxiety-disordered parents (Keller et al., 1992; Turner, Beidel, & Costello, 1987; Weissman, Leckman, Merikangas, Gammon, & Prusoff, 1984) and parents of anxiety-disordered children (Last, Hersen, et al., 1987) have been found to have far higher rates of anxiety disorders than controls. Finally, the concordance rates of anxiety symptoms and disorders has been shown to be higher among MZ than DZ twins (Kendler, Neale, Kessler, Heath, & Eaves, 1992; Thapar & McGuffin, 1995). Although these studies support a familial transmission of anxiety, the difference in concordance rate among MZ twins relative to DZ twins is low compared with other disorders, suggesting the importance of shared genetic and environmental factors. It has been suggested that a general predisposition for the development of anxiety-based disorders may be genetically based (Turner, Beidel, & Epstein, 1991).

The exact nature of this predisposition is not fully understood, although data suggest that the temperamental characteristic of behavioral inhibition to the unfamiliar may be genetically based, and may be a risk factor for the development of anxiety. In a series of longitudinal studies by Kagan and colleagues (e.g., Garcia-Coll, Kagan, & Reznick, 1984; Kagan, Reznick, & Snidman, 1988), behavioral inhibition was shown to be a stable temperamental characteristic with physiological correlates that are evident in infancy. In one study, children (2 to 7 years old) of parents with panic disorder were found to be more likely to demonstrate this characteristic than children of parents with depression or other psychiatric disorders (Rosenbaum et al., 1988). Moreover, children identified as behaviorally inhibited were found to have higher rates of anxiety disorders than uninhibited children (Biederman et al., 1990). These studies show that the characteristic of behavioral inhibition is evident during infancy, relatively stable, more common among children of parents with panic, and more commonly associated with anxiety disorders in childhood. It is possible that this temperamental characteristic may be a marker for a predisposition that is genetically based and may increase vulnerability for anxiety-based disorders.

While it is clear that anxiety disorders are familial, and possible that a general predisposition for anxiety (rather than predispositions for specific anxiety disorders) is genetically based, the expression of anxiety disorders is undoubtedly related to an interaction between life circumstances and developmental processes that occur throughout the life span. As noted previously, children universally experience different transient fears over the course of development (Marks, 1987a). It is possible that as this developmental process unfolds, the risk for the emergence of certain pathological fears changes concurrently. These developmental periods of increased vulnerability, in combination with certain life events may lead to the expression of specific anxiety disorders (Ollendick & King, 1994).

Although life events and experiences may affect, and are undoubtedly affected by, these developmental processes, they can result in learning experiences that shape anxious behavior. Through the processes of classical, operant, and vicarious conditioning, children may learn that certain stimuli are associated with aversive consequences, and that fearful and avoidant behaviors result in certain consequences that are sometimes reinforcing. In addition to their increased risk due to genetically-based factors, children of anxious parents may be more likely to observe overly-anxious behavior in their parents, and more likely to have fearful behavior reinforced by their parents (who may be more averse to unpleasant and embarrassing situations than less anxious parents). As the child's fearful behavior is inadvertently shaped by the parent, the parent's behavior may, in turn, be negatively reinforced by the anxious child becoming calm (Ginsberg, Silverman, & Kurtines, 1995; Hagopian & Slifer, 1993).

The expression of anxiety-based disorders in childhood is believed to be a function of familial, developmental, and environmental processes that interact synergistically. There may be a general predisposition for the development of anxiety disorders that is genetically based. Vulnerability for the development of specific types of anxiety disorder may then vary over the course of development and across the life span. Finally, life circumstances and events, in combination with the individual's predisposition and developmental status, may then determine the behavioral expression of anxiety disorders.

IMPEDIMENTS TO INTERVENTION IN THE REAL WORLD CONTEXT

While the efficacy of behavioral approaches for the treatment of disorders in children and adolescents has been demonstrated in the research literature (Weisz, Weiss, & Donenberg, 1992), practitioners often find such research of little use to them (Strupp, 1989). This state of affairs may be partly related to the failure of psychotherapy research to reflect the complexities of providing services in a purely clinical setting (Kazdin, Bass, Ayers, & Rodgers, 1990). Generally, little attention is given to factors that may influence treatment outcome, such as the characteristics of the child, family, and therapist, as well as the circumstances under which treatment is administered.

Perhaps the most frequently encountered impediments to treatment involve some aspect of the broader context interfering with achieving the goals of treatment. The broader context includes the physical and social setting in which the child lives, as well as the resources, values, beliefs, and goals of the child, family, school, and community. Graziano and Bythell (1983) described failures in child behavior therapy of this type as "contextual failures." Failure to address conflicts about whether a child's anxiety is a problem that warrants treatment, to identify realistic goals, to prescribe acceptable assessment and treatment procedures, and to work within the limits of the available resources may seriously impede the intervention process.

Communities, schools, and families may have different norms than the therapist about what constitutes an anxiety problem and warrants intervention. Unlike externalizing disorders, which are highly disruptive and frequently annoying to parents and teachers, the child who is withdrawn or quiet may be viewed by the community and school as "just shy" and certainly not as a troublemaker. Further, parents with psychopathology may distrust teachers or therapists who express concerns about their child's anxiety, or may not recognize their child's anxiety as important. For many such parents, recognition and acceptance of such a possibility often confirm their worst fears and lead to misattribution of cause. Educating individuals who will be involved in the assessment and treatment process regarding what is normal anxiety versus clinically significant anxiety warranting treatment may be needed to enlist their cooperation and consent for treatment.

Since children rarely refer themselves for treatment, and may be embarrassed about their fears or worries, assessing their attitude about the importance of receiving treatment is critical. Children who do not recognize their fear as unreasonable (which is not uncommon) may participate in the assessment and treatment process in only a limited way. In the case of school refusal, for example, it may be necessary to inform the child that going to school is absolutely essential, and that treatment will make it easier and less unpleasant to attend. In other cases, it may be appropriate for the therapist to work toward helping the child develop a desire to overcome fears by recognizing how decreasing anxiety could have positive effects. Yet, we must acknowledge that this is not an easy or straightforward process. Recently, we were working with a school-refusing child who had a long history of school avoidance. Tearfully, he explained, "You just don't understand . . . I'm scared . . . I don't know of what . . . but whenever I think of going to school this dread comes over me . . . my heart beats faster and I begin to sweat . . . it is like I'm going to die or something . . . I don't know why . . . if you felt this way you wouldn't go, would you?" Much reassurance and acceptance of him and his panic-like response were necessary to get beyond his initial refusal to view his petrified state as unreasonable.

The therapist must also carefully consider whether there are conflicts in the goals of treatment held by the child, parents, school, and community. A frequently reported conflict with respect to goals occurs when the context dictates goals for treatment that are more in the interests of the context than the child (see Graziano & Bythell, 1983). The therapist should guide the parents to develop realistic goals about treatment, informing them that changing the child's anxious disposition is not a reasonable goal from the onset. Additionally, it is advisable to inform parents that changing parental behavior will most likely be a goal of treatment. Failure to specify these goals may lead to noncompliance and dissatisfaction that could result in early termination.

Prescribing unacceptable assessment and treatment procedures will often impede the intervention process and undermine the therapist's credibility. Procedures may be unacceptable from the point of view of the child, parents, school, or community because of their values, misunderstanding, fear, or limited resources. While a comprehensive and functional assessment is critical for developing an effective intervention, the use of intrusive and time-consuming procedures over the course of several sessions—while the anxiety problem remains untreated—may be unacceptable. In addition, failure to advise those involved (i.e., child, parents, insurance carriers) of the assessment process or of the preliminary results may lead to dissatisfaction and decreased compliance.

Since treatment of anxiety disorders in children invariably requires the child to be exposed to the feared stimulus, concerns about the safety and acceptability of treatment procedures are commonly expressed by both parents and children. The use of graduated exposure procedures are generally viewed as more acceptable than those involving exposure to the feared stimulus at the outset of treatment (Reed et al., 1995). Since parents of anxious children are often quite sensitive to their children's level of anxiety, they may be somewhat reluctant to continue treatment if it is unpleasant for their child. In general, it is advisable to minimize the child's level of anxiety during the exposure process with the use of relaxation, cognitive self-instruction, or other coping strategies. The rate of progress of treatment is often an issue with parents which, if not addressed, can have serious implications for treating anxious children. We have worked with parents who have unsuccessfully attempted to move their child prematurely beyond the prescribed level of exposure (this typically occurs after some progress has been made). Frequently, this "impatience" leads to failure or at least disruption in the treatment program.

Failure to assess the resources available in the context required to carry out treatment procedures also can significantly interfere with progress. The therapist must assess the ability (i.e., time available, skills required, materials needed) of the child, parent, or teacher to carry out prescribed procedures. Since changing parent (or teacher) behavior is often an important component in altering the child's anxious behavior, identifying and dealing with limited resources in these settings is critical. It is advisable to take time to work with these individuals to develop procedures that are applicable in their respective settings. Probably the most significant impediment to parental compliance with procedures that we have encountered is parental psychopathology. Whereas mildly anxious parents tend to be quite reliable, parents suffering from depression, panic, or personality disorders tend to be much more limited in their ability to follow through on recommendations. Failure to deal with parental psychopathology may seriously impede progress, sometimes requiring the therapist to insist that the parents seek treatment for themselves.

Broader contextual issues that may impede interventions for treating anxiety in children are related to current societal realities such as the effects of poverty and the increased probability of experiencing or witnessing violence—particularly among inner-city children. According to some estimates, in 1993 over 3 million children in the United States were exposed to some type of man-made traumatic event, such as sexual and physical abuse, or community and family violence (Schwarz & Perry, 1994). We were recently consulted on a case of a young inner-city child who developed posttraumatic symptoms after witnessing a murder from his bedroom window. Arguably, the best intervention for this child would have been to move to a safer neighborhood; however, that was not an option for his family. This case illustrates probably the most serious contextual impediment to intervention: when the context itself is the direct source of the problem. Changing the broader societal context, however, is beyond the scope of the single therapist's influence. At that point, the intervention must focus on accessing available resources and on working with the family and child to promote effective coping skills that are realistic and embedded in the contextual framework in which the child and his or her family exist.

TREATMENT

Assessment Strategies

While the behavioral perspective emphasizes the role of classical, operant, and vicarious conditioning in the acquisition and maintenance of anxiety-based disorders in children, there is growing recognition of the importance of developmental, constitutional, familial, and other contextual variables in the assessment process (Ammerman & Hersen, 1994; Ollendick & Hersen, 1984). In particular, the assessment of anxiety disorders in children should take into consideration the developmental changes in the way children perceive and express anxiety, as well as the normal developmental progression of fearful behavior in childhood (Marks, 1987a). Constitutional factors should also be considered in light of the growing body of evidence suggesting that early temperamental characteristics of increased inhibition may be a risk factor for the development of anxiety-based disorders (Biederman, Rosenbaum, Bolduc-Murphy, Faraone, 1993). Moreover, assessment of parental anxiety and its impact on parent-child interactions is important given the high concordance rates of anxiety-based disorders among parents and children (Turner, Beidel, & Costello, 1987).

In general, child behavioral assessment can be characterized as an ongoing multimethod, multimodal process designed to identify and define target behaviors, determine controlling variables, and select and evaluate intervention strategies. This involves the use of empirically validated methods and instruments that are sensitive to developmental changes (Mash & Terdal, 1985; Ollendick & Hersen, 1984). A multimethod approach, involving the use of behavioral interviews, structured clinical and diagnostic interviews, self- and other-report measures, physiological measures, and direct behavioral observation has received widespread endorsement for the assessment of anxiety in children (Morris & Kratochwill, 1983; Ollendick & Francis, 1988). Because the anxiety response can occur across response modalities, a multimodal assessment of behavioral, cognitive, and physiological domains is highly recommended (Beidel, 1991; Lang, 1977).

Behavioral Interview

The behavioral interview is typically the first step in the assessment process. The goals of the interview include defining the problem, identifying the controlling variables, determining the broader context in which the anxiety is occurring, assessing the family's resources, selecting additional assessment procedures, and formulating treatment plans (King, Hamilton, & Ollendick, 1988). Although children are usually referred by their parents, the children themselves should be involved in the interview process to the extent that their abilities permit. This allows the therapist to obtain information from their perspective and to enlist their cooperation for additional assessment procedures, the development of treatment goals, and active participation in treatment.

In defining the problem, it is important to determine the nature and topography of the anxious response itself, including the response modalities that are most relevant. Detailed information about the frequency, severity, and duration of fearful behavior should be obtained. As noted, it is important to consider the child's developmental status when selecting target behaviors and determining the need for treatment. In conducting a functional assessment during the interview, asking highly specific questions is necessary to identify the antecedent and consequent variables; for example, "Under what conditions does he get anxious? . . . how do you usually respond—what do you say or do? . . . then what happens?" (see King et al., 1988).

Since anxiety problems in children tend to co-occur with other problems such as depression (Bernstein, 1991), detailed information about other nonanxious behavior problems (and their controlling variables) should be obtained as well. In addition to determining the onset of the problem behaviors, it is also useful to question parents about the child's temperamental characteristics, how siblings are similar to or different from the targeted child, and whether the parents themselves or other members in the family experience anxiety or other difficulties. Finally, it is important to elicit information about the child's strengths and interests from both the parents and the child to provide a more complete overall picture of the child (Ollendick & Cerny, 1981).

In general, it is desirable to interview the child separately from the parent. Where the child's participation is hampered because of shyness, embarrassment, or limited verbal skills, it may be useful to start by obtaining general information about the child (e.g., likes and dislikes, siblings) followed by a brief discussion of the presenting problem and description of additional assessment procedures. As will be discussed, more detailed information about the anxiety can often be obtained during subsequent interviews in the structured context of reviewing completed self-report measures or self-monitoring forms with the child. In general, using the child's own terms when discussing the anxiety and phrasing direct questions (e.g., "What do you do when you're scared?") will help minimize confusion.

Structured Diagnostic Interviews

A number of structured diagnostic interviews have been developed for use with children for diagnostic and research purposes. These allow for standardized administration of a set of specific questions to determine the presence of symptoms that constitute the criteria for a particular disorder. The more commonly used interviews include the Diagnostic Interview for Children and Adolescents (DICA-R; Reich & Welner, 1988), Diagnostic Interview Schedule for Children (DISC; Costello, Edelbrock, Dulcan, Kalas, & Klaric, 1984), the Children's Assessment Schedule (CAS; Hodges, Cools, & McKnew, 1989; Hodges, McKnew, Cytryn, Stern, & Kline, 1982), and the Schedule for Affective Disorders and Schizophrenia for School-Age Children (Kiddie-SADS; Chambers et al., 1985). The Anxiety Disorders Interview Schedule (ADIS-IV; Silverman & Nelles, 1988; Silverman & Rabian, 1995) and the Children's Anxiety Evaluation Form (Hoehn-Saric, Maissami, & Wiegand, 1987) have been developed for the diagnosis of anxiety disorders in children in particular. Although these interviews are broad in scope and can help arrive at a reliable diagnosis, they are generally time consuming and are often not as useful as a behavioral interview in the selection and evaluation of treatment.

Self- and Other-Report Instruments

A number of self- and parent/teacher-report measures designed specifically for the assessment of anxiety in children have been described in the literature (for a review, see King et al., 1988). The psychometric properties of these measures vary, as does the degree to which they attend to developmental issues (in terms of administration and availability of normative data). Careful attention should be given to the child's understanding of the directions and individual items when administering self-report measures to younger children. If it is necessary for the clinician to read each item to the child, then the child should be provided with an additional form to mark his or her responses. After the measure is completed, a discussion of some of the child's responses can sometimes provide detailed information that might have been difficult to obtain otherwise. It is advisable to begin with either positive or neutral items (e.g., "I like to read books"), and then move to items more relevant to the child's anxiety. This strategy should be used with caution as some children may become embarrassed by a discussion of their responses, and underreport concerns on subsequent measures.

Since anxiety tends to co-occur with other behavior problems, the use of general behavior problem checklists that include a subscale for anxiety problems is recommended. The Child Behavior Checklist (CBCL; Achenbach & Edelbrock, 1983) and Revised Behavior Problem Checklist (RBPC; Quay & Peterson, 1983) are widely used parent/teacher-report instruments that have good psychometric properties, extensive normative data, and sample a broad range of potential behavior problems (including anxiety). Since the comorbidity between anxiety and depression is particularly high, use of the Children's Depression Inventory (CDI; Kovacs, 1981) should be considered on a routine basis. Although the CDI is limited psychometrically (Kazdin, 1981), this self-report measure may provide useful clinical information that is difficult to obtain otherwise.

The most frequently used self-report measures of global anxiety and fearfulness in children include the Revised Children's Manifest Anxiety Scale (RCMAS; Reynolds & Richmond, 1978), the Trait Form of the State-Trait Anxiety Inventory for Children (STAIC; Speilberger, 1973), and the Fear Survey Schedule for Children-Revised (FSSC-R; Ollendick, 1983). These three measures possess good psychometric properties and extensive normative and cross-cultural data (see King et al., 1988, for a review). The State Form of the STAIC (Speilberger, 1973) is designed to provide a measure of the child's state anxiety. A number of studies have supported the validity of this instrument. This measure can be used for the assessment of any anxiety-based disorder by administering it when exposing the child to the feared stimulus (in vivo, or imaginally), or instructing the child to complete it when he or she experiences an anxious episode (e.g., for children with generalized anxiety or panic disorder). In addition, the State Form of the STAIC is a particularly good measure to use during treatment to monitor the child's ongoing subjective anxiety.

Physiological Assessment

Although the validity of physiological measures for the assessment of anxiety in children has been supported in a number of experimental studies using clinical populations, their widespread use in clinical settings has lagged considerably. This is unfortunate because physiological measures may be critical for both assessment and treatment evaluation in cases where physical sensations are a prominent feature of the anxious response. Cardiac measures (e.g., heart rate variability, and blood pressure with weight covaried) have been demonstrated to be most stable over time and most highly correlated with other measures of anxiety (Beidel, 1988, 1989; Kagan et al., 1988). Other physiological indices that have been used include heart rate, electrodermal responding, respiration, and urinary cortisol levels (see King, 1994; Ray & Raczynski, 1985, for reviews).

The relatively infrequent clinical use of physiological measures is most likely due to practical limitations (i.e., expensive instrumentation, time-consuming procedures, requirements of technical expertise, and children's noncompliance with sitting still). Where physiological data cannot be directly obtained, observational, self-report, and self-monitoring data should be collected on physiological sensations experienced during an anxious episode or when the feared stimulus is encountered.

Self-Monitoring

Self-monitoring procedures require children to observe and record aspects of their behaviors, thoughts, feelings, and physiological sensations during anxious episodes as well as the antecedent stimuli and consequent events. Such data can provide information about the topography and function of the child's anxiety, and help in the design and evaluation of treatment. Monitoring forms should use the child's own terms, be clear and uncomplicated, and be designed in close cooperation with the child (King et al., 1988). While a diary record can provide detailed information, it may be too time consuming and unstructured for younger children to complete adequately. It may be more effective to use monitoring forms that require children to answer three to five specific questions with a brief statement following the occurrence of an anxious episode (e.g., "What happened? . . . how did you feel? . . . what did you do/say? . . . what did your parents do?"). It is often helpful to include an item for the child to rate the duration and intensity of the anxious episode (using a 3-point Likert scale). Having the parents complete a similar monitoring form can serve both as an alternative source of information and as a reliability check for the child's report. In general, the parent and child should complete their monitoring forms independently, and the clinician should also review them with the parent and the child separately) to obtain independent reports.

Behavioral Observation

Behavioral observation, the hallmark of child behavioral assessment, is the least inferential and most direct method of assessing anxiety, determining its controlling variables, and evaluating an intervention. Observations can be conducted in the actual setting in which the behavior occurs or in structured analogue settings. Although direct behavioral observation may produce greater reactivity in the child than other indirect measures, it has the potential to provide information not attainable using other methods. Behavioral observation may be particularly useful for younger or lower functioning children for whom other methods of assessment (other than parent report) may not be possible. In general, it is advisable to inform children and obtain their consent prior to conducting the observation in the natural setting (e.g., in the classroom).

It is useful to begin with a brief informal observation of the child before establishing formal observation procedures. Developing precise, objective, and complete operational definitions of the target behaviors (with consideration of developmental issues) is the first step in the process (Kazdin, 1985). If avoidance of a particular stimulus is a problem, then recording approach or adaptive behaviors which will be targets of treatment, as well as fearful behaviors (e.g., crying, clinging, shaking) may be required. Next, a measurement system must be designed (e.g., frequency, duration, or interval recording), based on the nature of the target behaviors (e.g., discrete responses vs. ongoing behaviors). Finally, it is important that adequate levels of interobserver agreement be maintained to ensure reliable data collection.

The Behavioral Avoidance Test (BAT; Lang & Lazovik, 1963) is a behavioral observation method that can be used to assess avoidant behaviors in an analogue situation. The BAT involves exposing the child to the feared stimulus while recording approach and avoidance behavior. Hamilton and King (1991) illustrate the use of these procedures with dog phobic children. They generated a list of 14 steps ranging from "walk up to the playpen" (where a dog was enclosed) to "open the door of the playpen" to "stay here with the dog for a minute while I go inside the house." Each step was carefully graded and the child's willingness to complete each step was monitored.

In situations where a BAT is not possible, behavioral observations during imaginal exposure may be appropriate for some children. This involves guiding the child to imagine an encounter with the feared stimulus or the experiencing of an anxious episode; the child then describes or acts out what was imagined (Smith & Sharpe, 1970). The child can provide information about the controlling variables as well as a potentially detailed description of their own responses. Overt signs of fear, as well as physiological measures may be observed as well. This may also provide an opportunity to have the child practice completing self-monitoring forms.

Treatment Approaches

Treatment strategies based on the principles of classical, operant, and vicarious conditioning have been developed for the treatment of anxiety disorders in children. The more commonly used strategies with children include systematic desensitization, graduated exposure, flooding, contingency management, modeling, and cognitive-behavioral approaches. While these treatment strategies have been described extensively in the literature, few experimental studies have been conducted with children. Based on this limited information, it appears that the most effective and enduring treatment effects are obtained when interventions involve multiple components drawing from all these principles, including exposure to the feared stimulus (King et al., 1988; Marks, 1987b; Ollendick & Francis, 1988).

Therapeutic exposure requires that the feared stimulus is encountered in a controlled manner such that avoidant behavior does not occur *and* that aversive events previously associated (either vicariously, imaginally, or actually) with that stimulus are not experienced. In the case of dog phobia, for example, this would involve having the child encounter a dog without engaging in avoidant behavior and not experiencing any aversive event, such as being bitten. Exposure to the feared stimulus in the absence of avoidant behavior and aversive events involves extinction of both negatively reinforced avoidant behavior and the association between the feared stimulus and the aversive event. Thus, the processes believed to underlie therapeutic exposure are both classical extinction and operant extinction of avoidant behavior. The various behavioral strategies differ primarily in the techniques used to facilitate these extinction processes (e.g., relaxation, coping strategies, response prevention, reinforcement), and the method by which exposure occurs (e.g., in vivo, imaginal, vicarious, graduated).

Systematic Desensitization and Graduated Exposure

Developed by Wolpe (1958), systematic desensitization (SD) was originally conceptualized as involving the classical conditioning process of reciprocal inhibition, whereby anxiety is suppressed by an incompatible response (relaxation) in the presence of the feared stimulus. Systematic desensitization consists of three components: relaxation training, construction of an anxiety hierarchy, and systematic desensitization proper (for a detailed description of SD with phobic children, see King et al., 1988). An obvious consideration is whether the child is capable of learning relaxation (for a discussion of relaxation training with children, see Ollendick & Cerny, 1981). Construction of an anxiety hierarchy involves working with the child to develop a series of stimuli related to the feared stimulus and which are ranked from least to most anxiety evoking. The child should be involved in this process as much as possible, since the arrangement of items in the hierarchy should be based on the degree of the child's subjective anxiety. If desensitization is conducted in vivo, items from the Behavioral Avoidance Test can be used in the treatment process.

Systematic desensitization proper begins with having the child become and remain relaxed while being guided to imagine or encounter the least anxiety-evoking stimulus in the hierarchy. The child is instructed to calmly indicate (e.g., by lifting a finger) if he or she begins to experience excessive anxiety at any time. If this occurs, then the therapist immediately returns to lower hierarchy items so the child maintains a relaxed state. The higher hierarchy item that resulted in increased anxiety is later presented again, initially for a shorter duration. This graduated process of presenting increasingly higher hierarchy items until the child can maintain a relaxed state is continued until the highest item is presented. While SD can be performed imaginally or in vivo, younger children may benefit more from in vivo SD due to their limited imagery abilities (King et al., 1988).

A variant of SD, developed for children by Lazarus and Abramovitz (1962), involves the use of emotive imagery. Rather than relaxation to achieve reciprocal inhibition, the child is guided to imagine a positive story involving a hero who encounters the hierarchy items with the child. Emotive imagery has not been examined in a controlled group study, however, some case studies have achieved encouraging results (e.g., King, Cranstoun, & Josephs, 1989).

Although graduated exposure was originally introduced as a component of SD, it has been used more recently in combination with other treatment strategies (the use of relaxation training to achieve reciprocal inhibition is not involved). Other than flooding, all fear reduction strategies can incorporate graduated exposure to the feared stimulus. Graduated exposure may be particularly important for treating children for whom intense exposure may not be acceptable to the parent or child.

Flooding and Response Prevention

Flooding involves sudden and prolonged exposure to the feared stimulus and prevention of avoidant behavior. Avoidant responses must be prevented so that they will not be negatively reinforced by relief that would be experienced if avoidance were allowed to occur; and the feared stimulus must be presented in the absence of the unconditioned aversive stimulus to eliminate the association between these stimuli. Careful consideration should be made prior to attempting flooding with children because failure to complete a session may have the potential to worsen the child's fearfulness. That is, if avoidant behavior cannot be prevented (e.g., because of the intensity) or the child has an intense emotional or physical response that is aversive (e.g., the child vomits), the association between the feared stimulus and aversive events could be strengthened, and avoidant behavior reinforced.

Exposure and response prevention with obsessive-compulsive disorder (OCD) involves blocking the child from engaging in the compulsive behavior that occurs following exposure to the stimulus which leads to obsessions. Exposure to the feared stimulus can be performed either by flooding, graduated exposure, or vicarious exposure (Pinto & Francis, 1994). Exposure with response prevention allows the child to learn that failure to engage in compulsive behavior following exposure does not lead to an aversive outcome. As with prevention of avoidant behaviors, prevention of compulsions is believed to result in extinction of the negatively reinforced compulsive behavior (Foa, Steketee, & Milby, 1980).

Contingency Management

Contingency management procedures, which are based on the principles of operant conditioning, attempt to alter the child's anxious behavior by manipulating its consequences. Reduction of avoidant behavior and acquisition of approach behavior toward the feared stimulus—not a reduction of subjective states of anxiety—are the goals of treatment. Specific treatment programs using operant-based procedures can be derived based on the results of a functional assessment of the anxious behavior. Once the function of the anxious behavior is determined, then the reinforcer responsible for behavioral maintenance can be withheld (extinction) or provided contingent on an alternative response (differential reinforcement).

In terms of operant conditioning, extinction involves withholding the reinforcer responsible for maintaining the behavior. Identifying and eliminating all sources of reinforcement for the anxious behavior may be particularly difficult, however. Intensive training and monitoring may be required for parents or teachers to consistently withhold reinforcement (such as attention) from an anxious child. When possible, it is advisable to use extinction in combination with differential reinforcement procedures (see Sultzer-Azaroff & Mayer, 1977).

Positive reinforcement procedures involve presentation of a stimulus contingent on a behavior, which increases the probability that the behavior will occur again. In the case of anxiety-based disorders in children, which typically involve avoidant behavior, positive differential reinforcement procedures are typically used to increase approach behaviors toward the feared stimulus or to increase alternative or incompatible behaviors. The identification of effective reinforcers, either those maintaining the anxious behavior (e.g., attention) or other reinforcers (e.g., tangible items), is the most critical element in a reinforcement-based procedure. Additionally, the approach or alternative target behavior must be precisely defined (for the child as well as parent); the reinforcer should be provided as soon as possible after the target response; and reinforcement for competing anxious behaviors should be minimized or extinguished if possible (Ollendick & Cerny, 1981).

An additional consideration with any operant-based procedure is that the treatment contingencies are designed so that the child comes into contact with them. Where the target approach behavior cannot be reinforced because of extreme avoidant behavior, shaping procedure may be necessary to achieve a successful outcome. Shaping of approach behavior, which involves reinforcement of increasingly closer approximations to the desired response, is procedurally similar to (and may share similar theoretical underpinnings with) graduated exposure (Hagopian & Slifer, 1993). Response requirements for reinforcement are initially easy to assure success and are gradually increased so that the probability of obtaining reinforcement remains high (see Ollendick & Cerny, 1981).

Modeling

Modeling procedures, which are based on the principles of vicarious conditioning (Bandura, 1969), are designed to achieve fear reduction and skill acquisition in anxious children. Typically, the child observes another engage in nonfearful approach behavior toward the feared stimulus in a graduated fashion while showing appropriate coping behavior (Ollendick & Francis, 1988). In live modeling, the child directly observes another child interacting with the feared stimulus, whereas participant modeling also involves having the model guide the child to engage in successively increased interaction with the feared stimulus. The effects of characteristics of the model, observer, and presentation format have been described elsewhere (Perry & Furukawa, 1980). Participant modeling is considered the most effective modeling procedure in reducing fears in nonclinical children; however, few controlled studies on children with anxiety disorders have been reported (Ollendick & Francis, 1988).

Cognitive-Behavioral Procedures

Cognitive-behavioral procedures include strategies that attempt to alter behavior by restructuring children's maladaptive cognitions. These strategies are typically used in combination with other procedures, primarily those based on operant and classical conditioning principles. Cognitive self-instruction (Meichenbaum & Goodman, 1971) teaches children to generate positive self-statements using cognitive modeling and rehearsal. Positive self-statements typically include instructions to aid the child in developing a plan to deal with feared situations, coping with anxiety by using relaxation and other problem-solving strategies, and evaluating performance. In a controlled study involving 47 anxious children, Kendall (1994) demonstrated that a treatment program involving cognitive as well as behavioral strategies resulted in significant improvements, relative to a control group, at the end of the 16-session intervention and at 1-year follow-up. It has been suggested, however, that cognitive-behavioral procedures, in the absence of reinforcement for approach or alternative behavior, may not be sufficient to reduce avoidant behavior in some children (Hagopian, Ollendick, & Weist, 1990; Kane & Kendall, 1989; Ollendick, Hagopian, & Huntzinger, 1991). It is recommended that self-instructional and other cognitive-based strategies are integrated into other interventions to provide the child with a means of coping during exposure or other distressing situations.

Behavioral Family Interventions

While the behavioral assessment and treatment approaches previously described require intensive parental involvement, the "transfer of control" model (Ginsberg et al., 1995) and Family Anxiety Management (FAM; Dadds, Heard, & Rapee, 1992) emphasize the role of the family to an even greater extent. The transfer of control model emphasizes the gradual fading of control from the therapist to the parent, and to the child. Both approaches involve training parents in contingency management strategies to deal with their child's anxiety and to facilitate the child's exposure to the feared situation. Self-control strategies involving self-instruction and relaxation are taught to children so that they can control and manage their own anxiety and exposure to the feared situation. These approaches explicitly recognize and target parental anxiety, problematic family relationships, parent-child communication problems, and parental problem-solving skills. In a controlled group study involving 79 anxious children, FAM was found to be superior to a waiting list control group and a cognitive behavior therapy group after treatment and at 1-year posttreatment (Barrett, Dadds, & Rapee, 1996).

Pharmacological Interventions

While the scope of this chapter is limited to behavioral treatment of anxiety disorders in children, the use of pharmacological interventions should be noted. In contrast to the literature on the use of medications for the treatment of anxiety in adults, only a few controlled studies have been conducted with anxious children. There is some evidence indicating that tricyclic antidepressants are somewhat effective in treating separation anxiety disorder and panic disorder, and that benzodiazepines are helpful in reducing anxiety symptoms; however, it has been recommended that pharmacotherapy be used as an adjunct with other interventions (see Bernstein & Shaw, 1993).

SUMMARY

Anxiety disorders are believed to be one of the most common types of psychiatric disorder experienced by children and adolescents. An anxiety disorder is said to exist if the anxiety is extreme and of greater severity and duration than would be expected to occur as part of normal development to the extent that the child's functioning is impaired. The *DSM-IV* classifies anxiety disorders in children based on the type of feared stimulus or situation (e.g., social phobia) or the nature of the anxious response (e.g., panic disorder). The expression of anxiety disorders in childhood is believed to be a function of familial, developmental, environmental processes that interact synergistically. A general predisposition for the development of anxiety disorders may be genetically based, while vulnerability for the development of specific types of anxiety disorders may vary over the course of development and across the life span.

The behavioral assessment of anxiety disorders in children can be characterized as an ongoing multimethod, multimodal process that is developmentally sensitive and is designed to identify and define target behaviors, determine controlling variables, and select and evaluate intervention strategies. Strategies based on the principles of classical, operant, and vicarious conditioning have been developed for the treatment of anxiety. Therapeutic exposure, a common element in behavioral treatment approaches, requires that the feared stimulus is encountered in a controlled manner such that avoidant behavior does not occur *and* that aversive events previously associated with that stimulus are not experienced. The various behavioral treatment strategies differ primarily in terms of the use of other techniques to facilitate these extinction processes (e.g., relaxation, coping strategies, response prevention, reinforcement), and the method by which exposure occurs (e.g., in vivo, imaginal, vicarious, graduated).

Although the efficacy of behavioral approaches for the treatment of disorders in children and adolescents has been demonstrated, failure to identify and deal with impediments to the assessment and treatment process may interfere with achieving the goals of treatment. The effects of the social context in which the child lives, as well as the resources, values, beliefs, and goals of the child, family, school, and community must be considered when assessing and treating anxious children. Failure to address conflicts about whether a child's anxiety is a problem that warrants treatment, to identify realistic goals, to prescribe acceptable assessment and treatment procedures, and to work within the limits of the available resources may seriously impede the intervention process

Since changing parent (or teacher) behavior is often an important component in altering the child's anxious behavior, identifying and dealing with parental anxiety or psychopathology may be critical to achieving a successful outcome with the child. In cases where the broader context itself is the direct source of the problem, interventions must focus on accessing available resources and promoting effective coping skills that are realistic and embedded in the contextual framework in which the child and his or her family exist.

REFERENCES

Achenbach, T. M., & Edelbrock, C. (1983). *Manual for the Child Behavior Checklist and Revised Child Behavior Profile.* Burlington: University of Vermont Department of Psychiatry.

American Psychiatric Association. (1987). *Diagnostic and statistical manual of mental disorders* (3rd ed., rev.). Washington, DC: Author.

American Psychiatric Association. (1994). *Diagnostic and statistical manual of mental disorders* (4th ed.). Washington, DC: Author.

Ammerman, R. T., & Hersen, M. (1994). Developmental and longitudinal perspectives on behavior therapy. In R. T. Ammerman & M. Hersen (Eds.), *Handbook of behavior therapy with children and adults* (pp. 3–10). Boston: Allyn & Bacon.

Anderson, J. C. (1994). Epidemiological issues. In T. H. Ollendick, N. J. King, & W. Yule (Eds.), *International handbook of phobic and anxiety disorders in children and adolescents* (pp. 43–65). New York: Plenum Press.

Anderson, J. C., Williams, S. M., McGee, R., & Silva, P. (1987). DSM-III disorders in preadolescent children: Prevalence in a large sample from the general population. *Archives of General Psychiatry, 44,* 69–76.

Bandura, A. (1969). *Principles of behavior modification.* New York: Holt, Rinehart and Winston.

Barrett, P. M., Dadds, M. R., & Rapee, R. M. (1996). Family treatment of childhood anxiety: A controlled trial. *Journal of Consulting and Clinical Psychology, 64,* 333–342.

Barrios, B. A., & O'Dell, S. L. (1989). Fears and anxieties. In E. J. Mash & R. A. Barkley (Eds.), *Treatment of childhood disorders* (pp. 167–221). New York: Guilford Press.

Beidel, D. C. (1988). Psychophysiological assessment of anxious emotional states in children. *Journal of Abnormal Psychology, 97,* 80–82.

Beidel, D. C. (1989). Assessing anxious emotion: A review of psychophysiological assessment in children. *Clinical Psychology Review, 9,* 717–736.

Beidel, D. C. (1991). Determining the reliability of psychophysiological assessment in childhood anxiety. *Journal of Anxiety Disorders, 5,* 139–150.

Bell-Dolan, D. J., Last, C. G., & Strauss, C. C. (1990). Symptoms of anxiety disorders in normal children. *Journal of the American Academy of Child and Adolescent Psychiatry, 29,* 759–765.

Bernstein, G. A. (1991). Comorbidity and severity of anxiety and depressive disorders in a clinic sample. *Journal of the American Academy of Child and Adolescent Psychiatry, 30,* 43–50.

Bernstein, G. A., & Borchardt, C. M. (1991). Anxiety disorders of childhood and adolescence: A critical review. *Journal of the American Academy of Child and Adolescent Psychiatry, 30,* 519–532.

Bernstein, G. A., & Shaw, K. S. (1993). Practice parameters for the assessment and treatment of anxiety disorders. *Journal of the American Academy Child Adolescent Psychiatry, 32,* 1089–1098.

Biederman, J., Rosenbaum, J. F., Bolduc-Murphy, E. A., & Faraone, S. V. (1993). A 3-year follow-up of children with and without behavioral inhibition. *Journal of the American Academy of Child and Adolescent Psychiatry, 32,* 814–821.

Biederman, J., Rosenbaum, J. F., Hirshfield, D. R., Faraone, S. V., Bolduc, E. A., Gersten, M., Meminger, S. R., Kagan, J., Snidman, N., & Reznick, S. (1990). Psychiatric correlates of behavioral inhibition in young children without psychiatric disorders. *Archives of General Psychiatry, 47,* 21–26.

Bird, H., Canino, G., Rubio-Stipec, M., Gould, M. S., Ribera, J., Sesman, M., Woodbury, M., Huertas-Goldman, S., Pagan, A., Sanchez-Lacay, A., & Moscoso, M. (1988). Estimates of the prevalence of childhood maladjustment in a community survey in Puerto Rico: The use of combined measures. *Archives of General Psychiatry, 45,* 1120–1126.

Chambers, W. J., Puig-Antich, J., Hirsch, M., Paez, P., Ambrosini, P. J., Tabrizi, M. A., & Davies, M. (1985). The assessment of affective disorders in children and adolescents by semistructured interview. *Archives of General Psychiatry, 42,* 696–702.

Costello, A. J., Edelbrock, C. S., Dulcan, M. K., Kalas, R., & Klaric, S. H. (1984). *Report on the NIMH Diagnostic Interview Schedule for Children (DISC).* Amherst: University of Massachusetts Medical School.

Crowe, R. R., Noyes, R., Pauls, D. L., & Slymen, S. (1983). A family study of Panic Disorder. *Archives of General Psychiatry, 40,* 1065–1069.

Dadds, M. R., Heard, P. M., & Rapee, R. M. (1992). The role of family intervention in the treatment of child anxiety disorders: Some preliminary findings. *Behavior Change, 9,* 171–177.

Flament, M. F., Whitaker, A., Rapoport, J. L., Davies, M., Berg, C. Z., Kalikow, D., Sceery, W., & Shaffer, D. (1988). Obsessive Compulsive Disorder in adolescence: An epidemiological study. *Journal of the American Academy of Child and Adolescent Psychiatry, 27,* 764–771.

Foa, E. B., Steketee, G., & Milby, J. B. (1980). Differential effects of exposure and response prevention in obsessive-compulsive washers. *Journal of Consulting and Clinical Psychology, 48,* 71–79.

Francis, G., Last, C. G., & Strauss, C. C. (1987). Expression of Separation Anxiety Disorder: The roles of age and gender. *Child Psychiatry and Human Development, 18,* 82–89.

Francis, G., Last, C. G., & Strauss, C. C. (1992). Avoidant Disorder and social phobia in children and adolescents. *Journal of American Academy Adolescent Psychiatry, 31,* 1086–1089.

Garcia-Coll, C. G., Kagan, J., & Reznick, J. S. (1984). Behavioral inhibition in young children. *Child Development, 55,* 1005–1019.

Garrison, C. Z., Bryant, E. S., Addy, C. L., Spurrier, P. G., Freedy, J. R., & Kilpatrick, D. G. (1995). Posttraumatic Stress Disorder in adolescents after Hurricane Andrew. *Journal of the American Academy of Child and Adolescent Psychiatry, 34,* 1193–1200.

Ginsberg, G. S., Silverman, W. K., & Kurtines, W. K. (1995). Family involvement in treating children with phobic and anxiety disorders: A look ahead. *Clinical Psychology Review, 15,* 457–473.

Graziano, A. M., & Bythell, D. L. (1983). Failures in child behavior therapy. In E. B. Foa & P. M. G. Emmelkamp (Eds.), *Failures in behavior therapy* (pp. 406–424). New York: Wiley.

Green, B. L., & Lindy, J. D. (1994). Posttraumatic Stress Disorder in victims of disasters. *Psychiatric Clinics of North America, 17,* 301–309.

Hagopian, L. P., Ollendick, T. H., & Weist, M. W. (1990). Cognitive-behavior therapy with an 11-year-old girl fearful of AIDS and illness: A case study. *Journal of Anxiety Disorders, 4,* 257–265.

Hagopian, L. P., & Slifer, K. J. (1993). Treatment of Separation Anxiety Disorder with graduated exposure and reinforcement targeting school attendance: A controlled case study. *Journal of Anxiety Disorders, 7,* 271–280.

Hamilton, D. I., & King, N. J. (1991). Reliability of a behavioral avoidance test for the assessment of dog phobic children. *Psychological Reports, 69,* 18.

Hanna, G. L. (1995). Demographic and clinical features of obsessive-compulsive disorders in children and adolescents. *Journal of the American Academy of Child and Adolescent Psychiatry, 34,* 19–27.

Harris, E. L., Noyes, R., Crowe, R. R., & Chauldry, D. R. (1993). Family study of agoraphobia. *Archives of General Psychiatry, 40,* 1061–1064.

Hodges, K., Cools, J., & McKnew, D. (1989). Test-retest reliability of a clinical research interview for children: The Child Assessment Schedule. *Psychological Assessment, 10,* 173–189.

Hodges, K., McKnew, D., Cytryn, D. K., Stern, L., & Kline, J. (1982). The Child Assessment Schedule (CAS) Diagnostic Interview: A report on reliability and validity. *Journal of the American Academy of Child and Adolescent Psychiatry, 21,* 468–473.

Hoehn-Saric, E., Maissami, M., & Wiegand, D. (1987). Measurement of anxiety of children and adolescents using semistructured interviews. *Journal of the American Academy of Child and Adolescent Child Psychiatry, 26,* 541–545.

Kagan, J., Reznick, J. S., & Snidman, N. (1988). The physiology and psychology of behavioral inhibition in children. *Child Development, 58,* 1459–1473.

Kane, T., & Kendall, P. C. (1989). Anxiety Disorder in children: A multiple-baseline evaluation of a cognitive-behavioral treatment. *Behavior Therapy, 20,* 499–508.

Kashani, J. H., & Orvaschel, H. (1988). Anxiety disorders in mid-adolescence: A community sample. *American Journal of Psychiatry, 145,* 960–964.

Kazdin, A. E. (1981). Assessment techniques for childhood depression: A critical appraisal. *Journal of the American Academy of Child Psychiatry, 20,* 358–375.

Kazdin, A. E. (1985). Behavioral observation. In M. Hersen & A. S. Bellack (Eds.), *Behavioral assessment* (pp. 101–124). New York: Pergamon Press.

Kazdin, A. E., Bass, D., Ayers, W. A., & Rodgers, A. (1990). Empirical and clinical focus of child and adolescent psychotherapy research. *Journal of Consulting and Clinical Psychology, 58,* 729–740.

Keller, M. B., Lavori, P. W., Wunder, J., Beardslee, W. R., Schwartz, C. E., & Roth, J. (1992). Chronic course of anxiety disorders in children and adolescents. *Journal of the American Academy of Child and Adolescent Psychiatry, 31,* 595–599.

Kendall, P. C. (1994). Treating anxiety disorders in children: Results of a randomized clinical trial. *Journal of Consulting and Clinical Psychology, 62,* 100–110.

Kendler, K. S., Neale, M. C., Kessler, R. C., Heath, A. C., & Eaves, D. K. (1992). Generalized Anxiety Disorder in women: A population-based twin study. *Archives of General Psychiatry, 49,* 267–272.

Keppel-Benson, J. M., & Ollendick, T. H. (1994). Posttraumatic Stress Disorder in children and adolescents. In C. F. Saylor (Ed.), *Issues in clinical child psychology: Children and disasters* (pp. 29–43). New York: Plenum Press.

King, N. J. (1994). Physiological assessments. In T. H. Ollendick, N. J. King, & W. Yule (Eds.), *International handbook of phobic and anxiety disorders in children and adolescents* (pp. 365–379). New York: Plenum Press.

King, N. J., Cranstoun, F., & Josephs, A. (1989). Emotive imagery and children's nighttime fears: A multiple baseline design evaluation. *Journal of Behavior Therapy and Experimental Psychiatry, 20,* 125–135.

King, N. J., Hamilton, D. I., & Ollendick, T. H. (1988). *Children's phobias: A behavioural perspective.* New York: Wiley.

Kovacs, M. (1981). Rating scales to assess depression in school-aged children. *Acta Paedopsychiatrica, 46,* 305–315.

Lang, P. J. (1977). Physiological assessment of anxiety and fear. In J. D. Cone & R. P. Hawkins (Eds.), *Behavioral assessment* (pp. 178–195). New York: Brunner/Mazel.

Lang, P. J., & Lazovik, A. D. (1963). Experimental desensitization of a phobia. *Journal of Abnormal and Social Psychology, 66,* 519–525.

Last, C. G., Francis, G., Hersen, M., Kazdin, A. E., & Strauss, C. C. (1987). Separation anxiety and school phobia: A comparison using DSM-III criteria. *American Journal of Psychiatry, 144,* 653–657.

Last, C. G., Hersen, M., Kazdin, A. E., Francis, G., & Grubb, H. J. (1987). Psychiatric illness in the mothers of anxious children. *American Journal of Psychiatry, 144,* 1580–1583.

Last, C. G., Perrin, S., Hersen, M., & Kazdin, A. E. (1992). DSM-III-R anxiety disorders in children: Sociodemographic and clinical characteristics. *Journal of the American Academy of Child and Adolescent Psychiatry, 31,* 1070–1076.

Lazarus, A. A., & Abramovitz, A. (1962). The use of emotive imagery in the treatment of children's phobias. *Journal of Mental Science, 108,* 191–195.

Macaulay, J. L., & Kleinknecht, R. A. (1989). Panic and panic attacks in adolescents. *Journal of Anxiety Disorders, 3,* 221–241.

Marks, I. (1987a). The development of normal fear: A review. *Journal of Child Psychology and Psychiatry, 28,* 667–697.

Marks, I. (1987b). *Fears, phobias, and rituals.* New York: Oxford University Press.

Mash, E. J., & Terdal, L. G. (1985). Behavioral assessment of childhood disturbance. In E. J. Mash & L. G. Terdal (Eds.), *Behavioral assessment of childhood disorders* (pp. 3–76). New York: Guilford Press.

McGee, R., Feehan, M., Williams, S., Partridge, F., Silva, P., & Kelly, J. (1990). DSM-III disorders in a large sample of adolescents. *Journal of the American Academy of Child and Adolescent Psychology, 29,* 611–619.

Meichenbaum, D. H., & Goodman, J. (1971). Training impulsive children to talk to themselves: A means of developing self-control. *Journal of Abnormal Psychology, 77,* 115–126.

Milne, J. M., Garrison, C. Z., Addy, C. L., McKeown, R. E., Jackson, K. L., Cuffe, S. P., & Waller, J. L. (1995). Frequency of phobic disorder in a community sample of young adolescents. *Journal of the American Academy of Child and Adolescent Psychiatry, 34,* 1202–1211.

Morris, R. J., & Kratochwill, T. R. (1983). *Treating children's fears and phobias.* Elmsford, New York: Pergamon Press.

Ollendick, T. H. (1979). Fear reduction techniques with children. In M. Hersen, R. M. Eisler, & P. M. Miller (Eds.), *Progress in behavior modification* (Vol. 8, pp. 127–168). New York: Academic Press.

Ollendick, T. H. (1983). Reliability and validity of the Revised Fear Survey Schedule for Children (FSSC-R). *Behaviour Research and Therapy, 21,* 685–692.

Ollendick, T. H., & Cerny, J. A. (1981). *Clinical behavior therapy with children.* New York: Plenum Press.

Ollendick, T. H., & Francis, G. (1988). Behavioral assessment and treatment of children's phobias. *Behavior Modification, 12,* 165–204.

Ollendick, T. H., Hagopian, L. P., & Huntzinger, R. M. (1991). Cognitive-behavior therapy with nighttime fearful children. *Journal of Behavior Therapy and Experimental Psychiatry, 22,* 113–121.

Ollendick, T. H., & Hersen, M. (1984). An overview of child behavioral assessment. In T. H. Ollendick & M. Hersen (Eds.), *Child behavioral assessment* (pp. 3–19). Elmsford, New York: Pergamon Press.

Ollendick, T. H., & King, N. J. (1994). Diagnosis, assessment, and treatment of internalizing problems in children: The role of longitudinal data. *Journal of Consulting and Clinical Psychology, 62,* 918–927.

Ollendick, T. H., King, N. J., & Frary, R. B. (1989). Fears in children and adolescents: Reliability and generalizability across gender, age, and nationality. *Behaviour Research and Therapy, 27,* 19–26.

Ollendick, T. H., Matson, J. L., & Helsel, W. J. (1985). Fears in children and adolescents: Normative data. *Behaviour Research and Therapy, 23,* 465–467.

Ollendick, T. H., Mattis, S. G., & King, N. J. (1994). Panic in children and adolescents: A review. *Journal of Child Psychology and Psychiatry, 35,* 113–134.

Perry, M. A., & Furukawa, M. J. (1980). Modeling methods. In F. H. Kanfer & A. P. Goldstein (Eds.), *Helping people change* (2nd ed., pp. 131–171). Elmsford, New York: Pergamon Press.

Pinto, A., & Francis, G. (1994). Obsessive-Compulsive Disorder in children. In R. T. Ammerman & M. Hersen (Eds.), *Handbook of behavior therapy with children and adults* (pp. 155–166). Boston: Allyn & Bacon.

Quay, H. C., & Peterson, D. R. (1983). *Manual for the Revised Behavior Problem Checklist.* Unpublished manuscript.

Ray, W. J., & Raczynski, J. M. (1985). Psychophysiological assessment. In M. Hersen & A. S. Bellack (Eds.), *Behavioral assessment* (pp. 175–211). New York: Pergamon Press.

Reed, L. J., Carter, B. D., & Miller, L. C. (1995). Fear and anxiety in children. In C. E. Walker & M. C. Roberts (Eds.), *Handbook of clinical child psychology* (pp. 237–260). New York: Wiley.

Reich, W., & Welner, Z. (1988). *Revised version of the Diagnostic Interview for Children and Adolescents (DICA-R).* St Louis, MO: Washington University School of Medicine, Department of Psychiatry.

Reynolds, C. R., & Richmond, B. O. (1978). "What I think and feel": A revised measure of children's manifest anxiety. *Journal of Abnormal Child Psychology, 6,* 271–280.

Rosenbaum, J. F., Biederman, J., Gersten, M., Hirshfield, D. R., Meminger, S. R., Herman, J. B., Kagan, J., Reznick, S., & Snidman, N. (1988). Behavioral inhibition in children of parents with Panic Disorder and agoraphobia. *Archives of General Psychiatry, 45,* 463–470.

Schwarz, E. D., & Perry, B. D. (1994). The post-traumatic response in children and adolescents. *Psychiatric Clinics of North America, 17,* 311–326.

Shannon, M. P., Lonigan, C. J., Finch, A. J., & Taylor, C. M. (1994). Children exposed to disaster: 1. Epidemiology of posttraumatic symptoms and symptom profiles. *Journal of the American Academy of Child and Adolescent Psychiatry, 33,* 80–93.

Shaw, J. A., Applegate, B., Tanner, S., Perez, D., Rothe, E., Campo-Bowen, A. E., & Lahey, B. L. (1995). Psychological effects of Hurricane Andrew on an elementary school population. *Journal of the American Academy of Child and Adolescent Psychiatry, 34,* 1185–1192.

Silverman, W. K., & Nelles, W. B. (1988). The Anxiety Disorders Interview Schedule for Children. *Journal of the American Academy of Child and Adolescent Psychiatry, 27,* 772–778.

Silverman, W. K., & Rabian, B. (1995). Test-retest reliability of the *DSM-III-R* childhood anxiety disorders symptoms using the Anxiety Disorders Interview Schedule for Children. *Journal of Anxiety Disorders, 9,* 139–150.

Smith, R. E., & Sharpe, T. M. (1970). Treatment of school phobia with implosive therapy. *Journal of Consulting and Clinical Psychology, 35,* 239–243.

Speilberger, C. D. (1973). *State-Trait Anxiety Inventory for Children.* Palo Alto, CA: Consulting Psychologists.

Strauss, C. C., & Last, C. G. (1993). Social and simple phobias in children. *Journal of Anxiety Disorders, 7,* 141–152.

Strauss, C. C., Lease, C. A., Last, C. G., & Francis, G. (1988). Overanxious Disorder: An examination of developmental differences. *Journal of Abnormal Child Psychology, 16,* 344–443.

Strupp, H. H. (1989). Psychotherapy: Can the practitioner learn from the researcher? *American Psychologist, 44,* 717–724.

Sultzer-Azaroff, B., & Mayer, G. R. (1977). *Applying behavior analysis procedures with children and youth.* New York: Holt, Rinehart and Winston.

Thapar, A., & McGuffin, P. (1995). Are anxiety symptoms in childhood heritable? *Journal for Child Psychology and Psychiatry, 36,* 439–447.

Turner, S. M., Beidel, D. C., & Costello, A. (1987). Psychopathology in the offspring of anxiety disorder patients. *Journal of Consulting and Clinical Psychology, 55,* 229–235.

Turner, S. M., Beidel, D. C., & Epstein, L. H. (1991). Vulnerability and risk for anxiety disorders. *Journal of Anxiety Disorders, 5,* 151–166.

Warren, R., & Zgourides, G. (1988). Panic attacks in high school students: Implications for prevention and intervention. *Phobia Practice and Research Journal, 1,* 97–113.

Weissman, M. M., Leckman, J. F., Merikangas, K. R., Gammon, G. D., & Prusoff, B. A. (1984). Depression and anxiety disorders in parents and children. *Archives of General Psychiatry, 41,* 845–852.

Weisz, J. R., Weiss, B., & Donenberg, G. R. (1992). The lab versus the clinic: Effects of child and adolescent psychotherapy. *American Psychologist, 47,* 1578–1585.

Whitaker, A., Johnson, J., Shaffer, D., Rapoport, J., Kalikow, K., Walsh, B. T., Davies, M., Braiman, S., & Dolinsky, A. (1990). Uncommon troubles in young people: Prevalence estimates of selected psychiatric disorders in a nonreferred adolescent population. *Archives of General Psychiatry, 47,* 487–496.

Wolpe, J. (1958). *Psychotherapy by reciprocal inhibition.* Stanford, CA: Stanford University.

CHAPTER 18

Posttraumatic Stress Disorder and Acute Stress Disorder

MICHAEL D. DEBELLIS

DESCRIPTION OF THE DISORDERS

Traditionally, posttraumatic stress disorder (PTSD) has been studied in male soldiers and combat veterans. However, it is now known that PTSD may arise from a variety of traumatic events in both males and females and in children, adolescents, and adults. It is estimated that 4 out of 10 American adults have experienced trauma (Breslau, Davis, Andreski, & Peterson, 1991). The trauma may have interpersonal origins if the cause of the trauma is of human design. Examples of this include military combat, violent personal assault (child abuse and neglect, kidnapping, incarceration as a prisoner of war, mugging, rape, robbery, terrorist attack, or torture), and witnessing domestic or community violence. The trauma may be of noninterpersonal origin such as experiences of natural or human-caused disaster(s) (floods, earthquakes, hurricanes), diagnosis with a life-threatening illness, and/or an accident. PTSD from human causes is more common than from natural disasters. In the real world, war experiences, child maltreatment, and domestic and/or community violence may be the most common causes of interpersonal trauma in children and adolescents. When the trauma is of interpersonal origins, the disorder is thought to cause more severe and long-lasting symptoms. The *Diagnostic and Statistical Manual of Mental Disorders,* Fourth Edition (*DSM-IV;* American Psychiatric Association, 1994), states that the following constellation of symptoms occur more commonly in association with an interpersonal stressor: anxiety, a loss of previously sustained beliefs, depression, dissociation, feeling permanently damaged, hostility, hopelessness, self-destructive and impulsive behaviors, somatization, shame, and personality and relational disturbances. These associated sequelae of symptoms may represent a distinct subtype of PTSD that is termed *complex PTSD* or *disorder of extreme stress not otherwise specified* (DESNOS; Herman, 1993). This is important to keep in mind when treating the child and adolescent patient, who may likely be a victim of interpersonal traumatic experience(s).

Concepts of the relationship of stress to mental illness are in a state of change. The *DSM-IV* has four diagnoses in which a stressor precipitates the mental illness: adjustment disorder(s), acute stress disorder (ASD), reactive attachment disorder of infancy or early childhood, and PTSD. In this area, there have been four major changes from the *Diagnostic and Statistical Manual of Mental Disorders,* Third Edition-Revised (*DSM-III-R;* American Psychiatric Association, 1987). First, ASD is a new *DSM-IV* anxiety disorder diagnosis. Making the appropriate *DSM-IV* diagnosis depends on severity of the stressor, severity of the symptoms, and length of time of the illness. Tables 18.1 and 18.2 list the *DSM-IV* criteria for PTSD and ASD. ASD is thought to distinguish acute and severe short-term from long-term posttraumatic stress reactions.

Second, criterion A, the traumatic experience(s), is the same in both ASD and PTSD, and includes both objective and subjective features. In the *DSM-III-R,* criterion A, the traumatic experience was an event outside the range of usual human experiences that would be markedly distressing to almost anyone. The *DSM-III-R* did not include subjective reactions to the trauma nor did it include more common events such as child maltreatment, domestic or community violence, or civilian war experiences. The essential feature (criterion A) of PTSD and ASD in the *DSM-IV* is the development of characteristic symptoms following exposure to an extreme traumatic stressor in which the person experienced, witnessed, or was confronted with an event or events that involved actual or threatened death or serious injury, or a threat to the physical integrity of self or others; and responded with horror or disorganized behavior (American Psychiatric Association, 1994). The *DSM-IV* diagnosis of PTSD is made when criterion A is experienced and when three clusters of categorical symptoms are present for more than one month after the traumatic event(s):

1. Intrusive reexperiencing of the trauma(s) (criterion B).
2. Persistent avoidance of stimuli associated with the trauma(s) (criterion C).
3. Persistent symptoms of increased physiological arousal (criterion D) (American Psychiatric Association, 1994).

The third change in the *DSM-IV* diagnosis of PTSD is that symptom 6 of criterion D in *DSM-III-R* (physiological reactivity upon exposure to events that symbolize or resemble the traumatic event) was moved from criterion D (persistent symptoms of increased arousal), to criterion B, intrusive reexperiencing of the trauma(s). Fourth, in *DSM-III-R,* the duration of symptoms needed to be present for at least 1 month. In the *DSM-IV,* PTSD symptoms must be present for more than 1 month, whereas, ASD symptoms are present for 2 days to 1 month. Based on the *DSM-IV* criteria, PTSD may also have delayed onset (i.e., symptoms occur at least 6 months after the stressor).

In ASD, the essential features are the presence of three or more dissociative symptoms such as numbing or detachment, "being in a daze," derealization, depersonalization, and dissociative amnesia as well as symptoms seen in PTSD such as intrusive thoughts of the trauma, persistent avoidance of traumatic reminders, and increased physiological arousal (criteria B, C, and D of *DSM-IV* PTSD). For children, sexually traumatic events may include developmentally inappropriate sexual experiences without threatened or actual violence or injury. The symptoms must cause clinically significant impairment in social or school functioning. In younger children, it is more common to see disorganized and/or regressive behavior or agitated, oppositional, and irritable behavior in response to a severe stressor. If a person experiences ASD for more than 1 month, but less than 3 months, the *DSM-IV* diagnosis is then changed to PTSD, acute.

For example, 8-year-old April, who witnessed her alcohol-dependent father's frequent verbal and physical assaults against her mother, has nightmares, clings to mother, will not leave her alone with father, and is unable to focus or concentrate in

Table 18.1 *DSM-IV* **Diagnostic Criteria for 309.81 Posttraumatic Stress Disorder**

A. The person has been exposed to a traumatic event in which both of the following were present:

    (1) The person experienced, witnessed, or was confronted with an event or events that involved actual or threatened death or serious injury, or a threat to the physical integrity of self or others.

    (2) The person's response involved intense fear, helplessness, or horror. *Note:* In children, this may be expressed instead by disorganized or agitated behavior.

B. The traumatic event is persistently reexperienced in one (or more) of the following ways:

    (1) Recurrent and intrusive distressing recollections of the event, including images, thoughts, or perceptions. *Note:* In young children, repetitive play may occur in which themes or aspects of the trauma are expressed.

    (2) Recurrent distressing dreams of the event. *Note:* In children, there may be frightening dreams without recognizable content.

    (3) Acting or feeling as if the traumatic event were recurring (includes a sense of reliving the experience, illusions, hallucinations, and dissociative flashback episodes, including those that occur on awakening or when intoxicated). *Note:* In young children, trauma-specific reenactment may occur.

    (4) Intense psychological distress at exposure to internal or external cues that symbolize or resemble an aspect of the traumatic event.

    (5) Physiological reactivity on exposure to internal or external cues that symbolize or resemble an aspect of the traumatic event.

C. Persistent avoidance of stimuli associated with the trauma and numbing of general responsiveness (not present before the trauma), as indicated by three (or more) of the following:

    (1) Efforts to avoid thoughts, feelings, or conversations associated with the trauma.

    (2) Efforts to avoid activities, places, or people that arouse recollections of the trauma.

    (3) Inability to recall an important aspect of the trauma.

    (4) Markedly diminished interest or participation in significant activities.

    (5) Feeling of detachment or estrangement from others.

    (6) Restricted range of affect (e.g., unable to have loving feelings).

    (7) Sense of a foreshortened future (e.g., does not expect to have a career, marriage, children, or a normal life span).

D. Persistent symptoms of increased arousal (not present before the trauma), as indicated by two (or more) of the following:

    (1) Difficulty falling or staying asleep.

    (2) Irritability or outbursts of anger.

    (3) Difficulty concentrating.

    (4) Hypervigilance.

    (5) Exaggerated startle response.

E. Duration of the disturbance (symptoms in Criteria B, C, and D) is more than 1 month.

F. The disturbance causes clinically significant distress or impairment in social, occupational, or other important areas of functioning.

Specify if:

Acute: if duration of symptoms is less than 3 months

Chronic: if duration of symptoms is 3 months or more

Specify if:

With Delayed Onset: if onset of symptoms is at least 6 months after the stressor

Table 18.2   *DSM-IV* Diagnostic Criteria for 308.3 Acute Stress Disorder

A. The person has been exposed to a traumatic event in which both of the following were present:

    (1) The person experienced, witnessed, or was confronted with an event or events that involved actual or threatened death or serious injury, or a threat to the physical integrity of self or others.

    (2) The person's response involved intense fear, helplessness, or horror.

B. Either while experiencing or after experiencing the distressing event, the individual has three (or more) of the following dissociative symptoms:

    (1) A subjective sense of numbing, detachment, or absence of emotional responsiveness.

    (2) A reduction in awareness of his or her surroundings (e.g., "being in a daze").

    (3) Derealization.

    (4) Depersonalization.

    (5) Dissociative amnesia (i.e., inability to recall an important aspect of the trauma).

C. The traumatic event is persistently reexperienced in at least one of the following ways: recurrent images, thoughts, dreams, illusions, flashback episodes, or a sense of reliving the experience; or distress on exposure to reminders of the traumatic event.

D. Marked avoidance of stimuli that arouse recollections of the trauma (e.g., thoughts, feelings, conversations, activities, places, people).

E. Marked symptoms of anxiety or increased arousal (e.g., difficulty sleeping, irritability, poor concentration, hypervigilance, exaggerated startle response, motor restlessness).

F. The disturbance causes clinically significant distress or impairment in social, occupational, or other important areas of functioning or impairs the individual's ability to pursue some necessary task, such as obtaining necessary assistance or mobilizing personal resources by telling family members about the traumatic experience.

G. The disturbance lasts for a minimum of 2 days and a maximum of 4 weeks and occurs within 4 weeks of the traumatic event.

H. The disturbance is not due to the direct physiological effects of a substance (e.g., a drug of abuse, a medication) or a general medical condition, is not better accounted for by Brief Psychotic Disorder, and is not merely an exacerbation of a preexisting Axis I or Axis II disorder.

---

school secondary to poor sleep and constant worries about mother's safety. Since April's school report card grades have dropped and children no longer consider her "fun," a diagnosis of PTSD would be appropriate. April's symptoms may additionally meet *DSM-IV* criteria for a comorbid diagnosis of separation anxiety disorder. However, meeting criterion A (exposure to trauma) does not mean that a person has a diagnosis of PTSD or ASD. If a person's experience meets criterion A, but does not have other symptoms of PTSD or ASD, then a diagnosis of adjustment disorder is more appropriate. In the *DSM-IV* diagnosis of adjustment disorder, it is now specified whether the stressor is acute (less than 6 months), or chronic (more than 6 months; American Psychiatric Association, 1994). If April were not having symptoms of reexperiencing, avoidance, and increased arousal, a diagnosis of adjustment disorder with anxiety, chronic, would be more appropriate. Similarly if a child has symptoms of PTSD in response to a non-life-threatening traumatic event, such as parents' mutual and nonviolent marital separation, a diagnosis of adjustment disorder is more appropriate. Thus, 11-year-old Robert, who is chronically worried about his future, is irritable, oppositional, has difficulty concentrating in school, and has frequent nightmares of monsters stealing his daddy in response to his parents' separation and ensuing 1-year custody battle, most likely has an adjustment disorder with mixed disturbance of emotion and conduct, chronic.

The clinical picture of PTSD in children is similar to that of adults (Eth & Pynoos, 1985; Goodwin, 1988; Lyons, 1987; Pynoos et al., 1987; Terr, 1991; Wolfe, Gentile, & Wolfe, 1989). There is little information on the new diagnosis of ASD in children and adolescents. However, this diagnosis is similar to the diagnostic criteria for PTSD as listed in the *DSM-III-R*. Therefore, any research or clinical studies that reported PTSD symptoms and prevalence rates for 1-month duration or less are, for practical purposes, also giving the reader useful information about ASD. In this chapter, the assessment and treatment of PTSD will be discussed, keeping in mind that the assessment and treatment of ASD is similar except for the duration of symptoms. Childhood trauma has a traumatic and a developmental impact. There is little published information on PTSD in children and adolescents (Amaya-Jackson & March, 1995). This is especially true of interpersonal traumatic experience(s). The epidemiology, causes and consequences, interventions, and treatment(s) of PTSD and ASD in the real world will be reviewed. The review will include information from the adult PTSD literature. Then, practical clinical information on PTSD in children and adolescents will be presented.

EPIDEMIOLOGY

Community-based studies reveal current lifetime prevalence rates for adult PTSD that range from 1% (Helzer, Robins, & McEvoy, 1987) to 14% (American Psychiatric Association, 1994). The true lifetime PTSD prevalence rate may be as high as 9%, a number suggested by a study of young adults enrolled in a health maintenance organization of Detroit (Breslau et al., 1991). However, studies of individuals at risk from interpersonal and non-interpersonal traumas have yielded rates ranging from 3% to 58% in adults (American Psychiatric Association, 1994). PTSD lifetime prevalence rates for adults are greater for prolonged and complex trauma(s) (i.e., from interpersonal traumas). For example, Goldstein, van Kammen, Shelly, Miller, and van Kammen (1987) found a current prevalence rate of 50%, and Kluznik, Speed, Van Valkenburg, and Magraw (1986) found a rate of 47% in former World War II prisoners of war approximately 40 years after combat duty and prison camp confinement. Kilpatrick, Saunders, Veronen, Best, and Von (1987) found a lifetime rate of PTSD postcrime victimization of 27.8%, with a current prevalence rate of 7.5%, after a mean postassault time of 15 years. Rothbaum and Foa (1993) found that at 1 month, 65% of rape victims met *DSM-III-R* PTSD criteria; at 3 months, 47%; and at 6 months, 41.7%. For non-interpersonal traumas, prevalence rates of PTSD in adults are lower. For example, McFarlane (1988) found a *DSM-III* PTSD prevalence rate of 14% of a community sample of brushfire disaster survivors at 29 months follow up. However, this may not be true for children. Child survivors of the Australian brushfire evidenced rates of *DSM-III* PTSD of 53%, 6 months after the trauma (McFarlane, 1987).

In contrast to adult PTSD research, there are no epidemiological studies and hence no published community lifetime prevalence rates for PTSD in children or adolescents to date (Amaya-Jackson & March, 1995). However, PTSD lifetime prevalence rates for children and adolescents are thought to be similar or higher than those of adults.

Hence, a recent community sample estimated a *DSM-III-R* PTSD prevalence rate by use of the NIMH Diagnostic Interview Schedule Version III-R (DIS-III-R) of 6.3% in adolescents (Giaconia, Reinherz, Silverman, Pakiz, Frost, & Cohen, 1995). Studies of PTSD prevalence rates of at-risk children and adolescents will be reviewed. The stressor(s) will be arbitrarily divided into interpersonal and non-interpersonal traumatic experience(s).

Interpersonal stressors, such as child maltreatment, criminal victimization, and war, are thought to be more likely to be chronic and more severe than non-interpersonal traumas. An interpersonal stressor likely involves the child losing faith and trust in an authority or parent figure. Thus, this child will be more difficult to treat in psychotherapy because the establishment of a therapeutic alliance will take more time. On the other hand, a child who experiences a non-interpersonal stressor such as an earthquake, but otherwise grew up in a stable community with stable bonds to authority figures, and did not suffer a traumatic loss, will have more social and community supports. This child should be easier to treat because therapy is free to focus on the non-interpersonal trauma and does not involve repairing the wounds of an interpersonal trauma. Terr (1991) has divided all trauma stress conditions of childhood into type I or one-time sudden traumas and type II or repeated traumas. Type I traumas most likely have non-interpersonal origins, while type II traumas are usually caused by interpersonal stressors.

McNally (1993) reviewed the current research and clinical literature on the diagnosis of PTSD in childhood, based on the stressor. He found that PTSD was common in children and adolescents after warfare, where rates as high as 27% to 48% have been reported. In a study of Cambodian adolescents three years after survival from the Pol Pot Regime, 50% had persistent symptoms of PTSD as well as depression and anxiety symptoms (Kinzie, Sack, Angell, & Clarke, 1989). McNally (1993) also reported PTSD rates of 27% to 100% for those children exposed to criminal violence. Pynoos et al. (1987) reported that 60% of schoolchildren exposed to a sniper attack continued to meet *DSM-III-R* criteria for PTSD one year later. Child maltreatment is defined as physical, sexual, and emotional abuse, neglect, and exposure to domestic violence. A recent report by the National Research Council (1993) suggests that the combined incidence of all forms of child maltreatment ranges from 9.4 cases per 1,000 children per year to as high as 107 cases per 1,000 children per year. This wide range of estimates reflects the uncertainties inherent in the survey methodologies and different sources of data brought to bear on the epidemiology of maltreatment. PTSD prevalence rates from child maltreatment range depending on the nature of the study and type of assessment measures used. Neglect is the most frequent (63%) form of child maltreatment (National Research Council, 1993). There are no studies that specifically examine neglect as a stressor that produces PTSD. PTSD resulting from physical abuse ranges from 11% (Pelcovitz et al., 1994) to 50% (Green, 1985). McNally (1993) found that PTSD prevalence rates from sexual abuse range from 0% to 90% depending on the assessment measures used. However, a recent study found that 42.3% of sexually abused children met *DSM-III-R* diagnostic criteria for PTSD and further suggested that sexually abused children are at heightened risk for PTSD compared with physically abused children (McLeer, Callaghan, Henry, & Waller, 1994). As of 1980, the reported number of homicides per year was 23,967 and of aggravated assaults exceeded 265,000; 40% of these homicides were the result of domestic violence (Centers for Disease Control, 1984). It is currently estimated that 4 million women are battered by their partners each year (Sassetti, 1993). Therefore, the risks of exposure to children from parental violence have substantially increased. *DSM-III-R* PTSD rates from witnessing domestic violence are similar to those of sexual abuse (Pynoos & Nader, 1989). Thus, the reported rates of PTSD in maltreated children may be similar to those of children traumatized by war.

The prevalence rates of PTSD from stressors from non-interpersonal traumas are less than those of interpersonal stressors (McNally, 1993). It has been estimated that there are 400,000 injuries and 8,000 deaths per year in the United States attributed to natural or human-created disasters (Logue, Melick, & Hansen, 1981), a rate far less than that from interpersonal traumas. Non-interpersonal trauma(s) may involve secondary interpersonal traumatic experiences, such as painful medical procedures in the treatment of a life-threatening medical illness or the death of a family member in a natural disaster. A recent review reports percentage rates of 9% to 50% of PTSD in children who have experienced natural disaster(s) (Vogel & Vernberg, 1993). Severe burns were associated with PTSD rates of 30% (Stoddard, Norman, & Murphy, 1989), and 1-year post-bone-marrow transplantation rate of 50% (Studer, Nader, Yasuda, Pynoos, & Cohen, 1991). Although the nature of these initial stressors are non-interpersonal, the event may be associated with secondary interpersonal trauma(s). Also, depending on the developmental stage of a child or adolescent, the stressor may be subjectively interpreted as interpersonal. For example, a 3-year-old child with acute leukemia may believe his illness is a punishment for wishing his newly born sibling died ("imminent justice").

Causes and Consequences

Etiology

Many factors are thought to be associated and possibly etiologically related to PTSD. These risk factors are divided into three categories: (a) factors prior to (b) factors relating to and (c) factors after the traumatic experience(s). Factors that increase the risks of having PTSD prior to the traumatic experience include a family history of psychiatric illness (genetic risk factors), parental poverty, history of childhood maltreatment or childhood psychiatric or behavioral disorder prior to the traumatic experience that was etiological to PTSD, introversion or extreme behavioral inhibition, adverse life events before the trauma, being female, and poor health (Davidson & Fairbank, 1993). Of these, genetics may play a critical role. In a twin study, True et al. (1993) found that genetic factors accounted for 13% to 30% of the variance in the reexperiencing cluster, 30% to 34% in the avoidance cluster, and 28% to 32% in the arousal cluster of PTSD symptoms in Vietnam veterans with combat-related PTSD.

Risk factors for PTSD associated with the traumatic experience(s) itself are the degree of exposure to the trauma and an individual's subjective sense of danger. This includes proximity to the impact zone, witnessing of injury or death, witnessing the death of a loved one or peer, sustained personal injury, physical handicap or noticeable scar secondary to the injury, use of a deadly weapon, length of time of the trauma, and being trapped (such as by a fallen piece of a building after an earthquake; Pynoos & Nader, 1990). Rescue workers who may not be directly exposed to the trauma may be traumatized by the exposure to the mutilation and death of others (Jones, 1985). In studies of interpersonal and non-interpersonal trauma(s), it has repeatedly been found that onset and chronicity of psychiatric impairment increase with the dose of traumatic exposure(s) (Pynoos & Nader, 1990). Pynoos et al. (1987) found that the degree of exposure in school-children to a life threat of sniper attack was associated with severity of PTSD symptoms 14 months later. Green, Grace, and Gleser (1985), found that the degree of exposure to the Beverly Hills Club fire was the main factor associated with psychiatric impairment. Shore, Tatum, and Vollmer (1983) demonstrated that onset of psychiatric disorders after the Mount St. Helens volcanic eruption followed a dose-response exposure pattern. Any of these traumas can result in PTSD in a susceptible individual. However, severe trauma such as being a prisoner of war or experiencing sexual assault may override any genetic, constitutional, social, or psychological resiliency factors. These may heighten the risk for childhood PTSD and its associated psychosocial, learning, and developmental impairments.

Risk factors associated with the diagnosis of PTSD after the traumatic experience(s) include the diagnosis of ASD, lack of social supports, secondary stressors such as change of school, change of residence, destruction of a home, chronic illness, handicapping condition, or death of a family member or pet, and continued adverse events such as repeated threats and fear of the perpetrator (of child abuse), financial problems, or serious property destruction (Pynoos & Nader, 1993). Retrospective data from psychiatric adult patients suggest that traumatic events prior to age 11 are thought to be three times more likely to result in a later diagnosis of PTSD (Davidson & Smith, 1990). The experience of multiple life adversities may have more than an additive effect in increasing psychiatric morbidity (Rutter, 1985). Therefore, trauma in childhood may have a more severe and lasting effect on mental health functioning than trauma experienced in adulthood.

The Psychobiology of Trauma

Trauma causes activation of behavioral and biological stress response systems. This is called the "fight-or-flight reaction." There are multiple, densely interconnected, neurobiological systems that are likely impacted by the acute and chronic stressors associated with any life-threatening trauma experienced in childhood and/or adolescence (De Bellis & Putnam, 1994). PTSD is thought to be a disorder of dysregulation of the stress response systems (Charney, Deutch, Krystal, Southwick, & Davis, 1993). The locus ceruleus-norepinephrine/sympathetic nervous system or catecholamine system, the serotonin system, and the hypothalamic-pituitary-adrenal axis, are three major neurobiological stress systems that significantly influence arousal, stress reactions, physical and cognitive development, and emotional regulation. It is believed that many of the acute and chronic symptoms associated with child and adolescent trauma arise in conjunction with disturbances and dysregulation of these systems. Trauma in childhood may be more detrimental than trauma experienced in adulthood secondary to interactions between trauma and neurodevelopment. A brief review of these major stress systems is important because (a) these are the major systems implicated in mood and anxiety disorders (Goodwin & Jamison, 1990); (b) there are pharmacological treatments to target these systems; (c) alcohol and various illicit substances will also "self-medicate" or target these systems by damping down hyperarousal or dysregulated stress system(s); and (d) a hyperaroused stress system may lead to behavioral manifestations of motor restlessness and learning and memory deficits that may be secondary to anxiety. Thus, children with PTSD may be more likely to be also diagnosed with other psychiatric disorders because of related attentional problems, oppositional behavior, depressive symptoms, poor impulse control, and difficulty trusting authority figures. Early diagnosis of PTSD and an understanding of the psychobiology of trauma may lead to early psychotherapeutic interventions and early psychopharmacological treatment(s). This may lead to secondary prevention of the psychiatric chronicity and comorbidity commonly seen in PTSD.

The locus ceruleus is the major catecholamine- or norepinephrine-containing nucleus in the brain. Activation of locus ceruleus neurons increases norepinephrine in specific brain regions (locus ceruleus, hypothalamus, hippocampus, amygdala, and cerebral cortex). These brain regions are associated with regulation of stress reactions, memory, and emotion (reviewed by De Bellis & Putnam, 1994). Stress also results in simultaneous activation of another very basic and ancient cell body, the paragigantocellularis (Aston-Jones, Valentino, Van Bockstaele, & Meyerson, 1994). The paragigantocellularis has major inputs to the locus ceruleus, but also controls and activates the sympathetic nervous system causing the biologic changes of the "fight-or-flight reaction," or of lifesaving responses to an acute threat (Aston-Jones et al., 1994). Direct and indirect effects of the fight-or-flight reaction include increased heart rate; increased blood pressure; dilated pupils; sweating; inhibition of renal sodium excretion; redistribution of the blood to the heart, brain and skeletal muscle and away from skin, gut, and kidneys; enhanced blood coagulation by increasing platelet aggregability; increased glycogenolysis; and increased metabolic rate and alertness. The locus ceruleus via indirect connections through the limbic system results in activation of the hypothalamic-pituitary-adrenal axis. Combat-related PTSD is consistently associated with hyperactivity of the locus ceruleus/ sympathetic nervous system and increases in circulating catecholamines. Combat-related PTSD is associated with increased heart rate, systolic blood pressure, skin conductance, and other sympathetic nervous system responses to adrenergic or traumatic reminder challenge (reviewed by Charney et al., 1993; Murberg, McFall, Ko, & Veith, 1994; Pittman, 1993), decreased sleep latency and efficiency (Ross, Ross, Sullivan, & Caroff, 1989), and elevated 24-hour urinary excretion of catecholamines (Kosten, Mason, Giller, Ostroff, & Harkness, 1987; Yehuda, Southwick, Giller, Ma, & Mason, 1992). Chronic activation of the catecholamine system may also cause permanent cardiac changes (Perry, 1994) as well as suppression of immune function (reviewed by De Bellis & Putnam, 1994).

The hypothalamic-pituitary-adrenal axis, like the catecholamine system, is a major stress response system. Acute stress produces activation of the hypothalamic-pituitary-adrenal axis. Corticotropin-releasing hormone or CRH, a hypothalamic peptide, selectively stimulates and regulates pituitary adrenocorticotropin (ACTH). CRH promotes hypercortisolism, stimulates the sympathetic nervous system, and causes behavioral activation and intense arousal. Functionally, CRH and the locus ceruleus/sympathetic nervous system seem to participate in a positive, nonlinear feedback loop (reviewed by Chrousos & Gold, 1992). Plasma ACTH, in turn, stimulates adrenal secretion of glucocorticoids or cortisol which causes increases in gluconeogenesis, inhibition of growth and reproductive systems, and containment of the inflammatory or immune response (Chrousos & Gold, 1992). These functions enhance survival during a life threat. Hypothalamic-pituitary-adrenal axis abnormalities have been noted in adult PTSD. It is hypothesized that a central suppressive/inhibitory mechanism or down regulation mechanism involving supersensitivity to cortisol may be operating in PTSD (Yehuda, Giller, Southwick, Lowy, & Mason, 1991). Low urinary cortisol excretion, increased number of glucocorticoid receptors on lymphocytes, and suppression of cortisol with low dose dexamethasone (Yehuda et al., 1993) in combat-related PTSD subjects compared with control subjects supports this hypothesis. Although glucocorticoid activity is necessary for life, elevated levels may have neurotoxic effects and result in learning and concentration impairments secondary to damage to the hippocampus (Edwards, Harkins, Wright, & Menn, 1990), the principal neural target tissue of glucocorticoids (Sapolsky, Uno, Rebert, & Finch, 1990). Down regulation of this system in response to chronic stress may be adaptive and prevent neurotoxic effects. Accordingly, Bremner et al. (1995) have found decreased hippocampal volume in the right hemisphere in adult combat veterans who suffer from PTSD. Bremner et al. (1993) have also found short-term memory deficits in these adult PTSD subjects.

The serotonin system, another stress response system, plays important roles in the regulation of mood, aggression, impulsivity, and compulsive behaviors and has been implicated in a number of psychiatric disorders (Benkelfat, 1993; Siever & Trestman, 1993). In animal studies of unpredictable and uncontrollable stress (e.g., inescapable shock), serotonin levels decrease in the brain (Southwick, Krystal, Johnson, & Charney, 1992). Drugs that increase brain serotonin (serotonin agonists) prevent some of the behavioral changes seen in stressed animals (Southwick et al., 1992). Because of serotonin's interdependence with the catecholamine system (Sulser, 1987), it is believed that the serotonin system is different in children and adolescents who experience trauma. Low serotonin function is associated with suicidal and aggressive behaviors in adults, children, and adolescents (Benkelfat, 1993; Siever & Trestman, 1993). These are common behaviors seen in victims of childhood maltreatment and in adults and children with histories of sexual abuse (National Research Council, 1993), which is one form of an interpersonal traumatic experience(s) that may result in PTSD. However, very little is known about serotonin function and trauma in humans (De Bellis & Putnam, 1994).

Animal studies of the effects of trauma during early development have demonstrated permanent changes in the sympathetic nervous system and the hypothalamic-pituitary-adrenal axis of developing mammals (reviewed by De Bellis & Putnam, 1994). Dysregulation of the catecholamine system has been found in maltreated children with PTSD (Perry, 1994). Dysregulation of the catecholamine and hypothalamic-pituitary-adrenal axis system has been found in sexually abused girls (De Bellis, Chrousos, et al., 1994; De Bellis, Lefter, Trickett, & Putnam, 1994). Recently, Yehuda et al. (1995) found that adults with PTSD from surviving the Holocaust as children had lower urinary excretion of cortisol than the non-PTSD Holocaust survivor group and the normal controls. Consequences of childhood PTSD may include permanent changes or dysregulation of a child's neurobiological stress systems. More research on the psychobiology of trauma in childhood is needed and may lead to more effective clinical treatments.

Consequences

PTSD involves traumatic consequences, the psychopathology or signs and symptoms of ASD or PTSD as discussed above, and developmental consequences. Trauma in children and adolescents may disrupt developmental achievements and may cause delays in, deficits of, or failures of multisystem developmental achievements in motor, emotional, language, psychosocial, social, and cognitive skills. Trauma may also impact psychosexual and moral development (see Tables 18.3 & 18.4). Thus, PTSD in childhood can lead to many psychiatric, psychosocial, social, cognitive, and medical consequences.

Accordingly, PTSD is associated with a high comorbidity with other psychiatric diagnoses in children, adolescents, and adults. In a study by Kulka et al. (1990); comorbid alcohol abuse, major depressive disorder, and generalized anxiety disorder were most common among adult males with PTSD. Major depression, generalized anxiety disorder, alcohol abuse, and panic disorder were most common among adult females with PTSD (Kulka et al., 1990). A study by the Centers for Disease Control (1988) also found high rates of comorbid major depression, generalized anxiety disorder, alcohol and substance abuse in adult PTSD patients. Currently, there are only a few studies of co-morbidity of PTSD in childhood. In these studies, comorbid major depression, dysthymia, disruptive disorders, separation anxiety disorder, generalized anxiety disorder, and in younger children attachment disorders are also commonly seen. In the Kinzie, Sack, Angell, Manson, and Ben (1986) study of Cambodian adolescent refugees, significant rates of comorbidity were seen between PTSD and major depression, depressive disorder not otherwise specified (NOS), and generalized anxiety disorder. Increased rates of alcohol and psychoactive substance abuse have been reported in maltreated adolescents (Van Hasselt, Ammerman, Glancy, & Bukstein, 1992), who were not assessed for PTSD. Clark (1994) reported substantially higher rates of adverse life events such as sexual abuse and of the diagnosis of PTSD (made by structured interview) in adolescents with alcohol abuse disorders.

Childhood sexual abuse is a model of chronic and interpersonal trauma (Putnam & Trickett, 1993). It has estimated prevalence values ranging from 6% to 33% in females and 3% to 31% in males (Conte, 1991). It is a stressor commonly associated with PTSD (McLeer et al., 1994). Childhood sexual abuse will be used as an example of the impact of trauma on developmental achievements (see Tables 18.3 & 18.4). Victimization by caregiver(s) can be thought of as the traumatic event. PTSD from an interpersonal trauma is especially handicapping because the nature of the stressor or trauma reflects conflicts in primary interpersonal relationship(s). This may lead to impaired social skills, impaired social problem-solving abilities, and inability to generate alternative solutions to conflicts, to plan ahead, and to solve interpersonal conflicts (Perry, 1993a, 1993b). Poor coping skills may also result in feelings of hopelessness, comorbid major depression, and suicidal ideation. Children and adolescents with PTSD may be more likely to be diagnosed with other psychiatric disorders because of related deficits in developmental achievements. In retrospective studies, adults with histories of childhood sexual abuse manifest high rates of major depression, suicidality, somatization disorder, anxiety disorders, personality disorders, PTSD, and alcohol and substance abuse (National Research Council, 1993; Putnam & Trickett, 1993). These symptoms may represent failures of developmental achievements of security and trust, self-regulation, and emotional expression in language (inability to verbalize and label feelings rather than acting out). These achievements are normally present prior to age 6 years. Accordingly, aggressive and inappropriate sexual behavior (Friedrich, 1993), as well as major depression, dysthymia, suicidality, somatic complaints, and anxiety disorders are commonly reported in sexually abused children (Conte, 1991; de Wilde, Kienhorst, Dickstra, & Walters, 1992; McLeer et al., 1994). Adolescents also manifest

Table 18.3 Normal Multisystem Developmental Stages and Associated Achievements that May Be Delayed or Deficient as a Result of Trauma

Age (years)	0–.5	.5–1	1–2	2–3	3–6	7–11	12–12+
Motor and Physical Development (Gesell, 1968)	Sits alone Commands trunk and fingers Begins to crawl	Stands alone First steps Plays pat-a-cake	Begins to walk, walks up stairs, jump in place, scribbles	Runs Begins to be potty trained	Matures, hops, skips	Adrenal androgens increase and then puberty begins	Puberty begins, cortical glial development is completed
Emotional Development (Bandura, 1986; Bowlby, 1980)	Social smile, expresses discomfort, is sensitive to emotional cues	Begins to express anger and fear, learning to self-regulate extreme emotions	Empathy and self-consciousness begins	Capacity for empathy and ability to develop strategies self-regulation of emotions begins	Empathy increases and ability to self-regulate emotions is present	Can express and verbalize more than one emotion at a time	Adolescent has internal standards of behavior
Language Development (Gesell & Amatruda, 1974)	Phonemics, babbling with preference to native language	Verbal exchanges	Simple sounds, first words, turn-taking conversation, Pronunciation and vocabulary improve with increasing age	Sentence structure learned; begins to tell stories with beginning, middle, and endings (narrative coherent)	Pronunciation improves; understands several hundred words and understands metaphors Asks questions and stops baby talk	Understands 14,000 words, pronunciation subtleties and humor based on shadings of intent	Adolescent understands 30,000 words, abstract meanings, and references
Psychosocial Development (Erikson, 1963)	Trust vs. mistrust	Trust vs. mistrust	Autonomy vs. shame	Autonomy vs. shame	Initiative vs. guilt	Industry vs. inferiority	Identity vs. confusion
Cognitive Development (Piaget, 1952)	Sensorimotor-Reflexive and Primary Circular Reactions substages: Baby imitates, begins to play	Sensorimotor-Secondary Reactions and Coordination of Secondary Circular substages: Baby begins to learn goal-directed actions, plays peekaboo	Sensorimotor-Tertiary Circular Reactions and Mental Representation substages: Joy in dropping things, make-believe friend; memories of events and objects	Preoperational Stage: Egocentrism, animistic thinking perception-bound thought; centration—one aspect of a situation to neglect of others	Preoperational Stage: States vs. transformation, irreversibility, transductive reasoning, lack of hierarchical categories	Operational Stage: Conservation, decentration, reversibility, hierarchical classification; seriation, syllogisms, logic	Formal Operations: Hypothetico-deductive reasoning, propositional thought

466

Psychosexual	Innate predispositions (gender and sexual identity)	Gender identity is firmly established	Gender identity is expressed in play	Knowledge of gender roles and stereotypes begins	Knowledge of gender roles and stereotypes established	
Social	Undifferentiated	Undifferentiated	Undifferentiated: Confuses own thoughts with others and assumes others feel what the child is feeling	Social-Information: Different views come from different experiences	Self-Reflective: Able to see others thinking, viewpoints, and motivations	Third Party: Observes social interactions and understands a third party's motivations and behaviors
Moral (Kohlberg, 1964; Piaget & Inhelder, 1969)			Thinks in terms of good or bad. Focus is on self	Preconventional Level-Egocentric Stage: Imminent justice	Conventional Level-Incipient Cooperation: Respect for rules, social approval, and social systems	Postconventional level: Adolescent learns universal ethics based on justice and interpersonal obligations

Table 18.4   Likely Trauma (anxiety) Related Developmental Deficiencies in Learning and Achievement of Developmental Stages: Behavioral Problems and Symptoms

Age (Years)	
0–.5	Anxious infant—difficulty feeling safe.
.5–1	Anxious infant—afraid to explore, verbalize, express anger.
1–2	Anxious infant—afraid to explore or extreme motor restlessness, failure or delays in developing self-regulation, self-consciousness, verbal skills, empathy, and internal memories of events or objects.
2–3	Anxious toddler—regression in motor and verbal skills, bed wetting, fecal soiling, deficiencies in self-esteem, and in ability to empathize, self-regulate emotions, inability to develop coherent narratives, believes he/she is bad.
3–6	Anxiety-regression in motor and verbal skills, ability to empathize, self-regulate emotions and self-esteem, and may manifest extremes of psychomotor retardation (freezing) and restlessness. Believes he/she is bad, may feel guilty or not develop capacity for guilt, which may lead to violence, cruel behavior, and conduct disorder symptoms.
7–11	Androgens are associated with increased aggressive behaviors and inability to self-regulate emotions and verbalize feelings. Failure to enjoy work and play. Failure to develop appropriate social gender roles (e.g., sexually abused girl may be flirtatious or have masculine behaviors). Failure to appreciate social rules and need for hierarchical authority may lead to oppositional behavior, conduct symptoms, and peer rejection.
12–12+	In adolescence, trauma may impact on identity formation, separation-individuation, future goals and values, intimate relationships, parental relationships, and current motivational states. Thus failure to be empathetic with others, to understand others' motivations, failure to be considerate and thoughtful of self and others may lead to victim behavior, peer rejection, social isolation, self-destructive behaviors, and oppositional and conduct symptoms.

high rates of delinquency, violence, running away, substance abuse, and teenage pregnancy (National Research Council, 1993). These behavioral symptoms can be thought of as developmental failures to appreciate social rules, need for hierarchical authority, social and cultural values, and intimate relationships. There are failures of identity formation and separation-individuation. Thus, PTSD in children and adolescents is an area where appropriate clinical intervention has important practical, theoretical, economical, and societal implications.

IMPEDIMENTS TO INTERVENTION IN THE REAL WORLD CONTEXT

Impediments to intervention in the treatment of PTSD are human or cultural, financial, family, and therapeutic factors. Human or cultural factors include the ability of a society to prevent premorbid risk factors such as decreasing rates of child maltreatment, community and domestic violence, and undertaking appropriate and effective treatments for parental psychopathology and child premorbid psychopathology.

For some interpersonal trauma(s) and especially non-interpersonal trauma(s) (e.g., natural or human-made disasters), prevention may not be possible. However, quick and effective intervention in the form of critical stress incident debriefing or psychological debriefing, the currently accepted state of professional practice, is recommended. Impediments to quick intervention include lack of specially trained mental health workers available immediately during and after the trauma. In the case of trauma inflicted from being diagnosed with a life-threatening illness, it is important for the treating pediatrician to utilize mental health professionals to help both the child and family to cope with the overwhelming nature of lifesaving procedures or the child's impending death. This is a highly specialized area of mental health that encompasses special expertise in treating children, families, and patients with serious medical illness. Although most university settings have special multidisciplinary teams of professionals to treat this type of trauma, not all smaller community hospitals have these services available. These psychiatric consultation liaison services are also one of the first services to be cut during the current health care crisis.

Another human impediment to intervention is social stigma against psychiatry and mental health workers among families and professionals alike. This social stigma results in devaluation of a "talking cure" as a way of coping. One symptom of this social stigma is the common myth that talking about the trauma (or about the medical procedure the child will undergo in a few days) will heighten fear and anxiety; when in reality if professionally guided, debriefing and desensitization methods will lessen anxiety. Discussion of PTSD arising from a life-threatening illness is beyond the scope of this chapter and the reader is referred elsewhere (Glazer, 1991; Nir, 1985). Another major and critically important impediment to treatment in the real world is cultural glorification of violence. Children need protection from unnecessary exposure to the injured, mutilated, and dead. If at all possible, they should not be involved in disaster rescue work or exposed to inappropriate media coverage such as exhibiting of corpses or mutilated bodies (Pynoos & Nader, 1990).

Family dysfunction is another important impediment to treatment. The family is the key setting in which feelings of vulnerability can be mitigated and a sense of safety and security restored. Whenever possible, the family should participate in some aspects of the treatment. Family members often need support, guidance, and therapeutic intervention to reduce their own levels of stress or PTSD symptoms before they can effectively help the children. Family members need information about children's response to trauma, the effect of traumatic reminders, the presence of arousal behavior, realistic but hopeful expectations regarding recovery, and the need for developmentally appropriate open communication with their children (Pynoos & Nader, 1993). It is a recent and most likely very positive trend in nonprofit mental health agencies and state community mental health centers to not treat a child or adolescent unless the family (if present in the child's life) is also in treatment. The family is the therapist's strongest ally in the successful treatment of the child. Whatever gains a child makes in therapy can be unintentionally undermined by dysfunctional family dynamics at home.

Lastly, an often overlooked major impediment to treating trauma in children and adolescents is professional burnout on the part of the treating therapist, supervisor, and/or treatment team. Mental health professionals begin their careers with high energy, high ideals, and a goal is to help make a better world. However, some authors believe that the first 10 years of a therapist's professional life is his or her most clinically productive and rewarding (Grosch & Olsen, 1994). When clinicians fail to maintain balance between work, family, and leisure, they are vulnerable to inappropriate management of their countertransference reactions and to burnout. Countertransference refers to the feelings triggered in the clinician by the patient. Burnout is a form of depression. Grosch and Olsen (1994), in their book *When Helping Starts to Hurt,* point out that the current medical and mental health financial crisis is resulting in more professional demands for individual practitioners to take on increased numbers and more complex caseloads in both the private and public sectors. Complex cases usually involve the care of patients with histories of traumatic experiences. Learning about a child's trauma may lead to rescue fantasies, inappropriate anger directed at former therapist(s), child protective worker(s), and the child's caretaker(s). Listening to trauma is traumatic in and of itself. Primary therapists are encouraged to seek individual or group, formal or informal supervision which will help them function effectively and prevent burnout. Complex cases should be managed in a team approach, where team leaders foster cooperation and mutual respect of colleagues. Burnout is a painful erosion of the spirit in response to the pressures of work and an insufficiently sustaining personal life that shortens the work cycle of dedicated and needed clinicians. Burnout, although not a clinical diagnosis, has symptoms similar to that of PTSD (anhedonia, restricted range of affect, diminished interest, irritability, difficulty concentrating, and insomnia). Readings on the origins, prevention, and treatment of burnout in mental health professionals (Berkowitz, 1987; Grosch & Olsen, 1994; Stevenson, 1989) are recommended to prevent burnout and PTSD in those of us who choose to treat traumatized children and adolescents. Clinicians, no matter how dedicated, always need to step back and to prioritize taking care of their own mental health needs. In this way, the clinician will not only be better equipped to listen, observe, and treat themselves, their colleagues, and patients with respect and compassion, but will also be a role model of the importance of self-care to their child and adolescent patient(s) and their families.

TREATMENT

Assessment Strategies

A child or adolescent may present for clinical evaluation and treatment of ASD or PTSD in various settings. The child or adolescent may be referred immediately following a traumatic event such as in the case of an isolated trauma or disaster. The child or adolescent may be referred immediately following disclosure of chronic traumatic experiences such as ongoing sexual abuse by a caregiver. The child or adolescent may be referred for another psychiatric disorder or behavioral problems as listed in Table 18.4. Children may disclose past traumatic experiences as part of an ongoing empathetic and trusting relationship with a therapist, teacher, school counselor, trusted family member, or friend. These children may have had previous mental health treatment. In such cases, the evaluating clinician needs to be a bit of a detective in evaluating the traumatic reminders that may trigger school difficulties, peer rejection, and/or disruptive (oppositional or impulsive) behaviors.

To make an appropriate diagnosis, it is important for the assessing clinician to be familiar with the literature on traumatic reactions in childhood and the clinical diagnosis of PTSD and ASD as discussed previously. However, it is equally important for the assessing clinician to be very familiar with normal child development as reviewed in Table 18.3. The assessment and treatment of traumatic stress responses in children and adolescents raises issues that transverse the disciplines of cognitive, psychological, neurobiological, psychosocial, behavioral, and social development (Pynoos & Nader, 1993). Practical experience with children in clinical and nonclinical settings as well as theoretical knowledge of child development will obviously enhance an interviewers' skill in obtaining the appropriate information, and in making accurate diagnosis(es), treatment recommendations, or recommendations for further evaluation and assessment(s). Developmental issues also influence the child's and adolescent's clinical presentation, emotional and cognitive means of coping in their psychosocial environment, processing of treatment, and course of recovery.

Goals of PTSD prevention immediately after a traumatic stress experience(s) include ameliorating traumatic stress reactions and facilitating grief work, preventing interferences with child development and resulting maladjustments, promoting competence in effectively adapting to the crisis situation, and identifying children and adolescents at risk for ASD, PTSD, or other psychiatric illnesses such as depression or suicidality in order to quickly institute clinical treatment (Pynoos & Nader, 1993). Goals of treatment include bolstering the child's or adolescents' reality testing functions, encouraging active coping skills, identifying traumatic reminders that elicit PTSD symptoms (intrusive imagery, intense affective responses, hyperarousal symptoms), helping the child or adolescent anticipate, understand, and manage everyday traumatic reminders to decrease the likelihood of disruption of daily functioning, and lastly assisting the child or adolescent to make distinctions among current and ongoing life stressors from the past trauma that will decrease the impact of the past trauma on present experience (Pynoos & Nader, 1993). During the initial evaluation or ongoing treatment, it is important for the mental health professional to help maintain the safety of the child or adolescent, assist in legitimizing feelings and reactions, assist the child in maintaining self-esteem, and prepare the child to anticipate and cope with unresolved feelings and symptoms over time (Pynoos & Nader, 1993).

In this section, trauma work conducted as debriefing (psychological "first aid"), the trauma consultation child interview, the general psychiatric or clinical mental health assessment, methods for the elicitation of symptoms for major categories of ASD and PTSD criteria, brief psychotherapy, long-term pulse intervention, long-term therapy, and psychopharmacology will be discussed. Clinical examples will be provided.

Debriefing and Psychological First Aid

Critical stress incident debriefing or psychological debriefing immediately after an acute traumatic experience is the hallmark of adult trauma work. It is based on work with disaster workers and emergency personnel (Mitchell & Dyregrov, 1993). Debriefing may be done in individual sessions but is usually undertaken in group formats with trained group leaders. Debriefing involves seven phases: introduction of ground rules and assurance of confidentiality; objective discussion of the traumatic experience(s); the individual's thoughts about the experience(s); individual's feelings about the experience(s); a review of signs and symptoms associated with the distress of the traumatic experience(s); education in the normal nature of stress, stress reactions, and the fight-or-flight reaction; and a question phase to clarify any additional or unsettled issues. For individuals who are suffering from an ASD or who have latter symptoms of PTSD, information for further treatment and appropriate referrals are made. These techniques may limit the impact of the trauma and decrease the likelihood of or degree of impairment from PTSD. Pynoos and Nader (1988) adopted this technique for children in crisis centers and classrooms. It serves both as an intervention and screening tool for at-risk children. In the context of a classroom discussion of the traumatic experience(s), a drawing and storytelling technique is used to express feelings, clarify confusions, and identify needs. The classroom is an excellent site for addressing issues of dying and loss. However, it is not a substitute for needed individual or family treatment. It should not be used to delve into highly emotionally charged issues, such as intrusive thoughts of grotesque images or revenge fantasies. A child should be redirected to draw a more pleasant picture to bring proper closure, and arrangements should be made with the child's guidance counselor and parent (or caretaker) for needed individual treatment (Pynoos & Nader, 1988).

Trauma Consultation Child Interview

The child interview technique or trauma consultation interview is based on psychodynamic and debriefing techniques. It was developed by Pynoos and Eth (1986) and intended for individual intervention. This interview incorporates a review and reprocessing of the traumatic experience(s). The emotional meaning as well as the personal impact is embedded in the details of the trauma experience(s) (Pynoos & Nader, 1993). The therapist must be prepared to hear everything, no matter how horrifying or sad (Pynoos & Nader, 1993). This interview was developed for children and adolescents, aged 3 to 16 years. It is applicable for the child who has witnessed murder, suicide, rape, accidental death, assault, kidnapping, natural or human-made disasters, and school and community violence. It may be used for victims of child maltreatment or criminal assault with modifications. It differs from the usual child psychotherapy session or initial psychiatric or mental health assessment interview because it has a stated focus of discussing the traumatic experience(s) (Pynoos & Nader, 1993). It takes 1 to 2 hours to permit sufficient time to explore the child's traumatic experience(s).

Prior to the child interview, it is important to obtain information about the trauma and the child's response to the trauma, his or her behavior after the trauma as well as the premorbid functioning from family members, medical records, the police, the school, or other appropriate sources of information. Methods for information gathering are discussed in the section "General Psychiatric or Clinical Mental Health Assessment," later in this chapter. This interview may be adapted as an initial clinical assessment interview when the trauma (Criterion A of ASD or PTSD) is known and the therapist will continue to treat the child or adolescent. This interview technique may also be helpful in ongoing therapy when traumatic experience(s) have been newly disclosed. As long as the child or adolescent is not in distress at the time of the disclosure, the interview can be scheduled for a later date for 1 to 2 hours in order to fully explore the issue(s). If the child is in distress by the disclosure, it is best to reschedule your next patient, and provide the necessary treatment or needed emergency evaluation. However, if a child or adolescent discloses ongoing or past history of physical and/or sexual abuse, assessment techniques incorporating this technique and other specialized methods are needed (for review, see National Research Council, 1993). An imminent assessment of the child's safety and mental status, as well as a Child Abuse and Neglect Report needs to be considered. These methods are discussed elsewhere in this text.

Pynoos and Eth (1986) designed a specialized interview for use in an initial meeting with a recently traumatized child or adolescent. The optimal time for intervention is during the acute period after the trauma experience(s) when intrusive phenomena and incident-specific traumatic reminders are most identifiable and the associated affect is most available (Pynoos & Nader, 1993). The interview involves a three-stage process: opening, trauma, and closure (Pynoos & Eth, 1986). In the opening stage, it is the interviewer's job to establish the focus and a working relationship (therapeutic alliance) with the child or adolescent in a nonthreatening and empathetic manner. Telling the child that you have experience in talking with children who have "gone through what you have gone through" is a suggested method of establishing focus (Pynoos & Eth, 1986, p. 307). If you have spoken with other sources such as a parent, teacher, police, or read medical, mental health, or police report, it is a good time to tell the child that you know something about "what you went through" and that you "are interested in understanding with him/her what it was like to go through what he or she has been through" (Pynoos & Eth, 1986, p. 307). In this way, the traumatized child or adolescent does not have the opportunity to avoid discussing the trauma by denying its existence nor does the child feel as if he/she is telling a total stranger. The child is given paper and crayons, and is asked to "draw whatever you'd like but something you can tell a story about" (Pynoos & Eth, 1986, p. 307). The interviewer expresses interest, playfulness, and reassurance to encourage the child to elaborate and become more spontaneous. The interviewer needs to observe for traumatic references and symptomatic issues. For the 3- to 8-year-old child, major issues are helplessness and passivity, generalized fear, cognitive confusion, difficulty identifying feelings, lack of verbalization, magical reminders of trauma (omens), sleep disturbance, separation anxiety, regressed behavior, and anxieties about death (Pynoos & Nader, 1993). For the 9- to 12-year-old child, major issues include responsibility and guilt, reminders that trigger fear response, traumatic play and retelling, fears of extreme feelings, difficulties with concentration and learning, sleep disturbance, safety issues, changes in behavior, somatic complaints, hyperviligance to parents' anxieties, overconcern with others' behaviors, and disturbing grief reactions (Pynoos & Nader, 1993). For the adolescent, major issues include detachment, shame, guilt, self-consciousness, acting out, life-threatening reenactment behaviors, abrupt shift in relationships, desire for revenge, intense anger, changes in attitudes about life, and premature entrance into adulthood (Pynoos & Nader, 1993). These issues reflect the developmental stages that the child or adolescent is striving to achieve (refer to Table 18.3).

Preadolescent children regulate their anxiety about the trauma experience in many ways (Pynoos & Eth, 1986). "Denial-in-fantasy" allows the child to mitigate painful circumstances by imaginatively reversing the violent outcome or by providing a story with a more acceptable outcome (Pynoos & Eth, 1986). Some children inhibit spontaneous thoughts. Some children are so fixed on the trauma that they draw the actual scene in free play and give a rational or unemotional journalistic account. It is very important to get to the affect in those children who use rationalization and isolation of affect as their major defenses, as these defenses can lead to remorseless destructive reenactment behavior to others in the future. These defenses are also antithetical to empathy. For example, a child who has been kidnapped, beaten, and raped may become the adolescent abuser of younger children when these strong emotional reactions are not processed. On the other hand, the child who witnessed the murder of his or her mother, by an alcohol-dependent father, who is able to process the intense emotional reaction and reestablish empathy (a major developmental task at this time period), may become a future mental health care professional or prosecuting attorney. Some children are in a constant state of anxious arousal. These children are restless and hypervigilant. They may be further helped with adjunctive treatment with medications (see pharmacotherapy section) as well as with psychotherapy. Verbalization of the interviewer's astute and gentle observations can lead to a transition to the second stage of the interview, discussion of the traumatic experience(s). Sometimes, an empathetic statement such as "I'll bet you wish that . . . your father could have been saved at the end like the clown" or "your father were still here to protect you" may provide for needed emotional release (Pynoos & Eth, 1986, p. 308). It is important to offer a crying child appropriate and professional physical comfort. As long as children or adolescents are not feeling threatened by their emotional responses, they can then proceed with a verbal description of the trauma, the next stage of the interview (Pynoos & Eth, 1986).

From discussions of aspects of the drawing that can be directly related to the traumatic experience(s), the child is then asked to draw and to tell "what he/she has gone through" (Pynoos & Eth, 1986, p. 307). With some very constricted or mute children, another attempt at free drawing with techniques such as the squiggle game (Winnicott, 1971) may lead to helpful discussion of the traumatic experience(s). It is important to give the child enough time to feel comfortable with the interviewer and the reconstruction of the traumatic event. During reconstruction of the traumatic event, the interviewer will also be able to learn and document if the objective and subjective features of the child's traumatic experience satisfy Criterion A for ASD or PTSD. In this way, this interview can also be diagnostic. The interviewer's role is to function as a "holding environment" in order to provide a safe and protected setting so that the child can reconstruct the traumatic experience(s) despite rising anxiety (Pynoos & Eth, 1986). The interviewer does not allow the child to digress from this task of mastery of the trauma. The interviewer may need to question the child to ensure that the circumstances are completely reviewed. It is important to pay attention to the details the child provides and ask their significance. This will also help the child sort out any cognitive confusions about the traumatic experience(s). The interviewer then proceeds to ask what the worst moment was for the child. It may not be what the interviewer would assume (Pynoos & Eth, 1986). This exchange may provide a particularly empathic moment for the child. It is also important to guide the child to approach the impact of the violence and physical mutilation witnessed. Some children need, for example, to restore an image of, for example, the murdered parent as physically intact or undamaged (Pynoos & Eth, 1986). Inquiries about the funeral of a murdered parent may be especially therapeutic. Having the child bring a photo of, for example, a murdered parent or a pet lost in a disaster may also aid in the grief process by balancing the intrusive traumatic memories with happier images. Explanations of death that agree with the child's culture and developmental stage as well as explanations and empathy for the child's trauma and resulting grief may provide the child with a sense of not being alone and of being understood. This intervention may also provide some symptomatic relief. For interpersonal trauma(s), the child's and adolescent's sense of justice and of human accountability will also need to be addressed in a culturally and developmentally appropriate manner (Pynoos & Eth, 1986).

For the 3- to 8-year-old child, it is important for the interviewer to provide support, safety, repeated and gentle clarifications of aspects of the story or the trauma that do not make sense, and to provide emotional labels for experiences (Pynoos & Eth, 1986). Because of their limited cognitive skills and sense of helplessness, the 3- to 8-year-old children have difficulty imagining alternative actions that they may have taken to reverse the trauma (Pynoos & Eth, 1986). They tend to fantasize about third-party intervention, choosing to flee, look away, or sleep (Pynoos & Eth, 1986). Providing labels for emotions and strengthening the children's active participation in seeking help will strengthen ego defenses. For example, in response to a 6-year-child's utterance, "My heart felt like it would jump out of my body" the interviewer may say, "You must have been really scared! It must be comforting to know that a heart can't jump out of a body." It is also important to make plans with the child and caregivers for the child's future emotional support. The interviewer may say, "The boy in your story must have been really frightened. When I feel really scared, I tell myself I am safe and when that doesn't work, I tell my friends I need to talk and they calm me down. What can you do when you are scared? . . . [give the child time to verbally respond]. That's a good idea, you can tell your mother (or current caregiver) or your teacher how you feel." Letting the preadolescent child regress for a time-limited period while in the interview may also be helpful. However, it is equally important to tell the child, "It is okay to cry or scream or throw things for a while in the office as long as no one and nothing gets hurt because this is a special place and a special interview; but other children may not like you if you do this in public places like school or the playground. It would make me and your mom sad if children didn't like you and you had to play alone, because I think you are special. It must be scary to feel out of control. What else can you do when you feel out of control? . . . [give the child time to verbally respond]. That's a good idea! Tell your teacher or your mom that you need help to feel in control again."

For 9- to 12-year-old children, it is important for the interviewer to (a) allow expression of imaginings; (b) help them identify reminders; (c) listen and understand their feelings; (d) provide support; (e) provide realistic information; (f) help them control their impulsive drives and behaviors; (g) form mental links between symptoms and the trauma; (h) urge them to engage in constructive activities; and (i) assist them to grieve with positive memories (Pynoos & Eth, 1986; Pynoos & Nader, 1993). School-age children tend to defend against their helplessness by imagining themselves to be not a witness of the trauma, but a participant. Some children may show violent or aggressive behaviors as a psychological defense (identifying with the aggressor). These inner plans of action include imagining calling the police, locking the doors, grabbing a weapon, and offering help to the victim (Pynoos & Eth, 1986; Pynoos & Nader, 1993). Short- and long-term group treatments such as child abuse survivor groups take these developmentally appropriate defenses into account by teaching the child to recognize precipitants to abuse. Recommendations of self-defense classes also strengthen this defense and help provide mastery of the traumatic experience(s).

For adolescents, the interviewer should (a) discuss feelings and human limitations; (b) provide support; (c) provide realistic information; (d) address impulse control and reckless behaviors; (e) form mental links between symptoms, angry and depressed feelings, or acting-out behaviors, and the trauma; (f) learn and understand about the stress response and normalize an adolescent's reactions; (g) suggest that they engage in constructive activities and positive life decisions; (h) assist them to grieve; and (i) help them to forgive (Pynoos & Eth, 1986; Pynoos & Nader, 1993). Adolescents tend to implicate their own actions in a more realistic fashion and over a much longer period of time. For example, an adolescent may painfully regret not unloading her father's gun 2 weeks before he murdered her mother; or an adolescent boy may continue to make plans to kill the man who raped his mother (Pynoos & Eth, 1986, p. 310). Some clinicians who work with urban adolescents have found that the beliefs espoused by Martin Luther King, Jr. (1963), in *Strength to Love*, to be helpful especially with angry adolescents who are victims of interpersonal trauma(s) or by-standers to violence. King states, "It is necessary to realize that the forgiving act must always be initiated by the person who has been wronged . . . Forgiveness does not mean ignoring what has been done or putting a false label on an evil act. It means that the evil act no longer remains as a barrier to the relationship . . . that the evil deed is no longer a mental block impeding a new relationship" (1963). This philosophy encourages em-powerment, does not deny or ignore the need for the child or adolescent to be coopera-tive in legal proceedings against a perpetrator or in making plans and building strategies for their own safety, but lifts the burden when justice is not a possibility; such as in the case of a child whose father killed his mother and siblings and then him-self or the case of repairing a relationship with an abusing parent who is remorseful and committed to participating in treatment, stopping the abusive behavior, and re-gaining a relationship with the child. With younger children, this philosophy is es-poused and modeled with the "emotionally corrective experiences" (Alexander & French, 1946) that take place between the therapist and child in individual psychother-apy. A preadolescent child is not developmentally ready to understand abstract philo-sophical and social concepts.

Issues of human accountability add considerably to the child's or adolescent's dif-ficulty over mastery. It is important for the interviewer to understand whom the child holds accountable for the violent act and what the motive was. Paramount questions to ask a preadolescent are "How come it happened?" and "What would make some-body do something like that?" (Pynoos & Eth, 1986, p. 309). The child may blame him- or herself. For example, a very depressed and constricted 7-year-old girl said, "Mommy killed herself because she said I was a rotten kid. She said she didn't want to live with me and that she wished I had never been born." She then cries, "If I were a good girl, my mommy would still be here." An 8-year-old boy may say, "Mommy yelled at Daddy and made him mad . . . so he hurt her." In these circumstances, it is important to comfort and educate the child. It is also important to discuss punishment and retaliation by giving children permission to express these feelings; for example, by allowing them to draw a picture of "What you'd like to see happen to the person who upset you" (Pynoos & Eth, 1986, p. 310). Anger at God, parents, or a helping professional, may also be expressed by a child who is the victim of non-interpersonal trauma such as a life-threatening illness or a disaster. It is important to allow the child to express these feelings. Then statements such as "I see it feels good to imag-ine getting back at the bad man who stabbed your father" . . . when you really couldn't have stopped him at the time"(Pynoos & Eth, 1986, p. 310); or "It must feel good to imagine stabbing the doctor with a needle so that he[she] understands that it hurts." The child's ego and superego (sense of right and wrong) needs to be sup-ported. It is important to explore the child's own impulse control by asking the child what he or she does when angry. The child may need to hear from the interviewer for example, that people are in charge of their own actions, that no one can make another do something he/she feels is wrong, that depression and alcoholism are illnesses that need treatment and that it was sad that their parent did not get treatment. It is impor-tant to let children know that because individuals do not control their anger or their bad emotions or fail to get help, when they cannot control themselves, some of these bad things happen. It is important to always stress to children that they do not have to be alone with their bad feelings and to explain how to obtain that needed help. A child may also be afraid of revenge from the perpetrator of the traumatic experience. It is important to inquire from the child and caregivers if violent threats to the child are a realistic concern. Reassurance and plans for safety need to be addressed. Sometimes a visit with the police officer or prosecuting attorney is helpful for the child who may be in danger or who needs to testify in court.

After trauma has been discussed in detail, the interviewer needs to be sensitive as to how physically and emotionally exhausting this was to the child or adolescent. Relaxation time and snacks should be offered (Pynoos & Eth, 1986). It is then important to ask the child about current stressors and functioning. In asking these questions, the interviewer will be diagnostically evaluating criteria for ASD and PTSD. Questions such as, what worries you most now? What are you looking forward to? What do you think your life will be like in 10 years? Will you get married? Have children? What type of job will you have? What do you do for fun? How is school going? These are important questions. The trauma experience may permanently change a child's view of the world. Childhood trauma studies have consistently found changes in orientation toward the future including negative expectation, a foreshortened future, and altered attitudes towards marriage, career, and having children (Eth & Pynoos, 1985; Terr, 1991). These attitudes have prognostic significance. The traumatized child needs to learn to re-experience hope, joy, and regain motivation to work and play for completion of the grieving and healing process. The clinical interviewer's review of the child's or adolescent's symptoms will determine the need for and type of future treatment(s).

The last stage of this trauma consultation interview is closure. The interviewer reviews with the child or adolescent what they have discussed and emphasizes how understandable, realistic, and universal the child's feelings and thoughts are. It is important to discuss the following with the child:

1. It is normal to have felt helpless, sad, scared and angry.
2. There may be times when something will remind you of these feelings and you may feel this way again.
3. Trusted adults are available who can help you with your feelings.
4. The child's bravery both in surviving the traumatic experience(s) and in talking with the interviewer about it should be acknowledged.
5. The child shall be asked to describe what was helpful and what was upsetting about the interview (Pynoos & Eth, 1986).

Some interviewers will give the child his or her professional card and telephone number and so leave the door open for future contact (Pynoos & Eth, 1986). Once the interview with the child has ended, the interviewer should summarize the interview, diagnosis, and recommendations to the parent or current caregiver. Some interviewers will allow the child to be in the room so that the child can participate in future treatment planning. For example, "One of the things Bobbie learned today, is that it is okay to feel afraid and angry when she thinks about her mother's murder. She also learned that it is helpful to come to you or her teacher when she is upset so she can talk about it. Bobbie also taught me a lot today about how cooperative and brave she is." When the interviewer feels the child will need further treatment, arrangements should be made and this issue should be addressed in closure. If the interviewer will not be the treating therapist, it is important for the interviewer to make a follow-up telephone call or to be present for a brief introduction to the new therapist.

General Psychiatric or Clinical Child Mental Health Assessment

The initial mental health assessment involves a structured interview for information gathering on the following critical topics. It is briefly presented here with special attention to red flags that may give the interviewer clues to the child's trauma and severity of response. This is an important time to remind the reader that children and adolescents usually do not present with a chief complaint of PTSD. Children, adolescents, and their families may pathologically deny the impact of interpersonal traumatic experiences as a way of coping. Red flags only mean more details need to be gathered. Red flags are not proof that a previously denied trauma occurred (such as child abuse). The reader is referred to other references (Lewis, 1991) for more details on the art of interviewing and assessing the child and adolescent patient. In the evaluation of preschool and school-age children, the parent may initially be seen alone. The child can be left with another caretaker in a playroom area. For older children, self-report instruments such as the Youth Self Report (Achenbach & Edelbrock, 1981), The State/Trait Anxiety Scale (Fox & Houston, 1983; Spielberger, 1973), and the Child Depression Inventory (Kovacs, 1985) can be given while a history is being obtained from the parent(s). It is helpful to have adolescents present while a history is being taken from the parent(s); unless an adolescent requests to be seen alone first. When parents and adolescents are seen together, it is important not to ignore the adolescents, but to always ask them if they agree with the parents' statement(s) and if they have anything else to add. Some adolescents request not to be present when asked. If this is the case, they can be given the self-report measures to fill out in the waiting room. Parents of adolescents should be given the opportunity to be seen alone to provide further and possibly important private and needed information on the family. The interviewer's clinical judgment on the parent-child relationship needs to be taken into account. Some clinicians find it helpful to obtain the following information on a one-page sheet to construct a time line of symptoms and life events:

- *Identifying information.* Child's name and names of current members of the household, telephone numbers of parents' work and residence, current grade, name, telephone number, and address of school, including name of homeroom teacher or guidance counselor. For children who do not live with two legally married parents, it is important to ask who has legal custody of the child and who is responsible for consent to treatment. Documentation of custody is needed for the medical or mental health record. The clinician can now start a timeline beginning with the oldest sibling and other siblings' dates of birth, the child's date of birth, and the parent and family social supports at the time of the child's birth.
- *Problem for Which the Child or Parent Is Seeking Help.* Take 15–20 minutes to understand the problem in the child's and parent's own words and then tell the parent, child, or adolescent that this will be explored in more detail later. The onset of and type of symptoms or behavioral problems should be added to the timeline.

- *Past History of Psychiatric, Family, or Mental Health Treatment(s).* Gather information on the type of treatment (inpatient, outpatient, school counseling), the age of the child when treatment started, the name of mental health provider(s), the place of treatment, reason for treatment, diagnosis(es) made, type of therapy undertaken and/or medications used, and the parent and child's understanding of their clinical effectiveness. This is a good time to get parent(s) and adolescent(s) to sign consent for previous medical and mental health records. Ask whether the child has ever been suicidal, homicidal, had or has a legal problem, or alcohol and/or substance problem(s). Details about these need to be obtained as well as current suicidal and homicidal risk(s). Put this information on the time line.

- *Past Medical and Developmental History.* Ask mother about her pregnancy with the child. Were there any complications? What was the child's birth weight? When did the child start babbling, crawling, saying his or her first words, walking, speaking two or more words at a time, and was toilet trained? Were there any accidents (bed-wetting or soiling) since successful toilet training? What was the child's infant and toddler personality like? Were there any personality changes? Were there any major family stresses at the time? Also, were there any separations from the parent and/caregivers and did any other family member have primary responsibility for the care of the child during the early years (e.g., grandmother)? If you refer to the developmental chart (Table 18.3), red flags are regression in developmental achievements and may include a previously outgoing curious child who becomes sullen, irritable, and mute, or a previously toilet-trained child who begins to have accidents, or a child who never had a problem sleeping alone, who has a period of months of night terrors.

  It is important to know whether the child ever had any medical problems. Ask specifically about hospitalizations, medical illnesses, surgeries, broken bones, failure to thrive, and accidents. Ask how the child's medical health has been in the current year. Who is the current pediatrician, including address and telephone number? Releases of information for previous medical records and for the child's pediatrician should be obtained at this time. Add all this to the time line.

- *School History.* When did the child start kindergarten or preschool? How did he or she adjust? Were there any separation problems? What were the child's grades in major subjects for each grade since starting school? Was he or she ever held back? Did he/she ever have problems with teachers or peers? Get details and add these to the time line. Red flags for trauma or stress symptoms may be a drop in grades, a previously well-behaved child who is now aggressive and oppositional or who displays signs of sexual acting out, or a child with separation anxiety disorder who is afraid to leave his or her mother because of fears of domestic violence. Also, ask about school functioning in the current year.

- *Child's Strengths and Weaknesses.* Ask the parent what they like most about their child, what their child's hobbies and interests are, who their friends are, and what they would like to see improve in their child's behavior. Add to the bottom of the time line page.

Depending on the amount of time left, ask more about the current problem presented. Then interview the child or adolescent alone for understanding of the current problem, to obtain psychiatric symptoms, and to obtain a mental status exam. When the child is being seen alone, it is a good opportunity to have the parent fill out self-reports on the child such as the Child Behavior Checklist (Achenbach & Edelbrock, 1983), the State/Trait Anxiety Scale (parent version; Fox & Houston, 1983; Spielberger, 1973), the Child Dissociative Scale (Putnam & Peterson, 1994), and the Conners Rating Scale (parent version; Conners & Barkley, 1985). Unless there is sufficient time, it is not recommended to have the child undergo the trauma interview. This interview should be explained to the parent and child or adolescent in a developmentally appropriate fashion and rescheduled at a convenient date. This does not mean that the child should not be allowed to talk about the trauma; but it is not fair to the child or wise to go into trauma details that may bring out the emotional impact of the trauma without appropriate time for closure. Sufficient time will be needed to briefly go over the self-reports, summarize your clinical findings or the child's history from your timeline, answer questions, and make recommendations.

Methods for Elucidation of Symptoms of ASD and PTSD

The evaluation of Criterion A of ASD and PTSD will be assessed during the child trauma interview and from discussions with parent(s) or current caregivers. It may also be assessed by reviewing previous medical and mental health records, school records, police reports, child protective services reports, and/or newspaper articles. In some cases, the interviewing clinician may suspect that traumatic experiences have occurred, but they are denied by the child or the parent. In these cases, structured interviews may be helpful. Semistructured interviews that may be used to assess for anxiety symptoms and trauma history include the Anxiety Disorders Interview Schedule for Children, the Child and Adolescent Psychiatric Assessment (for review, see Stallings & March, 1995), and the PTSD Reaction Index (Pynoos et al., 1987).

Dissociative Symptoms

These symptoms are included as part of Criterion B in the *DSM-IV* ASD diagnosis. These symptoms include detachment, "being in a daze," derealization, and dissociative amnesia. Detachment or numbing, means that the child has an absence of emotional responsiveness such as joy when given a favorite toy or lack of anger when insulted, teased at school, or threatened. Children with these symptoms usually have constricted affect and a limited sense of humor. "Being in a daze" means the child has periods of reduction in awareness of his or her surroundings. Teachers may notice that children with this symptom "stare into space" and have difficulty paying attention in school. The therapist may notice that a child stares and becomes mute when aspects of the trauma are discussed in therapy. Children may be having frightening flashbacks during this time period. For example, 14-year-old Kevin was noted to be staring into space for 20 minutes during a very intense adolescent group therapy session. When asked later what he was experiencing, he stated he saw his and his sister's past abuse "as if it were on film." Derealization is a difficult symptom to elicit. Sometimes children will say that "it was so horrible that it did not seem real." Billy, an adolescent with a history of documented severe emotional and physical abuse, continues to have difficulty believing "that my mother was that cruel and that my memories are real." Billy sometimes has brief periods of believing that his "life is not real and that I do not exist." Depersonalization is another painful negative symptom that is hard to elicit. Figuring out if the child or adolescent is denying his or her human needs for comfort, love, attention, and expression of feelings may be one method of eliciting these symptoms. Depersonalization, derealization, and numbing are symptoms that seem to occur together. These are emotionally painful and may trigger self-destructive behaviors such as self-mutilation and alcohol and substance abuse. For example, Billy had a brief problem with alcohol abuse during a stressful period in his life. Billy's clinician felt that mother's intense denial of the abuse precipitated increased symptoms of depersonalization and detachment that triggered this behavior.

Dissociative amnesia is another important symptom that is difficult to elicit and should never be taken at face value. Children with histories of trauma will frequently tell the therapist that they do not remember as a way to avoid talking about the trauma. This is an avoidance symptom and not a dissociative symptom. When conducting the trauma interview, if the child has clear gaps in memory it will become obvious to the interviewer in the reconstruction of the traumatic event. It is always helpful to clarify with the child, "whether they don't remember or they just don't want to talk about it." Honesty in therapy needs to be addressed while still respecting the child's fears. Children will usually cooperate if asked to tell only what they are comfortable with or if asked how would they feel more comfortable in talking about the trauma. In some cases, when the trauma consultant is not an ongoing member of the child's treatment team, children will feel more comfortable if their treating therapist can be present in the interview. Self-report instruments are often helpful in assessing these symptoms. While some adolescents and parents find questions about dissociative experiences "silly," others find relief in learning that others feel the same way. It is always important to review the completed dissociative experiences self-reports with the parent or child and to clarify any positive responses. Self-report instruments that may be used to assess dissociative symptoms include the Child Dissociative Checklist, a 20-item parent report measure (Putnam & Peterson, 1994), and the Adolescent Dissociative Experiences Scale, a 30-item, self-report measure (Armstrong, Putnam, Carlson, Libero, & Smith, 1997). These are based on the Dissociative Experiences Scale (Bernstein & Putnam, 1986) and take less than 10 minutes to complete. They tap dimensions of amnesia, passive influence, depersonalization/derealization, identity disturbance, and absorption and enthrallment (Carlson et al., 1993).

Reexperiencing Symptoms

These symptoms are included as part of Criterion B in the *DSM-IV* PTSD diagnosis and Criterion C in the *DSM-IV* ASD diagnosis. Reexperiencing symptoms can best be conceptualized as a classically conditioned response. Something externally or internally (the conditioned stimulus) triggers unwanted and distressful recurrent and intrusive memories of the traumatic experience(s) (the unconditioned stimulus). These intrusive phenomena take the form of distressing nightmares or night terrors, dissociative flashback episodes, and psychological distress and physical reactivity on exposure to traumatic reminders. In young children, these intrusive thoughts may be part of repetitive play or trauma-specific reenactment(s). In eliciting these symptoms, it is important to try to reconstruct the child's state of mind and behavior prior to the symptom in an effort to isolate the traumatic reminder(s). The key to treating these symptoms is to identify and teach the child how to effectively deal with these traumatic reminders. Reexperiencing symptoms can be easily misdiagnosed as psychotic behavior. A few case examples will be presented to clarify these points.

Six-year-old Sarah has been a patient in a state mental hospital for 1 year. She was severely sexually abused by a mentally ill parent. In the daytime, Sarah functioned well at school and in group treatment(s). However, every evening Sarah heard voices of the abuser calling her "bad words." Sarah would then bang her head against the bed or wall and on occasion has caused herself injury. When an astute mental health worker noted that Sarah's behavior worsened when she did not have a roommate or when she was placed in seclusion, she asked Sarah what would help her regain control. Sarah reported that she wanted to sleep by the nursing station because she was afraid to be alone. This intervention resulted in Sarah's feeling safer, in exhibiting less self-destructive behavior, and in eventual tapering of her antipsychotic medications. Billy, who had multiple psychiatric admissions throughout his childhood, was reported to have multiple episodes of acting out "crazy behavior" at his group home. He would point at the wall and yell vulgar words at himself. These episodes were usually preceded by telephone conversations with his mother. Since mother frequently told Billy all of her problems, including her contention that his father's death was Billy's fault, it was felt that Billy might be reenacting his mother's behavior toward himself. This flashback was thought of as Billy's unsuccessful way to master his trauma. The next time, Billy had a flashback, staff surrounded him, told him who he was, how old he was, where he was, and that they were concerned and cared about him. He was then able to cry and discuss his mother's upsetting words. The next time his mother screamed at him on the telephone, Billy was instructed to tell her that he would talk to her another time when she had regained control. Two years after this intervention, Billy has had no further flashbacks or hospitalizations.

Avoidance Symptoms

These symptoms are included as part of Criterion C in the *DSM-IV* PTSD diagnosis and Criterion D in the *DSM-IV* ASD diagnosis. Avoidance symptoms can be thought of as ways to control painful and distressing reexperiencing of symptoms. Efforts to avoid thoughts, feelings, conversations, activities, places, people, and memories associated with the trauma help decrease the traumatic reminder(s). However, this also results in diminished interest in others, feelings of detachment from others, a restricted range of affect, and a sense of a foreshortened future. Avoidance feelings cause great psychosocial impairment and can lead to social isolation and comorbid major depression or dysthymia. In assessing for these symptoms, one needs to learn what changes occurred in the child's premorbid personality and psychosocial functioning. Avoidance of traumatic reminders of interpersonal trauma can cause a child to have difficulty handling strong emotions such as anger, joy, or intimate relationships because strong and out-of-control emotions may have precipitated the traumatic act. In children who have suffered multiple aversive experiences, reconstruction of their premorbid personality may be very difficult and will involve careful and detailed information on their developmental history.

Symptoms of Increased Arousal or Marked Anxiety

These symptoms are included as part of Criterion D in the *DSM-IV* PTSD diagnosis and Criterion E in the *DSM-IV* ASD diagnosis. These symptoms include difficulty falling or staying asleep, irritable mood or angry outbursts, difficulty concentrating, hypervigilance, and exaggerated startle response. These symptoms are part of the biological stress systems response, or the fight-or-flight reaction. It is important to be specific when eliciting these symptoms. In oppositional children and adolescents, who may be victims of interpersonal traumatic experience(s), it is better to ask open-ended questions about a symptom rather than to ask only if a symptom is present. For example, if you ask most children and adolescents how they slept last night, they will say "fine." It is better to ask about their sleep by asking the following: What time do you go to your room for the night? Do you share a room? What time do you get in bed and what time do you fall asleep? Do you ever get up during the night? Does your mother or sibling tell you that you wake up screaming? Have you ever found yourself waking up on the floor and do not remember how you got there? Do you feel rested when you wake up? Do you ever have bad dreams?

Most children and adolescents will tell you that they feel irritable or angry or mad. They will seldom tell you that they feel bad, sad, or depressed because they tend to perceive these questions as value judgments. Most parents or caretakers, and/or teachers will be able to give accurate reports of a child's angry outburst and difficulty concentrating. They may not be able to give accurate reports of internalizing symptoms. Children and adolescents will usually say that they can control themselves or pay attention if they want to. Some children will be able to spontaneously report difficulty concentrating because of intrusive thoughts. It is important not to take a child's or adolescents answer at face value, but to gently ask more detailed questions. Observing a child filling out a self-report assessment instrument in the waiting room will also give the clinician useful information about these symptoms as well as about hypervigilance. Hypervigilance and exaggerated startle response may be difficult to assess because most people are hypervigilant in a new situation and most people startle. Details and examples will help the clinician discriminate normal from exaggerated hypervigilance and startle. For example, some children will become frozen or jump at traumatic reminders such as loud noises that resemble gunfire.

Symptoms of increased arousal such as anxiety, insomnia, restlessness, and poor concentration are also included as symptoms in *DSM-IV* major depressive disorder and generalized anxiety disorder. Therefore, it may be helpful to have children and adolescents fill out self-reports on anxiety and depression. The Cognitive and Somatic State and Trait Anxiety Scale (parent and child versions; Fox & Houston, 1983; Spielberger, 1973), a 27-item self-report inventory designed to assess both state and trait anxiety, the Child Depression Inventory (Kovacs, 1985), a widely used 21-item self-report measure of depressive symptomatology, and the Conners Parent and Teacher Rating Scales (Conners, 1985), a self-report on restlessness and attention deficit disorder symptoms, each take less than 5 minutes to complete and provide useful clinical as well as research information.

Duration of Disturbance of Symptoms

As stated, the duration of symptoms of *DSM-IV* ASD is from a minimum of 2 days to less than or equal to 4 weeks. The duration of symptoms for *DSM-IV* PTSD is for 1 month or longer. Most parents, children, and adolescents can report whether a symptom occurred for a day, a week, a month, months, or a year or more. It is important to be specific about time periods. School-age children may be able to report the grade during which the symptoms started rather than their age or the month and year. Sometimes, a child will present with symptoms months or years after a trauma. It is important to be aware of this and to clarify whether or not there was a past diagnosis of PTSD that is now in partial remission versus making a new diagnosis of another anxiety disorder such as generalized anxiety disorder.

Symptoms Causing Clinically Significant Impairment

These symptoms are included as part of Criterion F in the PTSD and ASD diagnoses. Clinically significant impairment must occur in social, school, or family functioning. An interviewer may meet a resilient child or adolescent who has enough PTSD symptoms to make the diagnosis, but does not suffer from psychosocial impairment. A diagnosis of adjustment disorder may be more appropriate. However, therapy, if requested, needs to be trauma specific. The following self-reports are not only good for assessment of psychopathology, but also for psychosocial functioning: the Child Behavior Checklist (CBCL; Achenbach & Edelbrock, 1983) and the Youth Self Report (Achenbach & Edelbrock, 1981) are 113-item paper-and-pencil questionnaires to be filled out by the parental informant and by the child, respectively. These can be completed in 20 minutes or less. These reports yield social competency, externalizing, internalizing, and total behavioral scores, and are currently one of the most widely utilized instruments for the assessment of childhood psychopathology. The Children's Global Assessment Scale (Shaffer et al., 1983), was developed to reflect the lowest level of functioning for a child or adolescent during a specified time period. It is a quick assessment instrument (5 minutes) that can also be used periodically to monitor progress in treatment. It should be noted that whenever using self-reports, a clinician needs to assess a child's and parents' reading abilities. Having the child and parent read you the first few questions is a gentle way to assess their understanding of what is being asked and can be helpful.

Brief Psychotherapy

Trauma debriefing and trauma consultation will not be adequate treatment for many severely exposed children and adolescents. In this case, brief, focal individual psychotherapy or long-term therapy may be recommended. Brief therapy may require many months of treatment and may extend beyond the first anniversary of the traumatic event(s). It permits a contextual understanding of the trauma within the life situation and culture of the child and family. Brief psychotherapy has several goals: (a) to counteract traumatic hindrances to normal functioning and development; (b) to identify the child's ongoing processing of traumatic aspects of the event and its aftermath and to rework specific moments of the traumatic event; (c) to address ongoing issues of helplessness, self-blame, and passivity; (d) to enhance mastery of traumatic intrusive phenomena; (e) to monitor reactions to anticipated and unexpected traumatic reminders; (f) to address the dysregulation of aggression; (g) to explore the interaction between select existing intrapsychic conflicts on the emerging personality and specific features of the trauma; (h) to restore the capacity for normal play; and (i) to address secondary stresses subsequent to the trauma (Pynoos & Nader, 1993).

Traumatic experiences often lead to many changes in a child's life situation including medical treatment for injuries, relocation, school changes, loss of peers, separations, changes in parenting or guardianship, death of loved ones, and involvement in ongoing criminal procedures. The clinician must be prepared to monitor the child's mental activity, peer relationships, self-esteem, school performance, and be active with the family, school, medical, and judicial system, including improvising practical ways of helping the child and family cope with their current life situation (Pynoos & Nader, 1993). During brief therapy, the child may continue to play out a particular aspect of the trauma until further resolution. A clinician may note that certain details are omitted that may represent a disturbing aspect of the trauma. As the child continues to rework the traumatic experience(s), there should be a progression toward the most terrifying and irreversibly damaging moments. Moments of the traumatic event(s) may evoke conflicts related to maternal care and parental protection (Pynoos & Nader, 1993). The traumatic event(s) is a loss and needs to be grieved. The event may have resulted in the very real loss of a loved one or peer, or an injury that involves a temporary or permanent loss of function, or of a loss in faith and trust in a parent or in humanity. During therapy, children may process the event by undergoing stages of grief and bereavement: shock and denial, anger, bargaining, depression, and acceptance as described by Bowlby (1980) and Kubler-Ross (1969).

Family therapy may also be helpful after a traumatic experience(s). The primary goal is to educate family members about posttraumatic reactions and to validate and legitimize each other's psychological distress, to work through the trauma, and to provide mutual support. The goals to assist the child are: (a) restore the child's sense of security; (b) validate the child's affective responses rather than dismiss them; (c) anticipate and respond to situations in which the child will need added emotional support such as traumatic reminders and feelings of vulnerability; and (d) assist the family in minimizing secondary stresses and adversities (Pynoos & Nader, 1993).

Group intervention can also be an important therapeutic agent during the immediate weeks or months after traumatic experience(s). It also offers the opportunity to reinforce the normative nature of the child's or adolescent's reactions and recovery, to share mutual experiences and concerns, to address common fears and avoidant behavior, to increase tolerance for disturbing affects, to provide early attention to more severe depressive or PTSD symptoms, and to aid recovery through age-appropriate and situation-specific problem solving (Pynoos & Nader, 1993). Group treatment is especially valuable for adolescents by permitting the therapeutic working through of trauma-related conflicts in peer relationships.

Long-Term Therapy-Pulsed Intervention

Pynoos and Nader (1993) suggest a suspension of short-term therapy as an alternative to long-term therapy. It is based on the model of Wallerstein (1990) proposed to treat children of divorce. In such a strategy, an acute phase of treatment is followed by planned periods of consultation in accordance with the time trajectory of trauma recovery and projected achievement of developmental stages. It is designed to help maintain the child's normal development through ongoing communication with the family and the child. This treatment must be individually tailored and based on the treatment needs of the child and family. For certain children and adolescents, it may provide a cost-effective alternative to weekly individual long-term psychotherapy.

Long-Term Therapy

Indications for long-term treatment, or individual weekly psychotherapy for a period of 1 year or longer, include severe impact, intensity, and duration of traumatic experience(s).

If a child experiences multiple traumas, massive violence, loss of family members, friends, and/or multiple personal assaults, life-threatening injuries, and personal or health losses, the therapeutic processing of trauma and bereavement often require more extended treatment (Pynoos & Nader, 1993). Children with previous psychiatric problems will also likely require longer term treatment. For interpersonal trauma(s) such as domestic violence, child maltreatment, or death of a parent by suicide, longer term treatment is also recommended to address issues of the child's personality formation and to repair the ability to trust and form meaningful relationships. One major longitudinal concern is the dysregulation or impaired development of empathy and conscience that can accompany exposure to violence. There may be continued risk of life-threatening or violent behavior throughout adolescence. A major goal of therapy is to return the child to a normal developmental path with a mature conscience, and as a result, to alleviate dangerous self-destructive reenactment behavior (Pynoos & Nader, 1993). Principles, goals, and techniques of long-term child psychotherapy can be reviewed elsewhere (Pearson, 1968; Ruben, 1974). Long-Term Therapy-Pulsed Intervention therapy can also be utilized as an alternative to longer term therapy or individual weekly psychotherapy for a period of 2 years or longer.

Pharmacotherapy

Children and/or adolescents who have at least moderate psychosocial impairment from ASD, PTSD, and/or any comorbid psychiatric diagnosis that have not responded to brief (2 to 4 weeks) psychotherapy or are so severely affected as to require inpatient treatment, may be helped with psychotropic medication. Children should undergo a physical exam by a pediatrician for general health concerns. Sometimes, ASD and PTSD symptoms are the results of physical illness(es) that may require more detailed medical workup and treatment. Some children will need to undergo laboratory blood testing (including CBC with differential, thyroid function studies, electrolytes, BUN, creatinine, urinalysis, urine toxicology screen, urine pregnancy screen), and an EKG as part of a general health assessment and to screen out for contraindications for medication. Symptoms of dissociation, concentration problems, attentional deficiencies, and irritability can result from a partial complex seizure disorder or more rarely from a brain injury. More sophisticated neurological and neuropsychiatric testing such as a neurological exam, a sleep-deprived EEG, and an MRI scan of the brain, as well as complete psychoeducational and neuropsychological testing, may be indicated.

Psychopharmacological treatment is indicated for symptoms of hyperarousal or fight-or-flight reaction biological stress systems dysregulation such as reduced attention and learning, sleep disturbance, restricted affect, anxiety, and/or depression. To date, there are no published double-blind psychotropic treatment trials in children and adolescents who suffer from PTSD. Before choosing a psychopharmacological agent, it is important to identify target symptoms. It is also important to try to separate the psychiatric symptoms prior to and after the trauma. For example, a child with premorbid attention deficit disorder may best be treated with a tricylic antidepressant for target symptoms of sleep disturbance and difficulty concentrating. Tricyclic antidepressants have been shown to down-regulate the biological stress systems (De Bellis, Gold, Geracioti, Listwak, & Kling, 1993). Some have reported good clinical response in open trials with other psychopharmacological agents that down-regulate the stress systems, such as clonidine (Perry, 1994; Pynoos & Nader, 1993), propranolol (Famularo, Kinsherff, & Fenton, 1988), and benzodiazepines (Allen, Rapoport, & Swedo, 1993). These drugs however, need to be carefully monitored for side effects of sedation, orthostatic hypotension, memory and concentration impairments, and paradoxical behavioral disinhibition (Amaya-Jackson & March, 1995). Tricyclic antidepressants are effective in adult major depression (Goodwin & Jamison, 1990), but are somewhat less effective in adult PTSD (reviewed by Amaya-Jackson & March, 1995). Tricyclic antidepressants have not been shown to be effective in child and adolescent depression (Brent, Ryan, Dahl, & Birmaher, 1995). To date, the only antidepressant that has been proven to be effective in child and adolescent depression and anxiety disorders and in adult PTSD is the serotonin uptake inhibitor, fluoxetine (Birmaher et al., 1994; Emslie, Rush, Weinberg, Hughes, & Kowatch, 1995; Van der Kolk et al., 1994). Since fluoxetine will also down-regulate the biological stress systems (De Bellis et al., 1993) and does not have adverse cardiac effects, it may be a promising psychopharmacological treatment agent. The psychopharmacological treatment of child and adolescent PTSD is an area that needs further study.

SUMMARY

The description of *DSM-IV* PTSD and ASD was reviewed in children and adolescents. Traumatic experiences were arbitrarily divided into interpersonal and non-interpersonal traumas. Children are thought to be at greater risk for victimization by interpersonal than by non-interpersonal traumas. PTSD in childhood has psychopathological and developmental consequences. Developmental consequences may include biological changes in stress systems as well as failures to obtain important psychological developmental achievements. Current clinical treatments including psychological first aid, the trauma consultation child interview, the general clinical child mental health assessment, methods for elucidation of PTSD symptoms, brief psychotherapy, pulsed intervention therapy, long-term psychotherapy, and psychopharmacological treatments, were reviewed. Since there are no empirical studies evaluating treatment of children and adolescents with PTSD to date, current state-of-the-art treatment approaches presented were clinically derived. Although trauma in childhood may have a profound and long-lasting impact on development, it is always helpful and hopeful to note that individual children strive toward growth. Clinicians who struggle with these children as they work together through these children's traumatic experience(s), may be rewarded by their observations of an individual child's courage in undertaking each developmental stride.

REFERENCES

Achenbach, T. M., & Edelbrock, C. S. (1981). *Youth self-report for ages 11–18*. Burlington: University of Vermont.

Achenbach, T. M., & Edelbrock, C. S. (1983). *Manual for the Child Behavior Checklist*. Burlington, VT: Queen City Printers.

Alexander, F., & French, T. M. (1946). *Psychoanalytic therapy: Principles and application*. New York: Ronald Press.

Allen, A. J., Rapoport, J. L., & Swedo, S. E. (1993). Psychopharmacologic treatment of childhood anxiety disorders. *Child and Adolescent Psychiatric Clinics of North America, 2,* 795–817.

Amaya-Jackson, L., & March, J. S., (1995). Posttraumatic Stress Disorder. In J. S. March (Ed.), *Anxiety disorders in children and adolescents* (pp. 276–300). New York: Guilford Press.

American Psychiatric Association. (1987). *Diagnostic and statistical manual of mental disorders* (3rd ed., rev., pp. 247–251). Washington, DC: Author.

American Psychiatric Association. (1994). *Diagnostic and statistical manual of mental disorders* (4th ed., pp. 424–432). Washington, DC: Author.

Armstrong, J. G., Putnam, F. W., Carlson, E. B., Libero, D. Z., & Smith, S. R. (in press). Development and validation of a measure of adolescent dissociation: The adolescent dissociative experiences scale. *Journal of Nervous and Mental Disease.*

Aston-Jones, G., Valentino, R. J., Van Bockstaele, E. J., & Meyerson, A. T. (1994). Locus coeruleus, stress, and PTSD: Neurobiological and clinical parallels. In M. M. Murburg (Ed.), *Catecholamine function in Posttraumatic Stress Disorder: Emerging concepts* (pp. 17–62). Washington, DC: American Psychiatric Press.

Bandura, A. (1986). *Social foundations of thought and action: A social cognitive theory.* Englewood Cliffs, NJ: Prentice-Hall.

Benkelfat, C. (1993). Serotonergic mechanisms in psychiatric disorders: New research tools, new ideas. *International Clinical Psychopharmacology, 8*(Suppl. 2), 53–56.

Berkowitz, M. (1987). Therapist survival: Maximizing generativity and minimizing burnout. *Psychotherapy in Private Practice, 5,* 85–89.

Bernstein, E. M., & Putnam, F. W. (1986). Development, reliability and validity of a dissociation scale. *Journal of Nervous and Mental Disease, 174,* 727–735.

Birmaher, B., Waterman, G. S., Ryan, N., Cully, M., Balach, L., Ingram, J., & Brodsky, M. (1994). Fluoxetine for childhood anxiety disorders. *Journal of the American Academy of Child and Adolescent Psychiatry, 33,* 993–999.

Bowlby, J. (1980). *Loss: Sadness and depression.* New York: Basic Books.

Bremner, J. D., Randall, P., Scott, T. M., Bronen, R. A., Southwick, S. M., Seibyl, J. P., Delaney, R. C., McCarthy, G., Charney, D. S., & Innis, R. B. (1995). MRI-based measurement of hippocampal volume in patients with combat-related Posttraumatic Stress Disorder. *American Journal of Psychiatry, 152,* 973–981.

Bremner, J. D., Scott, T. M., Delaney, R. C., Southwick, S. M., Mason, J. W., Johnson, D. R., Innis, R. B., McCarthy, G., & Charney, D. S. (1993). Deficits in short-term memory in Posttraumatic Stress Disorder. *American Journal of Psychiatry, 150,* 1015–1019.

Brent, D. A., Ryan, N., Dahl, R., & Birmaher, B. (1995). Early-onset mood disorders. In F. E. Bloom & D. J. Kupfer (Eds.), *Psychopharmacology: The fourth generation of progress* (pp. 1631–1642). New York: Raven Press.

Breslau, N., Davis, G. C., Andreski, P., & Peterson, E. (1991). Traumatic events and Posttraumatic Stress Disorder in an urban population of young adults. *Archives General of Psychiatry, 48,* 218–222.

Carlson, E. B., Putnam, F. W., Ross, C. A., Torem, M., Coons, P., Dill, D. L., Loewenstein, R. J., & Braun, B. G. (1993). Validity of the Dissociative Experiences Scale in screening for multiple personality disorder: A multicenter study. *American Journal of Psychiatry, 150,* 1030–1036.

Centers for Disease Control. (1984). *Violent crime: Summary of morbidity.* Atlanta: Violence Epidemiology Branch.

Centers for Disease Control. (1988). Health status of Vietnam veterans: Psychosocial characteristics. *Journal of the American Medical Association, 259,* 2701–2707.

Charney, D. S., Deutch, A. Y., Krystal, J. H., Southwich, S. M., & Davis, M. (1993). Psychobiological mechanisms of Posttraumatic Stress Disorder. *Archives of General Psychiatry, 50,* 294–305.

Chrousos, G. P., & Gold, P. W. (1992). The concepts of stress and stress system disorders: Overview of physical and behavioral homeostases. *Journal of the American Medical Association, 267,* 1244–1252.

Clark, D. B. (1994, June). *Trauma and alcohol abuse in adolescents.* Paper presented at the meeting of the Research Society on Alcoholism, Maui, Hawaii.

Conners, C. K., & Barkley, R. A. (1985). Rating scales and checklists for child psychopharmacology. *Psychopharmacology Bulletin, 21,* 809–843.

Conte, J. R. (1991). Overview of child sexual abuse. In A. Tasman & S. M. Goldfinger (Eds.), *Review of psychiatry* (pp. 292–294). Washington, DC: American Psychiatric Press.

Davidson, J. R. T., & Fairbank, J. A. (1993). The epidemiology of Posttraumatic Stress Disorder. In J. R. T. Davidson & E. B. Foa (Eds.), *Posttraumatic Stress Disorder: DSM-IV and beyond* (pp. 147–169). Washington, DC: American Psychiatric Press.

Davidson, S., & Smith, R. (1990). Traumatic experiences in psychiatric outpatients. *Journal of Traumatic Stress Studies, 3,* 459–475.

De Bellis, M. D., Chrousos, G. P., Dorn, L. D., Burke, L., Helmers, K., Kling, M. A., Trickett, P. K., & Putnam, F. W. (1994). Hypothalamic-pituitary-adrenal axis dysregulation in sexually abused girls. *Journal of Clinical Endocrinology and Metabolism, 78,* 249–255.

De Bellis, M. D., Gold, P. W., Geracioti, T. D., Listwak, S. J., & Kling, M. A. (1993). Association of fluoxetine treatment with reductions in CSF concentrations of corticotropin-releasing hormone and arginine vasopressin in patients with major depression. *American Journal of Psychiatry, 150,* 656–657.

De Bellis, M. D., Lefter, L., Trickett, P. K., & Putnam, F. W. (1994). Urinary catecholamine excretion in sexually abused girls. *Journal of the American Academy of Child and Adolescent Psychiatry, 33,* 320–327.

De Bellis, M. D., & Putnam, F. W. (1994). The psychobiology of childhood maltreatment. *Child and Adolescent Psychiatric Clinics of North America, 3,* 663–677.

de Wilde, E. J., Kienhorst, I. C.W. M., Diekstra, R. F.W., & Wolters, W. H.G. (1992). The relationship between adolescent suicidal behavior and life events in childhood and adolescence. *American Journal of Psychiatry, 149,* 45–51.

Edwards, E., Harkins, K., Wright, G., & Menn, F. (1990). Effects of bilateral adrenalectomy on the induction of learned helplessness. *Behavioral Neuropsychopharmacology, 3,* 109–114.

Emslie, G., Rush, A. J., Weinberg, W. A., Hughes, C., & Kowatch, R. (1995). The frequency of remission, relapse and recurrence in children and adolescents with MDD. *Biological Psychiatry, 37,* 594.

Erikson, E. H. (1963). *Childhood and society.* New York: Norton.

Eth, S., & Pynoos, R. (1985). *Posttraumatic stress disorders in children.* Washington, DC: American Psychiatric Association.

Famularo, R., Kinsherff, R., & Fenton, T. (1988). Propranolol treatment for childhood Posttraumatic Stress Disorder, acute type. *American Journal of the Diseases of Children, 142,* 1244–1247.

Fox, J. E., & Houston, B. K. (1983). Distinguishing between cognitive and somatic trait and state anxiety in children. *Journal of Personality and Social Psychology, 45,* 862–870.

Friedrich, W. N. (1993). Sexual victimization and sexual behavior in children: A review of recent literature. *Child Abuse and Neglect, 17,* 59–66.

Gesell, A. (1968). *The mental growth of the preschool child.* New York: Macmillan.

Gesell, A., & Amatruda, C. (1974). *Gesell and Amatruda's developmental diagnosis: The evaluation and management of normal and abnormal neuropsychologic development in infancy and early childhood.* Hagerstown, MD: Harper & Row.

Giaconia, R. M., Reinherz, H. Z., Silverman, A. B., Pakiz, B., Frost, A. K., & Cohen, E. (1995). Trauma and Posttraumatic Stress Disorder in a community population of older adolescents. *Journal of the American Academy of Child and Adolescent Psychiatry, 34,* 1369–1380.

Glazer, J. P. (1991). Psychiatric aspects of cancer in childhood and adolescence. In M. Lewis (Ed.), *Child and adolescent psychiatry: A comprehensive textbook* (pp. 964–977). Baltimore: Williams & Wilkins.

Goldstein, G., van Kammen, W., Shelly, C., Miller, D. J., & van Kammen, D. P. (1987). Survivors of imprisonment in the Pacific Theater during World War II. *American Journal of Psychiatry, 144,* 1210–1213.

Goodwin, F. K., & Jamison, K. R. (1990). *Manic-depressive illness* (pp. 416–447). New York: Oxford University Press.

Goodwin, J. (1988). Posttraumatic stress symptoms in abused children. *Journal of the American Academy of Child and Adolescent Psychiatry, 22,* 231–237.

Green, A. (1985). Children traumatized by physical abuse. In S. Eth & R. S. Pynoos (Eds.), *Posttraumatic stress in children* (pp. 133–154). Washington, DC: American Psychiatric Press.

Green, B. L., Grace, M. C., & Gleser, G. C. (1985). Long-term impairment following the Beverly Hills Supper Club fire. *Journal of Consulting and Clinical Psychology, 53,* 672–678.

Grosch, W. N., & Olsen, D. C. (1994). *When helping starts to hurt: A new look at burnout among psychotherapists.* New York: Norton.

Helzer, J., Robins, L. N., & McEvoy, L. (1987). Posttraumatic Stress Disorder in the general population: Findings of the Epidemiologic Catchment Area Survey. *New England Journal of Medicine, 317,* 1630–1634.

Herman, J. L. (1993). Sequelae of prolonged and repeated trauma: Evidence for a complex posttraumatic syndrome (DESNOS). In J. Davidson & E. Foa (Eds.), *Posttraumatic Stress Disorder: DSM-IV and beyond* (pp. 213–228). Washington, DC: American Psychiatric Press.

Jones, D. R. (1985). Secondary disaster victims: The emotional effects of recovering and identifying human remains. *American Journal of Psychiatry, 142,* 303–307.

Kilpatrick, D. G., Saunders, B. E., Veronen, L. J., Best, C. L., & Von, J. M. (1987). Criminal victimization: Lifetime prevalence, reporting to police, and psychological impact. *Crime and Delinquency, 33,* 479–489.

King, M. L., Jr. (1963). *Strength to love* (pp. 49–57). Philadelphia: Fortress Press.

Kinzie, J. D., Sack, W., Angell, R., & Clarke, G. (1989). A three-year follow-up of Cambodian children young people traumatized as children. *Journal of the American Academy of Child and Adolescent Psychiatry, 28,* 501–504.

Kinzie, J. D., Sack, W., Angell, R., Manson, S., & Ben, R. (1986). The psychiatric effects of massive trauma on Cambodian children: 1. The children. *Journal of the American Academy of Child and Adolescent Psychiatry, 25,* 370–376.

Kluznik, J. C., Speed, N., Van Valkenburg, C., & Magraw, R. (1986). Forty-year follow-up of U.S. prisoners of war. *American Journal of Psychiatry, 143,* 1443–1446.

Kohlberg, L. (1964). Development of moral character and moral ideology. In M. L. Hoffman & L. W. Hoffman, (Eds.), *Review of child development research* (p. 383). New York: Russell-Sage Foundation.

Kosten, T. R., Mason, J. W., Giller, E. L., Ostroff, R. B., & Harkness, L. (1987). Sustained urinary norepinephrine and epinephrine elevation in Posttraumatic Stress Disorder. *Psychoneuroendocrinology, 12,* 13–20.

Kovacs, M. (1985). The Children's Depression Inventory (CDI). *Psychopharmacology Bulletin, 21,* 995–998.

Kubler-Ross, E. (1969). *On death and dying.* New York: Macmillan.

Kulka, R. A., Schlenger, W. E., Fairbank, J. A., Hough, R. L., Jordan, B. K., Marmar, C. R., & Weiss, D. S. (1990). *Trauma and the Vietnam War generation: Report of findings from the National Vietnam Veterans Readjustment Study.* New York: Brunner/Mazel.

Lewis, M. (1991). Psychiatric assessment of infants, children, and adolescents. In M. Lewis (Ed.), *Child and adolescent psychiatry: A comprehensive textbook* (pp. 447–463). Baltimore: Williams & Wilkins.

Logue, J. N., Melick, M. E., & Hansen, H. (1981). Research issues and directions in the epidemiology of health effects of disasters. *Epidemiology Review, 3,* 140–162.

Lyons, J. A. (1987). Posttraumatic Stress Disorder in children and adolescents: A review of the literature. *Journal of Developmental and Behavioral Pediatrics, 8,* 349–356.

McFarlane, A. C. (1987). Posttraumatic phenomena in a longitudinal study of children following a natural disaster. *Journal of the American Academy of Child and Adolescent Psychiatry, 26,* 764–769.

McFarlane, A. C. (1988). The longitudinal course of posttraumatic morbidity: The range of outcomes and their predictors. *Journal of Nervous and Mental Disease, 176,* 30–39.

McLeer, S. V., Callaghan, M., Henry, D., & Wallen, J. (1994). Psychiatric disorders in sexually abused children. *Journal of the American Academy of Child and Adolescent Psychiatry, 33,* 313–319.

McNally, R. J. (1993). Stressors that produce Posttraumatic Stress Disorder in children. In J. R. T. Davidson & E. B. Foa (Eds.), *Posttraumatic Stress Disorder: DSM-IV and beyond* (pp. 57–74). Washington, DC: American Psychiatric Press.

Mitchell, J. T., & Dyregrov, A. (1993). Traumatic stress in disaster workers and emergency personnel: Prevention and intervention. In J. Wilson & B. Raphael (Eds.), *The international handbook of traumatic stress syndromes* (pp. 905–914). Washington, DC: American Psychiatric Press.

Murburg, M. M., McFall, M. E., Ko, G. N., & Veith, R. C. (1994). Stress-induced alterations in plasma catecholamines and sympathetic nervous system function in PTSD. In M. M. Murburg (Ed.), *Catecholamine function in Posttraumatic Stress Disorder: Emerging concepts* (pp. 189–202). Washington DC: American Psychiatric Press.

National Research Council. (1993). *Understanding child abuse and neglect.* Washington, DC: National Academy Press.

Nir, Y. (1985). Posttraumatic Stress Disorder in children with cancer. In S. Eth & R. S. Pynoos (Eds.), *Posttraumatic stress in children* (pp. 121–132). Washington, DC: American Psychiatric Press.

Pearson, G. H. (1968). *Handbook of child psychoanalysis.* New York: Basic Books.

Pelcovitz, D., Kaplan, S., Goldenberg, B. A., Mandel, F., Lehane, J., & Guarrera, J. (1994). Posttraumatic Stress Disorder in physically abused adolescents. *Journal of the American Academy of Child and Adolescent Psychiatry, 33,* 305–312.

Perry, B. D. (1993a). Neurodevelopment and the neurophysiology of trauma: 1. Conceptual considerations for clinical work with maltreated children. *The Advisor, 6,* 1–18.

Perry, B. D. (1993b). Neurodevelopment and the neurophysiology of trauma: 2. Clinical work along the alarm-fear-terror continuum. *The Advisor, 6,* 1–20.

Perry, B. D. (1994). Neurobiological sequelae of childhood trauma: PTSD in children. In M. M. Murburg (Ed.), *Catecholamine function in Posttraumatic Stress Disorder: Emerging concepts* (pp. 233–255). Washington, DC: American Psychiatric Press.

Piaget, J. (1952). *The origins of intelligence in children.* New York: International Universities Press.

Piaget, J., & Inhelder, B. (1969). *The psychology of the child.* New York: Basic Books.

Pittman, P. K. (1993). Biological findings in Posttraumatic Stress Disorder: Implications for DSM-IV classification. In J. R. T. Davidson & E. B. Foa (Eds.), *Posttraumatic Stress Disorder: DSM-IV and beyond* (pp.173–189). Washington, DC: American Psychiatric Press.

Putnam, F. W., & Peterson, G. (1994). Further validation of the Child Dissociative Checklist. *Dissociation, 7,* 204–211.

Putnam, F. W., & Trickett, P. K. (1993). Child sexual abuse: A model of chronic trauma. *Psychiatry, 56,* 82–95.

Pynoos, R. S., & Eth, S. (1985). Witnessing acts of personal violence. In S. Eth & R. S. Pynoos (Eds.), *Posttraumatic stress in children* (pp. 17–43). Washington, DC: American Psychiatric Press.

Pynoos, R. S., & Eth, S. (1986). Witness to violence: The child interview. *Journal of the American Academy of Child and Adolescent Psychiatry, 25,* 306–319.

Pynoos, R. S., Frederick, C., Nader, K., Arroyo, W., Steinberg, A., Eth, S., Nunez, F., & Fairbanks, L. (1987). Life threat and posttraumatic stress in school-aged children. *Archives of General Psychiatry, 44,* 1057–1063.

Pynoos, R. S., & Nader, K. (1988). Psychological first aid and treatment approach to children exposed to community violence: Research implications. *Journal of Traumatic Stress, 1,* 445–473.

Pynoos, R. S., & Nader, K. (1989). Children's memory and proximity to violence. *Journal of the American Academy of Child and Adolescent Psychiatry, 28,* 236–241.

Pynoos, R. S., & Nader, K. (1990). Mental health disturbances in children exposed to disaster: Prevention intervention strategies. In S. Goldston, J. Yager, C. Heinicke, & R. S. Pynoos (Eds.), *Preventing mental health disturbances in childhood* (pp. 211–233). Washington, DC: American Psychiatric Press.

Pynoos, R. S., & Nader, K. (1993). Issues in the treatment of Posttraumatic Stress Disorder in children and adolescents. In J. Wilson & B. Raphael (Eds.), *The international handbook of traumatic stress syndromes* (pp. 535–549). Washington, DC: American Psychiatric Press.

Ross, R. J., Ball, W. A., Sullivan, K. A., & Caroff, S. N. (1989). Sleep disturbance as the hallmark of Posttraumatic Stress Disorder. *American Journal of Psychiatry, 146,* 697–707.

Rothbaum, B. O., & Foa, E. B. (1993). Subtypes of Posttraumatic Stress Disorder and duration of symptoms. In J. R. T. Davidson & E. B. Foa (Eds.), *Posttraumatic Stress Disorder: DSM-IV and beyond* (pp. 23–35). Washington, DC: American Psychiatric Press.

Ruben, M. (1974). Trauma in the light of clinical experience. *Psychoanalytic Study of the Child, 29,* 369–387.

Rutter, M. (1985). Resilience in the face of adversity: Protective factors and resistance to psychiatric disorder. *British Journal of Psychiatry, 147,* 598–611.

Sapolsky, R. M., Uno, H., Rebert, C. S., & Finch, C. E. (1990). Hippocampal damage associated with prolonged glucocorticoid exposure in primates. *Journal of Neuroscience, 10,* 2897–2902.

Sassetti, M. R. (1993). Domestic violence. *Primary Care, 20,* 289–305.

Shaffer, D., Gould, M. S., Brasic, J., Ambrosini, P., Fisher, P., Bird, H., & Aluwahlia, S. (1983). A children's Global Assessment Scale. *Archives of General Psychiatry, 40,* 1228–1231.

Shore, J., Tatum, E., & Vollmer, W. (1983). Psychiatric reactions to disaster: The Mt. St. Helens experience. *American Journal of Psychiatry, 140,* 1543–1550.

Siever, L., & Trestman, R. L. (1993). The serotonin system and Aggressive Personality Disorder. *International Clinical Psychopharmacology,* (Suppl. 2), 33–40.

Southwick, S. M., Krystal, J. H., Johnson, D. R., & Charney, D. S. (1992). Neurobiology of Posttraumatic Stress Disorder. In A. Tasman & M. B. Riba (Eds.), *Review of psychiatry* (pp. 347–367). Washington, DC: American Psychiatric Press.

Spielberger, C. D. (1973). *Manual for the State-Trait Inventory for Children.* Palo Alto, CA: Consulting Psychologists Press.

Stallings, P., & March, J. S. (1995). Assessment. In J. S. March (Ed.), *Anxiety disorders in children and adolescents* (pp. 125–147). New York: Guilford Press.

Stevenson, R. (1989). Professional burnout in medicine and the helping professions. *Loss, Grief and Care, 3*(1/2), 33–38.

Stoddard, F., Norman, D., & Murphy, J. (1989). A diagnostic outcome study of children and adolescents with severe burns. *Journal of Trauma, 29,* 471–477.

Studer, M. L., Nader, K., Yasuda, P., Pynoos, R. S., & Cohen, S. (1991). Stress response after pediatric bone marrow transplantation: Preliminary results of a prospective longitudinal study. *Journal of the American Academy of Child and Adolescent Psychiatry, 30,* 952–957.

Sulser, F. (1987). Serotonin-norepinephrine receptor interactions in the brain: Implications for the pharmacology and pathophysiology of affective disorders. *Journal of Clinical Psychiatry,* (Suppl. 3), 12–18.

Terr, L. C. (1991). Childhood traumas: An outline and overview. *American Journal of Psychiatry, 148,* 10–20.

True, W. R., Rice, J., Eisen, S. A., Heath, A. C., Goldberg, J., Lyons, M. J., & Nowak, J. (1993). A twin study of genetic and environmental contributions to liability for posttraumatic stress symptoms. *Archives of General Psychiatry, 50,* 257–264.

Van der Kolk, B., Dreyfuss, D., Michaels, M., Shera, D., Berkowitz, R., Fisler, R., & Saxe, G. (1994). Fluoxetine in Posttraumatic Stress Disorder. *Journal of Clinical Psychiatry, 55,* 517–522.

Van Hasselt, V. B., Ammerman, R. T., Glancy, L. J., & Bukstein, O. G. (1992). Maltreatment in psychiatrically hospitalized dually diagnosed adolescent substance abusers. *Journal of the American Academy of Child and Adolescent Psychiatry, 31,* 868–874.

Vogel, J. M., & Vernberg, R. M. (1993). Part 1: Children's psychological responses to disasters. *Journal of Clinical Child Psychology, 22,* 464–484.

Wallerstein, J. S. (1990). Preventive interventions with divorcing families: A reconceptualization. In S. E. Goldston, J. Yager, C. Heinicke, & R. S. Pynoos (Eds.), *Preventing mental health disturbances in childhood* (pp. 154–174). Washington, DC: American Psychiatric Press.

Winnicott, D. W. (1971). *Therapeutic consultations in child psychiatry.* New York: Basic Books.

Wolfe, V. V., Gentile, C., & Wolfe, D. A., (1989). The impact of sexual abuse on children: A PTSD formulation. *Behavior Therapy, 20,* 215–228.

Yehuda, R., Giller, E. L., Southwick, S., Lowy, M. T., & Mason, J. W. (1991). Hypothalamic pituitary adrenal axis dysfunction in PTSD. *Biological Psychiatry, 30,* 1031–1048.

Yehuda, R., Kahana, B., Binder-Brynes, K., Southwick, S., Mason, J. W., & Giller, E. L. (1995). Low urinary cortisol excretion in Holocaust survivors with Posttraumatic Stress Disorder. *American Journal of Psychiatry, 152,* 982–986.

Yehuda, R., Southwick, S. M., Giller, E. L., Ma, X., & Mason, J. W. (1992). Urinary catecholamine excretion and severity of PTSD symptoms in Vietnam combat veterans. *Journal of Nervous and Mental Disease, 180,* 321–325.

Yehuda, R., Southwick, S. M., Krystal, J. H., Bremner, D., Charney, D. S., & Mason, J. W. (1993). Enhanced suppression of cortisol following dexamethasone administration in Posttraumatic Stress Disorder. *American Journal of Psychiatry, 150,* 83–86.

CHAPTER 19

Mental Retardation and Developmental Disorders

G. STENNIS WATSON and ALAN M. GROSS

DESCRIPTION OF THE DISORDERS

Cognitive and social development follow remarkably similar courses in most children, so that parents, teachers, physicians and others frequently judge a child's health by achievement of developmental milestones. Some children, however, are delayed in achieving milestones, or never reach them. For a child who has substantial cognitive deficits and poor adaptive skills, a diagnosis of mental retardation is considered. For a child who has substantial social and language deficits, a diagnosis of autism is considered. The following discussion first considers mental retardation, then autism, and finally, the techniques of behavior analysis that have been used successfully in the treatment of mental retardation and autism.

Mental Retardation

Mental retardation (MR) is "characterized by significantly subaverage intellectual functioning, existing concurrently with related limitations in two or more of the following adaptive skill areas: communication, self-care, home living, social skills, community use, self-direction, health and safety, functional academics, leisure, and work. Mental retardation manifests before age 18" (American Association on Mental Retardation [AAMR], 1992, p. 1). Cultural and linguistic diversity are considered in assessment of MR, adaptive skill limitations are contextual and coexist with strengths, and life functioning of persons with MR can improve with appropriate supports (AAMR, 1992).

This definition reflects a current paradigm shift. MR, once seen as a permanent trait referenced primarily to an individual, is a descriptor of substantial functional limitations referenced to specific contexts. Environmental demands and supports interact with personal capacities to enhance or debilitate adaptive skills, thus altering the probability of a diagnosis of MR. A person with limited cognitive abilities may function well in one context and be substantially limited in another. The MR label, indicative of both personal and environmental deficiencies, is appropriate only when an individual is substantially limited in two or more life domains. If adaptive skills improve beyond this criterion, the label is removed; if adaptive skills deteriorate substantially, the label may be reapplied. A person living in a boarding home may lack the environmental support to shop, communicate effectively, or work, and a diagnosis of MR is made. Upon moving into a supervised apartment with strong support, the person gains adaptive skills, and the diagnosis is removed (see AAMR, 1992; Schalock et al., 1994).

Subaverage conceptual intelligence is necessary but not sufficient to diagnosis MR. Persons with limited cognitive capacity do not have MR if they function adequately in their life contexts. A high school student with an IQ of 70 would not be diagnosed with MR if she made adequate grades in school, demonstrated good interpersonal skills, assisted with domestic responsibilities, dressed like her peers, and expressed realistic vocational goals. A young adult with an IQ of 70 would be diagnosed with MR if he had difficulty maintaining employment, poor social judgment, few independent living skills, and little motivation to acquire adaptive skills.

Many children with MR evince delays in motor, language, sociobehavioral, and academic skills. Rate and degree of delay are idiosyncratic, and deficits may be latent until school age.

In general, children with MR display less accomplished motor skills than their age peers. Common motor deficits, such as poor balance, locomotion, and manipulative dexterity (Thomas & Patton, 1994) may be exacerbated by sensory deficits or physical illnesses. Epilepsy occurs in 15% to 30% of persons having MR, cerebral palsy and other motor impairments in 20% to 30%, and visual and auditory deficits in 10% to 20%. Severely impaired children may require special adaptive devices (e.g., braces, crutches, automated wheelchairs), physical or occupational therapy, medical interventions (e.g., a gastrostomy tube for feeding), or environmental alterations (e.g., ramps, railings) to facilitate adaptive skills (see Kobe, Mulick, Rash, & Martin, 1994; McLaren & Bryson, 1987; Nietupski & Robinson, 1994).

Speech and language disabilities are more prevalent among persons with MR than in the general population. Common impairments include delayed or limited production (especially poverty of vocabulary) and articulation errors, such as substitution, omission, addition, or distortion of sounds (Thomas & Patton, 1994). Severely impaired persons may have such poor articulation that they are comprehensible only to skilled and patient listeners, may speak in short phrases or single words, or may not speak at all (Nietupski & Robinson, 1994). Often, children with MR display deficits in receptive and expressive language. They focus on formal, sequential aspects of language and fail to employ strategies based on categorical, semantic, and conceptual properties of language (Abbeduto & Nuccio, 1991). When children with MR perceive that a listener has not understood them, they are capable of repair behaviors. However, their use of repair behaviors declines sharply relative to peers without MR as task demands increase (Scudder & Tremain, 1992).

Common maladaptive behaviors in persons with MR are disruptiveness, attention deficit, hyperactivity, distractibility, verbal and physical aggression, self-injury, and self-stimulation (Epstein, Cullinan, & Polloway, 1986; Nietupski & Robinson, 1994; Thomas & Patton, 1994). Persons with severe or profound MR often express extremely maladaptive behavior. Kobe et al. (1994) observed self-injurious behavior (SIB) in about 50% of persons with severe MR and aggression in about 25%. As inappropriate behavior increases, social rejection of children with MR increases (Thomas & Patton, 1994), compounding the difficulty that many of these children have establishing close interpersonal relationships (Polloway, Epstein, Patton, Cullinan, & Luebke, 1986). Their need for social attention may lead to increased disruptive behavior, which results in further neglect and rejection.

Children with mild MR experience learning-related problems (Thomas & Patton, 1994) because attention, metacognition, memory, and generalization may be delayed. Children with MR are more easily distracted from tasks than their peers; they lack focus, attention span, and selective attention to targets. Their ability to form and utilize learning strategies is poorly developed. Children without MR organize new information in efficient units and store new learning through rehearsal, classification, association, and imagery; they use prior learning to formulate rules and learning sets that facilitate new learning. Delay in these abilities is consistent with poor generalization and memory patterns observed in children with MR. For example, children with MR have impaired short-term memory (STM) but have long-term memory (LTM) patterns resembling LTM in children without MR. STM is highly dependent on metacognitive strategies (e.g., rehearsal or association), suggesting that children with MR have more difficulty with initial encoding than later recall. Inadequate learning sets hinder application of old knowledge to new tasks.

Epidemiology

MR occurs in approximately 2% of the population of North America and western Europe, with reported prevalence ranging from 0.7% to 3% (McLaren & Bryson, 1987; Schalock et al., 1994; Sonnander, Emanuelsson, & Kebbon, 1993). This is consistent with prevalence estimated from diagnostic criteria (American Psychiatric Association [APA], 1994) requiring an IQ of approximately 70 or below and concurrent deficits in present adaptive functioning in two or more areas. An IQ of 70 or below is observed in approximately 2.5% of the population, and a small proportion of these possess adaptive skills beyond diagnostic requirements.

Risk factors include gender, ethnicity, and socioeconomic status (SES). More boys than girls are diagnosed with MR (Epstein, Polloway, Patton, & Foley, 1989; Polloway et al., 1986; Thomas & Patton, 1994), and males with MR evidence more problem behaviors than females with MR (Epstein et al., 1986). Mild, but not severe, MR occurs more frequently among low-income families (Sonnander et al., 1993; Thomas & Patton, 1994) and among children who live outside traditional two-parent homes (Epstein et al., 1989). African-American children are more likely than Caucasians or Hispanics to be diagnosed with MR (Zigler, Balla, & Hodapp, 1984). Youth in the United States are 70% Caucasian, 12% African-American, and 13% Hispanic, but youth labeled with MR are 61% Caucasian, 31% African-American, and 5.6% Hispanic (U.S. Department of Education, cited in Thomas & Patton, 1994, p. 221). Epstein et al. (1989) described their sample of students with MR: 57.5% Caucasian, 38.7% African-American, 2.8% Hispanic, and 0.9% other.

Mental disorders are more prevalent in persons with MR than persons without MR (Bregman, 1991; Crews, Bonaventura, & Rowe, 1994; King, DeAntonio, McCracken, Forness, & Ackerland, 1994; Singh, Sood, Sonenklar, & Ellis, 1991), but estimates vary widely. Reports of dual diagnosis range from about 15% of all persons with MR (Crews et al., 1994; Jacobson; 1982) to 55% of persons with mild MR, 32% of persons with moderate MR, and 26% of persons with severe to profound MR (Iverson & Fox, 1989).

The most common mental disorders among institutionalized persons with severe to profound MR are impulse control, stereotypy, anxiety, and mood disorders (King et al., 1994). Schizophrenia occurs in 2% to 3% of persons with MR (Bregman, 1991). Crews et al. (1994) observed a 9% comorbidity of MR and affective disorders (especially bipolar disorder) in persons with MR, and increased prevalence of psychotic, affective, and personality disorders among persons with mild and moderate MR relative to persons with severe MR. Elevated risk of dual diagnosis is associated with genetic factors (e.g., fragile X, Prader Willi, and Down syndromes), cerebral abnormalities (e.g., severe head trauma, seizure disorders), and psychosocial factors (Bregman, 1991). (For a recent annotated bibliography of dual diagnosis literature, see Sturmey & Sevin, 1993.)

Causes and Consequences

AAMR (1992) has proposed a multifactorial etiology based on age of onset (pre-, peri-, postnatal) and causal factors: biomedical (e.g., genetic disorders, malnutrition), social (e.g., lack of infant stimulation), behavioral (e.g., injurious activities, maternal substance abuse), and educational (absence of educational supports that promote development of cognitive ability and adaptive skills).

MR etiological factors are myriad (AAMR, 1992, Table 7.3, pp. 81–91). Perinatal factors include chromosomal disorders (e.g., trisomy 21, fragile X), syndrome disorders, inborn errors of metabolism (e.g., phenylketonuria, Lesch-Nyhan syndrome), developmental disorders of brain formation (e.g., spina bifida), and environmental influences (e.g., intrauterine malnutrition, drugs, toxins, teratogens, maternal diseases). Perinatal factors include intrauterine disorders (e.g., placental insufficiency, abnormal labor and delivery, multiple gestation) and neonatal disorders (e.g., intracranial hemorrhage, respiratory disorders, infections, head traumas at birth, metabolic disorders, nutritional disorders). Postnatal factors include head injuries, infections (e.g., encephalitis, meningitis, fungal infections, parasites), demyelinating disorders, degenerative disorders (e.g., Rett syndrome, poliodystrophies, basal ganglia disorders), seizure disorders, toxic-metabolic disorders, malnutrition, and environmental deprivation.

A few risk factors account for a significant proportion of MR. Fetal alcohol syndrome (FAS), which occurs in 1 to 3 births per 1,000, is the most common cause of MR. Presence of FAS in an older sibling substantially elevates the probability of FAS in younger siblings. Primary FAS characteristics are subaverage intelligence (average IQ = 68–70), central nervous system dysfunction, craniofacial malformations, and low birth weight (Warren & Bast, 1988). Down syndrome (trisomy 21) accounts for 5% to 6% of MR. Down syndrome features include short stature; flat, broad face with small ears, nose, and mouth, and slanted eyes; reduced muscle tone; heart defects; and increased incidence of upper respiratory infections. Fragile X syndrome may be the second most prevalent genetic cause. Children infected with HIV or rubella (German measles) in utero are at high risk for MR. Premature delivery (less than 28 weeks) and perinatal anoxia increase risk for diminished cognitive capacity. Child abuse, lead poisoning, and malnutrition are common postnatal causes of MR. Finally, traumatic head injuries, which occur prior to age 18 in about 1 in 30 children, increase the risk of MR (see McLaren & Bryson, 1987; Polloway & Smith, 1994).

Impediments to Intervention in the Real World Context

Impediments to real world intervention begin with the complexity of the disorder. A single set of diagnostic criteria and a common label for all persons diagnosed with MR fail to portray the multitude of causes, symptoms, and needs associated with

MR. Broad intervention will require coordination of research and education by a variety of disciplines, supported by a commitment at all levels of society. A comprehensive MR policy must address factors as diverse as human genetics, social conditions, and medical conditions, as well as the traditional educational and vocational concerns of MR.

Public policy can be insensitive to family needs. Presence of a child with MR elevates a family's perceived financial stress; disrupts family routine, leisure, and social interaction; and exerts a detrimental effect on family mental and physical health (Singhi, Goyal, Pershad, & Singhi, 1990). Families who elect to maintain children with MR at home face a "social service system that financially values only out-of-home, medically oriented, and curative-rehabilitative services" (Birenbaum & Cohen, 1993; Hodapp & Zigler, 1993). Residential placement of a child with minimal social and self-help skills can reduce family stress, facilitate family support of the child, and provide essential services to the child (Blacher & Baker, 1994). However, many states are decreasing availability of residential placements (Derks, 1995).

African-American children are disproportionately diagnosed with MR. Scientists and laypersons argue whether this is a cultural artifact or a relevant scientific fact. As of yet, no consensus exists, and diagnostic disparity continues.

Mental health providers frequently underestimate the impact of psychological disturbances on the behavior of persons with MR *(diagnostic overshadowing),* and consequently, persons with MR may be substantially underserved (Crews et al., 1994). For example, anxiety and mood disorders (which are common in persons with MR) can be ameliorated by psychological and pharmacological interventions, but may go untreated because symptoms are misattributed to MR.

Pejorative labels can produce pervasive and detrimental effects (e.g., Darley & Gross, 1983; Rosenhan, 1973). The label "mentally retarded" has been associated with discrimination in employment (Langford, Boas, Garner, & Strohmer, 1994) and teachers' anticipation of student behavior (Jellison & Duke, 1994). Labeling of people with MR is necessary to delineate persons who qualify for special services. However, power of the label to harm should not be underestimated (Hastings, 1994).

Services for persons with MR are expensive. Families bear tremendous financial burdens when children with MR live at home. In 1985–1986 the average health care expenditure was about $4,000 for persons with severe MR maintained at home, whereas the average for all American children was $414; child care averaged about $950 per year for children with MR (Birenbaum & Cohen, 1993). Homes and automobiles must be modified to accommodate children with MR (sometimes costing in excess of $2,000), and property damage resulting from problem behavior is more expensive when children with MR are present. Mothers with a child 6 to 13 years old are employed at a rate 20% lower when a child with MR lives in the home than when a child with MR is not in the home (Birenbaum & Cohen, 1993). Income is lower, and costs are higher when a child with MR lives at home.

The cost of residential care is astronomical. In 1994, the average cost of maintaining one person at a regional center in Connecticut was $138,000–$182,000, and $70,000 in a group home (Sierpina, 1994). In 1995, Tennessee spent an average of $82,800–$123,360 for residential treatment, and Mississippi paid an average of $49,600, the least of any state. From 1990 to 1995, the average national cost for residential treatment rose from $75,051 to $99,254 (Derks, 1995).

Finally, crucial ethical issues arise in the treatment of children with MR. Selective termination of pregnancy (e.g., a fetus with Down syndrome) and right to life after birth of children who have disabling conditions (e.g., a neonate with brain damage secondary to perinatal anoxia) raise fundamental questions about the rights of women and parents to self-determination, the right of children with MR to live, and the responsibilities of the state to arbitrate difficult decisions. As children with MR mature, a different set of ethical issues emerges. Persons with MR have equal protection under the law, including rights to due process, privacy, least restrictive environment, and education. Cultural acceptability of intrusive or aversive training procedures has decreased (e.g., Grace, Kahng, & Fisher, 1994). Families and mental health officials must grapple with the rights of persons with MR to marriage and sexual expression, participation in treatment planning (including the refusal of behavioral or medical interventions), and choice of living arrangements.

Assessment

Assessment of MR consists of formal diagnosis and functional description of the person's strengths, weaknesses, and needs. Formal diagnosis is made by persons competent in psychological testing and interviewing. Functional description is best undertaken by multidisciplinary team.

Three diagnostic criteria exist for MR (AAMR, 1992; APA, 1994). First, significantly subaverage intellectual functioning must be established with a reliable and valid, individually administered IQ test. AAMR (1992) specifies an IQ of approximately 70 to 75 or below, and *DSM-IV* (APA, 1994) specifies an IQ of approximately 70 or below. The Stanford-Binet Intelligence Scale, Fourth Edition (SB:FE; Thorndike, Hagen, & Sattler, 1986a, 1986b), the Wechsler Adult Intelligence Scale-Revised (WAIS-R; Wechsler, 1981), the Wechsler Intelligence Scale for Children, Third Edition (WISC-III; Wechsler, 1991), and the Wechsler Preschool and Primary Scale of Intelligence (WPPSI-R; Wechsler, 1989) are recommended instruments (Sattler, 1992). One caution is that none of the four was designed for the assessment of children with severe or profound mental retardation (see Sattler, 1992, or individual test manuals for the psychometric properties). Second, deficits or impairments must exist in present adaptive functioning in at least two of the following areas: communication, self-care, home living, social/interpersonal skills, use of community resources, self-direction, functional academic skills, work, leisure, and health and safety. The breadth of this criterion necessitates multiple modes of assessment. Traditional behavioral rating scales can determine adaptive functioning globally or in specific areas. The AAMR (1992, p. 42) lists the following rating scales: the AAMD Adaptive Behavior Scale (ABS; Nihira, Foster, Shellhaas, & Leland, 1974), the AAMD Adaptive Behavior Scale-School Edition (ABS-SE; Lambert, Windmiller, Tharinger, & Cole, 1981), the Vineland Adaptive Behavior Scales (VABS; Sparrow, Balla, & Cicchetti, 1984), the Scales of Independent Behavior (SIB; Bruininks, Woodcock, Weatherman, & Hill, 1984), and the Comprehensive Test of Adaptive Behavior (Adams, 1984). (For a critical review of these and other behavioral rating scales, see Sattler, 1992.) However, no rating scales are comprehensive, reliability is no better than informants, and they are limited rather than general samples of behavior. Therefore, behavioral rating scales should be supplemented with methods that are flexible, broad, and ecologically valid. These methods include clinical interviews (with the person being assessed, primary caregivers, teachers, agency workers, health providers, employers, significant others), direct observation (e.g., at work, shopping, in a social setting), and archival data (e.g., medical records, school work, activities calendar). Finally, onset of cognitive and adaptive deficits must occur prior to age 18.

"Mental Retardation" is a global label that offers little guidance in individualized interventions. A thorough assessment of causes, impairments, and resources (personal and environmental) determines the nature of the intervention. *Primary prevention* checks the occurrence of MR. Examples are prevention of rubella (biological), maternal malnutrition (social), or maternal alcohol abuse (psychological). *Secondary prevention* limits the course of a disorder or reverses a problem post onset. Examples are dietary intervention in phenylketonuria (biological) or environmental enrichment (psychosocial). *Tertiary prevention* controls the adverse consequences of MR once it has occurred. Examples are vocational training (educational) or modification of aggressive behavior (psychological) (see AAMR, 1992).

Treatment

Often interventions target problems that coexist with, but are distinct from, MR. A person with physically handicapping conditions needs the same environmental and medical support as a person without MR. Depression, anxiety disorders, and attention deficit are common among persons with MR and may exacerbate maladaptive functioning. Generally, these can be remediated with the same psychological and pharmacological interventions in persons with or without MR. Pharmacological interventions are limited by individual medical conditions, and cognitive therapy is contraindicated when an individual lacks the language skills, motivation, or ability to change thought patterns.

Autism and Pervasive Developmental Disorders

Pervasive developmental disorders (PDD) comprise autistic disorder, Rett's disorder (RD), childhood disintegrative disorder (CDD), Asperger's disorder (AD), and pervasive developmental disorder not otherwise specified (PDDNOS), and are characterized by "severe and pervasive impairments in . . . reciprocal social interaction skills, communication skills, or the presence of stereotyped behavior" first evident in early childhood (APA, 1994, p. 65). Differential diagnosis is based on age of onset, gender prevalence, and specific inclusion criteria. Symptoms of autism include social, language, and behavioral impairments prior to age 3 years, and higher prevalence among males than females. In RD, normal development (5–30 months postnatal) precedes deceleration of head growth, loss of manual skill and social engagement, poor lower body movement, and impaired language; RD occurs exclusively in females. In CDD, substantial normal development (2–10 years) precedes social, communicational, and behavioral symptoms. In AD, social and behavioral symptoms appear, but language development is spared. PDDNOS is a developmental delay failing to meet criteria for a specific PDD.

Two views exist of PDDs: discrete disorders and a continuous entity. The *DSM-IV* (APA, 1994) describes PDDs as separate disorders with discriminant validity. (PDD field studies are reported in Volkmar et al., 1994.) However, data are equivocal (see Gillberg, 1990, 1993). Discriminant validity is supported for PDDNOS (Mayes, Volkmar, Hooks, & Cicchetti, 1993) and CDD (Volkmar, 1992; Volkmar & Cohen, 1989), and contradicted for AD (Ehlers & Gillberg, 1993) and RD (Ghaziuddin, Butler, Tsai, & Ghaziuddin, 1994; Gillberg, 1994; Tsai, 1992).

Relatively little research exists for PDDs other than autism. Discussions of AD are found in Gillberg and Gillberg (1989), Ghaziuddin, Tsai, and Ghaziuddin (1992), Rickarby, Carruthers, and Mitchell (1991), and Simblett and Wilson (1993). Discussions of RD are found in Garber and Veydt (1990), Van Acker (1991), and Wenk, Naidu, Casanova, Kitt, and Moser (1991).

Autism as a diagnostic category was proposed by Kanner in 1943. In a study of 11 autistic children, he abstracted the following common behavioral characteristics: inability to develop normal social relations, language acquisition delay, mutism or the inability to use language to communicate, extreme perseveration in activities, fascination with objects, lack of imagination, need for a highly stable environment, normal physical appearance, good psychomotor skills, and good cognitive potential, especially rote memory. Subsequently, behavioral characteristics of autism were reduced to three broad impairments: social, speech and language, and behavioral. Wing and Gould (1979) coined the term "triad of social and language impairment" to describe characteristics of autistic children.

Pervasive social impairment is the hallmark of autism. Autistic children prefer objects to persons, resist human contact, fail to make direct eye contact, and lack functional communication even when speech sounds are developed. Parents may describe autistic infants as "good babies" because they do not cry or demand attention from caregivers. The earliest symptom may be the parents' sense that they have not bonded with their baby and that the baby does not need their affection. Severely autistic children are aloof and cry when others make physical contact. Less severely autistic children may allow social contact when approached, but never initiate interaction. In the least severe form, autistic children approach others, but contact is odd or awkward, because they do not adhere to rules of social interaction. Often, older autistic children are loners, apathetic to the absence of caregivers, and resistant or indifferent to affection. They prefer solitary play to peer contact and do not seek consolation from others. They objectify other persons and relate to inanimate objects.

Autism is characterized by severe impairments in expressive and receptive speech and language, including elective mutism, echolalia, perseveration, literalness, and dysprosody. However, the fundamental problem is not linguistic failure, but a failure to grasp social reciprocity. "Most people with autism do not understand the meaning of language and its function as a *tool* for communication" (Gillberg, 1993). For a person with autism, language is a self-directed sensory experience rather than a means of relating to another person. In the most severe cases, there are neither verbal nor nonverbal attempts to communicate. As autism becomes less severe, children may attend and respond to other persons but not initiate communication, initiate communication as self-stimulation rather than social reciprocity, or use instrumental gestures. Verbal and nonverbal communication are self-referenced.

Repetitive or ritualistic behavior is characteristic of autism. Complex play sequences are performed repeatedly. Play may be dull and lack imagination—a banana is never a telephone, a cardboard box is never a house. Autistic children may insist on numerous repetitions of particular sensory experiences, such as watching a spinning top, hearing a particular sequence of sounds, stroking a furry animal, or smelling a flower. They may develop an overwhelming attachment to a specific object or class of objects, and incorporate it in ritual behavior, such as compulsively placing stones in a row. They may become obsessed with dates or numbers. Environmental stability is critical, and tantrums may result from minor alterations in travel route or furniture arrangement.

Self-stimulation is common. Odd self-referenced behaviors include stereotypic rocking (from foot-to-foot or of the upper body), hand flapping, jumping, gazing into lights, subtle body motions, and repetitive vocalizations or sensory experiences. Unusual eating patterns and destructive behavior may be symptoms of self-stimulation. Lack of response to environmental stimuli (e.g., startling noises, one's name spoken, or bright flashes) may be a negative sign of self-stimulation. According to some authors, the most extreme form of self-stimulation is SIB, such as head banging, self-biting, hair pulling, self-scratching, or self-hitting.

Epidemiology

Estimates of the prevalence of autism vary widely. The consensus prior to 1990 was 4 to 6 cases of autism per 10,000 children (Gillberg, 1990). Smalley, Asarnow, and Spence (1988) summarized 10 epidemiological studies in which the mean incidence per 10,000 persons was 3.44 ($SD = 1.75$), and six of the studies reported 4.3–5.6 cases per 10,000. Recent studies have proposed a higher incidence rate (7–21 cases per 10,000, Gillberg, 1993; Wing & Gould, 1979), which may reflect increased prevalence, more sensitive diagnostic criteria, or decreased reluctance to diagnose autism.

Autism is more prevalent among males than females, but estimates vary widely. In 10 epidemiological studies, autism was 1.3–15.2 times more frequent in males than in females ($M = 4.5$, $SD = 4.4$; Smalley et al., 1988). According Gillberg (1993), the most frequently reported male:female ratio is 3–4:1, but variability between studies results in a much wider range of 1.4–5.4:1. The ratio is lowest among children with severe and profound MR (Gillberg, 1993). Males are rated by parents to be more severely autistic in early social development, and older females are rated as having more severe deficits. Otherwise, male–female patterns of autistic behavior do not differ (McLennan, Lord, & Schopler, 1993).

Most autistic children score within the MR range on individual intelligence tests. Only 20% of autistic children have observed IQs above 70, and 60% have IQs below 50 (Schreibman, 1988). Cognitive abilities are not uniformly depressed among autistic persons. Wechsler performance IQ is better than verbal IQ, block design performance may be superior, and picture arrangement, comprehension, and similarities poor (Gillberg, 1993). These patterns of abilities are consistent with increased attention to internal stimuli and poor comprehension of social or environmental relations. A very few autistic children possess exceptional mathematical, musical, or mechanical skills.

Epilepsy is common in persons with autism. About 20% of autistic persons develop nonfebrile seizures before age 3 years, and another 15% to 20% develop seizures around the age of puberty (Gillberg, 1993; Gillberg & Schaumann, 1989). Complex partial seizures and tonic-clonic seizures are most common. Anecdotal evidence suggests that all symptoms of autism may disappear in a few persons when seizures are controlled completely. However, treatment of epilepsy in autism has been neglected in the research and clinical literature (see Gillberg, 1991b).

Hearing and visual deficits are common in children with autism. Moderate to severe hearing loss (> 25-dB) occurs in 5% to 20% (Jure, Rapin, & Tuchman, 1991; Klin, 1993; Steffenburg, 1991). At least 20% of autistic children have reduced visual acuity (Gillberg, 1993). Furthermore, assessment of children with autism is difficult because of their unusual response patterns. Relative to children without autism, a child with autism may be hyposensitive to most sounds and hypersensitive to a few sounds. Therefore, a child with suspected autism should be examined by a clinician with experience in autistic disorders.

The comorbidity of autism and mental disorders (other than MR) is poorly reported. Case histories and small studies document the dual diagnosis of autism and depression or anxiety disorders. No population-based studies were found in the recent literature.

Some data suggest that immigrants to western Europe from parts of Asia (excluding Japan), Africa, and the Caribbean bear children with a prevalence of autism higher than western Europeans (Gillberg, 1990, 1993).

Causes and Consequences

Twin and sibling studies suggest a strong genetic component to autism, perhaps, with a heritability of 90% (Piven & Folstein, 1994). Autism appears in about .10% of the general population. Smalley et al. (1988) reported a 2.7% incidence of autism among siblings of autistic probands (summary of six studies totaling 285 families and 886 siblings), an adjusted concordance of 9% among 36 pair of dizygotic (DZ) twins, and an adjusted concordance of 64% among 45 pair of monozygotic (MZ) twins. No source study (of single cases and three groups) reported a DZ concordance rate above 24% or an MZ concordance rate below 36%; three MZ concordance rates were 78% or greater. Steffenburg et al. (1989) reported a concordance rate of 91% for 11 pair of MZ twins and no concordance for 10 pair of DZ twins, and they argued persuasively that pre-, peri-, and postnatal suboptimality alone could not explain their data. The causal role of suboptimality is minimized in Lord, Mulloy, Wendelboe, and Schopler (1991), and Piven et al. (1993).

Autism is a biological disorder, but its causes remain obscure. Fragile X is the chromosomal disorder most closely associated with autism, occurring in about .9% of the general population, 4.4% of autistic females, and 7.4% of autistic males. However, reports vary widely (0%–16% for autistic males), and samples are small (Hagerman, 1989). Furthermore, the relationship among fragile X, autism, and MR obscures the relationship between fragile X and autism, as studies cited in Piven and Folstein (1994) illustrate: Fragile X is more common among persons with autism than MR, equally common in both, and more common among persons with MR. Trisomy 21 is associated with autism, but the relationship is far from clear. Polygenetic etiology is more probable than monogenetic. Collectively, neurofibromatosis, tuberous scerlosis, and hypomelanosis account for about 12% of autism (Gillberg, 1993). Metabolic disorders associated with autism include phenylketonuria, lactic acidosis, and hypothyroidism; infectious disorders include postnatal herpes encephalitis and interuterine rubella. (For comprehensive lists of medical disorders associated with autism, see Gillberg, 1990, 1993; Hagerman, 1989.)

Originally, theories of autism assumed environmental causation, particularly parental personality. In 1960, Leo Kanner stated in *Time* magazine "that children with infantile autism were the offspring of highly organized professional parents, cold and rational, who just happened to defrost long enough to produce a child" (cited in Steffenburg & Gillberg, 1989, p. 63). In the extreme, this hypothesis asserts that deviant parents create autism in a biologically normal child. A moderate version says that deviant parents can affect only children who have a biological vulnerability. Research has refuted parental genesis and its corollary that autism appears most frequently among upper SES children. Only one English language population-based study found a social class bias for autism, and at least 10 epidemiological studies failed to support social class as a determinant (Gillberg, 1993). When McAdoo and DeMyer (1978) compared an average Minnesota Multiphasic Personality Inventory (MMPI) profile of parents with autistic children to an average MMPI profile of parents with (nonautistic) children seen at a child guidance clinic, the profiles were in the subclinical range and remarkably similar (see also DeMyer et al., 1972; Pitfield & Oppenheim, 1964). Data do not support any theory (including psychodynamic or learning) that presupposes primary environmental causality.

Two important social cognitive abilities are absent in persons with autism: processing of affective stimuli and attribution of beliefs to other people. Hobson (1986a, 1986b) and others have demonstrated affective deficits across contexts: matching emotion to pictured context, discriminating facial emotional expressions, matching facial gestures to context, and comprehending affective terms (see Green, Fein, Joy, & Waterhouse, 1995). However, affective theory alone cannot explain autistic behavior because autistic affective deficits are seen in a wide variety of clinical populations, and some interpersonal emotional responsivity may be present in an autistic individual (Baren-Cohen, 1989).

Theory of Mind describes the attribution of cognitions to another person. Four-year-old children with normal social cognition can answer a question such as "What is Johnny thinking?" (a first-order attribution); normal 7-year-old children can answer a question such as "What does Mary think that Johnny is thinking?" (a second-order attribution). Persons with autism often lack the ability to make first-order attributions. When children with Down syndrome were compared with autistic children (who had higher mental ages), the children with autism, but not the children with Down, failed to make first-order attributions, indicating that this attributional deficit is specific to autism and not evidence of general cognitive delay (see Baron-Cohen, 1989; Happé & Frith, 1995).

Theory of Mind is consistent with behavioral and cognitive deficits observed in autism. When a child lacks the capacity to attribute thought to another person, communication is meaningless and social behavior hopelessly complex. Without thoughts, the other person is an object, and an object such as a toy is no different from a person. A game like chess is impossible because the autistic child cannot anticipate an opponent's next move. The Wechsler Picture Arrangement requires that the child attribute thoughts to another person and sequence the cards accordingly. Both Similarities and Comprehension measure social judgment, which makes no sense to the child who has no social reference. Block Design requires no social reference, only internal stimulation.

Impediments to Intervention in the Real World Context

The most damaging impediment is the historic residue of Kanner and therapists who told a generation of parents that they had defrosted just long enough to produce autistic children. This approach fostered guilt among parents, impeded the search for accurate causality, and perhaps, decreased the probability that children were diagnosed with autism (see Fong, Wilgosh, & Sobsey, 1993).

Late diagnosis of autism is common. *DSM-IV* (APA, 1994) diagnostic criteria specify onset before 36 months. However, Vostanis, Smith, Chung, and Corbett (1994) reported a mean age of 44 months at diagnosis when based on the first diagnostic referral, and a mean age of 82 months when based on two or more referrals. Therefore, many autistic children and their families do not benefit from early delivery of medical, psychological, educational, and social services.

The nature of the disorder impedes treatment. The autistic child does not reach out to others. Early in life, autism may be ignored; the child is seen as a "good baby" (no crying, no demanding), or parents blame themselves for their child's aloofness. Child rearing is a demanding task, requiring mutual affection between caregiver and child; the child may be incapable of giving sufficient rewards to sustain caregivers. A child's noncompliance with a professional (e.g., a psychologist or psychiatrist) makes evaluation difficult or impossible. In a crowded classroom, a teacher may turn to a more reinforcing student. Comorbidities of autism and other disorders (e.g., poor vision and hearing, epilepsy, and mental retardation) reduce the effectiveness of interventions.

Family life is taxed. Families of autistic persons report increased emotional strain, guilt, and depression. A parent may have to defer career plans to care for the child, and freedom to socialize or travel is diminished. Sibling conflict is increased in families of autistic children. Families feel abandoned by social service agencies and society (Fong et al., 1993; McCallion & Toseland, 1993). No cure for autism exists, and families face a lifetime of supporting a person who shows little progress and gives little in return for family efforts. Two-thirds of all autistic persons never lead independent lives (Gillberg, 1991a), and the costs of maintaining an autistic person can be tremendous.

Assessment

Initial evaluation of autism consists of interviews with parents and direct observation of the child for delayed language and lack of social behavior. Gillberg (1989b) suggested that preliminary screening for infants (aged 10–18 months) include assessment of eye contact, attention to parents, hearing, feeding behaviors, reaction to proximity/body contact, interest in surroundings, smiling or laughing, preference for human company, and resemblance of behavior to other children. Research has discriminated autism from mental retardation and normal functioning in children under 3 years old on the basis of five behavioral domains (social, communication, play-behavior, perception, and rhythmicity). Behaviors with the greatest discriminatory power were apparent isolation from surroundings, lack of attempts to attract adult attention, dislike for play with other children, suspicion of deafness, and empty gaze (Gillberg, 1989b).

Rating scales augment direct observation in diagnosing autism by providing structure and comprehensiveness. However, they should not be the sole basis for diagnosis. The most widely used autism rating scales are the Autism Behavior Checklist (ABC), the Autism Diagnostic Interview (ADI, and the revised version, ADI-R), the Behaviour Rating Instrument for Autistic and Atypical Children (BRIAAC), the Checklist for Autism in Toddlers (CHAT), the Childhood Autism Rating Scale (CARS), and the Ritvo-Freeman Real Life Rating Scale (RFLS). (For brief descriptions of each, see Campbell, Kafantaris, Malone, Kowalik, & Locascio, 1991; Vostanis et al., 1994.)

Once autism is suspected, medical, cognitive, psychosocial, and educational evaluations are requisite (Campbell et al., 1991; Gillberg, 1990, 1993; Steffenburg, 1991). The high comorbidity of autism and sensory deficits necessitates visual and auditory examinations; the exceptionally high coincidence of autism and epilepsy impels a comprehensive neurological examination. Screening for genetic and metabolic disorders may be indicated. In all cases, the child should be examined by a physician well acquainted with biological causes and effects of autism. Because as many as 80% of autistic children have MR, cognitive assessment is an important component of the evaluation. Standard instruments include the Bayley Scales of Infant Development (BSID; Bayley, 1969), WPPSI-R, WISC-III, SB:FE. A caution is that autistic children are difficult to test, and results may not be valid. Psychosocial evaluation will facilitate provision of support services for child and family. Psychoeducational testing should explore three broad areas: content (skills and concepts previously acquired), autistic behaviors and behavioral deficits, and techniques that improve attention, motivation, and learning (Lansing, 1989).

Treatment

Pharmacotherapy for autism and its symptoms is far from satisfactory. Neuroleptics, especially haloperidol, have been effective in reducing such conspicuous behaviors as stereotypy, SIB, and social withdrawal. However, neuroleptics have been prescribed reluctantly because of deleterious side effects. Fenfluramine, a serotonin reuptake inhibitor, has produced mixed results that appear to be confounded with IQ. Vitamin B6, naltrexone (an opioid antagonist), and lithium may prove useful in treatment of autism, but data are inconclusive (Handen, 1993; Jakab, 1993). Many autistic children require anticonvulsant pharmacotherapy. Benzodiazepines, phenytoin, and barbiturates can produce behavioral deterioration in autistic individuals, while valproic acid and carbamazepine can often be used without behavioral side effects (Gillberg, 1991a).

Educational models, which are integral to treatment of autism, emphasize the need for a structured learning environment, the value of parents and nondisabled students as "cotherapists," and integration of autistic children into regular classes and community (Haring & Breen, 1992; Harris, 1995; McClannahan, Krantz, & McGee, 1982). Educational goals concentrate on development of language, speech, and social communication, and treatment utilizes behavioral principles. TEACCH, a structured educational approach, assumes that the primary education mission is to improve an individual's adaptive functioning and that the environment should accommodate an autistic person. Space, schedules, work systems, and tasks are carefully organized to provide structure by minimizing distractions, optimizing communication, fostering independence, and raising motivation (see Schopler, 1989; Schopler, Mesibov, & Hearsey, 1995). Other educational approaches are reviewed in Gillberg (1989a).

Autism outcome studies offer little hope for children diagnosed with autism (Gillberg, 1991a). Fewer than 10% will be well integrated into adult society, and 60% will be totally dependent on others to meet basic needs. Therapeutic modality has not been associated with improved adult functioning. The only clear predictor of adaptive functioning as an adult is IQ. Children with low IQs have a uniformly poor prognosis for improvement; children in the average range have a variable prognosis. Consequently, goal clarification is essential in the treatment of autism. Prevention, cure, and functional improvement are all desirable, but not equally plausible goals. At present, there is no cure for autism, and prevention is limited to medical causes implicated in a small proportion of pathogenesis (e.g., phenylketonuria, rubella embryopathy, hypothyroidism). Current functioning can be improved with behavioral interventions.

While cognitive deficits of MR and autism are unremitting, adaptive skills can be improved with continuous evaluation and data-based interventions. Applied behavior analysis (ABA) is a highly effective tool for altering maladaptive behaviors across many domains. The basic tenet of ABA is that consequences control behavior. A clinician intervenes by consequating undesirable behaviors or substituting desirable behaviors that earn satisfying rewards. Whether target behaviors are idiosyncratic or common, a single-case approach is used: Targets are operationalized; antecedents, consequences, and contexts observed; interventions selected and employed; and data analyzed to assess treatment effectiveness.

Problems can be conceptualized as behavioral excesses or deficits. Excesses are present behaviors that should be inhibited partially or completely. Deficits are absent or incomplete behaviors that should be increased. In autism, primary excesses are self-stimulation and aggression toward others (e.g., tantrums, frustration, noncompliance), and many deficits (e.g., gross inattention, deficient social behaviors, inadequate communication, poor self-care). In MR, excesses and deficits are abundant. Excesses are vulnerable to reinforcement schedules that ignore maladaptive behaviors (extinction), reward low rates of behavior (DRL) or behaviors other than the problem (DRO), and punish maladaptive behaviors (e.g., time-out, restraint, overcorrection, physically aversive stimuli). Deficits are responsive to shaping procedures, positive reinforcement for desired behavior, and modeling of appropriate behavior. For example, a person who bites and kicks peers (behavioral excess) may be placed in seclusion for aggression (punishment) and rewarded for notifying staff when peers are irritating (DRO). A person who communicates poorly (behavioral deficit) may be rewarded for successive approximations of good communication (shaping) and placed with persons who communicate well (modeling).

Token economies develop and maintain behavior effectively. A target behavior is selected, the person earns secondary reinforcers (tokens) for compliance with normative behavior, and tokens are exchanged for primary reinforcers. Token economies possess ecological validity: A person working in a sheltered workshop receives money (tokens) for productivity (behavioral compliance) and uses the money for shopping, entertainment, or dining (primary reinforcement).

Contingency management programs (CMP) are similar to token economies, but address global functioning with reinforcement and punishment. Target behaviors are selected, and performance ratings are assigned at regular intervals. At larger intervals, ratings are compiled, and the person is rewarded or punished according to global rating. For example, adolescents in a treatment center begin each day with specified behavioral norms (e.g., social, academic, domestic) and privileges (e.g., access to snacks, social interaction, leisure). Every 30 minutes, staff evaluate individuals across domains and record 0–3 according to behavior. At the end of the day, ratings are compiled and privileges assigned for the next day according to the ratings. Thus, a number of separate domains (e.g., social interaction, academic behavior, personal hygiene, personal responsibility, cooperation with treatment protocols) can be incorporated into a single program and both appetitive and aversive consequences utilized.

Self-management has been used to teach appropriate play behavior (Stahmer & Schreibman, 1992), increase frequency of response to verbal initiations (Koegel, Koegel, Hurley, & Frea, 1992), and perform daily living activities without supervision (Pierce & Schreibman, 1994). The paradigm consists of teaching persons adaptive behavior in the presence of discriminative stimuli (SD) and fading the stimuli upon complete acquisition of learning. Stahmer and Schreibman (1992) treated three autistic children who lacked appropriate play behavior. The children were taught to discriminate appropriate from inappropriate behavior and then were rewarded for recording appropriate behavior on self-management forms. Gradually, the children's trainer (SD) was faded, and finally, the self-management materials (SD) were faded. Posttreatment probes and 1-month follow-ups showed maintenance of appropriate play.

Complex behavioral sequences can be parceled into small units, and behavior analysis applied to each unit, or sequences can be approached with multicomponent interventions. For example, a shopping trip includes communication, social behavior, merchandise choice, awareness of time, and actual buying behavior. Persons can be trained on each task, or trained with multiple schedules to develop integrated competency. Carr and Carlson (1993) treated three group home residents excluded from community activities for serious problem behavior. Five procedures (choice making, embedding, functional communication training, building tolerance for delay of reinforcement, presenting discriminative stimuli for nonproblem behavior) were used to increase adaptive supermarket shopping behavior. Training resulted in increased task completion and decreased problem behaviors. Multicomponent procedures have been used successfully to train children to complete activities of daily living (Matson, Taras, Sevin, Love, & Fridley, 1990) and school-related activities (Bambara, Mitchell-Kvacky, & Iacobelli, 1994).

Nevin's study of behavioral momentum has demonstrated that "learned behavior varies in its resistance to change and that resistance to change depends lawfully on the rate of reinforcement across a wide variety of procedures" (Nevin, Mandell, & Atak, 1983, p. 49). Mace et al. (1990) trained two men with MR to sort plastic dinnerware, using popcorn and coffee reinforcers on concurrent variable interval and variable time schedules. Following behavioral acquisition, attempts were made to distract the men with video programs. Results indicated that resistance to distraction was dependent on frequency of reinforcement signaled by task-related stimuli, but independent of baseline response rate and response-reinforcer contingencies.

Behavioral momentum has been applied effectively to child noncompliance (Davis, Brady, Williams, & Hamilton, 1992), fading (Ducharme & Worling, 1994), self-injury, and extinction (Zarcone, Iwata, Mazaleski, & Smith, 1994). Davis et al. (1992) used an antecedent high-probability request procedure to treat two boys with MR who were noncompliant with certain requests (e.g., Come here. Sit down in your chair. Stand up), and compliant with others (e.g., Touch your head, hand, eyes, or ears). When trainers issued high probability requests prior to low probability requests, compliance with low probability requests increased, compliance was maintained in return to baseline, and patterns of compliance were generalized to trainers issuing only low probability requests. Results suggest that behavioral momentum can be established, is resistant to extinction, and generalizes beyond SDs (trainers who issued antecedent requests).

The resistance of SIB to behavior modification led to the development of functional analysis (FA), a powerful operant model (Iwata, Dorsey, Slifer, Bauman, & Richman, 1982). FA emphasizes the functional and contextual nature of behavior. A single behavior can serve different functions for different individuals in one context, or different functions for one individual across contexts (Carr, 1977; Day, Horner, & O'Neill, 1994). In their analogue study of SIB, Iwata et al. (1982) identified two functions of maladaptive behavior, escape and social attention seeking. Of nine participants, two increased SIBs during academic tasks (escape from task demands), four during isolation (social attention seeking), and one during social disapproval; three showed undifferentiated patterns of SIB. The results were replicated by Carr and Durand (1985) in a school setting. Current research suggests four functions of behavior: attention seeking, escape from tasks, sensory reinforcement, and access to tangible events or items (Carr, 1994; Horner, 1994).

FA comprises five phases: (a) initial data collection; (b) hypothesis generation; (c) intervention formulation; (d) treatment implementation and data collection; and (e) data analysis (Foster-Johnson & Dunlap, 1993; Horner, 1994). As in ABA, problem behaviors are operationalized, and antecedents, consequences, and contexts are described. Indirect methods (e.g., rating scales and interviews), direct observation, and experimental methods provide initial data (Mace, 1994). Hypotheses are generated regarding the function of target behaviors, and interventions are developed from hypotheses. For example, if the behaviors correlate with attention seeking, interventions may utilize positive reinforcement of an alternative behavior (DRA); if the behaviors correlate with escape from task demands, intervention may increase adaptive skills (skills training). Following intervention, data (baseline, treatment, control) are analyzed to determine treatment effectiveness and accuracy of hypotheses.

The foremost use of FA has been intervention in SIB (Day et al., 1994; Durand & Carr, 1992; Hagopian, Fisher, & Legacy, 1994; Iwata et al., 1982; Iwata, Pace, Cowdery, & Miltenberger, 1994; Iwata, Pace, Dorsey, et al., 1994; Lerman, Iwata, Smith, Zarcone, & Vollmer, 1994; Shore, Iwata, Lerman, & Shirley, 1994). In a summary of 152 single-subject analyses of reinforcing functions of SIB among persons with MR, Iwata, Pace, Dorsey, et al. (1994) observed differential or uniformly high responding in 145 cases: social-negative reinforcement (escape) accounted for 38% of cases, social-positive reinforcement (attention, food, or material objects) for 26%, sensory (automatic) responding for 26%, and multiple controlling variables for 5%. Differential treatment response was observed across groups. The social-positive group responded well to noncontingent reinforcement, extinction (attention), differential reinforcement, and time-out, but poorly to verbal reprimand and response interruption. The social-negative group responded well to noncontingent reinforcement, task modification, extinction (escape), and differential reinforcement, but poorly to extinction (attention), verbal reprimand, and time-out. Response rates for the automatic groups were inconsistent, but best to noncontingent reinforcement and poorest to extinction (attention), verbal reprimand, and time-out. Response among multiple control and undifferentiated persons was often good to noncontingent reinforcement, but poor to extinction (attention), verbal reprimand, and time-out. These data suggest that SIB in some persons with MR may be maintained by social reinforcement, and effective treatment depends on replacing SIB with an alternate socially reinforcing behavior. For example, aberrant escape behavior may be effectively reduced by "increasing the density of positive reinforcement for compliance, . . . gradually increasing response requirements during training, . . . teaching individuals to request help when faced with difficult tasks, . . . and strengthening alternative escape behaviors" (Iwata, Pace, Dorsey, et al., 1994, p. 236).

The conclusion of Iwata, Pace, Dorsey, et al. (1994)—that the primary function of SIB in MR is social reinforcement—may not apply to autism. Children with autism find physical contact with other humans (and even social attention) aversive, and they self-stimulate excessively. Thus, sensory stimulation may be the primary reinforcer. Planned ignoring (extinction) may never be an effective strategy for some autistic individuals. If a problem behavior delivers self-stimulation, then the options may be to replace it with a self-stimulatory behavior, to punish it out of existence, or to restrain the individual. The function of behavior in autistic persons needs thorough study. (For an application of FA to autistic children in a classroom setting, see Sasso et al., 1992.)

FA can be formidable. It is a scientific treatment modality, emphasizing application of experimental methods in clinical settings. Data are collected and analyzed; hypotheses are formed and tested. Interventions are fit to hypothesized functions of behavior (see, e.g., Iwata, Pace, Cowdery, et al., 1994). Based on its intense and complicated nature, one may question the value of FA for practitioners.

FA has been effective in applied settings. FA has been used with tantrums (Repp & Karsh, 1994), mild disruptive behaviors (Carr & Durand, 1985; Durand & Carr, 1992), feeding problems (Munk & Repp, 1994), stereotypy (Crawford, Brockel, & Schauss, 1992), and noncompliance in children without retardation (Rortvedt & Miltenberger, 1994), and FA has been recommended in practitioner journals (Cooper, Peck, Wacker, & Millard, 1993; Dadson & Horner, 1993; Foster-Johnson & Dunlap, 1993). When Repp and Karsh (1994) treated tantrum behavior in two female students with MR, all phases of the study were conducted in a classroom under normal teaching conditions. Two certified special education teachers and two instructional aides administered all interventions. Initial data collection suggested that problem behaviors were maintained by attention seeking, and interventions were based on a social reinforcement hypothesis. Redirection of teacher attention from inappropriate to appropriate behavior resulted in a substantial reduction of problem behavior.

FA has been effective in outpatient treatment of SIB and aggression (Derby et al., 1992; Harding, Wacker, Cooper, Millard, & Jensen-Kovalan, 1994; Wacker et al., 1994). Harding et al. (1994) described a brief functional assessment consisting of parent questionnaires and interviews, child preference assessment, and a 90-minute analogue assessment utilizing eight procedures (free play, general directions and discussion, specific directions, choice making, differential reinforcement of appropriate behavior, differential reinforcement of communication, preferred activities, and time-out and guided compliance). An interdisciplinary team reviewed data and recommended treatment. Six months after treatment, the parents of six of seven children in the study were contacted. All six parents appeared to have implemented treatment suggestions with reasonable integrity, and all reported "high" satisfaction with treatment.

In Functional Communication Training (FCT), a derivative of FA, disruptive behaviors are replaced with verbal behaviors that decrease task demand or increase social reinforcement (Carr & Durand, 1985; Durand & Carr, 1992). Carr & Durand (1985) treated children with disruptive behavior in a classroom. Initially, children were observed in easy and difficult task conditions, and disruptive behavior was rated as escape-related or social attention-seeking. Then, children were taught three classes of verbal responses: (a) easing task demand, (b) eliciting positive teacher attention, and (c) nonfunctional control. Attention-seeking children showed decreased disruption in the presence of attention-eliciting responses. Escape-oriented children showed decreased disruption in the presence of task demand responses. Control responses had no effect on behavior. Subsequently, Durand and Carr (1992) treated disruptive behavior in schoolchildren with time-out and FCT. Disruptive behavior responded to both interventions, but reduced disruption was generalized to a new teacher, naive to treatment conditions, only with FCT.

The intensity of FA may suggest that it is not a cost effective intervention. FA requires knowledge of learning theory and application of experimental methods in a clinical setting. However, there are decided benefits. FA is a individualized approach, it provides a theoretical base for selecting least invasive treatments from among potentially effective interventions, and it is effective in a naturalistic setting with relatively short initial data collection. Therefore, functional analysis is a preferred approach to treating the problems of persons with mental retardation and autism.

SUMMARY

MR is diagnosed when persons have substantial deficits in cognitive abilities and adaptive skills that affect two or more life domains; onset must precede age 18. Prevalence, which is about 2% of the general population, increases among males, African-Americans, and persons of low SES. MR is associated with impairments in learning, speech, language, social behavior, sensory perception, and motoric functioning, and with increased risk for emotional disturbances, especially mood, anxiety, and attentional disorders. Origin can be biomedical, social, behavioral, or educational, and onset can be pre-, peri-, or postnatal. The most frequent causes are fetal alcohol syndrome, trisomy 21, fragile X, and childhood head trauma. Real world impediments to treatment include the complex nature of the disorder and the need for an integrated social policy, lack of family support, financial costs, diagnostic overshadowing, and labeling. Assessment must include a standardized, individually administered IQ test and evaluation of adaptive skills.

Autism is characterized by pervasive social impairment; onset precedes age 3 years. Typically, autistic persons display social withdrawal and resist human contact, lack social communication skills, and engage in odd, repetitive, or ritualistic behavior. *Theory of Mind* suggests that autistic behaviors reflect an inability to attribute thoughts to other persons. Self-stimulation and self-injurious behavior are commonly observed. Prevalence, which is 5–15 in 10,000 persons, increases among males. Autism is associated with increased incidence of MR (about 70%), epilepsy (about 40%), and auditory-visual impairment. Risk of autism increases with degree of genetic relationship, and heritability may approach 90%. However, no single cause is known to account for more than 8% of autism. Impediments to real world intervention include the residue of early attempts to explain autism as a failure in parenting, late diagnosis of autism, the nature of the disease, and lack of family support. Diagnosis is based on direct observation of the child, clinical interviews, and rating scales. Once a diagnosis has been established, physical, neurological, cognitive, sensory-perceptual, and psychosocial evaluations are essential.

No cure exists for autism or cognitive deficits in MR, but improvements in adaptive skills are possible. Educational and psychopharmacological interventions may be helpful. Applied behavior analysis has been effective in improving current adaptive skills. Techniques include positive reward, punishment, extinction, token economies, contingency management, and self-management. Functional analysis is a hypothesis-driven derivative of behavior analysis. Maladaptive behaviors, assumed to provide escape from task demands, social reinforcement, or sensory reinforcement, are replaced by adaptive behaviors serving equivalent functions.

REFERENCES

Abbeduto, L., & Nuccio, J. B. (1991). Relation between receptive language and cognitive maturity in persons with mental retardation. *American Journal on Mental Retardation, 96,* 143–149.

Adams, G. L. (1984). *Comprehensive Test of Adaptive Behavior.* Columbus, OH: Merril.

American Association on Mental Retardation. (1992). *Mental retardation: Definition, classification, and systems of support* (9th ed.). Washington, DC: Author.

American Psychiatric Association. (1994). *Diagnostic and statistical manual of mental disorders* (4th ed.). Washington, DC: Author.

Bambara, L. M., Mitchell-Kvacky, N. A., & Iacobelli, S. (1994). Positive behavioral support for students with severe disabilities: An emerging multicomponent approach for addressing challenging behaviors. *School Psychology Review, 23,* 263–278.

Baron-Cohen, S. (1989). The autistic child's theory of mind: A case of specific developmental delay. *Journal of Child Psychology and Psychiatry, 30,* 285–297.

Bayley, N. (1969). *Bayley Scales of Infant Development: Birth to two years.* San Antonio, TX: Psychological Corporation.

Birenbaum, A., & Cohen, H. J. (1993). On the importance of helping families: Policy implications from a national study. *Mental Retardation, 31,* 67–74.

Blacher, J., & Baker, B. L. (1994). Family involvement in residential treatment of children with retardation: Is there evidence of detachment? *Journal of Child Psychology and Psychiatry, 35,* 505–520.

Bregman, J. D. (1991). Current developments in the understanding of mental retardation: Part 2. Psychopathology. *Journal of the American Academy of Child and Adolescent Psychiatry, 30,* 861–872.

Bruininks, R. H., Woodcock, R. W., Weatherman, R. F., & Hill, B. K. (1984). *Scales of Independent Behavior (SIB).* Allen, TX: DLM/Teaching Resources.

Campbell, M., Kafantaris, V., Malone, R. P., Kowalik, S. C., & Locascio, J. J. (1991). Diagnostic and assessment issues related to pharmacotherapy for children and adolescents with autism. *Behavior Modification, 15,* 326–354.

Carr, E. G. (1977). The motivation of self-injurious behavior: A review of some hypotheses. *Psychological Bulletin, 84,* 800–816.

Carr, E. G. (1994). Emerging themes in the functional analysis of problem behavior. *Journal of Applied Behavior Analysis, 27,* 393–399.

Carr, E. G., & Carlson, J. I. (1993). Reduction of severe behavior problems in the community using a multicomponent treatment approach. *Journal of Applied Behavior Analysis, 26,* 157–172.

Carr, E. G., & Durand, V. M. (1985). Reducing behavior problems through functional communication training. *Journal of Applied Behavior Analysis, 18,* 111–126.

Cooper, L. J., Peck, S., Wacker, D. P., & Millard, T. (1993). Functional assessment for a student with a mild mental disability and persistent behavior problems. *Teaching Exceptional Children, 25,* 56–57.

Crawford, J., Brockel, B., & Schauss, S. (1992). A comparison of methods for the functional assessment of stereotypic behavior. *Journal of the Association of Persons with Severe Handicaps, 17,* 77–86.

Crews, W. D., Bonaventura, S., & Rowe, F. (1994). Dual diagnosis: Prevalence of psychiatric disorders in a large state residential facility for individuals with mental retardation. *American Journal on Mental Retardation, 98,* 688–731.

Dadson, S., & Horner, R. H. (1993). Manipulating setting events to decrease problem behaviors: A case study. *Teaching Exceptional Children, 25,* 53–54.

Darley, J. M., & Gross, P. H. (1983). A hypothesis-confirming bias in labeling effects. *Journal of Personality and Social Psychology, 44,* 20–33.

Davis, C. A., Brady, M. P., Williams, R. E., & Hamilton, R. (1992). Effects of high probability requests on the acquisition and generalization of responses to requests in young children with behavior disorders. *Journal of Applied Behavior Analysis, 25,* 905–916.

Day, H. M., Horner, R. H., & O'Neill, R. E. (1994). Multiple functions of problem behaviors: Assessment and intervention. *Journal of Applied Behavior Analysis, 27,* 279–289.

DeMyer, M. K., Pontius, W., Norton, J. A., Barton, S., Allen, J., & Steele, R. (1972). Parental practices and innate activity in normal, autistic, and brain-damaged infants. *Journal of Autism and Childhood Schizophrenia, 2,* 49–66.

Derby, K. M., Wacker, D. P., Sasso, G., Steege, M., Northup, J., Cigrand, K., & Asmus, J. (1992). Brief functional assessment techniques to evaluate aberrant behavior in an outpatient setting: A summary of 79 cases. *Journal of Applied Behavior Analysis, 25,* 713–721.

Derks, S. A. (1995, July 15). Tennessee lags in group homes for retarded. *The Commercial Appeal,* pp. A1, A6.

Ducharme, J. M., & Worling, D. E. (1994). Behavioral momentum and stimulus fading in the acquisition and maintenance of child compliance in the home. *Journal of Applied Behavior Analysis, 27,* 639–647.

Durand, V. M., & Carr, E. G. (1992). An analysis of maintenance following functional communication training. *Jounral of Applied Behavior Analysis, 25,* 777–794.

Ehlers, S., & Gillberg, C. (1993). The epidemiology of Asperger syndrome: A total population study. *Journal of Child Psychology and Psychiatry, 34,* 1327–1350.

Epstein, M. H., Cullinan, D., & Polloway, E. A. (1986). Patterns of maladjustment among mentally retarded children and youth. *American Journal on Mental Deficiency, 91,* 127–134.

Epstein, M. H., Polloway, E. A., Patton, J. R., & Foley, R. (1989). Mild retardation: Student characteristics and services. *Education and Training of the Mentally Retarded, 24,* 7–16.

Fong, L., Wilgosh, L., & Sobsey, D. (1993). The experience of parenting an adolescent with autism. *International Journal of Disability, Development and Education, 40,* 105–113.

Foster-Johnson, L., & Dunlap, G. (1993). Using functional assessment to develop effective, individualized interventions for challenging behaviors. *Teaching Exceptional Children, 25,* 44–50.

Garber, N., & Veydt, N. (1990). Rett syndrome: A longitudinal developmental case report. *Journal of Communication Disorders, 23,* 61–75.

Ghaziuddin, M., Butler, E., Tsai, L., & Ghaziuddin, N. (1994). Is clumsiness a marker for Asperger syndrome? *Journal of Intellectual Disability Research, 38,* 519–527.

Ghaziuddin, M., Tsai, L., & Ghaziuddin, N. (1992). Brief report: A comparison of the diagnostic criteria for Asperger syndrome. *Journal of Autism and Developmental Disorders, 22,* 643–649.

Gillberg, C. (Ed.). (1989a). *Diagnosis and treatment of autism.* New York: Plenum Press.

Gillberg, C. (1989b). Early symptoms in autism. In C. Gillberg (Ed.), *Diagnosis and treatment of autism* (pp. 23–32). New York: Plenum Press.

Gillberg, C. (1990). Autism and pervasive developmental disorders *Journal of Child Psychology and Psychiatry, 31,* 99–119.

Gillberg, C. (1991a). Outcome in autism and autistic-like conditions. *Journal of the American Academy of Child and Adolescent Psychiatry, 30,* 375–382.

Gillberg, C. (1991b). The treatment of epilepsy in autism. *Journal of Autism and Developmental Disorders, 21,* 61–77.

Gillberg, C. (1993). Autism and related behaviors. *Journal of Intellectual Disability Research, 37,* 343–372.

Gillberg, C. (1994). Debate and argument: Having Rett syndrome in the ICD-10 PDD category does not make sense. *Journal of Child Psychology and Psychiatry, 35,* 377–378.

Gillberg, C., & Schaumann, H. (1989). Autism: Specific problems of adolescence. In C. Gillberg (Ed.), *Diagnosis and treatment of autism* (pp. 375–382). New York: Plenum Press.

Gillberg, I. C., & Gillberg, C. (1989). Asperger syndrome—Some epidemiological considerations: A research note. *Journal of Child Psychology and Psychiatry, 30,* 631–638.

Grace, N. C., Kahng, S. W., & Fisher, W. W. (1994). Balancing social acceptability with treatment effectiveness of an intrusive procedure: A case report. *Journal of Applied Behavior Analysis, 27,* 171–172.

Green, L., Fein, D., Joy, S., & Waterhouse, L. (1995). Cognitive functioning in autism: An overview. In E. Schopler & G. B. Mesibov (Eds.), *Learning and cognition in autism* (pp. 13–31). New York: Plenum Press.

Hagerman, R. J. (1989). Chromosomes, genes and autism. In C. Gillberg (Ed.), *Diagnosis and treatment of autism* (pp. 105–131). New York: Plenum Press.

Hagopian, L. P., Fisher, W. W., & Legacy, S. M. (1994). Schedule effects of noncontingent reinforcement on attention-maintained destructive behavior in identical quadruplets. *Journal of Applied Behavior Analysis, 27,* 317–325.

Handen, B. L. (1993). Pharmacotherapy in mental retardation and autism. *School Psychology Review, 22,* 162–183.

Happé, F., & Frith, U. (1995). Theory of mind in autism. In E. Schopler & G. B. Mesibov (Eds.), *Learning and cognition in autism* (pp. 177–197). New York: Plenum Press.

Harding, J., Wacker, D. P., Cooper, L. J., Millard, T., & Jensen-Kovalan, P. (1994). Brief hierarchical assessment of potential treatment components with children in an outpatient clinic. *Journal of Applied Behavior Analysis, 27,* 291–300.

Haring, T. G., & Breen, C. G. (1992). A peer-mediated social network intervention to enhance the social integration of persons with moderate and severe disabilities. *Journal of Applied Behavior Analysis, 25,* 319–333.

Harris, S. L. (1995). Educational strategies in autism. In E. Schopler & G. B. Mesibov (Eds.), *Learning and cognition in autism* (pp. 293–309). New York: Plenum Press.

Hastings, R. P. (1994). On "good" terms: Labeling people with mental retardation. *Mental Retardation, 32,* 363–365.

Hobson, R. P. (1986a). The autistic child's appraisal of expressions of emotion. *Journal of Child Psychology and Psychiatry, 27,* 321–342.

Hobson, R. P. (1986b). The autistic child's appraisal of expressions of emotion: A further study. *Journal of Child Psychology and Psychiatry, 27,* 671–680.

Hodapp, R. M., & Zigler, E. (1993). Comparison of families of children with mental retardation and families of children without mental retardation. *Mental Retardation, 31,* 75–77.

Horner, R. H. (1994). Functional assessment: Contributions and future directions. *Journal of Applied Behavior Analysis, 27,* 401–404.

Iverson, J. C., & Fox, R. A. (1989). Prevalence of psychopathology among mentally retarded adults. *Research in Developmental Disabilities, 10,* 77–83.

Iwata, B. A., Dorsey, M. F., Slifer, K. J., Bauman, K. E., & Richman, G. S. (1982). Toward a functional analysis of self-injury. *Analysis and Intervention in Developmental Disabilities, 2,* 3–20.

Iwata, B. A., Pace, G. M., Cowdery, G. E., & Miltenberger, R. G. (1994). What makes extinction work: An analysis of procedural form and function. *Journal of Applied Behavior Analysis, 27,* 131–144.

Iwata, B. A., Pace, G. M., Dorsey, M. F., Zarcone, J. R., Vollmer, T. R., Smith, R. G., Rodgers, T. A., Lerman, D. C., Shore, B. A., Mazaleski, J. L., Goh, H. L., Cowdery, G. E., Kalsher, M. J., McCosh, K. C., & Willis, K. D. (1994). The functions of self-injurious behavior: An experimental-epidemiological analysis. *Journal of Applied Behavior Analysis, 27,* 215–240.

Jacobson, J. W. (1982). Problem behavior and psychiatric impairment within a developmentally disabled population: 1. Behavior frequency. *Applied Research in Mental Retardation, 3,* 121–139.

Jakab, I. (1993). Pharmacological treatment. In V. B. Van Hasselt & M. Hersen (Eds.), *Handbook of behavior therapy and pharmacotherapy for children: A comparative analysis* (pp. 171–193). Boston: Allyn & Bacon.

Jellison, J. A., & Duke, R. A. (1994). The mental retardation label: Music teachers' and prospective teachers' expectations for children's social and music behaviors. *Journal of Music Therapy, 31,* 166–185.

Jure, R., Rapin, I., & Tuchman, R. F. (1991). Hearing-impaired autistic children. *Developmental Medicine and Child Neurology, 33,* 1062–1072.

Kanner, L. (1943). Autistic disturbances of affective contact. *Nervous Child, 2,* 217–250.

King, B. H., DeAntonio, C., McCracken, J. T., Forness, S. R., & Ackerland, V. (1994). Psychiatric consultation in severe and profound mental retardation. *American Journal of Psychiatry, 151,* 1802–1808.

Klin, A. (1993). Auditory brainstem responses in autism: Brainstem dysfunction or peripheral hearing loss? *Journal of Autism and Developmental Disorders, 23,* 15–35.

Kobe, F. H., Mulick, J. A., Rash, T. A., & Martin, J. (1994). Nonambulatory persons with profound mental retardation: Physical, developmental, and behavioral characteristics. *Research in Developmental Disabilities, 15,* 413–423.

Koegel, L. K., Koegel, R. L., Hurley, C., & Frea, W. D. (1992). Improving social skills and disruptive behavior in children with autism through self-management. *Journal of Applied Behavior Analysis, 25,* 341–353.

Lambert, N. M., Windmiller, M., Tharinger, D., & Cole, L. J. (1981). *AAMD Adaptive Behavior Scale-School edition.* Monterey, CA: CBT/McGraw-Hill.

Langford, C. A., Boas, G. J., Garner, W. E., & Strohmer, D. C. (1994). Selecting clients for supported employment: Functional criteria or categorical labels. *Journal of Applied Rehabilitation Counseling, 25,* 37–41.

Lansing, M.D. (1989). Educational evaluation. In C. Gillberg (Ed.), *Diagnosis and treatment of autism* (pp. 151–166). New York: Plenum Press.

Lerman, D. C., Iwata, B. A., Smith, R. G., Zarcone, J. R., & Vollmer, T. R. (1994). Transfer of behavioral function as a contributing factor in treatment relapse. *Journal of Applied Behavior Analysis, 27,* 357–370.

Lord, C., Mulloy, C., Wendelboe, M., & Schopler, E. (1991). Pre- and perinatal factors in high-functioning females and males with autism. *Journal of Autism and Developmental Disorders, 21,* 197–209.

Mace, F. C. (1994). The significance and future of functional analysis methodologies. *Journal of Applied Behavior Analysis, 27,* 385–392.

Mace, F. C., Lalli, J. S., Shea, M. C., Lalli, E. P., West, B. J., Roberts, M., & Nevin, J. A. (1990). The momentum of human behavior in a natural setting. *Journal of the Experimental Analysis of Behavior, 54,* 163–172.

Matson, J. L., Taras, M. E., Sevin, J. A., Love, S. R., & Fridley, D. (1990). Teaching self-help skills to autistic and mentally retarded children. *Research in Developmental Disabilities, 11,* 361–378.

Mayes, L., Volkmar, F., Hooks, M., & Cicchetti, D. (1993). Differentiating Pervasive Developmental Disorder not Otherwise Specified from autism and language disorders. *Journal of Autism and Developmental Disorders, 23,* 79–90.

McAdoo, W. G., & DeMyer, M. K. (1978). Personality characteristics of parents. In M. Rutter & E. Schopler (Eds.), *Autism: A reappraisal of concepts and treatment* (pp. 251–267). New York: Plenum Press.

McCallion, P., & Toseland, R. W. (1993). Empowering families of adolescents and adults with developmental disabilities. *Families in Society: The Journal of Contemporary Human Services, 74,* 579–587.

McClannahan, L. E., Krantz, P. J., & McGee, G. G. (1982). Parents as therapists for autistic children: A model for effective parent training. *Analysis and Intervention in Developmental Disabilities, 2,* 223–252.

McLaren, J., & Bryson, S. E. (1987). Review of recent epidemiological studies of mental retardation: Prevalence, associated disorders, and etiology. *American Journal of Mental Retardation, 92,* 243–254.

McLennan, J. D., Lord, C., & Schopler, E. (1993). Sex differences in higher functioning people with autism. *Journal of Autism and Developmental Disorders, 23,* 217–227.

Munk, D. D., & Repp, A. C. (1994). Behavioral assessment of feeding problems of individuals with severe disabilities. *Journal of Applied Behavior Analysis, 27,* 241–250.

Nevin, J. A., Mandell, C., & Atak, J. R. (1983). The analysis of behavioral momentum. *Journal of the Experimental Analysis of Behavior, 39,* 49–59.

Nietupski, J. A., & Robinson, G. A. (1994). Severe and profound mental retardation. In M. Beirne-Smith, J. R. Patton, & R. Ittenbach (Eds.), *Mental retardation* (4th ed., pp. 242–278). Englewood Cliffs, NJ: Macmillan.

Nihira, K., Foster, R., Shellhaas, M., & Leland, H. (1974). *AAMD Adaptive Behavior Scales* (Rev. ed.). Washington, DC: American Association on Mental Deficiency.

Pierce, K. L., & Schreibman, L. (1994). Teaching daily living skills to children with autism in unsupervised settings through pictorial self-management. *Journal of Applied Behavior Analysis, 27,* 471–481.

Pitfield, M., & Oppenheim, A. N. (1964). Child-rearing attitudes of mothers of psychotic children. *Journal of Child Psychology and Psychiatry, 5,* 51–57.

Piven, J., & Folstein, S. (1994). The genetics of autism. In M. L. Bauman & T. L. Kemper (Eds.), *The neurobiology of autism* (pp. 18–44). Baltimore: Johns Hopkins University Press.

Piven, J., Simon, J., Chase, G. A., Wzorek, M., Landa, R., Gayle, J., & Folstein, S. (1993). The etiology of autism: Pre-, peri-, and neonatal factors. *Journal of the American Academy of Child and Adolescent Psychiatry, 32,* 1256–1263.

Polloway, E. A., Epstein, M. H., Patton, J. R., Cullinan, D., & Luebke, J. (1986). Demographic, social, and behavioral characteristics of students with educable mental retardation. *Education and Training of the Mentally Retarded, 21,* 27–34.

Polloway, E. A., & Smith, J. D. (1994). Causes and prevention. In M. Beirne-Smith, J. R. Patton, & R. Ittenbach (Eds.), *Mental retardation* (4th ed., pp. 136–201). Englewood Cliffs, NJ: Macmillan.

Repp, A. C., & Karsh, K. G. (1994). Hypothesis-based interventions for tantrum behaviors of persons with developmental disabilities in school settings. *Journal of Applied Behavior Analysis, 27,* 21–31.

Rickarby, G., Carruthers, A., & Mitchell, M. (1991). Brief report: Biological factors associated with Asperger syndrome. *Journal of Autism and Developmental Disorders, 21,* 341–348.

Rortvedt, A. K., & Miltenberger, R. G. (1994). Analysis of a high probability instructional sequence and time-out in the treatment of child noncompliance. *Journal of Applied Behavior Analysis, 27,* 327–330.

Rosenhan, D. L. (1973). On being sane in insane places. *Science, 179,* 250–258.

Sasso, G. M., Reimers, T. M., Cooper, L. J., Wacker, D., Berg, W., Steege, M., Kelly, L., & Allaire, A. (1992). Use of descriptive and experimental analyses to identify the functional properties of aberrant behavior in school settings. *Journal of Applied Behavior Analysis, 25,* 809–821.

Sattler, J. M. (1992). *Assessment of children* (3rd ed., rev.). San Diego, CA: Author.

Schalock, R. L., Stark. J. A., Snell, M. E., Coulter, D. L., Polloway, E. A., Luckasson, R., Reiss, S., & Spitalnik, D. M. (1994). The changing conception of mental retardation: Implications for the field. *Mental Retardation, 32,* 181–193.

Schopler, E. (1989). Principles for directing both educational treatment and research. In C. Gillberg (Ed.), *Diagnosis and treatment of autism* (pp. 167–183). New York: Plenum Press.

Schopler, E., Mesibov, G. B., & Hearsey, K. (1995). Structured teaching in the TEACCH system. In E. Schopler & G. B. Mesibov (Eds.), *Learning and cognition in autism* (pp. 243–268). New York: Plenum Press.

Schreibman, L. E. (1988). *Autism.* Newbury Park, CA: Sage.

Scudder, R. R., & Tremain, D. H. (1992). Repair behaviors of children with and without mental retardation. *Mental Retardation, 30,* 277–282.

Shore, B. A., Iwata, B. A., Lerman, D. C., & Shirley, M. J. (1994). Assessing and programming generalized behavior reduction across multiple stimulus parameters. *Journal of Applied Behavior Analysis, 27,* 371–384.

Sierpina, D. (1994, February 13). How the care of retarded people is changing course. *New York Times,* p. 13CN1.

Simblett, G. J., & Wilson, D. N. (1993). Asperger's syndrome: Three cases and a discussion. *Journal of Intellectual Disability Research, 37,* 85–94.

Singh, N. N., Sood, A., Sonenklar, N., & Ellis, C. R. (1991). Assessment and diagnosis of mental illness in persons with mental retardation. *Behavior Modification, 15,* 419–443.

Singhi, P. D., Goyal, L., Pershad, D., & Singhi, S. (1990). Psychosocial problems in families of disabled children. *British Journal of Medical Psychology, 63,* 173–182.

Smalley, S. L., Asarnow, R. F., & Spence, M. A. (1988). Autism and genetics: A decade of research. *Archives of General Psychiatry, 45,* 953–961.

Sonnander, K., Emanuelsson, I., & Kebbon, L. (1993). Pupils with mild mental retardation in regular Swedish schools: Prevalence, objective characteristics, and subjective evaluations. *American Journal on Mental Retardation, 97,* 692–701.

Sparrow, S. S., Balla D. A., & Cicchetti, D. V. (1984). *Vineland Adaptive Behavior Scales.* Circle Pines, MN: American Guidance Service.

Stahmer, A. C., & Schreibman, L. (1992). Teaching children with autism appropriate play in unsupervised environments using a self-management treatment package. *Journal of Applied Behavior Analysis, 25,* 447–459.

Steffenburg, S. (1991). Neuropsychiatric assessment of children with autism: A population-based study. *Developmental Medicine and Child Neurology, 33,* 495–511.

Steffenburg, S., & Gillberg, C. (1989). The etiology of autism. In C. Gillberg (Ed.), *Diagnosis and treatment of autism* (pp. 63–82). New York: Plennum Press.

Steffenburg, S., Gillberg, C., Hellgren, L., Andersson, L., Gillberg, I. C., Jakobsson, G., & Bohman, M. (1989). A twin study of autism in Denmark, Finland, Iceland, Norway, and Sweden. *Journal of Child Psychology and Psychiatry, 30,* 405–416.

Sturmey, P., & Sevin, J. (1993). Dual diagnosis: An annotated biography of recent research. *Journal of Intellectual Disability Research, 37,* 437–448.

Thomas, C. H., & Patton, J. R. (1994). Characteristics of individuals with milder forms of retardation. In M. Beirne-Smith, J. R. Patton, & R. Ittenbach (Eds.), *Mental retardation* (4th ed., pp. 205–240). Englewood Cliffs, NJ: Macmillan.

Thorndike, R. L., Hagen, E. P., & Sattler, J. M. (1986a). *Guide for administering and scoring: The Stanford-Binet Intelligence Scale* (4th ed.). Chicago: Riverside.

Thorndike, R. L., Hagen, E. P., & Sattler, J. M. (1986b). *Technical manual: The Stanford-Binet Intelligence Scale* (4th ed.). Chicago: Riverside.

Tsai, L. Y. (1992). Is Rett syndrome a subtype of pervasive developmental disorders? *Journal of Autism and Developmental Disorders, 22,* 551–561.

Van Acker, R. (1991). Rett syndrome: A review of current knowledge. *Journal of Autism and Developmental Disorders, 21,* 381–406.

Volkmar, F. R. (1992). Childhood Disintegrative Disorder: Issues for DSM-IV. *Journal of Autism and Developmental Disorders, 22,* 625–642.

Volkmar, F. R., & Cohen, D. J. (1989). Disintegrative Disorder or "late onset" autism. *Journal of Child Psychology and Psychiatry, 30,* 717–724.

Volkmar, F. R., Klin, A., Siegel, B., Szatmari, P., Lord, C., Campbell, M., Freeman, B. J., Cicchetti, D. V., Rutter, M., Kline, W., Buitelaar, J., Hattab, Y., Fombonne, E., Fuentes, J., Werry, J., Stone, W., Kerbeshian, J., Hoshino, Y., Bregman, J., Loveland, K., Szymanski, L., & Towbin, K. (1994). Field trial for autistic disorder in DSM-IV. *American Journal of Psychiatry, 151,* 1361–1367.

Vostanis, P., Smith, B., Chung, M. C., & Corbett, J. (1994). Early detection of autism: A review of screening instruments and rating scales. *Child: Care, Health, and Development, 20,* 165–177.

Wacker, D. P., Berg, W. K., Cooper, L. J., Derby, K. M., Steege, M. W., Northup, J., & Sasso, G. (1994). The impact of functional analysis methodology on outpatient clinic services. *Journal of Applied Behavior Analysis, 27,* 405–407.

Warren, K. R., & Bast, R. J. (1988). Alcohol-related birth defects: An update. *Public Health Reports, 103,* 638–642.

Wechsler, D. (1981). *Manual for the Wechsler Adult Intelligent Scale* (Rev.). San Antonio, TX: Psychological Corporation.

Wechsler, D. (1989). *Manual for the Wechsler Preschool and Primary Scale of Intelligence* (Rev.). San Antonio, TX: Psychological Corporation.

Wechsler, D. (1991). *Manual for the Wechsler Intelligence Scale for Children* (3rd ed.). San Antonio, TX: Psychological Corporation.

Wenk, G. L., Naidu, S., Casanova, M. F., Kitt, C. A., & Moser, H. (1991). Altered neurochemical markers in Rett's syndrome. *Neurology, 41,* 1753–1756.

Wing, L. (1981). Language, social, and cognitive impairments in autism and severe mental retardation. *Journal of Autism and Developmental Disorders, 11,* 31–44.

Wing, L., & Gould, J. (1979). Severe impairments of social interaction and associated abnormalities in children: Epidemiology and classification. *Journal of Autism and Developmental Disorders, 9,* 11–29.

Zarcone, J. R., Iwata, B. A., Mazaleski, J. L., & Smith, R. G. (1994). Momentum and extinction effects on self-injurious escape behavior and noncompliance. *Journal of Applied Behavior Analysis, 27,* 649–658.

Zigler, E., Balla, D., & Hodapp, R. (1984). On the definition and classification of mental retardation. *American Journal of Mental Deficiency, 3,* 215–230.

CHAPTER 20

Conduct Disorder

MARK R. DADDS

DESCRIPTION OF THE DISORDER

The term conduct disorder (CD) refers to a persistent cluster of antisocial behaviors occurring in approximately 5% of school-age children and adolescents. The disorder appears in various forms at different times throughout childhood and adolescence, but the most common behaviors include antisocial behavior and aggression to others, oppositional behavior to caregivers, theft, vandalism, firesetting, truancy, and lying. Throughout history, this cluster of behaviors has attracted various names, such as delinquency and antisocial behavior, and has been approached from several perspectives, ranging from a failure of moral development to a sociopolitical problem. Current parlance assumes the cluster can be thought of as a psychological or behavioral "disorder" and thus, the phenomenon has largely now become the domain of mental health professionals, and the term conduct disorder is a formal diagnosis specified by the *Diagnostic and Statistical Manual of Mental Disorders (DSM-IV)* of the American Psychiatric Association (APA, 1994).

The use of the formal diagnostic category of CD carries certain advantages, allowing clinicians and researchers a common language and facilitating the interpretability and generalizability of clinical studies of children thus diagnosed. However, it has inherent problems. CD is a subset of a wide range of behavior problems in children that can be referred to as disruptive behavior problems. The extent to which a child has disruptive behavior is a dimensional phenomenon. That is, children vary in the type, frequency, and severity of their behavior that causes problems to parents, teachers, peers, and society in general. Many children are referred for treatment of disruptive behavior problems who do not meet the formal diagnostic criteria. The formal term CD is used to identify a subset of disruptive children who show severe and persistent behavior problems. The cutoff point between those who attract a formal diagnosis and those whose behavior problems are subclinical is largely arbitrary. While research indicates that referred and nonreferred samples are readily distinguishable (e.g., Forehand & Long, 1988), there are few studies documenting differences between children referred for disruptive behavior problems with and without a formal diagnosis of CD other than the severity of their problems.

A major problem in interpreting the literature in this area is that many studies have used broad samples of children referred for disruptive behavior problems, or children selected from nonreferred samples who are found to have disruptive behavior problems on the basis of a screening measure. Only a subset of recent studies have used children specifically diagnosed with CD. A review limited to these latter studies would lose much of the richness of accumulated evidence about the characteristics of disruptive children. Thus, this review will cast the net widely. In this chapter, conduct problems and disruptive behavior problems will refer to the general population of children who are referred for disruptive behavior problems common in CD. Where the literature being referred to has specifically used a diagnosed sample, the term CD will be used.

The behaviors characteristic of the disorder can vary in frequency and severity, and can cluster in various combinations, but a formal diagnosis is not made unless they cause significant impairments to the daily functioning of the child and his or her social environment. For example, the *DSM-IV* (APA, 1994) requires the following criteria be met for a formal diagnosis:

- A repetitive and persistent pattern of behavior in which the basic rights of others, or major age-appropriate societal norms or rules are violated.
- Three or more behaviors from the following categories must be present sometime during the past 12 months, with at least one behavior occurring during the past 6 months: aggression to people and animals, serious violations of rules, destruction of property, and deceitfulness or theft.
- Disturbance must cause clinically significant impairment in social, academic, or occupational functioning.

While reasonable consensus now exists on the diagnostic features of the disorder, there is still some disagreement as to the central characteristics that are hypothesized to underlie the disorder. Further, if it is assumed that there are one or more such characteristics, the behavioral manifestations vary across specific children and their developmental stage (Loeber, 1990). The good news about CD is that it has been the subject of a large research effort over the past several decades. There is now reasonable consensus among scientists on the developmental patterns of the disorder and the risk factors for its persistence. Further, several treatments have been developed and evaluated that can minimize the problem during its early stages. The bad news is that if CD is not effectively treated, it often represents a lifetime of social impairment and distress for the person with the disorder as well as for others in his or her social environment.

EPIDEMIOLOGY

Rates of CD in the general population vary between 2% and 6% (Kazdin, 1993). For example, Rutter, Tizard, Yule, Graham, and Whitmore (1976) found that 4% of 10- to 11-year-old children had a diagnosable CD and that 70% of children who had any type of psychiatric disorder were diagnosed with CD. The frequency of children referred for disruptive behavior problems more generally would be even higher (Anderson, Williams, McGee, & Silva, 1987). Thus, conduct problems represent one of the most common child mental health problems.

The rates of CD and disruptive behavior in general are much higher in boys than girls. Speer (1971) found that approximately two-thirds of children diagnosed with CD were boys, a percentage that corresponds closely with Forehand and Long's (1988) data on children referred for disruptive behavior problems. Rates of CD are generally higher in families and geographic areas marked by low socioeconomic status (West, 1982). Low SES is a marker for many possible risk factors including genetic, environmental toxicity, poor educational opportunities, poverty, social isolation, lack of employment, and modeling of violence. In addition to being a clear risk factor for CD, it has been identified as a risk factor for many other forms of behavioral disturbance and psychopathology.

The age of onset of CD can range from early childhood to the teenage years, and there is evidence to suggest that early onset is associated with a poorer prognosis (Loeber, 1990). Similarly, the extent to which the problem behavior is expressed across multiple settings (i.e., in the home, school, community) is also a predictor of severity and durability of the CD (Kazdin, 1993; Loeber, 1990).

Comorbidity is a critical factor in CD. Kazdin, Siegel, and Bass (1992) found that 70% of youth aged 7 to 13 referred for CD met criteria for more than one disorder, with the mean number of diagnoses per case at slightly over two. Disorders such as depression, substance abuse, learning difficulties, and adjustment problems co-occur with CD, but the most common comorbid conditions are oppositional defiant disorder (ODD) and hyperactivity or attention-deficit/hyperactivity disorder (ADHD). In fact, the degree of overlap between these disorders is so high as to call into question their independence. Estimates of co-occurrence of ODD and CD range from 20% to 60%, and co-occurrence of CD and ADHD from 60% to 90% (Abikoff & Klein, 1992). The current wisdom is that ODD is probably a milder form of and, in many cases, a developmental precurser to CD, leading many authors to group them together in diagnostics (e.g., Abikoff & Klien, 1992) and treatment (e.g., Dadds, Schwartz, & Sanders, 1987) studies.

The relationship between CD and ADHD is more problematic. Hinshaw (1987) concluded that the dimensions of hyperactivity-inattention and conduct problems-aggression are moderately correlated (mean $r = .56$) even when attempts are made to remove overlapping assessment items. In studies of nonclinic populations using cut-off scores to classify children, between 30% and 90% of children classified in one category of CD or ADHD will also be classified as the other. However, children classified as CD are more likely to be also classified ADHD than vice versa, and this is true for clinic-referred samples as well (Hinshaw, 1987). For example, Reeves, Werry, Elkind, and Zametkin (1987) found that "pure" ADHD children were easy to identify whereas the vast majority of CD children had ADHD features in the home or school or both.

These patterns of comorbidity may be influenced by adult rating and referral factors as well as the actual nature of the disorders. One important and replicated finding is that teachers' ratings of hyperactivity in a child will be inflated if the child displays conduct problems, but ratings of conduct problems are not similarly inflated by displays of hyperactivity (Abikoff, Courtney, Pelham, & Koplewicz, 1993; Schachar, Sandberg, & Rutter, 1986). These effects have not been tested in parents as yet but they indicate that the covariance of CD and ADHD contains a complex mix of actual manifest and adult rating phenomena.

When children display ADHD as well as conduct problems, there is an increased risk of persistent CD in adolescence (Loeber, 1990). Moffitt and Silva (1988) compared delinquents with and without ADHD. The former scored worse on tests of verbal and visual integration, but children with ADHD who did not develop CD were less impaired on measures of verbal memory. Thus, it is important to consider the early presence of ADHD symptoms and other cognitive deficits in the development of CD.

Causes and Consequences

Based on the seminal work of researchers such as Patterson, Loeber, Farrington, Rutter, and others, a reasonably clear picture of the developmental course of CD has developed. In its most severe and persistent forms, CD takes an identifiable path from childhood to adulthood. Along this path, different causal factors can emerge. The prescription of a developmental course refers to a commonality among groups of CD children and it is easy to think of exceptions to that general pattern: youths who, after years of being well behaved showed the first signs of conduct problems in adolescence, and children who were highly oppositional and difficult as children but "grew out of it" by adolescence.

Notwithstanding these individual differences, it is crucial that CD is conceptualized as a developmental sequence involving multiple causative factors that interact at critical points or transition phases to produce the more chronic possibilities of this disorder. In this conceptualization, there can be no one cause or treatment of choice for CD. Rather, windows of opportunity exist, corresponding to the developmental progress of the disorder and the settings in which it occurs, at which time different interventions may ameliorate current problems in the child's life, or prevent potential problems from developing. This developmental perspective on the disorder blurs the usual distinction between treatment and prevention. That is, the treatment of current problems can and should be seen as a preventive strategy against the next stage or transition in the chronic potential of the disorder (e.g., Conduct Problems Prevention Research Group, 1992). As Loeber (1990) points out, given the early detectable signs of the disorder, pure primary prevention efforts are only possible in the earliest stages of child development.

Early Biological Markers

Children vary in their vulnerability to behavioral and emotional problems. The review by Rutter et al. (1990) indicated that the evidence of genetic vulnerability differs across different disorders, but the evidence with regard to oppositional, conduct, and hyperactivity disorders in children is currently too weak to make any definitive conclusions (although being male is a genetic risk factor for CD). Among other factors that may have a genetic component, numerous authors have pointed to "temperamental" difficulties (high activity level, feeding and sleeping difficulties) as a precursor to disruptive behavior problems (Loeber, 1990; Thomas & Chess, 1977). These temperamental difficulties, themselves related to parental adjustment problems (Zeanah, Keener, Stewart, & Anders, 1985), mark a pattern of parent-child conflict and high punitive/low nurturant parental discipline strategies that characterize the early stages of the disruptive behavior problems of childhood (Patterson, 1982).

As noted earlier, the presence of ADHD and other cognitive deficits significantly contributes to the persistence of CD, and so any factors that predict ADHD and other learning problems need to be considered. The presence of neurotoxic chemicals such as lead in the blood of children is significantly associated with ADHD and other cognitive deficits (Needleman & Bellinger, 1981), as are early malnutrition, low birth weight, and substance abuse by the mother during pregnancy (Loeber, 1990). These factors are easily but mistakenly interpretable as genetic factors across generations and are also linked with low SES. Thus, the early biochemical environment may make the child vulnerable to cognitive and behavior problems predictive of ADHD and CD.

Early Family Influences

The first definite signs of disruptive behavior problems can be observed and measured in the toddler years as the child learns to walk and speak and interact with others socially. Child characteristics such as irritability, noncompliance, inattentiveness, and impulsivity measured as young as 2 and 3 years of age are predictive of later CD (e.g., Campbell, 1991). These behavioral characteristics are reliably associated with family characteristics such as marital conflict and divorce, parental psychopathology, punitive discipline and low nurturance, and low SES and social isolation (Dadds, 1987, 1995). At extremes, the presence of physical abuse and neglect of the young child may also be associated with the development of conduct problems (Cicchetti, 1984).

Case studies have been fairly consistent in describing the families of these children as aggressive; disorganized and chaotic; economically stressed; marked by parent rejection, harsh discipline and abuse; and disrupted by divorce and separation (Kazdin, 1987a). At the systemic level, case descriptions of these families have stressed power imbalances and chaotic, disengaged relationships (e.g., Minuchin, Montalvo, Guerney, Rosman, & Schumer, 1967). Correlational studies have tended to confirm this pattern of aggression and disruption. Group comparison studies have confirmed a pattern in which a range of risk factors are associated with increased risk for aggression and conduct problems. These include marital distress, parental depression, paternal antisocial problems, socioeconomic stress and social isolation, harsh punishment, insufficient parental monitoring, abuse and neglect (Hetherington & Martin, 1979; Kazdin, 1987a). Perhaps one reason for this plethora of risk factors is that conduct problems are a diverse group of behaviors that, in a categorical sense, coexist with so many other forms of child disturbance. Conduct problems are found in approximately 70% of children with any psychiatric diagnosis (Rutter, Cox, Tupling, Berger, & Yule, 1975) and many different forms of child psychopathology contain similar discrete behavior problems. For example, aggression is commonly associated with CD, attention deficit disorder with hyperactivity, some forms of developmental delay, adjustment disorders and depression (Kazdin, 1987a).

The case studies and correlational designs previously referred to leave little doubt that these associations exist between conduct problems and a range of family factors. Studies demonstrating that experimental manipulations of parent behavior result in concomitant changes in aggressive, noncompliant child behaviors have been common in the child behavior therapy literature (Lochman, 1990). The most important parenting behaviors are harsh discipline, lack of modeling and positive attention to prosocial behavior, and deficits in monitoring in the child's activities (Loeber, 1990; Patterson, 1986). These clinical trials have typically involved the modification of parent behavior through parent training programs and behavioral family therapy (Miller & Prinz, 1990) and have provided strong evidence of the dependent relationship between oppositional child behavior and interactional patterns with parents. These interactional patterns involve the direct contingencies that parents provide to aggressive and oppositional child behavior. It appears that disturbed children tend to come from families who engage in relatively high rates of the disturbed behavior themselves in their day-to-day interactions. The aggressive child is regularly exposed to conflicts among family members, is likely to receive high rates of aversive instructions, and many of his or her behaviors will be followed by aversive consequences regardless of their appropriateness.

There may also be evidence to support the systemic hypothesis that children with conduct problems come from families with deviant or reversed family hierarchies in which the child has more power than parents (Haley, 1976; Minuchin, 1974). Green, Loeber, and Lahey (1992) showed that these structures appear to be specific to families of children with CD (compared with overanxious, oppositional disorder, depression, and attention-deficit/hyperactivity). However, examination of their longitudinal data revealed that CD in the child predicted a deviant family hierarchy one year later, but the reverse was not true. Thus, it appears that the family system organizes itself into this reversed hierarchical form because of the child's aggressive behavior, and is not a causal factor.

One of the most productive areas relating the family to the early development of conduct problems focuses on the actual moment-to-moment interactions that the family provides as a learning context for children (e.g., Patterson & Reid, 1984). Interactions are conceived and measured as sequences of discrete but interdependent communicative behaviors. Some important methodologies and findings have emerged from this approach. For example, observations of families of disruptive and aggressive children in natural environments have shown members of families that contain aggressive and conduct problem children are more likely to initiate and reciprocate aggressive behaviors than members of families of nonproblem children (Patterson, 1982; Sanders, Dadds, & Bor, 1989). Thus the families of conduct problem children provide their child with an environment conducive to learning a repertoire of aggressive behavior.

Studies demonstrating that experimental manipulations of parent behavior result in concomitant changes in aggressive, noncompliant child behaviors have been common in the child psychotherapy literature (Lochman, 1990). These clinical trials have provided strong evidence of the dependent relationship between oppositional child behavior and interactional patterns with parents. Patterson (1982) has developed a model for understanding these repetitive family interaction patterns. Coercion or reinforcement traps can occur in two ways. First, parents often inadvertently reinforce problematic child behaviors because doing so is, in itself, reinforcing to the parent as the child's problem behavior temporarily ceases. Second, reinforcement traps work by diminishing the contrast between problematic and desirable child behavior. The more a child engages in problem behaviors, the less likely the child will be reinforced for positive behaviors. Parents who feel they are spending hours engaged in unpleasant interactions with a child (sorting out fights, arguing over chores, having attention demanded) are less likely to notice and attend to the child's positive behaviors. Thus, a vicious circle entraps the parent and the child in which the parent has a "break" whenever the child is not misbehaving, and the child must escalate problem behaviors to obtain the parent's attention. The examples considered here refer to problem interactions between two persons; however, reinforcement traps can occur in considerably more complex forms (see, e.g., Sanders & Dadds, 1993).

The Development of Social Cognition

Other interpersonal models of parent-child interactions have come from attachment theory and the development of social cognition. Bowlby (1973, 1969/1980, 1982), the prominent attachment theorist, integrated the clinical observations of the psychoanalysts with an ethological approach usually used by evolutionists and biologists. He drew upon observations of children reared under different degrees of attachment to parental figures such as in orphanages and intact families. He argued that infants are driven to form a small number of stable attachments with other people and that the creation and maintenance of these bonds are necessary for healthy human development. Disruption of these bonds results in displays of ethologically fixed behaviors patterns of fear, anger, and despair.

The idea that loss of attachment bonds is central to the development of psychopathology has met with both theoretical and empirical difficulties (Rutter, 1972). Evidence shows that although loss of significant parental figures poses a general risk for child behavior problems, it does not appear to be differentially associated with different forms of child psychopathology, and its effect size is generally small compared with other psychosocial factors. However, attachment bonds can vary in many ways other than simply losing them through separation or death of the parent(s).

As Brewin (1987) has pointed out, Bowlby's model of how attachment leads to the development of self-esteem is highly consistent with current thinking in experimental cognitive psychology. Bowlby argued that the child appraises new situations and develops behavioral plans guided by mental models of him- or herself and his or her main attachment figures. In healthy human development, these models are gradually integrated into a stable and confident sense of self. Thus, Bowlby argued that disruption of these bonds leads to expectations of self and others based on anger, fear, and despair, laying the foundation for many forms of emotional disturbance.

Such mental models or cognitive styles appear to characterize various forms of behavioral disturbance. Research has shown that conduct problem adolescents may be less skilled at interpreting social messages, tending to expect and thus overdetect and elicit hostility and rejection in other people (Dodge, 1985; Rutter, 1989). Most research has examined these cognitive styles in the individual, but increasingly attention is being paid to the interpersonal context of these cognitive styles. That is, researchers are focusing on how individuals learn to interpret social meaning from early family experiences. The study by Barrett, Rapee, Dadds, and Ryan (1996) showed that the plans of conduct problem and anxious children for responding to an ambiguous but potentially threatening social situation were heavily influenced by the way the family discussed the particular problem. Conduct problem children and their parents were more likely to perceive threat in ambiguous social situations and to respond to this perceived threat with aggression. Further, the level of aggression in the child's responses increased when children were given the opportunity to discuss their responses with their parents.

The idea that the child internalizes his or her early social context into an emerging cognitive model of reality that is used to interpret and respond to future realities is the hallmark of social developmental theorists such as the Vygotsky (1960). Developmentally, the child passes through stages in which behavior is fully dependent on the social context (e.g., child is often lifted up by parents for cuddling and feeding), to an interactional stage in which the child behavior is reciprocal with context (e.g., child can lift arms in anticipation of being lifted up), to a stage when reality is fully internalized into a utilizable verbal, mental model (e.g., child can abstractly communicate or initiate being picked up by approaching parents with arms raised or using verbal forms).

Stressful Environments and Events

The literature on stress and coping and their relationship to the development of psychopathology is complex, in part due to inherent ambiguities about the meaning of the terms. It is very difficult to differentiate between stressful events, the stress effects they produce, and the coping strategies that are thought to mediate the relationship between the two. Generally, researchers think about a stressful event as one that produces a stress reaction because the event demands more coping skills than the person has at his or her disposal (Lazarus & Folkman, 1984). Rather than review the large range of possible environmental events that can have adverse effects on children (see Goodyer, 1990), the effects of one common stressor consistently associated with the development of CD will be used as an example.

The impact of parental divorce or separation on the child has been relatively well researched, and marital breakdown affects a substantial proportion of families in most developed countries (Emery, 1982). Children from separated households are at greater risk to develop disruptive behavioral and emotional problems than children from intact households (Emery, 1982). Further, evidence indicates that re-formation of an "intact" family through remarriage of the sole parent places even further risk for the behavioral and emotional adjustment of children (Fergusson, Horwood, & Shannon, 1984). The effects of divorce on children are largely mediated by the amount and type of conflict between the parents. Children from broken or intact homes characterized by open marital discord are at greater risk to develop a behavioral disorder than children from relatively nondiscordant broken or intact homes.

Hetherington and Martin (1979) found that the likelihood that the child's behavior would deteriorate following divorce was related to observed changes in the custodial parent's discipline practices. After separation, parents tended to show decreases in their limit setting, maturity demands, affection, and clear communication. These were accompanied by increases in disturbed child behavior that tended to peak approximately one year after the event. Further, boys were exposed to more of this inconsistency than were their sisters, and were observed to have the most behavioral adjustment problems. Thus, the effects of divorce as a stressor largely impact on the child through changes in the parental/family processes described in Patterson's (1982) coercive family process model.

There is also evidence that the effects of severe economic hardship on developing children are mediated by changes in the interactional patterns of parents and their children (Elder, Nguyen, & Caspi, 1985). Similarly, the relationship between parental psychopathology and child behavior disorders may also be mediated by the impact of the parent's psychopathology on the marital relationship and related parenting styles (Billings & Moos, 1983; Emery, 1982).

It is clear from the preceding studies that significant amounts of the variance of the effects of disruptive events on children may be accounted for by changes in the interactions the child has with parents concomitant with the event. In the words of Hetherington and Martin (1979):

The artificiality of separating social learning experiences in the family from extrafamilial social factors, specific traumatic experiences, and hereditary or constitutional factors must be emphasized. Although any one of these factors may initiate a developmental process, unidirectional causality quickly gives way to an interactive process between the child and other family members. (p. 72)

Structural Characteristics of Families

One of the most consistently documented risk factors for pathology, whether physical or psychological, is low socioeconomic status. Poverty is a major health hazard. Its effects do not appear to be specific to any specific form of distress, it is a generally noxious factor for ill health. However, one of the most extensively studied relationships is that of low socioeconomic status (SES) to conduct problems in children. Major steps toward understanding the development of childhood problems, in particular CDs, have been made by clarifying the mechanisms by which low SES affects children and families. While several factors, such as urban crowding, poor educational resources, lack of employment opportunities and unemployment, community violence, and social isolation and disempowerment, may be important, the social support available to parents may be an important variable mediating the relationship (Lamb & Elster, 1985; Wahler, 1980; Webster-Stratton, 1985).

Factors discussed earlier, such as parent-child interactions, maternal depression, marital discord, and a parent's personal adjustment may need to be seen in the context of the family's interactions within the system and with the local community. The observation that day-to-day social contacts and subjective evaluations of social support are predictive of a range of parent-parent and parent-child interaction patterns is an excellent example of clinical and research approaches the analysis of interacting hierarchical systems (Wahler & Dumas, 1984) and emphasizes the relationship between "molar" (e.g., SES delinquency) and "molecular" (e.g., parent-child interaction) variables (Patterson & Reid, 1984).

Although the evidence from controlled studies is generally not available, a number of other characteristics of family systems are hypothesized to be important in the development of child psychopathology. One promising construct is the family systems idea of deviant family hierarchies (Haley, 1976; Minuchin, 1974) in which the parents appear to have less power in the family than one or more of the children. Using a self-report measure of family structure, the Family Hierarchy Test (Madanes, Duke, & Harbin, 1980), research has shown that families of persons with substance abuse and conduct problems tend to have more deviant family hierarchies (Green et al., 1992; Madanes et al., 1980). However, the ability of this measure of hierarchy to discriminate between other forms of psychopathology is in doubt and the evidence for its reliability and validity is tenuous (Green et al.).

Importantly, Green et al. (1992) found that conduct problems in a child was predictive of a deviant family hierarchy one year later; however, the reverse was not true. Thus, it is likely that family hierarchies become deviant (i.e., reversed: the child has more power) because of the child's problems. This is a more simple and appealing explanation than the reverse logic that a deviant family hierarchy somehow leads to conduct problems in children. Anyone who has either tried to care for or work clinically with the families of teenagers who are on a delinquent or drug-abusing path will know that their destructive behavior can bring them enormous interpersonal power, and their parents are often unable to influence them despite continuous and extreme attempts to do so.

School Factors

School failure, dropping out of school, identification with a deviant peer group, and lack of adult supervision are all potential contributors to the development of CD (Loeber, 1990). Although many of these factors may themselves be driven by the behavior of the child, his or her learning potential, and early family environment, any characteristics of school environments that exacerbate their likelihood must also be seen as potential contributors to the development of CD. Little research is available to support speculation, but it is possible that school environments marked by poor supervision and teaching, lack of educational resources and opportunities, the availability of drugs, weapons of violence, and antisocial gangs, may facilitate a child's transition in to the later and more severe forms of CD.

Social Factors

As already noted, one of the risk factors for CD is low SES. Thus, any societal factors productive of poverty and all its corollaries can be seen as risk factors for CD. Urban crowding, poor educational resources, lack of employment opportunities and unemployment, community violence, and social isolation and disempowerment, have all been identified as risk factors.

Conclusions

The causes of CD are best seen as a set of systems, subsystems, and components of systems interacting at the biological, interpersonal, family, and social levels. Further, the importance of any one factor will vary according to the developmental stage of the child. Authors tend to think of these causes as additive risk factors (e.g., Loeber, 1990). Developmentally, the literature indicates clusters of risk that also may be seen as windows of opportunity for establishing comprehensive intervention programs. Table 20.1 summarizes the developmental sequence of risk with some potential interventions at each point. In the next section, interventions will be reviewed within this developmental framework, highlighting the impediments and difficulties faced by clinicians in typical clinical practice.

IMPEDIMENTS TO INTERVENTION IN THE REAL WORLD CONTEXT

Before reviewing the potential assessment and treatment strategies for CD, some of the real world impediments to treating this disorder will be reviewed. To make this discussion useful, it will be necessary to limit the focus to interventions that are commonly attempted and that have been shown to have some success with this disorder. Many of the broader preventive strategies that may be useful, such as reducing lead poisoning in our environments, are beyond the scope of clinicians and this chapter.

Table 20.1 Developmental Risk for Conduct Disorder and Associated Intervention Opportunities

Developmental Phase		Risk Factors	Potential Interventions
Prenatal–infancy	Child	Environmental toxicity Temperamental difficulties	Environmental safety (e.g., lead minimization) Early infant care programs
	Family	Poverty/low SES/social isolation Family violence/conflict/separation Parental psychopathology Poor health/nutrition	Social equality/support/community connectedness Family support, education, and therapy services Premarital and preparenting education programs
	Social	Economic hardship/unemployment Family breakdown/isolation Cultures of violence	Adequate healthcare/parental and infant support programs
Toddler–late childhood	Child	Learning and language difficulties Impulsivity	Early remediation of learning and language difficulties Parent training and broader family interventions
	Family	Coercive family processes/violence Low care and nurturance Inadequate monitoring of child	Family and marital support programs After-school care and monitoring Peer social skills programs
	Social	Inadequate child care and parental support Lack of educational opportunities Negative or no parent–school relationship	
Teenage years	Child	School-employment failure Cognitive bias to threat/hostility Peer rejection/deviant peer group Substance abuse/depression	Cognitive behavioral skills programs for teenagers Academic and work transition skills programs Crisis support for family/youth individuation problems, breakdown, and homelessness
	Family	Conflict/individuation problems Rejection/homelessness	Family-adolescent therapy services Substance abuse prevention
	Social	Lack of education/employment Cultures of violence	Cultures of community respect and connectedness

Thus, this section will limit itself to clinical interventions that can be used in typical community health and education settings.

Clinical Access and Referral Factors

In most tertiary clinical settings, clinicians rely on clients themselves seeking help. It is rare that children and adolescents seek help themselves for conduct problems and thus referral is usually made by parents and teachers. This carries with it inherent problems. First, many families with children at risk for CD may not seek help as part of a larger isolation or marginalization from traditional health services. This is often associated with low SES, low education, poverty, cultural and racial isolation, the lack of services in rural regions and urban areas of poverty, and general disempowerment in society. Thus, the very families at highest risk for CD may be ones least likely or able to access the services that can potentially help.

Second, where families or teachers do refer, the child, especially the adolescent, may be hostile to the service because it represents the social context that he or she has been marginalized from. This is less of a problem for younger children where a parent's intervention can often produce change. With adolescents, however, their involvement becomes increasingly important for treatment success, and clinicians working in settings that rely on parent and teacher referrals may often find their inability to form a relationship with the adolescent to be a frustration.

In rural and poor urban areas, special attention may need to be given to making contact with high-risk groups and (a) designing services so they are culturally appropriate, and (b) empowering client groups to maximize access and cooperation with available services. Where the main client population is older adolescents, services may need to be designed so that contact is made with clients outside home and school referrals, for example through schools and youth groups, so that services are not always seen as a part of a punitive adult system.

The Design of Mental Healthcare Facilities

Much of our mental health system has been designed for the individual. Only the past few decades have seen the recognition that much of our health is firmly embedded in the quality and quantity of our intimate social relationships. With CD, much of its early variance comes from family factors and comprehensive assessments and treatments need to take a broader parent training and family focus. This is very difficult if mental health teams do not have (a) physical structures (e.g., child-care facilities, group work consultation rooms, home visit services, to allow for comprehensive family services); or (b) political structures that allow clinicians to consult with the entire family versus the individual client. Many clinics still focus on individual pathology or assign various problems within a child or family to different professionals who may have little or no case coordination with each other.

Mental health services need to embrace a more systemic view of health and illness. This is particularly true for CD where major influences are the family, and then later the school. Services need to be structured so that consultations can be effective with broader groups of people, and cases need to be coordinated so that various aspects of a child's problem can be conceptualized within the broader family context.

Family Breakdown

Because family intervention is a core treatment for CD, especially in its early stages of development, the stability and availability of cooperative parents is important. Family breakdown is thus a major impediment to successful treatment where it is associated with frequent geographic moves, disrupted routines, changes in caregivers, school transfers, and—with the increasing number of blended families—changes of family composition. Approximately one in three parental relationships ends in separation in the Western world and the difficulties of blended families for parents and children are now well documented, as well as presenting a further risk factor for CD (Fergusson et al., 1984).

Any preventive or remedial intervention that increases the stability of family structures, without increasing the conflict and violence within them, may be an important contextual factor in improving the outcomes for children with this problem.

Dropout from Treatment

Dropout from treatment, usually meaning from a family-based intervention, is a common problem for clinicians working with CD; dropout rates can be as high as 50% of initial starters (Kazdin, 1990; Miller & Prinz, 1990). Factors affecting the likelihood of dropout include environmental stressors such as poverty, interpersonal factors such as low family or social support, low expectations of treatment acceptability or effectiveness, therapist interpersonal and cultural sensitivity, skill, and peer support (Prinz & Miller, 1991). Methods of maximizing family and adolescent engagement in the early stages of therapy are thus crucial to the effectiveness of tertiary treatments and a number of authors have written about process models of engagement processes (e.g., Chamberlain, Patterson, Reid, Kavanagh, & Forgatch, 1984; Dadds, 1989; Kanfer & Schefft, 1988).

Early versus Late Intervention

The interventions for CD with the strongest research support so far are family interventions in which caregivers are trained to provide effective, noncoercive discipline, acknowledgment, and reward of the child's prosocial behavior and achievements, and effective family problem-solving and communication styles (Miller & Prinz, 1990). Emerging evidence reveals that the age of the child is associated with the potential effectiveness of these interventions. With younger children, evidence for these interventions is strong. However, as children move into the teen years, evidence for the effectiveness of these interventions becomes weaker. Thus, early detection and intervention is a major factor in the prevention and treatment of CD. Clinical settings in which the most common referral of CD is for teenagers, especially those who are well established into a pattern of antisocial behavior, will have relatively little success with the sole use of these family interventions.

Therapist Expertise with Multiple Stressors in Families, Schools, and Society

As CD is frequently associated with multiple disruptions and stressors in families, schools, and their societal context, delivery of comprehensive interventions presents a major challenge to the skill level of the clinician. Providing a "state of the art" behavioral family intervention requires multiple therapist skills associated with individual and family assessment, behavior change strategies, family engagement and therapy process skills, communication and interagency liaison skills (Sanders & Dadds, 1993).

The extent to which therapists are trained and skilled in these areas greatly varies, and it cannot be guaranteed that any particular mental health setting will have clinicians who can provide these interventions. Areas of urban poverty become increasingly bereft of many important community and health services as the professional classes flee, and the treatment of CD often is left to mental health workers who are not equipped to offer such difficult but potentially effective treatments.

Violence, Individualism, and the Culture of Greed

On a more controversial note, voices in the media and popular literature often point to the cultural context of youth violence and antisocial behavior. Despite the appealing face validity of attributing high rates of youth antisocial behavior and violence to modeled violence in films and television, it has been difficult for researchers to establish clear links between the two. However, cross-cultural comparisons have related a cultural emphasis on individual gain and the lack of community values to the escalation of violence in society. Many who work with CD youths find it disturbing to view widely attended films such as *Pulp Fiction,* in which lead characters engage in extremes of violence with no emotional reaction, and are seemingly rewarded for their behavior. Where youths see little future for themselves as worthwhile contributors to a peaceful society, it is understandable that many might be tempted to follow such readily available, violent, and antisocial models.

Interagency Communication and Cooperation

Given that the development and effective treatment of CD can involve the interplay of multiple child, family, school, and societal factors, a common impediment to intervention is lack of communication and coordination between different health and educational agencies. The extent to which the caregiving systems in a child's life present a united cooperative front has been argued to be a major factor in the development of prosocial potentials in young people (Bronfenbrenner, 1977). Where families have little contact with schools and healthcare agencies, or worse where hostility exists, children are more likely to turn to deviant peer groups for a sense of belonging and support.

Often this lack of coordination can be seen in healthcare agencies. It may be difficult for clinicians in a mental health outpatient clinic, school guidance staff, and court-appointed welfare officers, to communicate and coordinate their efforts even though they are all involved with the same client. Thus, the likelihood of success of home-school monitoring and rewards programs and other interventions that require multiple setting cooperation is greatly reduced. In some instances, clinicians in different settings may even be using intervention strategies that are positively contradictory. For example, treatment of a recent case at the Griffith Psychology Clinic was greatly compromised when a psychologist in the clinic was teaching anger control techniques while the school guidance officer was encouraging the same youth to express and rehearse his anger in safe settings.

It is highly advisable for clinicians to establish positive links with other clinicians and agencies that are likely to have contact with their clients in other settings, and to minimize bureaucratic and other barriers to effective interagency liaison.

TREATMENT

Assessment Strategies

There are a number of caveats for the value of any psychological assessment with children and adolescents. First, the assessment should be in the spirit of scientific (as well as empathic) inquiry. Thus, it should be theory driven and premises and questions should be operationalizable into testable hypotheses. Second, it should be comprehensive in terms of measuring multiple domains of the disorder (child cognitive, behavioral, biological, and emotional factors; family, school, and social factors) using multiple informants (child, parents, teachers, peers), and multiple methodologies (self-report and rating scales, interview, direct observation). Third, the assessment should involve measures of change potential as well as status quo. For example, even in the area of educational testing, research within an interactive framework (Haywood & Tzuriel, 1992) shows that intelligence tests afford greater predictive accuracy when the tester assesses the client's ability to learn and improve rather than just using the test as an indicator of static IQ.

The developmental model that is now appropriate to CD requires viewing assessment as an ongoing and goal-directed process. Any objective measure represents a culmination of historical forces; it is a frozen snapshot of the current child and social context, but more importantly, an indication of what he or she may or may not become and the factors that will shape this future. The assessment should thus include: (a) a conceptualization of the stage and likely progression of the disorder given no change; and (b) an evaluation of how much the child and his or her system can change. To this end, our clinic often includes a child and family change exercise (e.g., a simple behavioral contract to reduce one area of conflict) in the early stages of intervention to assess the potential in the system for change. This is not a new idea, but one sadly lacking in traditional clinical models where assessment and intervention are separate phases. An intervention is probably the best way to test an hypothesis and assessment should be an ongoing process integrated with intervention.

A common problem in mental health assessment is the "treatment of choice" approach in which the clinician makes a diagnosis and then treats the diagnosis. Thus, the clinician might conclude on a basis of an assessment that the child has a severe CD for which there exists a standardized treatment of choice. This comes from the nomothethic group treatment outcome studies where this method is highly appropriate in developing and evaluating treatments. At the clinical level, however, it may be inferior to the method of individual assessment that while, guided by treatment of choice models, recognizes that clinicians do not treat disorders but rather individuals who will show very different patterns of personal, familial, school, and family characteristics.

Diagnostic Interviews

A number of semistructured interviews have been designed for use with young people and caregivers to facilitate a formal diagnosis and associated factors that are hypothesized to maintain the disorder (Edelbrock & Costello, 1988). The most well known and evaluated of these are the Child Assessment Schedule (CAS; Hodges & Fitch, 1979), the Child and Adolescent Psychiatric Assessment (CAPA; Angold, Cox, Prendergast, Rutter, & Simonoff, 1987), the Diagnostic Interview for Children and Adolescents (DICA; Herjanic, Herjanic, Brown, & Wheatt, 1975), the Diagnostic Interview Schedule for Children (DISC; Costello, Edelbrock, Dulcan, Kalas, & Klaric, 1984) and its revisions (DISC-R: Schaffer et al., 1988; DISC-2: Fisher et al., 1991), and the Schedule for Affective Disorders and Schizophrenia for School-Age Children (K-SADS; Puig-Antich & Chambers, 1978). All of these were designed to generate diagnoses based on the *DSM* system and all have parallel child and caregiver versions.

Reviews by Hodges (1993) and others have pointed to a number of findings that are common to all these diagnostic interviewing strategies. First, interviews with young people and their caregivers are not interchangeable because reliability between the two is often low. However, the highest rates of reliability between parents and children have been found for disruptive behavior problems compared with depressive and anxiety disorders, and notwithstanding, parental reports tend to be more informative for disruptive behavior problems (Loeber, Green, Lahey, & Stouthamer-Loeber, 1989).

Interrater reliability studies have generated kappas ranging from .31 to 1.00 with a mean in the .5 to .6 range for the diagnosis of CD, indicating moderate to good reliability (Hodges, 1993). Similarly, validity and test-retest reliability of diagnoses based on these interviews is acceptable for CD.

Self-Report Measures

A range of self-report measures are available for assessing disruptive behavior problems in children with the most common and well researched being the Child Behavior Checklist (Achenbach & Edelbrock, 1991), the Revised Behavior Problem Checklist (Quay & Peterson, 1983), and the Conners Parent and Teacher Rating Scales (Conners, 1969, 1970). These measures do not produce a diagnosis; rather they assess the child's behavior on a number of (usually empirically derived) dimensions of dysfunction (e.g., aggression, depression, inattention, social problems) allowing comparison of the child with normative samples. The Child Behavior Checklist has parallel forms for parents, teachers, and a youth self-report form that can be used with young people of 11 years and older. Self-report forms for disruptive behavior are not available for use with younger children, assuming that these would be reliable and valid.

Generally, checklists show reasonable convergence with interview-derived diagnoses for CD and other disruptive behavior problems (Hodges, 1993). However, which informants are used is important. For example, Brunshaw and Szatmari (1988) found that the best agreement occurs when parents' checklists are compared with parent interviews, and the lowest occurred between teacher checklists and parent and child interview. Generally, however, the ability of these checklists to discriminate between specific diagnostic categories is low. Further, because they do not include objective criteria relating to the durability or severity of symptoms, they are highly vulnerable to subjective biases in the rater and from the situation in which they are used.

Direct Observation

Some of the most important theoretical advances in our understanding of the interpersonal processes characterizing disruptive behavior problems have come from direct observations of family processes characteristic of these problems. Patterson and Reid's observations of family processes in the home led to the development of coercion theory, a range of useful clinical and research observation methodologies, and a replicable treatment program for CD (Patterson, 1982; Patterson & Reid, 1984). Similarly, Minuchin's (1974) observations of low SES families with CD was an important factor in the development of structural family theory and therapy.

Both assessment methodologies are based on the premise that a substantial variance in children's aggression and antisocial behavior can be accounted for by the interactional style of their families. Patterson's (1982) methodologies are readily utilizable in clinical settings. Assessment involves careful observation of the antecedent and consequential control that each family member's behavior has over other family members' behavior. Thus, as a basic example, the clinician would observe the way parents respond to displays of aggression versus prosocial behavior by the child. Common to families with CD, aggression results in escalating aggression and general attention whereas prosocial behavior is inadvertently ignored (Patterson, 1982; Sanders, Dadds, & Bor, 1989). The assessment directly guides interventions for reversing the interactional cycles that maintain the disruptive behavior.

To conduct such observations, a family task that approximates a realistic interaction is arranged. With young children, this usually involves free play time and tasks that prompt disruptive family processes such as cleaning up toys, taking a meal, or completing a task of attention (e.g., a jigsaw puzzle). With older children and adolescents, natural behavior is unlikely to occur in these situations so family problem-solving discussions are often used instead. This useful procedure is now commonly used in clinical research into marital distress, parent-adolescent conflict, and family factors in severe psychopathology (Miklowitz, Goldstein, Falloon, & Doane, 1984). Family problem-solving discussions are appropriate for children of approximately 7 to 8 years and older. A number of authors (e.g., Blechman & McEnroe, 1985) emphasize the role of problem-solving competence in protecting a family against conflict and breakdown. The major points for observation are the extent to which family members actively listen to each other's point of view, take time to agree on a problem definition, generate solutions and action strategies, or conversely, interrupt each other, criticize, talk tangentially, and prevent problem-solving through vagueness, concreteness, and expression of hopelessness and despair. The Issues Checklist (Robin, 1981) can be used to generate problems for discussion and is filled out by both parents and child. An example of its use was published by Sanders, Dadds, Johnston, and Cash (1992). They compared the discussion in families of depressed, CD, mixed, and nonclinic children and were able to discriminate between the different families on the basis of these family discussions.

Behaviors vary greatly in their amenability to direct observation. Oppositional behavior in young children, such as crying, noncompliance, and aggression, can be readily observed in the family home or clinic if the setting is selected appropriately. In the home, such behavior tends to escalate when parents attempt to engage young children in routine activities such as bathing, bedtime, getting ready to leave on outings and mealtimes (Sanders, Dadds, & Bor, 1989). In clinic settings, oppositional behavior will similarly tend to occur when the parent tries to engage the child in structured teaching tasks or when compliance is enforced (e.g., cleaning up toys). Many problem behaviors however, cannot be so readily observed. For example, stealing and fire setting tend to be secretive and relatively infrequent behaviors.

A number of formal systems for conducting systematic observation of the child, family, and classroom have been developed that allow clinicians to interpret assessment findings to clinical populations described in the scientific literature. Readers interested in more comprehensive accounts are referred to Touliatos, Perlmutter, and Strauss (1990).

Cognitive Approaches

Attention has increasingly been given to the styles of social cognition that appear to characterize CD, and these can be useful clinically in terms of programs that focus on individual and group work with CD youths themselves (e.g., Kazdin et al., 1992). Assessment focuses on the youths' appraisals and self-statements regarding their own behavior and other people's responses in various situations. Research has shown that CD children are prone to unrealistic expectations of hostility from others (Dodge, Price, Bachorowski, & Newman, 1990) and formulate aggressive response plans (Barrett, Rapee, et al., 1996), especially when there is ambiguity in the social setting. Barrett, Rapee, et al. (1996) further showed that that cognitive processes are part of a more general family processing style. Other evidence has shown that CD children have poor problem-solving skills (Rubin, Bream, & Rose-Krasnor, 1991) and again this is related to a more general deficits in the family (Sanders et al., 1992).

Typically, the cognitive assessments with the child involve the discussion of real day-to-day events in the child's life and hypothetical situations that elicit the characteristic aggressive or ineffectual problem-solving style (Dodge et al., 1990). But recent research is emphasizing that a more comprehensive approach is to assess these styles as early as possible within the broader family context (Dadds, 1995).

Community Outcomes

At a community level, a number of products of antisocial behavior can serve as a useful, if indirect and approximate, quantification of youth disruptive behavior problems in their most severe form. These include juvenile offense and recidivism rates, school attendance and achievement rates, and community vandalism.

State of the Art Assessment

A number of principles can be derived from this brief review of assessment strategies. Accuracy of information can be enhanced by the use of multiple informants and assessment formats. A developmental perspective needs to be taken in which disorder is seen as an unfolding set of potentialities, with associated risk and protective factors. Assessment should focus on a comprehensive range of cognitive and behavioral characteristics of the child seen within the common family, school, and community contexts that help maintain antisocial behavior.

Treatment Approaches

Excluding potential primary prevention interventions, treatments can be categorized into three basic groups: parent training and family interventions, individual or group social-cognitive work with the child, and miscellaneous other treatments. The latter are really distinguished from the former by the relative lack of research attention they have received. As such, little is known about their effectiveness.

Family Intervention

Research evaluating treatments for child CD has supported the efficacy of behavioral family interventions (BFI) in the short term and over follow-up periods of years after the termination of treatment (Miller & Prinz, 1990). The field has been reasonably responsive to the data that has emerged on the strengths and limitations of interventions and so the past few decades have witnessed continual refinement of the BFI approach. Research suggesting that some parents have difficulties in generalizing their parenting skills across settings or over time led to several clinical strategies designed to promote better generalization and maintenance effects (e.g., Forehand & Atkeson, 1977; Koegel, Glahn, & Nieminen, 1978; Sanders & Glynn, 1981). Research has shown that parents undergoing behavioral parent training are also generally satisfied consumers and view the specific behavioral techniques (e.g., praise, time-out) taught in these programs as both effective and acceptable (McMahon & Forehand, 1983; Webster-Stratton, 1985). Much less is known about how children view the treatment process although Dadds, Adlington, and Christensen (1987) found that both nonclinic and oppositional children rated time-out as an acceptable strategy for parents to use.

Empirical evidence and clinical experience suggested that not all parents or families benefit to the same extent from treatment (Miller & Prinz, 1990), and difficulties are commonly encountered when there are concurrent marital problems, parental depression, and other family difficulties such as economic hardship. Several authors have made various proposals to improve the outcome of treatment by expanding the focus of treatment (Miller & Prinz, 1990; Wahler, 1980). These suggestions have included providing additional skills training to overcome problems that are hypothesized to be related to their child management difficulties. Such adjunctive interventions include teaching parents self-management skills (Griest et al., 1982) providing concurrent marital therapy (Dadds, Sanders, Behrens, & James, 1987; Dadds, Schwartz, & Sanders, 1987), providing training in the selection and arrangement of activities for children in high-risk situations (Sanders & Christensen, 1985; Sanders & Dadds, 1982), anger management (Goldstein, Keller, & Erne, 1985), social support training (Dadds & McHugh, 1992), and the development of better home-school liaison for the management of school-based behavioral problems (Blechman, 1984). Although each of these suggestions has merits with selected cases, efficiency dictates that it is better to include only those components that are required to achieve the therapeutic objectives negotiated with a family. One of the challenges facing behavioral family therapy over the next few decades is to develop models of family process and intervention that are not so piecemeal, but rather flow from a more integrated model of the family.

Of the different approaches encompassed by behavioral family intervention, parent training has the most accumulated evidence regarding its therapeutic value (Kazdin, 1987b). This is due substantially to numerous studies that demonstrate its efficacy in the treatment of oppositional behavior disorders and CD in (young) children (e.g., Forehand & Long, 1988). Intensive behavioral parent training programs typically teach parents a variety of interactional and child management skills, as well as focus on additional family problems such as marital difficulties, social isolation, parents' psychological state (e.g., problems of depression, anger and irritability), financial difficulties, household organization, and division of labor. Examples of interventions at this level include work by Wahler and Dumas (1984) and Blechman (1984) with multiproblem parents, by Lutzker

(1984) with abusive parents, and by the author and colleagues with maritally distressed couples of oppositional children (Dadds, Sanders, et al., 1987; Dadds, Schwartz, & Sanders, 1987).

Another area of evaluation in family therapy for CD is with parent-adolescent conflict. Studies such as those by Robin (1981) and Alexander and Parsons (1973) have shown that combinations of behavioral parent training and family communication and problem-solving training are effective in ameliorating these problems in the majority of cases. Educative interventions of this type have also been shown to be effective with families in which a member has a diagnosed psychotic disorder. Falloon et al. (1985) have shown that psychoeducational family interventions are effective in reducing the return of psychotic symptoms and subsequent hospitalization in such cases.

Several studies have examined the durability of treatment effects of BFI (Forehand & Long, 1988; Sanders & James, 1983). The treatment program employed by Forehand and his colleagues represents the most thoroughly evaluated parent training program. A large number of studies with acting-out children whose primary presenting problem is one of noncompliance, have shown that immediately posttreatment, target children display reduced levels of oppositional behavior; their parents increase positive attention and decrease aversive attention; and parents also perceive their children as better behaved, evaluate the intervention (e.g., time-out) as being effective and acceptable, and are satisfied with the treatment they received. In a long-term follow-up study of adolescents who had been treated through this program 4 to 10 years previously, results showed that on most measures of adolescent functioning, treated children were indistinguishable from a comparison group of nonclinic adolescents. However, one-third of the treated group had received other treatment since leaving the program and were performing significantly more poorly academically at school. These findings highlight the importance of school-based intervention with disturbed children. The parents of the treated children were functioning just as well as parents of nonclinic adolescents on measures of depression, marital adjustment, and parenting competence.

As argued by Sanders and Dadds (1993), much of the research in BFI has focused on the reduction of behavioral excesses such as noncompliance with parental instructions, aggression, and demanding and tantrum behaviors. Meanwhile, relatively little work has focused on using family interventions to promote socially competent or prosocial behavior in children. Aversive interchanges with parents represent only a small proportion of family interactions (Sanders, Dadds, & Bor, 1989). Using home observations, Gardiner (1987) found that preschoolers with conduct problems spent significantly less time than nonproblem children in cooperative activities, joint activity, and conversation with their mother. They also watched more television or spent more time doing nothing, and spent less time in constructive play.

The importance of the therapist-client relationship in behavior therapy has received increased attention (e.g., Dadds, 1989; Sweet, 1987; Twardosz & Nordquist, 1988). The technological descriptions of parent training as reflected in scientific journals and books on the subject have largely ignored important process variables that affect the acceptability (to parents) of the behavior change techniques advocated by therapists. These techniques include a diverse range of clinical and interpersonal skills that provide the relationship context within which family intervention takes place. There is little doubt that therapists differ markedly among themselves in their effectiveness as parent trainers. For example, some therapists develop techniques of providing negative feedback that prompts parents to seriously question how they currently manage family problems. Other therapists might attempt to convey the same message; however, the parent feels criticized, devalued, and fails to return for her next appointment. Therapist variables for delivering effective behavioral family services involve more than simply having liberal doses of empathy, humor, warmth, and genuineness. These characteristics do not lead to replicable descriptions of specific clinical skills that exemplify competent clinical offerings to families.

BFI from a therapist's perspective involves a series of interrelated consultation tasks that occur within an interpersonal context of a therapeutic relationship. Kanfer and Schefft (1988) described a seven-phase therapeutic process model that outlines the specific tasks to be accomplished in therapy. These phases were role structuring and creating the therapeutic alliance; developing a commitment for change; undertaking behavior analysis; negotiating treatment objectives and methods; implementing treatment and maintaining motivation; monitoring and evaluating progress; following through with maintenance, generalization, and termination of treatment. Recently, other BFI process models have appeared that specifically focus on the consultation process involved in working with children and their families.

Evaluations of other forms of family intervention with CD are rare; however, a handful of studies have compared different types of family therapy for disruptive behavior problems, and the quality of these studies tends to be relatively high. Robin (1981) compared a "behavioral-systems" family therapy for parent-adolescent conflict with alternative treatments that included a mix of systemic, eclectic, and psychodynamic family therapies. The outcome measures included a mix of self-report and observational measures. Both groups showed reductions in parent-adolescent conflict immediately posttreatment on the self-report measures. However, the behavioral-systems group showed superior outcome on the measures of problem-solving, communication, and self-reported satisfaction with therapy.

Szykula, Morris, Sudweeks, and Saygar (1987) compared the effectiveness of strategic and behavioral family therapy for a mixed sample of behaviorally and emotionally disturbed children and their families. Only self-report measures were used to evaluate treatment. Although a t-test comparison showed that the outcome was similar and positive for both therapy groups, an analysis of outcome by severity of presenting problem showed that families with more severe problems responded more favorably to the behavioral intervention. Wells and Egan (1988) compared behavioral family therapy with systems family therapy in the treatment of child oppositional disorder. Their study was well controlled in that it employed a crossover design that controlled for therapist effects. Advanced clinical students undertaking courses in systemic and behavioral family interventions were assigned to referred families while undertaking each course and were supervised by the teaching staff in each of the courses. The results showed no differences between the two therapies on measures of parental emotional and marital adjustment; parents in both groups showed a decrease in anxiety and depression. Direct observations of the family, however, showed that the behavioral intervention was superior in producing improvements in parental positive attention and child compliance (the presenting problem).

Barkley, Guevremont, Anastopoulos, and Fletcher (1992) compared structural family therapy, behavioral parent training, and problem-solving and communication training, in the treatment of adolescents with attention-deficit/hyperactivity problems. Many of the children also had oppositional behavior problems. Dependent measures were both self-report and observational. Parents were equally and highly satisfied with all three treatments, and all three treatments were associated with improvements in parent-adolescent conflict and communication, and personal adjustment of the adolescent at home and at school. Finally, Brunk, Henggeler, and Whelan (1987) compared behavioral parent training presented in a group format to parents, with an individualized systems intervention for parents at risk for child abuse and neglect. The latter intervention included individualized behavioral parent training given in the home, counseling, interpersonal problem-solving, and a host of other interventions tailored to the individual needs of the parent. As expected, both interventions produced positive changes but the individualized multisystemic therapy produced a better outcome on a subset of the observational measures.

Social-Cognitive Interventions with CD Children

Social-cognitive interventions (SCIs) are based on the finding that CD is characterized by a tendency to overinterpret threat and hostility in others, and poor social problem-solving skills. Thus, these interventions aim to help the child to more accurately interpret the behavior of others, and formulate nonaggressive, prosocial responses in common social situations that would usually provoke them to aggression. The emphasis on abstract cognitive and social analysis means that SCIs with CD youth are generally limited to older children and youth who can operate at abstract cognitive levels (i.e., approximately 7–8 years and older).

According to Kazdin (1993), variations on SGI are numerous but these interventions share some central features. First, SCIs focus on the (cognitive) processes that are hypothesized to underlie children's responses to social situations. Second, children are taught to employ a step-by-step approach to solving interpersonal problems. Effective problem-solving can be seen as involving the steps of defining the problem accurately, generating alternative solutions, weighing up likely outcomes of each solution and choosing the most likely to produce desired (prosocial) outcomes, devising a specific plan and criteria for judging the success of the plan.

Third, to train these skills, clinicians use a range of activities that are engaging and understandable to the developmental level of the target CD children. These often involve working through hypothetical social situations framed as games, stories, and didactic tasks. Over the course of treatment, the social situations move from hypothetical to real examples from the child's life as problem-solving competence increases. Fourth, the therapist usually takes an active role in SCIs, and although time is allocated to nondirective exploration of the child's problems and cognitive style, the emphasis is on the directed learning of skills. Finally, diverse learning processes are used in the training of skills and thus therapists need to be skilled in providing clear information, modeling skills, role-playing with the provision of feedback, and shaping strategies applied to the child's behavior.

SCIs are a relatively recent development and less research into therapeutic outcomes and processes has been undertaken in comparison with BFI. Reviews of treatment outcome (e.g., Baer & Nietzel, 1991; Durlack, Furhman, & Lampman, 1991; Kazdin, 1993) are generally positive. Reductions in antisocial and aggressive behavior have been reported for both clinically referred samples and aggressive children selected from nonclinic samples, usually on the basis of high scores on self-report and parent or teacher report measures. However, a number of qualifications to these positive findings have been noted. First, the treatment effect size associated with SCIs is often not of clinically significant magnitude. Second, these interventions are limited to older children who can engage in and benefit from abstract social problem-solving. Third, the putative relationship between therapeutic change and the development of cognitive skills has not been established; that is, it is not clear that improvement in social problem-solving skills is the crucial mechanism that leads to behavior change. Experimental studies supporting the underlying premises of BFI—that changes in parental discipline strategies lead directly to change in childhood aggression—are common. Parallel studies have not been reported for SCI. Finally, variables influencing the effectiveness of SCIs have not been undertaken: Factors such as characteristics of the child and his or her behavioral profile, characteristics of the family, and variations in treatment content and format, have not been studied as they affect treatment outcome for SCIs.

Combined Behavioral Family Interventions and Social Cognitive Interventions

Given the potential effectiveness of BFI and SCI, an important direction for future research will be delineating the parameters for utilizing one or both of these interventions. Kazdin (1993) describes a series of studies in which the individual and combined effects of these treatments are being evaluated. A sample of 97 children aged 3 to 13 meeting criteria for CD or oppositional disorder were randomly assigned to a BFI alone, a SCI alone, or a combined treatment. Results at posttreatment and 1-year follow-up on parent and teacher completed standardized report forms showed that all treatments produced change; however, the combined treatment produced the overall best results.

At this point, little is known about the predictors of responsiveness to either treatment alone or the combined treatment, and Kazdin's analysis of the longer term outcomes and predictors is eagerly awaited. Similarly, results of the FAST TRACK (Conduct Problems Prevention Research Group, 1992) program for the prevention of CD will provide important data on the factors that are best associated with change for BFI and SCI. In the meantime, it appears that the provision of BFI and SCI together constitutes the most comprehensive treatment currently available for CD, especially in older children and adolescents.

Other Potential Interventions

A number of other interventions for CD and related disruptive behavior problems are yet to be evaluated in controlled trials. Minuchin's development of structural family therapy was closely associated with his work with ghetto children and their families in which disruptive behavior problems and aggression were common, and this approach has been popularly embraced throughout the world. Despite this, little research has been conducted into its efficacy with CD. One of the main reasons for this is that the intervention does not easily lend itself to standardization (i.e., into a replicable therapy manual). The same limitation has often characterized psychodynamic interventions. However, there is hope that this approach can be evaluated for CD in the near future as standardized treatment manuals have now started to appear (e.g., Kernberg & Chazan, 1991; see also Fonagy & Moran, 1990). Finally, while no form of medication has been shown to be effective with CD, its frequent comorbidity with ADHD points to the importance of considering stimulant medication in the treatment of comorbid children.

SUMMARY

CD is a complex and often severe behavioral disturbance that, in its most chronic forms, is characterized by a predictable developmental progression from oppositional behavior in the home, to aggression, peer rejection, and academic failure in schools, to antisocial behavior in the community. Risk factors for the development and maintenance of CD include temperamental and cognitive factors in the child, the stability and effectiveness of family structures and processes, school opportunities, and community stressors and values.

This developmental model and its emphasis on the multiplicity of risk factors indicates that treatments need to be conceptualized in terms of the developmental stage of the child and the specific pattern of risk factors he or she displays and is exposed to. A number of critical opportunities for intervention can be identified. The most well evaluated of these involves early intervention with the families of CD children in which parents of CD children are trained to provide effective, nonaversive discipline and communication with their children, and parents are empowered to constructively deal with other stressors that may compromise family stability, discipline and communication. As children approach the teen years, family interventions become increasingly difficult, and a combination of a family approach and a social problem-solving intervention for the teenager become increasingly important.

Several impediments to the utilization of these interventions in typical clinical settings have been identified. These include difficulties engaging CD youths and their families, high dropout rates, the lack of facilities in many health centers that are designed for family consultations, the high level of therapist expertise needed with multiply distressed families, lack of interagency communication and cooperation, and cultural and community factors that model and reinforce antisocial behavior as a problem-solving strategy.

REFERENCES

Abikoff, H., Courtney, M., Pelham, W. E., & Koplewicz, H. S. (1993). Teachers ratings of disruptive behavior: The influence of halo effects. *Journal of Abnormal Child Psychology, 21,* 519–533.

Abikoff, H., & Klein, R. G. (1992). Attention Deficit, Hyperactivity and Conduct Disorder: Comorbidity and implications for treatment. *Journal of Consulting and Clinical Psychology, 60,* 881–892.

Achenbach, T. M., & Edelbrock, C. S. (1991). *Manual for the Child Behavior Checklist and the Revised Child Behavior Profile.* Burlington, VT: University Associates in Psychiatry.

Alexander, J. F., & Parsons, B. V. (1973). Short-term behavioral intervention with delinquent families: Impact on family process and recidivism. *Journal of Abnormal Psychology, 81,* 219–225.

American Psychiatric Association. (1994). *Diagnostic and statistical manual of mental disorders* (4th ed.). Washington, DC: Author.

Anderson, J., Williams, S., McGee, R., & Silva, P. A. (1987). The prevalence of DSM-III disorders in a large sample of preadolescent children from the general population. *Archives of General Psychiatry, 44,* 69–76.

Angold, A., Cox, A., Prendergast, M., Rutter, M., & Simonoff, E. (1987). *The Child and Adolescent Psychiatric Assessment (CAPA)*. Unpublished manuscript.

Baer, R. A., & Nietzel, M. T. (1991). Cognitive and behavior treatment of impulsivity in children: A meta-analytic review of the outcome literature. *Journal of Clinical Child Psychology, 20,* 400–412.

Barkley, R. A., Guevremont, D. C., Anastopoulos, A. D., & Fletcher, K. E. (1992). A comparison of three family therapy programs for treating family conflict in adolescents with ADHD. *Journal of Consulting and Clinical Psychology, 60,* 450–462.

Barrett, P. M., Dadds, M. R., Rapee, R. M., & Ryan, S. (1996). Family treatment of childhood anxiety disorders: A controlled trial. *Journal of Consulting and Clinical Psychology, 64,* 333–343.

Barrett, P. M., Rapee, R. M., Dadds, M. R., & Ryan, S. (1996). Family enhancement of cognitive style in anxious and aggressive children. *Journal of Abnormal Child Psychology, 24,* 187–204.

Billings, A. G., & Moos, R. H. (1983). Comparisons of children of depressed and nondepressed parents: A social environmental perspective. *Journal of Abnormal Child Psychology, 11,* 463–486.

Blechman, E. A. (1984). Competent parents, competent children: Behavioral objectives of parent training. In R. F. Dangel & R. A. Polster (Eds.), *Parent training: Foundations of research and practice.* New York: Guilford Press.

Blechman, E. A., & McEnroe, M. J. (1984). Effective family problem solving. *Child Development, 56,* 429–437.

Bowlby, D. (1973). *Attachment and loss: 2. Separation.* New York: Basic Books.

Bowlby, D. (1980). *Attachment and loss: 1. Attachment.* New York: Basic Books. (Original work published 1969)

Bowlby, D. (1982). *Attachment and loss: 3. Loss.* New York: Basic Books.

Brewin, C. R. (1987). *Cognitive foundations of clinical psychology.* London: Erlbaum.

Bronfenbrenner, U. (1977). Towards an experimental ecology of human development. *American Psychologist, 32,* 513–531.

Brunk, M., Henggeler, S. W., & Whelan, J. P. (1987). Comparison of multisystemic therapy and parent training in the brief treatment of child abuse and neglect. *Journal of Consulting and Clinical Psychology, 55,* 171–178.

Brunshaw, J. M., & Szatmari, P. (1988). The agreement between behavior checklists and structured psychiatric interviews for children. *Canadian Journal of Psychiatry, 33,* 474–481.

Cambell, S. B. (1991). Longitudinal studies of active and aggressive preschoolers: Individual differences in early behavior and outcome. In D. Cicchetti & S. L. Toth (Eds.), *Rochester Symposium on Developmental Psychopathology: Vol. 2. Internalizing and externalizing expressions of dysfunction* (pp. 57–90). Hillsdale, NJ: Erlbaum.

Chamberlain, P., Patterson, G. R., Reid, J., Kavanagh, K., & Forgatch, M. (1984). Observation of client resistance. *Behavior Therapy, 15,* 144–145.

Cicchetti, D. (1984). The emergence of developmental psychopathology. *Child Development, 55,* 1–7.

Conduct Problems Prevention Research Group. (1992). A developmental and clinical model for the prevention of conduct disorder: The FAST Track Program. *Development and Psychopathology, 4,* 509–527.

Conners, C. K. (1969). A teacher rating scale for use in drug studies with children. *American Journal of Psychiatry, 126,* 884–888.

Conners, C. K. (1970). Symptom patterns in hyperkinetic, neurotic, and normal children. *Child Development, 41*, 667–682.

Costello, A. J., Edelbrock, L. S., Dulcan, M. K., Kalas, R., & Klaric, S. H. (1984). *Report on the NIMH Diagnostic Interview Schedule for Children (DISC)*. Washington, DC: National Institute of Mental Health.

Dadds, M. R. (1987). Families and the origins of child behavior problems. *Family Process, 26*, 341–357.

Dadds, M. R. (1989). Child behavior therapy and family context. *Child and Family Behavior Therapy, 11*, 27–44.

Dadds, M. R. (1995). *Families, children, and the development of dysfunction*. New York: Sage.

Dadds, M. R., Adlington, F., & Christensen, A. (1987). Children's perceptions of time out and other parental disciplinary strategies. *Behaviour Change, 4*, 3–13.

Dadds, M. R., Barrett, P. M., Rapee, R. M., & Ryan, S. (in press). Family processes and child anxiety and aggression: An observational analysis. *Journal of Abnormal Child Psychology*.

Dadds, M. R., Sanders, M. R., Behrens, B. C., & James, J. E. (1987). Marital discord and child behaviour problems: A description of family interactions during treatment. *Journal of Clinical Child Psychology, 16*, 192–203.

Dadds, M. R., Schwartz, S., & Sanders, M. R. (1987). Material discord and treatment outcome in the treatment of childhood conduct disorders. *Journal of Consulting and Clinical Psychology, 55*, 396–403.

Dadds, M. R., & McHugh, T. (1992). Social support and treatment outcome in behavioral family therapy for child conduct problems. *Journal of Consulting and Clinical Psychology, 69*, 252–259.

Dodge, K. A. (1985). Attributional bias in aggressive children. In P. C. Kendall (Ed.), *Advances in cognitive-behavioral research and therapy* (Vol. 4, pp. 73–110). Orlando, FL: Academic Press.

Dodge, K. A., Price, J. N., Bachorowski, J., & Newman, J. P. (1990). Hostile attributional biases in severely aggressive adolescents. *Journal of Abnormal Psychology, 99*, 385–392.

Durlak, J. E., Furhman, T., & Lampman, C. (1991). Effectiveness for cognitive-behavioral therapy for maladapting children: A meta-analysis. *Psychological Bulletin, 110*, 204–214.

Edelbrock, C., & Costello, A. J. (1988). Structured psychiatric interviews for children. In M. Rutter, A. H. Tuma, & I. S. Lann (Eds.), *Assessment and diagnosis in child psychopathology* (pp. 87–112). New York: Guilford Press.

Elder, G. H., Nguyen, T. V., & Caspi, A. (1985). Linking family hardship to children's lives. *Developmental Psychology, 56*, 361–375.

Emery, R. E. (1982). Interparental conflict and the children of discord and divorce. *Psychological Bulletin, 9*, 310–330.

Falloon, I. R. H., Boyd, J. L., McGill, C. W., Williamson, M., Razani, J., Moss, H. B., Gilderman, A. M., & Simpson, G. M. (1985). Family management in the prevention of morbidity of schizophrenia: Clinical outcome of a two-year longitudinal study. *Archives of General Psychiatry, 42*, 887–896.

Fergusson, D. M., Horwood, L. J., & Shannon, F. T. (1984). A proportional hazards model of family breakdown. *Journal of Marriage and the Family, 46*, 539–549.

Fisher, P., Shaffer, D., Piacentini, J., Lapkin, J., Wicks, J., & Rojas, M. (1991). *Completion of revisions of the NIMH Diagnostic Interview Schedule for Children* (DISC-2). Washington, DC: National Institute for Mental Health, Epidemiology and Psychopathology Research.

Fonagy, P., & Moran, G. S. (1990). Studies of the efficacy of child psychoanalysis. *Journal of Consulting and Clinical Psychology, 58*, 684–695.

Forehand, R. L., & Atkeson, B. M. (1977). Generality of treatment effects with parents as therapists. *Behavior Therapy, 8,* 575–593.

Forehand, R. L., & Long, N. (1988). Outpatient treatment of the acting out child: Procedures, long-term follow-up data, and clinical problems. *Advances in Behavior Research and Therapy, 10,* 129–177.

Gardiner, F. E. M. (1987). Positive interaction between mothers and conduct-problem children: Is there training for harmony as well as fighting? *Journal of Abnormal Child Psychology, 15,* 283–293.

Goldstein, A. P., Keller, H., & Erne, D. (1985). *Changing the abusive parent.* Champaign, IL: Research Press.

Goodyer, I. N. (1990). Family relationships, life events and child psychopathology. *Journal of Child Psychology and Psychiatry, 31,* 161–192.

Green, S. M., Loeber, R., & Lahey, B. B. (1992). Child psychopathology and deviant family hierarchies. *Journal of Child and Family Studies, 1,* 341–349.

Griest, D. L., Forehand, R., Rogers, T., Breiner, J., Furey, W., & Williams, C. A. (1982). Effects of parent enhancement therapy on the treatment outcome and generalisation of a parent training program. *Behaviour Research and Therapy, 20,* 429–436.

Haley, J. (1976). *Problem-solving therapy.* New York: Harper Colophon.

Haywood, H. C., & Tzuriel, D. (1992). *Interactive assessment.* New York: Springer-Verlag.

Herjanic, B., Herjanic, M., Brown, F., & Wheatt, T. (1975). Are children reliable reporters? *Journal of Abnormal Child Psychology, 3,* 41–48.

Hetherington, E. M., & Martin, B. (1979). Family interaction. In H. C. Quay & J. S. Werry (Eds.), *Psychopathological disorders of childhood* (pp. 30–82). New York: Wiley.

Hinshaw, S. P. (1987). On the distinction between attentional deficits/hyperactivity and conduct problems/aggression in children with attentional deficits. *Journal of Clinical Child Psychology, 20,* 301–312.

Hodges, K. (1993). Structured interviews for assessing children. *Journal of Child Psychology and Psychiatry, 34,* 49–68.

Hodges, K., & Fitch, P. (1979). *Development of a mental status examination interview for children.* Paper presented at the meeting of the Missouri Psychological Association, Kansas City.

Kanfer, F. H., & Schefft, B. K. (1988). *Guiding the process of therapeutic change.* Champaign, IL: Research Press.

Kazdin, A. E. (1987a). *Conduct disorder in childhood and adolescents.* Newbury Park, CA: Sage.

Kazdin, A. E. (1987b). The treatment of antisocial behaviour: Current status and future directions. *Psychological Bulletin, 102,* 187–203.

Kazdin, A. E. (1988). The diagnosis of childhood disorders: Assessment issues and strategies. *Behavioral Assessment, 10,* 67–94.

Kazdin, A. E. (1990). Childhood depression. *Journal of Child Psychology and Psychiatry, 31,* 121–160.

Kazdin, A. E. (1993). Treatment of Conduct Disorder: Progress and directions in psychotherapy research. *Development and Psychopathology, 5,* 277–310.

Kazdin A. E., Siegal, T., & Bass, D. (1992). Cognitive problem-solving skills and parent management training in the treatment of antisocial behavior in children. *Journal of Consulting and Clinical Psychology, 60,* 733–747.

Kernberg, F. P., & Chazan, S. E. (1991). *Children with conduct disorders: A psychotherapy manual.* New York: Basic Books.

Koegel, R. L., Glahn, T. J., & Nieminen, G. S. (1978). Generalization of parent training results. *Journal of Applied Behavior Analysis, 11,* 95–109.

Lamb, M., & Elster, A. B. (1985). Adolescent mother-infant-father relationships. *Developmental Psychology, 21,* 768–773.

Lazarus, R. S., & Folkman, S. (1984). *Stress, appraisal and coping.* New York: Springer.

Lochman, J. E. (1990). Modification of childhood aggression. In M. Hersen, Eisler, R. & P. Miller (Eds.), *Progress in behavior modification* (Vol. 2, pp. 47–85). New York: Academic Press.

Loeber, R. (1990). Development and risk factors of juvenile antisocial behavior and delinquency. *Clinical Psychology Review, 10,* 1–41.

Loeber, R., Green, S. M., Lahey, B. D., & Stouthamer-Loeber, M. (1989). Optimal informants on childhood disruptive behaviors. *Development and Psychopathology, 1,* 317–337.

Lutzker, J. (1984). Project 12 ways: Treating child abuse and neglect from an ecobehavioral perspective. In R. F. Dangel & R. A. Polster (Eds.), *Parent training: Foundations of research and practice* (pp. 260–291). New York: Guilford Press.

Madanes, C., Duke, J., & Harbin, H. (1980). Family ties of heroin addicts. *Archives of General Psychiatry, 37,* 889–902.

McMahon, R. J., & Forehand, R. (1983). Consumer satisfaction in behavioral treatment of children: Types, issues, and recommendations. *Behavior Therapy, 14,* 209–225.

Miklowitz, D. J., Goldstein, M. J., Falloon, I. R. H., & Doane, J. A. (1984). Interactional correlates of expressed emotion in the families of schizophrenics. *British Journal of Psychiatry, 144,* 482–487.

Miller, G. E., & Prinz, R. J. (1990). Enhancement of social learning family interventions for childhood conduct disorder. *Psychological Bulletin, 108,* 291–307.

Minuchin, S. (1974). *Families and family therapy.* Cambridge, MA: Harvard University Press.

Minuchin, S., Montalvo, B., Guerney, B., Rosman, B., & Schumer, F. (1967). *Families of the slums.* New York: Basic Books.

Moffitt, T. E., & Silva, P. A. (1988). Self-reported delinquency, neuropsychological deficit, and history of Attention Deficit Disorder. *Journal of Abnormal Child Psychology, 16,* 553–569.

Needleman, H. L., & Bellinger, D. C. (1981). The epidemiology of low-level lead exposure in childhood. *Journal of Child Psychiatry, 20,* 496–512.

Patterson, G. R. (1982). *Coercive family process.* Eugene, OR: Castalia Press.

Patterson, G. R. (1986). Performance models for antisocial boys. *American Psychologist, 41,* 432–444.

Patterson, G. R., & Reid, J. B. (1984). Social interactional processes in the family: The study of the moment-by-moment family transactions in which human social development is embedded. *Journal of Applied Developmental Psychology, 5,* 237–262.

Prinz, R. J., & Miller, G. E. (1991). Issues in understanding and treating childhood conduct problems in disadvantaged populations. *Journal of Clinical Child Psychology, 20,* 379–385.

Puig-Antich, J., & Chambers, W. (1978). *The Schedule for Affective Disorders and Schizophrenia for School-Age Children (Kiddie-SADS).* New York: New York State Psychiatric Institute.

Quay, H. C., & Peterson, D. R. (1983). *Manual for the Revised Behavior Problem Checklist.* Coral Gables, FL: University of Miami, Applied Social Sciences.

Reeves, J. C., Werry, J. S., Elkind, G. S., & Zametkin, A. (1987). Attention deficit, conduct and anxiety disorders in children: 2. Clinical characteristics. *Journal of the American Academy of Child and Adolescent Psychiatry, 26,* 144–155.

Robin, A. L. (1981). A controlled evaluation of problem-solving communication training with parent-adolescent conflict. *Behavior Therapy, 12,* 593–609.

Robin, A. L., & Foster, S. (1989). *Negotiating parent-adolescent conflict: A behavioral family systems approach.* New York: Guilford Press.

Rubin, K. H., Bream, L. A., & Rose-Krasnor, L. (1991). Social problem solving and aggression in childhood. In D. J. Pepler & K. H. Rubin (Eds.), *The development and treatment of childhood aggression* (pp. 219–245). Hillsdale, NJ: Erlbaum.

Rutter, M. (1972). *Maternal deprivation reassessed.* Middlesex, England: Penguin.

Rutter, M. (1989). Pathways from childhood to adult life. *Journal of Child Psychology and Psychiatry, 30,* 23–51.

Rutter, M., Cox, A., Tupling, C., Berger, M., & Yule, W. (1975). Attainment in two geographical areas: 1. The prevalence of psychiatric disorder. *British Journal of Psychiatry, 126,* 493–509.

Rutter, M., McDonald, H., LeCouteur, A., Harrington, R., Bolton, P., & Bailey, A. (1990). Genetic factors in child psychiatric disorders: 2. Empirical findings. *Journal of Child Psychology and Psychiatry, 31,* 39–83.

Rutter, M., Tizard, J., Yule, W., Graham, P., & Whitmore, K. (1976). Isle of Wright studies 1964–1974. *Psychological Medicine, 6,* 313–332.

Sanders, M. R., & Christensen, A. P. (1985). A comparison of the effects of child management and planned activities training in five parenting environments. *Journal of Abnormal Child Psychology, 13,* 101–117.

Sanders, M. R., & Dadds, M. R. (1982). The effects of planned activities and child management training: An analysis of setting generality. *Behavior Therapy, 13,* 1–11.

Sanders, M. R., & Dadds, M. R. (1993). *Behavioral family intervention.* New York: Allyn & Bacon, Longwood Division.

Sanders, M. R., Dadds, M. R., & Bor, W. (1989). A contextual analysis of oppositional child behavior and maternal aversive behavior in families of conduct disordered children. *Journal of Clinical Child Psychology, 18,* 72–83.

Sanders, M., Dadds, M., Johnston, R., & Cash, R. (1992) Child depression and Conduct Disorder: Cognitive constructions and family problem-solving interactions. *Journal of Abnormal Psychology, 101,* 496–504.

Sanders, M. R., & Glynn, T. (1981). Training parents in behavioral self-management: An analysis of generalization and maintenance. *Journal of Applied Behavior Analysis, 14,* 223–237.

Sanders, M. R., & James, J. E. (1983). The modification of parent behavior: A review of generalization and maintenance. *Behavior Modification, 7,* 3–27.

Schachar, R., Sandberg, S., & Rutter, M. (1986). Agreement between teachers' ratings and observations of hyperactivity, inattentiveness, and defiance. *Journal of Abnormal Child Psychology, 14,* 331–345.

Schaffer, D., Schwab-Stone, M., Fisher, P., Davies, M., Piacentini, J., & Gioia, P. (1988). *Results of a field trial and proposals for a new instrument (DISC-R).* Washington, DC: National Institute of Mental Health.

Scholom, A., Zucker, R. A., & Stollack, G. E. (1979). Relating early child adjustment to infant and parent temperament. *Journal of Abnormal Child Psychology, 7,* 297–308.

Speer, D. C. (1971). The Behavior Problem Checklist. *Journal of Counseling and Clinical Psychology, 36,* 221–228.

Sweet, A. A. (1987). The therapeutic relationship in behavior therapy. *Clinical Psychology Review, 4,* 253–272.

Szykula, S. A., Morris, S. B., Sudweeks, C., & Saygar, T. V. (1987). Child focussed behavior and strategic therapy: Outcome comparison. *Psychotherapy, 35,* 546–551.

Thomas, A., & Chess, S. (1977). *Temperament and development.* New York: Brunner/Mazel.

Touliatos, J., Perlmutter, B., & Strauss, M. (Eds.), (1990). *Handbook of family measurement techniques.* Newbury Park, CA: Sage.

Twardosz, S., & Nordquist, V. M. (1988). Parent training. In M. Hersen & V. B. Hasselt (Eds.), *Behavior therapy with children and adolescents: A clinical approach* (pp. 75–105). New York: Wiley.

Vygotsky, L. S. (1960). *Development of the higher mental functions.* Moscow: Nauk, RSFSR.

Wahler, R. G. (1980). The insular mother: Her problems in parent-child treatment. *Journal of Applied Behavior Analysis, 13,* 207–219.

Wahler, R. G., & Dumas, J. E. (1984). Changing the observational coding style of insular and noninsular mothers: A step toward maintenance. In R. F. Dangel & R. A. Polster (Eds.), *Parent training: Foundations of research and practice* (pp. 379–461). New York: Guilford Press.

Webster-Stratton, C. (1985). Predictors of outcome in parent training for conduct disordered children. *Behavior Therapy, 16,* 223–243.

Wells, K. C., & Egan, J. (1988). Social learning and systems family therapy for Childhood Oppositional Disorder: Comparative treatment outcome. *Comprehensive Psychiatry, 29,* 138–146.

West, D. J. (1982). *Delinquency: Its roots, careers and prospects.* Cambridge, MA: Harvard University Press.

Zeanah, C. H., Keener, M. A., Stewart, L., & Anders, T. F. (1985). Prenatal perception of infant personality. *Journal of the American Academy of Child and Adolescent Psychiatry, 24,* 204–210.

CHAPTER 21

Attention-Deficit/Hyperactivity Disorder

ARTHUR D. ANASTOPOULOS

DESCRIPTION OF THE DISORDER

Over the past 10 years, a tremendous amount of media attention has been focused on what we now know as attention-deficit/hyperactivity disorder (ADHD; American Psychiatric Association [APA], 1994). In addition to the countless times that ADHD has been the topic of interest in local newspaper articles and on radio talk shows, it has also received coverage from the national media, including the Public Broadcasting Service (PBS), *Time, Newsweek, The Wall Street Journal, 60 Minutes, Dateline, Good Morning America, Geraldo,* and *Sally Jesse Raphael.* Most of what has been presented has centered around the controversy over using Ritalin in the treatment of ADHD. Some of this same media attention, however, has raised questions about its legitimacy as a disorder.

In all likelihood, this surge in media coverage has contributed greatly to the public's perception that ADHD is a relatively new condition, "the disorder of the 90s" as some have described it. Although this particular labeling is relatively new, by no means is this a newly discovered clinical entity. On the contrary, accounts of its existence have been appearing in the scientific literature for nearly 100 years now, albeit under different names. Among the many diagnostic labels that previously have been applied are *Attention Deficit Disorder with Hyperactivity, Hyperkinetic Reaction of Childhood, Hyperactive Child Syndrome,* and *Minimal Brain Dysfunction.*

Confusion about this disorder has not been limited to its historical roots. Nor has it been confined to the public. Within professional circles as well, confusion and controversy have far too often swirled about, which in turn may be responsible for some of the difficulty that the public has had in understanding the historical background, the presentation, and clinical management of ADHD.

It is with this state of affairs in mind that this chapter has been written. To provide readers with a comprehensive overview of ADHD, this chapter begins with a detailed description of its primary features, its epidemiology, its etiology, and its psychosocial consequences. This is followed by a brief review of commonly employed assessment techniques and treatment strategies. As part of this discussion, mention is made of the many potential obstacles that practitioners face when providing clinical services to children and adolescents whose life circumstances are dysfunctional, or at the very least, nonsupportive. Including such a perspective will provide readers with an overview of ADHD that is not only comprehensive in its scope, but also practical and clinically useful.

Primary Symptoms

In clinical practice, it is not uncommon for parents or teachers to be unclear about what constitutes an ADHD diagnosis. For example, when asked to identify those behaviors that lead them to believe that their child may have ADHD, many parents cite noncompliance, emotional immaturity, or unsatisfactory academic progress. While such characteristics certainly can be associated with an ADHD diagnosis, they are by no means the core features of this disorder.

Within the child healthcare field, most professionals agree that ADHD is a chronic and pervasive condition characterized by developmental deficiencies in sustained attention, impulse control, and the regulation of motor activity in response to situational demands (APA, 1994). Clinical descriptions of children with ADHD frequently include complaints of "not listening to instructions," "not finishing assigned work," "daydreaming," "becoming bored easily," and so forth. Common to all of these referral concerns is a diminished capacity for vigilance; that is, difficulties sustaining attention to task (Douglas, 1983). Such problems can occur in free-play settings (Routh & Schroeder, 1976), but most often surface in situations demanding sustained attention to dull, boring, repetitive tasks (Milich, Loney, & Landau, 1982).

Clinic-referred children with ADHD may exhibit impulsivity as well. For example, they may interrupt others who might be busy, or display tremendous difficulty waiting for their turn in game situations. They may also begin tasks before directions are completed, take unnecessary risks, talk out of turn, or make indiscreet remarks without regard for social consequences. When hyperactivity is present, this may be displayed not only motorically but verbally. Descriptions of physical restlessness might include statements such as "always on the go," "unable to sit still," and so forth. As for the verbal component, more often than not these complaints center around the child's "talking excessively" or being a "chatterbox or motor mouth." Whether mild or severe, what makes all these behaviors manifestations of hyperactivity is their excessive, task-irrelevant, and developmentally inappropriate nature.

Although not yet widely accepted, difficulties with rule-governed behavior and excessive performance variability may also represent primary deficits (Barkley, 1990; Kendall & Braswell, 1985). Several studies have demonstrated that children with ADHD display significant problems adhering to rules or complying with requests (Barkley, 1990). In line with these findings are the clinical reports of parents and teachers, who commonly voice concerns about the inability of children with ADHD to "follow through on instructions." Such difficulties may arise in a variety of contexts, but most often occur when adults are not present, which increases the demand for behavioral self-regulation.

Children with ADHD may also display tremendous inconsistency in their task performance, both in terms of their productivity and accuracy (Douglas, 1972). Such variability may be evident with respect to their in-class performance or test scores, or it may involve fluctuations in their completion of homework or routine home chores. Although all children display a certain amount of variability in these areas, clinical experience and research findings have shown that children with ADHD exhibit this to a much greater degree. Thus, instead of reflecting "laziness" as some might contend, the inconsistent performance of children with ADHD may represent yet another manifestation of this disorder. To the extent that it does, this allows for a characterization of ADHD as a disorder of variability, rather than inability.

Future descriptions of ADHD may indeed include performance variability and deficiencies in rule-governed behavior as defining features. In the meantime, however, most professionals in the field today regard inattention, impulsivity, and hyperactivity as the primary symptoms of ADHD. Although these symptoms traditionally have been viewed as distinct and separate components of the disorder, the validity of this assumption has been called into question. At a theoretical level, Barkley (1995) has proposed that all three primary symptoms, as well as many of its associated features, may stem from an underlying deficit in behavioral inhibition processes. From a strictly empirical point of view, recently reported factor analytic results have further suggested that whereas inattention symptoms tend to cluster apart from symptoms of impulsivity and hyperactivity, these latter two symptoms nonetheless routinely cluster together (DuPaul, 1991).

Situational Variability of Symptoms

Contrary to the belief of many, ADHD is not an all-or-none phenomenon, either always present or never. Instead, it is a condition whose primary symptoms show significant fluctuations in response to different situational demands (Zentall, 1985). One of the most important factors determining this variation is the degree to which children with ADHD are interested in what they are doing. ADHD symptoms are much more likely to occur in situations that are highly repetitive, boring, or familiar, versus those that are novel or stimulating (Barkley, 1977). Another determinant of situational variation is the amount of imposed structure. In free play or low demand settings, where children with ADHD have the freedom to do as they please, their behavior is relatively indistinguishable from that of normal children (Luk, 1985). Significant ADHD problems may arise, however, when others place demands on them or set rules for their behavior. Presumably due to increased demands for behavioral self-regulation, group settings are far more problematic for children with ADHD than one-to-one situations. There is also an increased likelihood for ADHD symptoms to arise in situations where feedback is dispensed infrequently or on a delayed basis (Douglas, 1983).

Being aware of the situational variability of ADHD symptoms is central to understanding the frequently irregular clinical presentation of this disorder. There are numerous examples of how ADHD symptoms might occur in one setting but not another. One of the more common discrepancies that can arise is when teachers observe the symptoms in school, but parents report no such problems at home. At face value, this might cause parents a tremendous amount of difficulty in accepting their child's ADHD diagnosis, not to mention anger and mistrust toward the teacher. By pointing out that ADHD is not an all-or-none clinical phenomenon and that the conditions at school (e.g., less interesting activities, large groups) are more conducive to eliciting the symptoms, clinicians very often can replace faulty assumptions with more accurate beliefs, thereby facilitating not only parental understanding and acceptance of the disorder, but also their willingness to work cooperatively with their child's teacher.

Diagnostic Criteria

The currently accepted criteria for making an ADHD diagnosis appear in the fourth edition of the *Diagnostic and Statistical Manual of Mental Disorders* (*DSM-IV;* APA, 1994). At the heart of this decision-making process are two 9-item symptom listings—

one pertaining to inattention symptoms, the other to hyperactivity-impulsivity concerns. Parents and/or teachers must report the presence of at least 6 of 9 problem behaviors from either list to warrant consideration of an ADHD diagnosis. Such behaviors must have an onset prior to 7 years of age, a duration of at least 6 months, and a frequency above and beyond that expected of children of the same mental age. Furthermore, they must be evident in two or more settings, have a clear impact on psychosocial functioning, and not be due to other types of mental health or learning disorders that might better explain their presence.

As evidenced by these criteria, ADHD varies in clinical presentation from child to child. For some children with ADHD, symptoms of inattention may be of relatively greater concern than impulsivity or hyperactivity problems. For others, impulsivity and hyperactivity difficulties may be more prominent. Reflecting these possible differences in clinical presentation, the new *DSM-IV* criteria not only allow for, but require, ADHD subtyping. For example, when more than six symptoms are present from both lists and all other criteria are met, a diagnosis of ADHD, Combined Type is in order. If six or more inattention symptoms are present, but less than six hyperactive-impulsive symptoms are evident, and all other criteria are met, the proper diagnosis would be ADHD, predominantly inattentive type. Those familiar with prior diagnostic classification schemes will quickly recognize these *DSM-IV* categories as similar, but not exact, counterparts to what previously was known as attention-deficit hyperactivity disorder and undifferentiated attention deficit disorder in *DSM-III-R* (APA, 1987) and attention deficit disorder with or without hyperactivity in *DSM-III* (APA, 1980). Appearing for the first time in *DSM-IV,* however, is the subtyping condition known as ADHD, predominantly hyperactive-impulsive type, which is the appropriate diagnosis to make whenever six or more hyperactive-impulsive symptoms arise, less than six inattention concerns are evident, and all other criteria are met. Along with these major subtyping categories, *DSM-IV* also makes available two additional classifications that have primary bearing on adolescents and adults. For example, a diagnosis of ADHD, in partial remission, may be given to individuals who have clinical problems resulting from ADHD symptoms that currently do not meet criteria for any of the preceding subtypes, but nonetheless were part of a documented ADHD diagnosis at an earlier point in time. In similar cases where an earlier history of ADHD cannot be established with any degree of certainty, a diagnosis of ADHD, not otherwise specified, would instead be made.

EPIDEMIOLOGY

Depending on the criteria employed, estimates of the incidence of ADHD may vary a great deal, ranging from as low as 2% up to as much as 25% to 30%. Using the diagnostic criteria put forth by *DSM-IV,* approximately 3% to 5% of the general child population will meet criteria for some type of ADHD diagnosis (APA, 1994). Although its actual incidence may fluctuate somewhat within the general population, ADHD is by no means specific to any particular subgroup. It may be found among the rich and the poor, as well as among those with either very little or very high levels of education. It also cuts fairly evenly across diverse ethnic, racial, and religious lines. As with other externalizing problems, however, ADHD occurs much more often in boys than in girls. The ratio within clinic samples, for example, has been reported to be as high as 6:1, whereas in community samples it occurs on the order of 3:1 (Barkley, 1990). This may represent a real difference as a function of gender, but other factors may also mitigate this outcome. Due to their normally higher levels of physical activity and aggression, boys who display ADHD symptoms may get noticed more readily by teachers and parents and therefore get referred to clinics more often and sooner than girls with similar problems. To the extent that this might be true, it may also help to explain why girls who have ADHD symptoms do not get referred to clinics as often or as fast; what is abnormal for a girl may look tame relative to abnormal behaviors displayed by boys. In the absence of any empirical validation, such statements should be viewed as speculation at best. What remains certain in the meantime, however, is that boys currently outnumber girls by a wide margin when it comes to carrying an ADHD diagnosis.

CAUSES AND CONSEQUENCES

Etiology

Within the field today, there is consensus that neurochemical imbalances play a central role in the etiology of ADHD. More specifically, there may be abnormalities in one or more of the monoaminergic systems, involving either dopamine or norepinephrine mechanisms (Zametkin & Rapoport, 1986). The locus of this dysfunction purportedly lies within the prefrontal-limbic areas of the brain (Lou, Henriksen, Bruhn, Borner, & Nielsen, 1989). For a majority of children with ADHD, such neurological circumstances presumably arise from inborn biological factors, including genetic transmission, pregnancy, and birth complications (Biederman et al., 1987; Deutsch, 1987; Edelbrock, 1995; Streissguth et al., 1984). For relatively smaller numbers of children carrying this diagnosis, it can be acquired after birth, through head injury, neurological illness, elevated lead levels, and other biological complications (Ross & Ross, 1982).

Despite their widespread public appeal, there is relatively little support for the assertions of Feingold (1975) and others that ingestion of sugar or various other food substances directly causes ADHD (Wolraich et al., 1994). Likewise, although a few environmental theories have been proposed to explain ADHD (Block, 1977; Willis & Lovaas, 1977), these have not received much support in the research literature. Thus, there would seem to be little justification for claiming that poor parenting or chaotic home environments are in any way causally related to ADHD. When ADHD is found among children who come from such family circumstances, one might reasonably speculate that parents of such children may themselves be individuals with childhood and adult histories of ADHD. If so, this would help to explain why their homes might be so chaotic and, at the same time, provide support for a genetic explanation for the child's ADHD condition. Under this same scenario, the resulting chaos in the home might then be viewed as a factor exacerbating, rather than causing, the child's preexisting, inborn ADHD condition.

One of the first questions that many parents ask after learning of their child's ADHD diagnosis is, "What caused this?" Although clinicians generally cannot supply a definitive answer to this question, they can at least speculate about possible causes based on their knowledge of whether or not the child has any of the etiologic risk factors noted earlier. Emphasizing the biological nature of this disorder very often serves to help parents see their child's problems in a different light. This in turn sets the stage for them to let go of any faulty beliefs that they may have had (e.g., "I must be a bad parent"), thereby reducing any associated guilt feelings or other types of personal distress.

Impact on Child and Adolescent Functioning

In addition to their primary symptoms, children and adolescents with ADHD frequently display secondary or comorbid difficulties. For example, noncompliance, argumentativeness, temper outbursts, lying, stealing, and other manifestations of oppositional-defiant disorder and conduct disorder may occur in up to 65% of the clinic-referred ADHD population (Barkley, Anastopoulos, Guevremont, & Fletcher, 1991; Loney & Milich, 1982). Virtually all children with ADHD experience some type of school difficulty. An especially common problem is that their levels of academic productivity and achievement are significantly lower than their estimated potential (Barkley, 1990). Depending on the definition used, as many as 20% to 30% may also exhibit dyslexia or other learning disabilities (Barkley, DuPaul, & McMurray, 1990). As a result of such complications, a relatively high percentage typically receives some form of special education assistance (Barkley, 1990). Significant peer socialization problems may occur as well (Pelham & Bender, 1982). At times, such difficulties involve deficiencies in establishing friendships (Grenell, Glass, & Katz, 1987). More often than not, however, maintaining satisfactory peer relations is of even greater clinical concern. Due to their inability to control their behavior in social situations, children and adolescents with ADHD frequently alienate their peers, who in turn respond with social rejection or avoidance (Cunningham & Siegel, 1987). During adolescence, additional problems may arise in pursuit of meeting occupational responsibilities. Moreover, teens with ADHD are at increased risk for becoming involved in automobile accidents and for committing traffic violations (Barkley, Guevremont, Anastopoulos, DuPaul, & Shelton, 1993). Possibly as a result of such behavioral, academic, social, and/or vocational problems, children and adolescents with ADHD often exhibit low self-esteem, low frustration tolerance, symptoms of depression and anxiety, and other emotional complications (Margalit & Arieli, 1984).

Impact on Family Functioning

As noted earlier, ADHD is frequently accompanied by various behavioral, academic, social, and emotional complications. Together, such difficulties can have a significant impact on the psychosocial functioning of parents and siblings. Research has shown that parents of children with ADHD very often become overly directive and negative in their parenting style (Cunningham & Barkley, 1979). In addition to viewing themselves as less skilled and less knowledgeable in their parenting roles (Mash & Johnston, 1990), they may also experience considerable stress in their parenting roles, especially when comorbid oppositional-defiant features are present (Anastopoulos, Guevremont, Shelton, & DuPaul, 1992). Teens with ADHD are at increased risk for experiencing significant conflict with their parents, especially when oppositional-defiant disorder features are present (Barkley, Anastopoulos, Guevremont, & Fletcher, 1992). Depression and marital discord may arise as well (Lahey et al., 1988). Whether these parent and family complications result directly from the child's or adolescent's ADHD is not entirely clear at present. Clinical experience would suggest that they probably do, at least in part, given the increased caretaking demands that children and adolescents with ADHD impose on their parents. These include more frequent displays of noncompliance, related to difficulties in following through on parental instructions (Cunningham & Barkley, 1979). In addition, parents of these children often find themselves involved in resolving various school, peer, and sibling difficulties, which occur throughout childhood (Barkley, 1990) and into adolescence as well (Barkley et al., 1991).

Developmental Course

Some children begin to show evidence of ADHD in early infancy (Hartsough & Lambert, 1985). Most, however, first display clear signs of developmentally deviant behavior between 3 and 4 years of age (Ross & Ross, 1982). For a smaller number of children, ADHD symptoms may not surface until 5 or 6 years of age, coinciding with school entrance.

During middle childhood, ADHD symptoms often become more chronic and pervasive, even though they may appear somewhat improved at times. It is during this same period that secondary complications, such as academic underachievement or oppositional-defiant behavior, frequently arise. Contrary to popular opinion, most children do not outgrow their ADHD problems on reaching adolescence. As many as 70% will continue to exhibit developmentally inappropriate levels of inattention and, to a lesser extent, symptoms of hyperactivity-impulsivity during their teen years (Weiss & Hechtman, 1986). Of additional clinical significance is that the pattern of secondary complications accompanying ADHD in adolescence is highly similar to that found in younger ADHD populations (Barkley et al., 1990). Although adolescent and adult outcome data are scant, what research is available suggests that, while many children with ADHD continue to display these symptoms well into adolescence and adulthood, the vast majority will learn to compensate for these problems, and therefore make a satisfactory adult adjustment (Weiss & Hechtman, 1986; Wender, 1995). For those who do not, their comorbid problems, such as depression or alcoholism (Farrington, Loeber, & van Kammen, 1987), are of relatively greater clinical concern than their ADHD symptoms.

IMPEDIMENTS TO INTERVENTION IN THE REAL WORLD CONTEXT

Those familiar with the history of ADHD are well aware that much progress has been made in the evaluation and treatment of children and adolescents with ADHD. Despite these enormous strides, room remains for improvement in the rendering of clinical services. This is particularly true for children and adolescents with ADHD who come from economically disadvantaged or dysfunctional home situations. This is also problematic for children and adolescents with ADHD who come from ethnically, racially, or culturally diverse family backgrounds.

For many families with limited financial resources, for example, getting to a clinic to have a child or adolescent evaluated for ADHD may not be feasible. Even if they have the means to transport themselves to such a facility, they very likely may not have the necessary health insurance coverage or out-of-pocket monies to pay for the overall cost of a comprehensive multimethod evaluation. To the extent that highly specialized multimethod assessments can be streamlined to reduce their cost and/or delivered in community settings, higher percentages of economically disadvantaged children and adolescents may then have access to such services.

For those families who can get such services for their child or adolescent, additional obstacles may arise. Parents with limited education, for example, may have a great deal of difficulty reading and completing all the forms and questionnaires that so often are a part of multimethod assessments. Similar comprehension difficulties may occur among parents for whom English is not their primary language. When such situations arise, clinicians must then try to identify family friends or relatives who are willing to provide assistance as translators or interpreters. This introduces the risk that something may "get lost in the translation," thereby complicating the assessment process. To address such problems, researchers need to develop questionnaires and rating scales that have appropriate readability levels, as well as alternative forms written in languages other than English.

A related problem stems from cultural diversity issues. Many readily available assessment procedures for identifying ADHD do not include adequate ethnic and racial representation in their norms. Assessing the behavior and performance of children and adolescents from such backgrounds, therefore, runs the risk of unfair and inappropriate developmental comparisons. This, in turn, makes it more likely that children and adolescents from culturally diverse backgrounds may be overidentified as having ADHD, not to mention various other internalizing and externalizing conditions. More research is once again needed, this time for developing culturally sensitive norms that allow for more accurate developmental comparisons. In the meantime, clinicians would be well advised to consider employing only those ADHD assessment procedures that have some degree of sensitivity to these cultural diversity issues.

Dysfunctional home settings pose additional challenges to the assessment process. Many times, children and adolescents are not living with their biological parents. When such a situation arises, obtaining clinically relevant historical information can be next to impossible. More often than not, whatever information is obtained tends at best to be scanty and limited. This type of problem is exacerbated even further when children and adolescents move about from one foster care placement to the next. Along the way, their histories become less and less clear to those far removed from their pasts. Moreover, those currently responsible for their caretaking often have limited knowledge of their recent functioning, due to the typically brief and temporary nature of their contact. There is not an easy solution to this type of assessment problem. To whatever extent possible, the success of any evaluation conducted under these and similar circumstances rests on the clinician's ability to track down and review prior social service agency and school records that may shed light on the onset and course of ADHD type problems.

All these considerations—cultural diversity, economic disadvantage, and dysfunctional homes—also come into play and exert their influence on the intervention process. Trying to provide ongoing treatment to children and adolescents who move about from one caretaker to the next seriously compromises any chance for successful therapeutic outcome. Although many a clinician might be tempted to resist selecting such a case, most instead adjust their expectations for change and accomplish whatever they can under these adverse circumstances. Another commonly encountered situation is when a decision must be made as to the appropriateness of putting a child or adolescent with ADHD on a stimulant medication regimen, when the clinician knows full well that the youngster's parent has a history of substance abuse, and therefore may abuse what was legally prescribed for their child. Completing 10 sessions of parent training can also be rather costly for families without health insurance. Even when cost is not an issue, many parents are unable to comply with the demands of the program for the very same reasons that they are unable to keep their personal and family lives under satisfactory control. The solutions? Again, little research is available to guide such clinical decisions, which instead rest on the intuition and creativity of the practitioner.

CLINICAL EVALUATION AND TREATMENT

Assessment Strategies

Despite relatively clear diagnostic guidelines (APA, 1994), establishing an ADHD diagnosis remains a difficult matter. A factor contributing to this situation is the availability of an enormous number and variety of clinical assessment procedures on the market. Because detailed information about the reliability and validity of such measures is not always readily available, clinicians frequently have little to go on in trying to determine how best to obtain a representative sample of a child's or adolescent's real life behavior. The special nature of the ADHD population also presents many other assessment obstacles. An especially important consideration is the degree to which ADHD symptoms vary as a function of situational demands. Recognizing that this occurs, clinicians must try to obtain information from individuals who observe identified children across different settings. At the very least, this should include input from parents and teachers. When appropriate, other significant caretakers, such as day-care providers, should provide similar input. Another critical factor affecting the evaluation process is the increased likelihood that children with ADHD will display comorbid conditions. In view of this possibility, clinicians must incorporate assessment methods that address not only primary ADHD symptoms, but also other aspects of the identified child's psychosocial functioning. Of additional importance is the need for gathering assessment data pertaining to parental, marital, and family functioning. Although this type of information may not shed much light on whether or not an ADHD diagnosis is present, it nevertheless provides a context for understanding how problem behaviors may be maintained. Moreover, such information often serves as a basis for determining how likely it is that parents and other caretakers will implement recommended treatment strategies on behalf of their child.

Implicit in the preceding discussion is that clinical evaluations of ADHD must be comprehensive and multidimensional, so as to capture its situational variability, its comorbid features, and its impact on home, school, and social functioning (Barkley, 1990). This multimethod assessment approach may include, not only the traditional parent and child interviews, but also standardized child behavior rating scales, parent self-report measures, direct behavioral observations of ADHD symptoms in natural or analogue settings, and clinic-based psychological tests.

Interviews

Because of their flexibility, unstructured and semistructured interviews with parents and children can yield a wealth of information pertaining to a child's psychosocial functioning. They do not, however, allow for accurate normative comparisons, which complicates documenting developmental deviance. An alternative to these traditional approaches is the structured interview. In addition to avoiding documentation problems, structured interviews allow for standardized administration across children, which facilitates data collection and research. Among the many procedures of this sort that have been employed in ADHD research are the Diagnostic Interview Schedule for Children (DISC; Costello, Edelbrock, Kalas, Kessler, & Klaric, 1982) and the Diagnostic Interview for Children and Adolescents (DICA; Herjanic, Brown, & Wheatt, 1975), both of which are currently undergoing revision to be compatible with *DSM-IV.* While offering many advantages, structured interviews nevertheless possess certain limitations (Edelbrock & Costello, 1984), which makes them cumbersome to employ in typical clinical situations.

Behavior Rating Scales

Standardized behavior checklists and rating scales are often an indispensable part of the assessment of children and adolescents with ADHD. Their convenience, applicability to multiple informants, ability to gather information collapsed across long time intervals, and provision of normative references have led to their widespread application in clinical practice. Although a large number and variety of such questionnaires are now available, most have not yet been adequately validated against the new *DSM-IV* criteria for ADHD. Among those having documented diagnostic utility with the *DSM-III-R* version of ADHD are the Child Behavior Checklist (Achenbach, 1991), the Behavioral Assessment System for Children (Reynolds & Kamphaus, 1992), the Revised Conners Parent and Teacher Rating Scales (Goyette, Conners, & Ulrich, 1978), the ADHD Rating Scale (DuPaul, 1991), the ADDES (McCarney, 1989), and the ADD-H Comprehensive Teacher Rating Scale (ACTeRS; Ullmann, Sleator, & Sprague, 1984). A particular strength of these measures is their provision of norms, which allows for statistical comparison of identified children against normal children of the same age and gender. This facilitates documentation of the degree to which primary ADHD symptoms, as well as other symptoms of concern, deviate from developmental expectations.

In view of the relatively high incidence of parenting stress, marital discord, and psychopathology that exists among parents of children with ADHD, clinicians often incorporate parent self-report measures into the assessment process. This may include, but certainly is not limited to, such measures as the Symptom Checklist 90—Revised (SCL 90-R; Derogatis, 1986), the Parenting Stress Index (Abidin, 1983), the Beck Depression Scale (Beck, Rush, Shaw, & Emery, 1979), and the Locke-Wallace Marital Adjustment Scale (Locke & Wallace, 1959).

Clinic-Based Measures

Laboratory measures of sustained attention and impulsivity are commonly included in ADHD evaluations. Perhaps the most widely used instrument for assessing these particular ADHD features is the continuous performance test (CPT). Numerous versions of the CPT exist, including the Conners (Conners, 1994), the Test of Variables of Attention (Greenberg & Waldman, 1991), and the Gordon Diagnostic System (Gordon, 1983). This widespread usage may have developed because of their success in differentiating groups of children with ADHD from normal controls. Despite such success at a group level, many of these measures produce unacceptably high false negative rates when applied to individual children or adolescents (DuPaul, Anastopoulos, Shelton, Guevremont, & Metevia, 1992; Matier-Sharma, Perachio, Newcorn, Sharma, & Halperin, 1995). Although the exact reasons for this discrepancy are unclear, a possible explanation is that these procedures are typically administered in clinic settings under relatively novel, one-to-one, high feedback conditions, which greatly reduces the likelihood of eliciting ADHD symptomatology.

Direct Observational Procedures

Also available are various observational assessment procedures, which more directly assess the behavior problems of children with ADHD, as well as their interactions with others. Among these are systems for observing behavior in classroom settings (Abikoff, Gittelman-Klein, & Klein, 1977; Jacob, O'Leary, & Rosenblad, 1978), systems for examining child behavior in clinic analogue situations (Roberts, 1987), and systems for assessing the clinic-based interactions between ADHD children and others (Mash & Barkley, 1987). Many of these coding systems target behaviors reflecting specific ADHD concerns, such as off-task behavior, fidgeting, and so on. Because they attempt to capture behavior under conditions more representative of real life circumstances, such procedures often are more reliable and valid than clinic-based laboratory assessment devices.

Other Procedures

Information about intellectual functioning, level of academic achievement, and learning disabilities status needs to be incorporated into the assessment of children and adolescents suspected of having ADHD. Such information usually can be obtained through review of prior school and medical records. If for some reason this is not available at the time of the ADHD workup, additional testing of this sort must then be conducted.

Practical Considerations

As noted, the clinical evaluation of children and adolescents suspected of having ADHD generally requires a comprehensive multimethod assessment approach. As part of the evaluation process, clinicians must focus diagnostic attention not only on those behavioral difficulties suggestive of ADHD, but also on various other aspects of the child's or adolescent's psychosocial functioning that are at increased risk. Moreover, they must incorporate assessment procedures that yield information about parental, marital, and family functioning, so as to understand more fully the psychosocial context in which the child or adolescent functions.

The intuitive appeal of this rationale notwithstanding, many parents find such an assessment approach incompatible with what they thought might be done to determine the presence or absence of ADHD. "After all," they might reason, "if you're trying to find out whether my child has ADHD, why are you spending so much time interviewing me and having me fill out questionnaires . . . why aren't you spending more time testing my child?" Left unanswered, such matters can cause parents to feel threatened or to question the competence of the evaluating clinician. This in turn can interfere with their acceptance of any diagnostic feedback, as well as their willingness to implement treatment recommendations.

In anticipation of such problems, clinicians must explain the rationale for their assessment approach. In particular, they need to mention that direct testing involves relatively novel and interesting psychological test materials that are administered under closely supervised, high feedback, one-to-one conditions. Such circumstances decrease the likelihood that ADHD symptoms will surface. For this reason, therefore, a relatively more accurate sampling of a child's or adolescent's behavior stems from parent and teacher input, based on observations occurring in situational contexts (e.g., large group setting) that are more likely to elicit ADHD symptomatology. This type of explanation very often alleviates any parental concerns or doubts that might interfere with their receptivity to diagnostic and treatment feedback.

Although not previously discussed, clinical use of assessment procedures should not be limited to the diagnostic phase of the assessment process. In many cases, these same procedures can serve as outcome measures in assessing the efficacy of various treatment approaches (e.g., stimulant medication trials), many of which will be discussed in the following section.

Treatment Approaches

Many of the same factors that complicate the assessment process can affect treatment outcome as well. Foremost among these are the cross-situational pervasiveness of primary ADHD symptoms and the relatively high incidence of co-occurring or comorbid conditions. Such circumstances make it highly unlikely that any singular treatment approach can satisfactorily meet all the clinical management needs of children with ADHD. For this reason, clinicians must often employ multiple treatment strategies in combination, each of which addresses a different aspect of the child's psychosocial difficulties.

Among those treatments that have received adequate, or at the very least preliminary, empirical support are pharmacotherapy, parent training in contingency management methods/parent counseling, classroom applications of contingency management techniques, and cognitive-behavioral training. Despite such support, these interventions should not be viewed as curative of ADHD. Instead, their value lies in their temporary reduction of ADHD symptom levels and in their reduction of related behavioral or emotional difficulties. When such treatments are removed, ADHD symptoms very often return to pretreatment levels of deviance. Thus, their effectiveness in improving prognosis presumably rests on their being maintained over long periods.

Pharmacotherapy

For many years, clinicians and researchers have employed medications in their management of children with ADHD. The rationale for doing so rests on the assumption that neurochemical imbalances are involved in the etiology of this disorder. Although the exact neurochemical mechanisms underlying their therapeutic action remain unclear, research has shown that at least two classes of medication—stimulants and antidepressants—can be helpful in reducing ADHD symptomatology.

Numerous studies have consistently demonstrated that stimulant medications are highly effective in the management of ADHD symptoms in a large percentage of the children and adolescents who take them (Taylor, 1986). According to some estimates, as many as 80% to 90% will respond favorably, with a majority of these displaying behavior that is relatively normalized (Rapport, Denney, DuPaul, & Gardner, 1994). In addition to bringing about improvements in primary ADHD symptomatology, these medications often lead to increased child compliance and decreased aggressive behavior (Hinshaw, Henker, & Whalen, 1984). Although certain side effects can arise from their use (e.g., decreased appetite), these effects tend to be mild, and most children tolerate them without great difficulty (Barkley, 1990), even over extended periods (Zeiner, 1995). For reasons such as these, many child healthcare professionals have incorporated stimulant regimens into their clinical practices.

The most commonly prescribed stimulants are methylphenidate (Ritalin), d-amphetamine (Dexedrine), and pemoline (Cylert). Of these, Ritalin is most often the medication of choice. Unlike many other types of medication, Ritalin acts rapidly, producing effects on behavior within 30 to 45 minutes after oral ingestion, and peaking in its therapeutic impact within 2 to 4 hours. Its utility in managing behavior, however, typically dissipates within 3 to 7 hours, even though minuscule amounts of the medication may remain in the blood for up to 24 hours (Cantwell & Carlson, 1978). More often than not, it is prescribed in twice daily doses, but recent research has suggested that adding a third dose to the daily regimen can be tolerated fairly well by most children (Kent, Blader, Koplewicz, Abikoff, & Foley, 1995). Although many children take this medication exclusively on school days, it can also be used on weekends and during school vacations, especially where ADHD symptoms seriously interfere with home functioning.

Despite their overall utility, stimulants may not be appropriate for some children with ADHD, who nevertheless require a medication component in their overall clinical management. As a way of meeting the needs of such children, child healthcare professionals have recently turned to the use of tricyclic antidepressants, such as imipramine. Most often, these medications are employed in situations where certain side effects (e.g., motor tics), known to be exacerbated by stimulants, are present, or where significant mood disturbances accompany ADHD symptomatology (Plizska, 1987). As a rule, antidepressants are given twice daily, usually in the morning and evening. Because they are longer acting than stimulants, it takes more time to evaluate the therapeutic value of any given dose (Rapoport & Mikkelsen, 1978). Despite this limitation, recent research has suggested that low doses of these medications can produce increased vigilance and decreased impulsivity, as well as reductions in disruptive and aggressive behavior. Mood elevation may also occur, especially in children with significant pretreatment levels of depression or anxiety (Plizska, 1987). Such treatment effects, however, can diminish over time. Thus, antidepressants frequently are not the medication of choice for long-term management of ADHD.

Parent Training

As discussed earlier, ADHD is characterized by deficiencies in regulating behavior in response to situational demands (Barkley, 1990). Such "demands" include not only the stimulus properties of the settings in which children function, but also the consequences for their behavior. To the extent that these situational parameters can be modified, one might reasonably anticipate corresponding changes in ADHD symptomatology. Assuming this to be valid, it provides ample justification for utilizing various behavior therapy techniques in the clinical management of children with ADHD.

Despite the plethora of research on parent training in behavior modification, very few studies have examined the efficacy of this approach with children specifically identified as having ADHD. What few studies exist can be interpreted with cautious optimism as supporting behavioral parent training with such children (Anastopoulos, Shelton, DuPaul, & Guevremont, 1993; Pelham et al., 1988; Pisterman, McGrath, Firestone, & Goodman, 1989). Most of these interventions involved training parents in general contingency management tactics, such as positive reinforcement, response cost, and/or time-out strategies. Some, however, combined contingency management training with didactic-counseling, aimed at increasing parental knowledge and understanding of ADHD (Anastopoulos et al., 1993). In addition to producing changes in child behavior, parent training interventions have also led to improvements in various aspects of parental and family functioning, including decreased parenting stress and increased parenting self-esteem (Anastopoulos et al., 1993; Pisterman et al., 1989).

Classroom Contingency Management

In comparison with the parent training literature, relatively more research has addressed the use of behavior management methods for children with ADHD in the classroom. Such studies suggest that the contingent use of positive reinforcement alone can produce immediate, short-term improvements in classroom behavior, productivity, and accuracy (Pfiffner & O'Leary, 1993). For most children with ADHD, secondary or tangible reinforcers would seem to be more effective in improving their behavior and academic performance than would teacher attention or other types social reinforcement (Pfiffner, Rosen, & O'Leary, 1985). The combination of positive reinforcement with various punishment strategies, such as response cost, typically leads to even greater improvements in behavior than either alone (Pfiffner & O'Leary, 1987). Despite the promising nature of such findings, many of these reported treatment gains subside when treatment is withdrawn (Barkley, Copeland, & Sivage, 1980). In addition, these improvements in behavior and performance seldom generalize to settings where treatment is not in effect.

Cognitive-Behavioral Therapy

Over the past 20 years, clinicians and researchers have employed many and varied cognitive-behavioral interventions with children who manifest ADHD symptomatology including self-monitoring, self-reinforcement, and self-instructional techniques. Much of the appeal for their clinical application stems from their apparent focus on some of the primary deficits of ADHD, including impulsivity, poor organizational skills, and difficulties with rules and instructions. Also contributing to their popularity is their presumed potential for enhancing treatment generalization, above and beyond that achieved through more traditional contingency management programs.

Research on self-monitoring has shown that it can improve on-task behavior and academic productivity in some children with ADHD (Shapiro & Cole, 1994). The combination of self-monitoring and self-reinforcement can also lead to improvements in on-task behavior and academic accuracy, as well as in peer relations (Hinshaw et al., 1984). As for self-instructional training, the picture is less clear, with many recent studies (Abikoff & Gittelman, 1985) failing to replicate earlier reported successes (Bornstein & Quevillon, 1976; Meichenbaum & Goodman, 1971).

Readily apparent in these studies are several potential limitations. For example, to achieve desired treatment effects in the classroom, children with ADHD must be reinforced for utilizing self-instructional strategies. Hence, contrary to initial expectations, this form of treatment apparently does not free children from control by the social environment. Instead, what it seems to accomplish is to shift such external control to a slightly less direct form. Another limitation is that treatment effects seldom generalize to settings where self-instructional training is not in effect, or to academic tasks that are not specifically part of the training process (Barkley et al., 1980). In this regard, self-instructional training apparently does not, as had been hoped, circumvent the problem of situation specificity of treatment effects, which has plagued the use of contingency management methods for many years.

Combined Interventions

What should be evident from the preceding discussion is that singular treatment approaches—whether they be pharmacological, behavioral, or cognitive-behavioral—are not, by themselves, sufficient to meet all the clinical management needs of children with ADHD. In response to this situation, many child healthcare professionals have begun to employ multiple ADHD treatments in combination.

Despite the intuitive appeal of this clinical practice, there presently exists little empirical justification for utilizing such combinations. Although limited in number, studies generally have shown that regardless of which combination is used, the therapeutic impact of the combined treatment package typically does not exceed that of either treatment alone. This would certainly seem to be the case when stimulant medication therapy is combined with classroom contingency management (Gadow, 1985). Similar findings have emerged from studies examining the use of stimulant regimens in combination with cognitive-behavioral interventions (Hinshaw et al., 1984).

From a somewhat different perspective, there have been attempts to evaluate, retrospectively, the long-term effects of individualized multimodality intervention on ADHD outcome (Satterfield, Satterfield, & Cantwell, 1980). Such multimodal interventions included medication, parent training, individual counseling, special education, family therapy, and/or other treatments as needed by the individual. The obtained results suggested that an individualized program of combined treatments, when continued over a period of several years, can produce improvements in the social adjustment of children with ADHD, in their rates of antisocial behavior, and in their academic achievement. Similar prospective multimodal intervention research is currently in progress under the sponsorship of the Child and Adolescent Branch of the National Institutes of Mental Health. Thus, in the not too distant future, additional light will be shed on this matter.

Adjunctive Procedures

Discussed in the preceding sections were numerous treatment strategies, directly targeting the needs of children with ADHD. What was not covered was the manner in which various comorbid features are typically addressed. When certain types of comorbid features, such as aggression, are present, often they too will diminish in frequency and severity when targeted ADHD symptoms come under the control of various interventions. This does not always occur, however. Moreover, there are numerous occasions when secondary emotional or behavioral features arise independent of the primary ADHD diagnosis, and therefore are unresponsive to ADHD interventions. In such situations, it becomes necessary to consider adjunctive intervention strategies (e.g., individual therapy may assist children or adolescents in their adjustment to parental divorce).

Due to the increased incidence of various psychosocial difficulties among the parents of such children, clinicians must sometimes recommend that they too receive therapy services, such as individual or marital counseling. In addition to providing therapeutic benefits for the parents themselves, these adjunctive procedures can produce indirect benefits for their children. When parental distress is reduced, parents frequently become better able to implement recommended treatment strategies, such as parent training, on behalf of their child. Although intuitively appealing and sound on the basis of clinical experience, such adjunctive procedures within an ADHD population have yet to be addressed empirically. Thus, this would seem to be an area fertile for further, clinically meaningful research.

SUMMARY

Within the field, there is a consensus that ADHD is a chronic and pervasive condition characterized by developmentally inappropriate levels of inattention, impulsivity, and/or hyperactivity. Most children and adolescents with ADHD presumably acquire this problem through inborn biological mechanisms. One of the more intriguing, and yet confusing, aspects of ADHD is that its primary features are subject to situational variation. Although it can occur alone, ADHD often is accompanied by other educational, behavioral, emotional, social, and family complications.

Clinical evaluations of children and adolescents suspected of having ADHD must be multidimensional, so as to capture its situational variability and its secondary child features. Moreover, some attempt must also be made to assess the extent to which parental and family functioning may be disrupted by its presence. For many of the same reasons, the clinical management of children and adolescents with ADHD must be multidimensional. Among the many treatments available for dealing with this disorder, stimulant medication therapy is perhaps used most often and most effectively. Although not yet empirically validated, combining stimulant medication therapy with other types of treatments, such as parent training or classroom modifications, is regarded to be acceptable and desirable clinical practice.

As is the case for other child mental health difficulties, economic disadvantage, family dysfunction, and cultural diversity potentially complicate the assessment and treatment of ADHD. Until further research is conducted to clarify such matters, practitioners must rely on their creativity and intuition to guide them in their clinical management of children and adolescents with ADHD who come from such backgrounds.

REFERENCES

Abidin, R. R. (1983). *The Parenting Stress Index.* Charlottesville, VA: Pediatric Psychology Press.

Abikoff, H., & Gittelman, R. (1985). Does behavior therapy normalize the classroom behavior of hyperactive children? *Archives of General Psychiatry, 41,* 449–454.

Abikoff, H., Gittelman-Klein, R., & Klein, D. (1977). Validation of a classroom observation code for hyperactive children. *Journal of Consulting and Clinical Psychology, 45,* 772–783.

Achenbach, T. M. (1991). *Manual for the Child Behavior Checklist/4–18 and 1991 profile.* Burlington: University of Vermont, Department of Psychiatry.

American Psychiatric Association. (1980). *Diagnostic and statistical manual of mental disorders* (3rd ed.). Washington, DC: Author.

American Psychiatric Association. (1987). *Diagnostic and statistical manual of mental disorders* (3rd ed., rev.). Washington, DC: Author.

American Psychiatric Association. (1994). *Diagnostic and statistical manual of mental disorders* (4th ed.). Washington, DC: Author.

Anastopoulos, A. D., & Barkley, R. A. (1990). Counseling and training parents. In R. A. Barkley (Ed.), *Attention deficit hyperactivity disorder: A handbook for diagnosis and treatment* (pp. 397–431). New York: Guilford Press.

Anastopoulos, A. D., Guevremont, D. C., Shelton, T. L., & DuPaul, G. J. (1992). Parenting stress among families of children with Attention Deficit Hyperactivity Disorder. *Journal of Abnormal Child Psychology, 20,* 503–520.

Anastopoulos, A. D., Shelton, T., DuPaul, G. J., & Guevremont, D. C. (1993). Parent training for Attention Deficit Hyperactivity Disorder: Its impact on parent functioning. *Journal of Abnormal Child Psychology, 21,* 581–596.

Barkley, R. A. (1977). A review of stimulant drug research with hyperactive children. *Journal of Child Psychology and Psychiatry, 18,* 137–165.

Barkley, R. A. (1987). *Defiant children: A clinician's manual for parent training.* New York: Guilford Press.

Barkley, R. A. (1990). *Attention Deficit Hyperactivity Disorder: A handbook for diagnosis and treatment.* New York: Guilford Press.

Barkley, R. A. (1995). *Behavioral inhibition and executive functions: Constructing a unified theory of ADHD.* Unpublished manuscript, University of Massachusetts Medical Center.

Barkley, R. A., Anastopoulos, A. D., Guevremont, D. C., & Fletcher, K. E. (1991). Adolescents with AD/HD: Patterns of behavioral adjustment, academic functioning, and treatment utilization. *Journal of the American Academy of Child and Adolescent Psychiatry, 30,* 752–761.

Barkley, R. A., Anastopoulos, A. D., Guevremont, D. C., & Fletcher, K. E. (1992). Adolescents with Attention Deficit Hyperactivity Disorder: Mother-adolescent interactions, family beliefs and conflicts, and maternal psychopathology. *Journal of Abnormal Child Psychology, 20,* 263–288.

Barkley, R. A., Copeland, A. P., & Sivage, C. (1980). A self-control classroom for hyperactive children. *Journal of Autism and Developmental Disorders, 10,* 75–89.

Barkley, R. A., DuPaul, G. J., & McMurray, M. (1990). A comprehensive evaluation of attention deficit disorder with and without hyperactivity defined by research criteria. *Journal of Consulting and Clinical Psychology, 58,* 775–789.

Barkley, R. A., Guevremont, D. C., Anastopoulos, A. D., DuPaul, G. J., & Shelton, T. L. (1993). Driving-related risks and outcomes of Attention Deficit Hyperactivity Disorder in adolescents and young adults: A 3- to 5-year follow-up survey. *Pediatrics, 92,* 212–218.

Beck, A. T., Rush, A. J., Shaw, B. F., & Emery, G. (1979). *Cognitive therapy for depression.* New York: Guilford Press.

Biederman, J., Munir, K., Knee, D., Armentano, M., Autor, S., Waternaux, C., & Tsuang, M. (1987). High rate of affective disorders in probands with attention deficit disorders and in their relatives: A controlled family study. *American Journal of Psychiatry, 144,* 330–333.

Block, G. H. (1977). Hyperactivity: A cultural perspective. *Journal of Learning Disabilities, 110,* 236–240.

Bornstein, P. H., & Quevillon, R. P. (1976). The effects of a self-instructional package on overactive preschool boys. *Journal of Applied Behavior Analysis, 9,* 179–188.

Cantwell, D., & Carlson, G. (1978). Stimulants. In J. Werry (Ed.), *Pediatric psychopharmacology* (pp. 171–207). New York: Brunner/Mazel.

Conners, C. K. (1994, August). *The Continuous Performance Test (CPT): Use as a diagnostic tool and measure of treatment outcome.* Paper presented at the annual meeting of the American Psychological Association, Los Angeles, CA.

Costello, A., Edelbrock, C., Kalas, R., Kessler, M., & Klaric, S. (1982). *The NIMH Diagnostic Interview Schedule for Children (DISC).* Pittsburgh: National Institute of Mental Health, Author.

Cunningham, C. E., & Barkley, R. A. (1979). The interactions of hyperactive and normal children with their mothers during free play and structured task. *Child Development, 50,* 217–224.

Cunningham, C. E., & Siegel, L. S. (1987). Peer interactions of normal and attention-deficit disordered boys during free-play, cooperative task, and simulated classroom situations. *Journal of Abnormal Child Psychology, 15,* 247–268.

Derogatis, L. (1986). *Manual for the Symptom Checklist 90 Revised (SCL-90R).* Baltimore, MD: Author.

Deutsch, K. (1987). *Genetic factors in attention deficit disorders.* Paper presented at the symposium on Disorders of Brain, Development, and Cognition, Boston, MA.

Douglas, V. I. (1972). Stop, look, and listen: The problem of sustained attention and impulse control in hyperactive and normal children. *Canadian Journal of Behavioural Science, 4,* 259–282.

Douglas, V. I. (1983). Attention and cognitive problems. In M. Rutter (Ed.), *Developmental neuropsychiatry.* New York: Guilford Press.

DuPaul, G. J. (1991). Parent and teacher ratings of ADHD symptoms: Psychometric properties in a community-based sample. *Journal of Clinical Child Psychology, 20,* 245–253.

DuPaul, G.J, Anastopoulos, A. D., Shelton, T. L., Guevremont, D. C., & Metevia, L. (1992). Multi-method assessment of ADHD: The diagnostic utility of clinic-based tests. *Journal of Clinical Child Psychology, 21,* 394–402.

Edelbrock, C. E. (1995). A twin study of competence and problem behaviors of childhood and early adolescence. *Journal of Child Psychology and Psychiatry, 36,* 775–785.

Edelbrock, C., & Costello, A. (1984). Structured psychiatric interviews for children and adolescents. In G. Goldstein & M. Hersen (Eds.), *Handbook of psychological assessment* (pp. 276–290). New York: Pergamon Press.

Farrington, D. P., Loeber, R., & van Kammen, W. B. (1987, October). *Long-term criminal outcomes of hyperactivity-impulsivity, attention deficit and conduct problems in childhood.* Paper presented at the meeting of the Society for Life History Research, St. Louis, MO.

Feingold, B. (1975). *Why your child is hyperactive.* New York: Random House.

Gadow, K. D. (1985). Relative efficacy of pharmacological, behavioral, and combination treatments for enhancing academic performance. *Clinical Psychology Review, 5,* 513–533.

Gordon, M. (1983). *The Gordon Diagnostic System.* Boulder, CO: Clinical Diagnostic Systems.

Goyette, C. H., Conners, C. K., & Ulrich, R. F. (1978). Normative data on Revised Conners Parent and Teacher Rating Scales. *Journal of Abnormal Child Psychology, 6,* 221–236.

Greenberg, L. M., & Waldman, I. D. (1991). *Developmental normative data on the Test of Variables of Attention (TOVA).* Unpublished manuscript.

Grenell, M. M., Glass, C. R., & Katz, K. S. (1987). Hyperactive children and peer interaction: Knowledge and performance of social skills. *Journal of Abnormal Child Psychology, 15,* 1–13.

Hartsough, C. S., & Lambert, N. M. (1985). Medical factors in hyperactive and normal children: Prenatal, developmental, and health history findings. *American Journal of Orthopsychiatry, 55,* 190–201.

Herjanic, B., Brown, F., & Wheatt, T. (1975). Are children reliable reporters? *Journal of Abnormal Child Psychology, 3,* 41–48.

Hinshaw, S. P., Henker, B., & Whalen, C. K. (1984). Self-control in hyperactive boys in anger-inducing situations: Effects of cognitive-behavioral training and of methylphenidate. *Journal of Abnormal Child Psychology, 12,* 55–77.

Jacob, R. G., O'Leary, K. D., & Rosenblad, C. (1978). Formal and informal classroom settings: Effects on hyperactivity. *Journal of Abnormal Child Psychology, 6,* 47–59.

Kendall, P. C., & Braswell, L. (1985). *Cognitive-behavioral therapy for impulsive children.* New York: Guilford Press.

Kent, J. D., Blader, J. C., Koplewicz, H. S., Abikoff, H., & Foley, C. A. (1995). Effects of late afternoon methylphenidate administration on behavior and sleep in Attention-Deficit Hyperactivity Disorder. *Pediatrics, 96,* 320–325.

Lahey, B. B., Piacentini, J., McBurnett, K., Stone, P., Hatdagen, S., & Hynd, G. (1988). Psychopathology in the parents of children with Conduct Disorder and Hyperactivity. *Journal of the American Academy of Child Psychiatry, 27,* 163–170.

Locke, H. J., & Wallace, K. M. (1959). Short marital adjustment and prediction tests: Their reliability and validity. *Journal of Marriage and Family Living, 21,* 251–255.

Loney, J., & Milich, R. (1982). Hyperactivity, inattention, and aggression in clinical practice. In D. Routh & M. Wolraich (Eds.), *Advances in developmental and behavioral pediatrics* (Vol. 3, pp. 113–147). Greenwich, CT: JAI Press.

Lou, H. C., Henriksen, L., Bruhn, P., Borner, H., & Nielsen, J. B. (1989). *Archives of Neurology, 46,* 48–52.

Luk, S. (1985). Direct observations studies of hyperactive behaviors. *Journal of the American Academy of Child Psychiatry, 24,* 338–344.

Margalit, M., & Arieli, N. (1984). Emotional and behavioral aspects of hyperactivity. *Journal of Learning Disabilities, 17,* 374–376.

Mash, E. J., & Barkley, R. A. (1987). Assessment of family interaction with the Response Class Matrix. In R. Prinz (Ed.), *Advances in behavioral assessment of children and families* (Vol. 2, pp. 29–67). Greenwich, CT: JAI Press.

Mash, E. J., & Johnston, C. (1990). Determinants of parenting stress: Illustrations from families of hyperactive children and families of physically abused children. *Journal of Clinical Child Psychology, 19,* 313–328.

Matier-Sharma, K., Perachio, N., Newcorn, J. H., Sharma, V., & Halperin, J. M. (1995). Differential diagnosis of ADHD: Are objective measures of attention, impulsivity, and activity level helpful? *Child Neuropsychology, 1,* 118–127.

McCarney, S. B. (1989). *Attention Deficit Disorders Evaluation Scale (ADDES).* Columbia, MO: Hawthorne Press.

Meichenbaum, D., & Goodman, J. (1971). Training impulsive children to talk to themselves: A means of developing self-control. *Journal of Abnormal Psychology, 77,* 115–126.

Milich, R., Loney, J., & Landau, S. (1982). The independent dimensions of hyperactivity and aggression: A validation with playroom observation data. *Journal of Abnormal Psychology, 91,* 183–198.

Pelham, W. E., & Bender, M. E. (1982). Peer relationships in hyperactive children: Description and treatment. In K. D.Gadow & I. Bialer (Eds.), *Advances in learning and behavioral disabilities* (Vol. 1, pp. 365–436). Greenwich, CT: JAI Press.

Pelham, W. E., Schnedler, R. W., Bender, M. E., Nilsson, D. E., Miller, J., Budrow, M. S., Ronnel, M., Paluchowski, C., & Marks, D. A. (1988). The combination of behavior therapy and methylphenidate in the treatment of attention deficit disorders: A therapy outcome study. In L. Bloomingdale (Ed.), *Attention deficit disorders* (Vol. 3, pp. 29–48). New York: Spectrum.

Pfiffner, L. J., & O'Leary, S. G. (1987). The efficacy of all-positive management as a function of the prior use of negative consequences. *Journal of Applied Behavior Analysis, 20,* 265–271.

Pfiffner, L. J., & O'Leary, S. G. (1993). School-based psychological treatments. In J. L. Matson (Ed.), *Handbook of hyperactivity in children* (pp. 234–255). Boston: Allyn & Bacon.

Pfiffner, L. J., Rosen, L. A., & O'Leary, S. G. (1985). The efficacy of an all-positive approach to classroom management. *Journal of Applied Behavior Analysis, 18,* 257–261.

Pisterman, S., McGrath, P., Firestone, P., & Goodman, J. T. (1989). Outcome of parent-mediated treatment of preschoolers with Attention Deficit Disorder with Hyperactivity. *Journal of Consulting and Clinical Psychology, 57,* 636–643.

Pliszka, S. R. (1987). Tricyclic antidepressants in the treatment of children with Attention Deficit Disorder. *Journal of the American Academy of Child and Adolescent Psychiatry, 26,* 127–132.

Rapoport, J., & Mikkelsen, E. (1978). Antidepressants. In J. Werry (Ed.), *Pediatric psychopharmacology* (pp. 208–233). New York: Brunner/Mazel.

Rapport, M. D., Denney, C., DuPaul, G. J., & Gardner, M. J. (1994). Attention Deficit Disorder and methylphenidate normalization rates, clinical effectiveness, and response prediction in 76 children. *Journal of the American Academy of Child and Adolescent Psychiatry, 33,* 882–893.

Reynolds, C. R., & Kamphaus, R. W. (1992). *BASC: Behavior Assessment System for Children Manual.* Circle Pines, MN: American Guidance Service.

Roberts, M. A. (1987). How is playroom behavior observation used in the diagnosis of Attention Deficit Disorder? In J. Loney (Ed.), *The young hyperactive child: Answers to questions about diagnosis, prognosis, and treatment* (pp. 65–74). New York: Haworth Press.

Ross, D. M., & Ross, S. A. (1982). *Hyperactivity: Current issues, research, and theory* (2nd ed.). New York: Wiley.

Routh, D. K., & Schroeder, C. S. (1976). Standardized playroom measures as indices of hyperactivity. *Journal of Abnormal Child Psychology, 4,* 199–207.

Satterfield, J. H., Satterfield, B. T., & Cantwell, D. P. (1980). Three-year multimodality treatment study of 100 hyperactive boys. *Journal of Pediatrics, 98,* 650–655.

Shapiro, E. S., & Cole, C. L. (1994). *Behavior change in the classroom: Self-management interventions.* New York: Guilford Press.

Streissguth, A. P., Martin, D. C., Barr, H. M., Sandman, B. M., Kirchner, G. L., & Darby, B. L. (1984). Intrauterine alcohol and nicotine exposure: Attention and reaction time in 4-year-old children. *Developmental Psychology, 20,* 533–541.

Taylor, E. A. (1986). Childhood hyperactivity. *British Journal of Psychiatry, 149,* 562–573.

Ullmann, R., Sleator, E., & Sprague, R. (1984). A new rating scale for diagnosis and monitoring of ADD children. *Psychopharmacology Bulletin, 20,* 160–164.

Weiss, G., & Hechtman, L. (1986). *Hyperactive children grown up.* New York: Guilford Press.

Wender, P. H. (1995). *Attention-deficit hyperactivity disorder in adults.* New York: Oxford University Press.

Willis, T. J., & Lovaas, I. (1977). A behavioral approach to treating hyperactive children: The parent's role. In J. B. Millichap (Ed.), *Learning disabilities and related disorders* (pp. 119–140). Chicago: Yearbook Medical.

Wolraich, M. L., Lindgren, S. D., Stumbo, P. J., Stegink, L. D., Appelbaum, M. I., & Kiritsy, M. C. (1994). Effects of diets high in sucrose or aspartame on the behavior and cognitive performance of children. *New England Journal of Medicine, 330,* 301–307.

Zametkin, A. J., & Rapoport, J. L. (1986). The pathophysiology of Attention Deficit Disorder with Hyperactivity: A review. In B. Lahey & A. Kazdin (Eds.), *Advances in clinical child psychology* (Vol. 9, pp. 177–216). New York: Plenum Press.

Zeiner, P. (1995). Body growth and cardiovascular function after extended treatment (1.75 years) with methylphenidate in boys with Attention Deficit Hyperactivity Disorder. *Journal of Child and Adolescent Psychopharmacology, 5,* 129–138.

Zentall, S. S. (1985). A context for hyperactivity. In K. D. Gadow & I. Bialer (Eds.), *Advances in learning and behavioral disabilities* (Vol. 4, pp. 273–343). Greenwich, CT: JAI Press.

CHAPTER 22

Eating Disorders

J. SCOTT MIZES and TONYA MIZELL PALERMO

DESCRIPTION OF THE DISORDERS

The August 8, 1994, issue of *Sports Illustrated* featured the story of Christy Henrich, a 22-year-old aspiring Olympic gymnast who met her untimely death from complications arising from anorexia nervosa (Noden, 1994). At the peak of her career, the 4'10" Henrich weighed 95 pounds. When she died on July 26, 1994, of multiple organ failure, she was down to 61 pounds. This actually represented improvement from July 4 when she had weighed merely 47 pounds. Christy's family traces inception of her eating disorder in part to an incident at a meet in March 1988, when a U.S. judge remarked that Henrich would have to lose weight if she wanted to make the Olympic team. At that time, she began eating less and less (an apple a day at first) while continuing to work out 6 to 8 hours a day. In 1993, Christy told an interviewer: "My life is a horrifying nightmare. It feels like there's a beast inside me, like a monster. It feels evil."

Despite the sadness of the story of Christy Henrich, some people are not surprised by it. Cathy Rigby, who fought bulimia for 12 years during her gymnastic career, related: "This sort of thing has been going on for so long in our sport, and there's so much denial." In fact, eating disorders are much more common in women athletes who participate in appearance sports (such as figure skating and gymnastics). According to a 1992 NCAA survey of women's gymnastics programs reported in *Sports Illustrated,* 51% of respondents identified eating disorders among their team members, a far greater percentage than in any other sport (Noden, 1994). The article pointed out that gymnastics has evolved over the past several decades in a direction that is incompatible with a woman's mature body. The average size of a woman on the U.S. gymnastics team has shrunk from 5'3", 105 pounds in 1976, to 4'9", 88 pounds in 1992.

Because of the importance attached to weight and appearance in some sports, it is not surprising that eating disorders are common among athletes. However, the significance of various forms of eating pathology is only partly conveyed by prevalence of clinically severe anorexia and bulimia nervosa. From children in elementary school to college students, many young women and men express dissatisfaction with their body shape and weight, and place undue emphasis on food and weight. Thelen, Lawrence, and Powell (1992) found that older elementary school girls (Grades 3–6) are concerned about becoming overweight and are dissatisfied with their bodies, with over half reporting that they want to be thinner. What is even more alarming is that as many as

40% have already attempted to lose weight. Similarly, many adolescents aspire to be thin and experiment with weight control. While all adolescents must adjust to the physical changes of puberty and growth, older adolescents are considered significantly more likely to engage in inappropriate weight control methods (Phelps, Andrea, Rizzo, Johnston, & Main, 1993; Whitaker et al., 1989).

Dieting is a common practice in the general population. In a sample of university students, Klesges, Mizes, and Klesges (1987) found that 89% of women and 54% of men had engaged in some form of dieting in the previous 6 months. However, only 20% of these students were actually overweight by medical criteria. The psychological effects of dieting and weight concerns for these many young women and men are self-criticism, low self-esteem, a sense of failure, and feelings of depression. Lawrence and Thelen (1995) found a negative association between overweight concerns and general self-worth in third- through sixth-grade students; children who were more worried about becoming overweight felt a low level of general self-worth.

Clinical anorexia nervosa and bulimia nervosa may represent extreme ends on a continuum of disturbed eating in our culture. Drewnowski, Yee, Kurth, and Krahn (1994) found that college women shifted over a 6-month period along a continuum of disordered eating ranging from casual dieters, intensive dieters, dieters at risk, and bulimics. However, new cases of bulimia nervosa were drawn exclusively from the intensive dieters and dieters-at-risk groups, suggesting a progression from general dieting to more pathological eating.

Diagnostic Criteria

Anorexia Nervosa

The most prominent diagnostic feature of anorexia nervosa is severe weight loss (body weight reduction of 15% or more), and due to weight loss, in women, amenorrhea (at least three consecutive menstrual periods have been missed; American Psychiatric Association [APA], 1994). Despite being clearly underweight, anorectics intensely fear weight gain or obesity and explicitly refuse to gain weight. In addition, women with anorexia nervosa are more focused on their weight in their self-evaluations. They often wish to weigh 30 pounds less than their medically accepted ideal weight, and often their actual weight is a few pounds below this critically low self-ideal weight (Mizes, 1992a). Clinically, anorectics have long been subdivided into "restrictor" versus "bulimic" subtypes; the Diagnostic and Statistical Manual of Mental Disorders (DSM-IV; APA, 1994) now formally incorporates these two subtypes of anorexia nervosa into binge-eating/purging type or restricting type.

Bulimia Nervosa

The defining features of bulimia nervosa are frequent binge eating and purging behaviors to prevent weight gain (APA, 1994). Frequency of binge eating and inappropriate weight control behaviors are defined as occurring at least twice a week for at least three consecutive months. Although many people binge eat at times, such frequency and duration criteria appear best to distinguish clinical bulimia nervosa (Kendler et al., 1991). Furthermore, for an episode of overeating to be considered a "binge," it must meet two criteria: (a) the person consumes much more food than most people would in similar circumstances and in a similar period; and (b) the person feels that the eating is out of control. The bulimic repeatedly controls weight gain by inappropriate means, such as skipping meals or fasting, self-induced vomiting, excessive exercise, or abuse of laxatives or diuretics. Bulimic women also show a consistent overconcern with body weight and shape. While normal women on average wish to weigh 11 pounds less than their medically ideal weight, bulimic women want to weigh nearly 18 pounds less (Mizes, 1992a). In the *DSM-IV*, two subtypes (purging type or nonpurging type) of bulimia nervosa are also specified to distinguish bulimics by presence or absence of purging (i.e., vomiting, laxatives, and diuretics).

Women with bulimia nervosa experience marked disruption in their eating. Although binging and purging one to two times per day is common, some patients report as many as 30 to 40 bulimic episodes per week. Binges also vary in size. A typical binge is 1,300 kilocalories of grains, cereals, snack foods, and desserts (Davis, Freeman, & Garner, 1988), with carbohydrates as the primary choice of binge foods (van der Ster Walling, Norring, & Holmgren, 1994). Most bulimic episodes occur while the woman is at home alone, and tend to occur in late afternoon or early evening. Binge episodes are often preceded by strong negative emotions, such as feeling depressed or "stressed out" (Mizes & Arbitell, 1991). Aside from their eating binges, bulimics tend to eat only 70% of what normal women eat in a day (Arbitell & Mizes, 1988).

Eating Disorder Not Otherwise Specified

This classification is used to diagnose problems related to appetite, eating, and weight, which do not meet criteria for anorexia nervosa or bulimia nervosa. Persons diagnosed as NOS have been found to cluster in two groups: "near bulimics" and "near anorectics" (Mitchell, Pyle, Hatsukami, & Eckert, 1986). *DSM-IV* gives several examples of these groups; for example, individuals who meet criteria for anorexia nervosa but have normal menses or are low normal weight may be considered "near anorectics." Women who meet the criteria for bulimia but have infrequent binges or who do not swallow their binge foods may be considered "near bulimics." In addition, binge-eating disorder is listed as an example in this category and as a "provisional diagnosis requiring further study" in the Appendix.

Binge eating disorder (BED) has previously been referred to as compulsive overeating. The defining features of BED include recurrent episodes of binge eating not associated with inappropriate compensatory behaviors (as seen in bulimia nervosa) occurring at least two days per week over a 6-month period. Binge eating includes both the ingestion of an unusually large amount of food and a feeling of loss of control over the eating episode, as reflected through behavioral indices, such as eating rapidly, eating until uncomfortably full, or feeling disgusted with oneself, or depressed after overeating (de Zwaan, Mitchell, Raymond, & Spitzer, 1994). Although the majority of individuals with binge eating disorder are obese, they are distinguishable from obese nonbinge eaters by impairment in work and social functioning, overconcern with body shape and weight, amount of time spent dieting, and history of treatment for emotional problems (de Zwaan et al., 1994).

Changes in *DSM-IV*

With the recent publication of *DSM-IV* (APA, 1994), it is important to recognize changes in the diagnostic criteria for eating disorders in response to debate and confusion over the criteria used in *DSM-III-R* (e.g., Cooper & Fairburn, 1993; Wilson & Walsh, 1991). First, the classification "eating disorders" now includes only anorexia nervosa and bulimia nervosa; these disorders are now separate from feeding disorders of children (e.g., pica, rumination disorder) because it is now generally acknowledged that there is no connection between the feeding disorders of children and the eating disorders of older children and adults. Second, two subtypes of anorexia nervosa and bulimia nervosa based on presence or absence of purging are now used so that dual diagnoses of anorexia and bulimia do not have to be made for patients who show signs specific to each disorder (e.g., anorectics who have daily binging and purging episodes). Third, binges have now been defined as comprising both a "large" amount of food and sense of lack of control. Lastly, the category eating disorder not otherwise specified (eating disorder NOS) has been elaborated to include preliminary criteria for binge eating disorder.

Associated Psychopathology

In addition to the clinical diagnostic features of anorexia and bulimia, both disorders are associated with specific psychological characteristics (e.g., fear of weight gain) as well as global pathology (i.e., comorbid conditions). Bulimics and anorectics have similar cognitive distortions (Mizes, 1992b). They tend to be concerned about receiving approval from others, have high personal expectations for achievement or performance, and have excessive self-control as a component of their self-esteem. However, anorectics tend to be more socially and emotionally withdrawn, and they often deny the presence of an eating problem thus resisting or refusing treatment.

Initial research suggests that eating disorders often co-occur with other specific disorders, such as depressive disorders, anxiety disorders, substance abuse, and personality disorders. Bulimics often experience dysphoria as well as clinically severe major depression. Most evidence suggests that depression is secondary to the eating disruption (Hinz & Williamson, 1987). Anorexia nervosa has also been associated with depression (Swift, Andrews, & Barklage, 1986); depression can occur as a clinical problem independent of anorexia, or can be a direct result of the effects of starvation and weight loss. Among sixth- and seventh-grade girls, dysphoria and greater feelings of inadequacy and personal worthlessness were associated with eating pathology (Killen et al., 1994). Some recent research suggests that eating disorders and seasonal affective disorder (SAD) have similar physiological markers, possibly related to serotonin dysregulation. In one study, 13% of women with eating disorders also met criteria for winter SAD (Brewerton, Krahn, Hardin, Wehr, & Rosenthal, 1994).

Anxiety disorders have also been found in bulimics and anorectics. Bulimics experience significant anxiety (Mizes, 1988), which may be due to fear of weight gain or general anxiousness in response to life events (Shatford & Evans, 1986). Moreover, obsessive-compulsive disorder has been found to be prevalent in both anorectics and bulimics, in particular, in those women with more severe eating disorders (Thiel, Broocks, Ohlmeier, Jacoby, & Schufler, 1995). Several personality disorders have been identified in patients with eating disorders, including borderline, avoidant, and depressive personality disorders (Wonderlich, Ukestad, & Perzacki, 1994).

Eating disorder features and clinical eating disorders are common in individuals with alcohol problems (e.g., Taylor, Peveler, Hibbert, & Fairburn, 1993). Also apparent in adolescent girls, symptoms of eating disorders appear to be associated with problem drinking (Striegel-Moore & Huydic, 1993). Case studies have highlighted the potential for histories of sexual and physical abuse among bulimics and anorectics (e.g., Sloan & Leichner, 1986), which suggests the possibility of posttraumatic stress disorder. Histories of childhood sexual abuse were found to range from 16% to 30% in women bulimics and anorectics in one study (Schmidt, Tiller, & Treasure, 1993). The secondary diagnosis of borderline personality disorder has been associated with childhood sexual abuse in women with eating disorders (Waller, 1994). However, despite histories of physical and sexual abuse and speculations about posttraumatic stress disorder (PTSD), there is not yet empirical evidence of the comorbidity of PTSD in eating-disordered women.

EPIDEMIOLOGY

Due to the change to more stringent diagnostic criteria in recent years, prior estimates of the prevalence of bulimia nervosa have been modified from rates of 20% to about 1% of adolescent and young adult women (Fairburn, Phil, & Beglin, 1990). One study identified the current prevalence of women who ever had bulimia nervosa as 2.8%, and the lifetime risk of eventually developing bulimia nervosa as 4.2%, with another 4% of women developing near-bulimia symptoms (Kendler et al., 1991). Prevalence rates among adolescent junior high and high school students have been found to be slightly higher. Among female junior high students, it is estimated that 2% have bulimia, whereas 4% of female high school students can be diagnosed with bulimia (Stein & Brinza, 1989). In a county-wide high school population, 1.2% of girls had bulimia nervosa and another 1.2% of girls had subclinical bulimia nervosa (Stein & Brinza, 1989). Although bulimia nervosa most often occurs in females, studies have found that the disorder also occurs in males. The prevalence rate of bulimia nervosa in high school boys was found to be 0.4% and subclinical bulimia nervosa was also estimated at 0.4% for boys (Whitaker et al., 1989).

Since anorexia nervosa is rare in the general population, epidemiological studies of anorectics primarily report investigations of incidence per year. Most studies estimate incidence per year between 0.37 and 1.6 cases per 100,000 people (Szmukler, 1985). Although not as prevalent as bulimia, anorexia nervosa may affect more young women in its subclinical form. Five percent of young adolescent women may have subclinical anorexia nervosa (Szmukler, 1985). In a high school population of nonreferred adolescents, the prevalence rate for anorexia nervosa was 0.2% in girls, and subclinical anorexia nervosa was found in 7.6% of girls. No cases of anorexia nervosa were found in high school boys in this study; however, prevalence of subclinical anorexia nervosa was 0.6% in boys (Whitaker et al., 1989).

Because binge eating disorder (BED) is a recent diagnostic category not yet formally adopted into the *DSM-IV,* prevalence rates for BED are more difficult to ascertain. In the majority of prevalence studies of BED, samples have not been representative of the general population. For example, most women in these studies have been moderately to severely obese and many included obese women in weight loss programs. Therefore, prevalence rates have varied greatly according to the sample from 2.6% in college students, 4.6% in community samples, 29.9% in weight loss treatment groups, to 71.2% in Overeaters Anonymous (de Zwaan et al., 1994).

Despite frequent onset of eating disorders in adolescence, most epidemiological studies have included college students and young women; only a few have focused exclusively on children and adolescents. The average age of first onset of anorexia nervosa is 17 years, with 68% of the cases beginning between ages 14 and 20 (Willi, Giacometti, & Limacher, 1990). In fact, age of onset has remained relatively constant over the past 30 years (Hindler, Crisp, McGuigan, & Joughin, 1994). Bulimia nervosa has a slightly later average age of onset at about age 21 (Kendler et al., 1991); however, approximately 68% of cases of bulimia nervosa start between age 15 and 27. Adults with BED have been found to have significantly earlier age of onset of binge eating than adults with bulimia (14.3 years and 19.8 years respectively; de Zwaan et al., 1994).

Eating disorders have been documented in many countries, such as Japan, England, Italy, and Denmark, and have been found to cut across ethnic and socioeconomic groups. While previously anorexia nervosa was thought to exist exclusively in middle and upper economic levels, Kendler et al. (1991) did not find any relationship between prevalence of bulimia and participants' or parental educational or occupational level. Prevalence rates of anorexia nervosa and bulimia nervosa in Europe are very similar to those in the United States (e.g., Pagsberg & Wang, 1994). Moreover, studies of rural villages have found similar prevalence rates as urban settings. For example, in a rural Italian village, the point prevalence rate for schoolgirls 11 to 20 years of age was estimated at 1.3% for anorexia nervosa (Rathner & Messner, 1993). However, within ethnic groups in the United States, differences have been found to exist. African-Americans may comprise only 2% to 3% of all cases of anorexia nervosa (Andersen & Hay, 1985), and likewise fewer African-Americans than Caucasians also suffer from bulimia nervosa (Gray, Ford, & Kelly, 1987). African-Americans may be more accepting of heavier bodies; in one study African-American children showed less concern about weight and desired larger bodies than Caucasian children (Lawrence & Thelen, 1995).

Clinical descriptions of young women with diabetes and thyroid disease who manipulate their insulin or thyroxine to influence their body weight has raised questions as to prevalence of eating disorders in these populations. In one study concerning girls with insulin-dependent diabetes mellitus (IDDM), Striegel-Moore, Nicholson, and Tamborlane (1992) found that IDDM patients and controls had similar prevalence rates of eating disorders. These investigators note that in other studies there has been a confounding of food restriction for medical reasons and dieting for cosmetic reasons, which has inflated prevalence rates of eating disorders in women with IDDM. Among thyroid disease patients, however, prevalence of bulimia nervosa is almost twice that found in the general population (Tiller, Macrae, Schmidt, Bloom, & Treasure, 1994). Tiller et al. speculate that weight fluctuations or obesity may have been a risk factor for developing bulimia nervosa.

As previously mentioned, women athletes have disproportionately high rates of eating disorders. Women participating in activities emphasizing leanness (e.g., dancing, gymnastics, track) have estimated prevalence rates of eating disorders from 20% to 74%. This is much higher than athletes participating in activities without emphasis on leanness (e.g., tennis, volleyball) with prevalence rates of eating disorders of 0% to 24% (Constantini & Warren, 1994).

Little research exists on the course of bulimia nervosa in women. It appears that bulimia tends to alternatively worsen and abate over several years if left untreated

(Drewnowski & Garn, 1987). Among women who had received treatment for the disorder, over the course of 3 to 4 years 70% had at least one period of recovery. The course of anorexia nervosa has been better documented. Theander (1985) described the course of anorexia nervosa spanning a period of 30 years on average. From this study, anorexia nervosa appears to be a chronic and refractory disorder, though there is a trend toward gradual improvement over several years. The mortality rate that accompanies anorexia nervosa is remarkable; 8% of anorectics had died in the first 5 years and after 30 years 18% of anorectics had died either from complications of anorexia or from suicide.

Causes and Consequences

Causes of eating disorders are only beginning to be understood. As is true with all disorders, the causative factors include a complex synergy of sociocultural, biological and genetic, and psychological factors. The causes of eating disorders must also be viewed within the context of their associated conditions and their causative factors, as well as the interaction of eating disorders and other disorders and their reciprocal risk factors (Crowther & Mizes, 1992).

Discussions of the etiology of eating disorders usually emphasize, and perhaps overemphasize, sociocultural factors. Several authors have discussed the unique pressures on women to attain lower body weights, and how these conflict with biological factors, including increased weight and percent body fat during puberty for females, as well as the biological reality of higher percent body fat in postpubertal females versus males (Striegel-Moore, Silberstein, & Rodin, 1986). For example, heavier weight at menarche appears to be a risk factor for the development of bulimia (Lacey, 1992), increasing young girls' discrepancy between their actual weight and perception of cultural weight ideals.

Research has documented the societal overemphasis on thinness for females, such as the gradual lowering of relative ideal body weight over the 1960s and 1970s, as depicted by *Playboy* centerfolds (Garner, Garfinkel, Schwartz, & Thompson, 1980). Of note, toward the end of the years studied, centerfolds were approximately 85% of expected weight, which is the cutoff for anorexia nervosa. There are undoubtedly numerous sources of the societal overemphasis on thinness for females. Media images of idealized women who are excessively thin are rampant and are directed at primarily female audiences. More diet and shape-related content has been found in female versus male-oriented magazines, and an increase in weight-preoccupied content in women's magazines appears to parallel the previously rising incidence of eating disorders (Andersen & DiDomenico, 1992). Increased exposure to media images of thinness has been shown to be associated with females endorsing an extreme ideal body weight, thereby creating body image dissatisfaction that leads to increased eating disorder symptomatology (Stice, Schupak-Neuberg, Shaw, & Stein, 1994). On a somewhat encouraging note, over the period 1980–1991, there has been a decrease in weight-loss content in women's magazines, although women's magazines still overemphasize weight content relative to men's magazines (Nemeroff, Stein, Diehl, & Smilack, 1994). On the downside, there appears to be a modest increase in weight loss content in men's magazines over the same period.

Although feminist writers have emphasized characteristics of the traditional female sex-role and oppression of women as sources of societal pressures for thinness

(Fallon, Katzman, & Wooley, 1994), economic factors are likely to be important, particularly relative to media influences. Wolf (1991) has pointed out that female-oriented products for thinness and appearance are big business, thus creating strong inducements for companies to maximize or create markets. Promoting a female body ideal which suggests that women's bodies in their natural state are in some way defective creates markets for a potpourri of products to correct these presumed flaws. Targeting women for these media messages is not at all unexpected, since companies have long directed their advertising toward women, who are often the primary purchasers for the family. Indeed, there are numerous examples of non-weight-related advertising directed toward women to create new markets. An entire generation of women were exposed to messages on the importance of white collars for their husbands, increasing demand for washing machines and detergent products. A generation ago, it was common practice to wear a business shirt for a week; now it is expected that a newly cleaned dress shirt will be worn everyday (St. James, 1994).

Another expression of cultural valuation of thinness is to tease about body weight and shape. Teasing has been shown to be related to body dissatisfaction, global self-esteem, and eating disturbance in adolescent females (Fabian & Thompson, 1989). Effects of teasing during adolescence appear to be enduring. Among adult females, current body dissatisfaction, eating disturbance, and global psychological functioning have been shown to be related to previous weight-related teasing during adolescence (Thompson, Fabian, Moulton, Dunn, & Altabe, 1991).

Genetic factors also play an important etiologic role in eating disorders. Eating disorders tend to run in families, suggesting potential genetic factors (Strober, 1991). For example, female siblings of anorectics develop the disorder approximately 3% to 10% of the time. The genetic vulnerability for eating disorders appears to convey a shared risk for both bulimia and anorexia. Relatives of anorectics have an increased risk for both disorders, with 2% to 4% of first-degree relatives having had anorexia and a similar number having suffered with bulimia. Likewise, first-degree relatives of bulimics have shown an increased risk for both disorders, with 9.6% having had bulimia and 2.2% experiencing anorexia (Kassett, Gershon, & Maxwell, 1989). Twin studies strongly support a genetic vulnerability to eating disorders. Among monozygotic female twins, the concordance rate for anorexia is 44% to 50%, compared with 7% for dizygotic female twins, which is approximately the same rate as for nontwin sisters. In a large study of female twins ($n = 2,000$), the concordance rate for bulimia among monozygotic twins was 29%, compared with 9% for dizygotic twins (Kendler et al., 1991). These authors estimated that 55% of the risk for bulimia came from genetic rather than psychological or sociocultural factors.

A potential developmental and biological factor in the emergence of body dissatisfaction and disordered eating is the timing of pubertal maturation in females. Girls who experience a late menarche (after the age of 14) tend to have more positive body image than those who reach menarche early (before 11) or on time (between 11–14; Brooks-Gunn & Warren, 1985). There is some initial evidence that risk is conferred in part by teasing associated with early pubertal maturation (Cattarin & Thompson, 1994). Some authors have suggested that it is not pubertal timing that is important, but rather the co-occurrence of puberty and other stressful life events. Girls for whom menarche and dating co-occur have more body dissatisfaction and eating disturbance than girls experiencing menarche alone; and girls who experience a co-occurrence of early menarche and early dating have the most disturbance (Smolak, Levine, & Gralem, 1993). Additionally, a combined effect of the co-occurrence of puberty, dating, and academic stress has been shown to increase the risk for eating disturbance (Levine, Smolak, Moodey, Shuman, & Hessen, 1994).

Longitudinal studies of adolescent and young adult females have implicated weight changes, negative body attitudes, and dieting as risk factors for eating disturbance and disorders. Although most adolescent girls diet, few develop clinical eating disorders. However, girls who develop eating disorders pass through a period of dieting that is indistinguishable from the behavior of "normal" dieters (Patton, 1988). Moreover, weight gain is a strong predictor of eating pathology over time (Patton, 1988). Other research has shown that dieting behavior predicts future psychological symptoms, rather than the converse (Rosen, Tacy, & Howell, 1990). This implicates dieting as causal in the development of eating pathology, rather being one type of eating pathology resulting from psychological stress. Among freshman coeds, negative body attitudes have been shown to be associated with worsening of eating disorder symptoms (Striegel-Moore, Silberstein, Frensch, & Rodin, 1989), as have (to a lesser extent) feeling unattractive, increasing body weight, increasing body dissatisfaction, and feeling stressed and ineffective. In a study of adolescent girls, only negative body image predicted increased eating pathology over the course of 2 years (Attie & Brooks-Gunn, 1989).

Eating disorders have a comorbidity with several disorders, including depression, personality disorders, and anxiety disorders. Consideration of these comorbid conditions is important in understanding the causes of eating disorders. Crowther and Mizes (1992) have suggested that etiologic factors for eating disorders can be viewed in terms of variables that cause eating pathology versus those that cause associated comorbid conditions. Thus, "uncomplicated" cases of eating disorders are caused by eating disorder factors, while "complicated" cases are caused by eating disorder and "other" pathology factors that exert their influence in either an additive or synergistic manner. The etiologic role of family pathology and sexual abuse can be considered with this model in mind. Overall, families of eating-disordered persons tend to be more hostile, conflictual, isolated, noncohesive, and enmeshed, and less supportive and nurturant (Strober & Humphrey, 1987). However, no specific family functioning variable has been linked to specific eating pathology. In contrast, studies have shown that family pathology is related to personality disorder among eating disorders, with little association with level of eating disturbance (Crowther & Mizes, 1992). Likewise, histories of sexual abuse are common among eating-disordered persons. However, evidence suggests that sexual abuse is not a unique risk factor for the development of eating disorders, as normal populations and eating-disordered persons have equivalent rates of sexual abuse (i.e., 30%; Connors & Morse, 1993). However, among eating-disordered patients (mainly bulimics), history of childhood sexual abuse has shown a strong relationship to borderline personality disorder (Waller, 1994).

The most prominent consequences of eating disorders are medical complications, which are more severe and potentially life-threatening in anorexia nervosa. Among bulimics, general medical problems that occur include fatigue, lethargy, weakness, bloating while eating, dizziness, faintness, and puffy cheeks (Mitchell, Specker, & de Zwaan, 1991). Vomiting may lead to sore throats or occasionally ulceration, and chronic use of laxatives can result in laxative dependence and chronic constipation.

Purging behavior can result in potassium loss and hypokalemia, which most commonly leads to fatigue, but which can result in cardiac irregularities and cardiac arrest. Purging can also lead to dehydration, which can be medically serious. Increased dental enamel erosion is another effect of purging behavior (Philipp, Willershausen-Zonnchen, Hamm, & Pirke, 1991). Menstrual irregularity can also occur due to low body fat and irregular eating.

The preceding symptoms also occur in anorexia, bulimic/purging type. Additionally, both types of anorectic patients suffer from complications of starvation (Kaplan & Woodside, 1987). Heart rate is often slowed, and cardiac irregularities may develop. Blood pressure may be low, and orthostatic hypotension may occur. Delayed gastric emptying, especially upon refeeding, is a frequent problem, and constipation may occur. Due to reduced core body temperature and reduced blood flow to the extremities, coldness in the hands and feet is common. Loss of muscle tissue leads to fatigue and weakness. Amenorrhea and associated hormonal changes can lead to early osteoporosis and fractures. A fine, downy hair (lanugo hair) may develop on the body. Among adolescents, stunted growth may occur. Starvation also leads to pronounced psychological changes, including food preoccupation, irritability, fluctuating emotions and depression, and decreased concentration and alertness.

Although there is only initial research, eating disorders increase the risk for problem pregnancies. Despite altered menstrual function, some anorectic women do become pregnant. Pregnant anorectics gain less weight during pregnancy, deliver more low birth weight babies, as well as babies with lower APGAR scores (Franko & Walton, 1993). There is some suggestion that pregnant bulimics may have an increased risk of miscarriages (Mitchell, Seim, Glotter, Soll, & Pyle, 1991).

IMPEDIMENTS TO INTERVENTION IN THE REAL WORLD CONTEXT

There are numerous obstacles to successful and timely intervention for both treatment and prevention of eating disorders. These include problems with detection, barriers in healthcare delivery systems, resistance to treatment by patients, legal obstacles, and in the case of prevention, knowing who and what to target for intervention.

The first step toward adequate treatment is detection of an eating disorder, either by the person herself, or by concerned family or friends, or her doctor. Accurate detection by physicians has received surprisingly little research attention. One study presented pediatricians and primary care physicians with two case vignettes of children with anorexia, and asked them to indicate the differential diagnoses they would consider (Bryant-Waugh, Lask, Shafran, & Fosson, 1992). Only one-third of the pediatricians mentioned anorexia nervosa as a differential diagnosis; only 2% of the primary care physicians considered anorexia. Moreover, there was a low rate of recommendations for referral to a mental health practitioner, particularly among the primary care physicians. In another study of bulimia in a general practice population (King, 1989), physicians were not aware of existing cases of bulimia nervosa in their practice, even though symptoms of the disorder were documented in the medical record for many patients. The authors suggested that a reason for overlooking such clinical information was physicians' tendency to accept patients' comments about dieting as normal. Finally, in a study of consecutive general admissions to a psychiatric hospital, 80% of the bulimic patients had not been identified as such by their hospital diagnosis (Kutcher, Whitehouse, & Freeman, 1985). To be sure, bulimic patients in particular do not assist their doctor by fully informing the provider of their condition.

Identification of a person with an eating disorder is also problematic for family and friends. Despite extensive media coverage of both disorders, many individuals remain uniformed, especially about bulimia. One study found that almost all the participants had heard of anorexia, with far fewer being familiar with bulimia (Murray, Touyz, & Beumont, 1990). Although 70% of the females had heard of bulimia, only 16% of the males knew of the disorder. Moreover, most people were more familiar with the behavioral rather than psychological features of the disorders. This is important, because the psychological features (fear of weight gain, guilt after eating, etc.) may be the first warning signs for family and friends.

Once patients are diagnosed correctly, there are many obstacles to getting them involved in recommended treatment. One of the biggest barriers is the changing structure of healthcare delivery, specifically managed care (Wooley, 1993). Managed care has resulted in tremendous pressures to reduce or eliminate inpatient psychiatric treatment wherever possible. This paradigm shift has its potential benefits, with greater utilization of transitional care such as partial hospitalization. However, managed care in the extreme can result in denial of much needed care. This is most evident in chronic, treatment-resistant disorders such as anorexia nervosa. In a study of psychiatric inpatients in a non-managed-care environment (McKenzie & Joyce, 1992), over a period of 5 years the average cumulative length of stay of anorexia nervosa patients was exceeded only by patients with schizophrenia or organic disorders. The mean length of the first admission for anorexia nervosa was 64 days. This is contrasted with dramatic decreases in average lengths of stay in child and adolescent inpatient psychiatric units for all admission diagnoses, often down to only 14 days (Carek & Hand, 1995).

When considering the treatment needs of anorectics, we cannot ignore that it can be a fatal disorder, with the aggregate mortality rated estimated at .56% per year, or 5.6% per decade (Sullivan, 1995). The dramatically shortened hospital stays are a serious problem for attempts at weight restoration in anorectics. The usual recommended rate of weight gain in the hospital is 1–3 pounds per week. Many experts feel that restoring weight to at least 90% of medically expected weight is important, in part because this is a weight where menstrual functioning may begin to return. Many hospitalized patients need to regain 20–30 pounds, which cannot be accomplished in a 1- or 2-week hospitalization. A clinical study examined the outcome of anorectic women who were discharged at an average of 76% of recommended weight (average length of stay = 64 days) versus those who were fully weight restored at 98% of recommended weight (average LOS = 116 days; Baran, Weltzin, & Kaye, 1995). Admission weights averaged 64% to 68% of recommended weight. At follow-up, those discharged underweight maintained a lower weight (82% vs. 94% of ideal weight), and had a dramatically higher rate of rehospitalization (62% vs. 7%). Thus, short hospitalizations appear to increase the risk of a poor clinical course, and to not be cost-effective over the long term. The long-term effect on increased mortality is not known. Although we support increased use of transitional and outpatient care for anorexia, it should be noted that there is an extremely small body of research on outpatient treatment of anorexia, compared with an extensive body of research showing that weight restoration can be achieved on an inpatient basis (Hsu, 1986).

A 1985 survey of eating-disorder programs, administered before the current full development of managed care in many areas, found that 69% of programs experienced difficulties with insurance companies regarding recommended treatment (Kaye, Enright, & Lesser, 1988). Patients had been turned away from inpatient treatment in 28% of the programs. Additionally, 74% of programs reported having patients leave inpatient treatment prematurely due to inadequate insurance, and 20% reported early termination of outpatient treatment. Five programs reported that, in the previous year, deaths had occurred due to inability to hospitalize or treat on an outpatient basis due to lack of insurance benefits. One can only speculate about how these experiences have changed with the increased penetration of managed mental healthcare over the past 10 years.

One of the potential pluses of managed care is the increased importance of specifying concrete treatment goals. However, there are times when managed care reviewers focus on important, but not comprehensive, indicators of clinical improvement. For eating disorders, this often translates into an overreliance on number of binge-purge episodes or pounds gained as the criteria for improvement and treatment termination (Katzman, 1995). Even in the presence of improvement in eating and weight, continuing body image dissatisfaction (Freeman, Beach, Davis, & Solyom, 1985) and eating disorder attitudes (Fairburn, Peveler, Jones, Hope, & Doll, 1993) have been shown to be related to relapse. Thus, therapists and managed care reviewers need to incorporate broader criteria into treatment goals and treatment determinations.

Mental health providers have not helped their case with managed care reviewers by failing to show consensus on recommendations for treatment, and failing to quickly adopt empirically validated treatments as standards. In a survey of eating disorder clinicians, over 60% did not believe that there was a professional consensus as to appropriate treatment of anorexia and bulimia (Herzog, Keller, Strober, Yeh, & Pai, 1992). Additionally, clinicians showed a strong tendency to endorse treatments not necessarily supported by clinical outcome studies, and treatment preferences were influenced by the clinicians' professional discipline. In terms of professional consensus, perhaps the situation will improve given recent publication of standards of practice for eating disorder by the American Psychiatric Association (1993).

Patient resistance to treatment is another crucial barrier to effective intervention. Treatment resistance is usually thought of relative to anorexia nervosa, especially in life-threatening cases. However, resistance is a management issue for many bulimics as well. For adolescents under the age of 18, parents are in the legal position to "mandate" treatment on either an in- or outpatient basis, although adolescents can still resist treatment even in a treatment setting. Since average age of onset of anorexia is 17, many parents are acutely aware that there is a limited amount of time remaining before their daughter turns 18 and can make her own treatment decisions. For severely impaired, resistant anorexics over 18, at times the only recourse is involuntary psychiatric hospitalization. Viability of this option is greatly influenced by differing criteria in the commitment statutes of various states, as well as variations in implementation of statutes by judges and officers of the court.

For example, one of the authors (JSM) practiced in Pennsylvania, and experienced much success in involuntarily hospitalizing resistant anorexics with comparatively moderate weight loss. In the language defining "clear and present danger to self," the Pennsylvania law states that one evidence of this is inability, without care, to provide oneself with adequate nutrition such that there is a reasonable probability of serious physical debilitation in the next 30 days. With such language, we were able to successfully argue that an anorectic with low food intake was not maintaining nutritional status due to a psychiatric disorder, that the patient's physical state was already beginning to deteriorate, and that it would only worsen. Moreover, we argued that allowing the patient's weight to become extremely low before intervening would seriously hamper chances for recovery. The author (JSM) now practices in Ohio, which has a much more restrictive law, and has found it extremely difficult to involuntarily hospitalize even severely emaciated anorectics. The Ohio law's language states that the patient must show a substantial and immediate risk of serious physical impairment or injury and is unable to provide for basic physical needs due to a mental disorder. This leaves open what constitutes "basic physical needs," especially since patients are usually eating something, if only small amounts. Also, in practical terms, the phrase "immediate risk of serious physical impairment" results in the court asking for likelihood that the patient will die in the next few days. Not only is this extremely difficult to predict, it results in the patient being in an extremely grave condition before anything can be done.

Reasons for eating-disordered patients' resistance or interventions for their resistance have received little direct empirical study. Among cognitive behavioral treatment outcome studies for bulimia, dropout is usually 15% to 35%, with some studies reporting as high as 40% to 60% dropout (Garner, Fairburn, & Davis, 1987). This does not include those persons who did not enter the studies by choice or due to exclusion criteria. Failure to enter the study occurs for 25% to 50% of potential participants. Drug studies also experience high rates of dropout, ranging between 4% and 54% (Mitchell, Raymond, & Specker, 1993). As an illustration of the problem, we recently completed an internal retrospective chart review in our Eating Disorders Clinic, which is based in an tertiary teaching hospital with a significant Medicaid patient base. We found that 50% of patients did not attend past the second outpatient appointment before dropping out.

To date, there have been only a few studies of attempts to prevent eating disorders. Some have attempted to change attitudes and knowledge (e.g., Huon, 1994; Shisslak, Crago, & Neal, 1990); others have attempted behavioral change (Killen et al., 1993; Rosen, 1989). Regardless of stated goal, the overall effect to date has been to increase knowledge and modestly change attitudes, with little corresponding behavioral change. One of the challenges to prevention efforts is the attempt to change dieting and weight preoccupation when it is culturally supported (central to many females' self-esteem), and pervasive. Indeed, Killen and associates (1993) have questioned the viability of prevention efforts directed at all females in broad groups, and suggest targeting high-risk groups. However, who represents a high-risk group is not without its problems (Striegel-Moore & Silberstein, 1989). Although some high-risk groups are known (dancers, models, actresses), little is known about what constitutes high-risk behaviors, thereby identifying subgroups of at-risk females. Although it is known that persons who develop eating disorders pass through a period of dieting, only a small percentage of dieters will develop eating disorders. Little is known about what triggers certain dieters to develop clinical disorders. Thus, it is not known if reducing dieting behavior and weight preoccupation among broad groups of females will in fact prevent eating disorders. However, it can be argued that dieting, weight preoccupation, and negative body image have their own psychological and physical costs, and thus are legitimate targets of intervention in their own right. Targeting females during high-risk developmental periods has also been suggested. Prevention efforts have addressed middle school, high school, and university women. However, the high prevalence of weight dissatisfaction and dieting in the later elementary school years suggests the need for prevention efforts in the early elementary school years. Finally, current prevention efforts have utilized mainly school settings, which are already overburdened with numerous educational and societal missions.

TREATMENT

Assessment Strategies

Assessment of eating disorder cases ideally includes a clinical interview, self-monitoring of eating, binging, and purging behavior, questionnaire measures of eating-disorder and global psychopathology, an evaluation of body image, and an assessment of the actual avoidance of eating forbidden foods. Medical evaluations are often recommended that involve a routine checkup, consideration of medical risk (e.g., medical severity of weight problem, amenorrhea), and laboratory tests of electrolytes (Jacobs & Schneider, 1985). For bulimics, referral to a dentist may also be considered for problems with enamel erosion and dental caries.

Clinical Interview

Using a cognitive-behavioral orientation, the interviewer would obtain a functional analysis of binge-purge episodes, assessment of typical thoughts and emotions before and after binging and purging, typical precipitating events, typical times and places, rules about appropriate eating, and a clear delineation of the foods and amounts consumed during binges. A clear assessment of forbidden foods is also important because patients sometimes forget what foods they avoid. One way of questioning patients about this is to ask what foods make them so uncomfortable that they avoid eating them altogether, perhaps because they know they would have a hard time keeping them down.

Some writers describe the importance of obtaining a family history for eating disorders and other psychiatric disorders, as well as specific information from family members. Information may include family attitudes toward eating, exercise, and physical appearance; attitudes toward the patient; expression of negative and positive emotions in the family; and other family dynamics as they pertain to factors that may impede or facilitate recovery (Yager, 1994).

Assessment of Global and Specific Psychopathology

To assess global psychopathology, the Minnesota Multiphasic Personality Inventory (MMPI-2) is often used. The MMPI-2 is helpful in screening for depression, anxiety, and personality disorders. Similarly, for adolescents, aged 13 to 18, the Minnesota Multiphasic Personality Inventory-Adolescent version (MMPI-A) may provide useful information as to global psychopathology. Although the MMPI-A may provide useful descriptive and interpretive information, several cautions have been noted for use of the MMPI-A, including the lack of standardization on clinical populations and the questionable validity in using the code-type approach with MMPI-A interpretations.

The MMPI may also be used to assess outcome psychopathology in eating-disordered patients. The interrelationship at 10-year follow-up of anorectic patients between degree of general psychopathology on the MMPI and severity of eating disorder symptomatology was examined by Schork, Eckert, and Halmi (1994). These investigators found differences in mean MMPI profiles and correlations between MMPI clinical scale elevations and levels of eating disorder outcome. Subjects who had not recovered had significantly higher psychopathology on MMPI scales 1*(Hs)*, 2*(D)*, 3*(Hy)*, 4*(Pd)*, 6*(Pa)*, 7*(Pt)*, and 8*(Sc)*.

The best known structured interview for assessing specific psychopathology of eating disorders is the Eating Disorder Examination (EDE; Fairburn & Cooper, 1993). The Eating Disorder Examination is a commonly used semistructured interview for the assessment of psychopathology in anorexia nervosa and bulimia nervosa. The EDE is a 62-item interview that was designed to measure the full range of psychopathology and generates five subscales: restraint, bulimia, eating concern, weight concern, and shape concern. The EDE directly assesses the diagnostic criteria of all eating disorders.

A structured interview for children and adolescents that can be used for the assessment of both global and specific psychopathology is the Diagnostic Interview Schedule for Children, 2nd Edition (DISC-2.1). The DISC-2.1 has been found to have good sensitivity in the diagnosis of eating disorders in adolescents and appears to be more sensitive than the parent version (DISC-P) of the interview (Fisher et al., 1993).

Several questionnaires are available for assessment of eating-disorder-specific psychopathology. A well-known questionnaire is the Eating Disorders Inventory (EDI-2; Garner, 1991) which assesses behavioral and cognitive characteristics of anorexia and bulimia nervosa and associated psychopathology. The EDI-2 has norms for adolescents aged 13 and older. The Eating Attitudes Test (EAT; Garner, Olmsted, Bohr, & Garfinkel, 1982) is another commonly used self-report measure of disturbed eating habits and concerns about food, eating, shape, and weight. The Binge Eating Scale (BES; Gormally, Black, Daston, & Rardin, 1982) has been widely used to assess binge eating in obese patients. It can provide a general gauge of the overall severity of the symptoms of an eating disorder and can be useful in assessing therapeutic change.

Several other questionnaires have been developed specifically to assess eating attitudes and weight control behaviors in children and adolescents. Among these are the Body Image and Eating Questionnaire for Children (BIEQ; Veron-Guidry, Williamson, & Netemeyer, 1994) assessing three factors, diet, overweight, and restraint; the Eating Disorder Inventory for Children (EDI-C), a downward extension of the original Eating Disorder Inventory using the same subscales; the Children's Eating Attitudes Test (CHEAT; Maloney et al., 1993), assessing general eating attitudes and behaviors; and the Kids Eating Disorders Survey (KEDS; Childress, Brewerton, Hodges, & Jarrell, 1993), which contains child figure drawings to graphically assess weight and body dissatisfaction. Although these eating-disorder-specific scales have been found to have adequate reliability and validity, they are not able to provide differential diagnosis of eating disorders and are probably best viewed as supporting the diagnosis made from the clinical interview.

Questionnaires that measure specific eating-disorder cognitions are available. The Mizes Anorectic Cognitions Questionnaire (MAC; Mizes & Klesges, 1989) assesses cognitive variables related to anorexia and bulimia nervosa. The MAC has 33 Likert-type items that address three cognitive domains: perception of weight and eating as the basis of approval from others, the belief that rigid self-control is fundamental to self-worth, and the rigidity of weight- and eating-regulation efforts. Another questionnaire is the Bulimia Cognitive Distortions Scale (BCDS; Schulman, Kinder, Powers, Prange, & Gleghorn, 1986), which contains 25 Likert-type statements that assess two domains of cognitive distortions: those associated with eating and binging behaviors and those related to physical appearance.

One area of assessment which remains controversial because of problems with the validity, reliability, and practicality of various measures is the assessment of body image (Cash & Brown, 1987). Body image has been described as comprising two basic dimensions: perceptual and affective or attitudinal. Attitudinal perceptions of one's body are often referred to as body dissatisfaction. The attitudinal dimension of body image has proven to be more useful than perceptual distortion in discriminating eating-disordered from non-eating-disordered groups (Mizes, 1991, 1992a). The Body Dissatisfaction subscale of the EDI-2 is another measure used to assess body dissatisfaction.

Self-report assessment procedures of body image include the Body Image Assessment (BIA; Williamson, Kelley, Davis, Ruggerio, & Blouin, 1985), which uses nine cards that depict body silhouettes of various weights. Subjects pick one card to represent their perception of their actual weight and one card to represent their ideal weight. The discrepancy between the two represents the degree of body dissatisfaction. This method has been revised specifically for children and adolescents with cards validated for children in Grades 3–6 and Grades 5–7 (Veron-Guidry et al., 1994). Similar procedures have been used with children as young as 6 years to assess perceptions of body image (Ohtahara, Ohzeki, Hanaki, Motozumi, & Shiraki, 1993). However, a lack of empirical data limits conclusions that can be drawn about body image in children and adolescents. Although evidence suggests that body image during adolescence may be multidimensional, it is not clear whether body image in children is conceptually the same as body image in adults (Offman & Bradley, 1992). Moreover, because younger children tend to make global conceptualizations, it is difficult to separate the measurement of body image from that of other confounding variables such as self-esteem and depression.

Behavioral Assessment

Self-monitoring is a valuable method for examining the functional analysis of binge-purge episodes and covert behavior of the eating-disordered patient. Specially designed forms can be used that include the time, amount of food or liquid consumed, binges and purges, and feelings and thoughts before or after binging and purging, or a spiral notebook diary can be used just as adequately. Self-monitoring can also be valuable in helping patients to observe their own behavior. Self-monitoring can serve as an intervention itself when patients are highly reactive to it (e.g., a patient may reduce binge episodes because of embarrassment from recording them) and can provide patients with an increased awareness of their behavior and the effect of stimulus cues.

Because problems with body image are frequent among women with eating disorders, the assessment of body-image avoidance can be an important adjunct to a general assessment. The behavioral tendencies that frequently accompany body-image disturbance can be assessed using the Body Image Avoidance Questionnaire (BIAQ; Rosen, Srebnik, Saltzberg, & Wendt, 1991). This 19-item questionnaire measures avoidance of situations that provoke concern about physical appearance (e.g., avoidance of physical intimacy, avoidance of tight-fitting clothes).

A method of identifying forbidden foods is to use test meals as advocated by Williamson (1990). If purging is prevented, bulimics have been found to avoid consuming forbidden foods (Rosen, Leitenberg, Fondacaro, Gross, & Willmuth, 1985). Such behavioral avoidance can be assessed by presenting patients with standard meals with a strict prohibition on purging after the meal. Avoidance is measured in terms of the amount of the food consumed, and subjective measures of anxiety and the urge to purge are taken. The test meal procedure may be particularly helpful in the assessment of a patient who denies difficulties with eating behavior.

Treatment Strategies

A wide range of psychological therapies have been used to treat patients with eating disorders including cognitive behavioral therapy (CBT), behavior therapy, psychodynamic therapy, family therapy, and interpersonal therapy. In addition, a variety of pharmacological treatments have been used. Many of these treatments follow the recently developed practice guidelines for the treatment of anorexia and bulimia nervosa (APA, 1993). The majority of treatment studies have included adult eating-disordered patients; unless specified, the reader may assume that studies did not include children or adolescents.

Individual and Group Psychotherapy

Anorexia Nervosa.   Psychotherapy treatments of anorexia nervosa are advised to be considered within the context of a comprehensive overall treatment plan that includes medical management, psychotropic medications if indicated, and the appropriate use of dietary and rehabilitative services (APA, 1993). There are fewer controlled trials for treatment of anorexia nervosa (psychotherapy or pharmacological treatment) than for treatment of bulimia nervosa, with the focus of most techniques on achieving short-term weight restoration. A central goal in the early treatment of the seriously underweight anorectic is weight restoration. Weight restoration alone may improve several of the core physiological and psychological features of anorexia and bulimia nervosa, including endocrine abnormalities, obsessional thinking, depressed mood, irritability, emotional lability, and social withdrawal (Yager, 1994). Little is known about the long-term effectiveness of weight restoration although relapse occurs in about 50% of patients (Hsu, 1986).

Resistance is often identified as a barrier to psychotherapy of anorectics. Suggestions for engaging the anorectic in individual psychotherapy include focusing on her distress about the effects of the disorder, such as depression, physical problems, and the burden of extreme food and weight preoccupation rather than challenging her self-perception of fatness directly (Hsu, 1986). Behavioral techniques for anorexia nervosa often include the setting of specific expectations for weight gain and making contracts for rewards contingent on the patient's behavior. For example, a typical inpatient treatment includes weekly weight gain of 2–3 pounds per week to earn ward privileges (Yates, 1990). In other therapies such as ego-oriented individual psychotherapy, the therapy may focus on building the patient's ego strength, coping skills, individualization, reducing confusion over identity, and other interpersonal issues. Psychodynamic theorists recommend that treatment focus on the anorectic's pervasive perfectionism, extreme self-criticism and doubt, and her belief that her worth depends on others' approval (Hsu, 1986).

A cognitive-behavioral approach to treatment of patients with anorexia nervosa was described by Garner and Bemis (1982). They outlined an approach to treatment that emphasizes changing basic maladaptive attitudes, including beliefs about excessively rigid regulation of food and weight, the extreme importance of weight and shape to determining self-worth, and the need for exaggerated self-control over eating and weight.

Bulimia Nervosa. Cognitive-behavioral therapy (CBT) techniques have dominated the literature on treatment of bulimia nervosa. CBT approaches contain such elements as self-monitoring; cognitive restructuring; stimulus control measures including avoidance of binge-inducing settings and situations, and avoidance of hunger; exposure with response prevention, in which the anxiety associated with ingestion of forbidden foods is extinguished; relaxation training; and assertiveness training.

In a review of individual and group CBT of bulimia nervosa, mean reduction in frequency of binging and purging was 80% (Garner et al., 1987). At follow-up, 45% of patients were still abstinent from binging and purging. The typical duration of individual treatment in the reviewed studies was 15 to 20 weeks, usually with weekly sessions. Shorter versions of CBT have also proven to be effective; Fahy and Russell (1993) found an approximate 50% improvement rate in bulimia nervosa patients using an 8-week version of CBT. All studies reviewed by Garner and colleagues (1987) included some form of cognitive restructuring of distorted attitudes regarding food, weight, and body shape, and self-monitoring of binge-purge episodes. The majority of studies included specific meal planning and half of the studies included assertiveness and social-skills training, or relaxation training. The CBT technique of exposure and response prevention (ERP) has been reviewed as a separate treatment modality. Rosen (1987) suggests that ERP is an effective treatment, with 70% to 80% of patients experiencing some reduction in the frequency of purging and nearly half of patients becoming abstinent.

Other psychotherapeutic techniques, such as interpersonal therapy and psychodynamic therapy, have also received recent attention in the literature. Interpersonal therapy (IPT) focuses on coping with current life situations, in particular interpersonal conflicts, losses, role transitions, and interpersonal deficits. In one study, three psychotherapy treatments for bulimia nervosa (cognitive-behavioral, behavioral, and interpersonal psychotherapy) were found to reduce binge eating and depressive symptoms (Fairburn et al., 1991). However, CBT was more effective than the other two at modifying disturbed attitudes toward shape, weight, dieting, and the use of self-induced vomiting to control shape and weight (Fairburn et al., 1991). A follow-up study of the longer term effects of IPT, behavior therapy, and CBT revealed different results. Although a temporal effect was found for IPT in which it took longer to achieve effects, at the 12-month follow-up, CBT and IPT made equivalent changes across all areas of symptoms (Fairburn, Jones, Peveler, Hope, & O'Connor, 1993). Therefore, it appears that successful intervention with bulimics does not have to include direct attention to the patient's eating habits and attitudes regarding shape and weight.

Group treatment of bulimia nervosa has not been as well investigated as individual treatment. Studies have shown that cognitive-behavioral group treatment is successful in decreasing the symptomatology of bulimia nervosa (e.g., Childs-Clarke & Farmer,

1994; Kettlewell, Mizes, & Wasylyshyn, 1992). However, there seem to be insufficient data concerning whether group or individual treatment is more effective (Garner et al., 1987). Often, individual sessions are conducted prior to or concurrent with group sessions, so it is difficult to ascertain the independent effects of group CBT. In a review of group treatment for bulimia nervosa (Freeman & Munro, 1988), in which most groups had a cognitive-behavioral orientation, the most effective appeared to be combined group sessions with individual therapy. However, there was a higher percentage of dropout compared with other forms of psychotherapy. The authors conclude that overall improvement for patients receiving individual therapy was slightly greater than for those in group treatment.

Family Therapy

Anorexia Nervosa. The benefit of family therapy in the treatment of anorexia nervosa has emerged in the clinical literature in recent years. Moreover, the benefit of providing this treatment to adolescents has been empirically tested with controlled trials. Family treatment approaches vary, but most consist of three standard phases in which the family or parents take charge of the patient's eating and weight gain, the role of the anorectic's symptoms in maintaining family homeostasis and dysfunctional patterns of family interaction are managed, and the return of control over eating is given to the adolescent when target weight is achieved. Other variations of family treatment include focus on the adolescent's ego development in which the anorexia is believed to be a response to the strains of adolescent development. Family treatment has been described as lasting from as few as 12 sessions to 18 months (Crisp et al., 1991; Robin, Siegel, & Moye, 1995).

Family treatment for adolescents with anorexia nervosa has frequently been believed to be effective in weight restoration and improved psychological functioning (e.g., le Grange, 1993). Family variables, such as level of aggression, have been shown to influence therapy outcome. Shugar and Krueger (1995) found that greater weight gain occurred in anorectics whose families had low levels of covert or indirect aggression during systemic family therapy. Because family therapy includes multiple components, investigators have tried to separate the relevant dimensions. In one study, two forms of family treatment were compared: family therapy conjoint with patient and parents, or family counseling with separate supportive sessions for the patient and parents (le Grange, Eisler, Dare, & Russell, 1992). The two family treatments resulted in similar benefits in weight gain and psychological functioning; however, conjoint family therapy was not always effective in reducing high levels of family criticism and dissatisfaction.

Treatment comparison studies have also been conducted between family therapy and individual therapies for anorexia nervosa (some with controlled trials). In one treatment comparison study of family therapy versus nonspecific individual therapy for eating-disordered patients, Russell, Szmukler, Dare, and Eisler (1987) found strong support for family therapy in younger patients. Patients whose anorexia nervosa began at or before age 18 with less than 3 years' duration of illness improved more with family therapy than with individual psychotherapy. Another finding was that individual treatment led to higher weight gain than family therapy in patients over 18 years (Russell et al., 1987).

In a comparison of three therapies (inpatient, outpatient individual and family, and outpatient group) for anorexia nervosa patients, all treatment groups improved significantly more than a no-treatment control group (Crisp et al., 1991). These authors noted that early dropout occurred most frequently in the outpatient group therapy condition, although weight gain in the three therapies was equivalent. Behavioral family systems therapy has been compared with ego-oriented individual psychotherapy in adolescents with anorexia nervosa. Results demonstrated that 82% of the family therapy patients met target weight and resumption of menstruation, whereas 50% of individual therapy patients met target weight and resumption of menstruation (this difference was not statistically significant). Both groups had a large reduction in conflict over eating in the family which was maintained one year following treatment (Robin et al., 1995).

Bulimia Nervosa. Few family therapy studies have included patients with bulimia nervosa in their samples. In the investigation conducted by Russell and colleagues (1987), a subgroup of bulimia nervosa patients received either individual or family therapy. Only a few of the patients improved significantly by the end of the follow-up treatment period to be classified as having a good or intermediate outcome. Furthermore, bulimia nervosa patients had similar results with both individual and family therapies (Russell et al., 1987).

Pharmacological Treatment in Bulimia Nervosa

Drug trials for patients with bulimia nervosa have generally found positive results with various antidepressants. Antidepressants may be used with bulimics to reduce binging and purging and/or to treat concurrent depression. In a review of drug treatments for bulimia nervosa (Freeman & Munro, 1988), a modest but definite effect of antidepressant drugs was shown. However, some investigators have noted that long-term outcome relapse rates are high, and only a small portion of bulimics remain symptom-free. A long-term outcome study of antidepressant treatment for bulimia nervosa revealed that desipramine had a beneficial effect on bulimia symptoms when compared with placebo in the initiation phase (Walsh, Hadigan, Devlin, Gladis, & Roose, 1991). Patients taking desipramine had a 47% mean reduction of binge frequency. However, there was high relapse in the maintenance phase, which suggests serious limitations in the long-term effectiveness of a single antidepressant trial in treating bulimia nervosa (Walsh et al., 1991). Other studies have found the best overall gains in reducing bulimic symptoms with combined treatment of desipramine and CBT for a 24-week period (Agras et al., 1994). Conversely, others found no benefit from the combination of cognitive-behavioral therapy and desipramine, CBT alone had the best treatment outcome (Leitenberg et al., 1993). Double-blind placebo-controlled studies have demonstrated efficacy of fluoxetine in reducing bulimic symptoms (Fluoxetine Bulimia Nervosa Collaborative Study Group, 1992). Whereas dosages of other tricyclic and MAOI antidepressants parallel those used to treat depression, higher doses (60 mg/day) of fluoxetine seem more effective in reducing bulimic symptomatology than the lower dose (20 mg/day) used to treat depression (Fluoxetine Bulimia Nervosa Collaborative Study Group, 1992).

Outcome and Prognostic Factors in Anorexia and Bulimia Nervosa

Follow-up studies reveal recovery rates for anorexia and bulimia nervosa patients and rates of psychiatric diagnoses. Rates of recovery vary according to whether partial or full recovery or presence of clinical eating disorders are examined. Many investigators have used the Morgan-Russell Assessment Schedule, which indicates good, intermediate, and poor response. In a sample of eating-disordered patients followed after 6 years, 77% had no eating disorder diagnosis, while 40% were fully recovered (Norring & Sohlberg, 1993). Almost 50% of adolescent-onset anorexia nervosa patients showed recovery in spite of still having some abnormal eating behaviors (Gillberg, Rastam, & Gillberg, 1994). Other studies including adolescent eating disorders have found similar recovery rates. Steinhausen and Seidel (1993) found a recovery rate of 68% in a sample of adolescents with anorexia and/or bulimia at a 58-month follow-up.

The prognosis for bulimia nervosa patients appears to be considerably better than for anorexia nervosa or mixed patients. In one study, bulimics had a full recovery rate at one year of 56%, while mixed patients had a full recovery rate of 18%, and anorectics had a 10% full recovery rate (Herzog et al., 1993). Likewise, in a 10-year follow-up study of bulimic patients, over half of the subjects were fully recovered (Collings & King, 1994).

Similarities in the psychiatric diagnoses at follow-up have been found between anorectics with an average age of onset in adolescence and those with an average age of onset in early adulthood. In one study, 35% of subjects were free of any psychiatric disorder at follow-up 6 years after presentation with adolescent anorexia nervosa (Smith, Feldman, Nasserbakht, & Steiner, 1993). Of the remaining subjects, 43% continued to experience eating disorder symptoms, 30% were diagnosed with an affective disorder, and 40% with an anxiety disorder.

Prognostic factors, including personality disorders, duration of illness, age of onset, and percent ideal body weight, have been identified as related to treatment outcome of eating disorder patients. Cluster B personality disorders (antisocial, borderline, histrionic, and narcissistic features) predicted poor outcome in the treatment of bulimia nervosa patients in one study (Rossiter, Agras, Telch, & Schneider, 1993). In a sample of women with anorexia, bulimia, and mixed disorders, percent ideal body weight (IBW) was found to have the strongest predictive value (Herzog et al., 1993). The lower a subject's weight the less likely she was to achieve recovery within the follow-up period. Poor short-term treatment response was predicted by greater pretreatment symptom severity and presence of personality disorder in a sample of women with bulimia nervosa. In addition, outcome at one year was poorer in patients with personality disorders, a longer history of bulimia, and greater pretreatment symptom severity (Fahy & Russell, 1993). Other variables, including parent-child relationships, duration of symptoms, duration of inpatient treatment, and number of readmissions, were reviewed as significant prognostic variables by Steinhausen, Rauss-Mason, and Seidel (1991).

Prevention Programs

Although prevention has been advocated to decrease the number of new cases of eating disorders that develop in children and adolescents, there are few empirical data on the efficacy of prevention programs. Prevention programs have typically developed curricula focused on the general characteristics of eating disorders, physical development in adolescence, the effects of extreme weight regulation, and promotion of healthy weight regulation, through the use of videotapes, slide shows, workbooks, and discussion sessions. Several pilot projects developed for high school students (Rosen, 1989; Shisslak, Crago, & Neal, 1990) proved to be effective in disseminating information about weight-reducing behaviors and general information about eating

disorders (e.g., symptoms, psychological characteristics). However, there was no reduction in incidence of dieting, fasting, and other weight-reducing behaviors. Likewise, in a younger population of junior high school students, a prevention program
focused on eating attitudes and behaviors revealed that the program had a substantial
effect on children's dieting views, decreased their concerns about body weight, and
increased knowledge of the harmful effects of purging for weight control (Moreno &
Thelen, 1993). This study did not measure behavioral indices of change in weight regulation methods. One author noted that prevention efforts have to address the beliefs
that are most salient to teenagers (Rosen, 1989), which may not include the general
knowledge covered in these types of prevention programs.

The only large-scale prevention project conducted with a longer follow-up period
targeted young (6th and 7th grade) adolescents (Killen et al., 1993). The project included a curriculum of 18 lessons and measured students' knowledge, attitudes, and
behaviors concerning weight regulation over a 24-month period (Killen et al., 1993).
Results demonstrated minimal gains in adolescents' knowledge over the follow-up period and no significant changes in weight-regulation behaviors. These authors questioned the wisdom of providing a curriculum directed at all young adolescents because
it is unlikely to be cost-effective. However, the project was able to identify a subgroup
of at-risk students based on higher prevalence of substance use, unhealthful weight
regulation strategies, and more depressive symptoms who appeared to benefit slightly
more from the prevention program. Thus, prevention programs targeted at appropriate
subgroups may prove to be more efficacious and cost-effective than wide-scale prevention efforts.

SUMMARY

Eating disorders captivate our cultural attention, most likely for a variety of reasons.
It is a rare month that goes by without some media coverage about eating disorders.
Often it is the revelation of yet another public figure who suffers with an eating disorder, such as the disclosure by the singer and dancer Paula Abdul that she has struggled with bulimia nervosa. Perhaps one reason that we are fascinated with eating
disorders is that many of us recognize that we share much in common with eating-
disordered sufferers, as the data on the high prevalence of dieting and weight preoccupation strongly suggest. As the continuum hypothesis suggests, perhaps many
women realize that they are only a few steps away from their sisters with clinical eating disorders, and they fear that some unknown factor will lead them down that slip-
pery path. Many an anorectic has commented that the disorder started with a simple
diet, and for reasons that she cannot understand, quickly began to snowball and got out
of control, while at the same time creating the illusion of control. One would be hard
pressed to identify any other psychiatric disorder that has so consistently over the past
several years generated media and cultural attention. Against this backdrop, it is difficult to understand the serious lack of research funds for eating disorders, as well as
the diminishing resources for treatment. Considering that anorexia and bulimia nervosa were only formally identified as specific diagnoses in 1980 and that there is a
paucity of research funds, the amount of research generated in a short period of time
is amazing. Could it be that researchers are fascinated with these disorders for the
same reasons as the wider culture?

Eating disorders, particularly anorexia nervosa, are devastating, not only for the patient, but for family and friends as well. Bulimics tend to suffer in isolation, becoming progressively more deeply consumed with their disorder, increasingly becoming ashamed and embarrassed, withdrawing deeper into their own world of weight preoccupation and self-hatred, isolated from others. For anorectics in treatment, we often describe the terrible no-man's land that they are caught in by referring to the proverbial "between a rock and a hard place." On one side is their recognition that if their weight gets just a few pounds lower, they may die. However, just a few pounds above this point, they run headfirst into their overwhelming fear of gaining weight. For anorectics, that means losing their total self-esteem, sense of control, and an intoxicating feeling of being special. Added to this is the fear of disapproval from themselves and others for being fat. The entrenched resistance of the anorectic patient in particular is the desperate attempt to hold on to her sense of her very being. People working in the eating disorders field often hear joking comments from female acquaintances: "I wish I could be anorectic for a few months and lose some weight." Little do they know that the internal mental battle of an anorectic's life is a hell you would not want to wish on anyone.

When considering the causes of eating disorders, it is all too easy to point suspecting fingers at our culture in general, the perceived male-dominated society, media, parents, or other targets of our dissatisfaction or political agendas. It is important to maintain a balanced view, and realize that eating disorders are like all other disorders, in that they are a complex mix of sociocultural, biological, genetic, and psychological factors. Some of these variables are better defined and understood than others; the interrelationship among these factors at this time is poorly understood. Research is just beginning to look at these interrelationships, as illustrated by the work examining the biological variable of menstrual timing and the concurrence of certain psychological milestones or stressors. New, high-quality research on the genetic contribution to eating disorders is also causing us to rethink previous views on the etiology of eating disorders.

Eating disorders are not easy to treat. Reading research reports of treatment outcome studies for eating disorders can lead one to conclude that treatment is straightforward and that treatment will often be beneficial, if not curative. To be sure, an impressive body of treatment research for bulimia nervosa has mushroomed in a brief period. However, the clinician practicing in the real world trenches can easily and mistakenly get the impression that he or she is doing something wrong because his or her treatment results do not match those of the published outcome studies. The practicing clinician has to deal with poor detection and lack of appropriate referral, resulting in a worsening of the patient's symptoms or a lack of appropriate care. All too often, the skilled eating disorder clinician has to address a patient's history of inappropriate treatment, and the patient's resulting hopelessness or anger. Dramatic changes in healthcare delivery have had a substantial impact on provision of eating disorder services, including excessively short hospital stays for anorectics, inadequate or lacking insurance coverage or denial of coverage by managed care reviewers, and limited views of the parameters of clinical outcome that need to be assessed. These problems in the mental healthcare delivery system have led many eating disorder programs, especially inpatient units, to completely close. The resulting lack of services is not due to a lack of persons needing services, as the remaining eating disorder programs are able to attest.

The remarkable and rapid strides in the assessment and treatment of eating disorders provide one clear, bright beacon of optimism. One of the authors (JSM) recalls seeing his first woman with bulimia in 1979 while in graduate school. No one on the clinical faculty had heard of this problem of binging and purging, and there were only a handful of articles on the topic. It is impressive how far we have come since then! Our own research article database numbers over 1,700 articles, books, and chapters, and it is far from complete. Although treatment results are far from perfect, we can firmly state that cognitive-behavioral treatment is effective in the treatment of bulimia nervosa, and we can assert that behavioral interventions in inpatient settings are effective in weight restoration over the short term for anorexia nervosa. Also, antidepressant medication has positive effects on binging and purging, even though there is much to learn about long-term effectiveness, susceptibility to relapse, and the combined use of medication and cognitive behavior therapy. New research has strongly suggested that interpersonal therapy has much potential as an effective therapy for bulimia nervosa, and merits additional investigation. Much less is known empirically regarding effective therapies for anorexia nervosa, although many clinicians utilize adaptations of cognitive-behavioral treatments for bulimia. Recent research has scientifically investigated various forms of family therapy for anorexia, with the strong suggestion that it is likely to be an effective treatment for adolescent, recent onset patients.

We have learned much—we have much more to learn. Talented therapists have helped many; we look forward to helping more people, more completely, and more long-lastingly. Eating-disordered patients wait for us to become better as therapists and as a society in helping them let go of the incessant battle with their own body and own sense of self.

REFERENCES

Agras, W. S., Rossiter, E. M., Arnow, B., Telch, C. F., Raeburn, S. D., Bruce, B., & Koran, L. M. (1994). One-year follow-up of psychosocial and pharmacologic treatments for bulimia nervosa. *Journal of Clinical Psychiatry, 55,* 179–183.

American Psychiatric Association. (1993). Practice guideline for eating disorders. *American Journal of Psychiatry, 150,* 212–228.

American Psychiatric Association. (1994). *Diagnostic and statistical manual of mental disorders* (4th ed.). Washington, DC: Author.

Andersen, A. E., & DiDomenico, L. (1992). Diet vs. shape content of popular male and female magazines: A dose-response relationship to the incidence of eating disorders? *International Journal of Eating Disorders, 11,* 283–287.

Andersen, A. E., & Hay, A. (1985). Racial and socioeconomic influences in anorexia nervosa and bulimia. *International Journal of Eating Disorders, 4,* 479–487.

Arbitell, M. R., & Mizes, J. S. (1988, March). *Typographical and descriptive variables in bulimia nervosa: A controlled comparison.* Paper presented at the Southeastern Psychological Association Convention, New Orleans.

Attie, I., & Brooks-Gunn, J. (1989). The development of eating problems in adolescent girls: A longitudinal study. *Developmental Psychology, 25,* 70–79.

Baran, S. A., Weltzin, T. E., & Kaye, W. H. (1995). Low discharge weight and outcome in anorexia nervosa. *American Journal of Psychiatry, 152,* 1070–1072.

Brewerton, T. D., Krahn, D. D., Hardin, T. A., Wehr, T. A., & Rosenthal, N. E. (1994). Findings from the Seasonal Pattern Assessment Questionnaire in patients with eating disorders and control subjects: Effects of diagnosis and location. *Psychiatry Research, 52,* 71–84.

Brooks-Gunn, J., & Warren, M. P. (1985). Effects of delayed menarche in different contexts: Dance and non-dance students. *Journal of Youth and Adolescence, 14,* 285–300.

Bryant-Waugh, R. J., Lask, B. D., Shafran, R. L., & Fosson, A. R. (1992). Do doctors recognize eating disorders in children? *Archives of Disease in Childhood, 67,* 103–105.

Carek, D. J., & Hand, L. D. (1995). Current child and adolescent inpatient psychiatric treatment: Evolution or regression? *Journal of the South Carolina Medical Association, 91,* 5–8.

Cash, T. F., & Brown, T. A. (1987). Body image in anorexia nervosa and bulimia nervosa. *Behavior Modification, 11,* 487–521.

Cattarin, J. A., & Thompson, J. K. (1994). A three-year longitudinal study of body image, eating disturbance, and general psychological functioning in adolescent females. *Eating Disorders: Journal of Treatment and Prevention, 2,* 114–125.

Childress, A. C., Brewerton, T. D., Hodges, E. L., & Jarrell, M. P. (1993). The Kid's Eating Disorders Survey (KEDS): A study of middle school students. *Journal of the American Academy of Child and Adolescent Psychiatry, 32,* 843–850.

Childs-Clarke, A., & Farmer, R. (1994). Nursing care of bulimia with cognitive behavioural therapy. *Nursing Times, 90,* 40–42.

Collings, S., & King, M. (1994). Ten-year follow-up of 50 patients with bulimia nervosa. *British Journal of Psychiatry, 164,* 80–87.

Connors, M. E., & Morse, W. (1993). Sexual abuse and eating disorders: A review. *International Journal of Eating Disorders, 13,* 1–11.

Constantini, N. W., & Warren, M. P. (1994). Special problems of the female athlete. *Bailliere's Clinical Rheumatology, 8*(1), 199–219.

Cooper, P. J., & Fairburn, C. G. (1993). Confusion over the core psychopathology of bulimia nervosa. *International Journal of Eating Disorders, 13,* 385–389.

Crisp, A. H., Norton, K., Gowers, S., Halek, C., Bowyer, C., Yeldham, D., Levett, G., & Bhat, A. (1991). A controlled study of the effect of therapies aimed at adolescent and family psychopathology in anorexia nervosa. *British Journal of Psychiatry, 159,* 325–333.

Crowther, J. H., & Mizes, J. S. (1992). Etiology of bulimia nervosa: Conceptual, research, and measurement issues. In J. H. Crowther, D. L. Tennebaum, S. E. Hobfoll, & M. A. P. Stephens (Eds.), *The etiology of bulimia nervosa: The individual and familial context* (pp. 225–244). Washington, DC: Hemisphere.

Davis, R., Freeman, R. J., & Garner, D. M. (1988). A naturalistic investigation of eating behavior in bulimia nervosa. *Journal of Consulting and Clinical Psychology, 56,* 273–279.

de Zwaan, M., Mitchell, J. E., Raymond, N. C., & Spitzer, R. L. (1994). Binge Eating Disorder: Clinical features and treatment of a new diagnosis. *Harvard Review of Psychiatry, 1,* 310–325.

Drewnowski, A., & Garn, S. M. (1987). Concerning the use of weight tables to categorize patients with eating disorders. *International Journal of Eating Disorders, 6,* 639–646.

Drewnowski, A., Yee, D. K., Kurth, C. L., & Krahn, D. D. (1994). Eating pathology and DSM-III-R bulimia nervosa: A continuum of behavior. *American Journal of Psychiatry, 151,* 1217–1219.

Fabian, L. J., & Thompson, J. K. (1989). Body image and eating disturbance in young females. *International Journal of Eating Disorders, 8,* 63–74.

Fahy, T. A., & Russell, G. F. M. (1993). Outcome and prognostic variables in bulimia nervosa. *International Journal of Eating Disorders, 14,* 135–145.

Fairburn, C. G., & Cooper, Z. (1993). The Eating Disorder Examination (EDE, 12th ed.). In C. G. Fairburn & G. T. Wilson (Eds.), *Binge-eating: Nature, assessment, and treatment* (pp. 333–360). New York: Guilford Press.

Fairburn, C. G., Jones, R., Peveler, R. C., Carr, S. J., Solomon, R. A., O'Connor, M. E., Burton, J., & Hope, R. A. (1991). Three psychological treatments for bulimia nervosa: A comparative trial. *Archives of General Psychiatry, 48,* 463–469.

Fairburn, C. G., Jones, R., Peveler, R. C., Hope, R. A., & O'Connor, M. (1993). Psychotherapy and bulimia nervosa: The longer-term effects of interpersonal psychotherapy, behaviour therapy and cognitive behaviour therapy. *Archives of General Psychiatry, 50,* 419–428.

Fairburn, C. G., Peveler, R. C., Jones, R., Hope, R. A., & Doll, H. A. (1993). Predictors of 12-month outcome in bulimia nervosa and the influence of attitudes to shape and weight. *Journal of Consulting and Clinical Psychology, 61,* 696–698.

Fairburn, C. G., Phil, M., & Beglin, S. J. (1990). Studies of the epidemiology of bulimia nervosa. *American Journal of Psychiatry, 147,* 401–408.

Fallon, P., Katzman, M., & Wooley, S. C. (1994). *Feminist perspectives on eating disorders.* New York: Guilford Press.

Fisher, P. W., Shaffer, D., Piacentini, J. C., Lapkin, J., Kafantaris, V., Leonard, H., & Herzog, D. (1993). Sensitivity of the Diagnostic Interview Schedule for Children, 2nd edition (DISC-2.1) for specific diagnoses of children and adolescents. *Journal of the American Academy of Child and Adolescent Psychiatry, 32,* 666–673.

Fluoxetine Bulimia Nervosa Collaborative Study Group. (1992). Fluoxetine in the treatment of bulimia nervosa. *Archives of General Psychiatry, 49,* 139–147.

Franko, D. L., & Walton, B. E. (1993). Pregnancy and eating disorders: A review and clinical implications. *International Journal of Eating Disorders, 13,* 41–48.

Freeman, C. P. L., & Munro, J. K. M. (1988). Drug and group treatments for bulimia nervosa. *Journal of Psychosomatic Research, 32,* 647–660.

Freeman, R. J., Beach, B., Davis, R., & Solyom, L. (1985). The prediction of relapse in bulimia nervosa. *Journal of Psychiatric Research, 19,* 349–353.

Garner, D. M. (1991). *Eating Disorders Inventory: 2. Professional manual.* Odessa, FL: Psychological Assessment Resources.

Garner, D. M., & Bemis, K. M. (1982). A cognitive-behavioral approach to anorexia nervosa. *Cognitive Therapy and Research, 6,* 123–150.

Garner, D. M., Fairburn, C. G., & Davis, R. (1987). Cognitive-behavioral treatment of bulimia nervosa: A critical appraisal. *Behavior Modification, 11,* 398–431.

Garner, D. M., Garfinkel, P. E., Schwartz, D., & Thompson, M. (1980). Cultural expectations of thinness in women. *Psychological Reports, 47,* 483–491.

Garner, D. M., Olmsted, M. P., Bohr, Y., & Garfinkel, P. E. (1982). The Eating Attitudes Test: Psychometric features and clinical correlates. *Psychological Medicine, 12,* 871–878.

Gillberg, I. C., Rastam, M., & Gillberg, C. (1994). Anorexia nervosa outcome: Six-year controlled longitudinal study of 51 cases including a population cohort. *Journal of the American Academy of Child and Adolescent Psychiatry, 33,* 729–739.

Gormally, J., Black, S., Daston, S., & Rardin, D. (1982). The assessment of binge eating severity among obese persons. *Addictive Behaviors, 7,* 47–55.

Gray, J. J., Ford, K., & Kelly, L. M. (1987). The prevalence of bulimia in a black college population. *International Journal of Eating Disorders, 6,* 733–740.

Herzog, D. B., Keller, M. B., Strober, M., Yeh, C., & Pai, S. Y. (1992). The current status of treatment for anorexia nervosa and bulimia nervosa. *International Journal of Eating Disorders, 12,* 215–220.

Herzog, D. B., Sacks, N. R., Keller, M. B., Lavori, P. W., von Ranson, K. B., & Gray, H. M. (1993). Patterns and predictors of recovery in anorexia nervosa and bulimia nervosa. *Journal of the American Academy of Child and Adolescent Psychiatry, 32,* 835–842.

Hindler, C. G., Crisp, A. H., McGuigan, S., & Joughin, N. (1994). Anorexia nervosa: Change over time in age of onset, presentation and duration of illness. *Psychological Medicine, 24,* 719–729.

Hinz, L. D., & Williamson, D. A. (1987). Bulimia and depression: A review of the affective variant hypothesis. *Psychological Bulletin, 102,* 150–158.

Hsu, L. K. G. (1986). The treatment of anorexia nervosa. *American Journal of Psychiatry, 143,* 573–581.

Huon, G. F. (1994). Towards the prevention of dieting-induced disorders: Modifying negative food-and-body-related attitudes. *International Journal of Eating Disorders, 16,* 395–399.

Jacobs, M. B., & Schneider, J. A. (1985). Medical complications of bulimia: A prospective evaluation. *Quarterly Journal of Medicine, 54,* 177–182.

Kaplan, A. S., & Woodside, D. B. (1987). Biological aspects of anorexia nervosa and bulimia nervosa. *Journal of Consulting and Clinical Psychology, 55,* 645–653.

Kassett, J. A., Gershon, E. S., & Maxwell, M. E. (1989). Psychiatric disorders in the first-degree relatives of probands with bulimia nervosa. *American Journal of Psychiatry, 146,* 1468–1471.

Katzman, M. (1995). Managed care: A feminist appraisal. *The Renfrew Perspective, 1,* 1, 9.

Kaye, W. H., Enright, A. B., & Lesser, B. A. (1988). Characteristics of eating disorders programs and common problems with third-party providers. *International Journal of Eating Disorders, 7,* 573–579.

Kendler, K. S., MacLean, C., Neale, M., Kessler, R., Heath, A., & Eaves, L. (1991). The genetic epidemiology of bulimia nervosa. *American Journal of Psychiatry, 148,* 1627–1637.

Kettlewell, P. W., Mizes, J. S., & Wasylyshyn, N. (1992). A cognitive behavioral group treatment of bulimia. *Behavior Therapy, 23,* 657–670.

Killen, J. D., Hayward, C., Wilson, D. M., Taylor, C. B., Hammer, L. D., Litt, I., Simmonds, B., & Haydel, F. (1994). Factors associated with eating disorder symptoms in a community sample of 6th and 7th grade girls. *International Journal of Eating Disorders, 15,* 357–367.

Killen, J. D., Taylor, C. B., Hammer, L. D., Litt, I., Wilson, D. M., Rich, T., Hayward, C., Simmonds, B., Kraemer, H., & Varady, A. (1993). An attempt to modify unhealthful eating attitudes and weight regulation practices of young adolescent girls. *International Journal of Eating Disorders, 13,* 369–384.

King, M. B. (1989). Eating disorders in a general practice population: Prevalence, characteristics and follow-up at 12 to 18 months. *Psychological Medicine, 14*(Monograph suppl.), 1–34.

Klesges, R. C., Mizes, J. S., & Klesges, L. M. (1987). Self-help dieting strategies in college males and females. *International Journal of Eating Disorders, 6,* 409–417.

Kutcher, S. P., Whitehouse, A. M., & Freeman, C. P. (1985). "Hidden" eating disorders in Scottish psychiatric inpatients. *American Journal of Psychiatry, 142,* 1475–1478.

Lacey, J. H. (1992). A comparative study of menarcheal age and weight of bulimic patients and their sisters. *International Journal of Eating Disorders, 12,* 307–311.

Lawrence, C. M., & Thelen, M. H. (1995). Body image, dieting, and self-concept: Their relation in African-American and Caucasian children. *Journal of Clinical Child Psychology, 24,* 41–48.

le Grange, D. (1993). Family therapy outcome in adolescent anorexia nervosa. *South African Journal of Psychology, 23,* 174–179.

le Grange, D., Eisler, I., Dare, C., & Russell, G. F. M. (1992). Evaluation of family treatments in adolescent anorexia nervosa: A pilot study. *International Journal of Eating Disorders, 12,* 347–357.

Leitenberg, H., Rosen, J. C., Wolf, J., Vara, L. S., Detzer, M. J., & Srebnik, D. (1993). Comparison of cognitive-behavior therapy and desipramine in the treatment of bulimia nervosa. *Behaviour Research and Therapy, 32,* 37–45.

Levine, M. P., Smolak, L., Moodey, A., Shuman, M. D., & Hessen, L. D. (1994). Normative developmental challenges and dieting and eating disturbance in middle school girls. *International Journal of Eating Disorders, 15,* 11–20.

Maloney, M., McGuire, J., Daniels, S., Specker, B., Smolak, L., Levine, M. P., & Gralen, S. (1993). The impact of puberty and dating on eating problems among middle school girls. *Journal of Youth and Adolescence, 22,* 355–368.

McKenzie, J. M., & Joyce, P. R. (1992). Hospitalization for anorexia nervosa. *International Journal of Eating Disorders, 11,* 235–242.

Mitchell, J. E., Pyle, R. L., Hatsukami, D., & Eckert, E. D. (1986). What are atypical eating disorders? *Psychosomatics, 27,* 21–28.

Mitchell, J. E., Raymond, N., & Specker, S. (1993). A review of the controlled trials of pharmacotherapy and psychotherapy in the treatment of bulimia nervosa. *International Journal of Eating Disorders, 14,* 229–247.

Mitchell, J. E., Seim, H. C., Glotter, D., Soll, E. A., & Pyle, R. L. (1991). A retrospective study of pregnancy in bulimia nervosa. *International Journal of Eating Disorders, 10,* 209–214.

Mitchell, J. E., Specker, S. M., & de Zwaan, M. (1991). Comorbidity and medical complications of bulimia nervosa. *Journal of Clinical Psychiatry, 52*(10, Suppl.), 13–20.

Mizes, J. S. (1988). Personality characteristics of bulimic and non-eating-disordered female controls: A cognitive behavioral perspective. *International Journal of Eating Disorders, 7,* 541–550.

Mizes, J. S. (1991). Validity of the Body Image Detection Device. *Addictive Behaviors, 16,* 411–417.

Mizes, J. S. (1992a). The Body Image Detection Device versus subjective measures of weight dissatisfaction: A validity comparison. *Addictive Behaviors, 17,* 125–136.

Mizes, J. S. (1992b). Validity of the Mizes Anorectic Cognitions Scale: A comparison between anorectics, bulimics, and psychiatric controls. *Addictive Behaviors, 17,* 283–289.

Mizes, J. S., & Arbitell, M. R. (1991). Bulimics' perceptions of emotional responding during binge-purge episodes. *Psychological Reports, 69,* 527–532.

Mizes, J. S., & Klesges, R. C. (1989). Validity, reliability, and factor structure of the Mizes Anorectic Cognitions Questionnaire. *Addictive Behaviors, 14,* 589–594.

Moreno, A. B., & Thelen, M. H. (1993). A preliminary prevention program for eating disorders in a junior high school population. *Journal of Youth and Adolescence, 22,* 109–124.

Murray, S., Touyz, S., & Beumont, P. (1990). Knowledge about eating disorders in the community. *International Journal of Eating Disorders, 9,* 87–94.

Nemeroff, C. J., Stein, R. I., Diehl, N. S., & Smilack, K. M. (1994). From the Cleavers to the Clintons: Role choices and body orientation as reflected in magazine article content. *International Journal of Eating Disorders, 16,* 167–176.

Noden, M. (1994). Dying to win (anorexia nervosa). *Sports Illustrated, 81,* 52–58.

Norring, C. E. A., & Sohlberg, S. S. (1993). Outcome, recovery, relapse, and mortality across six years in patients with clinical eating disorders. *Acta Psychiatrica Scandinavia, 87,* 437–444.

Offman, H. J., & Bradley, S. J. (1992). Body image of children and adolescents and its measurement: An overview. *Canadian Journal of Psychiatry, 37,* 417–422.

Ohtahara, H., Ohzeki, T., Hanaki, K., Motozumi, H., & Shiraki, K. (1993). Abnormal perception of body weight is not solely observed in pubertal girls: Incorrect body image in children and its relationship to body weight. *Acta Psychiatrica Scandinavia, 87,* 218–222.

Pagsberg, A. K., & Wang, A. R. (1994). Epidemiology of anorexia nervosa and bulimia nervosa in Bornholm County, Denmark, 1970–1989. *Acta Psychiatrica Scandinavia, 90,* 259–265.

Patton, G. C. (1988). The spectrum of eating disorders in adolescence. *Journal of Psychosomatic Research, 32,* 579–584.

Phelps, L., Andrea, R., Rizzo, F. G., Johnston, L., & Main, C. M. (1993). Prevalence of self-induced vomiting and laxative/medication abuse among female adolescents: A longitudinal study. *International Journal of Eating Disorders, 14,* 375–378.

Philipp, E., Willershausen-Zonnchen, B., Hamm, G., & Pirke, K. M. (1991). Oral and dental characteristics in bulimic and anorectic patients. *International Journal of Eating Disorders, 10,* 423–432.

Rathner, G., & Messner, K. (1993). Detection of eating disorders in a small rural town: An epidemiological study. *Psychological Medicine, 23,* 175–184.

Robin, A. L., Siegel, P. T., & Moye, A. (1995). Family versus individual therapy for anorexia: Impact on family conflict. *International Journal of Eating Disorders, 17,* 313–322.

Rosen, J. C. (1987). A review of behavioral treatments for bulimia nervosa. *Behavior Modification, 11,* 464–486.

Rosen, J. C. (1989). Prevention of eating disorders. (1989, April/June). *National Anorexic Aid Society Newsletter,* 1–3.

Rosen, J. C., Leitenberg, H., Fondacaro, K. M., Gross, J., & Willmuth, M. (1985). Standardized test meals in assessment of eating behavior in bulimia nervosa: Consumption of feared foods when vomiting is prevented. *International Journal of Eating Disorders, 4,* 59–70.

Rosen, J. C., Srebnik, D., Saltzberg, E., & Wendt, S. (1991). Development of a body image avoidance questionnaire. *Psychological Assessment: A Journal of Consulting and Clinical Psychology, 3,* 32–37.

Rosen, J. C., Tacy, B., & Howell, D. (1990). Life stress, psychological symptoms and weight reducing behavior in adolescent girls: A prospective analysis. *International Journal of Eating Disorders, 9,* 17–26.

Rossiter, E. M., Agras, W. S., Telch, C. F., & Schneider, J. A. (1993). Cluster B personality disorder characteristics predict outcome in the treatment of bulimia nervosa. *International Journal of Eating Disorders, 13,* 349–357.

Russell, G. F. M., Szmukler, G. I., Dare, C., & Eisler, I. (1987). An evaluation of family therapy in anorexia nervosa and bulimia nervosa. *Archives of General Psychiatry, 44,* 1047–1056.

St. James, E. (1994). *Simplify your life: 100 ways to slow down and enjoy the things that really matter.* New York: Hyperion.

Schmidt, U., Tiller, J., & Treasure, J. (1993). Setting the scene for eating disorders: Childhood care, classification and course of illness. *Psychological Medicine, 23,* 663–672.

Schork, E. J., Eckert, E. D., & Halmi, K. A. (1994). The relationship between psychopathology, eating disorder diagnosis, and clinical outcome at 10-year follow-up in anorexia nervosa. *Comprehensive Psychiatry, 35,* 113–123.

Schulman, R. G., Kinder, B. N., Powers, P. S., Prange, M., & Gleghorn, A. (1986). The development of a scale to measure cognitive distortions in bulimia. *Journal of Personality Assessment, 50,* 630–639.

Shatford, L. A., & Evans, D. R. (1986). Bulimia as a manifestation of the stress process: A LISREL causal modeling analysis. *International Journal of Eating Disorders, 5,* 451–473.

Shiffman, S., Read, L., Maltese, J., Rapkin, D., & Jarvik, M. E. (1985). Preventing relapse in ex-smokers. In *Relapse prevention* (pp. 475–520). New York: Guilford Press.

Shisslak, C. M., Crago, M., & Neal, M. E. (1990). Prevention of eating disorders among adolescents. *American Journal of Health Promotion, 5,* 100–106.

Shugar, G., & Krueger, S. (1995). Aggressive family communication, weight gain, and improved eating attitudes during systemic family therapy for anorexia nervosa. *International Journal of Eating Disorders, 17,* 23–31.

Sloan, G., & Leichner, P. (1986). Is there a relationship between sexual abuse or incest and eating disorders? *Canadian Journal of Psychiatry, 31,* 656–660.

Smith, C., Feldman, S. S., Nasserbakht, A., & Steiner, H. (1993). Psychological characteristics and DSM-III-R diagnoses at 6-year follow-up of adolescent anorexia nervosa. *Journal of the American Academy of Child and Adolescent Psychiatry, 32,* 1237–1245.

Smolak, L., Levine, M. P., & Gralen, S. (1993). The impact of puberty and dating on eating problems among middle school girls. *Journal of Youth and Adolescence, 22,* 355–368.

Stein, D., & Brinza, S. R. (1989). Bulimia: Prevalence estimates in female junior high and high school students. *Journal of Clinical Child Psychology, 18,* 206–213.

Steinhausen, H., Rauss-Mason, C., & Seidel, R. (1991). Follow-up studies of anorexia nervosa: A review of four decades of outcome research. *Psychological Medicine, 21,* 447–454.

Steinhausen, H., & Seidel, R. (1993). Outcome in adolescent eating disorders. *International Journal of Eating Disorders, 14,* 487–496.

Stice, E., Schupak-Neuberg, E., Shaw, H. E., & Stein, R. I. (1994). Relation of media exposure to eating disorder symptomatology: An examination of mediating mechanisms. *Journal of Abnormal Psychology, 103,* 836–840.

Striegel-Moore, R. H., & Huydic, E. S. (1993). Problem drinking and symptoms of disordered eating in female high school students. *International Journal of Eating Disorders, 14,* 417–425.

Striegel-Moore, R. H., Nicholson, J., & Tamborlane, W. V. (1992). Prevalence of eating disorder symptoms in preadolescent and adolescent girls with IDDM. *Diabetes Care, 15,* 1361–1368.

Striegel-Moore, R. H., & Silberstein, L. R. (1989). Early identification of bulimia nervosa. In W. G. Johnson (Ed.), *Advances in eating disorders* (Vol. 2, pp. 267–281). Greenwich, CT: JAI Press.

Striegel-Moore, R. H., Silberstein, L. R., Frensch, P., & Rodin, J. (1989). A prospective study of disordered eating among college students. *International Journal of Eating Disorders, 8,* 499–509.

Striegel-Moore, R. H., Silberstein, L. R., & Rodin, J. (1986). Toward an understanding of risk factors for bulimia. *American Psychologist, 41,* 246–263.

Strober, M. (1991). Family-genetic studies of eating disorders. *Journal of Clinical Psychiatry, 52*(10, Suppl.), 9–12.

Strober, M., & Humphrey, L. L. (1987). Familial contributions to the etiology and course of anorexia nervosa and bulimia. *Journal of Consulting and Clinical Psychology, 55,* 654–659.

Sullivan, P. F. (1995). Mortality in anorexia nervosa. *American Journal of Psychiatry, 152,* 1073–1074.

Swift, W. J., Andrews, D., & Barklage, N. E. (1986). The relationship between Affective Disorder and eating disorders: A review of the literature. *American Journal of Psychiatry, 143,* 290–297.

Szmukler, G. I. (1985). The epidemiology of anorexia nervosa and bulimia. *Journal of Psychiatric Research, 19,* 143–153.

Taylor, A. V., Peveler, R. C., Hibbert, G. A., & Fairburn, C. G. (1993). Eating disorders among women receiving treatment for an alcohol problem. *International Journal of Eating Disorders, 14,* 147–151.

Theander, S. (1985). Outcome and prognosis in anorexia nervosa and bulimia: Some results of previous investigations, compared with those of a Swedish long-term study. *Journal of Psychiatric Research, 19,* 493–508.

Thelen, M., Lawrence, C. M., & Powell, A. (1992). Body image, weight control, and eating disorders among children. In J. H. Crowther, D. L. Tennebaum, S. E. Hobfoll, & M. A. P. Stephens (Eds.), *The etiology of bulimia nervosa: The individual and familial context* (pp. 82–102). Washington, DC: Hemisphere.

Thiel, A., Broocks, A., Ohlmeier, M., Jacoby, G. E., & Schufler, G. (1995). Obsessive-Compulsive Disorder among patients with anorexia nervosa and bulimia nervosa. *American Journal of Psychiatry, 152,* 72–75.

Thompson, J. K., Fabian, L. J., Moulton, D. O., Dunn, M. F., & Altabe, M. N. (1991). Development and validation of the physical appearance related teasing scale. *Journal of Personality Assessment, 56,* 513–521.

Tiller, J., Macrae, A., Schmidt, U., Bloom, S., & Treasure, J. (1994). The prevalence of eating disorders in thyroid disease: A pilot study. *Journal of Psychosomatic Research, 38,* 609–616.

van der Ster Walling, G., Norring, C., & Holmgren, S. (1994). Binge eating versus nonpurged eating in bulimics: Is there a carbohydrate craving after all? *Acta Psychiatrica Scandinavia, 89,* 376–381.

Veron-Guidry, S., Williamson, D. A., & Netemeyer, R. G. (1994, November). *Measurement of body image and eating concerns in third through seventh graders.* Poster presented at the Association for the Advancement of Behavior Therapy, San Diego.

Waller, G. (1994). Childhood sexual abuse and borderline personality disorder in the eating disorders. *Child Abuse & Neglect, 18,* 97–101.

Walsh, B. T., Hadigan, C. M., Devlin, M. J., Gladis, M., & Roose, S. P. (1991). Long-term outcome of antidepressant treatment for bulimia nervosa. *American Journal of Psychiatry, 148,* 1206–1212.

Whitaker, A., Davies, M., Shaffer, D., Johnson, J., Abrams, S., Walsh, B. T., & Kalokow, K. (1989). The struggle to be thin: A survey of anorexic and bulimic symptoms in a nonreferred adolescent population. *Psychological Medicine, 19,* 143–163.

Willi, J., Giacometti, G., & Limacher, B. (1990). Update on the epidemiology of anorexia nervosa in a defined region of Switzerland. *American Journal of Psychiatry, 147,* 1514–1517.

Williamson, D. A. (1990). *Assessment of eating disorders: Obesity, anorexia, and bulimia nervosa.* New York: Pergamon Press.

Williamson, D. A., Kelley, M. L., Davis, C. J., Ruggerio, L., & Blouin, D. C. (1985). Psychopathology of eating disorders: A controlled comparison of bulimic, obese, and normal subjects. *Journal of Consulting and Clinical Psychology, 53,* 161–166.

Wilson, G. T., & Walsh, B. T. (1991). Eating disorders in the DSM-IV. *Journal of Abnormal Psychology, 100,* 362–365.

Wolf, N. (1991). *The beauty myth: How images of beauty are used against women.* New York: Morrow.

Wonderlich, S., Ukestad, L., & Perzacki, R. (1994). Perceptions of nonshared childhood environment in bulimia nervosa. *Journal of the American Academy of Child and Adolescent Psychiatry, 33,* 740–747.

Wooley, S. C. (1993). Managed care and mental health: The silencing of a profession. *International Journal of Eating Disorders, 14,* 387–401.

Yager, J. (1994). Psychosocial treatments for eating disorders. *Psychiatry, 57,* 153–164.

Yates, A. (1990). Current perspectives on the eating disorders: 2. Treatment, outcome, and research directions. *Journal of the American Academy of Child and Adolescent Psychiatry, 29,* 1–9.

CHAPTER 23

Substance-Related Disorders

JOSEPH WESTERMEYER

Description of the Disorders

Diagnostic Criteria

Diagnoses of substance-related disorders in the fourth edition of the *Diagnostic and Statistical Manual of Mental Disorders* (*DSM-IV;* American Psychiatric Association, 1994) and ICD-10 are the same for children and adults. The *DSM-IV* criteria for substance abuse involve a maladaptive pattern of use leading to clinically significant impairment or distress manifested by one or more of the following over a 12-month period: failure to fulfill major role obligations at work, school, or home; use in situations where it is physically hazardous; legal problems; and social or interpersonal problems. *DSM-IV* criteria for substance dependence include a maladaptive pattern of use leading to clinically significant impairment or distress manifested by three or more of the following over a 12-month period: tolerance (i.e., need for more or diminished effect from same dose); withdrawal (i.e., characteristic syndrome or use of substance to relieve symptoms); use of larger amounts or longer use than intended; persistent desire or unsuccessful attempts to reduce or control use; much time spent obtaining, using, or recovering from effects of substance; important social, occupational, or recreational activities given up or reduced because of substance use; and persistent use despite exacerbation of physical or psychological problems. ICD-10 uses the term "harmful use" rather than "abuse." The ICD-10 category for "dependence" overlaps considerably with the *DSM-IV* criteria (collapsing a few of the preceding items into single categories and adding the category of "craving-compulsive use").

Types of Drug Use and Patterns of Abuse

Alcohol has been the most commonly used and abused substance among American adolescents in recent decades. Cannabis has been the next most commonly used and abused substance; about 75%–85% of adolescent substance abusers have reported cannabis use. Cocaine use has increased dramatically among adolescent substance abusers in recent years. Although opiate dependence is infrequent among adolescents, opiate use has occurred in 10%–20% of this population (Klinge & Vaziri, 1977; Patterson, Myers, & Gallant, 1988; Westermeyer, Specker, Neider, & Lingenfelter, 1994). Substance use and abuse among 100 of the author's patients (Westermeyer et al., 1994), aged 13 to 18, are shown in Table 23.1.

Table 23.1   Rates of Substance Use and Abuse among Adolescents

Type of Substance	Lifetime Use (%)	Current Diagnosis (%)	Ratio of Use/Diagnosis
Alcohol	100	72	1.4
Cannabis	91	45	2.0
Tobacco*	88	0	—
Amphetamine	70	10	7.0
Hallucinogens	51	5	10.2
Cocaine	44	9	4.9
Inhalants*	40	—	—
Mixed*	—	32	—
Sedatives	32	1	32.0
Opiates	24	2	12.0
PCP	11	—	> 11

* See text discussion of this substance.

This table indicates that the most commonly used substances among adolescents are also the most abused substances (i.e., a direct correlation between rates of use and abuse). Cocaine and opiates both have ratios that are less than half those of those substances just above them, suggesting that these substances are more prone to abuse among adolescents. Tobacco dependence was not diagnosed in this group due to the unusual criteria for this diagnosis (i.e., dependence + biomedical consequences + recommendation by a physician to cease use + failure to be able to cease use). Inhalant diagnoses were not assessed separately since such diagnoses are included under "mixed" substance use. "Mixed" diagnoses are made when use of any one substance cannot be considered excessive, but combined use leads to substance-related consequences. Although anabolic steroid use is not included in this list, this form of substance use can also produce psychosocial, psychiatric, and medical complications (Clancy & Yates, 1992).

Volatile inhalant use and abuse have occurred more frequently among children and adolescents than among adults—a pattern opposite to that of most substances. Several factors probably account for this particular pattern: their virtual universal presence in the home, school, and community; their low cost; their availability in nearby stores (grocery stores, hardware stores, gas stations); the ease and rapidity of administration; the short-lived nature of acute intoxicant effects and absence of strong, characteristic odors (reducing the likelihood of detection). Use may vary from brief experimentation on one or a few occasions, to daily administration throughout the day over years. Inhalant abuse may also occur among adults, especially those who have used these substances during childhood; circumstances associated with later adult use include the military, certain office and industrial settings, jail or prison, and use as "emergency" intoxicants when unemployed (Levy & Pierce, 1989; Miller & Gold, 1990; Oetting, Edwards, & Beauvais, 1988; Schwartz, 1988; Westermeyer, 1987).

Course

Adolescents coming to treatment for a substance-related disorder (SRD) differ from those first coming as adults to SRD treatment in two ways. First, those adolescents tend to have begun using licit and illicit psychoactive substances at an earlier age than those coming to treatment as adults. Usually, adolescent patients have begun use during later childhood or early adolescence, whereas adult patients have generally begun use during mid or later adolescence (Smart, 1979). Second, adolescents with SRD also have had shorter duration of heavy and/or problematic substance use at the time of presenting to treatment (i.e., a more rapid course), compared with adults. Adolescents enter treatment relatively soon after beginning heavy use (i.e., within a few to several years) no matter at what age substance use is initiated (Smart, 1979; Westermeyer et al., 1994), whereas adults have typically been abusing substances for several to a dozen years before their first treatment episode. These findings suggest that SRD beginning at an early age tends to undermine coping skills and precipitate crises, compared with SRD beginning later in life.

The postadolescent course of SRD is not as benign as was hoped a decade ago. Since adolescents come to treatment earlier, some clinicians believe that adolescent SRD might be merely a "developmental phase," or at least not presage SRD in adulthood. To assess the course of adolescent-onset substance abuse, several longitudinal studies have been conducted. These studies have revealed the following patterns of continuing and exacerbating problems among adolescents:

- Persistence (rather than amelioration) of problematic drinking patterns with increasing age (White, 1987).
- Persistence of heavy cannabis use with increasing age (Haas, 1987).
- Increased use of cocaine, but not other substances, with age (Reveis & Kandel, 1987).
- Later postadolescent onset of health problems during young adulthood (Newcomb & Bentler, 1987).

Frequency of substance use has often been considered low among adolescents. Although this may be true for those coming to SRD treatment as adults, it has not been true of adolescents with SRD. In one study of adolescents with SRD, younger adolescents used substances just as many days in the previous year as older adolescents, with younger adolescents using some substances even more frequently than older adolescents (Westermeyer et al., 1994). The authors compared days of use during the previous year between 100 adolescents and 200 young adults in their 20s for commonly used substances (using only those substances being abused by the patient in the preceding year, plus tobacco).

Table 23.2 shows that adults used four of the five drugs more days per year, on average, compared with the adolescents. However, only one of these substances—alcohol—showed a significantly greater frequency of use among adults. Adolescents showed significantly more amphetamine use in the previous year compared with adults.

Clinical Manifestations

The manifestations of SRD among adolescents are qualitatively similar to those experienced by older persons. The following symptoms were reported by 99 adolescents in treatment for SRD (Westermeyer et al., 1994): using to relieve psychological

Table 23.2   **Frequency of Substance Use in Adolescents and Adults**

Substance	Adolescents: n, mean days (sd)	Adults: n, mean days (sd)	Stat. Signif.
Alcohol	84 ss, 89 days (85)	166 ss, 131 days (113)	$p < .005$
Cannabis	70 ss, 126 days (137)	162 ss, 162 days (117)	ns
Amphetamine	43 ss, 68 days (117)	119 ss, 28 days (67)	$p < .01$
Cocaine	37 ss, 27 days (60)	120 ss, 39 days (81)	ns
Tobacco	88 ss, 299 days (124)	172 ss, 310 days (119)	ns

symptoms—83%; previous attempts at controlling use—75%; increased tolerance—70%; amnesia ("blackout")—69%; using alone—68%; ashamed or guilty regarding use—67%; morning use—66%; secretive use—66%; needs substance to relax or enjoy—64%; craving (strong frequent desire to use)—61%; keeps a hidden supply—59%; preoccupied with use—56%; occasional loss of control over use (uses higher doses or for a longer time than intended < 50% of use occasions)—55%; decreased tolerance—53%; rapid or "priming" use—52%; suspicious, mistrustful in association with use—52%; using at school or job—51%; self-pity—50%; unreasonable resentments—50%; suicidal ideas—46%; using to relieve physical symptoms—45%; using to feel normal—43%; late for appointments—42%; panic attacks—35%; regular loss of control over use (≥ 50% of use occasions)—32%; nightmares—32%; harassing or disturbing others via telephone—28%; night terrors—20%; using "emergency" intoxicants (e.g., vanilla extract, rubbing alcohol)—17%. Thus, these adolescents reported the same types of SRD-related symptoms and experiences as those reported by adults.

Severity

Conventional wisdom among some psychiatrists holds that adolescents may misuse psychoactive substances, but rarely manifest substance abuse and certainly not substance dependence (Carter & Robson, 1987; Peele, 1987; Seligman, 1986). Other reports suggest that adolescents may actually have a more malignant form of disorder, such as the "Type II alcoholism" described by Cloninger and others (Czechowicz, 1988; Von Knorring, Oreland, & Von Knorring, 1987). In one study of SRD severity, 83 SRD patients aged 17 to 20 completed the self-rated Modified Michigan Alcohol-Drug Screening Test (Westermeyer & Neider, 1988). Their average score was 21.2 (standard deviation 12.7)—a score well into the pathological range (normal is 0 to 5, borderline is 6 to 8, with scores 9 and above in the abnormal range). Within this sample of 83 older adolescents, there was a borderline trend for older patients to report greater severity of substance disorder ($r = .17$, $p = .06$) (Westermeyer et al., 1994).

Type and Number of Substance Disorder Diagnoses

Despite considerable overlap between adolescent and adult patients, adolescents with SRD appear apt to have relatively more substance abuse and less substance dependence, compared with older patients. For example, among 100 of the author's adolescent patients, 58% had substance abuse only, 42% had one or more substance dependence diagnoses. By contrast, among 200 young adults in their twenties, 33.5% had abuse diagnoses only, and 66.5% had one or more substance dependence diagnoses. This difference was statistically significant at $p < .001$ (chi-square = 15.47).

EPIDEMIOLOGY

The Pandemic of Substance Use among Youth

Cameron (1968) wrote his seminal article on the substance abuse pandemic among the young almost three decades ago, although Heilbrunn had written a brief commentary in the previous year (Heilbrunn, 1967). Prior to that time, adolescent substance abuse had occurred only sporadically. Since 1970, scores of articles on adolescent substance use and abuse have appeared. A large percentage of these reports are based on anecdotal clinical cases and subjective clinical experience bolstered by literature reviews (Amini, Salasnek, & Burke, 1976; Baumrind & Moselle, 1985; Bean, 1982; Bernstein, 1984; Blum, 1987; Coupey & Schonberg, 1982; Czechowicz, 1988; Easson, 1976; Griffin, 1981; Hennecke & Gitlow, 1983; MacDonald & Newton, 1981; MacKenzie, 1982; Masland, 1972; Niven, 1986; Rosenberg, 1971, 1972; Solow & Solow, 1986; Wells, 1985). Beginning in the early 1980s, almost 15 years after the initial clinical reports, reports appeared on drug use (but not diagnosed abuse) in a variety of adolescent groups, including students, "street" youth, and incarcerated adolescents (Anderson, 1984; Dias & Polvora, 1983; Kandel, 1982; Keyes & Block, 1984; McKirnan & Johnson, 1986; McLaughlin, Baer, Burnside, & Pokorny, 1985; Smart & Adlaf, 1991). Treatment outcome and comorbidity studies of adolescents with substance use disorders exist but tend to be few in number (Kashani, Keller, & Solomon, 1985; Smart, 1979).

Surveys of Drug Use

An abundance of surveys regarding childhood and adolescent drug use have appeared over the past few decades. One federally funded school-based survey has been repeated over the years. Although these surveys have provided a useful picture of child and adolescent drug use, they have not always agreed with clinical and mortality studies. For example, surveys have shown decreases in use at the same time that clinical events and mortality rates have persisted and even increased. It is likely that survey populations themselves have changed over time as more deviant or less able students have left school, perhaps leaving a newly biased, low drug-using group behind.

Despite these limitations in sampling methods, the surveys still provide much valuable information. For example, two research teams have noted increased cocaine use with age in the adolescent population (Johnson, O'Malley, & Bachman, 1987; Newcomb & Bentler, 1986). Although cannabis, PCP, and heroin use had been falling, use of these drugs appears to be increasing among youth in some areas. If a fall in general use is a harbinger of eventual decrease in SRD, the youth pandemic is not even close to a resolution.

Clinical Epidemiology

The male-to-female ratio among adolescents with SRD is more nearly one-to-one than it is among adults (among whom it tends toward one-to-three and higher). It is difficult to ascertain a precise gender ratio, however, in view of the difficulty in ascertaining a true population-based rate. In the author's treatment program, the adolescent SRD ratio has been around 1.4 males to 1 female.

Young males with SRD are more apt to appear in jails, courts, residential facilities, or the morgue (through violent death). Young females with SRD are more apt to be run-aways, illegitimately pregnant, or hospitalized on psychiatric wards. Traditionally, fe-males with SRD have been more apt to use licit drugs (e.g., alcohol, tobacco) and safer routes of administration (i.e., avoiding intravenous use)—although this may be chang-ing in some quarters, especially as large numbers of young women have become in-volved with cocaine use.

In clinical settings serving children and adolescents, the number of patients in-creases with age. Cases aged 13 and below have continued to be sporadic. In one series of consecutive adolescent patients (Westermeyer et al., 1994), the mean number of pa-tients per year of age was as follows: aged 14 to 16: 5.7 patients; aged 17 and 18 years: 14.5 patients; and 19 and 20 years: 27 patients. These data indicated a doubling (or more) of patients from the age group 14–16 years to the age group 17–18 years, and then another doubling of patients from the age group 17–18 years to the age group 19–20 years. (After age 19 until age 27, the number of patients per year of age re-mained stable.) These clinical data suggest a notable increase in clinical cases from early to middle adolescence, with another notable increase from middle to late adoles-cence, but with a leveling off in clinical prevalence from late adolescence to early adulthood.

Use of Indicators to Assess Rates

Many of the epidemiological indicators of SRD in adults occur too infrequently among adolescents to be of value (e.g., death by cirrhosis of the liver). Some indicators, such as suicide, may be related to various other factors besides SRD (such as mood and anx-iety disorders, availability of lethal means for committing suicide), thereby limiting its utility as an indicator. Still, attempts have been made to relate various indicators to substance use or abuse among adolescents. One of these has been the relationship of certain kinds of music to substance use, but not to SRD (Dent et al., 1992).

Psychiatric Comorbidity

Virtually any psychiatric disorder that occurs during adolescence can accompany SRD in the adolescent patient. Conduct disorder occurs often, especially among adolescent males who are in difficulty with the law, such as sex offenders (Kavoussi, Kaplan, & Becker, 1988). Conduct disorder may not be so frequent in other settings (Westermeyer et al., 1994). Perhaps most common is major depression and other forms of mood disor-der, which have been widely reported (Kashani et al., 1985). Eating disorders are espe-cially prevalent among older teenage females, in whom SRD often postdates the eating disorder (Katz, 1990). The opposite sequence prevails among males with combined SRD and eating disorder. Mental retardation, usually mild in degree, has become more frequent in the past decade or two (Westermeyer, Phaobtong, & Neider, 1988). Some of the latter cases were probably fetal alcohol effect from maternal drinking during preg-nancy, and several were acquired either through chronic inhalant abuse (younger onset, during childhood) or through alcohol- or drug-related violence, especially motorcycle and car accidents (later onset, during middle and late adolescence). Suicide must be carefully assessed in adolescent SRD patients in general (Runeson, 1990), but especially in those with comorbid conditions.

CAUSES AND CONSEQUENCES

Causes of SRD in Adolescents

Family History of Substance Disorder

Alcohol and drug abuse among adolescents has been associated with several family factors including the following:

- Family history of psychiatric and substance disorders (Schuckit & Chiles, 1978).
- Parental use of substances and parental attitude toward their adolescents' substance use (McDermott, 1984; Smart & Fejer, 1972).
- General family disruption and chaos (Burnside, Baer, McLaughlin, & Pokorny, 1986).

A study of 100 adolescent patients with SRD (Westermeyer et al., 1994) revealed that 10% of them were adopted—notably more than the expected 0.5% in that particular population. Those subjects whose mother had a SRD came to treatment with SRD significantly younger than those whose mother did not have a SRD ($p < .02$). Likewise, those subjects whose fathers had a SRD came to treatment for SRD significantly younger compared with those whose father did not have a SRD ($p < .01$). However among the 90 nonadopted patients, rate of SRD in first- and second-degree relatives was comparable to that reported in the literature for adults (i.e., mother—21%; father—36%; any sibling—38%; any grandparent—37%; and any aunt or uncle—32%).

Socioeconomic Status

The literature regarding socioeconomic status (SES) and adolescent SRD is confusing. On one hand, poverty and lack of opportunity have been posited as causes of adolescent substance abuse. However, disposable income and too many choices have also been suggested as causes (Newcomb & Bentler, 1986). Studies on this topic have been complicated by the skewing effect of virtually all sampling methods on SES. Perhaps higher SES acts to delay the onset of SRD, or to protect the adolescent from the consequences of SRD, or to lead to crisis and treatment at an earlier point in its course. At this time, it appears that neither high, middle, or low SES confers any notable degree of immunity against adolescent SRD.

Use of "Gateway" Drugs

Kandel's theory of gateway drugs (Kandel, Davies, Karus, & Yamaguchi, 1986) suggests that early use of licit substances (e.g., alcohol, tobacco) paves the way to use of "softer" illicit drugs (e.g., cannabis), which in turn conduces to use of "harder" illicit drugs (e.g., heroin, cocaine). It is not clear that Kandel's posited progression holds at all times and in all places (Reuband, 1995). Nonetheless, there is a homey appeal in adolescents' being urged to avoid milder substances so that they will not be "trapped" or "sucked" into SRD. Certainly for those at high risk to SRD, such advice is appropriate.

Peer Influence

The data on peer influence on adolescent SRD bears a similarity to the data on SES. One can find reports stating that peer influence dwarfs family influence, or that family factors ameliorate risk factors associated with peer group drinking (Brook, Whiteman, Gordon, Nomura, & Brook, 1986). It seems likely that factors related to sampling explain these divergent conclusions, although modes of data collection could also play a role. It may be that peer influence waxes if family influence wanes (through parents with active SRD, uninvolved parents, or other factors), and likewise that peer influence dwindles in the presence of a strong, supportive, intact family. In any event, further work will be required to solve this conundrum.

Consequences of SRD in Adolescents

Effects on Normal Development

Haas has suggested that adolescent substance use may foster detachment from the necessary but painful realities that shape normal adolescent development (Haas, 1987). Such substance-facilitated detachment may so impair the adolescent that the necessary and relatively rapid adjustments needed during the several years of adolescence cannot be accomplished. Adolescent substance abuse may also precipitate inordinate, mutually detrimental parent-child discord (Barnes & Windle, 1987). Under optimal circumstances, family members may discern that the adolescent is causing an abnormal and destructive level of discord, leading to more rapid detection by family members than would occur with young adults who are less close to their families of origin. Perceived "loss of control" and "meaninglessness" in the lives of adolescents have also been suggested as causes (Newcomb & Harlow, 1986). Absence of structure and meaningful consequences, especially among adolescents in lower socioeconomic or lower achievement groups, may also be operative (Brook et al., 1986; Newcomb & Bentler, 1986). From positing these theories to achieving successes through their implementation is a long process, and the expense of testing them adequately, as well as lack of resources or will to do so makes it unlikely that we will appreciate the utility of these hypotheses in this generation. Nonetheless, they provide hope for addressing the current, ongoing pandemic.

Criminality

Substance use and abuse can bear various relationships to adolescents' criminal behavior. First, the need for money to purchase alcohol or drugs can lead to property crime, and to crimes against person if assault or threat is employed during property crime (e.g., robbery, mugging). Second, crimes against person may result if the adolescent with SRD is sufficiently disinhibited by substances to act violently. Third, crimes against person and/or property may result if the adolescent with SRD, failing to mature as a result of SRD, employs violent means for dealing with problems. And fourth, SRD and crime may coexist in a given individual without having any causal relationship.

Klinge and Vaziri (1977) studied a large number of adolescent subjects ($n = 143$) in a state-run inpatient setting. They found a correlation between increasing age of adolescent substance abusers and the presence of any legal problems. In another study of 100 adolescents with SRD, the following legal problems were reported: "other" misdemeanor, such as disorderly conduct—17%; property misdemeanor—15%; driving while intoxicated (DWI)—11%; personal misdemeanor—9%; liquor-drug felony—4%; property felony—4%; personal felony—4% (Westermeyer et al., 1994). These latter data revealed only a borderline correlation between age and the presence of a legal problem (i.e., $p = .09$). In addition, these included property and liquor-drug law offenses to obtain the substance, personal crimes and felonies, disorderly charges, and DWI offenses.

Academic-Occupational Problems

For adolescents, school attendance is an occupation. In addition, adolescents often begin working part-time or seasonally at the same time that they are attending school. Later in adolescence, full-time work may displace school. To assess effects of SRD on school and/or work, 100 adolescents with SRD were asked about problems that might occur either at school or work (Westermeyer et al., 1994). Rates of problems associated with substance use among these 100 adolescents were as follows: decreased work productivity and/or academic grades—51%; decreased time spent at work and/or school—49%; confronted by teacher or supervisor regarding substance use—47%; missed promotion and/or graduation to the next grade—22%; and quit or changed job or school—20%. The total number of academic-work problems for each individual bore only a borderline relationship to age ($p = .09$).

Problems with Family and Friends

Among adults, SRD-related problems in the home often predate those in the school and workplace. Thus, it was of interest to study these types of problems in a sample of adolescents (Westermeyer et al., 1994). Problems with family and friends occurred with the following frequencies: confronted by a relative regarding substance use—77%; arguments with family members—64%; most friends have drug problems—60%; arguments with friends—50%; alienated from family members—45%; stealing from family members to obtain psychoactive substances—44%; loss of friends—33%; physical fights with friends—32%; physical fights with family members—25%; permanent separation (including divorce) from family members—10%. The number of family problems per individual bore no correlation to age of the adolescents.

Illegitimate Pregnancy

Illegitimate pregnancy during adolescence is often, but not inevitably associated with SRD (Amaro, Zuckerman, & Cabral, 1989; Gilchrist, Gillmore, & Lohr, 1990; Kokotailo & Adger, 1991). Birth outcomes from adolescent mothers with SRD have led to a high number of damaged children (Deisher, Litchfield, & Hope, 1991). Although efforts have been made to reduce the extent of this problem (Mercer, 1991), it has primarily been a matter to too-little, too-late. Once pregnancy has been established in the SRD adolescent, the clinician now perforce has two patients rather than one. Certain ethical, legal, and practical issues arise. Depending on the state and its laws, the clinician may have to take certain steps vis-à-vis the adolescent patient, the parents, and/or special state agencies.

IMPEDIMENTS TO INTERVENTION IN THE REAL WORLD CONTEXT

Parental Reactions

An almost universal obstacle is the parents' fear at what may happen to their off-spring—the child that they only recently (or so it seems) held as a helpless infant. They typically fear that their child will end up as one or more of the following: homeless, a hobo, a prostitute, a criminal, or dead. The clinician's first task is to recognize the parents' fears are not groundless: any or all of these tragedies can and sometimes do occur. Untreated, SRD in childhood or adolescence has a poor prognosis. Even when treated (at our current state of art and science), the prognosis is only fair—some will succeed grandly and others will die despite everyone's best efforts. Once the reality basis of the parents' dread is acknowledged, the clinician can proceed with helping the parents cope with this major obstacle.

Sometimes the parents' dread is paved over by a focus on the child's coping and ability. For example, a 17-year-old high school senior was brought to evaluation after she had mentioned a suicidal plan to one of her teachers. Evaluation revealed active alcohol abuse, bulimia nervosa, and major depressive disorder. Her parents wanted to delay entry into treatment for several weeks, as their daughter was to lead the high school prom (as one of the class officers), give the graduation address (as the class valedictorian), and compete in a 4-H contest with a prize bull. Only when the daughter promised them that they would have her funeral rather than any of these celebrations would they consent to her immediate treatment. (Although she did none of the activities for which she had prepared and her parents had long dreamed, she did recover from her three conditions, entered college two years later, and was the first member of her extended family to become a college graduate.)

Parental Substance Abuse

Perhaps the most common impediment to a successful outcome is alcoholism or drug abuse in one or both parents. A successful recovery by the adolescent would threaten the continued substance use of the parent. In some cases, the parent is so appalled at the adolescent's SRD that this discovery serves as a crisis inducing the parent to attempt recovery. Even under such circumstances, the clinician should not rest the adolescent's treatment plans on whether or not the parent does eventually recover—a process that will require at least a few, and possibly several years.

In some cases, the parent is a heavy user who has been functional and does not meet diagnostic criteria for SRD. The parent may permit, or even support the child in using a similar amount of psychoactive substance. However, the adolescent may encounter academic, social, and other problems at the same dose of substance. The parent may believe that normal function is possible for everyone at such a dose and therefore not accept the diagnosis of SRD. For example, a solo mother (who sold cannabis on the side to supplement her AFDC income) consumed a few cannabis cigarettes every evening. She permitted her eldest son to smoke cannabis in the evening along with her. Within several months, his behavior at school had become intolerable, and he was referred for a psychiatric evaluation. In another instance, a solo working father drank a six-pack of beer every weekday evening, and a case of beer per day over the weekend.

He tolerated his son's drinking, beginning with a few beers daily in early adolescence and progressing to his own six-pack daily by mid-adolescence. The son was referred due to increasing solitary behavior in school, a drop from A and B grades to failing, and deteriorating physical condition (e.g., weight loss, skin abscesses, bloated face and hands, incoordination).

Some parents have previously recovered from SRD and are sober at the time that the clinician is evaluating the adolescent. Recent sobriety and recovery may have led to the parent becoming newly aware of their offspring's alcohol- or drug-centered lifestyle. In other cases, the parent may have been recovered for years or even decades. Such parents can prove a great resource to the clinician in helping the adolescent, but they may also require special attention:

- The recovered parent may experience profound grief and irrational guilt regarding the development of SRD in his or her offspring. These strong feelings could lead to antitherapeutic behaviors and decisions, such as rescuing. If adequately attended in a timely fashion, with support and grief work, such parental responses should not be pathogenic for the adolescent.

- The parent may expect the adolescent to recover in the same fashion and through the same methods as the parent. While this could happen, it is not likely. The parent must realize that he or she must remain a parent, and not attempt to be an Alcoholics Anonymous (AA) sponsor for the adolescent.

- The offspring may have a comorbid psychiatric disorder, whereas the parent might not have had such a disorder. It may be very difficult for the parent to accept that the adolescent has another disorder, which will also require its own treatment. For example, two recovered parents—both educated, employed, and successful as alcohol-drug counselors—could accept their adolescent son's SRD, but not his psychosis. They delayed adequate care for the latter until he was dehydrated, malnourished, and suffering from pneumonia.

- Many recovered parents have had their SRD and recovery during their adult years, not during adolescence. They do not have an adequate store of information regarding the special needs and problems of the recovering adolescent. The clinician must inform them about their adolescent's recovery and not assume knowledge that the parents might not have.

- For the nonrecovered (or nonalcoholic) spouse of an alcoholic parent, the adolescent's SRD may stir up memories and feelings regarding the spouse's earlier behaviors, crises, and recovery—all very difficult times in the lives of most people. These memories and feelings may give rise to several responses: grief, anger, denial, escape, separation. The clinician can help this parent remain supportive to the adolescent by clarifying this spouse's memories and feelings, and the ways in which he or she is coping with them.

Single-Parent Families

The clinician should first ascertain the reason for single-parent status. Why is the other parent absent? Where is he or she? Did the absent parent have a SRD or other psychiatric condition, leading to the absence? If alive and accessible, can this parent be involved in the offspring's recovery process? Has the solo parent had SRD in the past? Might the solo parent have SRD now? Once this information is known, the clinician will be in a better position to guide the patient, the parent, and possibly social agencies toward an appropriate recovery plan. The child might remain in the home, or live for a time with the other parent or in residential care.

The most common solo parent dyad is a solo mother with a SRD son. This scenario can carry considerable risks for both members. The son may boss, threaten, and steal from the solo mother. The mother may seek to keep the son in the relationship with her, using him to serve as the new "man of the house" (so long as he remains an ineffectual and dependent "man"). If this is the case, the mother may undermine her son's recovery by providing him with money to continue his substance abuse. The latter process is termed *enabling*. The mother may also try to gloss over school problems or extricate the son from legal difficulties. This process is termed *rescuing*.

Financial Problems

One kind of financial problem is poverty. This problem can impede the family in its efforts to provide intervention and help for their SRD offspring. Since helping an SRD offspring to recover requires great effort and is emotionally draining, the parents need respite activities, with recreation, quiet, and support. Grinding poverty and long work hours may sap the parents of the morale, energy, and strength needed to cope with both offspring and SRD.

Another and just as serious (but less common) problem is great wealth, which the parents and the SRD offspring may employ to ameliorate the problems precipitated by the disorder. One parent hired attorneys to get her son out of trouble with the law, bought him new cars when he smashed them driving while legally drunk, and paid various private schools larger and larger sums to keep him enrolled. She lessened the stress on herself by engaging in projects designed to occupy her attention (e.g., building a new house, taking an extended trip around the world).

Even for middle-class people, the financial drain of providing care for a dependent child with SRD can be overwhelming. Distraught parents may become destitute if they pay for services that provide even the glimmer of a hope that their child might be made whole again. Struggles with third-party payers, social agencies, corporate insurance officers, and others may become a way of life for parents over several years.

Absence of Trained Professionals

For the past few decades, the usual treatment program for SRD adolescents has consisted of a combination of (a) staff members knowledgeable about alcoholism and drug abuse, but not about child psychology and psychiatry; and (b) staff members knowledgeable about child psychology and psychiatry, but not about alcoholism and drug abuse. Although it may seem reasonable to bring such people together to serve a single patient population, in fact it has ordinarily not resulted in increased skill and knowledge within either group. At best, the two groups work out an uneasy peace. At worst, they engage in a power struggle with each other, often to the detriment of their patients' care.

This situation has been resolving gradually as professionals are being trained both in child-adolescent psychiatry and in substance disorders. These newly trained professionals must integrate the two fields themselves, since there is no one to do it for them. Although this may be inefficient, it has the advantage of leading to innovation and creativity. Few resources exist for this training; it has depended mainly on professionals following their own career paths, driven by the obvious need and anguish in our families, communities, and society.

Ignorance

An impediment obvious to clinicians in the field is the lack of knowledge. Many practical questions must be answered before the effective prevention and care of SRD in adolescents can become a reality. What works in treatment, and for whom? If the clinician follows the "conventional wisdom" in the field, what outcomes can be anticipated? What approaches are cost-effective and which are not? Which patients have excellent prognoses with minimal therapy, and which patients are virtually doomed despite our best efforts? Does earlier recognition and entry into treatment carry a better prognosis? If the prognosis is better, how can we facilitate earlier recognition? Perhaps most importantly, how can we develop means of preventing child-adolescent SRD?

Power of the Psychoactive Substance and the Burden of Recovery

Clinicians must beware of underestimating the grip of a drug or alcohol on the child or adolescent patient. Those naive to this disorder may assume that it is simply a matter of will power for the patient to change, or that merely expressing concern for the patient will induce change, or that therapies can effect cures without the patient's willing participation. The clinician should assume instead that the substance has facilitated patients in coping with themselves and their lives. More than likely, the substance has become like a best friend, a reliable support, a necessary solace. Giving it up will require consummate effort and much loss. Grieving may be necessary, as though a death has occurred. Then, as the adolescent patient recovers, new onslaughts, injuries, and insults often appear. Often, recovering patients view with horror and dismay their SRD-wrought losses and injuries—some never to be regained or healed.

TREATMENT

Assessment Strategies

Rapport in Relation to Age and Phase of SRD

Developing rapport with children requires time, empathy, respect, and a willingness to understand the child's point of view. With SRD patients, this may take longer than with non-SRD patients. SRD youth may have more to hide and have more reasons to distrust adults (especially authoritative or "helping" adults). Due to delays in their psychosocial development, they may have more difficulty participating in a relationship with a nonfamily adult. Their model for adolescent-adult relationships may be one of mutual manipulation, rather than mutual benefit.

The context in which the clinical consultation occurs can also influence the clinician-child relationship. Older children and younger adolescents may not personally be in a crisis. In fact, they may be quite satisfied and nonambivalent regarding their continued substance use. In these cases, it is the parents who are in a crisis and distraught. Clinicians often find it easy to develop rapport with these parents, but not their children. Older adolescents are more typically in a personal crisis at the time that clinical consultation occurs. They may have been suspended from school, kicked off an athletic team, turned away by a boyfriend or girlfriend, in trouble with the law, or incarcerated. Rapport comes more quickly and easily with the older, distraught SRD adolescent. Those in their middle years, aged 15 and 16, can fall anywhere between these two extremes.

Some clinicians attempt to facilitate rapport by dressing, speaking, or acting like adolescents. This may gain some early rapport, but with an ultimate cost. The clinician is not an adolescent, after all, and the goal of the interchange is not simply friendship (although elements of that may evolve). More sophisticated patients may be put off by such a charade. Manipulative patients may play on the clinician's apparent identity confusion, seeking special favors or considerations.

History-Taking Techniques

Early in the development of rapport, it is best to remain with open-ended questions and not press for answers. It is better to have no information than misinformation or disinformation. With experience, the clinician may inquire more directly for any of several reasons: a sense that the patient is ready to communicate, an interest in the patient's handling of a certain question or topic, a signaling of the patient's willingness to discuss certain topics. In general, however, the clinician new to this kind of work should avoid putting the patient in a position of lying or otherwise compromising him- or herself. Patients often view this as a disrespectful and clumsy tactic—and rightfully so.

In discussing alcohol and drug use early on, the clinician should evidence an appreciation of the patient's experience and viewpoints regarding such use. Terms such as "use" and "high" should be employed, rather than "abuse" or "drunk." Adapting the patient's terms for psychoactive substances and experiences can facilitate mutual understanding, especially if the clinician otherwise remains "in role" and spontaneous in the dialogue. Likewise, the patient should gradually become familiar with certain of the clinician's jargon to facilitate the therapeutic process.

Physical Examination

On average, little can be discerned on physical examination of the child or adolescent coming to evaluation during the early phases of SRD. Later in the course, the nature and sometimes the extent of SRD can be appreciated through physical examination. Medical problems associated with SRD include the following:

- *Infections.* Low respiratory (bronchitis, pneumonia), sinusitis (especially if the patient is snuffing the drug), urinary tract, sexually transmitted diseases (especially if prostituting or trading sex for drugs), hepatitis, AIDS, and skin infections (e.g., cellulitis, abscesses).
- *Malnutrition.* Cheilosis, anemia, muscle wasting, stunted growth, sallow appearance.

- *Trauma.* Abrasions and bruises to the lower legs (from falling and bumping into objects), and more serious injuries (fractures, severe lacerations, head injuries) from fights, falls, vehicular accidents, and assaults.

Particular substances can give rise to special physical findings. Correction fluid, glue, or other hydrocarbons about the face or nares can indicate the recent use of volatile inhalants. Acute intoxication as well as withdrawal may provide telltale signs and symptoms, depending on the substance. Changes in pupils, skin color, pulse, blood pressure, bowel sounds, tremors, incoordination, and nystagmus should be noted. A formal mental status can also contribute to the diagnostic formulation.

Chronic administration of a drug through a particular route can also produce physical signs and symptoms. A raspy voice or chronic bronchitis may indicate heavy use of the respiratory tract as a means of drug administration. Parenteral administration of drugs can give rise to scars and bruises over veins, referred to as "tracks." Snuffing can produce nasal mucosal ulcers, sinusitis, and ultimately perforation of the nasal septum.

Laboratory Findings

As with physical exam, laboratory findings are often normal in early phases of SRD. Abnormal findings may be nonspecific, indicating poor nutrition (e.g., low B vitamins, low serum protein), chronic stress (e.g., high cholesterol, high triglycerides), or chronic infection (e.g., elevated white blood count, pyuria on urinalysis). Other findings may relate specifically to organ damage from chronic use of the substance, such as abnormal liver enzymes (from abuse of alcohol and certain solvent-inhalants), abnormal renal function (from certain solvent-inhalants), and abnormal electrocardiogram (from certain stimulants, solvents). Toxicological studies can reveal recent abuse of most psychoactive substances. Some drugs, if chronically abused in high doses, can produce positive test results even after several days (e.g., certain benzodiazepines) or several weeks (e.g., cannabis).

Collateral Sources

Information should be sought from as many sources as time, resources, and ethical and legal considerations permit. The following list of questions should aid in understanding the patient from developmental, constitutional, genetic, familial, and social perspectives:

- What were the health of the father and mother at the time of conception, as well as the health of the mother during pregnancy?
- Did either the father or the mother abuse alcohol or drugs prior to conception, during pregnancy, or in the child-raising years?
- Did either parent have a psychiatric condition that was disabling or required treatment?
- At what age did the various stages of development occur during infancy and early childhood?
- How did the developing child cope with peers, parents, teachers, siblings, and neighbors?

- What has been the patient's academic progress over the years?
- In what sports, hobbies, or extracurricular activities did the child participate?
- What have been this child's obstacles, successes, and failures?
- What have been his or her expressed plans, hopes, dreams, and expectations?

Family Assessment

A psychiatric and social history should be obtained for both parents, and for other significant persons in the patient's social network. Some clinicians and programs collect certain routine psychometrics, such as the Minnesota Multiphasic Personality Inventory-2 (MMPI-2), the Michigan Alcoholism Screening Test (MAST), or one of the symptom checklists. Although physical and sexual abuse are by no means universal in the families of SRD children and adolescents, the rates of such abuse greatly exceed those of the general population. The clinician should routinely inquire about such abuse in a matter-of-fact way.

Rating Scales

The Michigan Alcoholism Screening Test (MAST) can be used effectively with older adolescents. Some adolescents 13 to 16 years can complete it, although their honesty with the test might be an issue. The MAST is about as useful for those aged 17 or older as it is with adults (Westermeyer et al., 1994). Patients take the test in about 5 to 10 minutes by themselves, and it can be scored in less than a minute. The individual items are rated, with scores of 1, 2, or 5 per item. A modification of this test to include drug use can greatly extend the utility of this instrument, especially among those using drugs or combining alcohol and drugs (Westermeyer & Neider, 1988).

False Positives and False Negatives

Clinicians must be prepared for both false positive and false negative diagnoses of SRD in adolescents brought to them for alleged substance abuse. For example, a physician brought his 17-year-old son in for SRD evaluation after his son returned home from a summer job wearing "hippie" clothes. In another case, a 15-year-old girl left cannabis stashed around the house after her parents refused to let her attend parties or talk over the phone with boys. Initial evaluation as well as periodic reassessments of these patients failed to reveal any evidence of SRD. (In both these cases, family therapy alleviated the crisis produced by the adolescents' "offending" behaviors.) Besides such "false positive" cases, clinicians must be prepared to encounter "false negative" cases. For example, an ophthalmologist and a pediatrician opined that an 18-year-old college freshman did not have SRD after she had enucleated one of her eyes while intoxicated on cannabis and amphetamine. When her substance abuse resumed after hospital discharge, they referred her for SRD evaluation.

Treatment Approaches

Helping the Parents

Unless the SRD offspring presents a life-threatening crisis, the first step often lies in attending to the parents, especially if they are in greater crisis than their child. Paramount in importance is the following principle: Parents are unlikely to deal effectively with their SRD offspring until they cope with their own fears regarding their son or daughter's condition and ultimate prognosis. The clinician's first therapeutic step, once the diagnosis has been made, often consists of helping parents with this critical step. Acceptance of reality and recognition of their own limited ability to control the situation are often powerful first steps in setting a therapeutic course.

The clinician must discuss frankly the poor prognosis without treatment and the guarded-to-fair prognosis even with treatment. Parents must have adequate time and support to express their worst dreads. It is often useful to guide the parents in undertaking a kind of grief work, in which they surrender their idyllic hopes for their child, recognize the reality of the situation, and undertake an "anticipatory grieving" for both their own dreams and for their child. Once they have faced and acknowledged the possible deterioration and even death of their beloved child, they can then deal with their feelings. After experiencing their anguish and loss, they are usually able to act supportively and appropriately. This may require that they refuse enabling and rescuing requests from their own child, realizing that the child may die or become disabled as an immediate consequence of their refusal. However, supporting them in this decision is the knowledge that cessation of enabling and rescuing behaviors offers a promise of eventual recovery, whereas continued enabling and rescuing delays recovery at best or guarantees the child's eventual destruction at worst. Parents can be guided in making decisions that they can live with, even if their child dies.

Parental support and recovery to the recovering adolescent are possible under all socioeconomic circumstances. With poverty, the clinician must guide parents in seeking recreation, support, and respite, perhaps through church activities, local associations, community centers, and extended kin networks. With wealth, the clinician must guide parents in facing their grief as well as in avoiding the destructive use of wealth to enable or rescue their offspring, to escape the problem, or attempt to delegate it to others. Clinicians can orient middle-class patients to the methods and means of coping with case managers.

Families may need more than counseling to make it through periods of extended care. If the child dies or becomes chronically disabled, the marital relationship may not survive either. Marital/couples therapy can aid the couple, the recovering child, and the entire family.

Detoxification

Detoxification and early stabilization requires at least a few weeks for most drugs, and may require a few months for longer-acting drugs (such as some benzodiazepines), fat-stored drugs (such as cannabis), or drugs with enterohepatic recirculation (such as PCP and methaqualone). Generally, this requires good nutrition and hydration, safety away from access to drugs and alcohol, and a minimum of support while assisting the patient to assess his or her current condition. Some adolescents require a withdrawal medication over a period of days or weeks, although this is less common than among adults. Children who have been using large daily doses of certain inhalants or solvents may need a withdrawal regimen; a course of medication cross-tolerant with alcohol (e.g., benzodiazepines) usually proves satisfactory.

Establishing Abstinence

Some adolescents can maintain abstinence without hospitalization or residential treatment, especially if an intensive day program or evening program is provided. Some school systems have worked out arrangements by which recovering students can attend school in the morning and a recovery program in the afternoon. Most patients can maintain abstinence for several weeks to a few months. Failure to maintain abstinence for even such brief periods often indicates the presence of other psychopathology (e.g., major depression, panic disorder, mental retardation, dementia).

Return to substance abuse is most apt to occur some time between six weeks and six months after sobriety has been established. Some continued recurrence takes place between six months and two years postsobriety. Beyond five years of sobriety, recurrences do occur but are infrequent (probably no more frequent than in the general population). If recurrences last only hours or a few days, followed by a rapid return to treatment and recovery activities, these are often referred to as "slips." If slips are occurring less frequently over time and lasting for ever-shorter periods, they might not warrant a basic change in the treatment plan. If recurrences last weeks or longer, or result in a return to treatment or recovery only when crises recur, these are generally referred to as relapses. They are marked by every more frequent and longer periods of recurrence, until the downhill course of SRD continues uninterrupted. Relapses call for a change in strategy. This may consist of more extensive treatment (e.g., moving from a family home to a halfway house) or more intensive treatment (e.g., changing from an evening program to a day program). It may also consist of abandoning treatment for a time, especially if treatment activities are serving enabling or rescuing functions.

Phases of Recovery

Patients can be in treatment for months or even years without getting beyond the initial phases of recovery. Patients must open themselves to the recovery experience, be able to stand the difficult and lonely course of recovery, and evidence faith in their own strength and hope in their future. Many different recovery phases can be identified, but the following schema is simple, applicable, and easy to remember:

- *Abstinence Phase.* Continues for the first few months; involves detoxification and remaining safe from alcohol-drug access; depressive and anxious symptoms are abnormally high but resolve steadily and notably; patient begins to realize his or her problems and the contribution of substance use to these problems.
- *Stabilization Phase.* Begins after a few months of sobriety and continues for a few years; involves avoiding alcohol-drug use; 12-step self-help activities may be a central commitment; begins "rebuilding bridges" to those who have been hurt by the SRD; identifies with other recovering persons; invests time and effort in self-understanding and self-coping.
- *Comfort Phase.* Begins after a few years of sobriety and continues for several years; craving for alcohol-drug recedes greatly or disappears; sobriety becomes comfortable and life becomes rewarding; begins to branch out socially into non-recovering society; can tolerate the social use of alcohol by others; may enter psychotherapy during this period; may undertake commitments beneficial to the family, extended kin, or community.

Family members also encounter a kind of recovery of their own. Gradually with time and support, they learn surrender, acceptance, forgiveness, and a new level of understanding and comfort. They may accomplish this through the help of a supportive clinician, or through one of the family support groups now in existence. In addition to the parents' recovery, the need for recovery among siblings and other household members should be appreciated. In this era of widespread divorce and remarriage, recovery may involve more than one family.

Self-Help Groups

Adolescents may engage in such 12-step work with adult-supervised groups, sometimes called "teenage AA," "teen recovery," or other names. These groups may take place after school or in the evening, in a room within the high school, in a nearby church, or in a community center. An AA member familiar with adolescents and their special recovery issues usually leads the group. For example, a newly recovering 17-year-old who has been abusing substances heavily since age 14 may be unable to undertake an age-appropriate conversation with an attractive member of the opposite sex or to ask a person to high school prom. Other problems faced by recovering adolescents may include the ability to conduct a respectful, appropriate confrontation of teachers and parents, or to assert oneself in a discussion or debate without having to either win or leave the discussion. Group guidance and support can assist greatly with these age-appropriate tasks.

Psychoeducation

Psychoeducation involves more than simply providing adolescents and family members with information about SRD. It involves providing them with the *right information* (i.e., useful, appropriate information) at the *right time* (i.e., when it can be put to good effect). Often this educational process involves the learning of new skills. A parent may need to learn how to listen respectfully to an adolescent, not assuming that he or she knows what the adolescent is thinking. Or an adolescent may need to learn how to negotiate with a parent or teacher. Psychoeducation typically involves the acquisition of new *attitudes*. For example, a parent who is an AA member may develop new attitudes toward use of psychotropic medication for a recovering son or daughter who has a comorbid psychiatric condition.

Changing Residence and/or School

For years, clinicians have considered changing residences or school to be simply "running away from the problem." This can indeed be the case. Many SRD adolescents simply find drug suppliers and drug-using peers in their new neighborhood or school. By the same token, every experienced clinician has observed remarkably good outcomes in certain cases when a change has been made in residence or school. The following factors appear congenial or mutually beneficial to a school or residence change:

- The SRD child or adolescent and the family have begun treatment around the same time as the change.
- Other, less intrusive measures have not proven successful; the patient continues to have relapses.
- The recovering child or adolescent continues to be the recipient of social expectations or assigned roles as a "druggie" or "dopehead" even though actively involved in recovery.

- High access and availability in the environment result in strong pressures to resume substance use.

Families should be counseled not to destitute themselves financially on the thin hope that a miraculous change will occur with an adolescent who is not collaborating with treatment.

Special Considerations: The Young Child with a Substance-Related Disorder

Preschool children with evidence of chronic substance abuse are rare, but such cases do occur. These cases consist of parents giving sedatives, opiates, or alcohol to infants or preschool children to quiet them. Most of these parents have SRD themselves, although a few have other problems that impair judgment (e.g., mental retardation, borderline intelligence, schizophrenia or other chronic mental illness, antisocial personality disorder). These cases require careful supervision and education of the parents. Placement of the child outside the home, either temporarily or even permanently, may be necessary.

School-age children may begin to actively pursue substance use on their own. Such cases may occur after the age of 5, but are not typically encountered until around the age of 7, 8, or 9. Virtually all these cases involve chaotic family situations, often in a family rife with SRD. The alcohol or drug is usually available in the home. Parents may proffer the substance to the child, but more often the child simply takes it, either openly or surreptitiously. Children in this age group may also begin abusing volatile inhalants or solvents, which can be obtained in the home, school, local stores, or elsewhere (e.g., gas tanks of cars, construction sites). Chronic administration of certain solvent-inhalants can destroy brain tissue. Such cases usually involve a family-wide assessment and intervention. Although older preadolescents may be treated within more intact families, such cases often require agency supervision, temporary placement of children, and treatment of the entire family.

Epidemics of childhood substance abuse within entire schools or neighborhoods have been reported in certain areas of Canada, the United States, and Mexico with high rates of adult alcoholism (Beauvais, Oetting, & Edward, 1985; Goodwin, Geil, & Grodner, 1981; Oetting et al., 1988; Padilla, Padilla, & Morales, 1979; Schottstedt & Bjork, 1977). These epidemics require special public health and community-wide approaches. Restrictions regarding sale and access of inhalants and solvents may be undertaken.

Special Considerations: Early versus Late Adolescents with SRD

Treatment of adolescents between the age of 13 and 15 (sometimes even 16) usually requires that their parents have a major commitment to the treatment process. If they do not or cannot, some out-of-home placement for the adolescent will probably be necessary. Recovery of the child in this age group must occur within a context of a "recovering" family, whether that be the family of origin or a foster family.

For most patients aged 17 and older (and for some healthier 16-year-olds), recovery independent of the family may be feasible. This can be a great relief for clinicians, especially with patients who have entrenched psychopathology, social dysfunction, and near-fanatical commitment to chaos. "Parent-ectomy" in such cases can even be fostered by the courts and social agencies, if necessary. For early cases, it may be possible for the adolescent to remain at home while actively in treatment such that the treatment team and recovering peers become an artificial or "fictive" family for a period of months or a few years. In some cases, such recovering adolescents can stimulate remarkable improvements in the level of function among other family members.

Resuming Psychoactive Substance Use

Some recovered persons, treated for SRD in childhood or (more often) in adolescence will inquire about resuming licit substance use (if they had been abusing illicit substances) or attempting controlled drinking (if they had been drinking excessively). Some recommendations are as follows:

- It would be better for them to settle on lifelong abstinence from any and all self-administered psychoactive compounds.
- If their course of abuse was short and they did not become dependent on the substance, controlled use may be feasible after a period of abstinence and recovery. However, few such cases occur, and the risks are high.
- They should reenter treatment during a period of controlled use if they are committed to trying this (rather than try it on their own). They should attempt this in their 20s or later, at a time when their life is relatively stable and free of crisis.

SUMMARY

Prior to the mid-1900s, substance abuse among children and adolescents was rarely seen, and only in sporadic cases. Since 1950, and especially since 1970, large numbers of clinical cases have been reported. Epidemiological studies since 1980 have documented the widespread and early use of recreational psychoactive substances among older children and adolescents. Almost three decades ago, Cameron, a WHO official, first identified the pandemic of substance abuse among youth.

Studies among adolescents and among adults with SRD have indicated considerable similarity in the types of substances used, frequency of use, SRD diagnoses, and manifestations of SRD. Major differences also obtained, for example are, adolescents show more abuse and less dependency, a shorter duration of abuse prior to entering treatment, stifling of psychosocial maturation, and more comorbid psychiatric conditions. Youthful patients are more apt to abuse inhalants and less apt to abuse opiates. Cocaine abuse has been increasing among adolescents with SRD. Loss of a father or mother is associated with earlier onset of SRD. These differences demonstrate conclusively that clinicians cannot simply extrapolate from knowledge regarding SRD adults to SRD adolescents.

As with healthcare of children and adolescents in general, two critical factors must be considered in the assessment and treatment of SRD youth. One of these is the family. The other is the impact of youthful SRD on development, including biological development, but also psychosocial development and maturation. Unlike numerous other health problems affecting the young, the influence of the community is a crucial factor in permitting, facilitating, and ameliorating SRD among children and adolescents. Peers, schools, the police, and courts (in reducing drug-alcohol availability to youth), the legislature (in reducing risk while making treatment available), and the healthcare system all play critical roles in addressing SRD among children and adolescents.

REFERENCES

Amaro, H., Zuckerman, B., & Cabral, H. (1989). Drug use among adolescent mothers: Profile of risk. *Pediatrics, 84,* 144–151.

American Psychiatric Association. (1994). *Diagnostic and statistical manual of mental disorders* (4th ed.). Washington, DC: Author.

Amini, F., Salasnek, S., & Burke, E. (1976). Adolescent drug abuse: Etiological and treatment considerations. *Adolescence, 11,* 281–299.

Anderson, P. (1984). Alcohol consumption of undergraduates at Oxford University. *Alcohol and Alcoholism, 19,* 77–84.

Barnes, G. M., & Windle, M. (1987). Family factors in adolescent alcohol and drug abuse. *Pediatrician, 14,* 13–18.

Baumrind, D., & Moselle, K. A. (1985). A developmental perspective on adolescent drug abuse. *Advances in Alcoholism and Substance Abuse, 4,* 41–67.

Bean, M. (1982). Identifying and managing alcohol problems of adolescents. *Psychosomatics, 23,* 389–396.

Beauvais, F., Oetting, E. R., & Edward, R. W. (1985). Trends in the use of inhalants among American Indian adolescents. *White Cloud Journal, 3,* 3.

Bernstein, J. G. (1984). Kids and drugs: Part 1. Recreational use. *Clinical Therapeutics Drug Therapy, 14,* 59–72.

Blum, R. W. (1987). Adolescent substance abuse: Diagnostic and treatment issues. *Pediatric Clinics of North America, 34,* 523–537.

Brook, J. S., Whiteman, M., Gordon, A. S., Nomura, C., & Brook, D. W. (1986). Onset of adolescent drinking: A longitudinal study of intrapersonal and interpersonal antecedents. *Advances in Alcohol Substance Abuse, 5,* 91–110.

Burnside, M., Baer, P., McLaughlin, R., & Pokorny, A. (1986). Alcohol use by adolescents in disrupted families. *Alcoholism: Clinical and Experimental Research, 10,* 274–278.

Cameron, D. C. (1968). Youth and drugs. *Journal of the American Medical Association, 206,* 1267–1271.

Carter, Y. M., & Robson, W. J. (1987). Drug misuse in adolescence. *Archives of Emergency Medicine, 4,* 17–24.

Clancy, G. P., & Yates, W. R. (1992). Anabolic steroid use among substance abusers in treatment. *Journal of Clinical Psychiatry, 53,* 97–100.

Coupey, S. M., & Schonberg, S. K. (1982). Evaluation and management of drug problems in adolescents. *Pediatric Annuals, 11,* 653–658.

Czechowicz, D. (1988). Adolescent alcohol and drug abuse and its consequences—An overview. *American Journal on Drug and Alcohol Abuse, 14,* 189–197.

Deisher, R. W., Litchfield, C., & Hope, K. R. (1991). Birth outcomes of prostituting adolescents. *Journal of Adolescent Health, 12,* 528–533.

Dent, C. W., Galaif, J., Sussman, S., Stacy, A. W., Burton, D., & Flay, B. R. (1992). Music preference as a diagnostic indicator of adolescent drug use [Letter]. *American Journal of Public Health, 82,* 124.

Dias, C., & Polvora, F. (1983). Drug addiction among adolescents. *Bulletin on Narcotics, 35,* 81–86.

Easson, W. M. (1976). Understanding teenage drug abuse. *Postgraduate Medicine, 59,* 173–177.

Gilchrist, L. D., Gillmore, M. R., & Lohr, M. J. (1990). Drug use among pregnant adolescents. *Journal of Consulting and Clinical Psychology, 58,* 402–407.

Goodwin, J. M., Geil, C., & Grodner, B. (1981). Inhalant abuse, pregnancy and neglected children. *American Journal of Psychiatry, 138,* 1126.

Griffin, J. B. (1981). Some psychodynamic considerations in the treatment of drug abuse in early adolescence. *Journal of the American Academy of Child and Adolescent Psychiatry, 20,* 159–166.

Haas, A. P. (1987). Long-term outcomes of heavy marijuana use among adolescents. *Pediatrician, 14,* 77–82.

Heilbrunn, G. (1967). Comments on adolescent drug users. *Northwest Medicine, 66,* 457–460.

Hennecke, L., & Gitlow, S. (1983, June). Alcohol use and alcoholism in adolescence. *New York State Journal of Medicine, 83*(7), 936–940.

Johnson, L. D., O'Malley, P. M., & Bachman, J. G. (1987). Psychotherapeutic, licit, and illicit use of drugs among adolescents: An epidemiological perspective. *Journal of Adolescent Health Care, 8,* 36–51.

Kandel, D. (1982). Epidemiological and psychosocial perspectives on adolescent drug use. *Journal of the American Academy of Child and Adolescent Psychiatry, 21,* 328–347.

Kandel, D., Davies, M., Karus, D., & Yamaguchi, K. (1986). The consequences in young adulthood of adolescent drug involvement. *Archives of General Psychiatry, 43,* 746–754.

Kashani, J., Keller, M., & Solomon, N. (1985). Double depression in adolescent substances users. *Journal of Affective Disorders, 8,* 153–157.

Katz, J. L. (1990). Eating disorders: A primer for the substance abuse specialist: 1. Clinical features. *Journal of Substance Abuse Treatment, 7,* 143–149.

Kavoussi, R. J., Kaplan, M., & Becker, J. V. (1988). Psychiatric diagnoses in adolescent sex offenders. *Journal of the American Academy of Child and Adolescent Psychiatry, 27,* 241–243.

Keyes, S., & Block, J. (1984). Prevalence and patterns of substance use among early adolescents. *Journal of Youth Adolescence, 13,* 1–14.

Klinge, V., & Vaziri, M. (1977). Characteristics of drug abusers in an adolescent inpatient psychiatric facility. *Diseases of the Nervous System, 38,* 275–279.

Kokotailo, P. K., & Adger, H. J. (1991). Substance use by pregnant adolescents. *Clinical Perinatology, 18,* 125–138.

Levy, S. J., & Pierce, J. P. (1989). Drug use among Sydney teenagers in 1985 and 1986. *Community Health Studies, 13,* 161–169.

MacDonald, D., & Newton, M. (1981). The clinical syndrome of adolescent drug abuse. *Advances in Pediatrics, 28,* 1–25.

MacKenzie, R. (1982). The adolescent as a drug abuser: A paradigm for intervention. *Pediatric Annals, 11,* 659–668.

Masland, R. P. (1972). Drug abuse: A symptom of adolescent unrest. *Postgraduate Medicine, 55,* 227–230.

McDermott, D. (1984). The relationship of parental drug use and parent's attitude concerning adolescent drug use to adolescent drug use. *Adolescence, 19,* 89–97.

McKirnan, D., & Johnson, T. (1986). Alcohol and drug use among "street" adolescents. *Addictive Behaviors, 11,* 201–205.

McLaughlin, R., Baer, P., Burnside, M., & Pokorny, A. (1985). Psychosocial correlates of alcohol use at two age levels during adolescence. *Journal of Studies in Alcohol, 46,* 212–218.

Mercer, R. T. (1991). Adolescent pregnancy: Nursing perspectives on prevention: Introduction. *Birth Defects, 27,* 1–8.

Miller, N. S., & Gold, M. S. (1990). Organic solvents and aerosols: An overview of abuse and dependence. *Annals of Clinical Psychiatry, 2,* 85–92.

Newcomb, M. D., & Bentler, P. M. (1986). Longitudinal associations with social context, psychopathology, and use of other substances. *Addictive Behaviors, 11,* 263–273.

Newcomb, M. D., & Bentler, P. M. (1987). The impact of late adolescent substance use on young adult health status and utilization of health services: A structural-equation model over four years. *Social Science and Medicine, 24,* 71–82.

Newcomb, M. D., & Harlow, L. L. (1986). Life events and substance use among adolescents: Mediating effects of perceived loss of control and meaninglessness in life. *Journal of Personality and Social Psychology, 51,* 564–577.

Niven, R. G. (1986). Adolescent drug abuse. *Hospital and Community Psychiatry, 37,* 596–607.

Oetting, E. R., Edwards, R. W., & Beauvais, F. (1988). Social and psychological factors underlying inhalant abuse. *NIDA Research Monograph, 85*(172-203, 1988).

Padilla, E. R., Padilla, A. M., & Morales, A. (1979). Inhalant, marijuana and alcohol abuse among barrio children and adolescents. *International Journal of the Addictions, 14,* 945–964.

Patterson, E. W., Myers, G., & Gallant, D. M. (1988). Patterns of substance use on a college campus: A 14-year comparison study. *American Journal on Drug and Alcohol Abuse, 14,* 237–246.

Peele, S. (1987). What can we expect from treatment of adolescent drug and alcohol abuse? *Pediatrician, 14,* 62–69.

Reuband, K. H. (1995). Drug use and drug policy in western Europe. *European Addiction Research, 1,* 32–41.

Reveis, V. H., & Kandel, D. B. (1987). Changes in drug behavior from the middle to the late twenties: Initiation, persistence, and cessation of use. *American Journal of Public Health, 77,* 607–611.

Rosenberg, C. (1971). The young addict and his family. *British Journal of Psychiatry, 118,* 469–470.

Rosenberg, C. (1972). Drug and alcohol use by young people attending a psychiatric emergency service. *British Journal of the Addictions, 67,* 189–194.

Runeson, B. O. (1990). Psychoactive Substance Use Disorder in youth suicide. *Alcohol and Alcoholism, 25,* 561–568.

Schottstedt, M. F., & Bjork, J. W. (1977). Inhalant abuse in an Indian boarding school. *American Journal of Psychiatry, 134,* 1290–1293.

Schuckit, M., & Chiles, J. (1978). Family history as a diagnostic aid in two samples of adolescents. *Journal of Nervous Mental Disease, 166,* 165–176.

Schwartz, R. H. (1988). Deliberate inhalation of isobutyl nitrite during adolescence: A descriptive study. *NIDA Research Monograph, 83*(81-5, 1988).

Seligman, P. (1986). A brief family intervention with an adolescent referred for drug taking. *Journal of Adolescence, 9,* 231–242.

Smart, R. G. (1979). Young alcoholics in treatment: Their characteristics and recovery rates at follow-up. *Alcoholism: Clinical Experimental Research, 3,* 19–23.

Smart, R. G., & Adlaf, E. M. (1991). Substance use and problems among Toronto street youth. *British Journal of the Addictions, 86,* 999–1010.

Smart, R. G., & Fejer, D. (1972). Drug use among adolescents and their parents: Closing the generation gap in mood modification. *Journal of Abnormal Psychology, 29,* 153–160.

Solow, R. A., & Solow, B. K. (1986). Mind-altering drugs: Effects on adolescent sexual functioning. *Medical Aspects of Human Sexuality, 20,* 24–34.

Von Knorring, L., Oreland, L., & Von Knorring, A. L. (1987). Personality traits and platelet MAO activity in alcohol and drug abusing teenage boys. *Acta Psychiatrica Scandanavia, 75,* 307–314.

Wells, L. A. (1985). Chemical dependence among adolescents. *Mayo Clinic Proceedings, 60,* 557–561.

Westermeyer, J. (1987). The psychiatrist and solvent-inhalant abuse: Recognition, assessment, and treatment. *American Journal of Psychiatry, 144,* 903–907.

Westermeyer, J., & Neider, J. (1988). Social networks and psychopathology among substance abuse. *American Journal of Psychiatry, 145,* 1265–1269.

Westermeyer, J., Phaobtong, T., & Neider, J. (1988). Substance use and abuse among mentally retarded persons: A comparison of patients and a survey population. *American Journal on Drug and Alcohol Abuse, 14,* 109–123.

Westermeyer, J., Specker, S., Neider, J., & Lingenfelter, M. A. (1994). Substance abuse and associated psychiatric disorders among 100 adolescents. *Journal of Addictive Disorders, 13*(1), 67–83.

White, H. R. (1987). Longitudinal stability and dimensional structure of problem drinking in adolescence. *Journal of Studies on Alcohol, 48,* 541–550.

Author Index

Subject Index